The
AUSTRALIAN
WINE
COMPENDIUM

The AUSTRALIAN WINE COMPENDIUM

JAMES
HALLIDAY

ANGUS
& ROBERTSON
PUBLISHERS

ANGUS & ROBERTSON PUBLISHERS

Unit 4, Eden Park, 31 Waterloo Road,
North Ryde, NSW, Australia 2113, and
16 Golden Square, London W1R 4BN,
United Kingdom

First published in Australia
by Angus & Robertson Publishers in 1985
First published in the United Kingdom
by Angus & Robertson (UK) Ltd in 1985

Copyright © James Halliday 1985

National Library of Australia
Cataloguing-in-publication data.

Halliday, James, 1938– .
  The Australian wine compendium.

  Includes index.
  ISBN 0 207 15137 7.

  1. Wine and wine making — Australia.
  2. Wineries — Australia. I. Title.

663'.2'00994

Typeset in Garamond by
ProComp Productions Pty Ltd, South Australia
Printed in Tokyo, Japan

Acknowledgements

All base maps except those on pages 124 and 254 are Crown Copyright and have been reproduced by permission of the Director, Division of National Mapping, Department of Resources and Energy, Canberra, Australia.

The publishers gratefully acknowledge the co-operation of the following individuals and organisations who have given permission for photographs to appear in the book.

Australian Picture Library, *pp. 8–9, 278–9*

Berri Estates Pty Ltd, *p. 441*

Bleasdale Vineyards Pty Ltd, *p. 428*

W. H. Chambers & Son, *pp. 151, 217*

Houghton Wines, *pp. 488, 492–3, 516*

Kay Brothers Pty Ltd, *pp. 399, 447, 456*

Stephen Lambert, *pp. 552–3*

Lilydale Historical Society, *pp. 187, 237, 243, 253*

Lindemans, *pp. 11, 15, 83, 97, 194–5*

McWilliam's Wines, *pp. 112, 119*

Robert Wayne, Thomas Hardy & Sons Pty Ltd, *pp. 536–7*

National Library of Australia, *pp. 79, 126–7, 165, 175*

Orlando Wines Pty Ltd, *pp. 308, 324–5, 341, 355*

Photographic Library of Australia, *pp. ii*

Sevenhill Cellars, *p. 361*

S. Smith & Son Pty Ltd, Yalumba, *p. 351*

Tollana Wines, *p. 346*

Gil Wahlquist, *pp. 530–1, 542–3*

Weldon Trannies, *pp. 134–5, 474–5*

Woodley Wines Pty Ltd, *pp. 296–7, 302–3, 315*

Contents

CONTENTS

Foreword

Australia seems to be a series of endless contradictions: it is a vast continent yet, somehow, a small place; it exudes the enthusiasm and excitement of the new world yet harbours surprisingly old and conservative institutions. The inhabitants revel in an open-air life yet most live in the big conurbations; sun, sea and frolic on the one hand, desert, bushfires and other climatic excesses on the other. But it is fun, it is exhilarating, and great things are happening in the world of wine.

If ever there was the right man in the right place at the right time, it is James Halliday. As a practising lawyer he has the intellectual capacity to martial the facts and present them logically and dispassionately; as a practical winemaker he understands the problems, techniques and components; as a gifted and experienced taster his judgement can be relied upon; and as a much travelled wine and food man, an *amateur* in the French sense, he has an intimate knowledge of the great wines of the world which enables him to keep his views of Australian wines in perspective. Happily, he can also write—though how he finds the time I do not know.

It is a pity that Australia is so far away. I have been only twice and loved every minute. I find the Australians warm and hospitable, yet surprisingly and comfortingly English in some ways. But, of course, I am biased for, being a keen wine buff myself, I meet mainly fellow enthusiasts.

When I made a late start in the wine trade some 32 years ago, Australian wine had a rock-bottom reputation. No self-respecting London or county town wine merchant listed any. There were relics of the trade in very cheap iron-tonic "burgundy", and little else. Mind you, California was nowhere and Spanish wine was, at that time rightly, also vying for the bottom of the vinous pile. My wise old predecessor André Simon made a point of visiting Australia and I am sure the branches of the Wine and Food Society he founded behaved like the seeds of gum trees germinated, as it were, by the raging bushfire of wine in the late 1960s and '70s. It was, however, Hugh Johnson who introduced me to the great glories of Australian wine. I remember him coming to Christie's with samples of Grange Hermitage and Mick Morris's old muscats. Then I met Len Evans, and through him a galaxy of wine people, professional and amateur: all, it seemed to me, imbued with not only enthusiasm but a burning desire to know, to understand and to excel.

Who would have thought, 20 years ago, that young French and Californian winemakers would flock over to do a *stage*, apprenticed to an Australian winemaker. Yet at vintage time only a few months ago I visited Petaluma and was delighted to find a team of young vignerons working under Brian Croser, the French members including the son of a major *deuxième cru* Bordeaux chateau, a young French lady winemaker, and even someone from the Napa Valley. My son Bartholomew came of age in Australia, being burnt to a frazzle picking grapes at Rothbury, learning wine wisdom from Max Lake and then being stained purple cleaning vats at Yalumba. It did him a world of good!

The world, including Australia, is passing through troubled times. But you only have to read the papers and magazines of 50, 100 and 150 years ago to see there is nothing new in all this. It is amazing how we all manage to survive. What is different, I think, is an awareness of the past and its problems—possibly even a conscious desire to avoid the errors and excesses, though it is depressing to see how these recur and even more, a great desire to harness modern technology to tradition, not to supplant it. I find the most exciting thing of all is the way that, despite the difficulties, the perennial struggles with nature, and finances, new bright young (and not so young, even retired) vine growers and winemakers continually enter the field, striving for quality. But there is an important corollary: without the willingness to pay for quality and without intelligent appreciation, top-class wines will not be made. For the former we must hope for a continuously improving economic climate and greater support for the fine wine trade, and for the latter, skilled guidance. This James Halliday amply provides.

MICHAEL BROADBENT
Christie's, London

Introduction

As the Bicentennial approaches, the Australian wine industry mirrors many of the paradoxes of the country as a whole. The range and quality of Australian wine is far superior to that of 10 or 20 years ago, and consumption has increased to the point where wine can truly be said to be part of our way of life. Yet, the industry is going through a traumatic period in the aftermath of the excesses of the late 1960s and early 1970s.

The major wine companies have embarked on a process of rationalisation which is yet to run its course. Most industry experts predict there will be a maximum of six large companies—possibly less—by the turn of the century. Such a restructuring would mean the demise of many of the medium-sized family-owned companies which presently make an important contribution to both quality and choice.

An integral part of this rationalisation is the ever-increasing power of the wholesale distributors. Wine has ceased to be a speciality product; more than 80 per cent of Australian wine production is now marketed in precisely the same way as cornflakes, baked beans or any other grocery product. Casks and flagons account for 74.3 per cent of annual sales (for the year up to 30 June 1984), and it is generally agreed that brand loyalty runs a distant second to price in determining choice. It is many years since the recommended retail price had any meaning, with the "real" price almost invariably 20 per cent (or even more) under the recommended retail.

The quality of the average cask wine is exemplary, and it is indeed curious that wine should sell for less per millilitre than do lemonade or beer. There are several contributing factors to this state of affairs. Firstly, the Riverland areas of New South Wales, South Australia and Victoria are highly efficient grape producers, among the most efficient in the world.

Second, the collapse of the dried-fruits market has diverted enormous quantities of sultanas to winemaking at a price at or below the cost of their production, itself a low figure. Sultanas (known as Thompson's Seedless in California, where they also produce what the Americans call jug wine) are the ultimate dual-purpose grape, providing juice which is very well suited to bulk-wine production.

Thirdly, the major companies have seemingly been intent on maintaining their market share. They profess to resent the buying power of the wholesale distributors, but nonetheless do business with them on their (the distributors') terms. Thus wine retailing has become wine discounting. What is more, discounting has now moved upwards to permeate the entire industry, including quality bottled wine. A few brave and skilful marketers such as Wolf Blass remain Canute-like, but they are exceptions.

This has had a most unfortunate side effect on the major companies, which also happen to produce the lion's share of the best bottled wines made in this country. A major consumer research report commissioned by *Time* magazine in 1983–84 revealed that only six per cent of regular wine-drinkers thought that the big companies produced the best wines. Discounting must be largely responsible for this abysmal response. The truth is that, in terms of total volume, the major companies produce a large proportion of the country's best wines.

Importantly, however, the last two decades have witnessed the birth of the boutique winery. Max Lake established Lake's Folly in the Hunter Valley in 1963, the same year as Reg Egan founded Wantirna Estate on the outskirts of Melbourne. As the polarisation between the big companies and small ones intensifies, we have already reached the situation where the biggest 65 wine companies produce 98 per cent of the nation's wine, and the remaining 450 companies the other two per cent. I say the remaining 450, but no-one is quite sure just how many wine producers there are in Australia. Estimates vary between 450 and 550 in total; new wineries open their doors every day, while others quietly fade away.

The small winery is, almost by definition, family-owned. There the similarity between one and another ends: the families range from those of leading Melbourne and Sydney doctors and lawyers, to those seeking alternative lifestyles, to the Yugoslavs of the Swan Valley, the Italians of the Riverlands and the descendants of the German Lutherans in the Barossa Valley.

The wines produced by the small company range from the most sophisticated and expensive to bulk wines made under primeval conditions, which are palatable only to the ethnic communities who consume them. Prices range from sky-high to rock-bottom, with no necessary relation to value. Nonetheless, the two per cent produced by those small companies is of totally disproportionate importance. Firstly, it represents around 10 per cent of the total bottled-wine market, and substantially more of the portion selling for above $5 a bottle. Secondly, with one major exception, the small makers have been in the forefront in the development of cool-climate viticulture.

That exception has been the development of viticulture in the south-east of South Australia, at Coonawarra and Padthaway/Keppoch. This has been the virtually exclusive preserve of the biggest companies. However, the small winemakers have opened up the Margaret River and Mount Barker areas of Western Australia; the Adelaide Hills (though not the Eden and Barossa Ranges); Tasmania; virtually the whole of central and southern Victoria; the Australian Capital Territory; and the Granite Belt in Queensland.

More than this, the best of the small makers have pushed back the frontiers in the introduction of noble grape varieties. They have not hesitated to incur the expense of the best winemaking equipment and the best new, small oak barrels. More recently they have joined with the more progressive companies in re-appraising viticultural methods in an attempt to maximise grape quality.

The sad thing is that a fair proportion of these brave ventures is doomed to failure. Their cost of production is very high, and sophisticated marketing techniques beyond the capacity of many small wineries would be necessary if they were all to survive.

All of these developments have occurred in the space of 20 years. The rate of change during this time in the industry as a whole cannot be over-emphasised. In 1960 less than 300 tonnes of cabernet sauvignon (the equivalent of 22,500 cases) were crushed each year. Today Wynns crushes four times that amount at just one of its wineries, Coonawarra. Fifteen years ago there was virtually no chardonnay on the market; five years ago no sauvignon blanc.

In 1960 table-wine consumption was around two litres per capita per annum, chiefly of red wine. Fortified wine still accounted for 70 per cent of all wine sales; 10 years earlier the figure must have been over 90 per cent (although detailed statistics were not then kept). Even in 1970–71 sales of sherry were more than twice those of dry white wine, while dry red sales were almost twice those of dry white. The graph produced opposite shows just what has happened in the intervening 15 years. The soaring white-wine sales have been closely associated with that of the wine cask. Once again the graph below speaks for itself. But in truth these dry statistics do not tell all. Underlying these changes in consumption patterns have been fundamental changes in wine styles. These changes have occurred as part of a matrix involving equally important changes in the circumstances in which wine is consumed.

The Australian red table wine of 1960 was notable chiefly for the fact that it tasted much the same regardless of where the grapes had been grown or who had produced it. It was almost inevitably made from shiraz, perhaps with a little grenache or mataro thrown in; it was certainly high in alcohol and equally high in pH; new oak would have played no part in its composition, and it smelt and tasted more as if it had been baked than fermented. Australians were used to the roasted, leathery aromas and flavours, whereas they came as a considerable shock to the few intrepid visitors from overseas who came to our shores.

AUSTRALIAN WINE SALES
1970/71–1983/84

Source: Australian Bureau of Statistics

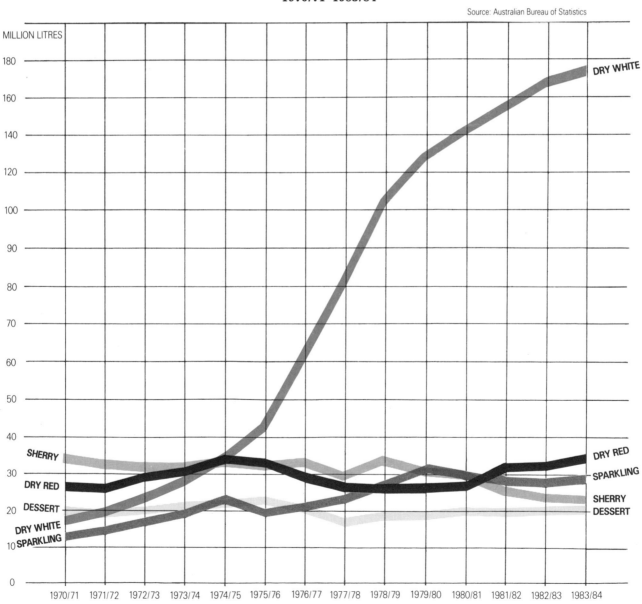

SALES OF AUSTRALIAN TABLE WINE BY TYPE AND CONTAINER SIZE
1978–1984

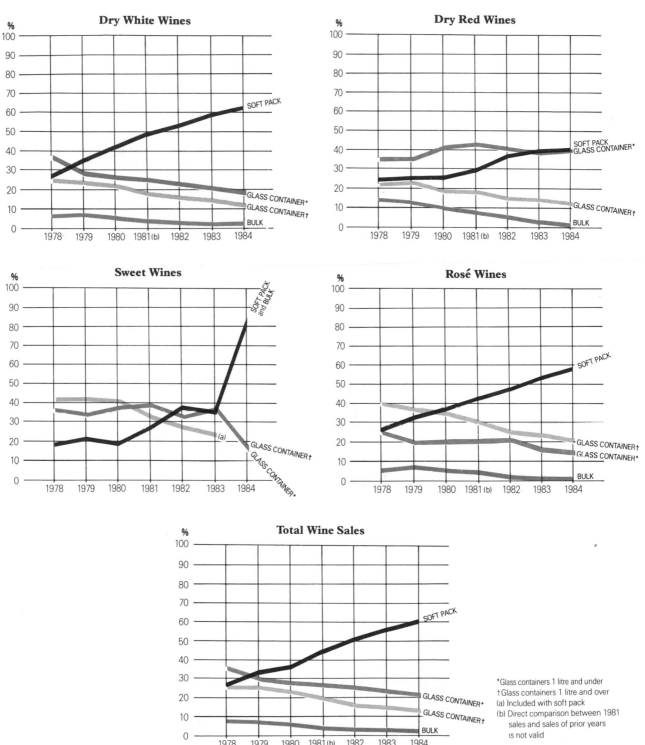

Clearly that description is something of a caricature; certainly there were small quantities of high-quality table wine which in no way resembled the mass. Maurice O'Shea in the Hunter Valley with the Mount Pleasant reds, Colin Preece at Great Western, Max Schubert with the early Grange

Hermitages, and Bill Redman at Coonawarra were among those producing wines of great individuality, finesse and style. Nonetheless, these were pin-points on a sea of otherwise unrelieved boredom.

Progressively throughout the 1960s, and even more in the 1970s, the pattern has changed. Cool-climate areas (chiefly the south-east of South Australia), the cabernet family (cabernet sauvignon, cabernet franc, merlot and malbec), cool fermentations and new oak have all come together to transform the style of Australian red wine. Shiraz has become an innocent and undeserving casualty; but grenache and mataro have been rightly sentenced to extinction. Pinot noir has had more chances than it deserves, but in the "cool corner" of Australia will in all probability ultimately prove its worth.

The two most important architects of current red-wine style have been Max Schubert and Wolf Blass. Curiously they have approached wine with radically different philosophies: Schubert always wished to make wines which demanded 10 years and would benefit from 20 years in bottle; Wolf Blass wanted to produce a wine which would be close to its peak when released at four or five years of age. Despite this divergence of approach, both believe that the greatest red wines are blends of varieties from different districts; and both see the role of the new oak barrel as an integral part of red winemaking and not simply to impart flavour. Thus both used oak barrels to finish the primary fermentation, a technique practised by relatively few other Australian red winemakers.

Not only has cabernet sauvignon become far more common, but its taste has changed too. In the mid-1970s leafy, herbaceous cabernets (with an edge of green stalkiness) became common for the first time. At first winemakers and wine judges were entranced to see these overtones of Bordeaux; but it was then realised that these characters were often obtained at the expense of mid-palate fruit flavour and undermined the cellaring potential of the wine. Early picking of cabernet sauvignon was not in itself the answer. Nonetheless, it acted as a catalyst for the re-appraisal of cabernet sauvignon (and indeed all grapes) grown in warmer areas, and for a growing appreciation of the role of pH in determining red-wine quality. Instead of automatically aiming for a wine with 13 degrees of alcohol, winemakers began to consider the 11.5 and 12-degree options. The result: fresher wines, with more fruit flavour, better acidity, and sometimes better cellaring potential.

Then came the mid-Victorian mint characters, and more recently the stewed plum pudding/mulberry/meaty flavours of Coonawarra; these have presented the consumer with an ever-widening range of choice. While in the long term certain of the flavours may be seen as undesirable, we have certainly reached the stage where no longer do all Australian red wines taste the same.

The last and most recent development has been that of the light red. Efforts to produce a light red, largely aimed at bolstering the declining consumption of red wine, started in the mid-1970s with such offerings as Rosemount's Melon Creek, Peter Lehmann's 1976 Saltram Carbonic Maceration Cabernet Sauvignon, April Red, Summer Red, Beauvais . . . a host of hopefuls appeared, to flicker briefly and then disappear from sight. At long last Hickinbotham Winemakers, with Cab Mac, appear to have produced on a consistent basis a light red with all of the necessary qualities. The marketplace is still to make up its mind finally; if it rejects Cab Mac, light-red winemaking must surely be at an end.

Overall, the red-wine market appears at long last to be on the road back. It reached its nadir in 1978–79, and since that year consumption has steadily increased. That of 1983–84 was identical to that of 1975–76, having increased every year since 1979–80. What is more, the rate of increase in the last year was virtually the same as that of dry white, which is flattening out at last.

Flattening out the white-wine market may be, but it has been a white-wine boom (and nothing else) which has seen per capita consumption increase from 12.3 to 20.5 litres per capita per annum in the last 10 years. There have been four distinct phases in the development of Australian white-wine style leading up to and then forming part of this explosion.

The first, and in many ways the most important, occurred in the period 1953 to 1960, when fermentation in stainless steel under pressure (and thereafter with temperature control replacing pressure) was introduced into Australia. Prior to that time white wines were fermented in old oak vats in much the same way as red wines. Together with the development of the new fermentation techniques came a move to early bottling within months of the end of fermentation. Prior to that time the tendency had been to leave white wines in large, old oak for at least 12 months after vintage.

The new wines bore little or no resemblance to those that had preceded them, and were undoubtedly very much better, but the public was by and large unimpressed. By the end of the 1960s the Australian Wine Board was running campaigns to try to persuade people to drink more white wine in an endeavour to relieve some of the pressure on red-wine stocks.

It was at this time that, quite coincidentally, the second of the four changes in white-winemaking techniques occurred. As filtration technology improved, and techniques for chemical analysis likewise, the practice of leaving a certain amount of unfermented sugar in white ceased to be the hazardous course it had once been. From the mid-1960s winemakers gradually increased the residual sugar in the aromatic varieties, headed by rhine riesling and traminer. This had a dramatic effect on the bulk end of the market in particular: the sugar not only filled out the flavour of otherwise bland and uninteresting wine, but also gained access to a vast section of the public that had never before consumed wine. Ben Ean Moselle at one time dominated the bottled-wine market like no other wine before or since. It is no longer Australia's largest-selling wine, but still accounts for 300,000 cases a year. So when one sees statistics that indicate that 175 million litres of dry white table wine have been sold in the year 1983–84, read 150 million litres of moselle-style wine, probably packaged in a cask, and 25 million litres of dry white wine in bottles.

The third major development has been associated with the appearance of chardonnay and sauvignon blanc; that is, the emergence of the wood-matured white burgundy style of wine made from either those two varieties or from semillon (or from a blend of several). These are very complex wines which, with their generosity of flavour, are food wines. It is these which more often than not accompany the upwardly mobile businessperson's lunch.

Finally, in the last few years white-wine technology has taken another quantum leap with a winemaking regime which starts at the time the grapes are harvested in the vineyard and continues until the wine is bottled and has a single purpose in mind: to rigorously exclude oxidation in any form. This has resulted in white table wines with aromas and flavours which had previously been lost but which are legitimately part of grape flavour. Also, botrytis has become a frequent visitor in many of the cool areas, and particularly Coonawarra. This microscopic mould, known as noble rot, modulates and intensifies grape flavour in many ways, which are later discussed at some length in this book.

Where, then, is the future of Australian wine headed? At least at the quality end, it is headed back into the vineyard. The great advances of the last 20 years have all taken place in the winery; the great advances of the next 20 will be among the vines.

Terroir is a word which the French understand very well and frequently use. I have unashamedly borrowed it for the purposes of this book. It is a single word which connotes altitude, slope, aspect, surface-soil composition, subsoil composition and soil structure. The French have not been clever enough to devise a special word for climate, but if they had it would encompass annual rainfall, growing season rainfall, relative humidity, day/night temperature range, mean January temperature, and heat-degree days from October to March. These are all fundamentally important component parts of viticultural climate, so it is "climate" that I shall use.

The dual effect of *terroir* and climate is of critical importance in determining grape quality. Modern viticultural techniques are able to modify and control significantly major components of both *terroir* and climate, principally through soil-management techniques, and through trellising and vine-training systems which bear no resemblance to those of years gone by.

Good though the Australian wines of 1985 may be, those of the year 2000 will be better.

New South Wales

It is virtually impossible to visualise the hardships and difficulties that confronted the first settlers in Australia. The meagre supplies of food which survived the long trip from England were quickly exhausted, and for decades a subsistence-style self-sufficiency was the aim of all farmers. It was inevitable that grape vines would figure in the inventory of plants carried by the First Fleet, and not surprising that right from the outset attention would be paid to vine propagation and winemaking.

By the standards of today, public support for winemaking (and drinking) came from an extraordinarily diverse range of viewpoints. Most surprising was that of some temperance activists, who promoted wine as a healthy and sober alternative to fiery home-brewed and imported spirits. This theme runs right through the nineteenth century, and naturally was enthusiastically adopted by those with a vested interest in the wine industry. So it was that James Busby dedicated his *Manual of Plain Directions for Planting and Cultivating Vineyards*, published in 1830, with these words:

> The design is to increase the comforts, and promote the morality of the lower classes of the colony; and more especially of the native-born youth.
>
> Those who have witnessed the temperance and contentment of the lowest classes of people in the Southern Countries of Europe, where wine is the common drink of the inhabitants . . . will appreciate the importance of introducing the one beverage, and diminishing the use of the others, in a community constituted like New South Wales, in which the high price of labour is calculated to allow the almost unlimited use of ardent spirits, and where the excitement they produce, is more likely than in most other countries to terminate in mischievous results.

Spirits—and the Rum Rebellion—did indeed dominate proceedings for a brief time, but beer (rather than wine) became "the one beverage", the national drink. Nonetheless, wine soon became a staple commodity, its production spreading like ripples from the stone dropped on the shores of Farm Cove in the vicinity of what is now Government House, which is where vines were first grown.

Gregory Blaxland produced the first commercial wine at Brush Farm on the banks of the Parramatta River near what is now Ermington. His, too, were the first wines to be exported to England, in 1823 and again five years later. Another famous pioneer family, the Macarthurs, also figured prominently in the early development of vineyards. Captain John Macarthur assembled a large collection of cuttings in Europe during an 18-month trip in 1815 and 1816; not many survived, but those which did formed the basis of a substantial vineyard and winery operation which the family established at Camden Park.

With the exception of Camden Park, Rooty Hill (Penfolds) and Smithfield (Laraghy's Kaluna) the vineyards of the Sydney metropolitan area did not survive for long. But before the Hunter Valley was established vines were tried in all sorts of strange places. In the first few years of the 1800s Bathurst had as many hectares of vines as did Sydney. One can only speculate that spring frosts quickly deterred the aspiring vignerons, for subsequent census statistics make no reference to the area.

Vines arrived in the Hunter Valley at the end of the 1820s; in May 1825 James Busby acquired a property halfway between Branxton and Singleton which he named Kirkton. He installed his brother-in-law William Kelman as manager. Given Busby's consuming interest in viticulture, it seems highly likely a few vines would have been established immediately, although the first recorded plantings were in 1830, expanded to four hectares in 1834. George Wyndham was the other pioneer, and he also planted vines in 1830. The 600 cuttings which were given to him by James Busby failed to take, so he tried again (with greater success) the following year. By 1832 there were 10 vineyards in existence, varying in size from less than half to little over one hectare.

From these humble beginnings the Hunter Valley industry grew rapidly, and I follow its course in Chapter 2. In 1849 George Wyndham took vine cuttings to a large holding he had acquired at Inverell, known as Bukkulla. By 1870 the Bukkulla vineyard was producing 50,000 litres of rich, dark, full-bodied wine per year which—in a foretaste of the 1970s—was blended with the lighter-bodied Dalwood reds to produce a much-esteemed, rich, full-flavoured burgundy. It remained in production until 1890 and the economic depression which led to the great bank crash of 1893.

In 1858 Adam Roth planted vines at Mudgee; and around the same time a number of small vineyards were commenced at Corowa on the Victorian border just to the west of Albury, where J. T. Fallon established a famous vineyard which remained in production until destroyed by phylloxera in 1906. The McWilliam family planted vines at Junee in 1895, while back on the outskirts of Sydney an Italian-born doctor, Thomas Henry Fiaschi, established a vineyard at Sackville Reach on the Hawkesbury River in the 1880s.

Thus by the end of the 1800s vines had been planted across much of the State; only the hot and dry western half remained untouched.

Yet notwithstanding that it has always been an important winegrowing State, and while the Hunter Valley has always had an enviable reputation for producing extremely fine table wine, the State has never assumed the dominant position one might have expected of it. What is more, only the Hunter Valley, Mudgee and the Murrumbidgee Irrigation Area have changed significantly in the aftermath of the wine boom.

Nor has there been any exciting new area to which aspiring vignerons have flocked. If anything, the scope of the viticultural map has shrunk: Junee went out of production in the 1950s, and Rooty Hill in the mid-1970s. Admittedly neither of these two regions was ever particularly significant commercially, but both produced some remarkable wines.

I do not see this situation changing, particularly if one excepts the Australian Capital Territory and its surrounds. The difficulties of establishing a viable vineyard and winery operation in a new and relatively isolated region are immense. The distances, and the size of the land holdings, militate against a concentration of viticultural activities in a new area unless it is seen to have outstanding potential. True enough, the major wine companies found Padthaway/Keppoch in an as seemingly remote and featureless place as one could imagine, while the doctors of the Margaret River have created a legend in a few short years. But these are exceptions, and in each case there were powerful climatic and geological reasons pointing to viticulture.

If there is to be a new area of real promise established, it is likely to be somewhere on the slopes of the Great Dividing Range. Because of the latitude, the climate of New South Wales is now generally regarded as being too warm unless one goes up the mountainside. The Catch 22 is that if one does this, spring frosts become a major viticultural hazard. Perhaps the Armidale/Glen Innes/

Inverell region has the most potential in the north. Inverell was a significant wine producer in the last century, and Keith Whish has made wine at his Gilgai vineyard for the past 17 years.

Further south, there are a surprising number of areas—principally on the inland slopes of the Great Dividing Range—in which grapes are grown and wine is made. In the hills, as it were, are Mudgee, Wellington, Molong, Bathurst, Cowra, Young and Junee, all of which either presently or in the past produce or have produced grapes. But only Mudgee, and to a lesser degree Cowra, have any real commercial significance; and, as we shall see, even these are really too warm to meet the criteria of contemporary viticultural thought.

So it is that the future of winemaking in New South Wales is likely to remain where it is concentrated today: the Sunraysia area around Mildura; the Murrumbidgee Irrigation Area around Griffith; Mudgee; and of course the Lower and Upper Hunter Valley.

LINDEMANS CELLARS, LATE NINETEENTH CENTURY

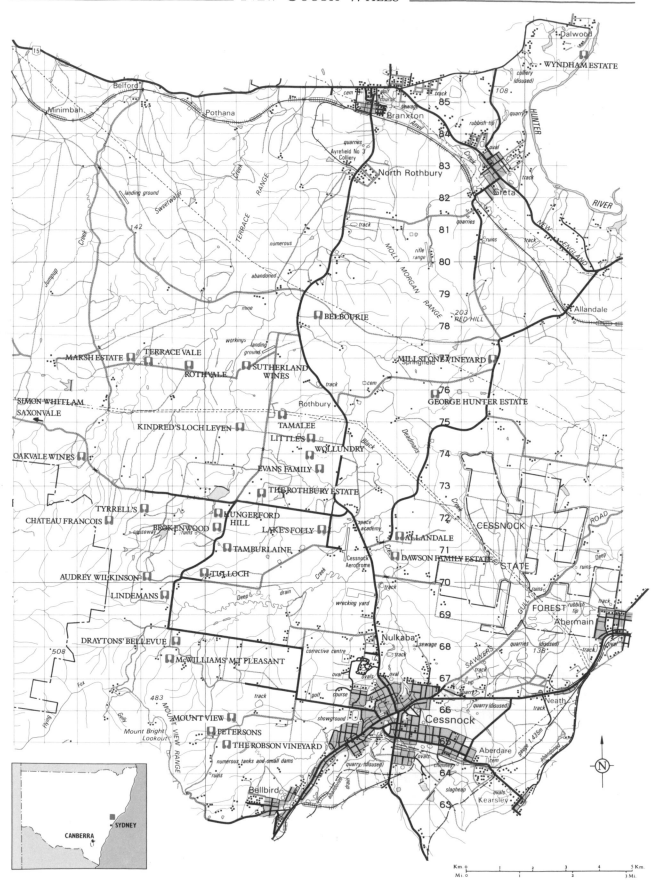

Dalwood

WYNDHAM ESTATE

colliery (disused)

Belford

Minimbah

Pothana

cem golf course

sewage

85

track

108

Branxton

84

rubbish tip

quarry

HUNTER

quarries
Ayrefield No 3
Colliery

North Rothbury

83

82

oval

Greta

track

NEW ENGLAND

RIVER

landing ground

Sweetwater

142

TERRACE RANGE

numerous

track

quarries

81

ruins

track

80

rifle range

79

MOLLY MORGAN RANGE

203 RED HILL

Allandale

abandoned

moe

BELBOURIE

78

workings

landing ground

MARSH ESTATE

TERRACE VALE

MILLSTONE VINEYARD

Springfield

ROTHVALE

SUTHERLAND WINES

track cem

76

GEORGE HUNTER ESTATE

SIMON WHITLAM
SAXONVALE

Rothbury

75

KINDRED'S LOCH LEVEN

TAMALEE

LITTLE'S

Deadmans

WOLLUNDRY

Black

74

OAKVALE WINES

EVANS FAMILY

73

CESSNOCK

THE ROTHBURY ESTATE

72

Creek

ROAD

TYRRELL'S

HUNGERFORD HILL

space academy

CHATEAU FRANCOIS

BROKENWOOD

LAKE'S FOLLY

ALLANDALE

STATE

Deep

causeway

ruins

ruins

TAMBURLAINE

Cessnock
Aerodrome

DAWSON FAMILY ESTATE

71

AUDREY WILKINSON

TULLOCH

track

70

ruins

FOREST

LINDEMANS

Deep

drain

wrecking yard

69

rubbish tip

track

Abermain

DRAYTONS' BELLEVUE

508

Nulkaba

sewage

68

quarries (disused)

138

oval

track

Neath

corrective centre

McWILLIAMS' MT PLEASANT

track

67

tip

quarry

Fox Gully

Flying Gully

483

track

golf course

oval

ovals

66

showground

quarry (disused)

track

gauge 1,435m

MOUNT VIEW RANGE

MOUNT VIEW

Cessnock

PETERSONS

65

Aberdare

cem

abandoned

THE ROBSON VINEYARD

Mount Bright
Lookout

numerous tanks and small dams

quarry (disused)

64

ruins

ovals

chimney

slagheap

ovals

Kearsley

Bellbird

63

N

Km. 0   1   2   3   4   5 Km.
Mi. 0   1   2   3 Mi.

Lower Hunter Valley

From the earliest days vines flourished in the Hunter Valley, and it quickly became the most important winemaking region in the State. Vineyards were spread north from the outskirts of Newcastle towards Clarence Town; north-north-west along the course of the Paterson River; in a complex skein running west by north along the Hunter and its tributaries past Branxton to Singleton and beyond; and finally in an arc around the north of Cessnock.

In 1847 the Hunter Valley Viticultural Association was formed; that decade saw plantings increase from 80 to 200 hectares spread over more than 50 vineyards. While the properties were generally large, each devoted only a small area to grape growing and many did not possess a winery. Relatively few vineyards exceeded 10 hectares, and most were only one or two hectares in extent.

In the light of subsequent developments it is curious that most of these early vineyards and wineries were all established north of the Maitland to Singleton road, and that the first vignerons did not come to the Cessnock-Pokolbin area until the 1860s. The names of most of the wineries have long since passed into history: Lewinsbrook, Trevallyn, Gostwyck, Glen Oak, Brandon, Irrawang, Kinross, Tomago, Oswald, Gostforth, Luskintyre, Cornhill, Bebeah and New Freugh. Only Cawarra, Kirkton and Porphyry (all preserved by Lindemans as brand names) and Dalwood have survived.

From the very start a wide variety of wines and wine styles was produced, employing an impressive array of grape varieties. At the inaugural tasting organised by the Viticultural Association, held in 1848, W. Burnett showed a pink-and-white champagne; Edwin Hickey an 1846 Hock from an unspecified blend of grapes; James King an 1844 Semillon (then called shepherd's riesling, and in due course Hunter River riesling) and a sweet dessert wine made from raisined grapes; while William Kelman provided an 1845 Red Hermitage and a White Burgundy said to be made from white pinot (the last presumably chardonnay, but possibly pinot blanc).

A few years later James King was among a number of New South Wales exhibitors who entered wines in the great Paris Exhibition of 1855, which led to the classification of the wines of Bordeaux, a classification which remains in force to this day. The official report of the judges on the New South Wales entries said:

> The wines included white wines akin to those of the Rhine; red light wines like those of Burgundy; Musseux varieties with a bouquet, body and flavour equal to the finest champagnes; Muscats and other sweet wines, rivalling the Montignac of the Cape.

King was the only exhibitor of sparkling wines, and one of his medal-winning entries (along with one of Macarthur's) was selected to be served to Napoleon III at the banquet which marked the end of the exhibition.

Yet another exhibition, held in Bordeaux in 1882, provides a wealth of information about the progress of viticulture in the Hunter Valley. Most noteworthy is the wide range of grape varieties represented in the entries, and the predominance of varietal rather than brand labelling. H. J. Lindeman won a silver medal for the only Australian Lachrymae Christi I have ever heard of, and there was a fair sprinkling of hocks and clarets throughout the entries. But far more numerous were wines labelled as hermitage, black pineau (the old spelling of pinot noir), verdelho, white pineau and verdot (short for petite verdot); an 1882 vintage from Dalwood made entirely from the latter variety won a gold medal. Of the noble grape varieties, only cabernet sauvignon and rhine riesling were missing.

Between 1866 and 1876 the Hunter Valley wine industry grew at a rate as spectacular as the boom which followed almost exactly 100 years later. The number of wine presses increased from 116 to 339;

production from 756,000 litres to 3.75 million litres; and the area under vines rose from 860 hectares to 1800 hectares. 1876 appears to have been the peak; by 1882 plantings had declined to 1630 hectares, although by and large the industry remained fairly prosperous until the economic woes of the 1890s. Both Victoria and New South Wales had placed prohibitive duties on wines from other States, effectively locking out South Australia. Federation, and Section 92 of the Constitution, changed all that; and the first 50 years of the twentieth century saw the Hunter drawing in on itself.

This was due not only to the removal of trade barriers but also to the marked change in both production and consumption. The two largest and most successful Hunter Valley companies (Lindemans and McWilliam's) depended principally on their fortified-wine sales: these came not from the Hunter but from Corowa and north-eastern Victoria in the case of Lindemans, and from Griffith and Yenda in the case of McWilliam's. Even then success was heavily qualified: Lindemans spent two decades (from 1923 until 1947) in the hands of a receiver appointed by the Commercial Banking Company of Sydney. By 1950 there were only eight wineries in operation: Lindemans, McWilliam's, Tyrrell's, Tulloch's, Draytons, Elliotts, Wilkinsons and Phillips. In 1956, close to the nadir of the Valley, there were only 466 hectares of vines in production, a year in which fortified-wine sales accounted for 81 per cent of total Australian sales.

Just how fine the wines of the last century were is a challenge to the imagination of all wine lovers. The absence of diseases (and in particular downy and powdery mildews) must have been an enormous advantage, and certainly facilitated the making of a wide range of styles. One of the best guides comes from the performance of Alexander Munro of Bebeah Vineyard, who consistently won gold medals in the major international shows which were so much a part of the growth in international commerce in the second half of the nineteenth century. In the Melbourne International Exhibition of 1881 he fought a battle royal with Hubert de Castella's St Hubert's Winery (from the Yarra Valley). St Hubert's was awarded the prize for the most successful exhibitor in the wine section by the barest of margins; it went on to win the prize for the most meritorious exhibit in the entire show, competing against felt hats and steam engines in so doing. In the light of the cool climate/warm climate debate of today, it was hardly a convincing demonstration of the superiority of the former.

The virtual disappearance of the fortified-wine market, and the subsequent domination of the table-wine market by whites, has worked in favour of the Hunter Valley. It will doubtless remain the most important quality-wine area in New South Wales for the next century at least. Just how much it will owe to the proximity of the vast markets of Sydney and Newcastle, and how much to the inherent quality of its wine, is a matter which is likely to be fiercely debated over that century.

Hunter Valley vignerons react with extreme vigour when the question of cool-climate winemaking is raised. But in truth the debate is illusory. The undeniable facts are that the Hunter has an extremely hot climate, but that a series of compensating factors (coupled increasingly with clever winemaking and improved viticultural practices) result in the production of table wines of a highly individual style and undoubted quality.

That is particularly true of the dry white semillons of the region: given a minimum of three years bottle age (and up to 20 or more) a well-made Hunter semillon has all the complexity of a high-quality French burgundy. Indeed, I have seen more than one eminent English wine writer confuse two such wines when placed next to each other in a "blind tasting". On each occasion the Australian wine was Lindemans 1964 White Burgundy Bin 2510; the French a distinguished white burgundy of the same vintage. And one might imagine that with the wholesale advent of chardonnay, the scope for confusion will increase.

I will come back to consider the style of Hunter wines (both white and red) in a moment, but before I do so, it is necessary to consider the climate and the *terroir*. *Terroir*, as I mentioned before, is a word I have unashamedly borrowed from the French, and it indicates not only soil, but subsoil, aspect and slope; that is, situation in its broadest sense. And when one looks at the climate and the *terroir* of the Hunter Valley objectively, the only possible conclusion is that one ought to forget vineyards and graze cattle instead.

Why? First, because the Hunter has what has been classified as a very hot climate; other Australian wine-producing regions falling in this group are Mildura, the Swan Valley, Angle Vale (near Adelaide), Griffith and Loxton. It has a centigrade heat-degree day summation of 1874, compared with 1517 for Nuriootpa in the Barossa Valley, 1259 for Coonawarra, 1158 for Healesville in the Yarra Valley and 981 for Launceston. (Bordeaux has 1238, Dijon 1115 and Reims 1065.)

Second, many of the vineyards are established on relatively poor and unsuitable soils, principally heavy and poorly drained clays. There are four main types of soil in the Hunter, classified according to their geological origin. The commonest are the brown to grey-brown soils deriving from the Lower Marine Series of agglomerates, shales, tuffs and sandstones. Their texture and fertility vary greatly, from sandy to heavy clay loam and from fertile to barren. Some of the best white-wine vineyards were established on fertile sandy loams, such as the old Sunshine Vineyard of Lindemans.

Then there are the red to red-brown loams that occur in hillside patches which are volcanic in origin, deriving from carboniferous lavas, tuffs, shales and limestones. These well-drained, friable soils are the site of the greatest red-grape vineyards; Lake's Folly, McWilliam's Rosehill Vineyard and Draytons' Lambkin share one notable outcrop as one moves off the valley flat towards the foothills of the Brokenback Range, while many of Tyrrell's vineyards have such soils. The Mount View area, too, has more than its fair share of these.

The third group derives from Upper Marine Series sandstones, shales and conglomerates. They are characteristically poor, shallow soils, often low in humus and minerals with impervious yellow-orange clay subsoils only a few centimetres below the surface. Many of the vineyards established in the wine boom of the 1960s were established on these basically unsuitable soils.

Finally, there are the fertile alluvial sands and silts occupying the flats of major stream courses, from Recent and Pleistocene deposits. Fertile and free-draining, they nonetheless hold moisture well and are ideally suited to white-wine grapes. McWilliam's Lovedale Vineyard near the Cessnock airport and some of the old Wyndham Estate vineyards are established on such soils.

But overall yields (without irrigation) have been derisory. In 1956, 468 hectares of grapes then in production produced 945 tonnes of grapes, or almost exactly two tonnes per hectare (or 0.8 tonnes per acre). This was close to the low point in terms of acreage for the Hunter Valley in this century, and it is reasonable to assume that a process of natural selection had by and large eliminated the less suitable vineyards, leaving only the best in production.

When vineyard plantings exploded in the second half of the 1960s it was inevitable that many of them

VINTAGE TIME, HUNTER RIVER VINEYARDS, 1912

should be made on unsuitable *terroir*, and equally inevitable that within 10 or 15 years many of those boomtime babies should be abandoned—more of which anon. And while low-yielding vineyards may produce grapes of extremely high quality, we do not yet have in this country a price-fixing system which in any way reflects grape quality.

The third principal disadvantage of the Hunter Valley comes in the shape of a two-edged sword. The ideal rainfall pattern for vineyards is said to be winter/spring dominant, but with evenly distributed follow-up rain through the growing season. Drive through any of the great wine districts of France in summer and autumn, and the grass along the roadsides will always be a lush green. This is a sure sign that the vine has adequate moisture to ensure proper maturation and ripening of the grapes. The old idea that the drought years make great wines is arrant nonsense.

The Hunter has an annual rainfall of 740 milli-metres, of which two-thirds (433 millimetres) fall between October and March; worse still, it tends to be concentrated in the latter part—between January and March—just when the harvest is getting under way. I will never forget the agony of the 1976 and 1978 harvests at the vineyard of which I was at the time part-owner; my only consolation was that I missed the worst vintage of all (1971) by two years. More recently the 1984 vintage in the Hunter was largely spoilt by excessive rain, whereas for the rest of Australia it was one of the greatest in living memory. On the other side of the ledger, the drought years of 1979 to 1982 averaged only 614 milli-metres. Yet this high summer rainfall is a very necessary counterbalance to the extremely high water requirement of the vine in this hot climate. The growing-season water usage has been calculated at 450 millimetres, giving rise to a negligible deficit of 18 millimetres. In Griffith the deficit is 705 milli-metres, hence the absolute need for irrigation in that district.

How then, you ask, was the Hunter Valley chosen in the first place? The answer is, at least in part, by a process of elimination. The Sydney metropolitan area was too wet and humid, Bathurst (where a number of small vineyards were planted between 1800 and 1810) too prone to spring frosts. But there are a number of tangible compensations for the Hunter Valley.

First, it has the least number of sunshine hours per day during the growing season: 7.3 hours, a figure it shares with Launceston. Griffith has 9.3 hours, and even Bordeaux has more at 7.6 hours.

This is in part due to the rainfall I have discussed, but more importantly to the hazy afternoon cloud cover which comes with the sea breezes which temper the after-lunch heat. It is without question one of the major factors in the Hunter's otherwise inexplicable ability to produce such lovely wine.

Secondly, when the Hunter Valley was established none of the major vine diseases was in existence, either in Europe or Australia. In particular, downy mildew and powdery mildew (the latter called oidium in Europe) were the first introductions from America; phylloxera followed a few decades later. The first outbreak of powdery mildew struck France in 1854; phylloxera and downy mildew followed over the next 20 years.

The first record I have been able to find of oidium in the Hunter Valley is in 1896 when H. M. Mackenzie, reporting in the *Maitland Mercury*, wrote:

> Referring to that baneful disease oidium, which luckily has not been so widespread this year as last, Mr. Scobie (a vineyard owner) informs me that it swooped suddenly on the vines one memorable year, distributing itself all over the place—a strange feature being that its presence previously was unknown to vignerons.

Downy mildew, now the major scourge, did not become a significant problem until well after the Second World War. As late as 1949 Lindemans were making their Porphyrys from genuinely late-harvested, raisined fruit—they were able to leave the grapes on the vine long after normal harvest because mould was not the problem it is today. In a wet, humid climate the absence of these fungal diseases was of enormous significance. As Karl Mollenhauer, Lindemans' winemaker until 1959 and something of an amateur historian, put it: "The wetter the season, the bigger the crop." And indeed, the yields of those days were very much greater than most of today. As in many parts of Australia, soil fertility had built up over thousands of years, and whatever was planted grew readily. Thus in 1830 George Wyndham at Branxton was able to grow wheat, tobacco and maize, peach, lemon, loquat, olive, fig, quince and pome-granate trees; and an endless variety of vegetables. Hail, flood and fire wrought their toll, but the soil was there.

But in the Hunter, no less than elsewhere, the soil was not looked after properly: fertilisers were all but unknown, and in this land of plenty there was always another opportunity, another place to go to. Who would imagine, looking at the Wollombi Valley today, that it was once an extremely rich wheat- and crop-growing area, intensively cultivated and inhabited.

Thus Wyndham's Dalwood Vineyard at Branxton in 1886 produced over 11 tons to the acre (27.6 tonnes per hectare) from its 26-year-old white hermitage vines, and 5.5 tons (13.8 tonnes) from its shiraz. True enough, the district average was lower. The official government report on the showing of the wines of New South Wales in the 1882 Bordeaux International Exhibition said:

> The production of the vineyards exhibiting at Bordeaux was ascertained to be an average of 395 gallons per acre [4440 litres per hectare] with a minimum of 125 gallons [1405 litres per hectare] and a maximum 660 gallons [7417 litres per hectare], save on the Dalwood vineyard, where it attains 800 gallons per acre [8990 litres per hectare].

Given that (particularly in those days) no more than 150 gallons (682.5 litres) of wine would be made from a ton of grapes, the average yield was over 2.6 tons to the acre (6.5 tonnes per hectare). A century later, in a 1975 study of the economics of wine-grape production in the Lower Hunter Valley, the New South Wales Department of Agriculture calculated the average yields for a typical large (115-hectare) vineyard to be 3.7 tonnes per hectare (1.5 tonnes per acre) for cabernet sauvignon; 4.3 tonnes per hectare (1.75 tonnes an acre) for rhine riesling and shiraz; and five tonnes per hectare (two tonnes per acre) for semillon.

The conclusions drawn by that study were little short of devastating. They were:

1. Although the hypothetical study vineyard was large and reasonably efficiently managed, it showed a negative return on capital invested of 1.3 per cent before any allowance was made for interest on borrowed funds, let alone capital repayments. There was, in other words, no ability to service any debt.
2. Because efficient management was predicated, increased yields were the only way to increase financial returns.
3. For the capital investment to yield a 10 per cent return (before tax and interest) the average yield had to rise by 65 per cent.
4. Labour costs accounted for approximately 60 per cent of total production costs. Thus any changes in the cost of labour would have a substantial effect on profitability.
5. If mechanical harvesting were to be prevented by unfavourable conditions (too wet), total production costs would rise by up to 20 per cent, with a consequent effect on profitability.

I have dwelt at some length on these rather gloomy aspects of viticulture because they explain the vast changes, not to mention the trauma, which have occurred in the aftermath of the wine boom, and are an essential part of putting the Hunter Valley into its true perspective.

The Valley in 1956 was a rather sleepy place: it was about that time I made my first visit to it, and I remember it well. Only Lindemans and McWilliam's were selling labelled wine on a commercial level, and Tulloch had recently been persuaded to follow suit by Harry Brown, who then worked for Johnnie Walker at Rhinecastle. Tyrrell, Drayton, Elliott and Tulloch (the other four producing wineries) sold their output to either Lindemans or McWilliam's, or to interstate wine companies (notably Mildara and Thomas Hardy) or to wine merchants such as Rhinecastle and Caldwells. Winery tours and cellar-door sales as we know them today were non-existent.

Overall table-wine consumption was minuscule: although separate figures for dry white, dry red and fortified-wine sales were not kept at that time, table-wine consumption was less than two litres per capita per annum, compared to the present figure of close to 20 litres. But the first stirrings of change were in the air; the complex web of social, racial and economic factors, which I discuss elsewhere in this book, was beginning to take effect. The first tangible sign was the bulky figure of Dr Max Lake prowling the hillsides and flats with a posthole digger, looking for land suitable for a vineyard on which he intended to fly in the face of contemporary wisdom and plant that odd grape, cabernet sauvignon.

His search over, Lake planted the bright-red soils of Lake's Folly with his beloved cabernet sauvignon in the winter of 1963. A few years later Cessnock medical practitioner Dr Lance Allen followed suit at Tamburlaine, and across the Valley Jim Roberts did the same at Belbourie. It is curious that it was the amateurs who provided the spark which quickly became a blaze, rather than the big companies already established or the big names soon to appear. In any event, what 70 years earlier had been described by a reporter observing the Clare Valley as "vine mania", took hold. I was one of the small fry infected, and commenced a search for suitable land at the end of the 1960s, a time when activity was nearing its peak.

Coincidentally, in June 1970 the Australian Wine Board released the first national statistics covering all of the major winegrowing regions in Australia. These gave details of the acres of vines in bearing as at 30 June 1969; the acres of vines planted at that date but not in bearing; and the acres of new vines planted between 30 June and 30 September of that year. (Vines are always planted in the second half of winter: in other words, between those two dates.) If ever a snapshot of a wine industry in a state of frantic change was to be taken, this was the time.

There were 591 hectares of bearing vines in the Hunter Valley as at 30 June, with 282 hectares not yet in bearing. In that one winter 550 hectares of new vineyards were planted; and, in what turned out to be a tragic misreading of future market trends, 420 hectares were planted to shiraz (90 to semillon, 17 to cabernet sauvignon, and buried in the catch-all of "all others", less than one hectare of chardonnay).

The high-water mark was reached with the plantings in the winter of 1976. At the end of that year total hectares under vine reached 4137, twice the peak of the last golden age of the 1870s and 1880s, and almost 10 times the area of 20 years earlier. (All of the figures, incidentally, take in both the Lower and Upper Hunter.)

By 1981 the figure had decreased to 3479 hectares; two years later only 3169 hectares remained, although there are indications that the rate of decline has been arrested. But even here the statistics tell only half the story. Most ominous of all has been the wholesale vacation of the Lower Hunter by the major companies. Prior to its eventual sale to Allied Vintners Limited, Gilbeys had sold off virtually all of Tulloch's Hunter Vineyards. Seppelt, who established a large vineyard on the outskirts of Cessnock in the early 70s, sold it late in 1982 to a wealthy investor who wished for a pretty location for a weekend home. McWilliam's sold their One Hundred Acre Vineyard (next door to Rothbury) in 1983; Lindemans has over the past few years quietly disposed of most of its Lower Hunter vineyards and established new ones on the fertile river flats at Broke, halfway between the Lower and Upper Hunter; while first Hungerford Hill and then Rothbury sold a significant portion of their vineyards, in addition to placing large areas (presumably unsalable) on a care and maintenance basis.

These changes have by no means invariably reflected themselves in reduced plantings; the purchasers have in many instances kept the vineyards in production, seemingly hoping to prove their erstwhile owners wrong. While the sales have been at a fifth (or even less) of the replacement cost, it seems to me only a matter of time before many of these vineyards, too, go out of production. Many of the companies I have mentioned (along with Arrowfield and Penfolds in the Upper Hunter, Saxonvale, Hermitage Estate, Wyndham and others in the Lower Hunter) had already accepted that reality with vineyard land they had either planted or acquired, and which they recognised was simply not marketable at any price.

The reasons are, obviously enough, economic. Much of the land which has been in effect abandoned was capable of producing grapes of excellent quality if the vintage conditions were not too unkind. But most of it was planted to shiraz with the balance to semillon, and the yields were far too low. The cost of grape production has exceeded the price for the grapes in what has been since the latter part of the 70s a substantially oversupplied market.

Perhaps a real-life example will best explain what is at once the weakness and the strength of the Lower Hunter. Prior to the 1978 vintage the winery of which I was then a part-owner took an option over 16 hectares of vineyard adjoining the four hectares it already owned. Brokenwood had done very well since it established that initial four hectares, but it needed more grapes. Hungerford Hill, by contrast, was in the middle of a major surgery exercise, and so it was that for $1500 an acre ($3705 per hectare) (with the 1978 crop included if we exercised the option) we were able to buy that 16-hectare block. It is a block which is unlikely to produce more than four tonnes per hectare (unless irrigated), and the annual running costs back in 1975 were over $1100 per hectare on the Agriculture Department study, and have since risen to at least $1800 per hectare. With shiraz bringing less than $250 per tonne in 1978 (and not a great deal more now), it is obvious why Hungerford Hill were sellers at almost any price. It is perhaps not so obvious, however, why Brokenwood was a willing purchaser.

The answer is two-fold. Firstly, any winemaker prefers to have control over all aspects of the growing and harvesting of the grapes that will be used. Secondly, we were not in the business of selling grapes but of making wine, and a great deal of synergy exists. Part at least stems from the expectation the public has that great wine will be estate-grown. Robert Mondavi of California has developed a ready-reckoner for grape prices: for every $100 per tonne you pay for your grapes, you must receive back $1 in retail value. In other words, at $800 per tonne you must receive $8 per bottle. And the simple fact was that Brokenwood could command far closer to $8 per bottle for its wine (and sell it far more quickly) than could Hungerford Hill.

Put simply, the Lower Hunter is a high-cost area which depends to a considerable degree on the marketing skills of its wineries to harness the enormous buying power of the Sydney and Newcastle markets. For the boutique wineries, this was relatively easy until the last few years; the public enjoyed visiting and discovering such places, and conversely still has the overwhelming perception that the big companies do not make the best wine. Over the past few years the level of competition between "boutiques" across the length and breadth of Australia has increased very sharply, and no longer does the consumer necessarily believe that what is small is beautiful. So it is that the small winery which produces good wine (and makes a reasonable marketing effort) will do quite well in the Hunter Valley, but the others will not. Further up the scale, marketing still becomes all-important, and the great success stories of the past 10 years—Tyrrell's and the Wyndham group in the Lower Hunter and Rosemount in the Upper Hunter—owe that success to the markets they have created, both nationally and overseas.

But enough of dry economics and of travelling salesmen: the Hunter happens to make some marvellous wine, none better than its semillon, for long known as Hunter River riesling (the table below shows the plantings as at 1 January 1984 of this and the other varieties I discuss). Traditionally made in large oak vats without any semblance of temperature control, and probably having been pressed in an old-style basket press, semillon always took a number of years for the initial hardness to soften and for the bouquet to build.

GRAPE VARIETIES	HECTARES
Cabernet sauvignon	227.7
Chardonnay	132.2
Chasselas	7.0
Clairette	36.3
Colombard	3.0
Frontignan	1.9
Marsanne	4.2
Mataro	9.4
Palomino	0.9
Pinot noir	23.3
Rhine riesling	32.0
Crouchen	3.0
Semillon	793.0
Sauvignon blanc	10.0
Shiraz	1099.0
Tokay	5.0
Traminer	78.0
Trebbiano	56.4
Verdelho	30.0
Others	71.0

One of the great white wines of the early 60s for those in the know was Lindemans' so-called London Hock. Shortly after the Second World War a consignment of Cawarra Hock had been sent to London. (A humble-enough middle-of-the-range commercial wine, it was at that time still made only from Hunter Valley grapes.) There it remained unsold and forgotten, until its importers found it 15 or so years later. They offered it back to Lindemans at cost, and so it came back to Australia, a glorious developed white wine at the peak of perfection.

One of the great pleasures of show judging, for me at least, is to judge the old white-wine classes. It is in these that the unique character of the 10- and 15-year-old Hunter semillon stands out. At their best—and in these old show classes Lindemans are rarely seriously challenged—these wines acquire an aroma of well-browned buttered toast, with perhaps a light helping of honey and nuts. Not surprisingly, the same characters come through on the velvety/biscuity/nutty palate; while the warm, rich, golden-yellow colour of the wine is entirely in keeping with its aroma and taste. The aftertaste is soft and languorous, and the acid is never assertive. These are the ultimate food wines, with enough structure and complexity to stand up to almost any dish.

This character and complexity were obtained without the use of any new oak, and without any of the aids of modern white-winemaking which are now regarded as quite essential. But there can be no doubt that for the first one or two years of their life such wines would have offered very little, whereas the dictates of financial managers and bankers now insist that almost all white wines be on the market within 12 months of their birth. This leads to the suspicion that such wines will not age well, but it by no means necessarily follows. The full force of modern technology (centrifuging of the juice before cold fermentation in stainless steel and relatively early bottling) was applied to the Rothbury Estate whites made by Gerry Sissingh between 1971 and 1979, and the oldest of those wines—particularly the '72 and the '73—are going from strength to strength.

The ever-increasing use of new oak adds yet a further dimension, and, to a degree, a further imponderable in the ageing equation. But for the life of me, I cannot see well handled oak maturation doing anything other than prolonging the life of the wine. For one thing, some oak tannins are imparted, which will have a preservative effect, while the careful winemaker will take every precaution to prevent oxidation. Certainly some of the newest semillons (made under the influence of the Oenotec team of Brian Croser and Dr Tony Jordan) show unfamiliar grassy/grapefruit aromas when young, but I have every confidence district character will assert itself in these wines given time.

Semillon is alive and well in the Hunter. It continues to make great wine which has a quite distinctive character. It would be a very great shame if the chardonnay and sauvignon blanc craze were to lead to its eclipse, in the manner of rhine riesling in South Australia, and shiraz all over the country. If you have never tasted an old Hunter semillon, try one on the next special occasion and I believe you will see what I am carrying on about.

Which leads me, obviously enough, to chardonnay and to the pioneering work of Murray Tyrrell emulating that of Max Lake with cabernet six years earlier. Chardonnay had been in existence in Australia since the earliest days; its progress in New South Wales has been documented well enough, appearing at Col Laraghy's Kaluna Vineyard at Smithfield on the outskirts of Sydney, then Alf Kurtz' vineyard at Mudgee, and finally at Penfolds HVD Vineyard in the Hunter. In other words, chardonnay was grown; it was left to Tyrrell to market it as such, although (with some degree of obstinacy) he still insists on labelling it Pinot Chardonnay. The grape is not a member of the pinot family, and the double-barrelled name is quite incorrect.

The first wine marketed by Tyrrell was his Bin 63, which took the mislabelling onto another plane, calling the blend of chardonnay and semillon, from which it was made, Pinot Riesling (riesling being the old fashioned abbreviation of Hunter River riesling, itself a completely incorrect name). That appalling Hunter vintage, 1971, saw the first Vat 47, his 100 per cent chardonnay. The last time I drank that wine—not so long ago I might add—it was thoroughly enjoyable, even if not in the same Olympian class as his 1973 and 1976 versions of the same wine.

The success of the chardonnay in the Hunter Valley puts the adaptability of the variety beyond doubt. Curiously, neither Lindemans nor McWilliam's have been especially successful with it, but numerous other makers in both the Upper and Lower Hunter have succeeded admirably. I remain to be convinced, however, that it is as suited to the climate of the Hunter as is semillon. Certainly it shouldn't be: chardonnay is classified as an early ripener, semillon a late ripener, and therefore suited to warmer climates. But these theoretical issues are less important than the wine in the bottle, and if you accept that one of the primary indicia of a truly great wine is its capacity to grow and improve in the bottle with age, semillon has proved itself and chardonnay certainly has not.

It is true that '73 and '76 and Vat 47 are great wines (although I am sure they will not improve further) but most of the chardonnays so far to come from the Hunter appear to reach their peak within two or three years of vintage, and to have little or none of the ageing capacity of their French counterparts. No less an authority than Murray Tyrrell throws in the further wild card, asserting that as the vines mature, the varietal definition of the grapes (and the wine) diminishes.

A host of other white grapes are grown in the Lower Hunter (clairette, traminer, rhine riesling, trebbiano, verdelho, sauvignon blanc and chenin blanc, in roughly that order) but with the exception of verdelho, none has any particular merit. Verdelho is grown in tiny quantities, chiefly by Lindemans but also by Harry Tulloch, and only 61 tonnes were crushed in the 1979 vintage (the last year for which I have detailed figures, but I am confident the acreage has not increased since). In 1968, 1972 and 1974 Lindemans made some remarkable wine from this grape; the 1968 Bin 3465 is my favourite, and I am currently drinking my way through my last case—I think the corks will expire long before the wine. But it seems to be an unfashionable variety, and I guess that it may be on the way to oblivion, pity though that may be.

Despite the fact that shiraz (or, as it is called in the Hunter, hermitage) has almost single-handedly born the brunt of the reduction in vineyard area, it remains by far the most important red grape. Just as in the case of Coonawarra, it was upon this grape—and this grape alone—that the reputation of the district was built. And at least so far as the residents of Sydney are concerned, Coonawarra and the Hunter Valley are the two finest wine districts in Australia.

The great wines of McWilliam's Maurice O'Shea, made between 1930 and 1956, were almost exclusively wrought from shiraz (pinot noir made a sporadic and usually minor contribution). These wines still fetch astronomical prices when they come up at auction, and the more cynical observer might say that this was due to the fact that no mention is made of the grape variety on the label. Rather there was simply the Mount Pleasant name followed by cryptic names such as Mountain C, Henry III, Richard, TY, and so on, which in fact indicated the source of the wine.

Traditional Hunter shiraz was never particularly deep in colour, big of body, or heavy in tannin, although alcohol levels could be impressive. When tasted at four or five years of age it was often difficult—if not downright impossible—to imagine that they would have the capacity to age gracefully in bottle for decades more. The other rather more controversial feature of those traditional red wines was their very distinct regional character, variously described as "cowshed", "sweaty saddle" and "tarry". I even heard one senior wine man, who really should have known better, once solemnly enunciate the theory that the particularly strong tarry aroma and taste that characterise many of McWilliam's wines were due to the roots of the old vines having reached the seams of coal which lie under much of the Hunter Valley.

I have long since made myself thoroughly unpopular with many Hunter vignerons by making clear my view that this character is nothing more or less than hydrogen-sulphide-derived mercaptan. While I remain unrepentant in my belief, I must admit it is fascinating to watch the development of Hunter shiraz in bottle. Those wines in which the mercaptan is particularly obvious (and obnoxious) at the outset seem to absorb and integrate the aroma gradually until it becomes part and parcel of an old wine with great character and individuality. Conversely, those wines which start out life with vibrant fresh fruit and no hint whatsoever of district character, seem to conjure some up magically as they age. I know, because I made 13 vintages, and have watched with something approaching awe as they have developed regional characteristics.

As with semillon, it seems to me that adolescent shiraz is a decidedly awkward customer, full of unpredictable temperament and not always terribly attractive: the vinous equivalent of a teenage face with a bad case of acne. Murray Tyrrell said to me recently: "I think the wines are some of the worst young wines in the country, full of H_2S [hydrogen sulphide] and so on." They gradually soften and open up; the more aged, the more graceful they become. An old Hunter shiraz of quality is a joy to drink; almost ethereal, gently velvety, with an immensely complex amalgam of animal, vegetable and fruit aromas and flavours. That description may sound implausible, if not downright unpleasant, but those who have extensive experience of these old wines will know it is true.

It highlights the fact that old wines are an acquired taste; Hunter reds likewise; and old Hunter reds doubly so. Far easier to come to terms with are the new-generation cabernet sauvignons, oak-matured and often looking not so different from the cabernets of many other regions. But do not think that I am decrying cabernet because of that; it is an accomplished traveller, and seems to assert its varietal character wherever it goes. What is more, its relatively loose bunch configuration, with its small berries and tough skins, enable it to withstand the rigours of a wet Hunter vintage far better than any other variety.

Cabernet franc, merlot and malbec are at present grown in tiny quantities only. Merlot, in particular, resolutely refuses to produce a meaningful crop two years out of three, and in some vineyards (notably Rothbury) has refused altogether. It is curious, because in Bordeaux it favours the clay soils above the gravels, and there is an abundance of the former in the Hunter. Nonetheless, I think these three varieties will make a greater (if still modest) contribution in the years to come.

Notwithstanding the apparent success Murray Tyrrell has had with the variety, I am absolutely convinced pinot noir has no place in the Hunter Valley. In exceptional years it can make a respectable regional light to medium red, but I defy anyone to say it has the least thing to do with pinot noir, if one accepts as the yardstick the red wines of Burgundy. McWilliam's reckoned it made a satisfactory wine on its own one year in 10; for the other nine they were content to blend it with shiraz. Lindemans had a small planting for many years; the only straight pinot they ever released was Bin 1600 from the exceptional red-wine vintage of 1959.

I may have left the Hunter Valley, but I wish it no harm. It has a proud history and a great reputation still. Its wines are different, but that is all to the good. We may need a world car; we most certainly do not need a world wine. The soft, velvety, fragrant reds and the voluptuous, honeyed whites are unmistakably the product of a warm climate, but that is no reason to denigrate them. If you do not like the style, so be it. There are sufficient (myself included) who do.

ALLANDALE
ALLANDALE ROAD, POKOLBIN

Allandale's unusual approach to making and marketing wine is a direct result of the initial training of winemaker-owner Ed Jouault as a chartered accountant, and of his initial involvement with the wine industry. Throughout the first part of the 1970s he worked successively for Saxonvale, Rothbury, McPhersons and Robsons in a management/accounting function. This gave him a unique insight into the economics of grape growing and winemaking, and determined the future structure of Allandale.

Jouault planned his entry into the industry with considerable care. In 1974 he enrolled as a student at the then-recently established wine course at the Riverina College of Advanced Education, learning his winemaking under the direction of Brian Croser. In 1978 he bought a 12-hectare property on the Allandale Road, not far from Cessnock airport, which had supported George Kime's vineyard in the latter part of the nineteenth century. The present Allandale winery is also adjacent to the site of one of the largest wineries in the Hunter Valley in the 1890s, also called Allandale.

When H. M. Mackenzie of the *Maitland Mercury* visited it in 1896 he had this to say:

> The Allandale cellars contained perhaps the largest stock of clarets and hocks in the Colony . . . The Allandale Claret, amongst other consumers, is highly appreciated by the Austrian Imperial Family—a scion of that family having, on a recent visit to Australia, carried away an immense quantity in his ship, moreover leaving Mr. Green [Allandale's owner] with orders to supply the Austrian warships with the best in his cellars. A wine-drinking Archduke's opinion should be worth something!

In another reminder that there is nothing new in sudden swings in consumption patterns, he noted that:

> Taking things altogether it is evident that the demand for claret holds its own well, a matter that cannot be said to apply to hock, which of late years seems to have become less sought after. Proof of this lies in the fact that one thousand gallons [4550 litres] of claret are annually sent away from Allandale to one hundred gallons [455 litres] of hock.

The winery had a capacity of 518,000 gallons (2.35 million litres) and quite evidently included some fine wine:

> Some of the six-year-old claret is as good as anything yet tasted. The first sampled [apparently from cask] was between five and six years, very dry, soft on the tongue and with a beautiful bouquet, and pleased me more than a sample of older wine which Mr. Green is maturing for an old customer, whose taste seems to lie in the direction of a rather full-bodied claret. The last, however, was a 9-year-old claret, as velvety on the tongue as milk, with a distinct flavour all of its own.

In 1891 Allandale was awarded the champion medal for New South Wales, and by that time had received over 70 awards in exhibitions around the world. It was technologically advanced for the time: it boasted "a machine used for the purpose of separating immediately the stalks from the fruit before finding its way into the presses"; a steam-engine was used for driving the crusher and cleansing casks; and centrifugal pumps were used for racking the wine.

Ed Jouault followed in the footsteps of his forebears by equipping the new Allandale with the latest plant when it opened its doors (just) in time for the 1978 vintage. His crusher had been offloaded at the wrong port, and arrived simultaneously with the first load of grapes. Jouault had in fact taken the decision that Allandale would make wine but not grow grapes, a decision which he modestly admits "worked nicely for Allandale". Given the economics of grape growing, and the prices prevailing through the late 1970s and early 1980s, that would seem to me to be a masterly understatement.

There is, of course, nothing new in buying in grapes from contract growers. But alone in the Lower Hunter, Allandale relied solely on outside growers. Even more unusually, the grape grower was clearly identified on the label, and each batch of grapes was kept separate. This inevitably led to a large number of releases in each year, and to a diversity of style within each varietal release. The system works well to this day, but the increasing marketplace competition and rising grape prices caused Jouault to think again in 1982. In that year he decided to plant two hectares each of chardonnay, semillon and pinot noir on his winery property. The pinot noir is established on the hill in front of the winery, while the chardonnay and semillon are across the road on the flats running down to a nearby creek.

As one would expect, it was a carefully thought-out decision. Jouault received Department of Agriculture confirmation that the alluvial soil on the creek flat was well suited for white grapes, and the creek provided a ready source to fill the 10-million-litre dam used to provide drip irrigation for the plantings. Jouault sees no reason why the yield should not reach between 10 and 12.5 tonnes per hectare, providing him with grapes at a significantly lower cost than the market would permit. The 1985 yield, in the third growing season, was between three and four tonnes per hectare, an encouraging start.

The pinot noir will no doubt yield less, but it is a variety that is virtually unprocurable from contract growers. While I have reservations about its suitability for red winemaking in all the exceptional years, it has already proved its worth as a sparkling wine base, and Jouault has demonstrated his skill in producing this kind of wine in the small batches he has so far produced.

Indeed, Jouault has shown his skill (and versatility) in making all kinds of wines, from dry white to red to sweet white to sparkling. Thus by the end of 1982 he was able to claim that all the chardonnays and cabernet sauvignons produced by Allandale since its inception had won gold or silver medals at Australian wine shows (including the Hunter Valley Wine Show, of course). At the 1984 Hunter Valley Wine Show Allandale was awarded a trophy, two gold, three silver and three bronze medals, which lifted its cumulative haul to four trophies, 14 gold, 28 silver and 55 bronze medals in seven years. The greatest success came at the 1982 Canberra National Wine Show. The 1980 Chardonnay from the Dawson Vineyard won the important Farmer Brothers' Trophy for the champion two-year-old chardonnay. The 1980 Cabernet Sauvignon was the top-pointed wine in the two largest red-wine classes in the show (with 137 entries), winning the 1980 and older Premium Dry Red (firm finish) Class with 56 points out of 60.

Yet I must be honest and say that not all of Allandale's wines have suited my palate. The whites, particularly, have been variable in quality, due (I suspect) in part to unsuccessful forays into "dirty French" winemaking techniques (including deliberately fermenting unclarified juice), and in part to some unsatisfactory grape sources. Thus some of the semillons have been rather coarse and heavy (particularly those from Leonard's Vineyard) while the more recent Dawson chardonnays have lacked the varietal fruit flavour of the great 1980 wine.

I think that this variability is accepted by Jouault. Together with the changing demands of the marketplace, it has led to the production of some varietal wines which are no longer from a single vineyard source, allowing greater flexibility in determining style, and also permitting larger quantities to be made to service the year-round needs of restaurants and the export market. It is the latter two markets which are supplementing the main sales source: cellar door and mailing list.

Over the years Jack Leonard, Petersons, George Hunter Estate (of Oliver Shaul), Dawson, Sutherland, Schlesinger, Oakdale and Trevina have all supplied grapes which have been made into vineyard wines. The number of names (and batches) will, as I say, reduce somewhat in future years, but contract-grown grapes will still account for 80 per cent of Allandale's production of around 7500 cases a year, even when the home vineyard is in full bearing.

AUDREY WILKINSON
DE BEYERS ROAD, POKOLBIN

The beautiful Oakdale Vineyard (often confused with Elliotts' Oakvale, and partly for that reason producing its wines under the Audrey Wilkinson label) is not only one of the most beautiful in the Hunter Valley, but also one of the most historic. It was established by Frederick Wilkinson in 1866, one of numerous vineyards with which members of the family were associated during the nineteenth century. These included Cote d'Or, Mangerton (replanted by Max Drayton), Maluna (replanted by Don Maxwell) and Coolalta and Catawba (both of which passed to Lindemans).

In a paper delivered to the Cessnock branch of the Australian Historical Society not long before his death, Audrey Wilkinson gave a vivid picture of Cessnock at the turn of the century:

> During the 1901–02 drought starving cattle were driven along Vincent Street (the main street), then an extremely dusty road between bare paddocks, to graze on Hector McDonald's property Barraba, which then comprised about 16,000 acres [6480 hectares] . . . As the starving cattle were travelling, wallabies hopped across the road in numbers; and near the site of the present railway station stood a stake with an application for the mineral lease of the present Aberdare Extended Colliery attached to it . . .

Wilkinson also recalled how Colonel Carew Reynell of Walter Reynell and Sons of South Australia visited the Oakdale Vineyard during the First World War (he died in action not long after):

> And as he arrived in our cellar he said to me, "Have you any of the hock you have been beating us with at all the shows?", and when I produced a glassful he buried his nose in it for some seconds and then looking at me said, "I say, old man, get me a chair and let me sit down beside it".

Wilkinson continued to make small quantities of wine in a fairly desultory fashion until his death in 1962. By the time the vineyard and old wooden winery were acquired by the Oakdale syndicate of 19 Sydney lawyers and businessmen in 1969, both were in a state of total neglect. The vineyard was entirely replaced to 24 hectares of shiraz, 22.5 hectares of semillon, 6.2 hectares of cabernet sauvignon, 2.3 hectares of chardonnay, 1.2 hectares of traminer and 0.8 hectares of malbec. No attempt was made to rejuvenate or rebuild the winery; the purpose was simply to grow grapes for sale to other makers in the district.

But even though it is an excellent vineyard, with

red-brown volcanic soil, it was not a financial success. Given the economic profile of the typical Lower Hunter vineyard, which I dwelt on at such length in my introduction to the Hunter Valley, this was hardly surprising. Tax losses are all very well, but they have to stop somewhere. So in the mid-1970s the decision was taken to buy back some of the grapes in the form of wine.

The first wine offered for sale was a 1977 Audrey Wilkinson Hermitage, and a 1978 Hermitage followed. As from 1979 the decision was taken to expand the range of wines significantly, all of which were made for Oakdale Vineyards Proprietary Limited by Reg and Trevor Drayton at Draytons' Bellevue. A 1979 Cabernet Sauvignon, 1980 and 1981 Traminers, a 1980 Hunter River Riesling (tradition runs rich at Oakdale), and a 1981 and 1982 French-oak Chardonnay followed over the next years.

The chief attraction of the wines was their modest price; it would not be too unkind to say this accurately reflected their fairly modest quality. Even this faint praise could not be extended to the 1982 Chardonnay, offered early in 1984 for just on $13 retail. It really was a poor wine, thin and devoid of any varietal character. The 1981 Gewurztraminer was no better, nor was the 1979 Hermitage.

BELBOURIE
BRANXTON ROAD, ROTHBURY

Jim Roberts was next in line after Max Lake when he planted the first hectare of grapes in 1964 on the 700-hectare grazing property which his wife had inherited. Even at the height of its prosperity wine-wise Belbourie remained predominantly a grazing property, and now that the scene has changed so much, grazing is more important than ever.

Roberts has always been a lateral thinker, eschewing convention. For a start his choice of grape varieties was little short of startling by the standards of the day: at various times he has propagated chardonnay, crouchen, montils, rhine riesling, sauvignon blanc, semillon, sylvaner, traminer, trebbiano, cabernet sauvignon, malbec, mataro and shiraz. He designed a mobile field-crusher (drawing on his skills as a Bachelor of Science from Sydney University and his time as an oil geologist), utilising carbon dioxide gas cover to prevent oxidation. He was one of the first—if not *the* first—vigneron to experiment with carbonic maceration on a commercial scale. He pioneered the mailing list/wine society concept so successfully utilised by Rothbury, and which plays an ever-increasing part in the marketing strategy of the boutique winery born in the 80s. He designed and painted some of the most striking, innovative (and beautiful) wine labels ever put on a bottle—the fact that they failed totally to comply with the bureaucratic requirements of the Pure Foods Act regulations was quite beside the point.

Above all else, he made wine in his way, in his own concept of things—it was very, very different from the wine made by others. Quite apart from the use of carbonic maceration with white wines as well as reds, he also employed a modified solera system with his white wines, topping up the cask with the current vintage as he bottled the wine for that year. Thus "Belah" was at one time a white wine comprised of four vintages with an average cask age of two and a half years, while super Belah spanned five vintages and had an average age of three and a half years.

These wines were made in a winery built from stone removed from the remains of the original Dalwood winery. Jim Roberts has a remarkable sensitivity and talent, which shows in the design of the building, the labels and, indeed, in his face. He once took exception to my somewhat clinical (and no doubt insensitive) criticism of the undoubted technical faults evident in many of his wines, taking it as a personal attack and affront. It was not, and I am sorry that we are not on speaking terms, for Roberts has contributed far more to the wine industry than he has received in return. Most importantly, he has given something different, something original, something from his heart.

BROKENWOOD
McDONALDS ROAD, POKOLBIN

Ask any father whether his daughter is beautiful, and he will honestly answer yes. It is now two years since I parted company with Brokenwood and moved to Melbourne, and its memory is as fresh as this morning's sunrise. Despite my lifetime training as a lawyer, I suspect that no matter how many years pass I will always find it difficult to be dispassionate about the winery and its achievements. But I suppose those achievements have been well-enough chronicled by other wine writers and industry observers for my own (still hopelessly biased) views to become redundant.

Tony Albert, John Beeston and I purchased a four-hectare block of scrub at the end of McDonalds Road in the latter part of 1970. The trees—spindly spotted gums and a sprinkling of steel-tough ironbarks of massive size—were bulldozed and pushed into windrows. Murray Tyrrell was the local fire-brigade captain and also our viticultural consultant, which gave rise to a momentary conflict of interest as the first match was struck towards the end of the summer of 1971.

By July of that year the land had been worked after a fashion, and the local conviction that we were going to erect a multistorey motel (we had paid an extremely high price for the land) had finally turned to pity as the broken humps of orange clay which we were about to plant with vines were contemplated. Despite all the odds, the vines grew; a vineyard formed and the first wine was made at the Rothbury Estate in 1973 (utilising our equipment). A temporary winery followed in 1974; another much larger one in 1975 with a great deal of aesthetic charm but decidedly impractical; and finally a totally functional and aesthetically unmentionable winery has replaced the "old" building as from the 1983 vintage.

In the intervening years the partners (first three, then nine and now 11) pruned the vines, picked the grapes, and made, bottled and marketed the wine. Between us we had a lot of friends, although not all of those could quite come to grips with the fact that on weekends and during holidays (at vintage) everyone was expected to work far harder than they did at their weekday jobs.

Finally, with the new winery on the drawing-boards and ambitious plans to turn the operation from a loss-making weekend diversion into a profitable enterprise, Brokenwood took on its first full-time employee and its first formally audited winemaker, Iain Riggs. It was a happy choice, for Riggs has rapidly built upon the red-wine reputation Broken-wood had gained over the years, with several outstanding white wines. That reputation derived from a series of red wines which differed quite radically from the (then) standard perception of Hunter Valley wine. My misgivings about my impartiality to one side, I really believe that the wines of Brokenwood are a classic example of changes which have swept across the industry as a whole (and not just in the Hunter) in the course of the last decade.

So it was that the Brokenwood reds of the mid-1970s had better colour, fresher fruit and a firmer structure than many of their contemporaries. The current vintages still retain those qualities, but many other Hunter reds have moved along the same path and the difference is accordingly less obvious. These characters were derived from a number of factors.

First, and as always, the soil. Both the original

four hectares and the adjoining 16 hectares purchased from Hungerford Hill in 1978, share the poor infertile clay I described at page 15. Over the 11 vintages I helped make at Brokenwood, the average yield was less than 2.5 tonnes per hectare. A night-mare economically, but the quality of the fruit was very good indeed. The small berries and scraggly bunches gave a high skin-and-pip ratio to juice. Anthocyanins, so important to red-wine quality, were produced in abundance, while tannins (not always evident in Hunter reds) were there in quantity.

Second, we picked our grapes far earlier than did our neighbours. Brokenwood was convinced that acid and pH levels were far more important than sugar. It was quite evident that flavour built to a satisfactory degree relatively early on in the ripening curve, and that all one was chasing by leaving the grapes on the vine was alcohol. The downside in our case was a rapid loss in acid, an equivalent rise in pH and only a modest increase in sugar. This whole issue, and the corrective use of tartaric acid, is a hotly debated one; all I can say is that the Brokenwood approach worked very well, gaining the winery successive trophies at the Hunter Valley Wine Show for best small makers' red, numerous gold medals and a consistent stream of praise from other wine writers.

Thirdly, we completed the last stages of the primary fermentation in small oak barrels (barriques, hogs-heads and puncheons). Again a technique with its detractors, it certainly is a time-consuming and messy one. In the Hunter it exacerbates the H_2S (hydrogen sulphide) problem, and generally requires a lot of extra handling in the initial stages. But I am convinced that it adds to complexity if both this and the malolactic fermentation take place in the barrel. It is also the method used in the making of Penfolds' Grange Hermitage and many of Wolf Blass's top reds. That is good-enough company for Brokenwood.

Next, we bottled the wine far earlier than contemporary wisdom dictated. Most winemakers like to bottle their reds in the winter of the following year (typically around July); we bottled over the Christmas/New Year following vintage. Again, the logic of that decision is both complex and not free from argument. But it undoubtedly captured more fruit and better colour, even if the wines then needed rather longer in bottle to reach their peak.

Finally, right throughout the winemaking process we waged an unremitting war against the propensity of all Hunter reds to develop H_2S, which, if left in the wine at the time it is bottled, produces mercaptan. This in turn is the source of the tarry/burnt rubber/

bitter aromas which (with age) modify into a slightly more genteel "sweaty saddle" or "cowshed" character. Others have accepted this as a simple manifestation of regional character; I do not, although I must admit that aged Hunter reds do develop aromas which are not far removed, even if in their youth they were devoid of any H$_2$S.

As I say, many other makers are now producing wines in similar style, none more so than Robsons Vineyard; Murray Robson's approach developed in parallel to that of Brokenwood, and while there was certainly no conscious copying of each other's wines, at times they can be hard to tell apart. But I am sure that Robson, a staunch defender of the Hunter Valley faith, looks with decidedly mixed feelings at the other Brokenwood innovation.

In 1978 a 16-hectare vineyard next door, owned by Hungerford Hill, was purchased. It was planted to 1.5 hectares of cabernet sauvignon, with the balance to shiraz. This presented us with a vast surplus of shiraz, and an urgent need of more cabernet sauvignon. 1978 was not a good Hunter vintage (thanks to heavy vintage rain) and Hunter cabernet was in any event unprocurable. So we were forced to look elsewhere, and our thoughts turned to Coonawarra and to some of the great Hunter and Coonawarra blends made in the 1950s. So cabernet—in the form of wine—was purchased from Eric Brand at Laira, and the Hunter-Coonawarra blend was born.

Since that time the Coonawarra component has come variously from Hungerford Hill, and more recently Petaluma. Changes to the licensing laws in New South Wales in 1983 removed the restriction which had existed up to that time requiring 70 per cent of the wine to have been fermented at the home winery, that is, Brokenwood. Until that year only one blend was produced—typically containing 30 per cent Coonawarra cabernet, 20 per cent Hunter cabernet and 50 per cent Hunter shiraz. In 1983 a 100 per cent cabernet sauvignon was released comprised of 60 per cent Hunter cabernet, 30 per cent Coonawarra cabernet and 10 per cent Margaret River cabernet—the last 40 per cent having made (and blended) at Petaluma. A Hunter-Coonawarra cabernet shiraz (following down the same track as previously) was also made.

There is a great tradition of blending in Australia, and many of the greatest reds of this century were area blends. Max Schubert, without argument the greatest red-winemaker in Australia in the period 1950 to 1980, is a passionate supporter of such blends. But in this age of varietal purity (a cabernet must always be better than a cabernet shiraz) and regional integrity (down with dishonest labelling and wine fraud), a long shadow has been cast over blends, and the belief is actively cultivated by some that they (blends) are necessarily inferior. It is not so.

The 1983 winery, and the arrival of Iain Riggs as winemaker, also saw another great change at Brokenwood. We had made a couple of casks of white wine on an experimental basis in 1982, but to all intents and purposes Brokenwood's first 10 vintages had been exclusively red. In 1983 almost as much white wine was made as red; for the first time significant grape purchases were made. A replanting programme since 1978 had seen much of the shiraz on the Hungerford Hill block replaced by cabernet sauvignon and, to a lesser degree, by chardonnay, so that by 1984 Brokenwood had become self-sufficient for reds. Inevitably, however, the white grapes had to be purchased and will for the foreseeable future.

But it really does not matter who grows the grapes, so long as appropriate viticultural practices have been followed. Riggs combed the district, and was successful in locating high-quality semillon and chardonnay. The grapes were picked into small slatted baskets, and chilled for 24 hours in the new cool-room before being crushed and given varying periods of skin contact. The chilled juice was then allowed to cold-settle for a prolonged period (up to a month) before fermentation commenced, partially in stainless steel and partially in new-oak casks stored in the by-now vacant cool-room.

Some of the steel-fermented wine was subsequently matured in small oak and some was kept in steel. In this way three separate batches of the same base wine, all with markedly differing characteristics, were made, allowing great flexibility in determining the style of the finished wine. There is nothing especially innovative in all of this: it simply represents the state-of-the-art of white-winemaking in the mid-1980s. But it does produce white wines which, while retaining maximum freshness and fruit aroma and flavour, have the capacity to become very complex with some bottle age.

In March 1984 Len Evans summed up Brokenwood and its wines this way, and I think it is a fair appraisal: ". . . Their wines are sturdily independent, and in less than 10 years have assumed an important place among those aiming for the highest quality."

CHATEAU FRANCOIS
BROKE ROAD, POKOLBIN

Dr Donald Francois has for many years been the Director of Fisheries in New South Wales. I think it is no secret that he looks forward with considerable anticipation to the day when he can retire and move to live in his beautiful, although not well-known, vineyard nestling at the very foot of the Brokenwood Range.

Limited production has been mainly responsible for the absence of a cellar-door sales operation (the wine is virtually all sold through a mailing list, although a few more adventurous restaurants offer Chateau Francois wines), but the relative isolation of the vineyard has also played a part. To reach it one proceeds along the Broke Road past Tyrrell's, and at an unmarked gate one turns left to drive up a dirt road skirting fields and vineyards. Once there, a foothill of the Brokenback Range rises sheer from behind the winery: I once scrambled up it, a far harder and longer task than I had imagined. The view, ample from the house and winery below, takes on another dimension. The entire sweep of the rolling plains of the Valley spreads in front of one, until in the distance one sees the smoky-blue outline of the ranges leading to the Barrington Tops.

But Francois's winemaking experience long antedates the establishment of his vineyard in 1970. From the mid-1960s he experimented with a variety of fruit- and grape- (sometimes table grape) based wines in the cellar of his Chatswood home. It was in part the detached interest of a scientist: his knowledge of wine in general was at that time not great (he had been born and raised in America), and grew hand-in-glove with his winemaking experience.

Francois's first Hunter vintages were carted back to Sydney and, like his earlier experimental wines, made there. But he had served his apprenticeship well, for his 1973 Shiraz won the trophy for the best Museum Class red at the Hunter Valley Show in both 1983 and 1984, competing against wines from companies such as Tulloch, McWilliam's, Rothbury, Hungerford Hill, Saxonvale and Wyndham. Indeed, Francois wins trophies and gold medals with almost nonchalant ease at the few shows he is able to enter with his restricted output. He professes disenchantment with the show system, but I am not sure why. Perhaps he does not realise that nobody is perfect 100 per cent of the time, show judges included. His success is all the more impressive given that the vineyard is one of the smallest in commercial production in Australia.

The property is 36 hectares overall, but only 2.4 hectares are planted: there are 1.2 hectares of shiraz, 0.8 hectares of pinot noir and 0.2 hectares each of semillon and chardonnay. A few cabernet vines go to make the occasional bottle of port for Francois's own consumption. His neighbour Murray Tyrrell has been a close friend and adviser over the years, and they share a healthy disrespect for cabernet sauvignon in the Hunter, a disrespect which only just falls short of outright dislike.

Whether it is the fine, sandy loam or the microclimate or a combination of both, I do not know, but Chateau Francois's plantings of pinot noir are among the very few worthwhile patches in the district. The resultant wine is not rich or robust, but it does have marked fragrance and elegance, and—rarer still—authentic varietal character. Sometimes Francois releases a 100 per cent pinot noir, but more often than not he elects to blend it with his shiraz. It is a testimonial to the pinot that even though (as with the '83) it may constitute only 33 per cent of the blend, its strawberry aroma and slightly sappy flavour dominate the finished wine.

Just as the overall style of the reds is light, fresh and elegant, so that of the whites is decidedly full-flavoured, reflecting the fact that relatively few of the solids (the suspended particles in the juice) are removed before fermentation. Francois's intake of semillon and chardonnay is substantially increased by grapes grown on an adjoining block of land owned by Christine Rethers—these vineyards were established with the specific intention of providing grapes for Chateau Francois.

While the winemaking techniques adopted with the whites are distinctly traditional, so is the ability of these wines to improve in bottle. The 1982 Chardonnay won the Small Winemakers' Trophy at the 1983 Hunter Valley Show, while the semillons have performed with great distinction over the years. The quite lovely 1977 Semillon, having won its Class Trophy at the 1978 Hunter Show, travelled to Mudgee in 1979 and was judged the best wine in the entire show.

Don Francois is a highly intelligent winemaker who sets high standards for himself. His strict attention to detail, and to cleanliness in his winery, have resulted in a stream of wines of which he should be proud.

DAWSON FAMILY ESTATE
HARPER'S HILL ROAD, POKOLBIN

Ben Dawson was responsible for negotiating the acquisition of the Hungerford Hill property from the Hungerford family in 1967; it was he who agreed that the property should retain the Hungerford name, thereby clinching the deal. His daughter Anne married Simon Currant who was for many years general manager at Hungerford Hill, and who was chiefly responsible for the development of the Hungerford Hill entertainment village.

In 1977 Ben Dawson decided to establish his own small vineyard at Lovedale, just to the east of Black Creek and only a small distance from Ed Jouault's Allandale winery. He planted several hectares of chardonnay but, at the urging of one of his sons, also included a token quarter of a hectare of traminer. He laments the fact that he did not plant more: made bone-dry, the tiny production sells out almost immediately it is released.

But the speciality of the estate is, without doubt, its chardonnay. In the early years part of the production was sold outright, and part repurchased as wine for release under the Dawson label. In 1980 a third variant appeared: the Dawson Vineyard Chardonnay made by Jouault and released under the Allandale label. It was this wine which brought fame to both Allandale and Dawson by winning the Farmer Brothers' Trophy at the Canberra National Wine Show in 1982.

In 1981 the Dawson Estate wine was made by Ralph Fowler at Hungerford Hill, and it won the top gold medal (against 42 producers) in Melbourne, demonstrating once again that the lighter, sandy sedimentary soils of the Lovedale area do produce some of the best white grapes in the Hunter Valley. This was Maurice O'Shea's view four decades earlier when he first established Lovedale Vineyard for McWilliam's.

With the 1984 vintage, winemaking returned to Ed Jouault on a contract basis. Dawson would like eventually to build a maturation cellar so that he could take delivery of the juice at the end of fermentation, then oak-mature and bottle it himself. He cannot see the justification for the cost of the highly sophisticated winemaking equipment necessary to crush, press and ferment chardonnay properly, and I think he is right.

In early 1984 the 1980 Dawson Estate was still a marvellous wine. While the colour is full, it retains some of the green tints which are so exciting to find in a mature wine. The bouquet is a lovely combination of grapefruit aromas and charred oak, while the palate has great balance and style, with outstanding varietal character and flavour. It remains comprehensively the best of the Dawson chardonnays to date.

The 1981 wine has a complex burgundian aroma, with the suggestion of some sulphide characters which no doubt contribute to that complexity and are far from unpleasant. The palate starts well, with soft full fruit on the front, but finishes a little hard. The 1983 Dawson, tasted in July 1984, was a most peculiar wine: it may conceivably have been an off bottle, but it had a curious medicinal/aniseed aroma and flavour, and an oily texture.

DRAYTONS' BELLEVUE
OAKEY CREEK ROAD, POKOLBIN

When Joseph Drayton set sail from England at the age of 27 with his wife Anna and two young sons he little suspected the tragedies which were to befall him. His two-year-old son Charles died on the journey; Anna gave birth to a daughter, Emily, shortly thereafter, but both mother and daughter died in quarantine after their arrival in Sydney in February 1853.

Joseph, with his eldest son Frederick, settled at Lochinvar where he met and married Mary Anne Chick. A few years later they moved to Pokolbin and acquired a thickly timbered 32-hectare property at the foothills of the Brokenback Range. Having cleared the land and built a homestead which they named Bellevue, Joseph Drayton began wheat farming. By 1860, however, he had planted his first vines and the Drayton winemaking dynasty had begun.

Joseph and Mary's second son, William, bought 16 hectares of land next door and he, too, planted vines before taking over control of Bellevue on the death of his parents. William married Susan Lambkin, whose family had at one time owned part of the hill on which Lake's Folly is situated. They had nine sons and a daughter before William died in 1945, having established W. Drayton & Sons Proprietary Limited, which operates the vineyards to this day.

As a gift to his wife, around the turn of the century William repurchased the Lambkin Estate at auction after a battle royal with an exceedingly stubborn neighbour, which saw the property change hands at £1000 an acre, a price which (in real terms) will never be equalled. After such a struggle it is perhaps surprising that until 1967 it was used solely to raise cattle. There are now 14 hectares of vines established on the striking red basalt soil, shiraz, semillon, rhine riesling and clairette (known in the Hunter as blanquette).

The home vineyard, Bellevue, still possesses many vines planted by Joseph Drayton over a century ago on the fertile heavy grey loams which surround the winery. The old shiraz, semillon and trebbiano vines were joined by cabernet sauvignon and rhine riesling in the 1960s, and over the past five years by chardonnay and traminer.

In 1969 the company acquired the Ivanhoe vineyard at auction from the Phillips Estate. The Drayton family still remembered the marvellous wines which had once come from the rich, red, volcanic soil of the steep hillsides running up into the Brokenback Range above and behind the Bellevue property, and they were determined bidders, just as William Drayton had been 70 years before. The heavy soil is given over exclusively to shiraz and cabernet.

Pokolbin Hills Estate, privately owned by Reg Drayton, is planted solely to semillon. Mangerton Estate, also owned by members of the family, is planted principally to white varieties. Yet another property to enjoy the red basalt/volcanic soil, it is best noted for chardonnay.

It is a tightly knit family: Bill, Max, Ron and Jock look after the viticultural side, while Reg and Trevor (the latter a Roseworthy gold medallist and a member of the fifth generation) run the winery and wine-making side. They also contract-make the Audrey Wilkinson Estate Wines, and over the years used to buy grapes regularly from six local growers. The situation has changed markedly over the past four years. The bulk of the grapes from the independently owned family vineyards is sold to other makers in the district, and little or no grapes are acquired from contract growers. The size of the crush has declined substantially in consequence.

For whatever reason, the wines have never enjoyed effective distribution, with cellar-door sales and Newcastle being the major outlets. The wines have always been modestly priced and soundly made, and their apparent lack of popularity remains something of a mystery. The whites, based on semillon, are quite distinctive: they are lean, with rather tart apple-like flavours, and age slowly. Even at 10 or more years they seldom develop the honeyed fruit/butter characteristics of Lindemans, looking more like the Anne and Elizabeth Rieslings of McWilliam's and some of the early-picked semillons made by Murray Tyrrell in the 1960s.

In more recent years the range has expanded, with Mangerton Estate Chardonnay sometimes excellent.

The 1979, in particular, was an outstanding wine. Some attractive spatlese semillons have been made, while in 1980 Trevor Drayton showed his technical expertise by marketing a Bellevue Traminer Riesling in March, just four weeks after the conclusion of vintage.

The red wines have, by and large, been even more successful. The Ivanhoe Estate has produced some deep, rich, full-flavoured reds evocative of the wines of bygone decades; while at the other end of the spectrum in 1983 Trevor Drayton made one of the best carbonic maceration reds I have seen.

Nonetheless, the image of Draytons has slipped considerably in recent years, and it is commonly known in the district that they have been finding the going very difficult. It has been recorded that it was the dedication of the family which pulled the company through the 1920s and 1930s when vintage wine sold for a paltry ninepence a gallon. Many lovers of Hunter wine will hope that the same tenacity carries the battle of the 1980s.

EVANS FAMILY
PALMER'S LANE, POKOLBIN

Even before it was finished, Len Evans's house in the Hunter Valley was legendary, the source of numerous stories, most of which were true and only a few embellishments of the truth. It is built on the top of a hill with sweeping views out over the rolling plains leading to the Brokenback Range. At the bottom of that same hill is the immaculately laid-out four-hectare planting of chardonnay which constitutes the Evans Family Vineyard. In 1985 two hectares of pinot noir joined the chardonnay; Evans, it seems, has a similar view to that of Murray Tyrrell when it comes to noble varieties in the Hunter Valley. To be fair, he has been a long-term vocal supporter of semillon, and no doubt figures that Rothbury can satisfy his needs for wine made from this variety.

The first experimental vintage was made at Rothbury by Murray Tyrrell in 1980; the first commercial release came in 1981. All of the wines have been made at Rothbury, and Len Evans has not the slightest intention of building a winery of his own. No expense has been spared either with the new French oak in which the wine is fermented and matured, or in the immaculate presentation of the French dead-leaf burgundy bottles and striking though simple label.

The wine is sold chiefly through a mailing list based on Evans's enormous circle of friends, through his retail establishment in Bulletin Place, and to a few selected restaurants. All so far released have shown rich and generous flavours; the 1981 is at its peak, while the 1982 and 1983 look like developing maximum character at some stage over the next two or three years. As one might expect, these are handsome chardonnays, full of character and with that touch of breeding to underpin their cellaring capacity.

GEORGE HUNTER ESTATE
WILDERNESS ROAD, POKOLBIN

George Hunter Estate was established by the well-known Sydney restaurateur Oliver Shaul in 1972. It came by its name in what can only be described as unusual circumstances. Shaul was standing by the traffic lights near the Australia Square building in Sydney (the Summit is but one of numerous successful restaurants under his umbrella) and turned to his accountant, saying, "We really do have to decide on a name for this property of mine." He looked up, and his eyes caught the street signs at the corner of George Street and Hunter Street. You know the rest.

The property is a very substantial one, with over 60 hectares under vine. The plantings comprise semillon (18.2 hectares), trebbiano (eight hectares), clairette (six hectares) and chardonnay and chenin blanc (four hectares each). The 20 hectares of red vineyard is planted exclusively to shiraz.

The major portion of the production has always been sold to major makers in the district. However, since 1975 small quantities of grapes have been retained by Oliver Shaul and vinified under contract for the George Hunter label. The chenin blanc has always been made at Mount Pleasant, initially under the direction of Brian Walsh. One is left in little doubt that the wine has been made by a thoroughly professional organisation; the only possible criticism stems from the somewhat vapid character of chenin blanc, although this is almost turned to an advantage in the chablis style in which it is made: The label, indeed, reads Chablis Chenin Blanc. Shaul waves his hands in half-hearted apology at the use of the name, but he is in most excellent company. Chablis in Australia is made from everything from rhine riesling to colombard to semillon to trebbiano to chardonnay; why not chenin blanc? And, as I say, the wine does have some chablis overtones in its fairly neutral fruit characteristics.

The other white wines are usually made by Ed

Jouault at Allandale. The 1983 Semillon and 1983 Chardonnay were at total contrast in style: the 1983 Semillon was made in the big old-fashioned style, heavy and broad, and needing much time to acquire any elegance. It seemed to me to have been deliberately fermented on only partially clarified juice. The 1983 Chardonnay, on the other hand, is a quite lovely wine with beautifully integrated oak, and most attractive peachy varietal fruit evident both in the bouquet and the palate. Oliver Shaul is backing his judgement about the cellaring capacity of these wines (and their predecessors) by keeping back between 200 and 300 cases each year for extended maturation. The wines are sold principally through Shaul's chain of restaurants, but are also supplied to other restaurants and a very little makes its way to the public through Sydney's Camperdown Cellars.

At the end of 1984 Shaul was seeking to dispose of some of the unplanted and subdividable land forming part of George Hunter Estate. He has no intention of selling the vineyard or the house, but if an offer came along which he could not refuse, he would at least ensure a continued option over the grapes so as to preserve the George Hunter Estate label as a permanent addition to the ever-widening choice of Hunter Valley wine.

HUNGERFORD HILL
BROKE ROAD, POKOLBIN

Six years ago I wrote that "Hungerford Hill is a cameo portrait of the changing face of the Hunter". If those words were true then, they are even more apposite today. In its 15 or so vintages Hungerford Hill has been subjected to enough change to last a corporate lifetime, although following its recent absorption into the Hooper Bailie Industries Limited group, one can but hope for a period of stability.

Established in 1967 at the height of red-wine fever, vineyards were planted at a furious pace, reaching a high-water mark of 235 hectares in the early 1970s. The miseries which were to follow were exacerbated by the fact that a considerable part of this was shiraz; and as if that were not bad enough, shiraz established on poor, low-yielding soils. Rationalisation was inevitable, but its scale was nonetheless breathtaking.

To all intents and purposes Hungerford Hill started again in the late 1970s. Large areas were sold off; others were allowed to revert to pasture, the vines having been cut off at ground level; yet other blocks were replanted; while more recently, grafting techniques have improved, allowing large-scale conversion of shiraz and other varieties to chardonnay. At the end of the 70s Hungerford Hill had almost no chardonnay; in 1984 it crushed more chardonnay than any other Lower Hunter winery, with the exception of the Wyndham group.

These changes were assisted by the creation of a second major dam, just across the road from the vast lake which has become so much part of the Hunter landscape. The first lake was established with the primary purpose of providing water for the Hungerford Hill Village, and the drought of 1981 very nearly emptied it. The second dam has ensured sufficient water to permit irrigation of a substantial portion of the vineyard also.

So it is that the Hunter vineyards of Hungerford Hill as at December 1984 total only 40 hectares, planted to chardonnay (11.33 hectares), semillon (6.87 hectares), traminer (4.97 hectares), verdelho (2.77 hectares), sauvignon blanc (one hectare), shiraz (seven hectares), cabernet sauvignon (3.43 hectares), pino noir (one hectare), merlot (0.89 hectares) and malbec (0.52 hectares). In the winter of 1985 a further 3.25 hectares of chardonnay, three hectares of pinot noir and 1.2 hectares of merlot will have been established, but these plantings are a far cry from the heady days of the late 1960s. They now count for approximately 60 per cent of the crush, the remaining 40 per cent being purchased from local vineyards.

At one time Hungerford Hill held very substantial vineyards in Coonawarra in its own right. As part of the reorganisation following the takeover of the company and the acquisition of the Hunter operation by Hooper Bailie, Hungerford Hill lost those vineyards, although it retained a right to buy grapes for a five year period. A further term of the arrangement was that Hungerford Hill would have control over the viticultural practices adopted to ensure a continuity of style (and quality). At the end of 1984 it moved to ensure its long-term position by buying back the farm, as it were. It acquired from the Abbey family 80 hectares of prime land situated on the northern outskirts of Penola. Once again the battle cry goes out: "One of the last pieces of Terra Rossa available in Coonawarra." I have now lost track of how many press releases I have received from various companies claiming to be the purchaser of the last block. Be that as it may, it is a prime piece of viticultural land, which manager Doug Balnaves rates more highly than the original block — and that is praise indeed.

Planting was due to commence in July 1985 to

cabernet sauvignon (32.4 hectares), merlot and cabernet franc (6.5 hectares each), pinot noir (4.85 hectares), rhine riesling (10 hectares) and chardonnay (four hectares). When completed, it will become the largest area in Coonawarra to be "close-planted", following Hungerford Hill's decision to reduce row separation to 2.75 metres. The theory behind close spacing is that the greater number of vines per hectare effectively compete against each other for available nutrients and water, reducing overall vigour but increasing the quality of the grapes. The spacing chosen is by no means as close, nor the vine population as dense, as the European model, nor as dense as some other cool-climate plantings presently under way. It will undoubtedly have a beneficial effect, however, and Hungerford Hill are understandably looking forward with some anticipation to the first commercial vintage expected in 1988.

A sophisticated frost-control system will also be installed; when temperatures drop to three degrees, eight pumps will automatically switch on a fine mist spray which will continue until turned off manually. The same system will no doubt come in very useful in summer heat to alleviate vine stress.

The sole purpose of these vineyards is to produce high-quality wines positioned towards the top end of the market, a true reflection of the fact that the Hunter is and always will be a high-cost area in which to produce wine. In Ralph Fowler, Hungerford Hill has a winemaker who has shown he can take full advantage of the wide range of fruit available to him, for he not only has the Hunter grapes to work with each vintage, but also an equal quantity of material from Coonawarra.

Trained at Tyrrell's, Fowler came to Hungerford Hill with a reputation for great chardonnay (thanks to Tyrrell's Vat 47), and a deep understanding of pinot noir and shiraz. Neither rhine riesling nor cabernet sauvignon figures large in Murray Tyrrell's view of things, yet it has been precisely with these varieties that Fowler's greatest successes have come. The rhine riesling is grown at Coonawarra but, like the Coonawarra cabernet sauvignon, is brought as juice to the Hunter in a refrigerated tanker, and is fermented there. The Hungerford Hill plantings in Coonawarra were established on some of the best country in the district, and the quality of the grapes (and the resultant wine) has always been extremely high, but in 1983 Fowler achieved a miracle.

It was a year in Coonawarra which most vignerons would prefer to forget: persistent rain leading up to and continuing through vintage saw botrytis spread at an alarming rate through both white and red grapes. Many were forced to pick before the grapes were properly ripe. With this unlikely scenario, Fowler made one of the most successful white wines in show history. The 1983 Coonawarra Rhine Riesling won four major trophies in its first year in the show ring, and six gold medals at successive shows. By the end of 1984 it had increased its gold medal tally to 11. Like many other wines of the year, it was picked relatively early, yet it has quite astonishing flavour, in which the influence of botrytis is evident yet not aggressive. The legitimacy of the role of botrytis in assisting the flavour of dry rhine rieslings is a fiercely debated issue; all one can say is that with some wines it is successful, and occasionally (as in this case) magnificently so.

It was a great wine to launch the new high-profile package for the top-of-the-line Collection Series; time alone will show whether the ultra-bold "HH" label, looking more like an artist's concept sketch than a finished product, will be successful. It was no doubt specifically designed to counter the fairly humble reputation which Hungerford Hill had held up to that time, and should at the very least create a new brand awareness.

The other three wines forming the first new label release are also indicative of the future direction for Hungerford Hill: a 1983 Pokolbin Chardonnay, a 1980 Pokolbin Shiraz, and a 1981 Coonawarra Cabernet Sauvignon. Between 3500 and 4800 cases of each wine were produced, underlining the fact that Hungerford Hill is by no stretch of the imagination a volume producer. On those figures it only just makes the medium-sized winery classification.

The success of (and publicity for) the 1983 Coonawarra Rhine Riesling should not obscure the fact that it is but one of a long series of excellent Coonawarra rhine rieslings, or that the Hungerford Hill Coonawarra cabernets have since 1978 been at the very forefront of Australian cabernet styles. Indeed, I would be surprised if any one label has had greater success in the major red-wine tastings organised each year by the leading Australian wine magazine, *Wine and Spirit Monthly.* The 1978 was a prolific medal-winner, while both the 1979 and 1980 wines were placed top of their classes in at least one major tasting I can remember.

But Coonawarra does not have a monopoly on success. In 1983 Fowler made one of the best red wines to come out of the Hunter Valley for many years. A blend of cabernet sauvignon, merlot and a little cabernet franc, it has already won five gold medals. It is no doubt this wine which has prompted the 1985 plantings of merlot, a variety which other Hunter vignerons have been unsuccessful in growing.

Equally, the Hungerford Hill Pokolbin chardonnays have grown from strength to strength in recent years. The 1981 vintage had the distinction of being the only Australian wine on the list of the prestigious London wine merchants, Corney & Barrow, and subsequently being selected in a blind tasting of wines from around the world for inclusion in the *Sunday Times* Wine Club Dozen. Fowler ferments these wines in new French oak barrels, which results in great richness and complexity, and should also hold the wine in good stead as it ages in bottle. As ever with Australian chardonnay, however, it is necessary to watch how each wine develops: the blithe assumption that chardonnay will necessarily repay cellaring has caught many an unwary wine lover.

The restricted output also emphasises the importance of the Hungerford Hill Wine Village in the overall scheme of things. There is no question that Hungerford Hill has been the principal catalyst for the development of tourism in the Hunter Valley, nor that it presently offers unrivalled facilities for the visitor, whether staying for a day or a week. The 72-room motel—the Village Inn—is the largest in the region, yet seems almost insignificant as it meanders its way through the spotted gums. It links up with palatial convention facilities in the village proper: the Wine Pavilion will accommodate 400 people in theatre seating, host a banquet for 320 or cocktails for 500. A series of smaller rooms provides the same facilities for fewer numbers. The wine cellars—modelled on the underground cellars of Chateau Reynella—are among the most attractive in the district. A series of smaller shops and kiosks is spread out throughout the trees, serving the thousands who visit the village every weekend. Hectares of picnic grounds overlooking the twin lakes, horse riding and a large children's playground make it the ideal location for a family outing.

Last, but by no means least, is the Pokolbin Cellar Restaurant where Robert and Sally Molines have presided for over ten years. The restaurant consistently produces the best food in the district amid a garden-like setting which is as welcoming in winter with its glowing braziers as it is in the height of summer, when it becomes a veritable oasis.

Wine-tasting and wine-drinking should be fun. At Hungerford Hill they invariably are.

KINDRED'S LOCH LEVEN
PALMERS LANE, POKOLBIN

Kindred's Loch Leven Estate is situated on the western prolongation of Palmers Lane after it crosses McDonalds Lane. Ian Kindred acquired Loch Leven, like so many others, with the dual purpose of grazing cattle and growing grapes. Planting commenced in 1973, and two substantial vineyards (Homestead and Loch Leven) have since been established. Almost 20 hectares are in full bearing at Loch Leven (semillon, marsanne, traminer, cabernet sauvignon, shiraz and pinot noir) with a further 10 hectares on the Homestead block (semillon, chardonnay, traminer, trebbiano and black muscat). Supplementary water is available to the Homestead Vineyard, which averages 10 tonnes to the hectare, compared with the dry-land average of five tonnes at Loch Leven.

Kindred has resisted the temptation of establishing his own winery, preferring instead to take back part of his grapes in the form of wine from the various companies to which he has sold his production over the years. Until late 1984 he had not made any move to sell the wine he had so accumulated, with the result that he was then able to offer an unusual range of red and white wines going back over the years. At that time he had over 30,000 bottles in stock, and given his plan to open for cellar-door sales on Sundays only between 10 a.m. and 4 p.m., it seems reasonable to assume these stocks will last for some time to come.

The wines included some rather tired 1976 Shiraz made by Andrew McPherson on sale at $36 per case; an untried 1975 Shiraz at $18 per case, the price suggesting it was even more tired; a 1980 Cabernet Sauvignon made at Tyrrell's, showing clean, light varietal character; a 1981 Semillon ($36) made by Ed Jouault, rather hard, green and with chalky austerity; and two excellent 1982 white wines made, at all places, in the Barossa Valley by Saltrams' Mark Turnbull.

The 1982 Semillon ($54) was showing the first signs of developing classic Hunter honeyed-toast aromas and flavours, while a 1982 Traminer ($72) deserved the high price placed on it. With pungent lime/spice aroma and excellent mid-palate richness (but no hardness on the finish), it is the best Lower Hunter traminer I have tasted.

Rhine Rieslings from 1981 and 1982, and 1982 Pinot Noir, 1982 Shiraz and 1982 Cabernet Sauvignon make up the balance of the bottled-wine stocks presently held for sale. In 1983 and 1984 grapes were sold variously to Rothbury, Murray Robson and Max Lake. It is not a bad system, although clearly it pays to pick the right winemaker.

LAKE'S FOLLY
BROKE ROAD, POKOLBIN

Always there is the problem of dealing with a man who has become a legend in his own lifetime, who is in so many ways larger than life and yet who in the end proves that nobody is perfect. But first it is necessary to pay unstinting homage to the man who had the courage and foresight to show others that it was indeed possible for a dedicated amateur to plant a vineyard, erect his own winery and, without any outside technical assistance, proceed to make great wine.

In so doing, Max Lake opened the way for the revolution which has done so much to transform the style and quality of Australian wine over the past 20 years. The boutique winemaker may not always make good wine, but it will not be for the want of trying; and, more often than not, nor for the want of expenditure. It is absolutely fundamental to the small winemaker that he or she is totally dedicated to quality. There are two reasons for this: firstly, there are a hundred easier ways to make a living and/or spend a weekend; secondly, unless that dedication is absolute, the winemaker will quickly fail and be driven out of business. Dedication therefore assumed, the next characteristic is a willingness to experiment, to test conventional wisdom, and to look beyond the narrow confines of contemporary practice. He or she fills the role of Socrates dissatisfied; let the large wine company be the pig satisfied if it must.

Lake has shown all of these attributes, and more, since he selected the small hill of bright-red soil in 1963 which was to become Lake's Folly. A gifted surgeon, he had had a lifetime love affair with wine, and had already declared his sympathies with the first of what was to be many books, simply entitled *Hunter Wine*. But his tastes were catholic and he was also thoroughly acquainted with the wines of France.

So it was that he compounded the folly of establishing the vineyard in the first place by determining to plant cabernet sauvignon, a variety which had disappeared from the Valley around the time of the Second World War. It was indeed a 1930 vintage blend of 50 per cent cabernet sauvignon and 50 per cent petite verdot grown at Dalwood and bottled by Matthew Lang & Co., which Lake drank with Douglas

Crittenden in 1960, which led him to plant cabernet. Lake recalls it was the best red he had drunk up to that time.

Having taken the decision to plant cabernet sauvignon, the logical corollary was to make it in the manner of the Bordelaise, using new hogsheads to mature the wine. At least in this respect Max Schubert had shown the way, but such use of new oak was still very uncommon. It led to Hector Tulloch complaining that Lake was trying to change the style of Hunter wine; Lake responded he was merely trying to create his own style of wine, but whether he intended to or not, he did provide a model for those who followed.

Lake's Folly Cabernet Sauvignon has been widely accepted both in Australia and overseas as one of the great classics. It is a tribute to Lake's charisma that it sells out every year, seemingly without effort. It is never advertised, never submitted to wine writers for appraisal, and has never been entered in wine shows. Any such scrutiny or publicity would, it seems, constitute a form of lese-majesty. It perhaps also explains why the wines are never criticised, not-withstanding that a number of older vintages suffered from an excessive amount of tarry, mercaptan-derived aromas and flavours.

In much the same way—indeed, if it were possible, more so—there has been an absolute prostration at the altar of Lake's Folly Chardonnay, first made in 1974. I cannot claim any great personal knowledge of these wines, but have encountered them from time to time in masked comparative line-ups of chardonnay, in which the consensus of the judges was that the wine was of average quality. Now that may be a harsh judgement, and it may be that if I knew the wines better I would revise my judgement. But I have always thought the masked line-up the fairest and most accurate assessment, and can but rest on it.

Max Lake has in recent years handed over the primary winemaking responsibility to Stephen, replacing Andy Phillips who had assisted in the winery since the first vintage as well as being responsible for the 1970s; the style of Lake's Folly has subtly changed and, in particular, those worrying tarry characters of earlier years seem to have diminished. The colour of the wine, too, seems to be better, holding its red-purple hues for longer.

It is difficult to be dogmatic, because Max Lake has always preferred to keep his winemaking methods and philosophies to himself; his statements and explanations would invariably do the oracle of Delphi proud, so obscure are they. If my judgements are correct, and some of the Lake's Folly wines have been less than perfect, it should not obscure the indestructible contribution Max Lake has made to the world of wine. *Bon vivant*, author, but above all else a creative genius, we—all of us—owe him a lasting debt of gratitude.

LAKE'S FOLLY: SUMMARY OF WINES

VINEYARD SEASON	YEAR	CABERNET SAUVIGNON	FOLLY RED OR CABERNET HERMITAGE	HVE & EXPORT	CHARDONNAY
Dry, hot	1966	Foot-stamped*	–	Supple*	–
Good	1967	First release, fine*	Good*	–	–
Wet vintage	1968	Chosen Ritz, London*	Good*	–	–
Bushfires	1969	Big, balanced*	Very good*	O'Shea Memorial*	First planted
Good	1970	Long palate, soft finish*	Good*	–	–
Very wet	1971	Light "burgundy"*	–	Senior rosé*	–
Good	1972	Outstanding*	Good*	Robust*	–
Good	1973	Good*	Good*	–	–
Wet	1974	Fair*	Fair*	Good*	Big, superb‡*
Cyclone loss	1975	Good, not great*	Good*	–	Coarsening‡*
Gale loss	1976	Good†*	Very good*	Good*	Fine*
Hail	1977	Elegant*	Light*	Light, good*	Good, not great now*
Drought	1978	Outstanding†	Very good*	–	Good*
Dry, good	1979	Stylish, balanced†*	Very good*	–	Very good†*
Dry, very good	1980	Finesse†	Balanced†*	–	Elegant†
Drought	1981	Balanced, fine†	–	Very good†	Outstanding‡
Top	1982	Elegant†	–	Very good†	Rich†‡
Excellent	1983	Elegant†	–	–	Big, balanced†
Good rain	1984				

* Drink   † Keep   ‡ Not stabilised—may throw natural tartrate crystal

I should allow Lake the last say, one in which his utterances are cryptic but hardly Delphic, and admitting no room for self-doubt. In 1984 he provided the summary of his wines and their future (assuming cool cellaring conditions) in the table opposite.

LINDEMANS
McDONALDS ROAD, POKOLBIN

In 1840 a Royal Navy surgeon named Henry John Lindeman resigned his commission to make his way to Australia. He continued on to the Hunter River, and in 1842 purchased a property near the Paterson River which he named Cawarra, an Aboriginal word meaning "Running Waters". In 1843 he planted the first vines, and within a few years had erected a winery and commenced winemaking operations. The success of the enterprise can be gauged from the 1861 vintage report in the *Sydney Morning Herald*.

> At Cawarra, near Paterson, Dr Lindeman has produced this year about 5000 gallons [22,750 litres] from his own vineyard and about 30,000 gallons [136,500 litres] from grapes purchased of other growers in the neighbourhood. Dr Lindeman's wines are made from the German Riesling, and from the Verdelho grape; the dark wines are made from the small black Hermitage. The average produce of the Cawarra vintage this year has been about 400 gallons [1820 litres] to the acre. On particular portions of the vineyard an average of 800 gallons [3640 litres] have been obtained.

Nine years later the business had grown to the point where Dr Lindeman judged it necessary to establish a head office, and storage and bottling facilities at Sydney. Lindemans was the first company to take this step, setting itself up at the Exchange Cellars in Pitt Street, Sydney. It subsequently moved to the Queen Victoria Building, where its administration and bottling plant remained until the second half of the 1930s. It was here that my father bought his table wine and in later years it was my introduction to the world of wine.

Dr Henry Lindeman died in 1882, aged 71, having established the foundation of the company which was to dominate the wine industry in New South Wales for significant periods in the following century, and which is still one of the largest enterprises in the field. Needless to say, it has had a special role and influence in the Hunter Valley. In 1896 H. M. Mackenzie, writing in the *Maitland Mercury*, observed:

> It is a recognised fact that Cawarra is the best vineyard in this district, the wine, especially a light claret which I tasted and found excellent, being bottled on the premises. About 25 acres [10 hectares] are devoted to vine culture on level ground bordering the river, the soil of which, according to Mr Lindeman, is a little too rich if anything . . . In order that no immature wine may be put on the market or, worse still, forced on the people at the hotels, it is an invariable rule . . . that none be sent away until at least 4 years have expired, which is increased in the Exchange Cellars for at least another year . . . In speaking of the claret made at this estate, I found it to be light, sound and free from acid, and by no means, as so many Colonial clarets are, rough on the tongue.

Following the death of Dr Henry Lindeman, the business was carried on by his three sons, Arthur Henry as winemaker, Charles Frederick as manager, and Herbert as wine-taster. In 1906 a major restructuring saw the partnership converted into a limited liability company; the retirement of Herbert Lindeman from the business; the retention of the Cawarra vineyards by Arthur Lindeman in his own right (although for some time he continued to sell the grapes to the Lindeman company); and in the following year the move to the basement of the Queen Victoria Building.

The coming of Federation in 1901 and the opening up of the New South Wales market to South Australian wine spelt disaster for many of the smaller wineries which had flourished at the end of the nineteenth century. But it presented Lindemans, with Penfolds the best-organised company, unparalleled opportunities for expansion. In 1895 C. F. Lindeman had written to Sir Henry Parkes saying:

> We have been established 45 years, we have three vineyards in the north and one on the Murray, but they are not very extensive; but in good vintages we buy all the good grapes in the districts and have them carted to our cellars. We have very large stocks of wine, having seven cellars full, the smallest holding 30,000 gallons [136,500 litres] and the largest about 80,000 gallons [364,000 litres].

At that time in the early years of the twentieth century, the opportunity to consolidate and secure their own vineyard sources (and a new winery) presented itself. The first and most important acquisition was of Ben Ean from John McDonald, whose name the road running past Ben Ean to the Hungerford Hill corner takes. Ben Ean had been established in 1870, and McDonald erected a substantial winery which forms the central part of the present-day complex at which all Lindemans' winemaking is carried out. This 1912 acquisition was followed by the purchase of Coolalta from the Wilkinsons; Catawba from the Cappers; Warrawee from unknown vendors; and Kirkton from the Kelmans in 1914.

Kirkton was in a sense in the family, anyway. Henry Lindeman's daughter Matilda had many years before married James Kelman, and just to complete the oenological knot, James Kelman's mother was Busby's sister. In 1924 100 gallons (455 litres) of chablis and 100 gallons of burgundy were made from the remaining Busby vines (planted in 1830) and were served at the centenary celebrations of Kirkton in 1930, organised by Lindemans. I would sell my soul for a bottle of such wine. It is a macabre fact that 1924 was Kirkton's last vintage, the vineyard being abandoned in that year.

The remaining purchase was not of a vineyard, but of a brand name—Porphyry. Porphyry was the wine served to Queen Victoria in 1851; it had been planted in 1838 by the Reverend Henry Carmichael, who was very active both as a member and president of the Hunter River Viticultural Association. The vineyard remained in the Carmichael family, but during the First World War, in the absence of Gavin Dixon Carmichael in France, the stocks of wine and brand name were sold to Lindemans and the vines were abandoned.

John McDonald is claimed by Lindemans to be the first winemaker at Ben Ean, which is true in one sense: it just happens that Lindemans did not own the winery during his stewardship, which lasted from 1870 to 1911. Subsequent winemakers have been Ron Wilkinson (1912–22), Eric Lindeman (1923–38), Ross Miller (1939–52), Gerry Gerathy (1953), Hans Mollenhauer (1954–59), Karl Stockhausen (1960–80 and 1982 to the present time) and Chris Buring (1980–81).

The Ben Ean Winery has been renamed Lindemans' Hunter River Winery: although Lindemans does not admit it, one of the main reasons for the change (if not the sole reason) was the success of Ben Ean Moselle. The first Ben Ean Moselle was indeed made at Ben Ean from Hunter Valley material, but it has long since ceased to have the least connection with the Hunter Valley. In a classic tail-wagging-the-dog exercise, the winery (rather than the wine) has been renamed so that some consumerist guardian of the innocent public cannot visit the wrath of God on Lindemans for misrepresenting its products. What nonsense.

But if the name of Ben Ean has changed, the feel has not. The original winery still forms the main part of the existing complex, mercifully free from the refinery-like tank farms and vast Colorbond sheds which mark the sterile confines of the typical

modern winery. One of the greatest sights of the Hunter Valley is to be had by driving 400 metres past Lindemans (travelling north towards Hungerford Hill) and, at the crest of the hill, pulling onto the picnic area provided by the local council. The view back down the hill is unequalled, with Ben Ean (I still know it as that, whatever the sign at the gate may say) nestling at its base, and thence to the vine-clad foothills of the Brokenback Range rising skywards.

Nonetheless, the acquisition of Ben Ean and the other vineyards proved overly ambitious, particularly given the difficult conditions of the times. While Lindemans had built up a substantial business at Corowa to meet part of the demand for fortified wine, this did not alter the fact that much of its capital was tied up in an area suited to the production of fine table wine, a style for which there was little or no demand.

In 1923 the Commercial Banking Company of Sydney (which had provided the company with all its loan funds) insisted that its nominee be appointed manager. That manager was none other than Leo Buring, and he remained in sole command until 1930. Whether through bad luck or poor management, the intervening years saw Lindemans' indebtedness to the bank double. The bank could finally take no more; in 1930 it removed Leo Buring and formally appointed a receiver, a Mr Nelson. Nelson promptly fired two-thirds of the staff, and in a short time had the company operating profitably. The after-effects of the Depression, the Second World War and the size of the accumulated debts combined to make his receivership a lengthy one, however, and he remained in that role until 1947.

For his part, Leo Buring had immediately formed his own company and purchased all of his opening stock from the receiver who had so soon before replaced him. If that twist were not enough, Lindemans eventually took over the flourishing business of Leo Buring, and it is today one of the operating divisions of the Lindemans group.

When the company came out of receivership it was agreed between the bank and the Lindeman family that the several outside shareholders should be compensated for the fact that they had received no dividends for 25 years, and they were issued with shares credited as fully paid. At the same time a substantial issue of shares was made to senior members of the staff; the net result was a substantial dilution of the Lindeman family control, although they remained the major shareholders.

In 1953 the company floated to the public. After a

major reconstruction in 1959 it was eventually taken over by Philip Morris Limited in 1971, and is now a wholly owned subsidiary of that company.

In the past 30 years Lindemans has produced more great white wines—almost exclusively from semillon, with touches of trebbiano, verdelho and chardonnay here and there—than all of the other Hunter producers put together. My personal involvement commenced with Bin 591 of 1956, a wine which my father bought in quantity, and which I clearly remember. (I had drunk many of the preceding vintages, but have no particular recollection of them.) Whether by coincidence or otherwise, 1956 was the year in which stainless-steel fermentation tanks (with pressure facilities) were introduced by Ben Ean.

At 10 years of age the wine had developed that glowing yellow-gold colour, which so distinguishes the great semillons of Lindemans, but it still had great freshness. The supple honey-nut aromas and flavours had also built and blossomed: in short, the wine was perfection. Bin 850 followed in 1957, then 1170 (1958), 1333 (1959), 1575 (1960) and 1616 (1961). From this point on I still have more than a few bottles of each vintage in my cellar, and take great pleasure in opening these old vintages for unsuspecting visitors from overseas.

There is limited point in talking about old wines which no-one is likely to taste, but with Lindemans it is a different story. Thanks to the far-sighted policy of managing director Ray Kidd, for the past 20 years or so Lindemans have kept back part of each release, partly for show purposes and partly simply to allow the wines time to reach the optimum point of maturity before their final commercial release. This policy started with 1960 Hunter River Riesling Bin 1616, which continued its show career until the mid-1970s (winning gold medals at the Sydney shows of 1972, 1973 and 1974) when its last commercial release took place. It ranks with Bin 591 of 1956 and Bin 3455 of 1968 as the greatest of Lindemans' white wines, and one of the all-time great Australian white wines. 1960 was overall a disastrous vintage in the Hunter: a series of hailstorms throughout the growing season reduced the crop to next to nothing, and the cool overcast conditions at vintage led to widespread rot and mould, with some botrytis cinerea. It was a baptism of fire (or hail, if you prefer) for Karl Stockhausen, a first vintage he will never forget. So few grapes were harvested that all the varieties went in together—chiefly semillon, with some verdelho and traminer, and even a few bits and pieces of other varieties.

This strangely conceived wine went on to win three championships at the Adelaide show (1961, 1967 and 1970), two trophies (Sydney 1962 and Adelaide 1971) and 20 gold medals. It always had an extraordinary concentration of flavour; I last tasted it when it was more than 20 years old in the company of Karl Stockhausen. He thought the wine was beginning to show signs of age; I thought that it was nectar of the gods.

The 1962 Bin 1930 was very nearly as successful, although it did not have the longevity of the Bin 1616. My remaining bottles suffer from the problem that has afflicted so many of these great Lindeman whites: poor corks, resulting in excessive ullage. Bin 2222 of 1963 was yet another wine of outstanding quality, even though it was overshadowed by the great reputation of the 1964 vintage whites. My recollection is that this wine had an accidental touch of residual sugar, which filled out the mid-palate. Bin 2464 of 1964 contained a small percentage of traminer, which came from an interplanted block at Ben Ean, and was another wine which stood a little to one side of the mainstream.

The 1965 Bin 2760 was a 100 per cent Sunshine Vineyard wine. Sunshine (first planted in 1910 on the sandy flats towards Branxton) and Ben Ean produced almost all the grapes used in this marvellous series of wines. 1965 was the great drought year, renowned for its reds, and one might have thought these 1965 whites would have had a fairly short lifespan. It seems Lindemans' did, for the wine had a very short show career (1965 to 1967) during which time it won two gold and three silver medals. But Lindemans did keep some wine back for re-release in 1981. By that year the wine was at last starting to show its age: the toasty characters were starting to dominate, and alcohol, more than fruit, was holding the wine together.

1966, another hot though less droughted year, produced Bin 2955, which was a blend of Sunshine and Ben Ean grapes. Together with the '69, the '66 was the least of the Hunter River rieslings of the decade. If it had come from any other maker, it would no doubt be regarded with awe. Against Lindemans' own Olympian standards it suffered a little, although it was included in the Classic Wine Series.

1967, a great all-round vintage in the Hunter, saw a welcome return to form with Bin 3255. This was a wine which taught me more than any other about the evolution of Hunter semillons, and in particular those of Lindemans. As a young wine, released in 1969, it had fresh, lively fruit and a crisp finish. It was delicious. From around 1972 it entered a phase in which it became thoroughly unapproachable: the fruit seemed to disappear, the wine became stolid and sullen, and I opened several bottles which ended up in the soup or down the sink. Then from the mid-1970s it blossomed into one of the more lovely Lindeman whites, a white burgundy by any other name. It commenced to win gold medals at will in shows, and was re-released as a Classic Wine in early 1979 at the (now) mouth-watering price of $6 a bottle. It still retained green tinges to its colour; and the luscious, honeyed fruit was freshened and lifted by lively acid on the finish.

This wine showed two things. First, the transformation from a young, crisp wine to a fully mature white burgundy style can be as difficult a transformation as that of any adolescent entering his or her adult life. Second, whatever the validity of the distinction between Hunter River riesling, chablis and white burgundy as young wines, it disappears once the wines are fully mature. They then all become one family, a truly unique wine style made in the Hunter Valley but nowhere else in the world.

Unlikely though it may seem, the wines of 1968 were even more successful than 1967. I say wines, because there were two bin numbers released in that year: Bin 3450 and Bin 3455. I encountered the wines next to each other in a major masked (or blind) tasting of Hunter semillons organised by *Winestate* magazine in mid-1983. Up to that time Bin 3450 had the more illustrious show record (seven trophies, two championships and nine gold medals), and on the day it carried its form with it. Deep buttercup-yellow, the very complex and rich buttered-nut bouquet led into a wine which was perfection on the palate: long in flavour, with a soft, rich middle balanced by excellent acid on the finish. I gave it 19 points out of 20, and felt churlish about not awarding it more.

Bin 3455 was slower to develop, but in recent years has swept all before it in the show ring. It is not always easy to identify which wine Lindemans has entered (only the Canberra National Show gives a full "commercial" description of the entries in the show results catalogue), but on looking back over my judging sheets for the past four years, I can say that on every occasion Lindemans has entered a 1968 Semillon I have given it a gold medal.

I did the same in the *Winestate* tasting, although at 18.5 points 3455 was just behind the 3450. Slightly lighter in colour, but still showing that glowing buttercup-yellow, the bouquet was as fresh as a daisy. My notes read "glorious Peter Pan, smooth and lively", and the same character came through on

the palate. I encountered the wine again at the Canberra National Show in November 1984. It won the top gold medal in Class 38 (Museum Class; 1979 and older—soft fruity and flinty varieties). We three judges awarded it 19 points (57 out of 60), and it duly went on to win three trophies at the show: the Margaret Hunter Trophy for best dry white table wine, soft fruity and flinty varieties (any vintage); the James Fabrication Proprietary Limited Trophy for best dry white table wine of show; and the ACI Trophy for best white table wine of show. My notes read "full yellow colour; strong honeyed/toast with a touch of camphor; dry, long flavour and great style". Despite this astonishing success, I think the wine has changed considerably over the last year and a half, and that from here on the fruit will start to subside and eventually break up. Keep it if you will, but do not expect miracles to go on forever.

1969 (or, to be precise, December 1968) was the year of the bushfires: a hot, dry smoky vintage, characteristics which seem to permeate each and every white wine made by Lindemans in that year. Others seem to be far more tolerant of the aromas and flavour: I have never liked them, and reacted with consistency when Bin 3655 came up (masked, of course) in the *Winestate* tasting of May 1983. I gave it 14 points, noting it was dark yellow in colour, with an exaggerated burnt-rubber/raincoat aroma, and similarly excessive burnt-toast characters on the palate. (My fellow judges, Len Evans and Karl Stockhausen, were not much kinder, I should add.)

Since 1970 the star which shone so brightly has dimmed somewhat, although Lindemans may yet have a few surprises in store. The wines ran Bin 3855 (1970), Bin 4055 (1971), Bin 4255 (1972), Bin 4655 (1973), Bin 4855 (1974), Bin 4959 (1975), Bin 5255 (1976), Bin 5355 (1977), Bin 5455 (1978), Bins 5615 and 5655 (1979), Bin 5755 (1980), Bin 5855 (1981), Bin 6055 (1982), Bin 6255 (1983) and Bin 6455 (1984).

Of these, only the Bin 4255 has so far merited re-release, in November 1980. Its modest show success of three bronze medals showed in the wine: it had some developed honey-toast characters but lacked the life and zest on the finish of the wines of the second half of the 1960s. Indeed, it was not until 1979 that any of these wines showed any real potential. Bin 5655 was a pleasant, full-flavoured wine, while Bin 5615 really does have a touch of class. In mid-1983 it had good depth of colour, still with some green tinges, an aromatic bouquet with vanillan characters and a crisp finish to the palate— something missing from many of the other wines. I also liked the 1980 Bin 5755, which had a clean, fresh bouquet followed by a long palate again with excellent acid on the finish.

Unhappily, there has not been much since. The 1982 had more than its fair share of the volatility which all but destroyed that vintage for Lindemans. Where the line goes from here is not certain. By rights the option of oak ought to be limited to the white burgundy (and possibly the chablis) range, and I am not convinced the Broke Vineyards will produce the fruit to make wines of the stature or style of the 1960s.

In each year Lindemans has also produced a white burgundy and a chablis, a practice going back into the mists of time. In some years these wines have outperformed the Hunter River riesling release: theoretically the chablis is picked earlier, the white burgundy later; the chablis crisper and flintier, the white burgundy richer and rounder. As I have said earlier, these distinctions—tenuous enough when the wines are young—disappear altogether with age.

The white burgundies I am familiar with run from 1963 Bin 2240, followed by Bin 2510 (1964), Bin 2790 (1965), Bin 2970 (1966), Bin 3270 (1967), Bin 3470 (1968), Bin 3670 (1969), Bin 3870 (1970), Bin 4070 (1971), Bin 4270 (1972), Bins 4670 and 4/88 (1973), Bin 4870 (1974), Bins 4970 and 4971 (1975), Bin 5170 (1976), Bin 5370 (1977), Bin 5470 (1978), Bin 5670 (1979), Bin 5770 (1980), Bin 5870 (1981) and Bin 6070 (1982).

Of the older wines the outstanding vintages were the '64, '67, '68 and '70, with the '65 and '66 not far behind. Bin 2510 is a magnificent wine, recognised as such by Lindemans early in its life, because uniquely among these wines it was not released as a young wine (and then re-released when mature). Made from semillon grown on the Sunshine Vineyard, it won a championship and 11 gold medals in a show career spanning the years 1964 to 1973. The very hot conditions in January of 1964 reduced the moisture content of the grapes by stress evaporation, concentrating the flavour. It was first released in 1975, with further releases up until the late 70s. As with any old wine, bottle variation must be expected, a difficulty compounded by those appalling Lindeman corks. On its day, the wine is still perfection, with a surprising freshness and only moderately pronounced honeyed-toast characters. The lesser bottles have lost that freshness, and the fruit is noticeably flattening and drying out.

Over the past few years I have drunk Bins 2790, 2970 and 3270 on a number of occasions, and think pride of place goes (just) to Bin 3270. But it really is a case of greatest among greats. The '65 Bin 2790 was at last showing some signs of age at the _Winestate_ tasting in mid-1983. The glowing golden colour was still there, but the fruit was showing some signs of hardening and dropping out. Despite this, it still had an abundance of flavour.

What is more, an ullaged bottle of Bin 2790 opened in December 1984 while these notes were being written proved once again the magnificent overall quality of these wines. Despite the ullage, the wine's gleaming yellow-gold colour was still tinged with green; the bouquet was remarkably fresh, with no sign of breaking up or drying out; the palate was likewise fresh, with a honeyed middle and a light touch of drying toastiness married with acid on the finish.

My most recent encounter with Bin 3270 was at the Canberra National Show in November 1984 and Class 38: the 19 wines in this Museum Class (1979 and older vintages) were awarded four gold, four silver and four bronze medals, marking it the greatest class of the show and one of the greatest classes I am ever likely to judge. Entry 18 (which turned out to be Bin 3270) was deep yellow in colour, with an enormously rich toasty-honeyed aroma and an identical palate, rich and very toasty. There is no question that this style of wine requires understanding, and will not be to everyone's taste. I am glad of that, because it is to mine.

1970 Bin 3870 was by far the most successful of the Lindemans' reserve bin releases of that year. It won a trophy, a championship and more than 10 gold medals in an illustrious show career. Nonetheless, it does not appear to be showing the extreme longevity of the great wines of the 1960s: the last bottle I tasted (_Winestate_ May 1983) was showing definite signs of age on the bouquet, with some curious camphor characters. The palate was much better, smooth and well balanced.

In the younger wines, the '72, '73, '75, '79, '81 and '83 have been the most successful. The '72 Bin 4270, which was a somewhat coarse and uninspiring wine in its youth, was re-released in November 1983 and once again showed how these wines almost invariably repay cellaring. True enough, the wine had no further improvement in front of it (indeed it seemed to be on the wane), but it had that rich toasty aroma and flavour which are so much the hallmark of the style, and which make these the ultimate food wines.

1973 produced very full-bodied whites, and both of Lindemans' releases from the year reflected this. As a relatively young wine, Bin 4670 was extraordinarily precocious, looking and tasting like a wine 10 years older. Bin 4788 was the second release (in 1977) at the princely sum of $3.25; it, too, had great vanillan-buttery richness to the mid-palate, even if it was a little short on finesse.

Bin 4911 of 1975, a 100 per cent Ben Ean Vineyard wine, was held back for its initial release in September 1979; a wine with considerable weight and firmness, it has a number of years left in front of it yet.

The wines of 1976, 1977 and 1978 were un-inspiring, but 1979 saw a partial return to form and the first appreciable introduction of new oak into the flavour and character of the wine. Karl Stockhausen, who made virtually all these wines, is a reluctant celebrant when it comes to the marriage of oak with semillon. He can (and does) point with obvious justification to the wines he made in the 1960s without any new-oak influence whatsoever. But I think that in the final analysis there is no choice. First, the marketplace today expects, indeed demands, oak in the make-up of semillon- and chardonnay-based wines. Second, semillon (wherever grown) does not produce a generous wine in its youth, unless the flavour is filled out by a little residual sugar or some oak. Third, Lindemans is now sourcing its grapes from Broke and from other Hunter River vineyards which are higher yielding than were the old Sunshine and Ben Ean Vineyards. The resultant flavour is less concentrated and, as I say elsewhere, it seems highly unlikely the wines will be as long-lived.

So it is that the 1979 had some oak in the back-ground, and that subsequent vintages have shown increasing levels. 1979 Bin 5670 has a considerable depth of fruit, and I was greatly taken by the wine when it was first released. Since then I have seen in the wine some evidence of the yeast-derived volatility which so bedevilled the industry in the early 1980s (Lindemans included). For the time being I reserve judgement: there may well be enough stuffing in the wine to push the volatility into the background.

The spicy vanillan oak aromas and flavours of the 1981 Bin 5870 are pronounced to the point where they tended to dominate the wine when it was first released, but are now settling back into the wine. Both the '82 White Burgundy Bin 6070 and the Chablis Bin 6075 suffered badly from volatility, which I presume derived from faulty yeasts.

The roll call of chablis from the 1960s is every bit as impressive. My last bottle of '60 Bin 1530 was a little tired at more than 20 years of age, and drank more like a white burgundy; the '63 Bin 2250 showed far more life when drunk around the same

time. The line comes alive with the '65 Bin 2755; that and the following three vintages produced magnificent wines, Bins 2975, 3275 and 3475.

Of these, '68 Bin 3475 was (and is) the greatest. Without the warmth and alcoholic strength of the '65 and '66 vintages, perhaps, but a marvellously rich and complex wine for all that. It was yet another gold medal-winner in Class 38 at the 1984 Canberra National Wine Show. It still retains the marvellous green-tinged colour it showed when a few years old; for many years it remained amazingly fresh and youthful, but has at last joined the white burgundy camp, with rich honeyed/toast/vanillan flavours which border on being thick.

From 1969 (Bin 3675) the line went into some-thing of an eclipse: the '69 showed the exaggerated toasty/burnt characters of the vintage, which I simply do not like. Indeed, looking at my notes of the wines of the 70s, there is little to be excited about. 1974 Bin 3875, tasted in mid-1983, had strange chalky/cheesy aromas and lacked fruit on the palate; the '78 Bin 5476 tasted at the same time was also hard and somewhat dirty, although it could have been a poor bottle. Bin 5676 of 1979 (again the same tasting) was distressingly volatile, while Bin 6075 of 1982 had been stripped of fruit aroma and flavour by excess sulphur dioxide. I simply do not know why the chablis line should have suffered so much in comparison to the others.

I have dwelt at such length on these wines because they represent an era of Australian winemaking of which we should be proud. To those readers (and there must be many of you) who have bottles of these great wines in your cellars, check the ullage levels. If they are poor, you should think carefully about having them recorked. Hand-corkers can be obtained from winemaking shops for a small outlay, and treated corks likewise. It is essential that you taste the bottle you use to top up with, but it is not strictly necessary to taste the others (although good fun, no doubt).

Over the years Lindemans has also released reserve bin riesling-traminers, verdelhos, verdelho-semillons, chardonnays and chardonnay-semillons. Of these the 1968 Verdelho Bin 3465 stands out: released in 1978 for a pittance, I purchased four-dozen bottles, so impressed was I with the wine. I am still drinking my way through it. The perennial cork problem to one side, it is still a gloriously honeyed wine with an exceptional generosity of mid-palate flavour. Sub-sequent releases (in 1969, 1972 and 1974, sometimes blended with semillon) were not in quite the same class.

The other great white line is provided by the Reserve Bin Porphyrys. Over the years I have drunk Lindemans' Porphyrys from before 1920 and from 1923. The first came from a friend's cellar (and in turn from his grandfather), the second bought at an auction at Len Evans Wines of a remarkable cellar discovered in a stone house at Hunters Hill in the early 1970s. In each case I have shared in a number of bottles, and every one was exceptional, still retaining luscious sweet fruit.

Perhaps the most remarkable tasting was the last bracket of wines at a great Australian Wine Dinner I attended in May 1983. We finished with Lindemans' Porphyrys from 1937, 1949 and 1956. The 1937 was bright deep yellow, still with green tints, and was incredibly fresh. It had been kept in a cellar at Bungendore (near Canberra) which partly explains its condition, but it had also evidently been helped by a fairly high dose of sulphur, which reduced the lusciousness the wine might have otherwise developed.

The 1949 wine shared with '53 Grange Hermitage my highest points of the night (19.5 out of 20). Dark burnished gold in colour, the orange-peel aroma was intensely rich and deep, and the palate of quite exceptional power and intensity, with a soft but lingering finish. 1956 Bin 1270 had some of the same orange-peel aroma in the bouquet, with some fresher vanillan characters. While not as intense as the 1949, the palate showed a remarkable combination of freshness and lusciousness, and was in superb condition.

The two subsequent vintages to equal very nearly the quality of the '56 were 1962 Bin 3080 and 1967 in 4180. None of these wines owes any of its character to botrytis or to new oak, these days considered absolute prerequisites to a sauterne-style wine of any pretension to quality. They were made by adding mistelle (concentrated grape juice) to a full-bodied (and very probably slightly coarse) base wine containing a considerable quantity of pressings, and then relying on vat and bottle age to do the rest. The '62 Bin 3080 shows just what age can do; it was originally released under the commercial Bin 36 label for around $1 a bottle. It was hurriedly withdrawn around 1965 and commenced a show career which netted it 16 gold and 19 silver medals between then and 1977. Its price had increased proportionately when it was finally re-released in mid-1979 to $21.70 a bottle. Both it and the '67 Bin 4180 show rich complex vanillan/camphor aromas and flavours which are purely and simply the product of bottle age. The newer Porphyrys derive substantial additional complexity from new oak, but are still deprived of botrytis influence. It will be extremely interesting to see whether time, instead of making it great, will simply pass it by.

These white wines, both dry and sweet, are in many ways red wines dressed up as whites. They have the complexity of flavour and structure one normally finds only with red wines; they are in so many ways Australia's answer to the great white wines of Burgundy. Here, too, the whites can sometimes show greater muscle, greater flesh, greater complexity, and greater longevity than their pinot noir counterparts.

All of which is not to deny that, just as Lindemans has produced sublime semillons, so it has produced some astonishingly great Hunter shiraz — which, with age, assumes a velvety sheen, a structure and a flavour almost exactly halfway between a great old Rhone Valley red and a great old French burgundy.

If my memories of Lindemans' whites start with Bin 591 of 1956, the red wines go back a little further to Bins 145, 146 and 147 of 1953. I drank the last of these — a half-bottle of Bin 147 — in the late 1960s, and my tastebuds still water at the recollection. Then followed Bin 1111 of 1957 and, with Bin 1590 of 1959, we move into the present tense, as it were.

This supreme wine ranks with the great wines of Maurice O'Shea, Colin Preece, Roger Warren and Max Schubert. Because of the handover of wine-making responsibilities from Hans Mollenhauer to Karl Stockhausen, Ray Kidd had a substantial personal involvement in the making of the wine. 1959 was a low-yielding vintage and a late harvest delayed by pre-vintage rain, but the grapes were nonetheless fully ripe when harvested. The outstanding quality of the wine was recognised while it was still in cask, and a decision was taken to use a special high-quality bottle when it was bottled on 21 October 1960. The only distinctive receptacle available was an imported bordeaux bottle, so this was used.

This in turn no doubt influenced the label for the token release made in the early 1960s, and which described it as Bin 1590 Claret (hastily changed to Burgundy a few years later). In an 11-year show career from 1964 to 1974 it amassed one championship, three trophies and 15 gold medals. When finally released (at a fully commercial level) in the mid-1970s at around $26 a bottle, I had not the least hesitation in buying a case — a wise-enough decision because by the time of its final re-release a few years later the price had reached $40 a bottle. Equally I have been in no rush to drink the wine: while it will not improve, it is on a plateau which it will hold for many years yet.

Light to medium garnet-red in colour, the aroma is unequivocally that of the Hunter, with a soft but infinitely complex amalgam of leather, earth, and vegetative aromas, yet with the fruit to carry all those things. The palate is a logical extension of the bouquet: the velvety softness gives an illusion of lightness, but the wine has both the alcohol and the structure to go on almost indefinitely. What tannin there is is almost imperceptible—these wines ensnare you by stealth; their capacity to age gracefully is by no means obvious when they are young.

But just as the style of the white wines has changed, so has that of the red wines. A retrospective tasting in the second half of 1982, covering the years 1961 to 1980, threw those changes into high relief. The change seems to have come somewhere between 1970 and 1973: I lead into my notes from those two tastings with some of the comments I made at the time.

> These 'new generation' wines show greater attention to pH; a more rigorous exclusion of extraneous odours and flavours; and a modest but nonetheless increased oak influence. The still-to-be-answered question is what will happen to these wines with age. At the moment the young and the old appear as different as chalk and cheese. But the Hunter does exert a regional influence quite separate from the effect of the mercaptan/H_2S. It is starting to show in Brokenwood's reds, and as young wines these were quite definitely free from H_2S.

> Because the regional influence is always present (and other influences sometimes) it is not always easy to tell where one finishes and the other starts. For me (although not for all tasters) the two 1970 wines provided a graphic contrast: one fell on one side of the line, the other on the other side.

> Bin 4103 had enormous regional complexity on the bouquet; certainly, it is a wine which requires an understanding of the district to be fully appreciated, but I would defend the intrinsic quality of the wine against all-comers. On the other hand I found both the bouquet and the palate of 1970 Bin 4000 quite objectionable, and virtually exclusively deriving from mercaptan.

> Possibly partly because of the extra tannin that the Bin 4000 had, it quite clearly had its supporters; a significant number of those present must have placed it somewhere near the top. I am not necessarily saying that they were wrong in so doing, but my personal preferences clearly lie elsewhere.

> The foregoing apart, the 1965 Bins 3100 and 3110, the 1966 Bins 3300 and 3310, the 1967 Bin 3565 and 1980 Bin 4103 showed the extraordinary cellaring potential that these wines have. Because they are all relatively low in tannin, and all have that velvety burgundy structure, the temptation is

to look at the young wines and say that they have a short span in front of them only. My guess is that the '79 Bin 5190 will be in every respect the equal of the 1967 in 12 years time, and may even rival the '65.

My notes (and points) were as follows:

1960 Bin 1970 *Colour:* medium red, with a tawny rim. *Bouquet:* complex camphor/straw/oxidation characters. *Palate:* that same straw oxidation character yet not at all unpleasant. Nice fruit still there, but wine clearly past its best. (17.5/20)

1965 Bin 3100 Immense colour, deep and dark. A very, very big wine with considerable tannin and, for me at least, a faint hint of volatility—but acceptable given the vast total flavour, and the overall finesse and balance. (19/20)

1965 Bin 3110 Again has extraordinary colour for a 15-year-old Hunter red. Very generous soft fruit dominates both bouquet and palate. A complete wine, absolutely perfection to drink now, although it will undoubtedly hold together for many years. One of the best Hunter reds—if not the best—of the last 20 years. (19.5/20)

1966 Bin 3300 An attractive wine, if the trace of volatility is ignored. Fresh, and with a lifted fruit character on early and middle palate. Perhaps a little sharp on the finish. (17.5/20)

1967 Bin 3565 *Colour:* reddish, still with some purples, of medium depth. *Bouquet:* tocacco/oak/lifted fruit aromas; smooth and complex. *Palate:* rich smooth fruit with considerable lift and life. At its peak; a most appealing wine. (18/20)

1968 Bin 3710 *Colour:* shows distinct browning. *Bouquet:* complex; pencil shavings/vegetable/fruit aromas. *Palate:* cabbagey/tobacco flavours to fruit, which is not particularly deep. (15/20)

1970 Bin 4000 *Colour:* deep red. *Bouquet:* sweet smelly mercaptan. *Palate:* heavy, tannic and aggressive. All in all, quite out of style (and out of class). (13.5/20)

1970 Bin 4103 *Colour:* tawny red. *Bouquet:* immensely complex blend of tobacco/vegetable/vanillan/camphor aromas. *Palate:* long flavour but slight bitterness detracts. A pity after that superb bouquet. (17.5/20)

1973 Bin 4810 *Colour:* strong red, good for age. *Bouquet:* clean, firm full and fruity; nice oak. *Palate:* lifted sweet cherry fruit. Overall a most attractive soft burgundy style. (17.5/20)

1975 Bin 5103 _Colour:_ red of medium depth. _Bouquet:_ big, round smooth fruit with a hint of aniseed. _Palate:_ big soft chocolatey/caramel flavours. A ripe wine. (16/20)

1977 Bin 5600 _Colour:_ youthful red-purple, light to medium depth. _Bouquet:_ light and fruity; clean, nice touch of oak. _Palate:_ light lifted cherry fruit; trace of bitterness on finish. As with most of the wines, low tannin. (17/20)

1978 Bin 5700 _Colour:_ light reddish. _Bouquet:_ some fruit complexity; not H₂S, rather a smoky/regional character. _Palate:_ medium-ripe fruit, slightly chewy. Fairly light and soft in structure. Drink-now style. (16.5/20)

1979 Bin 5910 _Colour:_ excellent deep purple-red. _Bouquet:_ riper and fuller with considerable glycerine 'legs'. _Palate:_ very ripe generous fruit, yet not jammy or coarse. First-class fruit wine; should cellar very well. (18.5/20)

1980 Bin 5900 _Colour:_ very youthful light purple-red. _Bouquet:_ rather aggressive stalky character. _Palate:_ light/stalky fruit; low tannin. Not my style at all. (14.5/20)

There is an ever-present danger in bemoaning that the wines of today are not up to the quality of those of yesterday. In the case of Lindemans' Hunter River wines I think that many of the changes are for the better. Certainly the changes in the winery are all to the good; but one cannot help but worry that these gains are being more than offset by a diminution in fruit quality as the old, low-yielding vineyards are being replaced by "economic" high-yielding ones which satisfy the criteria of parent-company finance directors, but have little else to commend them. Time alone will tell.

LITTLE'S
PALMERS LANE, POKOLBIN

Little's is the newest arrival in the Hunter Valley, its first vintage coming in 1984 not long after the acquisition of the property from Quentin Taperell, and the first wines going onto the market in mid-1984. Yet already Little's has gained a reputation for itself, and by the end of the year was in the happy position of being able to post the "sold out" signs against a number of the wines made in that vintage.

Winemaker Ian Little obtained a degree in biochemistry from Surrey University in England, but moved back to his native Australia at the end of the 70s to take up a position as assistant brewer at Tooths' Sydney brewery. After 18 months he moved to Rothmans and was seconded by Reynella, where he arrived shortly before commencement of the 1981 vintage. He stayed at Reynella until mid-1982, when he moved back to Rothmans' Sydney operation following Hardy's acquisition of Reynella.

During his time in Adelaide he and his Finnish-born wife Tulla had talked to his parents about the long-term possibility of acquiring a Hunter Valley vineyard and winery. His return to Sydney prompted a closer look and Quentin Taperell's "second" vineyard and winery in Palmers Lane was looked at as a possible acquisition. The thinking was still a leisurely weekend-type development, but in 1983 the family decided to go into the venture on a full-time basis. First the Taperell vineyard, and then the Honeytree Vineyard of Maurice Schlesinger, were acquired and the Taperell winery was upgraded and equipped for the '84 vintage.

Taperell, whose first winery had been sold to Peter Marsh and is now known as Marsh Estate, had established his second vineyard and embryo winery with the intention of making sparkling wine (and only that). The vineyard was accordingly planted to chardonnay and pinot noir, and a spray-insulated Colorbond winery shed had been erected. A single fermentation tank, numerous champagne racks and tables, and a hand-operated basket press were as far as Taperell had gone when the Little family company acquired the land and winery.

The vineyard around the winery had one hectare of pinot noir and a little over three hectares of chardonnay, nowhere near enough to sustain the winery's planned output. Negotiations commenced for the acquisition of Maurice Schlesinger's Honeytree Vineyard, and a fair proportion of its 1984 production went to Little's. The purchase of the vineyard, planted to two hectares of traminer, 2.85 hectares of semillon, 2.6 hectares of shiraz and 2.25 hectares of cabernet, was finalised in the second half of 1984.

The Honeytree Vineyard had been allowed to run down over the past three years, and Ian and Tulla (who is doing the viticulture course at Riverina while Ian finishes his winemaking course, both by correspondence) believe it will take some time before it is restored to full health. The soils at both vineyards are brown and red clays, but that at the winery (known by the Littles as Little Constantia Vineyard) has a permeable loose shale subsoil which should assist yields. Those yields are nonetheless likely to remain modest, chardonnay producing around six to seven tonnes per hectare, and pinot a little less. The yield from Honeytree is uncertain, although some earlier vintages made for Schlesinger by Murray Tyrrell produced some most interesting wine—a spicy '76 Shiraz stands out in my memory.

The strength of Little's will obviously be in the winery. Ian Little installed a refrigerated cool-room within the confines of the winery where the entire 1984 crush of 36 tonnes of grapes (27 tonnes from Honeytree and nine tonnes from Little Constantia) were processed. The fruit, hand-picked into small baskets, was chilled before crushing, and technically perfect wines were made in what was not an easy vintage. Two chardonnays, one with a longer period in oak than the other, a bone-dry traminer, a semillon with appreciable residual sugar (14 grams per litre) and a light, fresh, fragrant cabernet sauvignon were produced. In every case maximum fruit flavour had been retained, and wines conforming in every way to the demands of today's market were produced.

Careful winemaking, a bold label design, and up-market packaging will all help to continue to produce wines well suited to the cellar-door trade which is and will remain an important part of the business. Visitors to the winery will usually meet the winemaker (in the form of Ian) or Tulla, or other members of the family. That personal contact is one of the important weapons in the armoury of the small Hunter Valley maker as he or she struggles for that all-important market share.

McWILLIAM'S MOUNT PLEASANT
MARROWBONE ROAD, POKOLBIN

The Mount Pleasant Vineyard was established by Charles King in 1880 on some of the best red volcanic soil in the Hunter. Early in the following century it was purchased by the O'Sheas; O'Shea senior was Irish and his wife French. It was no doubt her influence which led to their son Maurice being sent to Montpellier in France to study viticulture and oenology. He returned to Australia in 1921 and took over as winemaker in 1925. He renamed the vineyard Mount Pleasant and the winery L'Hermitage, and proceeded to expand the vineyards.

It has been suggested that he was not a good business manager and that it was this which led him to sell a 50 per cent interest to McWilliam's in 1932, marking that company's entry into the Hunter Valley. He may indeed have lacked business acumen, but it is hard to imagine a more difficult time in which to build a business. The market of the day resolved almost entirely around fortified wine, which O'Shea had no interest in making, and the Great Depression respected no-one.

Whatever be the truth, there has never been any doubt about O'Shea's genius as a winemaker. Over the 40 years he was winemaker at Mount Pleasant, a constant stream of magnificent white and red wines were produced. It has been said more than once that these were all made in small quantities (often there would be only one 500-gallon (2275-litre) cask of a given wine, producing 250 dozen); that these wines represented the pick of the vintage, and that much more wine of lesser quality was made; and that many of his greatest wines were not vinified by O'Shea, but were purchased shortly after vintage and taken to Mount Pleasant for maturation and bottling.

That is all true, but in my opinion serves only to underline his brilliance. His ability to recognise a great wine immediately after the end of its primary fermentation, coupled with his skill in getting the wine into the bottle at the right moment, can only be properly understood with the wisdom of hindsight that we now have. Those privileged few who at any time in the past decade have drunk O'Shea wines made in the 30s and 40s, will be only too glad to join with me in praising one of the four greatest wine-makers of the twentieth century. The rather greater number who during the same time have drunk Mount Pleasant '52 Pinot Hermitage or '54 Richard Hermitage will be no less fulsome in their praise.

During 1983 and 1984 I had the opportunity of tasting a number of O'Shea's great wines. At the 1984 Single Bottle Club Dinner (which I also describe in the chapter on Seppelts' Great Western) we drank two whites from the early 50s and two Mountain Reds of the 30s. 1953 McWilliam's Mount Pleasant Florence Riesling, made from semillon, had aged to the point where there were orange tints in the colour, and the aroma showed distinct oxidation; the palate, however, was extraordinary, fine and rich, with the long finish sustained by the considerable alcohol evident in the wine. 1952 Mount Pleasant Light Dry White Bin 54/13 was even darker in colour; made from trebbiano (or, as it used to be then called, white hermitage), the aroma was rich, sweet and full, and the palate likewise—here there was a touch of orange-peel character, unusual but most attractive.

1939 Mountain C Dry Red was, so I am told, made in one of the great bushfire years. Appropriately, but unhappily, the wine showed some traces of burnt/Marmite character on both bouquet and palate, although the evident alcohol and fruit sweetness had preserved it to a degree, and there was none left in my glass at the end of the evening. 1937 Mountain A Dry Red will live with me for the rest of my days. The colour had faded almost to the point of being orange, but that was the only hint of senility. The bouquet was ultra-smooth, fragrant, distinctively and finally regional, yet not tarry or sour. The palate was ethereal in its delicacy, light and smooth and with a softly intense lingering finish. O'Shea would have been proud of it.

In 1983 I shared several bottles of 1954 Richard Hermitage. One, quite badly ullaged, had collapsed, showing both mushroom and volatile characters. The other was exceptional. These old Hunters are not powerhouses; the colour was light to medium red-brown, muted but clear; the bouquet smooth, clean and gently fruity; the palate distinguished by its great length, the flavour lingering in the mouth long after the wine was swallowed. Yet neither alcohol nor tannin was the least bit aggressive.

The fairly obvious point about all this is that these wines have aged with infinite grace for 30, 40 or 50 years. If there is to be a single attribute pointing to a great wine it will be its capacity to grow and develop in bottle for such extended periods. It is common in the great wines of France—particularly those of Bordeaux and the Rhone Valley—and relatively rare in Australia. The Woodley wines from Coonawarra made between 1930 and 1956; Penfolds' Grange Hermitage; and most of the Penfolds show blends made by Max Schubert up to 1967 . . . it is easy to exhaust the list. It may well turn out that some of the wines being made today (Balgownie, Virgin Hills, Yarra Yering and Taltarni spring to mind) will show the same capacity, but they have many years to go before their claims can be substantiated.

This is not to say that very good wine needs to demonstrate such longevity, nor that more than a small percentage of each year's production should be made with such aspirations. The overall thrust of current technology for top-of-the-range reds is to produce full-flavoured wines with good fruit character and some (probably oak-derived) complexity which will be most attractive four or five years after vintage.

Reverting to the wines of O'Shea, it is all the more remarkable that these wines were made almost exclusively from hermitage (some with a little pinot) or semillon; and that oak played no role at all in their creation. They were wines of finesse, of elegance and of charm; neither the sinews of cabernet nor the tannin of oak are to be found in their structure. Little wonder that the voice of Murray Tyrrell booms across the Valley urging winemakers and drinkers alike not to forget these two great classic varieties.

O'Shea was well known for his cerebral sense of humour and for his at times cryptic utterances. Part of that attitude comes through on the labels of his best wines: Mountain A, Mountain C, Henry I, II and III and then TY and Richard (in fact denoting Tyrrell wines), HT (Tulloch's) and Charles (Elliotts). In more recent years OP (Old Paddock) and OH (Old Hill) have appeared alongside Frederick (simply a blend) and Philip (likewise).

It has from time to time been suggested that the truckloads of Alan Bailey's wine shipped from Glenrowan to McWilliam's in the 40s and early 50s found its way into these wines. I do not doubt that O'Shea (and others) found blending useful; in the absence of O'Shea or his blend books to prove to the contrary, I think it mere supposition that Rutherglen material (or Tahbilk, for that matter) found its way into these top wines. Most significantly, I see no evidence of it in the bouquet or palate of the wines. The commercial blends were, no doubt, a different matter.

In 1956 O'Shea died and Brian Walsh took over as winemaker, a position he held for more than 20 years. In that time McWilliam's fortunes—and its vineyards—waxed and waned. In 1950 O'Shea had planted Rosehill (the other half of the old volcano shared by Lake's Folly and Draytons' Lambkin) and in 1959 Walsh made his greatest red, 1959 Rosehill RH, a wine very much in the style (and class) of O'Shea. In the 1960s McWilliam's developed its One Hundred Acre Vineyard, next door to Rothbury, but like so many other vineyards of its era it simply was not an economic proposition, and was eventually sold in 1983.

I wish I could be more enthusiastic about the wines of Mount Pleasant. Elizabeth Riesling is one of the leading brand whites in Australia, enjoying nationwide distribution, and with reported sales of around 75,000 cases per year. If that figure is correct (and if anything it may be conservative) it would account for upwards of two-thirds of the 1500 tonne crush at Mount Pleasant, which seems improbably high. It is likely that McWilliam's purchases bulk white wine from other producers in the Hunter which would go to swell the volume of Elizabeth, but which would not reflect itself in the crush given for Mount Pleasant. Elizabeth is a very well-made commercial wine; what it lacks in flair, it makes up in reliability.

In some vintages McWilliam's keeps back a parcel which it markets under the Anne Riesling label. Both these wines, incidentally, are made from semillon, the use of the word riesling being more a brand nomenclature although it did originally derive from Hunter River riesling. Anne, even more than Elizabeth, develops very slowly but seldom acquires the honeyed toasty richness of the Lindeman whites. A 1979 Anne Riesling on sale at the end of 1984 was a classic Hunter white, showing more toasty/ honeyed characters than one usually finds in McWilliam's wines, and with another 10 years in front of it.

In recent years some interesting traminer rieslings have come out from time to time: originally the riesling in this blend denoted semillon, but reference to the fine print discloses it is now rhine riesling. Such a wine was among the initial releases under a new McWilliam's label launched in mid-1984. This retains the Mount Pleasant badge (though not the name) and, perhaps significantly, only one of the four wines (a 1979 Cabernet Sauvignon) specifically states that the grapes were grown in the Lower Hunter.

Going back yet further, McWilliam's has made some truly obscure whites, including such rarities as aucerot riesling and montils shiraz. In fact aucerot and montils are one and the same variety (one of the most obscure in the wine world, grown in tiny—and declining—quantities in Cognac), while the shiraz is a shortening of white shiraz, a misnomer for trebbiano. The 1974 Montils Shiraz was excellent.

Last, but by no means least among the whites, is the Mount Pleasant Sauterne. The 1956 vintage of this wine was freely available towards the end of the 60s at around $7 a bottle, and was then (and indeed still is) a lovely, old-fashioned, fresh, clean, sweet white, made without the benefit of botrytis but seemingly none the worse for that. Other vintages (notably the '67 and '75) have also been most attractive.

It is the reds which have disappointed most. It is true that I have an intense dislike of mercaptan; it may be also true that I am not prepared to give Hunter reds the benefit of the doubt and attribute so-called regional characteristics to the district. Finally, I have to admit that a considerable number of consumers relate positively to the particular tarry bouquet and taste of the Mount Pleasant reds. All of that said and done I simply cannot bring myself to accept, let alone like, the style. I find that whatever fruit is in the wine is lost in a sea of rubbery/tarry flavours, while the top-of-the-line bins of OP, OH, Robert and Pinot Hermitage are almost invariably flawed by it. The pity is that there is some magnificent material here, coming from very old vines grown in

exceptional soil. 1959 Rosehill, 1961 Richard Hermitage and 1975 Cabernet Hermitage are among a handful of wines to rise above these difficulties.

The wines come up in wine shows and regularly cause heated discussion. It is not the job of show judges to guess which company might have made a particular wine—indeed one endeavours positively to exclude such thoughts—but these wines are so distinctive that recognition is inevitable. More than once the argument has been resolved by the production of a copper coin (copper will remove H_2S and reduce mercaptan) which has demonstrated that indeed something other than regional character has manifested itself in the wine.

MARSH ESTATE
DEASEYS ROAD, POKOLBIN

Peter Marsh had been one of the enthusiasts who had formed Terrace Vale. Between 1971 and 1978 he had come to known the Hunter well, and by 1978 he learnt that Dr Quentin Taperell, who had established nearby Quentin Estate in 1971 and erected its winery in 1976, was thinking of selling and moving to another vineyard in the area to make champagne. Events moved quickly; Marsh bought Quentin Estate late in the year, and in 1979 found himself as winemaker at the hastily renamed winery. It was an experience which Marsh and his family will not quickly forget.

Peter Marsh's training as a pharmacist gave him a head start in the tasks of juice analysis, the addition of sulphur dioxide and tartaric acid and so on, but winemaking is neither learnt from a textbook nor overnight. Nonetheless, his wines are solid if somewhat conservative citizens, based as they are on the stalwarts of the district—semillon and shiraz.

The 1983 Pokolbin Riesling (made from semillon) has an odd medical/plasticine aroma; some of the same medicinal characters come again on the broad, soft palate. A 1983 Traminer was more successful, with marked varietal spice on the bouquet. The 1981 red wines, on sale at the end of 1984, were ultra-traditional styles, free from any major fault but likewise soft and broad.

The vineyard is a fairly substantial one for a single-family operation: seven hectares of semillon, seven hectares of shiraz and three hectares each of cabernet sauvignon and traminer. With three sons, Simon, Nicholas and Andrew, Peter Marsh has long-term plans for Marsh Estate.

MILLSTONE
TALGA ROAD, ALLANDALE, via MAITLAND

Peter Dobinson is part-potter, part-winemaker. He leaves one in little doubt that he would rather be a full-time winemaker, even though he fills both occupations on the fairly remote vineyard which he and his wife Vivienne purchased in 1973. These days he does one firing a year in the adjacent kiln; it takes about a month to make a kiln load, and Dobinson says "whenever I'm in the pottery, I get pretty edgy thinking I should be out cultivating or suckering".

Right from the outset the Dobinsons have done things their own way, at their own pace. "If we wanted to get rich we would buy a fast-food chain, not a winery." In particular, they would not operate a vineyard and winery which produces only 1650 cases of fairly unusual wine a year. The emphasis is on the quality of life, which clearly suits the family, for elder son Craig joined the business in 1984 and younger son Matt was due to join it in 1985.

The first commercial release did not eventuate until 1979, when three wines (a 1978 Cabernet Sauvignon, a 1979 Shiraz and a 1979 Sauvignon Blanc) were offered. What is more, those wines and almost all those subsequently sold were made using the carbonic maceration process. Dobinson explains that "I didn't have a wine background, so I didn't have any preconceived ideas as to how the wine should taste". What ideas he did have were fashioned by some of the early releases from Jim Roberts's Belbourie Vineyard, which were also made using carbonic maceration principles. Peter Dobinson recalls being particularly taken by a 1976 Homestead Shiraz, and a 1972 Rhine Riesling, which had "cigar-box character", from Roberts.

So Dobinson commenced his winemaking in 1976 using carbonic maceration with 70-litre polythene containers doubling up as fermenters. While the size of the operation has grown to the point where in 1984 just under 32 tonnes of grapes were crushed, the basic winemaking process has not. Both whites and reds are left uncrushed for a week or more in the specially built two-tonne fermenters which line one wall of the winery. One was made commercially, the other half-dozen by a friend of the family.

The use of one form or another of carbonic maceration with reds is common enough, but it is distinctly uncommon with white wines. It is an extreme and extended form of skin contact, which is practised widely with varieties such as chardonnay. Normal skin contact, however, extends for between four and 24 hours in an inert atmosphere, at low temperatures and before fermentation commences. If extended for a week or more, and in the higher ambient temperatures of fermentation, it has a very different effect. The young wines are deep yellow, and rapidly turn gold; they tend to be tannic; the fruit aroma is markedly diminished; and the middle palate is usually lacking, although there is reason to suppose it may build back up after several years bottle age.

Peter Dobinson is the first to admit that not all of his white wines have pleased him, so much so that in 1984 he made part of his sauvignon blanc by using conventional winemaking methods. But he also made a small quantity employing carbonic maceration, and prefers the latter wine.

I cannot admit to being specially taken by the white wines, although I freely admit they are different, and are certainly not undrinkable. But I think he has been far more successful with his reds, with some attractive meaty/spicy carbonic maceration flavours in both his nouveau and conventionally matured wines. Dobinson likes the flexibility of the process, in which the wine can be removed from the skins at the end of the carbonic maceration (at around seven beaume) to make a nouveau style, or left with the skins until the end of the primary fermentation, to make a full-bodied, long-lived red.

So he will continue experimenting and refining the process (he devised an effective cooling method in 1984) and thereby to produce highly distinctive wines. Which, after all, has always been his professed aim. He says: "Perhaps I've got a cellar palate now, which I know is a bad thing. But I can't see the point in making the same wine as Hungerford Hill, or Tyrrell's, or Rothbury or whatever."

MOUNT VIEW
MOUNT VIEW ROAD, MOUNT VIEW

It is no coincidence that one of the foremost viticulturists of the Hunter Valley region should have established his own vineyard on the red basalt slopes of the Mount View area. This small side valley, shared with Robsons and Petersons, would have an entirely different appellation to the Hunter Valley proper if the two were magically transposed to France.

The atmosphere of the Mount View area is quite different. The flowers beside the roadside seem to bloom more profusely, more brightly. Throughout the growing season the vines are greener, lusher and more vigorous, the leaves gleaming against the dark-red crumbly soil. Partly because of the extra vigour (and the far greater yields of grapes which follow) vintage comes rather later than in the Hunter Valley proper. Yet on all the evidence to date the quality of the grapes is exemplary: the wines of these three vineyards have all of the flavour and varietal character one could possibly wish for.

Although not related to the J. Y. Tulloch family who established Tulloch's, Harry Tulloch has had a long involvement with the Hunter. His father was in charge of Tulloch's Fordwich Vineyard, while Harry is an expert in the clonal selection of grape varieties, and a vineyard layout expert. He was responsible for the Hollydene and Seppelt Vineyards: anyone who has driven out from Cessnock along the airport road must have seen the military precision of the rows and posts of the Seppelt Vineyard. That it was not successful was in no way Harry Tulloch's fault.

The 12-hectare property was first planted by Harry and Ann Tulloch in 1971; from 1973 until 1979 most of the grapes were sold to McWilliam's. Between 1977 and 1979 a certain amount of grapes were contract-made for Mount View at other wineries, but since 1980 all the wine has been made by Harry Tulloch (with assistance from his son Keith, a recent Roseworthy graduate).

The list of wines available in December 1984 had two most unusual features: the heavy reliance on verdelho, and the number of old wines available, with semillon-verdelho blends going back to 1977. I wholeheartedly share Harry Tulloch's enthusiasm for verdelho, which in bygone days was often called madeira in the Hunter. Particularly in the last century it was a highly regarded grape, while Lindemans released some lovely wines made from the variety between 1968 and 1974 which came off old plantings—in earlier decades the identity of the wine was lost in blends with semillon. The problem is that verdelho is a relatively low-yielding variety, a difficulty compounded by the fact that only its free-run juice can be used in dry whites: the pressings are too heavy and oily, being suitable only for sweet wines.

Not that the Mount View plantings of a little over one hectare of verdelho are of any statistical importance in the overall scheme of things. Mount View Wines had only seven hectares of grapes in 1984 (a little over one hectare each of verdelho, chardonnay and semillon, a little under three hectares of chardonnay, and less than half a hectare of cabernet sauvignon) with merlot (for blending with the cabernet) and pinot noir (for blending with the shiraz) planned for the not-too-distant future.

The development of Mount View Wines has taken place at a very leisurely rate, reflecting Harry

Tulloch's full-time involvement as a viticulturist in other vineyards. Thus even though the winery was erected in 1980, Mount View Wines did not open its doors to the public until 1983, and did not send out its first mailing-list offer until April 1984. It was largely due to this that the range of old wines was still available at the end of 1984. Now that Keith Tulloch has returned from Roseworthy, it is a fair bet that the pace will quicken.

A tasting of the semillon-verdelho blends back to 1977 showed that the blend is a very logical one: when the wine is young, the greater weight and flavour of the verdelho fills out the semillon; while with age the semillon builds around the verdelho smoothly and coherently. This is not a case of opposite characters tempering each other, but of similar ones building on each other. The most attractive of the older wines were the 1980, with the verdelho influence to the fore showing in the honeyed aroma and flavour, and the 1982, in which nicely integrated oak (used for the first time) added a further dimension to what is a richly flavoured and complex wine.

In 1983 and again in 1984 Tulloch also made small quantities of a straight verdelho, which not surprisingly sells out almost immediately on release. The 1984 was the most successful wine in that somewhat difficult year: its honeyed/melon aroma, and the slightly grassy but strongly flavoured palate augur well for more propitious vintages.

Vintage imperatives to one side, Mount View's shiraz-based wines reflect Tulloch's leaning towards softer reds, particularly those with good fruit flavour, rather than big, full bodied high-alcohol wines. This is manifested in his tendency to pick a little earlier than usual, and his desire to have some pinot noir available in the future. But just as 1984 produced light-bodied wines, so 1981 gave powerful, solid ones, and the '81 Mount View (with 13.2 degrees of alcohol) reflects this. It is a richly flavoured wine, with strong leathery regional character, yet it is devoid of objectionable tarry/mercaptan aromas. I liked it very much.

As one would expect, the wine was very well received by that sector of the market that looks to big-bodied reds. His 1982 and 1983 Shiraz are closer to his own preferences, and to those who look for elegance and finesse. The '83 is a lovely wine with a nice touch of new oak to go with the sweet berry flavours which are the hallmark of that excellent vintage.

With a present production of around 1650 cases, Mount View wines are always going to be hard to find unless you visit the Hunter Valley or get onto the mailing list. But the fundamentals are all there: an excellent vineyard, immaculately maintained and yielding around 7.5 tonnes per hectares of red wines and 12.5 tonnes per hectare of white wines, and a family team with all of the requisite viticultural and oenological skills.

OAKVALE WINES
BROKE ROAD, POKOLBIN

The cold statistics of boom and bust tell little of the human suffering which lies behind them; of all the Hunter families, the Elliotts have been most affected. For almost a century the Elliott name stood proudly alongside those of Tulloch, Tyrrell and Drayton. The four families were the pillars around which the Hunter was built; only later did McWilliam's and Lindemans arrive on the scene to lend their not inconsiderable support. In the early to mid-1960s, when I commenced my regular buying trips to the Hunter Valley, the first port of call was Elliotts' Wine Saloon, just off Vincent Street in the centre of town. In July of each year that visit would assume particular importance: the shiraz of the previous year would be released, and invariably sold out within a month or so. It could become critical to leave Sydney before 7 a.m. on Saturday so as to arrive at Elliotts before the rush began. The white wines were in less demand, although I do not think it is with the wisdom of hindsight that I say I always had a particular love of the Belford Private Bin Semillons. These quickly developed an intense honeyed/buttery flavour and structure which set them apart from almost all other wines. In those days Elliotts had four vineyards, Belford, Fordwich, Oakvale and Tallawanta.

Oakvale had been acquired in 1893 by a Scottish coalminer, William Elliott, and converted from a dairy farm to a vineyard. The winery, the oldest remaining part of which was destroyed by fire in 1969, was erected on the spot where the present winery stands today. William's son Bob purchased the Belford property near Branxton in the 1930s, which was planted to semillon to supplement the semillon and shiraz grown on the Oakvale Vineyard.

A little later the Fordwich Vineyard was acquired, also planted to semillon, and finally in 1943 the Tallawanta Vineyard was bought from Stevens. Tallawanta, just off the Broke Road, produced some marvellous traditional Hunter River reds from the hermitage grown on its heavy clay soils. The 1965, some of which was sold to Rhinecastle Wines, was quite memorable.

Doug Elliott had taken over as winemaker following the death of his father Bob in 1959. A taciturn man, he never seemed to derive any enjoyment or amusement from winemaking, although he was not helped by indifferent health. It came as no great surprise that he sold the business to Hermitage Estate in 1974, retaining only the Belford Vineyard with the intention of selling the grapes to other makers. It was an ill-fated decision: the red-wine boom was faltering, and economic woes were about to descend on the Hunter Valley. Within a few years Hermitage had gone into receivership, and the Elliotts lost a substantial portion of their sale price.

Hermitage was ultimately absorbed into the Wyndham group. The Tallawanta Vineyard was sold to a group of Cessnock businessmen (who have had no particular cause to celebrate their purchase), and Fordwich went to a syndicate associated with Len Evans and the Rothbury Estate. The Elliott family repurchased the winery and the Oakvale Vineyard, leaving the Elliott brand name with Wyndham—who after a few short years allowed it quietly to disappear.

John Elliott, Doug's son, became winemaker and manager and set about restoring the by-now thoroughly tattered reputation of the winery. Very much the traditionalist, he believes that semillon and shiraz are the grapes which have proved themselves beyond doubt as most suited to the climate and soil of the Hunter Valley. While that is the way John Elliott sees it, the public does not altogether agree. In the long run he may well be proved correct, but that is of little comfort. The confusion with the Elliott brand name has not helped either. The net result is that Oakvale is finding the going so tough that John Elliott sold his grapes from the 1984 vintage, making relatively little wine at Oakvale, and the future of the winery was very uncertain as the 1985 vintage approached.

Recent vintages have been extremely disappointing, with harsh, heavy-solids fermentation characters in the semillons from Belford. Neither the 1984 nor 1983 Belford Private Bin Semillons was of acceptable quality, while the 1982 Oakvale Chardonnay was excessively volatile and devoid of varietal character. Unhappily the hermitage wines from 1982 to 1983 were no better; only the 1982 Hunter Valley Cabernet Sauvignon was free from major winemaking faults.

PETERSONS
MOUNT VIEW ROAD, MOUNT VIEW

If a note, indeed a tune, of pessimism has invaded some of my writings on the Hunter Valley, it should not intrude into these lines. When in 1964 Ian and Shirley Peterson bought 77 hectares of rolling hillside land tucked out of sight on the seldom-visited Mount View Road, grape growing—and winemaking—was the last thing on their mind. The beauty of the property, with its views out over the valley floor, and the richness of the soil, marked it simply as an ideal weekend retreat from the long weekday hours worked by Ian Peterson as a pharmacist in his Toronto pharmacy.

And so for the next five or six years it remained just that, supporting a small polled-Hereford stud to justify its existence in the eyes of our ever-vigilant revenue authorities. Then, in the steamy, heated days of the end of the 60s, estate agents and would-be buyers started to beat on the front door, apparently wishing to buy the property and plant a vineyard. Intrigued, the Petersons sought advice from the Department of Agriculture. That department, I can vouchsafe, was in no way responsible for promoting the boom. In most instances (my own included) it gave a realistic cold shower to the aspirations of would-be vignerons. But just as correctly, it advised the Petersons that patches of soil on the property were ideally suited for grape growing.

So in 1971 the Peterson family was mobilised, and they personally planted 4.5 hectares of semillon. In that same year I and two others planted a little less than one hectare at Brokenwood. So it was with no great surprise that I heard Shirley Peterson tell me that "in 1973 we sold eight tonnes of semillon to McWilliam's picked from those four and a half hectares. That was the day we decided to put a winery in; we had done all that work and there was nothing left to show for it."

It is a story which has been told many times, and which I hope will be told until the end of time. One grows wheat, drills for oil or makes machines, and all there ever is to show for it is (if one is successful) money in the bank. For most people, that is more than enough. But vines are different; they entwine you in their steel-tough tendrils, ensnaring heart and mind.

Admittedly the Petersons took their time. In 1972 they added another 4.5 hectares of shiraz, followed over the ensuing years by 1.2 hectares of chardonnay, 0.4 hectares of cabernet sauvignon and half a hectare of pinot noir. Until the 1981 vintage all their grapes

were sold variously to McWilliam's, Allandale and neighbour Murray Robson. But in 1980 the family had taken the plunge, and erected a modest but functional winery.

Ian Peterson made that first experimental vintage; it quickly brought home the realisation that grape growing was one thing, winemaking another altogether. So during 1981 the Petersons employed the first outsider, Gary Reid, as their winemaker. Reid has been with them ever since, and has obviously played a part in the phenomenal success which Petersons have achieved in the interim. Although without technical qualifications, he learnt his wine-making skills at Tulloch's under Patrick Auld.

Not that there is anything especially sophisticated about the Peterson wines. The Petersons, with modesty and realism, attribute their success to "good soil, good cultivation, good grapes and a clean winery", which, if you care to think about it, is as close to a universal formula for success as you are ever likely to find. That success has come in large licks: champion small winemaker, Hunter Valley Wine Show 1983 and 1984; gold medal and trophy, Royal Sydney Show for best small makers' white wine; trophy and gold medal, Hunter Valley Wine Show 1984—the walls are literally festooned with show awards, all won within the last three years.

The vineyard now produces between 110 and 130 tonnes per year from the 13.5 hectares, close enough to 10 tonnes per hectare. This is due solely to the perfectly drained, rich, red volcanic soil. The vines seldom show stress, and they even produced hand-some crops in the worst of the drought years. The winery has a maximum capacity of 70 tonnes, so the excess semillon and shiraz grapes are sold, and the Petersons have no intention of ever using anything but estate-grown grapes.

These days Shirley and Ian Peterson are employed full-time at the winery and vineyard; Ian returns to his pharmacy to relieve the manager every Saturday morning and every fourth Sunday. "It keeps us fed," says Shirley, with a wry grin. Son Colin works as a coalminer at night to earn extra dollars, dividing his days between his horse stud at Mulbring and the vineyard. "He thinks he's young, and doesn't need sleep," Shirley continues. Who said Australians had forgotten how to work?

THE ROBSON VINEYARD
MOUNT VIEW ROAD, MOUNT VIEW

Many people aspire to style, but only a few achieve it. Murray Robson is one of the few who has, and it all seems to come so effortlessly. The former co-owner of a chic menswear shop in Double Bay in Sydney (which for some time gave its name to the vineyard and winery, then called the Squire Vineyard), he came to the Hunter first as a member of the then Oakdale (now Audrey Wilkinson) syndicate. Shortly thereafter he became a director of Pokolbin Winemakers Limited, the flame of which flickered briefly around 1970 when a modest public flotation raised enough money to buy Barrie Drayton's Happy Valley Vineyard and winery. It was not a great success, even in those heady days, and was soon taken over by Saxonvale Wines, then a division of the ill-fated Gollin group.

Robson's entry into the world of wine was a pure investment. Not only did he know nothing about wine, but he was, indeed, a teetotaller. But he visited the district frequently and let it be known he was looking for other investments in the region. Towards the end of 1971 an estate agent showed him an 89-hectare block at Mount View, an obscure side valley tucked in a fold of the Brokenback Range which Robson had never visited. A climb to the top of the steep slope persuaded Robson to buy it, with the sole intention of building a holiday cottage for letting.

With his flair for marketing, Robson determined to establish vines in front of the wooden cottage then in the course of construction. It is the mark of the man that, rather than plant just any vines, he should retain a consultant (John Stanford) and decide to ignore shiraz and semillon. Instead he planted trial blocks of chardonnay, sauvignon blanc, traminer, cabernet sauvignon, pinot noir, merlot and malbec.

It was the beginning of the end; it hardly seemed worth selling the few hundred kilograms of grapes which the vines produced in 1974 so he determined to turn them into wine. I well remember discussing winemaking theory and practice with Murray Robson around that time when he dropped into Brokenwood for a chat. He had the rather naive and idyllic view that he could successfully make natural wine, using a minimum of equipment and a minimum of chemicals. His 1974 vintage comprehensively proved otherwise, a failure compounded by the fact that he still knew little about the taste of wine.

But he was quick to learn, very quick. His 1975 Chardonnay won five medals, including a gold medal at Brisbane and a silver medal at Melbourne. Success has followed Robson ever since. While it has not always been easy from a financial viewpoint, the Robson Vineyard must have been one of the few small wineries to produce an acceptable rate of return within five years of its establishment.

The immaculately groomed, quietly spoken Robson is the very essence of the country gentleman, and I was sure that one morning, sooner or later, I would find him at the head of the Cessnock Hunt Club, dressed in scarlet coat to go with his omnipresent white moleskins. But this is only a veneer; Robson has worked with a single-minded purpose to bring his wines to the point where they are equal to the best the Valley has to offer. Almost as importantly, he is an ambassador for the Hunter as a whole, fiercely rejecting any assertions that it is less than perfect for winemaking, holding that cool-climate viticulture is nothing more than a trendy cliché which will be dead and buried within a few short years.

His venture started off on the right foot: the Mount View soil is exceedingly fertile and well drained, and the side valley seems to get that little bit of extra moisture. Although the vineyard is only four hectares, it produces a substantial part of the annual crush (which is supplemented by grapes purchased in the Pokolbin district). Plantings comprise 1.4 hectares of chardonnay, two hectares of cabernet sauvignon, four hectares of traminer and merlot and two hectares of sauvignon blanc and pinot noir.

His red wines have been models of consistency; but not so his whites. The latter are not infrequently unbalanced when first released, with the oak rather angular and the fruit hard. The chardonnays, in particular, have lacked lusciousness and varietal character. The cabernet sauvignon and hermitage wines lack nothing—invariably spotlessly clean, with beautifully moderated fruit, sensitively handled oak, and a long, crisp finish. Robson is a painstaking winemaker, and he goes to considerable lengths to protect his grapes and fermenting wine from oxidation. It shows in the crisp, bell-clear flavours of the finished wines.

Late in 1984 Murray Robson provided the following chart, giving his views as to when the wines should be at their peak. Older wines not shown should be drunk now, Robson adds.

1976 Chardonnay . . . . Drink now
1977 Chardonnay . . . . Now
1978 Chardonnay . . . . Now
1979 Chardonnay . . . . Now

1980 Chardonnay	Leave for two years
1981 Chardonnay	Leave for two years
1982 Chardonnay	Leave for four years
1983 Chardonnay	Leave for five-six years
1984 Chardonnay	Now whilst fresh or five years

1978 Semillon, Traditional	Now
1979 Semillon, Traditional	Now
1980 Semillon, Traditional	Leave for two years
1981 Semillon, Traditional	Leave for four years
1982 Semillon, Traditional	Leave for five years
1983 Semillon, Traditional	Leave for five-six years
1984 Semillon, Traditional	Now whilst fresh or five years

1982 Semillon, Early Harvest	Now
1983 Semillon, Early Harvest	Now
1984 Semillon, Early Harvest	Later this year

1979 Semillon, Oak-Matured	Now
1981 Semillon, Oak-Matured	Leave for two years
1982 Semillon, Oak-Matured	Leave for two years
1983 Semillon, Oak-Matured	Leave for three years
1984 Semillon, Oak-Matured	Leave for four years

1979 Sweet Semillon	Leave for two years
1980 Sweet Semillon	Leave for two years
1981 Late Harvest Semillon	Leave for three years
1982 Late Harvest Semillon	Leave for five years

1983 Traminer	Too late
1984 Traminer	Now for one year

1982 Sauvignon Blanc	Leave for two years
1983 Sauvignon Blanc	Leave for two years
1984 Sauvignon Blanc	Four years

1976 Cabernet Sauvignon	Now
1977 Cabernet Sauvignon	Now
1978 Cabernet Sauvignon	Leave for two years
1979 Cabernet Sauvignon	Leave for three years
1980 Cabernet Sauvignon	Leave for five years
1981 Cabernet Sauvignon	Not before 1988
1982 Cabernet Sauvignon	1990
1983 Cabernet Sauvignon	1990

1980 Pinot Noir	Leave for a year
1981 Pinot Noir	Leave for three years
1982 Pinot Noir	Leave for three years
1983 Pinot Noir	Leave for four years
1984 Pinot Noir	Leave for three years

1983 Malbec	Leave for one year
1984 Malbec	Leave for six months

1978 Hermitage	Now
1979 Hermitage	Leave for two years
1980 Hermitage	Leave for one-two years
1981 Hermitage	Not before 1986
1982 Hermitage	1986–1900
1983 Hermitage	1986–1990

1979 Cabernet-Merlot	Now

1980 Cabernet-Merlot	Leave for two years
1981 Cabernet-Merlot	Leave for three years
1982 Merlot-Cabernet	Leave for three years
1983 Merlot	Leave for three years
1984 Cabernet-Merlot	Leave for four years

1981 Muscat	Now
1982 Muscat	Now
1983 Muscat	Now
1984 Muscat	Now

1978 Cabernet Port	Now
1979 Cabernet Port	Now
1980 Cabernet Port	Leave for two years
1983 Cabernet Port	Leave for three years

THE ROTHBURY ESTATE
BROKE ROAD, POKOLBIN

Rothbury, vision splendid; Rothbury, boomtime baby; Rothbury, child of Len Evans; Rothbury, adolescent victim of the wine slump; Rothbury, vision realised and set fair on the path to greatness. Flamboyant and poetic prose perhaps; if it is, it may give some of the flavour of a vineyard which is much more than that and which has no parallel in Australia (or, for that matter, anywhere in the world).

So went the introduction to an article I wrote for the _Epicurean_ magazine in November 1978. It was a fair summary of the spirit which conceived Rothbury, and of the hope and vision which has sustained it through so many difficult years. Yet while it seemed at the time that Rothbury's financial problems were behind it, no-one could have foreseen the worsening drought of 1980–81, the tragic death of Peter Fox, and the intensification of the discount war. Rothbury has undergone drastic surgery since, and continues to rely heavily on the personal commitment of Len Evans as it struggles to survive.

All looked well in 1968, when Murray Tyrrell conceived the idea of subdividing some of his surplus land to allow small syndicates the opportunity of establishing their own vineyards. In discussions with Len Evans the concept soon changed and expanded, and 11 friends came together to form the Rothbury Estate. They were J. H. McDowell, A. S. Burgess, J. S. Burgess, P. J. Davidson, E. J. Gowing, R. B. Sanders, F. H. Mills, R. J. Komon, A. Grainger, M. D. Tyrrell and L. P. Evans. The original members founded what is known as the Rothbury Vineyard. The word spread quickly, and they were inundated by requests from others wishing to participate. Between 1969 and 1970 three associate syndicates—

Herlstone, Homestead Hill and Brokenback—were formed and their vineyards established. Three hundred and twenty hectares were planted between 1968 and 1971, right throughout the time of the red-wine boom.

In retrospect, it is easy to say that much of this area should not have been planted at all; and that the vineyards which were established should not have been planted to 65 per cent shiraz and 35 per cent semillon. It is no more difficult to be wise after the event and say that the original concept of one Rothbury red wine and one Rothbury white wine each year was doomed to failure. But no-one in the Australian industry could have foreseen the vast changes that were to occur in the mid-1970s. Len Evans has always been the most sensitive and prescient of the industry star-gazers, and he had little inkling of what lay around the corner.

The Rothbury Vineyard was the largest of the areas established by the four syndicates. It in fact comprised three properties: Leaver's, Brickman's and Wills's. A 38.5-hectare grant to W. Leaver had been made at the end of the last century, extending from the Broke Road to the north and encompassing the site of the present Rothbury winery. Leaver, who had vineyards on either side of the Broke Road (including the remaining Hungerford Hill plantings on the southern side), had a substantial winery on the spot, and one of the fermenting vats used by him can still be seen just to the right of the entrance gate off Broke Road. In the early 1900s this block was recognised as a great red-wine vineyard, and to this day the Hungerford Hill Leaver's block produces some of their best red wine.

Sebastian Brickman learnt winemaking before he emigrated to Australia; when he received a grant of 36 hectares in 1870 he, too, grew grapes and made wine. The two properties were bought by Harold Bloomfield in 1920 and changed hands several times, being used as vegetable gardens in the meantime, until they were bought by the Tyrrell family in 1946 and used for cattle grazing until 1968. In the meantime a further 62 hectares had been added to the Bloomfield holdings, adjacent to the northern end of Leaver's block. Yet another 20 hectares were consolidated after being purchased from the Wills family.

Planting of the vineyard commenced in 1968 with 55 hectares of shiraz established between 1968 and 1970, mainly on the red-clay slopes around and behind the winery. Small blocks of cabernet sauvignon (six hectares) and 2.5 hectares of pinot noir were interspersed amongst the shiraz. Thirty-six hectares

of semillon were planted on light-textured soil along the creek at the bottom of the slope and the adjoining blocks on Brickman's.

Spread throughout the vineyard were trial plantings of chardonnay, clairette, sauvignon blanc, crouchen, traminer, sylvaner, pinot blanc, rubired and chenin blanc. Only chardonnay and clairette proved successful, and all of the remaining varieties were removed prior to 1981. Even by that time reshaping of the Rothbury Vineyard was well under way. A number of the shiraz blocks on the northern slopes and along the creek, as well as the two blocks immediately below the winery, had proved uneconomical and had been removed. The creek blocks were replanted with chardonnay and semillon, but the northern blocks were not replanted. Average yields had declined to 3.7 tonnes per hectare, reaching a disastrous low of 1.25 tonnes per hectare in the 1981 vintage. Nonetheless, the Brickman and creek blocks have consistently produced some of the best semillon, while some excellent red wine came from the blocks behind the winemaker's house to the rear of the winery.

Over the years the Rothbury Vineyards have produced some of the best individual vineyard and individual paddock wines in the Rothbury Estate range. They are usually more delicate, soft styles, yet with surprising intensity to their flavour. In many ways they are the most typical Hunter wines of all of those coming out under the Rothbury Estate labels. Ironically, this is partially attributable to the relatively poor soils of the Rothbury Vineyard: the quantities may not always be economic, but the quality is very good.

Perhaps the most picturesque of Rothbury's vineyards lies at the foot of the Brokenback Range, on the Broke Road just past Tyrrell's Vineyards. Almost 108 hectares of vines have been planted on Brokenback Vineyard since 1970, making it the second after the Rothbury Vineyard. The land was purchased from the Merewether Estate in 1893 by James Lynch, who was killed in a horse accident in the late 1920s. George Phillips bought the Lynch Estate at the same time as he acquired the Ivanhoe Vineyard (now owned by the Drayton family). Phillips planted white grapes on the rich alluvial Brokenback flat and was rewarded with a contract with Leo Buring who took the whole crop—"Rhinegold" was originally made from these grapes, as well as some other famous old whites of Buring's up to 1962.

Three hailstorms in five years and unhappy relations with Lindemans (who had taken over Leo Buring) influenced Phillips to plough the vineyards back into pasture. After the deaths of both Phillips brothers in the late 1960s, Brokenback was auctioned in 1969 and bought by the Rothbury group. The famous Rhinegold flat is now only partly planted with semillon, the remainder with cabernet sauvignon and to a lesser extent to chardonnay. Plantings of shiraz stretch away from the flat over gently rolling slopes as far as the eye can see from the old Phillips winery. Most of the semillon and cabernet is planted in high-watertable alluvial loams, while the shiraz is planted in soils ranging from black volcanic to rich red podsolic soil.

Once again decreasing yields had made their presence felt by the early 1980s. The cabernet blocks, which had previously yielded up to 10 to 12 tonnes per hectare, had declined to five tonnes per hectare, although the quality increased. Other cabernet sauvignon blocks have been removed and replaced by chardonnay, while various plantings of shiraz had been removed and the ground left fallow. A trial planting of sylvaner (not surprisingly) failed to produce a worthwhile wine, although traminer was rather more successful. The cabernet off Brokenback can exhibit marked grassy/varietal character. In 1983 Brokenwood purchased eight tonnes, and was more than pleased with the resulting wine.

The Homestead Hill Vineyard was purchased in 1980 by the Homestead Hill syndicate, and was planted between that year and 1972 with 46 hectares of shiraz and 12 hectares of semillon. The vineyard lies between Hermitage Estate and the famous HVD Vineyard, recently purchased by Tyrrell's from Penfolds. Homestead Hill formed part of the Merewether Estate, which was subdivided into soldier settlement blocks after the First World War. It was allotted to Clarence Matthews who established a vineyard and dairy. Recognised as one of the top white-wine vineyards in the Hunter, when Penfolds reduced the size of their Hunter operation in the 1930s, the Homestead Hill Vineyard and the Trevena Vineyard were the only two outside vineyards from which Penfolds purchased grapes.

The shiraz is planted on the rich, black volcanic slopes which form the northern part of the vineyard, while most of the semillon is planted on the alluvial, sandy creek flats.

In the early years Homestead Hill had problems with excess vigour, producing up to five tonnes per acre (12 tonnes per hectare), but giving wines with insufficient flavour and character. Some of the shiraz blocks on the lower ridges were removed and replanted with semillon, chardonnay and traminer; sod culture (inter-row grass growth) was introduced in the mid-

1970s, and was effective in controlling vigour. After a feast of plenty came famine. The drought progressively bit, until the 1981 yield produced 15 tonnes of hermitage for the whole vineyard, equal to less than one-sixth of a tonne per acre (0.4 tonnes per hectare).

Homestead Hill produced the biggest, softest and often the broadest wines of the entire Rothbury Estate. The red wines tend to have a rich, full-fruit character, almost burgundian in style, accentuated by the high, sweet alcohol. The white wines are full-flavoured, round and soft; the grapes from the lower volcanic blocks are often used to make the Rothbury Estate late-picked semillons.

The fourth and smallest vineyard is Herlstone Hill. Although not used in any of the Rothbury labelling, it in fact contains two vineyards, Herlstone and Peacock Hill. They were constituted by land grants to J. J. Peacock (hence Peacock Hill) and Thomas Wills. Wills purchased Peacock's land in the late 1830s to create the 67-hectare block. Peacock Hill was the site of a post office and general store until about 1920, while the Wills family planted shiraz on the higher portions of the block, selling their grapes to the McDonald Winery at "Weronga" until the onset of the 1930 Depression.

The vineyard consists of a U-shaped ridge enclosing a small valley, with the bottom of the U tapering steeply to a flat plain. The red-brown earth ridge is planted to hermitage, while the sandy loam flat is dominated by semillon. In 1973 two small unplanted blocks on the ridge were filled in with traminer. The hermitage, from the north-westerly section near Palmers Lane, produces a stronger, robust style of wine, mainly due to the red volcanic soil and westerly aspect. The semillons, from the sandy loam flats, are in some ways similar to the whites from the Rothbury Vineyard. They consistently produce wines with clean, delicate yet intense fruit, showing distinctive Hunter "straw" character. While yields have never been especially generous, Herlstone suffered least (relatively speaking) in the 1981 drought.

As from 1985 the shape and ownership of the Rothbury Estate Vineyards altered dramatically. Daniel Chen, who along with Len Evans has done more than anyone else to support Rothbury and whose companies remain major shareholders, acquired the Homestead Hill Vineyard, the Herlstone Vineyard and part of the Rothbury Vineyard. Homestead Hill has been effectively abandoned; part of the west-facing hill of Brokenback looking towards Burgess's Moon Mountain Estate has been leased by the Chen interests to Murray Tyrrell for a nominal

sum (the benefit to Chen being the meticulous care Tyrrell bestows on all his vineyards, and hopefully the return of the vines to full health and vigour); while Herlstone remains in full production and its grapes will be taken by Rothbury.

It is a much leaner and fitter Rothbury, with a substantially reshaped Rothbury Vineyard and the best of the Brokenback flats, which faces the future. From a negligible intake of chardonnay four years ago, that grape is now third in importance after semillon and shiraz. Over 60 per cent of the total crush will be of white varieties, and it will not be too long before the combined Hunter/Cowra intake of chardonnay will rival that of semillon.

Whether in the very long term this will be seen as the correct decision is beside the point. For the next 10 years at least, and almost certainly longer, chardonnay has infinitely greater market appeal than does semillon. But Rothbury's holdings of semillon in the Lower Hunter should be a great asset in the long term, because so many other companies have withdrawn from the district, giving up the unequal struggle against yields which remain at or below five tonnes to the hectare. The compensation is, of course, the outstanding quality and the longevity of these wines.

On the credit side, as it were, was the acquisition of the Cowra Vineyard in 1981. The varietal composition of the vineyard is now very different from that which obtained when it was purchased by Rothbury. There are now 20 hectares of chardonnay, four hectares of traminer and 3.25 hectares of sauvignon blanc. Here, the red-brown earth/sand soils and supplementary water produce consistent yields of grapes of very reliable quality. The main danger is frost, which wrought devastation in November 1984 and all but destroyed the 1985 vintage. Yet, contrary to public belief, Cowra (on the Lachlan River in central-western New South Wales) does not have a cool climate. Rather it produces grapes with a very high sugar content (and potential alcohol), with strong fruity tastes. The 1981, 1983 and 1984 Cowra Chardonnays were outstanding wines, the 1982 being the only failure.

But the heart of Rothbury's claim to greatness lies with its semillons, first made on an experimental basis in 1970, and with the first commercial vintage coinciding with that most appalling vintage of 1971. From 1972 until 1979 an unbroken stream of great wines came from Rothbury, coinciding with Gerry Sissingh's term as chief winemaker. Sissingh, Dutch by birth and initially trained in France, joined Lindemans in the late 1950s. He worked at their Sydney headquarters, overseeing the maturation, blending and bottling of the great Hunter wines of the 1960s made by Karl Stockhausen. It was a coup to gain his services, and a lasting tragedy to lose them.

Murray Tyrrell took over as de facto winemaker in 1980–81, while David Lowe has been winemaker since 1982. The style of the whites changed significantly in 1980, while the 1982 whites in particular suffered from yeast-derived problems of volatility. The 1983 whites were a vast improvement, almost back to the quality of the 1970s, while the '84s— within the limitations of the vintage—were also quite good wines, which may yet surprise as they develop. Before I go further I should repeat (with surprise and pleasure) a hard-headed and realistic appraisal of the Hunter vintages since 1970, prepared by David Lowe.

Extremely Wet Vintage: **Too much rain at harvest time, hampers picking—disease rampant. 1970, 1971.**
Wet Vintage: **Copious rainfall, slows ripening. With careful harvesting, wines of finesse, stability, and immense freshness are made. Good whites of maturing characters predominate. 1972, 1974, 1976, 1978 and 1984.**
Poor Growing Season: **Combinations of complete drought, very poor growth, absolute vine stress or long periods of dry, short periods of rain deluge, hail and wind damage. 1973, 1975, 1978, 1980, 1981, 1982 and 1983.**
Ideal Growing Season: **Balanced season and adequate rainfall, warm days, even growth, dry vintage period very hard to make bad wine. Immense potential. 1979.**

One ideal growing season in 15 years!

But, particularly with its white wines, the Hunter seems able to rise above the vicissitudes of nature. In the case of Rothbury this has been reinforced by two factors. First, the exceptional skill of Gerry Sissingh as a winemaker; second, and this factor continues to play a key role, the relatively low-yielding vineyards which produce grapes of great intensity of flavour capable of making long-lived wines.

I believe that 1970 was a watershed year in which Lindemans abdicated in favour of Rothbury as the outstanding producer of Hunter semillon. Tyrrell lays claims as the top all-round producer of white wines, with the extra dimension of Vat 47 Chardonnay and Vat 63 Chardonnay Semillon (or, as he quaintly calls it, Pinot Riesling) to accompany Vats 1 and 18.

The semillons of Rothbury are not quite as rich or full-bodied as the greatest Lindeman wines, but are fresher and fruitier. But as the '72 and '73s show, they promise to be every bit as long-lived.

Rothbury started off with the grand scheme of producing just one great white worthy of the name in each vintage. But even before the commercial folly of this approach had become apparent, small "private bins", vintaged from individual blocks (or paddocks, as they came to be known) were being made for the enjoyment of the directors and "friends of the family". By 1974 the flood gates had started to open, and in the ensuing years a plethora of labels appeared.

The quality tree is headed by the Black Label Directors' Reserve and Shareholders' Reserve wines; then come the Black Label Individual Paddock wines; then the four White Label Individual Vineyard wines; then the Rothbury Estate varietal wines; next the "diagonal slash" label range; then the Brickman range; and finally SDR (Soft Dry Red) and SDW (Soft Dry White).

Writing this chapter gave me an ideal excuse to arrange a vertical tasting from the wines in my cellar; unfortunately I could not find them all (as at the start of 1985 it was still spread from Sydney to Melbourne). But it was still an exciting tasting, confirming once again the quality of these great wines. (I have included a few chardonnay notes along the way.)

1984 Rothbury Estate White Label Chardonnay Semillon *Colour:* pale yellow with a hint of straw. *Bouquet:* soft light, buttery chardonnay aroma evident; clean; no oxidation. *Palate:* gently sweet fruit with a light touch of honey, and some crisp acid. (16.2/20)

1984 Rothbury Estate Black Label Semillon *Colour:* pale yellow-green. *Bouquet:* light to medium weight, already developing a slight hint of burnt toast. *Palate:* very well made; just a little light-bodied on the mid-palate; attractive grassy/lemony flavours. (16.6/20)

1984 Rothbury Cowra Black Label Chardonnay *Colour:* medium yellow with a touch of straw. *Bouquet:* full and clean with a touch of apricot/peach fruit aroma, well balanced by oak. *Palate:* a big and generous wine with similar peach/apricot fruit flavours to those apparent in the bouquet. Seemingly fairly soft and destined to develop quickly. (18/20)

1983 Black Label Wood-Matured Semillon *Colour:* excellent medium yellow. *Bouquet:* medium full weight; good oak integration; developing some early richness. *Palate:* a full wine; rich mid-palate flavour with some lift; excellent sweet fruit/oak integration. (17.6/20)

1983 Black Label Shareholders' Semillon *Colour:* medium full yellow-green. *Bouquet:* firm, deep and indeed robust fruit, with obvious concentration. *Palate:* a strong, firm wine with a slightly peppery finish and needing at leave five years to approach its best. (17.8/20)

1983 Black Label Individual Paddock Semillon *Colour:* medium to full yellow-green, already showing development. *Bouquet:* rich and already honeyed, languorous and soft. *Palate:* rich, ripe fruit, softer and fuller than the shareholders' wine, and will develop more quickly. (18/20)

1982 Black Label Individual Paddock Wood-Matured Semillon *Colour:* medium yellow with a hint of straw. *Bouquet:* full; a fraction of the lifted, slightly volatile yeast characters typical of the year, although less obvious because of the oak background. *Palate:* lots of flavour; good fruit oak integration; volatility evident but not destructive. (16.6/20)

1982 Black Label Cowra Vineyard Chardonnay *Colour:* medium to full yellow with a touch of straw. *Bouquet:* coarse, heavy malic/solids character. *Palate:* heavy, hard and harsh, although there is unmistakable chardonnay fruit present. (14.8/20)

1982 Black Label The Rothbury Estate Chardonnay *Colour:* full yellow, bordering on orange. *Bouquet:* firm but lacking varietal definition. *Palate:* much better than the bouquet suggests, rich, good firm structure and nice fruit. (17.2/20)

1981 Black Label Cowra Vineyard Chardonnay *Colour:* medium full yellow. *Bouquet:* soft rich and buttery, with full peachy aromas. *Palate:* soft, very rich and ripe, full peachy/buttery flavours, almost too much of a good thing. (17.4/20)

1981 White Label Semillon Chardonnay *Colour:* glowing yellow. *Bouquet:* rich, buttery and toasty; most attractive. *Palate:* soft, rich buttery/toasty wine at its peak now; a lovely drinking style. (17.4/20)

1981 Black Label Oak-Matured Semillon (commercial release through Davids Holdings) *Colour:* excellent strong yellow; still tinged with green. *Bouquet:* heavy, strong slightly coarse aggressive solids fermentation characters. *Palate:* a rather big, heavy wine, out of the Rothbury style, though has plenty of flavour and will probably live. (15.4/20)

1980 White Label Rothbury Estate Homestead Hill Vineyard *Colour:* full yellow. *Bouquet:* rather coarse and slightly smelly. *Palate:* coarse and smelly, the wine may have been slightly corked but again a complete (and unfortunate) break in style. (15/20)

1980 Black Label Wood-Matured Semillon _Colour:_ full yellow. _Bouquet:_ solid; some camphor/oak aromas. _Palate:_ big, rich, solid wine; oak has married well to give texture and depth. (16.6/20)

1979 Black Label Directors' Reserve Semillon (Wood-Matured) _Colour:_ yellow gold. _Bouquet:_ gloriously smooth, honeyed/buttery rich aromas. _Palate:_ mirrors the bouquet, honeyed fruit flavours, perfectly married with oak; soft, velvety and lingering finish. (19.2/20)

1979 Black Label Shareholders' Release Semillon _Colour:_ brilliant full yellow-green. _Bouquet:_ a classic, youthful wine, living up to the promise of its colour. _Palate:_ magnificently balanced and flavoured wine, still gaining in richness and texture; gentle honey, and some fresh lemony semillon still there. (18.8/20)

1979 Black Label Wood-Matured Semillon _Colour:_ yellow gold. _Bouquet:_ rich and full, with just a touch of lift from oak. _Palate:_ full of life and character; a slight tang from the oak gives grip and life to the fore-palate, yet there is no suggestion of hardness to the finish. (19/20)

1979 White Label Rothbury Estate Herlstone Vineyard Semillon _Colour:_ strong yellow. _Bouquet:_ outstanding lively wine, smooth and gently honeyed. _Palate:_ bell-clear honeyed fruit; lingering finish, gently crisp. An outstanding, classic Hunter semillon, which will hold its form for years. (18.6/20)

1978 White Label The Rothbury Estate Rothbury Vineyard Semillon _Colour:_ bright medium yellow. _Bouquet:_ corked. _Palate:_ well-balanced fruit lurked under corkiness. (It happens to the greatest; no care in the world can prevent the unpredictable mould character from a bad cork. Not pointed.)

1977 Black Label Individual Paddock Brokenback Semillon _Colour:_ yellow, with some distinct browning. _Bouquet:_ heavy straw oxidation. _Palate:_ heavy camphor oxidation. (Another mysterious, although less frequently encountered ailment. Somehow or other the bottle must have been exposed to extreme heat at some stage. Not pointed.)

1976 Black Label Individual Paddock Rothbury Vineyard E Block _Colour:_ full yellow. _Bouquet:_ aromatic, lemony/pineapple aromas, rich and voluptuous. _Palate:_ similar rich, tropical fruit-salad flavours; far from conventional but most attractive. A drink-now style. (18/20)

1975 Mundurra Semillon _Colour:_ striking bright yellow-green. _Bouquet:_ fresh, lively lemony wine still to develop any signs of richness or age. _Palate:_ lively fresh lemony wine, still to build mid-palate richness, and seemingly with an indefinite life in front of it. (A Colgate-Palmolive release, purchased by me for next to nothing in the early 1980s.) (17.8/20)

1974 White Label The Rothbury Estate Semillon _Colour:_ deep yellow. _Bouquet:_ strong tropical-fruit aromas. _Palate:_ ripe, rich and honeyed, some of the same tropical fruit; very full-bodied but with a slightly hard finish. Drink-now style. (A wine which had five per cent chardonnay included.) (17.6/20)

1974 Black Label Individual Paddock Rothbury Vineyard Blocks C and E _Colour:_ deep yellow, almost verging on orange. _Bouquet:_ enormous, pungent almost rhine-riesling-like with lime/pineapple characters. _Palate:_ has an extra dimension, suggestive of a little botrytis; some of the features of the 1976 Individual Paddock; altogether a curious wine. (17.8/20)

1973 Black Label Directors' Reserve Semillon _Colour:_ deep yellow with a glimpse of green. _Bouquet:_ classic, fine honeyed toast aromas, yet still fresh and youthful. _Palate:_ archetypal honeyed/burnt-toast flavours; magnificent structure, holding to perfection. Will not improve but should be like this for a number of years yet. (18.8/20)

1973 White Label The Rothbury Estate Semillon _Colour:_ full yellow, although still tinged with green. Quite outstanding. _Bouquet:_ firm, youthful and light with just a touch of toast and a flick of lemon. _Palate:_ a faint suggestion of chalky hardness; still very fresh, although I suspect it will not lose that chalky hardness. A wine which suggests it had a little too much sulphur dioxide when it was made. (17.6/20)

1972 White Label The Rothbury Estate Semillon _Colour:_ full glowing yellow. _Bouquet:_ smooth, honeyed and buttery, yet unbelievably fresh; great breed and style; no hint of drying out. _Palate:_ perfection; lingering honey with light toast flavours and a very, very long finish. Hunter Semillon at its greatest. (19.2/20)

Rothbury has elected not to show its wines, no doubt because of the pre-eminence of Len Evans as a show judge and chairman of judges. Had it done so, numerous trophies and gold medals must necessarily have come its way.

I wish I could have repeated the tasting for the red wines, or at least written notes as fulsome in their praise. I think that all that can be said for the hermitage-based wines overall is that they are typical of the Hunter, although by and large lighter in body; and that, consistently with the overall capacity of the district, several of the seemingly frail and light-bodied reds of the mid-70s have developed a soft, velvety fragrance which is quite beguiling. It is also true that recent vintages have shown more colour, flavour and style; I quite look forward to tasting the reds made between 1979 and 1983 in 10 years times. Until then, here is Rothbury's rating of the shiraz (with some cabernet here and there) reds. The points, incidentally, are out of a maximum of seven, while the subsequent column indicates when the wines are expected to be at their best.

ROTHBURY VINEYARD REDS

1971	–	–
1972	4	Passed
1973	5	Now
1974	4	Now
1975	5	Now
1976	4	Now
1977	4	Now
1978	4	1984
1979	6	1986
1980	6	1987
1981	6	1990
1982	5	1988
1983	6	1990

Finally, Rothbury has worked very hard since 1979 to produce high-quality pinot noir, with some measure of success. I certainly agree that the '82 and '83 were the best vintages, but was very disappointed with the green and stalky '84, a peculiar wine which had more flavour of cabernet than pinot noir.

ROTHBURY PINOT NOIR

1978	–	–
1979	3	Passed
1980	5	Now
1981	6	1985
1982	7	1985
1983	7	1986

The great strength of Rothbury lies in the 30,000-strong membership of the Rothbury Estate Society. Despite occasional ill-fated forays into the wholesale distribution market (the first in the mid-70s with Colgate-Palmolive, which gave birth to the Rothbury Mundurra label; the second in the early 80s with the fine wines division of Davids Holdings), the major portion of the 110,000-case output is sold by mail order to members of the society. This has in effect allowed the members to buy at wholesale prices (and less than that for the several thousand shareholders, for Rothbury is a non-listed public company), and the wines have offered unequalled value for money.

Rothbury also boasts a superbly designed and built winery; whatever may happen to the Estate as it is organised today, the winery buildings will be an ornament to the Hunter landscape for centuries to come. This is the focal point for intensive weekend activities organised for members of the society. There are the "Ribbon Dinners" held by candlelight in the Great Cask Hall, allowing members to progress from the novice (white) ribbon, to green, to red and finally purple ribbon. I have the fondest memories of countless such dinners; by chance I happened to be around to receive the first purple ribbon awarded, a wine-age ago. There are also weekend "Wine Schools", special pre-release tastings, the Annual Rothbury Auction and a host of special dinners offering music ranging from the operettas of Purcell to the jazz of Don Burrows. Finally there is the lavishly produced monthly newsletter, *Rothbury Pressings*. Had I allowed myself to read all my back issues of that magazine, this would have become a book on Rothbury rather than the wines of Australia.

ROTHVALE
FORDWICH

The Rothvale partnership of Pokolbin restaurateur Peter Meier, leading Sydney Queen's Counsel Russell Bainton, and Lang Walker was formed to acquire the old Elliott Fordwich Estate Vineyard which had passed briefly into the Rothbury orbit in the early 1980s. Initial plans to market extensively the wine produced from Rothvale were shelved, and the production is now sold to Tyrrell's, with Rothvale having the right to repurchase 10 per cent of the annual production in the form of wine.

The 32-hectare vineyard is planted to semillon (14.2 hectares), shiraz (10 hectares), chardonnay (four hectares), trebbiano (a little over two hectares) and traminer (a little over one hectare). The production averages around 260 tonnes per year, reflecting the excellent alluvial soil on which the vineyard is established.

Only small quantities of wine have so far been offered by Rothvale. As at 1984 a 1983 Semillon made at the Rothbury Estate was available together with a 1983 Trebbiano made at Tulloch. As from 1984 all of the wines have been made by Tyrrell's, and the next release will offer a 1984 Semillon and a 1984 Chardonnay. The wines are available at Peter Meier's superb Casuarina restaurant, and by mailing list.

SAXONVALE
HAPPY VALLEY VINEYARD, OAKEY CREEK ROAD, POKOLBIN; POKOLBIN ESTATES VINEYARD AND TASTING ROOM, McDONALDS ROAD, POKOLBIN; FORDWICH ESTATE, BROKE

The branches of Saxonvale's operations in 1985 spread far and wide, with wineries at Fordwich and Griffith, two sales outlets in the Pokolbin district, and vineyards in three distinct areas of the Lower and mid-Hunter Valley.

One of Saxonvale's roots goes back to 1866 when the Happy Valley Vineyard on Oakey Creek Road was planted by James Connolly. This property eventually passed into the hands of Barrie Drayton, yet another of those to receive an offer he could not refuse in the super-heated days of the late 1960s. From 1969 until 1971 the Happy Valley Winery was owned by a short-lived public company, Pokolbin Winemakers Limited. This company was the subject of a reverse takeover/merger with Saxonvale Vineyards Limited, itself a syndication-type venture and which had been responsible for the establishment of the Fordwich and Mount Leonard Vineyards. Within a short time the major Sydney trading company Gollin & Company acquired the group, and provided the funds for the erection of a large modern winery at Fordwich in 1974, with a capacity of 2.5 million litres of wine.

History now relates that in one of the most spectacular financial failures of the 1970s, Gollin & Company went into receivership later in 1974, and with it went Saxonvale Vineyards. Saxonvale remained in receivership, though actively trading, until August 1978 when it was sold. Lindemans had been regarded as the most likely purchaser, but once again it drove too hard a bargain, and a new face—or rather faces—entered the wine industry. Garry, Graeme and Stuart Macdougall, well known on Rugby League and Rugby Union football fields, and with a long-term association with the hotel, club and restaurant industry, were the surprise purchasers. Their rationale was simple: as major suppliers of hotel and restaurant equipment, marketing wine would come easily. At the time Garry Macdougall issued a press release in which he said: "Because our

representatives are calling at a wide variety of licensed outlets, they can very easily sell a range of wines while taking orders for other goods."

One of the major lessons learnt by the Macdougalls was that marketing wine is a highly specialised art, and that far from being "very easy", it is in fact very difficult. Indeed, even to this day Saxonvale's image does not do full justice to the quality of its wines, despite the consistent marketing and public relations efforts of the past few years. The fact is that since 1978 Saxonvale has consistently produced some of the most attractive white wines at the top end of the commercial market, but has received inadequate recognition for doing so.

The foundation for its winemaking success lies firstly in its major vineyards at Fordwich and Broke. Fordwich was first settled in 1830 by John Blaxland, brother of the explorer, who named the district after his birthplace in Kent, England. The property became well known for the quality of its cattle, and was used for grazing until its acquisition in 1970. To assist in the establishment of the newly planted vineyards, the then third-largest trickle-irrigation system in Australia was installed in 1971. In conjunction with the red-chocolate volcanic soils, it ensured that the wines grew vigorously, soon providing substantial crops.

In keeping with the attitudes and expectations of the times, the 100-hectare property was planted principally with shiraz and cabernet sauvignon. Quite apart from the changes in consumer demand, shiraz proved unsuited to the vineyard. Vigour was impossible to control, yields were excessive, and the bunches tended to collapse before they ripened properly. In the end result most of it has been grafted to traminer and chardonnay. Semillon plantings, too, replaced reds, so that from a red-dominant vineyard the plantings are now 60 per cent white and 40 per cent red. The principal varieties are cabernet sauvignon (27.75 hectares), semillon, chardonnay and traminer.

The Spring Mountain Estate (originally called Mount Leonard) was also used as a beef- and dairy-cattle property—by the Hewett family—before its conversion to vineyards. The soils vary from deep, fertile, sandy alluvials over clay to gravelly ridges, and the property produces some of the best grapes available to Saxonvale. Sugars reach high levels, yet the grapes retain excellent acid and correspondingly favourable pH levels. Here the principal varieties are semillon, chardonnay and traminer.

The Fordwich and Spring Mountain Estates together comprise 56.7 hectares of semillon, 27.75

hectares of cabernet sauvignon, 22.1 hectares of chardonnay, 16 hectares of traminer, 8.8 hectares of shiraz and 3.9 hectares of sauvignon blanc. At the time of its acquisition Saxonvale was the second-largest estate-owned vineyard operation in the Hunter Valley, and is still one of the largest.

Finally, there are the Happy Valley Vineyards with some shiraz vines that are 50 years old. The 24.3 hectares of vineyard are established on typical Pokolbin shallow grey-brown topsoils over clay. Shiraz is the principal variety, with smaller plantings of cabernet sauvignon, semillon, rhine riesling and pinot noir.

The other great strength of Saxonvale has been its winemakers. Mark Cashmore joined Saxonvale in 1974 after completing the two-year oenology diploma course at Roseworthy in one year: he had gained a remission from some of the subjects having earlier gained a Bachelor of Science degree and Diploma of Education from Adelaide University. Although only 26 years old, he had also done National Service and spent some time as a schoolteacher. Cashmore worked with Brian McGuigan, who was then consulting to Saxonvale, and when Cashmore finally left Saxonvale prior to the 1981 vintage, it was no surprise to see him go back into the Wyndham group.

Alasdair Sutherland, who had joined Saxonvale as assistant winemaker in mid-1978 after three years at Arrowfield, took over as chief winemaker on Cashmore's departure. The style of Saxonvale's white wines has evolved, but there has been no radical change. Cashmore introduced Bin 1 Chardonnay in 1977, a wood-matured chardonnay with just a little residual sugar, and (by the standards of the time) in stark contrast is the more conventional Bin 2 Chardonnay, fermented and matured in stainless steel and without sugar. Both Bin 1 and 2 were given 20 hours skin contact, the grapes having been chilled on arrival at the winery.

That many of these practices have since become standard industry procedure explains why the Bin 1 style was such a commercial success. By March 1981, when the 1980 Bin 1 Chardonnay was released, Bin 2 had been discontinued. The 1980 Bin 1 showed the evolution of the style; whereas the early vintages had been given only two months' maturation in German oak, the 1980 spent four months in new Limousin oak puncheons after a long, cold fermentation, and was bottled in December. At the time of its release it was a marvellous wine, showing superb oak handling and integration, rich fruit and a lingering acid finish. Both it and the 1981 Bin 1 were entirely sold on pre-allocation prior to retail release.

Bin 1 of 1982 took the process one step further. The influence of Oenotec, quiet behind-the-scenes consultants, was evident in the use of R2 yeast; 20-hour skin contact was continued; fermentation extended for six weeks at 12°C; 80 per cent of the wine spent six months in Limousin oak, and the remaining 20 per cent in Cognac oak; and the words "Limousin Oak" were added prominently to the label. The grafting programme at Fordwich also allowed the inclusion of 10 per cent Fordwich juice; previously the wine had been made solely from Spring Mountain material.

1983 saw the changes ring once again. Eighty per cent of the finished wine was matured for six months in a combination of 60 per cent Limousin and 40 per cent Cognac oak puncheons, while 20 per cent of the wine was kept in stainless steel for back-blending shortly prior to bottling. Sixty per cent of the wine came from Spring Mountain and 40 per cent from Fordwich. At the time of its release it had won five gold and six silver medals.

It epitomises the Bin 1 style: the oak is, of course evident, but is far from overwhelming; the predominant aromas and flavours are rich and buttery, while the five grams of residual sugar add more of the feel than the taste of sweetness to the wine. This use of a little residual sugar is deplored by some winemakers and wine judges, but it is very readily accepted by the public, and I cannot see why it should raise such strenuous objections. It is readily accepted as part of the make-up of rhine riesling and sauvignon blanc; why not semillon and chardonnay?

The 1981 Bin 1, released in December 1984, was inevitably lighter in style; in recognition of this only 65 per cent of the wine was matured in Limousin oak, and 35 per cent kept in stainless steel.

Bin 1 Chardonnay has been the glamour wine of the stable, but the Saxonvale Semillons have been a model of consistency. This was demonstrated, for me at least, when early in 1983 I assessed 39 semillons then on current release for one of my *National Times* Wine Surveys. All four Saxonvale Semillons were among the top wines selected for review, with the 1978 and 1979 wines sharing equal top place. These were my notes made at the time:

1978 Semillon *Colour:* deep buttercup-yellow with tints of gold. *Bouquet:* spotlessly clean with a honeyed edge to the round, smooth fruit. *Palate:* not particularly heavy, but very smooth and at its peak now. A classic developed semillon.

1979 Semillon *Colour:* deep yellow, with orange glints. *Bouquet:* big, clean soft-developed semillon.

Palate: quite gorgeous, with honey/fruit, sweet and soft on the mid-palate and finishing with crisp but gentle acid. The sweetness of the wine is noticeable but not the least off-putting.

1980 Semillon *Colour:* strong yellow-green. *Bouquet:* full and weighty with a suggestion of some fruit oxidation along with yeasty/vanillan fruit; good balancing acid. A wine which started life superbly, went through a flat spot and is now developing quite well.

1981 Semillon *Colour:* light to medium green-yellow. *Bouquet:* quite full and rich with some burnt/toasty overtones typical of the Hunter Valley. *Palate:* round, soft fruit with little or no oak flavour evident but nonetheless with both balance and length. While already full-flavoured, should develop further over the next two or three years.

It was perhaps a comment on the marketing success—or lack of it—that four vintages were available at the one time.

A year later I picked the 1982 Semillon in another large masked tasting. These were my notes:

1982 Semillon *Colour:* full yellow. *Bouquet:* rich and developed and toasty/honeyed aroma. *Palate:* soft, round, rich and chewy wine with good weight and complexity.

The 1979 Semillon appeared in the famous Class 38 at the 1984 Canberra National Show. Two of the three judges (myself included) gave it a gold medal—indeed I awarded it 19 points! The third judge objected to the touch of sweetness, so it had to be content with 54.5 points out of 60, and a strong silver medal.

Saxonvale's success with semillon makes the quality of the Limited Release White Burgundies no surprise, but its success with gewurtztraminer has been less predictable. The 1981 wine received a trophy and two gold medals at the Hunter Valley Wine Show in that year. In more recent vintages sauvignon blanc grown on the Fordwich Vineyard has been used with effect to make a fumé blanc. The '84 vintage showed quite remarkable varietal aroma and flavour, but was in my view marred by the marked residual sugar which was left in the wine.

The reds—with one notable exception—have not shown the same distinction. That exception was the 1981 Show Reserve Shiraz, a winner of eight gold and four silver medals, released in the second half of 1983 for around $11 a bottle. 1981 was the year of the vineyard workers' strike, which coincided with

an abnormally hot vintage. In the result the Pokolbin Happy Valley Vineyard shiraz was picked when far riper than normal; with some clever winemaking (mainly in the form of acid correction), a brilliant if somewhat unusual wine was made. Dense red-purple in colour, it showed all of the big, ripe fruit one would expect, but good oak and considerable tannin added complexity to a wine which will not draw breath before the year 2000.

Finally, another dimension came in 1983 with the botrytis-affected show sauterne. Luscious, lifted fruit, with well-handled oak, produced a very, very good wine.

By way of postscript, the Happy Valley Vineyard and winery were sold to the German wine company Pieroth in April 1985.

SIMON WHITLAM
WOLLOMBI BROOK VINEYARD,
BROKE ROAD, BROKE

At the end of 1982 well-known Sydney wine retailer Andrew Simon joined forces with the equally well-known Sydney banker Nicholas Whitlam to form Simon Whitlam. Late in 1984 another luminary, David Clarke, joint managing director of Hill Samuel Australia Limited, became a member of the grape-growing partnership.

The partners acquired the Yellow Rock Estate Vineyard established by Jamie Smiley in 1972. It is situated not far from the tiny township of Broke on rich alluvial soil fronting the Wollombi Brook. Plantings comprise 3.5 hectares each of semillon and chardonnay, the former in full bearing, the latter largely still to come into bearing, and most having been planted by Simon Whitlam.

Until 1981 the grapes were sold to Tyrrell's, and in 1982 to Hungerford Hill. Since the vineyard was acquired by Simon Whitlam all of its production has been contract-made into wine for release under their stylish label.

In 1983 a semillon and a semillon chardonnay were released; in 1984 1600 cases of semillon and 550 cases of chardonnay were made and sold. The 1984 Cabernet Sauvignon, with 10 per cent merlot (bought from France as wine), is scheduled for release in 1985. The cabernet sauvignon for this blend came from the estate manager's own property. The wines have been made at Arrowfield, and it is intended that this practice will continue for the foreseeable future.

SUTHERLAND WINES
DEASEYS ROAD, POKOLBIN

Neil Sutherland was a highly successful businessman when he and his wife Caroline decided to look for a vineyard site in the Hunter Valley to which they could eventually retire. Still youthful, Sutherland was in no great hurry when he found one of the McPherson vineyards which seemed to suit his longer-range plans. The vineyard was planted to 10 hectares of semillon, 4.85 hectares of chardonnay and two hectares of chenin blanc. However, in the dying moment of the McPherson cooperative the vineyards had been largely neglected and were in a sad state when he took them over in 1977.

The turning point in their resuscitation came in 1981, with the installation of a drip-irrigation system fed by two large dams Sutherland had constructed on the property. Until the vines had regained health and vigour, yields were very small, and the grapes were sold to Ed Jouault of Allandale. A number of Sutherland vineyard wines feature in the early Allandale releases.

Looking forward to the day when he would have his own winery and commence to make wine on the estate, Neil Sutherland attended several of the short courses at the Riverina College of Advanced Education. With the background of his science degree from Sydney University, he was able to assimilate fairly readily the basic chemistry involved in winemaking. His next step was to retain the services of Oenotec and Dr Tony Jordan, who designed and built the simple but functional winery at Sutherland. Not surprisingly, it has much of the feel of the new winery at Brokenwood, having come from the same source.

It has a capacity of at least 100 tonnes, but it is unlikely ever to be strained to capacity. Sutherland prefers either to sell grapes which he thinks are unlikely to produce first-class wine, or leave them on the vines. So it was that in 1984, when 60 tonnes were crushed, a significant quantity of semillon was left hanging on the vine.

The first wines released from the new winery were made in the 1983 vintage. The last touches were being put to the winery, and the last pieces of equipment arriving, as the vintage got under way. The wines were an unqualified success. While I remain unenthusiastic about the 1983 Chenin Blanc, it was an outstanding commercial success, and sold out first. In a major white-wine tasting I conducted at the end of 1983 both the 1983 Semillon and the 1983 Chardonnay stood out, leaving far better-known

wines far behind. The 1983 Semillon had pungent, grassy aroma and flavour, quite unlike traditional Hunter semillon, and very like that of Brokenwood in the same vintage. The '83 Chardonnay was no less striking; my tasting notes at the time read: "Pungent barrel-grapefruit ferment characters, almost oppressive. Very idiosyncratic style."

The cry inevitably goes up that these are Oenotec-clone wines, all smelling and tasting of R2 yeast, and little else. This is a nonsensical assertion. The truth is that Oenotec (and a number of other skilled white-winemakers around the country) is protecting the natural grape flavour far more successfully than has ever been done in the past. This is capturing aromas and flavours which were previously lost (primarily through oxidation); and if the tastes and flavours seem the same, it is only because the same grape variety has been used. It is true that yeast can have a positive flavour impact, but it does not necessarily do so, and it is certainly not part of Oenotec's winemaking technique to encourage it to do so. What is more, I am perfectly certain that these wines will develop their own identity as they age, and that part of this identity will be a re-assertion of district character.

Finally, Neil Sutherland has his own views on winemaking, and will likewise not hesitate to assert himself if the need arises. At the moment the arrangement works very well. While Sutherland carries out most of the winemaking, Jordan makes periodic visits to offer advice on the critical points in the life of the wine as it makes its way towards bottle.

Nor has the success stopped with the white wines. Sutherland has established an additional two hectares of shiraz, and slightly over one hectare each of cabernet sauvignon and pinot noir. I can remember my surprise at finding he had elected to plant shiraz, and making it clear to him I thought it was an unwise move. Sutherland has answered in the best-possible fashion, by producing a 1983 Shiraz which won four silver and five bronze medals in the first 12 months of its life, and which was picked as a top wine by both *Winestate* and *Wine and Spirit Monthly* magazines.

At the end of 1984 Neil and Caroline Sutherland moved full-time to the Hunter Valley, making only occasional visits back to Sydney to monitor their business interests there. They are off to a flying start in their new life.

TAMALEE
McDONALDS ROAD, POKOLBIN

Tamalee is the somewhat singed phoenix, arisen shakily from the ashes of McPhersons Winery which had been established in 1968 with the formation of the Pokolbin Cooperative Limited. The driving force then was the larger-than-life figure of Jock McPherson, while son Andrew was winemaker. The winery, with a gravity-flow system which owed more to the nineteenth than the twentieth century, was designed and built to take the produce of 10 satellite vineyards which formed the cooperative. These in turn had an unusual varietal mix: hermitage 40 hectares, semillon 40 hectares, cabernet sauvignon 16 hectares, marsanne six hectares, chenin blanc 4.8 hectares, traminer 4.8 hectares, sauvignon blanc 3.2 hectares, cinsault 3.2 hectares, colombard 2.8 hectares and verdelho one hectare.

By the standards of the early to mid-70s this was a decidedly eclectic choice. The impact was heightened by some of the more extraordinary packaging to have been devised in the wine industry, including a wrap-around label looking like a fugitive from a Lea and Perrin sauce bottle. This might all have worked if the wines in the bottle had been as exciting as the labels and the varieties promised. They were not.

After a long struggle for survival, and after a hiatus while the complex legal problems of untangling the component parts of the cooperative were sorted out, the vineyards and winery were sold. The best vineyards went to an assortment of local and Sydney syndicates; while the winery, wine stocks and some vineyard land went to a company controlled by a Sydney businessman, David Wilks.

Looking for a new identity, Wilks renamed the winery Tamalee (the original name of the property), and embarked on ambitious plans for a major accommodation centre around the winery. He also set about disposing of accumulated wine stocks with a high-profile advertising campaign. The problem was that neither the accumulated stocks nor the wine made by the new Tamalee winemaker, Bob Davies, was good enough. This chapter has been written at some distance from Tamalee, because on an ABC *Four Corners* programme I was given a wine to taste, and asked to comment on its quality. I genuinely had no idea who made it, or where it came from. It was a nasty moment: conceivably it could have been one I had made, or one from a good friend. My answer was decidedly uncomplimentary (wood and water, or words to that effect) and it turned out to be a Tamalee wine.

Inevitably Tamalee took considerable offence, although it was said their sales leapt briefly, proving the old adage that no publicity is bad publicity. In the longer term the public was less easy to satisfy. My views of the quality of the wine were widely shared, and at the end of 1984 the future of Tamalee hung delicately in the balance. Details of production, vineyard plantings and such matters are understandably hard to come by.

TAMBURLAINE
McDONALDS ROAD, POKOLBIN

Once again vine and scalpel intertwine. Tamburlaine was established in 1967 by Cessnock pharmacist-turned-medical-practitioner Dr Lance Allen. In 1966 he purchased a 34-hectare property fronting onto McDonalds Road, Pokolbin, and in 1967 commenced planting the vineyard. Very much later he acquired a second block, part of the once-famous Caerphilly Vineyard, which he named Rothbury Ridge, and extended the plantings. These now comprise 6.4 hectares of shiraz, 2.2 hectares of cabernet sauvignon and 2.8 hectares of semillon at the Tamburlaine Vineyard; and a further two hectares of semillon at Rothbury Ridge, together with 0.8 hectares of chardonnay and 0.2 hectares of sauvignon blanc. The first Tamburlaine wines were made in 1971, although not at Tamburlaine. The winery was partially completed for the 1974 vintage, and since 1975 all of the wines have been made on the estate.

The vineyards are not irrigated, and yields from the heavy clay soils are pitifully low, averaging less than 2.5 tonnes per hectare. Thus it was that production seldom exceeded 2500 cases per year: 1500 cases of red and 1000 cases of white wine.

Wine styles have always been very traditional. At their best the Tamburlaine semillons have been rich, full-flavoured and with some attractive honey characteristics. At their worst they show coarseness from fermentation on unclarified juice, and sulphidic aromas. Some lovely semillons were made in 1979.

The red wines, too, were very traditional in style, with fermentation in open concrete tanks plunged by hand. In 1983 Lance Allen made a beautifully full-flavoured wine which deservedly won a trophy at the Hunter Valley Wine Show.

Dr Allen had founded Tamburlaine for his family, and in particular his children. Sadly, the plan did not work and at the end of 1984 it appeared certain Tamburlaine would be sold. By the time this book is published it will almost inevitably be in new hands.

TERRACE VALE
DEASEYS ROAD, POKOLBIN

Terrace Vale was yet another boomtime baby, born in 1971 when Peter Marsh and Bruce Tyrrell acted as the catalyst to bring together a look-alike syndicate to that at Audrey Wilkinson Estate. Eminent Sydney lawyers, chartered accountants and businesspersons (together with their families) came together to establish first a vineyard and thereafter a winery.

The first vintage was made in 1974; in that and the following year the wine was made for Terrace Vale at Tyrrell's. Later in 1975 the winery was erected, and since 1976 the wines have been made on the estate by Alain le Prince. One suspects that overall, both financially and in terms of the personal involvement of the families, Terrace Vale has been considerably more rewarding than its twin at Audrey Wilkinson.

The vineyards comprise shiraz (12.75 hectares), semillon (9.3 hectares), chardonnay (4.85 hectares), traminer (2.6 hectares), cabernet sauvignon (two hectares), pinot noir (1.2 hectares) and sauvignon blanc (0.44 hectares). The quality of Terrace Vale wines has been extraordinarily variable, with dirty-oak flavours, oxidation and mercaptan being recurrent yet unpredictable problems. Just when one is about to despair, Terrace Vale comes up with a quite beautiful wine, attesting to the inherent quality of the fruit from the vineyard. This variability is extremely puzzling: the syndicate members have from time to time sought advice about the Terrace Vale wines, and have shown they are not hyper-sensitive to criticism. One would have thought, too, that ample local help and (constructive) criticism would have been available.

The best wine so far to come from the winery was the 1979 Bin 2 Chardonnay, a wine which was, in terms of style, a forerunner of the so successful Rosemount Chardonnays of the 1980s. It had a rich butteriness, a fruit/glycerol sweetness on the mid-palate which set it apart from the wines of the time. One of its many moments of glory came at a comparative tasting at Camperdown Cellars in Sydney in late 1979, featuring top-ranked chardonnays from Australia, France and California. In a masked tasting the 35 wine-lovers present rated it second out of 12, a whisker behind 1977 Tyrrell's Vat 47, then in the middle of its triumphant show career. (Tyrrell, incidentally, never liked the Terrace Vale wine, averring it had residual sugar.)

The '82 Terrace Vale whites were uniformly disappointing, and the '82 and '83 reds were almost all dominated by mercaptan. The Bin 2 Chardonnay has more or less consistently been disappointing since that marvellous 1979 wine, with the '84 no exception to the rule. The one attractive 84 white was Bin 1A Semillon, which had surprising depth of flavour given the vintage, and every indication that it would develop well over the next few years.

TULLOCH
DE BEYERS ROAD, POKOLBIN

In 1883 John Younie Tulloch, a Methodist store-keeper from Branxton, accepted a 17-hectare property situated at Pokolbin in satisfaction of an overdue debt. J. Y. Tulloch was evidently a practical man, and did not let religious beliefs deter him when he found 2.2 hectares of rundown shiraz on the property. He set about rejuvenating it, and in 1896 produced his first vintage of one hogshead (270 litres) of wine.

The wine sold readily within the Hunter district and, with family support and advice from the Department of Agriculture, the vineyards were gradually increased to 32 hectares with the purchase of adjoining land. The plantings included semillon and verdelho, as well as additional shiraz. Aided by coalmining, the Cessnock district was a prosperous one at the turn of the century, but the first two decades of the twentieth century foretold a prolonged period of decline for the wine industry. The government decided to step in, creating a large number of 20-hectare soldier-settlement blocks at Fordwich. John Younie Tulloch purchased the grapes from these blocks, but it soon became apparent that they were not of economic size, and before long Tulloch had purchased the freehold to six of them, making him the largest vigneron (though by no means the largest winemaker) in the Hunter Valley. At the inaugural wine show held by the Pokolbin and District Vine Growers in 1918, Tulloch's was the most successful exhibitor and a championship prize-winner.

Given the decline in demand for table wines, it is not surprising that the small to medium producers sought to market their wines through wine merchants based in the capital cities, or sold them in bulk to major companies such as Lindemans and McWilliam's. So it was that in the 20s and 30s much of the Tulloch wine was sold under the Caldwell label; while after the Second World War Douglas Lamb's St Patrice, Rhinecastle & Leo Buring all purchased wine from Tulloch (and also from Drayton and Tyrrell).

In 1940 J. Y. Tulloch died, and his eldest son Hector became managing director and winemaker. In the early 50s Johnnie Walker—aided by a youthful assistant called Harry Brown—persuaded Tulloch to design a label and to bottle and market the wines under that label. It was not so many years thereafter that I made the first of my countless trips to the Hunter Valley.

As with all of the smaller wineries, informality remained the order of the day for the next 10 years or so. At Tulloch's, tasting was always a casual affair: errant glasses hunted up and washed underneath the garden tap which emptied into an open drain; bottles produced from odd stacks and hiding places among the rows of large, old casks resting above earthen floors; and in the dim timber-framed and corrugated-iron winery the wine was leisurely assessed. Even on the hottest days it always seemed cool, an illusion heightened by the virtual absence of artificial light.

1958 was a poor Hunter vintage, with the wines made excessively light by prolonged vintage-time rain. Hector Tulloch decided to bolster his dry red with the use of some wine from McLaren Vale, starting a practice which was to continue throughout the next few decades and to set the Tulloch wines further apart in style from their contemporaries. With the influence of the Fordwich material, the standard dry red was already distinctive, although it is true that the Private Bin Dry Red usually came from the vineyards surrounding the Glen Elgin Winery and seldom contained any non-Hunter material.

Hector Tulloch died in 1965, and his younger brother Keith took over. In 1969 Reed International made an offer which the Tulloch family had little hesitation in accepting. While at the time it seemed that the new owners would provide the capital needed to upgrade the winery (and indeed did so), and provide the marketing expertise, it was to mark the start of a long period of decline for Tulloch's which has not yet run its course. Five years later Reed sold to Gilbeys Australia, and Gilbeys, having disposed of virtually all of the vineyards in the meantime, have now resold Tulloch's to the Allied Vintners group. Press releases from the Tulloch group companies have made much of the need to rationalise uneconomic vineyards so as to produce a satisfactory rate of return, but the fact remains that a once-great family winery and vineyard has been reduced to the status of a brand name.

Just how unfortunate the decline has been was emphasised by a marvellous retrospective tasting of half a century of Tulloch dry reds which I attended at Tulloch's Hunter Valley winery in mid-1982. These were the tasting notes I made on that occasion; the short summary of the vintage conditions was provided by Tulloch's. (Looking back at the points which I gave at the time, I seem to have been generous, but they will nonetheless give an accurate comparative yardstick.)

1982 Selected Vintage Hermitage (_Vintage:_ moderate but cool.) _Colour:_ Intense young purple-blue. _Bouquet:_ very smooth, ripe deep fruit. _Palate:_ sweet ripe fruit; a very big wine with good acid. Clearly the best of the '81 and '82 wines, all of which were tasted ex-cask. (18/20)

1982 Selected Vintage Cabernet Sauvignon _Colour:_ youthful purple. _Bouquet:_ marked berry fruit. _Palate:_ rich varietal character, with big middle-palate fruit and low tannin. A clean wine. (17/20)

1982 Pokolbin Private Bin Dry Red _Colour:_ youthful purple. _Bouquet:_ some tarry district character; quite complex. _Palate:_ the lightest of the '82s, with a fairly crisp finish. (16/20)

1981 Selected Vintage Hermitage (_Vintage:_ severe drought.) _Colour:_ purple-black. _Bouquet:_ enormous aggressive wine already quite developed, with very rich fruit. _Palate:_ sweet fruit, medium to full tannin and well structured. (17.5/20)

1981 Selected Vintage Cabernet Sauvignon _Colour:_ red. _Bouquet:_ clean and elegant with a touch of cigar box. _Palate:_ a much lighter style; seemingly set to develop fairly quickly; some cabernet varietal character evident. (16.5/20)

1981 Pokolbin Private Bin Dry Red _Colour:_ medium to full purple-red. _Bouquet:_ strong sweaty saddle/tarry mercaptan aromas. _Palate:_ fruit obscured by tarry mercaptan. (13.5/20)

1980 Selected Vintage Hermitage (_Vintage:_ dry.) _Colour:_ of medium depth, still retaining some purple hints. _Bouquet:_ clean, soft and smooth, basically undistinguished. _Palate:_ slightly hard finish and lacking fruit on the mid-palate. (15.5/20)

1980 Selected Vintage Cabernet Sauvignon _Colour:_ red-purple showing some brown tints. _Bouquet:_ medium weight with fair varietal character and smooth. _Palate:_ fairly light, lacking fruit and already very developed. (15.5/20)

1980 Pokolbin Private Bin Dry Red _Colour:_ medium red. _Bouquet:_ a big tarry style and rather coarse. _Palate:_ much better, with some fruit richness and complexity. (16/20)

1979 Selected Vintage Hermitage (*Vintage:* balanced and moderate.) *Colour:* light to medium red. *Bouquet:* light and slightly cabbagey. *Palate:* some sweet fruit characters with just a hint of tar; surprisingly light. (15.5/20)

1979 Selected Vintage Cabernet Sauvignon *Colour:* blackish-red. *Bouquet:* strong varietal aroma but spoilt by a hint of oxidation. *Palate:* enormous herbaceous cabernet fruit with some balancing tannin. A very assertive wine. (16.5/20)

1979 Pokolbin Private Bin Dry Red *Colour:* medium red-purple. *Bouquet:* in typical Glen Elgin style, but fairly light. *Palate:* smooth with light- to medium-weight fruit and low tannin. Disappointing for the vintage. (16/20)

1978 Selected Vintage Cabernet Sauvignon (*Vintage:* wet with a moderate growing season.) *Colour:* developed garnet-red. *Bouquet:* chalky, dusty. *Palate:* light herbaceous/sappy fruit with good mid-palate structure and a clean finish. A great success for a difficult vintage. (18/20)

1978 Pokolbin Private Bin Dry Red *Colour:* medium red-purple with some garnet tinges. *Bouquet:* medium-weight fruit with a touch of tar. *Palate:* one of the few wines to show some new-oak character; sweet minty fruit; smooth and long finish. (17/20)

1977 Selected Vintage Hermitage (*Vintage:* moderate.) *Colour:* deep and strong, retaining very good hue. *Bouquet:* full and quite generous, with just a touch of medicinal character. *Palate:* in the mainstream of Hunter tradition; excellent mid-palate fruit and some balancing acid on the finish. (17/20)

1977 Pokolbin Private Bin Dry Red *Colour:* good hue, although less depth than the Selected Vintage Hermitage. *Bouquet:* a solid wine with big fruit though not overripe or jammy. A whisper of regional character. *Palate:* held back by lack of mid-palate flesh to fruit; low to medium tannin on finish. (16.5/20)

1976 Pokolbin Private Bin Dry Red (*Vintage:* moderate growing season, very wet vintage.) *Colour:* medium garnet-red. *Bouquet:* touch of varietal pepper-spice. *Palate:* again some spicey character showing but marred by slightly sour, mouldy flavours. (15.5/20)

1975 Selected Vintage Hermitage (*Vintage:* moderate growing season, excellent red year.) *Colour:* deep red. *Bouquet:* lovely fruit/oak integration; smooth and rich. *Palate:* a very complete wine with good fruit, a firm tannin finish and overall excellent

structure. Will be long-lived. (18.5/20)

1975 Selected Vintage Cabernet Sauvignon *Colour:* very deep for year. *Bouquet:* fresh solid and clean although varietal character very subdued. *Palate:* similar full and smooth fruit with good mid-palate flesh; good structure and balance and a nice touch of acid on the finish. Not particularly varietal, however. (17.5/20)

1975 Pokolbin Private Bin Dry Red *Colour:* medium red. *Bouquet:* soft and with some soapy overtones. *Palate:* a much lighter wine, lacking fruit richness although bolstered by medium tannin on the finish. (16/20)

1974 Pokolbin Private Bin Dry Red (*Vintage:* moderate conditions; some vintage rain; good white year, poor red year.) *Colour:* red-brown, but of surprising depth. *Bouquet:* slightly sappy fruit and some minty oak-derived overtones. *Palate:* similar to bouquet with minty oak adding to flavour, and quite pronounced tannin on the finish. A success in a difficult year. (16.5/20)

1973 Selected Vintage Hermitage (*Vintage:* moderate growing conditions; heavy February rain.) *Colour:* medium red, touch of tawny on rim. *Bouquet:* developed Hunter aromas with cabbagey/velvety burgundian aromas. *Palate:* clean, medium to full in weight with excellent mid-palate fruit; a touch of mint and nice acid on the finish. (17.5/20)

1973 Selected Vintage Cabernet Sauvignon *Colour:* attractive red. *Bouquet:* clean, of medium weight and subdued varietal character. *Palate:* excellent sweet fruit and a lingering finish; only criticism is lack of varietal character. (18/20)

1973 Pokolbin Private Bin Dry Red *Colour:* excellent red. *Bouquet:* light, developed and with a touch of tar. *Palate:* very typical Hunter, with a touch of sweaty saddle characters and a slightly hard finish. (16/20)

1972 Pokolbin Private Bin Dry Red (*Vintage:* moderate and balanced.) *Colour:* red-brown of medium depth. *Bouquet:* fairly light fruit and strong regional tar aroma. *Palate:* light and thin. (13/20)

1969 Pokolbin Private Bin Dry Red (*Vintage:* very dry; the vintage of December bushfires.) *Colour:* deep red-brown. *Bouquet:* strong rubbery/tar aromas and some medicinal characters. *Palate:* exaggerated heavy, strong, rubbery/sweaty saddle; a concentrate of Hunter character. (15/20)

1968 Pokolbin Private Bin Dry Red (*Vintage:* moderate with some rain.) *Colour:* medium red-brown. *Bouquet:* light-toned with just a touch of oak. *Palate:* well balanced and aided by some new oak. (16/20)

1967 Pokolbin Private Bin Dry Red (*Vintage:* excellent growing conditions; good red year.) *Colour:* medium to deep red-brown. *Bouquet:* clean, firm fruit aromas holding freshness. *Palate:* good depth and structure; firm fruit and good acid on the finish. Will live for many years. (18/20)

1966 Pokolbin Private Bin Dry Red (*Vintage:* very dry and hot.) *Colour:* deep brown-red. *Bouquet:* enormous high alcohol and some rubbery overtones. *Palate:* very big, ripe style with high alcohol. Lacks finesse but makes up for that in flavour. (16/20)

1965 Pokolbin Private Bin Dry Red (A 100 per cent Glen Elgin Home Paddock wine served from magnum.) (*Vintage:* drought, great red year.) *Colour:* incredible red-black. *Bouquet:* immense, sweet, ripe fruit, clean and with enormous character. *Palate:* sensational velvety-sweet ripe fruit, yet not porty. A great wine which will live for another 30 years. (19/20)

1965 Private Bin Dry Red (commercial release) *Colour:* deep red-brown. *Bouquet:* ripe, dusty and slightly porty. *Palate:* a very big ripe and rather clumsy wine, lacking finesse although filled with character. (16.5/20)

1964 Private Bin Dry Red (*Vintage:* moderate.) *Colour:* medium to full red-brown. *Bouquet:* medium weight with just a touch of vegetable character. *Palate:* marred by some mouldy/vegetable characters; medium weight; not a good bottle. (15/20)

1963 Private Bin Dry Red (*Vintage:* moderate.) *Colour:* red-brown. *Bouquet:* most attractive sweet-fruit aromas and the suggestion of new oak (not in fact used). *Palate:* smooth with good mid-palate intensity and an attractive camphor overlay. A lovely wine. (18.5/20)

1962 Private Bin Dry Red (*Vintage:* moderate, wet harvest.) *Colour:* garnet-red. *Bouquet:* traces of tobacco and slight mouldy characters. *Palate:* much better; a trace of volatile lift on the finish though not unpleasant. (14/20)

1961 Private Bin Dry Red (*Vintage:* moderate.) *Colour:* deep red-brown. *Bouquet:* great density and strength, and extraordinarily undeveloped. *Palate:* outstanding; deep, rich flavour, very long and complex, and still fresh. Will live for another 20 years. (18.5/20)

1960 Private Bin Dry Red (*Vintage:* wet growing season.) *Colour:* garnet-red/brown of medium depth. *Bouquet:* light and fresh with a touch of camphor. *Palate:* gentle, clean and light again with that touch of camphor evident. (17/20)

1959 Private Bin Dry Red (*Vintage:* moderate.) *Colour:* red-brown. *Bouquet:* attractive fruit but a touch of regional tar obtrudes. *Palate:* fruit holding well on palate and balanced by firm tannin on finish. (17/20)

1958 Private Bin Dry Red (*Vintage:* moderate growing season.) *Colour:* red-brown. *Bouquet:* big medicinal/cough mixture aromas and a touch of oxidation. *Palate:* a big, slightly oxidised wine with strong tannin on the finish. (15/20)

1957 Private Bin Dry Red (*Vintage:* dry.) *Colour:* more brown than red. *Bouquet:* big, rather hard and lacking fruit. *Palate:* very hard, and harsh tannin on the finish. (14.5/20)

1955 Private Bin Dry Red (*Vintage:* very wet with record floods.) *Colour:* strong red-brown. *Bouquet:* complex with quite attractive slight vegetative overlay. *Palate:* sweet fruit holding on very well on mid-palate; firm tannin on the finish. Just a trace of volatility. (17.5/20)

1954 Private Bin Dry Red (*Vintage:* dry growing season and a wet vintage.) *Colour:* dark brown, almost black. *Bouquet:* strong robust fruit with coffee/chocolate aromas. *Palate:* smooth and ripe with full generous ripe fruit on mid-palate and considerable overall weight. (17.5/20)

1954 Dry Red *Colour:* red-brown. *Bouquet:* lighter than the sister wine with some caramel/oxidised characters and of medium weight. *Palate:* attractive, light- to medium-weight fruit and some balancing acid on the finish. (17/20)

1953 Private Bin Dry Red (*Vintage:* moderate.) *Colour:* red-brown of medium depth. *Bouquet:* some mushroom characters to big fruit aroma. *Palate:* rich and ripe, but volatility intrudes. (15/20)

1952 Dry Red (*Vintage:* dry.) *Colour:* deep, dark red. *Bouquet:* an enormous tarry, strong wine. *Palate:* big, dark chocolate fruit flavours and a high tannin finish. Strong as a horse. (18/20)

1947 Dry Red (*Vintage:* dry.) *Colour:* deep red-brown in superb condition. *Bouquet:* astonishing sweet/ripe fruit. *Palate:* quite magnificent. Rich, ripe velvety, indeed unctuous, fruit with sweet berry flavours. Tastes like a 10-year-old. (19.5/20)

1944 Dry Red (*Vintage:* moderate.) *Colour:* brown. *Bouquet:* tired, coffee essence oxidised characters. *Palate:* again tired with coffee essence flavours. The wine had gone. (13.5/20)

1931 Burgundy (bottled by Thomas Hardy 1933) (*Vintage:* dry.) *Colour:* excellent hue and depth for age. *Bouquet:* strong bottle-developed mushroom characters. A disappointment. *Palate:* extraordinarily strong fruit and huge tannin on the finish. (15.5/20)

It was, by any standards, a remarkable tasting, showing why Tulloch's had gained such a reputation as red-winemakers over the years. But they also produced some excellent white wines from the 1974 vintage: a semillon, a semillon-chardonnay and a semillon verdelho. Made by Ian Scarborough, they proved that great white wine could be made from mechanically harvested grapes, up to that time a hotly debated issue. The 1974 Semillon, a winner of numerous trophies and gold medals, is marginally the best of the three wines, but all are still capable of winning gold medals. They are very different in style, inevitably enough, from those of the '50s and '60s. I shared in bottles of the 1954 and 1956 vintages in 1983: the 1956 had retained remarkable fruit richness and weight, and the 1954, although marred by cork-derived mustiness, also had considerable richness.

In more recent years Tulloch has made some exceptional chardonnay, none better than the 1980. When it topped its class at the 1982 Sydney show with 57 points out of 60 it took its show record to two gold, five silver and one bronze medals. 1980 also saw an outstanding Private Bin Hunter Riesling, released in 1984 and exhibiting outstanding honeyed, burnt-toast aroma and flavour. In every way, a classic Hunter white.

The crush is still a substantial one, at around 400 tonnes, although only 25 per cent of this is provided by the remaining 32 hectares of vineyards owned by the company. The plantings are of cabernet sauvignon, shiraz, pinot noir, semillon and chardonnay. If Tulloch does fade further from the scene, it will have left a rich heritage.

TYRRELL'S
BROKE ROAD, POKOLBIN

When, in March 1847, the Archbishop of Canterbury wrote to the rector of the insignificant parish of Beaulieu in Hampshire, England, offering him a more senior position within the Church, it would

have taken more than an ordinary dose of divine inspiration to foresee that his invitation would lead to the founding of one of the great wine dynasties of Australia. History relates that William Tyrrell accepted the offer of the bishopric of the newly founded city of Newcastle, and that he arrived in Australia to be installed as bishop on 30 January 1848.

In 1850 three of his nephews arrived in Australia to further their education under his guidance. One was Edward Tyrrell, who was 15 at the time. His father was Frederick Tyrrell, a surgeon at St Thomas's Hospital in London and William's elder brother. Within a few years of his arrival, and while still a teenager, Edward moved to Singleton and started a dairy farm. It was not a success, and when in 1858 Edward Tyrrell heard that selections suited to vine growing at Pokolbin were available, he applied for and was granted one of the last available.

As luck would have it, the 330-acre (134-hectare) grant, nestling under the lee of the Brokenback Range, contained some of the finest red basalt soil in the district, with a limestone subsoil. First he had to clear by hand the spotted gums (not so hard) and ironbark (very hard) which forested the land, and then work up the soil for planting. In these days of bulldozers and tractors that is accounted to be hard work, a notion that Edward Tyrrell would find highly amusing.

He produced his first vintage in 1864 from the first few acres of vines. By 1870 he had planted 30 acres (12 hectares) of vines, half to aucerot (which the locals regarded very highly and which they used to pronounce "ocka"), and the rest to semillon and shiraz. In the meantime he had built (in 1858) the one-room slab hut which stands diminutively but proudly in the forecourt of today's winery complex, a building beyond price.

The first stage of the winery was completed just in time for the 1864 vintage; it, too, stands today at the core of the subsequent extensions, most of which look to be very nearly as old. About this time he married Susan Hungerford from Farleigh near Maitland, and thus I can claim relationship with the Tyrrells. My maternal grandmother was a Hungerford, and her home at Palm Beach near Sydney, at which I spent every summer holiday from the time I could walk, was also called Farleigh.

The second of their 10 children, Edward George Young Tyrrell, was born in 1873. He and his youngest brother Avery were to assume responsibility for the vineyard and winery following the ill health of their father in 1888. Edward George (known to all as

Dan, and eventually as Uncle Dan) assumed that responsibility immediately, although he was only 15 years old. His ensuing 70 vintages as winemaker (he was forced to suspend winemaking activities in 1958 when he fell off a ladder) certainly stands as an Australian record, and can have few parallels in wine history.

Not content with making the wine and managing the estate (Avery eventually assumed responsibility for viticulture) at Tyrrell's, Dan Tyrrell also took over the day-to-day winemaking operations of Doyle's Kaludah Winery at Lochinvar. This brought him into contact with Philobert Terrier, a French-born and trained winemaker who had been in charge at Kaludah before moving across the road to commence his St Helena Vineyard and winery. Terrier's house, still beautifully maintained, is now run as a restaurant.

Under Dan Tyrrell's stewardship all of the estate-grown grapes were made into wine, wine which gradually gained a reputation among wine merchants and other wine companies operating in and out of the region. From the 1930s Maurice O'Shea of McWilliam's became a regular customer, to the point where most of Tyrrell's best wines were bought by O'Shea. These were either blended with other wines from the district (including those made by O'Shea himself) or kept separate and released under the name Mount Pleasant Richard Hermitage.

Day Tyrrell died of a heart attack at the age of 89 in April 1959, and Murray Tyrrell—who had spent several years in the winery after the Second World War learning the trade—came back from his cattle business to take over Tyrrell's Ashmans Winery. Even at this time, virtually all Tyrrell's wine was sold in bulk. Anne Tyrrell (now Anne Ellis) recollects that in the late 1950s, at the age of eight or nine, she became a child typist. The odd person who called at the winery to purchase wine in bottle was as often as not cheerfully accommodated by means of syphoning the desired wine direct from the vat into bottles. Anne would then type up the necessary labels by inserting "claret" or "burgundy", and the year, under the maroon coat-of-arms design.

Murray Tyrrell did not have much of an opportunity to change things immediately, for 1959 saw virtually the entire vintage wiped out by hail, and in 1960 the after-effects were such that only 600 gallons (2730 litres or two casks) of wine were made. Hail struck again in 1961, and only three casks of wine were made in that year. So 1962 was the first year nature gave Murray a chance, and he took it with both hands. Vat 5 of '62 won a gold

medal at the Sydney Wine Show, and caused such a storm that the committee sent Hector Tulloch and the local police sergeant around to the winery to check—firstly that the show wine was indeed a Tyrrell wine, and secondly the quantity.

I remember visiting the winery in 1959 while I was still at university, and even by the standards of those days it was decidedly basic. But Murray's influence was immediate, and following that early show success he embarked upon a deliberate policy of publicising and establishing the vineyard name. Proper labelling and the commencement of the vat system saw cellar-door sales take off. By the mid-1960s over half the production was sold under Tyrrell's label, and by the early 1970s the major part of production was sold from the cellar door and by mailing list direct to the public.

The Tyrrell's operation of today is in turn unrecognisable from that of the early to mid-70s. In 1975 the crush was around 500 tonnes; in 1984 it was 2500 tonnes, and 1985 was projected to be 3000 tonnes. But it does not stop there: this crush will provide between 60 per cent and 65 per cent of total requirements, the remainder being purchased in the form of wine, and not necessarily from the Hunter (something I will come back to shortly).

The volume of cellar-door sales remains much as it was, but instead of accounting for more than 40 per cent of total sales, now accounts for less than 10 per cent. The gap has been filled largely by large commercial blends such as Long Flat Red (in 1984 75,000 cases were made) and by export sales, which are planned to reach between 25 per cent and 30 per cent of production within a very few years. Just as Day Tyrrell was the winemaker in the 1950s and McWilliam's the marketers, the roles have now been reversed. In 1984 and 1985 there was hardly a wine company in the Hunter which did not sell grapes or wines to Tyrrell.

Tyrrell has always made good wine, and he continues to do so. But so do many of those who sell to Tyrrell, and the price at which they sell provides cash flow but very little else. Tyrrell succeeds because he, and son Bruce, have learnt how to market wine, and how to produce it for a cost which is in line with the sale price. Overall, there is a marked similarity in both the methods and the success of Tyrrell's and Brown Brothers of Milawa. In both, the family influence has been of paramount importance, with a tradition extending back over a century. Both companies have grown at a phenomenal pace over the past two decades, and through sheer skill (and hard work) have managed to finance that growth internally to remain privately owned. Both have been innovative in developing new styles and introducing new varieties; and both have deliberately sought to go outside the confines of the area immediately around their wineries to source their grapes.

In Tyrrell's case this has not been free from controversy, and Murray Tyrrell's attitude to the question of "imports" is decidedly ambivalent. On the one hand he is a fierce champion of the district and of its fundamental need to maintain its identity. Putting his money where his mouth is, he has taken out a long-term contract with Chateau Douglas in the Upper Hunter and more recently purchased Penfolds' HVD Vineyard. He is none too impressed with the amount of Coonawarra wine sold by Hungerford Hill at its Pokolbin Wine Village, and privately expresses great concern about the activities of one or two other large companies in the region.

On the other hand it is no secret that at various times the "Long Flat" has stretched all the way to Adelaide—in other words, that it has contained a majority of South Australian wine—and that its present Hunter Valley composition is more an indication of the abundance of bulk Hunter wine at the right price than anything else. Nor is it any secret that Tyrrell buys substantial quantities of rhine riesling from Renmark and elsewhere in South Australia, which is sold in substantial quantities as "function wine" in Sydney. These bread-and-butter wines provide cash flow and profits. They are not said to be Hunter Valley wines, but neither are they said not to be. Short- to medium-term expediency points to the necessity of marketing such wines, but not even Murray Tyrrell would suggest that it is in the long-term interests of the Hunter Valley to do so.

On balance, however, Tyrrell's is very much in the interests of the Hunter Valley. Since the end of the boom in the mid-70s Tyrrell's has been one of the few stabilising influences. By 1979 it had 45 hectares of vineyard in the Lower Hunter, and a further 140 hectares under contract with independent growers. In December of the preceding year Tyrrell's had entered into a five-year contract to purchase the grapes from the 115-hectare Chateau Douglas Vineyard near the Glenbawn Dam in the Upper Hunter and a lease of the 585,000-litre winery.

Planted to semillon, chardonnay, rhine riesling, traminer, trebbiano, hermitage and cabernet, Chateau Douglas initially provided Tyrrell's with between 1000 and 2000 tonnes of grapes, but the yield has declined dramatically in recent years to little more than 200 tonnes. Tyrrell attributes this in part to the

viticultural practices of the owners, and also to doubts about the long-term viability of much of the Upper Hunter. These doubts stem from the sulphur and sulphuric acid levels in the soil, leaching from the abundant coal deposits which underlie so much of the area.

The decline in Chateau Douglas's production, contrasted with the continued growth in sales both on the local and export market, made Tyrrell's the logical purchaser once Penfolds decided to offer its HVD Vineyard for sale by tender in 1982. The vineyard was established by the Hunter Valley Distillery Company in 1908 to support its distillery operations. Those operations ceased during the Depression, and Penfolds leased the vineyard until they purchased the freehold in 1949.

The 162-hectare property is situated on a long, sandy, protected flat, once a creek bed. The vines seldom suffer any water or wind stress, and consistently produce good yields of high-quality grapes. So favourable are the conditions that many of the original 1908 vines are still in production. Of the 24 hectares under wine, the majority is semillon (17 hectares) with smaller quantities of chardonnay (two hectares), trebbiano (2.5 hectares) and clairette (two hectares) (known in the Hunter as blanquette).

HVD provides Tyrrell's with much-needed high-quality estate-grown white grapes to balance the predominantly red vineyards on the family property. It is instructive in the extreme to note that even in the height of the boom Tyrrell resisted the temptation to expand his own plantings significantly, notwithstanding the substantial area he had available devoted to cattle. So most of the vineyards (Contour Block, 1.6 hectares; Short Flat, 24 hectares; Long Flat, four hectares; NVC, two hectares; Winery Pinot Noir Block, 6.5 hectares; Eight Acre Paddock, 3.25 hectares; Four Acre Paddock, 1.6 hectares; and Baulkham, four hectares) are established on the rich, striking red podsols of volcanic origin and which have always formed the base for the best vineyards in the region.

It is these vineyards which have produced the "Vat" or private bin wines for which Tyrrell's have become famous since the early 60s. If Murray Tyrrell had to nominate a wine which best represented the vineyard in particular and the Hunter in general, year in, year out, it would undoubtedly be *Vat 1 Riesling*. In most (but not all) things Tyrrell is a traditionalist, and he doggedly continues to call the wines made from 100 per cent semillon, riesling. This in turn is simply an abbreviation of the old name for semillon, Hunter River riesling. For many years now, Vat 1 Riesling has been made from old, relatively low-yielding vines grown on the Short Flat Vineyard. The wine is cold-fermented and then matured in large, old German vats until bottling in late June or early July of the year of vintage. Tyrrell does not believe that the introduction of any new-oak character is either necessary or desirable, and I totally agree with him. Outstanding vintages of Vat 1 have been '62, '65, '67, '73, '75, '77, '79 and '83.

Over this period of time the style has changed quite significantly. Until the late 1960s the grapes were picked fairly early, and while extremely long-lived, the wines never developed the rich, buttery/honeyed characters of the Lindemans wines of the 1960s. I recently drank a bottle of '70 Vat 1 in company with some other great Australian white wines of the same era, and those present all preferred the Tyrrell wine over the others (a spatlese from Leo Buring and a verdelho from Lindemans). Nonetheless, the wine was fairly austere: it has developed some toasty characters, but without richness or fatness. A '72 Vat 1, drunk 18 months earlier, was also light and crisp, with an aroma of fresh oysters. The palate, too, was fresh and crisp, with just a touch of sweetness on the mid-palate, and was overall disconcertingly youthful. With '73 Vat 1 the wine picked up that little bit of extra flesh; this remains a quite magnificent wine and is one of my personal favourites in the line.

Not surprisingly, the wine has picked up innumerable show awards over the years. Thus the '74, which is not even one of Murray Tyrrell's favourites, was a dual trophy-winner in Sydney in 1975, including the trophy for the best one-year-old white wine of the show, and won 11 gold medals in a show career extending to 1979. Vat 1 of '76, even less favoured by Tyrrell, also won the Bert Bear Trophy at Sydney for best one-year-old white wine of the show (in 1977) and the Championship Award at Perth in 1979. It amassed eight gold medals.

All of the Vat 1 Rieslings will repay a minimum of three to four years' cellaring, and many will still be going strong after six to seven years. But the style is markedly different from that of the old Lindemans wines, and also different from that of Rothbury. The wines are crisper, more elegant perhaps, but shorter and less generous.

Vat 3 Blanquette Shiraz is a 50/50 blend of clairette and trebbiano although, as with most of Tyrrell's labels, one would never guess so. The blend is brought about by the fact that two of the old vine blocks on the Short Flat Vineyard are interplanted indiscriminately, with the two varieties in roughly

equal proportions. Murray Tyrrell has always been attracted to the combination of the attractive floral character of the clairette and the crisp acid and firm structure of the trebbiano. It develops into an excellent white burgundy style if given time in bottle. In April 1983 the '72 Vintage Vat 3 opened very well: light yellow-green in colour, it had a voluminous honeyed nose with just a touch of roast caramel; the palate thickened out slightly on the back, but it had great flavour and character. The 1970 was probably the best of the line and, while never a show wine, nor as expensive as Vat 1, some lovely wines have appeared under this label over the years.

Vat 4 Riesling was first vintaged in 1979, and again in 1980 and 1981. Made from semillon grown on the best block at Chateau Douglas, it was designed as an early-drinking style. The decline in Chateau Douglas production, and the subsequent acquisition of the HVD Vineyard, has resulted in the discontinuance of the line.

For many years now Tyrrell has managed and brought the production of the de Beyers Vineyard. Grapes grown on the sandy loam soils of that vineyard, and picked mid-vintage, provide a light- to medium-bodied wine released as _Vat 15 Riesling._ The crisp fruit puts it in a chablis classification; not designed for long-term cellaring, it usually drinks best between two and four years after vintage.

Vat 16 Blanquette is one of the relatively few wines made at Tyrrell's to rely on perceptible residual sugar. The style came into prominence in 1975 when a certain amount of botrytis affected the grapes, and an extremely successful show wine (in the moselle classes) resulted. In earlier vintages this wine came from two plantings on the Contour Block; since 1983 it has come from the HVD Vineyard.

If Vat 15 is the Tyrrell chablis-equivalent, _Vat 18 Riesling_ is the white burgundy-equivalent. The grapes come from old vines on the Long Flat Vineyard, and are always the last semillon harvested in each year. Notwithstanding the white burgundy tag, the wine is not given any new-oak treatment, and at times appears positively delicate when young. Outstanding vintages were made in 1968, 1969, 1975 and 1980. While not as potentially long-lived as the Vat 1, it will nonetheless improve for many years.

Vat 20 Blanquette Shiraz made its appearance until the end of the 1970s, coming variously from grapes grown on the Short Flat Vineyard and on the Weinkeller Estate. It was a fuller alternative to Vat 3, designed to be drunk at a younger age.

About the same time that Vat 20 disappeared, _Vat 30 Wood-Matured Semillon_ was first released.

Initially new German oak puncheons were used, but since 1981 French Limousin puncheons have been employed. The period of oak maturation has also been extended in deference to developing market tastes. Once again the contribution of the HVD Vineyard is seen; since 1983 Vat 30 has been made from HVD grapes. While Murray Tyrrell may not approve of the style, the marketplace certainly does.

In a parallel development, *Vat 31 Wood-Matured Sauvignon Blanc* first made its appearance in 1983. It is made from sauvignon blanc grapes grown on the She Oak and Chateau Douglas Vineyards. Fermentation in stainless steel is followed by four to six months in new Limousin oak. The first two vintages ('81 and '82) were rich and full, with little obvious sauvignon blanc character. The '83 and '84 versions have been far more assertive and grassy, with pronounced acid, although perhaps lacking the varietal intensity of some of the new-generation Victorian wines made from this variety.

Without question, *Vat 47 Pinot Chardonnay* is Tyrrell's most famous and prestigious wine. In 1968, inspired by numerous bottles of great French white burgundy shared by Len Evans and Rudy Komon, Tyrrell obtained chardonnay cuttings from Alf Kurtz at Mudgee, establishing a little over one hectare of vines in that first winter. In 1970 *Vat 63 Pinot Riesling* (for the uninitiated, a blend of semillon and chardonnay) made its appearance; and in 1971, the worst Hunter vintage in memory, Vat 47 appeared.

Neither 1971 nor 1972 Vat 47 had any new-oak fermentation or maturation. Notwithstanding this, Vat 47 of 1971 and 1972 is still drinking remarkably well. But *the* great wine was made in 1973: I suspect Murray Tyrrell believes the quality of this wine may never be exceeded. I am fortunate enough still to have a number of bottles in my own cellar, and I shared a bottle with Murray Tyrrell in the company of Len Evans, Brian Croser and others in December 1984, this time in the Hunter and from Tyrrell's own cellar. Glowing yellow-gold, and still with green tints, the wine is perfection. Aromas of peach, apricot and honey intermingle in the bouquet, while the wine retains both its flesh and its freshness on the palate. It is interesting for two things: firstly, the wine came from fairly young vines; and secondly, it had a percentage of semillon blended in. Murray Tyrrell is convinced that as chardonnay vines become mature (in the Hunter Valley, at least), the wines become fuller, fatter and richer; the added glycerol gives an impression of sweetness, and the wines show less varietal character and less elegance in consequence.

This, mind you, does not appear to have prevented Vat 47 from continuing to be recognised by wine-show judges, wine writers and the public alike as consistently one of the best Australian chardonnays. 1977 Vat 47 won 10 gold medals, a championship and a trophy in a four-year show career, but every vintage of Vat 47 has had outstanding show success. 1979 Vat 47 has won over 20 gold medals and three trophies, winning four gold medals in 1982, comprehensively putting the lie to the belief that the wine was a precocious, early-developing example.

The vinification techniques have altered over the years. New-oak maturation was introduced in 1973, and a few years later Tyrrell commenced to ferment part of the wine in new oak puncheons. In some vintages the juice was scrupulously clarified, and the wine fermented at very low temperatures. Those practices have been modified somewhat in more recent years; and, indeed, in 1984 only part of the wine was fermented in oak, and the rest in stainless steel. It is difficult to single out one Vat 47 from another; since 1971 the various vintages of Vat 47 have won 68 gold medals, 48 silver, 32 bronze, 11 trophies and two championship awards. Nonetheless, most would agree that the '73, '76, '77 and '79 vintages have been quite outstanding, with the '83 showing similar potential.

Vat 63 Pinot Riesling, first made in 1970, is a blend of semillon and chardonnay. Until 1984 equal quantities of the two varieties were blended at the crusher; in that year the percentage of chardonnay was increased to 60 per cent to compensate for the fairly light fruit character of the vintage. One imagines that the blend will revert to 50/50 in future years. The wine is conventionally fermented in the large old-oak vats which have served Tyrrell's so well for so many years, and then transferred to new oak hogsheads for two to three months until bottling in or around August of the year of vintage. Outstanding vintages have been '71, '72, '79, '81 and '82. Like so many of Tyrrell's wines, it has capacity for ageing, notwithstanding that it is relatively lighter than the Vat 47. A bottle of 1972 Vat 63, tasted mid-1983, showed light to medium yellow-green colour; a fresh light bouquet with overtones of honey and burnt toast; while the palate still retained fruit sweetness and had superb balance and weight.

Vat 91 Pinot Riesling made a brief appearance at the end of the 1970s; the last vintage was made in 1980. A "little brother" to Vat 63, it was made using similar principles, but lesser-quality fruit, and sold for commensurately less.

Tyrrell's also makes a range of varietal whites both under the _Old Winery_ label and under a straight varietal label. A chardonnay, traminer, traminer riesling, sauvignon blanc, semillon chardonnay, rhine riesling and (in 1984 for the first time) a verdelho have all appeared. A 1983 vintage also saw the first _HVD Semillon_ released onto the commercial market. Given that 4500 cases of the wine were made, the quality was extraordinarily good. The richness and depth of the wine reflects in part the influence of the old vines from which it was made, and in part the very favourable 1983 vintage conditions.

Shiraz is the logical partner to semillon in Murray Tyrrell's mind. It is true that pinot noir has caught the imagination of the public in much the same way as chardonnay, but there is no chance whatsoever of it challenging shiraz as the most important red grape in the Tyrrell armoury. In turn, the four top red wines, year in, year out, are Vats 5, 8, 9 and 11.

Vat 5 is made from Shiraz grapes grown on the HVD Vineyard and typifies the Tyrrell red-wine style. It is a wine that is uncompromising in its reliance on fruit flavour, and on its capacity to age gracefully into a soft, velvety burgundy style if given enough age. New oak has never played a role in shaping the wine, and so long as Murray Tyrrell has anything to do with it, never will. He looks back to 1962 Vat 5 as providing the perfect example of what Shiraz in the Hunter Valley can do; only the 1975 Vat 5 comes close to the superb style and quality of the '62. Other top vintages have been 1967, 1973, 1975, 1979 and 1983. Vat 5 achieved greatest fame in 1978 when, to Murray Tyrrell's everlasting joy, it won the trophy for the best red wine at the Adelaide Wine Show of that year. It is fair to say that Tyrrell and the Adelaide establishment do not see eye-to-eye on all matters relating to wine style, and Tyrrell regards that result with even greater satisfaction than the championship award given to the wine in Melbourne in 1981. It has won a gold medal in every year since it was first shown as a young wine.

Like all of Tyrrell's reds, the wines are uncompromisingly of the Hunter Valley. Earthy, "sweaty saddle" aromas at time take on a distinct "cowshed" edge, and are often dismissed at shows and technical tastings because of mercaptan. It is a character of which I have been severely critical over the years. Yet it must be admitted that, given sufficient age, these characters subside back into the wine and, as another experienced winemaker of the region (Karl Stockhausen) says, can actually add character and complexity. Certainly, however, the wines demand patience. Sometimes they demand even more: a 1973

Vat 5 opened while writing this chapter was (to my palate) simply not drinkable, so strong was the mercaptan.

Vat 8 is Murray Tyrrell's concession to contemporary red-winemaking philosophy. In 1977–78, and again in 1982, 15 per cent of cabernet sauvignon (a variety which Murray Tyrrell does not hold in high regard) was blended in; in some years part of the wine had finished its fermentation in new small oak, before being backblended with the finished wine; and in all years the entire blend is given at least some months in new small oak French casks. (In the early years German oak was used.) In the wet vintages of 1976 and 1978 the presence of cabernet and the additional flavour from the new oak stood the wine in good stead, and in those years it outperformed its more prestigious counterparts of Vats 5 and 9.

Vat 9 usually comes from the very old Four Acre Vineyard which was planted in 1879 and runs off the righthand side of the road leading up to the winery. In the late 1960s every second row was removed to enable the vineyard to be more effectively worked, and within a very short time the yield was back to precisely where it was before the old close-spaced vines had been removed. In the majority of years Vat 9 disputes with Vat 5 the honour of being the top wine of the vintage. Best years were '64, '65, '67, '73, '75, '77, '79 and '83.

Vat 11 is also sourced from the old Four and Eight Acre Vineyards adjacent to the winery drive. Unlike Vat 9, which is given a short period immediately after fermentation in new oak, Vat 11 is matured in large old-oak casks only, relying on the sheer power of the fruit coming from the old vines. It frequently has an extra dimension of district character, and is one of the longest-lived of all of the Tyrrell reds.

Other Vats are 7, a lighter, softer style from grapes grown on the Long Flat Vineyard; _10_, a full-bodied, riper style made from grapes grown on the Baulkham Vineyard and usually harvested late in the vintage; _12A_, a cabernet shiraz blend, usually from the Hunter Valley Weinkeller Vineyard, but in 1982 utilising cabernet from Peter Lehmann's Masterson Winery in the Barossa Valley; and _70_, a 100 per cent Hunter Valley cabernet given new-oak treatment. _Vat 12_, for many years a Hunter–Coonawarra blend, but from 1978 until its demise in 1980 a 100 per cent Short Flat Vineyard wine, has disappeared from the scene. So has _Vat 94_, a cabernet shiraz malbec of years ago, the blend which now goes to make _Long Flat Red_ the outstanding commercial success it deserves to be. Year in, year out, Long Flat Red stands at the head of wines of similar price.

Finally, there is the famous—indeed, some might say infamous—Tyrrell *Pinot Noir*. In June 1979 the '76 vintage of this wine was placed first in the pinot noir section of what was called the Paris Wine Olympiad, organised in Paris by Gault Millau with 62 judges from 10 countries. It was subsequently featured on the front cover of *Time* magazine as one of the 10 greatest wines of the world in company with Romanée Conti, Chambertin Clos de Bèze, Chateau Petrus, Chateau Mouton Rothschild, Chateau d'Yquem and a few other similar wines. In selecting it, the judges described it as being a "rich, superb wine able to stand comparison with the greats of the Côte de Nuits".

I have drunk the wine many times, and saw it as being a beautifully constructed red wine with only a passing hint of pinot noir and more than a passing hint of regional character. The last time I tasted it (several years ago) it was a little tired and roasted, but I understand it has made something of a comeback since. To my palate the '79, '81 and '83 have all shown greater varietal character, and these wines have done very well in Australian wine shows. The '81 won the inaugural Peaches Trophy for best three-year-old pinot noir at the 1983 Canberra National Wine Show, the trophy being awarded by none other than the co-owner of the Domaine de la Romanée Conti, Madame Lalou Bize-Leroy.

Notwithstanding all this success, I remain to be convinced that in the long run pinot noir will be seen to be successful as a red table-wine variety in the Hunter Valley. As the vineyards of the Yarra Valley, Tasmania and other genuinely cool areas grow in size and commence to show regularly, their wines are almost certain to dominate shows. While Murray Tyrrell does not see pinot noir as suited to the Hunter Valley as a whole, he disagrees with my view when it comes to the red podsols over limestone. He regards soil as all-important, and largely dismisses climate, saying that he can make great pinot noir seven years out of 10. Only time will tell who is right.

In the other three years, and in all vintages for pinot noir grown on the wrong (grey-black) soils, sparkling wine is an obvious fallback. Here, too, Tyrrell has had outstanding success, culminating in the '82 Pinot Noir Champagne winning the trophy for best sparkling wine at the 1984 Canberra National Show. The cunningly packaged Semillon Champagne, the Pinot Noir-Chardonnay Champagne, and the Chardonnay Champagnes (with their Veuve Cliquot look-alike labels) have also had consistent show success and critical acclaim. These wines are made for Tyrrell by Dominique Landragin at Yellowglen Vineyard from base wine supplied by Tyrrell's. Good though the '82 Pinot Noir Champagne may have been, Tyrrell believes the '84 will be better still, and faces a major task in gaining access to sufficient pinot noir grapes to service even partially the demand for the wine. This, despite the fact that in January 1985 the '82 had a recommended retail price of $16.40, making it the most expensive Australian sparkling wine.

Tyrrell's is a highly successful business. Not everyone approves of all of the methods adopted or all of the wines. But no-one can argue about the bottom line or seriously challenge Murray Tyrrell's concern for the future of the Hunter Valley.

WOLLUNDRY
PALMERS LANE, POKOLBIN

Ron and Kay Hansen had a decidedly unusual introduction to wine: it was a bottle of Bailey's Liqueur Muscat won by Ron at a snooker game in his snooker and billiard rooms in Sydney, which he ran in conjunction with his snooker supply business. Yet in other ways they were typical of the hopefuls who flocked to the Hunter Valley at the end of the 60s and early 70s seeking to escape the city and make an idyllic country life. The intervening 15 years have hardly been that, and there is little relief in sight.

The Hansens purchased Wollundry in 1971 on the advice of Andy Phillips, with the intention of grazing cattle and growing grapes. Growing grapes inevitably led to thoughts of winemaking, and Ron Hansen served his apprenticeship with Max Lake. The vineyard is planted chiefly to semillon, clairette, chardonnay (a more recent arrival), shiraz and cabernet sauvignon. Situated on Palmers Lane, the 25-hectare vineyard is off the main road, although it has recently been given some publicity with the establishment of Little's Winery. The Wollundry wines have never received much publicity or exposure, with sales largely restricted to cellar-door trade and a very limited mailing list.

Substantial stocks have accumulated, and regrettably many of these are not of a style which is accepted in today's marketplace. Hansen has always believed in returning a certain amount of pressings to his free-run semillon and clairette (or blanquette, as he calls it) juice; fermentation of heavy-solids juice at medium temperatures gives the wines coarse, heavy characters which do not seem to soften with age. At the major tasting of Hunter Valley whites organised by *Winestate* magazine in mid-1983, the Wollundry wines fared very poorly. All vintages between 1977 and 1982 were included: with the exception of the '79, which had some pronounced burnt-butter complexity, the wines were simply not of an acceptable commercial standard.

The chardonnays have been more successful (the '83 winning a gold medal at the Hunter Valley Wine Show) while the red wines have been adequate, if somewhat straightforward. A very attractive spicy '76 Hermitage and a light, well-balanced '78 Hermitage Cabernet stand out in my tasting notes.

In recent years winemaking activities have changed direction. In 1984 virtually the entire crop was sold to Lindemans, following on the last-minute failure of negotiations for the sale of the vineyard and winery to another well-known and highly successful district winemaker. But in turn Lindemans made the 1984 Wollundry white-wine releases, which were a vast improvement in quality and of radically different style from earlier vintages. Even though this presumably leaves the winery largely unutilised, it would seem a sensible course for Wollundry to follow in the future if the Hansens finally decide not to sell out.

WYNDHAM ESTATE
DALWOOD ROAD, DALWOOD, via BRANXTON

George Wyndham planted vines in his first year at "Dalwood" in 1830; none survived; so in 1831 he tried again, along with peach, lemon, loquat, olive, fig, quince and pomegranate trees. This time they flourished, but still success did not come easily. In 1835 Wyndham ironically observed that his first vintage "promised to make good vinegar". In common with almost all of his contemporaries, Wyndham was a farmer who devoted a relatively small part of his holdings to growing grapes and a relatively small part of his working year to making wine. Thus for many George Wyndham is better known as having been instrumental in establishing Hereford cattle in New South Wales, and subsequently building a grazing empire extending from Merriwa to Inverell.

Perseverance was the order of the day, and more often than not it was rewarded. In 1836 his second vintage produced 7425 litres of wine, and he and his son John went on to become leading vignerons in their time. Dalwood, with its rich alluvial soils, was ideally suited (by the standards of the time) to the growing of grapes: in 1886 its 26-year-old trebbiano vines averaged 14,900 litres per hectare (1340 gallons per acre) or over 27 tonnes per hectare. In the same

year its shiraz produced a more modest, but still substantial, 13.6 tonnes per hectare.

By the time of George Wyndham's death in 1870, 15.4 hectares were under vine, but son John Wyndham increased this substantially. The fruits of the planting were such that there were 31.5 hectares under vine in 1886, with production well in excess of 225,000 litres, and the wines were some of the best known in Australia. But John Wyndham's early death in 1887, coupled with the recession of the 1890s, saw Dalwood brought to its knees and foreclosure by the Commercial Banking Company of Sydney, which ran the business until it was sold to J. F. M. Wilkinson of Coolalta in 1901.

Writing in 1896, H. M. Mackenzie painted a vivid picture:

> The departed glory of Dalwood is a thing to be deplored. The place of recent times has undergone a vast change, and though the vineyard continues to flourish as of old, and the capacious cellars are stored with as much as 90,000 gallons [409,500 litres] of wine, there is an air of depression hanging over the place that is at once infectious.
>
> This estate is said to be the second-largest vineyard in this Colony, its cultivated area being 71 acres [29 hectares] out of a total of 276 [112], the largest vineyard, I believe, being in the neighbourhood of Singleton.
>
> The last three years have shown a falling off in quality owing to the unfavourable seasons, beginning with 1892, which was satisfactory, followed by 1893, a shade worse, and finally 1894, which was distinctly bad. The vines, too, suffered a good deal from oidium.
>
> To see these cellars with only three men employed at the present time—no less than 20, I am informed, being the number in former times—is a sufficient proof how stagnant trade is. The holding capacity at Dalwood . . . would accommodate 200,000 gallons [910,000 litres] . . . the actual amount in stock is from 90,000 to 100,000 gallons [409,500 to 455,000 litres], the bulk of which dates from 1891, although I believe there is some dating from 1882.
>
> When Dalwood was in a more prosperous condition than it is today, the Bukkulla vineyard near Inverell, owned by the same family, was worked in conjunction . . . the vines from Dalwood being delicate compared with the Bukkulla kind, a very good blend was the result, the latter being so syrupy, I am informed, that it would hardly run out of the casks. Since the loss of such an estate as Bukkulla the making of this class of wine has ceased . . .
>
> A very large amount of business in former times was carried on with the Castlemaine Brewery, who

were in the habit of buying up for 8 successive years the entire Dalwood vintage.

Wilkinson divided Wyndham into two properties. The house and 52 hectares of land were sold to a Mr McNamara, and in 1904 the vineyards of 56 hectares were sold to Frank Penfold Hyland of Penfolds Wines. Dalwood was already a well-known brand name, but over the next 60 years Penfolds was to make it a household name across Australia.

In the early 60s Penfolds made its ill-fated decision to move to Wybong and sold its Dalwood Estate (but not the name) to Perc McGuigan, its long-serving cellar master, for the princely sum of £12,000. Wyndham Estate Proprietary Limited, founded by Perc's son Brian McGuigan, together with Tim Allen and Digby Matheson, purchased this block and subsequently reunited the entire property by acquiring the house block in 1971.

In 1976 Australian Guarantee Corporation Limited acquired a substantial shareholding, and provided the financial backing necessary for the ambitious programme of expansion which followed. This was strengthened even further by a second corporate reconstruction some years later which resulted in Caldbeck MacGregor Proprietary Limited and Australian Guarantee Corporation each holding 44 per cent of the capital, with Brian McGuigan retaining the remaining 12 per cent.

The period from 1970 to 1980 saw Wyndham Estate move from being a relatively small Hunter Valley winemaker (its 1972 crush was around 300 tonnes) to being one of the major forces in the Australian wine industry, with a 1984 crush of over 5500 tonnes. It acquired the Hollydene Vineyards and Winery, the Hermitage Estate Vineyards and Winery (and with it, the major portion of Elliotts Wines and the Elliotts Wines name), and formed a joint venture with Richmond Grove. Labels and brands proliferated; Brian McGuigan in those days shared the view of Wolf Blass that a label should be as large and as brightly coloured as possible. The high point was the iridescent satin pink and green prototypes for Mistletoe Farm, a project which I think never quite got off the ground, although the labels were certainly prepared.

It may be easy to poke fun, but the fact is that the Wyndham group succeeded where others failed. What is more, its success was achieved on a grand scale. That success did not come without a great deal of hard work and many hard decisions along the way.

Thus the Hollydene label has to all intents and purposes been abandoned; a limited range of Hollydene wines is available for sale from the winery door, but nowhere else. It may safely be assumed that their twin sisters may be found somewhere else in the Wyndham range under a different label. The Hermitage Estate label, too, was buried, along with that of Elliott. The latter had a reputation with a small number of wine lovers, but meant nothing to the market which Wyndham has always been interested in exploiting.

The group now markets its wines under three labels. The top-of-the-range wines, produced in limited quantities and selling for appreciably more, come out under the Hunter Estate label introduced several years ago. Then come the Richmond Grove labels, largely but by no means exclusively varietal white and red wines; and finally the largest volume wines under the Wyndham Estate labels.

At the beginning of 1985 Hunter Estate offered a Fumé Blanc, a Gewurztztraminer, a Blanc de Blanc, a Sauterne, a Première White Burgundy, a Première Chardonnay, the President's Reserve Chardonnay, a Pinot Noir and a Cabernet Sauvignon.

Richmond Grove features a White Burgundy, a Sauvignon Blanc Fumé, a Sauvignon Blanc Sauterne, a French Colombard, a White Bordeaux, a French Cask Chardonnay, a Semillon Chardonnay, an Oak-Matured Chablis, a Sandy Hollow Dry White, a Rhine Riesling, a Cabernet Merlot and a Ruby Cabernet.

Those appearing under the Wyndham Estate labels are Traminer Riesling Bin TR2, Chablis Superior, Graves Exceptional Bin 777, Hunter Bin Rhine Riesling, Spatlese Rhine Riesling, Semillon, Chardonnay, Pinot Riesling, Classic Hock, Chardonnay Bin 222, Gewurztztraminer, Chenin Blanc, Jardine Fumé Blanc, Oak Cask Chardonnay, Auslese Rhine Riesling, Hunter Sauternes, Cabernet Sauvignon Bin 444, Hermitage Bin 555, Cabernet Shiraz, Homestead Ridge Claret, Hunter Hermitage and Pinot Noir.

What is the quality of these wines, and where does the base material come from? These are two interesting questions, the second of which is likely to cause an immediate increase in blood pressure in certain quarters. But let me dispose of the first question immediately. The wines are of excellent quality given the volume in which they are placed and the market to which they are directed. Wyndham Estate wines are made to be drunk, not laid down in a wine-buff's cellar. But using objective yardsticks, it is quite possible to argue that they should indeed be collected and laid down, or at least given more recognition.

In one of the more remarkable of the numerous press releases which issue forth from Wyndham Estate, either Brian McGuigan or Mark Cashmore stated that Wyndham had decided to concentrate on international shows because it was not given "a fair go" in Australian shows. Just how the judges were supposed to pick the Wyndham wines so that they could discriminate against them was not made clear. In any event, I think it can be regarded as a piece of poetic licence, because Wyndham has in fact entered the Hunter Valley Wine Show regularly, being the most successful exhibitor in 1981 and 1983, and running a very close second to Rosemount Estate in 1984. Certainly it had a large number of entries, but that is no assistance unless the wines are of above-average quality in the first place. In 1984 it won a gold medal and trophy for its 1984 Merlot, while its 1984 Traminer, 1984 Rhine Riesling and 1984 Semillon all won gold medals.

I cannot remember the time when I last saw a Wyndham group wine with a major winemaking fault. I conduct very regular masked wine tastings for a variety of purposes, both journalistic and professional, and the Wyndham wines are consistently awarded points in the top half of the range. But I would be less than honest if I said that I thought any showed overt Hunter River character. These are universal wines, very rich and fragrant, often with an almost perfumed aroma and taste; and, if they are reds, they frequently show outstanding colour.

This inevitably leads into the second question,

where does the wine come from? I think the company should have the first say, and I quote at length a very interesting press release put out by Mark Cashmore on 28 June 1983.

Thousands of litres of bulk wine are being transported into the Hunter Valley in tankers annually. But according to a leading winemaker, the consumer is the person to benefit from the massive movement of wine throughout Australia. Mark Cashmore, winemaker for the Upper Hunter vineyard, Richmond Grove, says it is time the Australian wine industry emerged from its 19th-century guise.

'Winemaking is a modern, high-technology industry far from the beaten earth image that many people may portray.'

Mr Cashmore's comments follow the release of details of a State Government report into the activities of some winemakers in NSW. The report compiled by the Newcastle office of the NSW Health Department is expected to be put before Health Minister, Laurie Brereton, next week. Cashmore says the secret to producing many quality wines is in the blending of the best grapes from specialist growing regions throughout the country.

'At the moment the wine industry is experiencing a discounting war with many wineries competing purely on price,' he said. 'The public has little loyalty to labels and only the strongest will survive. In the quality, middle to upper price levels wineries must use the best-possible grapes available. We are

WYNDHAM GROUP: HECTARES UNDER VINE

	WYNDHAM ESTATE	HUNTER ESTATE	HOLLYDENE	RICHMOND GROVE	TOTAL
WHITE					
Semillon	8.6	22	24.6	13.2	68.4
Traminer	16	16	6.5	25.3	63.8
Chardonnay	7.2	4.2	9*	33.6	54
Blanquette	2.4	1.3	3.23	3.3	10.2
Colombard	–	–	–	6.4	6.4
Riesling	7.8	0.8	–	9	17.6
Sauvignon blanc	8.5	6	3.2	8	25.7
Tokay	2.6	–	–	–	2.6
Sylvaner	1.2	2	–	–	3.2
Verdelho	–	–	6	–	6
				TOTAL WHITE	257.9
RED					
Shiraz	2.9	50.6	4.5	14.8	72.8
Cabernet sauvignon	4.9	10.0	8.0	2.0	24.9
Ruby cabernet	–	–	4.4*	1.2	5.6
Merlot	4.0	2.1	6.0	1.0	13.1
Mataro	2.0	–	–	2.3	4.3
Pinot noir	6.5	7.1	3.6*	–	17.2
Cabernet franc	–	–	3.6*	–	3.6
Frontignac	1.6	–	–	–	1.6
				TOTAL RED	143.1

* = _new plantings_

in the fortunate position of having vast Upper Hunter vineyard holdings and are able to sell bulk wine to other producers. But there is nothing sinister in bulk wine being bought for blending. The practice has been going on for many years in South Australia.'

The Health Department report is also believed to point to some labels which allegedly mislead the buyer as to the origin of the wine. One example of this is the number of German-style wines, with similar labels to their imported European counterparts. Last year Richmond Grove altered 9000 of its White Bordeaux labels after complaints from the Appellation Society of France that the wine could be taken as a product of France.

Cashmore says vineyards, like any other producer of consumer products, must use aggressive marketing to survive. This includes the use of highly visible labels designed to sell the product. 'It is no use producing wine which will not sell. And the simple fact is the product has to taste good or it won't sell.'

Of course it is very difficult to know precisely what the company is saying here. The table on page 77 shows that the Wyndham group has almost exactly 400 hectares of grapes under vine. Given that all of them are serviced by drip-irrigation; that the Richmond Grove Vineyard in particular is viticulturally outstanding; and that Wyndham has one of the most experienced and knowledgeable viticulturalists in Australia (Brian Sainti) as vineyard manager, there is no reason whatsoever to assume overall yields of less than 11 tonnes per hectare, making allowance for the new plantings. Once the new plantings come into bearing, the overall yield should be close to 15 tonnes per hectare. When you then look at the total crush of 5527 tonnes, and the statement that 83 per cent of the fruit is estate-grown, seven per cent bought in from other Hunter regions, and 10 per cent from elsewhere, the figures are perfectly consistent. (All figures are in hectares.)

The more astute reader will say that that is only part of the story. How much wine is bought in from other regions? Once again, I think the answer must be that substantial quantities are bought in, and that Wyndham Estate plays the 80 per cent/20 per cent rule hard. For a wine to be labelled Hunter Valley Cabernet Sauvignon it must be at least 80 per cent Hunter and contain at least 80 per cent cabernet sauvignon. But in fact it may only contain 60 per cent Hunter Valley cabernet sauvignon, and yet be properly labelled. Thus it could contain 20 per cent Hunter Valley shiraz and 20 per cent north-east Victorian cabernet, and be perfectly legally labelled.

I am not, of course, saying that this is necessarily what Wyndham Estate does, but simply pointing to the possibilities which exist for a company which does not engage in any illegal activity, and yet wishes to free itself from the constraints imposed by viticulture in the Hunter Valley.

And in the final analysis I think that what matters most is the quality of the wine in the bottle; if the legislators and regulators in our society wish to make the labelling laws very much stricter, I personally believe it will lead to a decline in quality or to a more expensive product. Integrity should not have to be created through a government certificate.

By the time this book is published, Wyndham will almost certainly have entered a new phase in its life, with a public issue of shares proposed for mid-1985. At the end of 1983 Brian McGuigan and Stanley Hamley bought out Australian Guarantee and Caldbeck MacGregor, each acquiring 50 per cent of the company. If the issue proceeds as planned, Wyndham will be placed to continue its expansion both on the domestic and export markets. I, for one, wish it well.

WINEMAKING, NEW SOUTH WALES, NINETEENTH CENTURY

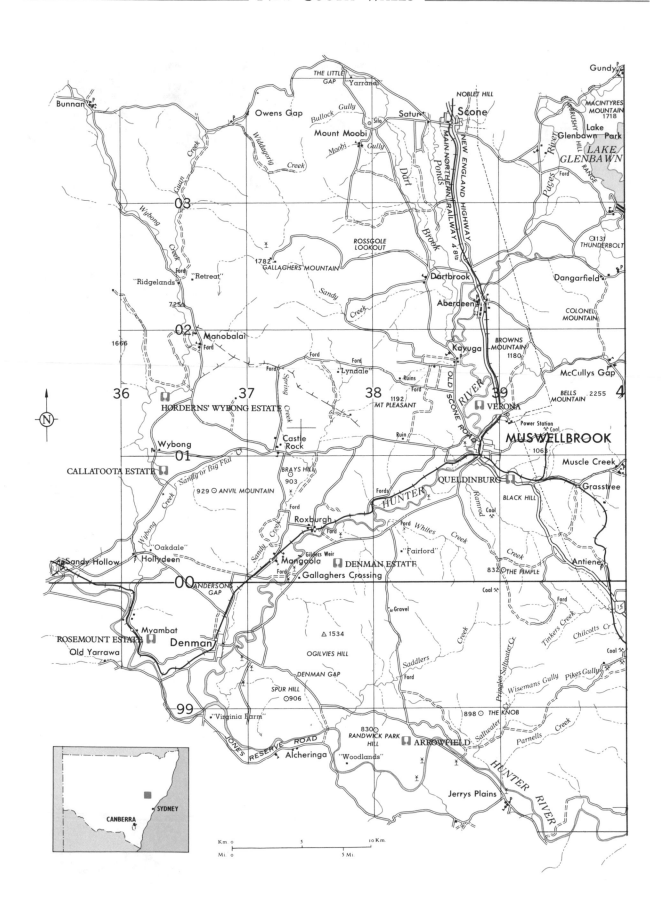

Bunnan

THE LITTLE GAP
"Yarrand"
Owens Gap
NOBLET HILL
Satur Scone
Gundy

Mount Moobi
Silo

Bullock Gully

Maobi Gully

MACINTYRES MOUNTAIN 1718

Lake Glenbawn Park

LAKE GLENBAWN

03

ROSSGOLE LOOKOUT

1782 GALLAGHERS MOUNTAIN

131 THUNDERBOLT

Dartbrook
Dangarfield

"Ridgelands" "Retreat"
Ford

Aberdeen

725

Sandy Creek

COLONEL MOUNTAIN

02 Manobalai
Ford

1666 Ford

Kayuga

BROWNS MOUNTAIN 1180

Ford Ford
"Lyndale"
Ruins
Ford

Spring Creek

McCullys Gap

36 .37 38

1192 MT PLEASANT

39 Verona

BELLS MOUNTAIN 2255 4

HORDERNS' WYBONG ESTATE

Ruin

Power Station Coal

MUSWELLBROOK

Wybong

Castle Rock

01

1063

CALLATOOTA ESTATE

BRAYS HILL 903

QUELDINBURG

Muscle Creek

Sandy or Big Flat

929 ANVIL MOUNTAIN

Ford

HUNTER

Ramrod

BLACK HILL
Coal

Grasstree

Roxburgh

Whites Creek

Ford
"Fairford"

Antiene

"Oakdale" Hollydeen
Sandy Hollow

Gilders Weir
Mangoola

DENMAN ESTATE

832 THE PIMPLE

Ford

00 ANDERSONS GAP
Gallaghers Crossing

Coal

Tinkers Creek

Chilcotts Cr.

Myambat

ROSEMOUNT ESTATE Denman
Old Yarrawa

1534

Gravel

Saddlers
Ford

Coal

15

OGILVIES HILL

Wisemans Gully Pikes Gully

DENMAN GAP

SPUR HILL 906

898 THE KNOB

99 "Virginia Farm"

830 RANDWICK PARK HILL ARROWFIELD

Parnells Creek

JONES RESERVE ROAD
Alcheringa "Woodlands"

Jerrys Plains

HUNTER RIVER

SYDNEY
CANBERRA

Km. 0   5   10 Km.
Mi. 0   5 Mi.

Upper Hunter Valley

While there were isolated vineyards in existence in the Upper Hunter Valley in the nineteenth and early twentieth centuries, its real viticultural history goes back only to 1960 when Penfolds made its ill-fated decision to quit Dalwood and open up a major vineyard at Wybong, directly north of Sandy Hollow and not far from Muswellbrook. The initial purchase was of 300 hectares (240 of which were considered suitable for planting), and this was soon followed by the acquisition of an additional 220 hectares of adjoining property.

Penfolds tackled the project with gusto, and by the standards of the day a vast sum was invested in it. Penfolds was particularly adventurous in the selection of varieties; crouchen, semillon, rhine riesling, clairette, trebbiano, chardonnay, chasselas and traminer were initially planted, followed by sylvaner and muller thurgau, and shiraz, cabernet sauvignon, malbec and pinot noir to make up the reds.

A large and modern winery was erected, and a substantial dam built with the idea of irrigating a small part of the vineyards. I remember some of those early wines quite well: the stark black-and-white labels and the unusual grape varieties commanded attention. One or two were truly excellent wines; I know Max Schubert has a fair collection in his private cellar to this day, and that is praise in itself.

But it was a project which never really got off the ground. While the soils were promising, the rainfall was significantly lower than that of the Pokolbin area, and only the irrigated sectors of the vineyard really flourished. By the time it was eventually sold to Rosemount Estate at the end of 1977, the vineyard area had been savagely reduced. Rosemount took the process further, simultaneously enlarging the dam and cutting back the vineyards yet again, leaving only a fraction over 50 hectares (all whites) in production.

But Penfolds' move acted as a catalyst for the development of the Upper Hunter by others. Not only were a number of major (and some much smaller) vineyard developments commenced, but also within a few years the first of the new wineries. One of the first vineyard developments was by local grazier David Hordern, who subsequently teamed up with Sydney orthopaedic surgeon and wine lover Dr Bob Smith to form Horderns' Wybong Estate.

Hollydene was founded in 1967, and then in 1969 the flood gates really opened. That year saw the commencement of the most ambitious undertaking of all (Arrowfield), the most successful of all (Rosemount), and one of the least successful of all (Denman Estates). Chateau Douglas (or Segenhoe, as it used to be called) followed in 1970, Verona in 1971 and Mount Dangar around the same time. In 1974 two members of the famous Sobels family of the Clare Valley—Kevin Sobels together with wife Margaret—opened Queldinburg Winery on the New England Highway at Muswellbrook. With his South Australian background, it was not surprising that he elected to build only a winery and to rely on the by-then ample supply of grapes in the district. Finally, and within the past few years, the Cruikshank family has opened Callatoota Winery, situated on Wybong Creek not far from Horderns' Wybong Estate.

If the Lower Hunter has been through a hard time in the past 10 years, the Upper Hunter has found the going even more difficult. In theory, the economics of grape growing were decidedly more attractive than in the Lower Hunter because virtually every vineyard (although not Penfolds) was established with drip-irrigation in place. With the course of the Hunter River never far away, and with a number of major tributaries fed by the nearby mountains of the Barrington Tops, water was far more plentiful than in the Lower Hunter. (In neither area is artesian water available from bores.)

In a companion study to that carried out for the typical Lower Hunter unirrigated vineyard, the

Department of Agriculture published in 1975 a profile of the economics of the typical (186-hectare) Upper Hunter irrigated vineyard, which concluded that the return on capital (before tax and interest) was between five per cent and 27 per cent, depending on the yields obtained. Looking at the estimated yields used, the higher level of income seems eminently reasonable and the lower level very pessimistic. The range was between five and 15 tonnes per hectare (two to six tonnes per acre); and on the rich soils and river flats of the Upper Hunter 15 tonnes to the hectare has never been difficult to obtain in practice.

Yet the pessimism was well founded. The two wild cards in the pack were the massive swing in consumption from red to white wine which manifested itself with increasing vigour throughout the 1970s, and the basic unsuitability of certain grapes (principally shiraz) to the rich soils and irrigation of the Upper Hunter. Indeed, if one lesson has been learnt it is that the region is basically a white-wine producer. Grown under standard conditions, shiraz is simply unable to ripen its grapes properly. The swollen bunches collapse into a pulpy mush once the yield goes above seven tonnes to the hectare, and the nature of the vine is such that yields quickly rise above this level. The solution is either to remove the vines altogether (frequently by grafting them over to another variety), or to turn off the irrigation, the latter being a solution adopted by Arrowfield for the few hectares of its shiraz it permitted to remain.

Cabernet sauvignon has fared considerably better. Genetically a more moderate yielder in any event, its far thicker skin means the bunches are more durable, and cropping at around 11 tonnes to the hectare, it produces an adequate if unexciting wine. Even here, though, some advances have been made in recent years, with both Arrowfield and Rosemount producing some very good cabernets in markedly different styles. Those of Arrowfield have been elegant, quite grassy wines, while Rosemount's have been surprisingly rich and textured, with minty overtones no-one else has been able to obtain. Again and again, Rosemount produces red wines which defy all the rules.

Nonetheless, the district is first and foremost a white-wine producer, and a producer of a wide range of varieties. Right from the outset it has been Rosemount Estate which has been the pacesetter, and the early vintages of Rosemount featured not, as one might have expected, semillon, but rather rhine riesling and traminer. The pendulum has swung back towards semillon, and of course chardonnay, but all four varieties are important. Sauvignon blanc,

too, is being grown in increasing quantities.

The rhine rieslings of the region are quite different in style from those of South Australia. Fleshier, softer and rounder, they develop fairly quickly and start to exhibit lime/camphor characters. Just as with red wines, the vignerons of the district have had to learn how far yields can be stretched without obvious adverse consequences for wine quality. After a promising start virtually every company encountered problems as their wines lost character, flavour and style; the 1977 and 1978 vintages were the low points of the evolution of the district.

More recently not only has quality come back for the dry styles, but some excellent late-harvest rhine rieslings have been made, culminating in the spectacular 1982 Trockenbeerenauslese Rhine Riesling from Rosemount Estate, a freakish wine by any standards. Such a wine will be exceedingly rare. The district is simply not suited to making heavily botrytised wines, although modern winemaking techniques can produce so-called late-harvest rieslings (in the spatlese/auslese range) at will.

Semillon seems to have been helped greatly by the increased use of new oak, both for fermentation and maturation. Inevitably, the concentration of grape flavour is ameliorated as the yield increases, and the semillon of the Upper Hunter will never have the strength nor the ageing capacity of that grown further down the valley from unirrigated vineyards. Indeed, that lack of cellaring potential—or, conversely, an ability to develop quickly—extends to all varieties. While it might be seen to be a disadvantage from a purist viewpoint, companies such as Rosemount, Wyndham (which draws an immense amount of fruit from the Upper Hunter) and also Arrowfield have turned it to their advantage. It enables them to market ripe, soft, flavoursome whites within nine months of vintage: if these wines have a maximum life-expectancy of two or three years, who cares? Certainly not the patrons of the restaurants in which the vast bulk of the wines was drunk long since. But reverting to semillon, the lack of mid-palate fruit flavour is compensated for by the buttery/nutmeg/vanillan characters one can gain from well-handled oak, and sometimes by a clever touch of residual sugar.

Chardonnay has gone down a similar track. A surprisingly late arrival (in any quantity) in the Upper Hunter, it has once again shown just how adaptable the variety is. Rosemount (consistently) and Arrowfield (intermittently) have had great success; the ultrasoft, rich and buttery texture and flavour of the wines, with liberal addition of oak-derived flavours, are extremely commercial. They may not be wines for cellaring, or for the purist, but they sell, and, most importantly, give uncomplicated pleasure.

As at 1 January 1984 the New South Wales Department of Agriculture recorded total Upper Hunter plantings of 1211 hectares compared with 2671 hectares for the Lower Hunter. (The aggregate of 3882 hectares is substantially higher than the Commonwealth Bureau of Statistics figures for the two regions, a discrepancy so far unexplained.) Those 1211 hectares were made up as follows (all figures are in hectares):

WHITE VARIETIES

Semillon 323
Rhine riesling 148
Traminer 139
Chardonnay 60
Clairette 33
Sauvignon blanc 19.2
Trebbiano 11
Colombard 5
Crouchen 3
Chasselas 2
Others 6.5

RED VARIETIES

Shiraz 243
Cabernet sauvignon 178
Pinot noir 7.9
Grenache 1
Mataro 0.4
Table grapes 26
Others 5.0

The Upper Hunter need have no fears nor make any apologies. It has undergone its hour of trial and emerged leaner and stronger. It will remain an important contributor of middle- to upper-middle-quality bottled white wines for a very long time to come, with Rosemount Estate at the helm. As each vintage of the 1980s passes, indeed, Rosemount seems to grow in stature, and with it, the district.

BULLOCK TEAM HAULING WINE, EARLY 1900s

ARROWFIELD
MUSWELLBROOK, JERRYS PLAINS ROAD, JERRYS PLAINS

Arrowfield has ridden the rollercoaster of the wine boom from the top to the bottom and back at least part-way to the top again. Its recovery from the viticultural, oenological and financial abyss of the mid-70s is one of the more remarkable stories of the decade.

In 1824 George Bowman was given several large land grants in the Upper Hunter by Governor Macquarie. He named them Archerfield, Arrowfield and Bowfield respectively and planted a vineyard on Archerfield. He made wine there; whether in recognition of its quality or for economic reasons history does not relate, but he subsequently applied for and obtained a distiller's licence. A sandstone homestead built by convict labour in 1832 still stands on Arrowfield; convict-irons dangle ominously from the walls of its underground cellars. The Moses family established a famous horse stud on Arrowfield during the 1920s, and when W. R. Carpenter & Company Limited bought the 1130-hectare property in 1969, it had never been used for viticulture.

W. R. Carpenter set about establishing a Charolais stud on 650 hectares of the property and a massive vineyard and winery operation on the remainder. An idea of the size of the development at its peak in the mid-70s can be gained from these statistics: a vineyard village of 21 houses accommodating many of the 80 or so employees, a number rising to 150 at the peak periods of pruning and vintage; 16 tractors and four mechanical harvesters; a private airstrip; six kilometres of frontage to the Hunter River; five million litres of stainless-steel storage capacity; 14 potter fermenters, each with a capacity of 45 tonnes; and eight million vines, making up 200 hectares of shiraz, 81 hectares of cabernet sauvignon, 81 hectares of semillon, 40 hectares of traminer, 40 hectares of rhine riesling, 20 hectares of chardonnay and 20 hectares of clairette. In 1977 it was the largest vineyard in production in Australia.

The 200 hectares of shiraz, and to a lesser degree the 81 hectares of cabernet, were at the heart of the massive problems which beset Arrowfield between 1975 and 1979. The market, of course, had turned away from red wine in favour of white. More importantly, however, Arrowfield had discovered what the other Upper Hunter producers had learnt: that irrigated shiraz, grown on rich soil, simply does not produce grapes of the quality which the competitive market of the 1980s demanded.

A veritable lake of wine accumulated: at first Arrowfield attempted to push it through the marketplace with a massive discount campaign. It did not succeed and the after-effects were felt for years as Arrowfield changed course with a then-youthful Garry Baldwin installed as winemaker and an equally youthful David Haviland as sales manager. Large quantities of substandard wine were disposed of, and to all intents and purposes Arrowfield started again. It was perhaps fortunate that it was owned by the substantial and proud W. R. Carpenter group: without the ability of its parent to absorb the large write-offs and losses which ensued, Arrowfield must have been sold or placed in liquidation.

The remedial medicine was strictly administered. Baldwin turned off the trickle-irrigation on the best of the cabernet: it received two brief waters in 1979 and none at all in 1980. The shiraz was given even harsher treatment: 128 hectares were cut off below the crown pending their removal. By early 1981 another 50 hectares of shiraz were earmarked for grafting to chardonnay and traminer following a successful trial grafting programme in 1980 of 2.5 hectares of shiraz to semillon. It was a programme which had a number of aims: to reduce overall plantings to a manageable size and to change radically the red/white balance by some increase in the plantings of white grapes; to increase the quality of the wine sold in bulk (then 60 per cent of total production) to achieve the maximum return; to sell only the top selections under the redesigned Arrowfield label; and to ensure that the small percentage of red wine made to meet the predicted market demand had adequate fruit flavour and colour.

There was a base to build on: the 1976 Semillon won two gold medals at the 1977 Sydney Show and the 1976 Rhine Riesling a gold medal at the same show. Indeed in the first year of their show life, the three 1976 white varietals (which also included a traminer) accumulated numerous show awards. This was only a foretaste of things to come under Garry Baldwin's stewardship.

Over the past few years I have had occasion to organise regular large-scale tastings of Australian wines as a consultant for retail organisations and/or newspaper reviews. The performance of Arrowfield white wines at those tastings bordered on the monotonous: time and again the wines would be at or near the top of their class, particularly when the very modest retail price was taken into account.

Arrowfield's finest hour came in the 1983 Canberra National Show, when the 1981 Bin G2 Chardonnay won the Farmer Brothers' Trophy for the best three-year-old chardonnay. This was Arrowfield's standard commercial release, made in substantial quantities and, like all Arrowfield wines, released at a very reasonable price.

The wines are neither especially complex nor long-lived, reaching a peak of smoothness at three or four years of age before the fruit starts to drop out slowly. Oak is used in the semillon, chardonnay and semillon-chardonnay blends to judicious effect, adding to the fruit flavour but not overwhelming it. Thus the trophy-winning 1981 Bin G2 Chardonnay spent only two months in new French oak puncheons before being transferred to one-year-old American oak puncheons where it spent a further five months.

The rhine rieslings, traminers and traminer-riesling blends are soft, gently aromatic wines; every now and then these surprise with the depth of their flavour and even their capacity to age for several years.

The 1984 wines were the last made by Garry Baldwin before he left to take up a position as group leader, extension services, with the Australian Wine Research Institute. In that position he will be able to bring a wealth of practical experience in advising commercial wineries on their more difficult and unusual technical problems.

1984 was not the easiest of vintages, with persistent rain leading up to and continuing through vintage, but the wines were—as ever—immaculate. The 1984 Chardonnay was quite outstanding: it had distinctive peachy fruit characters on the mid-palate which puzzled me until (well after the masked tasting in which it came top) I learnt that some Cowra chardonnay had been purchased and included in the wine. Four months' ageing in new Nevers casks and careful attention to acid levels resulted in a very attractive wine with ageing potential.

The management/winemaking team at Arrowfield remains strong. Richard Everett, the newly appointed Sydney-based general manager, is a Roseworthy graduate in oenology who had a distinguished career in both winemaking and marketing first with Kaiser Stuhl and then with Lindemans. At Arrowfield, Andrew Sheridan, also a Roseworthy graduate in oenology, has become vineyard manager after five years of working with Garry Baldwin as a winemaker. Thirty-year-old Boyes Simon Gilbert has been appointed chief winemaker, and must be wondering what there is left for him to do.

CALLATOOTA ESTATE
WYBONG ROAD, WYBONG

Callatoota Estate was established by the prominent Sydney management consultant John Cruikshank in 1974, when four hectares of clonally selected cabernet sauvignon were planted. The vineyard is situated near the Wybong Creek, not far from Horderns' Wybong Estate, and the vines have—as one would expect—flourished on their high trellises. The winery claims to be unique in being the only one in Australia to grow and make cabernet sauvignon exclusively. They may be right; I cannot think of another.

The winery was built in 1981 following extensive investigations of small wineries in Australia, the United States and Europe. It is sunk into the ground: only the roof of the cask storage area is above ground level, while the bottle store is completely underground. Although small, it is well equipped with the refrigeration and cooling necessary to enable it to make a rosé as well as a conventional dry red.

The non-vintage rosé is a very creditable wine: technically a very difficult style to handle, many small-winery rosés show bitter, oxidative characters which are then partially obscured by sugar. The Callatoota Rosé shows none of those faults: firm and dry, it has obvious yet not aggressive cabernet character. The dry red is also well made: the American oak in which it was matured is evident on both bouquet and palate, but there is ample sweet-berry cabernet fruit character to balance it up. The 1982 Bin II was a medal-winner at the 1982 and 1983 Hunter Valley Wine Shows. John and his son Andrew share the winemaking responsibilities (and the credit).

DENMAN ESTATE WINES
DENMAN ROAD, MUSWELLBROOK

The Denman Estate operations of today are a far cry from those of the 1970s. Founded in 1969, it was an ambitious undertaking with very substantial vineyards and a large winery (with a capacity of 1200 tonnes) designed to produce bulk wine for sale to other companies.

Its two principal vineyards were Mindaribba and Roxburgh, both of which produced substantial quantities of excellent grapes. However, crowding in the market place and significant production problems affecting the quality of the wine saw Denman Estate forced to completely change direction by the end of the 1970s.

Roxburgh was sold to Rosemount Estate outside wine consultants were retained; the crush was dramatically reduced; and the decision taken to concentrate on estate-bottled wines.

Denman Estate's subsequent profile has been extremely low. There has been a total absence of marketing or publicity, the wines seldom if ever being submitted to major magazine, newspaper or trade tastings, and equally rarely appearing on retailers' shelves.

Around 5000–6000 cases of wine are produced each year and apparently sold at the cellar door, although quite how that is achieved is not clear given the somewhat isolated location of Denman Estate and its practice of opening only on weekdays (other than by appointment). The crush is said to be around 250 tonnes, and whilst Denman Estate denies making bulk wine, that should produce over 18,000 cases a year, as opposed to the 5000–6000 stipulated by Denman.

The 80 hectares of vineyards likewise should produce very much more than 250 tonnes, even allowing for a substantial replanting programme which by 1987 is designed to change the balance to 85 per cent white varieties and 15 per cent red. At present, the ratio is 65 per cent white varieties and 35 per cent red. The principal white varieties grown are semillon, sauvignon blanc, rhine riesling, traminer and chardonnay (in that order).

All in all, Denman Estate is a somewhat shadowy and mysterious operation which bears many of the scars of a highly competitive and volatile wine market.

HORDERNS' WYBONG ESTATE
BROGHEDA STATION,
WYBONG via MUSWELLBROOK

Whereas the Lower Hunter Valley has innumerable weekend boutique wineries with the usual smattering of doctors, the Upper Hunter for many years had only one, Horderns' Wybong Estate—at least, a Sydney orthopaedic surgeon, Dr Bob Smith, had been responsible for its creation. Callatoota did not come onto the scene until many years later, and Queldinburg falls outside the usual profile of a boutique.

Bob Smith became interested in wine after a trip to the great vineyards and chateaux of Bordeaux in 1959. He subsequently wrote:

> Inspiration for the Estate came from the great wine-producing chateaux of Bordeaux where a small number of people are intimately involved from the first bud burst in spring to the final decorking years later, thus producing excellence and individuality. This is the system followed by Horderns' Wybong Estate.

His initial thoughts were to follow the herd, as it were, and establish a Pokolbin vineyard. A chance discussion with Brian McGuigan persuaded him he should look at the Wybong area of the Upper Hunter first. This he did and, after looking at a number of locations, found that David Hordern, a grazier and owner of the Brogheda Hereford stud, had become the first individual to plant grapes in the Upper Hunter, when in 1965 he established a three-hectare vineyard.

Two years later, in 1967, Bob Smith established Wybong Estate in the south-west corner of Brogheda. In 1969 he and David Hordern combined their interests to establish the beautiful and unusual Wybong Estate winery. Churches have been converted to wineries, but never before has a jail. The partners became aware of an old stone prison at nearby Bengala, long fallen into disuse and privately owned. After much negotiation both with the owner of the prison and with the local football team, who on weekends worked to dismantle and move the prison stone by stone from Bengala to Wybong Estate, the new winery began to take shape. The massive ironbark supports, bearers and joists came from 100-year-old Dalgety wool stores to support a cedar-lined roof. The winery complex was finished off with wine-maker's quarters made from ironbark slab, lined with handmade shingles wrought from King Billy pine.

It is a truly beautiful building in one of the most lovely parts of the entire Hunter Valley, Upper or Lower, and the amiable Bob Smith must have been more than content as he faced up to his first vintage in 1971. The practicalities of that first small vintage nonetheless convinced him he should learn more about winemaking, so in 1972 he worked a vintage as an apprentice in Wachenheim on the Rhine in West Germany and in the Napa Valley of California in the United States the following year. In 1973 he made a wine which won silver medals in the Brisbane and Melbourne National Shows and went on to be the top white in the Open Class in the Hunter Valley Wine Show. The 1974 wine was even more distinguished, winning the trophy in the Open White Class in the Hunter Valley show of 1976. Bob Smith, and Horderns' Wybong Estate, had truly arrived.

Subsequent vintages unhappily failed to fulfil the promise of those early years. The oak was not properly maintained, and sour, mouldy, oxidative characters adversely affected a number of the wines. In 1978 John Hordern, having completed a course in wine production and marketing at Roseworthy Agricultural College, joined the estate and has been winemaker since the 1981 vintage. In 1983 David Hordern sold his interest in the estate to Bob Smith who became sole owner, allowing his son Mark and daughter-in-law Fiona to return to assume responsibilities for the vineyard and become part of the family team.

The vineyard is planted to semillon (nine hectares), shiraz (six hectares), rhine riesling (two hectares) and traminer (one hectare). Fruit intake is supplemented by two hectares of chardonnay grown at Bob Hordern's Horseshoe Vineyard at nearby Martindale, which were the first chardonnay vines planted in the Upper Hunter. The now-mature vines produce excellent-quality fruit.

The more recent wines have largely eliminated the problems of the intermediate years. A surprisingly wide variety of wines is made. First is a Hunter Valley semillon grown on the sandy loam slopes of Wybong Estate, cold-fermented and bottled after brief oak storage. The 1984 vintage of this wine drank well: with some of the apple/straw characters of old-style semillons, it needs time to mature, but the wine does have the necessary richness on the palate to sustain it.

The Winemakers' Personal Selection Semillon is chosen in September of each year as the outstanding vat, and given a further six months in wood before release. The Wood-Matured Semillon is a similar wine, perhaps not with the same fruit character, but which is given additional bottle maturation as well as wood maturation prior to release. The Traminer Riesling is a 50/50 blend, fairly low in acid and intended for early drinking. The Chardonnay, and the Semillon-Chardonnay blend are recent additions to the range and invariably sell out quickly.

The Rhine Riesling Spatlese is made from the last rhine riesling grapes to be harvested, cold-fermented at 11°C for around three weeks, with the fermentation arrested while there is still one degree of residual grape sugar. I did not find the 1984 vintage particularly attractive, being rather hard and harsh and with the suggestion of a few fermentation problems. The last of the whites is a Semillon Sauterne, an adequate if unexciting wine.

There are only two reds: Bengala Light Red, which is non-vintage, and Shiraz. This is what the estate says about its Bengala:

Made from 100 per cent Shiraz taken off their skins as soon as adequate colour extraction is obtained and before the skin tannins have been completely extracted. It is then cold-fermented like a premium white wine but given sufficient oak treatment prior to bottling to enhance the flavour. We feel that this is as close to the Beaujolais style as any wine produced in Australia.

I purchased and tasted a bottle at the end of 1984; while quite delicious, it had absolutely nothing whatsoever to do with beaujolais, and was in fact like a very old Rhone Valley wine. Being non-vintage, there may well be variation from one batch to the next, but I seem to remember earlier releases being in very much the same style.

The shiraz can be very big, ripe and rich. The 1978 Shiraz was such a wine. One of the great attractions of Horderns' Wybong Estate — apart from the sheer beauty of the location — is the range of older vintages available, and the modest cost of the wines.

QUELDINBURG
NEW ENGLAND HIGHWAY, MUSWELLBROOK

Kevin Sobels is a member of the distinguished Sobels family of the Clare Valley; when he and his wife Margaret came to the Upper Hunter in the early 70s, it was not surprising that they should set up their winery in the South Australian fashion — in other words to rely on grapes purchased from independent growers in the region. Sobels had spent some years working as a winemaker in the Barossa-Watervale district, and the winery he designed and built on the New England Highway, 1.5 kilometres south of Muswellbrook, reflected his practical experience.

Refrigerated stainless-steel fermentation for the white wines is standard practice, while the red wines are all cask-aged. The wines released between 1974 and 1981 covered the main varieties — rhine riesling, semillon, traminer, chardonnay, shiraz and cabernet sauvignon. Of these the traminers were the best overall, with ample flavour, although they showed a certain amount of the hardness on the finish which so disfigures many Australian wines made from this variety. Probably the most distinctive aspect of the wines was the label, an unabashed copy of Chateau Filhot, a great sauterne property in France (with a little bit of German text thrown in to complete the spirit of ecumenism).

In 1982 Sobels, like his counterpart in the Lower Hunter, Ed Jouault of Allandale, changed direction, although Sobels took the course one step further. Queldinburg acquired an interest in a vineyard 3.5 kilometres north of Muswellbrook, and all of the Queldinburg wines have since come from grapes grown on that property.

The most recent releases have not been inspiring. The 1983 Cabernet Sauvignon showed strong mercaptan; the 1984 Pinot Riesling had tell-tale pink tints and some smelly, oxidative off-characters. The 1984 Chablis was the best: free from fault, although fairly bland and undistinguished.

ROSEMOUNT ESTATE
ROSEMOUNT ROAD, DENMAN

In just 10 years Rosemount Estate has come from obscurity to national—indeed, international—prominence in a period which has seen many companies fail altogether and others falter in their stride. Rosemount has gone from strength to strength. It has done so from a geographic base which can only be described as unfashionable; it has operated in a market (the bottled-wine market) which has shown little of the overall growth in wine sales, and which has experienced intense competition.

What, then, has been the basis of its success? A combination of first-class management at all levels (viticultural, winemaking, marketing and executive); of being predominantly in the white-wine market; of concentrating on the single sector of the market which has allowed reasonable profit margins; and by supporting its sales team with extensive advertising and careful attention to packaging and promotion.

When Bob Oatley, a highly successful New Guinea coffee and cocoa plantation owner, selected what was to become the nucleus of Rosemount Estate in 1969, he did so with the intention of grazing cattle. Indeed, Charolais cattle and thoroughbred horses still form a major part of the group's Upper Hunter activities. Moreover, neither he nor anyone else associated with the venture was aware that in the 1840s a young German settler, named Carl Brecht, had been brought to the area as a shepherd by William Dangar, one of the major pastoralists in the region. Brecht was ultimately granted land near the junction of Wybong Creek and the Goulburn River, and he planted grapes. He commenced making wine in the early 1860s, and throughout the 1870s he scored major successes in international shows. At the American Centennial in 1876 at Philadelphia one of his burgundies won a gold medal, while other gold-medal awards were won at Paris and Montpellier.

The vines fell to the cow, and the property became a dairy farm from the First World War until the Oatley family commenced to plant vineyards from 1970.

The first two varieties planted by Rosemount 100 years later were shiraz and traminer, the latter an unlikely choice because the grape was not widely propagated, nor was the wine particularly fashionable at the time. Nonetheless, the first vintage (1975) of the traminer started Rosemount on a spectacular show career, winning five gold medals in its first show entries, and contributing to an extraordinary tally of 58 medals won during the 1975 show year.

The first vintage, in 1974, had been made at another winery, but Rosemount built its own winery in time for the 1975 vintage. John Ellis joined as winemaker, and a national marketing campaign quickly established the Rosemount label. In 1977 the minnow swallowed the whale when Rosemount purchased the Penfolds Wybong Estate, signifying the beginning of the end for the New South Wales operations of Penfolds. Shortly afterwards, Rosemount purchased Roxburgh Vineyard from Denman Estates, and in 1983 purchased Mount Dangar from Adelaide Steamships. In the meantime it had established several new vineyards of its own.

The purchase of Wybong Estate from Penfolds was of enormous significance. The importance was not due to the vineyards (in fact Rosemount has removed almost 100 hectares of vines which either could not be reached by supplementary water or were on unsuitable soil), but to the large and efficient winery on the property. Thus, even though the annual crush has increased since 1979 from around 1000 tonnes to close on 4000 tonnes (Rosemount is reticent about disclosing the precise amount), no major winery extensions have been needed. Equipment has been progressively upgraded, the most recent acquisitions being two tank-presses and two Vinomatic fermenters, the product of the most advanced fermentation technology. It has never been doubted that Wybong Estate was purchased advantageously, and the relatively low capital base (given the size of the operation) has clearly helped.

One further acquisition might have been the crowning glory. Serious negotiations were under way at one stage for the purchase of Arrowfield, but agreement could not be reached. In some ways general manager Chris Hancock is glad. He points out that it places additional pressure on Rosemount to be the only clearly successful winery operation in the region, and that it would gain strength from another well-regarded operation. For this reason, if for no other, he wishes Arrowfield well, and privately admits that it remains one of the great vineyard properties in the region.

The jewel in the Rosemount crown is the Roxburgh property of some 270 hectares in all, with approximately 75 hectares of vines. Once again, Rosemount is cautious about detailed information, pointing out that the figures date very quickly as plantings are modified to meet changing demands in the marketplace and also the change in needs of winemakers. But as at 1984, at least, there were 28 hectares of chardonnay, 20 hectares of semillon, eight hectares each of rhine riesling and cabernet sauvignon, and four hectares of shiraz. There are insignificant (at least in the terms of size) plantings of sauvignon blanc and traminer.

When Roxburgh was acquired there were a little over two hectares of chardonnay, which was regarded as "experimental". In 1980 it yielded a little over 15 tonnes of fruit, and formed the basis of the Rosemount Show Chardonnay of that year. The blend was completed with grapes from Wybong and a certain amount from Craigmoor at Mudgee. Rosemount had no doubt that the quality of that very successful wine was primarily due to the Roxburgh fruit, and so a major grafting programme was undertaken.

In 1984 the first Roxburgh Vineyard wine was released under the Rosemount Estate banner. A 1983 Chardonnay, it had a recommended retail price of around $18.95. In the year or so since it had commenced its show career it had won gold medals almost at will.

The wine is at the far end of the spectrum of what I term the peaches-and-cream style. Rich to the point of being unctuous, and with a texture more akin to that of a sweet rather than dry wine, the flavour of the fruit (and to a lesser degree oak) coats the mouth. Not surprisingly, the Roxburgh label will be reserved for the very best wines from the Rosemount house. While it is intended that a chardonnay, and almost certainly a cabernet sauvignon or a shiraz, will be released each year under the Roxburgh label, this will depend on the quality of the vintage and thereby the wine. At this juncture the 1984 Chardonnay is certain to be released; although a more elegant and balanced wine, it is not as striking, but many might regard it as better. As at the end of 1984 no final decision had been taken on the first Roxburgh red, but a 1983 Cabernet Sauvignon still in oak looked very promising.

The extreme quality of Roxburgh is attributed to the red basaltic loam soil. The other Rosemount Estate vineyards do not share this soil, but general manager Hancock does not agree with the theory advanced that the soils of the Goulburn River system have any inherent advantage over those on the Hunter River side. The view has been put forward by some that the underlying coal seams on the Hunter River side have invested the soil with excess sulphur and sulphuric acid content, and it is for this reason that many of the vineyards have gone into decline. Hancock disagrees: he points out that the largest coalmine in New South Wales will be situated only two kilometres away from Roxburgh, and that the coal in the area is barely 30 metres below the surface. He prefers to point to a lack of understanding of the viticultural requirements of the region.

The 400-hectare Mount Dangar property currently has 113 hectares under vine, comprising semillon (44.5 hectares), chardonnay (36.4 hectares), rhine riesling (12 hectares), shiraz (eight hectares) and cabernet sauvignon (four hectares).

Edinglassie, which takes its name from the beautifully restored homestead and which has been the subject of much wrangling with the Wran New South Wales government, has 14 hectares of vineyard, roughly divided between chardonnay, traminer and rhine riesling. Alone among the Rosemount vineyards, it was devastated by the frosts of October 1984 and will produce next to nothing in 1985.

The "home" Rosemount Vineyard has had its varietal composition altered over the years, and will be reviewed once again after the 1985 vintage is over. Some of the Rosemount vines have successfully entered their third life, from shiraz to traminer to chardonnay. Presently it is planted to chardonnay (14 hectares), traminer (10 hectares), cabernet sauvignon (eight hectares), semillon (7.7 hectares), sauvignon blanc (5.7 hectares) and rhine riesling (4.85 hectares).

Roseglen Vineyard, established in 1978, next-door to the Rosemount Vineyard, has eight hectares of chardonnay, 3.2 hectares each of pinot noir and sauvignon blanc and two hectares of traminer.

Yarrawa, directly across the Goulburn River from the Rosemount Vineyard and Winery, is planted to 6.1 hectares of chardonnay and two hectares each of sauvignon blanc, merlot and cabernet franc.

Finally, there is the old Wybong Vineyard, or at least the remains of it. It has 16 hectares of traminer, 10 hectares of semillon, 8.1 hectares of rhine riesling, 17 hectares of blanquette and 6.1 hectares of chardonnay. There are also small plantings of chasselas, pinot noir, shiraz, cabernet and trebbiano, all survivors from the Penfolds days. The chasselas, a noted early ripener, performs an unusual task: the 13 or 14 tonnes to come from the few hectares of the variety are used to start the yeast propagations for the main ferment.

Rosemount was well served by John Ellis in its formative days. Some would say it has been even better served by Philip Shaw since his appointment as chief winemaker prior to the 1982 vintage. Shaw graduated from Roseworthy Agricultural College in 1969, and had a distinguished career with Lindemans, where he was in charge of the development of the premium wine range at Sydney prior to his appointment at Rosemount. He expressed his winemaking philosophy in these terms when he was appointed:

> I am very interested in what Rosemount are doing in the development of quality varietal wines, particularly with the different range of vineyards available. I believe in an emphasis on delicacy and fruit flavour. 'Elegance', combined with complexity, is what I am after in all wines. This may involve the utilisation of oak, plus different viticultural and district variations. I believe that in Australia in the past we have not emphasised fruit quality sufficiently.

There can be no doubting Rosemount's commitment to fruit quality and flavour. I have been a consistent admirer of its wood-matured semillons; winemakers from other areas tend to look down on these wines, with their unabashed use of a small amount of residual sugar, and the interesting glycerine texture that they acquire. A fair coating of new oak surrounds all of the other wine flavours. Purist wines they may not be, but they are outstandingly successful on the retail market, and a pleasure to drink with most food. This, surely, is what wine is all about. What does it really matter if after two or three years the wines start to become a little fat, clumsy and/or dry out. Many of the Rosemount wines do just that, but so what?

The chardonnays are built in a similar mould. At six months of age, when the wines first start coming into the show ring, they are a world apart from the wines of their competitors. Having been involved in the making of one or two Hunter chardonnays myself, I do not profess to understand how this is all achieved. Once again, I am not sure it really matters. I know from extensive personal experience that it gives wine-show judges much to agonise over when dealing with young chardonnay classes. Do you give the gold medal to the precocious youngster (which you cannot help but recognise as being a Rosemount wine, or at least very similar thereto) and which is clearly the best wine on the day, or do you give it to the wine which you believe is most likely to be at its best in six or 12 months time when the wine comes onto the market? Just as it is the function of judges

in a law court to interpret the law as it is, and not make the law, so I believe it is the function of the wine judge to judge the wines as he or she sees them on the day, and not try to second-guess the future. It is open to the show societies to amend the conditions of entry to provide that only wine in bottle is eligible for gold medals if they so wish.

A third string to the ultra-sophisticated, wood-matured, soft, white-wine range has been added with the development of Rosemount's Fumé Blanc. No sooner had the 1983 Show Reserve Chardonnay (next under the Roxburgh) been ranked by the prestigious English wine magazine *Decanter* as the outstanding buy on a quality/price basis of over 60 chardonnays assembled in London from around the world, than Terry Robards reviewed the 1983 Fumé Blanc in the *New York Post* on 7 November 1984, saying: "No sauvignon blanc that I have ever tasted from an American producer has reached this quality level."

If this were not all enough, in 1982 Rosemount made a Trockenbeerenauslese Rhine Riesling which I think is one of the most remarkable late-harvest wines ever made in this country. Explosively rich and luscious, it confounded all preconceived notions about the ability (or rather lack of ability) of the Hunter River to produce such wine styles. It is not likely to be repeated very often, but the fact is that it was at least done once.

If all of this suggests that Rosemount is primarily a white-wine company, that is indeed correct. But it has also achieved some remarkable results with its red wines, particularly given the major question which still hangs over the ability of the Upper Hunter to produce reds. Rosemount is unabashed in admitting that the 80 per cent rule (requiring that a wine be at least 80 per cent from the area designated on the label) is used in constructing the Rosemount reds. It believes that the reds of the Upper Hunter have excellent structure but lack middle-palate fruit. It was this in part which led Rosemount to purchase land in Coonawarra in December 1981: the 26-hectare vineyard, on the outskirts of Penola, has been slow to develop but is now planted to 10 hectares of cabernet sauvignon, six hectares of pinot noir, four hectares of chardonnay and two hectares each of shiraz, merlot and sauvignon blanc. In the meantime, until the vineyard comes into bearing, Rosemount buy significant quantities of shiraz and cabernet sauvignon from Coonawarra Machinery Company (which releases the Katnook wines) and also acquires red-wine material from Chateau Tahbilk. As little as three to five per cent in the final blend can add that extra bit of flesh to the mid-palate of the wine.

There is no difficulty in seeing the influence of these other wines in the Rosemount Estate reds. Once again, I am fully supportive of the Rosemount approach. What matters is the quality of the wine in the bottle, and not whether it is varietally or regionally pure. Obviously the 80 per cent rule should not be transgressed, but it makes no sense to suggest that a Coonawarra cabernet is being dressed up as a Hunter Valley shiraz.

Bob Oatley must be more than a little pleased with his small venture into viticulture.

VERONA
NEW ENGLAND HIGHWAY, MUSWELLBROOK

Verona remains as enigmatic as its name, which was given to a property at the northern end of Muswellbrook by two butchers, Joe Gillies and Abraham Clark, when they purchased it in 1890. It is said that they apparently considered themselves gentlemen and, having some knowledge of Shakespeare, they called the place Verona.

The property ultimately passed to Keith and Georgina Yore, who had a long-established farm machinery and irrigation business. The vineyard was started purely to demonstrate a new drip-irrigation system; in the manner of things, the vines grew and produced grapes, a few friends were invited in for a picnic day, the grapes were foot-stamped, and another winery was born (or at least conceived).

So, at least, the story goes: it may be apocryphal, but it is a fitting start to an enterprise which has since puzzled endlessly those who watch the Hunter Valley wine industry. The majority of the grapes in the early years was sold, but some wine was made for Verona from rhine riesling and from traminer by Rosemount. These wines—from the mid-70s— enjoyed great show success.

A winery was built at Verona (a 12-sided building, or dodecagon) and Rod Upton was installed as winemaker. A brief flurry onto the Sydney market ensued through AML & F (Australian Mercantile Land and Finance Company), but was not persevered with. In 1974 the vineyards were supposed to contain 23 hectares, in 1979 34 hectares, and they are now back to 21 hectares. At one stage an obscure Spanish variety called valdepenas made its appearance: the red wine from it was not attractive, and it has faded from the scene. Plantings now comprise five hectares of traminer (down from 12 in 1979), five hectares of

rhine riesling, four hectares of cabernet sauvignon, 3.5 hectares of chardonnay, 1.5 hectares of semillon and one hectare each of sauvignon blanc and shiraz.

From a 1979 crush of 150 tonnes, projected to increase to 500 tonnes, the 1984 crush declined to 40 tonnes (10 tonnes each of traminer, chardonnay, rhine riesling and semillon). All of this might not be so extraordinary were it not for Verona's activities in the Lower Hunter. In 1980–81 it purchased an abandoned Hungerford Hill vineyard in McDonalds Road directly opposite Brokenwood; an enormous turkey-nest dam was constructed on the top of the hill, and almost overnight a concrete pad and a stainless-steel fermentation tank made their appearance. The dam slowly filled with water pumped up from a creek at the bottom of a hill, and in 1981–82 a very large and not overly attractive red-brick winery was partially constructed.

After some months a violent windstorm demolished part of it, but it was eventually completed in 1982. In the meantime a desultory effort had been made to graft some of the ailing vineyard which, given the vineyard's condition and the largely empty dam, was predictably a failure. The building seems to serve chiefly as a cellar-door sales outlet (also offering excellent pecan nuts from the Upper Hunter) and as a source of endless gossip for bemused locals.

The Verona wines are, alas, not attractive. Hydrogen sulphide/mercaptan and oxidation are persistent faults, obscuring fruit flavour. ▯

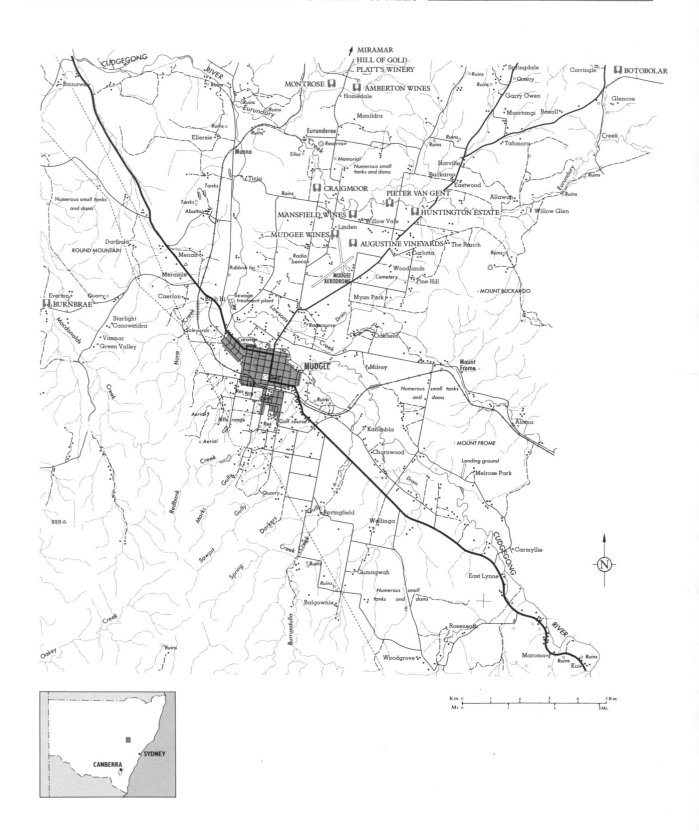

Mudgee

Mudgee was first settled in 1822 by George and Henry Cox, the year after James Blackman and William Lawson first entered the district. The village of Mudgee was gazetted on 12 January 1838, and is the second-oldest settlement west of the Great Dividing Range. Many of its National Trust classified buildings date back to the second half of the last century, the oldest to 1852.

Vines were first planted in 1858 by Adam Roth, one of a number of German "vine-dressers" who had been brought to Australia some years earlier as the result of the exhortations of William Macarthur, who needed skilled labour for his substantial vineyard at Camden. The German influence was as important in Mudgee as it was in the Barossa Valley, with the Roth and Kurtz families sustaining viticulture for a century or more; and others, such as Frederick Buchholz, making a major contribution in the last century.

Having served his time with Macarthur, Roth was given a 37-hectare grant on the banks of the Pipeclay Creek in 1858 and immediately planted part of it to vines. In 1872 gold was discovered at the quaintly named nearby settlement of Home Rule; the diggings quickly spread to within a kilometre of Roth's property which he had named Rothview. Once again gold and vines proved a symbiotic pairing; and once again the astute realised there was a more assured income to be made from feeding the miners than chasing the elusive pot of gold.

Grapes, wine and vegetables brought premium prices; by 1880 there were 13 wineries in the district, five of them owned and operated by Adam Roth's sons, while the sixth and youngest remained at Rothview to help his father. Andreas Kurtz was another German immigrant from Württemberg who followed closely on the heels of Adam Roth, planting grapes in the 1860s, and establishing one of the other wineries. The largest of all was that of Frederick Buchholz, who established his 80-hectare vineyard

and Fredericksburg Winery adjacent to Rothview. In 1888 he was a successful exhibitor at the Centennial Exhibition in Melbourne, but the bank crash and the depression of the 1890s badly hurt his business, and the property was sold in 1899.

Anti-German feeling during the First World War also paralleled that of the Barossa Valley, and Fredericksburg was renamed Westcourt. Either at that time or before, perhaps even 1899, it had passed to the Roth family, and was owned for many years by Bill Roth. In 1930 Colin Laraghy, winemaker at the then-famous Smithfield Winery on the outskirts of Sydney, came to Mudgee to arrange long-term contracts with the few local growers who were persisting with wine grapes. One such was Bill Roth at Westcourt, and Laraghy supplied him with cuttings to increase his range, including a white grape.

When Jack Roth married, and inherited his father's winery (by then renamed Craigmoor), he decided to expand the winery and its production, and purchased Rothview from his brother Bill. The white vines from the Laraghy cuttings had prospered, but Jack Roth never vinified them separately. All of his white grapes went together to make a dry white, released in an old-style green riesling bottle with a label in the shape of a grape leaf, and bearing neither vintage nor variety.

But they caught the attention (and respect) of Alf Kurtz, who worked on Craigmoor as well as tending to his own small family vineyard some distance down the road. When in the mid-60s he decided to establish Mudgee Wines, he obtained cuttings from the Craigmoor plantings and established them at his own vineyard. It was here that they were discovered and identified by a visiting French ampelographer, Dr Denis Bourbals, brought to Australia on a six-month study tour by the CSIRO. Bourbals in turn told Mildara's Bob Hollick of his discovery, adding that the clone was virus-free and one of the best he had seen anywhere in the world. The small planting was to become the source block for much of Australia's chardonnay, for this was the variety Bourbals had identified. It may not have come as any great surprise to Alf Kurtz, because he had labelled the wine made from it as white pineau, and had shared a bottle with Bourbals and Dr Peter May on the day they had visited his winery.

Back at the turn of the century winemaking (and grape growing) was on the wane in Mudgee as it was in so many other regions of Australia. One of Australia's most enterprising wine-medicos, Florentine-born Dr Thomas Henry Fiaschi, had gone against the trend and established a vineyard and winery at Buberra, three kilometres from Craigmoor, in the early part of the twentieth century. He died, aged 74, in 1927 at which time only his winery and that of Craigmoor remained in operation. It, too, passed into disuse, so that when Alf Kurtz established Mudgee Wines in 1964, his was only the second winery in the district. There are now 16 wineries selling to the public and more are planned; in 1983 there were 55 grape growers in the district, precisely the same number as in 1893.

Mudgee is to the Hunter Valley what Clare is to the Barossa Valley: it is quieter, more remote, less commercial, less aggressively tourist oriented, and far more personal. Here you will almost invariably be greeted by the winemaker, who equally is almost invariably the owner. There is only one large company (Montrose), and even it is very small by national standards. Thus even though Mudgee has expanded greatly since the days of Jack Roth and Alf Kurtz, it avoided altogether the broad acres of planting and excesses which caused so much trouble in the Hunter Valley. It is also a quietly beautiful place. The exquisite colour photographs taken by Gil Wahlquist of Botobolar show its many moods to perfection. These photographs appeared originally on the newsletter produced by him for his winery, the *Botobolar Bugle*.

Mudgee is an Aboriginal word for "nest in the hills", and that is precisely what Mudgee is. Situated on the western slopes of the Great Dividing Range, 275 kilometres from Sydney, the mountains on either side rise to almost 1000 metres. Most of the vines are planted at a height of 500 metres, although a few vineyards reach up to the 800-metre mark.

Mudgee, like most hilly regions, has an enormously variable microclimate. Certain slopes will favour one variety, others another. This also complicates the discussion of Mudgee's climate, a somewhat sensitive issue with some of the vignerons in the district. It is at the same latitude as the Hunter Valley, but thanks to its very cool nights and later spring, vintage takes

place one month later, getting into full swing in March. This has prompted some vignerons to claim that Mudgee should be regarded as a cool-climate region, but both the statistics and the style of its wines show otherwise. For a start, it has a centigrade heat-degree day summation of 1821, and it averages eight hours of sunshine per day compared with the Hunter's 7.3 hours. It has a mean January temperature (the average, in other words, for that month) of 22.7°C, precisely the same as that of Cessnock and Rutherglen.

So whatever the climate may be, it is not cool. The major compensations come through the cold nights, and from the fact that by the time the grapes are ripe, the worst of the summer heat has passed. Its summer rainfall, too, is less than that of the Hunter: 361 millimetres compared with 433 for the latter. Moreover, the heavy vintage-time rains which are so much part of the Hunter vigneron's life rarely upset the Mudgee vintage. 1984 was a classic case when Mudgee had an outstanding vintage. It shared in the cool summer conditions which prevailed over the whole of south-eastern Australia, but missed out on the heavy January–February rains which deprived the Hunter of the benefits of the cool summer.

The style of the wines also denies the cool-climate claim. While distinctly different from that of the Hunter, being richer, deeper and more robust, they have the unmistakable taste of sun. Thus the cabernets have flavours of dark chocolate and ripe plums, sometimes with a little mint, rather than grassy/green-leaf flavours. For some obscure reason shiraz seems determined to out-Hunter the Hunter, with persistent "sweaty saddle"/"cowshed" characters manifesting themselves in many vats.

Traditionally Mudgee was a red-wine producer. Like so many other areas, that reputation was in turn built exclusively on shiraz, for cabernet sauvignon was not introduced until 1961. Cabernet was first planted by Alf Kurtz, who obtained the cuttings from an experimental one-acre (0.4 hectare) vineyard at Molong owned by Jack Pride. Pride had been encouraged to start the vineyard by one of New South Wales's most far-sighted viticultural officers, Harry Manuel. Manuel had in turn obtained the cabernet rootstock from a special clonal selection in South Australia. These 100 cuttings provided the source of the cabernet sauvignon now established in the Huntington, Augustine, Glenroy and Botobolar Vineyards.

The ability of Mudgee to provide red wines with an immense depth of colour is nowhere seen to better advantage than with cabernet. I can remember with the utmost clarity during my first visit to the district over 10 years ago watching with amazement as Bob Roberts of Huntington Estate tipped some cabernet down the laboratory sink; the water took a seemingly interminable time to wash the stains away. Whether this is due to the soil, or the climate, or a combination of both, I do not know. The soils vary from red to yellow-brown in colour, and in texture from sandy loams through to clay loams; the subsoil is generally clay, and all soils have good water retention capacity.

While cabernet plantings are on the increase, and those of shiraz slowly declining, the table below shows that shiraz is still the dominant red variety, although over the past decade it has been used to make virtually every wine style: white wine, rosé, dry red and port. It has been asserted that Mudgee shiraz does not exhibit the same character as that from the Hunter: sometimes it does not, but far more often it does. I have seen the same character in shiraz from places as far away as Geelong, and I am coming slowly to the conclusion that it is in part a varietal character which may well be accentuated by fermentation conditions or some other winemaking practices. Certainly the winemakers with whom I have discussed the problem swear the character occurs naturally in the wine, and that none of the conventional methods for treating hydrogen sulphide has the least effect on it.

A number of growers, including Craigmoor, Edwards at Hill of Gold and Bob Roberts at Huntington, have struggled with pinot noir. Just as I believe it is unsuited to the Hunter Valley, so I

believe it is unlikely to be a viable variety in Mudgee. 1984 may yet prove the exception to the rule, but even if it does, one year in 10 is not an acceptable figure. In most years the wine looks like most Australian pinot noir: lacking in colour and tending to brown early in its life, and devoid of any of the intense strawberry/cherry/plum flavours which so distinguish the great wines of Burgundy.

Merlot is grown by Bob Roberts at Huntington Estate and blended with cabernet sauvignon to make one of Mudgee's most distinguished red wines. It has not been an easy task from a viticultural point of view: the variety has shown the same disinclination to set properly at flowering as in many other regions, and yields are generally very low. Improved clones would be a great assistance.

Finally, there is an exotic array of Italian grapes (barbera, sangiovese and nebbiolo) which have been planted and nurtured by Carlo Corino, the charming Italian-born and raised winemaker at Montrose. I say more of this when discussing Montrose Wines.

Mudgee has embraced chardonnay with the same fervour as most other Australian wine districts, but can at least claim a long courtship, which I described at some length earlier in this introduction.

One of the features of the Mudgee soil is that by and large it is too heavy and clay-impregnated to play host to a microscopic parasite called nematode which spreads many of the grape viruses. In contemporary Australian viticulture the nematode is a greater problem than phylloxera: in many districts it is this pest, and not phylloxera, which forces the grape grower to use grafted vines. The consequence is that the Mudgee chardonnay remained virus-free, and is still one of the most desirable selections in this day of advanced clonal selection and breeding.

The wines made in the region from the variety vary between solid, full-flavoured styles through to the almost riotous, rich essence-like grapefruit/melon aromas and flavours of the Miramar and Montrose wines. Bob Roberts at Huntington Estate takes an entirely contrary track, arguing that chardonnay has its own intense flavour which does not need the oak-fermentation techniques of the Miramar wine nor even the simple oak maturation of the Montrose.

Semillon is the next most important grape, although it was to all intents and purposes non-existent until the early 70s. An oddity of the region is that some of the plantings are interspersed with vines which produce fruit with a distinctly red skin. These rather unusual grapes are claimed by their growers to be "true" semillon (a claim of questionable validity). It does seem that they impart no unwanted

MUDGEE: GRAPE VARIETIES AND PLANTINGS

Variety	Hectares
WHITES	
Chardonnay	60.33
Semillon	47.63
Rhine riesling	15.24
Crouchen	10.16
Muscat gordo blanco	9.89
Traminer	5.87
Trebbiano	5.87
Frontignac	4.61
Sauvignon blanc	2.56
REDS	
Shiraz	158.22
Cabernet sauvignon	97.21
Pinot noir	14.12
OTHER	9.34

colour to the white wine, however. Because it is a relative newcomer to the district it is not possible to say whether the wine has the same ageing capacity as those of the Hunter Valley; but some of the Craigmoor semillons from the early 70s were drinking quite beautifully 10 years later.

Rhine riesling is something of a "sleeper"; with a wine-drinking public conditioned to believing it is little more than a bulk white with occasional aspirations to glory, there is little inducement to the growers and winemakers to pay much attention to the existing plantings, let alone increase them. But the fact remains that Montrose, Craigmoor and Miramar have produced some very, very interesting wines from the variety. With a year or two in bottle they develop a potent lime/passionfruit character which is subtly different from anything else I have encountered in Australia. The vines planted in the higher vineyards over the past 15 years have shown special promise.

Traminer, trebbiano, crouchen, frontignac, and muscat gordo blanco constitute the fruit-salad makings which are the inevitable mark of the willing-to-try-anything Australian vigneron. As the dedicated reader of this book will discern, I have no great love for traminer wherever it may be grown, and Mudgee seems unlikely to cause me to change my views. Nonetheless, Amberton and Montrose in particular have produced one or two quite serviceable wines from the variety. Most of the sauvignon blanc is going into sauterne-style wines, a decision I strongly support. The sauternes are extremely good (especially the Montrose Bemosa) and I very much doubt that the Mudgee climate will leave much worthwhile varietal character in the dry styles, although the '84 Amberton proves the exception to that rule. The other grapes are work-horses, pure and simple.

There was a time when it was fashionable to see Mudgee as the area of the future for New South Wales. I think commonsense has now prevailed, and it is simply regarded as a good viticultural region producing wines of quite different style from those of the Hunter—more nuggetty and chunky but with a little less finesse. Its one great strength may yet prove to be its appellation system, and it is to this which I now turn.

Appellation control is seen as so fundamental to the French system of wine marketing and control that it is easy to lose sight of the fact it is a creature of the twentieth century, and that most of the appellation systems were installed in the lifetimes of our parents. It is also salutary to remember that it was introduced to curb deceit and trickery on a scale way beyond anything contemplated, let alone executed, in this country. On the other hand, it is very much in tune with a society which seems hell-bent on regulation and protection, particularly when it concerns something we may wish to eat or drink.

So it will be apparent that I am lukewarm about the benefits of appellation. The fact is that there is a series of detailed regulations under the Pure Foods Act which, if enforced, would give 90 per cent of the protection which an appellation system offers on paper. But I fail to see the merit of replacing one set of unenforced regulations with another set of unenforced regulations, and if introduced on a national scale, I am sure that this would happen.

It is precisely here that the Mudgee scheme is different. It was a scheme set up voluntarily by all the wineries in the region, and they were careful firstly to limit the scope of the scheme so that it could be enforced, and secondly to provide the physical means of that enforcement. What does it certify? First, that the wine is of Mudgee origin; second, that the label faithfully represents the wine in the bottle; third, that the wine is free of objectionable faults at the time of assessment. These may seem modest guarantees, but as we shall see in a minute there is more substance than a cynical first reading might suggest.

The scheme is run, or enforced, by a controller who is a partner in a firm of chartered accountants. Vineyard plantings, grape yields and litres of wine produced are all registered with him. He has an absolute and unqualified right of inspection of vineyards, winery and wine stocks at any time he chooses. A winemaker desiring to use the Mudgee mark on a wine makes an application by way of a sworn declaration after the wine has been bottled. The controller then visits the winery, checks the quantities of the wine in stock, and selects random bottles from the stock which are subsequently tasted and assessed by the Wine Assessment Committee.

The committee is composed of the winemaker from each participating winery. All wines are assessed in the first instance anonymously; if the wine is considered to be *prima facie* acceptable, its identity (and in particular the variety) is then made known to the committee to enable a judgement to be made on the fidelity of the wine to its label. And it is not just varietal character which is considered. If, for example, the wine is said to have been aged in German oak, the committee must be satisfied that a German-oak influence can be detected in the aroma and/or the flavour of the wine. What is more, the Society for the Appellation of the Wines of Mudgee will not

PACKAGING PROCESS WORKERS

permit use of the "80 per cent rule" which governs the labelling of wine in Australia generally. The wine must be 100 per cent Mudgee wine, and if it is labelled as a varietal it must be composed 100 per cent of that variety. This contrasts with the 80 per cent requirement under the Pure Foods Act regulations in force in the various States.

The cynical will point out that a winemaker on the committee is very likely to recognise his or her own wine. Even if this be true he or she is but a minority of one; but having been in the position myself of searching for a wine I have made in a masked line-up, I can only say it is usually far more rewarding to forget who might have made what, and simply judge the quality of the wine in the glass. In any event, the selection committee has rejected 10 per cent of the wines placed before it, which is a high figure given the criteria set.

An unexpected bonus of the scheme has been the development of a far more questioning and critical attitude by the winemakers to their own wines (once unmasked), and a tangible increase over the years in the overall level of wine quality.

If, having run the gauntlet of the Wine Assessment Committee, the wine is passed, the controller then issues a certificate authorising the use of the Mudgee mark and the printing of numbered labels.

The society has considered, but (so far at least) considered too difficult and controversial, building in a quality grading scheme. As it points out, none of the appellation systems in the world has done so if one ignores the single-step "Superior Quality" rating given to some South African wines under its certification system. So it is that not all wines bearing the Mudgee mark will be of the same standard, nor should they be. But it remains the Achilles heel of this (and every other similar) system: the public expects more than the system promises, and believes it provides a positive guarantee of quality. It does not. Sylvaner might produce an excruciatingly ordinary wine in Mudgee, but as long as the wine is made from Mudgee sylvaner, is accurately described, free from objectionable (winemaking) faults, and is typical of this mediocre grape, it would be entitled to the mark.

In closing, I have yet to see a bad Mudgee wine with the mark; and if you have never tasted a Mudgee wine, but have been sufficiently interested to read these words, you owe it to yourself to do so.

AMBERTON WINES
HENRY LAWSON DRIVE, EURUNDEREE, via MUDGEE

Amberton is one of the newer vineyards in Mudgee, founded in 1975 by a group of wine- and food-loving doctors who frequented Manuel Damien's Little Snail restaurant at Bondi in Sydney. The major partners are Ted Jackson, Colin Franklin and Peter Kitchener. The vineyard was established on the gently rolling foothills of the Lowes Peak area. There are now 6.5 hectares of chardonnay, 5.8 hectares of semillon, 4.8 hectares of shiraz, 4.7 hectares of cabernet sauvignon, 2.3 hectares of traminer, 1.3 hectares of rhine riesling and 1.2 hectares of sauvignon blanc, all established on sandy loam soils. Only a small proportion of the 120-hectare property is planted, but the partners have no desire to increase significantly the size of the operation.

An experimental vintage was made in 1978; the first commercial vintage followed in 1979, made at a local winery under the direction of district identity Pieter Van Gent. The partners were sufficiently

encouraged with the results to proceed with the long-planned erection of their own winery, which was completed in time for the 1980 vintage. John Rozentals, a graduate of Riverina College of Advanced Education with a wine science degree, and a disciple of Brian Croser, was appointed winemaker, and made that and the ensuing three vintages.

During that period of time Amberton made a name for itself as a producer of high-class varietal white and red wines. In 1981 it received both trophies and seven of the eight gold medals awarded in the Medium Dry White Classes at the Mudgee Wine Show. Rozentals took a classically restrained view of the function of a winemaker: a quality-control officer, whose primary duty is to preserve all of the fruit character which the vineyard provides.

Rozentals suffered a degree of ill health during the latter part of his stay at Amberton, and it may well be for this reason that wine quality slipped somewhat; the drought-ravaged 1983 vintage was equally of no assistance. Prior to the 1984 vintage David Thompson was appointed winemaker: like Rozentals, he was a graduate from the winemaking course at the Riverina College of Advanced Education. This time the link with Brian Croser was even closer, as Oenotec was appointed as consultant.

The 1984 vintage was not only a very high-quality one in Mudgee, but bounteous into the bargain. Forty-five tonnes of semillon, 37 tonnes of shiraz, 36 tonnes of cabernet, 28 tonnes of chardonnay and 10 tonnes each of rhine riesling, traminer and sauvignon blanc were crushed. The small but functional winery was tested to its limits.

The first releases from 1984 bear the unmistakable stamp of Oenotec, and were rapturously received by the press. I classed these wines as "winemakers' wines", needing time to settle down and recover fully from the cold and slow fermentation, which not only results in every fraction of fruit character being retained in the wine, but also some fermentation characters. I was out of step in not particularly liking the wines when they were first released, but warmed to them greatly when I tasted them again three months later at the very end of 1984. The best of the four wines then released was the 1984 Sauvignon Blanc, the first major release of this variety from the Mudgee district. Like all of the Amberton wines, it was elegant to the point of outright delicacy; and again like all of the wines, it needed another year at least to allow the varietal character to express itself fully. Nonetheless, the unmistakable grassy-gooseberry aroma and flavour of sauvignon blanc was there to perceive.

The traminer and traminer riesling blends were fresh and light, with the traminer bolstered by a touch of residual sugar. They were extremely well made but not overly exciting wines early in their life.

The 1984 Semillon Classique is a most unusual wine. Twenty per cent was barrel-fermented late-picked material; the remaining 80 per cent was conventionally cold-fermented in stainless steel using earlier-picked grapes. The very cool ripening conditions of 1984 gave rise to some strange varietal characters, and certainly this semillon shows little or nothing of the character which we usually associate with the grape, either in Mudgee or the Hunter Valley. It does have considerable complexity, however, and it will indeed be interesting to watch the evolution of the wine over the next few years.

One can expect similar winemaking techniques to be used in 1985 and subsequent vintages, offering a radical departure from the more homespun traditional winemaking techniques hitherto employed in the district.

AUGUSTINE VINEYARDS
AIRPORT ROAD, MUDGEE

Augustine is the reincarnation of Dr Thomas Henry Fiaschi's vineyard, which had finally been abandoned in the 1940s. When Peter and Ken Spencer acquired the property in 1969 the only surviving vines were aleatico, an Italian variety. An extensive replanting programme was carried out, resulting in a 38-hectare vineyard including cabernet sauvignon, shiraz, pinot noir, semillon, traminer, chardonnay and trebbiano.

A range of varietal wines came out under the Augustine label, but the quality varied from indifferent to poor. The white wines were particularly unsatisfactory. The enterprise faltered and was virtually abandoned when two locals, Messrs Kerin and Murray, purchased Augustine. They have established a restaurant, opening seven days a week for lunch; and when John Rozentals left Amberton, he was appointed consultant winemaker. The revitalisation of Augustine should see some pleasant wines in the future; Rozentals has the necessary technical background, and knows the district well. He spends a fair proportion of his time as a journalist in Sydney, commuting to Mudgee as necessary to tend the wines.

The vineyard sources have now changed somewhat. Part of the Augustine Vineyard had been sold off separately, and the remaining portion has been joined by part of the Oakfield Vineyard purchased from the owner, Edgells.

BOTOBOLAR
BOTOBOLAR LANE, MUDGEE

Botobolar is home to Gil and Vincie Wahlquist and to a symbiotic population of weeds, grasses, plants, insects and birds which one would not normally expect to find in a vineyard, let alone encouraged. For over a decade the Wahlquists have been proponents of and ambassadors for organic farming principles. As Gil Wahlquist is at pains to explain, this is not a "do-nothing system": it calls for a great deal of management and the development of particular responses to the problems which do arise. On the other hand, it does keep both cultivation and the use of sprays to a minimum.

Once the vines are established, and into their second or third year, a grass cover is developed between the rows. Sheep are grazed during the winter months, and in the summer the grass cover is slashed. Downy mildew is controlled by Bordeaux spray (copper sulphate crystals applied shortly after the vines have flowered), while powdery mildew (the other great vineyard scourge) is controlled by lime sulphur. Neither of these sprays has any effect on insect or birdlife, which then live in natural balance without causing harm to the grapes or vines. Far from being discouraged, most birds are regarded as allies in effecting natural control of caterpillars and moths. Alternative food sources to the ripening grapes are supplied with the judicious planting of flowering gums and fruit trees. Exotic plants such as hyssop and penny royal also play a role in keeping the balance of nature. It all sounds easy, and quite romantic. In truth it is a very difficult viticultural regime, requiring great patience, skill and nerve. During the last 15 years the Wahlquists have mastered the technique, but they are among the very few to have done so.

The vineyard is planted to shiraz (7.6 hectares), crouchen (four hectares), cabernet sauvignon (3.2 hectares), rhine riesling (1.5 hectares), chardonnay (one hectare), marsanne (0.9 hectares) and mataro and traminer (0.2 hectares each). These grapes contribute 80 per cent of the annual crush, with the remaining 20 per cent (black muscat and muscat gordo blanco) bought in. It is a substantial operation: over 160 tonnes were crushed in 1984 in the old woolshed which has been converted to the winery.

From time to time Gil Wahlquist has also experimented with organically made wine, in which all chemicals (even sulphur dioxide) have been excluded. By and large, however, he leaves his organic principles in the vineyard and makes the wines using conventional methods. These in turn offer virtually every known wine style, and one or two not known outside of Botobolar. Gil Wahlquist is an ex-journalist and music critic; his sensitive, if not romantic, feelings towards wine and winemaking show not only in his viticulture but also in the names he gives to his wines.

Budgee Budgee has been a long-term favourite of the winery. An appreciably sweet and intensely fruity wine, the 1984 vintage was made entirely from muscat gordo blanco grapes grown on the Menah Vineyard. The name Budgee Budgee commemorates an old settlement near the intersection of Wollar and Muswellbrook roads, a few kilometres north-east of Mudgee. The sketch on the label shows an old hotel, closed but still standing in the settlement, believed to be the location of Henry Lawson's story "The Loaded Dog". Other unusual wines are the 1984 Rose of Shiraz (a completely dry rosé style); Vincentia Sauternes (named after Gil's wife) and Cooyal Port.

The exceptional 1984 vintage encouraged Wahlquist to experiment once again with making a sulphur-free wine. The major part of the 1984 Shiraz was made without the use of any sulphur dioxide, pasteurised at the end of fermentation and bottled immediately. This technique was developed by Dr Chris Somers at the Australian Wine Research Institute some years ago. To Gil's considerable pleasure, the wine won a silver medal at the Mudgee Wine Show, while the conventionally made remainder of the wine won a bronze medal.

All of this should not obscure the fact that Botobolar also releases a substantial number of "conventional" white and red varietal wines of considerable style and quality. Both the rhine riesling and chardonnay can be excellent, while the red wines (which are nearly always given three/to four years' bottle age before release) can be quite outstanding. The 1981 Cabernet Sauvignon and the 1981 St Gilbert Shiraz Cabernet were excellent, while the 1982 St Gilbert Shiraz Cabernet was one of the best wines made in the district that year.

All are clean, show excellent wood handling and have a richly textured fruit character. The *Botobolar Bugle*, a quarterly newsletter featuring Wahlquist's superb photography, has for years been distributed free to those on the Botobolar mailing list. The wines, the *Bugle* and Gil himself are outstanding ambassadors for the district.

BURNBRAE
THE HARGRAVES ROAD, MUDGEE

Burnbrae is one of the lesser-known Mudgee wineries, but has produced some of the district's outstanding red wines. Winemaker and part-owner Paul Tumminello had a family tradition of winemaking in Italy, but first became seriously interested in wine through wine appreciation courses and wine clubs in Sydney in the latter part of the 1960s. During the 1970s he attended many tastings which I conducted for a major Sydney retailer, and his consuming interest in and appreciation of wine was easy to see. He also obtained a Bachelor of Agricultural Science degree and spent the '75 vintage working with Gil Wahlquist at Botobolar. He was thus very well qualified to make the first vintage at Burnbrae in 1976.

The site, on the Hill End road 10 kilometres west of the town, was selected in 1971, and planting on the well-drained slate-shale soils commenced in 1972. The plantings have been increased at a leisurely pace, and even by 1980 the annual crush had reached only 18 tonnes with sales of 700 cases. The vines now comprise 11 hectares of shiraz, cabernet sauvignon, rhine riesling, semillon, trebbiano and chardonnay, with 130 malbec vines. Sauvignon blanc, pinot noir, merlot and durif (the latter for port) are presently under evaluation.

The emphasis of the winery is on dry reds and vintage ports. Over the years, the cabernet shiraz and cabernet shiraz malbec blends have been outstanding, always clean and with the depth of fruit one expects from the best wines of the district. In recent times the 1982 Shiraz (rich and peppery with vanillan/coconut oak flavours) and the 1982 Cabernet Shiraz (with crisp cherry/berry fruit flavours) have been equal to the best in the district.

The vintage ports can fairly claim to be the best, winning trophies and gold medals at the Mudgee Wine Show. Both the 1982 and 1981 Vintage Port show strong spicy fruit flavours well integrated with high-class brandy spirit, and they promise to be long-lived.

CRAIGMOOR
EURUNDEREE LANE, MUDGEE

The early history of Craigmoor is essentially that of Mudgee. When today you walk down the stone steps into the lower section of the winery built by Adam Roth before 1860, you enter not only the oldest working winery in Mudgee but also the second oldest in Australia, next after Olive Farm on the outskirts of Perth. It was to remain in the hands of the Roth family for over 100 years: in 1935 Alan (Jack) Roth, Adam's grandson, took over the winery, and ran it until his death in 1969.

It was then sold to interests associated with Cyrille and Jocelyn Van Heyst, a Sydney financier who shared with his wife a great interest in wine and food. The next 15 years were a time of turbulent change and controversy for Craigmoor, much of it taking place behind the closed doors of board rooms as financial arrangements were made, and (in the eyes of some) broken. At the very least, it can be said that not everyone agreed with Van Heyst's actions.

Craigmoor also changed its profile in the marketplace. Roth had made chiefly red wines, but had white varieties including the all-important source block of chardonnay. The Van Heysts set about developing a series of red and white varietal table wines under an entirely redesigned label, introduced new oak into the winery, and expanded the cabernet sauvignon, chardonnay and semillon plantings.

By the time the vineyard changed hands it comprised 10.5 hectares of shiraz, 7.2 hectares of semillon, 4.8 hectares of cabernet sauvignon, 4.3 hectares of chardonnay, two hectares of traminer, one hectare of pinot noir and 0.6 hectares of sauvignon blanc. These vineyards were established on soils varying from yellow-brown to red, sandy, clay loams through to heavy clay loam, and the quality of the Craigmoor fruit was demonstrated again and again.

The first varietal chardonnay was released in 1971, coincidentally the same year as Murray Tyrrell released his first Vat 47. It immediately became apparent that Mudgee was an excellent area for chardonnay of the fuller, richer style. Successive vintages varied considerably according to the oak treatment given to them, reaching a height in 1979 when four different chardonnays, each matured in different oak, were released. Throughout much of the 70s the Craigmoor chardonnays were highly regarded and sought after, but as other areas started to produce chardonnay in quantity and winemaking techniques became more sophisticated, the high reputation of Craigmoor slipped somewhat.

The semillon chardonnay blend, also first released in 1971, followed a similar track. These wines gradually built up body and richness in bottle, and at 10 or more years of age became spectacular, full-blown white burgundy styles. For many years the blend was the only wine released; by the second half of the 1970s, however, Craigmoor was also making

and releasing a wood-matured semillon, once again being one of the earliest wineries to deliberately induce oak flavour as part of the make-up of bottle-aged semillon.

The Craigmoor shiraz was the other particularly successful wine in the 1970s. The '71 was awarded a number of medals at national wine shows, including a gold medal; while the 1974 won the coveted Montgomery Trophy for best one-year-old red burgundy at the Adelaide Wine Show. With bottle age these wines achieved a soft, velvety structure very similar to Hunter Valley shiraz, with some of the same leathery, "sweaty-saddle" characteristics. The main difference is an extra degree of fruit sweetness on the mid-palate.

In the last few years under the Van Heyst stewardship some interesting pinot noirs were made by Barry Platt. While I hold to my reservations about the suitability of the variety for the district, several releases did show quite marked varietal character, and had surprising finesse into the bargain.

New labels and an aggressive marketing campaign adopted at the start of the 1980s failed to bring the sales needed. Negotiations for the sale of Craigmoor got under way, and Barry Platt—who, obviously enough, knew what was going on—agreed to purchase the entire 1983 production (decimated by drought and reduced to a mere 23 tonnes) for release under his own label. He made the wine at Craigmoor on a use-and-pay basis, supplementing the fruit with a small amount bought in from other regions. A complicated sale arrangement with Montrose was concluded, but not made public, in 1983. Part of the arrangement allowed the Van Heysts to dispose of their stocks of earlier vintages through the winery door as if Craigmoor were continuing in business.

The purchaser was in fact Montrose, which has subsequently released plans for a major expenditure programme at Craigmoor designed to establish it as a major tourist attraction and restaurant facility. The development, which was due to be completed in mid-1985, includes a wine-tasting hall with cellar-door sales and service; an à-la-carte restaurant and fully licensed bar; a banqueting hall, barbecue and outdoor dining area with no-charge picnic facilities; and ample parking and children's facilities, including a playground and games. The design of the new facilities retains the turn-of-the-century flavour of Craigmoor, including the use, wherever possible, of natural materials such as timber and stone.

The 1984 crush of almost 130 tonnes was processed at Montrose, and it is likely that most initial processing will take place there in future.

The ubiquitous Oenotec team was retained as consultants by Montrose/Craigmoor prior to the 1984 vintage, and its influence was obvious in the 1984 releases under the new Montrose-owned-and-run Craigmoor. While the traditional varietal releases will continue, the style will undoubtedly change. The '84 Craigmoor releases were some of the best of an outstanding vintage. At the end of 1984 they showed great elegance and finesse, with the 1984 Semillon Chardonnay reflecting to the utmost the cool ripening conditions and exhibiting some sauvignon-blanc-like grassiness. The 1984 Chardonnay had restrained but elegant fruit flavour, good oak handling and will undoubtedly develop magnificently over the next few years.

The acquisition of Craigmoor by Montrose (or, to be precisely correct, by Messrs F. Belgiorno-Nettis and C. Salteri) will ensure not only the future of this historic winery, but also bring new recognition to one of the more interesting wine regions of Australia.

HILL OF GOLD
HENRY LAWSON DRIVE, MUDGEE

Hill of Gold was established in 1974 by Peter Edwards, a professional engineer who, after a lifetime in industry, was approaching retirement. Both the name of the vineyard and the substantial plantings of pinot noir which commenced it indicated not only Edwards's intense interest in wine, but of burgundy in particular. (Hill of Gold is, of course, a loose translation of Burgundy's Côte d'Or.) There are now just under five hectares of pinot noir and 7.3 hectares of cabernet planted.

In 1977 and 1978 the wines were made for Peter Edwards at Miramar; by 1979, having read extensively and spent one vintage working with Gil Wahlquist, Edwards felt confident enough to tackle his first vintage.

While most of the grapes employed are estate-grown, Edwards has purchased merlot for the last four years (and made a straight merlot varietal in 1982, 1983 and 1984) and shiraz. In 1981 he purchased the entire production of the Edgell Vineyard, and made substantial quantities of a dry white frontignac. Basically, however, the output of the vineyard is of red table wine and of vintage port. Indeed, Edwards has achieved the greatest show success with his vintage ports, winning gold medals with each of his 1981, 1983 and 1984 vintages. They were made from cabernet sauvignon, and fortified with brandy spirit.

The early vintage pinot noirs released were not inspiring; if ever pinot noir were to succeed in the district it should be in 1984.

HUNTINGTON ESTATE
CASSILIS ROAD, MUDGEE

Over the past decade Huntington Estate has established itself as the maker of Mudgee's best red wines, and along the way has produced some very interesting semillons and chardonnays. Bob Roberts came to Mudgee (and winemaking) by a fairly circuitous route. By the time he became interested in the Mudgee area in 1967 he had acquired a diploma in agriculture from Wagga, a law degree from Sydney, and practical experience as a plantation owner and grower in New Guinea. He subsequently enrolled in a correspondence course run by the Oenological Research Institute in Surrey, England, and duly obtained his diploma.

The second half of the 1960s did not look to be a favourable time for Australian residents in New Guinea, and with a burgeoning interest in wine, Bob Roberts (then still in his 30s) and his wife Wendy started looking at vineyard possibilities. For a while they contemplated joining the original Rothbury syndicate, but when he shared one of Jack Roth's masterpieces in a blind tasting (it beat a classic Coonawarra and a classed-growth Bordeaux), he settled on Mudgee. In 1969 Roberts purchased 54 hectares of land in two parcels for the princely sum of $16,000.

In 1972 he designed a substantial but functionally simple and uncluttered winery, and called for tenders from local and Sydney builders. He and his vineyard manager, who knew a bit about building, were appalled at the prices, so they built the winery themselves for a cost of $30,000. It not only handles comfortably the annual crush, varying between 200 and 300 tonnes, but provides sufficient space to enable the red wines to be oak-matured for two years before bottling (and then to receive further bottle age), and to provide sufficient stainless-steel fermentation capacity to permit all whites and reds to undergo a long, cool fermentation.

The 1973 vintage was Roberts's first. At that time he had little interest in the production of white wines, and the vineyard was planted principally to shiraz and cabernet. Grafting and replanting has since altered the varietal mix somewhat, although the accent remains heavily on those initial varieties. There are 18.4 hectares of shiraz, 12.3 hectares of cabernet sauvignon, 3.6 hectares of semillon, 3.4 hectares of chardonnay, 1.5 hectares of pinot noir, 1.1 hectares of merlot and 0.5 hectares of sauvignon blanc. Yields from the basalt loam soils over a clay base vary from a low of four tonnes per hectare for merlot to nine tonnes per hectare for semillon. All of the fruit is estate-grown.

The "senior" wine is the cabernet sauvignon, although in each year there may be a number of separate releases. Roberts uses a bin-number system to differentiate different bottlings from different vats or casks. The first two letters of the bin number are usually MB, denoting a medium-bodied wine, or FB, denoting a full-bodied wine. These two letters are then followed by a number which simply represents the successive releases of the variety and style. Thus in September 1984 a 1980 Bin MB 9 Cabernet Sauvignon was on offer; this was the ninth release since 1973 of a medium-bodied cabernet. In a tribute to the capacity of the district, the FB Cabernet Sauvignon bin numbers had already reached 29 by 1979.

Keeping individual track of all of these wines is virtually impossible, but in March 1982 I was part of a group to taste a selection of cabernet sauvignons spanning the years 1974 to 1982. The 1974 Bin FB1 Cabernet Sauvignon was then holding its form exceptionally well. Deep red in colour, the bouquet was remarkably firm and fresh for its age, with a trace of mint, while the palate showed ripe berry/cassis flavours, and was every bit as fresh as the promise of the bouquet suggested. It was one of the outstanding wines in the line up and received 18 points out of 20. 1975 Bin FB9 was red-brown in colour with a clean bouquet showing good fruit and light minty overtones; the palate was fully developed, with light berry/camphor flavours in a wine at its peak (17/20). 1976 Bin MB19 was made in the worst vintage for Huntington; pale red/brown in colour, both the bouquet and palate were washed out and thin. 1977 Bin MB15 had a good red colour, a touch of coffee/caramel on the bouquet, but the palate was far more attractive with sweet strawberry/berry fruit flavours (17/20).

1978 was a fair year in the district, but Bin FB17 was starting to show its age. Brown-red in colour, the attractive soft fruit of the aroma showed tealeaf overtones, while the balance of the wine on the palate was upset by drying tannin on the finish (16/20). 1979 Bin FB24 was quite excellent, showing to the fullest the outstanding vintage which Mudgee enjoyed in 1979. Strong red-purple in colour, the bouquet was deep and clean with strong minty over-

tones; the palate followed on logically from the nose, with round and full, soft fruit, some mint, and the balance and depth to sustain it for many years (18/20). 1980 was a lighter vintage, and it showed in the wine; reddish purple in colour, the American oak was obvious on the bouquet, although the fruit was round and sweet. The tannin on the fairly soft and relatively light-bodied palate was in perfect balance; although I did not keep a note of the bin number I suspect this wine was released ultimately as Bin MB9 (16.5/20).

At 12 months of age the 1981 Cabernet Sauvignon (no bin number recorded) had all of the vibrant strength and youth one would expect from a top Mudgee cabernet. Vivid purple in hue, the very clean bouquet was redolent of minty fruit and oak. That distinctive minty flavour, which is apparent in so many of the Huntington wines, came through again on the palate, which finished with very soft tannin. It was my top wine of the tasting (18.5/20). Finally, the 1982 taken from cask showed strong rich fruit and no off-fermentation characters, even though it was at that time barely through the primary fermentation.

If all of this seems to be ancient history, it is not. The September 1984 newsletter from Huntington Estate offered 1980 Cabernet Sauvignon Bin MB9, 1981 Cabernet Merlot Bin FB12 and 1979 Shiraz Bin FB16. The most expensive of these was the 1981 Cabernet Merlot at $78 by the case, and the cheapest the 1979 Shiraz at $58.80. For years I have chided Roberts for underpricing his wines, and I still do so.

If the cabernet sauvignon is the senior wine, the cabernet merlot blend has probably created most excitement and attention since it was first released in 1977. The two varieties are picked together, and the blend usually comprises about 15 per cent merlot and 85 per cent cabernet sauvignon. The wine spends between four and six months in new oak casks, and is then transferred to larger older casks for the next 18 to 20 months. Partly because some of the best cabernet sauvignon is used with the merlot, this line-up has even more strength and ageing capacity than does the 100 per cent cabernet sauvignon. This is so despite the (theoretical) softening effect of the merlot. It is almost impossible to separate the quality of the wines so far released under this label, although to my palate the 1977 and 1979 probably just shaded the 1978 and 1981 wines. Certainly so far as the 1978 is concerned, Roberts would disagree. He may well disagree with my relatively low ranking of the 1980 Bin FB14.

I have never much liked the Huntington Estate shiraz, because so many of the releases appear to me to have mercaptan. If not—and Bob Roberts swears that they do not—then I simply do not like the regional character of the wine, at least as it manifests itself from the Huntington Vineyard. This, I freely admit, is a very personal viewpoint, and many of these wines have done well in shows, particularly at the Mudgee and Hunter Valley Wine Shows. When blended with cabernet sauvignon, the result is far more satisfactory. The 1979 Shiraz Cabernet Bin FB35, available in 1984, was a quite exceptional wine, firm and tightly constructed, with very rich yet smooth and deep flavour, and persistent soft tannin on the finish.

Since the end of the 1970s, when Huntington first started releasing white wines, Roberts has had considerable success with the practice of leaving some sugar in his semillon. He has now adopted this practice with one or two of his chardonnays, releasing a 1984 Medium Dry Chardonnay. Roberts has always had reservations about the use of much oak with chardonnay, and the small amount of residual sugar is no doubt intended as a different means to a similar end. All of the 1984 releases reflected the very cool ripening conditions. The 1984 Semillon Chardonnay was dominated by the semillon, which gave the wine a sauvignon-blanc-like character. The 1984 whites generally were in total contrast with the drought-reduced, concentrated richness of the 1983 whites.

The cellar-door range is rounded off with no less than four rosés (wood-aged, dry, medium dry and spatlese), a sauterne-style sweet white, and a vintage port.

Finally, Huntington Estate is one of the most reliable suppliers of wine for home-bottling enthusiasts. The quality of these wines can be astonishingly good, and the price no less astonishingly low. The wine is usually supplied in 25-litre containers, but is also available bottled at the winery for own-label purposes.

MANSFIELD WINES
EURUNDEREE LANE, MUDGEE

When Peter Mansfield established his vineyard in 1975, his great-great-grandfather would have undoubtedly approved. He was Andreas Kurtz, who commenced growing grapes in Mudgee in the 1860s after he arrived from Württemberg. Along with the Roth family, the Kurtz name is foremost in the viticultural history of Mudgee.

Peter Mansfield spent five years with his uncle, Alf Kurtz, at Mudgee Wines before purchasing land at Eurunderee, and establishing 22 hectares of vineyard planted to both table- and dessert-wine grapes. Mansfield Wines made its first wine in 1978, but then fire struck in October 1979 and destroyed all the maturing wine. Mansfield is now offering fortified wines and a few table wines, mostly purchased from outside the district, and of inconsequential quality.

MIRAMAR
HENRY LAWSON DRIVE, MUDGEE

Part-owner and winemaker, 45-year-old Ian MacRae is one of the relatively few formally qualified winemakers resident in Mudgee. Having graduated with honours from Roseworthy, he worked for Penfolds, Hardy's, Loxton Co-operative and Kaiser Stuhl before becoming involved in winery design. In this capacity he successively designed Hungerford Hill's winery at Buronga and Krondorf in the Barossa Valley, before moving to Pokolbin where he designed and supervised the construction of the Hungerford Hill, Tulloch, McPhersons and Hermitage Wineries.

He moved to Mudgee to become winemaker for Montrose between 1975 and 1976. Convinced of the long-term potential of the district, he formed a partership with Sydney architect Ken Digby, who had commenced planting a 15-hectare vineyard in 1974. There are 3.9 hectares of cabernet sauvignon, 3.8 hectares of rhine riesling, 3.4 hectares of semillon, 2.5 hectares of shiraz and two hectares of chardonnay. The soil is red clay loam over a deep clay base with outcrops of ironstone and quartz, and small patches of decayed quartz overlaying a similar deep clay subsoil.

The first vintage was made in 1977, and the following year MacRae planted a five-hectare vineyard (which he manages for the owner) with traminer, chardonnay, sauvignon blanc and muscadelle. This provides part of the 40 per cent of the annual 120-tonne crush which MacRae somehow handles in the small winery built as a temporary extension to his house. As a design exercise it is notable chiefly for its capacity to crowd angels on a pinhead.

Almost 90 per cent of the production of Miramar is of white wine, but one of Miramar's early show successes was a trophy for the best fortified wine at the 1980 Hunter Valley Wine Show. To prove its versatility, the year before Miramar had won the Australian Wine Consumers' Trophy for the best rosé at the Perth show. Between 1978 and August

1984 Miramar had won 29 gold medals, 72 silver and 113 bronze medals at Australian wine shows.

Digby sold his interest in Miramar to the MacRae family in 1981, although he has an association with geology professor Gordon Packham and Dutch mining engineer Maartin Velleboer, who are developing vineyards of their own which will provide a long-term supply base for Miramar.

Chardonnay has become an increasingly important wine for Miramar. Using barrel-fermentation techniques, MacRae has managed to make some astonishingly complex and full-flavoured wines. He rates his 1981 as the best up to 1983, but I would unhesitatingly pick the 1982. Early in 1985 it was still retaining the pungent grapefruit aromas and flavours which distinguished it when first released in mid-1983. Good acid was sustaining the rich flavours and, while a lushly rich wine, it was certainly not fat or coarse. The 1984 vintage will almost certainly produce greater wines, but to my palate the 1982 Miramar Chardonnay is the best Chardonnay so far to come from Mudgee.

The Miramar rhine rieslings have also shown great indivuality of style and richness of flavour. Whether it is soil or winemaking tecniques I am not sure, but the wines gain strong lime/tropical-fruit flavours and aromas which one normally associates with botrytis, an exceedingly rare visitor to Mudgee.

A wood-aged semillon, a semillon chardonnay blend, a traminer rhine riesling blend, a moselle (often of exceptional quality), a rose, two different shiraz reds and a cabernet shiraz complete the list of table wines usually on offer, with a 1981 Vintage Port and a 1980 Liqueur Muscat completing the 1984 list.

In early 1985 not all of the 1984 Mudgee wines had really come together, many still being relatively closed. The Miramar wines were a major exception: apart from a rather hard and austere rhine riesling, MacRae made a series of quite outstanding white, rosé and red table wines in 1984. At that early stage they had more flavour and finesse than any other wines from the region.

MONTROSE
HENRY LAWSON DRIVE, MUDGEE

Montrose is the most important winery in the Mudgee region, and seems intent on building on its position of pre-eminence. Yet another to be established in the mid-70s (1974), it is owned by Carlo Salteri and Franco Belgiorno-Nettis, Italian engineers who founded the highly successful construction company Transfield Limited in 1956.

As his name indicates, winemaker Carlo Corino is also Italian-born and trained, and has the distinction of having made wine in (amongst other places) Ethiopia before moving to Australia. The 1000-tonne winery was built with the long-term future in mind; so far the crush has never exceeded 400 tonnes, and even the prolific year of 1984 provided only 357 tonnes (if one excludes the Craigmoor-sourced wines).

In 1984, 85 per cent of the grapes crushed came from the three vineyards of Montrose (Stoney Creek, Poet's Corner and the Winery Block). These comprise chardonnay (12 hectares), cabernet sauvignon (nine hectares), rhine riesling (six hectares), shiraz (five hectares), traminer (four hectares), pinot noir (three hectares), semillon (2.4 hectares), barbera (1.5 hectares), nebbiolo (one hectare) and sangiovese (0.65 hectares). The last three grapes are Italian varieties, and have been introduced by Carlo Corino. It is not surprising that in 1984 he also purchased 6.4 tonnes of aleatico, another Italian variety, introduced into the district by Dr T. H. Fiaschi around the turn of the century.

Corino has been a long-term admirer of the carbonic maceration process for red wines, and was initially an opponent of the excessive use of new oak in any wine, white or red. This typically Italian approach to red-winemaking saw him get rid of most of the new oak in the winery when he joined in 1976. However, his attitudes have mellowed somewhat in the meantime, and restrained use is made of new oak both in whites (in particular chardonnay) and reds.

Chardonnay has rapidly become the most important variety for Montrose, with 85 tonnes crushed in the 1984 vintage. The chardonnays so far released conform very much to the district pattern: rich, luscious and full-bodied with flavours in the melon-grapefruit spectrum. Winemaker Carlo Corino did not hesitate to leave a small amount of residual sugar in one or two of the vintages, pleasing the public and most (but not all) of the critics. Nor in recent years has he hesitated to use new oak, something which did not work totally satisfactorily with the 1982 vintage. The oak was rather raw, and tended to dominate the underlying fruit. The wine came as something of a disappointment after the earlier successes. 1982, indeed, was not an outstanding year for Montrose's white wines, with the traminer riesling also being rather dull, flat and uninteresting.

Corino's best touch with whites has consistently come with the sweeter styles: some very good late-harvest rhine rieslings and an even better sauterne.

The 1980 Montrose Bemosa Sauterne was one of the outstanding sweet wines of its vintage, winning numerous gold medals and still drinking superbly. Complex oak integration and excellent acid balance were features of the wine. The 1981 Auslese Rhine Riesling was probably the best of the late-harvest rhine rieslings, developing great richness and lusciousness at its peak in 1984.

Over the years Montrose shiraz has impressed as a young wine, winning trophies at the Hunter Valley Wine Show, but it has seldom shown any capacity to live in bottle. The cabernet sauvignon, likewise, has been sound though not enthralling. It is with his beloved Italian varieties that Corino has had the greatest success. He is particularly enamoured of the barbera and nebbiolo grapes because of their very low pH and excellent acid. He blends the two, and the wine is released under the barbera nebbiolo varietal blend name. Both the 1981 and 1982 vintages (each released at two years of age) showed marvellous fresh, scented, grape aromas and flavours, and the low pH characteristics of the grapes were very evident. Both releases had firm tannin to provide some cellaring potential, although they probably offered most in the period three to four years after vintage.

1983 was hardly a year in which to attempt to make quality white wine seriously in Mudgee, so the contrast with the ideal conditions of 1984, and the arrival of Oenotec as consultants, should see a radical change in style and no doubt quality. Carlo Corino is a conscientious and clever winemaker, but he has not developed a consistent touch with the dry and semi-dry varietal white wines. This is an obvious area of strength for the Oenotec team, and the combination should be a potent one.

It will be particularly interesting to follow the Montrose wines from 1984 and subsequent vintages.

MUDGEE WINES
MUDGEE ROAD, MUDGEE

Mudgee Wines was established by Alf Kurtz in the mid-1960s; as I have recounted earlier, he played an important role in the development of chardonnay both in Mudgee and Australia generally. Right from the outset he believed in varietal labelling, and produced some lovely wines prior to his retirement in 1977. A syndicate then took over the vineyard, with Jennifer Meek as winemaker, and adopted the organic approach to viticulture practised at Botolobar and Miramar.

Unfortunately, neither the organic approach nor the winemaking techniques have proved successful, and Mudgee Wines has all but faded from the scene. Certainly I have not seen or heard of any worthwhile wines coming from the vineyard in the past few years.

PIETER VAN GENT
BLACK SPRINGS ROAD, MUDGEE

Pieter Van Gent can claim greater experience than any other person with winemaking in the Mudgee district, although before coming to Mudgee he had worked with Penfolds for 10 years, including a term at Minchinbury. His time at Craigmoor and his early experience with chardonnay instilled in him a lasting admiration for the variety. When he left Craigmoor to establish his own winery (an elegantly constructed and designed building in the style of an Australian colonial farmhouse, but curiously called De Windmolen, Dutch for windmill) he decided to concentrate on chardonnay and on fortified wines. The De Windmolen name, incidentally, has since been dropped.

Van Gent has 10 hectares of vineyards established, but is diffident about providing details of the plantings, and likewise about his overall source for the 50 to 100 tonnes of grapes crushed each year. The 1984 releases included a Mudgee mullerthurgau, an unusual variety at the best of times and particularly so in Mudgee.

Given the vast experience which Van Gent has, the chardonnay releases have been exceptionally disappointing: both the 1983 and earlier vintages were badly affected by mercaptan.

PLATT'S WINERY
MUDGEE ROAD, GULGONG

Barry Platt, who received part of his wine training at the famed wine school at Geisenheim in Germany, first came to prominence during his term as winemaker at the Hollydene Winery in the Upper Hunter. Here he produced the early vintages of the Richmond Grove wines. But notwithstanding his German training, and the range of wines he made at Richmond Grove, his interests always lay with the white burgundy style (semillons and chardonnays) rather than the floral aromatic styles of rhine riesling and traminer.

This was part of the reason for his early interest in Mudgee, and in 1978 he purchased a ten-hectare block fronting onto Mudgee Road, 20 kilometres from Mudgee and just short of the town of Gulgong. Before choosing this block he had looked as far afield as Molong and Wellington, and the decision to purchase was taken primarily because of the red basaltic soil, which runs in a band through Mudgee and is shared, among other vineyards, with Miramar.

The first plantings in 1979 were wiped out in 1980, and he started again in the winter of that year. Between 1980 and 1984 just under seven hectares of chardonnay have been planted, and the first commercial crop (between 10 and 12 tonnes) was expected in 1985. Although chardonnay remains the grape which most interests Platt, he also planted a little over one hectare of sauvignon blanc in 1982 which is yet to come into bearing.

At the end of 1982, realising that the end was at hand for the then-owners of Craigmoor where he worked as winemaker, Platt negotiated to buy the whole of the drought-reduced 1983 crop. It amounted to 23 tonnes, and he supplemented it with a few more tonnes purchased in from around the district. When he opened the door of Platt's Winery in April 1984 he had two 1983 Chardonnays (one from Craigmoor and the other from Gulgong), a 1983 Pinot Noir, a 1983 Shiraz and a 1983 Cabernet Sauvignon for sale. All were available in such a small quantities that they sold out within a few months.

In 1984 he was once again able to use the winemaking facilities at Craigmoor by arrangement with the new owners, Montrose, who processed the Craigmoor fruit at Montrose Winery in that year. The grapes were purchased in from the district, principally from Montrose and Craigmoor, and four wines were released in late 1984 and in 1985. These comprised a 1984 Chardonnay, a 1984 Semillon and two 1984 Traminers, one dry and one late harvest. All four were of excellent quality.

Platt's own winery was completed in time for the 1985 vintage, adding further to the standing of the district.

Murrumbidgee Irrigation Area

When, in the first half of the nineteenth century, the explorer John Oxley passed through the area now occupied by Griffith, he had no hesitation in classifying it as uninhabitable. Subsequent sparse settlement proved that to be an extreme view, particularly for those with land fronting the Murrumbidgee River. By 1890 the thought of using the vast flow of the river more efficiently had begun to take shape, and the first suggestion of a dam and irrigation scheme was made in 1891. In 1896 a survey was carried out, but nothing more was done until 1902 when a severe drought reawakened interest in the scheme, the feasibility of which had been proved on a pilot basis by Sir Samuel McCaughey at his North Yanko Estate. This led to the formulation by Robert Gibson of the Murrumbidgee Northern Supply and Irrigation Bill, which was placed before the New South Wales Parliament in 1904. A change of government prevented it becoming law, but by now it was only a question of time before a scheme was implemented.

The question was referred to the Parliamentary Standing Committee on Public Works in 1906, and in evidence before that committee McCaughey observed:

> In my opinion the waters of the rivers of the Commonwealth, if placed on the surface of the ground so that they could be utilised for irrigation, together with a supply for stock and household purposes, would be of more value to Australia than the discovery of gold; for gold will eventually become exhausted while water will continue as long as the world lasts.

With such eloquent testimony, it was not surprising that on 31 October 1906 the committee should approve the scheme and shortly after the Burrinjuck and Murrumbidgee Canals Construction Act was passed. Despite the immensity of the scheme—it involved the building of the Burrinjuck Dam 390 kilometres upstream with a number of intermediate weirs—it became operational in less than six years. The first water was supplied for irrigation on 13 July 1912, and within a month or so J. J. McWilliam had taken up a lease at Hanwood and planted 35,000 cuttings.

At that time McWilliam's main winemaking operations were based at Junee where there were extensive vineyards, and the first Hanwood vintage was crushed there. By 1917, however, they had erected a winery at Hanwood, followed by another at Yenda in 1920. As the Murrumbidgee Irrigation Area (MIA) prospered, so did the McWilliams: it was the start of a long association which was to make the family company one of the wealthiest in Australia. It is hard to say which has benefited the most from that association, so great has been the contribution of the McWilliam family to winemaking in the district (and indeed in Australia).

In 1913 control of the venture was passed to the specially created Water Conservation and Irrigation Commission, and by April 1914 over 600 farms covering 9700 hectares were in operation. (It was not until 1924 that it became possible to purchase freehold; all of the early farmers received perpetual leases, and the size of each holding was severely limited.) The First World War interrupted progress, but its cessation and the flow of returned servicemen seemed to present an ideal opportunity to give the scheme new impetus.

The theory was fine, but the reality less so. Many of the servicemen had no previous experience on the land (and certainly none of viticulture); the blocks were too small for economic operation; and those who decided to embark on grape growing often selected inferior grape types and inappropriate viticultural methods. On the other side of the ledger, the commission started a vine nursery in the early 1920s, while the first wave of Italian immigrants arrived around the same time. Many of these came from winemaking areas around Treviso in the north and Calabria in the south, and almost all had viticulture in their blood.

Then, as now, the farms tended to be mixed, with citrus trees, rice and wheat all forming alternative crops to grapes. By 1924, 48,000 hectares were occupied, and the towns of Leeton and Griffith were growing rapidly. By the following year rice-growing had been proved feasible, and in the 1925-26 season 1530 tonnes of rice were harvested.

In 1928 the Department of Agriculture assumed responsibility for the vine propagation nursery; it formed the genesis of what is now the main viticultural research station in New South Wales. Working in conjunction with the CSIRO, it has been at the forefront of developing the viticultural techniques which have so revolutionised the wine industry over the past 10 years. But well before this it had to meet a major challenge to the continued viability of the area, which occurred first just before the Second World War and which assumed major proportions in the 1950s.

One of the principal problems confronting the irrigation areas along the Murray River has been salinity, a problem which has steadily worsened over the years and for which there is no easy solution. The MIA had always been lucky, as there was very low salinity in the surface water. But extensive rice-farming in particular started to raise the underlying watertable (which was very salty), and by the early 50s salinity and waterlogging had become a major threat. A system of subsoil tile drainage was developed, which has since been installed on a massive scale, and the threat has been averted.

For the first 40 years of its existence the MIA produced virtually no table wine. The vast bulk of its production was of fortified wine (and between 1926 and 1938 much of this was exported), reflecting two things. First, and most importantly, it met the demands of the market place. Second, it was assumed that this was all, indeed, the district was suited to.

This belief was not unreasonable. The hot, arid climate has a centigrade heat-degree summation of 1953 (Rutherglen has only 1620) and an average rainfall of only 380 millimetres. Soils are varied, but basically sandy, and suited to the modified form of hydroponics which grape growing takes in the region. Quite high alcohol levels could be achieved notwithstanding the large crops carried by the vines, but all of this simply pointed to the production of a slightly common and coarse base ideal for fortification, and the large-scale production of the cheap cream sherry and tawny port consumed *en masse* at the time.

The ending of beer rationing in 1953 changed all that. Up until that time the Australian population, largely denied its national drink and desperate for alcohol in any form to help remind it that the horror of the war was indeed behind it, had accepted cheap fortified wine as an alternative. Once beer became readily available, these markets dried up overnight. Glen McWilliam, McWilliam's technical and production director and one of the unsung heroes of the Australian wine industry, determined that he would show that the area could indeed produce table wine of quality.

He tackled the problem both in the winery and in the vineyard. In conjunction with the Viticultural Research Station and the CSIRO, many new varieties and clones were imported and trialled; it was a slow process, and it was not until the end of the 50s that the first trickle of new varieties of wine became available, and not until 1963 that the first "new" wine (a cabernet sauvignon) was made. Meanwhile in the winery he had embraced the technology pioneered by Orlando and Yalumba in the mid-50s for the handling of white grapes, adapting it to the particular requirements of the region.

With an extraordinarily intuitive flair for design and a deep understanding of what can be done with stainless steel, he developed the peculiar elongated steel fermentation tanks which double as white-wine drainers and which are so much the mark of McWilliam's. Coupled with the increasing use of refrigeration and must-chilling, and later with the advent of mechanical harvesting at night, McWilliam's paved the way for the MIA to take the lion's share of the growth in table-wine consumption from less than two to almost 20 litres per capita per annum since 1960.

Over the same time the Viticultural Research Station has also contributed a great deal to the Australian wine industry. Its programmes have covered every conceivable aspect of grape growing—vine improvement; pruning techniques; harvesting methods; planting densities and trellising techniques; chemical growth regulators; and irrigation methods. Many of the programmes, while of great value, are highly technical and outside the scope of this book, but not so the work done on mechanical harvesting and mechanical pruning.

Labour has always been the major cost of the production of grapes, and in turn the principal contributor to those costs was pruning the vines and harvesting the grapes. By the end of the 1960s it had become clear that if production costs were to be kept within acceptable bounds, something had to be done.

In the traditional quality areas the pressure was by no means so apparent; the much higher return per litre of wine gave more scope for absorbing the costs, and, in any event, the real cost of labour was often ignored altogether by the farmer who provided it in producing grapes from his or her own land.

While the widespread commercial use of mechanical harvesting predated that of mechanical pruning, the two techniques have in truth been developed in tandem. There is a great art to cane-pruning a vine (it took me more years to learn how to prune than it did to make wine), and there is an instinctive opposition to tractor-mounted circular saws scything along the rows to produce an effect somethin akin to a ragged hedgehog. Likewise, the satisfaction and gaiety of a traditional vintage are sharply at odds with the menacing, rumbling monster with its gleaming dragon's eye piercing the dark as the mechanical harvester does its work between midnight and dawn.

When mechanical harvesting first made its appearance there were fierce opponents: it would oxidise all the fruit, destroy the vines and leave half the grapes behind. In fact in large commercial vineyards—and particularly in climates as hot as that of the MIA—it has led to a marked increase in wine quality. Instead of coming into the winery at more than 30°C the grapes came in at 15°C, and high temperature is the single most important factor in promoting oxidation.

Likewise, when mechanical pruning was introduced many experienced winemakers were convinced the vines would die within a few years. In fact it led to an initial sharp increase in yield, and over a longer period to lesser but still marked yield increases, and the vines have shown no sign of dying. More recently the research station has been conducting trials with what it is pleased to call minimal pruning, but which to all practical intents and purposes means no pruning at all. This flies in the face of 1000 years or more of experience, but its proponents argue that it is to be used in conjunction with a series of other novel techniques, and that it is the next logical step in the constant battle to keep labour costs within bounds. Pruning with lasers will be the next development, and it is not so far away as one might think.

Such techniques are fundamental to the role of the MIA, which contributes between one-fifth and one-sixth of the total Australian wine production, and more than 70 per cent of that of New South Wales. In 1983 that amounted to a little more than 71,000 tonnes of grapes (out of a total of 102,800), down sharply from the 1981 peak of 85,000 tonnes, due in part to the difficulties of the 1983 vintage.

The table on this page demonstrates both where the present strengths of the district lie and where it is headed in the future. First and foremost, it is a highly efficient producer of grapes: its 4694 hectares produced grapes at the rate of 15.37 tonnes per

MURRUMBIDGEE IRRIGATION AREA: VINE PLANTINGS AND PRODUCTION

GRAPE VARIETY	1969 HA	1979 HA	1980 HA	1983 HA	1979 T	1980 T	1983 T
Cabernet sauvignon	83	340	314	233	3203	3554	2658
Grenache	333	206	188	116	3586	3258	1805
Mataro	41	147	146	118	1866	2877	1910
Shiraz	730	1128	978	808	13,902	14,685	11,204
Other red grapes	605	247	238	186	2008	2205	997
Chardonnay	NP	NP	59	101	NP	375	558
Colombard	NP	NP	59	89	NP	151	1377
Doradillo	218	236	228	156	3968	3836	3046
Muscat blanc	76	61	58	77	823	674	939
Muscat gordo blanco	289	350	388	439	4557	5428	6563
Palomino, Pedro Ximinez	395	282	257	188	4315	4107	3012
Rhine riesling	NP	125	128	94	1509	1331	1262
Sauvignon blanc	NP	NP	21	37	NP	750	883
Semillon	731	978	1008	1031	15,631	17,910	18,799
Traminer	NP	NP	55	92	NP	750	883
Trebbiano	528	932	855	855	10,989	16,292	14,652
Other white grapes	534	236	96	75	1970	721	746
TOTALS	4563	5268	5076	4725	68,327	78,904	71,114

NP = not published

McWILLIAM'S WINES

hectare, compared with 3.52 tonnes per hectare for the rest of the State (excluding Sunraysia, which is principally a table-grape and raisin producer).

Secondly, it is primarily a producer of white wine, and by the turn of the century is likely to produce almost no red table wine if present trends continue. More particularly, two grapes which have underpinned the quality end of the wine market in other regions have been abject failures. Neither cabernet sauvignon nor rhine riesling have been able to produce grapes with any real varietal character or richness, and certainly not to compete with the same varietals grown in other regions. Indeed, given its lower yield and the depressed prices, the Viticultural Research Station a few years ago calculated that cabernet sauvignon produced the lowest dollar return per hectare ($1734) of any grape variety grown in the region. Given that 40 varieties (of which 23 produce more than 100 tonnes per year) are listed in the official returns, it is little wonder that after an initial burst of enthusiam cabernet sauvignon plantings have declined sharply over the past five years.

Finally, the MIA is an efficient producer of bag-in-the-box and cheap sparkling wine, interspersed with a few medium-quality white wines, and the occasional truimph such as the De Bortoli Sauterne. A number of the more progressive companies (and De Bortoli is foremost among these) has made a considerable effort to introduce top-of-the-line bottled wines as flagships to show just what the district can produce. But wine producers will deceive themselves (as well as the public) if they start to believe that such wines are typical of the region. They are not, simply because they are expensive to produce. Thus the Viticultural Research Station, which very properly had for many years carried out research into means of improving wine quality in the region, was able to take advantage of the glut of red grapes towards the end of the 70s. In 1979 a number of vineyards and wineries collaborated on a commercial scale to produce a series of red wines made from vines which had either been pruned far later than normal or had been pruned twice, once at the normal time in winter and then for a second time between 15 December and 8 January.

These techniques had been trialled by the station in 1975 and 1976, and both trials had resulted in grapes with better acidity and pH, yet unimpaired sugar levels. The resultant wine had better fruit flavour, a brighter colour and greater cellaring potential. The same results were obtained in the full-scale commercial trials of 1979, and Orlando, for one, released two 1980 vintage wines (a semillon and a

shiraz) using the late-pruning method. The problem was—and is—that yields are drastically reduced using these systems. The highest yield from double-pruned vines was only 2.8 tonnes per hectare; while late pruning reduced yields by 50 per cent.

While undeniably increasing quality, such techniques are commercially unacceptable. However unintentionally, they undermine the major strength of the district: the ability to produce wine more cheaply than any other. As one drives round the wineries this ability is immediately apparent. The Miranda Winery, for example, family-owned and operated, produces over one million flagons, one million casks and between three and four million bottles of sparkling wine each year. Its Golden Gate Spumante is one of Australia's top-selling branded wines, and yet it first entered the sparkling wine market only seven years ago. It is here that the future of the MIA lies.

CASELLA
FARM 1471, YENDA

Casella was established in 1965 and, like many of the wineries established in earlier decades, the first vintage was foot-crushed. Family-owned and run, son John Casella is winemaker for the crush of several hundred tonnes per year. Somewhat unusually, most of the crush comes from the Casellas' own 19-hectare vineyard, planted to shiraz (four hectares), trebbiano and grenache (three hectares each), pedro ximinez and semillon (two hectares each) and cabernet sauvignon and troia (one hectare each).

Most of the wine is sold in bulk to private customers for home bottling, but an increasing amount is marketed under estate-bottled, varietal labels.

DE BORTOLI
YENDA ROAD, BILBUL

The De Bortoli success story is second to none. If ever Australia is to build a family-owned and run colossus to rival (at least in relative terms) that of California's Gallo, it is surely De Bortoli. Victorio De Bortoli was born in 1900 in the Veneto region of northern Italy. Like almost everyone else in the region, his father was a farmer and small-scale wine producer. In 1924 he left Italy for Australia and arrived at Griffith later in the same year. He worked at various farms in the district, before moving to McWilliam's, working at their Beelbangera Winery until 1927, when he purchased the lease of a 22-

hectare farm at Bilbul, on which the De Bortoli winery of today is constructed.

The farm included three hectares of shiraz, which provided De Bortoli with 15 tonnes of unwanted grapes in 1928: the wine market had collapsed after the removal of trade preferences with the United Kingdom, and the major wineries in the region were taking grapes only from long-established contract growers. The solution was to turn the grapes into wine, and this is precisely what Victorio De Bortoli did. He established a market with Italian cane-cutters who returned from Queensland in the off season, and somehow or other survived the Depression years. By 1936 the winery had a total of 20 fermentation vats and a capacity of 12,500 litres. By 1959 Victorio's son Deen, who remains managing director to this day, had taken over the management of the winery and increased its capacity of 436,000 litres to 3.6 million litres.

In parallel with this development, Deen began to experiment with the new sparkling-wine methods which had been developed in the second half of the 1950s with the aim of bringing new wine styles onto the Australian market. One of these was Victorio Spumante, an Italian-style sweet, fruity, sparkling wine which became an overnight best-seller. The first of the style to come onto the Australian market, it still remains one of the largest-selling lines and was responsible for the prosperity which allowed De Bortoli to expand steadily throughout the 1960s.

Technical innovation has always been a hallmark of the De Bortoli operation; during the late 1960s foundations were set at the back of the winery to receive the first Potter fermenter installed in Australia. This Australian-designed fermenter is not only sold and used throughout Australia but also in numerous other countries.

The usual immense range of wines (table, fortified, flavoured and sparkling), spirits and liqueurs was produced. By the 1970 vintage De Bortoli had a capacity of 4.5 million litres; still the accent remained on innovation, and for those who had watched the progress of the winery, its subsequent outstanding success with its botrytised semillon came as no surprise.

De Bortoli currently has more than 60 different wines on sale. These range from bulk table wines sold in flagon and flask to fortified wines, through a full range of varietal whites and reds to the highly successful (and expensive) botrytised sauterne and chardonnay-based bottle-fermented champagnes. An idea of the extent and complexity of the vintage may be gained from the 1984 crush. It was as follows:

cabernet sauvignon 105 tonnes, chardonnay 96 tonnes, colombard 590 tonnes, doradillo 32 tonnes, frontignac 151 tonnes, muscat gordo blanco 1475 tonnes, grenache 374 tonnes, malbec 31 tonnes, mataro seven tonnes, merlot 34 tonnes, muscat hamburg 300 tonnes, palomino 334 tonnes, pedro ximenez 147 tonnes, rhine riesling 48 tonnes, semillon 1189 tonnes, sauvignon blanc 13 tonnes, shiraz 445 tonnes, sultana nine tonnes, tokay nine tonnes, traminer 307 tonnes, trebbiano 748 tonnes and troia 158 tonnes.

Victorio De Bortoli died in 1979, but in 1982 his grandson Darren graduated from Roseworthy and arrived to take up full-time work at the winery where he is now chief winemaker. It is a proud family tradition, yet still one which does not tolerate a sense of complacency.

The first four years of the 1980s saw significant grape surpluses in Australia and, in 1982, for the first time significant surpluses in Griffith. In 1981, conscious of the probability of continuing surpluses and noting what Orlando had been able to do with surplus semillon in the Barossa, De Bortoli had experimented by arranging for a contract grower to leave semillon on his vines long after normal maturity, with the hope of inducing botrytis. De Bortoli remembered that in 1958 McWilliam's had made a magnificent pedro sauterne from heavily botrytised grapes which had been blended in with some Hunter Valley material to make an outstanding show sauterne. In 1981 the grapes reached 16 baume before the botrytis infection dried up and ceased to operate in the absence of rain or sufficient humidity.

In 1982 the conditions were entirely different. The grape surplus increased significantly; semillon in particular suffered; and right throughout the late summer and early autumn months intermittent showers fell. By April, two months after the conclusion of the normal harvest, large patches of rotten semillon were spread throughout the district. Darren De Bortoli, just returned from Roseworthy, arranged for a trial patch to be hand-picked and processed. Word spread quickly among the growers and soon De Bortoli was inundated with offers (at extremely low prices) of rotten fruit. It accepted a large amount, and rejected even more.

Technically, the crushing, pressing and fermentation of grapes in this condition is extremely difficult. As they start fermentation no-one could imagine that the green-grey sludge could possibly make drinkable wine, let alone great wine. Least of all could one imagine that from this seemingly hopelessly oxidised and contaminated sludge would a glistening yellow-gold wine emerge. Little wonder that the first botrytised wines were made by accident and very much against the wishes of the proprietors of the time (over 150 years ago).

The finished wine had a chemical analysis of 10.35 grams per litre of acid, 12.4 degrees of alcohol and 7.5 baume (or 129 grams per litre) of residual sugar. In a show career of precisely two years it won 27 gold medals, achieving a higher success rate than any wine in Australian show history.

In November 1984 (outside that two-year period) I was one of the three judges who dealt with Class 33 (premium sweet white) at the Canberra National Wine Show. Entry number 10 was given 56.5 points (I in fact gave it 19/20) and the panel comments were "top award, magnificent balance of botrytis flavours with sugar and a touch of bitterness to dry out the finish". It was of course the 1982 De Bortoli Botrytised Semillon Sauterne. The only other wine in the class was very nearly as good, receiving 56 points. It was the sister wine: an even richer and sweeter wine made from pedro ximinez in the same year. The intensity of this wine is also searing; while it has even greater flavour and intensity, it does not have the superb balance of the semillon.

The '82 De Bortoli Semillon has been accepted overseas as an outstanding wine. Much of the remaining wine has been sold at high prices on the American market through Frank Stone, while the wine received the Wolf Blass Trophy at the 1984 Bristol competition in England for the top Australian entry of the show.

There were, of course, those who dismissed the '82 as a freak, a never-to-be-repeated quirk of nature. Nothing could be further from the truth. The 1983 vintage has already won nine gold medals, and in scoring 56.5/60 was 3.5 points in front of the next closest wine in Class 18 (1983 sweet white wine) at the Canberra National Wine Show, a class which the judges described as "very strong". That wine, incidentally, contained 20 per cent sauvignon blanc; although slightly lighter in body and richness than the 1982, it has outstanding complexity and superb acid balance. As at the end of 1984 De Bortoli was confident that the '84 Semillon Sauterne could rival the success of the '82; I have no reason to doubt what they say.

At the other end of the taste spectrum, as it were, De Bortoli has begun a series of experiments with bottle-fermented and tank-fermented dry sparkling wines, initially using a semillon trebbiano base (1981), but switching in 1982 to a chardonnay rhine riesling blend. The use of rhine riesling may cause a few raised eyebrows, but the answer is both interesting and compelling. Rhine riesling—especially when early-picked—produces a neutral wine, devoid of real character or varietal flavour when grown in the Riverland.

Having carefully selected its base wines, De Bortoli has then gone the whole way. Pupitres—those inverted-V-shaped hand-shaking trestles with the bottles inverted into the holes—feature in virtually every photograph one sees of the French champagne cellars. They are, to put it mildly, an unexpected sight in Griffith. While total production of wines made this way will only ever be a tiny part of the De Bortoli output, I imagine it will play an important role in De Bortoli's corporate image-building.

And there is no question that it is approaching the winemaking side very seriously: a part of the winery has been turned into an outsized cool-room in which the base wines will be matured (partly in oak) before being bottled at the first stage of champagne making, and in which the subsequent maturation on yeast lees in bottle will take place. The aim is to produce a French-style sparkling wine and to market it (no doubt) under the name champagne, at around $5 a bottle. Impossible? Well, chardonnay in Griffith costs around $220 a tonne, while in 1984 its French counterparts paid 17,000 francs a tonne—at then-current exchange rates, $2150 a tonne. That 10-times differential lies at the heart of the strength of Griffith; improbably, it is not so far away from the ratio between overall dry-land production per hectare in the Hunter and Barossa Valleys on the one hand, and Griffith on the other.

But these initiatives of De Bortoli might be seen as setting some kind of pattern for the district as a whole: accept the role as a bulk producer of value-for-money quaffing wine for say 90 per cent of total production, but use special selection and handling techniques for the remaining 10 per cent to produce wines—almost inevitably white—of real quality, and which will fulfil a valuable publicity function into the bargain.

FRANCO'S WINES
IRRIGATION WAY, HANWOOD

Franco's Wines had its origins in 1933 when the family purchased the fruit farm and vineyard on which the present winery stands. Until 1959 a small quantity of wine was made for the family's own needs and the remaining grapes were sold. In that year (in response to requests from relatives and friends) a fruit-packing shed was converted into a winery, and from 1964 the crush was supplemented by grapes bought in from adjoining properties.

Since that time the business has slowly expanded, but at nowhere near the rate of many other Griffith wineries. By the same token it is, by the standards of any other region, a large operation, crushing up to 1500 tonnes of grapes each year and with a storage capacity of 250,000 litres. There is the customary wide range of wines available at the cellar door; much of the wine, however, is sold in bulk to Italian communities in other parts of Australia. Quality is not outstanding.

JOLIMONT
BEELBANGERA ROAD, GRIFFITH

Jolimont was established on the site of the old Calamia Winery which shut down in 1978. Prior to the 1982 vintage it was purchased by the Shears Pastoral group, better known for its Uncle Toby's Oats, and recommissioned on a fairly modest budget. John Swanson was appointed winemaker for the 1982 vintage and crushed 130 tonnes of grapes. A graduate of the Roseworthy marketing course, Swanson had come to Griffith two years earlier, working first at San Bernadino and thereafter at Sergi Wines (now Riverina Wines) with Nick Guy.

The first two vintages saw some interesting varieties purchased: cabernet sauvignon came from the relatively low-yielding Cal Cal Vineyard, providing only five tonnes to the hectare (although the expectation was that with machine pruning this would increase somewhat). The cabernet sauvignon was blended with a small proportion of merlot to make one of 1983's outstanding light reds, a wine marketed in Sydney towards the end of that year for less than $4 a bottle, and which received unstinting praise.

The 1983 crush of just over 200 tonnes encompassed French colombard (to be given some oak maturation), and oddities such as all of the barbera available in the district. All of the wines were made in basic equipment: the reds in open concrete fermentation vats with header boards and a 15-tonne capacity; the whites in three stainless-steel fermenters. Jolimont plans to increase the crush eventually to around 800 tonnes per year (the winery has a theoretical capacity of 1800 tonnes) and to sell up to 70 per cent of the production in bulk to other wineries, picking only the top 30 per cent of each year's output for release under the Jolimont label.

Howard Anderson is now winemaker, John Swanson having moved to the Midas Tree at Orange in New South Wales. In a very short time Swanson created for Jolimont an enviable reputation.

Jolimont's winery is to be moved to Rutherglen in 1986, utilising the old Seppelt winery purchased by the owners of Jolimont in 1985.

LILLY PILLY ESTATE
LILLY PILLY ROAD, LEETON

Lilly Pilly Estate is the newest winery in the Murrumbidgee Irrigation Area. It is also one of the smallest, and although it will remain so, its operations received national publicity out of the blue in the early months of 1983. Unheard of outside of its local town of Leeton, the first wine made at the winery won the inaugural State Bank Trophy for best New South Wales small producers' dry white at that year's Royal Sydney Show. Earlier in the same week a hailstorm had decimated the family vineyard just before the commencement of the 1983 vintage. It was a bitter-sweet story which the nation's wine writers found impossible to resist.

The vineyard was established in 1972, the year of the tree, and was named appropriately—lilly pilly is a species of Australian native tree. The first plantings were to cabernet sauvignon and shiraz; in 1979 semillon, traminer and rhine rhiesling were added, while in 1981 11 additional varieties were planted on a trial basis for future evaluation. The total area under vine is only 12 hectares, and the winery is designed for a maximum production of only 200 tonnes per year. Hailstorms to one side, the winery is only intended to process estate-grown grapes. It is unlikely, therefore, that production will ever rise much above 12,000 cases a year.

The vineyard is run by Pasquale Fiumara, while the winemaking is carried out by son Robert. Trained at the Riverina College of Advanced Education, he graduated from the Bachelor of Applied Science (Wine Science) course in 1980, receiving the inaugural Ron Potter scholarship, and assisting the college winemaker in making the 1980 "The College" wines. Quietly spoken, shy and diffident, Robert Fiumara not only understands winemaking, but wine marketing too. He registered the trademark Tramillon for a traminer-semillon blend, and it was this wine which won the top gold medal and State Bank Trophy at the 1983 Royal Sydney Show.

The present plantings comprise cabernet sauvignon (2.6 hectares), shiraz (five hectares), rhine riesling (five hectares), traminer (1.6 hectares), muscat gordo blanco (1.6 hectares) and semillon (one hectare). The wines produced by Lilly Pilly reflect the plantings, with the addition of a small quantity of fumé blanc made from purchased sauvignon blanc grapes. The semillon is used in the Tramillon blend, and also to make a spatlese semillon, while the muscat gordo blanco is used to make a spatlese lexia. The other wines made include a dry rhine riesling, dry traminer, shiraz and a cabernet.

The whites reflect careful winemaking and the individual attention which a small volume permits. While the vineyard has been set out so as to allow mechanical harvesting, the grapes are (so far) hand-picked. Picking commences at dawn and finishes at midday before the grapes become too hot; the juice is chilled immediately the grapes are pressed and is then cold-settled before the commencement of fermentation. In 1983 the juice was held at 0°C until May and the fermentations were not completed until August. Not surprisingly, the wines are light-bodied, clean, very fresh and with gentle varietal character. The outstanding feature of the Tramillon was not so much its flavour as its balance, delicacy and freshness.

The 1983 white wines were adequate but not up to the exciting standard of those of '82. By far the best was the 1983 Spatlese Lexia, with all the fresh perfumed aroma and fruit one could wish for, and light cleansing acid on the finish.

The 1982 Cabernet, which like all of the Lilly Pilly reds spent three months in new American oak puncheons, showed light, crisp, varietal fruit with a touch of oak-derived astringency on the finish.

McMANUS WINES
FARM 1347, YENDA

McManus Wines was founded by local medical practitioner, Dr David McManus, in 1969 as what he described at the time as "a sort of commercial hobby". The small, indeed tiny, family vineyards and winery produce less than 1000 cases per year. All the grapes are estate grown, and the wine styles are, to put it mildly, highly individualistic. The labelling and description of the wine styles are no less unusual, taking as their theme the Christian names of the various members of the family involved in the operation.

In April 1985, McManus Wines was still offering (through the _Trade Liquor Magazine_, _Thomsons Liquor Guide_) 1974 and 1975 Shiraz, 1976 and

1978 Pinot Noir and 1977 Cabernet Shiraz Malbec (among other wines). Also available was 1978 Catherine Marie, a heat-treated cabernet sauvignon, described by Dr McManus as "a cross between a burgundy and a port".

These unusual wines are available only at the cellar door or by mail order.

McWILLIAM'S
HANWOOD WINERY
WINERY ROAD, HANWOOD
YENDA WINERY
WINERY ROAD, YENDA
ROBINVALE WINERY
MOORE ST, ROBINVALE
BEELBANGERA WINERY
WINERY ROAD, BEELBANGERA

The entire Australian wine industry, and not just the Murrumbidgee Irrigation Area, owes a lasting debt to the remarkable McWilliam family. In the course of building a vast company, successive generations have made unique and important contributions to all aspects of the industry—grape growing, winery design and operation, and marketing.

The company was founded by Samuel McWilliam when he planted vines at Corowa, on the Murray River, in 1877. The family then extended its operations to Junee and established a substantial winery there around the turn of the century. It is little known that the Junee vineyard (although not the winery) continued in production until the 1950s; the grapes were taken to Mount Pleasant in the Hunter Valley and the wine made there by Maurice O'Shea. I have shared more than a few bottles of the last vintage (a '52 red) and several bottles of a Junee white wine, both made by O'Shea, which in the 1970s was still most attractive.

As I have related earlier, Samuel's son, John James McWilliam, planted the first grape vines at Hanwood in the winter of 1912. The company's first winery was built at Hanwood in 1917, and in 1920 a second winery was built at Yenda. The third winery, at Beelbangera was acquired (fully operational) in 1944, while the fourth winery, just across the river at Robinvale in Victoria, was designed by Glenn McWilliam in 1961.

These wineries have crushed up to 50,000 tonnes in a single year, the equivalent of over 33 million litres of wine. Production has decreased somewhat from its peak at the end of the 1970s, but still exceeds 20 million litres a year, somewhere in the region of seven per cent of the total Australian production.

Hanwood is effectively the headquarters, and is certainly so for visitors to the region, thanks to the famous Hanwood Barrel, a giant tasting room in the shape of a wine cask. The size of Hanwood, old but scrupulously clean and carefully maintained, almost defies the imagination. It has storage for a total of 22.5 million litres of wine; the stainless-steel tank farm, stretching in endless rows, culminates in four 450,000-litre stainless-steel tanks; the Hanwood railway siding receives McWilliam's own stainless-steel railway tankers; and the 9000 wooden casks full of fortified wine are almost incidental in terms of volume.

The varietal whites and most of the fortifieds are made at Hanwood. The red wines are made at Beelbangera which has the capacity to crush 8000 tonnes of grapes per year. Yenda is the centre of the sparkling wine production, where the national best-seller Bodega is made. Capacity here is around 10,000 tonnes per year. Finally, Robinvale makes the other great money-spinner for McWilliam's, its celebrated cream sherry.

Companies the size of McWilliam's are reticent about providing too much detail on production because of competition in the marketplace. However, their entry into the cask market in the early 1980s can only be interpreted as a result of increasing competition to their long-established varietal white and red wines, which had had such success since their introduction in the early 1960s. Here once again McWilliam's had been the innovators, co-operating with the CSIRO and the Viticultural Research Station in introducing and evaluating classic grape varieties. It was responsible for the first varietal rhine riesling and for the first varietal cabernet sauvignon wines to be produced in the MIA. It followed on with traminer, chardonnay, colombard and, more recently, with the unusual Russian variety, rkatsiteli.

The subsequent relative failure of rhine riesling and cabernet sauvignon in the district is puzzling, although no fault of McWilliam's. As happens in so many regions, the grapes show excellent varietal character while the vines are young, but steadily lose that varietal definition as they mature. This, at least, is one explanation, given the outstanding show success which the early rhine rieslings achieved. The other explanation is the relative improvement in both the quality and range of style of these varietals grown in other (perhaps more suitable) regions.

Nor do I think that McWilliam's has helped its

own cause by retaining its red wines for three or four years before releasing them onto the market. A retrospective tasting in 1983 of all of the cabernets produced between 1970 and 1978 reinforced this view. On the other hand the '63 Cabernet, tasted a day or so earlier, had been absolutely magnificent: still retaining exceptional colour, body and richness. With the exception of the one- or two-year-old cabernets, it had more life and body than any of those made between 1970 and 1978. If ever the young vine theory is to be proved, the '63 must come close to doing so. Of those later wines the '72 was the best of the older half, and the '78 the best of the younger wines. The others showed gentle, aged characters at best, but really had insufficient complexity and flavour to warrant prolonged cellaring. I think it is new ventures, such as Jolimont, which have pointed the way for cabernet, releasing the wine within 12 months of vintage, and suggesting that it be drunk in the ensuing 12 months.

Traminer fares much better in the district than does rhine riesling, and perhaps the most reliable of the white wines from McWilliam's is the Traminer-Riesling Bin 77. This wine, along with the other whites, fully reflects the extremely high level of technology used by McWilliam's. Vast cool-rooms have been constructed for storing the white wines from the time the grapes are crushed until they go into bottle; centrifuges, earth-filters, and Brimstone desulphuring plants are used; modern presses and high-speed, inert-atmosphere bottling lines all play a role.

These white table wines are not for extended cellaring or even for detailed, critical examination. They are first and foremost drinking wines, economically produced, and selling at a very modest price. The red table wines are similar, although, as I have already said, I think they are kept too long by McWilliam's before release and are seldom, if ever, seen at their best. It follows, then, that I could never recommend cellaring them.

McWilliam's still has enormous reserves of old fortified wine. The best of these wines come together in its Tartan Vintage Port, a marvellous old Australian wine which is in truth a cross between a vintage and a tawny port in style. The 1971 was available not so long ago, and at 15 years of age provided a rich, complex, yet soft port style.

McWilliam's may have slipped somewhat from the position of pre-eminence which it once held, but it remains an extremely important Australian wine company.

McWILLIAM'S WINES

MIRANDA WINES
IRRIGATION WAY, GRIFFITH

It would be wrong to think that De Bortoli is the only success story in the Murrumbidgee Irrigation Area, or that it has a copyright on innovative technology. Other wineries have their own success stories, not the least being Miranda. Yet, like so many others, the beginnings were humble indeed.

Francesco Miranda and his wife Caterina left Naples in 1938 and established Miranda Wines in 1939. The first vintage was foot-crushed and then fermented in two open concrete tanks. Through the 1940s output averaged only 60,000 litres a year. But quality improved, and so did the market; in 1951 Francesco Miranda felt confident enough to employ a recently qualified winemaker, the then unknown Ron Potter. Potter has since become a major figure in the Australian wine industry, designing the Potter fermenter and becoming chairman of a major winery equipment fabrication company, which for a while was listed on the Sydney Stock Exchange. In 1958 he was instrumental in introducing the first ion-exchange column in Australia, a device that lowers pH.

Up until the end of the 1950s, however, Miranda was still producing only bulk wine, selling either to wholesalers or in kegs to the private trade. 1962 saw the first retail sales with hand-filled flagons. The trade grew rapidly (and the hand-filling was replaced by machines) until 1967 when Miranda was the first Australian company to introduce plastic PVC flagons. By 1968 almost 50 per cent of production was bottled at the winery.

A new bottling line introduced in 1975 meant that the entire production was packaged at the winery in either flagons or 750-millilitre bottles. Sparkling wines were then introduced, and were an overnight success. Within one year production was in excess of 100,000 cases a year, and 150,000 in the second year. A new half-million-dollar bottling line now sees 6000 bottles of sparkling wine come off the production line each hour, supplying annual sales of between three and four million bottles. Miranda Golden Gate Spumante is one of the top-dozen brand sellers in Australia, and has sales in excess of 150,000 cases.

Two qualified winemakers are employed to back up the Miranda family team. The 8000-tonne winery produces over one million flagons and one million casks each year, as well as very large quantities of table wine. A Brimstone desulphuring plant means that fermentation continues throughout the year,

with one-third of the total production being produced by this method.

At the other end of the scale Miranda has purchased grapes from the Clare Valley, the Hunter Valley and Swan Hill. The Clare and Hunter Valley grape wines were made separately and released under regional labels. The irony of that classic turning-of-the-tables is not lost on Sam Miranda, national sales director.

Production director, Lou Miranda, proudly asserts: "We are not a boutique winery—we are a bulk winery. We are second generation now and in a few years time we fully intend to be third generation winemakers. We aim to survive, and we believe we have the formula to do so."

ORLANDO WICKHAM HILL
HARRIS ROAD, GRIFFITH

Orlando did not plan its entry into Griffith, but inherited it. It must now be more than satisfied with that inheritance. In 1970 Reckitt & Colman bought both Orlando Wines and Morris Wines of Rutherglen. Charles Morris in 1954 had purchased a Griffith winery known as Dorrien Cellars, a small winery built in 1946 and equipped at that time only with open cement fermentation tanks.

With the rapid expansion of the cask and flagon market in the 1970s, Orlando had a ready-made base for operations on their hands, although the Wickham Hill Cellars of today bears no resemblance to that of 1970. It now handles an annual crush of around 7000 tonnes, with eight million litres of stainless-steel fermentation and storage capacity. A large Brimstone desulphuring plant ensures that wine is made continuously throughout the year to fill the unceasing flow of Orlando Coolabah casks which proceed out of the Barossa Valley Winery.

The Brimstone process is an interesting one. Grape juice may be kept for prolonged periods without deterioration either if kept very cold (around 0°C) or if treated with massive sulphur additions. The latter is a far more economical and practical way, requiring no cooling at all. To remove the sulphur prior to the commencement of fermentation, the wine is dropped down a column sparged with a blast of nitrogen travelling up the column. Once the sulphur is removed by this process, fermentation can commence. There is also extensive refrigeration enabling the juice to be chilled to 2°C as an alternative storage medium.

Wickham Hill makes more than one-third by volume of all Orlando's wine and, as I have said, most is dedicated to the Coolabah range. Orlando does have four hectares of its own vineyards, and has experimented on this with late-pruned semillon and late-pruned shiraz. These two wines, together with Wickham Hill Cellars Claret (a non-vintage wine), are the "local" wines, sold only through the cellar door at Wickham Hill. The wines show not only the extra structure and intensity of fruit one associates with late pruning, but also the impeccable wine-making technology which Orlando practises.

RIVERINA WINES
HILLSTONE ROAD, GRIFFITH

Riverina Wines is the new trading name for the old Sergi Wines. It takes no great imagination to guess the reason for the change of name.

The winery was constructed in 1975 to what can only be kindly described as a curious mixture of architectural styles. Somewhat unusually, the winery has always concentrated on dry table wines, both white and red. These are marketed almost exclusively to local areas and to Italian communities in other areas.

ROSSETTO'S WINES
FARM 576, BEELBANGERA

Rossetto's was founded in 1930 by Angelo Rossetto, who had emigrated from Treviso in Italy's north, and who purchased the site of the present winery at Beelbangera in 1928. While of substantial size (the crush has averaged 4000 tonnes per year over the last three years), both the winemaking methods and marketing techniques remained fairly traditional until the end of the 1970s. By far the major part of production was of fortified wine, and most was sold in bulk, principally to the Italian community living in Sydney.

But as with so many Griffith wineries, there has been a significant change due to the continued decline in the fortified-wine market. In 1980 the first "outside" winemaker was appointed: Peter Turley. Turley had spent five years at Roseworthy doing both the viticulture and oenology courses before working for San Bernadino for one year and McWilliam's for two years. He thus had an ideal blend of both practical and theoretical knowledge. With his assistance Rossetto's has moved into the premium white bottled market (under the Mount Bingar label), offering French colombard, traminer

riesling, chardonnay, traminer and white frontignac.

Fortified wines still account for more than 50 per cent of production (and are stored before bottling in open concrete tanks under a liquid paraffin seal) but they are steadily declining. Even in the cost-effective environment of Griffith, Peter Turley believes they are selling at less than the cost of production.

An unusual feature of white-wine production is the use of an ion-exchange column to treat the juice before fermentation to lower the pH to around 3.1, allowing the wines to finish with a pH of 3.25, retaining excellent acid levels.

In common with many winemakers in the district, Rossetto's thinks that chardonnay (and colombard) are particularly suited to the region, and that cabernet sauvignon and traminer are not.

The prices of the cellar-door price list read as if the list were printed 10 years ago; if the quality of the wines is modest, not even the most hard-hearted purchaser could complain about the prices.

SAN BERNADINO
LEETON ROAD, GRIFFITH

Once the high-flier of the Murrumbidgee Irrigation Area, San Bernadino suffered the ignominy of a two-year receivership between 1982 and February 1984. This followed a period of expansion in which production had been increased in leaps and bounds every year since its foundation in 1973 by the Pilloni and Aliprandi families. A newsletter written midway through 1981 carried the following banner headline:

Wine happenings from N.S.W. largest winery. YES — San Bernadino is now the PREMIER winery in "The Premier State". During the just completed, and excellent, 1981 vintage, San Bernadino produced 13,000,000 litres of wine, VINTAGED and PACKAGED at our own winery. All the fruit was selected by our production director, Aldo Pilloni, who supervised the vinification in conjunction with San Bernadino's chief winemaker, Scott Collett. This is far in excess of the total Hunter Valley production in a good year, and almost double the 1981 Hunter yield.

Pride before a fall? Perhaps, but the fact was that Stan Aliprandi and Aldo Pilloni were not about to give up all they had created, and after a dour struggle the company cleared all its debts and the receiver was triumphantly evicted.

The 1984 vintage may have been small in comparison with 1981, but it was very large when viewed against most other wineries in Australia — 4.7 million litres were made from 2420 tonnes of sultana, 2700 tonnes of trebbiano, 1450 tonnes of shiraz, 1350 tonnes of semillon, 1100 tonnes of muscat gordo blanco, 450 tonnes of cabernet sauvignon and 85 tonnes of sauvignon blanc.

An absolutely astonishing array of wines is produced and marketed by San Bernadino. The labels and names of these are unashamedly sourced from around the world, offering such bizarre delicacies as St Emilion Chablis Grand Cru NV, Rhine Steiner, Trevilini Australian Lambrusco, Trevilini Australian Chianti and such like.

One of the major contributors to the downfall of San Bernadino was their Emerald Cream, large quantities of which went onto a seemingly buoyant American market only to be impounded by customs officials. These troubles are now behind San Berna-dino, which is currently placing its up-market efforts in its Woodridge Estate 100 per cent varietal range. Several of these wines have been made without the use of sulphur dioxide before or during fermentation, a technique quietly used by some of the most famous winemaking names in the land, but requiring considerable skill and expertise to succeed. The Woodridge labels have had a mixed reception since their release, but few would wish to deny success to the revitalised San Bernadino.

STANBRIDGE ESTATE
GRIFFITH–LEETON HIGHWAY, LEETON

Stanbridge Estate is one of the few boutique wineries to survive in Griffith. Chateau Lysaght, as owners Roger and Rhonda Hoare laughingly refer to their winery, takes a small proportion of the annual production of the 18-hectare vineyards owned by the Hoares. Output usually varies between 1000 and 1200 cases per year, divided between semillon, chardonnay, traminer, rhine riesling and sauvignon blanc. The actual quantity of each varietal made depends, says Roger Hoare, on the sales of the prior year.

This seemingly casual approach should not fool anyone. Roger Hoare is chairman of the MIA Wine Grapes Marketing Board, representing all of the growers in the district. He also obtained a diploma in oenology from the Riverina College of Advanced Education before starting his winery.

Not having a press, and having an abundance of grapes, he uses enzymes to cold-settle the free-run juice after crushing, and follows modern technology in being in no hurry to commence fermentation. In 1982 and 1983 he made some quite excellent white varietal wines. The bright-yellow-green colours shown by his semillons, chardonnays and sauvignon blanc all attest to careful winemaking, as does the depth of fruit flavour.

Almost all the small output is sold through the cellar door, but the quality is such that it is surprising more does not find its way through the retail trade. Stanbridge may be very small, but it is nonetheless a credit to the region.

In 1985 Roger Hoare won a Churchill Fellowship to study grape prices in overseas countries, and in consequence made no wine. He is yet to decide the future of the Stanbridge label.

ST PETERS
ST PETERS ROAD,
OFF WHITTON STOCK ROUTE, VIA YENDA

St Peters Distillery Proprietary Limited was established with the utmost good taste and a seemingly limitless budget by Count Felice Sassoli d'Bianchi and his son Count Andrea Sassoli d'Bianchi in 1978. Its function was truly bizarre: to produce that most unwanted of all Australian alcohol commodities, brandy. Unwanted, certainly, following successive waves of government taxes. A few table wines came under its label, but it was a doomed venture from the start. In 1983 it was put out of its misery when the Saxonvale-Stanlee group purchased it. It now performs a most useful function for that group, because the winery itself was very well designed and lavishly equipped. Its output will see a significant extension of the range of wines to be made available by the Saxonvale group.

TOORAK WINES
TOORAK ROAD, LEETON

The name Toorak Wines, curious though it may be, is not a cosmetic facelift for one of the "kings in grass castles". When Frank and Vince Bruno founded Toorak Wines in 1975 that was the name they gave the business. Total crush in that year was only 50 tonnes; in 1984 1500 tonnes of grapes were converted into 700,000 litres of wine, principally table wine but with some fortified material. Storage capacity in the basic corrugated-iron winery is more than one million litres.

The Brunos have a small vineyard (10 hectares of semillon and five hectares each of cabernet and rhine riesling) which contributes around 10 per cent of the annual crush. Semillon, trebbiano, rhine riesling, muscat gordo blanco, muscadelle, white frontignac, cabernet sauvignon and shiraz are all purchased in some quantity, with lesser amounts of colombard and malbec.

The usual wide range of white and red varietals, together with a series of fortified wines, are made each year. It is a family operation from start to finish, and most of the wines (made by Frank Bruno) are marketed locally.

WEST END WINES
BRAYNES ROAD, GRIFFITH

Imaginative names seem to be one of the strong points of Griffith. The Calabria family gave the name West End to their winery because that was where it was situated—at the west end of the town of Griffith. Brothers Bill and Tony Calabria now run West End Wines, a business which their father had founded in 1948.

From that time until well into the 1970s almost all of the production was sold in bulk. Mr Calabria senior would despatch barrels of the wine on the goods train to Sydney, and follow on himself the next day, picking the wine up at Central Railway Station and then selling it through the inner-western suburbs. Thanks to their father's pioneering work, Sydney remains the main market for the Calabrias' wines, although Canberra is becoming increasingly important. The main sales these days are by mail order and the emphasis has changed to packaged wine in flagons and bottles. The latter now account for 60 per cent of the total production, and in turn most of that is sold in bottles.

Bill and Tony Calabria operate from a humble-enough base: a huge hangar-like corrugated-iron shed, with a smaller shed to one side. But they are acutely conscious of the need to upgrade both the quality of the wine and the image they project. They have recently installed refrigeration, enabling them to control strictly the fermentation temperatures of the white wines. Late pruning and bunch-thinning techniques are practised on their own 7.5-hectare vineyard, which provides around 10 per cent of the annual crush of 320 tonnes.

In 1984, 97 tonnes of shiraz, 57 tonnes of trebbiano, 45 tonnes of traminer, 23 tonnes of muscat gordo blanco, 22 tonnes of chardonnay, 16 tonnes of rhine riesling and 10 tonnes each of cabernet sauvignon and grenache were processed. West End has little

interest in producing casks, recognising that it cannot possibly compete with the economies of scale of the large producers in this market. It may well have positioned itself very nicely.

WYNNS' YENDA
MIROOL AVE, YENDA

David Wynn was not only the visionary who had the foresight and courage to take Wynns to Coonawarra, but also the visionary who realised the untapped market for cask and flagon wines which existed at the end of the 1950s. Against opposition from his father, Wynns acquired the old Caldwell Winery at Yenda, near Griffith, in 1959. (Caldwells had been one of the major wine merchants operating throughout Australia in the first half of the twentieth century.) Having acquired the winery, Wynns was the first to endeavour then to exploit the market which David Wynn had identified. Their first cask was a failure, not because David Wynn was wrong, but because of a design fault in the tap. The underlying rationale for Yenda was quickly proved correct, and the winery has been steadily expanded to the point where it is now the major production unit for the Wynn group, with a 13,000-tonne capacity.

Production is principally of white wine, with vast refrigeration systems, but significant quantities of fortified wine are also made and matured at the fairly unprepossessing but eminently functional winery. ◖◗

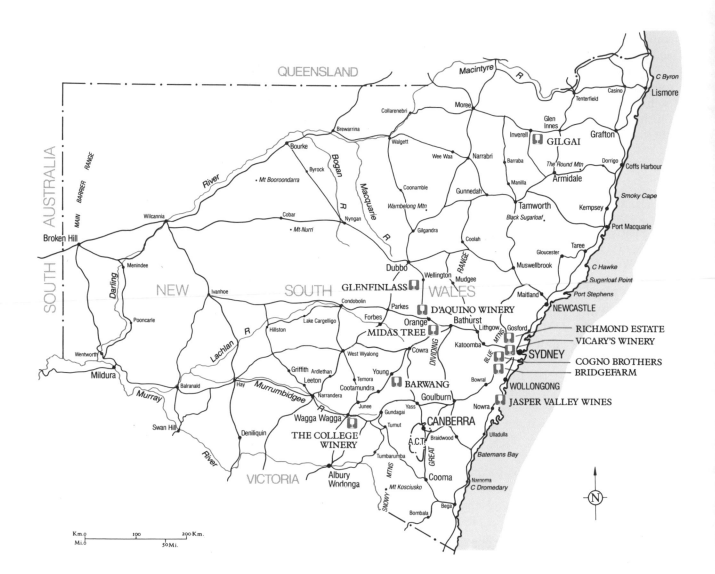

QUEENSLAND

Macintyre R

C Byron

Lismore

Casino

Tenterfield

Collarenebri

Moree

Glen Innes

Inverell

GILGAI

Grafton

Brewarrina

Walgett

Dorrigo

Coffs Harbour

Bourke

Wee Waa

Narrabri

Barraba

The Round Mtn

Byrock

Bogan R

Mt Booroondarra

Coonamble

Manilla

Armidale

Smoky Cape

SOUTH AUSTRALIA

MAIN BARRIER RANGE

River

Macquarie R

Gunnedah

Tamworth

Kempsey

Wilcannia

Cobar

Nyngan

Gilgandra

Black Sugarloaf

Port Macquarie

Mt·Nurri

Coolah

Taree

Broken Hill

Menindee

Dubbo

Wellington

Mudgee

Gloucester

Muswellbrook

C Hawke

Sugarloaf Point

NEW

Ivanhoe

SOUTH

GLENFINLASS

WALES

Maitland

Port Stephens

Darling

Condobolin

Parkes

D'AQUINO WINERY

NEWCASTLE

Pooncarie

Forbes

Orange

Bathurst

Lithgow

Gosford

RICHMOND ESTATE

Lake Cargelligo

MIDAS TREE

Katoomba

BLUE MTNS

VICARY'S WINERY

Hillston

R

Wentworth

Lachlan R

West Wyalong

Cowra

DIVIDING

SYDNEY

COGNO BROTHERS

BRIDGEFARM

Mildura

Balranald

Hay

Griffith

Ardlethan

Young

Temora

Bowral

WOLLONGONG

Murray

Leeton

Cootamundra

BARWANG

JASPER VALLEY WINES

Murrumbidgee R

Narrandera

Goulburn

Nowra

Swan Hill

Junee

Gundagai

Yass

Deniliquin

Wagga Wagga

Tumut

CANBERRA

Ulladulla

THE COLLEGE WINERY

A.C.T.

Braidwood

Batemans Bay

Tumbarumba

GREAT

Albury Wodonga

SNOWY MTNS

Cooma

Narooma

VICTORIA

Mt Kosciusko

C Dromedary

River

Bega

Bombala

N

Km.0   100   200 Km.
Mi.0   50Mi.

Other Districts

The vignerons of the "other districts" of New South Wales are a diverse group. They cast a spidery web from Inverell in the north; thence through Wellington, Orange and Cowra to Young in the west; and Wagga Wagga in the far south-west. Coming back to the coast, there is a vineyard at Nowra, and a spread of wineries on the western and south-western fringes of the Sydney metropolitan area.

As I have said earlier, it is difficult to see any one of these regions becoming an important viticultural area in the future. Those in the most likely viticultural regions, such as Young and Orange, suffer from the problems of isolation and lack of recognition. Those close to the major Sydney market suffer from a climate which is warm and prone to excessive vintage-time rain.

Nonetheless, modern viticultural and winemaking techniques are constantly making possible what was once considered impossible. In the final analysis I think it will be the marketplace (and tourism) rather than inherent wine quality which determines the success or failure of many of these enterprises.

BARWANG
BARWANG ROAD, YOUNG

Peter Robertson (together with sundry members of his family) planted his first vines 23 kilometres south-east of Young in 1975. The initial plantings were of rhine riesling (1.9 hectares), semillon (1.5 hectares), shiraz (1.4 hectares) and cabernet sauvignon (1.1 hectares). Established on deep-red granitic clays impregnated with basalt, at a height of 590 metres, the vines flourished.

The very cool ripening conditions mean that vintage does not start until late March, and often runs well into May for the late-harvest varieties. The rainfall of 675 millimetres is basically winter/spring

dominant, an ideal pattern, and supplementary water is not used. This rainfall pattern also ensures reliable harvest conditions, and the most successful wine made at the vineyard was a late-harvest botrytised semillon.

As Peter Robertson has discovered, winemaking on a small scale in a remote district is not easy. Some of the wines from Barwang have been good, one or two have been great, and others not of acceptable commercial quality. As I said, the best wine was the 1980 Late-Harvest Semillon which won a gold medal at the Canberra National Show. I was judging at that show, and well remember the stir the wine caused, coming as it did from the Small Producers' Class. None of the judges could imagine where the wine came from, and it caused great interest.

Notwithstanding the problems of consistency, Peter Robertson has been sufficiently encouraged to extend the plantings recently. One and one-third hectares of sauvignon blanc and 1.1 hectares of chardonnay are expected to produce their first crop in 1985, while two Hungarian varieties, furmint and harslevelu, have been planted on a trial basis and will produce their first crops in 1986. They will be accompanied by 0.65 hectares of pinot noir, 0.48 hectares of merlot and 0.2 hectares of cabernet franc.

There has never been much doubt that the vineyards will produce high-quality fruit; if some of the winemaking problems could be solved, and if the new varieties flourish as they should, Barwang could be a vineyard to watch.

BRIDGEFARM WINES
LOT 3, MACARTHUR ROAD, CAMDEN

Norman Hanckel was a member of the famous Roseworthy class of 1946–47, graduating in agriculture. For many years he was general manager and

NEW SOUTH WALES VINEYARD, NINETEENTH CENTURY

then a director of Hungerford Hill Limited before moving on to the Industries Assistance Commission in 1979.

In 1974 Hanckel planted vines on the banks of the Nepean River on the outskirts of Camden. The vineyards can be seen as one approaches Camden from Sydney on the lefthand side of the major overpass bridge. The vineyard is established on the site of the original 1812 Bridge Farm land grant, on the opposite side of the river to that on which Macarthur established his vineyard 140 years earlier.

There are 18 hectares of vines, principally planted to chardonnay, with lesser quantities of traminer, shiraz, trebbiano and cabernet sauvignon (in that order). The fertile sandy silt alluvial loams, assisted by the use of drip-irrigation, ensure vigorous growth and substantial yields. The major viticultural problems are excessive vintage-time rain and the humidity which necessitates constant spraying against downy and powdery mildew throughout the growing season. The Sydney metropolitan area is also a phylloxera region, and all of the vines are necessarily grafted onto American rootstocks.

Most of the production has been sold to other New South Wales wineries, chiefly Hungerford Hill and, more recently, Rosemount. In more recent years Bridgefarm has had wine made for it, not, as one would expect, by Norman Hanckel, but by his daughter Dr Sue Hanckel. The white wines have been made under her supervision at other wineries, with the 1984 Chardonnay showing all of the hallmarks of high-technology production. The labelling of the wine as "Le Docteur Hanckel" seems to me, to put it mildly, somewhat pretentious.

COGNO BROTHERS
COBBITTY ROAD, COBBITTY

The Cogno family has been making Italian-style wines at Cobbitty, eight kilometres north-west of Camden, since 1964. The 5.6-hectare vineyard is planted to barbera, muscat, trebbiano, shiraz and chardonnay, and substantial quantities of grapes are purchased from South Australia.

All sales are cellar door, and the clientele is largely Italian.

D'AQUINO WINERY
129–131 BATHURST ROAD, ORANGE

D'Aquino Winery is but part of a flourishing and diverse wine-and-spirit business which operates in the unlikely environment of the outskirts of Orange. The retail wine shop offers an array of wine equal to the largest specialised Sydney or Melbourne merchant; it incorporates a wine-and-spirit bond warehouse, entitling D'Aquino to import spirits in bulk for bottling and subsequent distribution. This in turn is the basis of an expanding wholesale enterprise; and finally, there is a 100-tonne winery.

The winery is run under the supervision of Rex D'Aquino, who graduated from Roseworthy Agricultural College in 1981. All of the grapes are purchased from other districts. At the premium end small quantities of traminer, cabernet sauvignon and rhine riesling are purchased from a grower in Cowra; while small quantities of high-quality grapes have also been purchased from time to time from McLaren Vale. These grapes go to make 300 or 400 dozen bottles of premium wine per year. The major part of the annual crush comes from grapes supplied from Hillston and various areas of South Australia. This wine is sold variously in bulk and in unlabelled bottles to other wineries. There is also a substantial business in supplying major companies wishing to do their own promotions: "special message" wines, as they are called in the trade.

Even though Orange appears to be one of the tableland areas of New South Wales with viticultural potential, Rex D'Aquino has no thought of establishing his own vineyards in the area. He is all too well aware of the difficulties and economic risks of such an undertaking.

GILGAI
TINGHA ROAD, NEAR INVERELL

Dr Keith Whish commenced his vineyard at Gilgai, 10 kilometres south of Inverell towards Tingha, in 1968 with cuttings obtained from Penfolds' Dalwood Vineyard in the Hunter Valley. It was a nice touch for, a little over 100 years earlier, George Wyndham had taken vines with him when he travelled north to establish his Bukkulla Station at Inverell in 1849.

The dark, rich and strongly flavoured Bukkulla wines were a very important part of Dalwood's production in the period 1860–90. Usually the wine was blended with the lighter Dalwood material, but occasionally it was bottled and sold under the Bukkulla label. An order taken in the 1860s shows the relative standing of the two wines: nine dozen Bukkulla Red was purchased for 60 shillings a dozen, while 36 dozen Dalwood Red cost a mere 26 shillings per dozen. Even the Fine Dalwood Red brought only 32 shillings per dozen. Production from the district peaked around 1890, and then entered a prolonged period of decline, the last remnants disappearing in the Second World War.

The new Gilgai vineyard is established on red volcanic laterite soil, with a little ironstone intermixed, at a height of 760 metres. Spring frost and summer humidity, the latter leading to all forms of mildew, are the main viticultural problems. In 1984 vintage-time rain was such that only 50 gallons (227.5 litres) of malbec were made, with all of the remaining grapes being left to rot on the vines. Although total rainfall is not high at around 700 millimetres, Dr Whish and his son Charles (recently graduated from Roseworthy) have introduced sod cultivation in an endeavour to control moisture and humidity in the growing season.

The six-hectare vineyard is planted to 1.6 hectares each of semillon, shiraz and cabernet sauvignon, and 0.4 hectares each of malbec and pinot noir. There are trial plantings of mataro, grenache, sauvignon blanc, rhine riesling and trebbiano. Yields vary from around 3.7 tonnes per hectare for cabernet sauvignon to 7.5 tonnes per hectare for semillon and shiraz.

Over the years wine quality has been variable, reflecting both the difficulties of small-scale winemaking and the lack of technical training. With the arrival of Charles Whish to take over winemaking, there is no reason to suppose the ability of the district to make deep and rich, red wines will not once again be realised.

GLENFINLASS
ELYSIAN FARM, PARKES ROAD, WELLINGTON

Wellington solicitor Brian Holmes has been making small quantities of wine at his Elysian Farm vineyard for over 15 years. The winery name Glenfinlass was adapted from that given by Lieutenant John Oxley in 1818. His diary gives a vivid description:

> It is impossible to imagine a more beautifully romantic glen than that in which we lay. There was just level space on either side of the stream for the horses to travel along, the rocks rising almost perpendicularly from it to a towering height, covered with flowering acacia of various species, whose bright yellow flowers were contrasted and

mingled with the more sombre foliage of the blue gum and Cyprus trees.

The winery, built from convict-made bricks, shelters under the trees which Oxley described. The vineyard is established on a mixture of red volcanic soil with rocky patches and alluvial clays. Two hectares of shiraz and half a hectare of cabernet sauvignon form the initial plantings; 0.2 hectares of sauvignon blanc was established in the early 1980s and will produce its first crop in 1985, while a trial planting of chardonnay was established in 1984.

Brian Holmes uses organic farming methods similar to those of Gil Wahlquist at Mudgee—he employs neither pesticides nor insecticides and uses only traditional sprays against downy and powdery mildew, principally Bordeaux spray. The same natural processes are applied to the maximum possible degree in the winemaking. No artificial yeasts are used, the wine is hand-plunged in an open fermenter, and is neither fined nor filtered.

These natural methods of viticulture and winemaking are far more difficult to handle than most people realise, and it is very easy to lose an entire vintage on the vine or in the vat. Three hundred millimetres of rain in January 1984 spelt the end of the 1984 vintage, but no amount of conventional viticulture could have averted that disaster. All things considered, Brian Holmes and his family have been very successful with their winemaking, and the tiny production (which never exceeds 500 cases a year) finds a ready market from the cellar door.

JASPER VALLEY WINES
CROZIERS ROAD, BERRY

When the late Sid Mitchell planted 5.5 hectares of grapes at Croziers Road, Berry (on the New South Wales South Coast near Nowra), in 1976, there was no little scepticism about the venture. The belief was that the climate was too warm and the rainfall too high. Subsequent events have proved otherwise.

Right from the outset the vines have flourished in the rich volcanic soils. The plantings comprise semillon (0.35 hectares), cabernet sauvignon and shiraz (0.25 hectares each), rhine riesling (1.1 hectares) and chardonnay (0.5 hectares). In 1984, a vintage many other small New South Wales wineries would prefer to forget, almost 50 tonnes of grapes were harvested in first-class condition, at an average yield of around 9.2 tonnes per hectare.

This was a far cry from the initial 1978 crush of three tonnes, made by Sid Mitchell with some help and advice from Dr Edgar Riek of Canberra. Mitchell had learnt the basic principles of winemaking by attending short courses run by the Riverina College of Advanced Education.

Sid Mitchell died suddenly in 1981, and his daughter and son-in-law, Ann and John Jorgenson, continued the vineyard and winemaking with help from Sid Mitchell's wife Daisy. The wines made by Mitchell prior to his death were commercially very acceptable, with the difficulties of small-volume white-winemaking largely surmounted. Most successful was a Semillon Bin AJ5, first made in 1979 and which has now been continued as a non-vintage white burgundy style. The one currently available in 1984 was a very creditable effort: full, soft and fleshy with some bottle-developed toasty-cheesy aromas.

Two 1982 red wines (a cabernet sauvignon and a cabernet shiraz) also show signs of careful and competent winemaking. They are not especially big wines, with soft, ripe and slightly sweet fruit flavours. The cabernet shiraz was distinctly the better wine of the two.

Cellar-door sales have always been brisk, and the locally made and produced wines were (and are) supplemented by the usual range of fortified, sparkling flavoured wines which—obviously enough—are bought in, along with a lambrusco. In 1983 and 1984 traminer grapes were also purchased to supplement the locally produced fruit, and to provide traminer and traminer riesling wines.

By 1984 it had become necessary to move the winery and equip it with larger, more efficient machinery. A larger cellar-door sales complex has also been constructed. These moves culminated in the appointment in mid-1984 of a full-time winemaker, Michael Kerr, a Roseworthy graduate. Kerr is confident that Jasper Valley can produce good-quality table wine with the use of appropriate vineyard management techniques to offset the high rainfall. The success of the 1984 vintage certainly gives support for that optimism.

MIDAS TREE
CARGO ROAD, LIDSTER, via ORANGE

Midas Tree has been established by Roseworthy graduate John Swanson on the outskirts of Orange. In 1984 he established four hectares of vineyards, planted to premium varieties, and plans to erect a winery eventually. In the meantime he fights a battle with the rabbits which threaten the young plantings,

and acknowledges that in future he will need to deal with the large resident bird population.

Nonetheless, Swanson believes the *terroir* and climate of his vineyard site are ideal for the production of high-quality wines, and that the difficulties and risks will be justified. In the meantime he markets wines bought in from other areas under the Midas Tree label, including those with which he is most familiar. Swanson is best known for having produced the excellent Jolimont wines in 1983. (Jolimont is one of the small wineries in the Murrumbidgee Irrigation Area.)

RICHMOND ESTATE
GADDS ROAD, NORTH RICHMOND

Sydney orthopaedic surgeon Dr Barry Bracken was among those who mourned the passing of Penfolds' Minchinbury Vineyard in 1956. He was also well aware of the proud history of the Sydney Basin area as the cradle of the Australian wine industry. Vines were grown in a circle from Ryde to Parramatta, to Windsor, Camden and Liverpool before commercial production commenced in the Hunter Valley. So when in 1967 he purchased a 24-hectare grazing property at Gadds Road, North Richmond, on Sydney's western outskirts, it was for the purpose of establishing a vineyard and ultimately a winery.

Being a phylloxera area, the initial 2.2-hectares planting in 1968 was of grafted vines. Over the next three years Dr Bracken watched as virulent soil fungus killed the vines. Realising that a skilled viticulturalist was required, in 1971 he employed Ferdnand (Mick) Lesnick as a full-time vineyard manager. Mick Lesnick had been trained in the Hunter Valley and came from a family which had been associated with viticulture there for generations.

Plantings commenced again in 1971 on the gentle slopes, contoured and banked, reaching a 1980 peak of just on nine hectares. Once the fungus problem had been surmounted, the red basaltic soil, mixed with some alluvials, produced good yields of high-quality grapes. Those initial plantings comprised 3.75 hectares each of cabernet sauvignon and shiraz, together with 0.25 hectares of malbec and 0.1 hectares of merlot. Since 1979 the shiraz plantings have been reduced somewhat, and early trials of chardonnay have not been persevered with, but the malbec plantings are being increased.

A token quantity of wine was made in 1972, and the first meaningful crush was made in 1973 (1800 litres). Production thereafter climbed steadily, peaking at around 22,500 litres in 1980. In 1974 Dr Bracken spent the best part of the year in Bordeaux with his family, studying the wines and winemaking of that region. Between 1974 and 1983 he shared the winemaking duties with Mick Lesnick, although Lesnick had the day-to-day winemaking responsibility.

1975 proved that Richmond Estate could produce wine of the highest quality. The shiraz of that year just missed out on winning the trophy for best red wine of show at Mudgee in 1976, and in 1979 won the only gold medal in the Shiraz Class at the Adelaide Wine show. I have tasted that wine on a number of occasions, and never failed to be impressed by its marvellous fruit quality and the excellent oak handling.

In January 1985 I assembled a retrospective tasting of shiraz from the 1979, 1980 and 1983 vintages, and cabernet sauvignon of 1983. The 1979 and 1980 Shiraz were both lovely wines, confirming an earlier tasting of 1979 Shiraz Malbec. This latter wine had abundant sweet, minty fruit and oak aroma and flavour, and with a soft almost chewy palate. The word "chewy" is not one I use frequently, yet it cropped up again in the January 1985 tasting without any reference to the tasting of the 1979 Shiraz Malbec some years earlier. Indeed, the tasting notes for the 1979 Shiraz and 1979 Shiraz Malbec are very similar, and I assume the malbec component in the latter wine was not significant. The 1980 Shiraz had more mint aromas and flavours; both had lovely fruit and structure. The 1983 and 1981 wines are unfortunately all marred by volatility. Quite obviously the oak casks have not been properly cared for, and lacto-bacillus has impregnated the wood and wreaked havoc on the wines.

No wine was made in 1984; 60 tonnes of rotten fruit were left on the vine, the legacy of the more or less continuous January-February rains. In 1984 Dr Bracken sold Richmond Estate to Tom Allen and his son, and Lesnick remains as vineyard manager and winemaker. I do hope they spend some money on new oak; the fruit quality from the vineyard certainly merits it.

THE COLLEGE WINERY
BAROOMA STREET, WAGGA WAGGA

The Riverina College of Advanced Education was established in 1972 and the wine course was commenced two years later. There are now almost 200 students studying for the Bachelor of Applied Science (Wine Science) degree, either full-time or by part-time correspondence study. The Riverina College and Roseworthy Agricultural College in South Australia are the only two tertiary institutions offering winemaking or viticulture courses.

Initially funded by a substantial grant from Ron Potter, the Ron Potter Centre, as it is commonly called, now includes a fully functioning commercial winery as part of the training course. Situated in a converted apple-packing shed, the 200-tonne winery (set up between 1976 and 1977) has a range of equipment second to none. The equipment includes extensive refrigeration and must-chilling facilities, a centrifuge, earth-filtration, a modern crusher and a modern press, air-conditioned wood- and bottle-storage facilities, and of course a very extensive laboratory. With such a range of equipment, skilled teachers and virtually unlimited labour provided by the students, it is hardly surprising that the College Winery has produced numerous high-quality white wines.

Approximately 70 per cent of the annual crush comes from the college's own Booranga Vineyard, planted to chardonnay (1.7 hectares), cabernet sauvignon (1.2 hectares), pinot gris (1.2 hectares), merlot (one hectare), rhine riesling (0.7 hectares), muscat frontignac (0.7 hectares), traminer (0.65 hectares), palomino (0.5 hectares), and cabernet franc, tinta amavella and touriga (0.3 hectares each).

For the remaining 30 per cent The College deliberately spreads its net as far as possible, so that wines can be made under identical conditions using grapes taken from widely varying climatic and soil conditions. This gives the students a unique opportunity to assess both the grape quality and the handling techniques appropriate for numerous Australian winegrowing areas. Thus between 1980 and 1982 quantities of Coonawarra cabernet sauvignon, Nagambie cabernet sauvignon, Cowra chardonnay, Griffith colombard and traminer, Eden Valley rhine riesling and Hill Tops (Young, New South Wales) rhine riesling and semillon were turned into wine and offered for sale on the commercial market. These wines were supplemented by pinot gris, traminer and cabernet sauvignon from the Booranga Vineyard.

Wagga itself is a warm to hot area, with vintage falling between the middle of February and the end of March. Chief viticulturalist is Max Loder, who in the 30 years since he came to Australia from Germany has built up a vast bank of experience. One of the more interesting techniques used in the Booranga Vineyard is a very high trellis with a double fruiting wire to provide a vertical foliage wall and yields of up to 10 tonnes per hectare.

The first winery director was Brian Croser, who spent several years at the college in between working for Thomas Hardy and setting up full-time operations at Petaluma. Under his direction some excellent varietal wines were produced; his responsibilities were assumed by Andrew Birks in 1980.

One of the most successful of the College Winery wines was a 1980 Oak-Matured Cowra Chardonnay which won numerous gold medals and several trophies in a distinguished show career. A sister wine, without oak, was also of very high quality. A 1980 Coonawarra Cabernet Sauvignon was also a startling wine, with an almost essence-like cool-climate cabernet aroma and flavour. Both of these wines were still available for sale at the end of 1984.

Some of the more recent College Winery releases have been far less exciting, with a number of the 1982 whites showing evidence of oxidation, which is not what one would really expect. Nonetheless, the range of wines is interesting, and at least some of the wines are of very high quality.

VICARY'S WINERY
NORTHERN ROAD, LUDDENHAM

Vicary's Winery, at Northern Road, Luddenham, on the western outskirts of Sydney, was established in 1923 with an extensive cellar-door trade in fortified wine. Owner Ross Carbery has recently moved to increase both the amount and quality of table wine offered for sale. Roseworthy graduate Chris Niccol is now winemaker, and 1.2 hectares each of rhine riesling and chardonnay have recently been planted. The original vineyard area was 2.5 hectares of muscat.

Vicary's own vines provide around 10 per cent to 15 per cent of the annual crush; the remainder comes from purchased grapes. In 1984 these included traminer (16 tonnes), cabernet sauvignon (10 tonnes), chardonnay, rhine riesling, shiraz and frontignac (eight tonnes each), and semillon and sauvignon blanc (four tonnes each). All of these came from the Upper Hunter Valley.

The 2500-case output is sold exclusively at the cellar door and by mailing list.

Victoria

Vines were established in New South Wales, Tasmania and Western Australia before they reached Victoria. Tasmania, indeed, was the source of the first vines to reach the colony, accompanying Edward Henty on board the schooner *Thistle* on 19 November 1834. History does not relate what happened to these vines, and indeed it seems they did not survive. In 1837 William Ryrie travelled overland from his home station on the Monaro plains near Cooma (in New South Wales) and took up a large grazing run in the Yarra Valley which became known as Yering. He brought with him vine cuttings, which were planted out in the following year.

By 1842 the *Statistical Record of Victoria* showed less than 1.5 hectares of vineyards. It seems that this must have been of vineyards in bearing, for in 1840 John Fawkner had established four hectares of vines at Pascoe Vale near Flemington, and by 1848 he was producing 10,000 litres of wine a year. The early 1840s saw the more or less simultaneous establishment of three districts which were each to remain of great importance until the 1880s or later: the Melbourne metropolitan area, Geelong and the Yarra Valley.

Phylloxera was to spell an abrupt end for Geelong, until then the most important table-wine-producing area of the State, while urban pressure caused the Melbourne metropolitan area to disappear as a wine producer between 1880 and the turn of the century. A mixture of government initiatives (to encourage dairy-farming) associated with rising land values and changing habits in wine consumption saw the progressive decline in the Yarra Valley between 1890 and 1921, when Yeringberg made its last vintage (until revived in the early 1970s).

The first plantings in Sydney failed because of the humidity and high rainfall, which led to fungal diseases such as anthracnose and black spot. The vignerons of Melbourne suffered no such problems: the metropolitan area was (and is) most suitable for viticulture, and vineyards flourished in numerous suburbs. Some of the first vineyards of significance included a five-hectare vineyard established by a Mr Gordon at Brighton, while David Ogilvy established a vineyard on the hillside running down to the Yarra River between Punt Road and Anderson Street in 1847. Portions of this vineyard, bounded by Alexandra Avenue and known as Airlie Bank, remained in existence until 1924. Francois de Castella records that its wine made from hermitage was celebrated.

T. J. Everist had a substantial vineyard and winery, situated between Hawthorn East and Kew, bounded by Auburn Road, Barkers Road, Kildare Street and Harcourt Street. In 1861 he was offering a selection of red and white wines priced betwen 12 and 30 shillings per dozen. John C. Allen had a vineyard immediately opposite on the southern side of Harcourt Street, while Bleasby's vineyards were a few kilometres to the north-east at Balwyn.

Numerous vineyards existed along Toorak Road, one of the largest lying between Auburn and Tooranga Roads. Count Alinant de Dollon had a 12-hectare vineyard here; he also bought in substantial quantities from other growers, and sold his wine from a depot established at 45 Swanston Street. On the opposite or southern side of Toorak Road was Edward Khull's Tooronga Vineyard; while J. C. Cole established his second vineyard on Tooronga Road, having moved from his first vineyard which became the site for Richmond Racecourse. Across the other side of the city Ngarveno Vineyard at Moonee Ponds remained in production until the 1890s when the last of the stock was purchased by Matthew Lang & Company.

Sunbury also fell in the County of Bourke, which covered the metropolitan area. Numerous vignerons established themselves there: Francis Bowie, F. Bubeck, R. F. Kurrle and J. S. Johnson. The latter owned Craiglee Vineyard, since revived by Patrick Carmody; a stock of Johnson's wine, from the 1872 vintage, was unearthed (literally) in 1951. Many of the bottles were in great condition, but unhappily the only bottle I shared had seen better days, although it was still possible to discern what had been there before.

In 1859 there were 36 hectares of vines in Bourke County and only two years later the vineyards had mushroomed to 136 hectares. The rate of growth then eased: by 1865 there were 241 hectares, while the 1871 total of 343 hectares was close to the high-water mark, a healthy proportion of the State total, then around 2000 hectares.

The first vines were planted in the Yarra Valley by William Ryrie in 1837; but both in this region and in Geelong the real impetus came from the Swiss settlers who played such an important part in the early colonisation of the State. This unlikely influence came through Charles La Trobe, who arrived as superintendent in 1839, and who became the first governor of the State following its separation from New South Wales in 1851. La Trobe had lived for a while at Neuchatel in Switzerland, and had married the daughter of the Swiss Counsellor of State. The de Castellas and the de Purys were to dominate viticulture in the Yarra Valley for the next half century. In Geelong, David Louis Pettavel, John Belperroud and Messrs Brequet established the first vineyards in 1842 and played an equally important role in that region.

In 1851 gold was discovered: at Wellington in New South Wales on 15 May and on 8 July at Clunes, near Melbourne. In September a 75-year-old John Dunlop walked beside a dray from Geelong to Ballarat, where he found gold in abundance lying under the wattle trees. Professor Manning Clark describes in picturesque terms the fever which gripped the Colony (Volume IV: _A History of Australia_):

> Another 'hot fit of the auriferous fever' took possession of the men in Melbourne and Geelong. As in _Macbeth_, men stood not on their social rank in going, but went at once. Painters put on a first coat, and then vanished; plasterers mixed their mortar, then threw away their trowels; bricklayers on scaffolding turned giddy with the thought of gold; carpenters shook with the fever till they flung their tools away and bolted for the fields; attendants at the lunatic asylum in Melbourne rushed off; teachers at the denominational schools dropped all pretence about their higher calling and made for the fields; capitalists saddled up horses and joined the army of prospective diggers on the road.

Gold was an ephemeral lure, but the effects of its discovery were to last forever. Quite apart from giving Australians one of the highest per capita incomes in the world, it led to the establishment of an enduring infrastructure of towns and support industries. Vines followed hot on the heels of the diggers, reaching Avoca in 1848, Bendigo in 1855, Great Western in 1858 and Ballarat in 1859.

By 1869, 1638 hectares were producing 2,018,458 litres; the 1890 vintage resulted in 7,103,655 litres, well over half the total Australian production in that year. But a prolonged period of decline had already commenced; phylloxera had been discovered at Fyansford near Geelong in 1875, and by 1881 over 218 hectares of the vineyards had been compulsorily removed and the once-proud district was headed to oblivion. The eradication of the vineyards was a futile and expensive exercise: phylloxera cut a swathe as it marched northwards over the next two decades, eventually reaching the Rutherglen area which the government had been so anxious to protect.

However, phylloxera was only partly to blame: the technique of grafting onto resistant American rootstock, first suggested in 1869, had become generally accepted by 1881. Thus it would have been possible for the devastated areas to be replanted had market conditions warranted it. But the dictates of both the domestic and the export markets required wines of a different style from those of central and southern Victoria: table wines high in alcohol and strong in extract, and sweet fortified wines. Hubert de Castella, who had recently visited the Rutherglen Wine Show, wrote in 1886:

> This state of things—a preponderant production of wines too strong for ordinary consumption—is due in a great measure to the influence of a certain commerce, which asks for a high degree of alcoholic strength in wine at a minimum of price, in order to effect manipulations afterwards. Alcohol is the virtue, or rather the vice, which the growers are advised to secure.
>
> Thus influenced, even in their local exhibitions, the vignerons who organised them, forgetful of past lessons and indulging in self-glorification, instead of favouring clean, dry wines, as light as their climate can produce, adjudicate the greatest number of prizes to what their list of awards calls sweet full-bodied red, and sweet full-bodied white—abomination of desolation.
>
> What will it serve them to fill their cellars with undrinkable wines, even if for a short time? Wine-sellers and grocers are ready to give a larger price for sweet and strong, which the prosperous Australian middle classes only prefer until they are educated to lighter wines—that consumption is limited, and that the market soon glutted. The trade in wine must, within the ten years that are to come, undergo as great a change as that of meat, of flour or wool have suffered in during the past ten. Two kinds of wines must disappear from the markets of the countries which do not grow the vine—the spurious strong ones and the weak mixtures.

Unhappily for de Castella, and for the Victorian industry as a whole, the trends continued, and by 1960 the viticultural map showed only two areas south of Rutherglen in production: the Goulburn Valley and Great Western.

Indeed, it seems clear that Victoria will never again assume the statistical importance it had at the end of the 1880s. Yet quantity is not the end of the matter. It is not upon the wines of the Midi and Provence that the reputation of France is founded, but upon that tiny percentage of total production which comes from the chateaux of Bordeaux and the domaines of Burgundy. So it is that in an altogether different way Victoria may yet come again to dominate the Australian wine industry.

The most exhilarating feature is that high-quality grapes can be grown across the length and breadth of the State. There is hardly a square centimetre of the central and southern regions which does not have the potential to produce great table wine, while the north-east needs no introduction as the producer of some of the world's finest fortified wines. The north-west may miss out in the quality stakes, but it is a significant producer of bulk wine, table grapes and dried sultanas.

One limitation is the prevalence of spring frosts in many areas, but even here modern viticultural techniques are pushing back previously accepted barriers. The vignerons of the Napa Valley in California have learnt to cope with this problem by using a combination of wind machines, smudge pots, overhead sprinklers and soil-management techniques. Few of these are at present used in Victoria, but they are available if the need should arise.

The great potential of Victoria stems from its much-maligned climate. One of the instant litmus tests for vineyard country is to observe whether the grass by the roadside is green; if it is, the vines are likely to be in good health, and the grapes likewise. The vine happens to be a drought-resistant species of plant. It also happens that in Europe the principal viticultural problem is not insufficient water but insufficient sun. So the myth of a drought year being a great year was born; but the truth is that a vine needs an adequate supply of water through the growing season to produce grapes which are chemically perfect for winemaking. Too much rain, particularly in the weeks leading up to and running through harvest, is obviously not desirable, chiefly because it is likely to promote the growth of moulds leading to rot. But outside the Hunter Valley, vintage problems of this kind are rare in Australia. The other characteristic of the vine is that it will ripen its fruit with a minimum of warmth and sunshine. Certainly there are no areas in mainland

Australia, and probably not even in Tasmania, in which there is insufficient warmth to ripen most grape varieties. Thus the coolest areas (coolest through the six months from October to March) in which grapes are presently grown in Victoria are all warmer than Dijon in Burgundy, though cooler than Bordeaux.

The so-called "cool-climate" debate has really only just begun in Australia. Vignerons from the traditional warm areas, such as the Barossa Valley and the Hunter Valley, have rushed in to protect their reputations, but the discussion has tended to degenerate into insupportable generalisations met by equally general and insupportable replies. Only when vignerons and wine consumers have agreed on what varieties they want, and what wine styles they wish those varieties to produce, can the debate come into any sensible focus.

This in turn necessarily predicates a balanced and mature appreciation of regional characteristics and qualities. It is legitimate—and necessary—to compare Australian wine styles with those of France; but it is neither feasible nor necessary for Australians to endeavour to make wines which taste the same as those of France. Australian wines may be seen by impartial judges as better or worse than those of France, but they should never be carbon copies.

In precisely the same way, a Coonawarra chardonnay will differ from one made in the Yarra Valley, and even more from one vintaged in the Hunter Valley. As one screws the microscope down further, differences continue to manifest themselves. A chardonnay made from grapes grown in Meursault will be quite different from one made a few kilometres south in Puligny-Montrachet, a difference stemming from *terroir* and climate, rather than winemaking techniques. In a few decades it will, I am sure, be accepted that a chardonnay made on one side of the Yarra Valley will be quite different from that made on the other side.

So it is that within the general umbrella of the cool (and often not so cool) climate Victoria is capable of producing an almost endless diversity of wine styles. Certainly there is not a single significant grape variety which does not thrive somewhere within the confines of the State. For all this, production in terms of quantity is minuscule as soon as one moves away from Sunraysia/Swan Hill. These Riverland areas produce over 75 per cent of the annual wine-grape crush. The available viticultural statistics lump the "rest of State" together, and the north-east (Rutherglen, Milawa and Glenrowan) in turn dominates the "rest of State".

Some interesting trends emerge, however. During the period 1979 to 1983, in which Australia-wide and, indeed, Victoria-wide plantings have declined, the "rest of State" vineyards have increased from 1973 hectares to 2425 hectares. Tonnage has varied from the drought-ravaged 1983 total of 6970 tonnes to a 1982 high of 11,988 tonnes, There can be no question that the figures will increase until the end of the 1980s at least, although what will happen thereafter is less certain. Here the success (or failure) of the boutique wineries will be the determining factor.

Finally, the extensive government initiatives announced in 1984 could prove of critical importance. So many initiatives of this kind have in the past been shown to be pre-election ploys, or have been abandoned on a change of government, that it is difficult to place any long-term confidence in the impact of the initiatives. But they do hold promise, and the authentication scheme (a form of appellation control) is of interest. An early byproduct of this is the division of the State into regions and subregions.

This classification was promulgated after the format of this book was determined, and my divisions do not conform precisely to those of the official break-up, which is as shown opposite. Some of these strange and unfamiliar names will become household names for the wine lovers of the twenty-first century.

MURRAY RIVER VALLEY

SUNRAYSIA REGION:
subregions:
Mildura
Robinvale
Merbein
Irymple
Karadoc
Lindsay Point

MID-MURRAY REGION:
subregions:
Swan Hill
Lake Boga
Beverford
Mystic Park
Barooga

GOULBURN VALLEY
subregions:
Shepparton
Nagambie
Tahbilk
Mitchelton
Seymour
Graytown
Picola
Katunga
Dookie
Murchison
Strathbogie Ranges
Yarck
Mansfield
Mount Helen

NORTH-EAST VICTORIA
subregions:
Milawa
Glenrowan
Rutherglen
Ovens Valley
King Valley
Wahgunyah
Barnawartha
Buckland River Valley

GREAT WESTERN

AVOCA
subregions:
Redbank
Moonambel

DRUMBORG

YARRA VALLEY
subregions:
Yarra Glen
Lilydale
Seville
Coldstream
St Andrews
Dixon's Creek
Steels Creek

BENDIGO
subregions:
Bridgewater
Big Hill
Heathcote
Harcourt
Mount Ida
Maiden Gully
Kingower
Baynton
Mandurang

GEELONG
subregions:
Anakie
Moorabel
Bannockburn

KYNETON

MACEDON
subregions:
Sunbury
Mount Macedon
Lancefield
Newham
Romsey

DANDENONG VALLEY

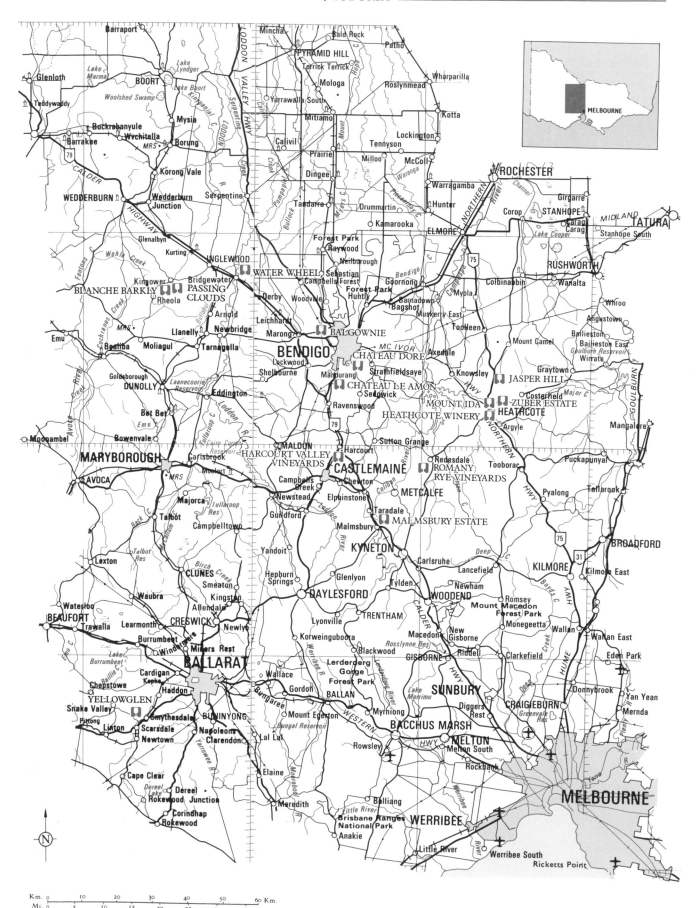

Km. 0   10   20   30   40   50   60 Km.
Mi. 0   5   10   15   20   25   30   35 Mi.

Bendigo and District

Francois de Castella places the arrival of vines in the Bendigo region (or Sandhurst, as it was then known) in 1855, a logical-enough date given the discovery of gold at the end of 1851. But Ebenezer Ward, who visited and described in minute detail so many of Victoria's vineyards in 1864, suggests a far earlier commencement. He wrote of vines at John Clement's vineyard on the Campaspe River "which cannot be less than fourteen or fifteen years old", while Yarraberb Station was said to contain more than two hectares of vines, up to 10 or 11 years of age.

Ward details more than 40 vineyards, most of which were still in their infancy, spreading from Bullock Creek in the west to the Campaspe River in the east. Three years earlier there were 50 hectares planted, but only 6800 litres of wine were made, and most of that was destined for home consumption. In 1862 a local vigneron named Klemm asserted that 20 hogsheads (5850 litres) were sold in that year; by 1869 there were 197 hectares, and production had soared to 240,000 litres. In 1880 the 216 hectares produced 273,000 litres, and there were more than 100 wineries in operation.

The 1873 Vienna Exhibition brought fame—indeed, notoriety—to the region. Henry Vizetelly, a leading wine authority and author in the latter part of the nineteenth century, was one of the judges and told of the competition in his book *The Wines of the World*. A jury, including a number of French experts, gave particular praise to several wines made from hermitage, but when it was discovered they were from Bendigo, the French jurors withdrew in protest, claiming that the wines must be French. Only after a substantial delay, and much reassurance, did they consent to resume judging.

In this golden age many different styles of wine were made: Ward lists a kaleidoscopic array of varieties, confused by the use of common names or nicknames and the intermingling of table-grape varieties. But in the light of today, white varieties were surprisingly common, with chasselas, gouais and verdelho the most common, and rhine riesling, white hermitage, aucerot and white pinot less so. Among the reds, hermitage, mataro and pinot meunière were frequently listed; carignan and petite verdot were rare; while cabernet sauvignon was conspicuous by its absence. Looking back, de Castella recalled that:

> Bendigo has produced a wide range of excellent wines, often attaining exceptional distinction, varying from light dry claret and hock types, through robuster Hermitage and full dry and semi-dry Verdelho and Pedro, to quite sweet wines, recalling Madeira in no small measure.

The end came with brutal suddenness in 1893 when phylloxera was discovered. Notwithstanding that the answer to the pest had been discovered over 15 years earlier, and that the attempt to contain it by the same methods at Geelong had proved totally ineffective, the government ordered the wholesale eradication of the vineyards. The £50,000 compensation paid added to the cost of what de Castella termed a farce.

When Bendigo pharmacist Stuart Anderson planted the first vines at his Balgownie Vineyard in 1969, it signalled the rebirth of this once-great wine-producing district. It also emphasised the diversity of climate in central Victoria: altitude plays an important role in determining climate, and areas such as Bendigo—at an altitude of 225 metres—are really quite warm. But even here one has to be careful: go just 100 metres up a mountainside, and the heat summation will rapidly decrease.

Obviously enough, the fruit flavour and wine style will reflect the climate, but there is a common thread which runs through virtually all the reds of the region: a particularly marked taste of mint, in the peppermint-spearmint spectrum, rather than garden mint. It extends across to Great Western and back to Tahbilk in the east, but is probably most intense in the wines of Bendigo. The cabernet sauvignons of

Chateau Le Amon and Passing Clouds have an extra ration; with Passing Clouds the same character even comes through in its pinot noir.

Francois de Castella records that the red wines of the nineteenth century were noted for a "faint curious character, resembling sandalwood", and that this same perfumed essence came through even in brandy distilled in Bendigo wine. It seems to be an inescapable conclusion that this is the same mint-eucalyptus character which is so much in evidence today. How much this character derives from the *terroir*—the soil, the subsoil and the aspect—and how much from the climate, I do not know. Certainly I unhesitatingly reject the fanciful suggestion that it comes from the surrounding eucalypts, an explanation sometimes advanced for the similar character evident in the Martha's Vineyard cabernets of the Napa Valley in California. Rather, I think it develops at a certain stage—usually late—in the ripening cycle of the grape. Vignerons tend to determine picking times by reference to sugar and acid levels rather than flavour. Depending on the season and the *terroir*, the mint character may or may not have developed. In this area, it appears more often than not.

It is rough country with scraggly gums attesting to the lack of rain, and hard red and yellow soils. "Passing Clouds" is a further testimonial to the modest rainfall, which should vary between 500 and 550 millimetres but by no means always does so. In the 1983 vintage year rainfall was a pitiful 160 millimetres; not surprisingly, even the drought-resistant vines failed to produce a crop in most vineyards. A compensation is that the soils tend to hold whatever moisture there is available; while some vineyards are established above a subterranean water drift, believed to be associated with the old goldmine workings spread throughout the district. Yields vary from low to moderate depending on the year; there is relatively little irrigation. The red basalts which abound in the Heathcote area are particularly suited to the production of intensely coloured, deep-flavoured and strongly structured red wines. The other perennial threat comes from spring frosts, which are particularly dangerous during the first week of November, and last for between seven and 10 days. Finally, in some vineyards birds are a pest, but not a major one.

Bendigo is a far-flung region, with a number of quite distinct subregions. These are Bridgewater, Big Hill, Heathcote, Harcourt, Mount Ida, Maiden Gully, Kingower, Baynton and Mandurang. The region's principal strength lies in its reds, with cabernet sauvignon to the fore. Since 1973 Balgownie's cabernet sauvignons have been at the very peak of Australian red-wine quality, and those early vintages—from 1973 to 1976—are still improving. Other makers have done better with shiraz, few better than Leonard French's Mount Ida Vineyard.

Both cabernet sauvignon and shiraz produce deep, richly textured wines, strong in colour and with that mint character in evidence to a lesser or greater degree. These are wines built to stay, seldom showing their full quality in less than eight years. For just how long they will improve is anyone's guess; we simply have not had time to test them fully so far.

Appropriately enough Stuart Anderson has also led the way with pinot noir and chardonnay. Both are made in tiny quantities; both are already legendary, with his pinot noir of undoubted class. An increasing array of white varieties is being attempted: chenin blanc, gewurtztraminer, rhine riesling, semillon and sauvignon blanc are all in evidence. But in the long term, and despite the success the district had in the last century with white varieties, I think the region will be remembered for its reds rather than its whites.

BALGOWNIE
HERMITAGE ROAD, MAIDEN GULLY

It is impossible not to compare Stuart Anderson with the Hunter Valley's Max Lake, the Yarra's John Middleton and Margaret River's Bill Pannell and Tom Cullity. Each have been the messiahs proclaiming the birth (or rebirth) of a great wine district; each has become a legend in his own lifetime; and each will leave behind him wines which will ensure his name is not forgotten by future generations.

Yet Stuart Anderson is very much his own man. For a start, he is (or was) a mere pharmacist, and not a doctor like the others. More obviously, he shrinks from any suggestion of hero-worship or divine infallibility. He knows too much about wine to doubt that it is made in the vineyard; understands too well the importance of *terroir*. With that understanding comes, on the one hand, an acknowledgement of the limited contribution of the winemaker; and, on the other, some singularly great wine.

His understanding of wine has been deepened yet further by a long-term association with Louis Vialard of Chateau Cissac; Stuart Anderson can probably claim to know as much about making wine in Bordeaux as he does in Bendigo. And that, it must be said, is a great deal. If all this were not enough, he has a magnificent cellar of great French wine, which he does not hesitate to share with his friends. It is customary, too, to pay homage to his professional skill with the bassoon and to his love of vintage Bugattis and Ferraris. However, one senses that Stuart Anderson is more than a little tired of hearing these things, and would prefer his privacy.

The Balgownie Vineyard is established on sand and clay loam, interspersed with gravel, overlying clay with quartz and ironstone gravel subsoils. Plantings comprise cabernet sauvignon (7.5 hectares), shiraz (four hectares), chardonnay (1.8 hectares), pinot noir (0.5 hectare) and rhine riesling (0.5 hectare) (or thereabouts, adds Stuart Anderson with a wry grin). The French influence comes to the fore with the neatly trimmed and hedged rows once the grapes have set, ensuring proper light penetration.

The task of writing a book such as this has (occasional) compensations. One such was the excuse to extract from my cellar a 10-year line-up of Balgownie cabernets covering 1983 to 1974. Tasted late in December 1984, these were my notes (and points).

1983 *Colour:* medium purple-red. *Bouquet:* clean, quite firm with fine berry characters and medium weight. *Palate:* a fine wine, not especially rich fruit, but with a long finish with soft, persistent tannin. (17.5/20)

1982 *Colour:* light to medium red. *Bouquet:* light to medium weight with a touch of leather/cedar/spice complexity. *Palate:* very similar, one of the most light-bodied wines in the line-up; attractive varietal fruit showing; some spicy/leather flavours. (17.2/20)

1981 *Colour:* medium to full red with just a touch of purple still showing. *Bouquet:* full, dense, solid and clean; will be very long-lived. *Palate:* solid and full with some mint/ripe-berry flavours and firm tannin on the finish. Needs many years. (17.8/20)

1980 *Colour:* dense purple-red. *Bouquet:* extremely complex, almost impenetrable depth to fruit and oak. *Palate:* very long carry to fruit; a powerfully elegant wine with cool-climate overtones; good balancing tannin. Has a minimum of 10 years in front of it. (18.4/20)

1979 *Colour:* medium red showing some development. *Bouquet:* light to medium with some complex cigar/leather aromas. *Palate:* a light smooth and gently sweet wine, rather in the style of the 1982. Very low tannin. Not far from its best. (17.4/20)

1978 *Colour:* medium to dark red, still with a hint of purple. *Bouquet:* firm fruit with excellent oak balance and integration. *Palate:* velvety rich fruit with some minty overtones; excellent length and balance. (18/20)

1977 *Colour:* fairly deep but showing definite tawny hints on the edge. *Bouquet:* lifted by volatility, and some bottle-developed camphor aromas also showing. *Palate:* a big wine but rather disjointed, with the flavour spoilt by that volatility. The least of the wines in the line-up. (16.6/20)

1976 *Colour:* deep, strong red. *Bouquet:* ripe, rich, dark fruit aromas. *Palate:* an enormous wine, round and complete, with ripe chewy/berry cabernet flavours. (18.8/20)

1975 *Colour:* excellent red with almost no sign of breaking. *Bouquet:* a magnificent wine with perfect weight/style to cabernet, holding its fruit to perfection. *Palate:* harmonious, round and balanced with a few bottle-developed camphor notes; softly sweet berry fruit with marvellous oak integration and balance. (19/20)

1974 *Colour:* full red with a touch of garnet. *Bouquet:* much riper style than the 1975; rich, soft, sweet berry, perhaps a touch of oxidation but no real sign of breaking up. *Palate:* smooth, soft, sweet berry flavours; low to medium tannin. Will not improve but a remarkable old wine. (17.8/20)

The most obvious thing about the tasting was the absence of the exaggerated mint characters which come through in so many of the district's wines. The other feature was the skilful use of oak, so consistently well handled that, on looking over my tasting notes, I find that I have almost never mentioned it, yet it is a constant accompaniment to the fruit. Anderson is a very fine winemaker, and he has had some marvellous cabernet from his vineyard.

Greatly though I admire the cabernet sauvignon, I simply cannot bring myself to like any of the Balgownie hermitage wines I have ever tasted. I would readily concede bias and preconceived ideas, except that I have come across them frequently in blind tastings, and my reaction has been consistent. I see mercaptan; Stuart sees only varietal character. I may well be wrong, but as I have said in relation to similar wines from other makers, the end result is the same: I do not like the wine. The two exceptions to my dislike of the hermitage are the 1973 (still a beautiful wine) and, to a lesser degree, the deep and rich 1981, although even there I see something lurking under the fruit.

Balgownie makes two other wines of magnificent quality in appropriate minuscule quantity. The almost unprocurable pinot noir probably reached its finest moment in 1980 with a magnificently sappy, burgundian wine of great texture and length. Great though the wine is, I have always thought it would have been greater still if taken out of oak a little earlier. Equally, I would travel a long way for the pleasure of sharing a bottle.

The similarly rare chardonnays have had reverential praise heaped on them by all and sundry. To leaven the loaf of the cabernet sauvignon tasting I committed vinicide and opened a bottle each of the 1981 and 1982 Chardonnay. The 1982 has the more obvious oak influence, with spicy/nutmeg aromas and flavours to go with the peachy fruit. The 1981 is a much bigger wine, with rich buttery characters and enormous strength. Anderson does not shrink from fermenting his white wines with the solids present. This leads to a certain heaviness when the wines are young, but certainly invests them with ageing capacity, and I think the 1981 Chardonnay has a number of years improvement in front of it.

Should Stuart Anderson ever tire of winemaking, Australia will be the poorer for it. Alas, since writing the foregoing, Stuart has—at least in part—done just that. Balgownie is now owned by Mildara Wines; Stuart Anderson remains as winemaker–manager for five years, but I cannot help but fear for the long-term future.

BLANCHE BARKLY
RMB 349, KINGOWER

Brothers David and Alvin Reimers established the tiny Blanche Barkly Vineyard on the western outskirts of the township of Kingower in 1972. Set in a picturesque gulley punctuated by old alluvial gold-workings, the vineyard (planted principally to cabernet sauvignon) grew ever so slowly in the dry climate which so distinguishes Bendigo. Eventually the vine roots penetrated to the water drift which runs beneath the vineyard at a depth of between three and four metres, providing a little extra sustenance in all but disastrous years such as 1983.

The Reimers family has lived in the district since the late 1860s, when their grandfather joined the goldrush and decided to stay on once the gold had been worked out. But the family had no prior experience with wine; David and Alvin picked up the basics by working at Reynella for several vintages. Alvin Reimers works full-time in the vineyard and winery, while schoolteacher brother David joins him on weekends and at vintage time. Subsequent to their time at Reynella, both have done several of the short winemaking and viticulture courses run by the Riverina College of Advanced Education.

While the main thrust of the production has been and will remain cabernet-based, the Reimers have at various times experimented with shiraz, rhine riesling, mondeuse and pinot noir. Mondeuse has fallen by the wayside, and chardonnay is now included in the projected plantings.

The shiraz is used to make a hermitage nouveau style, cool-fermented in the style of a white wine, taken off skins fairly early in the fermentation, and which then finishes in new oak. An adventurous way of handling the variety, which in 1984 worked very well, producing a lively, spicy pink fumé wine. It is almost certain the style will be continued in future years.

But it is with cabernet sauvignon that Blanche Barkly has had such outstanding success. The initial vintages, between 1975 and 1980, showed enormous depth of colour, rich texture and the strong mint/eucalypt character which is a recurrent theme throughout the district. More recent vintages have shown less minty and more herbaceous characters, and are all the better for doing so. The 1982 and 1983 Cabernet Sauvignons were quite outstanding.

The 1982 George Henry Cabernet Sauvignon has excellent red-purple colour, a complex bouquet of herbaceous and mint characters leading on to a crystal-clear palate with finely defined berry fruit, and a long clean finish. The 1982 Alexander Cabernet Sauvignon had even less mint and more herbaceous, crushed-leaf/crushed-pepper characters, with the finish aided by a touch of tannin.

The 1983 Johanne Cabernet Sauvignon was a triumph in adversity. Sixty-dozen bottles were made in that vintage, compared with 1000 dozen in 1984 from the same area of vines. Despite the extreme effects of the drought, the 1983 Johanne Cabernet was still a fine, elegant wine with clean, grassy cabernet and a pleasantly astringent finish.

Blanche Barkly took its name from that given to a 1800-ounce gold nugget found nearby in 1857; the nugget was itself named after the reputedly beautiful daughter of the then Governor of Victoria, Sir Henry Barkly. Rumour has it that the miners were disappointed when they actually saw Blanche, but there is no doubting the beauty of the cabernets which now bear her name.

CHATEAU DORE
MANDURANG, via BENDIGO

In 1866 Jean de Ravin built a large stone winery at Mandurang, eight kilometres south of Bendigo. He arrived only two years after Ebenezer Ward had toured the district and given such a detailed description of the vineyards of the time, so we have no contemporary record of de Ravin's activities. Nonetheless, the buildings survived and have now been restored by Ivan Gross, de Ravin's great-grandson. In 1975 he planted eight hectares to shiraz, cabernet sauvignon, rhine riesling and chardonnay, and reopened the winery in 1979.

Almost all sales are made from the cellar door, with the stone winery and the nearby lawn area for picnics being the principal attractions. Unhappily, the wines are not good, and certainly not representative of the mainstream of the district's style.

CHATEAU LE AMON
140 KM POST, CALDER HIGHWAY, BENDIGO

There is no mystery about the name here, nor, for that matter, is there any chateau either. The winery which Phillip and Alma Leamon established after Phillip's retirement from the Victorian State Electricity Commission is utilitarian, but hardly grand. One of the older (relatively speaking) Bendigo wineries, Chateau Le Amon is also one of the best. The home vineyard, planted to semillon (0.7 hectare), rhine riesling (0.7 hectare), cabernet sauvignon (1.4 hectares) and (transitionally) shiraz (1.4 hectares) supplies slightly less than half the total crush of around 70 tonnes. The balance comes in from a number of small independent growers who have sprung up around the Bendigo district.

Even though shiraz has grown well and produced a most attractive spicy style, the marketplace has other views. More than half the shiraz was top-grafted to cabernet franc in 1983 and the balance to merlot in 1984. As from 1985 a classic "bordeaux" blend will be available.

Crash-courses at Riverina College in winemaking and quality control, plus a knowledge of chemistry, put Phillip Leamon on course. Right from the first significant vintage (1977) outstanding show success has come his way. The cabernet sauvignon of that year won the top gold medal and small vineyard trophy at Canberra in 1978; the cabernet from the following vintage won a gold medal in the dry red (firm-finish) class at Melbourne and featured in the

final taste-off for the Jimmy Watson trophy; a 1979 Shiraz Cabernet won a gold medal at Lilydale in 1980; the 1980 Semillon Rhine Riesling won a gold medal and the Yeringberg trophy for the best dry white wine in the 1980 Lilydale Wine Show.

Subsequent wines have built upon and strengthened the reputation gained from those early successes. The regional mint character waxes and wanes with the vintage conditions. But the 1981 Cabernet Sauvignon showed strong grassy, varietal, herbaceous fruit on both bouquet and palate; crisp acid added to the elegance of a classically modulated wine. The 1982 shows yet another face of cabernet sauvignon: the aroma is redolent of sweet cassis/berry characters, leading through to a palate full of ripe blackcurrant/blackberry flavours. The 1983 was a firmer, more concentrated wine with its bouquet showing just a little mint, amongst a backdrop of oak, and a full, ripe, sweet palate with quite perceptible tannin, and again just a modicum of that regional mint character.

In many years I have placed the shiraz cabernet on a par with the cabernets because of the soft complexity of the fruit flavour, although I doubt that it will have the cellaring potential of the straight cabernet. However, shiraz has gone, and the many devotees of Chateau Le Amon will watch with great interest the evolution of the bordeaux blend.

I have never been an admirer of the semillon rhine riesling blend. The 1984 was typical: flowery and fragrant, and technically very well made (the juices were cold-settled with pectic enzyme, and the finished wine has only 1.6 grams per litre of sugar, in itself highly commendable), but they seem to me to lack character. Perhaps I am mentally put off by the unlikely blend of semillon and rhine riesling (a marriage of convenience if ever there was one), but the net result is the same.

HARCOURT VALLEY VINEYARDS
CALDER HIGHWAY, HARCOURT

I am never sure which is the chicken, and which the egg; which the horse, which the cart. Either way, the result is that the wine industry is thickly populated with people who are more than ordinarily pleasant. Ray and Barbara Broughton are among the nicest of them all. Ray Broughton was a senior mechanical engineer with TAA who, having passed the magic milestone of 50, decided there had to be more to life. On a spur-of-the-moment decision he quit his job and, with Barbara, started looking for an alternative lifestyle.

The possibility of an omelette restaurant considered and discarded, their thoughts turned to farming and in particular to viticulture. A six months' search led in 1976 to the purchase of a small weatherboard farmhouse and 10 hectares of an abandoned apple and pear orchard. Four hectares of grapes (principally cabernet sauvignon, with a little rhine riesling and shiraz) were planted, and a winery, built from locally hewn granite, slowly took shape. The first commercial vintage took place in 1980, and Harcourt Valley opened its doors to the public late in 1981.

Included in the wines from that vintage were 213 bottles made from a quarter of a tonne of grapes. Nothing so unusual in that, you might say, until you learn that all of the grapes (and of course all of the wine) came from a single vine. The precise age of the vine is not known, but it was planted within a few years of the construction of the 1849 cottage at Harcourt which the vine now surrounds. Hail wiped out the 1981 vintage, and drought took its toll of the 1983, but even in that year a substantial quantity of the wine was made. The vine is thought to have survived phylloxera because it was a single vine planted some distance away from the nearest vineyard.

A little distance away the Broughtons' niece Ruth Norris and her husband David have another four-hectare vineyard planted to 1.5 hectares of chardonnay and 0.25 hectare of pinot noir in bearing, with cabernet sauvignon, malbec and merlot planted recently. The Faraday Estate, as it is called, provided the fruit for Harcourt Valley's first chardonnay in 1984. Only 200 cases were made, but it was a creditable effort. The 1982 Rhine Riesling was even better: while showing just a very few signs of oxidation, it had rich, full, soft lime-camphor flavours on both bouquet and palate. Perhaps not surprisingly, the wine had some of the fruit character evident in the Balgownie rhine rieslings.

However, Harcourt Valley's strength lies with its cabernets. One or two have shown the variability that is part and parcel of the small winery, particularly where the winemakers are completely self-taught. Thus I did not like the 1981 Cabernet Sauvignon at all, but both the 1982 and 1983 were excellent wines. The 1982 won a silver medal at the 1983 Victorian Wines Show; the 1983 had the rich, deep, concentrated minty-cassis regional flavours which seem to develop if the grapes are allowed to ripen fully. Less than 1000 bottles were made, thanks to the drought, but the 1984 and subsequent vintages will be available in far larger quantities. A winery well worth a visit.

HEATHCOTE WINERY
183 HIGH STREET, HEATHCOTE

Heathcote was established in 1978 by Ken and Doris Tudhope. Right from the outset they set about things with both flair and purpose. The 14-hectare vineyard, established on a strip of excellent red volcanic soil, is planted to chardonnay, traminer, chenin blanc and pinot noir; while cabernet sauvignon and shiraz are purchased from local growers. A modern and well-equipped winery was built, with an ultimate capacity of 200 tonnes; and the Tudhopes' daughter, Elaine, commenced the Riverina College of Advanced Education wine diploma course by correspondence. Dr Tony Jordan of Oenotec was retained as consultant.

Although it was intended, fleetingly, as a retirement occupation for Dr Tudhope, a Melbourne veterinary surgeon, he was more than slightly surprised when the Commissioner of Taxation sought to treat the winery as a hobby only and disallow all of the deductions incurred in setting up the vineyard. That, at least, has been resolved satisfactorily, but Ken and Doris's retirement has now been postponed for 20 years at least as the reality of running a not-insubstantial winery has sunk in.

The somewhat unusual varieties established on the home vineyard were chosen in consultation with Allan Antcliff, a noted wine specialist with the CSIRO; this also led to the establishment of one of the rarest of all white grapes, viognier. Only 60 vines are planted, and a small quantity of wine will be made from them in 1985.

The Heathcote varietal white wines from the 1981, 1982 and 1983 vintage have been remarkably consistent. Overall the style is far lighter than the limited number of other white wines from the district. The traminer—as one would expect—shows the greatest varietal character, with crisply pungent spice on both bouquet and palate. Like all of the wines, it is nonetheless elegant and avoids the oily tannins which often plague the variety in Australia.

The 1981 Chardonnay was far too delicate, and gave the impression it should have been picked when more ripe. At 12 months of age the 1982 showed good varietal character, although it was rather light on the palate and seemed to need time. The 1983 Chardonnay at the same stage was rather swamped in oak, and difficult to assess. The 1982 Chenin Blanc was a clean, well-made wine which simply demonstrated that chenin blanc at the best of times lacks character. Something went awry with the 1983, and in an endeavour to invest the 1984 Chenin

Blanc with greater character, it was given some oak maturation.

The 35-tonne crush of 1984 was planned to become 60 tonnes in 1985. Heathcote is still to find its direction finally, but has every promise of becoming one of the more significant white-wine producers in the region. As at the end of 1984 it had not yet released any red wines.

JASPER HILL
DRUMMONDS LANE, HEATHCOTE

1979 was a crucial year in the life of Ron Lawton, then a successful food technologist and industrial chemist in the cheese industry. In his mid-30s, he and his wife Elva had two young daughters and the family was living the usual Melbourne suburban life. They decided to leave the city for good, to build a life together in the country. In that year they found a small vineyard near Heathcote which had been planted in 1976 to two hectares of shiraz and one hectare of cabernet franc. They purchased the block and, having sold their Melbourne house, used the proceeds to build an extremely handsome double-storey brick winery and cellars. Early in 1982 they acquired another vineyard planted to eight hectares of shiraz, three hectares of rhine riesling and 0.8 hectare of cabernet franc. The first block has now been named Emily's Paddock and the second Georgia's Paddock, both named for their two children.

1982 saw the first semi-commercial quantity of red wine made, with three tonnes of fruit crushed. Both in that and subsequent years part of the production has been sold to other wineries in the district, and only part turned into wine. Thus in 1984 more than half of the total tonnage was sold, with 1984 production limited to 1000 cases of wine (200 cases of rhine riesling, 600 cases of Georgia's Paddock Shiraz and 200 cases of Emily's Paddock Shiraz/ Cabernet Franc.

The first wine made (Georgia's Paddock Shiraz) won a silver medal at the 1984 Melbourne Wine Show in the open Victorian section for 1983 and older red wines. The first white vintage, 1984 Georgia's Paddock Riesling, sold out almost as quickly as the 1982 Georgia's Paddock Shiraz, in each case shortly after their vigneron's licence was obtained in May 1984.

The 1983 Georgia's and Emily Paddock wines are immensely deep and concentrated, opaque in the density of their colour, huge in their fruit. Yet they are not jammy. nor are they tannic.

MALMSBURY ESTATE
CALDER HIGHWAY, MALMSBURY

The Malmsbury Estate was established by Roger Aldridge as an adjunct to the Mill Restaurant on the Calder Highway just to the north to the township of Malmsbury. At one time Aldridge also had access to the Red Hill Vineyard, but that has now been sold to Rod Hourigan of Romany Rye Vineyards.

The Malmsbury Estate Vineyards produced their first small crop in 1983, and most of the wine is still sold through the restaurant. The Mill Winery, as it is called, will eventually process the fruit from five hectares of vineyards with cabernet sauvignon and shiraz accounting for three hectares and pinot noir and merlot the remaining two hectares. Only a token quantity of wine was made in 1984.

MOUNT IDA
HIGH STREET, HEATHCOTE

The famous Australian artist Leonard French purchased his Heathcote property over 25 years ago, but it was not until 1976 that, in conjunction with Dr James Munro and Mr A. Zuber, he decided to plant grapes on six of the available eight hectares. Four hectares of shiraz and two hectares of cabernet sauvignon were planted on the band of red soil which runs around the Heathcote area, and which has now proved itself without question to be magnificently suited to red varieties, and shiraz in particular. The adjoining vineyard of Flynn and Williams is another to share this red soil.

French and Munro endeavoured to make their own wine in 1980; since 1981 discretion has proved the better part of valour, and the annual production of between 1300 and 1400 cases has been made under the direction of John Ellis at Tisdall. The arrangements for the 1985 vintage were uncertain at the end of 1984 following the departure of John Ellis from Tisdall, but Leonard French hoped the wine would be made for Mount Ida at Tisdall for that vintage at least.

The 1982 Shiraz brought fame to Mount Ida when at the Victorian Wines Show of 1983 it won a gold medallion and trophy. I judged the class in which it won its medallion and my notes read "very, very rich oak magnificently integrated with and balanced by equally rich and deep fruit".

A subsequent tasting of the three wines made in 1981 and 1982 reinforced the outstanding quality of the '82 Shiraz with its voluptuous essence-of-mint characters. The 1981 Shiraz was a riper, more obvious style; while the 1982 Cabernet Shiraz is clean and full with some minty characters, but without the intensity of the 1982 Shiraz.

PASSING CLOUDS
KURTING ROAD, KINGOWER

Virgin Hills, Granite Hills and Passing Clouds: the names say much about the somewhat ungenerous, and at times inhospitable, climate and _terroir_ of the Bendigo region. Graeme Leith is a man of many parts—actor, writer, electrician, fly-fisherman and now vigneron, he also possesses the wry Australian humour necessary to withstand the vicissitudes of grape growing and winemaking.

The five-hectare vineyard was established in 1974 by Graeme Leith and Sue MacKinnon, on a coarse sand-loam river flat not unlike that of Blanche Barkly. The five hectares of vines are planted principally to cabernet sauvignon, shiraz and pinot noir, with lesser quantities of rhine riesling, chenin blanc and chardonnay.

As the name suggests, rainfall is very modest, seldom exceeding 475 millimetres and occasionally disappearing altogether, as it did in 1983. However, the vine roots penetrate deep into the alluvial drift in much the same way as at Blanche Barkly, and at long last the vines are starting to produce reasonable crops. The first commercial vintage was 1980, in which 500 cases of wine were produced. Production in 1984 was a respectable 1500 cases, and will increase further in the years ahead.

The Passing Clouds red wines are consistently at the far extreme of the peppermint-eucalypt style. The extraordinary thing is that the same (or, at least, similar) mint character pervades all three reds: the cabernet, the shiraz and—most unlikely of all—the pinot noir. I find this minty character increasingly difficult to evaluate: initially I was extremely attracted to it; now I am not so sure that it is not an unwelcome intrusion in many ways. Yet no sooner have I come to that conclusion, than I taste a wine such as the Passing Clouds 1982 Cabernet Shiraz: minty the wine may be, but it is also quite delicious. The 1981 was an equally outstanding wine; dense purple in colour in its youth, with smooth, intense, minty aromas leading through to a rich velvety-minty palate with superb weight, depth and varietal character. The 1980 and 1981 Pinot Noir also showed the vineyard/district mint. The 1981 was the better of the two, moving from a minty bouquet to a palate

which did show some varietally distinct strawberry fruit flavour.

Graeme Leith believes in a fairly warm, burgundian-style fermentation for his pinot noir, which in part accounts for the extraordinarily dense purple colour in all of the Passing Clouds pinots. New American oak is used throughout the winery which complements the sweet fruit flavours of the vineyard.

Anyone who is unfamiliar with the mint-eucalypt character of central Victoria, and who wishes to find out what I am talking about, can do no better than start with a Passing Clouds red.

ROMANY RYE VINEYARDS
METCALF POOL ROAD, REDESDALE

Romany Rye was established by Rod and Sue Hourigan in 1978. Since that time it has taken its fruit from a variety of sources, but the recent acquisition of the Red Hill Vineyard at Heathcote will both stabilise the source of supply and increase its quality. As at the end of 1984 Romany Rye had acquired the Red Hill Vineyard, a further 1.6 hectares at North Redesdale and 3.25 hectares at Redesdale. These sources provided a 1984 crush of 30 tonnes of semillon (with a little trebbiano), 15 tonnes of cabernet sauvignon and five tonnes of shiraz.

The Heathcote vineyard has the classic red loam over ironstone, while the Redesdale vineyards are volcanic basalt soils over gravel. Another eight hectares of vineyard are in the course of development, to be planted on close spacing to cabernet sauvignon, merlot, pinot noir and chardonnay.

The 2700 cases of wine produced in 1984 were sold chiefly through the cellar door, with some wholesale distribution through Woolcott Forbes. Wine quality has been variable, but this seemingly has had as much to do with the fruit quality as the winemaking. Hourigan has made some technically sound red wines, and once the new vineyards come into full production some interesting releases should appear under the Romany Rye label.

WATER WHEEL
CALDER HIGHWAY, BRIDGEWATER-ON-LODDON

Water Wheel takes its name from the water-driven turbine which until recently drove the flour-mill at Bridgewater-on-Loddon. Water Wheel Vineyards are a division of Water Wheel Flour Mills Proprietary Limited, the silos and mill of which rise above the flat vineyard surroundings and are still very much in operation.

When Water Wheel commenced replanting in 1972 the decision was taken to establish premium red varieties, with a selection of the best Portuguese port varieties. Cabernet sauvignon, hermitage, cabernet franc, ruby cabernet, mondeuse and pinot noir are familiar names; not so the port grapes mourisco preto, bastardo, souzao, trousseau and touriga. In 1975 further plantings of cabernet and hermitage were made, followed in 1977 by rhine riesling and chardonnay. All of the 10 hectares so far established are irrigated with water drawn from the adjacent Loddon River and yields average around 11 tonnes to the hectare for the reds.

A modern winery was constructed for the 1980 vintage with a capacity of 200 tonnes. German-trained winemaker David Von Saldern, who worked for a number of years with Yalumba, was responsible for the design, and it is, predictably, extremely functional.

The wines of Water Wheel have been consistently disappointing. The whites lack varietal character and flavour, with oxidation and stale characters also apparent. The red wines almost invariably show marked mercaptan and intermittent volatility. Looking from the outside in, as it were, it seems certain Water Wheel has major problems with its older oak casks.

YELLOWGLEN
WHITE'S ROAD, SMYTHESDALE

Yellowglen is at the furthest extremity of the area I have styled Bendigo and district. Situated at Whites Road, Smythesdale, just to the south-west of Ballarat, it is set in splendid isolation, although the Ballarat area did support grape vines in the last century. When Ebenezer Ward visited the region in 1864 he gave a detailed description of a flourishing vineyard owned by a Frenchman called Fleischhauer at Dead Horse Gully, seven kilometres east of Ballarat. About 1.5 hectares were planted in 1859, and had proved so successful that the vineyard was being extended to eight hectares in 1864 when Ward visited it. Plans were under way for a large winery and underground cellar, but the vineyard was apparently destroyed along with all the others in the Geelong and Bendigo areas when phylloxera arrived in the late 1880s. The only other present-day vineyard in the region is St Helena Sulky Vineyard which is now leased by Yellowglen.

Yellowglen was established in 1971 by Melbourne businessman and _bon vivant_ Ian Home. Home has been a long-term active member and office bearer of the Australian Wine and Food Society, and has a magnificent private cellar collection from all over the world.

Cabernet sauvignon (3.5 hectares) and shiraz (two hectares) were established between 1971 and 1975. Between that year and 1979 a little over one hectare each of chardonnay and pinot noir were planted, and a little under one hectare of merlot. In the early years the winery (completed at the end of the 1970s) had something of a split personality. The red wines were made by Gary Farr on secondment from Bannockburn (owned by Ian Home's close friend Stuart Hooper); while the sparkling wines were made by Neil Robb of Redbank. Back at his own vineyard Neil Robb made only red wines, although he had been well trained in the art of sparkling-winemaking during his time at Chateau Remy.

Despite quite considerable success with some fine, minty cabernet sauvignon and cabernet blend reds, and a few slightly less successful experiments with other varieties along the way, Ian Home was convinced that the area was particularly suited to making base wines for champagne styles, and equally convinced that the market for such wines was largely untapped and unsatisfied. Nonetheless, it came as a considerable surprise to the wine world when, in March 1982, Dominique Landragin left Great Western to join Ian Home as a partner at Yellowglen. It signalled a time of hectic growth for Yellowglen, and one of the most intensive and successful marketing and public relations campaigns ever waged in Australia. The success of that campaign is solely due to Ian Home; Dominique Landragin was fully occupied in endeavouring to satisfy the demand for the Yellowglen products which Home so quickly created.

The yellow label of Yellowglen swept across the country: in May 1982 the first release of the new _méthode champenoise_ sparkling wines (Brut NV and Brut '78 vintage) were released (wines, of course, which Landragin himself had no hand in making); in November 1982 the launch of Australia's first Brut Rosé in March 1983 the launch of Brut Cremant; in August 1983 the launch of Yellowglen's first 100 per cent Chardonnay (the wine entirely made and put together by Landragin); in November 1983 the launch of Australia's first Cuvée Tradition (a wine and a name conceived by Landragin); and then in November 1983 the release of the first Brut NV, Rosé and Cremant made completely at Yellowglen by Landragin.

The quantities of these wines were perilously small, particularly given the market demand. This of itself led to a finely balanced juggling act in the marketplace, but of course also placed enormous strains on the winery and its capital resources to expand production. In parallel with this Yellowglen had overnight become one of the more significant contract-makers for other wineries. The small- to medium-sized winery with high-quality base wine would send it to Yellowglen to be converted into champagne. Murray Tyrrell was one such, but there were numerous others. Tyrrell's pinot noir champagnes have received great recognition and show success, but many of the other better-class sparkling wines to come onto the market in the past few years have been made at Yellowglen. A rather larger customer was Mildara, although its use of Yellowglen was not widely known outside of the industry. The very successful Mildara Windsor Chardonnay Champagne was made at Yellowglen.

The decision to "merge" with Mildara in mid-1984 came as an even greater surprise than had Landragin's move to Yellowglen two years earlier, but in retrospect it seems to have been an inevitable move. The 1000 cases of the 1982 Chardonnay *Méthode Champenoise* sold out in two weeks when released at the end of 1983. That makes for good press, but for very bad on-going relations with restaurants and retailers—and the sparkling-wine market is very much a public relations market, with continuity of supply of paramount importance. For two individuals to finance the growth to meet the existing demand would have required enormous financial resources. While Ian Home was a wealthy man, Dominique Landragin was still at the start of his career. So, as I say, it had to happen.

Yellowglen is a tall poppy, and occasionally suffers from the Australian neurosis about the existence of such anomalies. But while other winemakers may occasionally criticise the wines, the fact remains that the public unhesitatingly puts Yellowglen first if there is ever a choice. There is no question that Landragin would dearly love to be in a position to allow his wines a longer time on yeast lees before disgorgement and sale; hopefully the Mildara merger will permit this in the years to come. In the meantime the wines run off the retailers' shelves and off the restaurant wine lists as quickly as they are placed there.

ZUBER ESTATE
HEATHCOTE

Mr A. Zuber has played a part in establishing a number of vineyards in the Heathcote region. He was for a brief time part of the Mount Ida partnership between Leonard French and Dr James Munro, but left that partnership to concentrate on his own three blocks, all situated within three kilometres of the town of Heathcote. The first of these was planted to two hectares of shiraz in 1972; the other two vineyards followed later and were also planted to shiraz and cabernet.

Zuber made the first wine in 1979 from shiraz, and persisted with his own wines for several vintages thereafter. Volatility was a major problem, and his subsequent decision to have the wine made for him (it is believed by Knights) seems a wise one. Wine quality should improve sharply as a result.

PICKING GRAPES, VICTORIA, c. 1920

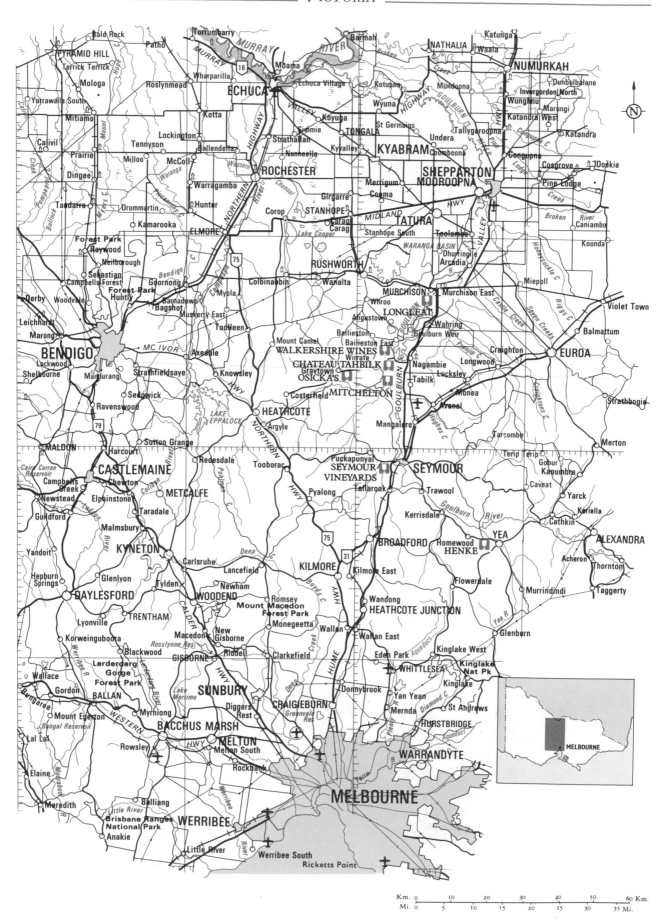

MELBOURNE

Km. 0   10   20   30   40   50   60 Km.
Mi. 0   5   10   15   20   25   30   35 Mi.

Central Goulburn Valley

The early history of the central Goulburn Valley is essentially that of Chateau Tahbilk; gold played no direct role for once. The area had been explored by Major Thomas Mitchell, who crossed the Goulburn River on 9 October 1836. Within a short time the first squatters arrived—then, and now, the fertile soils, abundant water and easy terrain of the Goulburn Valley made habitation easy. One of the first "runs" established was Noorilim, held by the Mantons from 1840. Noorilim was divided into two in 1842, and the number one run was named Tahbilk, the other retaining the Noorilim name.

Noorilim was subsequently purchased by Andrew Sinclair. In January 1860 he found himself on the provisional committee for the formation of the Goulburn Vineyard Proprietary, the prime mover of which was an energetic visionary named R. H. Horne. The proposal was that Noorilim Estate be purchased from Sinclair: a prospectus was prepared seeking to raise £30,000 by the issue of 6000 shares of £5 each, of which £6000 was the purchase price of Noorilim, the balance to be expended in developing the vineyard and winery.

The prospectus observed:

> That Victoria is a country eminently adapted by nature for the cultivation of Vines, is a fact that has long been generally known. The means we possess here of making wines of the most delicious quality, and better suited to the inhabitants of these colonies as a healthy beverage than most of the light wines which are imported, has also been equally well known to those who are conversant with the subject. The wines of the Rhine and the Moselle can certainly be equalled, but in some instances will probably be surpassed, by vintages of the Goulburn, the Loddon, the Campaspe, and, in fact, of the whole valley of the Murray . . . Besides the commercial benefits, the best sanitary and moral results may be anticipated, because a wine-drinking population is never a drunken population . . .

Prophetic words indeed, for Sinclair suddenly disappeared. Horne later gave this vivid description of the discovery of Sinclair's remains in May 1860:

> Nobody knew what had become of him. "Off on the spree!" it was said. At the end of two or three weeks the unfortunate gentleman's body, disfigured by insects, reptiles, and the native cat, and dissolving in the sun, was discovered in the scrub of the sea-shore near St. Kilda, where it appeared that he had wandered after having been hocussed by some brandy he had drunk at one of the evil villas of the suburbs.

The Goulburn Vineyard Proprietary was hastily terminated, and the promoters set about finding an alternative property. They lost little time; on 6 June 1860 the first committee meeting was held for the "purpose of forming the company to be entitled the Tahbilk Vineyard Proprietary"; by 1 August 1860 the company had been duly formed, £25,000 raised, and the Tahbilk run of 640 acres (259 hectares) purchased from its owner Hugh Glass for £5.10.0 per acre (0.4 hectare).

Once again, Horne had made much of the running (just what reward he received is not clear) but was joined by a successful merchant, John Pinney Bear, who like Horne did not believe in doing things by halves. At Bear's instigation Horne "advertised for one million of vine cuttings from all the Australian Colonies, which were obtained, the best of them planted by a highly competent vigneron, and 700,000 took root and produced grapes the first year".

By the following year 200 acres (81 hectares) were already under vine "all of them healthy and free from blight". The development continued throughout the 1860s; a corporate reconstruction in 1865 or 1866 saw the Australian Vineyards Proprietary Limited acquire all of the assets of the Tahbilk Vineyard Proprietary, with Glass and Bear having between them a controlling shareholding. After a number of further changes both ownership and management responsibility fell to J. P. Bear alone. Under his direction, and with Francois de Coueslant as winemaker and vineyard manager from 1877 until

1887, Tahbilk prospered mightily.

The "old" cellars had been constructed at the end of the 1860s: 300 feet (91.4 metres) long, they were built of stone quarried on the estate and timbered with beams hewn from the massive gum trees which flourished in the region. The "new" cellars were commenced at the end of 1875: the successful tenderer for the work was James Purbrick of Seymour, a nice coincidence as he was not related to the Purbrick family who ultimately acquired the property. It was essential the cellars be completed in time for the 1876 vintage as the previous two vintages had produced nearly 140,000 gallons (637,000 litres) of wine. In 1888 the company secretary wrote to T. A. Rattray (who had succeeded de Coueslant): "I am very sorry to hear that you estimate the vintage at only 60,000 gallons [273,000 litres]."

In fact between that vintage and 1925 the maximum production was 70,000 gallons (318,500 litres), but by the turn of the century phylloxera had started to take hold and production steadily declined. It did not devastate Tahbilk as much as surrounding vineyards because many of the plantings were on sandy soils. Francois de Castella, who was retained by the Purbrick family as a consultant after it purchased the property in 1925, subsequently wrote:

> There were at one time over 300 acres [120 hectares] of vineyard at Tahbilk. The stiffer soils succumbed early to phylloxera but the sandy lands long survived, and a considerable area had been reconstituted on resistant stocks. A nearby vineyard on stiff land that succumbed early to phylloxera was that of Frederick Egli, whilst at Nagambie, 6 miles [10 kilometres] downstream, were the several vineyards of T. Blayney, Brenzing, Braillard, and others that promptly fell victims to phylloxera.

For all that, Tahbilk had been a major producer of high-quality wine for 50 years or more. By 1890 50 hogsheads (1462 litres) a month were being exported to London, while the wines consistently won top awards at exhibitions both in Australia and abroad. Yet until 1955, when the Osickas arrived from Czechoslovakia and settled at Graytown, Chateau Tahbilk remained the only winery in production in the area.

Both the Tahbilk and Mitchelton Vineyards are established on rich alluvial soils, ranging from clays to sandy loams. It was the sandy soil which contained phylloxera at Chateau Tahbilk for so long, and which lulled both the Purbricks at Tahbilk and the Schelmedines at Mitchelton into a false sense of security as they respectively expanded and planted their vineyards in the early 70s . . . They took what was presumably a calculated risk, and planted ungrafted vines. Phylloxera has since taken hold and destroyed those plantings.

Rainfall is reasonable, but many of the Tahbilk vineyards are established above a readily accessible watertable, and yields from this vineyard are high. Vine vigour is indeed a problem in some areas, and a double-T trellis is extensively used. The Laradoc vineyards of the Schelmedine family are equipped with a variety of drip (30 hectares) and overhead spray (60 hectares) irrigation systems; with the well-drained soils, yields, particularly of whites, are substantial here too.

There are a large number of subregions in the district: Nagambie, Tahbilk, Mitchelton, Seymour, Graytown, Murchison, Strathbogie Ranges, Yarck, Mansfield and Mount Helen.

As with so many other districts an overall classification of the climate is highly contentious. With a centigrade heat-degree summation of 1548, and a mean January temperature of 21.2°C, Seymour falls towards the top end of the warm range in the Smart and Dry classification. It is true the Goulburn River has an ameliorating effect, particularly for those vineyards planted along its very banks, but with the notable exception of the Mount Helen Vineyard at an elevation of 500 metres above sea-level, the wines have a generosity in keeping with the abundant sunshine, which averages nine hours per day between October and March.

The Mount Helen Vineyard was established in the mid-1970s on the crest of a foothill of the Strathbogie Ranges. The grapes are harvested from between the end of February and mid-May, reflecting both the long ripening season and the range of wines produced, from a wooded early-picked sauvignon blanc through to botrytised rhine rieslings. The soils are fairly light and the very low rainfall makes drip-irrigation quite essential; but even with its aid, yields are low. By 1982, and the fourth vintage, average production had finally reached 5.5 tonnes per hectare, which Tisdall accepted as being close to the sustainable maximum.

The central Goulburn Valley produces a great range of wine styles from its eight vineyards; excepting Mount Helen, the red wines are both better and more plentiful than the whites, but generalisations stop here. Even though Chateau Tahbilk is but a stone's throw from Mitchelton, the red wines of each are radically different in style. This is due more to differences in winemaking techniques than to differences in the vineyards, although the latter do play a role.

The wines of Tahbilk are tannic, robust and at

times earthy reds which are in the mainstream of traditional Australian red-winemaking. The lighter reds of the winery require at least two years' bottle age, the biggest not less than 20 years. They are wines with lived-in faces, rugged and full of character and individuality. Those of John Walker at Walkershire, and those of Longleat, are cast in a similar mould, with the Walkershire wines quite outstanding. The wines of Mitchelton are poles apart: here highly sophisticated winemaking produces elegant, refined cabernet sauvignon which still has backbone but which slips like velvet down the throat three or four years after vintage.

This diversity does not diminish with the white wines: from the chalky and angular marsanne of Chateau Tahbilk through to the richly flavoured and cunningly wrought chardonnays of Mount Helen and back to the marvellous *tour-de-force* oak-matured whites of Mitchelton where marsanne, semillon and chardonnay all seem quite marvellous but disconcertingly similar.

CHATEAU TAHBILK
TABILK via NAGAMBIE

Chateau Tahbilk must have a special place in the heart and mind of any wine lover who has ever visited this most beautiful of wineries and vineyards. Set among the winding billabongs which run off the Goulburn River, it is an oasis in the hottest day of summer, and a somehow secure port on a cold winter's day. For those who have been lucky enough to experience the hospitality of the Purbrick family over the years, as I have, objectivity becomes quite impossible. Eric Purbrick, I suppose, must take the major part of the blame. Gentleman, scholar, lover of all things beautiful, he retains his impish sense of humour and the twinkle in his eye in this, his eighty-second year.

Yet a more unlikely figure to revitalise the decrepit and run-down winery he took control of in 1931 would be hard to imagine. His father, Reginald Purbrick, had a foot planted firmly in both Australia and England—even though he was the Conservative Member of Parliament for Walton, his son Eric was born in Sydney and educated at Melbourne Grammar. Eric returned to England for his university studies, graduating from Jesus College, Cambridge, in 1925 before being called to the Bar of the Inner Temple four years later. It was with this unlikely background that he arrived in time to preside over the 1931 vintage. Obviously enough, his technical contri-

bution was minimal, but he learnt quickly—from his winemaker called McDonald, from Arthur Pearson, and from Tom Seabrook and Francois de Castella. De Castella had already been retained as viticultural consultant, and had great faith in the ability of Chateau Tahbilk to assume once again its rightfully pre-eminent position. At that time the vineyards had shrunk to just 45 hectares, and the reputation of Tahbilk was such that Seabrook had initially refused to take on the distribution of its products. He soon changed his mind, but Eric Purbrick was still left with the task of driving around Victoria in an ancient utility selling wine in bulk from the casks in the back.

Both then and now Chateau Tahbilk was a major grazing property, which meant that Eric Purbrick was in charge not only of the cellars but also of the farming side. Life was made a little easier in 1936 when Sir Roy Grounds designed the present house, incorporating in one wing a still-surviving room from the homestead built in 1860 or thereabouts. The design of the "new" house is timeless, merging imperceptibly with the old, and featuring such extraordinary items as concrete bricks (of the kind made popular in the 1970s) manufactured on site. Quarry tiles on the floor were another touch 40 or 50 years ahead of their time.

With eldest son John running the farming side from 1955, Eric was able to devote more time to the affairs of the winery. Throughout the 1950s and 60s some extraordinary wines were made at Tahbilk; the private bin cabernets from 1962 and 1964 are still formidable wines with no hint of senility.

In the meantime in the early 1970s grandson Alister Purbrick had enrolled at Roseworthy Agricultural College, thereafter becoming the first formally qualified member of the family to preside over Australia's most beautiful family-owned winery. He gained practical experience with Mildara, working both at Coonawarra and at the head office at Merbein, before returning to Tahbilk to take over winemaking responsibilities in 1978. He immediately set about upgrading the virtually non-existent white-wine-making facilities. Tahbilk had always had a reputation for its marsanne, particularly after the 1953 vintage had been served to Queen Elizabeth II, and it was given various unusual epithets in consequence. Alister appreciated, however, that the facilities were quite inappropriate for the needs of the 1980s and, accordingly, a new white fermentation cellar was constructed in 1979 with a capacity of over 300,000 litres. Stainless-steel fermenters, refrigeration and all of the usual white-winemaking appliances were included, together with an airbag press.

The red-winemaking, however, continues to be made along deliberately traditional lines. The ferments still take place in 100-year-old open oak vats in the upper section of the old winery, and the wine is matured in aged 2250 litre oak vats in the below-ground section of the old original cellars. These wander catacomb-like into the arched drives, dating back to the 1860s and 70s, and in which the bottled wine is matured until its release up to six years after vintage.

The vineyards are not very much greater in size than they were when Eric Purbrick took over, but the varietal composition is very different and the yield very much better. There are 13 hectares of marsanne and shiraz, 12 hectares of cabernet sauvignon, six hectares of rhine riesling, five hectares of trebbiano, three hectares each of chardonnay and semillon, and two hectares of chenin blanc, all in bearing. New plantings, still to come into bearing, are of cabernet sauvignon (six hectares), rhine riesling (four hectares) and sauvignon blanc and semillon (three hectares each). All of the vineyards are established on old river alluvial sandy loam; it was this sandy nature which gave Tahbilk at least partial protection against the ravages of phylloxera.

The 1984 crush was 508 tonnes, and yields vary from seven to 12 tonnes per hectare. Although the rainfall is relatively low at only 558 millimetres, supplementary water is used sparingly and only on the white varieties. The older vines in particular have reached down to the underground watertable, and all of the vines show exceptional vigour.

For the third time in a decade Chateau Tahbilk has changed its label. The theory behind the new labels (the newest is no better than the one that preceded it) is that it differentiates the wine made in the old and new cellars. I do not follow the logic, and I like the new label no more than the two previous attempts. The original Tahbilk label, still happily continued with the reds after a brief aberration in the latter part of the 1970s, is a striking and original label. They should leave well alone.

These frivolities to one side, the white wines vary from serviceable to good. Marsanne is of course the vineyard speciality, and very occasionally rises to great heights. Of the recent vintages I was particularly attracted to the 1983; it may not be as long-lived as some of the other great wines that have preceded it, but it certainly has abundant honey. This characteristic flavour of marsanne, incongruously contrasted with a rather chalky texture when the wine is young, usually manifests itself only after a number of years

in bottle, and then only in the better vintages. I have no idea how the 1983 will mature. Prior outstanding vintages include 1975, 1969 and 1965; only the '65 has started to decline somewhat. In more recent years varietal semillon, rhine riesling and chardonnays have all made their appearance. The '79 Rhine Riesling was a quite lovely wine, which is now drinking at its peak. One or two very good semillons have also made their appearance.

The real strength of Tahbilk still lies with its red wines, however. Immense of structure, high in tannin, robust of fruit, these are archetypal Australian reds, yet in most years they avoid the baked/roast/jammy characters which so disfigure many of the red wines of earlier times. The peak of these are the special bin of either cabernet or shiraz selected each year. This simply represents the top vat selected more or less at the time the reds are due to be bottled; frequently it turns out to be a cask which has a substantial percentage of pressing returned to it. In consequence these highly individual wines are not always to everyone's palate. I—and I guess I am not alone in this—often find the tannin striking my back palate like a sledge hammer, successfully anaesthetising my tongue and gums for minutes thereafter.

At their best the voluptuous ripe fruit will live until the tannin softens, resulting in wines of extraordinary depth and complexity. Such vintages included 1962, 1964, 1965, 1968, 1971 and most recently (indeed currently) 1978. "Currently", because at the end of 1984 the 1978 Bin 65 had not been long released. Its gum-leaf/mint/leather aromas and flavours, followed by massive tannin, set it apart as one of the truly individual red wines available today. That tannin certainly needs to soften: I cannot see the wine approaching its best much before 1990, but I think it has the other characters there to do so if you do not mind the whisper of mercaptan which underlies that complexity.

Both the cabernets and the shiraz-based reds intermittently show central Victorian mint characters; the shiraz complicates the pattern further by every now and then exhibiting strong crushed-pepper spiced characteristics. These are marvellous wines; I remember one out of the early 1970s (not 1971, the allegedly great year) which I thought was absolutely outstanding, yet it was a wine which received little recognition elsewhere.

But whatever one's choice of style is, the Tahbilk reds cannot be ignored. Some people love them, others hate them. Because I love Chateau Tahbilk (and the Purbrick family) so much, I readily forgive the failures and glory in the successes.

HENKE
HENKE LANE, YARCK

Henke's Yarck Vineyards Estate was established in 1969 by H. C. Henke. It is situated near Yarck, a small town on the Goulburn Valley Highway near Seymour. The plantings, on hillside slopes, took a considerable period of time to take hold, and a number of the initial varieties tried have since been abandoned. The vineyard is now 4.8 hectares, with shiraz and cabernet sauvignon the most important.

In 1979 H. C. Henke's daughter Caroline and son-in-law Tim Miller took over the operation of Henke. A new winery has recently been constructed and future output will increase.

The first vintage was in 1974; the 1977 Shiraz Cabernet won the top gold medal in the Small Winemakers' Class at the 1978 Canberra National Wine Show, while more recently a very attractive 1980 Shiraz has been released.

This typifies the wines of the vineyard (and, indeed, of the district). It has strong peppery varietal fruit on the bouquet, followed by rich and strong mid-palate fruit with a very tannic finish. The colour is dense to the point of being opaque. A wine which certainly indicates a very low-yielding vineyard.

LONGLEAT
CEMETERY LANE, MURCHISON

Longleat was established in 1975 by Peter and Jenny Schulz, with their son Mark joining the venture in 1979. The vineyard is planted on the banks of the Goulburn River, 1.5 kilometres south of the township of Murchison. So far six hectares (shiraz, two hectares; cabernet sauvignon and semillon, 1.5 hectares each; and rhine riesling, one hectare) have been established, leading to the first substantial vintage in 1981. A further six hectares of vineyard are planned for the future, and the varieties will include pinot noir. Yields from the sandy loam over a clay base are good, ranging from nine tonnes per hectare for rhine riesling and cabernet sauvignon to 12 tonnes per hectare for semillon and shiraz.

The Longleat wines are made by Alister Purbrick at Chateau Tahbilk. Only a proportion of the annual production from the vineyard is turned into wine for Longleat, the balance of the grapes being sold. Thus 25 tonnes were crushed in 1984 and were expected to produce around 1350 to 1500 cases. Longleat did not commence selling its wine until the end of 1984, first releases being a 1981 Shiraz (85 per cent)/

Cabernet Sauvignon (15 per cent) blend, and a 1984 Semillon (70 per cent)/Rhine Riesling (30 per cent) blend.

As one would expect, the wines are very skilfully made. All of the reds show the pronounced tannin which mark the Tahbilk winemaking style, and also have rich mint flavours.

MITCHELTON
MITCHELLSTOWN
Off GOULBURN VALLEY HIGHWAY

I first visited Mitchelton in late 1975, not so long after the extraordinary winery complex had been built. The impact was profound; so profound, indeed, that I subsequently inadvertently described the top on the million-dollar observation tower as being like "an inverted witch's hat". Witch's hat it is, but inverted it is not. In this instance one man's poison was another man's meat, and it gave Mitchelton's indefatigable then marketing director, Brian Miller, a publicity opening he was not slow to seize. Many visits later the impact of Mitchelton is still substantial. Underneath the witch's hat is a seldom-used function room/restaurant with views out over the Goulburn River which runs next-door; there are two restaurants (underground, like so many of the facilities); a wildlife sanctuary; a walk-through outdoor aviary in the style of that favoured by zoos these days; swimming and wading pools; hostess winery tours (at least there used to be); barbecue and picnic grounds; and at one stage there was a chapel (again underground, but I did not see it last time).

Mitchelton was the creation of the late Ross Schelmedine. He was a man of enormous vision, but was somewhat unorthodox in his financial planning and dealings. Although some of his decisions were wrong, many were right. One of the inspired choices was the selection of Colin Preece to plan and lay out the vineyards, the planting of which commenced in 1969; a wrong choice was the decision to plant on direct-bearing rootstocks, ignoring the history of phylloxera in the region, and depending on the basically sandy alluvials on the Goulburn River flood plain to give protection.

Preece was instrumental in planting an enormous number of varietals for on-the-spot evaluation, a direct consequence of which has been the virtual flagship of the Mitchelton line, marsanne. Colin Preece was also at hand as consultant winemaker for the first few vintages. At his elbow was a then-young and inexperienced winemaker called Don Lewis;

Lewis has stayed with Mitchelton ever since, and is now its highly efficient and skilled chief winemaker. It is through his eyes that the history of Mitchelton since 1972 has been traced.

The first small vintage was produced in 1972. The fruit was sold to Brown Brothers, who released two individual vineyard wines, a shiraz cabernet and a trebbiano. 1973 was the first on-site vintage for Mitchelton, carried out in a partially completed winery, with no roof and tanks sitting wherever they had been unloaded from the trucks. The main wines made were a '73 Shiraz Cabernet and a '73 "Riesling", a blend of trebbiano, marsanne and semillon together with all of the other white bits and pieces from the 20-odd experimental varieties in the vineyard. Lewis recalls the wine as "delicate and soft, a little too much so for any long-keeping proposition, but showed potential".

1974 was the wettest vintage in the region for 50 years; somehow or other the winery was completed, but access was not easy. At one stage the mud on the front drive was 60 centimetres deep, and access past the front gate was impossible. Even the walk from the front gate to the winery was abandoned thanks to rising water, and for one week Lewis and Preece arrived for work by boat along the flooded Goulburn River. The nearly completed winery itself was totally flooded underground, not from the surface but from the underground sumps which were meant to act as drainage vents into the river. Not surprisingly, the wines were mainly light and mediocre, although the 1974 Cabernet won Mitchelton's first gold medal at a national show (Perth) with the assistance of some new oak. Two rhine rieslings were also made, one bone-dry and the other sweet; the latter was the better wine.

1975 was the year during which many long-term decisions were taken about the future of the 35 different white and red grape varieties then growing in the vineyard. The most promising were selected, and from that point onwards Mitchelton embarked on its policy of varietal labelling. The '75 Marsanne was matured in old oak and ultimately used as a sauterne base; a small quantity was kept unwooded and bottled for evaluation, developing the honeyed characters of a classic marsanne and encouraging Mitchelton to persevere with the grape as the source of a quality table wine. The rhine riesling was sold in bulk, while the cabernet sauvignon, bottled without the use of any new oak, was selected for *The Australian* Dozen. 1976 was the year in which the financial problems of Mitchelton were most acute: receivers, complex legal wrangles, and a continued absence of

the hordes of Melbourne buyers and tourists all meant that there was no money to make the wine, and the grapes were sold to other wineries.

If 1975 was the year of decision in the vineyard, 1977 marked the year of change in the winery. In that year juice filtration and clarification prior to fermentation, cold-fermentations and the use of carbon dioxide to prevent oxidation were all used far more extensively, and the first technically advanced wines were produced. The rhine riesling of that year was duly picked by the *Wine and Spirit Buying Guide* as one of the best new releases of the year. The '77 Cabernet Sauvignon and Shiraz were both light-bodied; any remaining bottles should be drunk now before it is too late.

1978 was an outstanding year, with perfect ripening weather. In the knowledge that the final decisions regarding the vineyard plantings had to be taken (decisions enforced in some instances by the then-rapid onset of phylloxera), a determined effort was made to keep every bit of varietal character in each of the wines. The rhine riesling scored the first major success for Mitchelton, winning the Clampett Trophy for best dry white wine at the Adelaide Wine Show of that year. Since South Australia regarded rhine riesling as its private monopoly, and also because no-one had heard of Mitchelton or of rhine riesling being successfully grown in Victoria, the award of the trophy to the somewhat germanic, richly flavoured wine (with just a little residual sugar) caused very considerable comment. The '78 Marsanne was bottled without wood maturation (finances were still on the tight side), but the remaining stocks held in the museum at Mitchelton have developed the typical varietal honey. The year also produced one of Mitchelton's best-ever cabernets. It has abundant varietal character on both bouquet and palate with gentle herbaceous overtones to the ripe, berry fruit flavours and well-handled oak. It won the gold medal at the inaugural Victorian Wine Export Awards in 1980, at which time it was readily available from retailers for $2.20. The story goes that at the time Roy Moorfield was negotiating to buy the balance of the winery stocks for his "Duke and Moorfield" house label.

The following year demonstrated that not all vintages are perfect. Light in both style and yield, it by and large provided better reds than whites. One notable exception was the 1979 Marsanne, the first commercial release to be given new-oak treatment. In August 1984 the wine showed most attractive rich, honeyed development on the bouquet and near-perfect fruit balance on the palate. It seemed to me to be at its peak. The '79 Rhine Riesling won six gold medals, and the remaining show stocks were released in 1984. The deep-yellow colour still retained some green tints, while there was big, soft, rich, developed fruit on both bouquet and palate. I could see none of the dreaded kerosene/flytox characters. The '79 Cabernet Sauvignon, while light, was very elegant and it, too, has aged well.

1980 marked a turning point in the fortunes of Mitchelton. The financial and legal impasse which had arisen was finally resolved with the purchase of the winery and surrounding vineyards by the Valmorbida family. Urgently needed money to upgrade the winery equipment was made available: a Willmes airbag tank press was purchased; the red fermenters were modified; other essential aspects of the winery were overhauled; David Traeger joined the winemaking team; and subsequently the Oenotec consulting team was retained.

The 1980 Marsanne proved that the '79 had been no fluke. My only complaint at the time was that, in Sydney at least, it was no more possible to purchase it than it had been to buy the '79. The subsequent arrival of Brian Miller in Sydney changed all that, but it was a frustrating period nonetheless. The rich, spicy, nutmeg-oak flavours blend so naturally with the honey character of the marsanne that I have always thought this line was more an exercise in oak handling than varietal definition. I cannot see that in the final analysis this matters very much. From the time the wine is released at around two years of age, the flavours have mellowed and integrated so that it is a harmonious whole, and one which has consistently shown the ability to improve in bottle for a further two or three years after its release.

The semillon of that year was a complete contrast, bottled without any oak influence whatsoever. It developed very well, but the decision now seems to have been fairly firmly taken to wood-mature this variety too. The 1980 Cabernet Sauvignon was a very rich, ripe wine, soft and with plenty of flavour. It probably should be drunk over the next year or two.

1980 also heralded the commencement of the Winemakers' Selection Range. Mitchelton has been fastidious in clearly identifying the source of all of the grapes used in its various wines; thus a 1980 Coonawarra Rhine Riesling (Winemakers' Selection) and a 1980 Coonawarra/Nagambie Cabernet Sauvignon blend came out under the Winemakers' Selection label of that year. Late in 1984 the Cabernet Sauvignon was still showing the influence of the two districts—the Nagambie fruit contributing some

spicy/leather aromas and softness to the palate; the Coonawarra a crisp lift of freshness and length.

1981 produced one of the best-ever rhine rieslings; due to continuing vineyard replanting, the quantity produced (and released) was very small, but the wine is packed with soft, albeit fairly advanced, flavour. The '81 Marsanne was also extremely successful. The nutmeg/spice characters of the oak are exemplary, and do not overshadow the fruit as in the case of the '82. The Coonawarra Winemakers' Selection Rhine Riesling is quite striking: a botrytis infection in the fruit resulted in an aromatic banana/pineapple/tropical-fruit wine of great style and richness. I am always doubtful about the long-term cellaring capacity of these wines; it was most attractive in early 1984, but I have not tasted it since. Of the two '81 Cabernets, I prefer the Coonawarra/Nagambie blend to the local wine, even though the latter has had the more successful show career (two gold, four silver and five bronze medals compared with one gold and four bronze medals). The Nagambie wine has a rather hard finish; the structure and flavour of the Winemakers' Selection blend is far fruitier and silkier.

Finally, the incidence of botrytis at Coonawarra gave rise to the first Winemakers' Selection Coonawarra Botrytis-Affected Rhine Riesling, a mouthful in more ways than one. Part of this wine has been held back for release (probably during 1985); towards the end of 1984 it was drinking beautifully with all of the depth, lusciousness and counterbalancing acid one could hope for.

1982 was a good, even vintage with moderate growing and ripening conditions throughout. The wines produced were generally a little bigger in style than those of 1981. As I have already commented, the '82 Marsanne has always been a little over-oaked to my palate; it will probably settle down given further time, but does not have the immediate charm of its predecessors. The '82 Rhine Riesling was basically harvested from 18-month-old vines, and once again showed that young vines, be they white or red, can produce floral, highly varietal aromas and flavours. A Wood-Matured Semillon was also released, and, like the Marsanne of the same year, shows more wood than fruit at this juncture. Without question the outstanding release of the vintage was the Coonawarra Winemakers' Selection Botrytis-Affected Rhine Riesling, which in 1983 won the Bert Bear Memorial Trophy for the best one-year-old white table wine at the Royal Sydney Show. It was magnificently intense, with acid, life and richness in abundance.

1983, and again 1984, saw the range of wines widen even further, with the Winemakers' Selection principle taken to its ultimate conclusion. In 1983 22 tonnes of rhine riesling grapes were purchased from the Pearce's Forest Hill Vineyard at Mount Barker, in the far south-west of Western Australia. The grapes were packed into small 12-sided cardboard boxes, specially constructed for the purpose, and transported in refrigerated trucks from Mount Barker to Nagambie where they were crushed and the wine was made. The journey took 32 hours, and I calculated that it was equivalent to driving grapes from the south of Spain to the centre of Norway. The resulting wine, I should add hastily, was worth the effort, with excellent fruit definition. Having mastered that exercise, to purchase semillon from the Hunter Valley was a mere morning's frolic, and this also was done in 1983. Mitchelton also buys selectively from regions in and around central Victoria. In 1982 it made a spectacular minty/spicy flavoursome cabernet from the Northwood Vineyard of Seymour Vineyards which is due for release at some future time.

1983 also produced the most successful Nagambie rhine riesling so far made, which has won two trophies, two gold and three silver medals. In spite of the much-publicised drought, the local vineyard was only marginally affected and the '83 Rhine Riesling shows none of the stress indications of some of the genuinely droughted vineyards. In consequence it is full-bodied but beautifully balanced, and it was this balance which led to its show success. I was judging at one of the shows at which it won a trophy, and it stood out as the unanimous choice of all the judges.

Mitchelton has established itself as a very reliable producer of high-class table wine, utilising a carefully thought-out strategy of sourcing its grapes from wherever it believes quality is available at the right price. Its future, as they say in banking parlance, is undoubted.

OSICKA'S
HEATHCOTE, NAGAMBIE ROAD, GRAYTOWN

The Osicka family arrived in Australia from Czechoslovakia in the early 1950s. Vignerons in their own country, they soon settled at Graytown, in central Victoria, and commenced planting vines in 1955. Their vineyard was the first new venture in central and southern Victoria for over half a century. The initial plantings were principally shiraz and cabernet sauvignon, with lesser quantities of crouchen and malbec. For many years plantings stayed at 15 hectares

but more recently rhine riesling and chardonnay have been established to extend the range of available wines.

The winery was substantially extended at the end of the 1970s, built into a hillside and constructed from handmade bricks. Small-oak maturation is extensively practised, although the majority of the casks are old.

The wines are pleasant, light- to medium-bodied and smooth. Seldom do they really excite, however. White-winemaking techniques have improved, and a creditable 1983 Crouchen was produced, holding out prospects for the rhine riesling and chardonnay releases of future years. Most of the reds released are cabernet-based, sometimes blended with shiraz and sometimes with shiraz and malbec. One of the very best was the 1978 Cabernet Malbec Shiraz which won two gold and two silver medals. The style of this and the other good reds from Osicka is diametrically opposed to that of Chateau Tahbilk.

Winemaker Paul Osicka has more recently shown his versatility by producing some very good vintage ports; at the 1981 Rutherglen Wine Show the trophy for best vintage port went to Osicka's, the first time in the history of the show that the award had been won by a winery from outside the Rutherglen area. Osicka repeated this success in 1982 and again in 1983.

SEYMOUR VINEYARDS
1 EMILY STREET, SEYMOUR

Seymour Vineyards had a turbulent history throughout the 1970s, with a number of changes of direction, name and ownership. The cellar-door sales outlet was situated on what was then the main highway, and the attractions of cellar-door sales were said at the time to have resulted in a number of wines of questionable parentage being sold. Even without these suspicions, the winery had diverse sources of fruit. The first vineyard, adjacent to the old Hume Highway, was originally called Glengariff, and has since been renamed Chinaman's Garden. At one stage it had 18 varieties planted, including rhine riesling, gewurtztraminer, sylvaner, semillon, sauvignon blanc, chardonnay and pinot noir. The second vineyard, some five kilometres away, is known as Northwood and is planted to cabernet sauvignon, shiraz, malbec, merlot and grenache.

The quality of the wines has been extraordinarily variable. The best put the worth of the vineyards beyond doubt; the worst raise substantial questions about the winemaking practices of the winery. The white wines frequently show marked volatile aroma and taste, with a very curious camphor overlay. Some of the reds are little better, stalky, harsh and aggressive, and utterly lacking in fruit. But Seymour can produce good wines. Its 1981 Auslese Rhine Riesling has considerable lusciousness and some evidence of botrytis. It is fairly soft on the finish, and does have a trace of that tell-tale camphor character which runs through so many of the wines. The 1982 Malbec is a very attractive wine, with typically soft, chewy fruit and a marked regional mint overlay. A 1981 Cabernet Sauvignon was of equal and not dissimilar style: rich, minty, berry aromas and flavours, with soft persistent tannin on the finish.

One thing is certain: taste before you buy.

WALKERSHIRE WINES
BAILIESTONE ROAD, NAGAMBIE

John B. Walker is one of those larger-than-life characters who seem to fill the room with their personality and to tower over mere mortals. Only the objective eye of the camera provides proof that he is not half a metre taller than anyone else, although it certainly confirms his wild and woolly visage. Absolutely no relation to the other well-known Walker wine family, he was born and raised in Yorkshire, England, although he roamed the world before settling in Australia and finding his way to a remote outpost beyond Nagambie towards the Rushworth Forest. Having grown tired of the construction industry in which he had made enough money to consider an alternative lifestyle, he purchased a 25-hectare block known as Grandma's Paddock on the Bailieston Road between Rushworth and Nagambie in 1975.

The following year he and his wife Megan planted one hectare each of cabernet sauvignon and shiraz. These have since been increased to 3.5 hectares, comprising two hectares of cabernet sauvignon, 0.4 hectare of shiraz, 0.2 hectare of merlot and 0.2 hectare of bastardo. The bastardo was planted in 1984 with the object of providing the base wine for a vintage port. If it grows well Walker will increase its plantings. A further 0.4 hectare of merlot is planned to be planted in 1987. Pinot noir was tried earlier and discarded.

The first wine, a 100 per cent cabernet sauvignon, was made in 1980. Walker made this and all of the subsequent wines at the small winery which he erected on the property, having learnt his wine-making from books, from part-time technical-school wine courses, and from attending seminars at Riverina College of Advanced Education.

The first commercial release from 1981 was a cabernet shiraz blend. Comprised of 60 per cent cabernet sauvignon and 40 per cent shiraz, this wine won a gold medal at the 1982 Victorian Wines Show. The surplus shiraz, made from grapes grown on an unirrigated vineyard at nearby Nagambie, was kept in cask and was entered in the 1983 Victorian Wines Show. I was one of the judges and well remember the discussion—if not excitement—which this massively rich and constructed wine caused. It went on to win the Hicks and Hayes Trophy for best varietal red wine in the show. At the 1984 Victorian Exhibition of Winemakers it was voted by the members of the public attending that exhibition to be the best red wine at the exhibition, winning the ACI Trophy for so doing. Given that Walkershire was a part-time exhibitor at the show, the win was all the more convincing.

In the beginning of 1985 that wine was still at the threshold of its life. Dense red-purple in colour, it has immense sweet and minty yet complex and deep aroma, and with a taste and structure which at first appears enormous but which really has quite delicate mid-palate fruit. There is a cocoon around that mid-palate of very soft, gently spicy tannin which provides the wine with its exceptional structure.

The beautifully designed labels, incidentally, feature *Rosa alba maxima*, the white rose of Yorkshire.

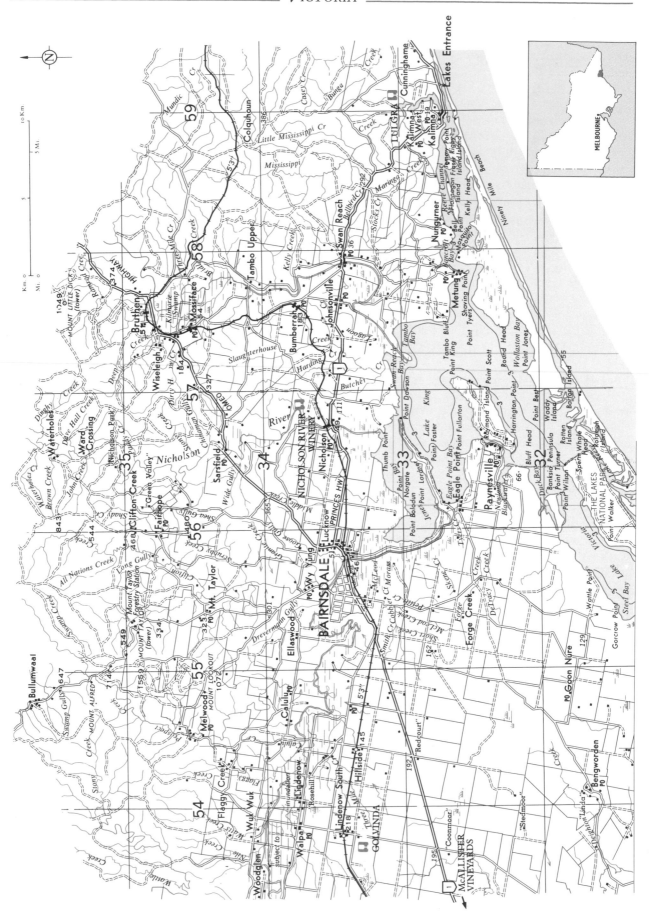

East Gippsland

The Gippsland region remains Victoria's most remote and least-known winegrowing region. Yet, as with so many other parts of Victoria, it produced fine table wine in the nineteenth century, and its rebirth in this century goes back to 1970. In the nineteenth century there were a number of vineyards, the most important of which were run by the Costellos and by Louis Wuillemin in the Maffra–Bairnsdale area. The Wuillemin cellars are still visible, although wine production had ceased prior to the onset of the First World War.

The East Gippsland region of today is a far-flung area, extending from Foster in the south west (just north of Wilsons Promontory) to Lakes Entrance in the east and Moe/Morwell in the north. As at 1984 there were 21 vineyards with a total of 41.5 hectares under vine. The doll's-house nature of the industry may be gauged from the fact that the largest vineyards are only six hectares in extent, and many are only 0.5 hectares. Four of the vineyards now have vigneron's licences, and several of the others have winemaking facilities.

The vines take a considerable time to become established, and the distance of the region from Melbourne (not to mention the scattered nature of the developments within it) seems to suggest it will be some time yet before its future can be regarded as assured. Nonetheless, it has demonstrated its capacity to produce wines of marked varietal character and considerable overall strength.

The first plantings (in 1970) were those of Pauline and Dacre Stubbs at Lulgra, followed by Robert and Ann Guy at Golvinda the following year. Travelling from Melbourne, the first vineyard in the district is Chris Hill's Carrick Springs Vineyard, commenced in 1978. With six hectares of vines (chardonnay, pinot noir, muller-thurgau, traminer, cabernet sauvignon and malbec) it is also one of the largest. It has its own winery but, as at the start of 1985, no licence had been obtained.

Due north of Carrick Springs at Moe, Stewart Mair has two hectares of cabernet sauvignon, merlot and cabernet franc at Galville Vineyard, previously called Coalville Vineyards. Dr Gordon MacIntosh has two hectares of chardonnay, sauvignon blanc and pinot noir near Briagolong, close to the site of the Wuillemin cellars. He has made several very good pinot noirs, one of which was the runner-up to the 1983 Yeringberg Pinot Noir at the 1984 Lilydale show. Dr MacIntosh produces under the name Parish Wines. Close by P. & M. Waters have a 0.5-hectare planting of rhine riesling, shiraz and cabernet sauvignon.

Due south of Briagolong is Maffra; here George and Jill Wisley have Tanjil Wines with two hectares planted to merlot and rhine riesling and a similar total area of merlot, cabernet franc and cabernet sauvignon. These grapes have been sold to Hickinbotham Winemakers, and a 1984 Rhine Riesling was released under the Hickinbotham Winemakers' label.

At the eastern end of the district is C. & M. Levis's Clifton Valley Vineyard with 0.5 hectare planted to pinot noir, merlot and cabernet sauvignon; I. & S. Roberts's vineyard near Nicholson with sauvignon blanc; and at Lakes Entrance M. & M. Winfield have one hectare planted to an extraordinary range of varieties.

At least one major Australian wine company has looked closely at the district with the thought of establishing a large vineyard there; others may do so in the future. Unless and until that happens it seems certain that the rate of development will be very slow, and that the wineries will be heavily dependent on cellar-door sales. Whether these will be sufficiently large to support a fully commercial operation is far from certain. The one saving grace is that wine quality is not in doubt.

GOLVINDA
RMB 4635, LINDENON SOUTH, via BAIRNSDALE

Golvinda was established in 1971 by Robert and Ann Guy. Guy is the only fully qualified winemaker in the district, but has always had a detached if not quixotic view of the region, and has been extremely reticent about promoting either his own wines or the potential of the district as a whole. Yet paradoxically he came to East Gippsland only after a long and painstaking search. He graduated from Roseworthy in 1965, and gained practical experience working at Kaiser Stuhl before setting sail on a 10-year trip around the wine world. In this time he worked in England, Switzerland and Russia before proceeding to oversee the building of a winery in Hyderabad, India. On returning to South Australia, where his family have grown grapes for generations, he carried out a painstaking analysis of meteorological data from all over Australia before choosing Gippsland.

Golvinda has in excess of six hectares planted including shiraz, semillon, cabernet sauvignon, rhine riesling and sauvignon blanc. Output of around 1500 cases a year is available only at cellar door and by mailing list. The quality of some of the early wines has attracted favourable comment.

LULGRA
LAKES ENTRANCE–BAIRNSDALE ROAD, LAKES ENTRANCE

As I have said earlier, Pauline and Dacre Stubbs were the first vignerons in the region (in 1970). However, it seemed almost certain at the start of 1985 that Lulgra would be sold to their next-door neighbours, Herbert and Andrew Smith, who have a separate four-hectare vineyard planted to traminer, pinot noir, chardonnay, rhine riesling and frontignac. These varieties will complement to perfection the 2.5 hectares of cabernet sauvignon, crouchen and sauvignon blanc comprising the original Lulgra plantings.

A 1979 Lulgra Sauvignon Blanc provided early evidence of the suitability of this variety to the Gippsland district.

McALLISTER VINEYARDS
GOLDEN BEACH ROAD, LONGFORD

Peter Edwards established McAllister Vineyards in 1975, planting two hectares to the classic Bordeaux mixture of cabernet sauvignon, cabernet franc, merlot and petite verdot. The last is an extremely rare variety in Australia, which has gone out of favour in Bordeaux, but which was once an important part of red-winemaking in that district.

All wines are sold by cellar door and mailing list.

NICHOLSON RIVER WINERY
LAKES ENTRANCE–BAIRNSDALE ROAD, BAIRNSDALE

Ken Eckersley and his family came to the Gippsland region in 1977, and planted the first of their four-hectare vineyard in 1978. Ken Eckersley, a science teacher (with a science degree) had been "fiddling around" with fruit-based wines for 12 years, and the possibility of grape growing was one of the reasons for the move to Gippsland.

Eckersley is now president of the Gippsland Viticultural Association, and will complete his wine science degree from Riverina College (undertaken by correspondence) in 1986. He candidly admits that he would have found things very difficult without the benefits of that course, pointing to the extra problems which confront the part-time vigneron in isolated areas. In fact since the start of 1984 he has been no longer part-time: he then gave up his position as a government social worker and his only interests outside the winery are as a part-time marriage guidance counsellor.

He has made some of the best wines so far to come out of Nicholson River. A beautifully flavoured 1983 Cabernet Sauvignon (matured in new French oak) and an equally attractive 1983 Chardonnay (likewise matured in new oak) were the high points of the 1983 vintage, while he is more than happy with his 1984 Cabernet Sauvignon and 1984 Semillon.

FORGE AND COOPERAGE, VICTORIA, 1880s

TARCOOLA

HICKINBOTHAM
WINEMAKERS

Lara
Lake

Lara

Kia Ora

Golf course

Sewerage
channels

Sewerage Farm

Ruin

Kirk Point

The Sand-Hummocks

BANNOCKBURN
CLYDE PARK

Bannockburn

Beulah

Moorabool

Sutherland Creek

Ballarat

Bruce

River

Geelong

Coutie

Gheringhap RAILWAY

Batesford

IDYLL VINEYARD

INNISFALL

Ruin

Subject
to inundation

Private railway

NORLANE

North
Shore

GEELONG
NORTH

GEELONG
WEST

Fyansford

Highton

GEELONG

BELMONT

Gnarwarre

"Airlie"

MOUNT
MORIAC

Waurn

"Waury"

Waurn Ponds
HIGHWAY

PRINCE ALBERT VINEYARD

Fire tower

Moriac

"Ellenbrae"

Modewarre

Paraparap

Merrigig

"Bongongo" Channel

Creek

Spring

Bellbrae

Golf links

BALD HILLS

Golf course

Fire tower

Anglesea

Urquhart Bluff

Aireys Inlet

Point Roadknight

Ingoldsby Reef

Black Rock

Point Addis

Bell Beach

Half Moon Bay

Rocky Point

Point Danger

Torquay

Zealy Bay

Lambidgee

Breamlea

Freshwater Creek

Mount
Duneed

MOUNT DUNEED

Grovedale

Marshall

Moolap

Leopold

Racecourse
(disused)

Reedy Lake

Lake
Conneware

Connewarre

Embankment

Levee

Ruin

CORIO

BAY

Avalon Airfield

Ruin

Corio

Subject to inundation

Salt
beds

Bird Rock

Point Lillias

South
Channel

South Channel

Hopetoun Channel
Point Henry

Stingaree
Bay

Beacon

Botanical gardens

Salt beds

Geelong

Point Wilson

Snake
Island

Beacon

Clifton Springs

Jetty
(ruin)

QUEENSCLIFF

Wallington

Reservoir

Reservoir

Fenwick

Marcus
Hill

Ocean
Grove

Barwor Heads

Point Flinders

BALLARATE

BARWON

HAMILTON

BARWON
RIVER

PRINCES

PORT FAIRY

Mount
Moriac

GEELONG

Duneed

Thompson

Channel

Km. 0   5   10 Km
Mi. 0   5 Mi

N

MELBOURNE

Geelong

The Swiss connection with viticulture in Geelong was evident from the very start. Ebenezer Ward opened the first of his essays in *Vineyards of Victoria* with these words:

> I cannot more appropriately commence the present series of articles upon the vineyards of Victoria than by a description of 'Neuchatel' (or, as it is perhaps better known, 'Pollock's Ford'), it being, in fact, if not the oldest vineyard in the colony, at all events, the oldest in the Western District. It is situate on the River Barwon, about ten miles [16 kilometres] from Geelong, between the Fyansford and Barrabool Hills roads. The present lessee of the property is Mr. Brequet, sen., of Geelong; but Mr. D. Pettavel was associated with him in the establishment of the vineyard. Planting was commenced there as early as 1842, and it will, therefore, be readily understood that many difficulties were encountered by the projectors of the enterprise. I shall presently allude to some of them, which it has required the labour of years to overcome. The extent of the vineyard is about fourteen acres [5.6 hectares], and there are besides six acres [2.4 hectares] of orchard and garden. The vines are planted on a hill, which rises in some places all but perpendicularly from the river flat. On the one side of the hill, the aspect is full eastern, and on the other south-eastern. The soil on the lower slopes of the eastern side is a red porous loam, sparsely intermixed with limestone. On the southern side the loam is blacker and richer, and the vines thrive more luxuriantly; but on the higher slopes throughout the vineyard, limestone is more abundant, and it is fair to infer that if quantity of produce decreases, their quality improves.

By 1861 Geelong had become the most important winegrowing region in the State: 225 hectares were under vine, compared with 136 for the Melbourne metropolitan area and 85 at Rutherglen. By the end of the 1860s both Rutherglen and Geelong had around 400 hectares of vineyards, twice as much as the next most important areas of Melbourne and Bendigo. Ebenezer Ward describes more than 50 vineyards, many of which had wineries. By that time

so much wine was being produced that a system of regular auctions was commenced. De Castella records that the first of these was held in October 1863; 100 hogsheads (2925 litres) of wine were sold, with prices ranging from three shillings and elevenpence to six shillings and ninepence per gallon (4.5 litres).

A peculiar feature of the vineyards was that many were held by absentee owners, who let them out on long-term lease to their frequently Swiss- or German-born operators. By 1875 the area had reached the peak of its success: vineyards extended along the valleys formed by the Moorabool, Leigh and Barwon Rivers; on the hillsides of Ceres and Waurn Ponds; and thence to German Town, or Marshall, as it is known today.

In that year (some say it was 1877) phylloxera was discovered at Fyansford, not far from the town of Geelong. Public agitation grew apace and, in a somewhat nervous response, the government ordered the progressive eradication of all the vines. The "Return of Vines Destroyed" reproduced on page 168 tells only part of the tale: every vine in the district was uprooted, and, as at Bendigo, compensation amounting to £50,000 was paid.

It is generally accepted that there were no attempts to re-establish vineyards until Dr Daryl Sefton and his wife Nini founded Idyll Vineyard in 1966. However, in his 1942 address to the Victorian Historical Society, Francois de Castella makes the interesting comment that "Pilloud and Deppler still own vineyards, replanted subsequently to the whole-sale eradication of the Geelong vineyards when phylloxera was found there in the seventies".

The Swiss and German vignerons of the 1840s must have felt thoroughly at home. Drawing upon the influence of the adjacent Port Phillip Bay, and with the Bass Strait only a few kilometres to the south, Geelong has a distinctly cool climate—cooler than that of Bordeaux in France and cooler than Mount Barker, Margaret River or Coonawarra.

1881.

VICTORIA.

VINES DESTROYED.

RETURN to an Order of the *Legislative Assembly*,
Dated 18th October 1881, *for*—

A RETURN showing—

(1.) The acreage of Vines destroyed in the Geelong district.
(2.) The area remaining and ordered to be destroyed.
(3.) The area not ordered to be destroyed.
(4.) The acreage destroyed in each vineyard, and the amount paid to each owner.

(Mr. Levien.)

Ordered by the Legislative Assembly *to be printed, 29th November* 1881.

(1.) The approximate acreage of Vines destroyed in the Geelong district :—527¾ acres.
(2.) The approximate area remaining and ordered to be destroyed :—16¾ acres.
(3.) The approximate area not ordered to be destroyed :—232 acres.
(4.) The acreage destroyed in each vineyard, and the amount paid to each owner :—

Name.	Area (approximate).	Amount. £	s.	d.	Name.	Area (approximate).	Amount. £	s.	d.
King and Son	2 acres	72	0	0	*C. Farroway	1½ acres	35	0	0
S. Andriske	5 ,,	60	0	0	*R. Williams	1½ ,,	20	0	0
W. Goldbach	6 ,,	25	0	0	S. Thompson	9 ,,	210	0	0
S. Kerger	4½ ,,	10	0	0	W. Guest...	5 ,,	85	0	0
J. Deppeler	18 ,,	180	0	0	*A. Shetig	½ ,,	15	0	0
W. Sohr	1½ ,,	10	0	0	‡A. Hobbs	½ ,,	4	0	0
C. Craike	25 ,,	456	5	0	‡J. Cummin	½ ,,	5	0	0
C. Marendaz	13 ,,	120	0	0	‡J. Kundell	¼ ,,	1	10	0
C. McFarlane	1¼ ,,	60	0	0	*R. Lehmke	5 ,,	150	0	0
M. Rossach	1¼ ,,	60	0	0	*M. Moodie	½ ,,	20	0	0
G. Bennett	3½ ,,	78	15	0	*J. McCarthy	8 ,,	30	0	0
P. Dietrich	6 ,,	90	0	0	*J. Pigdon	¾ ,,	20	0	0
J. Deppeler	5 ,,	130	0	0	*P. Pettit	¼ ,,	5	0	0
R. Amiet	14 ,,	70	0	0	G. Patcholke	2 ,,	50	0	0
*T. Adcock	2 ,,	185	8	1	*L. Pillond...	6 ,,	390	0	0
†M. Buchter	10 ,,	50	0	0	Mrs. Pegg	3 ,,	35	0	0
J. Crook	4 ,,	35	0	0	*N. Price	1½ ,,	5	0	0
J. C. Cochrane	8 ,,	20	0	0	*C. Petres	2 ,,	25	0	0
*C. Dahmke	1¼ ,,	75	0	0	R. Renzon	¾ ,,	25	0	0
*P. Dare	3 ,,	30	0	0	*F. G. Schultz	4½ ,,	85	0	0
*T. Dann	½ ,,	30	0	0	*D. Smith	8 ,,	130	0	0
W. F. Ducker	14 ,,	40	0	0	*G. Tanner	½ ,,	15	0	0
R. Fletcher	12 ,,	33	0	0	G. H. Tuffs	2 ,,	25	0	0
A. Fischer	1¼ ,,	30	0	0	*J. Weber	35 ,,	825	0	0
*J. P. Forster	½ ,,	22	10	0	*W. Winter	3 ,,	80	0	0
G. Hartley	4 ,,	5	0	0	T. Wadelton	7 ,,	175	0	0
*W. Herd	½ ,,	25	0	0	*H. Williams	1½ ,,	50	0	0
T. Harwood	6 ,,	30	0	0	R. Williams	3 ,,	60	0	0
G. Hope	6 ,,	125	0	0	*C. Wyatt	11 ,,	110	0	0
*W. Hunt	7 ,,	130	0	0	M. Aeschliman	15 ,,	350	0	0
G. Hill	2 ,,	35	0	0	F. M. Bregnet	9 ,,	110	0	0
G. E. Junod	20 ,,	150	0	0	Gugger Bros.	12 ,,	150	0	0
*H. Johns	¼ ,,	6	10	0	J. Henry	10 ,,	50	0	0
*H. Kossack	4 ,,	180	0	0	J. Hunt	4 ,,	35	0	0
E. Hopton	6 ,,	213	12	0	*F. Lovett	1½ ,,	60	0	0
*G. Clottu and Co.	20 ,,	300	0	0	*G. A. Martin	20 ,,	450	0	0
*L. S. Huginunin	4 ,,	30	0	0	*J. T. Mulder	10 ,,	350	0	0
C. Maurer	6 ,,	112	12	0	F. Parsons	6 ,,	30	0	0
D. Thompson	8 ,,	200	0	0	L. Schifferle	8 ,,	350	0	0
J. Jampen	9 ,,	180	0	0	G. Goldbach	2 ,,	...		
*J. H. Dardel	8 ,,	70	0	0	J. Ball	8 ,,	...		
H. Brocter	6 ,,	70	0	0	J. Hammerley	3½ ,,	90	0	0
J. Hammerly	7 ,,	210	0	0					
*J. Rau	1½ ,,	40	0	0		527¾ acres	8,996	2	1
*B. Evans	7 ,,	200	0	0					

* Included eradication. † Nursery stock exclusively. ‡ Principally garden vines.

[*Approximate Cost of Paper*.—Preparation, Nil: Printing (775 copies), £2 5s. 0d.]

By Authority: JOHN FERRES, Government Printer, Melbourne.

C.—No. 3.

Geelong's mean January temperature is a positively frigid 17.9°C (that of Launceston is 17.6°C) and its centigrade heat-degree summation is only 1193. Indeed, as anyone who went to school at Geelong College or who has lived in or frequently visited the area will tell you, it is a bitterly cold place for much of the year. Antarctic winds sweeping up from the south can cause havoc at flowering, with resultant crop losses; while even the sea breezes from Port Phillip Bay during the summer growing season mean a woollen jumper is never far from hand. Finally, a high incidence of cloud cover reduces average sunshine hours (October to March) to 7.8, notwithstanding the extremely long summer days.

The rolling hills and valleys of the Geelong area, bare of trees and more often than not barren brown in colour, provide an inevitable diversity of microclimate; the west-facing slope upon which the Prince Albert pinot noir vineyard is established receives afternoon sun long after most vineyards are in shade. Aspect, slope and surrounding terrain are also important in determining the impact of spring frosts which, in the low-lying areas around Moorabool and Lethbridge, can be a major problem.

Soils, too, vary considerably. The most common soil in the region is an alkaline, hard red duplex; but Hickinbotham Winemakers at Mount Anakie enjoy a deep, friable, black volcanic soil; while much of Bannockburn and Idyll Vineyards also have dark-black soils. The moisture retention capacity of such soil is of critical importance: despite the frequent cloud cover, annual rainfall is a low 530 millimetres, although almost half (249 millimetres) is usually received during the October to March growing season. Thus, while Mount Anakie provides sufficient moisture and nutrient to permit yields of between five and seven tonnes per hectare without irrigation, Bannockburn struggled for years to reach even two tonnes per hectare, and irrigation had to be installed to provide acceptable yields.

Partly because of diverse approaches to viticulture and to oenological practices, there is as yet no clearly defined "Geelong style" in either red or white wines. The winemaking philosophies of Hickinbotham Winemakers are far removed from those of (say) Tarcoola or Idyll, while the wide range of white and red grapes grown in the district adds further to the diversity of choice. The unifying feature is the depth and strength of flavour which all the wines exhibit: the long, slow ripening period invests the grapes with great flavour and — in the case of reds — colour.

On the evidence to date there appears no reason why white and red wines should not succeed equally well, with the styles extending from wooded chardonnay through to botrytised rieslings, from fragrant pinot noir through to robust cabernet sauvignon.

BANNOCKBURN
MIDLAND HIGHWAY, BANNOCKBURN

Bannockburn was established in 1973 by Stuart Hooper, a wealthy Melbourne businessman who had both the patience and the money to conceive and carry through to completion an enterprise which has more in common with the glamour of the Napa Valley in California than the rather spartan rolling hillsides on the outskirts of Geelong. Visiting it in the latter part of 1981 was one of the greatest surprises of many months' research for a book I was then writing on the wines and wineries of Victoria. I had heard little or nothing about the winery outside of the district, and even in the Geelong area it was shrouded in mystery.

Hooper had established his first vines within the confines of the tiny town of Bannockburn in 1973. In 1975 he planted eight further hectares on the rolling hillsides of his main pastoral property, some kilometres away. A sustained programme of replanting vines — which failed to survive the dry conditions of the area — persuaded Hooper a dam was essential to permit supplementary irrigation while the vines became established. Even with the benefit of supplementary irrigation to aid the annual rainfall of 500 millimetres, yields remain exceptionally low, varying from two to five tonnes per hectare.

The vineyards now comprise cabernet sauvignon (four hectares), chardonnay (three hectares), pinot noir (2.5 hectares), rhine riesling and shiraz (two hectares each), malbec (0.5 hectare) and merlot (0.4 hectare). All are established on black and red volcanic loam over limestone; visually, the soil is outstanding, and the persistently low yields even after the benefit of supplementary irrigation are something of a surprise.

Gary Farr has been winemaker since the late 1970s; he and I worked side by side at the Domaine Dujac in Morey-St-Denis during the 1983 vintage, as Farr attempted to come to grips further with that most elusive of varieties, pinot noir. The Bannockburn plantings are close-spaced, in the best French tradition, and it will be interesting to see what French influence (if any) comes to bear in the future vintages of this variety from Bannockburn.

The large winery is magnificently equipped with

rows of gleaming jacketed stainless-steel tanks and the best winemaking equipment money can buy. The 1984 crush of slightly less than 50 tonnes was handled with consummate ease in a winery with a capacity many times as great. The 1984 production was therefore only fractionally over 3000 cases, all of which will be released as varietal wines. (The merlot is not yet in bearing, and I imagine will be blended with the cabernet sauvignon and malbec when it does produce.)

Even though substantial quantities of wine had been made from the 1979 vintage and onwards, no wines were released until 1982. The policy always has been to allow the wines to have an absolute minimum of 18 months' bottle age before release, and some longer still.

My initial enormous enthusiasm for the wines has waned somewhat. They have not developed in bottle as I believed they would, but why this should be so, I simply do not know. In many ways Bannockburn remains as mysterious as it was before it had released wine. It has a low profile in the marketplace, does not enter its wine in wine shows, does not submit them to magazine or newspaper tastings, and has only limited retail distribution. The enormous potential remains, and it must be only a question of time before it is realised.

CLYDE PARK
MIDLAND HIGHWAY, BANNOCKBURN

Clyde Park was established by Bannockburn wine-maker Gary Farr in 1978, close to the site of one of the famous vineyards of the nineteenth century. The vineyard is on the Ballarat road, 23 kilometres out from the township of Geelong. A total of 1.8 hectares has been so far established; cabernet sauvignon and shiraz in 1978, and chardonnay in 1981 and again in 1983.

Established on very deep-black and brown loam soils on the flats of the Moorabool River, yields are reasonable, although spring frosts are likely to be an intermittent major problem. The protected nature of the valley may also give rise to the necessity to spray constantly against downy mildew—something which many Australian vineyards have to contend with.

The wines are made by Gary Farr at Bannockburn, but distributed under the Clyde Park label.

HICKINBOTHAM WINEMAKERS
STAUGHTON VALE ROAD, ANAKIE

The Hickinbotham family took over from Maltby's Anakie Winery just one week before the 1981 vintage. Since then they have done more than any other wine-maker or winery in the region to bring publicity to it.

The Hickinbotham family must lay claim to being one of the most distinguished in the history of oenology in Australia, notwithstanding its relatively late move to establish a family vineyard. Grandfather Alan Hickinbotham was largely responsible for establishing the oenology course at Roseworthy Agricultural College, and was responsible for world-pioneering research into the malolactic fermentation and its significance in determining pH levels in finished wine. Along with others, he also established the critical importance of pH in determining both wine quality and its capacity for bottle development.

Son Ian Hickinbotham made the first two vintages at Wynns' Coonawarra Winery, wines which will be long remembered by those lucky enough to taste them during the last 10 years or so. Grandson Stephen is another distinguished oenologist, with extensive experience both in Australia and overseas, particularly Alsace. Grand-daughter Jenny and other grandson Andrew are equally talented viticulturalists, who have contributed significantly to the understanding of cool-climate viticulture techniques in Australia.

The vineyards are established at the base of Mount Anakie on volcanic black basalt soil over a granitic base, running into grey loam at the very bottom of the hill. Quite apart from anything else, they afford spectacular views back over the valley to the north.

The first vines were established by Tom Maltby in 1968 when he commenced the cabernet plantings, which now comprise 6.1 hectares. This total was reached by virtue of further plantings in 1972, 1975 and 1978. Three hectares of shiraz were planted in 1968 and 1975 and 2.2 hectares of rhine riesling in the same two years. Dolcetto and biancone (0.7 hectare each) were planted in 1968 and, for reasons best known to the Hickinbothams, have been permitted to stay along with 0.5 hectare of mataro. Chardonnay (0.8 hectare) and cabernet franc (0.5 hectare) are more recent plantings (1979 and 1981 respectively), rounding off what can only be described as a catholic selection of varieties.

Unusual though the varieties may be, the Hickin-bothams have not rested on their laurels. While the estate-grown material provides 90 per cent of the annual crush (excluding for the moment Cab Mac), the remaining 10 per cent comes from sources as diverse and unusual as Meadowbank in Tasmania, the Mornington Peninsula in Victoria, and East Gippsland, again in Victoria. Indeed, the Hickinbothams are constantly experimenting with small batches of fruit grown in a wide range of cool-climate central and southern Victorian areas.

The vineyards are pruned according to the practices of Alsace, with a high vertical trellis and with summer thinning and hedging where necessary. Botrytis is a reasonably frequent late-season visitor to the vineyard, but the late-harvest wines made by Hickinbotham Winemakers have been unconventional in the extreme. The wine seems to become active without leading to the raisined aromas of other regions, and the late-harvest wines are allowed to ferment to natural dryness. For both these reasons the Hickinbotham late-harvest styles are set apart from other more conventional late-picked wines.

Stephen Hickinbotham has also provoked considerable discussion among winemakers and academics by his belief that a certain amount of botrytis is of advantage in red-winemaking. He stands Canute-like, with a rising swirl of contrary opinion surrounding him. I do not know whether he is right or wrong; I do know that I have not been able to see any detectable evidence (adverse or favourable) of botrytis in some of the very good Mornington Peninsula wines made by him from grapes grown on Baillieu Myer's Elgee Park Vineyard (and which are said by Hickinbotham to have been partially botrytised).

The 5000-case production is spread far and wide, both in terms of markets (both Australia and overseas) and in terms of the number of different wines produced. The style of these is not only unconventional but also diverse, and it is difficult to draw together any overall conclusions on style except to say that the fruit is usually very well protected, with varietal flavours clear. The one major exception is Hickinbotham Cab Mac. If the Hickinbotham family never produced another wine, its record with Cab Mac would still stand the test of time as a major contribution to the Australian wine industry. As the name suggests, Cab Mac is made using the carbonic maceration process. In its most technical sense carbonic maceration is (and I quote Dr Bryce Rankin of Roseworthy College) "a process for making red table wines by preliminary storage of whole grape bunches in an inert atmosphere".

In these days of mechanical harvesting, grapes come into the winery stripped from their stalks, split and with a very considerable amount of juice sloshing around in the bottom of the skip into which the fruit is flung by the harvester. With this head start the crusher's main task seems to be the removal of "mog"—material other than grapes. Apart from a liberal sprinkling of grape leaves, this consists mainly of canes (or branches) from the vine, although one story from the Riverland tells of a picker's bicycle attempting to pass through the crusher. But whether the grapes be hand-picked or mechanically harvested, the first step in making a conventional red wine is for those grapes to pass through the crusher, transforming them into a porridge-like much called must.

It is at this early stage that the carbonic maceration process diverges from the conventional one. The whole bunches are carefully preserved and are placed in an inert atmosphere. This can be achieved either by replacing the oxygen with carbon dioxide pumped in under pressure, or by the Hickinbotham method of using dry ice (solid carbon dioxide), or by placing the grapes into a container which already has a small quantity of vigorously fermenting wine in the bottom. Whatever method is used, there must be a positive displacement of the oxygen-containing air which otherwise would be trapped between the berries. If this does not take place acetobacteria will commence to work and the resultant wine will suffer acetic volatility, one of the main dangers with using this kind of technique.

Maceration then slowly starts. This is not, as the word might suggest, a form of mechanical change, a mincing of the grapes, but the changes are unseen, occurring inside the grape without any change in the exterior. When a bunch of grapes is harvested it is alive, in the sense that the grapes are still growing or, if not growing, changing their chemical composition. They contain an accumulated store of oxygen, which they consume over the day or so after they are harvested. Once this is exhausted the grapes turn to their own sugar, which is attacked by a naturally occurring enzymatic process designed to produce sufficient oxygen for the continued survival of the grape, a by-product of which is the creation of alcohol. This process is called intracellular fermentation anaerobic metabolism, and continues until the berry is killed by accumulated alcohol.

The length of time this process takes is dependent on the temperature at which the grapes are held. At 35°C it takes eight days after all the oxygen is consumed; at 23°C, 10 to 12 days; and at 15°C it takes two or more weeks. The secondary chemical changes which take place during this stage of fermentation are exceedingly complex, but are critical in developing the distinctive plum-cherry-spicy-meaty aroma which so distinguishes carbonic maceration wines from their conventionally made counterparts. At the end of the intracellular fermentation the whole grapes are pressed, and the real alcoholic fermentation starts to convert the last 10 degrees or so of alcohol. The resultant wine has brilliant colour, although less depth than conventional wines, and far less tannin. The fruit has a perfume both in its aroma and taste which can be quite beguiling.

Hickinbotham Winemakers, in conjunction with Australian Consolidated Industries (ACI), have taken out a series of patents around the world covering methods of employing the process, although obviously not the idea itself. The patents cover the special zip-up polythene bags inside the wooden crates into which the grapes are put when picked, and a gas-release valve to regulate the escape of the carbon dioxide produced by the dry ice in the polystyrene boxes in the bottom of the bag.

All of this is a twentieth-century gloss on a winemaking method which must surely stretch back into prehistory, although Bryce Rankin puts the modern-day origin of carbonic maceration as recently as 1934. In that year a French research team was experimenting with methods of conserving table grapes for sale long after vintage, and in one trial stored them under carbon dioxide. After two months they were found to be gassy, alcoholic and unfit for sale. Being French, the grapes were made into wine, which was considered unusual but very pleasant. A more scientific evaluation followed in 1935 in France, and further research was carried out in Switzerland in 1938. But as I say, it seems to me the method must have underlain the first wine ever made. Grapes ripen in autumn, and throughout much of the prehistoric world winter was a time without food other than that stored in the house or caves of the inhabitants. Grapes were stored like other food and, because they are easily crushed—and their precious juice lost—no doubt earthenware vessels were used to store them. Presto, carbonic maceration, and by the end of winter wine if you were lucky, vinegar if not.

It seems to me somehow fitting that the innovative and technically avant-garde Hickinbotham family winemakers should have reached so far back in time to come up with a wine such as Cab Mac.

IDYLL VINEYARD
BALLAN ROAD, MOORABOOL

Idyll Vineyard is well named. While Prince Albert is a beautiful place, and the views from the top end of the Anakie Vineyard are quite spectacular, by and large Geelong does not have the exquisite beauty of the Yarra Valley. Idyll is an obvious exception. The house and winery look out over the vine-clad hills running down to a bend in the Moorabool River. Poplars line one side, and the textures and colours change with the seasons, always adding interest.

The site was planted to vines in the nineteenth century, and the remains of the old blue-stone winery can still be seen set into the hillside among the vines. Indeed, part of the inspiration for Daryl Sefton (a hard-working veterinary surgeon) and his wife Nini (an equally hard-working ambassadress for Idyll in particular and the Geelong region in general) was the fact that his great-grandparents, Jacob and Rosina Just, were part of the Swiss community who turned Geelong into the greatest vineyard area in the State of Victoria until the onset of phylloxera.

The Seftons were the pioneers in the resurgence of Geelong as a viticultural region when they planted their first vines in 1966. They now have seven hectares each of cabernet sauvignon and shiraz, four hectares of gewurztraminer and two hectares of chardonnay yet to come into bearing. The vineyard is established on dark-brown to greyish light clay soils, with some organic matter present, overlying a limestone belt. As elsewhere in the Geelong district, rainfall is a miserable 524 millimetres, making the use of supplementary water essential to keep the vine in balance and to produce even modest yields.

These yields are indeed just that, even when frost has not interfered. Cabernet sauvignon and gewurztraminer average four tonnes per hectare, and shiraz seven to eight tonnes per hectare. 1984 was an exceptional year, with production reaching a record 6000 cases, substantially in excess of any prior vintage. In that year 17 tonnes of gewurztraminer, 25 tonnes of cabernet sauvignon and 60 tonnes of shiraz were crushed. Vintage runs from late March for gewurztraminer into early May for cabernet sauvignon and shiraz. It is expected that the chardonnay will ripen towards the end of March.

To date Idyll has produced only three wines, all highly individual in style. Idyll Blush is a rosé which the Seftons are fond of and of which I, in all honesty, am not. It certainly offers an alternative to the traditional blander, slightly sweet rosés, and it has its own band of loyal followers. The gewurztraminer is given 12 months' bottle maturation before it is released through the cellar door, and a further 12 months' bottle age before it is released into the trade. At any one time, therefore, there are likely to be two or even three vintages available from one source or another. Once again, they are wines which do not always please the purists. Flavour and body are the main attributes, delicacy and technical perfection sometimes absent. Of the 1982, 1983 and 1984 vintages, I thought those of 1984 were clearly the best, and should be most attractive by the time they are released in September 1985. When I say "those of 1984" I am referring to both the conventionally fermented and matured wine (stainless steel, then bottle) on the one hand, and the wood-matured version on the other. The wood-matured version was introduced in 1983, which produced the least satisfactory wines of the last three vintages. As at the end of 1984 the 1982 had full, soft, if somewhat broad character, and was ageing nicely.

The cabernet shiraz is sometimes split into two bins, one left in oak for longer than the other. Each, however, received extensive oak maturation: the "normal" release around 20 months, and the special bin around 30 months. The Idyll reds have always had great richness and complexity. A number of judges, myself included, have seen traces of mercaptan in some of the wines. On occasion this has positively detracted; in the majority of instances, however, the fruit richness more than compensates. What is more, it seems to be a problem which is largely behind Idyll.

In 1980, 1981 and 1982 the Seftons produced a series of clean, complex wines. The 1980 special bin had excellent fruit/oak integration and balance throughout, despite the extended period in oak. It by no means follows that leaving a wine in wood for this very long period will add overall complexity; loss of fruit and some degree of oxidation are always a risk. Likewise, the oak may overpower the fruit. Neither of those faults occurred with the 1980 wine, which has excellent balance, structure and astringency. It should be at its peak around 1990.

The 1981 version saw the cabernet component increase from 60 per cent (that of 1980) to 80 per cent. The extra volume of cabernet showed in the wine, with complex grassy/minty aromas and flavours. I like this wine very much. The 1982 Cabernet Shiraz (cabernet 70 per cent, shiraz 30 per cent and 20 months in oak) was clean, with the usual excellent fruit/oak integration, with some minty flavours on the palate with a slightly lifted finish.

Idyll is one of the small companies to explore actively the export market and, in a classic coals-to-Newcastle exercise, have established a market for their wine in Switzerland, as well as Germany and England. Their Swiss agent, indeed, recently entered the 1980 Shiraz Cabernet in one of the numerous European wine competitions where it received a gold medal. In 1984 almost 25 per cent of the total sales were achieved in the export market. The Commissioner of Taxation notwithstanding, more companies should follow the example set by Idyll.

INNISFALL
BATESFORD

Innisfall is one of the more recent vineyards in the Geelong area, and when the winery (presently in the course of construction) opens it will be the newest arrival on the scene. The vineyard was planted by Ron Griffiths near Batesford on a hillside slope with a south-westerly aspect: 3.6 hectares have been planted to the classic varieties of chardonnay, cabernet sauvignon, pinot noir and rhine riesling.

MOUNT DUNEED
FEEHANS ROAD, MOUNT DUNEED

Ken and Peter Caldwell commenced planting the Rebenberg Vineyard at Mount Duneed in the early 1970s. In spite of the winery name, the vineyard is only 50 metres above sea-level, the mountains of Geelong being more in the nature of hills. The vineyard is established on a north-facing slope, with the soil basically composed of volcanic clays. The initial plantings were 0.8 hectare each of semillon and cabernet sauvignon; further plantings of sauvignon blanc, malbec, merlot and shiraz bring the total vineyard area to 2.7 hectares.

The elegantly packaged and labelled wines are chiefly sold by cellar door and are obviously in very limited quantities. One or two spectacular late-harvest botrytised wines have been made at Mount Duneed.

PRINCE ALBERT VINEYARD
LEMINS ROAD, WAURN PONDS

Prince Albert was re-created on the site of one of the famous nineteenth-century vineyards owned and run by D. L. Pettavel, one of the most influential Swiss vignerons of the time. When Ebenezer Ward visited the vineyard in 1864 he had this to say:

This vineyard, also the property of Mr. Pettavel, is situate on the south of the Colac road, about seven miles [11 kilometres] from Geelong. The site of the vineyard rises gently from the road and the vines have a full northern aspect. Planting was commenced in 1858, and there are now eighteen acres [7.3 hectares] in bearing; twelve acres [4.8 hectares] more, making an aggregate of thirty acres [12.1 hectares], were planted last season. The soil is, for the most part, a rich chocolate loam with a limestone subsoil; the plough was used in trenching, and Mr. Pettavel strongly recommends the adoption of that course, where practicable, for its efficacy, expedition and economy. The vines are planted at five feet by three [150 by 90 centimetres] to enable plough cultivation to be resorted to. And Mr. Pettavel maintains that, by this means, as compared with hand labour, he can keep a vineyard in better order at half the cost. He uses a scarifier and a small vineyard plough.

The principal varieties at the Prince Albert vineyard are Burgundy, Miller's Burgundy and Hermitage, Pineau blanc, Riesling, Tokay and Rousset. The two Burgundies are mixed, and a pure wine made from each of the other varieties. Mr. Pettavel has imported for this vineyard a wine press similar to that he has in use at the Victoria.

The view to the north over the Waurn Ponds Valley is as beautiful as any to be had in the Yarra Valley. The soil is of course still the same: a rich red loam over a limestone base, providing owners Bruce and Susan Hyatt with large yields. Indeed, since an extremely promising start in 1978 Prince Albert has had more than its fair share of problems, and at least some of these seem to be stemming from excessive vine vigour and yields. The '78 and '79 vintages were excellent, but even the '79 was a forerunner of things to come, being distinctly lighter in colour and body than the '78. 1980 and '81 were troubled years, but in 1982 the vineyard started on the road back, with the '83 better again.

Competition is increasing as pinot noir wine from the Yarra Valley, Tasmania and the Margaret River becomes more plentiful. To retain the very high reputation Prince Albert had in the last century and briefly held at the end of the 1970s will require continuing effort. The Hyatts are absolutely committed to quality, and it will not be for the want of trying if they do not succeed.

TARCOOLA
MAUDE ROAD, LETHBRIDGE

Tarcoola has been in operation for a number of years now, but owners Alastair and Hermione Scott are content to take a low profile. The vineyard was purchased and established as a semi-retirement occupation for the Scotts, who came to Australia after running a tea plantation in Sri Lanka for 20 years. On the other hand, as Alastair Scott once said: "I'm sure our friends just think we sit here and watch the vines grow. No-one seems to realise how much unremitting work there is. But when the work is done at the end of a spring day and you can sit by the river with a glass of wine and watch the platypus—and there are even koalas in the trees—you realise that there's just nothing like it."

In truth, the vineyard is on a beautiful bend of the Moorabool River, even if the occasional late-spring frost does threaten the cabernet sauvignon plantings. The vineyard contains 3.5 hectares of shiraz, 2.5 hectares of cabernet sauvignon, with about one hectare in total of rhine riesling, chasselas and muller-thurgau. The sandy loam soils of the vineyard provide respectable cropping levels, with the annual crush usually more than 40 tonnes.

The wines are somewhat old-fashioned: the reds are soft, fairly light-bodied and easy-drinking; the whites showing evidence of solids fermentation. Chasselas and muller-thurgau are rare grape varieties simply because in most viticultural regions they produce indifferent wine—I wish I could say that Tarcoola proved the exception to the rule.

WORKING A PRESS, VICTORIA, 1884

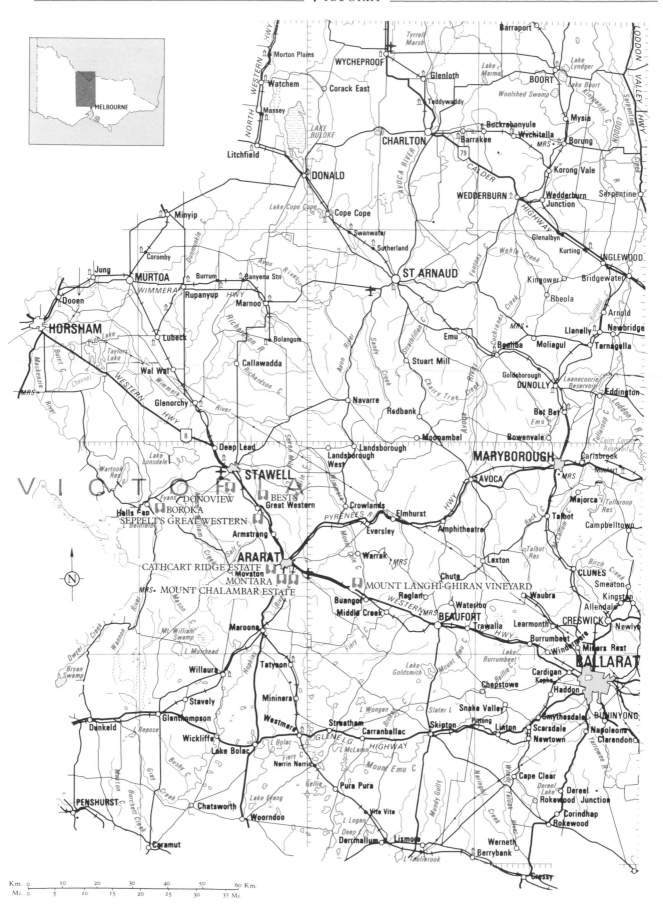

Barraport

Morton Plains

Tyrrell
Marsh

WYCHEPROOF

BOORT

Lake Lyndger

Watchem

Lake Marmal

Woolshed Swamp

Corack East

Mysia

Massey

LAKE BULOKE

Teddywaddy

Buckrabanyule

Borung

CHARLTON

Barrakee

Wychitella

Litchfield

79

Korong Vale

DONALD

AVOCA RIVER

CALDER

Serpentine

Cope Cope

WEDDERBURN

Wedderburn
Junction

Lake Cope Cope

HIGHWAY

Minyip

Swanwater

Glenalbyn

Sutherland

Kurting

INGLEWOOD

Coromby

Avon River

Kingower

Bridgewater

Jung

MURTOA

Burrum

ST ARNAUD

Emu

Rheola

Arnold

Banyena Stn

Newbridge

WIMMERA

Rupanyup

HWY

Marnoo

Llanelly

Tarnagulla

Dooen

Bealiba

Moliagul

HORSHAM

Lubeck

Bolangum

Stuart Mill

Goldsborough

DUNOLLY

Eddington

Callawadda

Navarre

Wal Wal

Redbank

Bet Bet

Glenorchy

Moonambel

Bowenvale

8

Deep Lead

Landsborough

MARYBOROUGH

Carisbrook

Lake
Lonsdale

Landsborough
West

Avoca

STAWELL

Majorca

DONOVIEW

BESTS

Crowlands

Elmhurst

Talbot

Campbelltown

Halls Gap

BOROKA

Great Western

PYRENEES R

SEPPELT'S GREAT WESTERN

Eversley

Amphitheatre

CLUNES

Armstrong

Warrak

Lexton

Smeaton

ARARAT

Kingston

CATHCART RIDGE ESTATE

Moyston

Chute

Waubra

Allendale

MONTARA

Raglan

MOUNT LANGHI-GHIRAN VINEYARD

MOUNT CHALAMBAR ESTATE

Buangor

Waterloo

CRESWICK

Middle Creek

BEAUFORT

Learmonth

Newlyn

Maroona

Trawalla

WESTERN HWY

Burrumbeet

Miners Rest

Mt William
Swamp

Lake
Burrumbeet

BALLARAT

Willaura

Tatyoon

Cardigan

Kopke

Stavely

Mininera

Chepstowe

Haddon

Glenthompson

Westmere

Streatham

Snake Valley

Smythesdale

BUNINYONG

Dunkeld

Wickliffe

Carranballac

Skipton

Linton

Scarsdale

Napoleon

HIGHWAY

Lake Bolac

GLENELG

Newtown

Clarendon

Norrin Norrin

Pura Pura

Cape Clear

Dereel

Penshurst

Chatsworth

Vite Vite

Rokewood Junction

Corindhap

Woorndoo

Werneth

Rokewood

Caramut

Lismore

Berrybank

Cressy

Km. 0   10   20   30   40   50   60 Km.

Mi. 0   5   10   15   20   25   30   35 Mi.

Great Western and District

Great Western was at the very centre of the gold rush which so altered the fabric of Victorian society. The lure of gold attracted hopefuls from all corners of the globe, and from all strata of society. The human amalgam which resulted brought a multitude of skills to the goldfields; while all were intent on amassing a fortune in the least-possible time, not all sought to do so by digging for gold. Others realised there was ample money to be made in filling the miners' stomachs and, above all, slaking their considerable thirst.

In the faraway district of Lorraine in France, 20-year-old Anne Marie Blampied and her 15-year-old brother Emile determined to run away and seek their fortune in Victoria. They arrived in Melbourne in 1853, and went first to Beechworth, where Anne Marie met and married Jean Pierre Trouette, a Frenchman from Tarbes. The three formed a partnership transporting supplies and provisions for the miners, and a few years later moved to Great Western where they acquired land and commenced a market garden.

Around the same time brothers Joseph and Henry Best moved to nearby Ararat, setting up business as butchers. De Castella comments that:

> Opinions differ as to who was the pioneer of the Great Western vineyards; some give the honour to Trouette and Blampied, others to Joseph Best. Records of early dates are lacking, but reference to the official list of exhibitors at the Melbourne Intercolonial Exhibition of 1870 gives priority to Trouette and Blampied, who showed wines of 1867 vintage, made from vines four to nine years old. At the same exhibition Joseph Best's oldest exhibit was 1869 vintage, made from vines five to seven years old. This would indicate that Trouette and Blampied's oldest vines were planted in 1858, and Best's oldest in 1862. It is held in some quarters, and seemingly with reason, that the real pioneer of the district was Louis Metzger, of Doctor's Creek, near Stawell, whose daughter Emile Blampied married.

Indeed, it seems clear that Blampied and Trouette obtained their cuttings from Geelong to establish their "St Peters" Vineyard, and that Joseph Best in turn obtained his cuttings from St Peters. In 1866 brother Henry took up 75 acres (30 hectares) fronting nearby Concongella Creek; he, too, planted vines. By 1869 the area under vine was 108 acres (43.7 hectares); Headdey and Salinger were other prominent growers. A few years later vines were established by Lorimer, Polo and Duver around the small settlement of Rhymney.

The gold soon ran out, but the vineyards prospered. Joseph Best built a substantial winery, and employed out-of-work goldminers to tunnel through the seams of soft decomposed granite under the winery to create the famous cellars of the Seppelt Great Western Winery of today. Best died intestate in 1887 while still relatively young at 57; his estate was auctioned, and the winery and vineyards were purchased by Hans Irvine for the considerable sum of £12,000.

Irvine was not only a skilled winemaker but also an astute businessman. He rapidly expanded the business, and was soon absorbing the entire production of the independent growers in the Great Western/Rhymney areas. But it was not until the early 1890s that he commenced making the style of wine for which the district became most famous: sparkling wine. Production started under the guidance of Charles Pierlot, a Frenchman who had learnt champagne-making in Rheims in France. Exports to the United Kingdom followed, but faltered and eventually ceased in the face of what de Castella describes as "unreasoned prejudice".

The Trouettes suffered a series of tragedies—coupled with a succession of poor vintages, their vineyard went into a period of decline before being sold in 1897 and eventually disappearing altogether. Another new arrival in the district soon took the place of St Peters: in 1892 William Thomson acquired a substantial property at Rhymney. Despite having no previous viticultural experience, he forthwith established a large orchard and vineyard, which he called St Andrews. By 1900 there were 23 hectares under vine; in that year William Thomson sold the property to his son Frederick Pinchon Thomson. In 1911 F. P. Thomson bought the adjoining Fairfield Vineyard, famous for its white grapes, and in 1920 added Best's Concongella Vineyard when it was offered for sale by Charles Best a few years after the death of his father Henry.

It was a time of change: in 1918 Hans Irvine sold his vineyard and winery to B. Seppelt & Sons Limited, concentrating winemaking in the hands of only two producers. The 1920s proved to be a very difficult time for Great Western: never a fortified-wine area, it found the market for its fine table wines had virtually disappeared overnight. With his back to the wall F. P. Thomson opened cellars in Melbourne and acquired a wine-and-spirit business in Ararat. His attempts to build a market were to no avail: St Andrews was sold and the vineyards pulled out, while Concongella went into the hands of a receiver. The Thomsons moved north to Lake Boga, but by 1931 were back at Concongella. The receiver had simply been unable to find a purchaser, and Thomson was able to redeem the property for a nominal payment.

For the next 40 years Seppelt and Bests had the region to themselves. Seppelt for much of this time was blessed with one of the greatest of all Australian winemakers, Colin Preece; and was of course but part of a winemaking empire which was centred on Seppeltsfield in the Barossa Valley. So the struggle was most fierce for Bests, who had to battle with a climate as indifferent as the market into which they endeavoured to sell their wine.

Lack of rainfall, spring frosts and soils of dubious generosity all combine to produce yields which can at best be described as meagre. Annual rainfall is 525 millimetres, with only 207 millimetres falling between October and March (less than half of the Yarra Valley). One of the saving graces is the surprisingly high relative humidity in the growing season, which goes some of the way to reducing the water deficit. Nonetheless, Bests averages only five tonnes to the hectare, a miserable yield given the average age of its vineyards and the care it takes of them. The soils on the flats are usually sandy clay loam overlaying clay, rising to gravel interspersed with sand on the hills. The climate is technically classified as warm with a centigrade heat-degree summation of 1551, compared with 1501 for

Margaret River, 1614 for Clare and 1548 for Seymour. The mean January temperature of 21.6°C is warm, but not overbearingly so. Its inland location, assisted by the hilly terrain which prevails through much of the region, ensures cold nights and cold early mornings, affording the grapes a respite from summer heat. Average daily sunshine hours amount to 8.3, putting any question of the grapes' ripening beyond doubt.

One of the most remarkable features of Great Western is the enormous diversity of grape varieties to be found there. This is due to two factors: firstly, the source of the cuttings was Geelong, which itself had a kaleidoscopic selection; secondly, phylloxera spared Great Western, leaving the original plantings unscathed, including the "Old Block" adjacent to Best's winery. Here a veritable fruit salad of 120-year-old vines provides a rich source of information for ampelographers such as Allan Antcliff, Australia's foremost expert in the field. He has identified numerous varieties, four of which are unknown elsewhere in Australia, and one of which still defies identification. These five are aubun, a black grape from the Mediterranean region of France; petit meslier, a white variety once grown in Champagne, and the few remaining hectares of which may still be used in champagne-making; piquepoul noir, from the Mediterranean region of France, producing a wine reminiscent of cabernet but which is used in Chateauneuf-du-Pape; troyen, which disappeared from Burgundy in the aftermath of phylloxera and which was called variously liverdun, la gloire or glory of Australia in Geelong, where it was widely grown; and finally a variety known only as "rough-leafed burgundy" which has defied all efforts at identification.

An oenological national trust treasure trove, the Old Block produces little fruit of commercial significance. But even in the main vineyards varieties are to be grown on a fully commercial scale which are all but unknown elsewhere. Thus Bests, Seppelt and Montara all grow chasselas (which is often labelled golden chasselas), a variety which is elsewhere in France and Australia regarded as a table grape.

Another "favourite son" is ondenc, a variety which is obscure even in its native France and which both there and in Australia travels under an amazing diversity of names. It used to be called sercial in South Australia and Irvine's white in Great Western, reflecting the fact that it was Hans Irvine who first established large plantings dedicated to providing the base for his sparkling wine.

Great Western also boasts the only commercial

plantings of pinot meunière in Australia; until the early 1960s it was almost invariably called Miller's burgundy, while the correct name is simply meunière, denoting "flour" in French culinary parlance. The name derives from the copious white hairs on the growing tips which give the impression the vine has been dusted with flour. It is, of course, the second red grape grown in Champagne, and together with pinot noir and chardonnay forms a part of almost all champagnes. Its use in Great Western has been for red table wine (Bests and Seppelt) and sparkling wine (Seppelt).

Mataro is a widely grown, high-yielding commercial variety given a special cachet in Great Western by the simple expedient of being called esparte. The foregoing varieties apart, Great Western runs the full gamut of the best varieties: chardonnay, rhine riesling and gewurtztraminer (although semillon and sauvignon blanc are so far missing); and in the reds, cabernet sauvignon, cabernet franc, merlot, malbec, pinot noir, shiraz and dolcetto.

From the cascading slopes of Montara to the wilderness of Boroka and Mount Langhi-Ghiran to the flats and gentle slopes of Seppelt and Bests there is an immense variety of topography and micro-climate to add to the diversity of the grape varieties. Yet by and large there is a coherent style, which gives de facto justification to the absence (so far) of any semi-official subregions. The white wines are long-lived, gradually gaining in stature and complexity as they age; the reds likewise, with a balance and equilibrium in the best vintages which come from perfect ripening. The wines have power and depth, yet usually show little or no aggressiveness when young.

Great Western deserves to be far better known and appreciated: Seppelt produces some marvellous regional wines, but these are lost in the plethora of wine labels that company has, and also suffer from the public's belief that the big companies do not make the best wines. At the other end of the scale Bests is a small to medium family-owned winery which has never sought a high profile and is content to market its wines in a conventional way. Perhaps the new arrivals of Boroka, Cathcart Ridge, Montara, Mount Chalambar and Mount Langhi-Ghiran will help lift the general awareness of the district and of its undoubted ability to make very good—indeed, great—wine.

BESTS
WESTERN HIGHWAY, GREAT WESTERN

Frederick Pinchon Thomson, the second-generation member of the family, did more than any other to establish the Bests of today. He was described as being "not merely energetic, but also a man of vision and ideas, unafraid of risks. A talkative man who made friends easily, he was fascinated by viticulture." "To my father," said Eric Thomson, "the sight of a row of vines was like honey to a bee."

In 1920 he took his biggest risk and purchased the Concongella Vineyard at Great Western. With the purchase of the vineyard came the name Bests; but before too long it appeared the gamble had misfired. A receiver took possession of Concongella, and the Thomsons were forced to leave. Eric Thomson picks up the story:

> 1928 and 1929 were very difficult years for my father, and he was forced to leave all his interests in Great Western. The Great Depression was now on. The fine old Concongella vineyard was still in the receiver's hands, but such was the lack of confidence anywhere, that nobody wanted it. Early in 1930, he went back to Lake Boga to see his now good friend Bill Milne, and bought a block of land from Australian Farms Ltd., through their agents Harwood and Pincott, solicitors of Geelong. It comprised some twelve acres [4.8 hectares] on the Kerang Road, covered with saltbush and carrying a dilapidated house, which was just habitable. The water supply came via a 'fluming', an open conduit from the Tresco pump. We called it 'Misery Farm', after the black-humour comic song of the depression years. I joined him at this time and we lived and worked there. The price was 140 pounds (280 dollars). The agreement was put in my name, although I had no worldly possessions, and was guaranteed by my father, who had no tangible assets. The terms were 10 pounds deposit, and the balance payable in 1935 at 6 per cent. These were generous terms, but in those times, agents were ready to obtain whatever money they could.

Before long Frederick Thomson and his son Eric had decided to move. Eric had located a far better six-hectare block near Lake Boga, which had a good house and available water rights. The price was £600, but only £20 were required as a down payment, with the balance being paid at the rate of £50 per year together with interest at six per cent. The block was initially called Evendens, but was soon renamed St Andrews, after the first vineyard at Rhymney. An unusual clause in the contract required the owner of Evendens to buy all of the available grapes from "the blockholders on the Scott area of the Tresco West Estate".

F. P. Thomson composed a couplet to summarise those years: "1929—not so fine; 1930—very dirty." That ironic sense of humour was to stand the Thomsons in good stead, but in fact by the end of 1930 things were improving once again. Concongella had not been sold, and somehow or other the Thomsons scraped together enough wine to satisfy the claims of the creditors who had installed the receiver in the first place. The family was able to return, and over the years built a substantial business from the two vineyards and two wineries which they now owned.

In 1960 E. V. (Viv) Thomson became the fourth generation to join the business, having graduated from Roseworthy Agricultural College. Viv and his uncle W. H. (Bill) Thomson run and own the business; Viv Thomson and Geisenheim-trained Trevor Mast share the winemaking responsibilities.

The Great Western Vineyards at Concongella have a splendid range of varieties. Those in bearing are shiraz (4.4 hectares), chardonnay (3.6 hectares), rhine riesling (2.5 hectares), chasselas and pinot meunière (two hectares each), ondenc (1.5 hectares), dolcetto (one hectare), gewurtztraminer (0.8 hectare) and mataro (0.4 hectare). New plantings of cabernet sauvignon (three hectares), merlot (1.3 hectares) and cabernet franc and pinot noir (0.8 hectare each) are yet to come into bearing. The vineyards planted on the flat lands around the winery are established on sandy clay loam overlying a heavier clay base, while the hill vineyards are almost pure gravel. The Thomson sense of humour came through in response to the question on the form I sent to all wineries: "Any special viticultural techniques?" The answer was "hard work".

St Andrews Vineyard plantings at Lake Boga reflect the very different climatic and soil conditions in that region, and also the different use to which most of the grapes are put. The plantings comprise muscat gordo blanco (seven hectares), sultana and grenache (4.2 hectares each), doradillo (two hectares), rhine riesling (1.7 hectares), grenache (1.6 hectares), chenin blanc and cabernet sauvignon (1.5 hectares each), frontignac (1.2 hectares), palomino and black muscat (1.1 hectares each) and colombard (one hectare).

Whereas virtually all (96 per cent) of the 170-tonne crush at Concongella is estate-grown, only 65 per cent of the substantially larger St Andrews crush is estate-grown. Here yields average 15 tonnes to the hectare with some varieties producing far more. It might be thought that St Andrews produces only bulk wine, but in fact it has provided Bests with a succession of very good cabernet sauvignon vintages, which have consistently shown up at comparative tastings to outperform far more expensive and theoretically more prestigious wines from the same vintage.

Concongella remains the focal point, however, of the quality-wine production. One of the more unusual wines of Bests, and—it must be admitted—hardly one of its highest quality, were the sparkling "Baby Cham" wines developed by Frederick Thomson in 1939 after he had noticed the habit of some drinkers of adding soda to their wine, particularly in summer. Baby Cham was a carbonated wine (the sparkle created by adding carbon dioxide under pressure to a still-based wine) and had no real pretensions to quality. Nonetheless, it was a major seller for Bests for many years.

The 1978 bottle-fermented sparkling wine produced by Trevor Mast from the tiny production of white wine left after spring frosts was a very different exercise, but in its own way no less successful. The '79 was made from ondenc, but in 1980 the base wine reverted to chardonnay; still only 200 cases were made, but this *méthode champenoise* wine is one of the first of Bests' wines to sell out on release.

There is invariably a tug-of-war with the chardonnay dedicated for the wood-matured table-wine version. First made in 1979 in tiny quantities, it was highly praised by wine writers and rapidly became something of a cult wine. None was made in 1980, but another very good wine (perhaps not quite in the class of the 1979) followed in 1981. The '82 was a fair wine, while the '83—drought-reduced—was fairly austere, and more in the chablis mould.

For as long as I can remember Bests has been producing its golden chasselas, as it is called on the label. In 1968 I purchased a few bottles of the excellent 1967 vintage from the winery; I still have the invoice which tells me that I paid 60 cents a bottle. The '62 Hermitage and Esparte was rather more expensive—70 cents a bottle. Both then and now the wine was matured for 12 months in old-oak vats before bottling; while not a truly distinguished variety, Bests makes an unusual—indeed, unique—wine from it. Outstanding vintages include the 1967 which I drank with enjoyment well into the 1970s; the '73, '77, '79 and '82.

In many ways Bests' Concongella Hermitage typifies the vineyard. The wine has never been particularly robust, although obviously some vintages have provided deeper, richer fruit than others, and the tannin levels are seldom high. The fruit has always had a special clarity, and in recent years that clarity has increased rather than diminished as wine-making techniques have improved and the use of new, small oak has made some contribution to the red wines. The 1976 and 1980 vintages have been the most outstanding in the last 10 years.

Finally, there are the St Andrews cabernets which, year in year out, provide perfectly made, smooth, easy-drinking wines, enhanced by a nice touch of sweet American oak, and show just what can be done with irrigated material.

BOROKA
POMONAL ROAD, HALLS GAP

Boroka was established in 1969 by B. E. Callaway and J. D. McCraken in the remote Halls Gap area in the lee of the Grampian Range. The winery was built in time for the 1976 vintage, and the very good medal-winning shiraz was made in that year. The winery then lost direction, and the vineyards were allowed to fall into disrepair until purchased by Bernie and Cordelia Breen in 1981.

The original plantings were limited to 4.5 hectares of shiraz with just a few rows of rhine riesling, trebbiano, malbec and pinot noir. The plantings have now been increased by three hectares of cabernet sauvignon (the first crop expected in 1985), 1.2 hectares of colombard (first crop expected in 1987) and half a hectare of chardonnay (first crop expected in 1988).

As these figures indicate, the vines grow slowly in the sandy loam over gravelly clay subsoils, notwith-standing the fairly high annual rainfall of around 900 millimetres. The 1984 vintage produced 20 tonnes of estate-grown shiraz; the equivalent of an additional six tonnes of grapes was purchased in the form of juice, and fermented at Boroka.

Breen, who has completed the wine corres-pondence course run by the Riverina College of Advanced Education, is not afraid to experiment with his wine style. In 1984 he produced a rosé which was 50 per cent red wine and 50 per cent white wine, with the red component given a fair degree of skin contact. It is best described as a rosé for real men. The red wines made from Boroka shiraz in 1981 and 1982 were not especially distinguished.

CATHCART RIDGE ESTATE
MOYSTON ROAD, CATHCART, via ARARAT

Cathcart Ridge is a new 4.5-hectare vineyard established in 1978 by local medical practitioner Dr Graeme Bertuch. It is planted principally to cabernet sauvignon and merlot, with a little cabernet franc, all designed to be blended together and made into the one classic Bordeaux-style red. Small quantities of rhine riesling and chardonnay have also been planted on a trial basis. The first wine released was a cabernet merlot blend from 1982, made in tiny quantities.

Cathcart Ridge also has released limited quantities of a straight shiraz, made from grapes grown at Bruce Dalkin's Westgate Vineyard in the hills at Rhymney. Established in 1968, the grapes from that vineyard have been sold in most years to Seppelt.

Cathcart Ridge wines are made jointly by Dr Bertuch and Trevor Mast.

DONOVIEW
POMONAL ROAD, STAWELL

Donoview was established by Peter and Brenda Donovan (and their three children Paul, Gina and James) in 1977. The eight-hectare property now has 4.6 hectares of vines. The plantings are cabernet sauvignon (1.9 hectares), shiraz (1.5 hectares), crouchen (1.4 hectares) and traminer (0.8 hectare). The shiraz and crouchen were the first vines planted on the sandy loam over clay, and other plantings have since followed progressively. Supplementary water is not used, and the vines have accordingly established themselves very slowly. Yields are still very small and are likely to remain low.

The first commercial vintage was in 1981, when 2.3 tonnes of shiraz were crushed under the supervision of winemaker Chris Peters. Peters, a science graduate, spent six years as chief chemist and trials winemaker at Seppelts' Great Western Champagne Cellars. He has since left the wine industry to become a science teacher at a local secondary school, but keeps his hand in with wine-making at Donoview. He is a firm believer in the winemaking methods of Leo Hurley, for many years Colin Preece's assistant at Great Western.

Both the 1981 and 1982 Bin B1 Shiraz have been excellent wines. The 1981 release was selected both by *Wine and Spirit Monthly* and by *Winestate* in their "Pick of the New Releases" sections at the end of 1982, while the 1982 vintage won a silver medal at the Victorian Wines Show of that year. The style of these wines is precisely what one would expect of the Great Western area when made in the Leo Hurley fashion: immensely deep and strong wines, with marked tannin, and needing many years in bottle.

Subsequent vintages are going to be in very short supply. The 1983 vintage was drought-affected, while in 1984 Donoview's own vineyards produced only 1.5 tonnes of grapes, supplemented by 2.5 tonnes purchased in from Dalkin's Vineyard at Rhymney.

MONTARA
CHALAMBAR ROAD, ARARAT

Montara is the largest of the new, family-owned vineyards and wineries in the Great Western district. Cascading down the side of Mount Chalambar, a name immortalised by the genius of Seppelts' Colin Preece, the vineyards and winery have a glorious view. The rolling foothills in the foreground, with twinkling blue ponds and lakes, lead out over the plains and eventually to the Pyrenees mountains. The blue ponds may look attractive from a distance, but they are also extremely functional. They are the settling system for the town's sewerage effluent, and also act as a source of the supplementary water used on the Montara vineyards.

The McRae family has been involved in every aspect of setting up the vineyard and winery. Father John McRae, a retired engineer, was responsible for much of the design and building of the winery; his wife Thelma runs the sales room, while son Michael is the winemaker.

The 12.5-hectare vineyard is planted to cabernet sauvignon, shiraz, pinot noir, chasselas, ondenc and rhine riesling. The mechanical ingenuity of the McRae family sees the mechanically harvested fruit transferred to a mobile tank which takes the grapes back to the winery in a very short space of time and in first-class condition. The slope upon which the vineyard is established means that frosts are never a problem, and yields are substantial.

The speciality of the vineyard is undoubtedly its pinot noir. While the quality has varied a little from one vintage to the next, there has never been any doubt about the varietal character, which is present in abundance. The '84 Pinot Noir was clearly the best for many years, and is in every respect an exemplary wine. The white wines, too, have been very well made in recent years. The 1983 Chasselas

had honeyed, malt flavours not unlike Loire Valley chenin blanc. Residual sugar added to the flavour and to the commercial appeal of the wine. A not dissimilar philosophy led to the wood-matured 1984 Ondenc, a very cleverly constructed wine of obvious commercial appeal. The cabernet usually shows good varietal character; some slightly bitter characters have manifested themselves in one or two releases. Montara also prides itself on its vintage port.

MOUNT CHALAMBAR ESTATE
Off TATYOON ROAD, ARARAT

Trevor Mast leads an active life. Not content with his winemaking responsibilities at St Andrews and Concongella, or his consultancy activities for several other vignerons in the district, he also has established his own vineyard at Ararat. Plantings commenced in 1980, and there are now two hectares each of rhine riesling and chardonnay. He runs yet another small vineyard at Ballarat where he has established two hectares of pinot noir on a stony loam soil at a height of 530 metres.

The chardonnay and pinot noir plantings are intended to provide base wine for the _méthode champenoise_ he appears so interested in. This interest was sparked in the first instance by one of his teachers at Geisenheim, a German who in the years before the Second World War had done pioneering research work into the yeast problems which were then causing the Champagne district in France many problems.

The rhine riesling reflects his other "inherited" interest from his time at Geisenheim. Utilising a double-arch trellis system, he hopes to modify the microclimate in the vineyard to produce distinctive wines with some input from botrytis. The 1984 release, the second from the vineyard, certainly showed abundant rhine riesling character and flavour, and was a first-class wine.

MOUNT LANGHI-GHIRAN VINEYARD
WARRACK–BUANGOR ROAD, via ARARAT

As the name indicates, this vineyard has been established on the slopes of Mount Langhi-Ghiran, due west of Ararat. Don, Gino and Sergio Fratin commenced the 15-hectare vineyard in 1971; it is now established to shiraz, cabernet sauvignon and rhine riesling, with small quantities of merlot and cabernet franc. For some years the grapes were sold, but the Fratin brothers then built a winery into the side of the hills. Gravity is used to assist much of the wine movement from the time the grapes are received into the winery until the wine reaches the underground storage area.

The white wines have not been good, oxidation and coarseness being major problems. The reds are variable, and at their best are quite magnificent. Trevor Mast has recently started to assist on a consultancy basis with the red wines, and although consistency is yet to be achieved, the base ingredients are there. Chief among these base ingredients are tannin, with fruit, colour and structure in close attendance. These wines are very different in style from what one normally expects from Great Western, no doubt reflecting the *terroir* of Mount Langhi-Ghiran. The 1982 Shiraz was a little clumsy, with big, sweet fruit flavours and some varietal spice. The '82 Cabernet Sauvignon was far better, a most impressive wine with great depth, complexity and balance; rich, firm cabernet fruit is well integrated with some nice oak. The '83s were less successful, with a harsh extractive tannic shiraz, and a far better-balanced cabernet with some attractive minty fruit flavours.

As young wines the 1984s were quite outstanding, with the 1984 Cabernet Sauvignon winning the gold medallion in Class 26 of the 1984 Seymour show. A wine of awesome proportions, with very high tannin (but the fruit to go with it), it epitomises the Mount Langhi-Ghiran style.

SEPPELT'S GREAT WESTERN
HIGHWAY 8, GREAT WESTERN

Joseph Best's first vintage in 1868 produced 38 gallons (173 litres) of wine. Like all people of his time he had faith in the future, but could not have visualised what that 38 gallons would eventually lead to. By the same token the enterprise soon flourished; by 1876 there were 50 acres (20 hectares) of vines, and the 1887 vintage yielded 7000 gallons (31,850 litres). Some time before 1870 Joseph Best conceived the idea of employing out-of-work goldminers to create underground cellars in the soft rock he had encountered when carrying out the excavations for his winery. In July 1870 the *Ararat Advertiser* carried this report:

> Mr. Best recently erected a fine wine press; adjoining the wine press house is the cellar, a large building lately put up, and it has two lofty stories sunk beneath the surface where the temperature cannot be but cool. The cellar will hold 20,000 gallons [91,000 litres] which Mr. Best estimates to be about two years' produce.

In August 1878 the same paper carried another report which gives a vivid picture of the winemaking methods of the time:

> Before reaching the cellar, the press room is passed, in which there is a large press worked by four, six or eight men on a capstan principle, in which 9 tonnes of grapes are treated at once . . . the Cellar comprises an upper storey . . . the ground floor in which there are twelve large oaken casks of a capacity of 500 gallons [2275 litres] each, and an underground floor containing, besides several smaller casks, three of 600 gallons [2730 litres] each, then a decline leads to a main storage cellar. This portion comprises four drives, 7 ft. x 4 ft. [210 by 120 centimetres], crossed and re-crossed by other drives of equal length.

By the time of Joseph Best's sudden death in 1887 at the age of 57, his wines had won numerous gold and silver medals at international exhibitions in London, Philadelphia, Bordeaux and Amsterdam, not to mention the 1875 Melbourne Intercolonial Exhibition, where he took first prize. A bachelor who died intestate, his estate was offered for sale and purchased by Hans Irvine, a Ballarat businessman. It comprised 22 hectares of vines, 182 hectares of grazing land and the cellars with a stock of around 70,000 gallons (318,500 litres) of wine. The purchase price was £12,000.

Irvine embarked on a major expansion programme immediately, planting another 16 hectares of grapes in the area surrounding the winery, and between 1880 and 1890 acquiring an additional 60 hectares of vineyard four kilometres to the south in a locality known as Arawatta.

In 1890 Irvine planted 21 hectares of a variety which he called white pinot, and which for many years was called Irvine's white, only to be finally identified as ondenc, a variety grown in the south of France. There can be little doubt Irvine thought he was planting chardonnay and one can only imagine what might have happened had he procured the correct variety, for these plantings were established with one thing in mind: to produce bottled fermented sparkling wine according to the *méthode champenoise*. In the same year he employed a French-trained champagne-maker who was born near Rheims in France and who had worked at Pommery. Charles Pierlot was joined shortly after by another Frenchman, Julian Grellet, who was in charge of the vineyards.

In 1892 new red-brick cellars were erected at a cost of £2000: 110 feet long and 60 feet wide (33.5 by 18 metres), the cellars had a capacity of 300,000 gallons (1.365 million litres) of wine. Specialised machinery was imported from France for the making of the sparkling wine, and Hans Irvine was in business. Pierlot left after an argument in 1896, but apparently returned two years later. Certainly the champagne-making flourished, and by 1907 over one mile (1.6 kilometres) of drives had been excavated which provided storage both for the bottles of sparkling wine and for the 300-gallon (1365-litre) oak vats for the storage of table wine.

Although he was married, Hans Irvine had no children. In his capacity as president of the Viticultural Society he had become close friends with Benno Seppelt of Seppeltsfield, as a consequence of which Benno Seppelt was given a right of first refusal to acquire the property if Irvine ever decided to sell. This occurred in 1918; Hans Irvine died four years later while on a visit to London at the age of 66.

The first manager/winemaker appointed by Seppelt was Reginald Mowatt, a Roseworthy graduate, who remained at Great Western until 1932. Between 1918 and 1923 an additional 50 hectares of vineyard were established, followed by 4.5 hectares in 1928. In 1932 Mowatt resigned, and was replaced by another Roseworthy graduate, Colin Preece, who had worked at Seppeltsfield since his graduation in 1923. It was the start of a glorious era for Great Western, for Preece turned out to be one of the most talented of all winemakers, and had a rare understanding of the rather particular style of Great Western fruit.

Preece's arrival did not presage any immediate changes, but between 1941 and 1961 a continuous programme of replanting and new vineyard establishment was undertaken. By 1961 the vineyards comprised almost 250 hectares, of which over 30 hectares had been replanted. Continued expansion in the sparkling-wine production meant that the drives were entirely given over to bottle storage, and all the oak vats were removed to the upper levels.

1953 saw the removal of beer rationing, the decline in the fortified-wine market, and the first beginnings of the new table-wine styles which were ultimately to transform the face of Australian winemaking and drinking. Between 1953 and 1955 Preece was responsible for developing and introducing four new styles: Moyston Claret, Chalambar Burgundy, Arawatta Riesling and Rhymney Chablis. Although "commercial" styles, between 1953 and 1963 (when Preece retired), these wines consistently reached levels of excellence which have never been surpassed in wines of comparable rank and style.

But Preece was also quietly producing small quantities (often single vats of only 250 dozen each, sometimes less) of private bin wines. Wine lovers were given an insight into these when two quite extraordinary private cellars were auctioned at Len Evans Wines in September 1982. I attended the pre-auction tasting, a subsequent tasting at Halvorsen Cellars of a number of the wines purchased at the auction, and in mid-1983 the Single Bottle Club dinner which featured five of the reds in a single bracket.

I make no apology for including these tasting notes: many wine lovers will have appreciated these wines over the years, and I have countless tasting notes scattered over that time. However, what is, to all intents and purposes, a single retrospective review of great old wines of this kind always seems to me to have a special value. Here then are the notes of the wines tasted on those three occasions. (The details of the varieties, the bottling dates and quantities produced came from the cellar books of Colin Preece.)

1949—Bin 80/84 Great Western Burgundy (hermitage and malbec, Arawatta Vineyard; mixed black varieties from Imperial and Flat). _Colour:_ deep red. _Bouquet:_ strong, smooth minty fruit with some camphor bottle-developed aromas. _Palate:_ rich, minty fruit, still fresh. (The bottle served at the Single Bottle Club dinner was nowhere near as good, marred by volatility. Yet another bottle, tasted at Halvorsen, had strong mushroom decay characters, highlighting the fact that there are no great old wines, only great old bottles.)

1950—Type G51 Burgundy (Bottled 29/8/51.) _Varieties:_ mixed black, Cellar Paddock, Bill Blass hermitage, esparte, Arawatta Vineyard; and hermitage, Imperial Vineyard.) _Colour:_ a strong red tinged with garnet. _Bouquet:_ a beautiful clean wine with fresh minty overtones. _Palate:_ big, rich fruity wine, still holding structure and style (Halvorsen).

1951—Type H66-68 Great Western Claret (An historic Moyston No. 1 blend assembled on 15 November 1950 from 400 gallons [1820 litres] of 1947 red pressings, 520 gallons [2366 litres] of 1946 red pressings, claret special blend 300 gallons [1365 litres] and Scaletti's dry red 180 gallons [819 litres]. How Preece concocted a 1951 vintage out of that assemblage is anyone's guess.) _Colour:_ excellent deep red with a touch of amber. _Bouquet:_ peculiar garlic aromas. _Palate:_ some of the same character comes through onto a meaty, fleshy wine (Single Bottle Club).

1953—Type J13 Great Western Burgundy (Bottled 15/10/54. _Quantity produced:_ 189 dozen. _Varieties:_ hermitage and Miller's burgundy, Arawatta

Vineyard.) *Colour:* dark with a suggestion of very ripe, high pH fruit. *Bouquet:* similar complex ripe aromas with a trace of tobacco, some mint and also bottled-developed camphor. *Palate:* very complex amalgam of minty fruit, oak and aged character with just a hint of pencil shavings. Nonetheless, an outstanding wine (Single Bottle Club).

1953—Type J34 Great Western Claret (Bottled 23/11/54. *Quantity produced:* 137 and five-twelfths dozen. *Varieties:* malbec and hermitage from Black Imperial, cabernet and malbec from St Ethel and Salinger. The greatest of all Preece's red wines, and a prolific show prize-winner between 1953 and 1961, taking numerous first prizes including Champion Claret in Sydney 1956.) *Colour:* superb lively red-purple. *Bouquet:* very full, deep and richly textured. *Palate:* rich and minty-sweet fruit, with light balancing tannin giving length. (Second bottle served at Single Bottle Club dinner; first bottle caramelised and oxidised. *Caveat emptor.*)

1954—Type 581 Great Western Claret (Bottled 11/11/55. *Quantity produced:* 198 and ten-twelfths dozen. *Varieties:* hermitage from St Ethel Vineyard.) *Colour:* dark red, still with purple-blue tinges. *Bouquet:* complex firm fruit with a touch of tobacco/leather and just a trace of aged mushroom character. *Palate:* enormously rich fruit on the mid-palate leading to a surprising soft finish. (Single Bottle Club: a great wine. Halvorsen Cellars bottle: oxidised, volatile and virtually undrinkable.)

1955—Type L34 Burgundy (Bottled 13/11/56. *Quantity produced:* 126 and a half dozen. *Varieties:* mixed black from St George and Rhymney Vineyards. Major show prize-winner.) *Colour:* strong red. *Bouquet:* crystal clear, vibrant, ripe fresh fruit. *Palate:* in superb condition; some camphor-mint flavours; a marvellously complex balance of fruit and tannin. Along with J34, the great wine of the tasting (Halvorsen Cellars).

1957—Moyston Claret (Blended 24/6/59. *Varieties:* 1954 Rutherglen red pressings, 1956 Rutherglen dry red, 1957 Great Western dry red hermitage plus Miller's burgundy, 1957 South Australia dry red hermitage and Miller's burgundy, 1957 Tahbilk dry red 450 gallons [2047 litres].) *Colour:* red, some browns showing. *Bouquet:* a touch of volatility with some nice fruit. *Palate:* marred by volatility (Halvorsen Cellars).

1958—Moyston Claret *Colour:* good hue, still predominantly red. *Bouquet:* smooth, aged and showing fairly high alcohol with some camphor characters.

Palate: rich, ripe soft mid-palate but a rather bitter finish detracts (a ring-in; tasted February 1983).

1960—Type Q58-61 Cabernet Malbec *Colour:* distinct browning. *Bouquet:* very ripe and slightly porty fruit with some minty overtones. *Palate:* a fairly ripe/sweet wine with low tannin. In remarkable condition given the ullage (another ring-in; tasted April 1983).

1961—Type MY17 Moyston Claret *Colour:* medium to full red, some tawny showing. *Bouquet:* chocolatey, ripe and warm. *Palate:* rich, soft, ripe style more in burgundy mould than claret (Halvorsen Cellars).

1962—Bin CH20 (Great Western—Barossa hermitage) *Colour:* medium red, some garnet hues. *Bouquet:* ripe, old Australian-style red with some old oak showing. *Palate:* full, fairly ripe and lacking structural complexity.

Preece also produced some outstanding white wines, as the Single Bottle Club dinner demonstrated.

1956—Type S14 Chablis *Colour:* extraordinary pale yellow-green, quite remarkable for age. *Bouquet:* crisp and slightly hard, reflecting the high sorbate and/or SO_2 additions which have kept the colour so good. *Palate:* exceptionally fresh and lively with good acid and crispness. Again the chemical protection shows through to slightly reduce the fruit, but it is a chablis style after all.

1959—Riesling Tokay *Colour:* vibrant light green-yellow. *Bouquet:* rich with some old-oak characters and remarkably full. *Palate:* in great, indeed perfect, condition with a long carry and soft finish.

1950—Arawatta Riesling *Colour:* light yellow-orange. *Bouquet:* a trace of volatility, with sweet fruit, but lacking depth. *Palate:* somewhat volatile and showing an odd varietal mixture (unlike the other two wines, somewhat tired).

At the risk of labouring the point, I have also taken part in a number of remarkable tastings of the old sparkling burgundies made by Preece between 1944 and 1963. I indeed possess many of these wines. The '44, '46, '53, '54 and '55 are still all glorious. The odd bottle will open with no gas left (and simply tastes like a lovely old hermitage), while others sometimes have a strong mushroom character. But largely they are far more reliable than the old still red table wines because of the preservative effect of the carbon dioxide in the wine. More recent wines of exceptional quality are the 1963 Bin 81A and 1964 Bin 85C, while the 1972 Bin 443/72 has excellent varietal shiraz flavour on the palate, if one ignores the slight leafy/mercaptan aromas. These wines are either due for release or have been recently released.

Many of these sparkling burgundies came to light during a reorganisation of the Great Western cellars in the early 1980s, and have prompted Seppelt to again lay down significant quantities for long-term cellaring and future release. One thousand dozen were made in 1982 from 100 per cent Great Western shiraz (following in the tradition of many of the old great wines) and 2000 dozen were laid down in 1983 from a mixture of Great Western shiraz and Keppoch material.

It is not easy to put the achievements of Colin Preece into perspective, even though his wines have survived as a lasting testimony. Obviously enough, many of them were produced in tiny quantities, representing the pick of each vintage. On the other hand, many winemakers lack the skill and foresight to be able to identify which batches of wine will turn out to be great. What is more, the winemaking equipment was antiquated in the extreme, and new oak was introduced only to meet increased production. By any standards he was a great winemaker; the only real debate is just how great, and where does he stand measured against the other great red-wine makers of his time, including Maurice O'Shea, Roger Warren and Max Schubert.

Preece's retirement in 1963–64 coincided with the start of the great red-wine boom. The next 10 years were a decade which—at least so far as the red wines are concerned—Seppelt would rather forget. It was faced with a choice of either introducing new brands underneath Moyston and Chalambar, or of vastly increasing the quantity of those wines (and thereby reducing the quality). It opted for the latter course, and the great reputation that Moyston and Chalambar once had was lost. In more recent years there has been an effort to restore some of the tarnished image, but inevitably it has only been partly successful. The production of sparkling wine, too, went through a difficult period with muscat gordo blanco joining trebbiano as the major component of the base wines.

Since the mid-70s things have greatly improved, although the labyrinth of the Seppelt table-wine-labelling system is enough to defeat the most ardent searcher of truth. Not that the labels are not explicit, they are, but there is (or was) such an incredible variety that it was very difficult to keep up with trends in style, quality and region.

Seppelt has the big-company mentality, and after its recent take-over battles, seems more than usually reticent to produce any hard statistics or facts. It contents itself with saying that approximately 50 per cent of the Great Western crush comes from company vineyards situated at Great Western, Drumborg, Keppoch and Barooga. The principal varieties processed are chardonnay, ondenc, rhine riesling, shiraz, pinot noir, pinot meunière and cabernet sauvignon.

Obviously enough, the major activity at Great Western is sparkling-wine production. In the late 1970s three large air-conditioned champagne tirage buildings were erected to complement the two kilometres of underground drives. The humidity in the underground drives can vary somewhat, and the temperature varies also by a degree or two. The totally sterile surroundings of the Colorbond triage buildings vary not one iota, and are therefore considered far preferable in these days of shining-bright technology.

The labels on the sparkling wines are, in the manner of the times, constantly being revised. As at the end of 1984 the hierarchy was Show Champagne (Seppelt's word, not mine), Fleur de Lys, Vintage Brut, Non-Vintage Brut, Imperial Reserve and Brut Reserve. The base wines are being progressively upgraded, with chardonnay and pinot noir now used almost exclusively in the younger show champagnes (with a little ondenc); the Fleur de Lys is substantially ondenc with some chardonnay; and from this point on the information becomes somewhat scanty.

The principal varieties grown by Seppelt of Great Western include ondenc, chenin blanc, chardonnay, rhine riesling, sauvignon blanc, gewurztraminer, chasselas and shiraz. The vineyards are established variously on brown earths and granitic sands, and rainfall is around 600 millimetres per year.

The most consistent wines from Great Western have been the shiraz (or, as they are labelled, hermitage) releases. The best of these have shown lingering soft, spicy aromas and fruit—shiraz at its best. There have also been one or two distinguished rhine riesling releases, although much of the better-quality output from the district is blended with Drumborg and/or Keppoch.

COOPER, VICTORIA, c. 1910

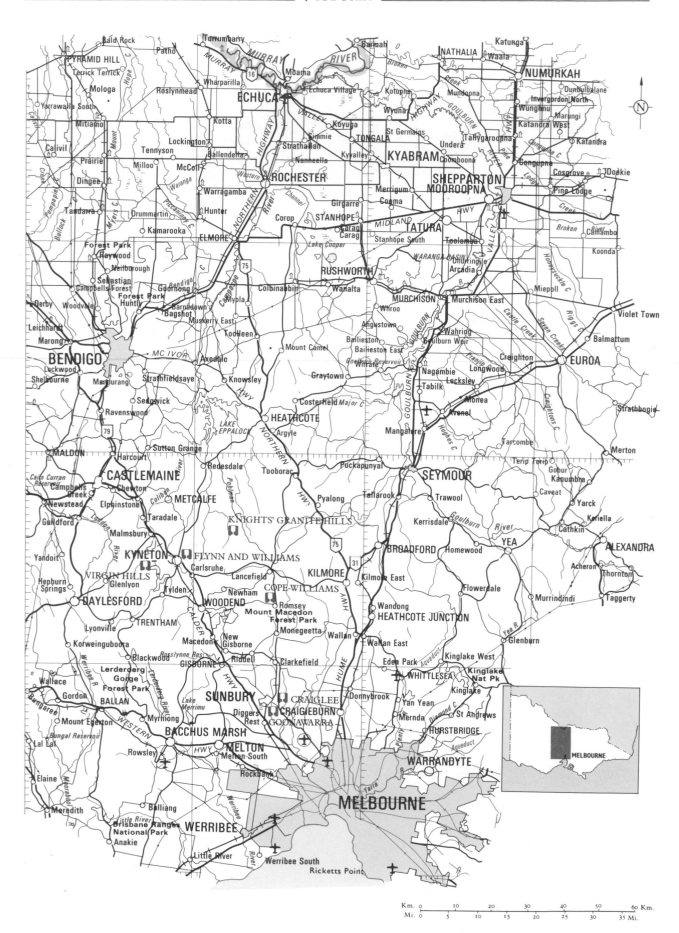

Macedon Region

The Macedon region encompasses five sub-districts: Sunbury, Mount Macedon, Romsey, Lancefield and Kyneton. As at the 1984 vintage 85 hectares of vines were spread across this geographically diverse area. These vineyards were held by no less than 28 growers supplying the five wineries which come within its confines.

The topography, soil and microclimate vary greatly, the one unifying factor being the difficulties posed to viticulture by wind. Not only does wind inhibit leaf growth and savagely impact on flowering and fruit set; but, particularly in areas such as Romsey, can significantly reduce the theoretical warmth in the growing season through the wind-chill factor.

The Shire of Gisborne falls in the centre of the Macedon region, and has embarked upon an active programme of encouraging grape growing in the region. Within the confines of the shire, special rate concessions and other inducements are offered to growers, while the shire has the grand ambition to see a major sparkling-wine house establish itself. Certainly the high country around Romsey and above Kyneton would seem ideally suited to the production of base wine for sparkling wine, provided steps are taken to combat wind successfully. Even then, growers must be prepared for years such as 1984 in which it proved impossible to ripen even pinot noir above 9.5 baume. For sparkling wine, this may be acceptable, but not for table wine.

Nonetheless, the two senior citizens of the Macedon region (Knights and Virgin Hills) have consistently made some outstanding red wines, if in somewhat different style. Flynn and Williams have proved themselves master winemakers, and have established the first "true" Kyneton vineyard within the past few years. Their earlier Heathcote wines were marvellously constructed, following closely in the tradition of Virgin Hills, where Laurie Williams worked for so many years.

COPE-WILLIAMS
GLENFERN ROAD, ROMSEY

Gordon Cope-Williams came to Australia 15 years ago to escape the rigours of the English winter. It also enabled him to realise a childhood ambition to grow grapes and make wine one day, instilled during an earnest conversation at the age of nine with his grandfather.

An architect who specialises in the design of country houses, it was inevitable Cope-Williams would himself settle in the country. He chose Romsey, in southern Victoria, and in 1977 planted Rocky Hill to 1.4 hectares each of pinot noir and chardonnay, including 300 vines each of rhine riesling and sauvignon blanc as a trial. At an altitude of 760 metres the vineyard struggled against winds and a climate which in some years was simply too cool to ripen the grapes. Cope-Williams has no doubt that the wind-chill factor reduces the temperatures at Rocky Hill by at least five degrees compared with temperatures two kilometres away (and at a lower altitude) where his more recent plantings have been established.

The Coniston Vineyard was planted three years ago to 1.6 hectares each of pinot noir, chardonnay and rhine riesling. With the experience of Rocky Hill, windbreaks were grown to protect the vineyard from the prevailing winds, and have been very successful until the effect of the shelter is lost. Here, at the end of the rows, the vines bear no resemblance to those sheltered by the windbreak. The Coniston Vineyard has been established with a traditional, very low European trellis and on a planting density of 5000 to the hectare. The rows are between 1.8 and two metres apart, with between one and 1.2 metres per vine.

A neighbour is establishing a further six hectares of vineyard on similar principles, planted to sauvignon blanc, chardonnay and merlot, with cabernet sauvignon scheduled for 1985. In all, Cope-Williams expects to have access to the production of around 12 hectares of grapes. Although he has sold Rocky Hill he has retained a long-term lease of the vineyard. With the planting densities chosen, yields are projected to be not less than 10 tonnes per hectare. Fifty tonnes will be processed in the winery planned to be erected prior to the 1985 vintage, the surplus grapes being sold to sparkling-winemakers. Cope-Williams sees the potential of the district lying primarily in this direction.

The Cope-Williams wines will include four table wines: a pinot noir, a chardonnay, a red (blended from cabernet sauvignon, cabernet franc and merlot) and a white (sauvignon blanc or largely sauvignon blanc).

Judy and Gordon Cope-Williams's son Michael is presently a third-year student at Roseworthy Agricultural College, and will eventually assume winemaking responsibilities. The Cope-Williams wines so far made have been made and blended at Tisdall, and are chiefly Goulburn River material, but incorporating some Romsey fruit. They are, as one would expect, extremely well put together and are very attractive commercially.

CRAIGLEE
SUNBURY ROAD, SUNBURY

Craiglee Vineyard was first planted in 1864 by James S. Johnston, a member of the Victorian Parliament and one of the founders of the _Argus_ newspaper. In those days Sunbury was no doubt reckoned to be a considerable distance from Melbourne, but now it is a mere 35 minutes' drive from the GPO.

Johnston established seven hectares of vineyard, initially to a large number of grapes, but eventually rationalised to concentrate on shiraz and riesling. After 12 years his son Wilfred succeeded him as winemaker, and continued to produce wine until the late 1920s when the vineyard fell, not to the cow, but to the sheep. The wine was made in a four-storey blue-stone winery, in the style of the times and designed to use gravity wherever possible. The building still stands in immaculate condition, but the ever-vigilant Department of Health has decreed that the present owners of Craiglee cannot make wine in it because it does not conform (strange though it may seem) to 1980 health regulations.

Much of the Craiglee production was exported, mainly to the United Kingdom but also to New Zealand. Again in the manner of the times it was entered in overseas competition, with the 1872 vintage gaining an award in Vienna. A cache of this wine was discovered in the 1950s, and came into the possession of Tom Seabrook. Various bottles were opened at wine dinners throughout the 1970s—I shared in one and, although it was showing rather more signs of age than many others, it still exhibited quite remarkable fruit.

The Carmody family purchased the property from the Johnstons in 1961, running it solely as a grazing and cropping farm until 1976, when it was decided to re-establish vines. Two hectares of shiraz were planted in that year, followed by 1.8 hectares of chardonnay and of cabernet sauvignon in 1977. The vineyard was extended slightly in 1980 with further small plantings of sauvignon blanc, cabernet sauvignon and pinot noir.

The two commercial releases presently available are a Craiglee hermitage (with a small amount of cabernet sauvignon) and a chardonnay. The wines are made by Patrick Carmody, an agricultural science graduate who has completed the wine science course at Riverina College. The Craiglee hermitage is a light-bodied red, with crisp varietal spice its principal attribute. Most of the wines so far released have been fairly delicate, with the 1982 already showing a touch of light leathery development in late 1984. The chardonnays, by contrast, have been much fuller and richer, exhibiting good varietal character, weight and richness. Carmody gives the wines some skin contact to enhance richness, and the juice is largely clarified before fermentation commences.

FLYNN AND WILLIAMS
FLYNNS LANE, KYNETON

John Flynn, a university student then completing a science degree, and Laurie Williams, a veteran farmer-turned-viticulturalist and cellar-hand, met at Tom Lazar's Virgin Hills. Laurie Williams had worked at Virgin Hills almost from its inception, helping to establish the vineyard and assisting Tom Lazar in the winemaking. John Flynn arrived during one vintage to gain experience and to help defray his education expenses. It led to a lasting friendship and ultimately to a partnership which acquired as its first asset in the 1970s a two-hectare vineyard at Heathcote, on its best red volcanic loam and ironstone soil and next-door to Leonard French's Mount Ida Vineyard. It was planted to 1.6 hectares of cabernet sauvignon, 0.4 hectare of shiraz with a few vines of malbec thrown in for good measure.

The Heathcote Vineyard was sold in 1983, following the establishment of a second 1.6-hectare vineyard at Kyneton on granitic sandy loam soils, which produced its first commercial crop (of two tonnes) in 1984. It is planted to 1.4 hectares of cabernet sauvignon and 0.2 hectare of gewurtztraminer.

Flynn and Williams have released three vintages from the Heathcote Vineyard—1980, 1981 and 1982. All have been of exceptional quality, and the tiny production sells out immediately it is offered to the few retail outlets which received an allocation. With a yield that reaches seven tonnes per hectare only in the best years, annual production has not exceeded 700 cases, and is usually less.

In January 1985 the five-year-old 1980 Cabernet Sauvignon looked and tasted like a six-month-old wine. Dense inky-purple in colour, it is a wine of enormous power and concentration, yet is neither tannic nor jammy. If there is to be a criticism it is a touch of leather in the aroma, perhaps indicating a little mercaptan. It is difficult to imagine when the wine might start to approach its peak. Nonetheless, I preferred the succeeding vintages. The 1981 Cabernet Sauvignon has excellent deep purple-red colour, a trace of regional mint on the bouquet, with full, deep and clean fruit; a lively, smooth and stylish wine on the palate, with clearly defined minty/berry flavours. The 1982 Cabernet Sauvignon is by far the most complex of the three wines, showing very sophisticated oak handling; the complexity is such that at three years of age it almost coated the tongue with its vanillan/mint flavours. This is Heathcote at its best, producing wines of enormous concentration and power, throwbacks to another era.

The drought completely decimated the 1983 vintage at Heathcote, so followers of the style will have to be patient. Future production will increase as John Flynn has purchased a 2.8-hectare block next to the Kyneton Vineyard, and this will be planted in 1985 to shiraz and chardonnay. Laurie Williams's years at Virgin Hills taught him that while the blend of shiraz and cabernet may be an unfashionable one, it makes great wine.

Winemaking is carried out at a small but functional winery on a property owned by the Flynn family on the outskirts of the historic town of Kyneton.

GOONAWARRA
SUNBURY ROAD, SUNBURY

Lest anyone should think that Goonawarra is a facile attempt to trade upon the fame of Coonawarra, this vineyard received its name in 1858 (or thereabouts),

long before the first vines were even planted at Coonawarra. It was established by a former Victorian Premier, James Goodall Francis, and produced wine until the early 1900s. Like so many other vineyards around Melbourne, it then went out of production, but the magnificent blue-stone winery complex remained.

It was purchased by Melbourne lawyer John Barnier and his architect wife Libby in 1982. With consultancy advice from Graham Durie, a Roseworthy graduate who is presently studying for his master's degree in vine physiology, they commenced the long process of re-establishing the vineyard and renovating the winery. Plantings so far comprise one hectare of chardonnay and 0.75 hectare each of semillon and cabernet franc. The plantings are on a closer-than-normal two-metre by 1.3-metre spacing.

The first small vintage is expected in 1985, and the first commercial harvest in 1986. In the meantime a separately labelled wine made from Cowra semillon will be sold. This wine was made at D'Aquino Winery at Orange, with the Barniers making the long car trip every three or four weeks to supervise its progress at the end of fermentation. Making wine in the old blue-stone winery on the premises will seem ever so easy after that introduction.

Unlike Craiglee, the Barniers have managed to satisfy modern-day Health Department needs, and received permission to use the bottom floor of the two-storey building for winemaking purposes. The upper storey will be turned into a restaurant in partnership with a restaurateur, while on the back of the property a thriving plant nursery is conducted.

KNIGHTS' GRANITE HILLS
BAYNTON WD 83, KYNETON

The Knight family had been graziers on the high hills above Baynton for many years before successive booms and busts in the cattle and wool industries led to the somewhat unlikely decision to plant grapes in 1970. Unlikely, because the Knights had no previous connection with viticulture and did not even drink wine, and because of substantial doubts as to whether the grapes would ripen at the vineyard height of 550 metres.

Experience has shown that the grapes do ripen, but only just: cabernet sauvignon from mid- to late April, shiraz late April to early May, and rhine riesling early to mid-May. This is around the same time as nearby Virgin Hills which is planted at an even greater height above sea-level. Knights also shares with Virgin Hills the granite-derived soils: coarse sandy loam over a clay base between 0.5 and two metres below the surface. All of these things considered, it is not surprising that the early production from Knights was sold in the form of grapes to Virgin Hills, and contributed substantially to the '73, '74 and '75 vintages of Virgin Hills. Nor, all things considered, is it surprising that since the first vintage in 1976 Knights has consistently produced first-quality white and red wines. All of the wine-making is now done at Knights by Lew Knight, but for many years there was a close working relationship with Tisdall. From 1979 and for several years thereafter the white wines were fermented at Tisdall and then brought back to Knights for maturation and bottling.

The vineyards are planted to two hectares each of cabernet sauvignon, shiraz, rhine riesling and chardonnay, 0.5 hectare of crouchen and 0.3 hectare each of merlot and cabernet franc. The chardonnay, merlot and cabernet franc are yet to come into bearing. Yields have always been rather better than one might imagine, and certainly far better than those at Virgin Hills. Cabernet and shiraz both yield in excess of seven tonnes per hectare, and rhine riesling yields eight. In recent years Knights has purchased shiraz and rhine riesling from Beverford in the Riverland, and has labelled and released separately the Beverford wines (at a far lower price than the Granite Hills wine). It also has purchased in traminer from Malmsbury, and shiraz and semillon from the Heathcote region from a contract-grower. Approximately 75 per cent of all its grapes are estate-grown.

The Beverford wines are adequate enough, and no doubt serve the purpose for cellar-door sales. But they prove (once again) that one cannot make silk purses out of sow's ears, no matter how skilled the winemaking. More constructively, they point to the infinitely superior quality of the estate-grown grapes.

The Knights rhine rieslings always exhibit strong varietal riesling character, with the richness of the wine depending on the year. Thus the '80 was very light-bodied, while the '82 showed far greater richness and depth of fruit character. The '83 was a curious wine: voluminous, germanic lime characters, presumably deriving from botrytis, were intermingled with the pepper/spice which one almost invariably finds in the Knights shiraz. It was not a wildly successful combination.

Knights' cabernet sauvignon is a consistently fine wine: contrary to what one might expect, it does not show exaggerated, herbaceous ultra-cool-climate characteristics. Although the grapes ripen late the wine achieves surprising body and smooth, ripe-berry characters which one would normally associate with a rather earlier vintage. That, I might say, is all to the good. The '82 is an exceptionally good wine, showing excellent balance between fruit, tannin and oak and correspondingly good structure. The cabernet sauvignon character is present throughout bouquet and palate, but not aggesssively so. At the end of 1984 it looked to have many years in front of it.

However, to my mind the outstanding wines from Knights are its shiraz-based reds. In a newspaper article towards the end of 1984 I had a momentary aberration, and suggested that the 1982 release did not show as much pepper/spice characters as earlier vintages. I must have been thinking of another wine, for that is simply not so. With remarkable consistency, this pungent, penetrating crushed-pepper/spice character comes through on both bouquet and palate. It is very much a hallmark of the best hermitage wines of the north end of the Rhone Valley, and is for me the ultimate expression of shiraz varietal character. The character is a relatively recent newcomer in Australia, and totally at odds with the flavour and style of the more traditional shiraz reds of the Hunter and Barossa Valleys. Perhaps for this reason it is not fully understood, and certainly not always appreciated. Little wonder that more dispassionate observers, such as American wine experts, are bowled over by the character and flavour, and far more interested in consequence in Australian shiraz (of this style at least) than cabernet.

Both the 1982 and 1983 wines are at least the equal of the great wines that have preceded them. I judged both wines at the Victorian Wines Show at the end of 1984, and consistently gave them gold-medals marks in the various classes in which they were entered.

Finally, Knights has also experimented with wood maturation of some of their rhine riesling, with more success than usually greets such attempts. It should be a useful learning curve for them as their chardonnay comes into production, and I await with considerable interest the first release of this variety.

VIRGIN HILLS
Off HONEYSUCKLE ROAD, KYNETON

One of the most fatuous questions a wine writer can be asked is: "What is your favourite wine?" The very fact that the question is asked in the first place indicates a total lack of knowledge on the part of the questioner. The great charm of wine is its infinite variability, its complexity, and its infinite capacity to surprise. There is not, nor can there ever be, any question of my favourite wine. But I suppose one could pose this question: to which vineyard would you point a French wine expert if you wished to impress on him or her the capacity of Australia to produce consistently fine wine over a decade? My answer would in all probability be Virgin Hills.

This may seem to be a very unconventional answer. If so, it is only fitting, for Virgin Hills was the creation of the highly unconventional, larger-than-life figure of Tom Lazar. Lazar came to Australia from Hungary via Paris, where he spent three years studying sculpture at the École des Beaux Arts. He first made his presence felt in Melbourne, establishing the Little Reata as the ultimate lunch-spot for the affluent in the mid-1960s, before moving to the other end of Little Bourke Street and opening a far larger Lazar's Restaurant. These were the days of success for Tom Lazar, and in 1968 he ventured to Virgin Hills, acquiring the timber-clad property for $30 an acre ($74 per hectare) on the strength of a most favourable report from the Victorian Department of Agriculture. This was despite the fact that there had been no previous history of winegrowing in the hill country above Kyneton where the vineyard was duly established.

Having selected the site and started to establish the vineyard, Lazar taught himself to make wine by reading textbooks and by spending the 1971 vintage with Owen Redman at Coonawarra. The first vintage was made in 1973, and immediately a legend was born. Lazar designed a label which simply said "Virgin Hills 1973"; in minute print at the bottom one learnt it was produced in Australia at Kyneton, Victoria, by Tom Lazar. He also procured the longest corks ever to find their way into a wine bottle—extravagantly and needlessly long, but a pointed comment on the parsimony of others.

Great red wine followed great red wine. But almost before the first wine was on the market, problems started to beset Lazar. He made a fateful decision to sell his Little Bourke Street restaurant and to turn Virgin Hills into a gastronomic and oenological Mecca. Just as was the case at Mitchelton, the expected crowds stayed away and the losses mounted. The most crushing blow came when the large restaurant he had built burnt down, never to be re-erected. A mortgagee's sale was averted at the last moment when Melbourne businessman Marcel Gilbert and his wife Renata bought Virgin Hills. Lazar stayed on for a number of years as winemaker,

but has now retired and Mark Shepherd has taken over.

Right from the outset the exceptionally high quality of the fruit was counterbalanced by the ludicrously low yields. The vineyard is established at a height of 594 metres above sea-level on fine, sandy clay loam over a light clay base. Rainfall is adequate at 760 millimetres, but the very cool growing and ripening conditions, coupled with the light soil, have meant that the vines have grown slowly. Nor was the vineyard helped by lack of attention during the difficult economic times which beset Tom Lazar in the latter part of the 1970s. Indeed, the precise varietal composition of Virgin Hills' red was always something of a mystery: Tom Lazar was not too sure just what the plantings were, and the yields from each varied substantially according to the vintage.

As at 1985 the plantings will comprise cabernet sauvignon and cabernet franc (8.5 hectares), shiraz (1.8 hectares), malbec (1.5 hectares), merlot (one hectare), gewurztztraminer (1.6 hectares) and chardonnay (0.4 hectare). But yields are still pathetically low. Even under optimum conditions they vary between four and five tonnes to the hectare, and 1984 production amounted to only 1500 cases. This will undoubtedly increase as the vineyards are revived and the replanting and grafting of varieties such as cabernet franc and merlot come into production. Nonetheless, one cannot cavil at the fact that Virgin Hills is a little more expensive than the average Australian red wine.

In the latter part of 1982, shortly after the release of the 1980 vintage, I attended a masked tasting of all the Virgin Hills wines released up to that time. The notes from that tasting follow; those for the 1982 and 1981 vintages were made at the end of 1984.

1982 *Colour:* purple-red. *Bouquet:* deep, fine fruit with superb oak balance, far better than the 1981. *Palate:* a marvellously textured and structured wine, not aggressive or jammy, yet with intense mid-palate fruit and soft lingering tannin. Oak evident but held well in restraint. (18.6/20)

1981 *Colour:* excellent youthful purple-red. *Bouquet:* oak tending to dominate but of excellent lemony style. *Palate:* fruit of light to medium weight and as yet dominated by oak; fine texture and should develop well. (17.4/20)

1980 *Colour:* strong purple-red of medium depth. *Bouquet:* strong unintegrated oak, very youthful. *Palate:* superb minty/berry fruit, with oak in much better balance; a complete, rich wine with a long future. (18/20)

1979 _Colour:_ purple-red of medium depth. _Bouquet:_ some minty fruit aromas with very well-handled oak. _Palate:_ excellent weight and structure with good length to the minty mid-palate fruit; good acid on the finish. An outstanding stylish wine. (18.6/20)

1978 _Colour:_ medium purple-red, very similar to that of the 1979. _Bouquet:_ peppery/powdery aromas in quite different style. _Palate:_ of medium weight and either showing some off-oak characters or traces of corkiness. (16/20)

1977 _Colour:_ medium red-purple, at last starting to show some signs of development. _Bouquet:_ very complex with some minty aromas but also a trace of cabbage. _Palate:_ sappy fruit; complex structure but again that touch of cabbagey character intrudes and detracts from the wine. Nonetheless, good acid on the finish helped. (16.4/20)

1976 _Colour:_ deep red-purple, extraordinary for age. _Bouquet:_ a veritable Peter Pan, still youthful, with the oak still aggressively evident but the fruit there to match it. _Palate:_ a youthful, potent wine with minty fruit on the fore-palate, and soft lingering tannin on the finish. (18.4/20)

1975 _Colour:_ medium purple-red, very little difference to the 1979. _Bouquet:_ seductive, round, sweet minty fruit with beautifully balanced and integrated oak. _Palate:_ a gloriously youthful minty wine with persistent flavour right throughout the palate and a long, clean, fruity finish. (19/20)

1974 _Colour:_ dense dark red-purple, almost opaque. _Bouquet:_ strong and deep with powdery oak and dense fruit. _Palate:_ strong pepper spice, rich and complex with Rhone-like overtones. Has another 20 years in front of it. Magnificent. (19.2/20)

1973 _Colour:_ red, but incredibly still with a few purple hues. _Bouquet:_ very clean, with oak still coming back into balance and integration. _Palate:_ smooth, crisp and long with fairly pronounced acid and one wonders whether the fruit will ever have sufficient body to outlive the oak. Nonetheless, a remarkable wine. (17.6/20)

There is no question that oak plays a persistent and at times dominant role in these wines. The balance of the 1982 suggests for this reason alone that it will be one of the great Virgin Hills wines. But the 1979, 1975 and 1974 have more than enough fruit to carry the oak, and the wines into greatness.

GRAPE-PICKERS, c. 1900

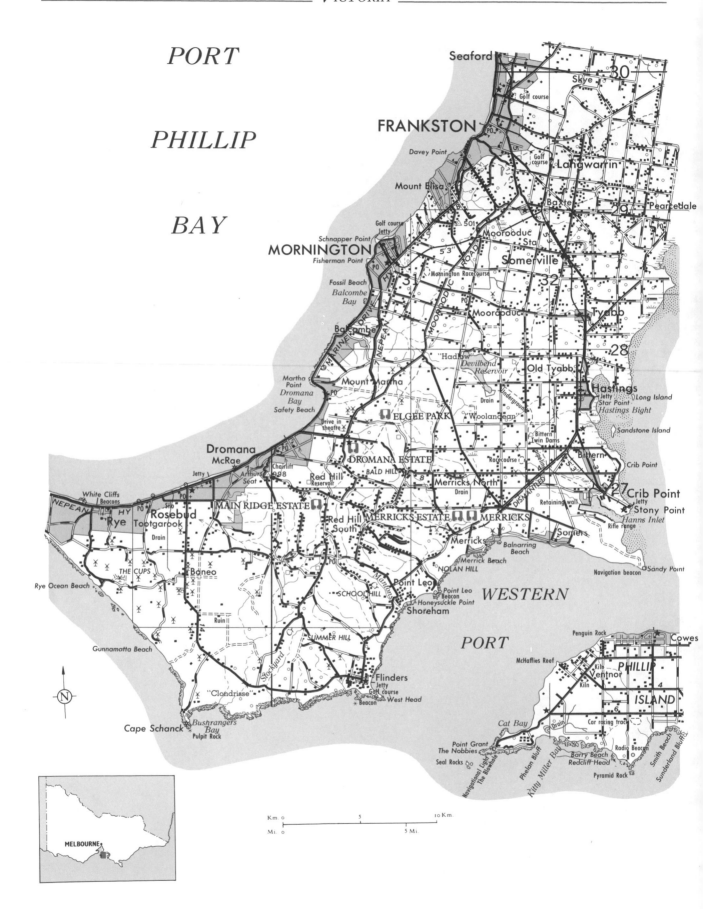

Mornington Peninsula

The Mornington Peninsula is one of the most recent to be accepted as a viticultural area. Yet back in the 1950s Douglas Seabrook planted vines on the lower slopes of the hill known as Arthur's Seat near Dromana. Douglas Seabrook was in many ways in advance of his time; he did not persevere and probably was discouraged by the difficulties which the district encounters.

As in other southern Victorian regions, wind is the major problem. Windbreaks are essential in many locations, but if the vines are able to establish themselves, growing conditions are excellent. With the influence of the sea ever present, it is an extremely cool, late-ripening area, with the earliest varieties seldom vintaged before the end of March.

As at 1985 there were 25 hectares of grapes grown by 22 growers. As these figures indicate, the industry in the area is still organised on a doll's-house scale, but it is most certainly an area we shall hear more of in the years to come.

DROMANA ESTATE
HARRISONS ROAD, DROMANA

Garry and Margaret Crittenden purchased their 11-hectare site in Harrisons Road, Dromana, in 1981 for the specific purpose of establishing a vineyard. They wasted no time in doing so, and at the end of the following winter planted 1.6 hectares of cabernet sauvignon, 0.2 hectare of merlot, 0.1 hectare of pinot noir and 0.1 hectare of chardonnay; a further 2.8 hectares of vines will be established in the future.

The vines are being established with the aid of trickle-irrigation on sandy loam overlying a well-drained and structured clay subsoil. The 18-month-old vines have grown well, producing 1.25 tonnes in their first vintage. The Crittendens are somewhat modestly aiming at an eventual yield of 7.5 tonnes per hectare, employing a vertical trellis system. I suspect that unless they deliberately reduce yields by bunch-thinning, they may well exceed expectations.

The first vintage was made for Dromana Estate by Nat White at Main Ridge. A winery is planned for 1986 or possibly 1987. The first vintage showed all the quality one would expect from a well-sited vineyard on the Mornington Peninsula.

ELGEE PARK
WALLACES ROAD, MERRICKS NORTH

When Baillieu Myer invited David Wynn to lunch at his Mornington Peninsula property in 1971, grape growing and winemaking had not entered into Myer's mind. But over lunch that day David Wynn told Myer of Doug Seabrook's efforts to establish a vineyard on the lower slopes of the hill known as Arthur's Seat in the 1950s. Wynn went on to say that he believed the site was ideal for viticulture, a view which had been confirmed by several wine visitors from Bordeaux.

The idea sown in his mind, Baillieu Myer turned first to Allan Antcliff of the CSIRO and thereafter to Ian Hickinbotham for further advice and help. The first plantings (two-thirds cabernet sauvignon and one-third rhine riesling) followed in 1972, and the first grapes were harvested in 1975.

The wine was made in fairly primeval conditions in an old shed on the property, with Ian Hickinbotham as consultant winemaker. Rhine riesling was made in 1975, 1976 and 1977, but it was so disappointing that Myer concluded the area was not suited to the variety, and grafted the rhine riesling plantings to cabernet sauvignon. The total quantity of wine produced was very small: the plantings are still modest, but at that stage were smaller still. Myer prefers to talk in term of numbers of vines, which as at 1984 amounted to 5500 in all. With a planting density of around 2500 vines per hectare, the vineyard is still little more than two hectares in extent. However, plans are under way to double the number of vines, if not the area of land planted. The decision has been taken to substantially increase the density of the plantings, although precisely what spacing will be used was still being determined early in 1985.

The existing plantings comprise chardonnay (0.6 hectare), rhine riesling (0.4 hectare), cabernet sauvignon (0.6 hectare), merlot (0.4 hectare) and cabernet franc (0.1 hectare). There are also some experimental plantings of viognier and one or two other white varieties provided by the CSIRO. The 1985 plantings will include 2000 sauvignon blanc vines (or a little under one hectare on a conventional spacing) and a _pro rata_ increase (totalling 3500 vines) of the chardonnay, rhine riesling, cabernet sauvignon and merlot plantings.

The rhine riesling exists because a number of the grafts failed to take, and the old rhine riesling plantings re-established themselves. With greater experience of the viticultural potential of the area, and with the better winemaking facilities at Anakie, it became apparent that rhine riesling was, after all, suited. Its initial failure was due in part to the grapes being picked too early, and in part to the limitations of the previous winery set-up.

Until the end of the 1970s all the wines were made at Elgee Park. Between 1980 and 1982 winemaking moved to the Hickinbotham Anakie Winery, and the 1983 Cabernet Sauvignon was also made at Anakie. Prior to the 1984 vintage a new winery was constructed at Elgee Park, designed and supervised by Oenotec. The 1984 wines were all made at Elgee Park under Oenotec's supervision, with Elgee manager Henk Vandenham's help.

Production is still minuscule: the Elgee Park vineyards provided five tonnes in 1984, and little more than 10 tonnes were expected for 1985. While Baillieu Myer is prepared to buy in grapes grown on the Mornington Peninsula for the Elgee Park label, he has no interest in going outside the district, either to the Yarra Valley or elsewhere. Thus for the foreseeable future distribution will be limited to the twice-yearly mailing list.

The Hickinbotham-made Elgee Park cabernet sauvignon left no doubt about the quality of the fruit from the vineyard. The only problem with the wine is that only 20-dozen bottles were released for sale each year, and it is accordingly exceedingly rare. The 1984 wines were, as one would expect, immaculately made, and reconfirmed the outstanding potential of the Mornington Peninsula for producing the finest of table wines.

MAIN RIDGE ESTATE
WILLIAM ROAD, MAIN RIDGE

Main Ridge Estate is the most senior of the Mornington Peninsula producers; while the vineyard (first planted in 1975) came after the initial experimental plantings at Elgee Park, the erection of the winery in 1980 came four years before the next commercial winery at Elgee Park. The first wine was made in that year, and the first Main Ridge Estate wine went on sale in 1981.

Nat White was formerly an engineer with the Public Works Department. His father-in-law, Gwyn Jones, helps with the winemaking, and for a basically self-trained team they have done exceptionally well. The vineyard is established on 2.8 hectares of cabernet sauvignon, 0.7 hectare of chardonnay, 0.5 hectare of pinot noir, 0.3 hectare of gewurztraminer and 0.1 hectare of pinot meunière, for a total of 4.4 hectares. The vines are established on large trellises and a modified form of Geneva double-curtain pruning is employed together with summer slashing to give fruit exposure. Despite the deep-red basalt soil, yields are not especially high, with 12.5 tonnes being produced in the 1984 vintage.

The quality is, however, exemplary. The 1982 Cabernet Sauvignon, at its only showing, won the St Hubert's Award and the Victorian Wine Centre Trophy for the best red wine at the 1983 Lilydale show; the 1983 Pinot Noir was likewise shown only once (at the same show) and also won a gold medal. Some equally good chardonnays have been made over the few years since Nat and Rosalie White hung up the "Wine for Sale" sign outside the winery in William Road, Main Ridge.

MERRICKS
THOMPSONS LANE, MERRICKS

One assumes that one of these days either Merricks or Merricks Estate will change its name. Until this occurs, endless confusion will ensure. Merricks, which takes its name from the locality in which it is situated, is the property of Brian Stonier and claims the largest plantings in the Mornington Peninsula area at the present time. The 4.85-hectare vineyard is planted to chardonnay (1.61 hectares), cabernet sauvignon and pinot noir (1.2 hectares each) and cabernet franc and merlot (0.4 hectare each).

The wines are made for Merricks by Stephen Hickinbotham at Anakie. As at 1985 they were sold through only two outlets, Gatehouse Cellars and Fannys Restaurant. Presumably as quantities increase, so will distribution.

A 1984 Cabernet Sauvignon from Merricks was absolutely stunning, with archetypal capsicum/bell-pepper flavours and yet exhibiting berry sweetness on the mid-palate.

MERRICKS ESTATE
THOMPSONS LANE, MERRICKS

George and Jacquellyn Kefford had shared a long-standing interest in wine and food when they purchased a 20-hectare property on the Mornington Peninsula in 1976. Nonetheless, it was not purchased for the specific purpose of commencing a vineyard; indeed, unaware that anyone else had established vines in the district, the Keffords were far from sure that it was suited to viticulture. In 1978 they determined to find out, and planted 50 vines as a trial. Nothing disastrous happened, so in 1979 they extended the trial plantings with 100 vines each of cabernet sauvignon, shiraz and rhine riesling. In 1980 they extended it even further, with an additional 100 vines of cabernet, 50 vines of rhine riesling and 100 vines of pinot noir. The resultant planting of 0.3 hectare, known as the "fruit salad" block, formed the basis of the first vintage in 1982. It has likewise produced the 1983 and 1984 vintages, the latter resulting in around 180 dozen bottles of wine.

By 1982 the Keffords had determined that, on the basis of their own experiments, cabernet sauvignon was suited to the region; and, on the basis of their next-door neighbour's property, that chardonnay was suited. So in the winter of 1982 they planted 300 chardonnay vines in the first of the "commercial" plantings which were to follow in the ensuing years. They ordered 1400 vines of chardonnay and of cabernet sauvignon for planting in the 1983 season, sufficient to establish 1.4 hectares of vines at a planting density of around 2000 vines per hectare. Due to problems at the nursery, they ended up with double the quantity of chardonnay and no cabernet sauvignon. The latter was eventually established in 1984 (0.6 hectare) and a similar 0.6-hectare planting of shiraz is planned for 1985. Total plantings of approximately 2.9 hectares at the present time will ultimately be extended to four hectares; any further increase would depend on circumstances at the time.

George Kefford learnt his winemaking the hard way, which was basically by trial and error. He was aided by the standard reference books and by short courses at Dookie Agricultural College. Nonethe-less, he freely admits to making mistakes; the first rhine riesling went down the drain, and other wines have been far from perfect.

As from 1984 he retained the consulting services of Alex White, with an immediate increase in wine quality. Merricks Estate produced a quite magnificent 1984 Shiraz, a richly deserved gold-medal-winner at the 1984 Victorian Wines Show. It has intense, fragrant, crushed-pepper/spice aroma and flavour; it is at the same time a very elegant wine. On the limited evidence to date it seems that Mornington Peninsula is singularly well suited to shiraz. One can only hope that the marketplace is prepared to recognise that quality.

The Keffords have recently increased their land-holdings by buying a further 20 hectares, so any future expansion will not be limited by availability of suitable land.

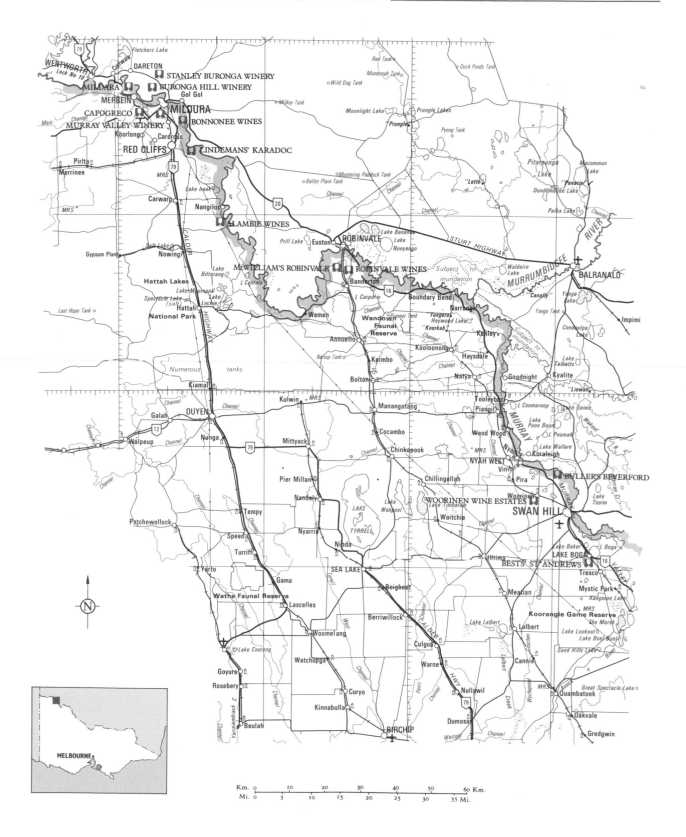

Murray River

The development of the Victorian riverlands was due almost entirely to the tenacity and vision of the brothers George and William Chaffey, who had played a leading role in the establishment of the first irrigation projects in California. Alfred Deakin, then a youthful politician, had persuaded the Victorian government of the feasibility and need to utilise the vast water supply of the Murray River, which then flowed through uninhabitable, parched desert. In the early 1880s he made a study tour of the Californian developments, and it was his interest which led to George Chaffey arriving in Melbourne in 1886.

Chaffey took one look at the Murray River, and the red sandy soil which spread out on the dead-flat plains on either side of it, and knew it was ideally suited for a major irrigation project. He immediately purchased the Mildura Station, then drought-ridden and virtually abandoned. Syd Wells, in *Fine Wines from the Deserts*, which tells the story of the establishment of Mildara, provides a vivid picture of the property which Chaffey purchased (and of his reasons for purchasing it):

> The Mildura Station had been one of the first selections on the Victorian side of the Murray, about 30 kilometres upstream from the Darling Junction on a river flat between white cliffs and the red which the Aborigines had named literally red-rock (Mil-dura). Separated from Melbourne by a wilderness of mallee—an insane monotony of sand, dwarf eucalypts, and saltbush plains—there was nothing to distinguish the homestead from any other, apart from its famous garden which produced abundant crops of whatever fruit or vegetable the Jamieson family cared to plant. The locals wondered why it flourished. When Chaffey saw it he knew he had found his Eldorado: the soil which needed only water to make it fertile and a climate similar to California which, with its low rainfall and abundant sunshine, was perfect for maturing and drying fruit naturally.

Confident that the government would welcome his expertise, George Chaffey arranged for his brother to sell all of their Californian landholdings in haste (sustaining substantial losses in so doing) and to join him in Australia. By the time William Chaffey arrived it had become apparent that they were to be entwined in a political and bureaucratic web. Instead of being granted the land (which no-one else wanted), the government decided an Act of Parliament was necessary, and that tenders for the land would be called for.

Disillusioned, the Chaffeys offered their services to the South Australian government and were welcomed with open arms. By the time the Mildura tenders had lapsed they had already selected and cleared much of the Renmark site in South Australia. When no other responses were received to the tender applications, a chastened Victorian government returned to the Chaffeys and offered them the land on substantially the same terms as those which the Chaffeys had originally sought. Somewhat surprisingly, the Chaffeys agreed to take on this major project as well as that at Renmark, dangerously stretching their resources in so doing. Notwithstanding this strain, between 1887 and 1890 the Mildura settlement was commenced and grew rapidly. Within months of its opening 200 hectares of land had been cleared for occupation, 27 kilometres of main irrigation channel constructed, temporary pumping plants installed, and a population of 270 had arrived with cottages, shops and offices in the course of construction.

Over the next few years development continued at the same hectic pace, and by 1893 the first vines and fruit trees produced the first commercial harvest. It was a disastrous year in Australia: on 28 January 1893 the great bank crash commenced, and with it came the end of the land boom which had been at the base of the speculation leading to the crash. By May even the country's largest bank, the Commercial Banking Company of Sydney, had been forced to close its doors temporarily. As if this were not enough, the Murray River dried up unusually early in that year, and the only means of transport to Melbourne was severely curtailed. The end result was that three-quarters of the crop rotted on the wharves at Mildura, or was found to be in unsaleable condition when it arrived in Melbourne. The *coup de grâce* came when it was discovered that yabbies were undermining the main irrigation channels, and that salt seepage was killing many of the newly established vines and trees.

The Chaffeys struggled on for two years, but in 1895 were forced to close their offices. A royal commission found them guilty of mismanagement (against all of the evidence), and George Chaffey returned to America, broken and bankrupt. William Chaffey, however, was made of sterner stuff and stayed on, determined to prove that the Mildura development was viable.

Right from the outset both table grapes and wine grapes had formed an important part in Chaffey's planning. In 1891 he had established Chateau Mildura; while the settlement had been founded on temperance principles, wine was considered a natural beverage and to be encouraged accordingly. The winery was constructed prior to the 1892 vintage, complete with large underground store-rooms and oak vats.

The difficulties of marketing the product became immediately apparent, and in the following year the restraint against spirits was suspended to allow wine from the 1892 and 1893 vintages to be distilled into spirit. The distillation was not carried out at Chateau Mildura, but the wine was supplied from there. This created a small but inadequate market and table wine continued to accumulate. No local market for table wine could be established and the cost of freight to Melbourne was prohibitively expensive. In 1897 half the vineyard area was grafted to table grapes and, bowing to the inevitable, Chaffey installed a still to permit the production of fortified wine, which the local population was prepared to buy. A steam-driven crusher was also installed, replacing the foot method of crushing. It was to no avail. The products could not be sold in sufficient quantity, and by 1908 the winery had closed, the remaining vineyards having been grafted to table grapes.

Almost immediately the situation changed once again. The vignerons in north-eastern Victoria were anxious to secure a cheap source of fortifying spirit, and a consortium involving several of those vignerons together with William Chaffey formed Mildura

Winery Proprietary Limited, which purchased the assets of Chateau Mildura and obtained a distiller's licence. The winery (situated at Irymple) was successfully reopened, and the guaranteed markets soon led to the establishment of a second operation at Merbein. Opened in time for the 1914 vintage, it soon became the centre of operations. The Irymple Winery was leased to Graham Brothers of Rutherglen from 1918.

The extravagant swings of fortune continued, however. The Returned Soldier Settlement Schemes sponsored by the New South Wales, Victorian and South Australian governments produced a sudden grape surplus; and discontent among the growers became acute when Mildura Winery was unable to honour certain of its grape-purchase contracts. An impasse developed, and in 1920 both the Irymple and Merbein Wineries were offered to the Growers' Association for $110,000. After lengthy deliberation the growers declined, and it was resolved to wind up the company but to incorporate a new company (bearing the same name) to acquire the assets of the old. The major shareholders included many of the larger growers and William Chaffey retained his position as chairman.

Between 1921 and 1924 the new company survived (just), but in the latter year events turned dramatically in its favour. In 1924 government-induced grape surpluses (in no small measure caused by the Soldier Settlement Schemes) were looming as a major economic and political problem. At Mildura the growers refused an offer of $4 a tonne for all grapes over the agreed contract intake, and it became evident that the government would have to take some action. Banking on rumours of a government bounty for exports, Mildura Winery recommissioned the then-idle Irymple plant, and made plans for a substantially increased intake.

Up until the end of 1924 exports to the United Kingdom had been largely table wine because the duty on fortified wine gave the Spanish and Portuguese exporters an inbuilt preference, due to their lower production and transport costs. In 1925 the Wine Export Bounty Act was passed by the Australian government, and in the following year the United Kingdom introduced preferential tariffs for British Empire countries. The combined effect of these two pieces of legislation was dramatic: in 1921 England had imported $9,342,000 worth of wine from France and $1,082,000 from Australia. In 1927 it imported $8,448,000 of wine from Australia and $7,082,000 from France. Although both pieces of legislation were repealed before the end of the

1920s, the value of Australian wine exports to England remained substantially greater than those of France right up to the outbreak of the Second World War.

At least until the onset of the Depression, and the removal of the preference and the bounty respectively, it was a time of great prosperity for most of the Riverlands of South Australia, Victoria and New South Wales. Curiously, the north-west had to wait until the latter part of the 1970s to come really into its own as a highly efficient producer of bulk table wine and fortified wine. Until the early 1960s Mildura Winery had to carry the torch on its own. I follow the development from 1935 of Mildara Wines (as it came to be known) in more detail a little later; suffice it to say here that until well into the 1950s Mildura was primarily a fortified-winemaker, and it was for this style alone that the region was known.

The vast changes in consumption (and production) which then swept across the country inevitably also had their mark on Sunraysia, as the district came to be known. It has always been the most important producer of table and dried grapes in Australia, and for no other area does the collapse of the dried-fruits market have such grim implications. Yet on the other hand it is one of the most efficient bulk producers in the country, rivalled only by the Murrumbidgee Irrigation Area of New South Wales.

The general introduction of tile drainage some 50 years ago, and the works programmes introduced up and down the length of the Murray by the three State governments concerned around 15 years ago, have done much to alleviate the problems of salinity which once threatened the irrigation areas. Salinity levels are still decreasing, and while pollution in the Murray remains a problem for some facets of the industry, it is having a minimal effect on viticulture.

The dark-red sandy soil of the region needs only water: plant literally anything in this sand, give it moisture, and it will grow luxuriantly. Mildura, Merbein and Irymple are truly garden cities (or towns, if you prefer), a verdant oasis year round. It is, in short, the perfect area in which to grow grapes such as sultana and muscat gordo blanco destined for bulk white wine.

It was not until 1964 that Hungerford Hill decided to establish a winery at Buronga, just across the river in New South Wales. Ten years later Lindemans followed suit and commenced the construction of the immense Karadoc Winery, which in 1984 crushed a record 44,000 tonnes of grapes. Until these two major wineries came into production much of the fruit was sent out of the district for processing both

upstream and in Griffith in New South Wales. Since that time Bonnonee Wines and Sunnycliff Wines have taken an increasing share of local production, producing both clarified grape juice and bulk wine for sale to other winemakers. Finally, there is a handful of small family-owned wineries run by Italian and Greek families, producing wine styles aimed specifically at the ethnic communities from which they spring.

Official production figures for the Sunraysia are, to say the least, puzzling. The Australian Bureau of Statistics figures show 30,930 tonnes crushed for winemaking in 1979; 38,778 in 1980; 32,388 in 1981; 26,404 in 1982; and 34,644 tonnes in 1983. Even allowing for the fact that substantial quantities of grapes are bought (*inter alia*) from Padthaway for Lindemans, the figures suggest very substantial grape movements in and out of the region. These figures, incidentally, are all dwarfed by table-grape production of 230,000 tonnes in 1982 and 254,000 tonnes in 1983. These are largely dried; about 10,000 tonnes a year are sold as fresh grapes.

Further upstream, due east, is the Swan Hill–Kerang area which produces substantial quantities of grapes under similar conditions and for nearly identical purposes. Although the scale of production is less (about one-third that of Sunraysia), far more of the grapes are used for winemaking. Production for this purpose has fluctuated around 24,000 tonnes a year.

A double threat hangs over the production of bulk wine in Australia early in 1985: the seeming inevitability in increases in the level of wine taxes, and the imminent total and final collapse of the dried-fruits market. No region can feel totally secure, but the inbuilt advantages of the Sunraysia/Swan Hill areas must give them a headstart over most other regions.

ALAMBIE WINES
NANGILOC ROAD, NANGILOC

Alambie is an interesting winery, which seeks to maximise the district propensity for highly efficient grape production and bulk-wine manufacture. Whereas almost all of the other modern wineries which either have been built or significantly expanded in recent years rely totally on independent growers, all of Alambie's 2000-tonne crush is estate-grown.

From this point on similar methods are followed: all of the 1.5-million litre production is sold within months of vintage, either in the form of juice or as bulk wine. The buyers are other major wineries, almost inevitably situated outside the district. Production is slanted towards better-quality varietals (cabernet sauvignon, shiraz, grenache, tarrango, rhine riesling, colombard, traminer and chenin blanc), although some muscat gordo blanco and sultana are produced. All of the grapes are machine-harvested at night, and winemaker David Martin has a well-equipped modern winery able to produce technically perfect bulk wine and clarified grape juice.

BESTS' ST ANDREWS
MURRAY VALLEY HIGHWAY, LAKE BOGA

Bests' St Andrews Vineyard is situated at Swan Hill, more than 200 kilometres upstream from Mildura. I trace the history of Bests, and the circumstances under which it acquired St Andrews, on pages 177 and 178.

St Andrews is now planted to muscat gordo blanco (seven hectares), shiraz and sultana (4.2 hectares each), doradillo (two hectares), rhine riesling (1.7 hectares), grenache (1.6 hectares), chenin blanc and cabernet sauvignon (1.5 hectares each), frontignac (1.2 hectares), black muscat and palomino (1.1 hectares each) and colombard (one hectare). At an average yield of around 15 tonnes per hectare, these plantings provide approximately 65 per cent of the annual crush, the remaining 35 per cent being bought in from other growers in the district.

Wine quality is exemplary.

BONNONEE WINES
CAMPBELL AVENUE, IRYMPLE

The Bonnonee operation of 1985 bears no resemblance to that of 1974, the year in which local growers Michael and his wife Sandi Fitzpatrick decided to join forces with Californian-born Richard Cirami and his wife to make a little wine on the side. Cirami was an amateur winemaker, and the partners decided to see what could be done on a rather larger scale.

Cirami has now left the partnership; in 1984 Bonnonee crushed 7500 tonnes of grapes, and was looking forward to a 9000-tonne crush in 1985. Ninety per cent of the intake comes from independent growers in the district, the remaining 10 per cent coming from the Fitzpatrick vineyards. These are planted to traminer, chardonnay, rhine riesling, colombard, ruby cabernet, shiraz, sultana, crouchen

and muscat gordo blanco. Other grapes (including barbera) are bought in.

Currently around 10,000 cases of wine (or 15 per cent) are bottled and sold under the three label ranges, the remaining 85 per cent being sold in the form of clarified juice (two-thirds) and bulk wine (one-third). The three-label range starts with flavoured and sparkling wines, featuring some of the labels which Bonnonee acquired when it purchased the remaining stock and goodwill of Mildura Vineyards, situated on the north side of the Murray River. Blue Party Girl and Red Cliffs Big Lizzie were two of the more memorable labels, both in terms of the names and the graphic illustrations. These days Mike Fitzpatrick settles for the more prosaic spumante, sparkling passion wine and sparkling strawberry wine under the Mildura Vineyard label. The Bonnonee range offers a Moselle, Sandalong Dry White, Traminer, Belara Light Red and a range of sweet and dry sherries and ports.

In December 1984 the third top-of-the-range wine was introduced under the Fitzpatrick Estate label. These comprised a chardonnay (very light-bodied and with obvious oak), a rhine riesling (full, soft and clean with quite good varietal character), a traminer (gently spicy and refreshingly dry), a rhine riesling/traminer (a very commercial, perceptibly sweet style), which were all from 1984; and two 1982 reds, a ruby cabernet/barbera blend (nondescript aroma, but a clean well-balanced palate), and a straight cabernet sauvignon (gently astringent and with good varietal character).

All of these wines were made by Neville Hudson, a native of Mildura but who learnt his winemaking during a six-year stint with Saxonvale. He returned to Mildura and joined Bonnonee prior to the 1983 vintage. Although he concedes that he would like Mike Fitzpatrick to spend a little more on some new oak, with the capital investment associated with the increase in Bonnonee's crush from 2700 to almost 9000 tonnes in four years he also concedes that it is not very likely. That capital investment has equipped Bonnonee with a formidable array of white-wine-making equipment, not to mention a vast investment in stainless-steel fermentation tanks and storage tanks. Nonetheless, a new $50,000 bottling line imported from Italy gives an indication of the seriousness with which Bonnonee is approaching its brand products.

BULLER'S BEVERFORD
MURRAY VALLEY HIGHWAY, SWAN HILL

Buller's Beverford is another Swan Hill winery, set up in 1952 and complementing Buller's Rutherglen operation in the same way as Bests' St Andrews complements its Great Western production. The 14-hectare vineyard is planted to cabernet sauvignon, shiraz, pedro ximinez, muscat of alexandria and semillon. These plantings contribute around 15 per cent of the annual crush, which has been as high as 1800 tonnes a year. A significant part of this was distilled, providing fortifying spirit both for Buller's dessert wines and ports, and also for sale to other makers of fortified wine throughout Victoria and South Australia.

A range of casks, flagons and bottled wine and red varietal table wine is produced. Overall the quality of the wines has been honest rather than outstanding.

BURONGA HILL WINERY
BURONGA

Buronga Hill Winery was established in 1984 by ex-employees of the Hungerford Hill Buronga winery who, in the aftermath of the sale of that winery to Stanley, decided to set up their own operation. Situated on the New South Wales side of the Murray River, it has been established with all the necessary modern winemaking equipment and was expected to crush several thousand tonnes in 1985. All of the production will be sold in bulk.

CAPOGRECO
RIVERSIDE AVENUE, MILDURA

Capogreco, established in 1976, is at the opposite end of the Sunraysia wine spectrum from Bonnonee, Alambie and Sunnycliff. All of the production comes from the family's 20-hectare vineyard, all is sold by cellar door in bottles or flagons, and none is sold in bulk.

What is more, winemaking techniques are uncompromisingly Italian-traditional. The winery prides itself in using "no unnatural additives", and in wood-ageing most white wines and all red wines for between six and 24 months. The cellar-door sales area in Riverside Avenue, Mildura, is within sight of the Mildura aerodrome, and attracts a steady flow of visitors. Here they taste wines which are as different as one could imagine from those of Bonnonee.

Prolonged wood-ageing of white wines, with little or no sulphur dioxide added to preserve the wines, inevitably leads to browning and oxidation; the red wines, likewise, inevitably pick up volatility. The resultant wines are something of an acquired taste. Far more successful are the herb-flavoured fortified wines; here any problem with the base wine is obscured by the fortifying spirit and the most attractive herb infusion. Rosso Dolce is really a very pleasant base for mixed drinks.

LINDEMANS' KARADOC
NANGILOC ROAD, RED CLIFFS

Lindemans purchased a remote 160-hectare dairy farm, north-east of the town of Red Cliffs, in late 1963. There it erected one of the largest and most modern wineries in Australia with a single object in mind: to produce what company executives call *vin ordinaire* at the lowest-possible cost. Such is the technology employed that, instead of being, as the French say, *très ordinaire*, Karadoc has excelled itself.

But first the *vin ordinaire*, or, as it is also known in the company, VO. This is provided through the medium of a crush which rose to a record 44,000 tonnes in 1984. The sources of the grapes for this massive intake were remarkably varied. Lindemans' own plantings of 110 hectares (principally rhine riesling, chardonnay and cabernet sauvignon) produce a token three or four per cent. The vast bulk comes from other growers in the district, although Karadoc is used increasingly to process surplus grapes from Lindemans' Padthaway Vineyard which the Rouge Homme Winery cannot handle, and also to ferment clarified juice emanating both from Rouge Homme and Chateau Leonay at Tanunda in the Barossa Valley.

Vintage extends for 10 weeks, and at the peak of the season 1200 tonnes per day are crushed, day in, day out. This is achieved in a 10-hour crushing day; the plant could work 24 hours, but the pressing facilities and the fermentation cellars already work a 24-hour shift. Not for Karadoc a lengthy cold-settling of juice, skin contact, and a leisurely commencement to white-wine fermentation. The white grapes are crushed, drained and centrifuged. The juice is then put through a heat exchanger to reduce the temperature to 18°C, before being transferred to the fermentation tank and the yeast cultures added, all by 2 p.m. on the day on which the grapes were harvested. The wines are then transferred to the tank farm, established in the open and of awesome size. There are 200 tanks, the largest of which hold 1.5 million litres of wine. The total of 200 tanks provides 47 million litres of storage. Not a drop of grape juice or wine lees is wasted. Earth-filters, centrifuges and pad-filters reclaim every last drop of wine; while the marc is carted off on an aerial automated overhead bucket system reminiscent of one of the rides at Luna Park, ultimately making its way to Tarac Distillery in South Australia where it is distilled into spirit.

The primary object of Karadoc is the production of soft-pack wine and, in the heady days of Ben Ean Moselle success, much of the material for it. The casks are packaged and stored in a large air-conditioned warehouse with a semitrailer seemingly constantly parked outside and being loaded. One hundred and twenty-five people are permanently employed on site, with another 40 casuals—casuals who work most days of the year.

In the midst of this sea of plenty there are two rather unexpected facets of Karadoc. First, and almost unseen next to the towering, monolithic tank farm, is "the winery". When Lindemans closed its long-established winery at Corowa in New South Wales, the old corrugated-iron winery was dismantled and largely re-erected at Karadoc. All of the old sweet, white, fortified-wine stocks followed, the ports going to Chateau Leonay. To walk into the corrugated-iron winery (which has been insulated on the ceiling and two of the side walls) is something of a culture shock. The smell and the feel of generations of winemaking, of wines 20, 30 and even 50 years old, have been magically transported to the unexpected surroundings of Karadoc.

The other unexpected facet of Karadoc is the range of varietal table wines released under the Matthew Lang label. In late 1979 Gerry Sissingh left the Rothbury Estate, and rejoined the Lindemans fold from whence he had come. He was appointed chief winemaker and manager at Karadoc, and was quick to realise that some first-class material was being lost in the anonymity of flagon and cask blends. He set out to prove that some of these wines could and should be bottled separately, and in November 1982 Lindemans announced the Matthew Lang range. For this purpose it revived the label of one of Victoria's foremost wine merchants, whose business it had acquired many years previously.

The three wines were a 1981 Chardonnay Chablis, 1982 Fumé Blanc and a 1980 Cabernet Sauvignon. The concept of a chardonnay chablis was and is a clever one: the vineyards of Sunraysia will never provide rich or luscious chardonnay, but can provide wines which legitimately aspire to the chablis name (whatever that may mean in Australia). Both this and the subsequent vintages, in 1982 and 1983, have maintained a consistency of style and quality which can only be admired. The first release of Fumé Blanc from the 1982 vintage showed an exemplary introduction of oak flavour and aroma to a wine which had surprising mid-palate fruit weight. It was these features which led the judges at the 1983 Victorian Wines Show to award it a gold medallion and trophy, an award I shared in giving and could hardly argue with.

Arguably, however, the greatest success has come with the two releases of Cabernet Sauvignon, the first from 1980 and the second from 1983. The 1980 was a gold-medal-winner at the Melbourne show and runner-up for the trophy for best Victorian red; it showed surprising herbaceous/green-leaf character in both its aroma and palate. The 1983 Cabernet Sauvignon is in many ways a better wine, with lovely cassis-berry aromas and flavours, and quite excellent structure. In early 1985 the colour was absolutely extraordinary for a warm-area wine—still a vibrant red-purple.

In 1983 rhine riesling also made its appearance under the Matthew Lang label; commercial expediency led to the inclusion of rather more residual sugar than seems to me to be absolutely necessary, and which detracted from a wine which had above-average fruit and varietal character.

McWILLIAM'S ROBINVALE
MOORE STREET, ROBINVALE

McWilliam's established its Robinvale Winery in 1961, the last of its network of wineries spread throughout the Riverland areas of New South Wales and Victoria. It produces white table wines from sultana, muscat gordo blanco, chenin blanc, rkatsiteli and italia, and fortifying spirit from a mix of varieties. Winemakers Max McWilliam and Jason Chester preside over a highly efficient operation in a winery which, inevitably enough, reflects the technological skills of the McWilliam family.

MILDARA
WENTWORTH ROAD, MERBEIN

The period from 1933 to 1937 was an extremely important one for Mildura Winery. Until 1933 it had lurched along from one crisis to the next, making fortified wine with equipment which, even by the standards of those days, could only be described as basic, and producing a mediocre product which was sold—not always successfully—into the bulk market.

In 1933 Gus Pegler was appointed chairman; he immediately made arrangements for Mildura Winery's products to be marketed in England through the Overseas Farmers' Cooperative Federation in place of the Emu Wine Company; commenced the design of wine labels; and initiated steps to obtain licences for cellar-door sales from the two wineries. While the change of English marketing agents was to prove advantageous in the long run, continued complaints regarding the condition of the product arriving in England led to the appointment of Ronald Haselgrove as technical adviser in 1935. This was to be the turning point for the company.

A graduate of Roseworthy Agricultural College, Haselgrove had started his career in the wool trade but quickly moved across to the wine industry. After gaining practical experience working for Buring and Sobels, he went to Europe in 1922 to study at Montpellier College, thereafter working firstly in Cognac and then Bordeaux. On returning to Australia he joined Angove's at Renmark, where he vastly improved the products of that company by reducing bacterial spoilage in its fortified wines and introducing pot-still brandy. Haselgrove's initial appointment to Mildura Winery was for a five-year term as technical adviser, and as a board member. At the subsequent expiration of his contract with Angove's, he joined Mildura Winery as sales and technical director, and embarked on a programme designed to produce the finest sherries and brandy available on the Australian commercial market.

In 1937 the Mildara trade mark was registered, and from that point of time onwards the old Mildura Winery name gradually disappeared. Initially domestic brand sales were restricted to the local market, with the bulk of production still being exported. Exports reached their peak in 1940 when the Second World War eliminated European competition, but rapidly dwindled thereafter as ships ceased to be available. During the war years Mildara's distilleries were largely directed to distilling brown sugar into methylated spirits, a project which not only helped the war effort but also contributed significantly to

profits through sales of the spirit to local transport and industry.

By the end of the Second World War the company's production was almost entirely given over to red and white sweet fortified wines, although a limited trade had developed for a lightly fortified sweet wine made from sultanas, sold in the Sydney market. With the gradual easing of the wartime restrictions, Ronald Haselgrove was once again able to take up his flor fino sherry project, and in 1949 the first Mildara Supreme Sherry was bottled, 350 dozen in all. The following year 10 dozen of an experimental bone-dry sherry were produced for its chairman, George Caro, who had a sugar-free diet. Thus Mildara's second major sherry, George, was created.

Until well into the 1960s Mildara was first and foremost a sherry company, and to this day derives a substantial part of its sales income from fortified wine and brandy. In 1949, however, the links with Gollin & Company, which had commenced before the Second World War, were strengthened. Gollin & Company was Mildara's sole agent in the eastern States, and in that year took up a major shareholding in Mildara. Gollin had an established market (although limited) for red table wine as well as fortified wines, and Mildara was unable to supply any part of this. So in 1950 Ronald Haselgrove went back to France to inspect winemaking equipment, secure supplies of oak (in fact intended principally for fortified winemaking) and to evaluate wine-making practices generally. His path must have crossed with that of Max Schubert, who was on a similar mission for Penfolds.

In 1951 the first Mildara red wine was made and released under the now-famous cabernet shiraz label. Bin 21 was unique in that it was a 100 per cent Chateau Reynella wine, all of the subsequent releases being area blends. In 1952 Mildara acquired a controlling interest in Walter Reynell & Sons, ensuring a continuing supply of red table wine under the Mildara "Yellow Label". For the next 15 years this wine was Mildara's flagship, until its Coonawarra plantings came into production and the Coonawarra label made its appearance on the market.

The Mildara Yellow Label Series is treasured by the majority of those who were introduced to red wine in the 1960s and early 1970s. It has had a chequered history since 1975, largely due to the Gollin collapse. No Yellow Label wine was made in 1976, or in 1978 or 1979. When Gollin & Company went into liquidation its vast stocks of Mildara wine flooded onto the market at very depressed prices. Merchants such as Crittenden in Melbourne bought semitrailer loads, offering the wine for as little as $1.25 per bottle if purchased by the case. To compound the problems a substantial part of the Gollin stock had been stored in a non-air-conditioned shed, and had deteriorated. The liquidator was understandably not concerned with such niceties, and the affected stock was sold along with the good stock.

For a number of years it appeared as if the reputation of the line had been irrevocably damaged. However, loyal customers kept demanding the wine, and it was reintroduced in 1980 with Bin 46. These days it is a curious, old-fashioned label to find amongst the razzle-dazzle of the Mildara Flower Label Series, and other such offerings by Mildara's energetic and effective sales director, Ray King. Nonetheless, as at 1985 Mildara intended to continue the line, and—hopefully—to leave the label untouched.

In January 1985 I attended a remarkable tasting of every table wine of significance made by Mildara since its inception, going back to that 1951 Bin 21. Missing were only the Golden Bower rieslings, a Doug Elliott-made semillon purchased by Mildara in bulk and bottled and labelled by them. (Before it faded from the scene Golden Bower had changed its composition substantially.)

It is always a question, and one with no absolute or invariable answer, whether one commences a retrospective tasting with the youngest wine or the oldest. In my tasting youth I preferred to start with the youngest wine and move to the oldest, and became quite disoriented if the reverse process was used. Now I no longer mind too much, and it gave no pain when tasting commenced with the first wine in the series, 1951 Bin 21. In retrospect this may not have been such a good idea: the wine was so perfect that inevitably those which came after were something of an anticlimax. The problem—if one can call it that—was exacerbated by the fact that it was an absolutely outstanding bottle of the wine, the best that Richard Haselgrove had seen in many, many years. In the interest of historical accuracy I accordingly report on the tasting as it took place on 15 January 1985.

1951 Bin 21 *Composition:* despite the label, 100 per cent Reynella shiraz. *Colour:* aged red, browning on the edges. *Bouquet:* rich, ripe fruit still lingers under complex cedar/tobacco/chocolate aromas; in superb condition. *Palate:* harmonious perfection, with gentle sweet fruit on the mid-palate and a soft, lingering finish. A freakish aged wine in which the structure has not broken at all. (19.2/20) (Richard Haselgrove remembers bottling this wine at Reynella during his school holidays. A bottling team of four

took several weeks to bottle the 3000 dozen made, everything being done by hand, and the wine being transported in wicker baskets from one point of the bottling line to another.)

1953 Bin 22 *Composition:* 35 per cent each of Coonawarra and Southern Vales shiraz, 25 per cent Southern Vales cabernet sauvignon, five per cent Coonawarra cabernet sauvignon. *Colour:* aged redbrown. *Bouquet:* still remarkably firm and rather closed; hint of medicinal/cough mixture. *Palate:* a firm and ripe wine, with a touch of mint, holding both fruit and structure. (17.6/20)

1954 Bin 23 *Composition:* 33 per cent Coonawarra and Southern Vales shiraz, 16 per cent Southern Vales cabernet sauvignon, 12 per cent Coonawarra cabernet sauvignon, six per cent Southern Vales mataro. *Colour:* aged red-brown. *Bouquet:* smooth, gently sweet aromas with a touch of caramel. *Palate:* fine, elegant and smooth, no jammy or tarry characters, and pleasant acid on the finish. (Second bottle opened: first bottle caramelised and oxidised.) (18/20)

1955 Bin 24 *Composition:* 50 per cent Coonawarra shiraz, 25 per cent Southern Vales shiraz, 20 per cent Southern Vales cabernet sauvignon, five per cent Coonawarra cabernet sauvignon. Not tasted on this occasion; on last occasion many years ago showed as a firm, quite astringent style.

1957 Bin 26 *Composition:* 55 per cent Southern Vales shiraz, 20 per cent Southern Vales mataro, 20 per cent Coonawarra shiraz, five per cent Langhorne Creek malbec. An experimental wine which did not succeed and which was not continued, nor tasted on this occasion.

1958 Bin 27 *Composition:* 50 per cent Coonawarra shiraz, 35 per cent Southern Vales shiraz, 15 per cent Southern Vales cabernet sauvignon. *Colour:* aged brick-red. *Bouquet:* firm, closed and still tightly structured. *Palate:* very clean, fine, fresh and, like the bouquet, surprisingly firm, with just a touch of leather; attractive fruit sweetness on the back palate. (18/20)

1958 Bin 27 *Composition:* 65 per cent Coonawarra shiraz, 33 per cent Southern Vales cabernet sauvignon, two per cent Southern Vales shiraz. *Colour:* light to medium in depth, very youthful and still retaining fresh red tinges. *Bouquet:* light and fragrant, with leathery/cedary/grassy aromas, with some similarities to the Bin 21 although less complex. *Palate:* full plummy fruit on the mid-palate, balanced by a touch of tannin and some complex bottle-developed cedar flavours. Opened magnificently. (18.6/20)

1959 Bin 28 *Composition:* 35 per cent Coonawarra shiraz, 25 per cent Southern Vales shiraz, 25 per cent Southern Vales cabernet sauvignon, 15 per cent Hunter Valley shiraz. Not tasted on this occasion; reputed to be a big, full wine but lacking richness and complexity.

1960 Bin 29 *Composition:* 55 per cent Southern Vales shiraz, 25 per cent Hunter Valley shiraz, 15 per cent Southern Vales cabernet sauvignon, five per cent Coonawarra shiraz. *Colour:* aged brick-red. *Bouquet:* strong and very complex with some mint and cedar notes, but overall a little baked and porty. *Palate:* a very big, robust wine, again with that slight baked character from the aroma showing up; marked tannin on the finish. Will certainly be very long-lived. (17.4/20)

1961 Bin 30 *Composition:* 50 per cent Coonawarra shiraz, 25 per cent Southern Vales shiraz, 17.5 per cent Hunter shiraz and 7.5 per cent Southern Vales cabernet sauvignon. *Colour:* dark red with some browning on the rim. *Bouquet:* complex leafy/cedar/leather aromas, full, rich and satisfying. *Palate:* firm and tightly constructed, with rich, fairly ripe fruit and years in front of it. Perhaps a little plain, lacking the almost ethereal complexity of some of the better older wines, but a marvellous 20-year old. (18.2/20)

1962 Bin 31 *Composition:* 55 per cent Coonawarra shiraz, 30 per cent Southern Vales shiraz, 7.5 per cent Southern Vales cabernet sauvignon, 7.5 per cent Hunter Valley shiraz. *Colour:* medium to full red-brown. *Bouquet:* another solid, rich wine, not as open or fragrant as the older wines in the line-up; touch of volatile lift evident. *Palate:* quite different from the bouquet, fragrant and lifted, and given an extra touch of life by that volatility. Some minty flavours also evident. (17.8/20)

1963 Bin 32 *Composition:* 35 per cent Southern Vales shiraz, 33 per cent Coonawarra shiraz, 25 per cent Hunter Valley shiraz and seven per cent Southern Vales cabernet sauvignon. *Colour:* strong red with some signs of browning. *Bouquet:* strong and youthful with a trace of attractive fresh gravel/earth aromas. *Palate:* superb, round and ripe fleshy fruit followed by soft but persistent tannin. A beautiful wine at its peak, but which will hold for many years yet. (18.4/20)

1964 Bin 33 *Composition:* 50 per cent Southern Vales shiraz, 20 per cent Coonawarra shiraz, 15 per cent Hunter shiraz, 10 per cent Southern Vales cabernet sauvignon and five per cent Coonawarra cabernet sauvignon. *Colour:* medium to full brick-red. *Bouquet:* soft, smoothly ripe, sweet fruit, holding well but without the complexity of the older wines. *Palate:* a trace of bottle-developed volatility with good fruit; lacks the complex structure of the older wines. (17.4/20

1965 Bin 34 *Composition:* 58 per cent Southern Vales shiraz, 15 per cent Coonawarra cabernet sauvignon, 13 per cent Hunter shiraz, 11 per cent Coonawarra shiraz, three per cent Southern Vales cabernet sauvignon. *Colour:* medium to full red with just a touch of brown. *Bouquet:* has developed surprising complexity, with rich, sweet, caramel/toffee overtones, though not at all unpleasant. *Palate:* a lively wine, combining freshness with elegance; a surprise given its poor reputation; has developed quite remarkably over the last 10 years. (18/20)

1966 Bin 35 *Composition:* 50 per cent Southern Vales shiraz, 36 per cent Coonawarra shiraz, 11 per cent Hunter shiraz, three per cent Southern Vales cabernet sauvignon. *Colour:* strong brick-red. *Bouquet:* strong, deep and robust with the suggestion of a touch of oak. *Palate:* a very big, solid, deep and ripe long-lived wine; will it ever gain fragrance or elegance though? (17.6/20)

1967 Bin 36 *Composition:* 44 per cent Southern Vales shiraz, 20 per cent Coonawarra shiraz, 13 per cent Coonawarra cabernet sauvignon, 11 per cent Merbein shiraz and grenache, eight per cent Hunter River shiraz, four per cent Southern Vales cabernet sauvignon. *Colour:* medium brick-red. *Bouquet:* light and fragrant, with some grassy cabernet sauvignon notes, a touch of mint and a background whisper of straw-oxidation characters. *Palate:* a much lighter, greener style; marked sappiness on the finish. (16.4/20)

1968 Bin 37 *Composition:* 61.5 per cent Southern Vales shiraz, 15 per cent Coonawarra shiraz, 10 per cent Coonawarra cabernet sauvignon, 6.5 per cent Hunter River shiraz, 3.5 per cent Southern Vales cabernet sauvignon, 3.5 per cent Southern Vales mataro. *Colour:* distressingly brown. *Bouquet:* smooth and clean holding fruit but rather simple and one-dimensional. *Palate:* a simple, slightly sweet aged red with a touch of caramel to the flavour. (15.8/20)

1969 Bin 38 *Composition:* 60 per cent Southern Vales shiraz, 18.5 per cent Coonawarra shiraz, 18.5 per cent Coonawarra cabernet sauvignon, 2.5 per cent Hunter shiraz, 0.5 per cent Merbein cabernet sauvignon. *Colour:* very pale red-brown, unimpressive. *Bouquet:* rather smelly with a touch of sulphide and some lactic characters. *Palate:* green lactic characters dominate. (14.6/20)

1970 Bin 39 *Composition:* 79.5 per cent Southern Vales shiraz, 12.5 per cent Coonawarra shiraz, six per cent Coonawarra cabernet sauvignon, two per cent Southern Vales cabernet sauvignon. *Colour:* light brick-red. *Bouquet:* light and thin, redeemed by just a touch of aged Rhone character. *Palate:* light, stretched and sweetish. (14.2/20)

1971 Bin 40 *Composition:* 57 per cent Southern Vales shiraz, 33 per cent Coonawarra shiraz, six per cent Coonawarra cabernet sauvignon, two per cent Southern Vales cabernet sauvignon, 1.5 per cent Hunter shiraz. *Colour:* dark red-brown. *Bouquet:* big, solid, ripe, plum/tobacco aromas, quite attractive. *Palate:* a fairly big wine with similar plum/tobacco characters; probably has improvement in front of it. (16.8/20)

1972 Bin 41 *Composition:* 45 per cent Coonawarra shiraz, 34 per cent Southern Vales shiraz, 14 per cent Coonawarra cabernet sauvignon, five per cent Southern Vales cabernet sauvignon, two per cent Hunter shiraz. *Colour:* medium red-brown. *Bouquet:* lively, fragrant, fresh, crushed-pepper/spice aromas. *Palate:* light, lively with spicy Rhone-like flavours; would have received higher points had it shown a little more weight on the palate. (16.8/20)

1973 Bin 42 *Composition:* 40.5 per cent Southern Vales shiraz, 32.5 per cent Coonawarra shiraz, 21 per cent Coonawarra cabernet sauvignon, four per cent Southern Vales cabernet sauvignon, two per cent Coonawarra malbec. *Colour:* medium to full red-brown. *Bouquet:* fairly simple, sweetish and with a touch of oxidation. *Palate:* a big, sweet, slightly baked old-style Australian red; simple fruit characters dominate. (15.2/20)

1974 Bin 43 *Composition:* 44 per cent Southern Vales shiraz, 38 per cent Coonawarra cabernet sauvignon and shiraz, 18 per cent Hunter shiraz. *Colour:* light to medium red with some browning. *Bouquet:* dusty/leafy aromas, then bitter mercaptan characters. *Palate:* soured by mercaptan. (14/20)

1975 Bin 44 *Composition:* 55 per cent Southern Vales shiraz, 25 per cent Coonawarra shiraz, 20 per cent Coonawarra cabernet sauvignon. *Colour:* medium red with some browns developing. *Bouquet:* fruit diminished somewhat by some dusty/chalky overtones. *Palate:* fairly light and simple, with some sweet lactic characters intruding. (14.6/20)

1977 Bin 45 *Composition:* 51 per cent McLaren Vale shiraz, 27 per cent Coonawarra shiraz, 22 per cent Coonawarra cabernet sauvignon. *Colour:* red with some browns evident. *Bouquet:* smooth; some gentle old-oak characters and not a great deal of fruit showing. *Palate:* a suspicion of mercaptan; certainly green/sour characters are evident in the fruit. (15/20)

1980 Bin 46 *Composition:* 55 per cent Coonawarra shiraz, 25 per cent Eden Valley shiraz, 20 per cent Coonawarra cabernet sauvignon. *Colour:* a radical colour change from the older wines, medium red still with a hint of purple. *Bouquet:* proclaims its Coonawarra origin with that peculiar grassy/stewed fruit/meaty aroma. *Palate:* a complex mixture of grassy/leafy Coonawarra flavours, a touch of mint and then pepper spice from Eden Valley. A fair wine, not a great one. (16.4/20)

1981 Bin 47 *Composition:* 55 Coonawarra shiraz, 25 per cent Eden Valley shiraz, 20 per cent Coonawarra cabernet sauvignon. *Colour:* medium red, showing greater development than Bin 46. *Bouquet:* smooth, full and clean with a most attractive overlay of pepper/spice aromas. *Palate:* big, soft peppery fruit with considerable richness and good balance. A real return to form for the line. (17.8/20)

In 1958 Ronald Haselgrove also assembled an experimental blend of 50 per cent each of Coonawarra shiraz (with just a little cabernet) and 50 per cent Hunter Valley shiraz. All of the Hunter Valley material, incidentally, came from Doug Elliott, and most of the Southern Vales material has come from Johnstone's Pirramimma. Bin 58 of 1958 has long been regarded as one of the greatest Australian red wines made in the last 30 years, and it fully lived up to its reputation at this tasting.

1958 Bin 58 *Colour:* full red-brown. *Bouquet:* superbly complex with finely counterpoised leathery aromas from the Hunter and sweet fruit from Coonawarra. *Palate:* shows extraordinary life and freshness right from the fore-palate through to the finish; intense yet soft, a wine of almost freakish elegance and finesse. (19.4/20)

In 1974 Richard Haselgrove valiantly attempted to repeat the exercise in honour of his father, who retired as chairman of Mildara in that year. A total of 960-dozen bottles were made from a blend of 50 per cent Elliott Tallawanta shiraz and 50 per cent Mildara Undoolya shiraz, the latter off an old planting of shiraz in Coonawarra restored by Mildara. 1974 was hardly an auspicious year from a viticultural viewpoint, being poor in both the Hunter Valley and Coonawarra, and although the wine tries valiantly to rise above the circumstances of its birth, it only partly does so.

1974 *Colour:* medium to full red-brown. *Bouquet:* full plum-spice aromas with some straw oxidation evident. *Palate:* full, soft and plummy; has come on very well since it was released in May 1981, but will never be a 1958 Bin 58. (16.4/20)

The significance of the Mildara Yellow Label Series goes beyond the wine in each bottle. Its genesis was that of the table-wine industry as a whole, reborn in the early 1950s after almost half a century in the wilderness. Its nadir was reached in the late 60s and early 70s as the red-wine boom peaked, and virtually all companies were forced to stretch dangerously their available material to meet the demand. Its irregular appearance at the end of the 1970s reflected problems peculiar to Mildara, and its rebirth in 1980 signifies the new direction of Mildara with almost all of its quality table wine coming from Coonawarra and the Eden Valley.

But more significantly still, the wines show both the importance and the skill of the blender's art. I have included the blend details not because I think the differences are significant, but rather because I believe they are not significant. It does not matter whether there is this percentage of cabernet sauvignon or that percentage, this percentage of Coonawarra material or that percentage. What matters is the quality of the wine in the bottle, the balance and harmony which the differing blends give. The blender's skill is but one of a number of arguments against an over-enthusiastic adoption of appellation control and/or labelling requirements which in effect put the cart before the horse. In other words, contemporary attitudes would have it that a wine with more Coonawarra cabernet sauvignon in it will be a better wine than one with less; the blender's art shows otherwise.

In the chapter on Coonawarra I trace the events leading to Mildara's first acquisition of land there in August 1955. Those vineyards now produce more than 90 per cent of the grapes which provide the premium table-wine releases of Mildara. In 1979 Mildara acquired the old South Australian winemaker, Hamiltons. With that acquisition came an Eden Valley winery (originally built by Penfolds in 1922 and purchased by Hamiltons in 1965) together

with a 45-hectare vineyard. While the Eden Valley winery has been substantially upgraded since its acquisition by Mildara, the annual crush is tiny compared with that of Coonawarra. Less than 100 tonnes are processed from the Eden Valley, compared with over 2000 tonnes at Coonawarra and 15,000 tonnes at Merbein.

The Eden Valley winery is little more than a fermentation cellar; immediately at the end of vintage the white wine is taken to Merbein, and the red wine to Coonawarra. At the present time all of the Eden Valley grapes are purchased from independent growers; the old Penfold vineyard has been disposed of; and an entirely new vineyard development started, planted to rhine riesling (18 hectares), chardonnay (four hectares) and traminer (two hectares). As at 1984 none of this vineyard was in bearing.

Since the 1979 acquisition Mildara has released an Eden Valley rhine riesling in each year since 1980. The 1980 and 1981 releases were under the Hamilton label, but since 1982 the wine has been released under the Mildara Eden Valley rhine riesling label. Whether the Hamilton label will be preserved remains to be seen: it still has commercial strength in a few specialty areas, but the once-strong profile of the company had been badly eroded during the 1970s. Of the five Eden Valley rhine rieslings so far released, the 1982 and 1984 vintages stand out. Both show marked Eden Valley fruit characteristics, with that totally distinctive touch of lime.

The 30 tonnes (or thereabouts) of shiraz crushed each year is put to very good use. In 1981 90,000 litres (equivalent to 10,000 cases) of a 66 per cent Coonawarra cabernet sauvignon and 34 per cent Eden Valley shiraz was assembled and put into a mixture of small oak casks for maturation. The equivalent of 3000 dozen was set aside as a special show blend, the difference stemming from the greater percentage of new oak used in that blend. It went on to win the Jimmy Watson Trophy at Melbourne in 1982; it and its sister blend subsequently made their appearance under the controversial Mildara J.W. Classic label. The controversy stemmed from the fact that the labels were largely identical; a small gold band in the corner of one, and the back labels of both, signified the different wines. The recommended retail prices of the two, however, were substantially different. The dual labelling underlined the difficulties inherent in awarding important trophies to wines which are still in cask and where, no matter what efforts the winemaker may make to avoid this, the wine which is ultimately released for commercial sale will necessarily be different from that which won the trophy. Mildara was castigated in all quarters (myself included), notwithstanding that it was an ethical decision to keep the two parcels separate and to release them accordingly. The arguments should not obscure the fact that both of the 1981 releases, and the 1982 release, were and are excellent wines. In January 1985 the new-oak influence in the trophy-winner was very evident; I pointed it fractionally higher than the 1981 standard J.W. Classic, with the 1982 vintage fractionally further behind. All have considerable complexity, although the 1982 has quite evident stewed-plum Coonawarra fruit flavours.

The arrival in 1982 of Ray King as sales director signified an aggressive and extremely successful change in direction for Mildara's marketing methods. The J.W. Classic was but one example; equally noteworthy were the 1983 Flower Label releases. These comprised a 1983 Coonawarra Fumé Blanc (a blend of sauvignon blanc, chardonnay and palomino), a 1983 Coonawarra Traminer Riesling blend, a 1983 Church Hill Chardonnay (from north-west Victoria) and a 1983 Chablis (of unspecified grapes and origin, but no doubt from the north-west of Victoria). A quite excellent 1983 Cabernet Merlot was subsequently released, a blend of Coonawarra cabernet sauvignon and north-west Victorian merlot. Fresh, clean and well made, the most striking feature of the wines was, nonetheless, the labels. These were said to have been inspired by Suzanna Haselgrove, Richard Haselgrove's wife, who is an acknowledged expert gardener, with a radio gardening programme to her credit. The labels were designed by a Mildura-resident artist, Joy Scherger, and feature flowers to be found in Suzanna Haselgrove's garden. Nonetheless, the similarity to the flower labels of the leading Beaujolais shipper Georges Duboeuf was all too obvious, and once again the hounds were baying. The labels are most attractive and, quite certainly, almost all of those who have flocked to purchase the wine would be blissfully unaware of the existence of Duboeuf or his labels. It is just a pity that they are so similar, but at least Georges Duboeuf could not complain about the quality of the wine in the bottle.

In 1984 Mildara, as it likes to put it, merged its operations with those of Yellowglen. In 1979 Mildara made its first release of a 100 per cent chardonnay sparkling wine (labelled Chardonnay Champagne) made from a base wine vintaged in 1978. So far as I know this was the first commercial chardonnay sparkling wine released onto the Australian market. It, and some earlier chardonnay blends, had been made for Mildara by the Wynn/

Seaview group under the direction of Norman Walker. The wine was an immediate success, but when the Australian Wine Company was unable to continue making the wine for Mildara, Mildara turned to Yellowglen. The Yellowglen-made wine was released in 1983 under the Mildara Windsor Imperial Chardonnay Champagne label; produced by the *méthode champenoise*, it was even more successful than its predecessors. This success, coupled with the enormous financial demands of the expansion programme made necessary by Yellowglen's success, led to the Mildara merger.

In March 1985 Mildara took the merger process one step further with its acquisition of Balgownie. The same rationale did not apply, and personally I have doubts about the long-term logic of the move. In the shorter term, it may well bring benefits to all concerned.

While Mildara must regard itself as one of the more vulnerable targets in the likely continued rationalisation of the Australian wine industry, it at least has the comfort of knowing, as it enters 1985, that it has a range of wines better than it has ever had in the past, effectively marketed, and covering all of the growth areas of the industry.

MURRAY VALLEY WINERY
FIFTEENTH STREET, MILDURA

Murray Valley Winery is the smallest and oldest of the family-owned and run Sunraysia wineries. The cellar-door sales area in Fifteenth Street, Mildura, is adjacent to the simple corrugated-iron winery established in 1920 by the Kalamastrakis family. Now owned and run by George and Nancy Kalamastrakis, it produces a range of basic table wines together with Greek-style wines such as retsina and kokinelli, the latter being a medium-sweet red wine. However, the main emphasis has always been and remains on the production of fortified wine.

The grapes come partly from the family's own five-hectare vineyard planted to shiraz, muscat gordo blanco, rhine riesling and cabernet sauvignon, but the major part of the modest crush comes from local vignerons. Sales are both cellar door and in bulk to the Greek community in Melbourne.

ROBINVALE WINES
BLOCK 436, SEA LAKE ROAD, ROBINVALE

Robinvale Wines is situated in one of the unusual wineries in Australia: the front facade is a replica of a Greek temple. Established by G. Caracatsanoudis & Sons in 1976 on the Sea Lake Road, five kilometres south of Robinvale, it offers the lot: white and red table wines, sparkling wines, fortified wines and a selection of Greek styles. These are all produced from the family's 20-hectare vineyard planted to muscat gordo blanco, sultana, waltham cross, mataro and purple cornichon. History does not relate whether the table-grape varieties (waltham cross and purple cornichon) are also pressed into service for winemaking.

STANLEY BURONGA WINERY
BURONGA, NSW

Although technically in New South Wales, the winery is very much part of the Sunraysia scene, and takes a large percentage of its grapes from the Victorian side. Set up in the open, much in the manner of Karadoc, Buronga was always an efficient producer of bulk wine. Since its acquisition by Stanley in January 1984 it has, however, been transformed beyond all recognition. In the first 12 months over $4 million were spent upgrading the winery and plant, with an ongoing five-year expenditure plan of $1 million per year designed to increase the crush by 30,000 tonnes, making it the largest and most modern winery in New South Wales.

All the bulk-wine operations, and in particular the cask operations, have now been transferred from Stanley's Clare Valley Winery to Buronga. The abundant grape supply, and the proximity to the eastern markets, are seen by Stanley as the major advantages.

WOORINEN WINE ESTATES
WOORINEN ROAD, SWAN HILL

Woorinen Wine Estates is the trading and brand name of the Mid-Murray Producers' Cooperative Society Limited. The 240 cooperative shareholders have approximately 2000 hectares of grapes, the most important varieties being rhine riesling, semillon, cabernet sauvignon and shiraz, all centred around the Swan Hill area at the eastern end of the Murray River wine areas.

The cooperative, like so many others, was formed during a time of deep trouble for the local growers. The cause in this instance was the collapse of the dried-fruit market, which gave rise to an enormous surplus of, among others, sultana grapes. This variety is the classic "dual-purpose" grape, producing both dried sultanas and very adequate bulk wine for flagons. Under the direction of Wallace Cockroft, one of the principal growers in the district, the cooperative was established in 1968 and produced its first vintage in 1969 from the Fairfield Winery. Initially all of the sales were in bulk to other winemakers, but before long the cooperative began to establish small sales of labelled branded wine. These were initially made under the Fairfield label, but around 1980 the trading name was changed to Woorinen Wine Estates.

With some very innovative and clever winemaking by Neil Jericho (who has since left Woorinen), some excellent varietal and other wines came out under the Woorinen label. These sales still account for little more than five per cent of the total production of around six million litres, but are of great importance for the cooperative.

The wines offered include the usual varietals: semillon (given six months in French oak), rhine riesling, cabernet sauvignon, spatlese riesling, and even a sylvaner. These are all well-made wines sold at attractive prices. But the real success for Woorinen has come with its cabernet rosé which has been consistently excellent, and, above all else, for its Mellifera. The latter wine is a sweet auslese style made from botrytised grapes using the rack inoculation method. Utilising old fruit-packing sheds, Neil Jericho harvested the grapes at normal maturity, placing them on the trays and inoculating them with botrytis mould. This system was developed in Australia by Tim Knappstein and Joe Grilli in South Australia, and utilised extensively by the Stanley Wine Company at its Clare Valley Winery. I describe the process in greater length in that chapter.

Jericho has used principally rhine riesling grapes in his Mellifera, and all of the releases so far made have showed marvellous intensity of flavour, with no off-characters nor the volatility which sometimes mars these styles. The 1982 Mellifera was particularly good.

In early 1985 Woorinen went into receivership, and the prospects for its future looked grim. ◪

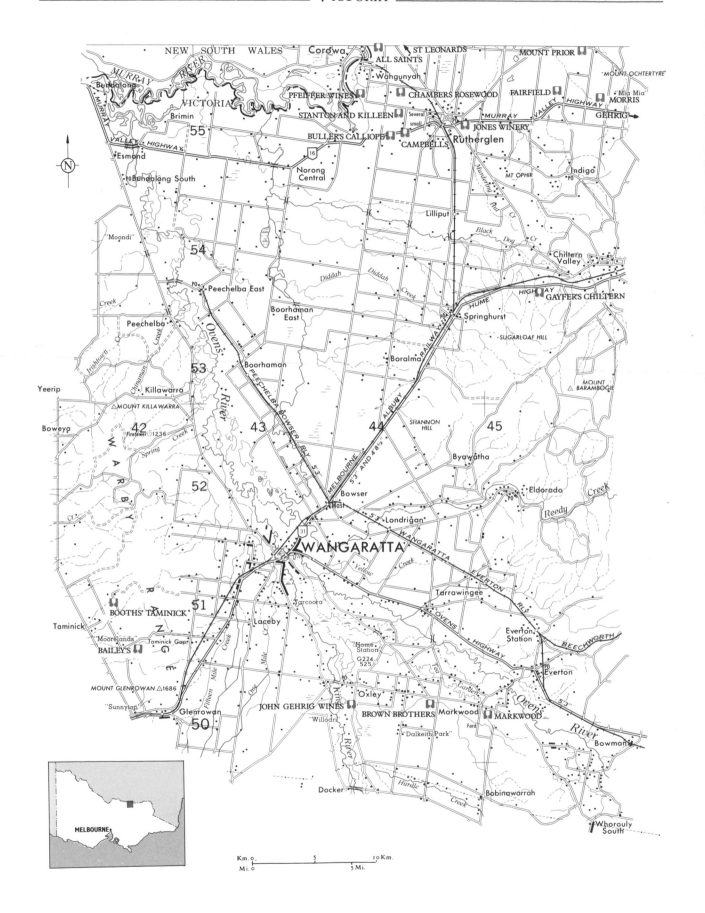

NEW SOUTH WALES

MURRAY RIVER

Corowa • ST LEONARDS MOUNT PRIOR
Bundalong ALL SAINTS 'MOUNT OCHTERTYRE'
Wahgunyah
VICTORIA PFEIFFER WINES CHAMBERS ROSEWOOD FAIRFIELD 'Mia Mia' MORRIS
Brimin STANTON AND KILLEEN Several small MURRAY VALLEY HIGHWAY GEHRIG
55 BULLER'S CALLIOPE JONES WINERY
CAMPBELLS Rutherglen
Esmond 16 Indigo
MT OPHIR PO
Norong
Bundalong South Central Lilliput
'Moondi' Chiltern
Valley
54 Diddah Diddah Black Dog Cr
PO Peechelba East GAYFER'S CHILTERN
Creek Boorhaman HUME HIGHWAY
Peechelba East Springhurst
Peechelba Ovens SUGARLOAF HILL
53 Boorhaman MOUNT
Yeerip BARAMBOGIE
Killawarra Boralma
MOUNT KILLAWARRA River SHANNON 45
Boweya 42 HILL
Firetower 1236 43 44
Spring Creek Byawatha
52 Eldorado
PEECHELBA BOWSER RLY 5'3" Reedy Creek
MELBOURNE 5'3" AND 4 8½ Bowser PO
Mast ALBURY
W A R B Y Londrigan 5'3"
31 WANGARATTA WANGARATTA EVERTON RLY.
Taminick BOOTHS' TAMINICK Yellow Creek OVENS HIGHWAY BEECHWORTH
51 Laceby Tarrawingee
'Moorelands' Taminick Gap Everton
BAILEY'S Home Station
Station PO Everton
G224 Ovens
MOUNT GLENROWAN 1686 525 PO
'Sunnytop' King 'Oxley' Markwood MARKWOOD River
Glenrowan JOHN GEHRIG WINES BROWN BROTHERS Ford 5'3" Bowman
50 'Willodri' 'Dalkeith Park'

Docker Hurdle Creek Bobinawarrah

Whorouly
South

Km. 0 5 10 Km.
Mi. 0 5 Mi.

North-East Victoria

Gold was to set the north-east aflame, but for once vines came first. Major Thomas Mitchell, who crossed the Goulburn River at what became the site of Tahbilk, performed the same service at Gooramadda near Rutherglen in 1836 when he crossed the Murray River. The Gooramadda run, as it came to be known, was taken up by Lindsey Brown in 1839. Three of his farmworkers were from Germany, and when they moved to nearby Albury they established vines. In 1851 they persuaded Brown that he should start a vineyard at Gooramadda. The vines flourished, and Brown became an instant disciple. De Castella records that "[Brown] was in the habit of settling miners' discussions as to the depth of which sinking should be carried. 'To get gold,' he would say, 'you need sink only about 18 inches [45 centimetres] and plant vines.'"

Others listened and soon followed. John Graham planted vines at Netherby in 1859, and in 1862 brought the first steam-plough into the district for the enormous cost of £1200. He faded from the scene, as did Roderick Kilborn (1863), Camille Reau at the Tuilleries, and Joseph Webster (1864), Alexander Caughey at Mount Prior (1868), then Anthony Ruche, Hugh Fraser, Joseph Pearce, James Prentice and William Cullen. While these names are represented no more, the Tuilleries and Mount Prior homesteads remain as magnificent reminders of the opulence of nineteenth-century Victorian living.

However, yet other vignerons came whose families have carried on: Campbell, Chambers, Gehrig, Morris and Sutherland Smith. Of these, George Frederick Morris had the greatest impact on the contemporary scene. He was an English bank clerk who unsuccessfully prospected for gold on the Ovens River, but who made sufficient money as a wholesale trader at Beechworth to move to Rutherglen in 1859 and buy a 100-hectare property. He planted four hectares as an experiment; pleased with the results, another 12 hectares followed soon after. But while the vines grew and the winemaking was accomplished without undue difficulty, the market was not there. So for a while Morris concentrated on other crops. Nonetheless, by 1869 Rutherglen was already the largest winegrowing area in the State, with 2407 hectares producing just under 800,000 litres of wine.

The 1870s, indeed, marked a low period in the north-east. Gold had been discovered in 1860 on what became the Main Street of Rutherglen, but by 1870 the surface gold had been largely worked out. There was a lull until 1886 when means were devised to work the deep alluvial leads, and prosperity returned. In the intervening 15 years the miners had largely drifted away and a mini-recession occurred. Some turned to viticulture, adding to the problems of finding a market.

Ironically, one man who made literally no attempt at all to dispose of his wine seems to have provided the spark which led to the major period of growth in the district. Hubert de Castella, in *Notes of an Australian Vine Grower*, first published in 1882, tells the story of Anthony Ruche who, 20 years earlier, had established a one-hectare vineyard. In 1880 he was persuaded to sell his entire stock to an enterprising Melbourne wine merchant. Hubert de Castella takes up the tale:

> Ruche, the wine grower, until then had clung to his casks like a hen to her chickens, and had never sold until his back was to the wall, in a few cases only because he was forced by the few creditors who supplied his humble needs. It was his mania. Selling his wine was a heartbreak for him. Consequently when one of his barrels was put up for sale it used to fetch a good price, even when other vine growers could not sell theirs. Besides, the man was an expert, and if he was so keen on keeping his wine it was because he rightly had a very good opinion of it.

Having cost the merchant four shillings and nine-pence a gallon (4.5 litres), the wine brought between six shillings and 21 shillings per gallon at auction. To what extent the ensuing publicity was responsible we will never know, but in the following six years plantings in the Shire of Rutherglen trebled, rising from 2770 hectares in 1880 to 7410 hectares in 1886. George Frederick Morris had jumped the gun, it seems; he had expanded his plantings to 250 hectares throughout the 1870s, and in the early 1880s he built the beautiful two-storey Fairfield Homestead. At the same time he constructed the largest wine cellars in the southern hemisphere, which held the equivalent of three vintages of one million litres each.

By far the greatest part of Fairfield's production was exported to London. In the latter part of the nineteenth century a very large trade in Australian wine was built up, with B. P. Burgoyne taking the lion's share. It was no doubt his success with the immensely rich and alcoholic burgundies, much appreciated in Victorian England, which led him to acquire Mount Ophir and to the long-term connection that company had with the London trade. Fairfield won 425 first prizes in a 20-year show career spanning exhibitions held in London, Amsterdam, Paris, Calcutta, New Zealand, South Africa, Perth, Melbourne and Sydney.

In 1883 the Murray District Vinegrowers' Association was formed with George Sutherland Smith as its first president. A powerful lobby group which represented a large source of income for the State, it was instrumental in securing the passage of legislation providing for a bounty of £2 for every acre of grapes planted. One does not have to be especially cynical, either, to believe it was behind the government decree ordering the destruction of the Bendigo vineyards when phylloxera was discovered there in 1893. Even if the vain hope of arresting the spread of the pest came to nought, the destruction would remove a source of competition in the same way as the removal of the Geelong vineyards had 10 years earlier.

The government bounty caused indiscriminate planting in several areas, not the least being the north-east. In 1895 there were 4340 hectares of vines in the Rutherglen shire, and of these 613 were still to come into bearing, attesting to the rate of planting. But troubled times lay ahead. In 1899 phylloxera was positively identified in the region. With nothing left to protect, the government finally adopted the action it should have taken in Bendigo (and arguably Geelong): it encouraged growers to replant with phylloxera-resistant rootstocks supplied by the government at a subsidised price.

Between 1890 and 1910 virtually every vineyard in the north-east was destroyed; a considerable number were replanted, but many were not. Those that were not replanted by the outbreak of the First World War disappeared from the scene permanently. Up to 1914, and in the period 1918 to 1925, much of the local production was exported to the United Kingdom. Local sales were largely effected through Melbourne merchants, with W. J. Seabrook and John Connell & Company being regular buyers. Wine was sold at cellar door through a two-gallon (nine-litre) licence, but little or none of it was bottled or labelled. You brought your own container and the vigneron filled it direct from cask. Prices ranged from three shillings per gallon for table wine through to six shillings per gallon for sweet fortified wine. W. H. Chambers at Rosewood had one of the rare single-bottle licences; here prices were sixpence per bottle for table wine and one shilling per bottle for fortified wine. Nonetheless, the same rules applied: you brought your own bottles.

The collapse of the export market in the late 1920s, and the onset of the Depression, brought even harder times to the north-east. Wine prices slumped to below the cost of production, the only comfort being that all of the other Australian regions suffered similarly. The Second World War and the period until 1953 saw relative prosperity return. The demand for fortified wine was great, and the north-east was well placed to supply it. The events of 1953, however, precipitated a further major decline in the fortunes of the district. The three largest vineyards, Mount Ophir (280 hectares), Fairfield (250 hectares) and Grahams (250 hectares) pulled out their vines in the second half of the 1950s as the demand for fortified wine disappeared and table wine took its place. Others, such as Morris, quickly turned to red-wine production. But it was basically due to the superb quality of its fortified wines, wines that have no peer, that the north-east survived first phylloxera, then the Depression, and finally the 1951 excise on fortified wine and the after-effects of the removal of beer rationing.

As with all great wines—table or fortified—the quality comes initially from the interaction of *terroir* and climate. If you prefer, the old adage that great wine is made in the vineyard is proved once again. The climate is perhaps obvious enough: while the nights and early mornings are cool even in the height of summer, the days are swelteringly hot, a dry heat which causes the red soil and the Warby Ranges rising above to shimmer and convulse in the heat-haze. In these conditions grapes ripen rapidly,

WILLIAM CHAMBERS OUTSIDE ORIGINAL CELLAR, ROSEWOOD

attaining 15, 16 or 17 baume with regularity, and every now and then reaching 20 baume.

But what about the *terroir*? Most of the vineyards are established on flat or nearly flat terrain, and surely the soil cannot be so important for fortified wines? It is in Portugal, it is in Madeira and so it is in north-east Victoria. There is a consistent soil profile throughout the district: a poor quartz gravel on the hilltops, then a band of red loam on the lower slopes of the hills, and finally grey sandy loam on the flats. The gravelly hilltops can produce great wine, and did so once. They are now abandoned as uneconomic, and the great fortified wines come from the red loam which snakes its way through and around Rutherglen. It extends 2.3 kilometres to the west, reaching as far as Morris's if not beyond, and five kilometres south. (A separate and indeed geologically unique variant is to be found at Glenrowan, where the Bailey vineyards are established. These soils are shared by Chambers, Morris, and Stanton and Killeen; All Saints, by contrast, is established on the sandy loam of the Murray River which runs not so far away. If anyone wondered why Chambers, Morris (and latterly Stanton and Killeen) can produce great fortified wine at will, while All Saints seems to struggle to do so, the answer lies in the soil.

The other great contributor to these wines is prolonged cask ageing. A great young muscat bears as much similarity to a great old muscat as does a six-month-old baby girl to an 80-year-old great-grandmother. The wine starts off life light red in colour, with tinges of pink and orange; it ends up an impenetrable dark brown, with olive-green hues on the rim. (It is a simple matter to gain a fairly accurate idea of the age of these wines by merely looking at their colour.) The wine also starts off with an intense but simple fruity aroma with a bracing edge of spirit; it ends up with unfathomable complexities of dark fruits, sombre wood and a softly warming back cut of spirit. Like Narcissus drowning in his reflection, one can lose oneself in the aroma of a great old muscat. All this, and one has not yet felt the necessity of actually tasting the wine. That moment destroys the calm which preceded it: an old muscat has an explosive intensity of luscious flavour, combined with high acid and a twist of wood-derived volatility, which strips the saliva from the sides of the taster's mouth, leaving the flavour in undiminished magnificence for minutes after the last millilitre has been swallowed.

Such a wine came before three of the judges at the 1984 Canberra National Show (of which I was one) in Class 94, Museum Muscat. This is one of a small group of classes for fortified wines which requires neither that the wine be commercially available, nor that it even be held in more than very limited quantities (the equivalent of 50-dozen bottles, I seem to remember). Each of us gave it 19.5/ 20, the first occasion anyone present could remember such a happening. It was a Bailey's muscat, no doubt drawn from the great-grandmother solera which is the font of the incomparable HJT Liqueur Muscat (the latter wine being placed first by a different panel in the Premium Muscat Class).

It was with such wines—and equally memorable fortified tokays—that the reputation of the district was founded. Mick Morris at Mia Mia and Bill Chambers at Rosewood complete the big three, a triumvirate which has not been allowed the luxury of complacency, thanks to the recent efforts of Campbells and Stanton and Killeen. It is due to these wines that north-eastern Victoria has the foremost entitlement to appellation control status in Australia, for no other district comes close in style, and only the Swan and Barossa Valleys even attempt (valiantly but unsuccessfully) to match the quality. Every other district in Australia has a clone somewhere or other, producing wines of similar structure and style. There are cogent reasons for saying that modern winemaking techniques are tending to draw wines closer together, as varietal purity is enhanced at the expense of district identity. Wines are losing their blemishes, and also their individuality. But no such accusation could ever be levelled at the great fortified wines of north-east Victoria.

Yet the district is turning its back on this unique heritage, partly inadvertently, and partly in response to market indifference. The "angel's share"—the annual evaporation loss—alone adds a significant additional cost which compounds over the many years that the wine stays in cask. Then there is the capital cost of prolonged cellaring of a wine which the Commissioner of Taxation has treated as trading stock, and pretended it was sold at the end of the financial year in which it was made. The net result is that income tax is paid on a wine which is not in fact sold for 10, 20 or even 30 years thereafter. The oak barrels in which the wine is stored, the winery space, the cost of the grapes, the cost of the pickers, the cost of the fortifying spirit: all these are outlaid for a future return which is pitifully inadequate by any normal financial criteria. So who can blame vignerons such as George Sutherland Smith at All Saints for arguing that the north-east should forget fortified wines, and get on with the business of copying the rest of Australia in producing light, fresh white wines? Mind you, I believe George Sutherland Smith has got it wrong both ways. If one is going to do that, one follows the example set by Brown Brothers which has used its Milawa Winery as a receiving base for grapes grown in altogether different climates and on altogether different *terroirs*. It draws its fruit from a series of vineyards, many of which are situated on mountainsides or in mountain valleys nominally in the north-east, but in truth having little or nothing in common with it.

Yet no sooner have I said this than I am confronted with the paradox of the white wines made by Morris, both for itself and for the Mount Prior label, and by Brown Brothers for St Leonards. These really are high-quality white wines. It is true that the greatest success comes with chardonnay (a notoriously adaptable variety) and semillon, which thrives in the equally warm climate of the Hunter Valley. Campbells excepted, success with rhine riesling has been very limited, and St Leonards gewurtztraminer is likewise an odd-man-out. One then gets into specialty areas such as late-harvest chenin blanc, orange muscat and the naturally high acid-retention properties of colombard. It is a complex argument, and one which will be resolved only in future decades.

The north-east of today is subject to the same economic pressures that are reshaping so much of the viticultural map in other areas. Seppelt has vacated, and Lindemans has done likewise at Corowa across the river. On the credit side, Mount Prior and Fairfield have been resuscitated, attesting to the very different market (that is, different from the market of Seppelt and Lindemans) directed to the tourist trade and cellar-door sales. Just as the Hunter Valley will rely increasingly on tourist support, so must many of the smaller ventures in the north-east. Its rich heritage is an asset beyond price, and it is to be devoutly hoped that the vignerons of the district continue to see fortified wine as an integral part of that heritage.

ALL SAINTS
ALL SAINTS ROAD, WAHGUNYAH

All Saints must have been to the 1880s what Mitchelton was to the 1970s: to the man who made it, the realisation of a dream; and to dispassionate onlookers, a magnificent folly. Let us simply hope that in 100 years' time Mitchelton is as impressive and imposing as All Saints is today, and that, like All Saints, it is classified by the National Trust. A first-time visitor to the north-east (and to All Saints) might well wonder how a turreted castle, erected

around an internal quadrangle, came to be erected at a place like Wahgunyah and, for that matter, how a flag flies proudly from the corner tower with its castellated parapet.

The answer lies in family tradition. The first George Sutherland Smith (the present incumbent is the third to carry the name) arrived in Australia in the 1850s. His family had worked for generations as carpenters and joiners at the castle of Mey at Caithness, Scotland, in the parish of All Saints. This ancient castle in Scotland is now owned and tenanted by Queen Elizabeth the Queen Mother.

It barely needs saying that, having made some capital with his brother-in-law John Banks plying the river trade on the Murray on 1860s, and having in 1864 purchased a large river-front block at Wahgunyah on which they planted the vines, George Sutherland Smith would want to build his own castle. This he literally did: a clay pit was dug on the river bank, and the kiln that he used to fire the bricks still stands today. First of all he built stables with an incongruous Spanish-style facade, and then in 1880 commenced to build the immense cellars and winery which—along with Fairfield, Mount Prior and the Tuilleries—are the great landmarks of the north-east today.

The vineyards flourished on the sandy loam of the Murray, and George Sutherland Smith and David Banks quickly learnt the art of winemaking, it would seem. In the manner of the day they were active exhibitors in overseas competitions and, while not challenging Morris at Fairfield, had many successes. The story goes that in 1876 a wine entered in a major competition at Brussels in Belgium was rejected because of its alcohol content, which the judges declared could not have occurred naturally and was due to the addition of fortifying spirit. (This was a fate which befell many Australian wines, and had led to a furious debate in England, where the consequence was not the withholding of prizes but the imposition of a higher rate of duty.) The Australian Ambassador in Brussels became involved, and after due enquiries and assurances the wine was once again (grudgingly) admitted to the competition as being one naturally high in alcohol.

The sandy soils of the vineyard did not stop phylloxera (even though other similar vineyards across the region were spared), and in the 1890s David Banks Smith, George's son, had to replant all of the vineyards with grafted phylloxera-resistant rootstocks. Notwithstanding the cost and disruption involved, the turn of the century was a time of expansion for the Sutherland Smith business. The winery capacity was extended on several occasions to feed the growing market, which had been served by the establishment of a Melbourne warehouse and bottling facilities at Selborne Chambers some 20 years earlier. All Saints remained at Selborne Chambers for over 80 years, finally moving to new premises in North Melbourne in 1960. For 100 years the Melbourne side of the business has been run by one of the sons, and the production side at Wahgunyah by the other son. Presently George Sutherland Smith (and his brother Peter) look after Wahgunyah, and Ian Sutherland Smith tends the Melbourne office and sales.

All Saints is in many ways a victim of circumstances. Its fortified wines have never been as rich and luscious as those of Rutherglen or Taminick. In a declining and highly competitive market these wines have proved very difficult to sell. Thus even the museum releases, containing significant proportions of very old wines, fail to impress the few people who understand, admire and—even more importantly—buy such wines. So for the past decade All Saints has been reshaping its 150-hectare vineyards, progressively removing or grafting varieties more suited to fortified-wine and red-wine production and replacing them with varieties such as chardonnay, traminer, semillon and rhine riesling. Shiraz is still by far the most important variety, accounting for more than 25 per cent of the total. Other varieties include cabernet sauvignon, pinot meunière, pinot noir, pedro ximinez, palomino, marsanne, trebbiano, chasselas, rhine riesling, tokay, crouchen and chardonnay. The estate plantings usually account for around 80 per cent of the annual crush of a little over 1000 tonnes.

Thanks to the efficient and energetic public relations and marketing systems of All Saints, I have tasted virtually all of the new releases from the vineyard over the past five years. It grieves me to be unable to find something truly complimentary to say. The plain fact of the matter is that the table wines are simple, dull and ordinary. They are not bad wines, in the sense that they do not show any marked winemaking faults; on the other hand, they invariably lack varietal definition and life on the palate. Thus a 1983 Premium Vintage Chardonnay showed that it had been fermented on solids, but ended up with no varietal character whatsoever and simply the hardness that this technique can give. Its 1981 Marsanne (also released in 1984) was equally unappealing. There was a slight suggestion of honeysuckle on the aroma, but nothing at all on the palate. The red wines vary between being light, thin and scrawny on

the one hand, and jammy and obvious on the other. There seems to be no happy medium.

The fortified releases are, relatively speaking, far better. They are light, but they do conform to style. Some of the old sherries are particularly appealing, although even here the problem is that other makers have better stocks of what is a lamentably neglected style—neglected, that is, by the marketplace.

How All Saints extricates itself, I do not know, but it does seem to me that a very close and hard look needs to be taken at both the quality of the fruit coming out of the vineyard and the winemaking techniques employed to deal with the fruit.

BAILEY'S
Cnr TAMINICK GAP ROAD & UPPER TAMINICK ROAD, GLENROWAN

The Bailey family were among the first settlers in Melbourne, having left Manchester in England in the 1830s. They continued their trade as cartage contractors, carrying the bricks which were used to construct the first Melbourne mint. In the 1840s they moved to the north-east of Victoria, and were well placed when gold was discovered. They established the first store at Glenrowan, and when the gold ran out and the miners dwindled they used their accumulated profits to buy the property now owned by Fielder Gillespie Davis and trading as Bailey's Bundarra Vineyards.

This is Ned Kelly country and the wines are constructed appropriately: rich, robust, strong and with fire in their loins. The unique character of Bailey's wines, both white and red, is due principally to the geologically unique soil upon which the 102 hectares of vineyards are planted. The belt of red granitic soil runs along the lee of the Warby Range underneath Taminick Gap for about five kilometres; it is only a few hundred metres wide, and the old plantings followed its boundary to within a few metres. It is very well drained and friable, encouraging the establishment of a massive root growth. Yields are not increased (at around 4.5 tonnes per hectare they are in fact extremely low), but the grapes can obtain exceptionally high sugar levels whilst still retaining very good acidity. More importantly still, they have an unequalled depth of flavour.

The property remained in the hands of the Bailey family for 102 years. I can still remember taking delivery of a consignment of wine at Darling Harbour Railway Station in 1964 which included three-dozen bottles of Bailey's 1953 Hermitage at a price of 45 cents a bottle. Half was mine, and half a friend's. There were also several cases of a 1958 Hermitage, much of which went into a Greek dish called *stiphado* of which I was very fond at the time and frequently cooked. The '53 Hermitage was despatched at barbecues and on other inconsequential occasions. Oh, for the innocence of youth!

I first visited Bailey's in 1968; while other wineries visited on that two-week trip have long since faded from my mind, the memory of Bailey's is indelibly printed. It seemed to me, looking at all the rusty bits of iron and scrap lying around the winery, that I had at last unlocked the secret of the extraordinary strength of the wine. What grieves me most is the knowledge that at that time I was interested only in table wine, and both at Bailey's and Morris I studiously ignored the fortified wines proffered me. Damn the innocence of youth!

In 1972 an ageing Alan Bailey, great-grandson of Richard Bailey, sold out to Davis Consolidated Industries, now merged with the Fielder Gillespie group. And thereby hangs a tale. Davis had made up his mind to diversify into the wine industry, and commissioned one of its brightest executives to carry out the search. Harry Tinson had taken an honours degree in physical engineering at Sydney University in 1951, and a master's degree in 1952, ending up in the corporate planning department of Davis. His Australia-wide search concluded, Tinson put before the Davis board a strong recommendation that it offer to acquire a 50 per cent interest in Bailey's Bundarra. While he considered it the best acquisition available, he also stressed the necessity of continuity in management and winemaking knowledge. He argued that the winery produced magnificent and unique table and fortified wines, and it was essential that the style not be altered. The board agreed, and Tinson went to Alan Bailey with an offer to purchase a half-interest in the winery and vineyard. To Tinson's dismay, Alan Bailey refused: he wanted to sell 100 per cent, and to be able to retire.

Defeated, Tinson returned to the board who promptly instructed him to proceed with the 100 per cent acquisition and to take over the winemaking responsibilities himself, retaining Alan Bailey as a consultant until a permanent winemaker could be found. Tinson realised he was trapped: he had done such a good job with his initial report that the board would not be deterred. The "temporary" winemaker, assisted by his wife Cath as assistant winemaker, is still happily in charge, and has enhanced the reputation of Bailey's even further.

This reputation is built fairly and squarely on the magnificent fortified muscats and tokays. These are released under three labels of increasing importance. The "basic" muscat and tokay come out under the Award Founder Series label. At the end of 1984 these had a retail price of around $7.90. Next is the Gold Label Muscat and the Gold Label Tokay, at around $13.30. Finally there is the HJT Liqueur Muscat and the HJT Liqueur Tokay, at just under $30. At long last some recognition is being given to the ultimate quality of the HJT range. Only four years ago these wines were retailing at around $14 for the muscat and $8.50 for the tokay. What is more, at that point of time there was never any restriction on availability. Now the trade price bible, *Thomson's Liquor Guide*, carries the warning "when available" against both the Gold Label and HJT Series.

Nothing can be said to praise the quality of these wines too highly. Whether one prefers the Bailey or the Morris wines it is not so much a question of which is better, but rather which style one prefers. Those of Bailey are slightly heavier, slightly more complex and slightly richer; those of Morris are slightly fresher, slightly more elegant but equally intense in flavour. In many ways the same considerations separate the bottom-of-the-range Founder's Liqueur Muscat from the top-of-the-range HJT. At the Canberra National Show in 1984 the HJT duly topped its class with 56.5 points out of a possible 60, but the Founder's Liqueur Muscat was only half a point behind, amassing 56 points. The next-nearest wine in the class was the Lindemans Reserve Old Liqueur Muscat Bin 1625A with 51 points, and a silver medal. (For some reason Morris was not an entrant in the class.) It was not until the Museum Class that Bailey's and Morris came face to face, with the Bailey's wine scoring at extraordinary 58.5 points, and the top Morris wine being content with 55.5 points and a gold (even Lindemans did better — their Reserve Liqueur Muscat Z295 scored 56.5 points).

I have participated in many discussions over the years during the course of show judging. There is not a show judge in Australia who does not rub his or her hands with joy at the prospect of being allotted one of the old muscat classes. Nor is there ever any substantial disagreement on what the judges see as the characteristics and style of the wines they are called upon to judge. But there is great disagreement between those who prefer the younger, fresher styles and those who glory in the intense, concentrated lusciousness of the very old blends, happily accepting the trace of volatility and the touch of oxidation that these very old (up to 30, 40 and 50 years average age) wines acquire. Thus the Canberra show judges were saying that the Founder's Liqueur Muscat was a magnificent example of a younger, fresher style, and that the HJT Liqueur Muscat was an even greater example of the older, richer style. Whether you think the $20 per bottle price differential is justified is a very personal decision: Bailey's has so little of the very old material that it would far prefer you to choose the younger wine.

The Bailey tokays live in the shadow of the muscats. Yet these, too, are of consistent top gold-medal standard: both Show Tokay entries won gold medals in the Premium Class at the Canberra National Show in 1984. The flavour is quite different from muscat, reminding me very strongly of cold tea. Made from the muscadelle grape, the wines tend to be slightly less viscous in texture and less complex in their structure. At times they can provide a welcome change from muscat.

Dry-red production still accounts for the major part of the annual output of around 315,000 litres. At times Harry Tinson achieves the best of both worlds: some of the finesse of modern red-wine-making techniques, with a touch of new oak, married with the immense power and strength of the traditional Bailey red. Perhaps my palate, and the palate of most other professional or semi-professional wine judges, has changed, influenced by the constant stream of new, light- to medium-bodied, astringent, cool-climate wines. Perhaps the quality and style of Bailey's reds has never changed. Perhaps in 20 years time I will eat (or, better still, drink) my words. Whatever be the true reason, some of the most recent red releases from Bailey's (particularly the '79 and '80 vintages) have seemed to me to contain just too much of everything, and every now and then a little bit of H₂S/mercaptan into the bargain. On the other hand the HJT Cabernet Sauvignon label almost invariably heralds a wine of high quality and even greater power and depth of flavour.

The muscats and tokays are next most important in terms of volume, followed ultimatey by the white wines introduced by Tinson in the 1970s to meet the demands of the marketplace. The first white varieties introduced were colombard, rhine riesling, aucerot, traminer, chasselas and chardonnay. As befits the region and the vineyard, the late-harvest (spatlese and auslese) versions of these wines have been far and away the most successful. A quite startling auslese aucerot was released some years ago, while the 1984 Auslese Rhine Riesling has marvellous honeyed/toffee aroma and flavour, yet had sufficient acid to prevent it cloying.

However, it is the fortified wines for which Bailey's will always be famous, even if an earthquake were to swallow the vineyard tomorrow.

BOOTHS' TAMINICK
TAMINICK via GLENROWAN

The Booth family has been making wine at Taminick, seven kilometres from the town of Glenrowan, since 1893. Despite a splendid photograph of some other company's gleaming stainless-steel tank farm (in the course of construction) attributed to Booths in the 1984 edition of Len Evans's _Complete Book of Australian Wine_, winemaking methods (and the wine styles produced) have barely changed in the last 90 years.

Foremost among the wines are the immense shiraz-based reds, high in alcohol, dense in colour and robust of palate, which for many years went to make the base for Wynns' Ovens Valley Shiraz. In 1972 that long-standing arrangement was terminated, and for the first time Booths' Taminick wines became generally available under their own labels.

The vineyard is planted to shiraz (11.5 hectares), cabernet sauvignon (5.6 hectares) and trebbiano (2.8 hectares). The soils are varied: some of the plantings are on the red soils to be found at Bailey's, others on brown sands. Interestingly, winemaker Cliff Booth finds that in some years the red soils produce higher-baume grapes, in other years the brown sands do so. The net result, however, is that the table wines regularly achieve 14 or more baume, while shiraz and cabernet destined for liqueur port can run up to 20 baume.

A welcome sign is that Booths is planting brown frontignac grapes with the intention of making a traditional Rutherglen muscat. It just may be that at long last the quality of these wines is being recognised by the public.

Production, which runs from between 4000 and 5000 cases a year, is all sold by cellar door and mailing list. Significant quantities are sold to the smaller wine clubs organised by major companies and government departments. None is sold through retail outlets.

BROWN BROTHERS
GLENROWAN–MYRTLEFORD ROAD, MILAWA

Brown Brothers seems to say to Tyrrell's: "Whatever you can do, we can do better." Murray Tyrrell might well counter that John Brown senior has an unfair advantage in having four sons to Murray's one. But in truth these two families have created magnificently successful operations, each finding ways and means to circumvent the limitations which other vignerons in their respective districts have accepted as inevitable.

The rich Brown Brothers story commences in 1852 when an 18-year-old law clerk named George Harry Brown arrived in Melbourne. Like so many others, he found the lure of gold irresistible and went to Bendigo to join the search. He was unsuccessful and joined with four others to travel further north and buy a property at Hurdle Creek near Milawa. Known locally as the "Farmers Five", they prospered sufficiently for each soon to acquire his own property. George Brown remained at Hurdle Creek and that property still remains in the Brown family with 18 hectares under vine. In 1857 a Scot named John Graham arrived at Milawa and purchased 50 hectares at the first land sale at Oxley Plains George Brown met and married his schoolteacher daughter, and on her father's death the couple moved to the Milawa property.

John Graham had planted table grapes, and George Harry Brown extended the plantings with wine-making varieties. His son John Francis Brown (born in 1867) made the first wine on the property, using an old Canadian-style barn which John Graham had built. It still stands and is used for maturing the fortified wines of Browns. In 1900 an additional winery was built, part of which still stands, and was incorporated into the winemaking complex which has grown, Topsy-like, over the ensuing 80 years.

In 1915 phylloxera finally made its way from Rutherglen to the Milawa region. The beginning of the First World War had meant the end of the export trade and had taken so many young Australians to the battlefield. Of the numerous vineyards then in existence around Milawa, only the Brown vineyard of 16 hectares was replanted.

John Charles Brown, eldest son of John Francis, left school in 1933 and made his first vintage in 1934. The 1984 celebrations of John Charles's fiftieth vintage were enjoyed by many, myself included, and all of us politely turned a blind eye to the fact that it was in fact his fifty-first vintage. For it has been due to the extraordinary foresight of this gentle, kind and compassionate man that Brown Brothers has been transformed from a quiet and sleepy family winery at the end of the 1950s to one which in 1984 produced 200,000 cases of premium wine from 2500 tonnes of high-quality grapes, not including the substantial bulk-wine production of the enterprise. There is a twinkle in John Charles's eyes, which at times gleams even more brightly in those of his son Ross, that is a telltale sign of the intelligence and ability of John Charles Brown. During a time in which all of the financial and taxation guns were aimed against private companies, and particularly private companies which attempted to reinvest the profits they earned back into the business, Brown Brothers has succeeded on a grand scale.

It started back in the early 1960s. Long before the red-wine boom took hold Browns decided to hold back part of the best red wines made in each year for release seven or eight years later, when they had reached their best. With the exception of Lindemans, I am unaware of any other wine company in Australia at that time adopting such a policy. Then, in 1962, John Brown recognised an outbreak of botrytis in a rhine riesling paddock similar to one he had seen in 1934, and made the first of the great rhine riesling spatlese wines, now renamed Noble Riesling. Next, and perhaps most importantly of all, he began an active programme of experimentation with a vast range of table grapes, both white and red but principally white, anticipating—and indeed making no small contribution to—the massive swing to white varietal table wines which occurred from the early part of the 1970s.

There was a continuity to all of these developments. When the original Milawa Vineyard was replanted in the aftermath of phylloxera, one of the varieties chosen was mondeuse, planted on the advice of Francois de Castella. De Castella said at the time:

> It is a grape which seems destined to play an important part in the vineyards of the future, especially for the production of light natural wines which will be sought in increasing quantities as the education of the public advances concerning the advantages that accrue from the logical and the reasoned use of wine of this type.

Only Brown Brothers heeded de Castella's advice, for even at that time it was chiefly a table-wine producer, taking a lone stand during a time in which the north-east produced fortified wine virtually exclusively. The reason for the stand lay partly in the climate and partly in the soil. Although Milawa is situated only 16 kilometres east of Wangaratta, due south of Rutherglen, its climate is distinctly cooler than that of Rutherglen due to the influence of the Victorian Alps. The deep-red loam soils, lying over river gravel containing large reserves of water and moisture, are also conducive to the growing of grapes. These moisture reserves allow the vines to offset naturally the water deficit which would otherwise arise from the modest rainfall of 625 millimetres.

Plantings at the Milawa Vineyard have increased from 12 to 72 hectares. Even though the climate is more moderate than the principal fortified-wine-producing sub-districts, the Milawa Vineyard is the main contributor to the dessert and fortified wines of Browns. It also contributes the botrytised rhine riesling which goes to produce Noble Riesling.

The proximity of the Alps means that the winters are severe, and spring frosts can at times be devastating. On 29 November 1967 a frost descended which completely eliminated the 1968 crop at Milawa. At that time John Brown was already buying in grapes from other growers, and had established a small vineyard at Everton Hills, which produced some of the marvellous early 1960s wines but which was eventually sold because the yields were so low. The 1967 frost may have been a blessing in disguise; it prompted the development of the first vineyard away from home at Mystic Park, to be followed by Hurdle Creek, King Valley and eventually Whitlands. At the same time John Brown set about encouraging farmers in the surrounding hills and valleys to plant grapes against the assurance of long-term contracts with Brown Brothers. These contract-growers now provide 50 per cent of the annual intake at Browns, and have been of critical importance in establishing the Individual Vineyard wine series.

Indeed, it is no easy task to list the diverse sources of grapes and the equally diverse number of labels for the Brown Brothers wines. Ignoring less important varieties (in terms of production) such as orange muscat (which makes a light though fragrant table wine utterly unlike the fortified wines from brown muscat) and rkatsiteli (an obscure Russian variety) the main varieties crushed each vintage create an imposing list. They are chardonnay, colombard, chenin blanc, rhine riesling, sauvignon blanc, gewurztraminer, crouchen, semillon, sylvaner, cabernet sauvignon, shiraz, malbec, merlot, ruby cabernet, mondeuse and tarrango.

The estate-grown grapes come from the 72 hectares at Milawa and from an identical area at Mystic Park. This was purchased as an established vineyard shortly after the disastrous frost of 1967, although since it was acquired virtually the entire vineyard has been

replanted with varieties more suitable to Browns' requirements. The soils are classed as red trachera sandy loam, with a content of limestone intermingled and overlaying a limestone base. Situated on the shores of Kangaroo Lake between Kerang and Swan Hill, supplementary water is essential to alleviate the totally inadequate rainfall of only 300 millimetres. The third "low-country" vineyard is at Hurdle Creek, where 18 hectares of vines are established on silted clay loam. Rainfall here is slightly higher than at Milawa, at around 675 millimetres.

The King Valley Vineyards are some of the most important. One hundred and thirty-five hectares are planted on a variety of soils varying considerably between the hilltops and the valley floor from residual volcanic soils to fertile river flats. In some places there are water-worn pebbles on hilltops. The vineyards are planted at varying heights from 230 to 560 metres, and the rainfall varies correspondingly from between 625 millimetres on the valley floor to 1250 millimetres on the high vineyards.

Yields from the established vineyards are remarkably consistent; not surprisingly, Mystic Park is the highest-yielding vineyard at around 12.5 tonnes per hectare, with the Milawa and King Valley vineyards each producing 10 tonnes per hectare. Hurdle Creek is still to reach full production, and the yields so far are not indicative of the potential of the vineyard.

The most recent and in many ways the most ambitious and interesting of the vineyard projects is that being undertaken at Whitlands, at a height of around 770 metres. The soil here is a striking, rich red clay of volcanic origin, deep and permeable, and is formed over a basaltic base. The extreme fertility of the soil coupled with the high rainfall of 1410 millimetres have led to an altogether different approach to viticulture. It is being established under the direction of Jim Hardie, who obtained his master's degree in viticulture at the Davis School of Oenology at the University of California, and subsequently worked with the Department of Agriculture as a viticultural research officer. The third factor dictating the choice of viticultural style is the very cool climate and thus the anticipated long ripening period. Snow falls frequently during winter, and in 1984 it fell in mid-October, after bud-burst on some of the vines.

All of these factors have acted together to dictate a European approach to vineyard layout and management. The vineyard is established in rows 1.7 metres apart with one metre between vines, giving a planting density of 6000 vines per hectare, compared with the typical Australian vineyard of less than 2000 vines per hectare. The vineyard is being laid out so as to utilise to the fullest the available radiation; this dictates the orientation of the rows, the height of the trellis, and the exposure of both fruit and leaves to air and sunlight. The high rainfall and correspondingly high humidity also require trellising and training methods which provide adequate exposure and ventilation of the foliage. The solution is a relatively high trellis with the vines being constantly trimmed throughout the growing season so that they take on the appearance of the hedge-like rows of vines that one finds across France.

The property was prepared for planting in the summer of 1981: photographs taken at the time show the extreme care used. The vineyard layout design was established and a substantial reservoir was constructed, fed by a nearby spring. Even though the rainfall is very high, prolonged dry spells in summer were known to be common, and an irrigation system was planned from the outset to combat the effects of this. Notwithstanding that the vineyard is outside the proclaimed phylloxera area, it was decided to plant grafted rootstocks, and to meet the very large requirements a grafting facility was established on the spot.

Ten hectares of vines were planted in the spring of 1982, only to be met by the worst drought ever experienced in the area. The drip-irrigation system was by then not commissioned, and was finally completed the day the drought broke. Not surprisingly, the vines did little more than survive and many failed even in that endeavour. In 1983 a further 10 hectares were planted and much of the original 10 hectares replanted; 9.2 hectares of merlot, six hectares of gewurztraminer, 2.1 hectares of pinot noir, 1.8 hectares of chardonnay and 1.1 hectares of rhine riesling were established at that stage. Eventually 58 hectares will be under vine.

In a most unusual experiment 60 fully mature vines of 15 varieties were transplanted from Mystic Park to Whitlands in October 1981. A very small crop in 1984 was picked from each of these vines, and the wines were made on the laboratory bench. The juice showed exceptional varietal character, and Browns is understandably excited about the prospects for this new vineyard.

Browns' innovation in the vineyard and winery has been matched by its adventurous approach to labelling. But by the end of 1982 one needed a computer to keep track of the styles, classifications, varieties, vineyards, vintage releases and a million other distinctions, a problem made worse by differing label designs. A decision was taken to standardise the label design at least, even if not to reduce significantly the number of wines. The distinctive "bow" label, produced in a Joseph's coat range of colours, was introduced. They are nothing if not distinctive, and I am sure Wolf Blass approves of them. At the same time I must admit to a sneaking admiration for them.

The basic wines are the traditional Milawa range of varietals typically comprising a White Frontignac, a Rhine Riesling, a Crouchen Moselle, a Spatlese Lexia, a Shiraz, a Cabernet Shiraz, a Shiraz and Mondeuse, a Shiraz Mondeuse and Cabernet, and a Cabernet Sauvignon. All of these wines are produced in sufficient quantity to be available for a full 12 months after their release through retailers and restaurants.

Moving up the line, and made in smaller quantities, are the Special Limited Production releases. Here the range widens even further. Over the past few years the Limited Production releases have included Sauvignon Blanc, Chenin Blanc, Gewurztraminer, Sylvaner, Flora, Orange Muscat, Emerald Riesling, Marsanne, Traminer Riesling and Trebbiano. The reds are only slightly less varied, including Ruby Cabernet, Barbera, and the CSIRO hybrid, Tarrango.

Then come the Individual Vineyard wines from the specialist long-term growers under contract to Browns. In years gone by these included the Delatite wines now made and released under their own label; currently they include Koombahla and Meadow Creek. Koombahla is one of the most important of the outside sources for Brown Brothers. Koombahla, an Aboriginal word for "gum tree", is situated in the beautiful King Valley at Whitfield, some 37 kilometres from Milawa, and under the lee of the new Brown Brothers Whitfield development. It was purchased in 1970 by Guy Darling and the first cabernet sauvignon vines were planted in that year. Rhine riesling and further cabernet sauvignon were planted in 1971, followed by shiraz in 1972, and ultimately towards the end of the 1970s by chardonnay, pinot noir, sauvignon blanc and merlot. The last two varieties are only now producing fruit in commercial quantities. While situated in a shallow valley, at a very much lower altitude than the Browns Whitfield Vineyard, the heat of the summer days is significantly ameliorated by the late rising and early setting of the sun, due of course to the nearby mountains. The Koombahla wines have always had an extra dimension of intensity and delicacy: the rhine rieslings have a hint of lime/tropical fruit; the cabernet sauvignons have an almost Bordeaux-like structure. Meadow Creek, situated on the steep sides of a narrow valley, with soils of gravelly hill loam, has proved itself especially suited to shiraz and cabernet.

Finally come the Classic Vintage releases, principally of red wines but also including the Noble Riesling. Some of the red wines are kept for unusually long periods of time. At the extreme end of the maturation range the wines are elevated even further to the status of Family Reserve. Thus in 1984 a 1970 Shiraz Cabernet from the old Everton Hills Vineyard was released as a Family Reserve wine.

With such a vast range of wines it becomes superfluous to go back over the hundreds of tasting notes I have accumulated over the years to single out particular wines for attention. But there is one ghost which should be laid to rest. Some years ago it was fashionable for wine writers and critics to say that all of the Brown Brothers wines tasted the same. Indeed, there was a period when the principal yeast used seemed to impose its own character on the different varieties; that is no longer the case. The wines are varietally distinct, and each release has its own individual character.

The one uniform characteristic is the quality: winemaker John Graham Brown has developed exceptional skills in dealing with the vast numbers of batches of wine that come through the winery each year, somehow keeping track of each and ensuring that not one of them shows any fault or off character. Tall, dark and quietly spoken, John Brown junior (as he is commonly called) would be one of the cult winemakers if he were employed at a commercial winery. Instead, he prefers to go quietly about his business, leaving the marketing to Ross Brown (who these days spends much of his time overseas building up the very successful export side of the business), the vineyards to Peter R. Brown, and vine breeding and propagation to Roger F. Brown. It is one of the great triumphs of the family, and one of its chief strengths, that each of the four sons has settled so inevitably and naturally into his chosen area of work. It would be difficult to imagine four brothers of more different temperament, and yet they work in perfect harmony together. Little wonder that John Brown senior and his wife Pat have such a look of contentment in their faces.

Like a small boy I have, however, left the best until last. I briefly related earlier how in 1934 the first incidence of botrytis was noticed by John Brown senior. In that year the wine was ultimately incorporated into one of Browns' fortified wines, as there was no market for and very little understanding of sweet botrytised table wine. It occurred again—naturally—in 1962. In that vintage, and in each year in which botrytis has occurred, the grapes have been handled and vinified separately, yet have always come from the same block.

The vines grow on heavier soil in one of the low-lying areas in the Milawa Vineyard; in autumn the fog hugs the ground, creating the necessary humidity for the botrytis to develop. The 1962 infection was the heavy one; 1963 saw a similar outbreak, but there was then effectively a gap until 1970. In 1964 and 1965 there was only a light infection; 1966 was simply a poor vintage, as was 1967; 1968 was the aftermath of the frost, and 1969 was ruined by heavy vintage-time rain. Since 1970, however, botrytis has occurred to a lesser or greater degree every year, and wines have been made in every vintage. On 14 January 1977 a cyclone hit Milawa, wiping out many of the vineyards, crumpling fermentation tanks like pieces of silver paper, tearing down 100-year-old trees and unroofing part of the winery, yet miraculously leaving the rhine riesling section of the Milawa Vineyard untouched. Despite that miracle for some reason botrytis failed to appear, as it had likewise failed in 1975. 1970, 1972 and 1978 were years of heavy botrytis infection, with 1978 the most affected. 1971, 1973, 1976, 1979, 1980 and 1982 were years of medium infection, while 1964, 1965, 1981 and 1983 were light.

Right from the outset Brown Brothers has exercised exemplary restraint in its labelling. The 1970 vintage was released under a Special Spatlese Rhine Riesling label; given the baume levels and the richness of the wine, and the use of the terms spatlese and auslese by other makers, by rights it should have been labelled beerenauslese. When the confusion became too great, it changed the label to Noble Riesling. Even then, when the 1977 vintage failed to produce any significant botrytis, it declined to use the Noble Riesling label, simply styling the wine Late-Harvest Rhine Riesling.

The 1970, 1972, 1976 and 1978 releases (the last not marketed until 1984) are generally regarded as the most successful. The '70 and '72 wines are still drinking marvellously well: for one reason or another I still have significant quantities in my cellar, and they are sheer pleasure to drink. Yet despite the major contribution of the botrytis, they seem to lack some of the freshness of life of the cool-climate botrytised wines which are now becoming more readily available. This is no doubt partly due to Browns' practice of leaving the wine in 500- to 900-gallon (2275- or 4095-litre) casks for up to a year before bottling, and then holding them in their cellar for a further four or five years before release. Indeed, I wonder whether we will not see a change in these practices in future. It is no doubt also due to the fact that botrytis significantly reduces varietal character, and inevitably leads to a degree of oxidation in the fruit before it is even processed. Ageing then only accentuates these characters further. These are perhaps carping criticisms of what is undoubtedly one of Australia's unique and great wine styles.

BULLER'S CALLIOPE
Off MURRAY VALLEY HIGHWAY, RUTHERGLEN

Buller's was founded in 1921 when Reginald Buller took up the property under a Soldier Settlement Scheme. It had been worked as a vineyard prior to the outbreak of phylloxera by the Callen family, and about 24 hectares of grafted vines were already back in production when Reginald Buller acquired the property. His son, Richard L. Buller, graduated from Roseworthy in 1947 and joined his father at Calliope. Richard and Andrew Buller are now the third-generation winemakers, with Graham and Andrew Buller in close attendance. Richard makes regular pilgrimages to Portugal to work with Taylors, and plays ready-host to return visits.

The 32-hectare vineyard is planted to varieties primarily aimed at making fortified wine (shiraz, brown muscat, frontignac, grenache, cinsaut and muscadelle). The Buller family is convinced the low-yielding, non-irrigated vineyards of their area are best suited to fortified wines, and they have no argument from me on that score.

The Calliope Black Label fortified wines are of a very high standard, the liqueur muscat and the liqueur frontignac being only very marginally behind the commercial releases of Bailey and Morris. They have also thought deeply about their vintage port style, drawing extensively upon Richard Buller's experiences in Portugal.

Production of the Calliope vineyard is very modest, with little more than 100 tonnes being crushed annually. The real volume comes from their Beverford Vineyard and winery, where substantial quantities of table wine are produced. While the quality of this does not approach that of Calliope, it produces the cash flow necessary to keep bank managers quiescent and to provide a reasonable standard of living for the family.

CAMPBELLS
MURRAY VALLEY HIGHWAY, RUTHERGLEN

Campbells has probably gone further than any other winery in the north-east in proving that it is possible to have the best of both worlds, and make both high-quality dessert wines together with above-average table wines from the same viticultural base. At the risk of appearing obstinate, I cannot help but speculate what would happen if it devoted its obvious intelligence and skills in developing a separate table-wine vineyard in one of the numerous cool mountain areas so readily identified by Brown Brothers. None-theless, one must pay tribute to the dedication and energy of the Campbell family, who have not always found things easy since 24-year-old John Campbell sailed on the _Merchant Prince_ on 5 December 1857. He arrived in Melbourne in March 1858 and almost immediately set out for Beechworth to prospect for gold. He returned to Melbourne to marry Jessie Robb on 13 December 1858, but then once again returned to the goldfields, this time to Rutherglen. For a while he worked on the Bobbie Burns lead, one of the richest deposits in the district, but also elusive and fragmented.

When the gold dwindled he selected 32 hectares of land adjoining the Bobbie Burns lead, and set about clearing the property, using the timber to erect a slab-and-shingle house and 120 chains (2414 metres) of post-and-rail fencing. When the Land Act was passed in 1869 he applied for and obtained title to the property he had named Bobbie Burns, and the following year was granted a further 48 hectares to the rear of the original block.

By 1874 the 16 hectares of cleared land had been sown to 15 hectares of wheat and oats, and a little under one hectare of vines had been planted. More vines were planted the following year, and plantings continued steadily until 1886 by which time there were almost 15 hectares of vineyard (producing around 12,000 litres of wine), and a 46-foot by 25-foot (14 metres by 7.6 metres) cellar built of sawn red-gum slabs erected. The plantings comprised shiraz, riesling, pedro and malbec together with a few brown muscat vines. There were also small plantings of table grapes, and at an 1889 exhibition a bunch was exhibited by James Campbell weighing 8.5 pounds (3.8 kilograms).

In 1891 Campbells was producing prize-winning wines, and the future looked bright. But by 1898 phylloxera had taken hold; and in 1909 John Campbell died, heartbroken and convinced that his vineyard had no future. Prior to the onset of phylloxera the vineyards had been extended to over 35 hectares, and the cellars had capacity for 53,000 litres of wine. John Campbell was survived by only three of his eight children. His land was split between his two surviving sons, with David retaining the whole of the original Bobbie Burns selection. It was he who determined to replant the vineyard on grafted rootstock and to refurbish the cellars.

In one of the curiosities of the times the Chinese population, who had arrived during the goldrush and stayed on afterwards, provided most of the labour force during vintage. The Campbells recollect that they were paid $1 per week for unlimited hours, and that as the time for picking grew near the Chinese could be heard approaching, their goods and chattels clanging together as they carried them across their shoulders on sticks. The grapes were picked into four-gallon (18-litre) tins and brought into the winery on horsedrawn drays. Power to drive the crusher was provided by a horse-operated windlass, while the hydraulic basket presses were hand-operated and all pumping was carried out with hand-pumps. Later the vineyard horses were replaced by a tractor, and the cellar horse was replaced first by a steam-engine and then by an oil-engine which drove the crusher and must-pump until electricity arrived in 1945.

David Campbell died in 1933 at the age of 58, following an accident in the cellar. His eldest son, Alan, who was only 18 years of age, found himself in charge of a winery at the tail-end of the Depression. He had 15,000 litres of wine but no purchasers for it, and a mortgage. The family struggled through: the money to buy a small flock of sheep was found, and gradually a small private trade was built up for the wine which had hitherto been sold in bulk.

In 1943 an additional 16 hectares were purchased, including four hectares of vines planted in 1912. A further 10-hectare vineyard was purchased in 1948 from John Stanton, and has since consistently produced the finest grapes. Yet another property followed in 1952, another in 1960 (of 80 hectares), and in 1966 a further 56 hectares. These later purchases were principally dedicated to the extensive farming operations which the Campbell family carry on to this day. Alan Campbell died in June 1974 and his sons Malcolm and Colin now carry on the business. Malcolm is the agriculturist and viticulturalist; Colin the winemaker, having gained a diploma of agriculture from Dookie College and a diploma of oenology from Roseworthy.

The 46 hectares of vineyards have been significantly reshaped over the past decade. Old dry-land vineyards have been abandoned, and new vineyards established in areas where adequate water was available for supplementary irrigation. The varietal mix, too, has now reached the point where over 50 per cent of the plantings are given over to table-wine production, and a substantial proportion of this to white-wine production. The varieties include chardonnay, pedro ximinez, rhine riesling, semillon, sylvaner, trebbiano, gewurtztraminer, cabernet sauvignon, durif, royalty, ruby cabernet, rubired, malbec and shiraz, all of which are given over to table-wine production, with some of the shiraz going to port. The port and fortified varieties include touriga, alvarello, muscadelle and brown muscat.

Campbells started to draw attention with its white wines in the second half of the 1970s as the new plantings came into bearing. The first rhine riesling was produced in 1978; in 1980 it won a gold medal in Melbourne, and followed up by winning the trophy for the best Victorian dry white table wine in the 1981 and 1982 shows. Probably the most consistent white wine of all has been the chablis, made—of all things—from pedro ximinez. The 1983 vintage was very good, and one or two outstanding wines were made in earlier years. The one problem with the white wines appears to be a tendency to oiliness, forcing Colin Campbell to do a balancing act between delicate, early-picked styles with insufficient varietal fruit and later-picked, richer styles which quickly became fat, flabby and oily. If only he would go to the high country.

Campbells also attracted attention with its 1983 Ruby Cabernet, which won a gold medal at the 1983 Melbourne show. The acid retention properties of this variety may prove to be of great worth. The traditional Bobbie Burns Shiraz is a good wine (with the '81 of outstanding quality), and once again Colin Campbell's thoughtful approach to winemaking can be seen. It has changed from a big, burnt style to one in which greater attention has been given to pH and freshness, together with some new oak lift.

The Collectors' Series tokays of 1964 and 1968 (straight vintage wines) were—and are—of extremely high quality. More recently the Merchant Prince bottling, with its striking label and packaging commemorating that voyage of John Campbell, was released and received high praise.

But what about the highlands? They are, after all, Campbell country.

CHAMBERS ROSEWOOD
COROWA ROAD, RUTHERGLEN

The Chambers family has been at Rosewood for over 100 years; if present incumbent Bill Chambers' grandfather were to walk into the winery tomorrow he would have little or no difficulty in finding his way around, and would even recognise the press he used, still kept in working condition in case the Vaslin breaks down. I have come to know Bill Chambers well over the years, and it is a friendship I value highly. The disconcertingly bright azure-blue eyes reveal the agile mind which Bill Chambers tries to hide from the casual observer. Laconic in the extreme, he seems to give the impression he would really rather not sell his wine at all, at the same time without giving the least offence to anyone. Marketing is not a word which looms large in his vocabulary.

He still has some very limited stocks of some magnificent old muscat and tokay made by his father, W. H. Chambers, in 1928 or 1929. The wines won first prizes at Sydney, Adelaide and Melbourne in 1939. They were left more or less untouched until the 1970s, when Bill decided they had become "too syrupy", so he topped them up with some 1952 vintage wines also made by W. H. Chambers. He then grudgingly let it be known that they were available for sale. The price started out at $10 a bottle and by the early 1980s had reached $25 a bottle. Every time someone bought a bottle, the price went up. It was not that Bill really wanted more money for his wine, he simply did not particularly wish to sell it. It came to the attention of Robert Chadderdon, a noted wine importer in New York who selected only the finest French and Australian wines. Chadderdon bought several cases (with no discount) and in 1984 his Melbourne agents asked for more samples; Chambers replied there was no need for samples, the wine was the same. Another 10 cases went on their way (untasted) to New York, where it sells for over $100 a bottle. Chambers also has some equally remarkable old sherries, the best of which he does not even list, preferring to give the odd bottle away to those he feels will appreciate them.

There are over 40 hectares of vines at Rosewood, but almost half of these are extremely old and slowly going out of production, having been planted by Bill Chambers' grandfather between 70 and 90 years ago. He had succeeded to the property which his father had purchased from Anthony Ruche, the German-born vigneron whose celebrated sale had been recorded by Hubert de Castella and had done so much to give publicity to the north-east. Ruche

apparently could not get over the loss of his treasured wine stocks, and sold the property to Chambers senior shortly thereafter. The oldest plantings which still survive date from the time of phylloxera at the end of the 1890s, when the vineyard was necessarily replanted. Thus some of the most unusual white wines in Australia have come from Rosewood. These include a rhine riesling and gouais blend and a chenin blanc and montils blend. The reds include a wine called blue imperial, which is the old Rutherglen name for cinsaut.

A substantial portion of each year's crush is provided from Peter Chambers' vineyard at Lakeside, where cabernet sauvignon, rhine riesling, alicante bouchet and cinsaut are planted. The vines here are irrigated and go to make the rosés and Lakeside beaujolais styles which are marketed each year.

FAIRFIELD
PALMER STREET, WOORINEN SOUTH

Incredible though it may seem, Fairfield was inhabited only for a brief time after it was sold in 1910. It was thereafter abandoned to the sheep and to the vandals; by 1970 it was virtually in ruins, the roof gone, the ceilings collapsed, the cellars flooded. Everything that could be removed or smashed had been so treated. Against all architectural advice Melba Slamen, granddaughter of C. H. Morris, purchased the house and determined to restore it.

Part of the subsequent successful restoration has been the establishment of eight hectares of vineyard planted to shiraz, cabernet sauvignon, durif, trebbiano, muscadelle and muscat. In turn, these wines are made at Fairfield using most of the winemaking equipment that was in place at the turn of the century. It had survived the vandals simply because it was too strong to wreck. Thus the fermenting must is cooled by one of the oldest methods devised: it is pumped up to a height of two metres above the concrete fermenting vats and allowed to run down sloping boards back into the tank. Theoretically the wine should be oxidised by the treatment, but the carbon dioxide present in the ferment largely protects it. This treatment also is very effective in getting rid of unwanted hydrogen sulphide formed during fermentation.

Melba Slamen is helped in the winemaking by estate manager Stephen Morris and with advice from Rick Morris of Markwood. Modern winemaking theory is not entirely ignored, and the wines made with the old equipment have been good enough to win medals at the Melbourne show. The label of the Fairfield wines is a replica of that of the original Fairfield, found by Mrs Slamen in a museum at Kyneton.

Fairfield will never reassume the importance it once had, but at least its past glories will not be forgotten.

GAYFER'S CHILTERN
HUME HIGHWAY, CHILTERN

The 12-hectare Chiltern Vineyard of Keith Gayfer has been on the market throughout much of 1984, and will almost certainly have been sold by the time this book goes to press. The purchaser will acquire one of the most extraordinary wineries in Australia, excelling even the stone jail of Dr Bob Smith at Wybong Estate. Until 1922 the corrugated-iron buildings that comprise the winery were perched 80 metres above the ground on top of head works of the great Chiltern Valley goldmine. Keith Gayfer bought the Chiltern Vineyard in 1948 and changed little. Whether it will be seen as a viable winery in today's market remains to be seen, but it would be a great pity if it were allowed simply to rust away.

GEHRIG
Cnr MURRAY VALLEY HIGHWAY AND HOWLONG ROAD, BARNAWARTHA

The history of this small vineyard goes back to the late nineteenth century when it was briefly owned by the Barnawartha Vineyard Company; shortly prior to the onset of phylloxera it was purchased by Phillip Gehrig, who increased the plantings from 20 to 40 acres (eight to 16 hectares), only to see them destroyed by the louse. His son Frederick replanted the vineyard, and it passed to one of the great district characters, Barney Gehrig. Barney died in early 1984, and his son Bernard now runs the operation.

The winery is one of the more unusual I have ever visited, seemingly totally disorganised, and little changed from the last century save for the stainless-steel tanks (with some refrigeration) used to make the white wines. Until the end of the 1970s the red wines were simply labelled claret, regardless of whether they were made from shiraz, cabernet sauvignon or a blend of the two.

In 1966 Barney Gehrig rather unexpectedly branched out, planting chardonnay obtained from the local Viticultural Research Station. A cuckoo got into the nest somehow, because the chardonnay vines were eventually identified as chenin blanc, a problem compounded by the fact that when some of the young "chardonnay" rootlings died, they were inadvertently replaced with pinot noir. This rather Gilbertian story had a happy ending when the pinot noir performed very well, producing wines of considerable colour and depth and encouraging Bernard Gehrig to extend the plantings. He believes the success of the variety is due to the microclimate of the vineyard which is significantly cooler than that of the Rutherglen area proper, so that vintage occurs up to two weeks later.

The Gehrig wines I have drunk over the years, to put it mildly, have been basic. I recently shared a bottle (or rather less than that) of the "chardonnay" purchased some years before by Tim Knappstein. It was rather tired and hard, with no discernible chardonnay varietal character—which is hardly surprising in the circumstances.

JOHN GEHRIG WINES
GLENROWAN–MYRTLEFORD ROAD, OXLEY

John Gehrig Wines is the newest winery in the north-east, established 13 kilometres south-east of Wangaratta on the main Glenrowan to Myrtleford road at Oxley. The vineyard was established in 1976 by John McKeone Gehrig, and is planted to rhine riesling, chenin blanc, pinot noir and merlot. All of the production is sold at the cellar door.

JONES WINERY
CHILTERN ROAD, RUTHERGLEN

The Jones vineyard was established by Frederick Ruhe in the 1860s. Les Jones still holds a medal awarded to Ruhe by the Rutherglen Agricultural Society in 1880 for a sweet, delicate white wine. According to local history Ruhe's vineyard suffered the dubious distinction of being the first recorded site of phylloxera.

The vineyard was purchased in 1927 by Les Jones senior, who sold his grapes to All Saints until 1930. In that year he established a winery and began marketing his wines through Melbourne merchants. 1933 saw the commencement of cellar-door sales, and Les Jones senior continued winemaking until 1977 when Les junior took over. The winery is virtually unchanged: the only concession to modernisation has been the placing of galvanised iron over the original bark roof. All of the original casks are still in use, as is all of the winemaking equipment other than the crush hand-press. Horses were still being used to provide the power for winery equipment until the early 1950s. The 12-hectare vineyard is planted to shiraz, pedro ximinez and trebbiano. Many of the vines are extremely old, dating back to the turn of the century.

Jones Winery has never made a white wine. It produces principally fortified wines, with limited quantities of dry red. The most extraordinary feature is the brilliantly coloured ultra-modern wine labels with their bold design printed in psychedelic colour. It is perfectly certain to me that the graphic artist who designed those labels had never been within 100 kilometres of the Jones Winery.

MARKWOOD
MORRIS LANE, MARKWOOD

When Reckitt and Colman took over Morris's Mia Mia Winery and Vineyard in 1979, Rick (F. J.) Morris decided it was time to leave. He had worked Mia Mia since leaving school but preferred the thought of being his own master to having a big brother watching over his shoulder. So he moved down the road from Brown Brothers, and gradually established his own vineyard and small winery devoted almost exclusively to table wine, but also producing a flor fino sherry. In due course he also hopes to release limited quantities of fortified wine, using the brandy he produces from a tiny pot-still established on the premises.

With only three hectares under vine, and yields of around 7.5 tonnes per hectare, output will always be very small because Morris relies exclusively on his own estate-grown grapes. The vineyards are planted to shiraz, cabernet sauvignon, chardonnay and palomino. 1982 saw the first small production of chardonnay, while the palomino is used both to produce the dry table wine and flor fino sherry.

With only 1000 cases of wine a year to dispose of, all sales are at the cellar door. It is a quiet life, but one which Rick Morris is evidently quite happy with.

MORRIS
MIA MIA VINEYARD, RUTHERGLEN, OFF MURRAY VALLEY HIGHWAY

Yet another to follow the siren-allure of gold to Australia was a young Bristol bank clerk, G. F. Morris. He left England in 1851 bound for Victoria and unsuccessfully mined for gold at the Reeds Creek diggings on the Ovens River. His training as a bank clerk must have stood him in good stead, for he quickly realised there was far more money to be made in trading with the miners, and he bought a share in a small wholesale business at Beechworth. Within a few years the company had expanded five-fold, and Morris was able to return with his young wife and family to England with the profit.

There his son C. H. Morris was born in 1859, but Morris returned to Australia that year to buy a 100-hectare property at Browns Plains, not far from Rutherglen. He was pleased with the results, and planted another 12 hectares. At first, however, he found it difficult to sell the wine for a reasonable price. It would bring no more than tenpence a gallon (4.5 litres), so for some time he concentrated on his other farming activities. Demand for wine increased, and Morris, at first slowly and then more rapidly, increased both the size of his vineyards and his land-holdings. The vineyard ultimately exceeded 250 hectares, making it one of the largest in the world.

In the early 1880s Morris built the glorious two-storey Fairfield mansion (now being restored by Melba Slamen) and constructed the largest cellars in the southern hemisphere—they held the equivalent of three vintages of one million litres each. Three-quarters of the annual production of Fairfield was exported to London from where it passed to Europe and the remainder of the British Empire. In 20 years Fairfield wines won 425 first prizes and innumerable medals at exhibitions in London, Amsterdam, Paris, Calcutta, New Zealand, South Africa, Perth, Melbourne and Sydney.

In 1887 Morris's 28-year-old son, C. H. Morris, purchased his own land at Mia Mia, three kilometres east of Fairfield, and planted 36 hectares to shiraz and muscat. Like other growers in the district, these were sold to his father's Fairfield Winery. Around the turn of the century C. H. Morris married, and left Fairfield to move into a far more humble house on his own property.

G. F. Morris died in 1910, and it was Mia Mia, not Fairfield, which survived. Phylloxera had devastated many of the Fairfield vineyards, and there was dissension and unhappiness in the family. Fairfield and the vineyards were sold to various buyers, and Fairfield itself entered a prolonged period of decline, with winemaking operations ceasing almost immediately. C. H. Morris, by contrast, went from strength to strength. Observing that phylloxera did not attack vines growing in sandy soil, in 1908 he acquired land at Balldale just across the Murray River in New South Wales. The 120-hectare Sandhills Vineyard indeed proved resistant to phylloxera, and gave Mia Mia a source of grapes to tide it over in the years following the First World War, when C. H. Morris and his three sons, Charles Tempest, Gerald and Frederick, replanted Mia Mia with resistant vines. Once Mia Mia came back into production the Sandhills Vineyard was used in part to supply the material for distillation in the still which the Morris family had installed; to this day they continue to make their own spirit for distillation.

The business continued in the hands of the family both before and after C. H. Morris's death in 1943. Until 1953 winemaking was carried out by Gerald Morris, and after his death by Charles Tempest and Frederick Morris. Charles's son, C. H. (Mick) Morris, was the first member of the family to obtain formal qualifications. Schooled at Scotch College in Melbourne, he then obtained a Bachelor of Science degree from Melbourne University before gaining his diploma in oenology from Roseworthy. When Mick Morris came back to the business around 1950 the output was almost exclusively fortified wines. He recalls that they were making about 300 gallons (1365 litres) of dry red wine a year but could not sell even that much. However, the events of 1953 soon had their effect, and by 1956 Morris was starting to make more and more dry red wine. A very few white wines were made, but there was little or no demand for them.

In 1970 the Morris family decided to sell to Reckitt and Colman; in the same year Reckitt and Colman also acquired Orlando, but it has been very careful to preserve the identity of both companies. Reckitt and Colman have been lucky to retain the services and wholehearted support of Mick Morris, who has continued on in exactly the same fashion as he would have were he the sole owner of the business. Mick is a working winemaker, and more than that, passionately devoted to defending the reputation and quality of the great fortified wines of the region, while at the same time finding the means of developing a remarkable range of white and red table wines. It is here that the Orlando technology has no doubt proved immensely useful, not to mention the substantial additional capital provided by Reckitt and Colman. In 1973 Reckitt and Colman provided the funds to acquire an additional 200 hectares of land nearby, and by 1980, 40 hectares had already been planted with tokay, muscat, shiraz, cabernet sauvignon and durif. Those plantings, together with the 40 hectares of the old Mia Mia Vineyard, represent the core of

the 80 hectares of unirrigated vineyard which provide the majority of the grapes for the fortified and dry red wines.

The majority of the white grapes come from long-term contract arrangements, chiefly with Mount Prior. The Mount Prior vineyards are an important source of chardonnay and traminer, and will provide chenin blanc and sauvignon blanc in the future. The few hectares of semillon and white hermitage owned by Morris make a further contribution.

By far the most exciting development for Morris is a long-term contract arrangement entered into with a grower in the highlands of the Buckland Valley, past Beechworth towards Bright. The soil, the climate, the rainfall and the viticultural techniques adopted are all very similar to those of the Brown Brothers' development at Whitlands. Ten hectares each of chardonnay and pinot noir have been established, and it is expected that with the close spacing, high fertility and high rainfall, yields will be not less than 15 tonnes per hectare, providing Morris with an additional 300 tonnes of very high-quality fruit. Rainfall is 1250 millimetres and the rich volcanic soil is tremendously deep. The development, which is under the control of Orlando's chief viticulturalist, Don Lester, is seen primarily as providing base wine for champagne.

Being part of a major winemaking group, Morris is not forthcoming with precise details of production. But it is known that in 1980 over 200,000 litres of wine were being produced annually, and it is unlikely that present production is less than 500,000 litres. When Mount Prior and the Buckland Valley come into full production, annual output should be in the region of 700,000 litres, although obviously not all of this will be released under the Morris label—the Buckland Valley base wine will no doubt largely go to Orlando.

The top-of-the-range wines are the Old Premium Liqueur Muscat and the Old Premium Liqueur Tokay, retailing for around $21 at the end of 1984. The real art in making a great muscat or tokay lies in the blending of old and younger parcels of material, an art as critical—and as difficult—as assembling a champagne cuvée. The Old Premium Liqueur Muscat is a blend of many vintages, with small parts going back 50 or more years. Mick Morris still has a tiny quantity of pre-phylloxera aucerot which he "freshened up" in 1952. Wines such as this—and I have tasted it—border on the undrinkable, so concentrated is the flavour, so searing the acid and so high the volatility. Even 0.5 per cent in a blend will make an enormous impact. But on the other hand, the contribution of young, fresh material is no less important. It is this which contributes much of the fruit aroma and the essential freshness and life on the palate to prevent the wine from cloying.

The Liqueur Muscat and Liqueur Tokay are little brothers (or little sisters, if you prefer) to the Old Premium range. They are less complex, less intense and very slightly lighter in body. But all things are relative: tasted on their own, the richness of the flavour astonishes those who have not encountered them previously. It cannot be said too often: for quality, and uncompromising purity of style, these wines rank with the very greatest wines in the world, sitting proudly alongside Chateau Latour, Chateau Petrus, Chateau d'Yquem, Romanée Conti, Montrachet _et al._

Since the late 1970s the varietal white table wines, and in particular the Morris semillon and the Morris chardonnay, have consistently been of the very highest quality. For some time their price was absurdly low; it has crept up somewhat over the past few years, but the wines still represent excellent value for money. The Mount Prior Vineyard, which has produced much of the fruit, quite clearly has something special about it, while the influence of the Orlando technology is also of critical importance.

The red wines, too, have been very interesting, with the Morris durif representing one of the atavistic throwbacks to the rock-solid reds of yesterday, tempered only by some attention to pH levels and possibly (although it is difficult to see in the wine) a token coat of new oak.

MOUNT PRIOR
HOWLONG ROAD, RUTHERGLEN

In the latter part of the nineteenth century there were five great wineries in the Rutherglen district: Fairfield, Netherby, Mount Prior, Mount Ophir and All Saints. Netherby and Mount Ophir have, it seems, gone for all time, but it must please all wine lovers and equally all supporters of the National Estate that Fairfield is being restored and that Mount Prior is once again a major contributor to the wine industry of the north-east.

Owner Dr Hugh Catchlove set about re-establishing the vineyards in the 1970s. There are now 14 hectares of chardonnay, six hectares of traminer, two hectares each of cabernet sauvignon, shiraz, malbec and durif, 0.8 hectare of cabernet franc and 0.4 hectare each of carignane and grenache, all in bearing. More recently, eight hectares of sauvignon blanc

and six hectares of chenin blanc have been planted on the red loam soils of the vineyard. This is the red loam, with its permeable base, which has supported all of the great vineyards of the region, and is no doubt largely responsible for the high quality of the grapes.

Most of the wines have been made by Morris, and the white wines will continue to be so made for the foreseeable future. In any event only a small percentage of the estate-grown grapes is made into wine for Mount Prior. Most are sold under the long-term arrangements to Morris. But consistent with his aims of restoring Mount Prior, Dr Catchlove has recommissioned the old winery. It presently has capacity for processing and storage of about 40 tonnes of grapes or 25,000 litres of wine. However, due to the arrangement of the tanks it is only possible to process three varieties. Thus the actual tonnage is determined by the yield coming from those varieties. In 1983 it amounted to only 10 tonnes of cabernet franc, carignane and grenache. The wines are made by Rick Kinsbrunner, and are basically sold at the cellar door, by mailing list and through the Australian Wine Club.

A substantial number of wines are available at the cellar door, sometimes covering more than one vintage. The reds offer varietal releases of durif, cabernet sauvignon, shiraz and carignane, with the grenache usually made into a rosé. The chardonnay is under such pressure that it is sometimes released under a non-vintage label; I have drunk more than my fair share of Mount Prior (vintage) chardonnay at Tsindos's Bistrot in Melbourne, and thoroughly enjoyed its rich flavour. The 1982 Cabernet Franc was another excellent wine, with very good green-leaf varietal flavour and intensity.

PFEIFFER WINES
DISTILLERY ROAD, WAHGUNYAH

Chris Pfeiffer was senior winemaker at Lindemans' Corowa Winery and Vineyards until they were closed early in 1984. While the option of a transfer to one of Lindemans' other winemaking centres was open, Pfeiffer had grown too fond of the area to contemplate leaving it. Seppelt was also moving out of the region, and having unsuccessfully attempted to sell the whole of their north-eastern vineyards and winery in a single line, offered them separately.

Pfeiffer purchased the so-called M and D Block, named after Masterton and Dobbin who had originally planted it. It now has 4.4 hectares each of chardonnay and pinot noir, and 0.4 hectare of gammay. Finally, there is a single row each of 26 different Portuguese port varieties, also making up 0.4 hectare. Pfeiffer's second acquisition was the old Seppelt distillery at Wahgunyah, which he has resurrected as his winery and cellar-door sales area. The fine old brick building is a handsome location for the north-east's newest winery. Pfeiffer also manages the 12-hectare Tuilleries Vineyard, owned by John and Anna Bryers, who run the very good Tuilleries restaurant. This vineyard is planted to muscat, tokay and cabernet sauvignon, and Pfeiffer has first call on the fruit from it.

For the foreseeable future Pfeiffer will concentrate on wines made from these two vineyards. The first wine to be released will be a 1985 Chardonnay, with both red table wines and traditional fortified muscats and tokays further down the track. If all goes according to plan Pfeiffer is hopeful he may be able also to gain access to some high-country grapes, grown in areas such as the Buckland Valley or Whitlands.

ST LEONARDS
ST LEONARDS ROAD, WAHGUNYAH

The long, low, whitewashed cellars at the beautiful St Leonards Winery give some clue as to the age and rich history of the St Leonards vineyards. Vines were first planted here in 1866 by James Scott, who quickly ran into financial difficulties and was forced to sell to a New Zealander named Henry Ireland. Ireland built up the business, both by increasing the plantings commenced by Scott and by buying adjoining vineyards and land. He erected a small winery, not far from the site of the present cellars, and by 1900 had 40 hectares of vineyard.

Phylloxera then struck as it did everywhere else in the district, forcing Scott to replant. This he did, taking the opportunity to increase the plantings to 95 hectares, and establishing many of the varieties which Francois de Castella brought to Australia for the express purpose of re-establishing the Victorian vineyards. Foremost among the de Castella varieties were durif, mondeuse and alicante bouchet; also planted were shiraz, aucerot, trebbiano, chasselas, touriga and bastardo.

The deep, rich alluvial soils, ranging from sandy loams through to red clay loams, have always yielded well. Supplementary water from the Murray River irrigation system is also readily available. The average crush in the early 1900s was around 400 tonnes per year, producing principally dry red wine, a little white wine and about 30 per cent fortified wine.

Much of the production was exported to the United Kingdom. In 1919 Ireland sold St Leonards to a syndicate of local vignerons and businessmen, Seppelt, Chambers, Masterton, Dobbin, Gehrig and Herman. From this point on much of the wine went to Melbourne merchants.

Between 1924 and 1928 St Leonards processed all of the Seppelt grapes, and made Seppelt's wine for that company, while it rebuilt its Clydeside Cellars. The Depression and the Second World War years saw production fall dramatically. In 1959 St Leonards was sold, and virtually all the vineyards were removed. The few remaining hectares produced grapes purchased by Italian tobacco growers at nearby Myrtleford.

In 1973 the artist John Darbyshire purchased the property and began to re-establish the vineyards. In 1978 Brown Brothers was asked to make the wine on a contract basis for St Leonards. Only two years later members of the Brown family formed the nucleus of a syndicate which purchased the property from Darbyshire and the St Leonards of today was born.

The vineyard is now planted to over 40 hectares of grapes, the most recent plantings being 1.5 hectares of merlot which is still to come into bearing. The principal varieties planted are chenin blanc, chardonnay, gewurztraminer, shiraz, cabernet sauvignon, semillon and sauvignon blanc. There are small plantings of orange muscat and trebbiano, and a very few fetayaska vines. St Leonards is managed by Rick Burge, one of whose major tasks is the marketing of St Leonards' wines. Although they are made by John Brown junior at Brown Brothers, the marketing is entirely separate (and, I might add, the wines are also kept entirely separate).

Right from the outset the quality of the St Leonards varietal whites (in particular), and to a lesser degree its reds, has been absolutely outstanding. The wines seem to have an extra dimension of flavour, structure and varietal character beyond any other wines produced in the north-east. They certainly complicate my idyllic picture of the north-east as being a fortified-wine area; one could hardly wish to improve on the white wines of St Leonards. The two varieties that have consistently stood out are the chardonnay and the semillon. Certainly the chardonnay is of the fuller style, but at the end of 1984 the 1980 had not fallen apart, as so many five-year-old Australian chardonnays tend to do. Some of the fresh-fruit flavours had diminished, but the wine still retained a tight, albeit full, structure. The St Leonards semillons, although varietally distinct and quite different in terms of flavour, show structural similarities. These are generous, round and full-flavoured wines, not infrequently filled out further with clever use of new oak.

Even the gewurztraminer, a variety I am not especially fond of, has distinguished itself. In the November 1983 *National Times* White Wine Survey I had this to say of it: "Shows all of the virtues and none of the vices of gewurztraminer; very well balanced, no hardness, clean, soft and full-flavoured with clearly manifested but not aggressive varietal character. A wine I would be happy to drink any time." By my book that is high praise indeed. I am not too sure that I would not be even happier to drink the orange muscat at any time, or at least any time I wanted a wine with an extra degree of aroma and fruit flavour without residual sugar. This little-known variety (no relation whatsoever to the grape which makes the great fortified wines of north-eastern Victoria) makes some very interesting table wine.

Not surprisingly, St Leonards has had outstanding success with some of its late-harvest styles. The 1982 Spatlese Gewurztraminer won major show awards for its rich, slightly sweet flavours. The 1980 Late-Harvest Semillon also received two gold, two silver and two bronze medals in its relatively short show career. But the one late-harvest wine of quite exceptional quality, equal to anything produced in Australia in the past five years, is the 1981 Late-Harvest Chenin Blanc. Early in its show career it won gold medals at Melbourne and Perth in the year of its vintage. Part of it was sold thereafter, restricting its entry to the smaller shows with lesser volume requirements. In 1983 at Lilydale, and in 1984 at the Victorian Wines Show, it took out multiple trophies for the best white wine in its class, for the best white wine of show, and for the best table wine of show. It has developed into a magnificently complex wine, showing true varietal flavour enhanced by the botrytis which occurred in that vintage. There is all of the honeyed, slightly malty flavour of chenin blanc, coupled with excellent balancing acid which will see the wine through the next few years, although it is hard to see it improving. While the red wines appear less exciting, it is only because of the excellence of the whites. Thus the 1982 Shiraz and 1982 Cabernet Sauvignon on release at the end of 1984 were both gold-medal-winners. The Shiraz had won two gold medals at Rutherglen (in 1982 and 1984, on each occasion topping its class) while the Cabernet Sauvignon had won a gold medal at Melbourne in 1984.

The beautifully packaged and labelled St Leonards wines are among my personal favourites. Any wine lover not on the mailing list should think again.

STANTON AND KILLEEN
MURRAY VALLEY HIGHWAY, RUTHERGLEN

The Stantons have always been a remarkably long-lived family; there was nothing unusual in 86-year-old Jack Stanton spending each day in the winery in the early 1980s, resulting in three generations being actively involved at the one time. Timothy Stanton and his son, John Lewis Stanton, had arrived in Australia from East Anglia, England, in the 1850s to search for gold, but turned instead to farming. They settled first at the picturesquely named Black Dog Creek near Rutherglen before moving in 1875 to the property they called Park View, where they established a vineyard. Timothy and John Stanton carried on the winery until the death of Timothy in 1895; when phylloxera struck, Timothy's grandson John Richard Stanton replanted the vineyard, but it was sold to the Campbells in the 1940s.

Meanwhile, in 1925, fourth-generation winemaker John Charles Stanton had established the Gracerray Winery on the site of a vineyard that had disappeared at the time of phylloxera. A winery had been in existence, and the new Gracerray Winery was built on the same site. It has been in continuous production ever since, and is still the Stanton and Killeen winery. During the 1930s the vineyards exceeded 40 hectares, but by the 1950s they were back to 12 hectares.

New plantings commenced at the Moodemere Vineyard in 1968, while in 1977 a new vineyard a kilometre away was commenced. The Quandong Vineyard, named after the first Stanton winery, is established on the prized red loam soil which is dotted throughout the district. Planted to brown muscat, muscadelle and durif, it is already producing the finest fruit to come into the Stanton and Killeen winery each year. The vineyards now comprise 34 hectares in total with 16 hectares of muscat, eight hectares of shiraz, four hectares of muscadelle, three hectares of cabernet sauvignon, two hectares of durif and one hectare of touriga.

The partnership became known as Stanton and Killeen in 1953 when Norman Killeen, who had married Joan Stanton in 1948, left the Department of Agriculture to join Jack Stanton at the winery. Norman Killeen has a Bachelor of Agricultural Science degree, and was for a number of years manager of the Rutherglen Viticultural Research Station. Nonetheless, from 1953 until the late 1960s Norman Killeen was chiefly concerned with the agricultural activities carried out on the 360-hectare farming property, and it was not until shortly before 1970 that he took over winemaking responsibilities from his father-in-law Jack Stanton.

In 1979 a new fully insulated building was added to the old winery, permitting longer-term storage of both bulk and bottled table wines under controlled temperature conditions. This was followed by a progressive upgrading of the winery itself, the installation of stainless-steel fermentation tanks, cooling, filters and the like. Christopher Killeen, who took over winemaking responsibilities in 1980, has been responsible for most of the more recent developments.

Stanton and Killeen carries a token range of white table wine made elsewhere to satisfy cellar-door sales, together with the usual bits and pieces of marsala, vermouth and the like. Its own production is centred exclusively on red table wine and on fortifieds. It is hard to say at which it succeeds best.

The Stanton and Killeen Moodemere reds, while showing all of the robust characters one comes to expect from the district, have an edge of elegance and finesse which is really quite unexpected. The 1980 Shiraz and the 1982 Shiraz were both marvellously full-bodied, fleshy, rich, red wines with happily restrained tannin. The 1980 Cabernet Sauvignon was another huge wine—rich, ripe and round, with firm tannin and yet avoiding clumsiness. It was released after the 1981, which was a far more pedestrian wine.

The Stanton and Killeen muscats have a far fresher, fruitier style than those of the big names. Stanton and Killeen frequently release single-vintage muscats at three or four years of age, arguing that at this point the wines have maximum fragrance, freshness and fruit characteristics. Some older blended vintage wines are available, again usually stipulating the vintages involved, and these represent a halfway house between the immense wines of Bailey, Morris and Chambers on the one hand, and the fresh delicacy of the young vintage wines of Stanton and Killeen on the other.

One has the strong feeling that Stanton and Killeen is here to stay.

KNOCKING-OFF TIME, VICTORIA, 1900

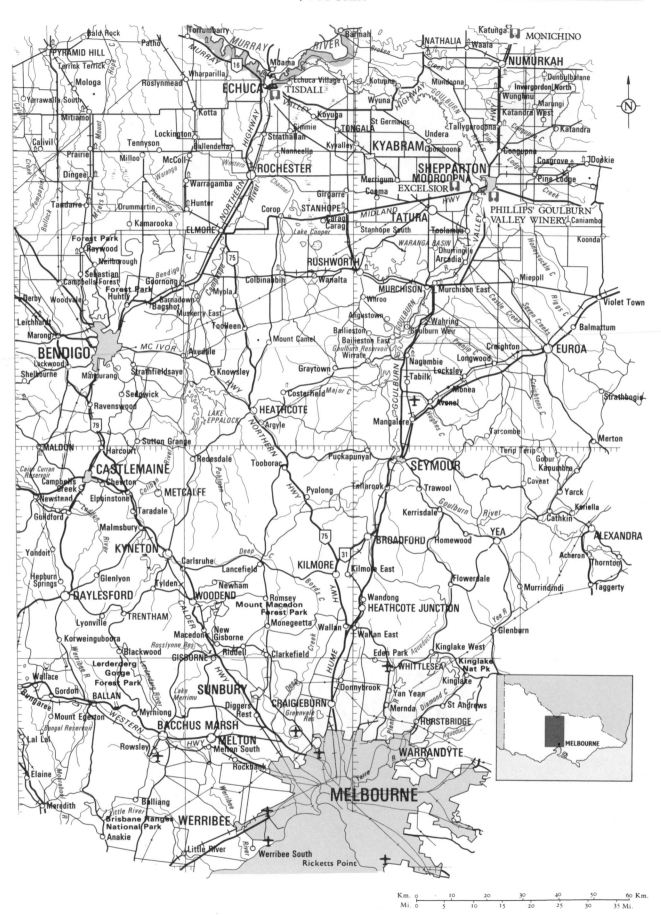

North Goulburn River

The vineyards and wineries at the northern end of the Goulburn River Valley are frequently regarded as being part of the Goulburn Valley proper, or, as I have called it in this book, the central Goulburn Valley area. In fact, they have little or nothing in common with the vineyards further south. Those of the north are established in a significantly warmer climate, and depend for their existence on extensive irrigation. In other words, they have far more in common with the wineries of the Murray River, and could equally well have been included in that chapter.

Tisdall is by far the most important winery in the region, demonstrating just what can be achieved with careful selection of grape types and high-technology winemaking. The area will never produce great wine, but can and does provide above-average wines at affordable prices.

EXCELSIOR
EXCELSIOR AVENUE, MOOROOPNA

Excelsior is now but a shadow of its former self. It was established at Mooroopna (near Shepparton) in 1868 by Trojan Darveniza, who jumped ship in Melbourne to become a gold prospector. With this unlikely start the vineyard went on to fame in the second half of the nineteenth century; the family still has the letter from the Governor of Victoria written in 1890 congratulating Trojan Darveniza on the 300 awards he had won in overseas competitions.

Only a few remnants remain of past glory. A few hectares of irrigated shiraz on the river flats, an ancient and run-down winery, and wine sold in bulk to the local Italian community.

MONICHINO
BERRY'S ROAD, KATUNGA

Carlo Monichino and his family established their Katunga Vineyard, north of Shepparton, in 1962. The site was chosen with Department of Agriculture advice, as were the varieties planted. A successful trial vintage in 1965 encouraged the family to expand the plantings and to erect a winery. This, and much of the winery equipment, were built by Carlo Monichino, his son Phillip, Lloyd Thomas and Keith Mellar, a retired engineer.

The winery was completed in 1972 and since that time the Monichinos have demonstrated unusual flair. Thus in 1975 they introduced a stainless-steel field-crushing unit, which they designed and built themselves, and which has the aim of protecting the grapes from oxidation by immediately crushing them and placing the must under a carbon dioxide blanket. As a further measure of protection, all of the picking is done by hand and ceases before midday. The 12-hectare vineyard is planted to cabernet sauvignon, malbec, rubired, troia, gewurtztraminer, chardonnay, rhine riesling, semillon, sauvignon blanc, chenin blanc and frontignac.

The white wines almost invariably reflect the extreme care taken with the grapes prior to fermentation, and the low temperatures (below 10°C) at which they are fermented. This is hot-climate fruit, heavily irrigated, and miracles cannot be expected. But the Monichinos are very careful not to lose what nature gives them, and wines such as their 1984 Basalt Estate Chardonnay amply reward them for the trouble they take. Some of the reds, too, show unusual depth and intensity of flavour for Riverland material. The 1982 Cabernet Sauvignon is a very acceptable wine, with some attractive leathery, astringent cabernet flavours.

PHILLIPS' GOULBURN VALLEY WINERY
48 VAUGHAN STREET, SHEPPARTON

The Goulburn Valley Winery was established in 1908 in what is now the commercial area of Shepparton. It ceased production in 1966 but continued to purchase wine made elsewhere, which it then released under the Goulburn Valley label.

The business was purchased by Don Phillips in 1978, who leased out most of the building but retained the winemaking and sales areas. With the help of Peter Hayes, lecturer at Dookie Agricultural College and enthusiastic judge of amateur wines, winemaking was recommenced in 1978 using material bought in from growers in the Shepparton area. Other vineyard sources have since opened up, but the winery has had a troubled history over the past few years.

TISDALL
CORNELIA CREEK ROAD, ECHUCA

The link between vine and scalpel has been such that it prompted a book by Max Lake devoted entirely to the subject and written before the events of the last 20 years. If Dr Lake were to rewrite that book, I venture to say its size would be doubled or even trebled. Medical practitioners have found the lure of the vine as irresistible as ever, and in areas such as the Margaret River have flocked in droves to establish a near-monopoly of winemaking in the region. But there is no true comparison between Dr Peter Tisdall and his contemporaries; one must go back to Dr Henry Lindeman and Dr Christopher Penfold to find kindred souls. On the other hand, the pace and flair of the Tisdall development is very much that of the twentieth rather than the nineteenth century.

In 1972 Peter Tisdall and his wife Diana decided they would become involved in viticulture, and established 80 hectares of vineyard at Rosbercon in the riverlands near Echuca. These vineyards were designed to produce large quantities of grapes at economical prices to support a mid-price range of bottled table wine and bulk-wine sales. Once established, Peter Tisdall turned his mind to a second vineyard site to produce the highest-quality grapes for the top end of the market.

After a search which started in the dry confines of government departments evaluating climatic and geological data, and which then moved out into the high country of central and southern Victoria, the property which came to be known as Tisdall Mount Helen was selected in the Strathbogie Ranges at a height of 450 metres. The development undertaken here was on an equally grand scale: a massive dam was constructed at the bottom end of the hilltop property to provide water for the supplementary irrigation system, essential given the low 600-millimetre rainfall. Plantings, too, were on a scale uncommon in central and southern Victoria.

At both vineyards great care was taken to select varieties suitable to the climate and site. The ongoing viticultural management of both properties has likewise been directed to maximising the potential fruit character in the grapes, and the winemaking techniques designed to protect that character.

The Rosbercon Vineyard is established on a mixture of hard, cracking clay requiring extensive use of mulching techniques, with patches of lighter-yielding sandy soil; irrigation is, of course, essential. The varietal mix has changed somewhat since the original vineyard was established, not so much because unsuitable varieties were chosen, but rather to reflect the continued surge in white-wine consumption. It now comprises cabernet sauvignon (15 hectares), malbec (nine hectares), merlot (eight hectares), shiraz (seven hectares), ruby cabernet (four hectares), chenin blanc (eight hectares), semillon (six hectares), colombard (six hectares), sauvignon blanc (five hectares), chardonnay and trebbiano (four hectares each), rhine riesling (three hectares) and emerald riesling (two hectares).

Mount Helen is planted to cabernet sauvignon and pinot noir (eight hectares each), merlot (three hectares), chardonnay (13 hectares), rhine riesling (six hectares), sauvignon blanc (five hectares), and traminer (four hectares). Here the soils are granitic podsols of relatively low fertility, with some clay interspersed in the subsoils.

In 1978 Tisdall decided the time had come to establish his own winery in the cheese factory he had hitherto operated at Picola. Prior to this time the grapes from Rosbercon had been sold to other winemakers, notably Brown Brothers. At that time John Ellis was riding the crest of a wave at Rosemount Estate in the Hunter Valley, having taken it from obscurity to national prominence within a few years. When it was announced he was joining an obscure operation in Victoria's north there was general disbelief. Within two vintages Tisdall was crushing 1200 tonnes of grapes a year, selling 25,000 cases of mid- to top-quality wines at commensurate prices through an Australia-wide network of distributors; and making an additional 600,000 litres of bulk wine for sale to other winemakers. Tisdall had demonstrated that Australia is no less the land of opportunity in the 1970s than it was in the 1870s.

Since that time the business has gone from strength to strength. Bottled-wine production has increased to 60,000 cases (20,000 cases from Mount Helen and 40,000 cases from Rosbercon), while the less profitable bulk market has decreased to 340,000 litres. But—particularly for a book such as this—it is not so much the quantity of the wine as its quality which matters. Quality has been little short of astonishingly good: astonishing not only for the inherent quality of the wines, given their price, but also their consistency. The wines from Rosbercon are labelled simply Tisdall, and are usually distinguished only by the variety used. Those from Mount Helen bear that name prominently. The original Tisdall label was an unashamed copy of Chateau Lynch Bages in the Médoc in France, radically different from the feel of the innovative and pleasing Mount Helen label. The latter remains the same, but Tisdall has been unable to resist changing the Rosbercon labels, for reasons which escape me. The white wines released under the Tisdall Rosbercon labels comprise a chenin blanc, a colombard, a traminer riesling, a white burgundy and a chardonnay riesling. The last-named wine perpetuates a 1979 winemaker's nightmare, when inexperienced night staff failed to realise an incoming load was half chardonnay and half rhine riesling. The grapes were crushed together and the only chardonnay riesling ever made on a commercial basis reached the market. It created a demand which continues to this day, so the wine follows suit.

Indeed, such is the winemaking skill and finesse of the Tisdall team that any wine released under the Tisdall label is going to appeal for its fruit freshness and flavour, and that is the first rule of successful white-winemaking.

Over the years the chenin blanc has been produced in a wooded form, a moselle style, and various other permutations and combinations, but finally Tisdall has settled on an unwooded wine with just a little residual sugar giving rise to sweetness which can be felt rather than tasted. The lovely 1984 wine showed just what can be achieved with this formula, with an almost smoky overtone to the aroma, followed by beautifully fresh and lively fruit on the palate, a hint of spice, and a lingering finish. With a retail price of around $5.50, it typifies the exceptional value that these wines offer.

Likewise, the 1984 Colombard, from a grape which I think has failed by and large to live up to the expectations held of it, showed rich gooseberry/

melon flavours, complex and satisfying. The traminer riesling, which each year is composed of traminer grown at Mount Helen and rhine riesling grown at Rosbercon, is an equally appealing wine, which in the skilled hands of Tisdall results in the synergy which the blend gives on paper but not always in practice. Perhaps part of the quality of the blend comes from the counterbalance between the fairly acid traminer from Mount Helen and the softer, fuller rhine riesling from Rosbercon.

But, year in, year out, it is the cabernet merlot of Tisdall Rosbercon which is my pick of this range. Since 1980 it has been in the top half-dozen of the value-for-money, fresh, early-drinking red wines to be released onto the Australian market. I have lost track of how many times I have selected it at the very top in large comparative tastings, and more than once placed it in front of the excellent Mount Helen cabernet merlot; it has won the Victorian Economic Development Corporation Export Award; been selected for service on Qantas; and received consistent praise from wine critics across the country. The fruit flavours are invariably clean and lively; the wine soft but full on the middle palate, followed by a gently acid finish virtually devoid of tannin. The wines are deliberately made to be at their best within one or two years of vintage, and should be drunk—and enjoyed—accordingly.

Obviously enough, overall pride of place goes to the Mount Helen range. The wines regularly released under this label comprise a cabernet sauvignon, a cabernet merlot, a pinot noir, a chardonnay, a rhine riesling and—more recently—a fumé blanc. These are not boutique wines made in 500-case lots, but wines which are nationally distributed. The first wines released from Mount Helen were made in 1979. Of these the two rhine rieslings, dry and late-picked, and the cabernet sauvignon were the most successful. The 1979 Cabernet Sauvignon won the Stodart Trophy for best one-year-old red at the Brisbane show as well as gold medals in Adelaide, Brisbane and Hobart. It was a wine of medium body which was always destined to rely on elegance rather than power, and is now at its peak.

1980 was as cool at Mount Helen as it was in most regions throughout Australia; the late-harvest rhine riesling was not picked until 18 May, but the dry version lacked the fruit of the 1979 and faded fairly quickly. This vintage saw the first Mount Helen cabernet merlot blend made (90 per cent cabernet sauvignon, 10 per cent merlot) and, like the straight cabernet sauvignon of that year, it was an outstanding wine: full, sweet berry fruit flavours married with the new oak which has always formed part of the Mount Helen cabernet-based reds. The 1980 Mount Helen Cabernet Merlot topped Class 22 at the 1981 Canberra National Wine Show, a class which chief judge Len Evans described as "one of the strongest classes of young red wines we have seen for 20 years". The 1981 reds were big wines, reflecting the year. The fruit was surprisingly soft, although there was more than usual tannin evident on the finish, and the 1981 will be one of the longest-lived Mount Helen cabernets so far made—reaching its peak between 1988 and 1990.

The 1980 Pinot Noir was by far the most successful of the pinots made between 1979 and 1983, but highlighted the problems that John Ellis had in dealing with the variety (he has now been succeeded by Jeff Clarke as winemaker). The wine had very good colour, generous flavour but really very little varietal character. The 1982 Pinot Noir had varietal character, but had neither the body nor the colour. John Ellis tried everything he knew during his time at Tisdall to make a great pinot noir. In 1982 one of the batches was made using a full carbonic maceration process, leaving the whole bunches in the tank for 25 days before they were pressed. Initially hopes ran high, but after a while in bottle it became apparent that any real varietal character still had eluded him.

Those early years also proved frustrating for the Mount Helen fumé blanc; while the wood handling was impeccable, the fruit character was less than perfect. Here, however, the winemaker has triumphed. The 1983 Fumé Blanc was a first-class wine, showing a complex blend of fruit with overtones of grapefruit, and a richly textured, complex palate in which the slight grassiness of the sauvignon blanc married to perfection with the oak. Good though that wine was, it paled into insignificance beside the 1984 Fumé Blanc, in which the varietal character was little short of explosive and the wood handling enormously sensitive. It is a quite startlingly good wine.

The 1981 Rhine Riesling saw John Ellis settle on a compromise between the dry and late-harvest styles he had experimented with in earlier years, and each subsequent release has shown a fair degree of fruit lusciousness and a little sugar on the palate.

1982, 1983 and 1984 ran the climatic changes at Mount Helen in no uncertain fashion. 1982 was mild, 1983 very hot and very dry late in the season after a cool start, while 1984 was exceptionally cool throughout. In the midst of all of this the Mount Helen chardonnay has continued to show the consistent high quality in evidence since the earliest vintages. The 1980 Chardonnay was a lovely wine with excellent acid and considerable intensity of flavour, characters which are still with the wine and making it exceptionally long-lived. The 1981 and 1982 wines were fuller and softer and are now at or about their peak. The 1981 vintage, a multiple gold medal- and trophy-winner (including the "Dinner at Eight Club" Trophy for best one-year-old white at the Brisbane show), demonstrates the rich fruit characters to be gained from fully ripe chardonnay. But John Ellis was not satisfied with his achievements, and with the 1983 vintage he used a variety of techniques borrowed unashamedly from the French to produce a quite lovely wine. The bouquet is ripe and fleshy, with rich, buttery, fruit aromas, the palate well constructed, again with some buttery characters coming from the oak and fermentation techniques used, and yet showing great depth of fruit flavour.

1984, not surprisingly, produced an excellent Mount Helen rhine riesling, fleshed out with just a little residual sugar, and with abundant fruit. The 1984 Chardonnay, a gold-medallion-winner at the Victorian Wines Show (amassing 56.5 points out of 60) showed superb charred-oak characters, some obvious barrel-ferment characters, and all of the citric/grapefruit chardonnay aroma and flavour one would expect from the very cold year. It will unquestionably develop into an outstanding wine.

As I have said, John Ellis has left Tisdall after a six-year term in which he has permanently established the reputation of Tisdall. Jeff Clarke, who worked with John Ellis for the 1983 and 1984 vintages, has a rich inheritance.

WINE WAGON LEAVING CELLARS, VICTORIA, 1900

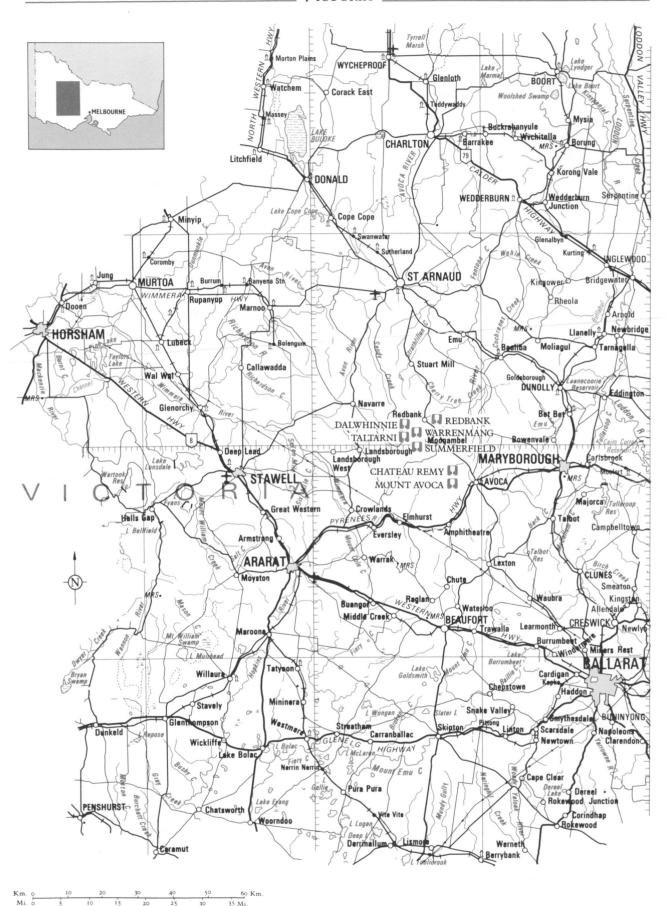

MELBOURNE

Km. 0   10   20   30   40   50   60 Km.
Mi. 0   5   10   15   20   25   30   35 Mi.

Pyrenees

The inhabitants of the mountain range marking the border between France and Spain would be more than slightly puzzled if they were to visit the vineyards centred around the towns of Redbank, Moonambel and Avoca. The gentle slopes upon which vines grow ultimately yield to a series of hills, rather than mountains, which would be utterly lost in the savage grandeur of the Pyrenees proper. Nonetheless, it is the name of the nearby "mountain" range, and is the name which the vignerons of the region have selected to group themselves under. It has never been particularly well known as a wine area, although Taltarni and Chateau Remy seem determined to alter that state of affairs in the very near future, if they have not already done so. Very little is recorded of early viticulture in the region: it was given only the briefest of mentions by de Castella (*Early Victorian Wine Growing*), and was at no time a significant producer in terms of volume.

The first vines were planted by a Mr Mackereth in 1848; as the number of his children grew, so did the size of his vineyard and winery. The winery passed to his sons, Edwin, John, Charles and Alfred; Alfred, at the age of 91, wrote to Dr W. S. Benwell in 1962, recalling the history of the vineyard, which met with great success in its heyday. An important red grape was "pinneau", which was used to make both red table wine and port. Whether this was pinot noir or pinot meunière is not certain: both were available and fairly widely propagated at Geelong, which would have been one possible source (the other being the commercial nurseries, such as Cole's, in the Melbourne metropolitan area).

The winery won numerous prizes: the certificates were sufficiently numerous "to paper a good-sized room", wrote Alfred Mackereth. Much of the wine was exported: "Local people used to drink it too, but few Australians were wine drinkers." The operation was sufficiently profitable for Edwin to leave the

Victorian police force and join his brother Charles in the day-to-day management of the vineyard. Following the death of Charles in 1908, at the age of 28, John — a music and drawing teacher — reluctantly assumed the role of vigneron. With considerable acumen, Alfred remained a bank manager, looking at the winery with increasingly jaundiced eyes as the market for its output progressively slipped away.

Towards the end of the First World War Edwin began negotiations to sell the winery and vineyards to Seppelt. At the time it was still a substantial operation, with a storage capacity in excess of 90,000 litres and supporting three wine shops in Avoca. The sale fell through at the last moment. Apparently Edwin wished to retain some of the winemaking equipment; Seppelt, suspicious that he might set up in competition, insisted on all or nothing.

Seppelt bought Hans Irvine's winery at Great Western instead, and Avoca's grip on oenological life slipped away. In a little-known postscript Seppelt eyed the district with some care and interest in the 1960s, but was unable to secure options over sufficiently large parcels to make the venture commercially viable, so it withdrew once again. Eventually Mackereth sold the property in 1929 to a Methodist minister named Dawson, who promptly closed the winery, smashed the cellars and pulled out the last 20 hectares of vines.

At Moonambel, north-east of Avoca, a Mr Adams established the first vineyards; these subsequently passed to J. Kofoed and became known as Kofoed's Mountain Creek. In 1941 de Castella wrote that the winery "still flourishes", but it went out of production in 1945. Dr Benwell wrote in *Journey to Wine in Victoria*: "There are still a few bottles of the old Avoca wine — like the Kofoed's dry White Muscat — in private cellars, bottled in heavy dark-green Champagne bottles, and still sound too."

Vignerons returned to the district in 1963 when

John Robb came down from the Hunter Valley (with his young son Neil in tow) to plant the extensive vineyards of Chateau Remy, a joint venture between Melbourne wine merchants Nathan and Wyeth and Remy. For a number of years Chateau Remy remained in splendid isolation, but the boom years between 1970 and 1974 saw first Mount Avoca and Summerfield, then Taltarni, Redbank and Warrenmang all come into the region.

It is an area which seems capable of producing almost any wine style one cares to think of: Chateau Remy was established with the aim of making high-class Australian brandy, and the grape varieties were selected accordingly, somewhat unfortunate given the change of direction to sparkling-wine manufacture halfway down the track (and the abandonment of distillation). Most of the other wineries started off with red wine as their sole or dominant objective, but in the wake of the upheaval in the wine market most are producing at least some white wine. Taltarni, in particular, has been very successful in this, most recently with sauvignon blanc.

Notwithstanding the single-minded determination of Chateau Remy, and the outstanding marketplace success of Taltarni's sparkling wines, I still feel the long-term potential of the region lies with its red wines. It certainly is on the cool side of warm (one source gives it a centigrade heat-degree summation of 1416, but I am not convinced it is at its best providing base wines for *méthode champenoise* sparkling wines. Overall the climate is temperate, and extremes are uncommon—a heavy snowfall in 1982 was the first in living memory—while spring frosts are rare, striking in 1980 but not since then.

The red wines, with the cabernet family and shiraz to the fore, have intense flavours with varying levels of tannin and extract according to the maker. Those of Taltarni are at one end of the spectrum; Summerfield and Redbank at the other end. That pervasive mid-Victorian eucalypt/ mint character comes through in the majority of the wines: only those of Taltarni seem to be able to avoid it. It is a character to which I was initially most attracted, but now feel it is best kept to a background level at most. In small doses it can be very attractive, and adds complexity. If allowed to run riot it threatens to turn wine into a toothpaste-flavoured mouthwash.

The vineyards of the region are established in a narrow rainfall belt, about 18 kilometres wide, which gives an annual rainfall of between 600 millimetres at Chateau Remy and 525 millimetres at Redbank. The rainfall pattern is near to ideal: it falls mainly in winter and spring, with "follow-up" rainfall during the remainder of the growing season at the rate of between 25 and 40 millimetres per month. Some of the vineyards have supplementary drip-irrigation, much needed in the drier years to keep yields at a viable level. Chateau Remy obtains part of its water requirements from a lake inadvertently formed during the goldmining days. An alluvial dredge bit into an underground stream, which promptly flooded the work area causing the "floating dredge" to sink, bringing mining operations to an unscheduled and permanent halt.

The gravelly-sandy topsoil, heavily interspersed with quartz and shale, is typical gold-country stock, supporting trees that are more frequently straggly than grand. The clay subsoil varies in colour from red at the subregion of Redbank, to yellow at Avoca and orange at the subregion of Moonambel. The clay holds the spring rainfall moisture well, but yields can still be pitifully low. Redbank, for example, produces less than one tonne to the acre on average (2.5 tonnes per hectare); even Taltarni averages little more than five tonnes per hectare. The ability of such areas to compete successfully in today's environment depends heavily on the marketing skills of the vignerons: it is one thing to make excellent wine, and another to sell it at a price which will provide an adequate return.

CHATEAU REMY
VINOCA ROAD, AVOCA

Chateau Remy must inevitably be suffering from an acute attack of schizophrenia, and it is hardly surprising that we are yet to see the best from it. Its origins go back to the founding of Nathan and Wyeth Proprietary Limited in Melbourne in 1913. For many years that company handled the distribution of the Remy Martin products imported from Cognac in France. When the Second World War broke out Nathan and Wyeth was unable to obtain further supplies. Showing great enterprise, it substituted locally made brandy, although history does not relate just how much it chose to reveal on the label. Remy Martin knew nothing of this initiative until after the war, when a large and totally unexpected cheque arrived by way of royalties.

Remy Martin was both grateful and impressed, and it led to a closer association between the two companies, culminating in a decision in 1960 that the two companies should join together to locate a suitable site for the establishment of vineyards to produce a truly high-quality Australian brandy.

Research ended two years later with the selection of a 365-hectare property near Avoca. In recognition of the intention to distil the production, the vineyards were planted chiefly to doradillo and trebbiano. Needless to say, the vineyards took some time to come into production, and the winemaking facilities required for making a base wine for brandy were not especially complex. So when in the 1970s the decision was taken to divert from brandy-making to champagne, it was necessary virtually to start all over again. Trebbiano makes an adequate base wine for champagne, but doradillo does not. It was removed accordingly and the overall vineyard area substantially expanded by, among other things, chardonnay. (For a time Chateau Remy flirted with red-winemaking in conjunction with brandy-making, and there are some shiraz and cabernet vines.)

Remy had assumed entire control of Chateau Remy in 1969 when its Australian holding company, Vignerons Distillers & Vintners Limited, acquired the issued capital of each of Buring and Sobels (Quelltaler), Nathan and Wyeth and Mac's Cider. So when the decision came to concentrate on the production of sparkling wine, all of the necessary capital was immediately available. A new champagne cellar was opened in 1981, and a few years later French-born and trained Christian Morlaes arrived to take over the champagne production.

The top wine—Cuvée Speciale Brut—is made strictly according to the *méthode champenoise* system (including hand-disgorgement), and is aged on yeast lees for three years. The base wine is a blend of trebbiano and chardonnay; it seems to me that the release is, up to and including 1984, largely trebbiano-based—certainly the contribution of chardonnay was not particularly obvious. One imagines that as the blend evolves with the increasing amount of chardonnay available, so the base fruit-flavour will improve.

The Cuvée Speciale available towards the end of 1984 was a solid if unexciting wine: the bouquet has some toasty aromas, and the palate was full and showing some bottled-developed characters. But the wine lacked the life and crisp lift that one expects in the very best sparkling wines.

DALWHINNIE
22 ERRAND STREET, NORTH BALLARAT

Dalwhinnie Vineyard is established on a 130-hectare property purchased by Ballarat architect Ewan Jones in 1974. Adjacent to Taltarni, it is situated at the head of a valley surrounded by mountains. The soil conditions vary from light-grey to rich-red loams with a clay base and a quartz gravelly mix. Drip-irrigation is installed, and the yields of around nine tonnes per hectare are very good. The vineyard is managed on a modified organic viticulture basis—there is strictly limited use of chemical sprays, and cover crops between the vines are ploughed back each year. It is also noteworthy as being the highest vineyard in the Pyrenees area (610 metres above sea-level) yet is virtually frost-free.

Plantings presently comprise 2.6 hectares of chardonnay, 2.5 hectares of merlot, 1.5 hectares of chardonnay and 0.5 hectare of merlot. The merlot and chardonnay are recent additions and are yet to come into full bearing; the cabernet, too, was marginally increased in 1983.

The first wines were made in 1980. Right from the outset Ewan Jones determined that he would have the wines made for him, rather than battle with the time and cost of erecting his own winery and hoping that somehow—by divine inspiration or other-wise—he might learn how to make red wine. Marketing of those first wines did not commence until September 1983, and is still restricted to private distribution and mailing-list sales. Production has risen from 2000 cases in 1980–81 to 3400 cases in 1984. The labels are an exercise in classic simplicity and overall the presentation and packaging is excellent. An attraction for some buyers is the ready availability of the wine in half-bottles. Perhaps as a consequence of the (financially) realistic approach adopted by Jones, all of the Dalwhinnie wines so far released have been well over two years of age at release time.

The 1980 Cabernet Sauvignon exhibited beautiful cedar/cigar fragrances intermingled with the fruit, with similar fragrant fruit and oak flavours on the palate. The shiraz of that year showed fairly pro-nounced central Victorian mint character, with very rich fruit. The '81s were not in the same class and were hard, tannic and with a trace of mercaptan evident in the cabernet sauvignon. In the long run they may well come together, but I simply did not like the style.

1982 saw a reversion to the style of 1980, but the wines were even better. The 1982 Hermitage is a most interesting wine. Both its colour—a vibrant youthful crimson-purple as at January 1985—and its smooth, crisp cherry-flavoured palate strongly suggest that the wine did not undergo a malolactic fermentation. There is a touch of astringency on the bouquet, which serves only to confirm this impression. Whatever be the answer, it is a very fresh, spotlessly clean wine which looks to have years and years in front of it. If the wine is to be criticised, it might be said it lacks the complexity which the 1982 Cabernet Sauvignon shows. The flavour and the style of the two wines are surprisingly close, but the cabernet has a little bit extra in its structure and complexity. There is also just a trace of regional mint character on the palate which does not intrude and simply adds to the attractiveness of the wine. Both are red wines of very high quality.

To date the wines have been made by Gary Farr at Yellowglen winery, but one imagines that different arrangements will need to be made in the future. Perhaps not; whatever occurs, Dalwhinnie has already shown it can produce the basic ingredients for first-class wine—first-class grapes.

MOUNT AVOCA
MOATES LANE, AVOCA

Wine has always been part of Melbourne stock-broker John Barry's life. He was introduced to it by his father, the distinguished Victorian judge and historian, Sir John Barry; and the books of Dr Sam Benwell and Walter James nurtured the idea that one day he might make his own wine. By the mid-1960s the idea had firmly taken hold, and together with his wife Arda he commenced the long search for a suitable vineyard site. Possibilities looked at and discarded included Whittlesea, just north of Melbourne, and once home to the famous Dawson Vineyard; McLaren Vale; and the Warby Ranges near Rutherglen. There the manager of the Rutherglen Viticultural Research Station suggested the Barrys take a look at the Avoca area.

The Barrys did this, and liked what they saw; climatic data backed up their judgement, and eventually a site was found and purchased in 1970. The original plantings comprised 10 hectares of shiraz, four hectares of cabernet sauvignon and one hectare each of trebbiano and semillon. More recently two hectares of chardonnay and two hectares of sauvignon blanc have been established, but are yet to come into full bearing. Drip-irrigation supplements the low rainfall of 525 millimetres, and average yields are very modest at around 6.25 tonnes per hectare.

A simple but functional winery was designed by architect Arda Barry, and built in time for the 1978 crush. John Barry had previously enrolled as a correspondence student in the oenology and viticulture course at Riverina College, where he met Guy Stanford (son of the distinguished Australian wine-maker and consultant John Stanford) who was also a student. This led to Guy joining John Barry as winemaker at the end of 1980; given the size of the Mount Avoca enterprise, I am not the least bit surprised that John Barry felt he needed some assistance. In 1984 Guy Stanford was replaced by Rodney Morrish, although as ever the winemaking is something of a joint effort with John Barry making a major contribution.

In the meantime John Barry had made some very attractive red wines. The early vintages had strong regional mint overtones; the '78 Cabernet Sauvignon won a number of medals before being bottled, when it suffered somewhat at the hands of the Melbourne-based contract-bottler. Since 1980 there has been a deliberate effort to tame the minty flavour and aroma, no doubt partly by earlier picking.

White-wine production will assume increasing importance in the years to come. New refrigeration facilities were installed in time for the 1984 vintage, and the two 1984 whites show the results of careful winemaking. (Morrish worked as a winemaker at Seppelt and is no stranger to modern white-wine technology.) As befits the relative standing of the two varieties, the '84 Semillon was far preferable to the '84 Trebbiano, with very well-handled spicy/lemony oak aroma and flavour adding complexity to the wine.

Cash flow not being of the essence, John Barry has been able to keep back his red wines for bottle maturation before release, and at the end of 1984 was still selling 1981 Cabernet Sauvignon and 1981 Hermitage. The 1979, 1980 and 1981 wines were virtually all of above-average quality. The only qualified exception was the 1981 Hermitage, which was rather simple and a little dull. Particularly with the '81 Cabernet Sauvignon, the strong minty characters evident in earlier vintages were muted, and pleasant leafy astringency was substituted.

REDBANK
SUNRAYSIA HIGHWAY, REDBANK

Neil and Sally Robb are now veterans, yet it seems only yesterday that I tasted wines from their first vintage made in 1976. I guess that part of my vivid memory stems from the fact that I had little or no previous experience with the mid-Victorian mint character which, to a lesser or greater degree, runs through all of the Redbank wines. That there is this continuity puts the regional source of the character beyond any shadow of doubt. Neil Robb has taken grapes from an amazing number of small vineyards dotted around the Pyrenees area (and down to Nagambie) over the years. All of these small batches are vinified and bottled separately. The districts or towns of Carisbrook, Marong, Maryborough, Myers Flat, Mugana, Mountain Creek, Nagambie, Ballarat, Avoca and Moonambel have all been mentioned at one time or another on Redbank labels.

The key to Redbank's production, however, is Sally's Paddock, named after Sally Robb. The four-hectare block is planted principally to shiraz, cabernet sauvignon and malbec, and produces what is appropriately Redbank's best wine, year in, year out. The Robbs have a further six hectares planted to cabernet franc, merlot and pinot noir, much of which is yet to come into bearing. All of the "home vineyards" are established on thin alluvial, gravelly soil over a friable red clay subsoil—hence the name Redbank. Yields are deplorably low, as Neil Robb eschews irrigation and the average rainfall is only 550 millimetres. The fully established vines average 2.2 tonnes per hectare, and it is hardly surprising that 65 per cent (or thereabouts) of the annual crush is bought in from other small growers.

Output has crept up from 1000 cases to 2000 cases a year, but it is just as well that Neil Robb has been able to gain some additional income as a consultant to various winemakers over the years. Interestingly, he has no formal qualifications, all his skills having been learnt the hard way, and his clients range from the big to the small. He started with Berri Cooperative, the biggest of them all, then moved to Hardy's, before coming back to Chateau Remy where he spent four years in the time leading up to the establishment of Redbank in 1973.

Redbank was established in time-honoured tradition: the winery was built first, or at least built to the point where it was feasible to conduct vintage operations in it. Then came the house, and finally the winery was finished. Even then it caused one visiting English journalist to ask politely: "And where do you actually make the wine?" Both house and winery are built from the most beautiful 100-year-old orange-red bricks, made in the district from its red clay.

Neil Robb has very positive ideas about winemaking, but at times his utterances on the subject take on a Delphic-like quality, rather similar to those of Max Lake, whom Robb much admires. Nonetheless, it is no secret that he believes in as natural a method of winemaking as is possible; open stainless-steel fermenters (usually cut-down dairy vats), hand-plunging, little or no cooling (the small batches and the ambient temperature make it largely unnecessary in any event) and finishing off the ferment in small oak casks. It is a method of winemaking which I think works admirably and this shows in his wines. All of them share a similar structure: smoothness and balance, gently crisp acid, and very soft tannin on the finish. The flavours run the gamut from mint to cassis, with stalky herbaceous characters rarely encountered. I suspect that Neil Robb likes to pick his grapes fairly ripe.

A confirmed red-wine drinker and red-winemaker, he has recently branched out into chardonnay, crushing 2.5 tonnes in 1984 out of a total crush of 32 tonnes. I did not greatly like the wine, a totally irrelevant judgement as it had sold out rapidly.

Neil Robb is yet another one of those gearing up to make sparkling wine: here he will bring a wealth of experience, not only from his time at Chateau Remy but also from his subsequent consultant winemaking at Yellowglen before the arrival of Dominique Landragin. Like the visiting English journalist, I am moved to enquire where the sparkling wine will be made.

SUMMERFIELD
MOONAMBEL–STAWELL ROAD, MOONAMBEL

The Pyrenees region has shown remarkable stability over the past decade. Each one of the seven wineries was established more than 10 years ago, if one treats the date of establishment as going back to the first vineyard plantings. Thus the Summerfield Vineyard was planted in 1970, even though the grapes were sold to other makers in the district until the building which serves as the winery was purchased in 1979.

Production remains very modest, and distribution is limited. But Summerfield has made some most attractive shiraz-based wines over the past few years. Ian Summerfield is winemaker, but shares the responsibilities with his Roseworthy-trained son who also works at Yellowglen. That Yellowglen experience has encouraged Summerfield to make and release its own estate-made and bottled sparkling wine. The first release was a blend of 1982 and 1983 base wines vintaged from trebbiano, and with 18 months on yeast lees they had developed rich bread/biscuity wholemeal characters on both bouquet and palate.

Nonetheless, it is the shiraz-based wines which have been most impressive. These have ranged between the very light and elegant '79 vintage through to the rich, dense, minty 1983 Hermitage, concentrated by spring frost and summer drought, and made from vines yielding barely one tonne to the acre (2.5 tonnes to the hectare).

TALTARNI
Off MOONAMBEL–STAWELL ROAD, MOONAMBEL

Taltarni grows in stature with every vintage. Right from the outset winemaker Dominique Portet, assisted now for some years by Greg Gallagher, has made massively constructed wines of exceptional style and vinosity. At times the sheer power of the wine, and in particular the tannin level, makes the young wines extremely difficult to assess. Even though Dominique Portet is very much his own man, his winemaking philosophies inevitably reflect the mixture of influences which lie behind Taltarni. His father André Portet was technical director of Chateau Lafite from 1955 until 1975, while Dominique's elder brother, Bernard Portet, established Clos du Val in the Napa Valley in California in 1972. Both Clos du Val and Taltarni are controlled by wealthy Californian businessman John Goelet who provided the money to establish the two brothers in their respective operations.

The selection of Taltarni came after a search which extended not only across Australia but also much of the western world. In choosing Taltarni they selected not simply a vineyard site, but a very large property which already had significant areas under vine. It had been developed by a local earth-mover, Wal Henning, with financial support from a Ballarat-based group of investors. The size of the venture they had undertaken apparently dawned on them fairly early, and in 1972 control passed to the present owner.

David Hohnen, then recently returned from the Davis Oenology School in California, was installed as the first manager, and oversaw the major part of the vineyard development which occurred between 1973 and 1978. Not only were substantial additional areas planted, but a number of lesser varieties established by the original syndicate were removed.

All of the vineyards are established on gentle slopes with an ideal soil structure: an oxidised clay top, with well-drained intermediate gravel rubble and quartz over a clay base. They are high in iron and low in potassium, which is conducive to low pH levels in the grapes. After considerable reshaping, new plantings and recent grafting the 108 hectares of vineyard now comprise cabernet sauvignon (28 hectares), chardonnay (18 hectares), sauvignon blanc (15 hectares), rhine riesling (12 hectares), merlot, malbec and shiraz (seven hectares each), cabernet franc and trebbiano (five hectares each) and chenin blanc (three hectares). Yields vary from 5.5 tonnes per hectare for cabernet franc and sauvignon blanc up to 10 tonnes per hectare for shiraz. Most varieties yield between 6.5 and seven tonnes per hectare. The resultant crush is around 700 tonnes, and output is a very healthy 38,000 cases a year.

Dominique Portet has degrees in oenology and viticulture from Montpellier, France, and gained experience working in wineries in the south of France and three years at Clos du Val, before coming to Australia and Taltarni. It is no doubt that American/ French training which instilled in him a respect for the ageing characteristics of wines with higher-than-usual levels of tannin, and to a lesser degree the extensive use of new, small oak barrels.

Since 1977 Taltarni's cabernet sauvignon has been the vineyard's *grande marque*. At virtually every *Wine and Spirit Monthly* buying guide new release tasting, at virtually every *Winestate* new release tasting, and in all of the major comparative tastings for the *National Times* which I conducted, the Taltarni cabernet sauvignon of the year in question received a high rating. Just as consistently, all of the judges and commentators pointed to the density of colour, the richness of structure and the immense tannin.

It is only in the last few years that it has been possible to obtain a limited perspective on the longer-term cellaring capacities of the early wines. This exercise has, however, been complicated by a subtle shift in both the varietal composition of the wine and, to a lesser degree, in the winemaking practices and philosophies of Dominique Portet.

As the plantings of cabernet franc and merlot have come into bearing, Portet has been able to increase the percentage of these varieties to go with the malbec in filling out the final blend. In the best French tradition he has no rigid formula, preferring to balance the amount of merlot (in particular) against the weight of the cabernet from each particular vintage. In some years he will use more, in others less. The one guiding rule is that the wine will always contain at least 80 per cent cabernet sauvignon, and always be labelled simply cabernet sauvignon.

This does not necessarily apply to the wines destined for the American market. The 1979 Special Reserve which was released in America, and which came top in one of the most prestigious comparative tastings involving Californian, French and Australian wines (held at the end of 1983), contained 73 per cent cabernet sauvignon, 20 per cent merlot and seven per cent cabernet franc. The sister wine, released in Australia in March 1984, (labelled 1979 Cabernet Sauvignon Special Reserve) had 90 per cent cabernet sauvignon, seven per cent cabernet franc and three per cent malbec (but no merlot) in the blend. It deserved every cent of its $18 release price. Strong purple-red in colour, the bouquet is clean and fine, with a superb balance between spicy and cassis-like aromas. The palate is rich and full, with generous berry fruit and the customary high tannin of the Taltarni wines. But instead of the tannin overwhelming the palate, it simply comes as an assertive reminder on the finish that this wine really is not ready to drink, and should be looked at again in five years' time.

Two years earlier when I tasted the 1977 Cabernet Sauvignon Special Reserve (in May 1982) I found the huge drying tannin on the finish out of balance and, while it had great minty fruit aroma and flavour, it was by no means my favourite wine. On that day the 1980 Taltarni Shiraz did battle with the 1979 Clos du Val Merlot for top honours, with the battle unresolved at the end of the tasting.

Curiously, Taltarni did not make an outstanding cabernet sauvignon in 1980, a vintage which smiled on virtually every other winemaker in the country. The wine is not bad, but at least in the first four years of its life was rather sullen and dumb. Nor do I think that the 1981 Cabernet Sauvignon is in the class of the 1982. In this latter vintage all the strands seem to me to have come together. Portet has progressively lightened the style, learning from the evolution of the earlier vintages, and I think learning that Australian tannins have a very different structure from those of France (albeit possibly with some similarity to those of California). At the end of 1984 the wine looks set to be a classic: a rich and deep bouquet, with smoky-oak characters intermingled with a hint of blackcurrant led onto a very clean, generous wine with lovely mid-palate fruit, and persistent lingering tannin in perfect balance.

These will always be masculine wines, upright and uncompromising. They will always have higher than usual levels of tannin. But tannin does have a place in every great red cabernet-based wine, and Portet is absolutely right in continuing to employ it.

Even though the Taltarni shiraz has been a consistently good wine over the years, and even though in 1981 (clearly) and in 1982 (marginally) it was in my view a better wine than the cabernet sauvignon, the marketplace no doubt will continue—relatively speaking—to ignore it. In recognition of this, and, if not quite in desperation, then in Gallic pique, the wine was solemnly relabelled "French Syrah" with the release of the 1982 vintage. This was allegedly an export-inspired move to differentiate the wine from California's petite sirah, which is in fact durif. One suspects that there may be a sideways look back over the shoulder to see what happens in Australia. The problem is the wine is so good that it just might carry the day on its own account.

With the notable exception of the 1983, which I thought was brown, thin and disappointing in the extreme, Taltarni's fumé blanc has gone from strength to strength. The 1980 vintage was good, the 1981 better still and the 1982 quite excellent, but all pale into insignificance compared to the 1984 Fumé Blanc. Whether the extreme pristine, grassy/gooseberry aromas and flavours will appeal to every palate is beside the point—clearly they will not. But if you like the flavour of sauvignon blanc, like a bone-dry green-flavoured wine to cool the tastebuds on a hot summer's day or provide a sparkling counter-point to fish and shellfish, there can be little better than wines in the style of Taltarni's '84 Fumé Blanc.

Dominique Portet is especially proud of his beautifully packaged and presented sparkling wines. With the exception of the Royale, with its flick of cassis and glowing pink colour, I wish I could say I shared his enthusiasm. I find the wines too aggressive, although the release of the 1984 Blanc de Blancs, with a 100 per cent chardonnay base and 21 months on yeast lees, at last started to show some softness. My problem with the wines has been their aggressiveness, but then Dominique Portet makes very masculine wines.

WARRENMANG
MOUNTAIN CREEK ROAD, MOONAMBEL

Wine and food have always loomed large in the lives of the two owners of Warrenmang, Russell Branton and Luigi Bazzani. Branton had a distinguished career as a hotelier before becoming a partner in the Melbourne wine merchant Duke and Moorfield; while Bazzani owns and runs one of the most prestigious and successful Victorian country restaurants, La Scala at Ballarat.

The Warrenmang Vineyard was originally planted by Wally Henning, the local earth-moving contractor who had been responsible for the initial development of the adjoining Taltarni Vineyard. Warrenmang was first planted in 1974, and Branton and Bazzani took over at the end of 1977. They retained Leo Hurley as their winemaking consultant—Hurley had been Colin Preece's cellar foreman at Great Western for 50 years, and knew more about winemaking than most people would forget in a lifetime. The first wines were made at Warrenmang in 1978, one of them appropriately labelled Leo Hurley's Blend. Hurley remained on until 1980, when Neil Robb took over the consulting role. However, it is strictly a consultancy; Russell Branton does most of the day-to-day winemaking work.

The vineyard is planted to five hectares of shiraz, 1.8 hectares of cabernet sauvignon, 0.6 hectare of merlot and two hectares of chardonnay, which provide Warrenmang with 75 per cent of its 55-tonne crush. The remaining 25 per cent (principally cabernet sauvignon) is purchased from other growers in the area. The fairly light soils, with a clay base, provide low yields of high-quality fruit: ignoring aberrations such as 1983, the yield is around 4.5 tonnes per hectare, a level not calculated to make the partners wealthy men.

A chardonnay was made in 1984 which reminded me very much of Neil Robb's chardonnay of the same year, which perhaps is not surprising given Robb's role as a consultant. As in the case of the Redbank wine, I found the evidence of solids fermentation obscured the varietal fruit in the bouquet, although the palate had some richness before that hardness came again on the finish.

It is the red wines of Warrenmang, and especially the cabernet sauvignon, which give most pleasure. At the start of 1985 I lined up the five cabernet sauvignons from the years 1979–83. While the quality was remarkably consistent, there were really three different styles represented. The 1982, 1981 and 1979 all show marked regional mint aromas and flavours, most marked in the 1982. The 1979 Cabernet is now at its peak, and should not be held much longer. The second style is the 1983 Cabernet Sauvignon, which shows all of the drought-concentrated characters of a very small vintage: dense purple, almost opaque, in colour; dense inky aromas,

with just a touch of mint; and a huge concentrated palate with powerful drying tannin on the finish. Whether the fruit in the wine will ever come up to match that tannin is questionable, but the answer will not be known for 10 years at least. The outstanding wine of the line-up was the leafy, herbaceous 1980 vintage, showing no regional mint whatsoever. Once again, it seems to me that these regional mint characters come in the warmer years and from fairly ripe grapes. Whether winemakers wish to encourage it or suppress it is very much a matter of personal choice.

The Warrenmang shiraz is no less generous in its flavour and colour. In early 1985 the 1981, 1982 and 1983 wines all showed good purple hues, becoming steadily stronger in the younger wines, and reaching a high point with the dense inky-purple of the 1983 vintage. This wine was the best of the three, without the mercaptan which is evident in the 1982, although with the same massive tannin and concentration of the 1983 Cabernet Sauvignon. Like that wine, it needs at least 10 years' cellaring. It will never be elegant, but then it does not aspire to be. ◪

WINERY HORSE AND CART, VICTORIA, c. 1910

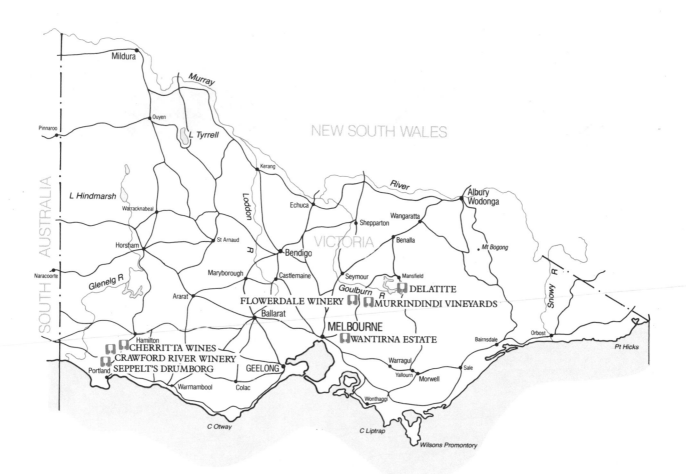

NEW SOUTH WALES

VICTORIA

SOUTH AUSTRALIA

Mildura

Murray

Pinnaroo

Ouyen

L Tyrrell

L Hindmarsh

Kerang

Watracknabeal

Echuca

River

Albury
Wodonga

Wangaratta

Shepparton

Loddon

Horsham

St Arnaud

Benalla

Mt Bogong

R

Bendigo

Naracoorte

Maryborough

Castlemaine

Seymour

Mansfield

Snowy R

Glenelg R

Ararat

FLOWERDALE WINERY

DELATITE

MURRINDINDI VINEYARDS

Goulburn R

Ballarat

Orbost

Bairnsdale

MELBOURNE

WANTIRNA ESTATE

Pt Hicks

Hamilton

CHERRITTA WINES

CRAWFORD RIVER WINERY

SEPPELT'S DRUMBORG

GEELONG

Warragul

Portland

Sale

Warrnambool

Colac

Yallourn

Morwell

Wonthaggi

C Otway

C Liptrap

Wilsons Promontory

Southern and Central Victoria

The wineries discussed in this chapter are isolated dots on the map, falling outside accepted viticultural boundaries. They are unified only by the fact that there is seemingly no part of central and southern Victoria which is unsuited to the growing of grapes.

The Melbourne metropolitan area is represented by Wantirna Estate; the high country above Mansfield by Delatite; the hills around Yea by Flowerdale and Murrindindi; and the far south-west by Cherritta, Seppelt's Drumborg and Crawford River.

Urban land values will prevent any significant plantings in the metropolitan area, although a surprising number of "vineyardettes" exist, varying in size from a few vines to 300 or more. These are tended by hobby winemakers whose products are never sold. By contrast, the hills around Yea and further north around Mansfield are bound to see further vineyards and wineries established in the coming decades. In the fullness of time both of these districts will form part of established viticultural areas and will merit chapters of their own.

CHERRITTA WINES
HENTY HIGHWAY, HAMILTON

Cherritta Wines was established in 1969 by the Sobey family. Four hectares of rhine riesling, shiraz, chardonnay and cabernet have been planted at the vineyard, which is off the Henty Highway 25 kilometres south of Hamilton. Rhine riesling is one of the main wines produced by the winery, usually left with a little residual sugar. The quality is not outstanding.

CRAWFORD RIVER WINERY
Off HENTY HIGHWAY, CONDAH

Crawford River Winery is situated halfway between Hamilton and Portland, not very far from Seppelt's Drumborg Vineyard. The first vines were planted in 1975 by local grazier John Thompson. In that year he established 0.8 hectare each of rhine riesling and cabernet sauvignon. The plantings now total 6.9 hectares, being cabernet sauvignon (3.3 hectares), rhine riesling (2.4 hectares), merlot (0.8 hectare) and sauvignon blanc (0.4 hectare). The sauvignon blanc will produce its first crop in 1986; if it is successful a further 2.4 hectares of this variety will be planted. The merlot, most recently established and not likely to come into bearing before 1988, will be used in conjunction with the cabernet sauvignon.

The first wines were made in 1981 by John Thompson on the property. He had learnt the basics of winemaking by taking the external winemaking course at the Riverina College of Advanced Education. The tiny production was all marketed locally, and it was not until the 1984 release of 400 cases of rhine riesling that limited retail distribution was commenced. In the same year a 1982 Cabernet Sauvignon was released, but only sold by mailing list and cellar door. The 1984 Rhine Riesling demonstrated both the potential of the area and John Thompson's expertise as a winemaker.

DELATITE
POLLARDS ROAD, MANSFIELD

The Delatite Vineyards were established by Robert and Vivienne Ritchie in 1968, 11 kilometres south-east of Mansfield. The Ritchies were one of the families who planted vineyards for the express purpose of supplying grapes to Brown Brothers of Milawa. Their property, situated in the hills around Mansfield, was and is one of the very cool-climate areas in which Browns was particularly interested.

Twenty hectares of vineyard have been planted on steep hills of ironstone origin to rhine riesling, gewurztraminer, pinot noir, chardonnay, shiraz, cabernet sauvignon, malbec, merlot and sylvaner. For a number of years the Ritchies were content simply to sell the grapes, and happy to see recognition given to Delatite by Brown Brothers in the fine wines that company produced from the grapes. But, as so often happens, the urge to make their own wine took hold. Looking forward to the day when they would eventually have their own winery, the Ritchies purchased back quantities of the Brown Brothers wine for ultimate release under the Delatite label. When they eventually obtained their licence and commenced trading, they were able to offer Delatite cabernet shiraz from five vintages—1977 to 1981 inclusive.

Their own winery was constructed prior to the 1982 vintage, and daughter Rosalind Ritchie—having undertaken the Riverina College course in wine-making—became winemaker with the assistance of Oenotec. A series of fine, delicate, and at times ethereal wines have since been released by Delatite.

As 1984 proved beyond doubt, the Mansfield Hills are an extremely cool area, and in years such as 1984 ripening is a problem. In that vintage the rhine riesling never really attained sufficient ripeness to produce a wine of distinctive varietal character, and it was blended with sylvaner. But there are exceptional years; in most vintages Delatite can and does produce wines of considerable finesse and quality. Thus the wines from that first vintage were enormously successful in the show ring. The 1982 Cabernet Sauvignon, 1982 Gewurztraminer, and 1982 Rhine Riesling won seven gold medals between them. The 1983 Rhine Riesling was even more successful, winning four gold medals and the trophy at the 1983 Melbourne show for best Victorian dry white.

Both the rhine riesling and gewurztraminer consistently show the effects of exemplary wine-making practices, in which oxidation is rigorously excluded from the fruit and juice, and the wine likewise jealously protected right until the time it goes into bottle. At times I wonder whether these wines are not overprotected, too elegant, too perfect. But I guess that is a very personal viewpoint. The pinot noir invariably exhibits clear varietal flavour, but has been rather light-bodied in some vintages. The cabernet sauvignon is a much fuller wine with

pristine berry characters, low tannin but a lingering, crisply acid finish. The clever use of French and American oak adds further authority to the wine.

FLOWERDALE WINERY
RMB 6513, YEA ROAD, FLOWERDALE

Flowerdale is the second of the two wineries established in the Yea district. Murrindindi is an equivalent distance due south-east of Yea, Flowerdale due south-west. Owner Peter Geary has planted one hectare of chardonnay, 0.5 hectare of chenin blanc, 0.4 hectare of traminer and 0.1 hectare of pinot noir on alluvial, gravelly clay soils. The winemaker is David Wakefield, and the first commercial vintage in 1984 yielded 350 cases in total. The 1984 Chardonnay and the 1984 Traminer had little or no varietal character, but coming from such young vineyards and made in such tiny quantities, it is probably unfair to make any final judgement. Certainly the area should produce high-class fruit.

MURRINDINDI VINEYARDS
RMB 6070, MURRINDINDI

Murrindindi Vineyards, a little over 10 kilometres south-east of Yea, were established by Jeanette and Alan Cuthbertson in 1979. So far two hectares of cabernet sauvignon, 1.6 hectares of chardonnay, 0.4 hectare of merlot and cabernet franc and 0.2 hectare of sauvignon blanc have been established on a mudstone/quartz gravel over a limestone-clay base. At a height of between 400 and 500 metres, the vineyards are in an uncompromisingly cool area, with chardonnay ripening in late March and the red varieties in late April.

One tonne of chardonnay and two tonnes in total of cabernet sauvignon, merlot and cabernet franc were harvested in 1984; winemaker is son Hugh Cuthbertson, better known as proprietor of Talavera Wines, the fortified-wine specialist. The 70-dozen chardonnay and 160-dozen red wines which eventuated will be consumed largely by family and friends; distribution will be by mail order and a few selected merchants. The Yea area is full of promise, and there are a substantial number of vineyards presently coming into production, with other wineries certain in the future.

SEPPELT'S DRUMBORG
HENTY HIGHWAY, PORTLAND

Seppelt's Drumborg Vineyard was first planted in 1964 as part of the company's drive to obtain access to greater quantities of early-ripening premium varietal grapes. The ultimate choice of Drumborg was in part the result of limitations elsewhere: because of quarantine restrictions designed to prevent the spread of phylloxera, suitable grape varieties were either unprocurable or in extremely short supply in South Australia; and in Seppelt's traditional home base in Victoria at Great Western, no large parcels of suitable land were available.

The prolonged search under the direction of Karl Seppelt came up with a totally untried area, one of the few Victorian regions not to have a history of grape-growing in the last century. A 190-hectare property was purchased in undulating country near the town of Portland. The red-brown volcanic earth soils, interspersed with ironstone gravel, coupled with the generous rainfall of 750 millimetres per year resulted in extremely vigorous vine growth. Moisture stress is seldom a problem, for follow-up rain throughout the summer months is common. Notwithstanding these advantages, however, the vineyard has proved viticulturally extremely difficult. For a start the area is extremely cool, and sunshine hours are low. Continued vigorous vine growth right throughout the growing season inhibited ripening, and the conventional viticultural techniques employed up to 1980 had only qualified success.

Recent viticultural developments have brought a greater understanding of the requirements of such areas, and the large vineyard is now assuming an ever-more important role in Seppelt's fine-wine production. There are more than 120 hectares of vines, planted chiefly to rhine riesling, traminer, sylvaner, pinot noir and cabernet sauvignon, with lesser quantities of ondenc, chasselas, muscadelle and chardonnay. An increasing proportion of the production is used in the making of Seppelt's best sparkling wines. Eighty-seven per cent of the base material for the newly introduced Fleur de Lys was provided by Drumborg ondenc.

Partly because of ripening problems, single-vineyard releases from Drumborg have been few and far between. However, two releases in early 1985 seem to indicate that future releases will be more common. The beautifully labelled and packaged wines add yet another line to the Seppelt's armoury, and are worth the effort to acquire.

The 1980 Cabernet Sauvignon won three trophies at its first showing at the Victorian Wines Show in 1981, including the award for best wine of show, and has since received silver and bronze medals at most of the capital city shows. A fresh and elegant wine, with lively, soft cherry/berry flavours and low tannin, it will no doubt hold in bottle, but really does not need further ageing. The 1981 Rhine Riesling, released at the same time, falls into a similar category.

WANTIRNA ESTATE
BUSHY PARK LANE, WANTIRNA SOUTH

Reg and Tina Egan established Wantirna in 1963, the year in which Max Lake first planted vines at Lake's Folly. In my book Lake still takes the honour of being the first weekend vigneron, making his first significant wine in 1966 and the first fully commercial release in 1967, substantially before Wantirna. Nonetheless, the Egans had remarkable foresight—and courage—even though others such as Dr John Middleton and Dr Peter McMahon were "playing around" with winemaking around the same time. Middleton, indeed, had made wine on an experimental basis in the late 50s. The fact remains that Wantirna is still able to show wine scribes wines going back to 1970 (cabernet sauvignon) and 1971 (clare/rhine riesling). I attended a remarkable tasting in mid-1984 sampling 36 different wines made by Reg Egan between 1970 and 1983.

These have all come from a remarkably small vineyard—remarkable, that is, given the number of wines produced—established within the confines of the Melbourne metropolitan area. It is a mere 20 minutes' drive from town, if traffic and the long arm of the law do not interfere. The vineyard was established, and the wines made, as an "out-of-hours" hobby for Reg Egan, who was then a solicitor (and who has since retired to the more gentlemanly pursuits of the Bar). He was aided in this by the happy fact that his house, winery and vineyard are all situated on the one property. With no prior experience to guide him Reg Egan planted a number of varieties on the vineyard, including some rather unexpected ones. Thus the early wines (and indeed up to the end of the 1970s) feature grapes such as crouchen, pedro ximinez, grenache, malbec and mataro. All of these fairly humble varieties have now gone in the interests of rationalisation, and the four-hectare vineyard is now planted to two hectares (in total) of cabernet sauvignon, cabernet franc and merlot, and one hectare each of chardonnay and pinot noir.

The thin topsoil and heavy yellow clay subsoil provide an unexpectedly hospitable environment for the vines: the girth of the older vines has to be seen to be believed. As so often happens in these cooler regions with adequate rainfall (800 millimetres), vine vigour is not always easy to control: the vine produces wood and leaf in abundance, often at the expense of grapes. Thus, despite the awesome proportions of the vines, yields seldom exceed five tonnes per hectare; and with the recent reshaping of the vineyard the overall average is decidedly less. The 1984 vintage provided only 15 tonnes of grapes to produce marginally over 1000 cases of wine. What the vineyard may lack in quantity, it certainly makes up in quality, particularly if it is judged by its red wines.

In 1983 Reg Egan, with help from Ian Deacon, who was then employed as assistant winemaker, made 25 dozen of a quite exceptional sparkling wine from a pinot noir/chardonnay base. I suspect this in future vintages will be kept as a house wine, and I think I would do precisely the same if I were in Reg Egan's shoes.

The white wines are led by the chardonnays, and if the 1984 retrospective tasting is any guide, considerable patience is required. The chardonnays tasted covered the years 1978 to 1982 inclusive, although the former wine had been blended with 40 per cent of pedro ximinez. This was the only wine available to fill up the partially empty single cask of chardonnay, first produced in that year. Not surprisingly, the pedro ximinez did not help the blend, and the wine remains a curiosity. The '79 Chardonnay was the best of the group, still surprisingly undeveloped on the bouquet, but with a rich, complex and weighty palate with nice, buttery fruit and oak flavours. Next came the 1980 Chardonnay, of medium weight, good fruit, still developing, and with a similar touch of buttery oak. The 1981 was rather hard and acid on the finish, and the 1982 similarly unapproachable with sharp, lifted, apple characters. Egan is confident that time will bring a miraculous transformation.

Other wines tasted included a 1983 Rhine Riesling/Crouchen blend (60 per cent/40 per cent), harsh, thin and unattractive; a 1981 Crouchen/Pedro Ximinez blend, demonstrating that even at Wantirna South these varieties remain very ordinary; a 1980 Trebbiano, rich and biscuity, but with some rather phenolic, heavy solids characters; a 1979 Rhine Riesling, oak-matured, showing great richness in the fore-palate but finishing hard, reinforcing the lesson that these are white wines made in the style of reds; a most interesting 1978 Riesling with voluminous Alsace overtones in the aroma, and a rich camphor/lime palate, jujube-like; 1977 and 1975 Crouchen/Pedro Ximinez blends, proving that these white wines are nothing if not durable; and finally a 1971 Crouchen/Rhine Riesling blend, which showed disconcertingly similar characteristics to the wines that had preceded it.

Five pinot noirs from 1977 to 1981 inclusive demonstrated that the Yarra Valley does not have this variety to itself. With the qualified exception of the 1978, in which some off-oak characters intruded, these wines all showed excellent, if varying, varietal character. The 1979 was the outstanding wine, with fine, elegant, sappy aroma and superb burgundian fruit on the fore-palate, intense and sappy, finishing with that seemingly inevitable trace of hardness. Whether time will soften it, I do not know, but equally it is at best a carping criticism. The 1977 Pinot Noir, too, was very good if one forgives the trace of volatility. It is a remarkably youthful wine, and has years in front of it. Both the 1980 and 1981 vintages show marked strawberry fruit aromas, with the 1980 far more elegant and fragrant; the 1981 richer, hotter and riper.

The shiraz and shiraz blend group was enormously variable in quality. The 1980 Shiraz is totally spoilt by mercaptan, and the 1978 lacks fruit, although the palate is heavy. The three exceptional wines were the 1979 Shiraz, 1977 Cabernet Shiraz and 1974 H and F Blend. The H and F Blend is named after the Egans' closest friends, Herman and Faye Schneider. A blend of shiraz, grenache and a little cabernet sauvignon, it is still a magnificent wine, with a rare amalgam of mint, spices and berries, with beautifully structured soft tannin running through the wine, and cherry-like fruit coming again at the finish. The 1977 Cabernet Shiraz shows more spicy shiraz character than any of the straight varietals, pungently rich and spicy, and yet not obscuring the touch of powdery green-leaf cabernet on the nose and some cabernet berry flavours on the palate. A wine as wonderful as the H and F Blend. Against these two the solid, honest and spicy 1979 Shiraz looks almost clumsy, but it simply needs another 10 years to gain age and grace.

The 11 cabernet sauvignon and cabernet blends covering every year from 1970 to 1982 (other than 1976 and 1981) were by and large magnificent. Of the younger wines only the '79 Cabernet Merlot disappointed, with strong, leathery, mercaptan aroma and flavour obscuring the fruit. The 1973 Cabernet Mataro was curiously disjointed, suggesting that the components parts had still not come together (and almost inevitably never will); the 1971 Cabernet Shiraz Malbec was big, rich, extractive, tannic and with a little mercaptan; and the 1970 Cabernet also showed some errant winemaking. But even in these wines the fruit quality shone through, and they suffered only in comparison with the quality of the other wines in the line-up.

The 1972 Cabernet Sauvignon is still a veritable child: clean, fruity and minty on the bouquet and with minty, slightly herbaceous, smooth and fresh fruit on the palate. It may not have much improvement in front of it, but it will be around for many years to come. The 1974 Cabernet Sauvignon is a much bigger wine than the 1972, showing some of the minty characters evident in the 1974 H and F Blend, a character which Egan has never liked but which seemed to me to fit very well in the wine. The 1975 Cabernet Sauvignon is simply a bigger, richer version of the 1974 vintage, being rich, fleshy and minty.

The 1977 Cabernet Merlot represents a complete break in style and was the wine of the night. Classic, powdery, Bordeaux-like fruit aroma on the bouquet, and an exquisite palate, sweet and rich on the mid-palate melding into a lingering, gently astringent Bordeaux-like finish—all contribute to one of the great Australian reds of the 1970s. A hard act to follow, but the 1978 Cabernet Sauvignon does the job. Clean and elegant, with perfectly modulated cabernet sauvignon character throughout, it balances berry flavours against a touch of green astringency and, finally, balanced tannin.

The 1980 Cabernet Pressings was a totally unexpected wine, with the pressings evident in the dense tannic aroma, but disappearing altogether on the voluminous though soft palate, with none of the tannin finish that one would expect. A most unusual and very successful wine. The 1982 Cabernet Merlot may well develop to challenge the sublime quality of the 1977: at the end of 1984 it was extremely youthful, with vibrant purple colour, youthful berry-fruit aromas, clean and gently sweet; cherry/berry flavours on the mid-palate but then finishing with delicate astringency. It is not an especially big wine, in spite of the propensity of 1982 to produce such wines, and is destined to become great. ♔

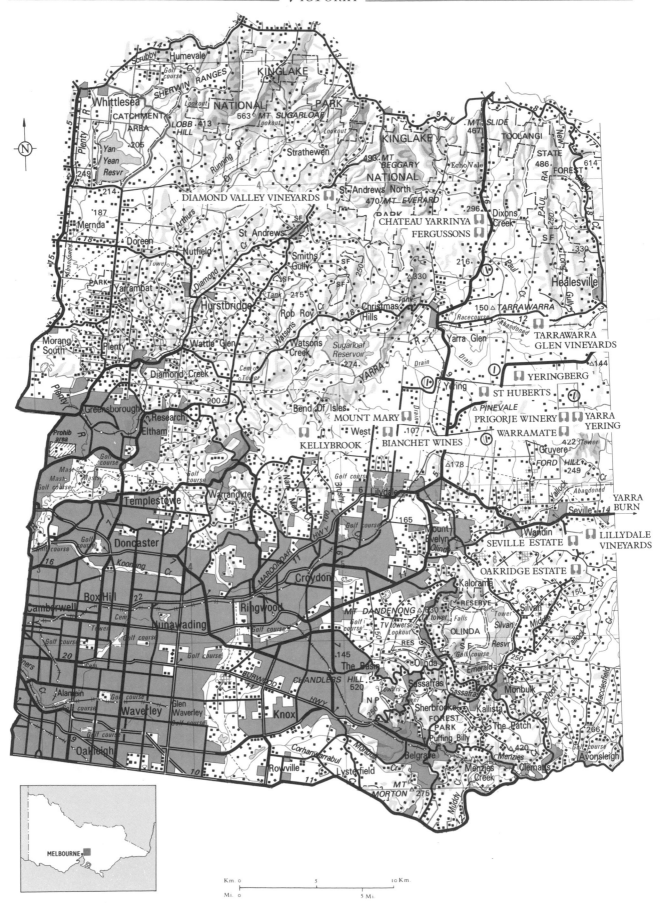

MELBOURNE

Km. 0   5   10 Km.

Mi. 0   5 Mi.

Yarra Valley

What became of William Henty's vines is not known, and William Ryrie can thus lay claim to being Victoria's first vigneron. He arrived in the Yarra Valley in 1837, having travelled overland from Arnprior Station in the Monaro, and set up a large grazing run. William Ryrie's brother, Donald, subsequently gave his recollections of the circumstances of the planting of the first vines in August 1838:

> They were taken from Arnprior and were the Black Cluster or Hamburg and a white grape, the Sweet Water. We afterwards had sent from Sydney other vines taken from MacArthur's vineyard at Camden. The first wine was made in March, 1845; a red wine resembling Burgundy and a white wine resembling Sauterne, and both very good. Dardel, a Swiss (afterwards at Geelong) used to come to prune the vines. He also put us in the way of making the wine.

The Swiss connection was soon further cemented. Paul de Castella left Gruyères in Switzerland in 1849 and landed in Victoria later that year. He purchased Yering Station from Ryrie and inherited the 0.4-hectare vineyard. Impressed with the quality of the wine it made, he arranged for a consignment of vine cuttings to be obtained from Europe; 20,000 cuttings, chiefly taken from Chateau Lafite, arrived in 1854 or 1855. They were packed in moss for the journey, and the vast majority survived. A plant nursery was quickly established, and in 1857 the bulk of the 40-hectare Yering Vineyard was planted. The vineyard development was carried out by Samuel de Pury, brother of Guillaume de Pury, the founder of Yeringberg.

Yering soon gained a reputation for its red wines. Because of the frequent misspelling of cabernet as carbinet, de Castella shortened the name to Yering sauvignon. In 1861 it was awarded a 100-guinea gold cup offered by the _Argus_ for the best Victorian wine; in 1889 it won a grand prix at the Paris Exhibition of that year, the only southern hemisphere wine to receive such an award, and one of only 14 given to wine entries at the exhibition.

Yeringberg and St Huberts were both founded in 1864, and it was these three vineyards which brought the Yarra Valley a reputation second to none for producing the finest table wine. Curiously, there were relatively few other vineyards. Samuel de Pury planted Cooring Yering, between Coldstream and Lilydale, in the late 1850s; when he returned to Switzerland in 1868 the purchaser of the property uprooted the vineyard in 1870. Auguste and Louis Deschamps planted two small vineyards near Lilydale in the late 1850s, which went out of production around the turn of the century when the land was sold for residential purposes.

Yeringa was planted near Yering by two of Auguste Deschamps's sons. Coldstream was planted by David Mitchell (Dame Nellie Melba's father) in the 1890s, and produced some wines which Francois de Castella described as "worthy of the district", but was uprooted in the 1920s, as was Chateau D'Yves which was established by de Bavay in the hills near Emerald in the 1880s. De Castella says that "recurring frosts were the cause of abandonment of this vineyard, which produced some wines recalling French medoc in a remarkable manner".

The Yarra Valley flickered briefly in the early 1890s, when the government of the day announced its intention to fund the erection of a cooperative winery, encouraging many of the farmers to plant grapes. A change of government, and a new Premier who preferred milk to wine, saw the promise revoked, and slowly but surely the Yarra Valley fell to the cow.

The vines have now returned; with the vines came wineries, and from the wineries have come wines which showed just why the Yarra Valley was so highly regarded in the nineteenth century. Yet in some ways the rate of development has been slower than one might have expected. After a rush of planting between 1968 and 1971, in which eight of the better-known wineries were established, the rate of planting and development slowed markedly until surging again in the early 1980s. As at June 1984 a report prepared by the Knoxfield Fruit and Vegetable Extension Group estimated that there were 118 hectares of vines (including non-bearing vines) in the Yarra Valley established by 60 growers and producing 470 tonnes a year. It also identified 13 wineries. I think it is almost certain that by the 1986 vintage production will exceed 1000 tonnes and will in all probability exceed 2000 tonnes by 1990. A major vineyard development on the site of the original St Huberts Vineyard was commenced in 1984 by a syndicate of investors with Tony Staley at the helm. Plantings of 20 hectares are projected. The number of wineries will also increase; this book lists 16, and there are a number of others at the planning stage. Just how many of these will proceed, and how many of both present and future wineries will still be in operation at the turn of the century, is far from certain.

The Yarra Valley has a number of advantages over virtually all other Victorian wine districts, but it will still face many of the same problems. Its greatest advantage is its proximity to Melbourne; as a district it has not so far effectively promoted itself or its tourist potential. That, however, is only a question of time. It is a place of great beauty with ever-changing scenery and mood. It is ideally suited to intensive farming (and viticulture), so that the distance between wineries is relatively short. Just as the Hunter Valley has transformed itself between 1970 and 1985, so will the Yarra Valley between 1985 and the turn of the century. In this period a full tourist infrastructure will surely be built up, providing a multiplicity of attractions for the whole family, adequate restaurant facilities and motel accommodation. Some of it is there already, but the rest will follow.

The next advantage is the exceptional combination of climate and soil. Inevitably, both vary across the length and breadth of what is a very large and open valley. There are five distinct subregions: Yarra Glen, Lilydale, Seville, Coldstream, St Andrews, Dixons Creek and Steels Creek. The soils vary from the rich red basalts of Seville Estate to the grey loam of Yeringberg, the latter so highly valued by the de Castellas. Climate—and microclimate—alter subtly with slope and aspect, but the entire area is well within the limits of Region One under the Davis California scheme of things, the coolest classification. Healesville has a centigrade heat-degree day summa-

tion of 1158, the coolest of all the major Australian mainland areas.

The Yarra Valley is not, however, without its viticultural problems; high summer humidity levels necessitate constant spraying against powdery and downy mildew; botrytis infections can break out at any stage of the growing season (with disastrous results for partially formed grape bunches); while late-summer drought can lead to substantial vine stress in unirrigated vineyards. But these problems are no greater than those confronted by any of the great winegrowing districts of the world, and the solution to all of them is readily at hand for the competent viticulturalist. The net result is, or should be, yields of the highest-possible quality grapes, of between eight and 12 tonnes per hectare in an established vineyard. It is true that some vignerons with established vineyards have lower yields, but modern viticultural thought is adamant that higher yields could be achieved without any diminution in wine quality.

Perhaps the greatest attribute of the Yarra Valley is its seeming ability to get the best out of virtually every variety vignerons have cared to plant. Chardonnay is an unqualified success; inevitably the style is more towards that of chablis, crisper and more elegant than that of warmer areas such as the Hunter Valley or McLaren Vale. The wines also take longer to develop in bottle. The net result is that, if hastily compared with the richer, peaches-and-cream style of the Hunter Valley, flavour and body can appear lacking. There will be those who will always appreciate the lusher, richer and more obvious styles, but there is equally no question that the finer chardonnays of the Yarra Valley will progressively come into their own. Rhine riesling has shown its versatility, producing the magnificent beerenauslese and trocken-beerenauslese wines of Seville Estate and more recently St Huberts at one end of the spectrum, and the delicate, elegant and fine rhine rieslings of Lilydale and Diamond Valley at the other end. Here there is a hint of spicy character almost suggestive of gewurtz-traminer, very much the indication of cool ripening conditions.

John Middleton finally pulled out his traminer, having tried a number of winemaking tricks including oak maturation to invest it with the authority and class he was seeking. Lilydale Vineyards has taken up the challenge, its 1982 Traminer being regarded as one of the best traminers so far made in Australia. Once again, the style is delicate, elegant and fragrant, with varietal spice evident but not the least bit aggressive. Semillon and sauvignon blanc are being grown, but little or none has been so far released as wine. I can see no reason why these varieties should not also be most successful, and with the botrytis option could well produce a magnificent sauterne-style wine in the years to come.

The main strength of the Yarra Valley to date has been its red wines, and it is hard to see this pattern changing much over the next 20 years. The cabernet family (cabernet sauvignon, cabernet franc and merlot) all flourish. The wines have brilliant, deep colour; magnificently structured berry-fruit aromas and flavours (generally in the blackberry/blackcurrant range) and great length to the finish. This seldom owes much to tannin; it is invariably present, but is very fine-grained. At their best these wines are disconcertingly similar to those of Bordeaux. Shiraz is as out of favour in the Yarra Valley as it is elsewhere in Australia, but Seville Estate, Yeringberg (until it was removed from the plantings there) and Yarra Yering have all demonstrated that superb wine can be made from it. Those of Seville and Yeringberg, in particular, intermittently show intense crushed-pepper/spice characters. But pinot noir has, relatively speaking, been the greatest success in the Yarra Valley. A difficult variety in most areas of Australia, all of the vignerons who grow it in the Yarra succeed. The style varies considerably from the almost delicate fragrance of Mount Mary to the opulent, strawberry richness of Yarra Yering. I suspect that winemaking techniques may also play a role in the differing style and structure. But, as I say, wherever one looks, pinot does marvellously well. David Fyffe, at Yarra Burn, makes a magnificent table wine, but has also recently demonstrated his capacity to make a sparkling wine full of character and style.

One this is certain: the Yarra Valley will never again fall to the cow.

BIANCHET WINES
LOT 3 VICTORIA ROAD, LILYDALE

Lou and Theresa Bianchet planted their small vineyard off Victoria Road, Lilydale, in 1976. Lou Bianchet, a builder by trade and who had worked for a number of years in Melbourne, had grown up amongst vines in Friuli in the north of Italy. There he helped his father and grandfather tend the family vineyard. But when he came to Australia he had no real winemaking experience, and his only formal training has been two winemaking courses at Dandenong Technical School.

The initial plantings were of a little less than half a hectare each of cabernet sauvignon, shiraz, pinot noir and merlot. These were followed by cabernet franc, traminer and a hectare of chardonnay. The traminer produced its first crop in 1984, as did the chardonnay, while the cabernet franc came into bearing in 1985. There is also a small planting of muscadelle. The first vintage was made in 1980; increasing production from the vineyards led to a new, larger winery being constructed in 1984.

The relatively few white wines so far released (a 1983 Muscadelle and a 1983 Chardonnay) have tended to be rather heavy and oily, with a certain amount of oxidation. They are wines which are fermented on unclarified juice, and subsequently spend seven or eight months in not-so-new oak. A degree of oxidation is almost inevitable.

The red wines show an extraordinary similarity of cellar style, with a peculiar resinous edge to the aroma, at times reminiscent of detergent, which I can only ascribe to old oak. I must admit it is not particularly marked; I would far prefer simply not to see it at all. It does not carry through to the palate of the wines, all of which show firm, deep, berry-fruit characters. Of the 1980, 1981 and 1982 Shiraz, I prefer the latter wine, with its touch of varietal crushed-pepper spice. All of the cabernets show some bitter astringency on the finish which needs time to soften; although it was particularly marked in the 1983 Cabernet Sauvignon, the wine nonetheless won a silver medal at the Lilydale show in 1984 and a bronze medal at Hobart in the same year. Once again the Yarra Valley has shown it is an ideal location for pinot noir: both in 1983 and 1984 Bianchet produced a very good wine from the variety. The 1983 has some strawberry aromas allied with a fairly firm, slightly sappy and astringent palate.

Bianchet produces honest wines. The fruit quality is there, they simply lack the sophisticated oak handling which the majority of the other Yarra Valley vignerons lavishly bestow on their wines.

CHATEAU YARRINYA
PINNACLE LANE, DIXONS CREEK

Graeme and Denise Miller purchased their 58-hectare property at Dixons Creek in 1967 with the intention of taking up dairy farming. Graeme Miller had studied agriculture at Dookie Agricultural College, and it was not until 1971 that they formed a partnership with Don and Jan Hall to plant grapes and eventually make wine. In 1971 two hectares of cabernet sauvignon and two hectares of shiraz were planted. Graeme Miller has never believed in irrigation, preferring to let the vines establish themselves naturally, and it was not until 1975 that a significant yield was obtained. That vintage produced 2200 litres of experimental wine, followed in 1976 by the first substantial crop. The 27,000 litres of wine were made under extremely difficult conditions in an old cowshed on the property. Notwithstanding the problems that this caused, the 1976 Shiraz won a gold medal at the 1976 Yarra Glen show.

The present "chateau" was erected in 1976, being completed in December of that year. Of quite extraordinary architectural style, complete with towers and battlements, it houses a conventional and functional winery on two levels. In it Graeme Miller has made some very good wines. The moment of glory that all winemakers dream of came at the 1978 Melbourne show, when the Yarrinya 1977 Cabernet Sauvignon won the Jimmy Watson Trophy for best one-year-old red of show. For reasons which can only logically be put down to some very clever promotion by the Royal Agricultural Society of Victoria, this trophy is regarded as the most significant in Australia, even though it is awarded to wines which are still in cask and which do not always make the transition to bottle on the retailers' shelves with grace.

The vineyard is planted to a classic mix of varietal white and red grapes: shiraz (2.2 hectares), cabernet sauvignon (2.1 hectares), chardonnay (1.6 hectares), pinot noir and traminer (1.2 hectares each), rhine riesling (0.9 hectare) and merlot and malbec (0.4 hectare in total). Because Graeme Miller declines the assistance of irrigation, yields vary substantially according to the dictates of the year, ranging between a low of three tonnes per hectare to a high of 8.5 tonnes per hectare. The estate-grown grapes account for around 60 per cent of the annual crush of slightly under 100 tonnes; the remaining 40 per cent is bought in, principally from Swan Hill, but also from areas such as Cowra in New South Wales. A small amount of grapes is also bought in from local growers in the Yarra Valley.

Chateau Yarrinya has received some criticism for its decision to buy grapes from outside of the Yarra Valley. This I think is unreasonable; at least some of the criticism comes from those who do not rely upon their winery for their major source of income. The fact is that both the labels and the sales literature clearly differentiate between wines which are made from estate-grown or Yarra Valley grapes on the one hand, and wines made from purchased-in grapes on the other. It can be said that it is not particularly edifying to see a Yarra Valley winery offering strawberry nip, blackberry nip, cream sherry, spumante and sparkling burgundy, and in a perfect world I would prefer not to see such wines sold. Thanks in part to State and Federal governments, it is not a perfect world, and so far as I am concerned the Millers are entitled to earn an income in such way as they see fit.

Chateau Yarrinya Cabernet Sauvignon has been their most consistent wine over the years. The 1980 was an extremely good wine, well deserving the trophy, three gold medals and six silver medals it won in its show career. The 1981 showed the density and strength of flavour that so many of the 1981 Yarra Valley wines show, reflecting the fairly hot year which produced wines very different in style from those of 1980. There is plenty of sweet-fruit flavour and firm tannin on the finish to allow the wine to improve for at least five years. The 1982, due for release in 1985, is dense and powerful and every bit as good as the 1980.

The first pinot noir was released in 1981; both it and the 1982 Pinot Noir won gold medals at capital city shows, while the 1983 followed up with two silver medals. The Chateau Yarrinya Pinot Noirs so far released have all had strong colour, good weight and plenty of fruit. Judged by the standards of any other area, they would be quite outstanding. Judged by that of the Yarra Valley, I think they lack a little varietal intensity.

The shiraz is a workman-like wine, and the small quantity of white wine (in 1983 limited to a traminer riesling blend) is adequate.

The 1984 vintage saw Graeme Miller joined by Lee Clarnette as winemaker after completing the degree course in oenology at Roseworthy College. A 100-tonne crush is a large one for one person, and the extra technical skills of Lee Clarnette will no doubt be very welcome.

DIAMOND VALLEY VINEYARDS
KINGLAKE ROAD, ST ANDREWS

In 1970 a group of professional scientists who were interested in wine decided to attempt some small-scale winemaking. Grapes were purchased from Mildura in 1971 and the first hogshead of "Greensborough Red", as it became affectionately known, was produced in David Lance's garage at Greensborough. A native of Ballarat, David Lance gained a diploma of applied chemistry from the

School of Mines in 1964, and thereafter spent four years in postgraduate studies in organic chemistry at Queens University, Canada, where he was awarded M.Sc. and Ph.D. degrees. On his return to Australia he took up a position with Carlton and United Breweries where he met his future partners in crime, Martin Grinbergs and Alex White.

In 1976 David and his wife Cathy Lance, together with their children, planted a 2.8-hectare vineyard at Kinglake Road, St Andrews, in the Diamond Valley, and commenced building their house on site. The Diamond Valley is adjacent to and is treated as forming part of the Yarra Valley. By this time Messrs Lance, Grinbergs and White were quite involved in their viticultural and oenological pursuits, being the unseen winemakers at St Huberts. Carlton and United Breweries turned out to be a less than sympathetic and understanding employer, not altogether surprising in the circumstances. David Lance retired in 1982 and is now a full-time vigneron and winemaker at Diamond Valley, and a partner in the viticultural and oenological consultancy service company with Martin Grinbergs and Alex White.

The Diamond Valley vineyard is established on grey silty clay loam over a mudstone base on a 20-degree hillside, with the vineyard contoured and terraced into the slope. In these circumstances cultivation is out of the question and herbicides are used to regulate weed growth. As ever, birds are a major pest, and the trio have developed a remarkable clear-span netting technique to combat the birds. Although the vineyard is very small, yields are generous, ranging between eight and nine tonnes per hectare. Output is nonetheless tiny at around 1500 cases per year. Three wines are produced, including a cabernet blend from the total of one hectare planted to cabernet sauvignon, merlot, cabernet franc and malbec. The pinot noir comes from the single hectare of that variety, and the rhine riesling from 0.8 hectare of those vines. A new planting of 0.8 hectare of chardonnay is planned.

Both the Diamond Valley wines and the Lilydale Vineyard wines are made on a use-and-pay basis at St Huberts. They also pool their resources in marketing, but the critical winemaking decisions are arrived at completely independently, and the Diamond Valley wines have their own particular style.

Both reds are equal to the best the Yarra Valley can produce. The 1981 Cabernet blend won a gold medal and medallion at the 1983 Victorian Wines Show; it happened to be a class that I judged, and the wine stood out like a beacon from the other 14 in its class with its fragrant-scented complex fruit, with

overtones of spicy nutmeg oak. The 1982 Cabernet shows very similar characters to the 1981. Sweet, spicy/mulberry aromas, and fragrant, spicy, sweet fruit with some vanillan oak flavours. Like its predecessors, it is a very gentle wine which may surprise with its capacity to live in bottle, but which is already very attractive, indeed, seductive.

The fragrance is a feature of the pinot noir too, which achieved even greater success at the 1984 Canberra National Show, winning the Peaches Trophy for the best three-year-old pinot noir. This followed on its earlier gold medal at Lilydale in the year of its vintage, when it overcame an active malolactic fermentation to win the Chateau Yerring Award for the best pinot noir of show.

FERGUSSONS
LOT 19 WILLS ROAD, YARRA GLEN

Peter Fergusson has been one of the more controversial figures in the Yarra Valley; like Graeme Miller of Chateau Yarrinya, he has not hesitated to buy in grapes from outside the region. The establishment has taken even greater exception to this because of his flamboyant marketing methods, which have seen Fergussons turned into a tourist Mecca centred on the riotous and communal Spit Roast Restaurant. Some would say that his labels have also been less than forthcoming in identifying the source of the grapes; it is not so much what the labels say, as what they do not say. The uninitiated might well believe that "Victorian Shiraz" or "Victorian Chenin Blanc" under the Fergussons' label might mean that grapes come from the Yarra Valley, when it does not necessarily mean this at all. I hasten to add that this is all perfectly legal, although in the minds of many it adds validity to the move towards a Victorian certification system.

The vineyards were established in 1968 on the Wills Road, Yarra Glen, seven kilometres along the Yea road towards Yea. The plantings, which have changed somewhat over the years as well as being increased, now comprise cabernet sauvignon (6.5 hectares), shiraz (four hectares), chardonnay (3.5 hectares), rhine riesling (two hectares) and chenin blanc (1.5 hectares). The soils are principally clay loam, with a heavy clay subsoil at a depth of between two and five metres.

Production is presently around 5000 cases, but is expected to increase substantially as the vineyards come into full bearing; this will also see the percentage of estate-grown fruit (currently 60 per cent) increase.

Some excellent, smooth and full cabernet sauvignons have been released under the Fergusson label and, as ever, I think the shiraz is underrated.

KELLYBROOK
FULFORD ROAD, WONGA PARK

Kellybrook was established in 1966 in the hills at Wonga Park, which is at the entrance to the Yarra Valley as one drives from Melbourne. It started off not as a vineyard and winery, but as an apple orchard with a difference—apples grown with the express purpose of making cider according to the traditional English methods. The orchard had in fact been planted in 1962, but owner Darren Kelly dates the establishment of the enterprise from 1966 when he first went to England and France to learn the techniques of cider-making (returning again for the same purpose in 1974). He points out that making both still and sparkling cider is similar to winemaking, but more difficult. These difficulties stem from the higher pH: apples are usually ripe at around 3.8 pH with six grams per litre of acid, which makes them readily susceptible to bacterial spoilage. There are other points of similarity with winemaking. Sparkling cider is made using the *méthode champenoise* technique, and the quality of the cider—whether still or sparkling—is directly dependent upon the quality of the base fruit. The normal commercial ciders are made from eating apples, the cider-equivalent of sultana or grenache. The best ciders are made from a number of varieties of non-table apples with names as fanciful as any grapes.

While Kelly has had every success with his ciders, he could not resist the temptation to make a little wine on the side. A little looks like growing into a lot. He has now planted chardonnay (2.5 hectares), cabernet sauvignon (two hectares), pinot noir (1.5 hectares), rhine riesling (one hectare) and half a hectare each of shiraz and traminer. This compares with two hectares of cider apples and two hectares of table apples. All of the vineyards are planted on fairly steep slopes of clay and ironstone. Until the vineyards come into full bearing Kelly has no option but to rely on bought-in grapes which currently account for 90 per cent of his crush; within three years he expects this to reduce to 25 per cent. The bought-in grapes come from Bail Brothers' Vineyard at Beverford, and the quality of the wine made from these grapes is limited by the circumstances of their parentage. But both with these grapes, and with the very small estate-grown production, Kelly has already

shown that cider-making is a hard task master, and that he will have no problem whatsoever in adjusting to winemaking.

This is a book about wine, not cider, but I must say that his range of cider—from dry still through to sweet still and to sparkling, thence to fortified cider and ultimately to calvados, distilled at the estate—is quite marvellous.

LILLYDALE VINEYARDS
DAVCROSS COURT, SEVILLE

Lillydale Vineyards was established in 1976 by Alex White and Martin Grinbergs. White and Grinbergs, it will be remembered, formed the second and third parts of the trio which terrorised Carlton and United Breweries for a number of years. Profiles of each of the partners appear in one of their newsletters, apparently each written by the other about the other, but no doubt containing the whole and nothing but the truth. So I quote:

> Martin Grinbergs landed on the Australian continent as a young lad at Fremantle in 1950. After a few months at Northam, he moved to Melbourne where he has lived ever since. His primary education was started in a forceful manner when his employer, the Post Master General, discovered that Martin was under age and should not have been delivering telegrams during school hours.
>
> At Yarra Park State School he was taught English as [it] is spoken but managed, more or less, to survive the experience. Rather than heading for Richmond Tech to do panel beating, Martin decided to be a white-collar worker and, having completed his secondary education at Melbourne High School, went to the University where he was awarded a B.Sc. degree with majors in biochemistry and microbiology. During his time at Melbourne University Martin married Anita who provided much-needed financial support.

As indicated, thereafter Carlton and United Breweries provided financial support while the burgeoning wine interests of Martin Grinbergs and Alex White grew. Like the others, he has now become a full-time winemaker and consultant, taking with him the expertise in various aspects of fermentation technology in which he specialised during his time at CUB. And so to Alex White:

> Alex White is a scientist by nature. His education started at Haileybury College, leading to a Fellowship Diploma of Applied Chemistry from RMIT followed by an M.Sc. degree from La Trobe University. Alex is an associate of the Australian Institute of Food Science and Technology, and a

professional member of the American Society of Oenology as well as of the Australian Society of Oenology and Viticulture.

Like Martin and David, Alex worked in the research laboratories at Carlton and United Breweries Limited, then moved to Red Tulip as technical manager. Although his passion for ginger chocolate soon waned his daughters were delighted with Dad's new job.

Against his daughters' wishes, Alex White became a full-time vigneron and consultant in July 1982. In recent years his wife Judith has gained her bachelor's degree in Applied Science (Wine Science) from the Riverina College of Advanced Education, adding to the formidable list of qualifications that the partners have.

The vineyard, situated at Davross Court, Seville, is planted to 2.4 hectares of chardonnay, two hectares of rhine riesling and 0.6 hectare of traminer. The chardonnay and traminer produced their first commercial crops in 1980, the rhine riesling (not planted until 1980) in 1984. Established on grey silty clay loam, the vines are extremely vigorous, yielding between 10 and 11 tonnes per hectare.

The viticultural techniques and vine-training methods used reflect the most modern approach to vineyard management, although one must have reservations about the insight into Alex White's character afforded by his use of predator mites. These microscopic insects scramble through the vines chasing three-spotted mites; having captured one, they bite off its legs, leaving the three-spotted mite immobilised until the hunt is over, whereupon the predator mites return to eat their prey. The enthusiasm Alex White has for these predators leaves much to be desired.

Lillydale Vineyards makes exemplary white wines. White and Grinbergs would be the first to admit that they have not yet finally determined their long-term approach to the making of chardonnay. The multiplicity of options continues to fascinate them, and with each of the vintages so far, some new techniques have been employed. Despite this, there is a basic continuity of style reflecting the high-quality fruit from the vineyard. Like most Yarra Valley chardonnays, they are finely structured and elegant—yet intense—wines which leave no doubt as to their cool-climate parentage. I remember on one occasion completely "missing" the 1982 Lilydale Chardonnay in a line-up of florid, peachy, warm-climate chardonnays. I cringe with the recollection of accusing the wine of not having sufficient varietal flavour. On the other hand, these are wines that are bred to stay. They need at least three years in the bottle and, on

the evidence to date, will benefit from five years. Oak handling is always sensitive, with a blend of French and American oak often employed.

The 1984 Chardonnay was entered in the Victorian Wines Show of the year, and we (the judges) had no hesitation in awarding it a gold medal. The wine had great depth to its flavour even at that early stage, and promises to be quite outstanding. (It subsequently won a Gold Medallion at the International View 85 exhibition in Melbourne in April 1985.) The traminers achieve remarkable intensity of varietal flavour, yet avoid the coarseness and oiliness of warmer-climate wines. The 1981 Traminer was a marvellous example of the style; intensely aromatic, clean and full with smooth spice, yet neither tannic nor oily. The 1984 Traminer follows very much in the pattern, perfumed and proclaiming its varietal ancestry loud and clear.

MOUNT MARY
COLDSTREAM WEST ROAD, LILYDALE

Dr John Middleton is to the Yarra Valley what Dr Max Lake is to the Hunter Valley. Comparisons between the two men are dangerous, but inevitable. Both are doctors who came into winemaking through an intense love and understanding of wine—wine in all its facets, wine as it is made and consumed throughout the western world. Both have a curious mixture of sensitivity and Olympian aloofness in their temperament. Both have led by example, scaling heights and breaking barriers, yet both have made wines which show distinctly human failings. Both are given to Delphic utterances of such obscurity as to defy questions regarding their meaning. But as is only right and proper, their wines have the last say, and those of John Middleton speak louder and more clearly. This, I am sure, is due to the accident of their birth: the Yarra Valley is a far kinder place in which to make wine than is the Hunter Valley.

John and his wife Marli Middleton moved to Lilydale in 1971. Prior to that time, and indeed for more than a decade, Middleton had grown grapes and made wine on an experimental basis. When the time came to become seriously involved, he exercised the same care and patience as did Max Lake in choosing the particular site—a north- and north-east-facing slope featuring the grey clay loam and sand soil classed by Hubert de Castella as the best in the Yarra Valley.

John Middleton has no time for shiraz, and regards my views on the subject as very mistaken, particularly when it comes to the Yarra. His initial plantings of red grapes were the cabernet family (cabernet sauvignon, cabernet franc, merlot and malbec) and pinot noir. He has had no regrets with that choice, and has no intention of changing it. His choice of whites was less inspired: of the initial three white varieties gewurztztraminer, chasselas and chardonnay, only the latter survives. The gewurztztraminer was finally removed after the 1983 vintage. For the future he has plans to make a sauvignon blanc, semillon and muscadelle blend to rival his "cabernets" blend. Being of impeccable parentage, Middleton does not believe in irrigation, and has adopted a fairly traditional approach to viticulture, rather like that of Graeme Miller at Chateau Yarrinya. In more recent years he has, however, altered his pruning system to give better fruit exposure in what is a modified form of the Geneva double-curtain system. Yields vary widely with the will of Allah, but vine vigour is never a problem: the beautifully drained soils encourage luxuriant growth.

John Middleton has made many exquisite wines. The 1978 Pinot Noir, the 1980 Pinot Noir, the 1980 Cabernets and the 1982 Cabernets stand out in my mind. Middleton has conjured up the term "cabernets" as a shorthand encapsulation of the complex cabernet-family blend. But he knows the wines much better than I do, and while I would not normally quote winemaker's notes, I think those of John Middleton (made at the end of 1984) are a special case. I do not agree with everything he has to say (I am, for instance, most concerned about the 1983 Chardonnay which seems to me to have pink-brown colours and little aroma at this juncture), but some points of disagreement are inevitable. Here, then, are his notes on the three main wines (I have omitted the gewurztztraminer, which has now gone to its maker in the sky in any event).

CHARDONNAY

1977. Still a good wine with food, crisp and flinty, probably will tire in the next couple of years.

1978. Good drinking now, complex, mature, still sound.

1979. Not ready yet, bright, nutty chardonnay flavour and aroma, crisp, finishes well, oak not yet totally integrated. New oak with young vines always predominates.

1980. Pale-yellow bright wine, delicate undeveloped aroma, bone-dry, clean and flavoursome, still needing some time yet.

1981. Golden, brilliant, warm, rich, chardonnay aromas, soft well-balanced luscious flavours without sweetness, coarseness or bitterness. Lots of complex flavours, toasted oak, butterscotch, hazelnuts. Wine from a warm, warm year, advancing more quickly

than the others. Good with red meat, but needs another few years.

1982. Deep golden wine, warm rich flavours again but with a much more delicate structure than the 1981. Luscious without the stainless steel 'baby fat' of the mass production wines here and overseas. No bitterness or sugar, delicate crisp finish, some oak evident still. Will need at least three years.

1983. Alcohol 12 per cent v.v. A young wine showing reflective brilliance in the glass. After about five months in bottle, this slow-maturing wine is still very aromatic and fruity needing lots more time before drinking. The year was bad, with severe water stress and defoliation of the vines. Acids were good, but sugars did not rise and grapes began to wrinkle so we picked before optimum levels for this variety. The wine is crisp and will be delicate and elegant. We kept botrytis out of the vineyard in order to protect aroma and flavour from the oily masking of varietal character that this organism produces. About 35 per cent of the casks were new, and this is evident in the toasted-oak overtones and palate firmness. The finish is harsh at present, which augurs well for later drinking; acids and tannin prevent dumbness and flatness in wine as it ages. It is good with food now, but should be kept.

PINOT NOIR

1977. Remember to decant this and all our older wines whether pinot or cabernets. I feel that this wine should now be enjoyed, and should be opened and decanted at least three hours prior to drinking. It has many beautiful flavours, mostly nuts and small fruit. Some bottles show a hint of ethyl acetate in typical Burgundian fashion. For the amateur chemists, the legal limit in Victoria for volatile acids, expressed as acetic acid, is 0.12 g/100 ml. This wine was bottled at 0.058. The threshold for the average human is 0.072. A great wine.

1978. A paler wine than the 1977 but more spirit is evident in the aroma and in the flavour adding that fiery sweetness that only comes in good pinots. Lots of strawberries and nuts. Still needing a few more years yet, but already outstanding in its richness and finesse.

1979. Brilliant garnet colour, still undeveloped, rich young pinot aromas and flavours. Spicy and starting to develop a middle palate sweet-soft quality. Finish is a bit bitter at present, so be patient. A wine that is confounding its detractors in no uncertain fashion, to our satisfaction. Well worth trying a bottle now, with food.

1980. Dark, brilliant garnet wine, strawberry aromas, mouth-filling soft, sweet, strawberries and cherries. There are even some herbaceous spicy qualities. Needs another three or four years at least. Acid and tannins are adequate for further development.

1981. Good pinot colour, sweet strawberry middle palate, some spice and some mushroom flavours. No stalkiness. Will develop yet, but might need watching, the year was hot and the vines very stressed, it may develop some plum qualities.

1982. A dark ruby wine, undeveloped but very powerful in aroma and flavour, but needs more time to allow the rather tannic finish to soften. Give it at least three years yet. It may rival the 1977 one day. Remember a good pinot needs at least five years to develop a good middle-palate richness.

1983. Alcohol 13 per cent v.v. Only recently bottled after slow cask maturation, it will need at least a year of bottle age before pulling the first cork. It reminds me of the 1981 in colour, aroma and flavour. The finish is a good deal crisper, and there are plenty of strawberry flavours and middle-palate complexities to ensure its place with our other pinots as it matures. Remember at least five years is needed in bottle for pinot to develop true character and richness.

CABERNET

1976. Still has young wine colour, classical cabernet aromas and flavours, cassis, fine resinous oak, herbaceous hints and violets. Tannins, acid and balance are good for many years yet. Has finesse ++. Worth sneaking the odd bottle for a try from now on.

1977. This wine still has a grassy aroma, it has great colour, it is still austere and undeveloped. Has great flavour and complexity. Good finish, plenty of acid and tannin for years to come. Leave three to five years at least.

1978. Very good colour, a fine elegant cedar-box aroma typical of cabernet, even better now than a year ago. We think this is a marvellous wine, but it will get better. So don't drink it all.

1979. Brilliant ruby wine, clean, rich, young cabernet aroma, mulberries, violets and cedar. Loads of blackcurrant flavours with fine tannin and a good clean acid finish. Rich and intense, yet elegant and not jammy. Keep, it needs time yet.

1980. Slightly lighter in colour, but richer in aroma than the 1978 and 1979. Soft mellow elegance with plenty of tannin despite all that. A great wine that we now realise is of international quality. It was rated the wine of the night at the I.W. & F. Society's Small Winemakers' Dinner in Sydney this year. In 1983, our 1978 Cabernets received the same accolade. The 1980 has a great future, so keep some for at least five years.

1981. The wine has surprised me in the way it has slowly come back into the style of our cabernets, despite its hot year origins. It is a big wine, but nevertheless it is now showing the elegance for which Mount Mary is becoming known. Leave it alone, it will last for years, but like a good young Bordeaux can be enjoyed as a young wine.

1982. 12 per cent v.v. A very dense ruby wine with brilliant colour at the edges of the glass. It has one of the most powerful aromas of young cabernet I have experienced from this vineyard. All the 'small fruits', as the French say, are there in abundance. The flavour of the wine matches the bouquet, and with good, fine tannins and plenty of acid this wine has great potential. For the *cepage* detectives, cabernet sauvignon was 65 per cent, cabernet franc 16 per cent, merlot 13 per cent and malbec 6 per cent. These are actual juice proportions prior to fermentation. Be patient and give this wine some five to eight years at least.

The 1982 Cabernets were shown as part of a masked tasting of a dozen 1982 Cabernet Sauvignons organised by the Yarra Valley Vignerons' Association. By common consensus, and certainly my vote, it was the wine of the night. It is astonishingly like a fine Bordeaux, with elegance, balance and finesse rarely encountered in Australian wines.

OAKRIDGE ESTATE
AITKEN ROAD, SEVILLE

Oakridge Estate is the newest arrival in the Yarra Valley, established by Jim and Irene Zitzlaff in Aitken Road, Seville. Two hectares of cabernet sauvignon have been established at the Aitken Road vineyard, with trial plantings of merlot, shiraz, rhine riesling and crouchen totalling a further half-hectare. A second 5.5-hectare property has been acquired on the Seville to Monbulk road, designed both for a cellar-door sales outlet and to accommodate further plantings.

The Aitken Road vineyard is established on the rich, startling red volcanic soil shared by (among others) Seville Estate, although not by Lilydale Vineyards. Even though some have expressed concern at the pH levels which these soils can give rise to, there is no doubting their capacity to produce first-quality red wine. The first vintage of Oakridge Estate — 1982 — demonstrated this. The cabernet sauvignon of that year is an enormous wine, powerful, deep and tightly structured, yet avoiding any suggestion of being extractive. At the end of 1984 the oak was still aggressive, but the wine has the components to come together.

The production of Oakridge will never be great, and it is expected that all of the production will be sold at cellar door and by mailing list.

PRIGORJE WINERY
MADDENS LANE, GRUYERE

Prigorje (pronounced preoria) is a town near Zagreb in Yugoslavia. Here Ivan Vlasic-Sostaric's family have made wine for five generations. When he came to Australia and bought a smallholding in the Yarra Valley in the late 1960s, it was inevitable he would wish to plant some grapes. Between 1970 and 1971 four hectares were established: 1.2 hectares of pinot noir and 2.8 hectares of shiraz. The vineyard is situated between that of Yarra Yering and Warramate on one of the best slopes in the entire Yarra Valley. Ivan Vlasic-Sostaric works for the Country Roads Board and many of the vineyard and winery chores are carried out by his wife and daughter.

Until 1984 the entire production was blended and released as a dry red burgundy. In that year he decided to keep part of the pinot noir separate, and it will be bottled after two years' oak maturation. All of the Prigorje wines are given an extended period of time in old oak, and unhappily they show the effects of it. The 1979 Burgundy had an aggressive pencil-shavings aroma and a distinctly volatile palate; while the 1980 Burgundy, much softer, had peculiar meaty/gamy flavours. Both of these wines were still available for sale at the end of 1984, with the 1982 vintage due for release at the end of January 1985.

SEVILLE ESTATE
LINWOOD ROAD, SEVILLE

When, in 1970, Peter and Margaret McMahon bought their property in Linwood Road, Seville, its physical beauty was the determining factor. After 20 years as a medical practitioner in the Yarra Valley, Peter McMahon had decided that his longer-term future lay in viticulture, although he had no intention of letting the more arcane aspects of soil analysis determine his choice. If he was going to grow grapes and make wine, he was going to do so in an environment which he thoroughly enjoyed. And at no time since has the smile gone off Peter McMahon's face; others may take themselves (and their wines) with the utmost seriousness, but never Peter McMahon.

The elevated hillside paddocks, with panoramic views out over the Yarra Valley, are established on extremely fertile red to grey volcanic soils over a clay base. The brilliance of the red loam is quite astonishing, but both soil types foster vigorous growth, and I am not certain that the traditional viticultural techniques employed at Seville have necessarily obtained the best results from the site. This, allied with Peter McMahon's determination not to lose sight of his enjoyment of life, may explain why some of the wines are variable in quality. Not, I hasten to add, that I am suggesting any want of care or attention; anyone who has visited the Seville Winery will know that Peter McMahon is as careful and dedicated as any winemaker. It is something more intangible, something which at the same time

has produced such astonishingly magnificent wines as his 1980 Rhine Riesling Trockenbeerenauslese.

The vineyard plantings comprise chardonnay (0.8 hectare), rhine riesling, pinot noir, shiraz and cabernet sauvignon (0.5 hectare each), merlot (0.2 hectare) and cabernet franc (0.1 hectare). These go to produce six wines: a cabernet sauvignon (in which the small percentage of merlot and cabernet franc is included), a pinot noir, a shiraz, a chardonnay and two rhine rieslings, one dry and the other a late-harvest botrytis-affected style. In spite of the vigour of the vines, yields are not particularly high as much of the vigour is diverted to vegetative growth rather than grape production. On average the vines yield around seven tonnes per hectare, giving rise to a tiny production of around 1000 cases of wine a year. Little wonder that it is all sold by mailing list and on a rigid quota system, usually offering only half a case of each variety to each mailing-list customer.

The Seville Estate cabernet sauvignon is probably its most consistent wine. Peter McMahon is not afraid to employ fairly lengthy maturation in basically new oak, and the wines are not infrequently somewhat disjointed in their youth, needing at least two to three years to gain harmony. The fruit flavours vary somewhat according to the vintage, from the hint of dark chocolate and caramel in the '79 through to the strongly herbaceous aroma and classic firm-berry palate of the 1980, which I think is clearly the best of the cabernet sauvignons so far released. The 1982, released at the end of 1984, undoubtedly has sufficient fruit, but the oak was raw and assertive at the time of release. It is difficult to see this wine even approaching its peak before 1990, but it should make a great glass at that time.

The pinot noir releases have varied substantially in terms of technical perfection (or rather, imperfection), but the majority have showed what I regard as true pinot varietal character in lesser or greater degree. These are not big, luscious, strawberry-jam wines—certainly some vintages have strawberry-like fragrances, but they are in the leaner, slightly sappy mould of Vosne-Romanée. Volatility has been one intermittent problem, but I think that a certain amount of this is part and parcel of the style of many great burgundies.

The shiraz is the unsung hero; it was obliterated by botrytis in 1984, and none was made in that year. It customarily stands in the shadow of the other Seville wines, yet in absolute quality terms it is very hard to see why. At its best it exhibits marvellously intense pepper-spice flavours and characters; the '79 and '80 vintages were such wines. At the beginning of 1985 a bottle of 1978 Shiraz opened beautifully: it certainly had far less spice than the two following vintages, but there was a touch there, along with leafy tobacco aromas and that classic velvety structure of shiraz on the mid-palate. In another year or two it will be at its best.

The chardonnays have been the most erratic of the Seville wines, although since 1980 Peter McMahon seems to have come to terms with the variety, and with the handling techniques to be used. That year, in particular, was quite outstanding, and the chalky/oxidative/solids-fermentation characters which marred some of the earlier vintages seemed to be a thing of the past.

In 1980 McMahon produced a sweet wine unlike anything that had hitherto been seen in Australia. One or two wines made since then have rivalled the explosive richness of the 1980 Rhine Riesling Trockenbeerenauslese, but with one exception these have been engineered in the artificial confines of cool-rooms. I have been present while technocrats have criticised the Seville wine for oxidation and volatility, and certainly there is an element of both characters in the wine. But one has to go hunting for them under the massive structure of opulent fruit, and almost searing acid, which distinguishes almost all of the ultimate, heavyweight, sweet dessert wines of the world, whether a 1976 German Trockenbeerenauslese, a Chateau St Jean Selected Late Harvest from the Napa Valley, or South Africa's Nederburg Edelkeur. A quite fantastic wine, and I guard the few bottles I have accumulated with great jealousy.

In subsequent years Peter McMahon has contented himself with making a beerenauslese rhine riesling, also almost invariably of very high standard. The dry rhine rieslings all show some lime characters typical of the very first stages of botrytis, and are very distinctive and enjoyable wines. Peter McMahon, for obvious reasons, has a very ambivalent attitude towards the botrytis which is an ever-present threat to his red wine and, to a lesser degree, to his chardonnay. But it most certainly allows him to scale the heights.

ST HUBERTS
ST HUBERTS ROAD, COLDSTREAM

The "first" St Huberts was established in 1862, when Hubert de Castella purchased a portion of Yering Station from his brother Paul de Castella. De Castella had previously lived in the Yarra Valley between 1854 and 1857, and returned to his native Switzerland in 1857, only to find the lure of Australia too strong. He had intended to establish a sheep station, but on returning found that sheep were too expensive and that his brother's wine made at Yering was in great demand. So it was to vines that he turned, quickly establishing 40 hectares and increasing total planting to 80 hectares by 1875. Massive cellars were built with the capacity to hold two or three vintages. But the establishment expenses were understandably very large, and sales lagged in the face of the poor reputation which "colonial" wine had at the time. This poor reputation was brought about by large quantities of wine being made by the numerous small vignerons. Businesses had sprung up across the length and breadth of Victoria, many of which had little or no idea about the basics of winemaking.

In 1875 the St Huberts Vineyard Company was formed to take over the enterprise, with Hubert de Castella retaining a major interest. The injection of new capital did little to alleviate the problems, and further reconstruction took place in 1879 when Hubert de Castella, in partnership with Andrew Rowan, repurchased St Huberts from the company. A period of prosperity followed; Rowan was an energetic and effective marketer.

Francois de Castella, put in charge of St Huberts between 1886 and 1890, recalled the 1880s in his paper delivered to the Victorian Historical Society in 1942. It is a remarkable near-contemporary record of a Yarra Valley which we may never see again. De Castella observed that:

> Rowan did much to put St Huberts on the map, and its wine on every restaurant's list. With the de Castella and Rowan regime, dawned an era of prosperity for St Huberts. The vineyard of 250 acres [101 hectares], then in its prime, produced several vintages of over 70,000 gallons [318,500 litres] each. Relieved of the worry of wine sales, my father could give all his attention to vineyard and cellars. Wines of exceptional quality resulted, most notable vintages being 1875, 1879, 1883 and 1887. Every four years was a vintage year, though several others were nearly as good.

The height of St Huberts' fame and success came in 1881, at the Melbourne International Exhibition. This was an exhibition of every type of agricultural and industrial product, and the wine section alone attracted 711 entries. The Emperor of Germany gave the judges of the numerous sections a major problem by offering a grand prize, a silver-gilt epergne, for the most meritorious exhibit in the show. A St Huberts wine won the wine section, and then competed against felt hats, steam-engines and sundry other items to take the Emperor's prize.

Despite an active export trade, with wine regularly leaving in consignments of 50 hogsheads (1462 litres) at a time, the end of the 1880s saw financial problems mounting once again for St Huberts. Disagreements between Hubert de Castella and Rowan (which had led to de Castella returning to Switzerland in 1886) did not help, and in 1890 Rowan purchased Hubert De Castella's share. The sale was organised through an attorney and did not meet with de Castella's approval when he learnt of it; but it turned out to be a wise decision for St Huberts slowly faded from the scene. It was subsequently purchased by David Mitchell, the father of Dame Nellie Melba, but went out of production in the early years of the 1900s.

It was replanted in 1968 by the Cester family, who had bought the property and who both then and now are major poultry and gamebird breeders. Hubert de Castella would no doubt be more than a little surprised to find the St Huberts wine of today made in a converted chicken shed, built of corrugated iron and (in a concession to the dictates of winemaking) spray-insulated inside.

The vineyard is planted to cabernet sauvignon (5.5 hectares), shiraz, pinot noir, chardonnay and rhine riesling (3.5 hectares each) and one hectare of trebbiano. The soils are the grey silt and loam over clay so favoured by de Castella. Yields range around the seven to eight tonnes per hectare range, with the more recently established pinot noir still to come into full bearing. As so frequently occurs in the Yarra Valley, vine vigour is very marked, and one of the techniques used at St Huberts to control excessive cropping is bunch-thinning. This involves the removal of a portion of the crop from the vine after bunches have been fully formed.

Peter Connolly was for many years treated as the winemaker, but in truth the Lance, Grinbergs and White trio had more than a little to do with the winemaking, and these days Oenological Services (Victoria) Proprietary Limited, the trio's consultancy company, is officially recorded as winemaker.

With a 9000-case production from a crush of over 100 tonnes, St Huberts is by far the largest of the existing Yarra Valley wineries and vineyards, and for this reason if for no other has been far more active in promoting its products on the retail market. This activity reached the point of outright notoriety with the retail release of its 1977 Cabernet Sauvignon at $17 a bottle in 1980. The wine was initially released at the cellar door at a fraction of that price, and when it did not sell particularly well the decision was taken effectively to double the price and offer it for retail sale at the new level. It worked wonders—the ensuing publicity ensured that the wine walked out the door. It also happened to be one of the very best of the St Huberts cabernets, a fact recognised by that discerning New York merchant, Robert Chadderdon, who took it to New York (at a cost of rather less than $17, although it retailed in New York for very much more).

The 1977, 1979 and 1980 vintage cabernet sauvignons were all of very high quality, with the 1980 showing marked sweet, cassis-berry flavours to its rich, soft fruit. As often throughout the Valley, the 1981 Cabernet Sauvignon was rather plain, dull and straightforward, but St Huberts returned to its best form with the 1982. Ripe-cherry/mulberry aromas and flavours are a feature of the 1982 wine, although not for the first time with a St Huberts cabernet sauvignon, I thought there might have been a trace of mercaptan.

The St Huberts shiraz can be a better wine than the cabernet sauvignon, as the 1981 vintage showed. A touch of varietal spice on the bouquet, allied with clear, rich fruit, led on to a powerful and lengthy palate. Contrary to some tasters, I also greatly liked the minty flavours of the 1980 Shiraz, even if it tended to be a little overripe and obvious.

The St Huberts chardonnay is a new arrival on the scene and has been enthusiastically received. Here the skills of the consultant winemakers come to the fore, with a stylish wine full of flavour. If one wants to find fault it is that the oak tends to dominate the fairly fine, elegant fruit (with its citric overtones) early in the wine's life.

Finally there are the striking rhine rieslings, usually very full-bodied and marked with lime/pineapple flavours suggestive of the botrytis. A touch of residual sugar fleshes the wine out further. Not a particularly elegant style, perhaps, but with abundant flavour and character. In 1984 St Huberts added an outstanding beerenauslese to its range.

TARRAWARRA GLEN VINEYARDS
HEALESVILLE ROAD, YARRA GLEN

Late in 1981 prominent Melbourne businessman and philanthropist Mark Besen purchased one of the most beautiful properties in the Yarra Valley. There are 315 hectares of rolling hills and valley flats, and while it will remain primarily a grazing property, 4.5 hectares of chardonnay and 1.5 hectares of pinot noir were planted in the winter of 1983 and will produce their first commercial crop in 1986.

A 150-tonne winery will be constructed prior to the end of 1985. This will be capable of handling the entire production of the vineyard, which will be increased over the next few years to approximately 12 hectares in all. A modified form of close spacing has been utilised, and there seems little doubt that yields will comfortably reach 10 tonnes per hectare.

David Wollan, formerly a winemaker at Arrowfield in the Hunter Valley, has been in charge of the development since its inception. Mark Besen is determined to produce the best-possible-quality wine, with expense of little concern. The overall size of the venture is a major one by any standards and particularly those of the Yarra Valley.

WARRAMATE
LOT 4, MADDENS LANE, GRUYERE

No sooner does the first-time visitor to the Yarra Valley think he or she has discovered its most exquisitely beautiful corner, than another even more beautiful one unfolds. The view from the hillside shared by Yarra Yering, Prigorje and Warramate is challenged only by that of Yeringberg and perhaps Seville Estate, although the latter two are quite different in their feel.

Warramate is the weekend and ultimately the retirement haven for Jack and June Church, and a weekend retreat for their two sons. The vineyard was planted in the early 1970s and the first commercial vintage was made in 1977. Jack Church had obtained a science degree in his youth, which stood him in good stead when he came to do the winemaking course at the Riverina College of Advanced Education.

Everything about Warramate is low key: Jack and June Church are a very nice but modest, if not shy, couple; the vineyard, planted to cabernet sauvignon, shiraz and rhine riesling, is only two hectares in extent; and the winemaking is conducted in the small basement underneath the weekender built at the top end of the vineyard. This utterly belies the quality of their cabernet sauvignon, which right from the outset has been of the highest order. The 1977 vintage won trophies at the Lilydale show in 1977 and 1978. The 1978 Cabernet Sauvignon had clearly marked varietal definition, in a lighter mould, and had great elegance. The 1979 was a much sweeter wine, tracking in style the other Yarra Valley cabernets of that year and augmented by well-handled oak. The 1980 was and is outstanding: firm varietal fruit, typical of the depth of the vineyard, allied with a nice twist of acid intermingled with strong oak aromas and flavours. It is a wine which will not begin to approach its best until the 1990s. The 1981 Cabernet Sauvignon was the only disappointment, still showing the deep fruit characteristics of the vineyard, but without the lift and life of the other years. 1982 saw the wine come back to its usual top form, with enormous plum/spice/meaty aromas and ripe-plum flavours on the palate. A super-heavy-weight wine, it has distinct similarities to some of the bigger Yarra Yering cabernets. The Warramate shiraz, too, can be very good, as the 1980 vintage showed.

I am not too certain that Jack Church's predilection for leaving the wine in stainless steel until at least 12 months after vintage and only then moving it into oak is the right way to go; it has in part been dictated by economic constraints, but it does mean that many of the wines are very disjointed when they are first released. Thus in the second half of 1983 the 1980 Shiraz really looked like a one-year-old wine.

The Warramate rhine rieslings are not successful; oxidation is endemic, reflecting to the fullest the great difficulties of satisfactorily making white wine in a very small winery with very limited equipment.

YARRA BURN
SETTLEMENT ROAD, YARRA JUNCTION

When David Fyffe planted the Yarra Burn Vineyard in 1976, he knew what he was letting himself in for, at least so far as wine marketing was concerned. For many years he had been a wine merchant, and knew well the perils. Yet one look at the blue-stone sales and restaurant complex which he has since built among the vines is sufficient to understand why he was prepared to run the gauntlet. For Yarra Burn is situated in yet another of the beautiful corners of the Yarra Valley, unique in itself and linked only by the imposing beauty and grandeur which surround it — here provided by the sheer wall of the Warburton Range which rises directly behind the vineyard, and which is sometimes covered in winter snow.

After a somewhat uncertain start, David Fyffe has produced a series of lovely pinot noirs, cabernet sauvignons and chardonnays. The vineyards, planted on rich loam and helped by a rainfall which usually exceeds 1000 millimetres a year, produce fruit with an extra dimension of flavour. It is hard to single out one wine, but if forced to do so, I would choose the pinot noir. These have depth and style of varietal character, second only to the great pinot noirs of Yarra Yering, and I find David Fyffe's qualified enthusiasm for the wine difficult to understand. That, at least, is how I interpret his 1983 decision to divert the major part of the crop to sparkling wine, made for Yarra Burn by Dominique Landragin at Yellowglen. The 1981, 1982 and 1983 wines all showed deep, sappy pinot with marked burgundian overtones.

The Yarra Burn chardonnays are typically among the richest in the Yarra, and are very well made. Here the flavours run through the peach/apricot spectrum, with much less of the citric/grassy overtones of others in the region. The oak is also well handled. The cabernets have a distinct style, with a bell-clear structure, smooth berry flavours and a touch of mint. The balance of these wines, both between fruit and oak, and in the actual composition of the fruit, is exceptional.

Yarra Burn is also a compulsory eating spot for weekend lunches: the beautiful blue-stone restaurant—with its spit-roast lunch cooked at the enormous fireplace at the end of the room, bush band and audience participation—livens up an often staid Yarra Valley.

YARRA YERING
BRIARTY ROAD, GRUYERE

If I had to content myself with the wines of only one Yarra Valley vineyard, not a situation that I would contemplate with equanimity, my choice would have to fall on Yarra Yering. The wines made by Dr Bailey Carrodus may not be the most elegant and sophisticated, but they are consistently the most substantial, complex and satisfying wines—wines with the added bonus of a 10 to 20-year cellaring capacity. Dr Carrodus is an intensely private individual, happy to look out on the world, and far less happy when it attempts to look in on him. Right from the outset he has followed the dictates of his own beliefs and conceptions, and found it completely unnecessary to share them with others, let alone convert others to his point of view. So he keeps himself aloof from the other makers in the Yarra Valley; politely turns aside impertinent questions about his winemaking practices; and declines even to tell me how the vineyard is made up. In response to the question: "What are the vineyards, hectares by variety?" came the answer: "Oh dear, total 12 hectares."

What is known is that the vineyard includes some very exotic varieties, including tiny quantities of viognier and other unspecified Rhone Valley varieties. The major plantings are more conventional, with cabernet sauvignon the most important, followed by shiraz, and then small plantings of pinot noir, malbec, merlot and cabernet franc. The two principal white varieties, although again the plantings are small, are semillon and chardonnay.

The silty clay loam soil, interspersed with gravel, typifies the best viticultural *terroir* in the Yarra. Bailey Carrodus came to the district in 1969, having carefully considered alternatives in a number of parts of Australia, and only choosing this part of the Yarra Valley after a lengthy search. Furthermore, he came with a degree in oenology from Roseworthy College, and a Ph.D. gained for a thesis on plant physiology, his specialty during a lengthy career with the CSIRO. Thus it is hardly surprising that his vineyards produce magnificent fruit, even if the yield at around five tonnes per hectare is surprisingly low.

Notwithstanding all of this, the Yarra Yering red wines made between 1973 and 1977 have never been accepted by the mainstream of Australian opinion. I, like almost every other critic or judge, found them excessively volatile. Bailey Carrodus swears he will make me recant one of these days, and maybe he will. He has yet to provide the proof. The problem of volatility was initially deliberately induced by leaving the bungs loose in the casks, but rapidly got out of hand as the lactobacilli infected the oak. 1978 was a watershed year, and since that time the wines have gone from strength to strength.

The labelling continues to reflect Carrodus's idiosyncratic approach to wine. His principal red is simply labelled "Yarra Yering Dry Red No. 1". Principally cabernet sauvignon, with a little malbec and merlot included, it is a majestic wine. I would rank the vintages 1980, 1982, 1978, 1981 and 1979. The 1982 Dry Red No. 1 is a full, ripe, chewy wine with vanillan oak flavours and aromas, showing the concentration which the dry conditions leading up to vintage caused. The 1980 Dry Red No. 1 is magnificent in its balance and depth of flavour. Someone once described these wines as being willowy and delicate; whatever they aspire to, it is not those two characters. The Dry Red No. 2 is principally composed of shiraz, but with Carrodus's Rhone varieties included, along with the white grape viognier. This is in the best traditions of the Rhone Valley. These are excellent wines, with soft velvety flavours, a hint of spice here, cherry there. I consistently rank them, however, behind the No. 1 Dry Red, a habit which Carrodus finds more than slightly irritating. He himself will not be drawn into comparisons, and least of all choices, but stoutly defends his No. 2 style. Interestingly, it was made neither in 1975 nor 1978, and even in the best years is dwarfed in terms of production by the No. 1 wine.

All of these wines, however, pale into insignificance against the magnificence of the Yarra Yering pinot noir. The vintages leading up to 1982 seem in retrospect to be limbering-up exercises, demonstrating the capacity of the vineyard to produce startling varietal character, yet faltering at the last. Thus the 1981 wine, while packed with ripe pinot flavour, fell away somewhat on the finish which was rather hard and unbalanced. The 1982 Pinot Noir, indeed, also falters a fraction on the finish, which is a little green and stalky, but the aroma and fore and mid-palate flavours are stunning. This is pinot noir at its aristocratic, powerful best, an Australian equivalent to Romanée Conti. The 1983 Pinot Noir is a wine of entirely different style, voluptuous in its sweet strawberry/plum richness, round, soft and mouthfilling to the very end. It has more pinot noir character than any other Australian wine I have seen made from the variety, and for that reason alone I have no hesitation in classing it as the greatest Australian pinot yet made at the time of its release in late 1984. With total production amounting to less than 300 cases, it did not last long.

The Yarra Yering white wines are made to live in bottle. The dry white, principally semillon, is often hard and rather closed when young, but blossoms with age. The chardonnay, made in tiny quantities (seldom more than 100 cases a year) has at times shown the opulent richness of the reds, at other times the vagaries of small-scale white-winemaking.

YERINGBERG
MAROONDAH HIGHWAY, COLDSTREAM

Guillaume, Baron de Pury, was a cousin of Governor La Trobe, and one of the foremost members of the influential and wealthy Swiss families who were responsible for the establishment of the Yarra Valley wine industry. In 1862 he purchased part of the vast Yering Station from Paul de Castella, and named it Yeringberg, in recognition of the fact that much of it comprised a large hill which looked out over the main bulk of the Yering Station. It was on top of this hill that the magnificent cellars were built, and likewise the house. The property has never passed out of the hands of the family, the present owners being Guillaume de Pury, grandson of the founder,

and his wife Katherine.

Much of the production of Yeringberg was destined for export: by the late 1860s almost 30 hectares of vineyard were established, and these were subsequently expanded. The first winery has long since gone, but the one erected in 1885 still stands in near-new condition. The striking two-storey wooden building, with some passing similarities to the architecture of Chateau Tahbilk, must have been a showpiece of technological design in its day. The grapes were carried to the top storey in a hydraulic lift and then crushed into railway trucks which ran in either direction along the top storey on a miniature railway line. From here on the winery operated entirely on gravity. The red grapes would be deposited from the trucks into the open wooden fermenters; the whites into the press. At the conclusion of fermentation the wine would be fed into the oak casks and the vast stone cellars underneath the wooden structure.

The original vineyard was planted to shiraz, pinot noir, marsanne, trebbiano, verdelho, pinot gris, pinot blanc and gouais. It was for the marsanne that Yeringberg was most famous. Francois de Castella commented that, "Yeringberg has produced some of the finest white wines ever grown in the southern hemisphere". Bottles of this wine dating back to 1901 are still held at Yeringberg, with good bottles of the 1915 vintage still showing exceptional freshness and youth.

When in 1969 Guillaume de Pury was persuaded by friends to re-establish a tiny portion of the vineyard on the exact spot planted by his grandfather 100 years earlier, the first grape chosen was marsanne. With seven varieties, and only 1.6 hectares of vineyard in total, it is all something of a doll's-house operation, singularly at odds with the massive winery towering above. The plantings are now chardonnay (0.39 hectare), marsanne (0.36 hectare), pinot noir (0.35 hectare), cabernet sauvignon (0.25 hectare), merlot (0.11 hectare), rousanne (0.09 hectare) and malbec (0.05 hectare). The second decimal place is of significance when each vine counts. The rousanne is a recent arrival, designed to complement the marsanne. (In the Rhone Valley the two grapes are grown in tandem.)

It hardly needs saying that with over 400 hectares of prime grazing land, winemaking is little more than a hobby. Guillaume de Pury stoutly resists the urgings of others to increase the size of his vineyards. When the pressure to produce more chardonnay became too intense, and the desire appeared to have a few rows of rousanne, he simple removed the shiraz which had previously flourished.

In August 1984 I attended a retrospective tasting of the majority of the Yeringberg wines made to date. A cold did not help my evaluation, but the character of all of the wines came through clearly enough. Neither then nor at any other time have I been able to become enthusiastic about the marsanne. Whether the clones of 100 years ago were better or whether attitudes towards white wine have changed dramatically in the meantime, I do not know, but neither the Chateau Tahbilk nor the Yeringberg marsanne appeals, while those of Mitchelton are so coated with oak that the variety is unimportant. The wines do have some honeysuckle aromas on the bouquet which are not unattractive but the palate is usually chalky and dry, needing years in the bottle to soften sufficiently in order to appear attractive. In a seeming denial of that general observation, the 1983 Marsanne was the most attractive of the three tasted, followed by the 1980 and with the 1981 (hard and harsh) a distant third.

De Pury has been making chardonnay since 1979, and it is not hard to see why this wine is one of the favoured children of the vineyard. Of the three years tasted at the dinner, the 1981 was easily the best, with rich peachy/apricot fruit lifting both bouquet and palate. The 1979 Chardonnay also appealed, with some heavy burgundian characters, but tending to cloy on the finish. De Pury explained that he did not correct the acid in that year, as he has done subsequently. The 1979 showed some of the green herbaceous characters encountered elsewhere in the Valley, and it suffered by comparison. The 1984 Chardonnay, when eventually released, looks likely to be one of the best yet. A gold-medal-winner in the Chardonnay Class of the 1984 Victorian Wines Show, it has marked varietal aroma, with overtones of both honey and grapefruit, excellent texture and structure on the palate, and with very attractive smoky-oak flavours, followed by a lingering finish.

Six vintages of shiraz (1975 to 1980) fittingly culminated in the magnificent 1980 wine, the last from the vineyard. Intensely rich, with cassis/berry/spice aromas and flavours, it is a wine of immense power and depth. If ever there is to be a wine from Yeringberg to live for the next 100 years, it is this.

On the other hand I have to admit that the six cabernet sauvignons (1974 to 1980 inclusive but omitting 1978) were far more impressive as a range. Only the 1977, suffering from a bad attack of mercaptan in the bouquet, and rather mawkish on the palate, was anything less than outstanding. Once again the 1980 was outstanding, with ripe cassis-berry aromas on the bouquet allied with fairly marked oak. The palate is very full, ripe and sweet, almost voluptuous in its richness, and again the oak is still to integrate fully—a truly striking wine. The 1974 Cabernet Sauvignon was in the same class. The colour is still strong, with no hint of browning; it has some cigar-box complexities but with lingering fruit, and the palate is seemingly still developing: lively, sweet, berry/cherry flavours dominate. Next came the 1979, with strong, slightly minty fruit and again some new oak yet to integrate fully. It was followed by the 1975 (seeming to be simply an older version of the 1980) and the immensely powerful and robust 1976, with strong tannin and great depth. The 1983, a gold-medallion-winner in its class of the 1984 Victorian Wines Show, will uphold the quality and style of the line.

Of the pinot noirs from 1975 to 1980, the younger wines stood out. Neither the 1978, 1977 nor 1975 is especially attractive. The 1979 Pinot Noir has strong spicy fruit with just a touch of burgundian sulphide-like characters, a feature that appears again to induce a little bitterness on the finish of an otherwise full and rich palate. Two pinot noirs were made in 1980, one left in wood for far longer than the other. The "wood-matured" wine shows greater complexity; the conventional wine far more strawberry/plum fruit. I preferred the latter wine. Once again the 1983 is quite outstanding, winning two trophies at the 1984 Victorian Wines Show, and entrancing all the judges with the depth and smoothness of the fruit.

With total production less than 500 cases a year, and with no more than 150 cases of any one wine produced, it is hardly surprising that Yeringberg wine is extremely hard to come by. It is virtually all sold on mailing list (the winery is not open for cellar-door sales) and through a very few retailers. The wines are worth the effort.

South Australia

The colony of South Australia was founded in 1836, and vines followed almost immediately. In 1837 J. B. Hack planted cuttings which he had obtained at Launceston in Tasmania on the way to South Australia; George Stevenson followed suit the next year. These small garden plantings led to the first commercial vineyards, and to the competing claims of John Reynell, Richard Hamilton, Walter Duffield and John White to have made the first wine. Duffield has the best reported claim. The *South Australian Register* of 25 June 1845 recorded that he had made six hogsheads (175.5 litres) of wine and congratulated him on producing the first wine on a fully commercial scale. Duffield capitalised on his success by sending Queen Victoria a case of an 1844 white made from grapes grown in the Mount Lofty Ranges, and was promptly prosecuted for making wine without the requisite licence.

Numerous others followed hot on his heels. By 1839 there were over 60 varieties of grapes in the colony, while in 1840 a public meeting resolved to seek funds for the importation of 500,000 vines from the Cape of Good Hope. Public subscriptions were matched by a £100 subsidy from the government. In October 1841 57,000 cuttings arrived, somewhat less than the half-million originally proposed, but nonetheless providing the industry with a real boost. Inevitably the early years were marked by trial and error. Captain William Macarthur of Camden Farm provided both cuttings and advice, favouring the establishment of the classic European varieties. John Reynell tried pinot noir, but found it unsuited and switched his attention to Spanish varieties which John Morphett had imported from Jerez. On the other hand, rhine riesling succeeded from the outset on the slopes of the Barossa Valley.

John Reynell established his vineyards at Reynella in late 1838 or 1839; Dr Alexander Kelly planted Trinity Vineyard near Morphett Vale in the early 1840s; Dr Christopher Rawson Penfold at Magill in 1844; Johann Gramp at Jacob's Creek in 1847; Samuel Smith founded Yalumba in 1849; while Joseph Seppelt arrived in the Barossa Valley in 1851 with the intention of growing tobacco, but soon switched his attention to wine.

By 1847 there were 80 hectares of officially recorded vineyards; in 1856 there were 305 hectares; and by 1862 when Ebenezer Ward toured the vineyards, recording them in minutest detail for posterity, the figure had soared to 1934 hectares. In 1860 820,000 litres of wine were made; only five years later production had increased to 3.78 million litres. It was a rate of growth which simply could not be sustained: no sooner had South Australian vignerons started to open up markets in the far more populous states of Victoria and New South Wales, than a preferential duty

of six shillings a gallon (4.5 litres) was imposed, effectively closing those markets altogether.

In 1862 Patrick Auld formed the Australian Wine Company in London to distribute his Auldana wines in England. A few years earlier in 1858 John Reynell had sent a consignment to a London wine merchant who pronounced the wine to be undrinkable. He advised Reynell to tell his friends not to waste their time and money on seeking a market in England, but to confine their attentions to the colonies. Reynell ignored this gratuitous advice, and a shipment the following year to another merchant was far more favourably received. But substantial markets are not built overnight. Unable to sell their grapes, the vignerons turned to making their own wine, only to find the cure worse than the illness: a flood of immature and often poorly made wine engulfed both the local and English markets. Great damage was done to the reputation of South Australian wine, which caught both large and small, good and bad winemakers in its backlash. Thus Edward Salter sent 50 hogsheads (1462 litres) of wine to London in 1864; after waiting two years for an account of sales, he finally received it—but instead of a cheque, he received a demand for payment of £50 to cover excess shipping and warehousing costs. By 1877 the State's vineyards had fallen from their 1865 peak of 2683 hectares to 1685 hectares, and production of wine had declined even more dramatically to 1,497,500 litres.

Inevitably it was the larger and better producers who survived the shake-out. By the late 1870s Thomas Hardy was buying grapes from over 40 growers, selling his wine through agents spread across the length and breadth of the State. In a letter written in 1890 Edward Salter observed that in the aftermath of the depression ". . . gradually the small growers gave up winemaking and sold their grapes to other large makers. For the past fifteen years nearly all the wine in the Barossa has been made by five firms." This trend saw a marked improvement in wine quality: in June 1875 the _South Australian Register_ reported that: "Nearly all the worthless stuff of which there was such a quantity a few years ago has been turned into spirit by the distillers, and the stocks of wine now on hand are for the most part of good sound quality."

In the 30 years from 1884 to the outbreak of the First World War, the South Australian industry enjoyed a period of remarkable (and this time sustained) growth, which saw it become Australia's premier wine-producing State. It was aided in this by four factors: the opening up of the London market on a large scale; the devastation of the Victorian vineyards by phylloxera; the introduction of free trade following Federation; and the swing from table- to fortified-wine production (to which areas such as the Barossa Valley were ideally suited). 1884 was a watershed year: for the first time in two decades new plantings exceeded vine removals. But the 1858 hectares of vines had soared to 7085 hectares 10 years later, and although the rate of growth then slackened somewhat, it nonetheless continued right through to 1914 by which time there were 10,875 hectares under vine.

In 1889 South Australia produced 2,298,033 litres against Victoria's peak of 7,103,655. Twenty years later the positions had been reversed: South Australia in 1910 made over 15 million litres compared with Victoria's 4.5 million litres and New South Wales's contribution of around 3.6 million litres. From here on South Australia's domination of the industry was unchallenged by the other States: in 1930 its production of 55.8 million litres was more than 75 per cent of the Australian total, while the 1946 contribution of 91 million litres represented 80 per cent of Australia's production in that year.

The 1920s had seen a rapid progression of boom and bust, culminating in the Great Depression. Grape prices fell as low as £2 per tonne, far below the cost of production, with most wineries eking out an existence and producing almost exclusively fortified wine. Recovery was slow in the years leading up to the Second World War; while 1940 once again signalled the end of the export market, it somewhat surprisingly heralded a vast surge in domestic consumption from 16 million litres in 1939 to 40.5 million litres in 1945. This was due to the shortage of beer, the rationing of all forms of alcohol, and the presence of foreign servicemen. The first two factors, at least, continued to underpin the continued prosperity of the industry until the removal of beer rationing in 1953.

With the growth of the Riverland areas in New South Wales and Victoria, and to a lesser degree the establishment of so many new areas in Victoria, Western Australia and elsewhere, the contribution of South Australia now varies between 58 and 65 per cent according to the vagaries of the vintage. The 1984 vintage resulted in 200,891,000 litres of table and fortified wine (and 33,608,000 litres of distillation wine) from 283,841 tonnes of grapes. Total Australian production in 1984 was 348,403,000 litres, 8.4 per cent higher than the previous record production of 321.5 million litres in the 1980 vintage. That of South Australia was also the highest on record, 1.6 per cent greater than the 1982 vintage of 197.7 million litres.

While the dramatic changes evident in Victoria have not occurred to the same degree in South Australia, there have been substantial shifts in emphasis over the past two decades. These changes will continue to run their course through to the end of this century and, in all probability, beyond. The most significant change has been the establishment of the vineyards at Padthaway/Keppoch and the increase in the plantings at Coonawarra. When Ronald Haselgrove conceived his vision splendid for Coonawarra in the mid-1950s, there were around 100 hectares of vines in the south-east, as the area is now called, and production was less than 1000 tonnes. By 1981 this had increased to 23,000 tonnes and is projected to reach 43,900 tonnes in the year 2001. By contrast, if current trends continue, in the same 20-year span production of the Barrossa Valley will decline from 46,500 tonnes to 9100 tonnes. These forecasts were contained in a paper delivered to the Roseworthy Centenary Grape and Wine Symposium in May 1983 by Dr Richard Smart. He was careful also to point out that it was a deliberately simplistic analysis which quite certainly would not all come true, but which nonetheless established certain basic trends.

If the salinity problems which have caused so much trouble in some of South Australia's Riverland areas can be overcome, or at least contained, the contribution of this region—and particularly the area between Renmark and Loxton—will continue to be massive. Half of South Australia's output comes from this area now, and at least half is likely to come in the year 2001. The reason for this is easy enough to comprehend: the region is a highly efficient producer of grapes destined to fill the casks and flagons which account for 70 per cent of the annual consumption of table wine.

It is with the production of premium grapes destined for bottled wine that the changes are occurring. The trend is clearly away from the warmer areas, such as the floor of the Barossa Valley, to the hillsides which surround it and to areas such as Padthaway and Coonawarra. The Adelaide Hills region, extending in an arc from Mount Lofty up to the sides of the Eden Valley, offers the very real prospect of a new viticultural region able to offer grapes of a quality equal to anything Victoria or Tasmania can produce.

Morgan
Cadell
Bower
Mount Mary
Saddleworth
Marrabel
Sutherlands
"Murbko"
RIVERTON
EUDUNDA
"Murbko"
Hamilton
Hansborough
"Craigie Plains"
"Haylands"
MURRAY RIVER
Alma
Tarlee
Bagot Well
Owen
Stockyard Creek
Stockport
Blanchetown
Lock No 1
Pinery
KAPUNDA
Fords
Dutton
Wild Horse Plains
Long Plains
Hamley Bridge
Light River
"Portee"
Caloma
Mallala
Freeling
Greenock
Stockwell
Truro
Parham
Windsor
32
Moculta
Dublin
Wasleys
NURIOOTPA
Sedan
Swan Reach
Red Banks
Shea Oak Log
TANUNDA
ANGASTON
HENSCHKE
"Punyelroo"
Roseworthy College
Roseworthy
ORLANDO
Keyneton
Ridly Conservation Park
Bakara
GAWLER
Rowland Flat
STEINGARTEN
Nildottie
Two Wells
20
Lyndoch
YALUMBA: HEGGIES AND PEWSEY VALE
Cambrai
Ridly Conservation Park
Gawler R.
WYNNS' HIGH EDEN
Wongulla
Port Gawler
Williamstown
Eden Valley
MOUNT ADAM
Black Hill
Forster
Conservation Park
Virginia
South Para Reservoir
HOLMES ESTATE
Springton
Sanderston
Walker Flat
Warren Reservoir
CRANEFORD
"Numerous"
Saint Kilda
Snaylers C.
Purnong
Outer Harbour
Mount Pleasant
Tungkillo
Milendella
Teal Flat
Kersbrook
Apamurra
Punthari
ADELAIDE
Houghton
Gumeracha
Birdwood
Palmer
MANNUM
Bowhill
Mount Torrens
Ponde
Lowan Conservation Park
LOBETHAL
Reedy
Caloote
ENTERPRISE LENSWOOD
Harrogate
"Rompoota"
ASHBOURNE
WOODSIDE
Tepko
PETALUMA
Balhannah
"Konetta Downs"
Holdfast Bay
NAIRNE
Brukunga
Pallamana
SAINT VINCENT
Littlehampton
Kanmantoo
Mypolonga
COOLAWIN
STIRLING
MOUNT BARKER
Echunga
Balyarta
Callington
MURRAY BRIDGE
CLARENDON ESTATE
Mt Bold Resvr
Warla
Monarto
Rabila
Port Noarlunga
Bogie Ranges
South
Kangarilla
Macclesfield
Hartley
Monteith
Monteith
Noarlunga
Meadows
Woodchester
Ferries McDonald
McLAREN VALE
Conservation Park
TAILEM BEND
Port Willunga
Aldinga
Willunga
Ashbourne
STRATHALBYN
8
12
Aldinga Beach
Langhorne Creek
Sellicks Beach
Coxs Scrub Conservation Park
Wellington
Aldinga Bay
Mount Compass
Sandergrove
Tolderol
Carrickalinga Head
Myponga
Finniss
Point
Milang
Pomanda I
Normanville
Myponga
LAKE
Low Point
Yankalilla Bay
Conservation Park
Currency Creek
ALEXANDRINA
Yankalilla
Middleton
GOOLWA
Point McLeay
Ashville
Rapid Head
VICTOR
Port Elliot
Hindmarsh
Narrung
Rapid Bay
HARBOR
Island
"Narrung"
Second Valley
Yilki
Granite I
Delamere
Seal I
FLEURIEU
Rosetta Head
Barrages
LAKE
Cape
West I
ENCOUNTER
Murray Mouth
ALBERT
Jervis
Newland Head
BAY
Youngbusband
MENINGIE
Deep Creek Conservation Park
BACKSTAIRS PASSAGE
Coorong
National Park
PENINSULA COORONG
PRINCES HWY
1

Km. 0   10   20   30   40   50   60 Km.
Mi. 0   5   10   15   20   25   30   35 Mi.

ADELAIDE

Adelaide Hills

Over the next two or three decades we may reach some consensus in Australia as to whether any form of appellation control is desirable on a national scale. Neatly defined regional areas with no boundary-definition problems, such as Mudgee and the Margaret River, have already answered that question in the affirmative. As I write these words, the Victorian government, no doubt from the best of motives, is pushing the whole of Victoria towards some form of appellation control. With an eye to its political antecedents, it prefers the more bourgeois term certification. The net result is the same: a committee, the ultimate form of democracy, which sits down and writes a set of rules. More often than not these rules are the product of the lowest common denominator, and serve much the same purpose as Linus's blanket.

So far there are no nice warm feelings in South Australia. Depending on one's viewpoint, there is either the free enterprise freedom of choice or virtual anarchy. Certainly when it comes to the question of defining the Adelaide Hills (and inevitably thereby the extremities of the Barossa Valley and the Southern Vales) there is endless disagreement. The absence of any authoritative pronouncement has led me to regard the Adelaide Hills as that remarkably coherent strip of land running from Keyneton in the north through the Eden Valley to Mount Pleasant, and thence south through Birdwood, Woodside, Bridgewater, Stirling and thence around through Mount Barker to Clarendon. Drawn on a large-scale map, the road connecting these points is a firmly drawn more-or-less straight line, wandering only between Mount Barker and Clarendon. It is an undeniable umbilical cord joining north and south.

The difficulty, of course, is that the Southern Vales wish to treat Clarendon as part of their inheritance, while the Barossa Valley squeals in rage at the thought of Eden Valley and Keyneton being excised from it. Yet in terms of *terroir* and climate, the Adelaide Hills have nothing in common with the grape-growing areas lying beneath them. The Hills area is unified by lying at an altitude of above 400 metres; the rainfall is far higher than that of the lowlands, as is the humidity. Most importantly of all, the centigrade heat-degree summation is below 1200 in most regions, with the grapes ripening up to three weeks after similar varieties grown in Coonawarra.

If one accepts my definition of the Adelaide Hills area, viticulture and winemaking have been carried out for decades at both the northern and southern ends. Indeed, at the northern end one of the outstanding nineteenth-century vineyards, that of Joseph Gilbert at Pewsey Vale, was established. Thus it is that the vineyards and wineries which I group in this area are a remarkably disparate lot. Viticultural practice and winemaking vary from traditional and basic to state-of-the-art high technology. But in the long term such divisions as may exist will be more than compensated for by the imperatives of climate, which will weld the region together. It is an exciting region, and one we shall hear much more of in the future.

ASHBOURNE
LENSWOOD

Ashbourne has had a somewhat peripatetic existence since its label first appeared with the 1980 vintage Coonawarra Cabernet Sauvignon. Ashbourne is owned by Geoffrey and Judith Weaver; Geoff Weaver is better known as Hardy's Siegersdorf winemaker, for many years in charge of its white wines.

Thomas Hardy has a singularly enlightened attitude to the extracurricular activities of its winemakers: Weaver has Ashbourne, Geoff Merrill has Stratmer Vineyards. The key to the seeming incompatibility is that both men keep the level of their own label production to an absolute minimum. Thus the greatest quantity of any of the Ashbourne releases so far was the 700 cases of the 1980 Coonawarra Cabernet Sauvignon. This goes a very long way to avoiding the conflict of interest which might otherwise occur, and is a very clever way from the Thomas Hardy viewpoint of allowing a winemaker to express his individuality, while at the same time conforming to large-company winemaking discipline.

At the outset Geoff and Judith Weaver were partners in the Forbes' Craneford Vineyard at Springton. When Colin Forbes married it was mutually agreed that the Weavers would establish their own business, and thus Ashbourne came to be.

Six hundred cases of a Clare Valley rhine riesling were made in 1982, and 530 cases of a Coonawarra rhine riesling made in 1983. All of the wines are made by Geoff Weaver at Petaluma, a 15-minute drive from home or work. But in February 1982 Ashbourne put down roots, when 27 hectares were purchased at Lenswood. In the lee of Mount Lofty, it is in the same subregion as that of Tim Knappstein's Enterprise Vineyard, and close by that of the Petaluma developments. Two hectares of rhine riesling were planted in 1982, and were expected to provide their first commercial crop of around 2.5 tonnes per hectare in 1985. With a planting density of 2700 vines per hectare, the ultimate yields will of course be much higher than this. The vines survived (just) the appalling 1983 bushfires, and a further 1.2 hectares of chardonnay, two hectares of cabernet sauvignon and 0.4 hectare of merlot were established in 1983.

Over 15 hectares of the block is suitable for planting but development will proceed slowly. For the foreseeable future the wine will continue to be made at Petaluma. 1985 was the first year in which Lenswood fruit was used, and the last in which grapes from other regions were employed, with a projected output of 500 cases of Coonawarra rhine riesling.

It barely needs saying that wine quality to date has been exemplary, and once Lenswood comes into full production even greater wines should be released under the Ashbourne label.

CLARENDON ESTATE
MAIN ROAD, CLARENDON

Clarendon Estate is one of the more ghostly inhabitants of the Adelaide Hills. It commenced business in 1983, offering a range of wines which it said "had been contract-made at various wineries

according to our negotiations and specifications". It also had established vineyards at Clarendon, with the intention to plant a new vineyard on a 30-hectare property at Echunga, near Mount Barker and just south of Bridgewater.

The principals behind Clarendon Estate include Nicholas Baranikow and Andrew Garrett. Their initial choice of wines was undeniably excellent, although precisely what connection they have with the Adelaide Hills in a viticultural sense is not clear. One can only take Clarendon Estate at its word and assume that it does intend to be a long-term bona fide resident of the area. To be fair, one can say the same of Ashbourne or Enterprise.

The initial Clarendon Estate releases comprised a 1982 Rhine Riesling (a clean, pleasant wine, although it lacked distinction, a view I must say was not shared by the judges of the 1982 Adelaide Wine Show who awarded it a gold medal); a 1982 Fumé, made from a blend of semillon and sauvignon blanc (an excellent wine with very sophisticated oak handling and attractive light, lemony fruit); a 1982 Beerenauslese (made from a blend of 90 per cent rhine riesling, sauvignon blanc and semillon, which won two gold medals and which was reviewed favourably, but which I found unattractive); and a 1980 Cabernet Sauvignon. This was said to be made from grapes harvested from the Clarendon Estate vineyards, and in a large masked line-up of cabernets it did show distinct cool-climate characters. The aroma is a complex amalgam of vanilla-bean/tobacco characters, while the palate had distinct grassy/wintergreen flavours. The wine was perhaps lacking a little generosity, but it was quite impressive.

Subsequent releases have also been well received, although the source of the grapes is a moving target. Time alone will tell where Clarendon Estate is finally headed.

COOLAWIN
WINDEBANKS ROAD, HAPPY VALLEY

The Adelaide Hills must seem more like those of the Shaky Islands, for Coolawin, a long-time resident winery, was sold at the end of 1984 to Norman's Wines of the Adelaide Plains. The Light family continues to own the vineyards, and in particular those situated at Bakers Gully, which have provided Coolawin with much of its excellent material.

It seems unlikely that the Coolawin label will continue to be marketed. For that reason alone I have not reviewed its many quite excellent wines. I wish its new owners well, but it does seem to me a pity that the industry—and in particular the retail industry—could not find an adequate place for Coolawin. For no-one could deny that the wine quality was there.

CRANEFORD
WILLIAMSTOWN ROAD, SPRINGTON

The Craneford Wine Company was established by Colin and Jenny Forbes in the latter half of the 1970s, releasing its first wine in 1978. Craneford produces around 60 per cent of its annual crush from three hectares of rhine riesling grown in the Barossa Ranges near Springton; the wine is made at Petaluma under Colin Forbes' direction. Forbes is yet another of the young brigade of winemakers who do their own thing as a sideline; in what might be termed real life, Colin Forbes is a winemaker at Saltrams.

As with many of his contemporaries, any conflict of interest is avoided by the tiny size of the operation. Less than 1000 cases of wine are made each year, and virtually all are sold by mailing list. A few of the more enterprising retailers occasionally carry small stocks.

As one would expect, the quality of the wine is exemplary, with the rhine riesling showing the intensity and depth of flavour of the best Eden Valley wines of this variety. One hectare of chardonnay yet to come into bearing will offer a second string to the Craneford bow, and will no doubt be eagerly sought after.

ENTERPRISE LENSWOOD
2 PIONEER AVENUE, CLARE

Tim Knappstein's Lenswood Vineyard, perched high in the Adelaide Hills, is climatically far distant from the Clare Valley. It was purchased several years ago but Knappstein is uncertain how many surface hectares are, so steep is the terrain. Nominally 18 hectares, it is probably more than 20 in size. Over 5.5 hectares had been planted by the end of 1984. The vines were planted on an eight-foot by four-foot (2.43-metre by 1.22-metre) spacing, utilising a vertical curtain trellis. "Rheinhessen rather than French", observes Knappstein.

The rate of development of the vineyard will depend on the demands on the Clare Valley Winery; the latter has a continuing capital investment pro-

gramme which has first call on cash flow. But Knappstein sees Lenswood (amongst other things) providing him with naturally botrytised grapes—sauvignon blanc, rhine riesling and even possibly semillon—to add flexibility to his options. It will also produce the classic red varieties, and these will be regarded, too, as providing flexibility. Knappstein explains:

> If I thought Lenswood added some desirable characteristics to our Clare wines, then sure, I would like to blend it. On the other hand, I want to keep some parcels of it quite separate. If something quite outstanding came along, I would market it, but the basis of Enterprise wines will always be the Clare Valley.

HENSCHKE
KEYNETON

Henschke underlines the immense variation in climate and *terroir* that one finds close to the Barossa Valley. Keyneton, where the Henschke winery and home vineyards are situated, is a little over 10 kilometres south-east of Angaston, and well within the boundaries of what has traditionally been regarded as the Barossa Valley. For the reasons I have explained earlier, I am nonetheless treating Henschke as within the Adelaide Hills.

Rainfall is still very sparse at around 500 millimetres a year, and the Henschkes do not use supplementary water. Yields from the Keyneton vineyards, with a soil of podsolic sandy loam overlying heavy clay, are extremely low. Shiraz produces three tonnes per hectare on average, and rhine riesling 2.6 tonnes per hectare. The family has two quite separate vineyards one at Keyneton (at 450 metres); the other smaller one at an even higher altitude in the Eden Valley. Shiraz (40 hectares) and rhine riesling (35 hectares) dominate the plantings. There are in addition four hectares of white frontignac, three hectares of semillon, and one hectare each of chardonnay, chenin blanc, gewurtztraminer, cabernet sauvignon and malbec.

Seventy-five per cent of the annual crush is produced from these vineyards; the remaining 25 per cent (chiefly cabernet sauvignon and smaller quantities of semillon, chenin blanc and gewurtztraminer) is bought in from contract-growers in the region. With a 1984 production of around 35,000 cases, the firm of C. A. Henschke & Company is a very important one, particularly given the high reputation in which the wines are held.

Its origins go back to the arrival of Johann Christian

Henschke, who came to South Australia in 1842, settling at Bethany near Tanunda. His son, Paul Henschke, first planted grapes on the small farm his father had started at Keyneton. Following Paul's death in 1914, *his* son Paul Alfred extended the plantings and also the cellars. For a time fortified-wine sales boomed, but in the 1930s and 1940s the scale of operations was substantially reduced. It was not until 1949, when 25-year-old Cyril Henschke persuaded his father to renovate and extend the winery, that winemaking once again became an important part of the family's activities. Until this time the limited output had been sold entirely in bulk, and, as well as extending the cellars, Cyril Henschke began to bottle and label the wine at the cellars.

By the time fifth-generation Stephen Henschke, who studied winemaking at Geisenheim, took control following the death of his father in 1979, Henschke's wines had a formidable reputation. Henschke had earlier obtained a Bachelor of Science degree from Adelaide University, majoring in biochemistry and botany. This reputation was built chiefly on two red wines: Hill of Grace, named after the nearby Gnadenberg Lutheran church, and Mount Edelstone, or Noble Stone. Of the two Hill of Grace is by far the most eagerly sought after. Made from very old shiraz vines, it is an immense and very traditional wine style. The black label with its silver lettering was decades in front of its time when first introduced, but I cannot count myself as one of its disciples. No matter, for it invariably sells out as soon as it is released. Outstanding vintages have been 1962, 1972, 1978 and 1980. Mount Edelstone is a slightly less massive and leathery style, with the 1980 the most impressive of the wines of recent years. I believe it may have had some cabernet sauvignon included in it; it is a beautifully elegant wine, with some grassy flavours and outstanding mid-palate structure.

The best of the 1980s is the 1981 Cyril Henschke Cabernet Sauvignon, a wine made by Stephen in memory of his father. Deep purple in colour, with an aromatic and scented minty, rich aroma, and a palate redolent of Ribena/plum/cherry flavours, it understandably had an illustrious show career. Some of the Henschke reds have worried me because of mercaptan, but this wine was (and is) beautifully clean, and has enough fruit to take it comfortably into the 1990s.

Henschke has also produced a wide array of white varietal wines over the years. The quality of these has varied from quite magnificent to somewhat less than drinkable, but happily with more successes than failures. Obviously enough, with the substantial plantings of rhine riesling, it has been this wine which has carried the banner. I drank my last bottle of 1964 Rhine Riesling late in the 1970s, the last reminder of a South Australian odyssey made in 1968. The wine was tiring but still gave great pleasure. The 1972 vintage was one of the outstanding Barossa rhine rieslings of that year, and at 10 years of age was still drinking quite beautifully. Other vintages seem to have suffered from an excess of sulphur dioxide, and more recently from what I take to be yeast-derived volatility.

Like many other South Australian makers in recent times, Henschke has produced some wood-matured semillon. The 1982 vintage was a lovely wine, with sensitive oak handling, good acid and enough mid-palate fruit to see the wine develop for at least four or five years. In the same year an attractive dry white frontignac was made, devoid of any sugar and with that marvellous spicy/grape flavour which frontignac alone can give.

HOLMES ESTATE
MAIN STREET, SPRINGTON

Leon and Leonie Holmes purchased a 40-hectare property at an altitude of 500 metres in the Springton Ranges, between the towns of Mount Pleasant and Springton in 1973. Ten hectares of vines were established the following year, and the plantings have now been built up to a total of 12 hectares comprising rhine riesling (six hectares) and cabernet sauvignon and shiraz (three hectares each). The mountain soils are a sandy loam over a gravelly clay base, and the lack of irrigation (coupled with the high winds which prevail in the area) keep yields down to a pitifully low level. Cabernet sauvignon averages one tonne per hectare, shiraz and rhine riesling 2.5 tonnes per hectare. The compensation is, as ever, in the high-quality fruit which results in most vintages.

With an annual crush which aspires to reach 40 tonnes but which in fact seldom exceeds 20 tonnes, production is tiny. Since the end of the 1970s it has been marginally supplemented by some merlot purchased from Langhorne Creek, to produce a very successful cabernet merlot blend. Nonetheless, even the biggest releases seldom exceed 500 cases. Amidst all of this it is somewhat strange to find that the Holmes have an extremely active and efficient mailing list, with a quite unique letter going out to their "dear friends" twice a year. Anyone who receives it has the distinct feeling that they must in some way be related or, at the very least, that they have known the Holmes family for a very long time. At a more practical level the Holmes also pioneered a wine futures offer. First used over five years ago, it offers wines of the current vintage at the time they are made, with delivery anything between six and 18 months thereafter. Thus the 1984 vintage wines were offered in May of that year for $35 a dozen. When the first of the 1984 releases was offered by the bottle at the cellar door in September 1984 (the so-called May wine, the late-harvest rhine riesling of that year) it was on sale for $6 per bottle. Fifty per cent of the wine of each year is sold this way, and it clearly is a system which works as well for the Holmes as it does for the members of their little club.

In 1978 the Holmes purchased an old stone blacksmith shop in the town of Springton which has for many years been their cellar-door sales area. Leonie Holmes runs a restaurant in the building, and food is available continuously from 10 a.m. to 5 p.m. Wine can be purchased by the glass (or, of course, by the bottle) with the meal. Prior to the 1984 vintage a new winery and laboratory were completed at the back of the tasting room.

The rhine rieslings are made with up to 24 hours' skin contact: they are picked and crushed in the vineyard, with the juice transported to the winery at Springton in a small stainless-steel tank with a drainer enclosed. The juice drains from the container into the stainless fermentation tank overnight. While the Holmes are confident this will overcome the problems of oxidation which have affected one or two of their earlier rhine rieslings, the wines will still be very big in body. Fermentation is lengthy, under strictly controlled temperature conditions.

The 1980 Cabernet Merlot was very attractive, and all Holmes wines are as honest as the day is long.

MOUNT ADAM
HIGH EDEN ROAD,
HIGH EDEN RIDGE, EDEN VALLEY

It may well be 100 years or more before the full importance of the contribution of the Wynn family to the development of the Australian wine industry is put into perspective. First Samuel Wynn and then David Wynn showed a breadth of vision and a depth of courage rarely encountered. It is true the family has left its name to Wynn Winegrowers, one of the largest and most successful Australian wine companies. It is also generally recognised that David Wynn

was largely responsible on the one hand for saving Coonawarra, and on the other hand for the commercialisation of the wine cask. But these are only points in a complex fabric of innovative thought and commercial acumen which spread across all facets of the Australian wine industry. What is more, the eagle of Mount Adam is only now emerging as a fledgling from its nest: third-generation Adam Wynn is at the commencement of a winemaking career which promises to add another dimension to the Wynn family story.

By the end of the 1960s David Wynn had fully understood both the limitations of many of the then-existing viticultural areas, and the prime importance of *terroir* and climate in determining wine quality. He could also see the day coming when he would wish to sever his connection with the company he had founded, which was headed towards public listing. So he commenced the search for a vineyard site for his family. It ended on the high Eden Ridge, at the top of the hills which separate the Eden Valley from the Barossa. In 1969 the property now known as Mount Adam was acquired, and three years later establishment of the vineyards commenced. The rootlings came from the Modbury Nursery which Wynns had established, and which was the commercial source of the first new clones of premium varieties to come into South Australia for more than half a century. As I have said elsewhere, the limitation then and now on new clones has cost South Australia dearly, even if it may have helped keep phylloxera out. I have heard it argued that South Australia would have been better served with phylloxera, if that were the price to be paid for improved clones. I should perhaps add that the situation has changed for the better since the start of this decade.

The rate of development at Mount Adam was leisurely. There are now 32 hectares of vineyard, of which only half were in bearing as at 1984. Because of the very cool climate and wind factor, the vines take far longer to become established than in most areas. It is not anticipated that full production will be reached until around 1990. The plantings comprise chardonnay (22 hectares in all, with seven hectares in bearing in 1984); rhine riesling (5.25 hectares, all in bearing); pinot noir (three hectares planted, of which 1.4 hectares are in bearing); and cabernet sauvignon (0.6 hectare, all in bearing).

While yields are very low— 100 tonnes of grapes were produced in 1984, and it is not expected that the estate-grown crush will ever exceed 250 tonnes— grape quality is excellent. The altitude ensures frequent mist and cloud cover, which keeps the soil moist; yet the afternoon winds tend to dry the bunches and foliage, eliminating unwanted moulds and infections. The vineyard slopes towards the east, thus exposing the vines to the morning sun, and reducing the impact of the hot afternoon sun. The vineyard did not produce a commercial crop until 1979. In that year, and in the ensuing years up to and including 1983, the wines were made at the Roseworthy Agricultural College with input from the Wynn family. Part of the wine was released under the Roseworthy label, and small quantities under the Mount Adam label.

Early in 1984 I tasted a range of these Roseworthy wines. The 1981 Riesling and the 1982 Rhine Riesling both showed intense fruit, with that typical lime-juice aroma and flavour which is vaguely suggestive of botrytis, but which is in fact nothing more than a regional (and climatic) manifestation. It is the same character as that produced by the slightly lower Eden Valley Vineyards, but in a more concentrated form. The only criticism of the wines was a slightly hard finish, a common-enough occurrence given the volume of mid-palate flavour.

The 1979 Chardonnay was soft, over-oaked and no more than gently pleasant. But the 1981 Chardonnay was quite outstanding—it has pungent, intense buttery/ripe aromas with a tang to prevent the bouquet from cloying; the palate shows rich varietal character, complex, long and full, with marvellous acid on the finish to give lift and balance. A rather curious blend of pinot noir and cabernet sauvignon made in 1980 was adequate but rather pedestrian, but the 1979 Cabernet Sauvignon showed all of the style and finesse one would expect from a cool-climate vineyard: an attractive touch of cedary/ leathery oak intermingled with gently herbaceous fruit.

While these wines were being made, Adam Wynn was in France studing at the University of Bordeaux for three years. On graduation he topped his class, and then gained further experience in Burgundy before moving to California to study the newest developments in winery equipment and winemaking technology. It was thus a formidably equipped young winemaker who returned to Australia to join with his father David in planning the winery, which was completed in time for the 1984 vintage. Opened with pomp and circumstance in the presence of virtually everyone of note in the Australian wine industry, the winery is a *tour de force* in planning, and immaculately equipped. It has one of the two Demoisey polygrap grape crushers in Australia (Jeffrey Grosset has the other), a marvellous machine

which I watched working in Burgundy in 1983; the ultimate in Willmes presses (the TP6 tank press); a must chiller, and special variable capacity stainless-steel tanks provide everything that is required for the highest-quality winemaking. The striking winery building is clad with a special steel designed to rust, with a subtly changing colour that blends in with the striking landscape. It is a winemaker's Garden of Eden.

At the end of 1984 a further release of Mount Adam wines was made, including the first release from the new winery. The three wines were a 1984 Rhine Riesling, a 1983 Pinot Noir and a 1982 Chardonnay. The two older wines were, of course, made at Roseworthy. The chardonnay is by far the most successful wine of the three, and is in the Olympian class of the 1981 vintage. Similar in structure, it has rather more melon/grapefruit aromas and flavours, with a potent and authoritative palate, and the oak held nicely in restraint. The pinot noir was disappointing, and the rhine riesling I found very curious. Against all the odds, there seemed to me to be some slight pinking or browning in the colour, a truly ominous sign. However, the wine gave no hint of oxidation in the aroma, with voluminous aromatic fruit in the tropical spectrum. The wine had a full palate but rather hard finish. The wine was assessed in November 1984; I do not think it is fair to make a final judgement.

ORLANDO STEINGARTEN
TRIAL HILL, EAST BAROSSA RANGES

The cash flow from wines such as Barossa Pearl allowed Orlando's managing director, Colin Gramp, to tackle in 1962 a hillside on the eastern face of the Barossa Range behind Rowland Flat. There was no earth to speak of, the surface (and the subsoil) being a decomposed schist rock, a form of soft shale and similar to many of the rocky vineyards of Germany. The Steingarten Vineyard (Garden of Stones) was painstakingly established at a height of 490 metres. The "soil" was created by breaking up the stone first with bulldozers and dynamite, and thereafter by hand with hammers.

Recognising the impact of the high altitude, poor soil and cooler growing season on vine vigour, ultra-close spacing was chosen. In the average Australian vineyard there are 1600 to 1700 vines per hectare; in Steingarten there are 6000 vines per hectare. This European spacing was carried further by the staking and pruning methods: a single stake for each vine, with two arms tied together at the top of the stake forming a heart shape. This proved unsuccessful because of the high winds, and eventually a conventional trellising system was installed, although the close spacing remained.

Vine vigour—or rather lack of it—has been all Orlando expected. Only in the most exceptional years had yield reached five tonnes per hectare; while in 1973, 1974, 1975 and 1977 no wine at all was made. Until 1976 only four vintages had been made in sufficient quantities to warrant a semi-commercial release—1968, 1970, 1972 and 1976. Yield overall has been less than 2.5 tonnes per hectare, and the quantities of wine made up to the end of the 1970s ranged between 50 and 250 cases per year.

Orlando, one suspects, has a love-hate relationship with the vineyard. The Orlando winemakers do not claim it produces their greatest white wine, but its very scarcity inevitably puts that suggestion into consumers' minds. Expensive it may be, but it will never be commercially self-supporting. The wind and hail which decimated almost half of the vintages of the 1970s will do so again in the future, and drought years such as 1983 will achieve the same result.

Steingarten's value lies as a loss leader; as a tribute to and a signal of Orlando's determination to produce high-quality wines of distinctly different character. In recognition of this Orlando increased the plantings at Steingarten at the end of the 1970s and future releases will increase to around 500 cases per year.

A few years ago I chaired a comparative tasting of all of the Orlando Steingarten wines made between 1966 and 1980. Three distinct styles emerged: the light-bodied wines of 1969, 1971, 1972 and 1980; the full-bodied, developed, basically dry wines of 1966, 1967, 1968 and 1970; and finally the spatleses made in 1976, 1978 and 1979. As from the mid-1970s Orlando felt that great though the intensity of wines such as the 1968 and 1970 was, the style would have been even more complete and better balanced had the grapes been picked later and residual sugar been retained. The tasting certainly proved this correct: the 1976 and 1979 wines are quite magnificent. Yet in ultra-cool years such as 1980 it is simply not possible to achieve sufficient ripeness to allow spatlese style to be made, so in that year a marvellously fine and elegant drier wine was made.

PETALUMA
SPRING GULLY ROAD, PICCADILLY

Others may vacillate, but the commitment of Petaluma to the Adelaide Hills is absolute and irrevocable. Yet it, too, in its formative days was little more than a pretty face, a label that was attached to bottles of wine made from diverse sources of grapes which were processed at the Riverina College of Advanced Education, where Brian Croser was at the time senior lecturer in oenology. The first Petaluma release was a spatlese rhine riesling made from grapes grown in the Mitchelton/Tahbilk region. A bottle tasted at the end of 1984 was in astonishing condition, causing me to regret my impetuosity in consuming most of my bottles many years ago.

A traminer followed in 1977; anyone wishing to unsettle the normally positive and aggressive Brian Croser should delicately raise the question of his seemingly high regard for that variety. More serious was the making in the same year of his first chardonnay, with fruit from Cowra. This wine has proved an object lesson in demonstrating that Australian chardonnay can, indeed, grow steadily in bottle; the wine is still fine, crisp and elegant with absolutely no indication of becoming coarse or flabby. A bottle included as a "wild card" in an extensive tasting in 1983 of French white burgundies from the 1978, 1979 and 1980 vintages was rated very highly by a group of experienced judges. The comment was that it needed more time.

1978 saw the second of the chardonnays made, again at a home away from home because the Petaluma Winery in Spring Gully Road, Piccadilly, was erected later that year. By far the richest of the Cowra chardonnays, it was one of the first wines to show the sophisticated oak handling which is the hallmark of Petaluma. Excellent though the wine is, there is little to be gained from cellaring it.

By 1978 Croser had left Riverina College and commenced the consulting business which has been so successful. One of the first clients was the Evans Wine Company, which had recently purchased vineyards in Coonawarra and in the Clare Valley. The death of Peter Fox led to a radical reorganisation of the fairly complex arrangements that had developed between Petaluma, the Evans Wine Company and Adelaide Holdings Limited. The net result was the partnership between Brian Croser, Len Evans and Denis Horgan (the owner of Leeuwin Estate), formed to acquire Adelaide Holdings' interests and to simplify the Petaluma structure. A fourth partner, Colin Ryan, joined in 1983; and in March 1985 the champagne house of Bollinger became a fifth (equal) shareholder.

A consulting business was separately established. Dr Tony Jordan became a partner with Brian Croser in Oenotec Pty Limited, which is run as an entirely separate business. But life, it seems, cannot stay simple for long with Brian Croser in the driving seat. The Coonawarra Vineyard, the Clare Vineyard and much of the development in the Adelaide Hills is now being undertaken by an associated company, Hills Vineyard Development Company.

It is this company, in conjunction with Brian Croser and Tony Jordan in their respective personal capacities, which is coordinating the extensive plantings in the Adelaide Hills around Piccadilly and Bridgewater. Thirty-six hectares of chardonnay, eight hectares of pinot noir and a little over one hectare of merlot have been established, all on the closest-possible spacing of over 3000 vines per hectare. Certain of the blocks have been chosen specifically for producing grapes to be made into table wine, but the majority of the plantings are dedicated to the highly ambitious sparkling-wine venture which Petaluma commenced.

In 1984 the old Bridgewater Mill was purchased, an historic stone building which during the course of 1985 will be converted into champagne cellars and cellar-door tasting facilities. It will ultimately incorporate a large restaurant. Cold-room facilities and presses will be established throughout the Adelaide Hills, with the grapes being picked into small plastic-lined containers and pressed immediately. The cold juice will then be taken back to Petaluma for fermentation and for bottling; thereafter the wine will be taken to Bridgewater for its second fermentation and yeast lees maturation.

Experimental quantities of sparkling wine made from Adelaide Hills fruit were laid down in 1984. The first commercial vintage is expected in 1985, for release in November-December 1986. The wine will spend between 18 and 30 months on yeast lees, depending on the character of the fruit and the style desired. Production is planned to increase ultimately to 20,000 cases per year.

The involvement of Bollinger as a partner will be of immense importance to Petaluma. It is very significant that Bollinger chose to become an equal shareholder—in Bollinger's terminology, an equal partner—in the overall operation, rather than simply forming a joint venture for the production of sparkling wine. Indeed, Bollinger made it clear that its role in the sparkling-winemaking would be limited to that of an adviser. Bollinger's chairman of directors, Christian

Bizot, was emphatic that just because Bollinger knew how to make fine champagne did not mean that it knew how to make fine sparkling wine in Australia. It looks to the Petaluma winemaking team, headed by Brian Croser, to do the job. Conversely, Bollinger can be expected to play a wider role, providing both marketing support overseas and no doubt adding significantly to the financial and other strengths of the Australian operations of Petaluma.

Ultimately the Petaluma Chardonnay, which I left in 1978, will be made exclusively from Adelaide Hills-grown grapes. But in 1979 it was still sourced from Cowra; a marvellously balanced wine, it is now reaching its best. The 1981 Chardonnay was 50 per cent Coonawarra and 50 per cent Cowra material; as each year passes, Petaluma appears to fine-tune and hone its winemaking procedures, with the oak handling becoming ever more sophisticated. A feature of this is the prolonged storage of the barrels in cold-rooms, still a fairly rare practice in Australia, but which radically alters both the rate of oak pick-up and the flavour extracted from the oak. The 1982 vintage is 80 per cent Coonawarra and 20 per cent Cowra, while the 1983, due for release in the second half of 1985, is 80 per cent Coonawarra, 10 per cent Clare Valley and 10 per cent Clarendon material.

Petaluma is also a very important contract winemaker for a surprisingly large number of winemakers throughout South Australia. It has very close ties with Wirra Wirra—most of the Wirra Wirra wine is made at Petaluma; similarly Santa Rosa in McLaren Vale, Jud's Hill in the Clare Valley, Ashbourne and Craneford all rely on Petaluma. The highly efficient and superbly equipped winery consistently produces wines of the very highest quality. (I discuss its Coonawarra-sourced wines at page 417.)

YALUMBA: HEGGIES AND PEWSEY VALE
FLAXMAN VALLEY ROAD,
EAST BAROSSA RANGES

When in 1961 Yalumba determined to plant a vineyard in the East Barossa ranges, there was no difficulty in choosing an appropriate name. Joseph Gilbert had established a magnificent vineyard and winery 100 years earlier, known as Pewsey Vale. When Joseph Gilbert commenced its development in the 1840s the area was considered to be wild and remote. By 1862, when Ebenezer Ward visited it in the course of writing his series on the "Vineyards and Orchards of South Australia" for the *Adelaide Advertiser*, he summarised Gilbert's achievements thus:

It may be a comparatively easy matter for a wealthy merchant, or gentleman of ample private fortune, to found, by the mere outlay of capital, a magnificent mansion and elegant pleasure-grounds in the vicinity of a centre of population, but it is a very different thing to establish all the useful and ornamental qualifications experience and taste can suggest upon no more convenient foundation than a rugged site in a mountain vastness of a comparatively young colony, 40 miles [70 kilometres] distant from its metropolis. Yet Mr. Gilbert has accomplished even more than this, for he has besides extended the influence of his enterprise and judgment to the remotest corner of an estate comprising something like 11,000 acres [4453 hectares] of land.

Ward went on to describe the vineyard in detail:

On the vineyard there is now about 16 acres [6.5 hectares] in full bearing. Mr. Gilbert commenced planting it to the north of the house in 1847, when about one acre [0.4 hectare] was put in with Verdeilho, Gouais, and Riesling for white wines, and Shiraz and Carbonet for red. In 1855, the bearing wood of all the vines was destroyed by frost on the 12th November, and the head had afterwards to be taken off with saws. Since 1847, Mr. Gilbert has almost every year increased the extent of his vineyard, planting Verdeilho and Riesling for the white wines, and Shiraz and Carbonet for the red. Although in the first instance many of the vines were planted at a less distance apart, they stand now throughout the vineyard at 8 feet by 4 [2.43 metres by 1.22]. The plough, horse-hoe,, and scarifier, are freely used between the rows to keep down the weeds, hand labour being largely employed for the same purpose between the vines. When Mr. Gilbert commenced planting he staked his vines, and pruned them short. Finding that system unsatisfactory in its results, he reared standards, but equally dissatisfied with that practice, he discarded it for trellising and long pruning. Now the whole of the vines are trellised upon wires, with the exception of about three acres [1.2 hectares] which will be trained in that way after the present vintage. The vineyard, being situated on the crown and highest slopes of what we have called the residence hill, is open to all aspects. On the north-west side an orchard has been planted to protect the vines from the influence of the rough winds which prevail from that quarter. On the south and east the vineyard is enclosed by a splendid white-thorn fence, about 12 feet [3.6 metres] high.

Large cellars had been erected, once again described by Ward in great detail:

The wine cellars are situated on the northern side of the vineyard. Like the lower apartments of the house, the lower floors of the cellars are excavated in rock, and thus the desirable degree of coolness has been ensured. The inner cellar on the lower storey is 67 feet [20.4 metres] long by 27 feet [8.2 metres] wide, and eleven feet [3.3 metres] high, but on the upper storey an additional foot [30 centimetres] of space is gained by reason of the decreased thickness of the upper walls. The wine is chiefly stored in the lower cellar, the upper apartment being used as the manufactory, if we may apply the term. The casks range from 100 to 550 gallons [455 to 2502 litres] in size, the latter being the largest Mr. Gilbert uses. Mr. Gilbert prefers vessels of from 200 to 500 gallons [910 to 2275 litres] for fermenting, as the weather is generally cool in the hills at vintage time, but if the weather was hot he would use smaller vats, because large bodies of must are apt to ferment too quickly and too violently, and it is then difficult to lower the temperature. He also objects to large vats on account of the difficulty of filling them on one day, and he objects to large store casks because he thinks the wine is not so likely to be properly attended to as it would be in smaller vessels. All the casks in the cellar are furnished with tin labels, on which the age, quality, and quantity of the contents are distinctly painted. There is a good deal of comparatively old wine in the cellar, and the three last vintages are largely represented. Indeed, it is Mr. Gilbert's custom not to sell his wines until they have attained three or four years' age, and we cannot help remarking that it would be extremely fortunate for the reputation of South Australian wines if the majority of our vignerons were in a position to follow such a judicious course. Here, as at Evandale, we considered the choicest wine to be the Riesling, thoroughly matured, fragrant, delicate, and pure. Mr. Gilbert has some of this of the vintage of 1852, and some of every vintage since. There are some persons, however, who would probably prefer Mr. Gilbert's red wines, made from the Shiraz and Carbonet, especially that of his earlier vintages, a wine that would fairly rival if not outvie the finest Burgundy. To return to the Riesling for a moment, we may mention that a short time since a number of gentlemen—all experienced connoisseurs—met together in Adelaide, for the purpose of testing the relative merits of this same Riesling (of the vintage of 1854, we think), and some choice Hock, considered to be the best wine of its class ever imported to this colony. The decision was in favour of the colonial product.

Mr. Gilbert uses a crushing mill in the manufacture of his wines, and presses the 'murk' in horsehair bags. In racking off the must he invariably uses canvas hose in preference to the guttapercha article, which he considers imparts an objectionable flavour to the wine. He is now building a new wing to the cellar on the east side. This will be 60 feet long by 27 [18.2 metres by 8.2], and will be chiefly used as a storeroom and cooperage, etc.

One hundred and twenty years later I came within the flick of a feather duster of tasting one of Joseph Gilbert's prize reds. Len Evans successfully bid for an 1864 red at Christie's auctions in London, but, while in the care of Michael Broadbent, the office cleaner knocked the bottle to the floor. The empty bottle, with a sad hole in the side, eventually made its way to Australia, an echo of what might have been.

Like cool-climate vineyards across the length and breadth of Australia, Pewsey Vale faded away around the turn of the century. When Yalumba moved back into the Hills in 1961, in partnership with Geoffrey Angus Parsons, the proprietor of Pewsey Vale Station, only the history books recorded the prior use as a vineyard. Rhine riesling was the principal variety planted, with lesser quantities of cabernet sauvignon and trial planting of a number of other varieties including semillon. Twenty years' experience has shown that the initial choice of rhine riesling and cabernet sauvignon was correct, but the vineyard is nonetheless well into a replanting programme turning on new and improved clones of both rhine riesling and cabernet sauvignon. These clones give better yields of grapes, with far greater intensity of flavour and varietal character, and preliminary results suggest even better wines are in store in the future. The rhine riesling is a German-bred clone with great aromatic quality.

A few years ago I shared a retrospective tasting of all of the Pewsey Vale rhine rieslings. These were my notes on that occasion:

1966 Cloudy orange colour—out of condition and obvious deterioration. Madeirised musty bouquet. Palate a surprise; still there with some real fruit retained. Nonetheless, overall a museum piece. (Made in tiny quantities and never commercially released.) (13/20)

1968 Bright, clear and youthful colour, very good indeed for a wine of this age. Curious oily medicinal overtones to bouquet, but palate in fine fettle with crisp acid, although fruit flavour is lacking on the mid-palate. If a bit more sugar had been left in the wine it might well have reached the heights of the '69. (17/20)

1969 Golden colour still tinged with green. Honeyed germanic style—rich pineapple/lime complex fruit flavours. Marvellous palate: soft, yet clean and intense. Tended to fade and break up in the glass as the evening wore on, but quite outstanding earlier on. (19/20)

1970 Golden yellow. Full bouquet with touch of developed "kerosene" character and also a trace of mercaptan. Fairly rich palate but flattening somewhat and obviously past its best. (16.5/20)

1971 Colour showing development; bouquet likewise, lacking aromatic rhine character although quite clean. A similar wine to the '70: a rather flat, hard palate with fruit distinctly drying out. Not a bad wine by any means, but past its best. (16.5/20)

1972 Golden colour with faintest hint of browning evident. A smooth old wine on both bouquet and palate which tended to fade fairly quickly in the glass. As it did so the latent hardness of the fruit and acid became more obvious. (16.5/20)

1973 Superb bright-green-gold colour. Bouquet muted initially by a touch of SO_2 but blossomed in the glass. Palate showing great balance and length, with particularly attractive fruit on the mid-palate. Soft developed rhine flavour showing the benefit a trace of residual sugar gives to the Pewsey Vale style. (18.5/20)

1976 Considerable variation between the two bottles on the table. This was the last Pewsey Vale to be released with conventional corks—and half the vintage was put out with the now mandatory (for Pewsey Vale, that is) Stelvin cap. A pity our bottles were not given Stelvins, as one was mouldy (the one I shared in) and the other was not. The good bottle was very good; my points and rank represented a compromise between the two bottles. Overall the group clearly had less problems with the "off" bottle than I did. (17/20)

1979 Good fresh colour. Excellent bouquet, complex and with marked rhine aromatics. Still developing character, and has all the fruit acid balance one could wish for. Overall flavour and structure very good indeed. (18.5/20)

1980 Pale colour but good hue. Intense lifted fruit aromatics to bouquet: grapey and with clear varietal definition (despite a yeasty off-flavour which will go as the wine develops). Lovely soft fruit a feature of the palate. (18/20)

The tasting underlined the capacity the best vintages have to age magnificently; of the releases between 1981 and 1984 the latter wine stands out both in terms of present quality and future potential. It is a wine of extraordinary aroma and fruit intensity, taking rhine riesling beyond its normal confines. Like its sister wine, 1984 Heggies Rhine Riesling, it has had a scintillating show career, winning a number of gold medals and trophies. It overshadows the 1981, 1982 and 1983 vintages; of these three wines the 1982 was the best, with firm, clean riesling flavour; the wine should be at its best in 1986 or

1987. It certainly needed some years for the latent fruit to develop.

Pewsey Vale has also produced some fine cabernet sauvignon. Not surprisingly, the fruit style of these wines is radically different from that of the other Yalumba reds. The oak treatment provides the connecting link, being quite distinctive and—I must say—at times threatening to swamp the fairly delicate and quite astringent cabernet fruit which the vineyard provides. Thus the 1981 vintage, available in late 1984, was a gold-medal-winner in the Adelaide show of that year, but I felt the aroma of the wine was unduly dominated by oak. I have no complaints about the palate, with a lovely touch of sweet berry on the mid-palate leading to a stylish, delicately astringent finish. Every Pewsey Vale Cabernet Sauvignon since the first release in 1972 has won at least one gold medal at Australian wine shows, with the exception of 1974, in which year the wine was not made—or at least not released under the Pewsey Vale label.

The second of Yalumba's high-country vineyards is Heggies. Here rhine riesling and cabernet sauvignon have been recently joined by sauvignon blanc, pinot noir and chardonnay, all of which are producing wines of great flavour and style. In 1984 some of the sauvignon blanc was sold and eventually appeared under a special merchant label, having been made by Petaluma. There were few better sauvignon blancs made in that year.

Heggies was purchased in 1971 from Colin Heggie, a well-known identity and grazier; the distinctive label pays tribute to that past. The 120-hectare property now has over 50 hectares of vines planted to rhine riesling, cabernet sauvignon, chardonnay, sauvignon blanc, pinot noir, merlot and traminer. As befits cool-country viticulture, the vines are close-planted on a high trellis; all of the material has been clonally selected through Yalumba's own extensive nursery system.

The Heggies rhine rieslings have had extraordinary success since 1979, when the wine was first made. Without question the 1982 and 1984 vintages have been quite outstanding, which is reflected in their glittering show career. The feature of Heggies dry rhine rieslings is the steely backbone to the wine, handsomely clothed with full-flavoured, estery aromatic fruit. It may be my sweet tooth, but I find the Heggies Rhine Riesling Botrytis-Affected Late Harvest a mouthful in many ways. The first heavily botrytised Heggies rhine riesling was made in 1982. It caused Yalumba to think hard about the label that was to be given to the wine, and they came up with the very honest but rather long-winded name which now appears on the label. Commendably, they did not borrow the beerenauslese tag from Germany. They did, however, borrow the idea of capsule identification, used by such famous vineyards as Schloss Vollrads to denote varying grades of quality. Using the German rules, Yalumba have come up with the scheme that wines with over 35 per cent residual sugar by weight (equivalent to German trockenbeerenauslese) are entitled to a gold capsule; and those between 28 and 35 per cent residual sugar by weight are entitled to a red capsule (equivalent to beerenauslese). Both the 1982 and 1983 releases were a little over 30 per cent residual sugar by weight, in the middle of the beerenauslese range—hence the red capsules. But I wait in awe for the day when a gold-capsule Heggies is released.

The 1982 and 1983 releases, multi-gold-medal-winners, are absolutely marvellous. By rights these wines should be very long-lived, yet the rate of development of the 1982 makes me wonder just how long-lived they will in fact be; I honestly do not know. It may well be that the development will slow down and the wine will hold its intensely rich fruit for many, many years. In that event we shall have the best of both worlds. These are magnificent dessert wines: the influence of botrytis is extremely pronounced, with intense pineapple/lime aromas, lifted by that touch of volatility which is part and parcel of the style, and which also gives lift and life to the softly intense fruit of the palate. The acid is pronounced though not mouth-puckering.

Yalumba has had considerable success in vineyard management, for the 1983 Heggies Rhine Riesling (dry) is a lovely full-flavoured conventional wine with no evidence of botrytis whatsoever. There is a hint of lime in the bouquet and fruit sweetness on the fore-palate, but the wine is conventionally flavoured with a long, beautifully balanced finish. Heggies is a vineyard to watch.

The third high-country vineyard is the new Hill-Smith Estate "Hills" Vineyard, diagonally opposite Heggies. These three vineyards now provide Yalumba with 200 hectares of high-country, cool-climate vines, making Yalumba a force to be reckoned with in the quality market in the years to come. []

Adelaide Metropolitan Area/ Adelaide Plains

With the exception of the Adelaide Plains area, and a few token vines left around Penfolds' historic Magill Winery, viticulture has come to an end in the Adelaide metropolitan area. A steadily declining number of wineries still have limited manufacturing or storage facilities, but these too are on the wane. It is a sad decline for an area which reached its peak in 1925, when 1570 hectares were under vine.

As with the other winegrowing States the first vineyards were established within the present city boundaries. Those in South Australia were planted at North Adelaide in 1837 by J. B. Hack and George Stevenson. A number of distinct subregions subsequently developed. In the West Torrens region the Hardy, Norman and Holbrook families planted vineyards in the 1850s. Norman's Wine Estates Proprietary Limited (now owned by the Horlin-Smith family) has its head office at Holbrooks Road, Underdale, at the core of what was once a 10-hectare vineyard. Thomas Hardy also established a large winery at Bankside, supplied in part by a surrounding 14-hectare vineyard. The Bankside Winery was destroyed by fire in 1904 and was never rebuilt. Hardy's Mile End Cellars continued as a landmark in Adelaide until the 1980s, but all of the company's operations are now centred on Chateau Reynella in McLaren Vale.

The Marion district was a major grape producer, both of table and wine varieties. The principal winery and vineyard was that of Hamiltons, whose Ewell Vineyards were of prime importance. Hamiltons is now no more than a label on a range of wines marketed by Mildara, and even that tenuous link with the past is threatened. Norman's, too, had a substantial vineyard at Marion established in 1911; the 25-hectare property was ultimately resumed for housing development, leading to the establishment of Norman's present vineyards in the Adelaide Plains region.

In the long term the most important sub-district was that of the Magill–Glen Osmond area. Dr Christopher Rawson Penfold established Penfolds in 1854, the same year as Patrick Auld established Auldana. Osmond Gilles followed in 1858, forming Woodley Wines; and in the same year Stonyfell was established by Henry Clarke. Wynns' Romalo Champagne Cellars were also to be found in this area. Woodley's remains at Glen Osmond, but has always been a wine merchant more than a wine producer.

The Tea Tree Gully and Hope Valley areas, on the north-eastern outskirts of the town, lasted longer. The Highercombe Cellars operated until 1925, but both Angove's Pty Limited and Douglas A. Tolley's Pty Limited remained important vignerons and winemakers for far longer. Until 1975 Angove's had over 100 hectares of vineyard at Tea Tree Gully, which were then resumed for a residential subdivision. The winery and cellars now serve duty as a tourist information centre, and yet another operating winery is lost to the Adelaide area. D. A. Tolley's once extensive Hope Valley and Tea Tree Vineyards are likewise no more, although the Hope Valley Winery remains in production.

Thus it is that the viticultural mantle has fallen on the Adelaide Plains winegrowing district. Here 650 hectares of vines are in production, approximately 75 per cent of which have been planted since 1969. The three surviving commercial wineries are Anglesey, Primo Estate and Norman's. The Gawler River Estate label of the Munno Para Cooperative is no more, this short-lived venture (formed in 1979) having gone into liquidation. The 42 grower members of the cooperative will in future sell their grapes to the Barossa Valley and other areas, as they did prior to the formation of the cooperative.

The main strength of the area stems from the very reliable growing-season conditions. Sea breezes from the nearby Gulf St Vincent reduce humidity to the point where it becomes unnecessary to spray for either fungus or pest control. Throughout the growing season there is an absence of rain and storm activity. The limitations in quality stem from the very warm climate (only partially alleviated by the cool nights and afternoon sea breezes) and, to a minor degree, by the necessity of irrigation. Rainfall of around 450 millimetres per year is winter dominant, making supplementary irrigation essential.

The two main soil types in the region, red-brown earths and heavy brown soils, are overlain by a top bank of sandy loam. This has led to the establishment of extensive market gardens throughout the region, and, of course, is also beneficial to vines. The subsoil is a limestone marl which provides excellent drainage. The net result is dependable yields of around 10 tonnes per hectare of shiraz, cabernet sauvignon, pinot noir, malbec, semillon, rhine riesling, sauvignon blanc, chardonnay and frontignac.

Progessive growers such as Primo Estate have adopted various viticultural and winemaking techniques to invest the grapes (and thereby the resulting wine) with greater flavour and character. Without these techniques the wines are soft, pleasant and bland, fitting into the lower to middle half of the market.

ANGLESEY
HEASLIP ROAD, ANGLE VALE

Anglesey was established by Sydney stockbroker Jack Minnett at the height of the red-wine boom in 1969. He planted the 44-hectare property principally to shiraz, with a little cabernet sauvignon. For a time it was part of an ill-fated consortium of Angle Vale Vineyards Proprietary Limited, but when that organisation ran into difficulties, Anglesey went its own way. Between 1972 and 1977 the grapes were sold to other wineries, both local and in the Barossa. In 1978 the first vintage was made at Anglesey under the direction of consultant wine-maker Lindsay Stanley.

The radically different shape of the wine market has now been reflected in the vineyards. Much of the shiraz has been removed, with plantings down to 12.5 hectares, almost matched by eight hectares of cabernet sauvignon and three hectares of malbec. The remaining vines have been replanted or grafted, with a total of 20 hectares coming into bearing progressively from 1984. These are semillon (4.5 hectares), rhine riesling (2.5 hectares), chardonnay and chenin blanc (two hectares each), sauvignon

ADELAIDE FROM ABOVE WOODLEY WINES, c. 1900

blanc (1.5 hectares) and colombard and merlot (one hectare each).

A variety of special viticultural techniques are used, the most notable of which is the organic style of farming which the district allows. Thus there are no chemical sprays used for disease or pest control, and no cultivation between the rows. The vines are mechanically pruned by what is said to be a special method, and are mechanically harvested. The only chemicals used in the vineyard are pre-emergents applied during the dormant period to control weed growth.

The winemaker is Christopher Hackett, who receives consultancy advice from Max Schubert. The attractively packaged wines are of adequate if unexciting quality. As at the end of 1984 the principal offerings were a 1983 Chablis, a 1983 Rhine Riesling, a 1982 Cabernet Sauvignon and a 1980 Cabernet Sauvignon. When the new plantings come into bearing the 10,000-case output of the winery may offer rather more than it does at the moment.

In future, releases will devolve around Anglesey QVS White (a blend of semillon, chenin blanc and sauvignon blanc) and QVS Red (cabernet sauvignon, malbec and shiraz). QVS signifies "quality very special", although it has unfortunate connotations of VDQS, a humble French appellation grading.

NORMAN'S
183–187 HOLBROOKS ROAD, UNDERDALE

Norman's has been making wine for 132 years. Jesse Norman, a brewer from Cambridge in England, planted a three-hectare vineyard at Underdale in 1853 and built a small winery. In 1911 the business was substantially expanded when Jesse Norman's son Arthur purchased a 25-hectare vineyard at Marion. Ten years later a new winery was built in Holbrooks Road, not far from the original winery, and the buildings erected there form the nucleus of the present operating winery and cellars. When the Marion vineyards were resumed the Norman family purchased land in the Adelaide Plains at Angle Vale, and these vineyards now provide 40 per cent of the annual production. As at Anglesey, an extensive replanting programme has been undertaken in the past few years to provide varieties more attuned to today's market conditions. However, right from the outset some unusual varieties were included, amongst them some of the earliest plantings of gewurtz-traminer in South Australia.

In 1982 Norman's was acquired by the Horlin-Smith family, a well-known South Australian wine family whose involvement up to that time had been limited to running hotels and liquor stores. It heralded a time of change for Norman's. Jim Irvine became consultant winemaker, and introduced a policy of selective purchasing of grapes and wine from other premium areas, notably Coonawarra. The wines were repackaged and the marketing became much more aggressive. So successful was the dual strategy that at the end of 1984 Norman's purchased the Coolawin Winery of the Light family in the Adelaide Hills. This will enable Norman's to make a far higher percentage of its wine, although there is little doubt that the policy of going to premium areas for a substantial part of the intake will continue.

The Evanston Vineyard in the Adelaide Plains, near the Gawler River, bears little resemblance to that of five years ago. The new plantings will progressively come into bearing over the next two or three years. The varieties planted are pinot noir (nine hectares), rhine riesling, gewurtztraminer, chenin blanc, chardonnay, cabernet sauvignon and shiraz (four hectares each), sauvignon blanc (three hectares), merlot and cabernet franc (two hectares each), and white frontignac and red frontignac (1.5 hectares each). Much of the vineyard is established on deep river alluvial sandy loam, eventually decreasing to five metres in depth with a limestone base. Yields are very good, ranging from 10 tonnes per hectare for pinot noir to 17 tonnes per hectare for shiraz.

The Norman's labels explicitly disclose the origin of the wine. They also show just how far afield it has gone in recent years to obtain the best available material. Thus the 1982 Pinot Noir was a blend of Hunter Valley and Barossa Valley material; two 1980 Cabernet Sauvignons were marketed, one from McLaren Vale and the other (quite outstanding) from Coonawarra. The 1983 Chardonnay (again an extremely good wine) came from the Barossa Valley, while the 1984 Chardonnay was a blend of Evanston Estate-grown grapes and Barossa Valey material. The 1982 and 1983 Rhine Riesling was sourced in Coonawarra, including a high-quality botrytis-affected wine; while the 1983 Gewurtztraminer was a blend of Coonawarra and Evanston material. The strength of these varietal releases may be judged from Norman's success at the 1983 Royal Sydney Show, where it received the Jones Steains & Waller Trophy for most successful exhibitor in the varietal wine classes.

The 1983 Chardonnay and the 1980 Cabernet Sauvignon were not only of high quality, but, like virtually all Norman's wines, were sold for a very modest price. If one can forgive the pun, Norman's Conquest Brut also offers excellent value in the sparkling-wine category, being one of the better non-vintage releases of the second half of 1984. The wide range is completed by a 27-year-old tawny port of extremely high quality, which won a gold medal and top points in its class at the 1983 Canberra National Wine Show.

PATRITTI
13 CLACTON ROAD, DOVER GARDENS

Patritti was established in 1926 at Dover Gardens, 14 kilometres south of the city, by Giovanni Patritti. Originally the vineyards were established around the winery, but following housing resumptions in 1952 new vineyards were established at Aldinga and Blewitt Springs.

Much of the wine is sold in bulk, with limited local distribution under the Blewitt Springs Estate label and the Patritti Aldinga label.

PENFOLDS' MAGILL
PENFOLD ROAD, MAGILL

Amid a major public outcry, dozens of protest meetings and the formation of numerous committees and subcommittees, Penfolds sold the major part of the Magill Vineyard on the outskirts of Adelaide in the latter part of 1982. The winery, administration centre and National Trust house, built by Christopher Rawson Penfold, are to be preserved, along with a token area of vineyard.

I believe Penfolds is seriously considering the production of a chateau-bottled style of wine, coming exclusively from Magill-grown grapes. Those who have a few remaining bottles of wine such as the 1956 Magill Burgundy (the show stocks of which were released by Penfolds in the late 1970s) will wish the project well. The wine is still a joy to drink, with a velvety elegance which is entirely seductive.

PRIMO ESTATE
PORT WAKEFIELD ROAD, VIRGINIA

Primo Estate is one of the most innovative small wineries in Australia. Instead of following the example of Norman's and going outside the Adelaide Plains area for much of its fruit, the Grilli family has developed techniques to modify radically the character and style of their estate-grown and made wines. Given that the enterprise was not established until 1973, and the first wines not made until 1979, the record of achievement is all the more impressive.

The vineyard was established by Primo Grilli and has now passed into the ownership and management of his sons, Joe and Peter. Much of the innovative impetus has come from Joe Grilli, who attended Roseworthy College between 1977 and 1980, graduating with the gold medal as dux of his class. The 18.9-hectare vineyard is planted to rhine riesling (six hectares), sauvignon blanc (three hectares), white frontignac (2.5 hectares), colombard and shiraz (two hectares each), semillon and cabernet sauvignon (1.2 hectares each) and chardonnay (one hectare). These provide the Primo Estate with 90 per cent of its annual crush of around 200 tonnes.

Substantial quantities of wine are sold to other wineries, with 7500 cases of premium-quality wines released under the Primo Estate label. These releases are headed by the cabernet sauvignon made from vines which have been double-pruned, and from the branch-cut artificially inoculated botrytised rhine riesling.

For many years now the CSIRO, the Viticultural Research Station at Griffith and Roseworthy Agricultural College have been interested in developing techniques to moderate the effects of very warm climates on premium-quality grapes. Many of these techniques remain at the experimental stage, but the late-pruning and double-pruning techniques have been translated into commercial reality, if on a small scale. Late pruning is practised by leaving the vines unpruned until long after normal bud-burst; at some time in December or early January all of the new growth is pruned off and the vines cut back in much the same way as if they were being pruned while dormant during winter. This forces the secondary buds (which would have otherwise remained dormant until the following year) to shoot. Double pruning involves an initial pruning at the conventional time, and a second pruning later in the growing season. The result is very much the same as late pruning. Yields are very significantly reduced; the ripening of the grapes is delayed until mid- to late May; and the flavour (and chemical composition) of the grapes is modified in consequence.

The system works well if wine quality is the sole determinant. The Primo double-pruned cabernets have the structure and style of cool-climate cabernet sauvignon, with marked astringent/herbaceous characters. The difficulty with the technique lies in the sharply reduced yields and the consequent increased cost of viticultural techniques. It is not a practice that Primo Estate carries out every year.

The greatest success has been achieved with the late-harvest rhine rieslings. Labelled beerenauslese, the wines have been produced each year since 1981, and immediately attracted national attention for both their concentration of flavour and quality. Only 1500 half-bottles of that initial vintage were made, and as at February 1985 it was fulfilling all of its early promise. A blend of 85 per cent rhine riesling and 15 per cent traminer, it retains eight degrees baume of sugar and has 11 degrees of alcohol. The colour is a glowing yellow-gold; the bouquet a rich amalgam of apricot and candied-mandarin-peel aromas, and yet is neither heavy nor cloying. The palate is rich and viscous, with tastes of honey and apricot; and the acid is well balanced and prevents the wine from cloying. At that time it was getting close to its best, although it will undoubtedly hold for many years to come. Subsequent vintages have followed very much in the same pattern, if anything showing a little more life and a little greater intensity. The technique used to make the wines is very complex; I describe it at length at page 386.

D. A. TOLLEY'S PEDARE
30 BARRACKS ROAD, HOPE VALLEY

D. A. Tolley Pty Limited is not infrequently confused with Tolley Scott and Tolley. While both companies were founded by members of the same family, they have long since gone their separate ways. Tolley Scott and Tolley markets its table wines under the Tollana brand label; Douglas A. Tolley under the Pedare brand. Over the past few years that brand has come into national prominence as wine quality has increased out of all recognition, but few wine lovers appreciate just how substantial this family-run and owned operation is.

Its vineyards have been rationalised somewhat in recent years, and are now concentrated in two areas: 100 hectares in the Barossa Valley, and a further 100 hectares at Qualco in South Australia's Riverland. These two sources provide 55 per cent of the annual crush of 3500 tonnes. The remaining 45 per cent is bought in, and, as in the case of Norman's, is used extensively in the production of the top-of-the-range wines. Much of the Riverland material goes to provide the 1,667,000 litres of bulk wine sold each year. The Barossa Valley vineyards, supplemented by the bought-in material, go to provide the 80,000

cases of wine produced under the Pedare label.

The white wines are undoubtedly the most successful, but it is remarkable that a wine of the quality of the Black Label 1980 Shiraz Cabernet could be sold for around $4.50 in late 1984. It is a very well-put-together wine, in the modern oaky idiom, and with attractive berry-fruit flavours (balanced by some astringency) on the palate. Nonetheless, it is the 1983 and 1984 vintage white wines which have really stood out. The chablis of both years is one of the few wines which really aspire to the characteristics of a classic chablis: crisp, reasonably austere fruit with some firmness on the finish. Early-picked grapes and rigorous protection of the juice and wine from oxidation are the keys to the success Tolley has had. Interestingly the 1984 Chablis was made not, as the palate might suggest, from sauvignon blanc, but from colombard grown at Qualco.

My reservations about Australian traminer do not need repeating, but when a wine of the quality of the 1984 Pedare Traminer comes along it is hard not to be impressed. The wine successfully negotiates the balance between being on the one hand too delicate, and overblown and blousy on the other, the two extremes which seem depressingly common. Frontignac is, by contrast, a relatively easy grape to handle, and it is hardly surprising that the Spatlese Frontignac of 1984 is a bell-clear example of the variety, proclaiming the grape from which it was made. These wines never fail to impress visitors from overseas; it is curious they are so little honoured in this country.

Tolley's has also turned its hand with great success to the wood maturation of semillon; I thought the 1983 vintage a marvellous example of the style. Some reviewers thought it too oaky; I do not agree.

All of this has been achieved by a winemaking team headed by Christopher Tolley, with Andrew Garrett as assistant winemaker, and with help from the ubiquitous Oenotec consultants. It is evidently a very successful combination.

WOODLEY WINES
BLYTH STREET, GLEN OSMOND

Woodley Wines has always had an air of fairytale romance about it. In 1838 J. W. Bull acquired an option to purchase the property on which the present cellars stand. He decided the rocky terrain was too difficult to build on, and gave the benefit of the option to a friend, Osmond Gilles, the first Treasurer of the colony of South Australia. Gilles was still contemplating building a residence when a large silver and lead deposit was discovered. A mining company was formed, and the substantial royalties paid to Gilles led to his premature retirement as Treasurer. He spent part of his wealth in establishing a vineyard on the property in 1858; when the deposit was worked out he was left with a series of underground drives extending for four kilometres which proved ideal for wine storage.

After Osmond Gilles's death the property passed through a number of hands, with several of the owners extending the plantings. In 1894 the then president of the Vignerons' Association, H. V. Pridmore, bought the property. In 1903 it produced 18,000 litres, making it one of the smallest of the then-flourishing Adelaide district vineyards. In 1922 the vineyards were sold for suburban building blocks, and for the next 60 years Woodley Wines became first and foremost a wine merchant, buying and blending wines produced by other makers. It was nonetheless a most important company, for its next two owners were men of unusual vision.

The first was Lieutenant-Colonel David Fulton, who purchased the business in 1924 and converted it to a limited liability company in 1926. It was he who formed the association which led to Woodley obtaining a very large portion of its red wine from Coonawarra for the next 30 years. He formed a close friendship with Bill Redman, and was instrumental in persuading Redman to make a lighter style of claret wine by picking the grapes earlier than was contemporary practice. In the 1930s Fulton introduced the St Adele Burgundy label, under which some of Redman's greatest wines were bottled and received first prizes at wine shows. The St Adele label has been revived, although the quality of the wine in the bottle is now very much more humble.

In 1940 an Austrian winemaker named Tony Nelson joined the company, and when Colonel Fulton retired Nelson became managing director. He introduced a light, sweet, table wine named Est, which was an outstanding success in the Second World War years, and which has also been revived (in 1984). For many years it was Woodley's largest-selling wine. In 1946 Nelson purchased Milne's Coonawarra vineyards and winery, at that time given over entirely to the production of brandy, and renamed it Chateau Comaum. With the Redmans in charge, the winery (built by John Riddoch) once again began producing quality red table wine. It was purchased by Wynns in 1952 and is now the best known of all the Coonawarra wineries. Nelson's other great

contribution was the development of the Treasure Chest Claret Series for Redman Coonawarra wines made between 1949 and 1956. The most exquisite—and certainly the most expensive—labels ever used in Australia, they adorned some suitably beautiful wines. In 1971 I attended a tasting of 16 vintages of the Woodley Coonawarra reds spanning the years 1930 to 1956. The 1930, 1941, 1943 and 1945 vintages were humbling in their magnificence.

In 1963 Woodley Wines was acquired by a Melbourne chain-store company, Crooks National; this was in turn taken over by Industrial Equity Limited in 1971. Industrial Equity's chairman, Ron Brierley, has shown no sentiment when it comes to disposing of unwanted bits and pieces acquired in the course of take-overs, but has kept a tight hold on Woodley. Brierley is known to be fond of the odd glass of fine table wine, and his New Zealand interests control Cooks Wines. The most successful reincarnation of all has been that of the Queen Adelaide label, which originally adorned the 1953 wine. It is used on Queen Adelaide Riesling, one of the top-10 selling brands in Australia with 1984 sales of 140,000 cases, and is also used on a rather less successful Queen Adelaide Claret.

In 1981 Woodley moved to bolster its own production capacity by commencing the construction of a large winery at Dorrien, with a capacity of 2000 tonnes and room for ultimate expansion to 5000 tonnes.

Virtually all of the 1984 crush of around 1300 tonnes was of grapes purchased from independent growers, principally in the Southern Vales region. The other important source is Coonawarra. The balance of the company's wine requirements came from contract-making and bulk-purchasing arrangements with other wineries. Given that around 1850 tonnes of grapes would be needed to service the Queen Adelaide Riesling sales, it is not surprising that a further 3000 tonnes are purchased in this way. Only a token quantity of grapes is grown on the nine hectares of vineyard surrounding Woodley's Dorrien Winery.

Around the same time Woodley also moved into the top end of the merchant market by purchasing small quantities of some very high-quality parcels of wine which they then wood-matured and bottle-developed. In 1984 a 1977 Cabernet Shiraz, a 1977 Cabernet, two 1980 Cabernet Sauvignons (one from McLaren Vale and the other from Coonawarra) and a 1981 Skeleton Cabernet Shiraz (another reincarnation from the Treasure Chest Series) were released. These are quite excellent wines, although they were

made in very small quantities. The outstanding wine was the 1980 McLaren Vale Cabernet Sauvignon, of which only 480 dozen were made. A marvellously soft yet concentrated wine, the palate has fine, perfectly ripened fruit with soft tannin, good acid and a touch of cedar and mint from the oak. It will be interesting to see whether the present-day Treasure Chest has other jewels in store.

EXCAVATING CELLARS AT WOODLEY WINES, c. 1900

ADELAIDE

BLASS'S BILYARA

BAROSSA VALLEY

ELDERTON
PENFOLDS
KAISER STUHL
TOLLANA

Nuriootpa

The Willows
Catrama
Light Pass
Plush Corner
Penrice Quarry
Penrice
Arcady
Tappa Pass

Ku-Ring-Gai
Maranarga

SEPPELT
PATTERSON HILL
Seppeltsfield

Dorrien

Nuraip

Abgaston

PETER LEHMANN WINES   HOFFMANS
BERNKASTEL   LEO BURING
VERITAS

Koemers Crossing

Barossa Valley
Vine Vale

YALUMBA
Lind

BASEDOW
Tanunda

ROSEWORTHY
Crayford
Bethany

MENGLER HILL

Gomersal

Schreiberau

HIGH WYCOMBE WINES

ST HALLETTS WINES

ROCKFORD
Krondorf   KRONDORF

CHATTERTONS
72

CHATEAU YALDARA
KARLSBURG
WILSFORD

RED GUM VINEYARD
Altoha

Warpoo WARD'S
GATEWAY
CELLARS
69
Lyndoch

SANDY CREEK
CONSERVATION
PARK

Moorooroo

Rowland Flat
ROVALLEY
ORLANDO

KAISERSTUHL
CONSERVATION
PARK

Mandalay

Hillanso

BAROSSA   RANGE

FOREST   RESERVE

MOUNT
CRAWFORD
FOREST

Piers Hill

17   18

Km. 0   1   2   3   4   5 Km.
Mi. 0   1   2   3 Mi.

Barossa Valley

The Barossa Valley is not simply a valley, or at least not just a valley floor. It has traditionally been regarded as covering an area measuring 35 kilometres north-south and 25 kilometres east-west, bounded by Springton, Williamstown, Sandy Creek, Daveyston, Koonunga, Truro and thence to Keyneton. It rises from a height of 250 metres above sea-level on the valley floor to 600 metres at Pewsey Vale. As I say in Chapter 1, I have elected to excise the Barossa Ranges around Pewsey Vale from the Barossa Valley. Perhaps there is historical precedent for this: while Captain Joseph Gilbert established his Pewsey Vale winery in 1847, it was on the floor of the Barossa Valley that almost all of the subsequent development took place.

Johann Gramp planted his vines at Rowland Flat later in the same year. In 1849 an English brewer named Samuel Smith settled at Angaston and founded Yalumba, starting a dynasty which proudly continues to this day; while J. E. Seppelt followed suit in 1851. Henry Evans, G. F. Angas's brother-in-law, planted Evandale, just to the north-east of Angaston, in 1842.

George Fife Angas played a central role in the development of the Valley. He was one of the promoters of the South Australian Company and became its chief executive. He settled in the Valley, taking up vast holdings, and in 1841 Angas Town (later Angaston) was surveyed and named after him. Needing labour for his substantial estates, he financed the immigration of three ship-loads of German Lutheran farmers from Silesia, who were then suffering oppression from King Frederick III. The first families settled at Bethany in 1842, and soon turned their attention to viticulture. Thus Johann Gramp was joined by Samuel Hoffman (also in 1847), followed by J. E. Seppelt and then William Jacob at Moorooroo in 1854.

Many of these enterprises flourished, but none more so than that of Seppelt at Seppeltsfield—by the late 1880s Seppeltsfield was producing more than any other winery in the colony. In 1888 the crush reached 1,215,000 litres, and Benno Seppelt built vast new cellars in which the 60 cement fermentation vats (ranged in serried rows down the side of the hill on which the fermentation house was erected) could handle 540,000 litres of wine at any one time. By 1900 Seppeltsfield had a 4.5 million litre storage capacity, but in 1908 the winery size was once again doubled to supplement the production from its own modest 50 hectares of vineyards. Seppelt's purchased grapes from 165 growers within a radius of over 20 kilometres around Seppeltsfield, providing employment for 1700 people in all. By 1903 Seppeltsfield was unchallenged as the largest winery in the State, with a make of 1,980,000 litres. Thomas Hardy & Sons Limited, which had thrown out a brief challenge in the 1890s, was way behind (with 765,000 litres), having been overtaken by Chateau Tanunda (1,462,500 litres) and Yalumba (810,000 litres). In that vintage the Barossa Valley contributed more than half of the State's total crush of 11,490,000 litres.

Chateau Tanunda had been formed in 1889, a joint venture between Adelaide merchant George F. Cleland and local growers who agreed to contribute to the capital of the company and to supply grapes, taking half the purchase price in shares and half in cash. Cellars that outshone even those of Seppeltsfield (at least as it stood in those days) were erected, and 99 growers, holding between them a little over 600 hectares of grapes, contracted to sell all their grapes to Chateau Tanunda for five years. Of the initial crush of 945,000 litres, 315,000 were distilled into brandy. Tolley Scott and Tolley were at that time the principal brandy-makers in the region, and in 1896 doubled their distilling capacity by purchasing Sage's Angas Park Distillery. Both then and for the ensuing 50 years distillation provided an essential safety valve in years of overproduction, and supported many of the vineyards which went out of production in the wake of the tax on brandy which was progressively increased throughout the 1960s.

The other two large wineries in the Barossa were the Kalimna Winery owned by D. & J. Fowler Limited (with a 1903 crush of 405,000 litres) and Saltram (292,500 litres). The other great name of the Barossa Valley today, Gramp's Orlando, was almost nowhere to be found: G. Gramp produced a mere 33,750 litres and J. Gramp produced 11,250 litres.

Much of the prosperity of the years up to 1914 was based upon exports to the United Kingdom. The First World War not only rudely interrupted this trade, but also spelt trouble for the descendants of the Silesian Lutherans who had populated so much of the Valley. Ill will reached such a level that an Act of Parliament was passed changing the name of Kaiser Stuhl to Mount Kitchener, Siegersdorf to Dorrien, and Gnadenfrei to Marananga.

Throughout the 1920s and right through until the mid-1950s the Barossa's *raison d'être* was the production of fortified wine. The records up to 1950 show the heavy emphasis on the high-yielding second-class varieties suited to the production of fortified wine but to very little else.

The Barossa suffered as much as any other region from the outset of the Depression: the formation of the Barossa Cooperative Winery on 4 June 1931 with eight shareholders and a paid-up capital of $116 was a sign of the times. But greater problems still have come in the aftermath of the red-wine boom of the 60s, as the public has turned its attention to white wine and redefined what it expects of its red wines. This will inevitably lead to a fundamental reshaping of the Barossa as it has traditionally been known, but by no means will it lead to its demise as the centre of the South Australian wine industry. The enormous fixed investment in its infrastructure will see to that: these days chilled juice and must can be rapidly moved hundreds of kilometres, and the area is within easy reach of Coonawarra/Padthaway in the south-east and the Riverlands of the north-east. In the end result 75 per cent of all grapes processed in Barossa Valley wineries comes from outside the region.

There is nothing sinister in all of this: the proponents of appellation control do not like it, as it sits uneasily with their neatly parcelled view of things. But it reflects economic commonsense—necessity, indeed—and is in truth in the interests of the consumer, who ends up with a better product at a better price through efficient plant utilisation. One of the great problems of the wine industry is the waste inherent in winemaking equipment sitting idle for 10 months in each year. By processing fruit harvested from the end of January in the Riverlands, through to the commencement of May from Coonawarra, far more efficient use is made of the plant. So the vast wineries of Penfolds/Kaiser Stuhl at Nuriootpa and Orlando at Rowland Flat, not to mention Lindemans at Chateau Leonay and Yalumba at Angaston, will continue to be the focal point of production for decades to come.

Nor should it be assumed the Barossa will become a viticultural desert, despite Dr Richard Smart's projections. Yalumba was one of the first companies to give practical recognition to the fact that the Barossa contains a great diversity of climate within its boundaries, and to the importance of site selection for varieties. Thus the Valley floor is indeed ideally suited to the production of fortified wine (with very real possibilities for the as yet sparingly propagated Portuguese port varieties), while the East Barossa ranges have left no-one in doubt that they can produce a range of high-quality white and red table wines.

Finally the fact remains that while there has been an inevitable reshaping of the vineyards since the swing to white wine, reflected in the following table, and while there has been a certain degree of geographic shift up into the hills, the Barossa remains a very important grape-growing region.

VARIETY		HECTARES		
		1969	1979	1983
WHITE				
Chardonnay		—	—	133
Crouchen		283*	458	448
Doradillo		460	282	126
Palomino and pedro ximinez		924	839	713
Rhine riesling		283*	988	1283
Semillon		283*	478	553
Trebbiano		215	175	141
	TOTALS	2448	3220	3397
RED				
Cabernet sauvignon		133	365	376
Grenache		1424	1688	1128
Mataro		848	564	248
Shiraz		1204	1669	1307
	TOTALS	3609	4286	3059

* The three varieties were counted as one up to 1970 because accurate identification of the plantings had not been made.

The above figures are only for selected varieties: as at 1983 there were between 7400 and 7700 hectares of vines (there is some disagreement among those responsible for the statistics) held by about 650 grape growers. Overall, red varieties accounted for 3250 hectares. As the figures show, rhine riesling is by far the most important premium white grape. Practically every winery in the region produces a rhine riesling, which vary in style from the soft, full-flavoured and fairly broad wines of the Valley floor through to the fine, aromatic and long-lived wines of the Eden Valley, exemplified by the magnificent Leo Buring wines made by John Vickery in the late 60s and early 70s. Indeed, I believe that on balance the greatest Australian rhine rieslings are made from Eden Valley grapes. The wines are notoriously slow developers, seldom developing real fruit character for two years after vintage, and improving for five, 10 or even 15 years. They have a distinctive lime flavour, which is a regional rather than botrytis-induced character, and they seldom suffer the kerosene/Flytox aromas of aged rhine rieslings from other areas.

In more recent times Yalumba with its Heggies and Pewsey Vale wines, Wynns' High Eden, David Wynn's Mount Adam, Orlando's Eden Valley, Tollana's Woodbury Estate and Kaiser Stuhl's Rogers Vineyard Green Ribbon have all added new and varying dimensions to dry and semi-dry rieslings from the Barossa. In the Heggies and Pewsey Vale Vineyards botrytis has made its appearance to add yet a further dimension, offering a clearcut alter native to the traditional auslese rieslings made by Orlando since 1970, and intermittently by Leo Buring and Kaiser Stuhl (particularly the 1976 vintage).

Rhine riesling has suffered a backlash from the sudden popularity of chardonnay and sauvignon blanc; the fact remains that if the wines of these three varieties are viewed dispassionately, those wrought from riesling frequently exhibit greater flavour and style, and certainly more varietal fruit character. I remain confident, therefore, that rhine riesling will continue to flourish in the Barossa, particularly on the hillsides and hilltops.

The sharp increase in rhine riesling plantings is, of course, a partial (indeed inadequate) reflection of the sevenfold increase in white-wine consumption. In this light the smaller increase in semillon plantings accurately reflects the reservations held by both vignerons and winemakers about the variety in the Barossa. It was long regarded as inferior, to the point where Orlando was able to enter into grape-purchase contracts at very low prices and then direct the growers to leave the grapes on the vine to ripen far beyond normal maturity. This is always a risky business, but Orlando (having pre-agreed the weight

of the crop and the price per tonne) was prepared to accept that risk as part and parcel of making sauterne-style wines. The first release (1978) came out under a gaudy and short-lived Goldberren label for around $2.85 a bottle. The wine deserved a far better fate (and higher price) and was re-released under a purple ribbon late-harvest semillon private bin label at $5.60 or thereabouts. A third and final facelift sees the wine (which now also receives expensive new-oak maturation) now marketed as a sauterne.

Orlando's success opened up new markets for semillon; others, notably Peter Lehmann's Masterson Winery, have followed suit and indeed surpassed the achievements of Orlando. Lehmann's sauterne has consistently ranked among the best in Australia, if the wine show results are any guide. Seemingly coincidentally there has also been a revival of interest in the use of the variety to produce a wood-matured dry white in the chablis to white burgundy spectrum. Smaller companies such as Basedow and Red Gum (formerly Karrawirra) have from time to time released most attractive examples. Semillon is a reasonably late-maturing variety, and should by rights be well suited to the warm to hot climate which prevails over most of the Barossa.

Chardonnay and sauvignon blanc are as yet largely unproved varieties. Because chardonnay has proved itself such an adaptable grape (as witness its success in the Hunter) it is impossible to say it will not succeed, but I have grave reservations about sauvignon blanc. There are at the moment only tiny plantings (62 tonnes were crushed in the '83 vintage), and if it is to succeed, microclimatic site selection in the hills will be essential.

The sharp decline in doradillo and trebbiano plantings only proves what everyone knows: the Barossa is no longer the place to produce second-class varieties for bulk (i.e. cask) wines. The 1983 vintage, affected by drought, yielded an average for all varieties of 4.12 tonnes per hectare; 1984, a record harvest, provided 5.06 tonnes per hectare. It is simply not economic to produce anything but the best grapes in these circumstances, and the old dry-land (i.e. non-irrigated) small vineyards are surely and not-so-slowly disappearing. That they have lasted so long is a tribute to what on one view is the courage and on another the intense conservatism (if not financial stupidity) of the typical Barossa farmer. Often with a Teutonic streak of stubbornness in their make-up, the farmers have a series of crops and farming activities and little or no idea of the relative profitability of each. With seemingly no alternative, they continue their traditional activities and are

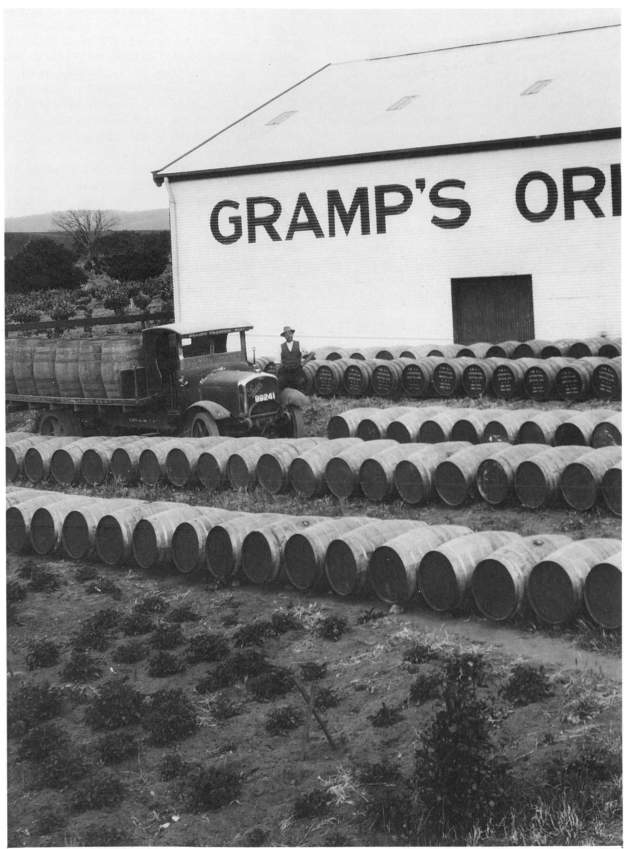

EXPORT BARRELS, GRAMP'S ORLANDO WINES, 1930s

simply thankful that at the end of the year their overdrafts are no greater. Such growers are at the very heart of the industry in the Barossa: of the 650 vineyards, 630 are in the hands of growers and only 20 or so are owned by wineries. It was these 630 growers whom Peter Lehmann was determined to protect, and for whom Masterson was set up.

If Leo Buring and Orlando have led the way in establishing the ability of the Barossa to produce fine white wines, Penfolds (for decades) and Yalumba (more recently) have led the way with red wines. Wolf Blass has been (and is) a high-profile inhabitant, but his wines come from far and wide, with the Barossa component providing only part of a complex mosaic. Guided by the practices and beliefs of that grand master of red-winemaking, Max Schubert, Penfolds has also engaged in a fair degree of blending. In years gone by that fact was not always fully reflected on the label, and some wines of seemingly 100 per cent Barossa provenance were not necessarily so. Nonetheless, Bin 28, Bin 389, Bin 708 and St Henri have always owed far more to the Barossa than any other region, while Grange Hermitage drew at least some of its base material from the district.

In the period from 1960 to the early 1970s, when Max Schubert retired from the day-to-day control of the winemaking team, these Penfold wines consistently ranked with the greatest Australian reds of their day. If public tastes have changed somewhat in recent years, and the wines no longer hold the glitter they once had, Yalumba (for one) has stepped into the breach to uphold the tradition and reputation of the Barossa. The reds, just as much as the whites, underline just how varied the *terroir* and climate of the Barossa are. The Valley floor is at an average of 250 metres above sea-level, while the ranges at Pewsey Vale rise to 600 metres. Rainfall on the Valley floor is a mere 520 millimetres, while on the hilltops and sides it rises to 700 millimetres. In both locations, and curiously even more so in the hills, supplementary water (or irrigation) has proved to be an essential step in securing reasonable yields in most years.

The soils on the Valley floor and the western side are red-brown earths with topsoil varying from sandy through loamy to clay-like. There are also patches of deep sands over dark-brown cracking clays. The ranges have a sandy topsoil over clays technically classed as solodised-solonetz, podsolic and solodic soils. Finally, there are strips of alluvial soil following the course of the Para River and its tributary streams.

Climate is an exceedingly vexed and complex issue. Some heat-summation figures suggest that Nuriootpa has a similar centigrade heat-degree summation to that of Margaret River in Western Australia (1517 for Nuriootpa and 1501 for Margaret River). October to March rainfall of 164 millimetres is very low, and sunshine hours correspondingly high at 8.8 hours per day. Arguments as to its suitability for fine table wine quickly degenerate into insupportable generalisations. The wines in the bottles provide the best answers, and here the skills of the winemakers become of paramount importance in shaping those wines to meet contemporary expectations.

The Barossa Valley has a feel all of its own. The German placenames returned after the end of the First World War; bienenstück and sauerbröten take the place of lamingtons and meat pies; while to this day the Lehmanns, the Hoffmans, the Seppelts, the Lindners and literally hundreds of others of similar ancestry grow grapes and make wine. As in so much of South Australia, century-old blue-stone houses abound in tree-lined streets, while a few hundred metres out of the small towns the rolling vistas of the Valley unfold, the colours and even the shapes changing dramatically with the seasons. All of this comes together in a joyous crescendo every two years with the Barossa Valley Festival. Anyone who enjoys wine and has not been to at least one Barossa Festival has missed one of the great wine experiences.

BASEDOW
161–165 MURRAY STREET, TANUNDA

The Basedow family has one of the great names in South Australian viticulture. Martin Basedow was one of the numerous German settlers who came to the Barossa Valley in the 1840s, settling in Tanunda in 1848. He became Minister for Education for South Australia, and in 1883 was one of the prime movers in the establishment of an agriculture college in association with the University of Adelaide, which was in due course to become Roseworthy Agricultural College. Martin Basedow joined his brother Johann to found Basedow Wines in 1896. Johann had been a major shareholder in Chateau Tanunda and had supervised the building of the winery.

Some of Martin Basedow's sons were prominent in winemaking—both Bernhard and Alfred studied winemaking in France. Bernhard was responsible for the establishment of Horndale Distillery, while Alfred was winemaker at the Stanley Wine Company during the years of its great expansion in the late 1890s.

Basedow grew rapidly, and by the turn of the century had become a significant producer of both red and fortified wines. Yet another of Martin Basedow's sons, Oscar, became manager; management then passed to _his_ two sons, Fritz and Hans, before going in turn to Fritz's son John. It was he who made the 1969 vintage wine which won the Jimmy Watson Trophy in 1970. I remember visiting the winery in 1968 and being unable to prise a single bottle of Basedow's eagerly sought-after red wines away from them. In 1972 Basedow became an unlisted public company, and both control (and winemaking) finally passed away from the Basedow family.

Douglas Lehmann, son of Peter Lehmann, has been winemaker at Basedow since the second half of the 1970s. Under his stewardship the range of wines made has substantially increased. Basedow grows only a small part of its intake, purchasing grapes from various parts of the Barossa and Eden Valleys. One of the innovations of Douglas Lehmann was the development of a wood-matured semillon at the end of the 1970s, well before such treatment had become fashionable, and at a time when semillon was not a widely utilised grape in the Barossa Valley for the production of quality table wine. This particular style has gone from strength to strength in subsequent vintages, although the 1979 vintage won two gold medals at the Melbourne show shortly after its release.

1984 was an extremely successful vintage for Basedow's white wines. The 1984 Semillon White Burgundy is quite outstanding, while the 1984 Eden Valley Rhine Riesling and the 1984 Spatlese Frontignac are both well above average quality. The frontignac, in particular, shows exemplary varietal flavour—in the manner of the variety the flavour of the grape is faithfully reproduced in the wine.

The red wines are traditional, richly flavoured Barossa Valley styles. The fruit is invariably ripe, but the wines gain distinction from the skilful (albeit fairly marked) use of oak. Basedow still has some very old fortified material, and occasionally make high-quality releases of a range of fortified styles, from liqueur frontignac through to tawny ports. These are complex old wines of great character.

BERNKASTEL
LANGMEIL ROAD, TANUNDA

Bernkastel's production is marketed under the Langmeil label, coming from the name of the street in which the principal winery is situated. Production is almost entirely bought in, both from the Barossa Valley and the Adelaide Plains. Winemaking methods are, to say the least, traditional; and the wines are not really able to compete in today's marketplace. Sales are principally cellar door and through a small private trade.

BLASS'S BILYARA
STURT HIGHWAY, NURIOOTPA

In 1961 a young German winemaker, who had worked for a time studying champagne-making at Rheims in France, was brought to Australia to assist Kaiser Stuhl in its then-developing sparkling-winemaking activities. On 9 May 1984 Wolf Blass Wines Limited issued its prospectus offering 31,399,944 shares of 50 cents each, capitalising the operation at just under $16 million. The stock market has subsequently said the company is worth more still, valuing it at $19.2 million. Wolf Blass has only recently turned 50, and one wonders what he will achieve in the next 30 years.

After arriving in Australia Blass spent three years with Kaiser Stuhl before moving on to Tolley Scott and Tolley. Here he made his first red wines, and with an unlikely background of a degree from a German wine school and sparkling-wine experience in France and Australia, he immediately achieved outstanding success. In 1966 he commenced to make small quantities of red wine for ultimate release under the Wolf Blass label. This was in truth more a blending than a making exercise; and in the fuller perspective of time Blass will surely take his place along with the great makers in the twentieth century, all of whom were consummate blenders. Blass's ability to visualise a finished blend comprising radically different component parts has been one of the two foundation stones for his success. The other has been a marvellously judged, although unashamedly obvious, use of new oak. In 1969 he purchased a two-hectare site, four kilometres outside Nuriootpa, on the main Adelaide to Riverland highway. This remained a part-time operation until 1973, when he left Tolley Scott and Tolley to commence full-time operations at Bilyara.

In 1974 Wolf Blass wines won the Jimmy Watson Trophy at the Melbourne show; he proceeded to win the trophy for three years in a row, making both Wolf Blass Wines and the Jimmy Watson Trophy household words in Australia. For if Wolf Blass is a master winemaker, he is also a master wine-marketer.

The company now has a totally disproportionate share of the top end of the quality wine market, yet has achieved this without ever discounting its products. No other wine company in Australia has gone close to matching this feat.

No less remarkable has been Wolf Blass's success in presenting his wines as his own. Until 1980, when Wolf Blass purchased a 49-hectare site in the Clare Valley and commenced to develop the company's own wines, virtually none of the crush was estate-grown. What is more, a substantial percentage of the annual production was made by other winemakers, and purchased in bulk as a young wine before incorporation into one or other of the Wolf Blass Bilyara wines. The public sees these wines as handcrafted in the style of a boutique winery. They may well be handcrafted, and enormous effort is put into the handling of the red wines in new small oak, but boutique winery it is not. The winery, now standing on a nine-hectare site, has the capacity for maturing 1,160,000 litres of wine in American, French and German oak; and it has stainless-steel storage for more than 3.2 million litres of rhine riesling and other dry white wines. The token vineyards around the winery have steadily fallen prey to modular expansion of the facilities, which include a large public relations centre, modern offices and a fully maintained laboratory with every piece of analytical machinery available today.

The success of Wolf Blass in the show ring borders on the indecent. The statistics roll on and on: most successful red wine exhibitor for the years 1980 to 1984; winner of the Montgomery Trophy for the best commercial red wine at the Adelaide Wine Show for six consecutive years (1978 to 1983); winner of the Dr Gilbert Phillips Trophy for best red wine in the Sydney show (1981 to 1983), thereby becoming the first outright winner of that trophy in the history of the Sydney show; and achieving an overall success rate in excess of 75 per cent for his show entries. No other exhibitor on the scale of Wolf Blass even goes close to challenging that success rate.

If this were not enough, Wolf Blass Wines is now one of the most important producers of rhine riesling in Australia; by the end of 1982 Wolf Blass Wines had almost four per cent of the total Australian bottled white-wine market, and its share has grown since. For a company basically known for its red wines, that was an outstanding achievement.

One of the popularly held beliefs in the early days of Blass's success was that the wines did not repay cellaring. In the second half of 1979 I attended a tasting featuring every wine made by Wolf Blass between 1966 and 1976. In the meantime, collecting complete sets of Wolf Blass wines has become a favourite occupation for many wine lovers, so I include very brief notes of those wines and of the characters they then showed. As the notes indicate, many wines have stood the test of time, some have not.

Yellow Label 1966 Shiraz grapes from Langhorne Creek, malbec from Great Western district (Bests). Matured in new French Nevers oak. Intriguing combination of big, old rich fruit and some cool-climate type characters. Holding very well. (17.5/20)

Yellow Label 1967 Sixty per cent cabernet and shiraz from Langhorne Creek, shiraz from the Clare Valley. Matured in oak for nine months prior to bottling. A very strong and clean wine; oak well balanced. Still outstanding. (18/20)

Grey Label 1967 Cabernet sauvignon and shiraz— grapes entirely from Langhorne Creek. Matured 15 months in new French Nevers oak hogsheads. Cheesy and broken; may have been a poor bottle. (12.5/20)

Yellow Label 1968 *(Second Release)* Cabernet sauvignon and shiraz from Langhorne Creek. Matured 12 months in new Nevers oak. Some camphor wood characters showing and also a touch of bottle-developed volatility but still quite pleasant. (Blass believes the wine was at its best in 1975.) (17/20)

Yellow Label 1968 Eighty per cent cabernet sauvignon and shiraz from Langhorne Creek— 20 per cent malbec from Great Western. Outstanding wine with fruit still holding to perfection; excellent oak balance. (18.5/20)

Grey Label 1968 Eighty per cent cabernet sauvignon from Langhorne Creek—20 per cent shiraz from Langhorne Creek. Old-style wine showing some chocolate/caramel/straw oxidation characters. (14.5/20)

Grey Label 1969 Seventy per cent cabernet sauvignon from Langhorne Creek—30 per cent shiraz from Langhorne Creek. Lovely bottle-developed aromas, quite delicate and scented; light fruit, nice flavour. (17.5/20)

Yellow Label 1970 Eighty-five per cent cabernet sauvignon and shiraz from Langhorne Creek—

15 per cent Wilton shiraz from Eden Valley. A poor corked and dirty bottle. (Not pointed.)

Yellow Label 1970 Eighty per cent cabernet sauvignon and shiraz from Langhorne Creek—20 per cent malbec from Great Western—40 per cent American oak used. Quite a complex wine with edgy fruit and a slightly hard finish. (16/20)

Grey Label 1970 Eighty per cent cabernet sauvignon from Langhorne Creek—20 per cent shiraz from Langhorne Creek. Matured in French Nevers oak for 12 months; smallest bottling—1200 dozen. Burnt-rubber aromas; better palate with some sweet fruit but showing definite signs of age. (13/20)

Yellow Label 1971 Eighty per cent cabernet sauvignon and shiraz from Langhorne Creek—20 per cent cinsaut from Langhorne Creek. A distinctly tired wine showing volatility and H_2S. (13/20)

Grey Label 1971 Eighty per cent cabernet sauvignon from Langhorne Creek—20 per cent shiraz from Langhorne Creek. Slightly dank, off characters in bouquet; palate better but fruit fairly light and wood starting to dominate. (14/20)

Eaglehawk 1971 One hundred per cent cabernet sauvignon from Eden Valley. Excellent bouquet, showing strong varietal cabernet aroma but a rather disappointing, flat, cardboardy palate. (15/20)

Grey Label 1972 Eighty per cent cabernet sauvignon from Langhorne Creek—20 per cent shiraz from Langhorne Creek. Mixture of new American and French oak casks. A fine and complex wine with lovely fruit and wood integration; good balance and length, with rich, ripe fruit. Years in front of it. (18.5/20)

Yellow Label 1972 Eighty per cent cabernet shiraz from Langhorne Creek and Barossa Valley—20 per cent cabernet sauvignon from McLaren Vale; 100 per cent American oak. Some mercaptan evident on bouquet which marred the wine; palate better. (14/20)

Yellow Label 1972 Eighty per cent shiraz from McLaren Vale and Clare Valley—20 per cent cabernet sauvignon from Langhorne Creek. Strong vanilla/caramel American oak on aroma and forepalate; rather thin finish. Plenty of total flavour though. (16/20)

Victory Claret 1972 Special selected 1972 vintage —80 per cent cabernet sauvignon from Langhorne Creek—20 per cent shiraz from Langhorne Creek. To commemorate the Federal election victory 1972 on behalf of Mr Young, Labor Party, Adelaide. Strong and rich wine with some volatile lift to both bouquet and palate. (17.5/20)

Grey Label 1972 Special release (experimental bottling)—95 per cent cabernet sauvignon and five per cent shiraz from Langhorne Creek. Very strong-flavoured, fresh and still fruity wine; a whisper of mercaptan evident. (17.5/20)

Black Label 1973 Eighty per cent cabernet sauvignon from Langhorne Creek—20 per cent shiraz from Eden Valley. American and French oak for over 16 months of maturation. (First Jimmy Watson Trophy winner.) Some aged caramel character showing on bouquet; palate outstanding with sweet fruit. (17.5/20)

Yellow Label 1973 Eighty-five per cent shiraz from McLaren Vale, Clare Valley and Coonawarra—15 per cent cabernet sauvignon from Hunter Valley. Matured in French oak for 12 months. A much lighter style, and a fraction hard on the finish. Lacked complexity. (15.5/20)

Eaglehawk 1973 Special release Eaglehawk Label—100 per cent shiraz, Murray Tyrrell and Wolf Blass Blend. Twenty-five per cent Hunter and 75 per cent Langhorne Creek shiraz—6000 bottles only. A very rich, ripe wine in which the Hunter component is not discernible. (15.5/20)

Eaglehawk 1973 Eric Brand and Wolf Blass Blend, 100 per cent shiraz; 20 per cent Coonawarra—40 per cent Eden Valley-Wilton—40 per cent Langhorne Creek—5000 bottles only. American oak dominates fruit. (14.5/20)

Yellow Label 1973 Thirty per cent shiraz from Langhorne Creek—25 per cent shiraz from McLaren Vale—20 per cent shiraz from Clare Valley—25 per cent cabernet sauvignon from Angle Vale (Adelaide Plains). Interesting estery bouquet with leafy herbaceous flavours. Lacks weight. (15.5/20)

Grey Label 1974 One hundred per cent shiraz from Angle Vale. Matured in American oak for eight months and then transferred into small French oak casks for a further 12 months. A very complex bouquet; rich almost thick palate; an enormous wine. (16/20)

Yellow Label 1974 Forty per cent Barossa Valley and 40 per cent Langhorne Creek shiraz, 20 per cent cabernet sauvignon from McLaren Vale. Predominantly matured in American oak. Marred by volatility. (14/20)

Yellow Label 1974 Thirty per cent cabernet sauvignon from Langhorne Creek, 70 per cent shiraz from McLaren Vale area. Matured in Nevers and American oak for 18 months. Sweet oak aromas; quite rich fruit but some off characters. Perhaps a poor bottle. (14.5/20)

Black Label 1974 Cabernet sauvignon 80 per cent from Langhorne Creek and 20 per cent shiraz from Coonawarra. (Second Jimmy Watson Trophy winner.) Cigar box/tobacco aromas; sweet fruit on palate with a touch of oxidation evident. (17/20)

Eaglehawk 1974 Special Duke of York Blend—80 per cent shiraz, 20 per cent cabernet sauvignon. Limited release—Kangaroo Island only. To commemorate Kangaroo Island settlement—140th anniversary. Pronounced minty oak the outstanding feature of a pleasant wine. (16/20)

Adelaide Club Cabernet Shiraz 1974 This extraordinary blend from the Bilyara Vineyards is a combination of 40 per cent Langhorne Creek Cabernet Sauvignon, Jimmy Watson Trophy 1975 Melbourne, and 60 per cent Angle Vale Shiraz which won the Arthur Kelman Memorial Trophy for the best exhibit in Class 5 Sydney 1975. Both wines matured in small American and French oak hogsheads. Despite its antecedents, jammy and with a volatile, crushed-ants aroma. (14/20)

Yellow Label 1975 Seventy-five per cent shiraz from Barossa Valley and Clare District; 25 per cent cabernet sauvignon from Langhorne Creek. Matured in Nevers and American oak hogsheads for 14 months. A firm wine with some astringency; surprisingly youthful. (16.5/20)

Grey Label 1975 Eighty per cent cabernet sauvignon; 20 per cent shiraz from Langhorne Creek. This wine has been matured 60 per cent in French Nevers oak and 40 per cent American oak. Rough-sawn new-wood characters were still to integrate fully in 1979. Very good potential, however. (16.5/20)

Eaglehawk Hermitage 1975 The first 100 per cent shiraz from the Langhorne Creek and Barossa Valley coming out of the Bilyara Vineyards. A big, solid one-dimensional wine. (16/20)

Yellow Label 1976 Sixty per cent shiraz from Barossa Valley and Clare District and 40 per cent cabernet sauvignon from Langhorne Creek. Matured

in Nevers and new American oak hogsheads for 16 months. A cool, clean, stylish wine with oak held well in restraint. (16.5/20)

Black Label 1975 Eighty per cent cabernet sauvignon from Langhorne Creek and 20 per cent shiraz from Barossa Valley. (Third Jimmy Watson Trophy winner.) Intense, aromatic, oaky nose; very good colour still; minty/raspberry fruit aromas and flavours. (18.5/20)

Yellow Label 1976 Seventy per cent shiraz from Barossa Valley and Langhorne Creek, 30 per cent cabernet sauvignon from Langhorne Creek and Coonawarra. Matured in Nevers and American oak from 18 months. A clean, balanced and stylish wine. (17/20)

The lessons learnt at that tasting were reinforced four years later, when in the second half of 1983 I confronted all of the Black Label wines. As the tasting notes indicate, I am in no doubt this line has gone from strength to strength. Since 1978 the blends have been stabilised around a Langhorne Creek/Barossa Valley/Clare Valley cabernet sauvignon blend (with a little shiraz from time to time), while the oak is American, matured as staves by Wolf Blass for over two years before being made into casks. The company has invested over $500,000 in its oak programme, Blass being very confident that the extra oak maturity avoids the astringent green characters which commercially purchased casks frequently have.

1973 *Colour:* excellent red-purple; just a touch of amber and very good for age. *Bouquet:* quite developed with complex vegetative characters overlying caramel/porty fruit. *Palate:* similar soft/porty/caramel flavour; holding reasonably well but a wine made in the old style and without the finesse of the younger wines in the line-up. (16/20)

1974 *Colour:* similar to the 1975; holding remarkably well and with only a touch of amber. *Bouquet:* developed fruit with light tea/tobacco aromas; pleasant but showing a touch of oxidation. *Palate:* the oxidation is more obvious, with some straw characters. Definitely starting to fade now. (16/20)

1975 *Colour:* red-purple with the first hint of amber. *Bouquet:* extremely smooth with lightly complexed minty fruit and oak. Quite outstanding. *Palate:* lovely sweet, minty fruit; nice balancing tannin on the finish; drinking superbly now. (18/20)

1976 *Colour:* good red-purple of medium depth;

first touch of ruby. *Bouquet:* well-integrated minty fruit and oak aromas holding very well. *Palate:* a big solid wine, with a slightly thick palate, although plenty of overall flavour. (16/20)

1977 *Colour:* strong purple-red—excellent for age, with little or no browning. *Bouquet:* slight vegetable/sappy overtones, with not enough fruit and a slightly smelly edge. *Palate:* a big wine with quite heavy tannin and some minty oak flavours. The fruit seems to be diminished in the wine in comparison with the others in the range. (15/20)

1978 *Colour:* virtually no difference from the younger wines, outstanding purple-red. *Bouquet:* rather dumb and closed after the younger wines; clean and well balanced; probably just going through a phase and should open up with age. *Palate:* lively fruit and good acid; oak beautifully balanced and integrated; great wine for drinking now but certainly seems to have development in front of it. (17/20)

1979 *Colour:* similar to the 1980—superb purple-red. *Bouquet:* minty/sweet oak; slight trace of fresh earth to the fruit; very complex. *Palate:* rich, deep sweet minty fruit and oak; very full-flavoured; low to medium tannin. Almost too big and needs to soften a little. (17.5/20)

1980 *Colour:* very good purple-red. *Bouquet:* smooth, rich, minty fruit/oak; spotlessly clean. *Palate:* very full but excellently balanced wine; smooth and minty; good tannin on the finish. Rich and with lots of character and flavour. (18.5/20)

1981 *Colour:* excellent deep purple with just a touch of red. *Bouquet:* tremendous complexity, weight, depth and style; full but not jammy fruit; nice deep oak. *Palate:* very lively; fresh acid lifts the fore-palate, then full, smooth, rich mid-palate and finish. Tons of flavour and style. (19/20)

Amid this feast of plenty it is very easy to lose track of Wolf Blass's achievements with white wines, which in fact outsell the Blass reds by a two-to-one ratio. After an uncertain start in the early 1970s, and a subsequent period during which he experimented with a number of alternatives, the white-wine releases have centred on two radically different styles: the Yellow Label Rhine Riesling, full-flavoured, soft and with appreciable residual sugar; and the wood-matured Classic Dry White.

The Yellow Label Rhine Riesling is produced in enormous quantities; in May 1984 sales were estimated at 145,000 cases a year and rising, placing it third in the table-wine stakes (still well behind Leo Buring's Leibfrauwine at 340,000 cases and Lindemans Ben Ean at 300,000) but rapidly closing the gap. In terms of the dollar value of the sales, the Wolf Blass rhine riesling must be the number one table wine. Guaranteed to be 95 per cent rhine riesling (with just a little Clare Valley crouchen) the wine comes from all over South Australia, but principally Coonawarra, the Barossa and Eden Valleys and the Clare Valley. One imagines that a certain amount of Riverland material may also find its way into the blend. It is a totally reliable wine which perfectly delineates the public palate.

In 1979 Blass made his first commercial blend of 7000 cases of what was then called Eaglehawk Dry White and is now called Classic Dry White. With that vintage and every subsequent vintage at least one gold medal has been won; the rate of success is increasing as the years go by. Thus both the 1982 and 1983 vintages won five gold medals each within the 12 months following vintage. The blend started off as a 40 per cent colombard, 50 per cent crouchen and 10 per cent tokay mix, with the colombard provided from the Victorian Sunraysia region and the crouchen from the Clare Valley. The tokay has since disappeared, and in its place has come McLaren Vale and Sunraysia chardonnay. A complex blend of German, French and American oak further enhances the sophistication of the blend.

In recent years Wolf Blass has become increasingly involved in administration and marketing; initially (and a number of years ago now) he handed over winemaking responsibilities to John Glaetzer, who joined the company in 1975. Glaetzer in turn is now director of operations for the group and chief red-winemaker, while David Wardlaw is senior winemaker and principal white-winemaker, having joined the company in 1981. Mike Fallon is general manager. It is a formidable array of talent.

LEO BURING
STURT HIGHWAY, TANUNDA

Leo Buring was born in 1876, the son of T. G. Hermann Buring who became one of the founding partners of Buring & Sobels, the original owners of Quelltaler Estate. He studied first at Roseworthy Agricultural College (where he graduated as dux and gold medallist) before continuing his studies in Geisenheim in Germany and Montpellier in France. In 1898 he returned to Australia to work for several vintages at Buring & Sobels before moving to

Penfolds' Minchinbury Cellars in 1902. He stayed with Penfolds until 1919, leaving to become one of Australia's first wine consultants. It was in this capacity that the Commercial Banking Company of Sydney appointed him as governing director of Lindemans' Wines in 1923. It was a de facto receivership, the fate which formally befell Lindemans when Leo Buring was removed by the bank in 1930, having failed to trade Lindemans out of its financial problems in the meantime.

The following year Leo Buring went into partnership with Reginald Mowatt of Great Western to form Leo Buring & Company, and began the Sydney-based wine-merchant business which built its success on the first semi-sweet white wine to be commercialised actively in Australia. Rhinegolde became a household name; produced from Hunter Valley semillon vintaged by the Phillips family, and bottled in a distinctive German flask-shaped bottle, its already substantial success grew further during the Second World War.

In 1941 Leo Buring took over the long-established Melbourne wine merchant Matthew Lang & Company, and in 1945 he moved to the Barossa Valley to purchase a small winery which had been built by Gottlieb Hoffman in 1897. This was to become Chateau Leonay, an extraordinary amalgam of architectural styles which stands as one of the more striking landmarks of the Barossa Valley today. The winery was substantially expanded by Leo Buring, who took the opportunity to add the strange turrets at the corners of the building. In 1955 John Vickery, then recently graduated from Roseworthy, joined Leo Buring as an assistant winemaker. The re-equipping of the winery was still proceeding and the grand schemes for its facade were incomplete when Leo Buring died in 1961, at the age of 85.

In 1962 the wheel turned full circle with the Lindemans acquisition of all the shares in the company. Lindemans immediately spent large sums in upgrading the winemaking equipment and substantially extending the winemaking facilities and storage capacity of the winery. Refrigeration was installed prior to the 1963 vintage, and from 1964

GRAPE-PICKERS, 1906

John Vickery and Reg Shipster commenced to make rhine rieslings of unequalled quality. No other company in Australia could produce a range of rhine rieslings of remotely comparable quality made between 1964 and 1975 (when John Vickery moved to Coonawarra, although he has since returned to Chateau Leonay).

The Chateau Leonay of 1985 bears no resemblance to that which Lindemans acquired in 1962. One of the more fascinating aspects of its development in the interim was the degree of autonomy with which it has been run and its products marketed. Since the mid-1970s the barriers have been broken down somewhat, and now there is clearly a substantial amount of product swapping among the various Lindeman entities. With only 40 hectares of vineyards around Tanunda, and a further 26 hectares at Watervale, Leo Buring derives the major part of its 10,000-tonne crush from independent growers spread throughout the Barossa, Eden and Clare Valleys. For some arcane financial or other reason, Buring is also the owner of the Lindemans group vineyards at Broke in the Hunter Valley, and releases a Wollombi Brook Estate Wood-Matured Semillon from grapes grown there. Its ever-expanding range of products also extends to wines coming from Lindemans' Coonawarra and Padthaway Vineyards, and at the bottom end of the range from Lindemans' Karadoc Winery.

Right from the early days Leo Buring has been known chiefly as a white-wine company. This is reflected in the composition of its own vineyards (over 90 per cent rhine riesling) and in its product range as a whole. The hierarchy of the Leo Buring labelling system sees the White Label Reserve Bin wines at the top; recently interposed under these labels have been the varietal/regional labels; then the Private Bin Black Label range; next the Chateau Leonay Extra Special range and finally the jewel in the crown—Leo Buring's Leibfrauwine, Australia's largest-selling still table wine in 750-millilitre bottles. In May 1984 its annual sales were estimated at 340,000 cases.

Its red wines have all tended to be pedestrian at best. Even the Reserve Bin White Label wines from Watervale (10 to 15 years old in some cases) have lacked any real redeeming features. The "new-generation" varietal labels offer a little more, but there are certainly better wines on the marketplace today.

The classic White Label Rhine Riesling releases fall into an altogether different category. I have collected various bottles over the years, and at the Barossa Valley Festival Wine Auction a few years ago I added substantially to my collection. These wines are truly extraordinary; they demonstrate an ability to age with grace equal to the greatest Hunter semillons. The 1964 Bin DW 57 can still open magnificently, with an almost Hunter honeyed character. One of the most disconcerting aspects of judging the Chablis Class at the Royal Sydney Show is never being quite certain whether you are judging a very delicate aged Hunter Valley semillon or one of the old Buring classics. I tend to get them sorted out these days, but when I commenced judging 10 years ago, I had little hope.

I last shared a bottle of 1966 DWV 12 two years ago; it was a freakish bottle, seemingly as fresh as the day it was bottled, and again showing some honeyed character. With white wines as old as this, there are good bottles and bad ones; that DWV 12 will stay in my memory for many, many years. The line probably reached its greatest expression with DWY 15 of 1969, DW 110 of 1970, DWA 15 of 1971 and DWC 17 of 1973. The extraordinary thing about these four wines is that none of them shows the kerosene/Flytox character which is a hallmark of so many aged Australian rhine rieslings, and that well into 1984 all of them were still superb. They have a steely raciness which sets them apart from all other Australian rhine rieslings; a crisp cleansing finish which is sheer class.

Almost all of those wines were Eden Valley sourced; however, there have been few better rhine rieslings than the Watervale DWB 13 of 1972. This wine in 1984 was flawless: magnificently powerful and combining fruit freshness with the suppleness of full maturity. If that seems an impossible balancing act, it is one which Leo Buring to the virtual exclusion of all others can achieve. Among the younger wines, Bin DWE 13 (Watervale) and DWE 17 (Eden Valley) both of 1975, Bin DWI 17 (Eden Valley) of 1979 and DWJ 24 of 1980 have been the most successful. Nonetheless, I think most judges would agree that the return of John Vickery from Coonawarra in 1983 was Chateau Leonay's gain, even if it was Coonawarra's loss.

Perhaps the most successful Leo Buring wine of recent years was the 1980 DWK 31 Auslese Rhine Riesling from the Barossa Valley. It is an exceptionally luscious wine and botrytis played no part in its formation, the grapes simply ripening and raisining in the extremely hot vintage conditions of that year. It is similar fruit which has gone to make the Orlando auslese wines over the years, but few of those (other than the 1976) have rivalled the lusciousness of the DWK 31.

CHATEAU YALDARA
GOMERSAL ROAD, LYNDOCH

In 1947 a German, who had been brought to Australia during the Second World War as an internee from Persia when that country was occupied by the British, purchased the ruins of a 100-year-old winery and flour mill at Schlenke's Gully. It was in an entirely derelict condition, a wilderness of weeds and nesting birds. Today it stands as one of the most extraordinary winery complexes and cellar-door sales areas in Australia. A magnificently opulent stone chateau, with an immense ballroom crammed with objets d'art, overlooks two ornamental lakes set among carefully tended gardens. The Thumm family have more recently completed a reception centre, and own and run the Barossa Motel.

Herman Thumm had gained a diploma in oenology in Germany; in 1930 he travelled to Persia to set up a number of business enterprises, including a winery. It was here he was interned, and upon his release in 1946 he worked as a winemaker in the Barossa Valley for a year before deciding to stay and establish his own business. Then and now his success has been based upon both white and red wines which have appreciable sugar. The sweet red table wine is an art form practised by few others. In the period from 1947 to 1960 (when the main beautification programme for the chateau began) his wines struck an especially responsive chord.

Thumm's eldest son Robert is also a German-trained oenologist, and has long since assumed winemaking responsibilities. He supervises an enormous crush, which at one stage reached 4000 tonnes per year.

A kaleidoscope range of wines is made. These are headed by the sparkling-wine range featuring Gold Label Brut, Gold Label Demi Sec, Fiesta Spumante, Brut Champagne, Demi Sec Champagne, Great Barossa Champagne Brut and Reserve Vintage Champagne 1979. There are two rosés, one conventional and the other Schillerwein Spatlese; and then a range of more conventional white table wine. The 1984 releases included a white burgundy made from colombard, a 1984 Chardonnay and a 1984 Lyndoch Valley Riesling. Naturally enough, there is also a range of spatlese and sauterne styles, these usually having bottle age. All the red wines offered have been cellared for substantial periods of time and they are sold at between three and seven years of age. Thus the 1984 list included a 1977 Cabernet Sauvignon, 1978 Cabernet Shiraz and the Chateau Yaldara specialty, a 1978 Spatlese Claret.

Overall the emphasis is on price rather than quality, the 1977 Cabernet Sauvignon having a recommended retail price of only $5.50. The quality of the wine usually reflects the price, although every now and then a very good red wine pops up.

CHATTERTONS
BARRITT ROAD, LYNDOCH

The Chatterton family had been grape-growers in the Barossa Valley for three generations before Roland, an architect and now winemaker, and brother Brian (South Australian politician) established Chatterton Wine Cellars on the northern outskirts of the town of Lyndoch. The North Para River wends its way close by, and the winery and cellar-door sales area were converted from a 100-year-old coach house by Roland Chatterton. The small production is virtually all estate-grown, and principally sold by cellar door. About 20 per cent of the total crush is sold in bulk.

The wines offered include white and red table wines, and unusual fortified wines, the latter matured in Australian hardwood casks.

ELDERTON
MURRAY STREET, NURIOOTPA

The vineyards that provide the wines for Elderton, one of the newest of the Barossa Valley labels, have been in existence since the turn of the century. For many years the vineyards were owned and run by Sam Tolley, of Tolley Scott and Tolley. Some time ago they passed into the ownership of Neil and Lorraine Ashmead, who have now determined to label and release their own wine.

The vineyards comprise shiraz (13.4 hectares), cabernet sauvignon (7.8 hectares), rhine riesling, crouchen and pinot noir (two hectares each) and colombard (0.8 hectare). All are established on red-brown alluvial river soil, and supplementary water is available and is used. Nonetheless, yields remain modest.

Elderton does not have its own winery; the wines are made for the Ashmeads by Peter Lehmann and James Irvine. Initially they will be sold by cellar door, but with a 1984 crush of 210 tonnes (or 140,000 litres), national distribution will inevitably follow. The initial release comprised a 1982 Hermitage, a 1983 Hermitage, a 1983 Cabernet Sauvignon and a 1984 Rhine Riesling. All of the red wines have been matured in new American oak hogsheads for in excess of 12 months, something very evident in the wines. The 1982 and 1983 Hermitage were both excellent, the older wine being the more elegant, with a beautifully balanced palate; the younger wine showing rich and lively minty/sweet fruit and oak flavours. Both wines were significantly better than the 1983 Cabernet Sauvignon, which was strong and robust, but rather obvious and lacked real varietal definition. The 1984 Rhine Riesling is a very traditional wine: generous, full and round with just a touch of lime/pineapple aroma and flavour.

Wine quality is certainly not in dispute. The success or failure of the venture will depend on the marketing skills brought to bear in offering shiraz and rhine riesling from the Barossa Valley.

HIGH WYCOMBE WINES
BETHANY

High Wycombe Wines is a tiny winery situated at Bethany, a German Silesian settlement established in 1843, three kilometres to the east of Tanunda. The winery was established by Colin and Angela Davis in 1976, with an initial crush which made them the smallest winery in the Valley. Twelve hectares of clonally selected cabernet sauvignon planted around the winery in the late 1970s have now added substantially to the crush, but all the wine is still sold by cellar door.

HOFFMANS
PARA ROAD, NORTH PARA

Hoffmans was established in 1847 by the son of Samuel Hoffman, one of the numerous Silesian settlers to arrive in the Barossa Valley in the 1840s. The vineyard and winery remained in the family for five generations, but in 1976 Andvin Pty Limited acquired a major shareholding, now holding in excess of 99 per cent of the issued capital of Hoffmans. Andvin is in turn owned by the Anders family, and has diversified wine interests. It has a shareholding in Masterson, Basedow and Chesser Cellars, as well as owning a large wine-storage facility in the Barossa Valley.

While Hoffmans has always had table wines available for sale, its real strength has rested with its fortified wines. It still has substantial stocks of old tawny port material, some dating back to 1933, all made and matured at Hoffmans. The table wines

have, however, been made under contract at other wineries. In 1979 Peter Lehmann of Masterson produced small quantities of table wine for Hoffmans, and his involvement has steadily increased to the point where all of the Hoffman wines are now made at Masterson. In earlier years Basedows and Tollana were among those to produce wines for the company.

Approximately 1000 tonnes of grapes are crushed each year to produce the Hoffman range. The major part of these comes from the 50 hectares of vineyards planted to rhine riesling, cabernet sauvignon, shiraz, frontignac, grenache and mataro. Other grapes, notably semillon, traminer and chenin blanc are purchased from local growers. The Hoffman product range is divided into three categories: commercial varietal releases under the standard Hoffmans label; the Sternagel Estate label for the premium releases; and the fortified wines.

The quality of the Hoffman table wines has improved dramatically over the past few years, with the 1984 white wines being outstanding. Prior releases of quality included a 1982 Chablis (a solid commercial wine with ripe, soft flavours and some oak) and a quite excellent 1982 Sternagel Estate Cabernet Sauvignon (rich minty/berry-fruit flavours, balancing acid and some soft tannin). This wine, made by Peter Lehmann, really does have great elegance and has been a consistent medal-winner at National shows. Foremost among the 1984 white wine releases are an Eden Valley rhine riesling (under the commercial label) and a 1984 Sternagel Estate Auslese Rhine Riesling.

The fortified wines are headed by the Old Tawny Port, a marvellous old wine with an average age of 15 years and part of the blend going back to 1933. It shows all of the developed, rancio characters one expects in an old tawny, yet has enough freshness to give the wine lift and elegance.

KAISER STUHL
STURT HIGHWAY, NURIOOTPA

Kaiser Stuhl was born in the depths of the 1931 Depression. The grape-growers of the Barossa Valley were in a disastrous economic situation, and the wine industry was facing ruin. In 1928 a meeting of growers had resolved not to accept prices lower than those paid in 1921; by late in 1930 it became apparent that worse was in store. A meeting was held on 9 January 1931 between the growers and the winemakers; the latter were represented by

Thomas Hardy, Hugo Gramp, Leslie Penfold Hyland, Sam Tolley and Oscar Seppelt. The winemakers, all of whom had grown up in the Valley and were close personal friends with the majority of the growers, explained their financial difficulties, and indicated that prices would have to be reduced by between 30 and 40 per cent if they were to make wine in 1931.

The growers retired to consider their position. The Barossa Wine Growers' Association had been formed in the early 1900s, and it was this body which had the task of deciding what should be done. Three general meetings of the growers were held before agreement was reached on 21 February 1931 "that we establish ourselves into a co-operative wine company". On 4 June 1931 the South Australian Grapegrowers' Cooperative Limited was incorporated. In anticipation of incorporation, the 1931 vintage was processed by Tolley Scott and Tolley and at Fowlers' Kalimna (now Penfolds' Kalimna). The same arrangements were made in 1932, the projected winery not having been built in time.

After much argument the present site at Nuriootpa was selected, and a winery with a capacity of 1500 tonnes was completed in time for the 1933 vintage. The wines made were almost entirely port, with a little dry red. The first export order was received in August 1931, for 2800 hogsheads (81,900 litres) and until 1940 virtually all the production was exported in bulk. The name Nurivin was branded on the casks, and indeed became the brand name for the company.

The Second World War meant the gradual loss of the export market, and in 1942 the cooperative was unable to process any grapes, having neither the cash nor the markets. Production commenced again the following year, and with the end of the war production slowly built up around bulk sales of port and other sweet wines to merchants and the larger established wine companies.

The events of 1953, and in particular the removal of beer rationing, plunged the cooperative into yet another crisis. Its problems were exacerbated by the fact that sherries based on muscat gordo blanco had become very popular, and it had no gordo available. 1956, and the appointment in that year of Ian Hickinbotham as winemaker, was to prove the turning point. The immediate decision was to commence the manufacture and marketing of dry red table wine. The wine was sold under the Nurivin label in half-gallon (2.25-litre) flagons from two trucks, which departed from the winery fully laden every Monday morning and returned only when they were empty — usually towards the end of the week. In that year

Orlando introduced Barossa Pearl, the first commercial sparkling wine of its kind. Hickinbotham quickly realised the potential for this wine style, and set about circumventing the lack of finance available to the cooperative for the purpose of setting up a conventional sparkling-wine plant.

Three pressure tanks with a capacity of 11,250 litres each were purchased from the Springfield Brewery for $200 each, and a semi-automatic filling machine was purchased from a mineral-water company at a cost of $260. A prefabricated cold-room in which the pressure tanks were housed was built by winery employees, and the project was under way. Sparkling wines, both for sale under the Nurivin label and made under contract for other wine companies, played an important part in the economic development of the company. It provided the cash flow necessary to support the increasing brand sales of the cooperative's products. The company was determined to build up its independence and to avoid the situation where the loss of a single customer or a single market could bring it to its knees.

An important part of this strategy was the development of a brand name with a little more elegance than Nurivin. The name Kaiser Stuhl was suggested by a friend of Hickinbotham, deriving from the largest of three hills on the edge of the Barossa Valley and so named by the early German settlers. Meaning "Emperor's Throne", it had been changed during the anti-German feelings of the First World War to Mount Kitchener, but changed back some years later. The move to establish Kaiser Stuhl as an important brand was an unqualified success. In 1961 Wolf Blass was brought from Europe to assist in the development of the flourishing sparkling-wine side of the business. By the time Ian Hickinbotham left in 1964 the future of Kaiser Stuhl was assured. His position was taken by George Kolarovich, an extroverted marketer who, with flair and enthusiasm, built on the foundation laid by Hickinbotham. In due course he became general manager and during the latter part of his term sales grew from $10 million in 1974 to just under $23 million in 1978.

By 1980 Kaiser Stuhl was one of the five largest-selling brands in Australia. Its intake in the 1980 vintage was 33,000 tonnes, one of the largest in the country. It had also in effect taken over management of the Waikerie Cooperative Winery in 1976, and in January 1981 entered into a similar arrangement with the Clarevale Cooperative Winery. Finally, it expanded its options even further in the late 1970s by commencing to buy quality grapes from other regions. It did this under the astute and energetic management of then general manager, Keith Smith, who was primarily responsible for making its grower members aware that it was essential for the cooperative to run on normal financial criteria.

All of this was not achieved without opposition or difficulty, but by 1981 Kaiser Stuhl had an immense range of base wines available to it, ranging from the most humble bulk material to some outstanding individual vineyard single-variety batches. The wisdom of keeping separate some of the best material had been recognised by Ian Hickinbotham, and small private bins date back to the early 1960s. Red Ribbon Shiraz was first produced from grapes grown on A. E. Materne's vineyard at Greenock in 1966. The Green Label Rhine Riesling was introduced even earlier, initially coming from Rogers' Eden Valley Vineyard. At the same time a substantial number of small show reserve bins was laid down, and many of these were ultimately released.

Slowly the image of Kaiser Stuhl as a bulk-wine merchant producing large quantities of very ordinary wine was changed. But given the capacity of the winery, and the interests of its growers, marketing still remained a problem. It was the recognition of this which led to the Barossa Cooperative Winery Limited agreeing to sell all of its assets and trade names to Penfolds in January 1982. From the outside, at least, it is an arrangement which seems to have worked very well. Penfolds has actively promoted the range of excellent wines produced by Kaiser Stuhl, and have substantially upgraded the massive Nuriootpa winery. Kaiser Stuhl Sparkling Summer Wine is one of the three largest-selling brands in the country, with sales of over 400,000 cases a year.

The Kaiser Stuhl releases over the past few years have gone from strength to strength. In 1981, to celebrate the fiftieth anniversary, four 1976 white wines were sold. Rhine Riesling Bin U24 from the Eden Valley had three trophies, 16 gold medals, nine silver medals and three bronze medals to its credit. Brilliant green-gold in colour, the clean, full and softly generous bouquet has vanillan overtones; the palate is long, full and rich. 1976 Bin U25 Rhine Riesling Traminer also comes from the Eden Valley. The 15 per cent of traminer in the wine adds just a little spiciness; otherwise it is very similar to the Bin U24. It collected one trophy, five gold medals, 15 silver and seven bronze medals in its show career. Probably the greatest of the four is Bin U29 Spatlese Rhine Riesling from the Eden Valley. A rich and voluptuous wine, its sugar/acid balance was nigh on perfect, inciting the show judges to award it two

trophies, 17 gold medals, 11 silver medals and seven bronze medals. The fourth release was Bin U31 Auslese Rhine Riesling, again from the Eden Valley, which is the sweetest and richest of the releases. By 1984 the wines had started to show their age a little, although the Bin U29 will live for many years yet.

Two remarkable red wines also formed part of that release, Rogers' Shiraz Bin EX24 of 1972, and Hermitage Bin 847 of the same year. Both were from the Eden Valley, but were radically different in style. The Bin EX24 from Rogers' vineyard had won two trophies and three gold medals, and was (and is) a big, rich, traditional Australian red. The Hermitage Bin 847 (like the Bin EX24 from the Eden Valley) was radically different in style, with a bouquet more reminiscent of a wine of Bordeaux, and a curious grassy/sweet palate.

In 1978 new oak became available to Kaiser Stuhl's red-winemakers on a planned basis, as did premium-quality fruit from the areas outside the Barossa Valley. With a quality vintage such as 1980, it was inevitable that some outstanding wines would be made. Four Red Ribbon wines were made in that year, between them winning 25 gold medals and two trophies in national shows. The wines were a cabernet sauvignon from Coonawarra; a cabernet sauvignon from the Barossa and Langhorne Creek areas; a cabernet sauvignon malbec blend from Coonawarra, Barossa and Langhorne Creek; and finally the Red Ribbon Shiraz. Even the latter won six gold medals. I believe the show record of these recent Kaiser Stuhl wines is important: the instinctive attitude is one of condescension or surprise, and it is even now hard to accept that Kaiser Stuhl is making wines which are truly at the peak of Australian wine quality.

The 1980 Red Ribbon Cabernet Collection, as it was called, shows a substantial new-oak influence. The wines were continuing to win medals at will after their release in 1984, and will continue to develop in bottle throughout the remainder of the 1980s. The Green Ribbon Rhine Riesling has likewise been a model of consistency. The 1978, 1980 and 1982 vintages have been especially successful; between 1957 (when the wine was first released) and 1982 succeeding vintages had won 25 gold medals. The 1978 Green Ribbon won the trophy for best white wine of show at Melbourne in 1984 and the trophy for best hock at the Sydney show in 1985. On that latter occasion it exhibited rich lime aromas and flavours balanced by unusual freshness for a seven-year-old wine.

The style of the Green Ribbon Rhine Riesling has always been full-flavoured; for many years now the sales of the wine have been such that the original individual vineyard concept has fallen by the wayside. No one vineyard, and certainly not the Rogers vineyard, could produce all of the grapes for such a major brand. The Eden Valley content, however, continues to be the most important, bolstered by Barossa and Coonawarra material.

It is the Red Ribbon wines since 1980 that have really caught the imagination: the 1980 Red Ribbon Shiraz was a very good wine; the 1981 absolutely outstanding. Released in 1984, it had already won two trophies, including the Stoddart Trophy at the 1982 Brisbane show for best one-year-old red wine of show. I have tasted it in masked line-ups on many occasions, both in wine shows and in trade tastings. Invariably it has been one of my top wines, with rich, sweet, fruit perfectly augmented by strong charred-oak aromas and flavours. A preview of the 1983 Red Ribbon, tasted at Kaiser Stuhl only five months after vintage, left no doubt that Penfolds is continuing to make the effort and monetary investment necessary to maintain the quality of the line.

As with any major company, Kaiser Stuhl has a large range of products on the retail market. Apart from the usual offerings of casks and flagons, the range starts at the bottom with Bin 44 Riesling, Bin 55 Moselle and Bin 33 Claret. Its Chablis Colombard is a large-volume mid-range product (virtually all of the material coming from Waikerie), while at the top of the range comes the Gold Ribbon Spatlese Riesling, Purple Ribbon Auslese Riesling and the Special Bin reds.

All of these wines are prey to the discount market, even the great 1980 Red Ribbon Cabernet Collection being so treated. I suppose it is part and parcel of big-company wine-marketing philosophy, but I believe the wines deserve better. They certainly need no apology.

KARLSBURG
GOMERSAL ROAD, LYNDOCH

In a valley abounding with rococo architecture, the spires and battlements of Karlsburg nonetheless give the impression that a piece of Disneyland had broken loose and resurfaced in the Valley. It is all the more extraordinary given that the building and its landscaped gardens were not completed until 1973. The 30 hectares of vineyards were commenced in 1971; the initial plantings were the traditional varieties (rhine riesling, cabernet sauvignon and shiraz), but by the end of the 1970s such exotic

varieties (by the standards of the time) as chardonnay, traminer, ruby cabernet, carignane and pinot noir had been added.

The treatment of the grapes was as idiosyncratic as the architecture; riesling traminer blends were oak-matured, perceptible (not subliminal) sugar was left in chardonnay which was blended with riesling, and other strange wine styles were made. The range of wines on offer now is rather more conventional: a chardonnay and gewurtztraminer riesling blend, spatlese frontignac, spatlese rhine riesling, Barossa rhine riesling, colombard, Cabernet Sauvignon Bin 117 of 1980, shiraz cabernet, a ruby cabernet carignane blend, pinot noir, a very old shiraz and a shiraz cabernet merlot blend.

A few years ago Karlsburg commenced its own marketing in the eastern States; I well remember tasting in 1982 a large range of Kalsburg wines, including several that were labelled pinot noir. They continue to market their wines in the eastern States, and the most recent releases suggest the effort may be worthwhile.

KRONDORF
KRONDORF ROAD, TANUNDA

Krondorf has been one of the fairytale success stories of the past decade. Although the history of the winery which forms the basis of the present-day Krondorf can be traced back to 1860 and to the arrival of yet another Silesian immigrant, Gottlieb Falkenberg, the Krondorf of today goes back only to 1978. In that year two young winemakers put their life savings (and substantial bank borrowings) at the core of a financial syndicate formed to purchase the Krondorf Winery from Dalgety Wine Estates. While Dalgety had spent considerable sums in virtually rebuilding and re-equipping the old winery (which had earlier travelled under a number of different names), marketing and promotion had been entirely neglected. It was generally agreed at the time of the acquisition that Grant Burge and Ian Wilson had paid a very low price for what was a very functional winery, but the question remained as to what would happen to the wine they made.

There was never any doubt that the quality would be high. Burge and Wilson had met at Southern Vales Cooperative in 1972, and, despite the antiquated winery, quickly established their reputation as first-class winemakers. In 1976 they formed a jointly owned company and in that year made their first red wine, which was ultimately released under the

Krondorf label. In 1977 they used the Krondorf Winery to make that year's vintage, culminating in its purchase from Dalgety Wine Estates in January 1978.

Dalgety had renamed the winery Krondorf, but had done little else. A distinctive, clean and uncluttered label was designed (which mercifully has so far remained unchanged) and Ian Wilson threw himself into the marketing of the wines, leaving Grant Burge to concentrate on the wine-making. It has been a potent partnership: within 12 months of the first release Krondorf's wines were known and respected across Australia.

One cannot help but admire both the strategies adopted by Krondorf, and the efficiency with which those strategies have been put into practice. The decision was to purchase selectively the highest-quality grapes available from the best South Australian regions, and to produce only bottled table wine falling in the middle/upper sector of the market. The wine would be offered at a price which would be sufficiently attractive to eliminate the necessity of discounting.

By constantly emphasising the personal involvement of Grant Burge and Ian Wilson, the image was built up of a small boutique winery producing very limited quantities of excellent wine. The quality was (and is) undoubtedly there, but the fact remains that it is a very substantial operation. By 1981 the crush had already reached 3000 tonnes, the maximum envisaged. Since that time the annual crush has fluctuated between 2500 and 3000 tonnes. A crush of this magnitude produces a great deal of wine: the 2500 tonnes in 1984 gave 1,625,000 litres, the equivalent of 180,000 cases. The grapes for this crush came from Coonawarra, McLaren Vale, Eden Valley, the Barossa Valley and the Clare Valley.

Since 1976 a seemingly unending stream of major show successes has been achieved by Krondorf; newspaper and magazine reviews have been no less consistently fulsome in their praise. In 1980 Krondorf released the first wines under the Burge and Wilson label, a 1979 Late-Harvest Rhine Riesling and a 1977 McLaren Vale Cabernet Sauvignon. These top-of-the-range releases have been consistently outstanding. The most recent addition to the Burge and Wilson range was the 1984 release of a 1983 Chardonnay, made from grapes grown in the Barossa Valley and McLaren Vale. A surprisingly elegant and fine wine, with delicate grapefruit flavours and nicely balanced oak, it looked to be one of the relatively few warm-area chardonnays which would repay cellaring.

Krondorf's most celebrated red wine was the 1979 Burge and Wilson Cabernet Sauvignon, winner of the Jimmy Watson Trophy at Melbourne in 1980. A blend of 50 per cent McLaren Vale, 30 per cent Coonawarra and 20 per cent Barossa cabernet sauvignon, it has developed into a rich, berry-flavoured wine with pronounced French oak. At six years of age it is showing no sign of breaking up. The 1980 Coonawarra Cabernet Sauvignon and the 1980 Burge and Wilson Cabernet Sauvignon (the latter from Barossa Valley cabernet) are of similar stature.

I have yet to see a faulty wine released under the Krondorf label. The large-volume lines of Barossa Valley rhine riesling, chablis, traminer riesling, spatlese frontignac, riesling (a blend of rhine riesling and crouchen and district varietals such as Coonawarra hermitage) are always well made, generously flavoured wines. The top-of-the-range wines such as the Eden Valley rhine riesling and the Burge and Wilson releases are, as I say, invariably excellent.

It is now ancient history, as it were, that Krondorf was the first of the "new breed" of companies to join the lists of the Stock Exchange; and that it has taken over the Ryecroft Winery in the McLaren Vale region to process its red-grape intake (accounting for around 25 per cent of the total crush). The Krondorf Winery has become exclusively a white-wine cellar with a capacity of around 2000 tonnes.

It is difficult to know what is left for Krondorf, or for Grant Burge and Ian Wilson, to achieve. With their flair and unquestioned skills, they will no doubt think of something.

ORLANDO
STURT HIGHWAY, ROWLAND FLAT

Orlando is not forthcoming about the size of its present-day production, but it may be safely assumed to be over 40,000 tonnes. This is a far cry from Johann Gramp's first vintage in 1850 of less than half a tonne of grapes. Gramp had arrived in South Australia at the end of the 1830s, working in a number of capacities before moving to Jacobs Creek in 1847. There he established a small vineyard, the first in the Barossa Valley, and only one kilometre distant from the present Orlando Winery. In 1887 Johann Gramp's son Gustav took control, re-establishing the winery at Rowland Flat where it remains to this day.

Growth was steady, but hardly spectacular. The 1903 vintage produced 34,000 litres, compared with 112,000 litres at Basedow, 810,000 at Yalumba and 1,980,000 at Seppeltsfield. The rate of development increased thereafter. In 1912 the business was incorporated as a limited company, and in 1920 Gustav's son Hugo became managing director. By the end of the Second World War Gramps' Orlando was firmly established as an important producer of table and fortified wine.

In 1953 Orlando triggered a technical innovation which was to revolutionise the Australian white-wine industry. Both Colin Gramp (Hugo's son), who was by then managing director, and the Hill Smiths of Yalumba, had been anxious to import newly designed German stainless-steel pressure ferment-ation tanks. These had been developed in Germany not so much for fermentation of wine as for the preservation of unfermented grape juice. With the after-effects of the Second World War still being felt by the Australian economy, only one import licence was immediately available. Orlando were the recipients. In August 1952 the tanks arrived, and the first vintage was made in 1953; that of Yalumba arrived a year later.

The style was so radically different from anything that had preceded it that it was inevitably misunder-stood (and rejected) by many in the industry. But the senior judges, headed by George Fairbrother, under-stood it well enough to award it first prize in both the Adelaide and Melbourne shows, and Orlando's Barossa Special Riesling was born. This wine has better claim than any other single wine to be the ancestor of modern-day aromatic white wines.

In October 1978 I was one of a group of wine judges and writers to attend a silver anniversary tasting of the Orlando Barossa Rhine Riesling spanning every vintage between 1953 and 1978. It was remarkable for two things: the sheer quality of many of the older wines; and in teaching me that even the most humble commercial rhine riesling can age magnificently if the vintage conditions were good and the wine well made. The outstanding wines in that line-up were the 1953, 1954, 1958, 1960, 1961, 1962, 1966, 1968, 1973 and 1977. The greatest wine of the tasting was a forerunner of things to come: 1954 Bin B was a blend of Barossa Valley and Eden Valley fruit. Gloriously fresh, and with that typical Eden Valley lime-juice character, it seemed more like a five-year-old than a 25-year-old. A foretaste of things to come, because after 1976 the wine became a regional blend before finally being overtaken by the marketers' desire for a 1980-style label and name.

The tasting tracked the developments in the handling of aromatic varieties such as rhine riesling and traminer. The initial vintages relied purely upon pressure to arrest the rate of fermentation; between 1957 and 1960 a combination of pressure and cooling was used; and from 1961 cooling gradually replaced pressure altogether. In subsequent years residual sugar also made its appearance, subtly changing the style further and also assisting its longevity.

In 1956 Orlando produced the first naturally fermented sparkling wine (made in horizontal pressure tanks) released in Australia, calling it Barossa Pearl. In this day and age Barossa Pearl may seem _passé_ (although it still enjoys solid sales), but here again the development was of immense significance to the industry as a whole. Over the years it has introduced countless drinkers to wine; some stay with it all their lives, but many others move on to bigger and better things. Certainly Barossa Pearl contributed greatly to the prosperity of Orlando over the next 20 years.

But Orlando was equally active in developing the premium end of the market. In 1962 it had com-menced the Steingarten Vineyard, which I discussed in Chapter 1. Steingarten has always been something of a whimsy, and in 1969 Orlando took what seems the obvious course of selecting a vineyard site between the extremes of Steingarten and the Barossa Valley floor. It purchased a 100-hectare property in the Eden Valley. The vineyards which it established here at a height of 400 metres are on a mixture of grey sandy loams and yellow to grey-brown podsolic soils. Even with the aid of drip-irrigation, yield is very modest at between five and 5.7 tonnes per hectare. The compensation is the extremely high quality of the fruit yielded by the 34.3 hectares of rhine riesling and 17.2 hectares of gewurztraminer.

While Orlando purchases by far the greater pro-portion of its annual crush, some of its very best grapes are inevitably estate-grown, and this certainly applies to the Eden Valley vineyards. These produced their first vintage of traminer in 1975, and since that year have produced an outstanding traminer/ riesling blend. Frequently with marked overtones of Alsace, successive releases of this wine have demonstrated an extraordinary capacity to improve in bottle.

In 1984 Orlando made the first public release of what will be a continuing series of Classic Maturation Releases, featuring wines which have been reserved for national wine shows and which are considered to have reached the peak of perfection. Included in that release was 1979 Eden Valley Traminer Riesling Bin 7901V102. The wine received five gold medals and a major trophy in a show career between 1979 and 1983. Its trophy and one of the gold medals was

COOPERAGE, ORLANDO, 1936

awarded in that latter year, underlining the benefits of bottle age. It is, quite simply, a very great wine: still retaining excellent green tints in the colour, it is classically restrained with definite nuances of Alsace in the bouquet, and a complex lingering finish. It has none of the oily coarseness of so many Australian traminers.

The 1984 Classic Maturation Release also featured a 1976 Eden Valley Rhine Riesling, Spatlese Bin 270. A winner of three gold and nine silver medals (and an outstanding merit award at the 1976 Expovin International), it retains great weight and richness on the palate, yet finishes without hardness.

In the year following the establishment of the Eden Valley vineyards, the Gramp family sold the company to Reckitt and Colman. In that same year Reckitt and Colman acquired Morris Wines, and with Morris Wines came what is now known as Orlando Wickham Hill Cellars at Griffith, in the Murrumbidgee Irrigation Area. These cellars, drawing on the vast surrounding vineyards, now provide Orlando with the material for its Coolabah casks and flagons. The acquisition also heralded significant expenditure in upgrading and expanding the rambling Rowland Flat Winery. Always a technically innovative company, Orlando was at the forefront in the development of the use of sophisticated winemaking equipment including centrifuges, gravity separators, the Brimstone de-sulphuring process (permitting grape juice to be kept unfermented at an ambient temperature until required for winemaking, extending the winemaking process over 12 months), and thermovinification (the flash-heating and pasteurisation of wine), not to mention considerable work in the development of yeast strains.

Since the middle of the 1970s Orlando has adopted a deliberate policy of sourcing its grapes from the area (and climate) which it considers most suited to the style of wine it wishes to make. It remains a Barossa Valley company first and foremost, but chiefly in the winemaking sense, and not nearly so much from a grape-growing viewpoint. It continues to look to the Barossa for two of its most famous white-wine styles. The first is its rhine riesling auslese. The first vintage was produced in 1964; that year also resulted in a once-only trockenbeeren-auslese wine which I was privileged to taste in late 1983. By that time it was dark brown in colour, but retained a rarely encountered lusciousness and acidity, typical of a great aged German trockenbeeren-auslesen.

Botrytis plays no part in the making of these wines: the grapes simply raisin in the six additional weeks they are left on the vine after the end of the normal rhine riesling vintage. A certain amount of mould and rot may develop, but it is not noble rot and, indeed, destroys the vintage in some years. Thus after the initial offering in 1964 Orlando was not able to repeat the style until 1971. Since that time the releases have been quite frequent. The 1972 and 1976 vintages were quite magnificent, while the 1977 vintage (still freely available in 1984) is only marginally behind in quality. The great strength of these wines is that the riesling aroma and flavour is not obscured by botrytis: while botrytis certainly increases the intensity of the flavour, it masks varietal character to the point where it can be exceedingly difficult to tell a rhine riesling and a traminer apart. The wines are softer in structure than those produced from botrytised grapes, but are nonetheless very long-lived. The 1971 and 1972 vintages are still lovely drinking wines, even if they have lost some of the freshness of youth.

The other style based firmly in the Barossa Valley is that of the late-harvest semillon, released variously under spatlese, auslese and sauterne labels. In 1977 Orlando took advantage of the fact that there was a significant surplus of Barossa Valley semillon which growers realised would not normally be salable. Orlando purchased the grapes on the vines, pre-agreeing both the weight and the price per tonne, and then instructed the growers to leave the grapes on the vine until Orlando decided the time had come to harvest them. The first semillon auslese was produced in 1977, and in 1978 a commercial release under a gaudy and transient label, Goldberren, was made. The recommended retail price was $2.95. Immediate show success and a consistently favourable reception by the wine press resulted in the substitution of the Purple Ribbon Spatlese Semillon (and a concomitant price rise to over $5).

The 1984 Classic Maturation Release included two late-harvest semillons. The 1978 Semillon Auslese (a multiple gold-medal-winner) has a glorious green-yellow colour, a rich buttery/vanillan bouquet, spotlessly clean, and a rich, peachy mid-palate with good balancing acid on the finish which prevents the wine from cloying. The 1979 Spatlese Semillon is a very different style. Glowing buttercup-yellow, it has distinct grassy/citric aromas intermingled with buttery characters, leading on to a soft vanillan wine with a rich mid-palate and soft finish. It had a far more successful show career than the Semillon Auslese, winning a trophy at the National Wine Show in 1981, and six gold medals.

Great though these two wines are, both are now overshadowed by the 1979 Semillon Sauternes. This wine has consistently improved since it was first shown; its complex toasty/oaky/vanillan bouquet leads into a wine with exceptional lusciousness on the palate and marvellous fruit/oak integration. Not surprisingly, its major show successes came late in its career, with three gold medals awarded during 1983 and 1984.

A retrospective tasting of Orlando Barossa Cabernet in the early 1980s (with wines from 1961, 1963, 1966, 1970, 1971, 1975 and 1978) showed just why Orlando has looked increasingly to Coonawarra and Padthaway for its cabernet sauvignon. The wines of the 1960s had not aged with grace; burnt-rubber characters and high alcohol were un-inspiring components. An outstanding exception was 1970 Cabernet Sauvignon Bin V62 (not released under the Barossa Cabernet label) which, like the 1970 Springton Shiraz, has retained freshness and elegance. Both of these wines have cigar-box/leather development, but are not tired.

In 1978 Orlando blended cabernet sauvignon from Coonawarra, Padthaway, McLaren Vale and the Barossa Valley, aged it in new Nevers oak hogsheads, and promptly won the Jimmy Watson Trophy at the Melbourne show in 1979. The wine won a further gold medal in Sydney in 1983, and at the end of 1984 was showing complex tobacco-leather aromas, with a lean, firm and fairly austere palate, with the oak delicately counterpoised to the fruit.

In 1983 Orlando released its first St Hugo Cabernet Sauvignon, vintaged from 1980 Coonawarra cabernet sauvignon. It was one of the top commercial releases of that year. I have heard the wine criticised for being too low in acid, and maybe its analysis says it is. All I can say is that in early 1985 there were few Australian wines of its vintage which were affording me greater pleasure. It has soft, sweet, cassis-berry characters; the oak is in perfect balance; and the wine is not too heavy. In mid-1984 it was succeeded by the 1981 St Hugo Coonawarra Cabernet Sauvignon, nearly as good as the wine which preceded it. Reflecting the warmer vintage, the wine is bigger, firmer and with rather more tannin than the 1980 vintage, and should be at its best around 1986/1987.

A concurrent release was the first vintage of St Helga Eden Valley Rhine Riesling, from 1980. It is a sad reflection on the current attitudes to rhine riesling that Orlando should have felt it appropriate to release such a wine under what is intended as a commercial label, and for less than $8 a bottle (recommended retail, with the true price no doubt

less). Its five gold medals (including two gold medals at the Sydney show of 1984) are in a sense incidental: it is one of the highest quality and most attractive rhine rieslings to be released in Australia over the past five years. Happily its quality was recognised (as was the ludicrously low price), for the wine sold out within one month of release. I shall watch for future releases of the St Helga with considerable interest.

In many ways Orlando has excelled itself with chardonnay. Its first vintage from this variety was 1979, composed almost entirely of Riverland fruit. Since that year Orlando has almost single-handedly kept sanity in the commercial chardonnay market, although it has more recently received great assistance from Seppelt with its 1983 and 1984 Chardonnays. Orlando and Seppelt have between them shown that first-class chardonnay can be made and marketed at a reasonable price: time and again their commercial releases, retailing for less than $5, came out at the very top of wine tastings which included numerous wines with retail prices twice as high. Orlando's commercial chardonnay has now had a label facelift and is one of the three wines in its excellent RF range (which also features a fine wood-matured semillon and a blanc fumé). perhaps the most successful of the commercial releases was the 1982, a trophy and gold-medal-winner at the 1982 Canberra National Wine Show.

Notwithstanding the humble provenance of most of the grapes, and even more significantly the propensity that most Australian chardonnays have to lose life and varietal character within three years of vintage, the 1984 Classic Maturation Release of the 1979 and 1980 Premium Show Chardonnays proved Orlando has somehow or other performed a miracle. 1979 Chardonnay Bin 7901V18A has amassed a trophy, eight gold medals and 13 silver medals between 1979 and 1983. It is still a quite lovely wine: the bouquet is toasty, rich and developed but the palate, with its touch of lemony oak, still has life and lift. The same lemony notes occur in the 1980 Chardonnay Bin 8001V42 (with five gold medals to its credit), veering to grapefruit flavours on the palate. The 1982 Show Chardonnay, due for release mid-1986, won two trophies and a champion-ship award at the 1985 State Bank Royal Sydney Show. I participated in the judging, and it richly deserved its success.

If I had to single out one wine made by Orlando in the past 10 years, it would not be a difficult task. 1977 Rhine Riesling Spatlese Bin 270 must be one of the greatest rhine rieslings ever made in Australia. Marvellous green-yellow in colour with crystal-clear citric/lime aromas, and still as fresh as the day it was made, this barely sweet wine has one of the most delicate yet intense riesling palates one could imagine. Its 18 gold medals (and a trophy) do it scant justice.

What a remarkable company Orlando is. Between 1978 and 1980 it won the trophy for most successful exhibitor at 10 successive Australian wine shows. Having made its point, it then deliberately turned its back on the near-certainty of continuing success by electing to concentrate on exhibiting only those wines which it had available in large commercial blends. While inevitably it no longer took the trophy as most successful exhibitor, it still won an inordinately large number of gold medals. Thus on these objective yardsticks it produces some of the greatest premium-quality wines in Australia, some of the best mid-range commercial bottled wines, and it demonstrably produces the best casks and flagons. Over the past five years I have at least once a year carried out a comparative tasting of all of the casks and flagons available — Orlando has without exception been the most consistent maker. And then of course there is Jacobs Creek, one of the top-selling brand wines in Australia, now encompassing both a red blend and a rhine riesling.

PENFOLDS
STURT HIGHWAY, NURIOOTPA

The Penfolds group is now the largest wine company in Australia. Its products range from the largest-selling brands (Minchinbury Champagne at 450,000 cases and Kaiser Stuhl Summer Wine, at 410,000 cases) to Australia's greatest red wine, Grange Hermitage. Its vineyards once extended from the Hunter Valley to Coonawarra; although their span has now contracted somewhat, they are still immense. The vast winery at Nuriootpa, consolidated with that of Kaiser Stuhl since 1982, is of almost incredible size. Yet large though the company is, its ultimate lord and master, Adelaide Steamships' managing director, John Spalvins, has made it very clear he is not yet finished with his rationalisation of the wine industry. As at the start of 1985 it seems that Seppelt had successfully warded off Penfolds' overtures, but we are yet to see the end of the story.

The beginning of the story is the arrival of an English physician, Dr Christopher Rawson Penfold, and his wife Mary Penfold in Adelaide in 1844. Before he left England Dr Penfold had purchased a land grant at Magill, on the outskirts of Adelaide and at the foot of the Mount Lofty Ranges. It was here that he planted the vine cuttings he had brought with him from England, their ends dipped in sealing wax to prevent them from drying out on the journey. The cuttings took; Penfold's aim was to produce wine for his patients, particularly those suffering from anaemia. A little wine for thy health's sake is an age-old prescription, and one which Dr Penfold frequently handed out. Before long winemaking had ceased to be an incidental adjunct to medical practice, the great soil of Magill working the same magic then as it did 100 years later. The Penfolds had built the low stone cottage which still stands at the Magill Vineyard and which they called The Grange, and Dr Penfold lived there until his death at the age of 59 in 1870.

Penfold's wife, Mary, outlived him by 25 years; together with her daughter and son-in-law, she ran and expanded the business, acquiring the neighbouring vineyards and cellars of Joseph Gillard in 1881. She installed Gillard as manager of The Grange, a position he held until 1905. In that year Leslie Penfold Hyland (Mary's grandson who, with his brother Frank, had changed his name by deed poll in honour of his grandfather) took over management of the South Australian branch. Frank Penfold Hyland had opened the Sydney branch one year earlier; he had entered the business in 1892, spending three years in France studying winemaking.

By 1903 Penfolds was by far the largest of the numerous wineries surrounding the Adelaide metropolitan area. In that year it produced 450,000 litres of wine, and was poised on the threshold of a programme of expansion which has not yet finished. In 1904 Frank Penfold Hyland bought the historic Dalwood Vineyards near Branxton; in 1910 the McLaren Vale Cellars were purchased; and in 1912 the Minchinbury Vineyards and cellars at Rooty Hill near Sydney were acquired, with Leo Buring installed as manager. In the middle of this the most significant expansion of all occurred. In 1911 Penfolds commenced operations at Nuriootpa, building a new winery to process a guaranteed 1000 tonnes of grapes to be provided by local growers, at a minimum price of £4 per tonne. The cellars were expanded in 1913, and the largest pot-still in Australia was installed to produce grape spirit. The same year Penfolds began construction of a large winery at Griffith, although the first vintage was not made until some years later. In 1920 yet another winery and distillery were built, this time in the Eden Valley, east of Nuriootpa. For some time the wine was made at Eden Valley and taken to Nuriootpa for maturing;

as road transport improved the roles were reversed, with Eden Valley being converted into maturation cellars for sherry.

For two decades Penfolds consolidated its position, but in 1942 commenced another round of acquisitions. In that year it acquired the vineyards of the old Hunter Valley Distillery; the HVD Vineyards, as they came to be known, were retained until 1982, when they were sold to Tyrrell's, marking the end of an 80-year Penfold involvement in the Hunter Valley. The following year, 1943, Penfolds acquired the historic Auldana Vineyards and cellars near Magill. These had been established 101 years earlier, when Patrick Auld purchased 93 hectares of land which he subsequently planted. Auldana became famous as the home of St Henri, made by Jack Davoren.

The style was created by Davoren about the same time as Max Schubert was creating the radically different Grange Hermitage at Magill. The label was a largely faithful copy of the old 1880s version, which had been discovered in a storage loft at Auldana. The first wine to be known as St Henri within the Penfolds group was made in 1956, although it was never commercially released. Indeed, the first fully commercial release was 1960. Up to that vintage the grapes were foot-crushed, and for many years (until the advent of mechanical harvesting) the ferment contained a large percentage of stalks. While it is common practice in parts of France (and particularly Burgundy), it has only rarely been used in Australia. This stalk-retention in part explains the distinctive character of St Henri. Contrary to public belief, St Henri has always been predominantly shiraz, with the cabernet sauvignon content varying between two and 19 per cent. In sharp contrast to Grange Hermitage, no new oak was used, the wine being matured in large, old-oak vats. The material principally came from Magill and Kalimna, although since the late 1970s an increasing percentage of Coonawarra material has been employed.

St Henri is the junior brother of Grange and has lived in its shadow. In the early 1980s I shared a tasting of all the St Henris made between 1967 and 1977. The overall quality was good, but there was little of the excitement which pervades any similar tasting of Grange Hermitage. As one might expect, the wines from 1967 to 1970 bordered on the pedestrian. These wines were made at the height of the red-wine boom, a period during which competition for top-quality grapes was at its greatest. It shows in the wines, which were the least of the entire range.

The 1971, by contrast, was quite outstanding,

with complex fruit, considerable acid, and still with excellent colour. The other good wines in the line-up were the 1973 (rich and with almost Californian overtones) and the immensely ripe, robust and deep 1976. The 1974 vintage was a great surprise, and an unqualified success in a very mediocre vintage. Subsequent releases have been variable. The 1979 St Henri was disappointing, but the 1980 much better. Even it is perhaps a little straightforward by the standards of today, and I think there will be more complexity evident in future releases. A preview of the 1983 vintage, tasted only three months after vintage, certainly suggested that this was so, with considerable complexity and charred-oak/chocolate flavours and aromas very evident.

If the 1943 acquisition of Auldana was of great importance at the time, the purchase of the 160-hectare Kalimna Vineyard in 1945 was to prove even more important. Kalimna had always been a major vineyard and winery, producing over 400,000 litres of wine at the turn of the century when it was run by William Salter. From that time on it was owned by D. & J. Fowler Limited, and virtually all of the production had been exported to the United Kingdom. The Second World War had interrupted that trade, and Fowlers Limited was a willing vendor. The winery is presently used only for oak storage and maturation, as is the Magill Winery. The principal varieties are cabernet sauvignon and shiraz, with mataro and cinsaut being progressively removed and replanted. The source block for Bin 28 Dry Red for much of its life, and likewise Bin 389, Kalimna has been of enormous importance in the Penfolds scheme of things.

In 1948 the already immense Nuriootpa cellars were extended further following the acquisition of an additional hectare of land adjacent to the main winery. The winery now covers three hectares, with a storage capacity of over 30 million litres.

In 1960 Penfolds made its ill-fated move from Wybong to the Upper Hunter. It marked one of the few obvious mistakes the company has made in a swashbuckling corporate career of more than 100 years. By the time Wybong Park was sold to Rosemount in 1977, hundreds of thousands of dollars had been written off. The move to South Australia's Riverland in 1973 was far more successful, although even here life has not always been easy. The property is at Morgan and has 520 hectares of vineyards including rhine riesling, sylvaner, traminer, muscat gordo blanco, colombard, doradillo, cabernet sauvignon, shiraz and pinot noir. It is a remote place, with unbelievably inhospitable saltbush plains on either side. It is only the Murray River which gives life to the vineyard, and even here there are mixed blessings. The production from this vineyard, processed at Nuriootpa, almost exclusively goes to cask and equivalent-quality bottled wine, although the traminer has been used for some years in Bin 202 Traminer Riesling.

The 1976 acquisition of Penfolds by Tooth & Company heralded a prolonged period of rationalisation. Minchinbury and Wybong Estate were sold in 1977; the following year the Griffith winery was closed down; in 1980 Auldana was disposed of; in 1982 the HVD Vineyard; and in 1983, amid great public controversy, almost all of the Grange vineyards around Magill were sold. To balance the ledger, as it were, a 164-hectare property was purchased in the Polish Hill River area of the Clare Valley. Under the direction of then vineyard manager, Diana Davidson, a showpiece vineyard employing all the latest techniques was established and planted to rhine riesling, traminer, sauvignon blanc, chardonnay, merlot, malbec, cabernet sauvignon, shiraz and cabernet franc. This was the realisation of a long-held dream nurtured by Max Schubert that one day Penfolds might have secure access to top-quality Clare Valley fruit. That acquisition paled into insignificance compared to the acquisition of the Kaiser Stuhl assets, brand names and goodwill in 1982. Tooth & Company had itself been taken over by Adelaide Steamships in the interim, and the Kaiser Stuhl acquisition was personally orchestrated by managing director John Spalvins. It certainly makes Penfolds the major force in the Australian market.

A large measure of Penfolds' pre-eminence in the public's mind can be traced to one man, and, through him, to one wine. The man is Max Schubert, and the wine is Grange Hermitage. For years the methods used to make Grange Hermitage were shrouded in corporate secrecy, but since 1979 more and more information has become available. The starting point was a lecture delivered by Max Schubert at the First Australian National University Wine Symposium held in September 1979. Schubert takes up the story:

It was during my initial visit to the major wine-growing areas of Europe in 1950 that the idea of producing an Australian red wine capable of staying alive for a minimum of twenty years, and comparable with those produced in Bordeaux, first entered my mind. I was fortunate to be taken under the wing of Monsieur Christian Cruse, one of the most respected and highly qualified wine men of the old school of France at that time, and he afforded me, among other things, the rare opportunity of tasting and evaluating Bordeaux wines between forty and fifty years old which were still sound and possessed magnificent bouquet and flavour. They were of tremendous value from an educational point of view, and imbued me with a desire to attempt to do something to lift the rather mediocre standard of Australian red wine in general at that time.

The method of production seemed fairly straightforward, but with several unorthodox features, and I felt that it would only be a matter of undertaking a complete survey of vineyards to find the correct varietal grape material. Then with a modified approach to take account of differing conditions, such as climate, soil, raw material and techniques generally, it would not be impossible to produce a wine which could stand on its own feet throughout the world and would be capable of improvement year by year for a minimum of twenty years. In other words, something different and lasting.

The grape material used in Bordeaux consisted of four basic varieties, namely cabernet sauvignon, cabernet franc, merlot and malbec, and these were used in varying percentages to make the Bordeaux wines. Only cabernet sauvignon and malbec were available in South Australia at the time, but a survey showed that they were in such short supply as to make them impracticable commercially—after all, the development of a new commercial wine, particularly in the high grade range, depends on the quality and availability of the raw material, the maintenance of standard, and continuity of supply.

I elected to use hermitage or shiraz only (which was in plentiful supply)—knowing full well that if I was careful enough in the choice of area and vineyard and coupled that with the correct production procedure, I would be able to make the type and style of wine I wanted. If necessary, I could always use a small percentage of cabernet malbec from our own Kalimna vineyard in the Barossa Valley as a balancing factor to lift flavour and character. As it happened, this was not necessary— at least, not in the early Granges.

It was finally decided that the raw material for the first experimental Grange Hermitage would be a mixture of shiraz grapes from two separate vineyards and areas consisting of Penfolds Grange vineyards at Magill in the foothills overlooking Adelaide and a private vineyard some distance south of Adelaide. I had already observed that both vineyards produced wines of distinctive varietal flavour and character with a great depth of colour and body weight, and felt that by producing them together, the outstanding characteristics of both vineyards would result in an improved all-round wine eminently suitable for my purpose.

During the 1951 vintage, the first Grange experimental wine was made, incorporating five new untreated oak hogsheads which I had observed were used to such good effect in France and other European countries. The objective was to produce a big, full-bodied wine, containing maximum extraction of all the components in the grape material used.

The procedure to be employed was first to ensure that the grape material was sound and that the acid sugar content was in balance, consistent with the style of wine as specified. Using the Baume scale, this was to be not less than 11.5 degrees and not more than 12 degrees with a total acidity of not less than 6.5 and not more than 7 grams per litre. With strict attention to detail and close surveillance, this was achieved.

Max Schubert is as atypical as the wine he made. He is, quite simply, a winemaking genius who had the courage and the imagination to ignore completely the conventional winemaking philosophies and techniques of his day. Geniuses are usually eccentric and egocentric; Schubert is as modest and as straightforward as it is possible to be. It is for this reason that he makes the conception and execution of those early Grange Hermitage wines seem so simple.

Yet when they were finally unveiled at public tastings arranged at the insistence of the Penfolds directors in 1956, the reaction of experts and critics was extreme. Even the stoical Max Schubert confessed that comments such as these caused him great pain and anguish: "A concoction of wild fruits and sundry berries with crushed ants predominating"; while another prominent wine man observed: "Schubert, I congratulate you. A very good dry port, which no-one in their right mind will buy—let alone drink."

A thoroughly disconcerted Penfolds board of directors issued a written directive just before the 1957 vintage that Schubert should forthwith cease production of Grange Hermitage. With support from Jeffrey Penfold Hyland in Adelaide, Schubert ignored those directions. Nonetheless, the quantity of wine produced was significantly reduced, and he was unable to purchase the new oak which was so essential to the style. The embargo continued until 1959, but by that time the tide of public opinion had started to turn. Just before the 1960 vintage Schubert received further instructions from Sydney head office, this time to recommence making Grange Hermitage; with funds officially available, new oak could once again be used.

The real turning point came in 1962 when, for the first time, Penfolds' administration permitted Schubert to enter the wine in the Sydney show. The 1955 vintage was duly entered and won a gold medal in the Open Claret Class. Between 1962 and 1979 Grange Hermitage won 117 gold, 63 silver and 34 bronze medals, together with 27 trophies and seven championship awards. No wine seriously challenges it as Australia's greatest red. Such is the longevity of Grange that it is not released until six years of age; the 1978 vintage was released at the very end of 1984.

Over the years I have attended many comparative tastings of Grange Hermitage, the most recent in December 1982. It covered all of the vintages from 1955 to 1976 inclusive, with the exception of the non-wooded years of 1957 and 1958. At a dinner held six months later, I had the great good fortune to share in a bottle of the 1953 Grange, and include the tasting notes from that dinner in this review:

1953 *Composition:* Magill shiraz 50 per cent, Morphett Vale shiraz 45 per cent, Kalimna cabernet sauvignon five per cent. *Colour:* astonishing dark, dense red-purple. *Bouquet:* rich and minty with quite incredible depth and character; will seemingly live for ever. *Palate:* giant blackberry-cassis; velvety fruit and oak. (19.5/20)

1955 *Composition:* Magill shiraz 60 per cent, Morphett Vale shiraz 40 per cent. *Colour:* medium-full red with just a touch of garnet. Excellent for age. *Bouquet:* free from any taints or signs of age; fresh fruit with just a touch of leather/cigar-box oak. *Palate:* marvellously smooth, only gently aged still retaining fragrant fruit; while rich, the overall impression is of elegance. (19/20)

1959 *Composition:* Magill shiraz 70 per cent, Morphett Vale shiraz 30 per cent. *Colour:* medium to full red-garnet, showing more age than the '55 and certainly than the '53. *Bouquet:* some volatile lift; oak a fraction dull, and some lactic characters evident. *Palate:* soft, rairly ripe fruit with low tannin; overall well balanced and holding well. (16.5/20)

1960 *Composition:* Magill shiraz 75 per cent, Morphett Vale shiraz 25 per cent. *Colour:* strong brick-red. *Bouquet:* camphor overtones to oak and a distinct trace of volatile lift, but eminently acceptable within the style. *Palate:* much more weight than the 1959, with more oak and more tannin, and also very strong fruit still evident. (18/20)

1961 *Composition:* Magill shiraz 65 per cent, Morphett Vale shiraz 20 per cent, Kalimna shiraz 15 per cent. *Colour:* dark brown-red, suggestive of high pH. *Bouquet:* porty and oxidised. *Palate:* caramel/oxidised. Definitely not a representative bottle. (10/20)

1962 *Composition:* Magill shiraz 65 per cent, Morphett Vale shiraz 20 per cent, Kalimna shiraz 15 per cent. *Colour:* medium to full red with just a hint of garnet; almost identical to the 1955. *Bouquet:*

glorious complex minty oak and fruit. *Palate:* full and long, with tremendous fruit on the mid-palate and persistent tannin on the finish. Still full of life; an outstanding bottle. (19/20)

1963 *Composition:* Magill shiraz 65 per cent, Morphett Vale shiraz 20 per cent, Kalimna shiraz 15 per cent. *Colour:* excellent full red, still with a tinge of purple. *Bouquet:* very full and rich with sweet, ripe fruit, though not jammy. *Palate:* rich and very complex; very sweet fruit, but, as in the bouquet, not jammy or overdone. A great fruit wine, though the oak is there to support it. (18.5/20)

1964 *Composition:* Magill shiraz 65 per cent, Morphett Vale shiraz 15 per cent, Kalimna shiraz 20 per cent. *Colour:* medium-full red-brown. *Bouquet:* strong fruit with a hint of cigar-box oak, though lacks the complexity of some of the other top wines. *Palate:* a fairly firm wine, almost sharp, and lacking the velvety richness of the top vintages. (17/20)

1965 *Composition:* Magill shiraz 65 per cent, Morphett Vale shiraz 15 per cent, Kalimna shiraz 20 per cent. *Colour:* dark brown-red. *Bouquet:* oxidised. *Palate:* oxidised. Most definitely an atypical bottle. Normally a very full-bodied rich wine, perhaps lacking in subtlety but very generously flavoured. (12.5/20)

1966 *Composition:* Magill shiraz 68 per cent, Morphett Vale shiraz 12 per cent, Kalimna shiraz 20 per cent. *Colour:* strong red. *Bouquet:* very youthful and robust; strong, sweet, minty oak and deep fruit. *Palate:* an enormous wine with strong drying tannin on the finish which threw it out of balance on the night. The fruit is there, but the tannin was more so. I have seen it show much better. (17.5/20)

1967 *Composition:* Magill shiraz 75 per cent, Kalimna shiraz 25 per cent. *Colour:* strong purple-red. *Bouquet:* full minty/camphor oak, and fruit still remarkably firm. *Palate:* outstanding balance, with rich fruit in typical style and pleasant lingering tannin on the finish. A complete wine, drinking superbly. (18/20)

1968 *Composition:* Magill shiraz 65 per cent, Kalimna shiraz 35 per cent. *Colour:* advanced brown-red. *Bouquet:* vegetative/aldehydic with evidences of oxidation. *Palate:* again signs of oxidation, although strong fruit lurks underneath. Probably not a good bottle, but Grange did go through a rough trot at this time. (15/20)

1969 *Composition:* Magill shiraz 60 per cent, Kalimna shiraz 40 per cent. *Colour:* acceptable red-brown. *Bouquet:* rather dull and flat, lacking life and complexity. *Palate:* a much more promising start with some freshness, but then drying tannin on the finish throws the wine out of balance. (15/20)

1970 *Composition:* Magill shiraz 40 per cent, Kalimna shiraz 50 per cent, Clare shiraz 10 per cent. *Colour:* medium deep red with just a hint of garnet; very good for age. *Bouquet:* lively fruit with just a trace of bottle-developed camphor; overall, fresh with lovely fruit/oak balance. *Palate:* fresh and lively fruit, with low to medium tannin. Again a hint of the camphor apparent in the bouquet. A wine which gives the impression of being close to its peak. (18.5/20)

1971 *Composition:* Magill shiraz 30 per cent, Kalimna shiraz 60 per cent, Clare shiraz 10 per cent. *Colour:* dark, deep red, with almost no browns at all. *Bouquet:* superbly rich and complex, with immense velvety depth. *Palate:* an enormous wine, with an almost chewy texture; pronounced tannin does not overwhelm the rich mid-palate fruit. A controversial wine which has from time to time been accused of excess volatility; certainly no excess was evident on this occasion (or on most others I have seen it). (19/20)

1972 *Composition:* Magill shiraz 25 per cent, Kalimna shiraz 60 per cent, Clare shiraz 15 per cent. *Colour:* deep red-brown. *Bouquet:* a touch of volatile lift followed by marked cassis-berry/oak aromas. *Palate:* another enormous wine with great fruit and equally impressive tannin. Still needs 10 years to reach its peak. (18.5/20)

1973 *Composition:* Magill shiraz 25 per cent, Kalimna shiraz 60 per cent, Clare shiraz 15 per cent. *Colour:* medium deep red. *Bouquet:* particularly complex, with sweet oak and ripe fruit, surprisingly attractive given the relatively mediocre reputation of the year. *Palate:* a much lighter style with quite sweet fruit and gentle tannin. (17/20)

1974 *Composition:* Magill shiraz 20 per cent, Kalimna shiraz 60 per cent, Clare shiraz 20 per cent. *Colour:* slightly lighter than the 1973, with just a touch of brown evident. *Bouquet:* rather chalky and flat, and disappointing. *Palate:* better than the bouquet, although the fruit is light and the main strengths lie in the structure of the wine. 1974 was an appalling vintage in South Australia, and basically the wine reflects this. (15/20)

1975 *Composition:* Magill shiraz 15 per cent, Kalimna shiraz 50 per cent, Clare shiraz 20 per cent, Kalimna cabernet sauvignon 10 per cent, Koonunga Hill shiraz pressings five per cent. *Colour:* immense purple-black. *Bouquet:* voluptuous deep spicy/peppery, very reminiscent of a big-year Rhone Valley wine. *Palate:* by far the biggest wine of the line-up, immense, chewy and tannic. Needs 10 and probably 15 years. May develop like the 1966. (18.5/20)

1976 *Composition:* Magill shiraz 15 per cent, Kalimna shiraz 60 per cent, Clare shiraz 15 per cent, Kalimna cabernet sauvignon five per cent, Koonunga Hill shiraz pressings five per cent. *Colour:* dense purple-red. *Bouquet:* pungent aromas with a twist of attractive volatility and some minty overtones. *Palate:* huge fruit, sweet and minty and beautifully balanced in a very ripe style. (18.5/20)

1977 Composition: Magill shiraz 15 per cent, Kalimna shiraz 55 per cent, Clare shiraz 25 per cent, Koonunga Hill shiraz pressings five per cent. *Colour:* excellent deep purple-red. *Bouquet:* complex fruit and oak aroma; medium to full weight, not overripe, but nonetheless a pale imitation of the 1976 vintage. *Palate:* solid fruit followed by very firm tannin on the finish, bordering on harshness. Needs years to soften. (Tasted July 1983.) (17/20)

1978 *Composition:* Magill shiraz 20 per cent, Kalimna shiraz 55 per cent, Clare shiraz 20 per cent, Koonunga Hill shiraz pressing five per cent. *Colour:* strong, deep red with no hint of browning. *Bouquet:* a very big, ripe wine with excellent oak; clean and deep-flavoured. *Palate:* in mainstream of Grange style, with almost thick, velvety fruit on the mid-palate, lifted by just a touch of volatility and balanced by tannin astringency on the back palate. (Tasted February 1985.) (17.5/20)

1979 *Composition:* Magill shiraz 20 per cent Kalimna shiraz 55 per cent, Koonunga Hill shiraz pressings five per cent. Wine neither released nor tasted by me.

1980 *Composition:* Magill shiraz 30 per cent, Kalimna shiraz 55 per cent, Clare shiraz 10 per cent, Koonunga Hill shiraz pressings five per cent. *Colour:* strong red-purple. *Bouquet:* beautifully balanced and structured, still opening up, with overtones of sweet minty oak. *Palate:* exceptional minty fruit/oak balance; very smooth, with less naked power than many of the previous releases, bordering on outright elegance. Outstanding potential. (Tasted July 1983 — not due for release until late 1986.) (18.5/20)

Controversy still surrounds Grange. Much discussed is the deliberate induction of volatile acidity into the wine, usually at levels of around 0.8 grams per litre, but occasionally going above one gram per litre. This level is far higher than that found in most quality wines, but Max Schubert and Don Ditter, who has succeeded Schubert as chief winemaker, argue that without it the wine would be too heavy and cloying. I agree. The other unusual feature is the addition of tannin in powdered form; while performing an essential part in extending the longevity of the wine, it seems to me that in one or two years the tannin is excessive. In July 1983 I was able to taste a three-month-old Grange, an experience I will not quickly forget. If the wines are robust at six years of age, they are positively frightening at three months. The last area of controversy turns on the exact percentage of cabernet sauvignon. The composition figures quoted were supplied by Max Schubert to David Farmer, and first appeared in a *Financial Review* article in 1981. They included the cryptic footnotes that: "We have only documented some of the years that contain Cabernet Sauvignon. Most years now contain at least five per cent Cabernet Sauvignon." It may safely be assumed, I think, that the operative words of this footnote are "at least".

For decades Grange Hermitage, St Henri Claret, Bin 707 Cabernet Sauvignon and Bin 389 Cabernet Shiraz (aided to a lesser degree by Kalimna Shiraz Bin 28 and Coonawarra Shiraz Bin 128) put Penfolds on a pedestal, unchallenged as the premier red-winemakers in Australia. Then, in 1969, production of Bin 707 was discontinued (until 1976), and between 1973 and 1978 the junior partners of Bin 389, Bin 28 and Bin 128 all slipped somewhat in quality. St Henri, too, went through a difficult period and, as the tasting notes indicate, even Grange reflected some poor to mediocre vintages in South Australia. Nor were there any of the magnificent small Show Bins such as those made by Max Schubert in 1962, 1963, 1966 and 1967. Directions had come from above to discontinue these. All in all, it was a worrying time, and the sight of Bin 389 being heavily discounted in the marketplace added nothing to the overall reputation of Penfolds.

Even if some of the woes of the marketplace continue, wine quality has taken a distinct turn for the better as from the 1980 vintage. Not only are all of the red wines of that year excellent, but it also marked the return of some of the special blends which had so enlivened the 1960s, and which are now doing wonders for Penfolds in the show ring. A range of these wines was shown to the New South

Wales Wine Press Club in May 1982. Foremost was a 1980 Coonawarra Cabernet/Kalimna Shiraz, a latter-day manifestation of Penfolds' greatest red wine — 1962 Bin 60A. It was this latter wine which caused the great American winemaker André Tchelistcheff, upon tasting the wine at a major wine dinner, to spring to his feet and proclaim to the startled room: "Gentlemen, you will all stand in the presence of this wine."

The 1980 vintage may not reach the sublime heights of the 1962, but it was quite magnificent at two years of age, with complexes of mint and spice, a very long finish to the palate, marked by beautifully handled fruit and oak. A very great elegant yet complex wine. As I say, the 1980 vintage of Bin 28, Bin 128 and Bin 389 fully reflected that outstanding year, while the 1981 vintages of the same wines rose above that difficult year. Once Penfolds' Clare Valley Vineyard comes into full production, we should see some quite startling red wines.

The strength of this renaissance was underlined at the 1985 State Bank Royal Sydney Wine Show, in which the 1983 Bin 707 Cabernet Sauvignon received a trophy and gold medal, and the 1984 Cabernet Sauvignon won top points (and a gold medal) in its class. The latter is destined to become a great classic. Penfolds' first chardonnay from the 1982 vintage was also full of promise. By early 1985 it was probably close to its peak, with full, soft, white burgundy flavours and structures and just a hint of cinnamon and peach.

PETER LEHMANN WINES
TANUNDA

Peter Lehmann is the personification of the Barossa Valley. He has devoted his life to its people and its wines; and he is a staunch and often outspoken defender of both. His credentials for this role are impeccable. He was born at Angaston in 1930, the son of a Lutheran pastor, and the fifth generation of German forebears who had moved to the Barossa Valley almost a century earlier. He worked first at Yalumba, where he spent 13 years, before moving to Saltram in 1960 where he remained until 1979.

In that year the largest wine agglomerate in the world, Seagram, acquired Saltrams from Dalgety. It was a time of particular problems in the Barossa Valley, with a large grape surplus and the probability of that surplus increasing. Lehmann felt keenly the plight of the numerous Barossa growers with whom he had dealt over the years, and was only too well

aware that if he stayed at Saltram he would have little or no power to help them. He also believed that the grapes produced by the growers were of worthwhile quality, and if turned into wine by a skilled winemaker using modern equipment, would produce a premium product with a ready market. So Masterson Barossa Vignerons Proprietary Limited was formed, inspired by Damon Runyon's great character Sky Masterson. It was indeed something of a gamble, but Lehmann took care to reduce the odds against the venture succeeding by enrolling as shareholders Cerebos (Australia) Limited and the Anders family company Andvin Proprietary Limited. The Anders family is a long-established Barossa family with widespread commercial interests and considerable financial strength. That company owns the massive stainless-steel tank farm used by Masterson Barossa Vingerons.

Masterson made its first vintage in 1980. Many industry observers predicted it would fail, arguing that Lehmann was trying to turn back the hands of time, supporting a sector of the industry which was simply not economic. For a while the fate of Masterson seemed to hang delicately in the balance; rumours circulated that the going was very difficult. So it may have been, but the efficiency of the operation and the sheer quality of the production soon carried the day. Initially the major part of the annual crush, which varies between 8000 and 10,000 tonnes, was sold in bulk. The operation was primarily intended as a source of contract-made bulk wine for on-sale to other wineries, shortly after vintage. Thus the total crush was linked (and still is to a degree) to the demand for contract-made wine. But in more recent vintages an ever-increasing portion of the 5.5-million to seven-million litre production is bottled under the Peter Lehmann and Masterson labels for conventional retail sale.

Consistent with its aims and philosophies, Masterson does not own any vineyards; equally consistently, it purchases fruit only from the Barossa and Eden Valleys. But the secret to the survival of the Barossa Valley is the immense diversity of *terroir* and climate. This diversity gives a far greater range of base material (both in terms of style and quality) than one would at first sight imagine. Thus frontignac, muscadelle and semillon are vintaged between late February and early March; chardonnay, pinot noir, gewurztztraminer and rhine riesling from early to mid-March; shiraz, grenache and chenin blanc from mid- to late March; cabernet sauvignon from late March to early April; and late-harvest semillon for sauterne in May.

The top-of-the-range products, released under the Peter Lehmann label, are very good. The 1982 Barossa Valley Rhine Riesling was typical of the style released under this label: a very rich, full-flavoured wine, with hints of tropical fruit, at its best within 12 to 18 months of vintage; an utterly reliable early-drinking style. 1982 also produced a dry semillon (so labelled to avoid confusion with the sauterne style at which Lehmann excels), which at the end of 1984 had developed into a first-class wine, equal to anything the Valley can offer. Although reasonably well developed, it still retained some grassy/lemony aromas and flavours, partially fruit-derived and seemingly partially coming from a little oak. With a true retail price of less than $5, it is difficult to think what more one could ask for. Also current at the end of 1984 were a 1982 Cabernet Sauvignon (fresh, vibrant in colour and with beautifully balanced and modulated fruit aromas and flavours in the blackcurrant spectrum, almost with a hint of wild flowers); and a 1981 Shiraz Dry Red (rich but not overripe with a hint of minty oak and a soft, velvety rounded palate balanced by soft tannin on the finish).

The high quality of those two marginally un-fashionable reds is inevitably overshadowed by the 1982 Pinot Noir. Lehmann has had consistent success with his pinot noir, defying the laws of gravity (in the sense that it is exceedingly difficult to obtain recognisable varietal character in warmer regions), and has won numerous gold medals since first making the wine in 1980. Lehmann manages to preserve recognisable varietal character and yet invest the wine with depth and structure; so many Australian pinot noirs either have good colour, flavour and depth but no pinot character, or show varietal character at the expense of body. The latter are exercises in pinot noir, but they are certainly not wines.

Great though the Lehmann success with pinot noir has been, his greatest achievements have come with his semillon sauterne. The 1981, still available at the end of 1984 for less than $10 a bottle, avoided the excess volatility of the very good 1980 vintage, although still shows some characteristic lift. There is no question that these wines need a little volatility to prevent them cloying; in 1981 Lehmann judged it to absolute perfection. A marvellously rich, intense wine with a long finish and subtle oak, it is one of the top late-harvest styles available in Australia today.

The Peter Lehmann and Masterson labels are gaining a major place in the Australian market, and are also flourishing in the American market. They deserve their success.

RED GUM VINEYARD
LYNDOCH TO WILLIAMSTOWN ROAD, LYNDOCH

In 1857 Reinholdt Kies migrated from Schwaben, now part of West Germany, to South Australia; like many of his countrymen he settled in the Barossa. The region he chose was named by the new settlers Hoffnangsthal Valley. Close to the base of the Barossa Hills, the good rainfall patterns, well-structured deep loam soils and good drainage supported a prolific growth of tall red gum trees.

Reinholdt Kies adopted the regional name Karra-wirra—Aboriginal for "forest of red gums"—for his vineyard; the initial label of some of the first wines produced depicted a sprawling, age-old red gum. For four generations the Kies family continued to produce wine under the Karrawirra label, but in November 1983 it sadly announced it had been forced to change the name because of confusion with the Wynns' brand, Killawarra. In a press release at the time Ken Kies, who has owned and run Karrawirra for the last 40 years, commented:

> We have tried to exist alongside this group, but to the consumer, there is not much difference on the shelf between Karrawirra and Killawarra. We have simply been discounted out of the market, and to survive, we have been forced to change our name. Our red gum tree insignia has been featured on our new labels—but this time it is twice as big.

So, I might add are the labels, vaguely reminiscent of the medicine bottle wrap-arounds of McPherson's wines in the Hunter Valley in the mid-1970s. I do not quarrel with the change of name, but I think the new labels do scant justice to the wine.

Killawarra, as it then was, and Red Gum as it now is, has in fact made some excellent wines over the years. Lindsay Stanley was winemaker throughout the latter part of the 1970s, and was succeeded in 1983 by Trevor Jones. Winery equipment has been substantially upgraded with the installation of a large refrigeration plant which enables must-chilling through a Spiroflo must-chiller and precise temperature control over fermentation. A new Miller grape-crusher with adjustable rollers was also acquired. This equipment goes alongside an already impressive array of equipment including a centrifuge and auto fermenters. The enterprise is in fact a very substantial one; the annual crush has reached 700 tonnes, virtually all drawn from the 70 hectares of family-owned vineyards. All of this has been achieved in a remarkably short space of time, given that until 1969 the Kies family sold virtually all its grapes to other makers. The range of wines produced is no less impressive, at one time offering such delicacies as Lubly Bubbly.

The 1983 Red Gum releases featured some very sophisticated oak handling. The 1983 White Barossa, made from a blend of unspecified varieties, was indeed virtually totally dependent upon spicy nutmeg oak aromas and flavours. While a purist might criticise the wine for lack of fruit, it was (and is) a very commercial style. Better still was the 1983 Fumé Blanc, in which citrus lemony flavours intermingle with nutmeg oak. With a retail price of less than $5 it was a great bargain. The 1980 Red Gum Cabernet Shiraz, also on release during 1984, was a good commercial wine showing sweet American oak and soft fruit.

ROCKFORD
KRONDORF ROAD, TANUNDA

Rockford opened its doors for business on 26 October 1984. After nearly two decades of making wine for others, Robert O'Callaghan opened his own winery in what used to be the township of Krondorf. The address now is Krondorf Road, Tanunda, simply because, with a few exceptions, the township is no more. One of those exceptions is the old free-stone cellars in which the Rockford wines are stored and offered for sale through the cellar door.

O'Callaghan entered the wine industry as a trainee winemaker for Seppelt at Rutherglen in 1966. Before long he had moved to the Barossa Valley as winemaker for a number of companies. Between 1980 and 1984 he was a consultant winemaker for Bernkastel, St Halletts and Gawler River (as well as several others). Wines made by him have won numerous gold medals over the years, including one Montgomery Trophy for the 1980 St Halletts Dry Red and the Frangos Trophy for vintage port.

O'Callaghan professes to be impressed by traditional winemaking methods and equipment. Over the years he has accumulated a collection of other wineries' discards, and has housed these at Rockford to make part of the red wine and fortified wine vintaged each year. The balance will be made at other wineries under O'Callaghan's supervision; all of the white wines are made, and will in the future be made, this way. The avant-garde label sits oddly with this highly traditional approach, but I must say I find it quite attractive. It is certainly different. It graces a wide range of wines comprising the original releases: a 1984 Rhine Riesling from the Eden Valley, a 1984 White Frontignac Spatlese, a 1984 Sauvignon Blanc

from the Adelaide Plains, a 1984 Alicante Bouchet from the Adelaide Plains, a 1983 Rhine Riesling Botrytis Cinerea, a 1981 Shiraz Cabernet from the Barossa Valley and McLaren Vale, a 1980 Cabernet Sauvignon from McLaren Vale, and an old tawny port.

The outstanding wine amongst the release was the 1980 McLaren Vale Cabernet Sauvignon. It puts me very much in mind of the Woodstock Cabernet Sauvignon of that year; certainly it has firm, astringent cabernet sauvignon aroma and flavour, with silky mid-palate fruit and sweet-berry tastes, with a lingering finish. Every now and then McLaren Vale comes up with wines which defy all of the rules. This is such a wine.

The 1984 Alicante Bouchet is a rare and interesting wine. This variety has red flesh, and produces red juice with minimal skin contact. It lends itself to a beaujolais style, with the wine removed from the skins early in the fermentation, retaining maximum fruit freshness and next to no tannin. This is precisely how the wine presents itself; fresh, crisp and aromatic, with a very light mid-palate and a crisp finish. The 1983 Rhine Riesling Botrytis Cinerea lives up to its name, with strong botrytis influence; it is a rich spatlese style, with pronounced acid on the finish which may well soften and permit the wine to develop further. A 1984 Sauvignon Blanc was also released showing ample flavour and nice oak but relatively little varietal character. The major part of the 5000-case output will be sold by cellar door and mailing list, with limited Melbourne distribution.

ROSEWORTHY
ROSEWORTHY AGRICULTURAL COLLEGE, ROSEWORTHY

Roseworthy was founded in 1883 and is the oldest agricultural college in Australia. Until 1936 oenology and viticulture were taught simply as subjects forming part of the main agricultural course. The first formal course (diploma in oenology) was commenced in 1936, and converted to a degree course (Bachelor of Applied Science in oenology) in 1978. Until the advent of the wine school at the Riverina College of Advanced Education, Roseworthy was the only wine school in Australia, and has produced the vast bulk of Australia's winemakers.

As at the Riverina College a fully operational commercial winery (with a capacity of 200 tonnes) is operated by Roseworthy. Again as with the College, grapes are purchased from a variety of sources within

South Australia, enabling students to monitor the performance of different regions under commercial conditions. Jeff Anderson has been resident winemaker for a number of years now, and the Roseworthy wines released onto the commercial market seem to go from strength to strength. A revamped label introduced in 1984 underlines the fact that Roseworthy is very serious about the making and marketing of its wines.

The standard of the 1984 releases, covering the 1982, 1983 and 1984 vintages, was consistently high. Roseworthy indulged in a small flight of fancy in releasing a 100 per cent varietal rkatsiteli from the Barossa Valley, using the remainder of the wine in a curious colombard, rhine riesling, rkatsiteli blend labelled as a chablis. It seemed to me the main point of this exercise was to prove that this Russian variety produces fairly ordinary wine when grown in warm climates.

The 1983 Eden Valley Rhine Riesling, 1983 Eden Valley Chardonnay and 1982 Eden Valley Chardonnay were wines in an altogether different class. I assume the Eden Valley Chardonnay came from the Mount Adam Vineyard; whether or not this be so, it is a marvellous wine, and the 1983 vintage is absolutely outstanding. If has fresh, lively grapefuit/melon flavours and aroma, with an elegant, lingering finish. The 1982 vintage was also very good, firm and deeper than the 1983, and without that sparkle which the 1983 possesses. The 1983 Eden Valley Rhine riesling is a rich, characterful wine with the strong lime-juice aroma and flavour that so distinguishes the region.

A 1982 Shiraz Cabernet blend from the Adelaide Hills was in the same gold-medal class as the 1983 Eden Valley Chardonnay. The wine shows excellent lemony oak handling, with good "cool" fruit, yet not green or astringent, with medium to full berry characters and just a hint of spice to round the wine off.

Roseworthy also has stocks of some marvellous old fortified wines, including an old fortified sweet white, a liqueur brandy and an old raisin liqueur frontignac. These wines are intermittently released in small quantities onto the market and all are worth waiting for.

ROVALLEY
STURT HIGHWAY, ROWLAND FLAT

Rovalley Wines is only a stone's throw from Orlando at Rowland Flat. It has been owned and run by the Liebich family since 1919, when Paul Benno Liebich started to produce small quantities of red wine and port. The vineyards grew more quickly than the winery, and for decades much of the production was sold in the form of grapes. That made at Rovalley was (to put it mildly) traditional, and enjoyed a limited regional market.

Paul Liebich died in 1941, and his three sons took over and expanded the business significantly. The winery was further modernised in the 1970s, after which output grew rapidly.

In early 1985 the third-generation members went their separate ways, with Dean Liebich selling his interest and moving to Merrivale in McLaren Vale. Dean Liebich was a prominent member of the team, and just where Rovalley will head in the future is uncertain.

ST HALLETTS WINES
ST HALLETTS ROAD, TANUNDA

The Lindner family was among those who left Silesia in 1845 to seek a new life, free from persecution, in Australia. Johann Lindner, his wife and six children settled in Bethany. It was left to his grandson, Karl Richard Lindner, to buy a property in the Halletts Valley in 1912 and plant vines. A small winery followed in 1918, producing dry red and dry white table wines.

Karl's grandson, also known as Karl, now runs the substantial enterprise. For many years the winemaker was Robert O'Callaghan, who recently established Rockford. Ninety per cent of the crush comes from the two family-owned vineyards, one at Gomersal planted on heavy red loam with a limestone underlay, and the other at Halletts Valley, on sandy river loam.

The vineyards comprise shiraz (9.85 hectares), grenache (7.4 hectares), pedro ximinez (six hectares), rhine riesling (5.6 hectares), muscat gordo blanco (3.3 hectares), cabernet sauvignon (3.3 hectares), tinta amarella (2.4 hectares), touriga (1.45 hectares) and muscadelle (0.2 hectare). Drip-irrigation has been installed, and yields are adequate, ranging from around seven tonnes per hectare for rhine riesling and cabernet sauvignon to between 12 and 15 tonnes for other varieties.

The St Halletts Winery is an excellent one, and

the acquisition of a Willmes tank-press assists in the production of a range of well-made varietal white wines. Most of these are offered with considerable bottle age: those available at the end of 1984 spanned the years 1978 to 1982, with most coming from the 1980 and 1981 vintages.

The greatest success, however, has come with St Halletts' red wines. It won the Montgomery Trophy in Adelaide in 1980 for the best one-year-old red, and followed this up with a well-made Barossa Valley Shiraz Cabernet in 1980. Spicy shiraz was balanced by strong smoky/charred-oak aromas and flavours, with full but soft tannin rounding the wine out. The label—and indeed the whole packaging—is most attractive. St Halletts Karl's Special dry reds, usually a blend of shiraz, cabernet and malbec, are sometimes excellent. The 1981 vintage was quite a good wine, with rich oak and mid-palate fruit.

The Portuguese varieties, tinta amarella and touriga, will form the base of some interesting fortified wines in years to come.

SALTRAM
ANGASTON ROAD, ANGASTON

Saltram was founded in 1859 by William Salter and his son Edward—the business was established under the name of W. Salter & Son. William Salter had arrived in South Australia from England 20 years earlier, and had turned his hand with great success to many activities (mostly in the Barossa) in the meantime. A religious man, he had named the property he bought and developed near Angaston "Mamre Brook", after a verse in Genesis describing some of Abraham's land.

The first vintage in 1862 was made in a cave-like cellar excavated in the side of the hill up which one still drives to reach the present-day Saltram Winery. Production was of red wine, usually fortified, and between 1859 and 1882 markets were gradually established, first in South Australia, then Melbourne and ultimately New Zealand. The latter market was opened up by Alfred Percy Birks, who was subsequently to found A. P. Birks' Wendouree Cellars in the Clare Valley. In 1882 Saltram entered into a marketing arrangement with Thomas Hardy & Sons, who undertook to purchase and then market all of Saltram's production. This led to the establishment of Saltram in the English trade.

By 1891 the vintage had reached 180,000 litres, and by 1903 it had reached 290,000 litres. Incredibly until 1891 all of the grapes were crushed in special treading boxes, with the workers wearing special knee-boots made by a local bootmaker. In that year a hydraulic press and pump driven by a four-horse-power steam-engine was purchased. To be more accurate two were purchased; the first was too big to fit between the vats, and was ultimately resold to A. P. Birks at Wendouree.

The winery passed through several generations until Leslie Salter was appointed manager in 1902. He became close friends with Ronald Martin of Stoneyfell, and when Saltram was converted to a company in 1920, Stoneyfell took a one-third interest with Ronald Martin as chairman and Leslie Salter as managing director. Following Leslie Salter's retirement in 1937, Saltram was managed by Stoneyfell and in 1941 became a subsidiary of that company. There was a close working relationship between the two companies: the winemaking was carried out at Saltram, and the maturation and bottling at Stoneyfell.

Throughout the 1950s Bryan Dolan was manager and winemaker; when he was transferred to Stoneyfell in 1959 Peter Lehmann became winemaker, a position he held until 1979. Dolan had created the Metala label; during Peter Lehmann's time Metala and Mamre Brook became two of the most eagerly sought-after red wines in South Australia. Both were immense wines when Lehmann assumed winemaking responsibilities; he lightened the style somewhat, but all things are relative. Metala remained a very big, old-fashioned wine, and Mamre Brook was not infrequently quite formidable. I must confess that with odd exceptions neither wine has ever appealed to me greatly, with mercaptan a recurrent problem in the Mamre Brook range. Nonetheless, the two labels remain an important part of the winemaking history of South Australia.

In 1972 Dalgety Australia Limited made its ill-fated venture into the wine industry. In that year it acquired Saltram, Stoneyfell, Krondorf and Roxton Estate. Like Reed International and Gilbeys, winemaking and the wine industry remained a closed book to Dalgety. Bruised and defeated, Dalgety sold Saltram to Seagram in 1979. Saltram is now a subsidiary of the world's largest wine and spirits company, and has changed radically over the past six years.

While some, such as Peter Lehmann, might disagree, those changes overall have been for the better. Saltram has followed the course of Orlando in seeking premium grapes from a variety of areas best suited to their production. The 20 hectares of vineyards surrounding the Saltram Winery (and a further five hectares in the Clare Valley) provide only five per cent of the annual crush which produces over four million litres of wine each year—this is in fact less than the quantity made in the latter part of the 1970s. Seagram has deliberately concentrated its attention on the top end of the market and recognised the near-impossible conditions under which Peter Lehmann was asked to make wine during his last few years at Saltram.

The changing attitudes at Saltram are reflected in the vineyards, which have been radically reshaped. Gone are the traditional Barossa Valley varieties, such as cabernet gros, dolcetto, grenache and mataro; and in their place are semillon, rhine riesling, shiraz, cabernet sauvignon, merlot, malbec and chardonnay. But, as I say, these provide only a minute part of the annual crush. Saltram is a major purchaser of grapes from districts as far away as the Hunter Valley (although buying less from that region than it did formerly), the Clare Valley, McLaren Vale and Coonawarra.

The emphasis is on the production of premium varietal table wines, with white wines in turn predominant. With the extensive refitting of the winery carried out prior to the 1982 vintage, it is not surprising that some excellent and sometimes outstanding wines have been released under the new Saltram labels. The top-of-the-range wines are the Pinnacle Releases. This label was conceived in 1982 and reserved for the best of the varietal wines. Releases include a sauvignon blanc, an auslese rhine reisling, a gewurztztraminer, a rhine riesling, a sauterne and an Eden Valley shiraz. In January 1985 recommended retail prices were between $10.80 and $14.40 and these wines should by rights be consistently excellent. The difficulty to date has been that some have been very good, others have not.

Thus the 1982 Pinnacle Gewurztraminer (made, surprisingly, from Hunter Valley grapes) was excellent, with a real touch of Alsace spice in the aroma, and rich, soft, peachy/spicy fruit flavours. The 1982 Pinnacle Coonawarra Rhine Riesling Auslese was if anything even better, with magnificent botrytis aroma and flavour resulting in a rich and luscious wine with an intense acid finish. The 1982 Pinnacle Rhine Riesling, however, suffered from volatility, a fault which crops up in a number of the 1982 white wines under the Saltram label, while the 1982 Pinnacle Fumé Blanc was too soft and had a suspicion of sulphide. The issue of volatility also dogged the 1982 Saltram Mamre Brook Chardonnay, introduced for the first time in that year. I do not doubt the volatility is present, but I nonetheless greatly like the

wine for its rich, full and soft peachy fruit. My only criticism was that the oak was very obvious when the wine was two years old.

The 1983 white wines reflected the difficult vintage; the 1984 releases to appear so far have been much better. The top-of-the-range wines are still to be released at the time of writing, but the basic varietals and generic releases have been quite attractive. The only real criticism of the 1984 Chablis is that it might equally well have been labelled white burgundy. Full, soft and oaky, it offers flavour rather than finesse. The 1984 Traminer Riesling is another very commercial wine; here the appeal lies in the residual sugar which fleshes out a soft, gently honeyed and aromatic wine. The 1984 Chardonnay is a logical conclusion; the wine derives its flavour more from oak than fruit, but the two are well integrated, and in commercial terms its full flavour is a success. The most recent releases of Mamre Brook Shiraz Cabernet from 1978 and 1979 have been solid wines in a fairly traditional style. The wines have been free from mercaptan, and the 1979 vintage in particular showed rich, soft, typically warm-area cabernet sauvignon fruit characters. The yet-to-be-released 1980 and 1982 vintages are said to be quite excellent.

Saltram gives the impression it is still to find its way after the rapid changes of direction which have occurred in the past five years. Once some stability returns, there is no reason why consistently first-class wines should not be produced.

SEPPELT
SEPPELTSFIELD via TANUNDA

Joseph Seppelt arrived in South Australia with his wife Johanna and two sons, Oscar and Hugo. The son of a wealthy factory owner, he brought with him adequate capital, and in February 1852 he purchased a number of blocks of land in the Tanunda district. The family business in Germany had involved the manufacture of tobacco snuff and liquor products; however, after finding that the district was unsuited to tobacco growing, Joseph Seppelt turned his attention to corn, wheat and grapes. He also persuaded his neighbours to plant grapes, and the first vintage was made in the family dairy.

In 1867 the nucleus of the present-day vast complex of stone buildings which constitutes Seppeltsfield was built. From this point on the business grew at a quite remarkable rate: by 1875 the estate was 225 hectares, and the 1867 winery had been doubled in size. Three years later a massive building programme

TRANSPORTING A BRANDY POT STILL, ORLANDO, c. 1920

quadrupled the capacity of the 1875 building, and in 1885 yet another winery was commenced. The 1887 vintage was 900,000 litres, with a very large portion of production being exported to England. Growth continued unabated: in 1903 two million litres of wine were produced; approximately one-third of this came from the Seppelt vineyards which by this time had grown to 600 hectares.

In 1914 Seppelt moved interstate, acquiring the Clydeside Vineyard and cellars at Rutherglen in Victoria. Two years later Chateau Tanunda was purchased; this was a major acquisition for Seppelt. The building itself was a magnificent one—erected in 1890, the winery was 240 feet (73 metres) long and 120 feet (36.5 metres) wide, with storage space for nearly five million litres of wine. The acquisition also included vast stocks of brandy: Chateau Tanunda at the time was operating four wineries (of which this was the most important) and held over half the total brandy stocks in Australia.

Another two years passed, and another acquisition of lasting importance was made. In 1918 Seppelt purchased Hans Irvine's Great Western cellars and stocks of table wine and champagne. In the same year Seppelt established yet another winery at Dorrien, close to Nuriootpa. At long last Seppelt's appetite was satisfied, and the company entered into a period of consolidation, notable only for the fact that it was during this time that the palm trees which so distinguish Seppeltsfield were planted.

It was not until the early 1960s that Seppelt made its next significant expansion moves. All the company's vineyards, and all its traditional independent grower sources, were situated in warm areas with the exception of those at Great Western. Lack of suitable soil, frost problems on the flats, and lack of water for drip-irrigation precluded any thought of significant expansion in that district. Seppelt needed substantial additional supplies of the earlier-ripening premium table-grape varieties for use both in sparkling-winemaking and table wine. The company accordingly turned its attention to what has become known as the cool corner of Australia and selected two vineyard sites, the first at Drumborg in the far south-west of Victoria, and the second at Padthaway/Keppoch in the far south-east of South Australia. The plan was that the Drumborg vineyard would produce the fine, aromatic white varietals and base wines for champagne; and that Keppoch would be planted to cabernet sauvignon and shiraz, for the purpose of producing fine table wines.

It is no secret that Seppelt has had an exceedingly difficult time viticulturally at Drumborg. The company's viticulturalists and winemakers are now quietly confident that after 20 years they have unlocked the secrets of this extremely cool area, and that with appropriate vineyard management techniques and fruit handling, it will fulfil the promise so far denied. Keppoch, too, has presented its share of problems, but none of the magnitude of Drumborg. The principal problem lay in the original decision to plant red grapes at Keppoch; before long it was recognised as a premium white area, and the vineyards were rearranged accordingly.

Seppelt has 124 hectares of irrigated vines at Barooga near Rutherglen planted to chardonnay, pinot noir, muscat of alexandria, ondenc and trebbiano on alluvial red sandy loam. The vineyard was established in the 1920s, primarily for the purpose of establishing phylloxera-resistant rootstocks. Until the closure of the Clydeside Winery, the grapes were processed there.

In December 1980 Seppelt purchased an historic property (and homestead) between Mount Pleasant and Springton, south of Eden Valley. Called Partalunga, the vineyards are established on podsolic soils at a height of between 400 and 500 metres above sea-level with an annual rainfall of 675 millimetres. Rhine riesling, chardonnay, sauvignon blanc and cabernet sauvignon have been planted, and the first significant crop was expected in 1985. Seppelt sees it as an important source of premium-quality grapes.

In the 1970s Seppelt made an ill-fated move to the Hunter Valley, establishing a large vineyard on the outskirts of the town of Cessnock. Beautifully laid out, and immaculately maintained, it was nonetheless planted on unsuitable soil. At no time were the yields economic, and to compound the problem, the wrong varieties were planted. It was sold in the 1980s and I believe it will quickly pass into oblivion.

Indeed, the most important development in that decade was the public listing of Seppelt in 1970. The Seppelt family continued to control a substantial portion of the issued capital and to run the company, but by early 1985 it had itself been taken over in a friendly merger designed to ward off the depredations of the Adelaide Steamship group, who had ambitions to merge its operations with those of Penfolds. The Seppelt family is now largely removed from the management of the company. The demands of the marketplace have seen some of the surgery which followed the acquisition of Penfolds. Seppelt's Rutherglen operations have been disposed of piecemeal; the Dorrien Winery is no more, and, as I say, the Hunter Valley vineyards have been disposed of.

The main processing and wine maturation function

in South Australia is split between the magnificent Seppeltsfield Winery and Chateau Tanunda. Seppeltsfield remains the showpiece of the Barossa; indeed, it remains one of the two showpieces of the Australian wine industry. Only Chateau Reynella competes with it in terms of grandeur and historical romance. The grounds are immaculately maintained, and the buildings likewise. Seppeltsfield's main function is the storage and maturation of the vast stocks of Seppelt's fortified wines, including the celebrated 100-year-old Liqueur Port Series. The size of these reserves is stupendous: in the late 1970s I calculated that the theoretical value of the 100-year-old ports (and those of progressively diminishing age) was more or less equal to Seppelt's market capitalisation at that time. The grape intake at Seppeltsfield is relatively small, concentrating on grenache from the company's Seppeltsfield vineyards together with shiraz and grenache from independent growers in the district. This is all used in the production of port, principally tawny.

The grapes for dry sherry and sweet fortified wines are processed at Chateau Tanunda, and the wine is sent to Seppeltsfield for maturation and blending once fermentation has finished. Seppeltsfield has a large insulated flor sherry store for the production of the flor fino, amontillado and oloroso sherries for which Seppelt is well known (and indeed should be better known, for they are truly outstanding).

Chateau Tanunda is the principal processing winery for the group. Like Seppeltsfield, it is run by James Godfrey (manager/winemaker Barossa) and Nigel Dolan (senior winemaker Barossa). It processes the material from the Seppelt vineyards in the Barossa, Keppoch and Qualco areas. Seppelt's Qualco Vineyard, on the River Murray in South Australia's Riverlands, was another development of the early 1960s. One hundred and sixty hectares of palomino and trebbiano (for use in sherry production) together with shiraz, doradillo, cabernet sauvignon, rhine riesling and muscadelle have been established. Grape intake at Chateau Tanunda is supplemented by purchases from independent growers in the Barossa Valley, Eden Valley, Southern Vales, Langhorne Creek and Murray River regions. The major varieties processed are semillon, muscadelle, chardonnay, palomino, rhine riesling, cabernet sauvignon, shiraz, grenache and pinot noir. All of the company's South Australian-sourced table wines are made at Tanunda, and all of its small-oak red-wine maturation is carried out there in a large lower-floor cool cellar in the main building. There is also a large brandy maturation warehouse. Curiously, no wine is bottled at either

Seppeltsfield or Chateau Tanunda—all of the wines are despatched either to Great Western or to the bottling hall at Braeside in Victoria for bottling and packaging.

Keeping track of the vast range of the Seppelt products is no easy matter. From time to time the company has endeavoured to rationalise the enormous number of products (and ever-changing labels), but no sooner has one label disappeared than another takes its place. One particularly ill-fated move was the Peter Ustinov venture in early 1983, which saw the creation and launch of the Seppelt Estate 1982 Riesling and Seppelt Estate 1980 Hermitage Cabernet Sauvignon. Very considerable sums of money were spent in trying to launch products which the retail industry studiously ignored. In more recent times a series of old-world labels have been re-created, vaguely reminiscent of those of the last century and which do nothing to aid the failing memory of wine writers.

These idiosyncrasies to one side, the range starts with the commercial releases, three of which are rich in history and memories for older wine drinkers: Arawatta Riesling, Moyston Claret and Chalambar Burgundy. The fourth, Rhymney Chablis, has disappeared from the scene. Other wines in this quality range (and price) include Muroomba Moselle, Spritzig Moselle and Spritzig Rosé.

Next up the quality tree come the so-called Bin range, distinguished by their labels borrowed from Chateau Mouton Rothschild (which is no doubt flattered, although it hardly needed the rams on top for the point to be made). These comprise Bin WB1 White Burgundy, CH2 Chablis, CB3 Rhine Riesling, SA5 Sauterne, EC4 Claret and BW6 Red Burgundy. These wines, with a recommended retail price of around $5.50 (and a real price at least $1, and probably $1.50, less than that), are typical of the technical excellence which the big wine companies can achieve. They lack the flair and individuality of the top 20 per cent of boutique-winery products, but placed in a masked line-up with the other 80 per cent they will come out on top more often than not. At half the price of the boutique wines, they start to look most attractive. Like the Reserve Bin wines (next up the quality tree, but only marginally so) the Bin wines are made to be consumed within a year or so of their release. With the immense diversity of vineyard sources, and the ability to blend as required, quality remains remarkably consistent from one year to the next. There is little more one can say about them or, for that matter, about the Reserve Bin range.

This latter range comprises chardonnay, rhine

riesling, sylvaner, frontignac blanc, spatlese rhine riesling, pinot noir, cabernet sauvignon and hermitage. Again, consistency of style and of quality are the major features of the wines. I have participated in a number of retrospective tastings of all these wines, and all one can say is that Seppelt does the job very well.

A recent introduction has been that of the varietal chardonnay, sitting to one side and not forming part of any range. It is this wine (and a sauterne) which was blessed with the old-world label. Both the 1983 and 1984 vintages of it were outstanding in their class, the 1983 particularly so. The winner of a substantial number of medals, its real price in the $5 mid-range linked it with the Orlando chardonnay as the best value-for-money chardonnay on the market. Impeccable oak handling linked with soft, very distinctive buttery chardonnay fruit in the peach-flavour spectrum, provide a wonderful wine.

Next come the Black Label varietal range of wines, usually good and sometimes great. There are three regular releases under this label. First, a Great Western Hermitage, soft velvety and spicy, and very often outstanding; second a rhine riesling, usually a blend of Keppoch Great Western and Drumborg material, with the percentage contribution varying from year to year. The 1981 was a marvellously aromatic wine with pungent fruit, and it won numerous gold medals and several trophies. 1982 was another successful wine, though it lacked the intense aroma of the 1981 vintage. The last release (1983) reflected the problems of the year. Finally there is the Black Label Cabernet Sauvignon: like the rhine riesling, this is usually sourced from the three cool-climate vineyards in the Seppelt armoury. Small oak plays an important part in the shaping of this wine, which is usually released with at least four years age. The 1979 vintage was an attractive wine with clearly marked varietal grassy aromas on the bouquet and a smooth, gently oaky palate with some ripe-berry flavours.

Next there come the Gold Label releases, featuring single varieties from single vineyards of outstanding quality, such as the marvellous 1976 Late-Harvest Rhine Riesling from Great Western and the even greater 1978 Traminer from Drumborg, and occasional Dorrien Cabernet Sauvignons. The 1976 Dorrien Cabernet Sauvignon, a winner of five gold medals, was an excellent wine for many years although is now starting to show its age.

Finally, and again not fitting easily into the structured hierarchy, are occasional show releases such as the 1982 Show Chardonnay, released in 1984. Full, rich and buttery, it is an excellent example of the ripe and generous Australian chardonnay style. Such wines are at their peak within two or three years of vintage, and should be drunk when young.

Seppelt is of course a market leader in sparkling wine. By the end of 1984 sales of sparkling wine under the Great Western label (in other words including all of the various manifestations of it) were at 475,000 cases and rising, putting the Great Western label at the head of the Australian sales charts. Once again there is a hierarchy under this label: Great Western Imperial Reserve Champagne and Great Western Brut Reserve have the same theoretical retail price, which, like the Bolivian peso, varies from one day to the next. As the name suggests, Imperial Reserve is a little sweeter than the Brut Reserve, which is a much drier style made employing the traditional French techniques of incorporating some red grapes in the blend, giving rise to a distinctive bronzed colour.

Rather confusingly, Great Western N.V. Brut is a superior wine to Brut Reserve, principally composed of ondenc, chardonnay and pinot meunière from Drumborg and pinot noir and ondenc from Great Western. Next come Seppelt's Great Western Vintage Brut and the newly introduced Fleur de Lys. Only one vintage of Fleur de Lys has so far been released, the 1981 wine, which was made from a blend of ondenc from Drumborg (83 per cent) and pinot noir from Rutherglen/Great Western (17 per cent). Like Great Western Brut, Fleur de Lys was left on yeast lees for three years before disgorgement. It is an elegant and fine style, which promises much for the future.

Finally within the champagne range there are the intermittent releases of the show champagnes. Very often these have considerable age: thus a 1963 and 1969 vintage were released in 1983, and a 1970 vintage in 1984. In that latter year a very interesting 100 per cent pinot meunière show champagne was also made available in very restricted quantities. It barely needs saying that these wines are magnificently complex, uniquely Australian sparkling wines.

Finally comes Seppelt's unequalled range of old fortified wines. The commercial solera releases of Extra Dry Sherry, Medium Dry Sherry, Cream Sherry, Semi-Sweet Sherry and Sweet Sherry commence the line-up. Then follows the range of DP44 Fino Gold Label, DP96 Amontillado Gold Label, DP20 Oloroso Gold Label, DP38 Oloroso Buff Label, DP116 Show Amontillado Buff Label, and DP117 Show Fino Flor Buff Label. These are all great wines. Except for a few aficionados, sherry is a dead letter in Australia, yet we make the greatest wines of the style outside of Spain. Those who know and appreciate the styles need no introduction from me; numerous exhortations to those who do not, made by myself and others over the years, have fallen on seemingly deaf ears, so I will pass on.

At the diadem of the fortified crown sit the Seppelt ports. The line commences with Mount Rufus Tawny Port, progresses through vintage ports (usually released at around 10 years of age), Para Liqueur Port, DP90 Port, thence to the Family Series ports and finally to the most exotic wine of any kind on commercial release in Australia, the 100-year-old tawny ports.

DP90 is a show tawny released in tiny quantities at irregular intervals. It was first blended from reserve stocks of tawny ports in 1948, overblended in 1963 and again in 1977. A release of 500 dozen is made every seven or eight years; the last retail release, some years ago, was at $25 per bottle. The quality of the DP90 is on a par with that of the Family Series port. The first release in the series was Camillo Pedro, the second Flora Eugenie, next Clara Blanca, with those to follow (at the rate of one a year) being Udo Waldemar, Selma Melitta, Xavier Arno, Leo Renato, Marco Dominico, Oscar Benno, Norbert Erno, Joseph Gerold, Vero Viola and Tuisko Turso. The names of the Seppelt children were fittingly exotic, as are these intensely flavoured aged tawny ports which include as part of the blend material that is older than 50 years and have an average age of 18 years. The extreme wood-age of the wines gives them a distinctive olive colour on the rim of the glass, ethereal spirit and strong rancio. Rancio provides that touch of oxidation and volatile lift which comes only in old fortified wines; it transforms the simple, cloying, sweet young base wine into a magnificently complex tawny with an almost dry finish. All of these characters come together in distilled form in the extraordinary 100-year-old liqueur tawny ports, first released in 1978—which was, needless to say, the 1878 vintage. Seppelt has an unbroken run of these wines, and is bottling off the old stocks at the age of 100 years, with a release each year of the equivalent 1800s wine.

I have been privileged to taste most of the releases so far made. Whether a bottle is worth $1000, $2000 or $3000 is academic: the wine is extraordinary, with no other fortified wine, in Australia or elsewhere, of similar style. After the first few releases twentieth-century technology came to the fore with a decision to cold-stabilise the wine immediately before bottling. This process freshened the wines greatly without in any way diminishing their exceptional intensity and character. Every millionaire should have a bottle in his or her cellar.

TOLLANA
STURT HIGHWAY, NURIOOTPA

Tollana's history can be traced back to 1858, when the East Torrens Winemaking and Distillation Company was formed. Until 1888 when Thomas Scott, Ernest Tolley and Douglas Tolley purchased the distillery and began trading as Tolley Scott and Tolley, the venture had a turbulent and unprofitable history. The new partners brought real expertise in distillation to the venture for the first time, and were immediately successful.

By 1961, when United Distillers Limited of the United Kingdom acquired Tolley Scott and Tolley, it was one of the largest distillers of brandy in Australia. Brandy production is still an important part of the group's business, but within a very short period of the United Distillers' acquisition it became apparent that the likely market growth lay with table wine rather than spirits. This view was reinforced as the excise on Australian made brandy rose rapidly throughout the late 1960s and 1970s. So it was that in 1966 the decision was taken to expand into the production of high-quality table wine. The group's existing 240 hectares of Barossa Valley vineyards were totally unsuited, both in terms of location and varieties planted, and new areas were sought. A 400-hectare vineyard was established at Waikerie (in the Riverland) and shortly thereafter the Woodbury Vineyard in the hills of the Eden Valley was commenced.

The Woodbury Vineyard is planted at levels of between 450 and 520 metres above sea-level, and contour-planted on the hillsides down which it cascades. One hundred and forty hectares are planted to rhine riesling, shiraz, cabernet sauvignon, traminer and chardonnay. The soils vary from podsolic sandy loam with outcrops of quartz and shale, to shallow loam with a clay-gravel subsoil on the upper slopes. Annual rainfall is 686 millimetres, but supplementary water has proved desirable in the area. The development of Roesler's Vineyard (in the same area) came later, planted principally to 20 hectares of rhine riesling and shiraz. The Waikerie vineyards provide both flagon and cask material and base wine for the brandy operations: the varieties grown include crouchen, trebbiano, white frontignac, shiraz, cabernet sauvignon and mataro.

TOLLEY'S WINES, c. 1920

Tollana not only chose its vineyard areas well, but also its first winemaker. Wolf Blass was winemaker between 1968 and 1973, placing his own highly individual stamp on the Tollana red-wine style. This reached a peak with the 1973 Shiraz Cabernet Malbec Bin TR222, which still bore its pedigree proudly in 1983. Blass was followed by the equally redoubtable John Glaetzer before he, too, left to join Wolf Blass. In due course Alan Hoey became chief winemaker, a position he held for many years before joining Yalumba as chief white-winemaker. Hoey did for the Tollana white wines what Blass did for the reds: the Woodbury releases have been consistently excellent wines, with a quite remarkable depth of flavour, and more often than not they repay handsomely extended cellaring.

Somewhat unexpectedly, Tollana has also been responsible for producing some of the best sparkling wines available on the commercial market in Australia over the past few years. Given the fairly ordinary base material from which the wine is made, the performance has been doubly commendable.

The 1982 Eden Valley Rhine Riesling, released in 1984, is typical of the Tollana wines at their very best. At that point it was only starting to open up, proving once again that Eden Valley Rhine Riesling needs at least two years in bottle. It has magnificent balance and intensity, with crisp acid on the finish balanced against the rich lime-juice fruit flavours on the mid-palate. It will surely develop in the same fashion as the 1979 Eden Valley Rhine Riesling, which in the early part of 1985 was approaching its peak, but giving every indication of living for another five years at least.

In the eastern states at least, little or no attempt is made to promote Tollana wine. I cannot remember ever having received a press release, let alone a wine sample, and am unaware that there have been any formal tastings of the wines. The net result is that Tollana has the lowest imaginable profile, and its white wines simply do not receive the recognition they deserve. Precisely the same situation also exists with its reds. 1977 Bin TR333 Shiraz Cabernet was available in May 1984 for a little over $6 a bottle. That price was little short of an insult to a beautifully balanced and mature red wine, with marvellously integrated fruit and oak. The wine was full without being heavy or jammy, and has marvellous texture. It seems to me that someone should tell the Distillers Company Limited that wine should be marketed and promoted in a manner different from Scotch whisky.

VERITAS
LANGMEIL ROAD, TANUNDA

Veritas was established by the Binder family, headed by Rolf Binder, in 1955, five years after Binder's arrival in Australia from Hungary. The winery, just north of Tanunda, was originally a transport and trucking shed. It had been converted into a small winery in the 1940s, but has been substantially expanded and upgraded since its purchase by the Binders.

A substantial part of the Veritas crush comes from estate-grown grapes. The vineyards comprise rhine riesling (four hectares), shiraz (four hectares), mataro (three hectares), cabernet sauvignon (2.5 hectares) and one hectare each of chardonnay, semillon, chenin blanc, white frontignac, merlot and pinot noir.

Production is virtually all sold by cellar door. Despite the rather odd names bestowed on many of the wines offered, some very pleasant wines are available under the Veritas label. The reds usually show rich, ripe, traditional Barossa fruit flavour and structure; while the white wines also show the flesh and richness of Barossa Valley floor fruit. Not surprisingly the late-picked rhine rieslings are often the best, with a well-made late-picked rhine riesling vintaged in 1982. With full, sweet fruit and richness, it developed fairly quickly in bottle, but then that is precisely what one would expect.

WARD'S GATEWAY CELLARS
LYNDOCH

Ward's Gateway Cellars owns what are claimed to be the oldest vines in the Barossa Valley: two hectares of shiraz, grenache and mataro. If true, it is somehow appropriate, because Ray Ward has spent a lifetime in the Barossa Valley wine industry, entering it at the age of 14, and interrupting his career only to spend three years with the navy and thereafter two years with Roseworthy Agricultural College. He worked at Woodley Wines, Yalumba, Renmark Growers and Angle Vale Vineyards for a total of 29 years before establishing his own small family winery at the very bottom end of the Barossa (between Sandy Creek and Lyndoch) in 1979.

Apart from the small output of the two hectares of family vineyard, the balance of the 50-tonne crush is purchased from growers in the Barossa and Adelaide Plains. The winery, an old converted cow barn, is insulated and adequately equipped. A number of varietal wines are made, as well as port.

WILSFORD
LYNDOCH

The Burge family have been Barossa grape growers and winemakers for over 100 years, but it is ironical that the name has become well known not through Wilsford, the family winery, but through Krondorf. Grant Burge is a member of the family that owns and runs the tiny Wilsford Winery on the outskirts of Lyndoch.

John Burge arrived from Wiltshire, England, in 1855, and took up the selection which the family still owns. He made wine for some time, but eventually sold his equipment and stock to Patrick Auld of Auldana fame, and the family's activities reverted to mixed farming and grape growing. In 1928 it became almost impossible for grape growers to sell their produce. Meetings were held resolving not to accept prices less than those of 1921, but the times were desperate. The export bounty had been removed, as had the British Empire Preference in London, and the export market had collapsed. To make matters worse, the Depression lay around the corner. Unable to sell his grapes, Percival Burge commenced to make his own fortified wine, and somehow or other he found a market for it.

His son Noel Burge enrolled at Roseworthy in 1936, the first year in which a formal oenology course was conducted. In 1938 he became one of the first four graduates in oenology from Roseworthy, and joined Berri Cooperative where he remained for the next 12 years. His brother Colin (Grant Burge's father) remained at the vineyard and winery, and was joined by Noel following the death of their father.

Wilsford has 36 hectares of vineyards planted to rhine riesling, semillon, chenin blanc, pedro ximinez, shiraz, cabernet sauvignon and grenache. None is irrigated, but modern viticultural techniques are applied where appropriate. All of the wine is sold by cellar door and the Burge brothers are outspoken opponents of discounting.

YALUMBA
EDEN VALLEY ROAD, ANGASTON

If rationalisation of the Australian wine industry is to take the course which many predict, Yalumba must be one of the companies which stand most threatened. Family-owned and family-run, it is vitally concerned with wine quality and with ways to increase quality. It has done more than countless boutiques in pointing the way to such improvement. Yet it is of such a size that its products are necessarily distributed nationally through a wide range of outlets; with this has come the seeming necessity of discounting, and with this has come the taint of the big company.

It is desperately important for the wine industry, and even more important for the consumer, that Yalumba—and half a dozen or so other companies like it—survive. Ironically the battle will not be won or lost in the vineyard or in the winery, but in the marketplace. Worst of all it will be decided without regard to the quality of the products which Yalumba produces. The only consolation is that the dilemma which the Hill-Smith family face in deciding the future course of the company is a pleasant one. It has a very high reputation within the industry, and if the decision finally comes to sell, the descendants of Samuel Smith will have cause to thank the foresight and courage of their forefather.

He was clearly no ordinary man. He was 35, with a wife, five children and a successful career as a brewer when he decided to leave the security and comfort of England to make a new home in Australia. Evidently he had accumulated little capital, for on his arrival in South Australia he moved to Angaston which was then being created by George Fife Angas. He worked for Angas by day establishing gardens and orchards; by night he commenced to establish a small vineyard in the 12 hectares of land he had purchased and called Yalumba, an Aboriginal word meaning "all the country around".

In 1852 Samuel Smith and his 15-year-old son followed the rest of Australia's male population to the Victorian goldfields. After sinking 15 barren shafts, they struck gold on the sixteenth attempt and returned to Angaston with enough money to purchase a further 32 hectares, a plough, two horses and a harness, and had some money left in the bank to finance the erection of a new house and wine cellars. By the time Samuel Smith died in 1889 Yalumba was a thriving business, with markets established both in Australia and England, and medals in international shows and exhibitions to its credit. Samuel's son Sydney built upon the base his father had left, building the imposing two-storey winery and clock tower of blue marble that stand today as part of the vast complex of buildings which are set in the spacious grounds. In 1903 the vintage produced 810,000 litres, and Yalumba was established as one of the principal producers in the region.

Expansion continued steadily through the first decades of the twentieth century: in one particularly bountiful year excess port was stored in the in-ground swimming pool, protected only by a coating of liquid paraffin wax. Indeed, while Yalumba made limited quantities of white and red table wine, it was primarily a fortified-wine producer, venturing into substantial brandy production shortly before the Second World War. It was also at this time that it established a substantial distribution business of wines and spirits, principally imported. But even at this time Yalumba was going where others feared to tread. Sydney Hill-Smith, one of those tragically killed in the Kyeemagh air crash of 1938, was responsible for introducing rhine riesling into the Eden Valley, and employed German-trained Rudi Kronberger as winemaker. Kronberger made some remarkable rhine rieslings, introducing early bottling 20 years before it became common practice.

Those who attended the tasting preceding the 1983 Barossa Valley Vintage Festival Wine Auction (and who were fleet of foot and tongue) were given a unique opportunity to assess the Yalumba rhine rieslings from this period. Very old white wines take considerable understanding on the part of the taster: inevitably one must look for the wine's good points, and forget the frailty of age. Like grandchild with grandparent, the relationship can be a marvellous one, but it takes a very special perspective. I think it can be fairly said that with very old white wines I am indeed a grandchild: I certainly treasure my memories of those wines at that tasting. 1934 G29 Riesling Bin CO46 is one of the oldest rhine rieslings still left in the Barossa Valley. Oldest it may be, but it was also one of the outstanding wines in the grandmother group. The bouquet was clean, with a touch of camphor (but no oxidation or volatility) and still retained fruit fragrance and aroma; the palate is drying but still firm, with identifiable riesling fruit flavour. It was a truly glorious bottle.

1939 M27 Riesling Bin CO51 proved that tasting wines as old as this is very much a matter of chance. This wine most assuredly showed its age, with the dry kerosene characters which are so frequently encountered in aged rhine riesling—although aged in the sense of 10 or 15 years, rather than 45. The wine was certainly drinkable, but had unfortunately given up the fight some years ago (the curious thing about wines of this age is that the next bottle is apt to be magnificent).

1940 Eden Valley Riesling Bin CO52 was the first of three from this region pioneered by Sydney Hill-Smith. Light orange-yellow in colour, the bouquet was drying out somewhat, but was free from taint. The palate was likewise still holding fruit on the mid-palate, but tended to trail away on the finish. If anyone cares to share a bottle with me, I shall cheerfully join him or her.

I was sufficiently seduced by 1942 Eden Valley Riesling Bin CO59 to join (successfully) in the auction bidding. Somewhere in my cellar I accordingly have a second bottle; one of these days I will see whether it is the same as that which I tasted in April 1983. That wine had orangey tints, but retained distinct fruit richness on the bouquet with just a touch of caramel. The wine really came alive on the palate with surprising depth to the fruit on the mid-palate, followed by a smooth, albeit soft, gently dry finish.

If it were possible, 1944 Eden Valley Riesling Bin CO99 excited me even more; certainly I ended up with both of the bottles auctioned that day. The colour was glowing yellow; the bouquet fresh and lively with minty/camphor bottle-developed aromas. The palate largely fulfilled the promise of the bouquet, holding well, with some of those camphor characters coming again. Like the 1942 vintage it was drying on the finish, but none of the dreaded kerosene/ Flytox characters was perceptible.

The question inevitably arises as to how the current vintage rhine rieslings will fare in 50 years' time. The answer is almost certainly not as well. While modern-day wines retain far more essential fruit flavour and aroma, they are fermented on very clean juice. This has great advantages while they are young (say in the first 10 years of their life), but it is most unlikely that the wines will have the body, the structural strength, to see them safely through 50 years. On the other hand the old Kronberger wines, while taken out of wood and bottled at about six months of age, thereby preserving some fruit freshness, would be rejected out of hand if offered as one-year-old wines in today's marketplace. They would be roundly condemned for being hard, harsh and phenolic, all telltale signs of fermentation at warmer-than-acceptable temperatures on unclarified juice. It is these very phenolic characters which contribute to the ability of the wine to age, however.

The rapidly changing circumstances of the 1950s made their impact on Yalumba just as much as any other major Australian wine company. Kronberger ordered one of the new German stainless-steel pressure fermenters for white-winemaking. It is a little-known fact that Yalumba placed its order before Orlando—Orlando receives all the credit in Australia because theirs arrived and was put into production first. Yalumba was also the first company to make a strategic reappraisal of the relative suitability of the traditional Barossa Valley floor grape-growing areas and those of the surrounding hills, and in particular in the East Barossa Ranges. In 1961 it commenced development of its Pewsey Vale Vineyard. With no real conviction, and realising that whichever way I choose to view the subject I would have opponents, I have elected to treat Yalumba's Pewsey Vale and Heggies Vineyards as falling within the Adelaide Hills area and discuss these two ventures in greater detail in Chapter 1. Suffice it to say here that Yalumba is very much of the view that the areas should be regarded as admittedly widely divergent parts of the Barossa Valley. It may well be right, and I justify my decision to include the high-country areas in the Adelaide Hills region simply to underline the difference.

Putting these areas into the context of the Barossa Valley, but segregating the vineyards by altitude, one arrives at three areas. Area one is the Barossa high country with seven vineyards scattered through the East Barossa Ranges at altitudes of between 400 and 560 metres above sea-level. Here the preferred grape varieties are chardonnay (cool-climate fine style with intense flavour); sauvignon blanc (distinct, grassy and intense); rhine riesling (fine, aromatic, high-acid styles with great ageing potential or botrytised late-harvest styles with very high sugar levels); pinot noir (destined for use with *méthode champenoise*); and cabernet sauvignon (fine styles, not unlike those of Coonawarra).

Area two can be described as the Barossa midlands or lower Barossa Ranges, falling between an altitude of 350 and 399 metres. There are a substantial number of private growers and also a number of company-owned but not separately identified vineyards in this area. The Yalumba Hill-Smith Estate vineyards are one of the few that are separately identified. Here the preferred grape varieties are rhine riesling (to produce a fuller, medium-dry style, destined for early consumption); semillon (an up-and-coming variety, particularly when augmented by new oak: like semillon elsewhere, it needs time in bottle); and shiraz (a variety which flourishes in this climate, showing good peppery richness, but retaining more acid and finesse than Valley-floor-grown shiraz).

Area three is the Barossa Valley floor at an altitude of less than 350 metres. Here the preferred grape varieties are shiraz (used for full, ripe, traditional dry-red styles or fortified wines); cabernet sauvignon (but only for use in vintage port); touriga and other Portuguese port varieties (experimental plantings are increasing and should continue to be so); and pedro ximinez and palomino (for sherry). Not only has Yalumba been at the forefront in the recognition of this delineation, but has carried the fight for

better wine quality to the very centre of the battlefield: to the vines and to the grapes which grow on them.

Yalumba has established its own nursery to provide the best-possible planting material. This extends to extensive research on the most suitable rootstock which will combine parasite resistance (chiefly nematode, as phylloxera is unknown in South Australia), with appropriate vigour characteristics; and to clonal selection of the grape variety to be grafted, with such selection very dependent upon *terroir* and climate. The nursery is established on a vast scale, and once all of the new plantings of Yalumba are complete it will become a commercial nursery supplying the industry as a whole.

Yalumba's viticultural programme is second to none in the country; it involves a fully integrated plan from management of the root system and soil moisture retention, to canopy control and shoot-placement techniques. The detail of this approach is a highly technical and sophisticated one, falling outside the scope of this work, but the net result is clear enough. Yalumba maximises the potential of each site to produce the most distinctive and the highest-quality fruit.

How, you might ask, can anyone be sure Yalumba has done this? Once again, the company has been at the forefront not only of Australian viticultural and winemaking practice, but indeed has also become a world leader, with its techniques now utilised in California and elsewhere. Some years ago it instituted a system whereby juice was taken from every load of grapes to come into the winery, and the unfermented grape juice was then subjected to a wide range of tests. These started with the traditional chemical analyses (although on a much more comprehensive scale than usual and involving a computerised laboratory), but most importantly they extended to a sensory evaluation of the juice. The winemakers treated the juice in exactly the same way as a wine-show judge would taste a wine at the show, minutely analysing it, marking it for flavour, balance and so on. Detailed records were kept and correlated against the wine ultimately made from that juice. Not surprisingly, a very close connection emerged. The process has now been refined even further by deep-freezing a portion of the juice for subsequent (face-to-face) evaluation with the wine later made from the juice. It has led to Yalumba being able to devise an extremely complex bonus payment scheme rewarding growers for producing higher-quality grapes, with the rewards announced at the time the fruit is brought into the winery, rather than months or years later. This approach is as far removed from

YALUMBA WINERY, 1925

that of the large wine companies as it is possible to conceive. I devoutly hope that the Yalumba team, as the family and winemakers like to call themselves, receives its rewards in this world and not in the next.

In spite of Yalumba's rapidly growing stature as one of the finest white-winemakers in Australia, it first came to prominence with its red table wines. There is no question that the wholehearted endorsement of a Prime Minister is more valuable than the wholehearted endorsement of a State Premier; and when that Prime Minister is one of the stature of Sir Robert Menzies at the height of his power and popularity, the effect can only be described as dramatic.

In 1966 Menzies was due to deliver a routine political speech at a forgettable lunch at the South Australian Hotel in Adelaide, which was attended by a group of stockbrokers. The press was there as a matter of routine, and the day would have passed into oblivion were it not for the fact that as Menzies got to his feet he picked up his glass of red wine and declared to the gathering: "Gentlemen, this is the finest Australian wine I have ever tasted." The wine was the 1961 Yalumba Special Reserve Stock Galway Vintage Claret, Yalumba's top-of-the-range red. In 1958 the company had decided to hold back quantities of their top red from each year for subsequent release under the Special Reserve Stock label. It was thus the fourth vintage of this wine which Menzies so praised.

It also followed that when managing director Wyndham Hill-Smith took the inevitable decision to capitalise on the publicity, he had substantial stocks of a 1962 vintage red waiting in the wings. The 1961 wine was always to be known as Menzies' Blend, although it was not labelled as such. It is a wine, incidentally, which proved that Menzies was not only a good judge of people and politics, but of wine too. To this day it remains an outstanding, if marginally old-fashioned, Australian red. If a tag is to be given to it, it is more a burgundy than a claret, but that is really beside the point.

Wyndham Hill-Smith hit upon the idea of creating the now-famous Signature Series, a personalised line of wines commemorating the contribution of the generations of Hill-Smiths and senior employees of the company. It rapidly established itself as one of the most highly rated dry reds of its time. The first wine was 1962 Samuel's Blend, appropriately enough celebrating the man who had started it all. A blend of 35 per cent cabernet sauvignon and 65 per cent shiraz from the Barossa and Eden Valley districts, it is now tiring but still offers soft, velvety, ripe-fruit

flavours with the shiraz component dominant. The 1963 Sydney's Blend (85 per cent cabernet and 15 per cent shiraz with 80 per cent coming from the Barossa Valley and 20 per cent from the Southern Vales) shows the delicate astringency of an aged cabernet but, like Samuel's Blend, has stood the test of time remarkably well. 1964 Oliver's Blend (38 per cent cabernet sauvignon and 62 per cent shiraz, all Barossa Valley) is a big, soft, oaky wine which can still open very well.

1964 saw a second release—until 1974 there was a practice of offering several wines in good years (and none in other years, notably 1965, 1969 and 1972). Since 1974 only one wine has been released each year under the Signature label, and it is intended that this practice will continue. 1964 Percy's Blend was very similar to Oliver's, both in terms of varietal composition and in terms of structure; it perhaps showed a little more acid.

1966 saw three releases, Alfred Wark's Blend, Harold Obst's Blend and Harold Yates's Blend. The latter two were 100 per cent cabernet releases, with 80 per cent coming from the Barossa and 20 per cent from Yalumba's Riverland Vineyard at Waikerie. The Obst and Yates Blends were, not surprisingly, very similar, the only difference stemming from the selection of oak. Both were fairly volatile. Wark's was a much bigger wine, although again some volatility showed.

1967 produced the Clair Chinner's Blend (50 per cent Barossa Valley cabernet sauvignon and 50 per cent Waikerie cabernet sauvignon) and Rudi Kronberger's Blend (70 per cent cabernet sauvignon and 30 per cent shiraz, both Barossa Valley). Clair Chinner, like the 1968 Mick Hungerford's Blend and 1968 Eric Mackenzie's Blend, continued to show volatility.

Yalumba both then and now had huge stocks of small oak barrels, and the problem of adequately maintaining them proved daunting. Lactobacilli permeated the casks, and volatility was the inevitable result. They eventually cured the problem by turning the casks on the quarter (or the shive). Instead of permitting air to enter, as is the case when the casks are stored with the bungs upright, the reverse happens and a vacuum is created. It eliminates the dual problems of oxidation and volatility, and is a technique now widely practised throughout the industry. Its only disadvantage is that it slows the rate of maturation somewhat and it can be argued (although not very convincingly) that the resultant wine is less complex.

The Les Falkenberg's Blend of 1970 (100 per cent

cabernet sauvignon) and the 1970 Paddy Fitzgerald's Blend (90 per cent Barossa cabernet and 10 per cent shiraz) were the last cabernets before three fairly ordinary wines made from 100 per cent shiraz were released—1971 Bruce Coulter's Blend, 1971 Alf Mader's Blend and 1973 Juan Prado's Blend. Juan Prado is notable chiefly for the fact that for the first time it honoured someone outside the immediate confines of the compound, as the Hill-Smith Estate is affectionately known. Prado is the chief executive of Bacardi Rum, which Yalumba distributes.

Since 1973 the quality of the wines improved once again. Wyndham Hill-Smith had the great advantage of choosing his own wine (the second 1973 release) which was to win 10 gold medals and a trophy. 1974 Christobel's Blend (60 per cent cabernet sauvignon and 40 per cent shiraz, both from the Barossa Valley) is probably the most distinguished of all of the Signature wines. Also released as Bin FDR1A, it won two trophies and 11 gold medals. Between 1979 and 1980 the wine was magnificent; I drank many bottles of it, and thought it destined to be a classic. But it was always elegant, and time has proved that it needed more body, for it has faded with surprising rapidity in the ensuing four years.

From this point on the cabernet component in the wines increased, as did the extent of the oak maturation. The period increased from 12 to 18 months, and the percentage of new oak likewise increased. I am not too certain that sometimes the oak is not a little obtrusive in the subsequent wines, although the show judges have certainly had no reservations. 1975 Walter's Blend (85 per cent cabernet sauvignon and 15 per cent shiraz, both Barossa Valley), 1976 Sid Hill-Smith's Blend (55 per cent cabernet sauvignon and 45 per cent shiraz, both from the Barossa Valley) and 1977 Harry Mahlo's Blend (65 per cent cabernet sauvignon and 35 per cent shiraz from the Barossa and Pewsey Vale areas) and 1978 Colin Hayes's Blend have all been prolific show winners.

Once again, nostalgia strikes with an extraordinary tasting of old Yalumba dry reds and ports at the 1983 Barossa Festival, and at the Yalumba Museum tasting of that year. Among the younger wines were the 1967 Rudi Kronberger's Blend which showed superbly: strong, firm, robust fruit and oak bouquet, with the rich, ripe fruit well balanced by soft though persistent tannin on the finish. 1961 Menzies' Blend again showed its class, although there was appreciable bottle-developed volatility on bouquet and palate. Curiously the standard 1961 Yalumba Galway Claret was more impressive, still very elegant, with

marvellous fruit-oak balance on both bouquet and palate, with soft tannin on the finish.

Yalumba 1919 Valley Claret Bin CO39 is thought to be one of the oldest Barossa Valley red wines in existence. The colour has faded to the point of that of a rosé, a light red-brown. The bouquet is light to the point of being ethereal, yet without oxidation or volatility. The palate likewise has declined, albeit with infinite grace, to the point where it really is simply a marvellous old curio.

Two 1920 reds were included in the Museum tasting: 1920 Old 4 Crown Claret Bin CO22 and 1920 Yalumba Cabernet-Shiraz Claret. Both of these wines were made at a winery which Yalumba established in the early part of the twentieth century in the Eden Valley, and which went out of use in the late 1930s or early 1940s. (Yalumba is not certain itself.) The cabernet shiraz had collapsed completely, being volatile in the extreme, but the 4 Crown still showed extremely sweet, almost sugary, port-like fruit on both bouquet and palate. It must have been an extraordinary wine when young. Two Barossa Valley clarets, from 1930 and 1935, again showed their age, or perhaps they were poor bottles. The 1930 was rather volatile, and the 1935 had some musty, corked characters.

The extraordinary wine of the tasting, which sold for a richly deserved $150 per bottle, was out of Yalumba's Museum Cellar, but unhappily for the Barossa Valley was made in the Hunter Valley and thought to be a Tulloch wine. Yalumba 1936 Caldwells' Sydney Claret was one of those freak wines: if properly corked and cellared it will live for another 50 years with ease. While distinctively regional, the fruit is rich and velvety with just the first signs of bottle-developed mint/camphor flavours. The wine still has fresh acid and perfect balance. (Caldwells was a Sydney-based wine merchant of some note.)

Then there were the old vintage and tawny ports. The oldest true vintage port was 1935 Yalumba Bin C120. The colour suggested the wine would be undrinkable, cloudy, dusty and totally out of condition. The bouquet and palate were a revelation: minty herbaceous aromas with very light but clean spirit, and a marvellously complex palate, again low in alcohol, with extraordinary minty/spicy/grassy flavours. A comfortable gold medal on my score-sheet. It was a sign of things to come. The 1950 Special Reserve Tawny Port Bin CO65, with marvellous complexity and strong rancio giving distinction to the sweet, slightly caramelised bouquet and leading on to a lively palate, with that marvellous twist of acid on the finish to dry the wine out, helped by the prolonged wood ageing, led to another gold medal. Then perhaps the most historic of all, Yalumba 4 Crown Port Bin C120—this was the blend Sir Douglas Mawson took on his Antarctic expedition of 1929–30 for service at the Christmas dinner. The Mawson expedition composed a drinking song which included the verse: "Put me down on the first bit of pack ice with Yalumba uncorked near my mouth, and leave me to die unmolested. For I see now we'll never get south." It is a very complex wine with some tea-leaf/tokay characters, and far more luscious than one would normally expect from a tawny port. It was a strong silver-medal-winner.

The last two were show-stoppers: 1927 Yalumba Adelaide Show Port Bin C42 (a blend of much older wine put together for that show) and 1896 Yalumba Old 4 Crown Port, made by Sydney Hill-Smith (son of the founder) from shiraz vines established from cuttings brought to Yalumba from the original Busby collection between 1849 and 1856. I have commented in other circumstances that drinking such wines is in truth drinking history, and so it is. In this instance, however, those who had the privilege of sharing the bottle had the best of both worlds. Both wines were in absolutely immaculate condition: the 1927 had a lifted, lively bouquet with excellent rancio and a long, softly intense palate with some minty notes. The 1896, bright golden in colour with a slight olive-green edge to the rim, was magnificently complex, yet light and subtle on the bouquet; it finished with a light but extremely long and smooth palate, showing all of the greatness of age and none of the faults.

If all of this leads you to believe that I have considerable affection for the wines of Yalumba, you would be correct. But I have equal affection for the people who have had the courage and vision to make Yalumba what it is. When Sydney Hill-Smith was killed in the Kyeemagh air crash, 28-year-old Wyndham was peremptorily summonsed back from Perth and shared the management responsibilities with his brother Donald, in due course becoming managing director. Windy, as he is universally known, is one of the great characters in the wine industry today, following in the footsteps of his father (or it may have been uncle—it is a confused family tree) Walter Hill-Smith. Walter was known as Tiger, in recognition of his passion for big-game hunting and travel, making Yalumba port a well known brand in India and the East. Wyndham's dual passions were cricket and horse-racing. His uncle was none other than Clem Hill, and Windy himself played cricket at both interstate and international level. In more recent

years horse-racing has become his passion; it was he who conceived the idea of the racehorse ports, and it was no doubt he who was instrumental in honouring his close friend Colin Hayes in the 1978 Signature Series clarets. Wyndham Hill-Smith and Hayes were among the partners who founded Lindsay Park, Australia's top thoroughbred horse stud.

In 1972 Wyndham handed over the role of managing director to his nephew, Mark Hill-Smith, and himself became chairman, the position he holds today. Wyndham's son Robert is now the company's marketing managing, while Mark's sons Michael and Matthew are both full-time employees, Michael ably discharging the duties of national publicity manager and occasional croquet umpire par excellence. Thus the fourth, fifth and sixth generations of the family are working with the winemaking team, headed by Peter Wall and Alan Hoey. Alan Hoey joined Yalumba from Tollana at the end of the 1970s, and has done much to contribute to the excellence of the Yalumba white wines.

With an annual crush of around 20,000 tonnes (30 per cent of which is grown on the family's own vineyards spread throughout the Barossa Valley, Barossa Ranges and at Waikerie), Yalumba is a very important Australian wine company. It deserves to be so for a long time to come.

BOTTLING LINE, ORLANDO, 1930s

ADELAIDE

JIM BARRY WINES
Atherley
Armagh
Clare
Wolta Wolta
Emu Creek
Kookynie
Lyndhurst

ENTERPRISE WINES
JUD'S HILL
Hill River
CLAREVALE COOPERATIVE
STANLEY LEASINGHAM
PETALUMA
Donnybrook
WENDOUREE
HERITAGE WINES
Roblyn

STONY POINT

56
55
54
52
51
50

74 75 76 77 78 79 80 81 82 83 84 85 86

Springs
Township
QUARRY
HILL

Neagles Rock
scramble track
Ohlmeyer Park
Donnybrook
showgrounds
Gillentown
49
Sevenhill
48
Sevenhill
SEVENHILL
oval
47

Billabong
Woodlands Brae
Creek
lookout
Gully
Spring Gully
Spring Gully
SPRING GULLY
CONSERVATION
MITCHELL'S
PARK
Killikanoon
Woodvale
Bryans Spring
TOWER HILL
MOUNT OAKDEN
SKILLOGALEE
Waninga
45
44
43
42
41

WILSON'S
POLISH HILL RIVER
VINEYARDS
MOUNT
RUFUS
Phaewyn
PAULETT'S
Holme Lacy
Nyora
TRILLIANS HILL
46
Wyndham Park
Penwortham
Kadlunga
Mintaro
slate quarry
Fairfield
MOUNT
HORROCKS
Mortlock
Experime
Station

Hughes Park
ford
yards
40
Carinya
THE PEAK
Peak Springs
39
Watervale
QUELLTALER
WATERVALE CELLARS
cemetery
38
LINDEMANS
AND LEO BURING
Leasingham
37
Narrawa
SKILLY
HILLS
36
HORROCKS WINES
FAREHAM ESTATE

JEFFREY GROSSET

TAYLORS

Clare Valley

The founding father of the Clare Valley was John Horrocks, who has given his name to the highest mountain in the district and to one of its newest wineries. He settled in the region in 1840, one year after it had first been explored by Eyre, and established a 400-hectare property which he named Hope Farm. It was here that he — or rather his manservant, James Green — first planted a few vines.

In 1842 Horrocks returned briefly to England and, while passing through the Cape of Good Hope on his way to England, arranged for a further consignment of vine cuttings to be sent to Hope Farm. He was to die in 1846 at the age of 28 from a gunshot wound accidentally sustained while exploring the country north of Spencer Gulf. Even in this short time he had had a profound influence on Clare Valley, with his leadership qualities attracting many settlers to the district.

One of the earliest other inhabitants was an Irishman by the name of Edmund Burton Gleeson, who established a property around two waterholes known as The Twins in 1840. In 1846 he laid out a township near his homestead which he called Clareville, in memory of his County Clare upbringing. Gleeson was to become the first mayor of the town of Clare, and for many years was a prominent figure in the district. Legend has it that, in his capacity as a magistrate, he was given to dispensing justice in the form of a whip wielded from horseback. Gleeson had attended a public meeting at Adelaide at 1840 called to arrange the importation of 500,000 vine cuttings, an ambitious project, partially funded by private subscription and partially by the government. Fifty-seven thousand vines in fact arrived, and Gleeson's share of these was 550, which he planted at his property called Inchiquin. Inchiquin wine was still being sold in the 1890s. In 1841 the Hawker brothers established Bungaree Station, a few kilometres north of Clare, and vines were planted here in 1842.

Over the next decades Clare was to become a thriving frontier town, servicing first the copper mines discovered at Burra in 1845 and at Wallaroo and Moonta between 1859 and 1861. When the mining boom waned, the wheat boom started. Vast wheat fields were established both in the Clare and Polish Hill areas, and further north towards Broken Hill. Small vineyards and tiny wineries sprang up all over the Clare Valley, producing wine by primitive methods, which was principally consumed within the region. Part of the wages of farmworkers was an annual wine ration, and the major wheat fields were significant employers of labour. The wheat boom was in full swing by 1874; in that year the *Northern Argus* reported that the main street of Clare was crowded with passenger vehicles and waggons loaded with farm implements all heading for the newly opened-up areas to the north.

Closer to home at the Hill River Station, a few kilometres east of Clare and owned by C. B. Fisher, one wheat field was five kilometres long. Thirty-four horse teams, each drawing a double-furrowed plough, covered from two to three acres (0.8 to 1.2 hectares) per day. Six 22-foot (6.7 metre) broadcast machines sowed 40 acres (16 hectares) of wheat each per day, while harvesting was carried out by 37 strippers each drawn by a four-horse team. Seventy people were permanently employed on the station, rising to 200 at shearing and harvest time. One hundred thousand sheep were shorn each year on Hill River Station.

The boom did not last for long: grasshopper plagues, red rust, rapidly falling soil fertility, declining yields and an Australia-wide wheat surplus all led to a rapid contraction of activity in the 1880s. The formation of The Broken Hill Proprietary Company Limited in 1885 led to brief hopes of recovery, as silver fever gripped the Clare Valley. Speculation was intense, but collapsed at the end of the year when the government geologist pronounced the area worthless. One of the initiatives taken to halt the decline was the establishment of a large fruit-processing factory to make preserves and jams. Between 1882 and 1883 it purchased and processed 70,000 kilograms of fruit, packed into 100,000 cans made by local tinsmiths. But technical problems, freight costs and a glut in the market led to the company going into liquidation in 1885.

From that year on newspaper editorials became increasingly interested in the prospects for viticulture; that of the *Northern Argus* of 22 December 1874 was typical:

> It is strange that the occupiers of the soil should devote nearly the whole of their time and attention to the growth of wheat, which is attended with a great deal of labour and risk while other industries that would yield a good return are all but neglected. On a great many homesteads there were, at one time, well-kept gardens, containing a variety of good fruit-bearing trees, besides a thriving vineyard; but now they are neglected, being left unpruned and impoverished with suckers and weeds.

The scene was set: what was then and many times since described as a vine mania gripped the whole of South Australia, and the Clare Valley in particular. In 1890 there were 100 hectares of vines in the Valley; by 1897 there were 580 hectares, a 480 per cent increase compared with a statewide increase of 300 per cent. The newspapers of the day tell the story. On 3 March 1892 the *Chronicle* contained an extremely lengthy report on a trip through the Clare district by the Central Agricultural Bureau. During the three-day visit Mr D. A. Crichton, a Victorian horticultural expert, addressed a large gathering of local farmers. The *Chronicle* summarised Crichton's speech:

> They [the farmers] could not go wrong also in growing wine grapes, as they could find a suitable market for years to come. Six million pounds sterling was expended annually in England in the import of wines, and, in this district wines of high character should be produced . . . He [Crichton] pointed out to the growers that they had large and unlimited markets in Europe for their wines, and he thought that by placing a good article before the public they might induce the European settlers in India to purchase their light wines. The future was bright before them and they need not hesitate in planting vines, and they could make it a much more thriving district if they did something of the land.

On 7 May 1892 the *Chronicle* reported an address given by Thomas Hardy to yet another large public meeting:

> At present the English market could absorb all the wine they could produce, while the Australian wine trade was gradually increasing. This he was sure would continue. It behoved growers, however, to see that none but first-class wines were placed on the English market, as an inferior wine would give people a well-founded prejudice against the wine produced in the country . . . Speaking of the possibility of a fall in the price of wine in the future, the speaker considered that if there was such a fall it would be the case with inferior wines, and he recommended the planting of high-class wine grapes. He thought, however, that a considerable quantity of inferior grapes could be used in distilling spirits . . . They need not be afraid that they would not find a market for their grapes should they go in for the industry extensively, as, should several vineyards be planted, there would soon be cellars for them. He suggested that every farmer should plant about 20 acres [eight hectares] with vines, and he maintained that they could be grown at small expense . . .

With exhortations such as this from one of the State's largest and most respected vignerons, it was hardly surprising that the farmers of the Clare Valley did exactly as they were told. But within two years concern mounted as farmers began to question just how and to whom they would sell their grapes. Meetings held throughout 1894 culminated in the formation of the Stanley Wine Company at the end of 1894. While not a true cooperative, it was nonetheless intended to have the same effect: guaranteeing the local growers a market for their grapes.

The owners of the Stanley Wine Company soon discovered that even turning grapes into wine was not enough; the potential buyers were not prepared to take raw, three-month-old wine, and it became necessary to store and mature the wine for at least two years before offering it for sale. Under these circumstances the size of Stanley grew in leaps and bounds, while another two substantial wineries—Koonawla and St Andrews—opened their doors. With the long-established Sevenhill Cellars and the Spring Vale Winery of Buring and Sobels the Clare Valley had become one of the major wine-producing regions of South Australia.

Just how important it was may be gauged from the figures for the 1903 vintage: in that year the Stanley Wine Company made 450,000 litres; Spring Vale 225,000 litres; St Andrews 126,000 litres; Wooroora 99,000 litres, Koonawla 67,500 litres, Sevenhill 27,000 litres and Birks Wendouree 5000 litres. By way of comparison Penfolds made 450,000 litres and Thomas Hardy & Sons 765,000 litres in the same vintage. By far the greatest part of this production was exported in hogsheads to London. In December 1890 the *Australian Vigneron and Fruit*

Grower baldly asserted: "Without London we need never plant another vine for a quarter of a century. With London we need have no fear what quantity our vintage reaches, the more the better." The truth probably lay somewhere in between, but nonetheless from 1890 to 1940 the London market was of major and at times quite critical importance to the South Australian industry in general, and to the Clare Valley in particular.

As the twentieth century arrived, and the years passed, the Stanley Wine Company came to dominate production totally. That of Sevenhill always remained small, and the only other major producer to survive the period from 1900 to 1930 was Buring and Sobels' Spring Vale or, as it came to be known, Quelltaler. The 1930s saw the establishment of the Clarevale Cooperative, but its products and its market were inevitably limited in range.

It is quite remarkable how the early plantings of the Clare Valley were dominated by cabernet sauvignon, shiraz and malbec. It is no less clear that in the first 60 years of this century those varieties were largely replaced by high-yielding types suited to fortified-winemaking. Thus grenache, pedro ximinez, crouchen, mataro, doradillo, muscadelle, gordo and frontignac were the most important varieties by 1941, with only shiraz remaining from the bold start of the 1890s. Cabernet sauvignon accounted for 12 hectares, and malbec had disappeared into the anonymity of the "mixed" category. The reshaping of the vineyards commenced in the mid-1950s, largely stimulated by the Stanley Wine Company. Clare riesling was by that time known to be something other than rhine riesling (although it was to be another decade before it was identified as crouchen), and Stanley actively promoted the planting of rhine riesling. (The Knappsteins had realised that the excellence of the Buring and Sobels hock stemmed from their holdings of the variety.)

On 1 January 1984 there were 748 hectares of rhine riesling in the Clare district, significantly more than twice as much as the next most widely propagated variety, shiraz, at 323 hectares. The table below gives a bird's-eye view of the vineyards as they stood during the 1984 vintage, and the production they achieved.

The dominance of rhine riesling reflects the fact that the Clare Valley is accepted as one of the classic areas for the variety; only the Eden Valley would be placed on a par or possibly in front. Just why the Clare Valley is so suited to rhine riesling is not easy to explain: all the official records credit the Clare Valley with a centigrade heat-degree day summation of around 1600. In 1981 it reached 1741, with a low of 1528 in 1980 and 1585 in 1984. These figures compare with 1517 for Nuriootpa in the Barossa Valley and 1620 for Rutherglen in north-east Victoria. The January mean temperature of 22°C and average of 8.8 sunshine hours all add to the confusion, proving once again that raw statistics on

CLARE VALLEY: GRAPE VARIETIES 1984

	BEARING	TOTAL AREA (HECTARES)			PRODUCTION (TONNES)
		NOT YET BEARING	ALL VINES	VINES 40 YEARS AND OVER	
RED GRAPES—					
Cabernet sauvignon	204	59	263	5	1012
Grenache	162	–	163	30	1221
Pinot noir	10	2	12	–	22
Shiraz	312	10	322	24	1570
Other red grapes	37	30	67	2	140
WHITE GRAPES—					
Chardonnay	47	80	127	–	179
Crouchen	130	2	132	8	1006
Doradillo	14	–	14	4	168
Palomino and pedro ximinez	237	8	245	41	2258
Rhine riesling	692	56	748	21	3630
Sauvignon blanc	28	5	33	–	103
Semillon	44	6	50	–	276
Traminer	54	10	64	–	295
Other white grapes	53	3	56	8	341
TOTAL	2024	271	2295	145	12,243

a piece of paper tell only part of the story. The style of rhine riesling is distinctively Australian and can only be described as traditional. While aromatic, the pungent botrytis aromas and the almost essency lime infusions of rhine riesling from areas such as Coonawarra are notably absent. While this may not presently be seen as an advantage, in the medium to long term I am certain it will. The best Clare rhine rieslings have only a few grams of sugar, and from the better vintages they will improve in bottle for a minimum of seven years, holding their form for far longer.

Quelltaler has led the way with semillon; over the years it produced one or two remarkably good (and extremely cheap) semillon-based chablis styles, pungent and grassy. More recently, since the arrival of Michel Dietrich, the marvellous Quelltaler Estate Wood-Matured Semillon of 1982 (and subsequent vintages) has made its appearance. Jeffrey Grosset, as winemaker for Mount Horrocks, has proved that he, too, can produce wine of very high quality in the same style. Being a late-ripening variety, there is every reason why semillon should produce high-quality wine; whether the public is prepared to see it in that light is another matter altogether.

Inevitably the attention of many of the wineries has turned to the darling of the 1980s, chardonnay. Knappstein and Stanley both made commercial quantities of chardonnay in 1984; Jeffrey Grosset made it one year earlier. Of all the vignerons he seems the most deeply committed to the variety. Equally he shares with Croser and Knappstein the view that the heavy, lush, rich, buttery/oily style is not the way to go. Whether microclimate, site selection, early picking and/or winemaking techniques will allow Grosset (and others) to master the propensity of the district to produce big, rich styles remains to be seen.

For many years Tim Knappstein had sauvignon blanc all to himself. Now once again others are starting to produce the wine, with Stanley and Quelltaler both making small quantities in 1984 which they intend to release commercially. I am a supporter of sauvignon blanc: I do not agree with Len Evans or Hugh Johnson when they dismiss it as a pedestrian, second-rate variety. But whether you see the Clare Valley as suited to the variety depends in no small measure on the style of sauvignon blanc you wish to drink. If it is that of the Loire Valley—crisp, flinty and pungent—look to New Zealand, or Tasmania perhaps, but not to Clare. But if it is the smoky, wooded fumé blanc style of California that you prefer then look to Clare, for Tim Knappstein

has done remarkably well since he introduced the style to the Clare Valley—and for that matter, to Australia.

The premium red grapes are headed by cabernet sauvignon, but it is interesting that right from the outset malbec and shiraz were grown in conjunction with it, and equally that in those early days the three varieties were invariably blended together. In the Clare Valley, no less than other regions, wine made exclusively from cabernet sauvignon tends to dip in flavour in the middle palate. It is precisely for this reason that the great wines of the Haut Médoc of France all have less cabernet franc, merlot and sometimes a little petite verdot blended in.

The style—and flavour—of Australia's cabernet sauvignon is in a state of flux. Twenty-five years ago there was almost no cabernet sauvignon grown; when it made its appearance (or rather reappearance) on a larger scale it was grown in warm areas, such as the Barossa Valley, and was allowed to ripen fully. The result was big, chocolatey wines with some sweet fruit and heavy tannin, a mile apart from the flavour and structure of a good bordeaux. Then from Coonawarra in particular the first of the sappy/grassy/green-leaf cabernets appeared in the mid-1970s. For a while they swept all before them, but those extreme styles have already been rejected as thin and lacking both mid-palate fruit and balance. Since then the plum/spice/stewed-prune cabernets have had a brief moment of glory, but again are likely to be found wanting in the long term.

The essential conflict in all of this stems from the desire to maximise elegance and finesse, without at the same time losing structure and flavour—to capture all the varietal fruit characteristics without producing a caricature of the variety. This conflict fully reflects itself in the cabernets of the Clare Valley. At the one extreme we have the cabernet sauvignon/cabernet franc wine of Jeffrey Grosset; at the other extreme the cabernet sauvignon and cabernet malbec of Wendouree. Knappstein's wines are somewhere in the middle; while the 1982 Mitchell veered to the lighter, more elegant style with overtones of a Bordeaux.

Cabernet sauvignon is one of the great travellers; if respected, it will produce a superior-quality wine wherever it is grown. But it should not produce the *same* wine wherever it is grown. The traditional red wines of Clare were robust, yet not coarse wines—big but delicate, to paraphrase Ray Kidd. The marvellous wines of Wendouree are prime examples of this style, and I hope that it is such wines which will be seen as the yardstick for the region, rather

VINEYARD HANDS, SEVENHILL, 1940

than an excessively fine and elegant copy of a light-bodied Coonawarra or mid-Victorian cabernet. Which is not to say that there is no room for improvement or refinement. There is, and it lies in the agency of malbec, cabernet franc and merlot. Malbec has been around longest, and has a large band of supporters for its being peculiarly suited to the Clare Valley. The figures given for Stanley on page 383 make interesting reading: less than half a hectare of malbec is in bearing and 10 are coming into bearing. The answer is that Stanley replanted all its malbec in 1980–81 because it felt its existing clone was an inferior one, a view reinforced by the outstanding quality of the clone at Birks' Wendouree. Poor clone or not, it resulted in the 1971 Bin 56 Cabernet Malbec, one of Brian Croser's all-time favourites among Australian reds.

Cabernet franc seems to hold out equal promise. Of many outstanding vats of red wine made by Knappstein in 1984, by far the most exciting was the cabernet franc. If ever I have seen a young Bordeaux style in Australia, this was it. The merlot suffered a little in comparison; although it was still very good, it did not have the intensity of flavour. Being an early ripener, there may be problems in retaining enough acid and achieving enough flavour; Croser certainly has reservations.

On the evidence to date pinot noir should not be planted other than in the Polish Hill area, where John Wilson has made some very interesting wines with excellent fruit character. The efforts of Stanley and Taylors have so far produced very little reward. On the other hand the region can and does produce superb shiraz—full of flavour, character and strength, yet not coarse. The export market may prove the ultimate salvation of these wines, because Australians seem absolutely determined to ignore them. More power to Andrew Mitchell, who was so impressed by the quality of his 1984 Shiraz that he has decided to bottle and release it (in previous years it was sold in bulk).

Then there is the Polish Hill River, which nestles under the lee of the hills running north-south forming the eastern wall of the Clare Valley. As one drives towards the Polish Hill area, vast plains stretch as far as the eye can see, past Mintaro and towards Burra. The atmosphere is totally different from that of the Clare Valley: no twisting streamlets, no folding hills, no cameo vistas. This is raw-boned Australia, and one can well imagine how it must have both impressed and awed the first Polish settlers who arrived in the region in the late 1850s. The Polish community remained the dominant force in the area

until the early years of the 1900s; thereafter it gradually disintegrated, but in recent years interest has returned with the restoration of the historic St Stanislaus church which had been consecrated on 30 November 1871.

A large vineyard was established in the region by Dr J. W. D. Bain on the main Sevenhill to Mintaro Road. In 1896 the 200-hectare property had over 40 hectares of wines and eight hectares of fruit trees in production. The Nyora Winery was built on the property in 1903 after it had passed into the ownership of the Main brothers. Production was between 45,000 and 50,000 litres a year, with storage capacity of 150,000 litres. It was a short-lived enterprise, seemingly going out of production in the First World War.

Viticulture has now returned in a major way, thanks to Penfolds and Wolf Blass. Yet the major publicity for the area comes not from these two companies, but from the two minnows: Paulett's and John Wilson's Polish Hill River Vineyards. Penfolds acquired its property in the late 1970s; despite its prior history of grape growing, the old hands of the Clare Valley all shook their heads, avowing that it was too far out on the plain, and that the rainfall would be far too low. But Penfolds had the answer: the 160-hectare property is served by two massive dams built by Penfolds and which hold 100 million litres and 50 million litres respectively. The first vines were planted in 1980, and all were served by drip-irrigation to provide the supplementary water so necessary in this admittedly dry climate. The vineyard is immaculately laid out and maintained, using the latest trellising techniques to facilitate mechanical harvesting once the vines are fully mature. Flexible steel uprights allow pulsator harvesting: the bunches are literally shaken off the vine, rather than being beaten off as in the case of conventional harvesters. There is accordingly much less skin breakage and juicing of the grapes, with a corresponding increase in juice quality once the grapes are processed.

The varieties planted include rhine riesling, traminer, chardonnay, muller-thurgau, sauvignon blanc, cabernet sauvignon, cabernet franc, merlot, malbec and shiraz. Overall the balance is about two to one in favour of the white-grape varieties, with rhine riesling being the major grape. The first commercial vintage was in 1983, when about 30 tonnes of rhine riesling were processed at Clarevale Cooperative Winery. The red grapes were sent direct to Nuriootpa and processed there. It will be interesting to see whether Penfolds releases wines made only from Clare fruit or whether the wines will be used for blending. Certainly if Max Schubert were still at the helm the major portion of the red production would be employed this latter way. Penfolds, incidentally, treats its vineyard as being in the Sevenhill region, and there appears a measure of agreement that, indeed, its vineyard is not in the core area of the Polish Valley—although to the casual observer it is quite unequivocally on the Polish Hill side.

The other major producer, Wolf Blass Wines, acquired its property in 1979. The 55-hectare property is now planted to capacity with 28.5 hectares of rhine riesling, half having been planted in 1980 and the remainder in 1981. (There is a token 1.25 hectares of chardonnay.) The vines are supported by supplementary irrigation from a 17-million litre dam; on the basis that a maximum of 160 millimetres of supplementary water will be given to the vines in any one year, the dam has a two-year capacity. This would lift the average rainfall of 600 millimetres to 750 millimetres, and should ensure vigorous vine growth.

The decision by Blass to plant rhine riesling to the virtual exclusion of all other varieties—and indeed to buy and develop the property in the first place—was a very interesting one. Wolf Blass Wines, it should be remembered, owns virtually no vineyards, relying instead on buying grapes and bulk wine from other producers. This approach has been enormously successful, both from the quality and financial viewpoints. As far as quality is concerned, the end result is testimony to the exceptional skills of the winemaking team headed by Wolf Blass and John Glaetzer. Financially it is a recognition of the fact that for many years now the return of the average grape grower has been woefully inadequate. Whatever real return there is in the industry stems from wine-making, not grape growing. So Blass has been more than content that others should do that part for him.

The *volte-face* in the Clare Valley came from a recognition of a number of factors. First, the very high regard that Wolf Blass Wines has for Clare Valley rhine riesling. Valley sources suggest that more than 50 per cent of all rhine riesling grown or made in the Valley is sold to Wolf Blass Wines, destined for Blass's Yellow Label Rhine Riesling. Second, Blass fully realised that the days of the small grower in the Clare Valley were numbered, and that continuity of supply—let alone growth in supply—could not be guaranteed. Thirdly, utilising the most recent viticultural techniques, it was reasonable to assume that Wolf Blass Wines would

in fact be able to turn the tables and produce rhine riesling for less than the district buying price. So it is that, like Penfolds, the vineyard has been trellised with flexiposts, fitted with drip-irrigation and so on. To the casual observer the military precision of the rows might simply appear to be a reflection of a Teutonic desire for absolute order, but it is more than that. The era of laser-pruning is at hand, and the dead-straight rows will permit pruning at tremendous speed and correspondingly low cost if the technique is perfected.

Blass expects to harvest between 11 and 12.3 tonnes to the hectare when the vines are fully established, and if this aim is realised, the cost per tonne will indeed be below the ruling Clare price. One hundred tonnes were harvested in 1984, and more than twice the amount is expected in 1985. It is unlikely that a 100 per cent Clare Valley rhine riesling will be released (all the fruit will go to the blended Yellow Label wine), although the first crop of 18 tonnes in 1983 did make an outstanding sweet white.

Such aims are far removed from those of the legally constituted association known (and registered) as the Vignerons of the Polish Valley Incorporated. Its foundation constitution records the aims of the association as being:

(a) to promote an awareness of the Polish Valley, its wines, history and environment;
(b) to encourage production of high-quality wine from the locality;
(c) to monitor the environment of the locality and to make representations to appropriate authorities on environmental matters; and
(d) to develop a system of integrity of labelling, for wines from the area.

These are in turn encapsulated in the stylised logo of a vigneron and his wine with the motto "Identity and Integrity". But of course there is something of a dilemma in all of this. Few people have ever heard of the Polish Valley and, at least for the time being, the vignerons in the area do not wish to cut themselves too far adrift from the better-known Clare Valley. Time alone will tell whether two distinct regions emerge, or whether the secessionist tendencies presently evident will wither on the vine.

I hope it prospers. There can be no doubting the integrity (or enthusiasm) of its leading winemaker, Dr John Wilson, and I am certain he sees the marketing advantages that also flow from the guarantees provided by an appellation control system. The difficulty will be that the major vignerons in both the Polish Hill and Clare Valley areas are implacably opposed to appellation.

JIM BARRY WINES
MAIN NORTH ROAD, CLARE

Jim Barry was the first qualified winemaker to practise in Clare. He spent 22 years at Clarevale Cooperative before taking on the task of creating Chateau Clare for the Taylor family. His four years there saw the establishment of the largest new vineyard development in the history of the area, and the erection of the striking winery.

While he remained on good terms with the Taylors, he had a growing family to consider. After nearly a quarter of a century working for others, he felt it was time to establish his own business, and it was hardly a surprising decision. In 1959 he had bought a house sitting on 40 hectares on the northern outskirts of the town. Even in those days the £14,000 purchase price was a bargain. Although they were once extensively planted, the vineyards had largely been removed by the previous owner, a wealthy grazier. A little under two hectares of prime vineyard remained, and over the following years Jim Barry progressively planted much of the remaining land. Three years later he purchased a further 26 hectares at Benburnie, and this too was gradually planted.

So by the end of the 1960s Barry was a significant grape grower in his own right. He sold most of the grapes, but in 1968, 1969 and 1970 he made limited quantities of rhine riesling, shiraz and cabernet sauvignon at Roly Birks's Wendouree Cellars. It was a good arrangement: Jim Barry put in a Wilmes press for Roly, and Birks let him use the winemaking and storage facilities at Wendouree. So in June 1973 he decided to leave Taylors, having taken it to the point where it was poised to make its first vintage, and set up his own operation. He had six months to design and build his winery, which he called St Clare Cellars. For once a winery due for completion by vintage was finished on schedule, and the first "homemade" St Clare Cellars wines were produced in 1974. With some stocks of mature wine immediately available for sale, St Clare Cellars was in business.

The winery is functional rather than beautiful, which is what one would expect from a thoroughly professional winemaker. Certainly it has none of the embellishments of Chateau Clare about it. Both the name St Clare Cellars and the somewhat psychedelic labels of those early years have gone. The winery now trades under the name of Jim Barry Wines, and the labels are an exercise in disciplined restraint. This, one suspects, reflects the influence of son Peter Barry, a Roseworthy graduate. While Peter did

the full wine course (as opposed to the marketing course), it is marketing that is Peter's forte. Curiously the eldest son, Mark, who is winemaker, has done only a short Roseworthy course. He learnt his winemaking the hard way—as cellar-hand—and is, in Jim Barry's words, "a very practical winemaker".

What will in the long term prove the most important acquisition was made seven years ago, when the property now called Lodge Hill was acquired. It used to be known as the Wolta Thoroughbred Stud, and Lodge Hill marks the highest point on the eastern ranges of the Clare Valley. There are two separate plantings on Lodge Hill: an eight-hectare rhine riesling vineyard, and a separate area of rhine riesling (7.7 hectares), together with traminer (3.6 hectares), merlot (1.3 hectares) and malbec (1.1 hectares). Eventually, this will become the principal—if not the sole—source of grapes for the winery. In the meantime the vineyard adjacent to the winery provides a valuable supplement to the crush, being planted with chardonnay (four hectares), sauvignon blanc (1.6 hectares), rhine riesling (2.6 hectares), cabernet sauvignon (4.7 hectares), shiraz (four hectares), cabernet franc (0.8 hectare), merlot (0.8 hectare) and malbec (0.6 hectare). These vineyards together produce virtually all of the 350-tonne crush which the winery handles in a normal year. More than three-quarters of each year's production is still sold in bulk, with companies such as Stanley and Wolf Blass being ready purchasers. The remaining wine is bottled under the Jim Barry label, and most is sold by cellar door and in Adelaide.

The Jim Barry Lodge Hill Rhine Riesling, like the Jim Barry Watervale Rhine Riesling, is a very soft, very full-flavoured and slightly broad style. It may not please technically minded winemakers, but I have always enjoyed the generosity of flavour. It is the sort of rhine riesling which will stand up to food.

The style of the Jim Barry reds has changed radically between 1971 and 1981. The older wines were traditional, chocolatey Clare Valley reds, with some slightly dusty, old-oak characters. The 1980 and 1981 Cabernet Sauvignons are wines of a very different style. The 1980 has intense grassy/green-leaf cabernet aroma and flavour; while the 1981 inevitably reflects the hot vintage conditions and shows diminished varietal character, but it is nonetheless a very commercial wine and well put together.

More recently Barry has produced a merlot and several chardonnays. The early releases of the latter showed very little varietal character; this will presumably build as the vines mature. The merlot had good depth of flavour and colour, although the grafted vines from which it was made have since faltered, and it may be some time before the replacement plantings come into bearing.

CLAREVALE COOPERATIVE
15 LENNON STREET, CLARE

Clarevale Growers Winery Limited was founded in the dark days of 1928. Following the removal of the export bounty by the Federal government, the grape surplus was such that a meeting of Barossa and Clare Valley growers held on 24 November 1928 resolved "not to accept any prices lower than those given in 1921, when shiraz was £12 per ton". That resolution led more or less directly to the incorporation of Clarevale Growers Winery Limited, which lasted for only two years before going into liquidation. In its place Clarevale Cooperative Winery Limited was incorporated, and started with a State government loan of £8000. That money was used to purchase the old depot and the stables of a coaching company, Hill & Company. It was a relatively simple matter to convert the building into a winery, and almost immediately Clarevale was producing substantial quantities of principally fortified wine.

As ever, the problem was not making the wine, but selling it. The two senior executives of the cooperative, Bill Quirke and Alan McAskill, became travelling salesmen, loading 1.5 tonnes of wine in casks into the back of an International utility and travelling over much of South Australia selling it door-to-door. Years later Quirke recalled: "If you had the wine with you, people would buy it." By this means, and by bulk sales to the major wine companies, Clarevale survived the difficult times of the 1930s and the Second World War years, with sales building up to the equivalent of 35,000 cases a year. In 1946 a recent graduate from Roseworthy College, Jim Barry, became Clarevale's (and the Clare Valley's) first qualified winemaker. The crush quickly built up to 2200 tonnes in the buoyant market between 1948 and 1952.

The collapse of the fortified-wine market brought problems to Clarevale once again. The bankruptcy of a major Sydney customer led to the enforced acquisition of his wine business and licence, and Clarevale Wines Sydney started trading in Little Riley Street, East Sydney. This in turn led to the involvement of the Taylor family: Bill Taylor had always had a regard for the Clare Valley, and throughout the 1950s and 1960s the Taylors bought large

quantities of Clarevale wine in bulk for their chain of Sydney hotels. The continuing decline in the fortified-wine market, and the changing style of table wines of the 1960s, made life increasingly difficult for Clarevale. Successful marketing became more and more difficult, and the stocks were accumulating to an unacceptable level when Clarevale entered into a marketing arrangement with its fellow cooperative, Kaiser Stuhl.

In 1980 a 10-year contract was entered into with Kaiser Stuhl which in effect placed Clarevale under Kaiser Stuhl management, both in terms of winemaking and marketing. With the subsequent Penfolds acquisition of Kaiser Stuhl, Clarevale's own labels have all but disappeared. It has become an important grape-processing plant for the production of bulk wine, most of which finds its way into casks and flagons. The old Clarevale labels linger on for the purpose of cellar-door sales, but have no significance in the marketplace as a whole.

The quality of the wines was utilitarian at best, and that of the wines today barely relevant to the Clare Valley.

ENTERPRISE WINES
2 PIONEER AVENUE, CLARE

Enterprise Wines was conceived in 1972. In that year Tim Knappstein received payment for his shares in the Stanley Wine Company which had been sold to H. J. Heinz. Knappstein wryly recalls that "in those days it was possible to actually make some money out of growing grapes". He accordingly purchased some high-country land to the south-east of Clare and set about establishing a vineyard. The gestation period was a lengthy one; it was not until 1976 that Knappstein finally left Stanley and, in partnership with his mother, formed Enterprise Wines.

In that year they purchased the marvellous old blue-stone building on the northern outskirts of the township of Clare, which was originally the Enterprise Brewery. In one of those twists of fate, the Enterprise Brewery had been owned by J. C. Christison, one of the founding shareholders of the Stanley Wine Company. Some years earlier it had become apparent to Tim Knappstein that, sooner or later, he would wish to part company with Stanley. He accordingly made wine in both the 1974 and 1975 vintages at other wineries in the district, forgoing sleep and weekends to do so. Thus, when Enterprise opened for business, it had wine for sale.

The first vintage made at Enterprise was in 1977: the 1977 Rhine Riesling won numerous gold medals and a trophy; while the 1975 red (released at the same time) was very nearly as successful. Enterprise was away to a flying start, and has not looked back since. That initial crush was 80 tonnes, and in the intervening years has risen to around 240 tonnes, which is as much as the present winery set-up will handle.

The vineyards are planted to rhine riesling (11.6 hectares), sauvignon blanc (3.8 hectares), gewurtz-traminer (3.3 hectares), chardonnay (1.2 hectares), cabernet sauvignon (8.2 hectares), shiraz (four hectares, but shortly to be grafted to merlot and sauvignon blanc), cabernet franc (1.5 hectares), malbec (0.8 hectare) and merlot (0.6 hectare). Not surprisingly, rhine riesling is the dominant variety in the vineyards and, together with cabernet sauvignon, is the flagship of the Enterprise range. These wines invariably show Knappstein's complete mastery of the varieties and are eloquent ambassadors for the district as a whole. Knappstein passionately believes in the entitlement of rhine riesling to pride of place in the Australian white-wine industry. He points out that despite the efforts of certain wine scribes, more rhine riesling is produced and bottled than all of the other premium white varieties put together. Equally importantly, its overall quality is at the very least the equal of any other variety. Finally, and most importantly of all, it is a wine to drink, a wine which tastes as good at the end of the bottle as it does at the start.

If ever a winemaker is to provide practical proof of his beliefs, it is Tim Knappstein. The Enterprise Rhine Rieslings made between 1977 and 1984 are absolutely exceptional. The most freakish feature of the wines is their elegance and finesse as young wines, balanced by their capacity to age with exceptional grace in the bottle. A tasting in mid-1984 of all of the wines made between 1977 and 1983 resulted in first place going to the 1980, only a shade in front of the 1977 vintage. Had the 1984 been included, I am sure it would have been somewhere at the top end of the tasting. All the wines, indeed, were of high quality and only the 1981 fell a little behind in terms of ultimate class. These wines really are the personification of Clare Valley rhine riesling at its greatest.

In 1978 the first Clare Valley Sauvignon Blanc was made by Tim Knappstein; he had recognised the potential of the grape before anyone else, and had planted it first. He also used the term fumé blanc before any other Australian winemaker; the currency

has been debased somewhat in the meantime, as other makers across the country have used the name with scant regard for variety or style. But Knappstein can hardly be blamed for that. Knappstein remains committed both to the variety and the style, as do his customers: the wine invariably sells out first. While I think the wines are good, and in 1982 and 1980 great, I do not think they consistently reach the same heights as the rhine rieslings. Put another way, while the Clare Valley is an outstanding rhine riesling area, I have reservations about its long-term suitability for sauvignon blanc.

When one listens to Tim Knappstein speak, one could be forgiven for thinking that his cabernet sauvignons have been little more than practice efforts, with all of the best still to come. In perspective, it is simply a case of Knappstein ever striving to improve the quality of the wine. In this context quality is heavily qualified by style: while Knappstein does not believe there is any merit in going too far in seeking elegance (particularly if this results in a loss of body, flavour and staying power), it is nonetheless something which he sees as being of great importance. It is in this context that the role of cabernet franc and merlot will be of great importance in the future. But even without their aid in the past, a tasting of Enterprise cabernet sauvignon in July 1984 showed a distinct evolution in style, with vintage variation playing its part. Of the wines made between 1978 and 1982, I think the 1979, 1980 and 1982 vintages are quite outstanding. The 1978 and 1981 vintages will improve for years, but are the heavier style which Knappstein wishes to avoid. The evolution of the other vintages follows the ever-so-difficult path of achieving elegance without diminishing the intensity of fruit flavour. The 1980 wine fully reflects the very cool conditions of that year, with obvious herbaceous characters. The 1982 vintage takes the whole process one step further; it has elegant, ripe yet not jammy fruit, with fragrances of mint, cassis and oak, and perfect balance, with soft but persistent powdery tannin on the finish. These are very great Australian red wines.

Over the years Knappstein has also made some excellent shiraz (although, bowing to the inevitable, that wine has now headed to extinction) and one or two shiraz cabernet blends when either one or other variety has not come up to his own high standards. The other regular Enterprise release has been of gewurtztraminer, a variety which I am quite certain is not suited to the Clare Valley in most vintages. The 1981 wine was, however, an exception to the rule.

Finally, Knappstein has made tiny quantities of some quite magnificent botrytised rhine riesling, made as either beerenauslese or trockenbeerenauslese. These have been made by artificially inoculating grapes placed on racks in a cool-room with the botrytis spore, and then precisely regulating temperature and humidity to achieve optimum mould growth over the ensuing two to three weeks. In this time the grapes lose moisture, gaining constantly in sugar and acid. It is an extremely expensive and risky method of production, and the market for such wines is a very limited one. Production will accordingly always be very small, and the wines will be appreciated only by a handful of wine connoisseurs who are happy to pay the price of $14 a half-bottle which (just about) returns to the winemaker the cost of production. When the Enterprise Vineyard at Lenswood, in the Mount Lofty Ranges, comes into full production, Knappstein will hopefully no longer have to rely upon the cool-room.

FAREHAM ESTATE
MAIN NORTH ROAD, LEASINGHAM

The wines of Fareham Estate are known to relatively few people, notwithstanding the fact that it has been in production since 1976, and that since 1976 it has run a highly successful business. That business was not, however, so much concerned with winemaking as contract wine-bottling. The substantial but plain buildings at Fareham Estate housed one of the most sophisticated bottling operations in Australia, which had its genesis when Peter Rumball left the Stanley Wine Company in 1976. He had worked there for three years following his graduation from Roseworthy Agricultural College, one of his chief responsibilities having been the elimination of problems which had plagued the Stanley bottling line.

Rumball correctly identified the need for contract bottling services in the Clare and Barossa Valleys, and the business grew quickly. His capital expenditure grew even more quickly, and despite the arrival of Stephen Elliott as a partner, financial constraints caused Fareham to curtail severely its winemaking activities. The releases under the Fareham Estate label were both sporadic and not always up to standard.

Those difficulties are now behind Fareham. The contract bottling plant has been transferred to new premises in the Adelaide metropolitan area; winery equipment has been upgraded (although in 1985 the crushing and pressing facilities at Grosset's were utilised); the vineyards have been rejuvenated; and the future crush will rise to nearly 100 tonnes, at which time the winery will be fully equipped.

Grape intake at the moment comes from the vineyard surrounding the winery and from a separate vineyard owned by Stephen Elliott's father. The winery block is planted to rhine riesling (3.2 hectares), sauvignon blanc (two hectares), cabernet sauvignon and traminer (0.8 hectare each). Elliott's block is planted to a total of eight hectares of cabernet sauvignon, cabernet franc, sauvignon blanc and chardonnay, all of which are progressively coming into bearing.

The 1983 releases from Fareham Estate comprised a blanc de blancs, a gewurztraminer, a fumé blanc and a rhine riesling. All were generously flavoured wines with a little bit of residual sugar to add both weight to the palate and to their commercial appeal. In the longer term Rumball has plans to install a sparkling-wine fermentation and maturation cellar in the now-capacious winery.

JEFFREY GROSSET
KING STREET, AUBURN

Jeffrey Grosset was born and raised in the Clare Valley, but took a circuitous route before returning to it after graduating from Roseworthy Agricultural College in 1975. He had spent five years there, taking first the diploma of agriculture and then the diploma of oenology courses. After graduation, he worked at Seppelt's Great Western for 18 months, gaining experience in the making of both still and sparkling wines. He then journeyed to Europe, and accepted a position as assistant winemaker at a German winery near Freiburg with a crush of 1000 tonnes. When the French head winemaker-designate failed to arrive, Grosset found himself in charge of the entire winery.

He returned to Australia in 1977, and worked at Lindemans' Karadoc Winery for the next three years. Karadoc was even then crushing over 30,000 tonnes of grapes a year. It was also handling overflow material from Lindemans' Padthaway Vineyards, and all in all it was an exciting place to be. Grosset had no real thought of leaving Karadoc when he learnt through his family that the Farmers' Union milk depot at Auburn was on the market for a virtually nominal price, but he purchased the depot regardless.

The building had started life as a butter and ice factory at the end of the last century, and had been extended and modernised by the Farmers' Union around 1960. This has resulted in the best of both worlds so far as Grosset is concerned: the quite lovely stone front section of the building remains untouched (except for Jeffrey Grosset's name in place of "Butter and Ice Works"), while the extensions were built to the clinical specifications necessary for a milk factory, from the steel tiles on the floor through to the insulated building and refrigeration capacity.

In the second half of 1980 Grosset left Karadoc to return to Auburn. His first vintage in 1981 amounted to 12 tonnes of fruit. This produced five wines, each made in tiny quantities: a Polish Hill Rhine Riesling, a Watervale Rhine Riesling, a Late-Picked Rhine Riesling and a Cabernet Sauvignon. The crush increased to a little over 20 tonnes in 1982, and again three rieslings were made, together with a cabernet sauvignon/cabernet franc blend. All of these wines were impeccably made; the cabernet sauvignon/cabernet franc was particularly well received by critics around the country, the whites only marginally less so. The "sold out" sign went up almost immediately, and despite steadily increasing production, the sign has remained more or less continuously displayed ever since.

In 1983 Grosset made his first chardonnay; initially extremely delicate, it developed quite extraordinary richness in bottle by the end of 1984. Seldom have I misjudged a young wine so much, for I simply could not see the development capacity it in fact had.

Grosset is a perfectionist who is absolutely committed to making the best wine he possibly can. By the same token, he makes his wines in his own style, and that may not please everyone. Indeed, I have heard the odd critical comment from other winemakers who feel he errs too far on the side of delicacy. I must confess I do not understand that criticism; I believe that the Polish Hill Rhine Rieslings from 1981–84, and the Watervale Rhine Rieslings from 1982 to 1984, are all excellent wines.

As one would expect, vintage variation has played a significant role in shaping style: the 1983 Polish Hill Rhine Riesling in particular is a far heavier wine than the other vintages from this interesting area. It is in marked contrast to the style of the 1982 and 1984 wines. 1983 was not an easy vintage in the Clare Valley, but the 1983 Watervale Rhine Riesling was a great success: a flavoury, flowery wine with full, rich fruit and excellent overall weight and style. Grosset finds the same ambivalent reaction to his late-harvest rhine riesling that other makers have to contend with. At the cellar door, where the wine is tasted as part of the range, sales outweigh all others.

Yet on the retailers' shelves the wine is ignored. It seems that the public will buy these wines on taste, but not on label. Specifically, the Grosset style is at the light end of the spectrum: the wines are neither especially sweet nor heavy.

Grosset's reds started in 1981 with a cabernet sauvignon; the 1982 and 1983 vintages were a cabernet sauvignon/cabernet franc blend in the proportion of 80 per cent to 20 per cent. The straight 1981 Cabernet is by far the biggest of the three wines, the 1982 the lightest. In 1983 Grosset achieved the balance and style he was looking for, and the 1984 wine should be outstanding.

HERITAGE WINES
WENDOUREE ROAD, CLARE

Heritage Wines is the reincarnation of Robertson Wines. Ex-Saltram winemaker (and Roseworthy-graduate) Stephen Hof has taken a lease of the winery, and expects to exercise his option to buy before the 1986 vintage. Robertson took the diverse stock he had on hand, and has set up a roadside stall in a disused garage from which he plies his trade on weekends.

With four years' experience at Saltram and the wine-marketing degree course at Roseworthy under his belt, Hof has no illusions about the difficulties confronting a new small winery seeking to establish its place in the market. Thus in 1985 the crush was a very modest 23 tonnes: the red wines (shiraz and cabernet sauvignon) were made at Heritage, the white wines (semillon and rhine riesling) under contract at Stanley.

Hof's first priority is to build markets rather than make large quantities of wine, and he expects it will take three or four years for the crush to reach the projected maximum of around 70 tonnes. In the meantime, he will spend much of each week "door-knocking" on Adelaide restaurants and retailers, and in mid-1985 was hopeful of concluding distribution arrangements with a Sydney wholesaler.

With an abundance of grapes in the district, Hof does not intend, or wish, to commence his own vineyards, and will rely on grape purchases in the Clare Valley, possibly supplemented by a small quantity from the Barossa Valley. Until the 1985 vintage wines become available, Heritage is offering a range of Barossa Valley wines made by or on behalf of Stephen Hof over the past few years.

HORROCKS WINES
MINTARO ROAD, WATERVALE

Horrocks Wines had made a name for itself before its winery came into existence, and before its production extended beyond a handful of restaurants and specialty fine-wine shops. It was one of those ventures in which everything seemed to go right: excellent label design and packaging, new-style wines which caught the eye of wine journalists and magazines, and that most important commodity of all—scarcity.

All of this came from a background which can only be described as unlikely. The Ackland brothers—Trevor, Roger and Lyall—were confronted with entering their father's butchery business when they left school, something which did not greatly attract them at the time. So they looked for additional seasonal work, vaguely hoping to find something more congenial. Pruning and grape-picking led to a more or less accidental share-farming arrangement on a block of vines owned by a friend of their father's, and that—as the saying goes—was the beginning of the end.

Their first vines were planted in 1967 on the foothills under Mount Horrocks, hence the name of the winery. Further plantings (on three more properties) have followed in the intervening years, and by 1982 the Ackland brothers were among the most important growers in the entire district. The Mount Horrocks Vineyard is by far the largest of the four properties, with 56 hectares of which 29 hectares are planted to nine varieties. The soils vary from red loam through alluvial to heavy clay, all with a slate/schist substratum. The heavy clay is planted to semillon, a variety which Lyall Ackland is particularly enthusiastic about, and which was one of the principal factors in the Acklands' eventual decision to commence winemaking. Other varieties planted are chardonnay, rhine riesling, crouchen, pedro ximinez, traminer, shiraz, cabernet sauvignon and merlot.

Eyre Creek bisects the middle of the 7.3-hectare Leasingham Vineyard, with soils varying from lime-stone-impregnated clays to heavy rich loam. This has one of the few plantings of chenin blanc in the district (one hectare), with three other varieties to make way shortly for chardonnay. The balance is planted to grenache. A second smaller block is almost fully planted to four hectares of shiraz.

Over the past five years the fourth vineyard has been established, fronting the Main North Road and towards Leasingham. Much of the 25 hectares is suitable for planting (the western extremity rises into scrub-covered foothills), but so far only 10 hectares is under vine, planted to rhine riesling, pedro ximinez and semillon. Finally, there is the six-hectare Winery Block, 300 metres off the Main North Road on the Leasingham to Mintaro road. The winery had been due for completion in time for the 1984 vintage but, almost inevitably, the builders fell behind schedule by eight weeks, and grapes wait for no-one.

The winery had been designed for the Ackland brothers by Jeffrey Grosset, who had contract-made the Horrocks wines in 1982 and 1983. In the event he did the same in 1984. He is to remain a consultant for future vintages, so the style of the wine should not change greatly. The first release, from the 1982 vintage, centred on an oak-matured semillon, a wine which combined elegance and generosity of flavour. It has developed beautifully in bottle, and deserved all the praise which was heaped on it.

The range of wines increased substantially in 1983, and in the early part of 1984 a 1983 Watervale Rhine Riesling, a 1983 Eyre Creek Semillon, a 1983 Chardonnay and a 1982 Cabernet Merlot were released. These continued the high quality evident with the first releases. The rhine riesling is a wine of abundant flavour and rich texture, aided by a touch of residual sugar. The semillon showed impeccable oak handling, good depth to the fruit and equally good acid contributing to a long, clean finish. The chardonnay seemed very light when first released, but if it follows in the track of the Grosset wine of the same year it will have already developed surprising depth. The 1982 Cabernet Merlot has the unmistakable stamp of the winemaker, Jeffrey Grosset, on it. Fresh cherry/berry-fruit aromas intermingle with a touch of buttery, almost caramelised, oak. The palate is light, fresh and vibrant, with crisp acid on the finish.

The limited output of Horrocks Wines is well worth chasing; cellar door or the mailing list are the most likely methods of securing the wines.

JUD'S HILL
FARRELL FLAT ROAD, CLARE

Brian Barry was chief winemaker at the Stanley Wine Company between August 1976 and the end of 1978. Prior to that time he had had a distinguished career at Berri Cooperative, and is, of course, one of Australia's senior wine judges.

His brother Jim Barry had been a long-term Clare

resident and vigneron. Not long after Brian Barry arrived in the district one of the best agricultural properties came onto the market—known as the Wolta Thoroughbred Stud, it included two separate titles. Because it was offered for sale in one line, Brian and Jim Barry purchased it jointly, but promptly split the property into the two separate blocks. Situated on the high hills on the eastern side of the Clare Valley, the 33-hectare property taken by Brian Barry is now almost fully planted. There are 25 hectares under vine, with 19 hectares in bearing. Rhine riesling is by far the most important variety, with significant quantities of cabernet sauvignon and merlot, and trial blocks of malbec and cabernet franc.

The property is named after Brian Barry's 16-year-old son, Judson. He, I understand, intends to do the wine marketing course at Roseworthy Agricultural College, so the family tradition will be continued. On the other hand, there is at present no winery, nor is any planned. Since 1984 all the wines have been made at Petaluma on a contract basis, with Brian Barry keeping a fatherly eye on proceedings. In prior vintages the red wines were made at Jim Barry's and the white wines at Petaluma.

The decision by a winemaker of the standing of Brian Barry to concentrate on the vineyard, and to allow outsiders to make his wine, is interesting. It reflects two main factors. Firstly, with a maximum yield of 7.5 tonnes per hectare the quantity of fruit is at the bottom end of the scale to justify the capital expenditure in setting up a winery. Contract-making is a far more profitable way to proceed at these levels, if a contract-maker can be found who is reliable. In Brian Barry's view (and indeed in the view of many others) Petaluma offers a great deal more than that. Brian Barry candidly says: "I put in an appearance when the grapes go through the crusher, but really I couldn't fault what the Petaluma team does. Croser's thinking is so close to mine, I just have to have total confidence." The other factor is that the lack of capital commitment on a winery has enabled more money to be expended on the vineyard with the aim of improving fruit quality. Perhaps a lifetime of working with grapes grown by others was the catalyst which persuaded Brian Barry to reverse the normal trend and establish a vineyard rather than a winery.

The Jud's Hill Rhine Rieslings of 1982, 1983 and 1984 are of the quality one would expect given this potent combination of forces. The non-irrigated vineyard certainly reflects the impact of varying vintage conditions, and the three rhine rieslings are

in markedly different style. The 1982 and 1984 vintages promise to be very long-lived; the 1983 should be at its best around 1985–86.

The Jud's Hill red wines are merlot/cabernet blends, elegant wines but nonetheless reflecting the view of both Brian Barry and Brian Croser that red grapes need to be fully ripe to permit full flavour development. Clever winemaking, and the sensitive use of oak, avoid any suggestion of jamminess.

LINDEMANS AND LEO BURING
FLORITA VINEYARD, MAIN NORTH ROAD, WATERVALE

The story of Lindemans' involvement in the Clare Valley is much more one of what might have been, rather than what is. Indeed, one of Lindemans' most significant continuing ties with the Clare Valley comes through Leo Buring's Florita Vineyard, purchased by Leo Buring himself from Malcolm Allen well before Leo Buring & Company was acquired by Lindemans. Yet on two separate occasions Lindemans came very close to acquiring the Stanley Wine Company; that it failed to do so is obviously a cause of regret to present managing director Ray Kidd. On the other hand by the time the shareholders of Stanley finally decided that the time had come to sell, the price had escalated well beyond that which Lindemans was prepared to pay.

Lindemans' association with Clare began in the aftermath of the removal of beer rationing, and the consequent collapse of the fortified-wine market. In 1953 Alex Knappstein of Stanley travelled to Lindemans' Sydney office bringing samples of red wine made in that vintage. Ray Kidd recalls that first tasting with clarity:

> I can remember being very, very impressed with the red wine. We always described them as having a delicate bigness, which isn't really the contradiction in terms it might seem to be. I recollect our purchasing lovely Clare Shiraz, big, full and astringent. Big, because they had picked the grapes fully ripe as they did when using them for fortifieds. We starting using the wines for blending—they were marvellous for this—but I do remember we bottled Bins 297 and 298 from the 1953 vintage, because they were so outstanding: beautiful big reds with great softness and fruit flavour.

Throughout the 1950s Lindemans' table-wine sales grew rapidly. In 1956 they introduced Ben Ean Moselle, which went on to become the largest-selling brand wine in Australian wine history. For a while it was composed almost entirely of Clare Valley pedro ximinez and some Barossa Valley material, but as sales continued to rise Lindemans was forced to look elsewhere. Grapes grown in the Riverlands south of Corowa in New South Wales were introduced into the blend, and finally in 1974 Lindemans' Karadoc Winery was built and thenceforth supplied all of the wine for Ben Ean. But in the meantime this wine alone had led to Lindemans becoming major purchasers in the Clare Valley area. It also soon learnt that Hunter Valley base material made a fine sparkling burgundy, but not a champagne-style wine. For several decades the major component of the base wine for Lindemans' Dry Imperator came from muscadelle and early-picked rhine riesling grown in the Clare Valley. But it was first of all the Clare Valley red wines and then the high-quality rhine rieslings made by Stanley which were the focus of Lindemans' attention. While Stanley always remained its principal source, Lindemans purchased its first reds from Roly Birks at Wendouree in 1954; in 1956 it purchased its first rhine riesling from Stanley; and in 1957 began buying bulk wine from the Clarevale Cooperative.

The latter part of the 1950s saw the development of the Lindemans cellar blends. While much of the Clare Valley material went into brand wines such as Cawarra Claret, Cawarra Hock, St Cora Burgundy and Kirkton Chablis, the demand for better-quality table wine was increasing all the time. As Coonawarra opened up, the three-area blend of Hunter Valley, Coonawarra and Clare was developed. The initial releases were under the Private Bin label, incorporating an old photograph of the Ben Ean Winery.

The first top-quality blends were released in 1962 with the bin numbers 1945 and 1950 of the 1960 vintage. By that time it had become apparent that a further grade of wine was needed, so in that year the Reserve Bins 2300 and 2305 were laid down, and the Private Bins became Bin 45 Claret and Bin 50 Burgundy. Halfway through 1966 the Reserve Bin blends were relabelled Nyrang Hermitage and Auburn Burgundy. The show record of these two great "cellar blends" speaks volumes for the quality Lindemans was able to achieve and maintain.

With the 1962 acquisition of Leo Buring & Company, Lindemans' links with the Clare Valley were forged even more tightly. However, at the insistence of Lindemans chairman, Leo Buring was run as a separate company, and Lindemans gained little access to the Florita Vineyard material. Thus right up until the time that H. J. Heinz acquired Stanley, and even thereafter, it was Stanley

which provided the material for the Lindemans Watervale Rhine Riesling and the cabernet shiraz releases.

A 1984 tasting of all of the Watervale Rhine Rieslings from 1982 to 1966 was full of interest. There is no question that the quality and style of the wines reflect the changing fortunes of the white-wine market in general, and rhine riesling in particular. The wines made between 1966 and 1974 were, with a few qualified exceptions, absolutely outstanding. 1972 Bin 4295 is the greatest, with a long, delicate and lingering palate, superbly structured and balanced, and showing no sign whatsoever of drying out. 1968 Bin 3495 is of the same quality, aromatic and scented, with lively, dancing fruit on the palate. It still has grip and freshness in its lingering crisp finish. 1970 Bin 3895 is only fractionally behind the top two wines, with its lively, fresh palate denying both its 15 years of age and the toasty development starting to show in the bouquet.

1966 Bin 2995 (a deep and concentrated wine, with good acid and strong mid-palate structure) and 1967 Bin 3295 (a quite lovely old wine, still retaining fruit freshness and considerable delicacy) were a triumphant conclusion to the tasting. Of this old bracket only 1969 Bin 3695 (a little thick and flabby) and 1973 Bin 4695 (full of flavour, but rather hard) were slightly less than Olympian in quality. 1974 Bin 4895 was the turning point. The wine has a rich fore-palate, but then falls away on the back-palate and finishes hard. 1974–75 was of course the year in which white-wine sales commenced to accelerate, overtaking those of red wines for the first time. From here on the quality of the release declined dramatically, reaching the bottom with 1978 Bin 5595, 1979 Bin 5695 and 1980 Bin 5795. The chief criticism of these wines is an absence of mid-palate fruit, and there is simply no way that prolonged cellaring will magically transform the wines. They are indeed already past their very modest best. 1981 Bin 5895 and 1982 Bin 6095 showed a partial return to form. The wines have a little more fruit although neither could really be classed as outstanding. The consolation is that some of the old wines are still available through the Lindemans' Classic Release programme.

A parallel tasting, again in 1984, of all of the spatlese rhine riesling bins from 1982 to 1965 showed a similar pattern. The striking thing about these wines was the relatively low residual sugar in all but the youngest wines, reflecting Ray Kidd's belief that a spatlese should by no means necessarily be sweet, but simply indicate very late-picked rhine riesling. 1968 Bin 3490 was the outstanding wine of the tasting, with long, deep, lime-camphor fruit flavours and superb balance. In close attendance was the 1965 wine, followed by 1971 Bin 4090 (luscious and developed with just a touch of rich camphor), and 1972 Bin 4290 (aromatic and intense, with excellent acid giving freshness and adding to the overall flavour).

Since 1973 the spatlese rhine riesling has made only an intermittent appearance. The 1975 Bin 5090 and 1977 Bin 5390 are wines made in the traditional Lindemans perception of the style, full-flavoured, but rather hard and not particularly luscious. 1982 Bin 6091 is in the modern idiom, with voluminous lime aromas akin to botrytis, and a rich and full, sweet palate, albeit with a little coarseness.

The other major release under the Watervale label has been the shiraz cabernet. First made in 1961 as Bin 2335, it was not until 1965 that the first major release under the Watervale label was made. Here first Wendouree and subsequently Taylors made a contribution to the blend, which has produced wines which were of good quality when judged against the standards of their time, but which for the most part now look decidedly pedestrian. The exceptions are the 1968 and 1971 which I ranked equally at the very top. This line, too, has seen troubled times in recent years, with none produced in 1976, 1977, 1980 and 1982, although the 1981 wine suggested that better times may be in store for it. One little-known fact is that most, if not all, of these wines underwent a substantial part of their oak maturation at Lindemans' Hunter Valley Winery, although the final blending and bottling was always carried out at Sydney.

1965 Bin 3115, like all of these wines (when tasted in 1984), was a very attractive old-style plummy/strawberry/cherry-flavoured wine. As the description suggests it is rather jammy, yet far from unattractive. 1966 Bin 3315 and 1967 Bin 3615 have not aged with grace, developing distinct volatility. 1968 Bin 3815 has a magnificent bouquet, with minty/berry aromas, but falls away a little on the palate which is dominated by astringent tannin. 1969 Bin 4015 was not good, and 1970 Bin 4215, while showing some attractive leather/cedar aromas, is not in the class of 1971 Bin 4315. This is now at its best, with rich, smooth, berry flavours, good balance and length to the palate. The tannin is in balance, and it typifies the Clare Valley and its traditional best.

1972 Bin 4615, 1973 Bin 4915 and 1974 Bin 5015 are rather overripe, roasted reds in a style which Australia no longer makes. The two 1975 releases, Bin 5140 (a one-off straight cabernet sauvignon) and Bin 5115, have a little more finesse, although the fruit is still fairly ripe. 1979 Bin 5815 is in the mould of the 1973 and 1975 wines, and has little positive to offer. The best of the younger releases are without doubt 1978 Bin 5715 (with attractive ripe-berry flavours, but quite firm and fresh) and 1981 Bin 6215. The latter represents the first wine in the entire line-up to reflect contemporary winemaking approaches. Far greater attention has been paid to pH; there are some herbaceous cabernet aromas and flavours; and new oak has been used in the wine for the first time.

The Reserve Bin White Label Leo Buring releases from Watervale, likewise tasted in 1984, followed a similar pattern to the Lindemans Watervale Rhine Riesling. Here the explanation may well lie in the fact that in 1974 John Vickery, long-standing master white-winemaker at Chateau Leonay, was moved to Lindemans' Coonawarra Winery. Certainly, the old wines were the outstanding ones. 1968 Bin DWX14 on its day is still magnificent, while 1972 Bin DWB13 is one of the all-time classics under the Leo Buring label, including the vaunted Eden Valley releases. It still has exceptional richness and freshness, sustained by a touch of residual sugar and none of the developed kerosene/Flytox characters which show in some old rhine rieslings. 1973 Bin DWC15 and 1975 Bin DWE13 are both excellent wines; Bin DWE13 has many years in front of it. (It is fair to point out that the latter wine was not made by John Vickery.)

Two releases in 1977 (Bin DWG41 and Bin DWG37) have developed into full-flavoured but slightly heavy wines; it is difficult to see them developing with any great distinction, although there is plenty of flavour present. 1978 Bin DWH21, 1979 Bin DWI6, 1980 Bin DWJ18 and 1981 Bin DWK7 are disappointing. The best of the four is without question Bin DWI6, which does have good balance and crisp flavour, although the fruit characters are rather thin and green. It would not be surprising if this release did develop well in bottle.

It is possible that I misjudged these young wines, and that they will prove me wrong with bottle-age. However, I cannot help but think that with the fine 1984 vintage and the return of John Vickery to Chateau Leonay, greater things are in store in the future.

MITCHELL'S
HUGHES PARK ROAD, SKILLOGALEE VALLEY
via SEVENHILL

Mitchell's was established by Andrew and Jane Mitchell in 1975. Andrew Mitchell's parents had been growing grapes in the Skillogalee Valley, which runs parallel to the main Clare Valley on the western side, for a number of years. Nonetheless, it was not until he had completed an economics degree at Adelaide University and spent a short time as a public servant that Andrew Mitchell changed course to become a winemaker. He considered and rejected the idea of attending Roseworthy Agricultural College; instead, he learnt in the hard school of necessity, aided by the correspondence winemaking course run by the Riverina College of Advanced Education. Jane Mitchell subsequently undertook the short Roseworthy wine production course. But for the first vintage in 1975 it was very much a case of going in the deep end.

The winery was established in an old stone apple-packing shed, built into the side of the slope (with substantial underground cellars) beneath the hill on which Andrew Mitchell's parents' house stood. Five tonnes of cabernet sauvignon produced a wine which won a gold and a silver medal in the Claret and Burgundy Classes of the first show in which it was entered. Kevon Kemp wrote in the *National Times* about the wine and its fairytale ancestry, and Mitchell's was established overnight.

1976 saw another five tonnes of cabernet sauvignon come into the still only partially equipped winery; in 1977 (and again in 1978) Andrew Mitchell crushed rhine riesling at Jim Barry's winery and transported the juice to the Riverina College of Advanced Education where it was made (under the direction of Brian Croser) as a project constituting part of Mitchell's winemaking course. By 1979 the crush had increased to 60 tonnes; the Mitchells had firmly decided on the style of the wines they wished to make and had assembled both the equipment and the expertise to realise their aim.

Grapes all come from the vineyards owned by the Mitchell family. These fall into two parts: firstly, a vineyard at Watervale planted to rhine riesling (10.5 hectares) and shiraz (1.7 hectares); secondly, the Skillogalee Vineyards surrounding the winery. These comprise cabernet sauvignon (two hectares) rhine riesling (1.7 hectares) and a further 3.2 hectares of cabernet sauvignon planted in 1982 and 1983 and 1.2 hectares of merlot planted in 1983. The latter plantings will make their first contribution of

significance in the 1986 vintage.

The most important wine is their Watervale Rhine Riesling. The Mitchells have played their part in establishing the Clare Valley as one of the greatest dry rhine riesling areas in Australia, and the swing away in public taste from rhine riesling only strengthens the Mitchells' resolve to make the best possible wine from the variety.

The grapes are chilled immediately they are crushed, and drained through an open Willmes press. All oxygen is quickly removed from the juice, which is allowed to cold-settle for four days before earth-filtration. Fermentation then commences, using the controversial R2 yeast developed by Mitchell's one-time teacher Brian Croser during a visit to Chateau Rahoul in France in 1979.

There are two schools of thought about the yeast: one thinks that R2 is less than perfect. Andrew Mitchell, however, is quite satisfied that, provided the fermentation proceeds quickly, albeit at low temperatures, R2 is the ultimate yeast leaving no impression at all on the natural flavour of the wine. In 1983 the wine took 20 days to ferment to dryness at 7°C, which Mitchell regards as perfection. For the non-technical reader, fermentation at this speed at such a low temperature is not easily done: the preparation of the yeast is a key element in its success. The aim is to produce a wine with clean, fresh and intense fruit flavour, with as little residual sugar as possible. In 1983 the wine was left with no sugar at all, in marked contrast to more conventional winemaking which leaves a barely perceptible six or seven grams of sugar per litre.

Given Andrew Mitchell's personal preference for rhine rieslings with some bottle-age—he thinks his 1979 is now at or about its peak—I have some reservations about the absolute exclusion of sugar. Its lack is not a problem in early years, indeed it helps the wine marry with food, but with seven or eight years' bottle-age I am not so sure. Back-tastings of other makers' rhine rieslings suggests a hardness or hollowness tends to develop after five years.

For all that the Mitchell rhine rieslings must rank along with those of Enterprise as the outstanding white wines of the Clare Valley. At five years of age the 1979 Watervale Rhine Riesling was perhaps getting close to its best, although it will clearly live for many years. There is just a suggestion of toasty development on the bouquet, while the marvellously balanced palate shows no sign of drying out. The 1980 is a much richer wine, with lime aromas and lime/pineapple flavours, in some ways reminiscent of the wines of the Eden Valley. It seems to be a character which intermittently appears in the Clare Valley, most frequently associated with cool vintages. The 1982 and 1984 vintages were both outstanding, the younger wine being quite magnificent in its youth. I have no doubt that over the next six years it will develop into a wine of similar stature of the 1979. The 1981 and 1983 wines were, to a degree, a reflection of the years in which they were made; nonetheless, the 1983, which was bone-dry, does show remarkable intensity, and was one of the best rhine rieslings to come out of the Clare Valley in that vintage.

Even though 80 per cent of Mitchell's production is of rhine riesling, I think the quality of the area, and of the Mitchells as winemakers, is equally well demonstrated in their Sevenhill Cabernets. Some absolutely magnificent wines have come out under this label; the Mitchells' decision to sell the 1978 vintage in bulk (as clean-skins) is a pointed indication of their integrity and dedication to quality. The decision to sell the wine came in the wake of the first three vintages (1975 to 1977) which had established the style of red wine the Mitchells desired to make. This is a wine of elegance, balance and structure, far lighter than the traditional full-bodied Clare red. The unusually hot 1978 vintage (in complete contrast to the ultra-cool previous year) caught Andrew Mitchell unprepared. The grapes ripened above the 12.5 baume level which experience shows is ideal, and a traditional, somewhat jammy/porty wine resulted. Mitchell looks back over his shoulder somewhat wistfully and concedes the wine has turned out very well, but still holds to his decision: "It just wasn't ready; the style was not what we were aiming for, and we couldn't afford to wait for the wine to come round."

While the 1980 vintage was (and is) a great wine, Mitchell sees the 1982 as coming closest to his perception of the ideal. Obviously the classic wines of Bordeaux are his inspiration, and not surprisingly he is eagerly awaiting the first harvest from the 1.25 hectares of merlot he has established in the Skillogalee Valley. This will definitely be used as a minor blend component rather than form the base of a separate wine. Like growers of cabernet sauvignon everywhere, Mitchell has discovered that not every year is there adequate mid-palate flavour, while merlot could be equally useful in cutting back the excesses of a year such as 1978. In the meantime the cabernet sauvignons are 100 per cent varietals, with an increasing influence of French oak adding to the inevitable changes in style wrought by the imperatives of different vintages.

PAULETT'S
POLISH HILL RIVER ROAD, SEVENHILL

Paulett's is one of the two wineries to be established in the Polish Hill River area, a district which sees itself as at once distinct from, but part of, the Clare Valley. Neil Paulett was winemaker at Penfolds' Wybong Estate when it was taken over by Rosemount; he stayed on after the take-over, and it was not until 1981 that he seriously contemplated leaving to start his own winery. After looking at the Great Western area in Victoria, his attention was directed to the Clare Valley by erstwhile boss Don Ditter of Penfolds. Penfolds had itself recently established its Polish Hill River Vineyard, and Ditter felt the area was full of promise.

It took almost a year for Paulett to find the right property and to complete the purchase. In the early months of 1982 he acquired a house set among a grove of pine trees, four hectares of long-established vineyard, and a hillside rising behind with sweeping views over the Polish Hill River area. He arrived in the second half of 1982; within two months the ancient pine trees were no more, destroyed by the Clare Valley bushfires of that December. Miraculously, the house survived, as did the vines.

The vineyard was not only old but also run down; care and attention have saved the little over one hectare of rhine riesling and half-hectare of shiraz, the other vines being of unsuitable varieties. In the drought-stressed conditions of 1983 the hectare of rhine riesling yielded a little over three tonnes of grapes, which Paulett crushed at Andrew Mitchell's winery and fermented at Fareham Estate. It was a traumatic time: no filtration was available, so after settling on enzyme for three days the wine was fermented on only partly clarified juice, and then racked and fined. It was finally filtered for the first time shortly before being bottled, on the day Australia won the America's Cup. Given all of the difficulties associated with the production of the wine, it was of high quality, and not surprisingly, the wine sold out quickly.

A winery has now been erected, and Paulett intends to make a wide range of varietals from Polish Hill River grapes. In 1983 he planted 0.6 hectare of chardonnay and 0.25 hectare of pinot noir adjacent to the winery, but will supplement this with sauvignon blanc, traminer, cabernet sauvignon, cabernet franc and merlot purchased on a long-term contract basis from a nearby vineyard.

PETALUMA
Off FARRELL FLAT ROAD, CLARE

The Hanlin Hill Vineyard was acquired by the Evans Wine Company from Bob Clampett in 1977, and in the reorganisation which followed the tragic death of Peter Fox in late 1981 it became part of Petaluma.

It is planted to rhine riesling (20 hectares), cabernet sauvignon, malbec and chardonnay—the latter grafted onto the shiraz vines which once bore fine but unwanted fruit. Right from the time of its acquisition the vineyard was managed by Brian Croser of Petaluma, and he purchased the fruit from it in the years leading up to its transfer from the Evans Wine Company to Petaluma.

Croser had recommended the acquisition of the vineyard from Clampett because he had been impressed with the quality of the fruit which it produced. Nonetheless, it was one of those acquisitions which had the locals rubbing their hands with satisfaction: the wine industry's whizz kid and the big-city money had bought a property which no-one else wanted. It would never yield enough grapes to make it worthwhile.

But Croser knew exactly what the Evans Wine Company was getting for its money. The vineyard clings to the side of a bare hill at an altitude of over 500 metres above sea-level overlooking the whole of the Clare Valley. Tim Knappstein's vineyard is not far distant, and he did not laugh at the purchase. But it is true that the skeletal soils, which peter out to exposed slate at the top edge of the planted area, support only stunted, low-yielding vines. The saving grace is that the vines are in balance with their environment, and the small crops achieve a high level of ripeness in terms of both flavour and sugar.

From 1979 the decision was taken that Hanlin Hill—and only Hanlin Hill—fruit would be used for Petaluma Rhine Riesling. It was one of the first wines made at the then newly completed Petaluma Winery at Piccadilly, high in the Adelaide Hills above Adelaide. Only the cream of the production from the 20 hectares of rhine riesling goes to the Petaluma label; the balance goes to "clean-skin" wines, at least some of which have been sold by Rothbury under a special regional label. Part of the cabernet sauvignon was used in the '79 Petaluma Red, but in subsequent years it has been sold as bottled clean-skin (i.e. unlabelled) wine.

The rhine riesling grapes are picked into wooden crates lined with a large polythene bag, and are transported to Piccadilly in those same wooden crates, virtually eliminating all breakdown and juicing.

Immediately after crushing (at night) the must is cooled to between 0°C and 5°C; draining is done under an inert gas cover from the Willmes tank-press. Only wine made from free-run juice is even considered for inclusion in the final Petaluma blend. The juice is cold-settled at −2°C until all of the suspended particles and solids have settled at the bottom of the tank; the crystal-clear juice is then ready for fermentation. In fact this may not commence for months as Croser conducts exhaustive—some might say exhausting—trials to determine the particular strain of Petaluma-propagated yeast most suited to each individual tank of juice.

The wine is fermented at between 10°C and 15°C over a period of four weeks. One of the many popular myths is that Petaluma always uses the same R2 yeast (not true) and uses prolonged ultra-cool fermentations (also not true). At the end of fermentation the temperature is once again reduced to −2°C and the wine naturally clarifies itself. This handling technique reduces filtration and wine movement to an absolute minimum, allowing far-lower-than-normal sulphur levels. Pasteurisation is also selectively used to ensure sterility without diminishing flavour.

One of the other great myths is that all Petaluma wines taste the same. Nothing could be further from the truth: while all of the Petaluma Clare Rhine Rieslings share the same strength and concentration—once described by Croser as dry spatlese styles—the vintage variation is particularly marked. The 1979, 1980 and 1984 vintages are exceptional wines; the 1984 may prove the greatest in a very distinguished line.

QUELLTALER
Off MAIN NORTH ROAD, WATERVALE

The Quelltaler story starts with Francis Treloar, a Cornish-born adventurer who commenced his wanderings in 1842. After 10 years of high adventure in the Cape of Good Hope, the goldfields of Victoria, and the copper fields of South Australia, he acquired a 47-hectare property near Watervale which he named Spring Vale. On 15 June 1853 he recorded in his diary that he had planted vines acquired from a neighbour, Mr Reuben Solly.

In 1860 he sold Spring Vale to Walter Hughes, another adventurer, who had captained a whaling ship and thereafter a trading ship in the Orient. Hughes had discovered the Wallaroo and Moonta copper mines on one of his pastoral properties in

1859, and rapidly acquired great wealth. In 1862 Treloar returned to the Clare Valley and acquired Prospect Farm, adjacent to Spring Vale. In July 1862 he planted two hectares of vineyard, and before long was managing not only his own plantings but also those of Hughes at Spring Vale. In 1868, on the recommendation of Treloar, Hughes employed Carl Sobels to supervise the erection of a winery and to make the wine from the 14 hectares of vineyard then coming into bearing. The first part of the vast cellar complex, which stands as the showpiece of the region today, was commenced in 1869.

By 1882 the vineyard had increased to 30 hectares of mataro, riesling, malbec, cabernet sauvignon, shiraz and two varieties known simply as red Spanish and white Spanish. By 1880 annual production was around 45,000 litres, or 5000 cases. The enterprise flourished over the next 10 years as the London market was developed.

Hughes died childless in 1887 and his nephew J. M. Richman inherited the property. In 1890 he accepted an offer to purchase Spring Vale made by Carl Sobels and Herman Buring. For the preceding 11 years Herman Buring, who had worked for a time at Seppeltsfield with Benno Seppelt, had run a flourishing wine-merchant's business in Adelaide. Buring and Sobels knew each other well, for they had married sisters. These family ties were further strengthened by the fact that Buring had been a major purchaser of Spring Vale wine. The purchase price for the then-substantial business was £9000, and the rapid growth of the business continued. Buring was an adept salesman who ran the Adelaide side of the business, while Carl was a highly skilled winemaker, not to mention a prolific father. He had 13 children, and four of them—Emil, Oscar, Talbot and Verno—all lived on the property, managing various aspects of its operation.

To this day the seven substantial stone houses which housed them remain at Quelltaler—all in superb condition and all still occupied. The oldest is Spring Vale House, now occupied by Jamie Sobels and built between 1854 and 1859. The next oldest is Prospect House, built by Francis Treloar in the early 1860s. The remainder were built in the second half of the nineteenth century.

By 1892 Spring Vale had 20 hectares of vineyard at Leasingham and 18.5 hectares at Watervale in bearing, while a further 13.8 hectares had been planted in the preceding 12 months. In 1891 81,000 litres of wine had been exported to England, more than the total 1982 vintage. But production grew apace: the 1895 vintage produced 225,000 litres,

the young vines having made great progress. The export market more than kept pace with the growth in production: a contemporary newspaper report observed: "The proprietors of Spring Vale find no difficulty at all in disposing of all the wine they make, Messrs. Burgoyne and Co. of London being so pleased with the sample that they have standing orders of any quantity of it to be shipped to them."

The Spring Vale cellars were expanded during 1895; by February 1896 the cellars had a storage capacity of 2.25 million litres of oak storage. The partnership had in the meantime opened Adelaide premises, and in June 1896 the extensions to these were also officially opened with pomp and ceremony. Two years later Herman Buring's son Leo returned from his studies at Geisenheim and Montpellier and briefly joined his elder brother Rudi, who was then sharing the management duties at Spring Vale. It was around this time that the Quelltaler name began to assume prominence. Originally spelt Quellthaler, it was nothing more or less than a German translation of Spring Vale. Many of these names were the invention of Rudi Buring: Quelltaler Hock, Quelltaler Sauternes and San Carlo Claret became national brands, of disproportionate fame given the size of the company. Rudi Buring, who doubled up as graphic designer for the labels, also introduced the Cachet d'Or and Cachet Vert (the latter for chablis) labels, providing a strong historical justification for the current Cachet Blanc label.

Leo Buring never became a full-time member of the team; perhaps he saw the writing on the wall with the vast number of Burings and Sobels there before him; but on the other hand he kept closely in touch with the firm. For a while he worked as a consultant, and when in the late 1920s he visited Spain and brought back the flor yeast spore in his handkerchief, it was to Quelltaler that the culture went, providing the means for that firm to dominate the flor fino sherry market for the next 30 years with its Granfiesta Sherry. Leo rejoined the company as a director in 1934, a position he held until five years before his death, and for decades he was the New South Wales agent (as was Matthew Lang & Company in Victoria).

The numerous show awards that Quelltaler won underline the fact that, except for a brief period around the Second World War, Quelltaler was primarily a table-wine producer with a specialty interest in sherry, and a minor producer of port. Initially, and indeed for much of its existence (and despite the enormous success of Quelltaler Hock), it was essentially a red-wine producer. It is only since the latter part of the 1970s that Quelltaler has become a specialist white-wine producer, concentrating on rhine riesling. Even here, though, history has much to say: for most of this century the fame of Quelltaler Hock rested on the for-long-unremarked fact that alone among Clare Valley vineyards it had substantial plantings of rhine riesling. Most of the "riesling" in the district was, of course, crouchen, known as Clare riesling.

In 1910 the partnership was converted to a proprietary company. It continued to be family-run and managed, with the Sobels family being by far the most active. The first half of the 1920s was a period of prosperity for Quelltaler, as it was for the rest of the industry; the problems of 1928–29 (followed by the Depression) were no less devastating. But the company quickly recovered after seeing sales for the 1929 year fall to pre-First World War levels.

In 1932 the cellars were expanded once again, when the large east wing was added for bulk-wine storage. Shortly thereafter a new warehouse was completed at the western end of the winery, with room for over 400,000 litres in bond. In 1934 Quelltaler House was opened in Gilbert Street, Adelaide; while 1936 saw the first sales of Granfiesta Sherry, which had been developed after years of work by Emil Sobels. Granfiesta was to win the Champion Flor Sherry Trophy on innumerable occasions, both at Adelaide and other capital city wine shows. It was also to provide Quelltaler with a substantial part of its income over the next 30 years. The Sobels family continued to be actively involved in all aspects of the management of the company, but by 1960 there was no longer a representative of the Buring family on the board. As the wine boom of the 1960s got under way, Quelltaler fell under siege. Jamie Sobels recalls: "It became impossible for us to operate effectively because we were receiving so many offers; the board had to shut up shop every time an offer was made, and it all became too much. Finally, therefore, we decided to amalgamate with Nathan and Wyeth." This was but an interlude before Remy Martin acquired full ownership of Nathan and Wyeth, and with it, ownership of Chateau Remy and Quelltaler.

Remy Martin incorporated an Australian holding company, Vignerons Distillers and Vintners Limited, which acquired Buring and Sobels, Nathan and Wyeth, and Macs Cider. Although the structure had long-term logic, there was little outward change in the activities of the subsidiaries. Right up to the end of the 1970s, indeed, Quelltaler continued much as it always had. The major labels continued to be San Carlo Claret, Quelltaler Private Bin Claret, Quelltaler Grande Reserve Hock, Grande Reserve Riesling, Granfiesta Sherry and Wyatt Earp Vintage Port.

The real changes at Quelltaler have come since 1980, and the arrival in Australia of group managing director, Francois Henry. The distinctive "Q" Quelltaler Estate label was introduced for the 1981 vintage wines, and Alsatian winemaker Michel Dietrich arrived to take control of winemaking. His family owns an impossibly beautiful winery in Alsace, where they have carried on winemaking for generations. Dietrich, however, decided that his interests lay outside Alsace, and studied both oenology and viticulture for a total of four years first at Dijon Wine College and thereafter at Bordeaux University. After graduation he worked for the Deutz House in Champagne before joining the Remy Martin group and working with Krug. The arrival of Dietrich signalled Quelltaler's intention to concentrate on the making of white wines, and rhine riesling in particular. His arrival also signified the application of the French view of _terroir_, in which the slightest difference in soil structure, aspect and slope is recognised as being of critical importance.

Applying these principles, Dietrich has divided the vineyard up into 37 small plots, with soil character, structure and aspect being the prime determinants. Conventional wisdom would divide it up according to grape variety, and most probably in far larger blocks. Right at the outset Dietrich observed a substantial difference in the soil at the top of the hills (with far more limestone apparent) than at the bottom (where heavier clays predominated). Soil analysis followed, and to his surprise Dietrich found the soil composition on certain upper slopes to be almost identical to that of his native Alsace. The pH of that limestone-rich soil is nine, compared with 7.5 for the clay at the bottom. In the three vintages Dietrich has supervised at Quelltaler he has found a consistent correlation between certain of these small sub-blocks and the resultant wine quality. He is convinced that in Australia, no less than Europe, terroir plays a major role in shaping wine quality (and style).

And indeed, why should it be otherwise? The problem is that in Australia there is little opportunity (or incentive) to observe these variations. Mechanical harvesters munch their way through hectares of grapes every hour; only in the small vineyards where hand-picking continues is there any hope of keeping separate small parcels. Even here one can be defeated by the very smallness of the operation: all the cabernet and all the chardonnay are needed, so the great and the good are blended in the interests of expediency. At Quelltaler they are kept separate because there is now a ruthless process of quality grading and selection. Only 10 to 15 per cent of the total production goes out under the premium Quelltaler Estate label. There are five wines under this label (Cachet Blanc, Wood-Matured Semillon, Rhine Riesling, Traminer Riesling and Late-Harvest Rhine Riesling) and usually between 1000 and 1500 cases of each are produced, amounting to 6000 cases in all. Around 55 per cent of total production goes to the Clare Valley Estate label, again centred primarily on white wines (85 per cent of total production), but with a shiraz and fortified wines making up the range. In technical terms the juice which goes to make these wines is "free-run"; the remainder (principally pressings) is either sold in bulk or used in diminishing quantities for the Grande Reserve and Private Bin labels.

All of the white grapes are chilled immediately after crushing to between 6°C and 8°C; only a minimal amount of sulphur (20 parts per million) is added; and the juice is cold-settled for 48 hours before being racked off to the tank where fermentation takes place. At between 11°C and 13°C, this usually takes around four weeks to complete. The wines are centrifuged after fermentation (special precautions are taken to hermetically seal the centrifuge and thereby prevent any oxidation), fined with bentonite and cold-stabilised before going through membrane filters at bottling.

All of this is standard large-winery practice, and it is in a way surprising that the Quelltaler wines made by Dietrich have been seen as outside the norm. But they have, and it is true that in comparative masked line-ups the wines do not always fare particularly well. Australian winemakers, in particular, have been outspoken in their criticism of the wines, describing them variously as heavy, coarse and oxidised. Yet when I tasted them at the winery in 1984 I thoroughly enjoyed the wines. I can only conclude that there is an extra dimension to the wines, a touch of Alsace, which differentiates them in the comparative situation. The other factor is that these wines all benefit substantially from bottle-age: I was one of those who did not like the 1982s when they came onto the market, but had a very different view a year later.

There is little argument about the quality of the wood-matured semillons of Quelltaler. The 1982 release was quite superb, winning gold medals and a trophy at major wine shows, and consistently high praise from wine writers and the major wine magazines. Despite the success of the 1982 wine, I

have the feeling the 1984 vintage will be even better. The wine for the wood-matured semillon comes from vines between 40 and 50 years old; the fruit is always picked at maximum ripeness. The wine spends approximately nine months in oak after barrel fermentation. About one-third of the casks are new, one-third one year old, and one-third two years old.

Quelltaler is absolutely committed to making great white wines, and it is at the point of achieving its ambition.

SEVENHILL
COLLEGE ROAD, SEVENHILL

The promise of religious freedom brought many races and creeds to South Australia in the 1840s. The success of the German Lutherans in settling in the Barossa Valley became well known in Europe, and in 1848 a wealthy Silesian farmer, Franz Weikert, determined to gather a band of his countrymen to emigrate to South Australia. Silesia, now part of Poland but then one of the provinces of Prussia, was predominantly Catholic; and Weikert applied to the Superior of the Jesuits of the Austro-Hungarian province for two chaplains. The Jesuits had themselves received an expulsion order from Emperor Leopold two weeks earlier, so the request was well timed.

Two priests volunteered. One returned to Europe through ill health shortly after his arrival; the other, a Tyrolese who had been ordained for only six weeks, was Father Kranewitter. The group landed in Port Adelaide on 8 December 1848. Dissension had broken out on the trip, so it was a relatively small party which accompanied Weikert to Clare, where he had decided to settle. Kranewitter accompanied Weikert, and settled nearby at Nagles Rock, south-west of the township of Clare. In April 1849 he was joined by Brothers George Sadler SJ and John Schreiner SJ. They worked day and night, walking overnight to Burra to sell butter to the miners until the purchase of a horse increased both their mobility and their earnings.

In January 1851 Father Kranewitter was able to buy the first parcel of land, part of a property known as Open Ranges, for the sum of £2 an acre payable by instalments over 20 years. He renamed the property Sevenhill (without an "s") because it was hoped it would become a centre of Catholicism in the North, a little Rome with its seven hills. With the marvellous sense of humour which continues to this day in the person of Brother John May, they named the tiny stream which (sometimes) flows through the property the Tiber. Their grand plans called for a college, a college-church, colonnaded walks around a paved quadrangle, and a village with broad streets—Industry Road, Commercial Street, College Street and so on.

Later in that same year the priests obtained cuttings from Hawker's property, Bungaree, for the purpose of establishing a vineyard to make sacramental wine. (These vines, to the west of the winery, are still in production.) Wine purchased in Europe for this purpose was not only expensive, but frequently arrived diseased and out of condition. The vineyards flourished, and Brother Schreiner (who, like Kranewitter, was an Austrian) is credited with having brought tokay and crouchen (or Clare riesling, as it was then called) to the district. The first wine press was built by Brothers Schreiner and Schneider in 1863, and was capable of processing four buckets of grapes at a time—hardly large-scale winemaking. Rough cellars had been excavated in 1851 and were covered by a lean-to. The magnificent underground arched stone cellars, still very much in use, were built in the early 1860s, and Mintaro slate fermentation tanks were installed, which remained in use until the 1970s.

While it has been suggested from time to time that Sevenhill made only sacramental wine until the 1950s, this is simply not so. Even as early as 1858 it seems they were not averse to selling a little brandy, while records from the 1890s show that the "best claret" was sold for six shillings a gallon (4.5 litres), "the keg to be returned as soon as possible".

In 1863 the decision was taken to build the splendid church which now dominates Sevenhill. The foundation stone was laid on 15 August 1864, and building operations commenced the following month. A year later, with the stonework only partially completed (and filled in with wood), building operations were halted owing to lack of funds. The Brothers had shown an all-too-temporal failure to control expenditure, and for several years Sevenhill battled to survive. This it did; building operations were resumed in 1870 and the church was completed in 1874.

Throughout this time Brother John Schreiner remained in charge of winemaking; indeed, in the 135 years there have been only seven winemakers at Sevenhill: 1850–84, Brother John Schreiner; 1884–89, Brother Francis Lenz; 1889–1916, Brother Patrick Storey; 1917–24, Brother Peter Boehmer; 1925–52, Brother George Downey; 1952–72, Brother John Hanlon; and since 1972 Brother John May has been winemaker. In 1925

Brother George Downey took up his position as winemaker, and immediately produced a wine which was to make Sevenhill famous and which is still remembered with awe and affection by wine lovers such as Max Lake, who has been privileged to drink it. The cellar book gives little hint of what was to come: after recording that all of the shiraz, tokay, grenache, pedro and frontignac were fortified with "fifteen proof gallons [68 litres] of spirit to every 100 gallons [450 litres] of wine" (and that only the mataro, doradillo and riesling were made as dry wine), it goes on: "There was three and a half press full's [*sic*] (little square press) of skins to 400 gallons [1820 litres] of liquid shiraz, a little bit too light in colour, for a good-coloured port." Evidently the pressings had done their work well, because the words "a little bit too light in colour" had been crossed out later and the concluding words, "for a good-coloured port", written in with the same hand (Downey's) but with a different pen. This became the 1925 Sevenhill Port, recognised as one of the greatest wines of its style ever produced in Australia, and on a par with the 1945 Stonyfell.

In 1952 Brother John Hanlon became winemaker, and for the first time Sevenhill bottled red wine became available through retail outlets. Brother John May records that: "During Brother John Hanlon's time the last horse was sold for 35 pounds, and two tractors were purchased to begin the era of mechanised vineyard farming at Sevenhill. He installed concrete Hume pipe fermentation tanks, a continuous press and numerous pumps to facilitate winemaking."

But in truth the real transformation, both in the vineyard and the winery, has occurred since 1972 when, following the sudden death of Brother Hanlon, Brother John May took over winemaking responsibilities. The annual crush has increased from 160 to 380 tonnes since 1972, and by the time the newest plantings come into bearing it will edge over the 400-tonne mark. When May commenced his replanting, accepted yields for cabernet were 1.25 tonnes per hectare; now they are closer to 7.5 tonnes. More importantly still, he has concentrated on establishing classic varieties: cabernet sauvignon, cabernet franc, merlot, malbec and rhine riesling. He is contemplating plantings of semillon, and has chardonnay stock available. The 70 hectares of vineyards, almost all in bearing, comprise shiraz (12 hectares), tokay (six hectares), crouchen (six hectares), pedro ximinez (5.7 hectares), grenache (5.4 hectares), cabernet sauvignon (five hectares), rhine riesling 2.9 hectares), frontignac (2.25 hectares), touriga

(1.5 hectares), merlot (one hectare), verdelho (0.8 hectare), cabernet franc, traminer and doradillo (0.5 hectare each) and malbec (0.4 hectare).

Like so many enlightened winemakers, John May has no doubt about the significance of grape quality in determining the quality of the finished wine. "One important thing so far as Sevenhill is concerned, and we are proud of it, is that we do not buy grapes. We can guarantee 100 per cent grown, vintaged and bottled at Sevenhill, so we've got complete control of the product." Winery development has gone hand-in-glove with that of the vineyard. John May numbers carpentry, concrete laying, welding, bricklaying (and anything else needed) among his various skills; with the help of the eight full-time (lay) employees, he has in effect hand-built an entirely new winery at the back of the historic buildings. The old winery, and in particular its beautiful underground cellars, are basically used for storage. Funded totally from cash flow—and even then after granting the Church its dues—the winery is now as well equipped as any in the Clare Valley. Recent years have seen the installation of temperature-controlled stainless-steel fermenters (being converted from skin cooling to brine); an earth-filter; cold-stabilisation tanks; an airbag press; a fully equipped laboratory; and a modern bottling line including bottle sterilisation and full gas cover during filling.

Obviously enough, this range of equipment makes John May confident he can make and bottle high-class white wines. So far these have come from unfashionable varieties—chiefly crouchen and tokay—but have always sold well. The first rhine riesling was made in 1982; both in that year and in 1983 the quantity was negligible, but since 1984 it has exceeded 5000 litres. Taking into consideration all these limitations, the white wines have been more than creditable, and a surprisingly wide range is available: a rhine riesling, a crouchen (or Clare riesling); a dry tokay; a white burgundy; a moselle; the College white; and a frontignac. Three of these are made bone-dry, a welcome change from the tendency to leave that little bit of residual sugar in every white of every style.

But it is for the red wines that Sevenhill is best known. The simply labelled dry red has never failed to win a medal at the Adelaide show and is a model of consistency. I have tasted all the vintages made since 1976, and they have invariably had excellent colour, a firm but fresh bouquet and a smooth flavoursome palate at around four to five years of age. These are not the blood-and-thunder reds of Sevenhill of the 1950s or the 1960s. They are wines

made in the modern way for modern tastes. The 1982 Merlot Cabernet Franc takes the whole process one step further. It is a wine which could come from any of the avant-garde Victorian wineries of today. Excellent purple-red in colour, with crisp, smooth fruit on the bouquet and similar sweet-berry flavours on the mid-palate (yet avoiding jamminess), it is a perfectly made wine with excellent fruit character.

SKILLOGALEE
Off HUGHES PARK ROAD, SKILLOGALEE VALLEY
via SEVENHILL

Spencer and Margaret George came to the Skillogalee Valley in 1970 on what was essentially a spur-of-the-moment decision. Having sold his Victor Harbour real estate business in the late 1960s, Spencer and his wife were looking for something which was in effect a retirement occupation, but which would keep their interest. The property in the Skillogalee Valley which they saw one weekend (and bought) seemed ideal, but it was not until they had arrived in the Skillogalee Valley that they thought of viticulture.

The Mitchell family vines growing next door acted as the spur. A report from the Department of Agriculture confirmed that, while the land varied from marginal to very good, overall it was well suited to grape growing. The Georges wasted no time. In 1970 and 1971 much of the present 22 hectares of vineyard was planted, principally to rhine riesling, shiraz and grenache. It was always their intention to make, or rather have made, their own wine, but in the early years all the grapes were sold to Stanley Leasingham. The Georges still do not have a winery: the 1976 Shiraz, the first from the property, was made by their Roseworthy-trained son Stephen at Robertson's; the 1977 and 1978 reds were made in the same way.

In 1977 the first rhine riesling was made for them by Tim Knappstein. The 1978 Rhine Riesling (again made by Knappstein) brought overnight fame to the then still obscure vineyard, winning trophies as best dry white in both Adelaide and Canberra National Wine Shows. In 1981 neighbour Andrew Mitchell took over winemaking responsibilities for both whites and reds, the Georges' son Stephen having gone off to follow winemaking pursuits at other wineries and to establish a vineyard in the Adelaide Hills.

In recent years Spencer George has spent much time and money in the vineyard, grafting over the grenache, and also establishing source blocks for the Department of Agriculture for cabernet sauvignon, cabernet franc, malbec and rhine riesling. He also established a small rhine riesling vineyard near Penwortham which supplies the material for the late-harvest rhine riesling. The basic (or dry) rhine riesling comes from the hillsides rising above the Skillogalee homestead—in remote and beautiful country, and wrinkled with thickets of gums and populated by kangaroos. These vineyards are at an altitude of almost 500 metres above sea-level and the fruit ripens late. The natural tendency to produce grapes with an added intensity of flavour is protected by Andrew Mitchell's careful winemaking. This is Clare Valley rhine riesling at its best.

All of the Rhine Riesling Bin 2 wines (as they are known) so far to come from Skillogalee have been firm, full-flavoured wines, which cellar extremely well. The red-wine releases, basically a blend of cabernet sauvignon (around 75 per cent) and shiraz (around 25 per cent), have been very nearly as impressive. They have the depth of flavour and the sinew to allow prolonged bottle-ageing; it is hard to see any of the releases so far made reaching their best in anything under eight years.

But the future promises even more. Commencing with the 1982 vintage, small quantities of malbec and cabernet franc have been used in the wine, and these percentages will increase in the years to come. As it is the wines are very impressive: the basic quality of the fruit is excellent and Andrew Mitchell is a talented winemaker. Skillogalee is also one of the relatively few makers of vintage port in the district. Despite its long tradition of fortified-winemaking, opinions are divided as to the suitability of the Clare Valley for vintage port. The Skillogalee Vintage Port of 1983 seems to provide clear evidence that it is suited, and with a small area being planted to the classic port variety touriga, the Skillogalee line could be one to watch.

STANLEY LEASINGHAM
7 DOMINIC STREET, CLARE

The Stanley Wine Company has so dominated the Clare Valley that in many ways the history of the company is that of the Valley. It is true that others, notably Sevenhill, had been making wine for over 40 years before the Stanley Wine Company was established, but within a few years of its foundation in 1894 Stanley was making more wine than the combined production of all of the other vignerons in the Valley. It has been thus ever since; indeed, in recent years Stanley has produced almost 80 per cent of the wine vintaged in the Clare Valley.

The Stanley Wine Company was formed at the end of 1894 largely to deal with what promised to be a rapidly mounting surplus of grapes from within the district. The founding shareholders were J. C. Christison, a local brewer; J. H. Knappstein, one of the largest vineyard owners in the district; Magnus Badger, a local solicitor; and Dr Otto Wein-Smith, the district medical practitioner. The syndicate purchased the Clare Jam Factory and the Stanley Wine Company opened its doors for business in March 1895.

Alfred Basedow, a member of one of South Australia's most famous winemaking families, joined as winemaker for that first vintage. Together with one of his brothers, he had completed the winemaking course at Montpellier in France, and had subsequently gained practical experience working as a winemaker in Germany, Spain and Portugal. Even though the winemaking facilities installed for that first vintage, which amounted to 18,000 litres, were very primitive, the wines took prizes at the Adelaide show. Production grew in leaps and bounds, and the size of the winery doubled and redoubled. By 1899 the vineyard had reached 162,000 litres, with 450,000 litres of wine in stock. Large quantities had been shipped to England in the previous six months.

Basedow was clearly a winemaker in advance of his time. In his post-vintage report for 1900 he said: "My refrigerator works very well. I have had a blower fixed up to blow a big draft of air onto the pipes, and I reckon I can now cool 1000 gallons [4550 litres] of wine 10° Fahrenheit in a little over an hour with 100 gallons of water." Another touch of the 1970s was the use of seaweed to insulate the ceiling of the winery.

By 1901 the vintage had reached 360,000 litres and two years later it was 450,000. In that year it was the sixth-largest winery in the State of South Australia, and by the time the 1903 vintage was completed more than two million litres of wine were in stock. This rate of expansion, obviously enough, was not sustainable; by 1907 the vintage had fallen to 250,000 litres and 900,000 litres were held in storage. The frantic pace of the development, and the accumulation of wine stocks up to 1903, had taken its toll of the shareholders. Christison had become involved in a bitter public brawl with B. P. Burgoyne, the London merchant who had up to that point in time purchased almost all of Stanley's production. J. H. Knappstein was forced to return from Perth, where he had a thriving ship's chandler business, to take control of the situation. He bought the shares of the now thoroughly nervous and dis-enchanted Magnus Badger and Otto Wein-Smith, and set off for London in 1903 seeking replacement markets for those lost through the argument with Burgoyne. He was sufficiently successful to return to South Australia in 1904 to collect his family, increase his shareholding in the company to 75 per cent, and return to England where he remained for the next three years. There he worked hard and successfully to build markets for Stanley's wines, principally its export burgundy.

When Christison died in 1911 his widow sold his interest to Knappstein, who remained in total control until his death in June 1919. He died intestate, and control of the business was vested in a trustee company. The family, headed by Mick Knappstein, remembers the period from 1919 to 1938 with great bitterness. Mick Knappstein boldly says: "They ruined us . . . we had a very strong case against the trustee company for mismanagement . . ." In the end a deal was done, with the trustee company relinquishing management in 1938 in return for a release from any claims against it by the family.

Mick Knappstein recalls that:

> Virtually all production up to the Second World War was of dry red table wine. It was classed as burgundy in those days. Most of it was exported to London to our agents, the Victoria Wine Company. We used to get an order for 100 or 200 hogsheads [2925 or 5850 litres] almost every month—of course in those days almost everything went out in wood. I can remember in my youth a whole trainload of wine going from Clare to Adelaide.

It was a very substantial business, with an annual production of almost 900,000 litres. After 1940 the export market disappeared with the trading ships, and Stanley turned to making fortified wine for the American and other soldiers. Knappstein says: "They all wanted sweet fortified wine. There was a tremendous beer shortage, of course, with beer tickets and so on."

Stanley moved swiftly with the events of 1953. In that year it sold one of its large old Clare vineyards which was becoming unproductive, and bought in its place land at Watervale which it planted to cabernet sauvignon, rhine riesling and grenache. Mick and Alex Knappstein made their historic pilgrimage to Sydney, and were successful in securing Lindemans as a major customer. As Lindemans' requirements increased each year, so did Stanley's production. Others came to buy too—Penfolds, Seppelt, Hardy's, Orlando and McWilliam's all bought significant quantities of wine—but Lindemans was the major

customer, and the two companies soon settled into a regular pattern of dealing. Knappstein would go to Sydney each January to establish Lindemans' require-ments prior to vintage, and a significant portion of the crush would be made to its requirements. Lindemans, with Ray Kidd at the helm, would then come down to Clare in May, as soon as the wines had been cleaned up after vintage, and taste them all. Its orders would be placed in writing, whether or not Lindemans had taken delivery of the wine (usually they had).

This system provided Stanley with an assured cash-flow base, and underpinned the growth of the company. This, in turn, meant an increasing involvement with the growers in the region. Between 1947 and 1971 Stanley established between 200 and 240 hectares of vineyards in the Watervale area, much of which was share-farmed for Stanley by trusted employees. It was an ingenious scheme which worked very well. Stanley established the vineyards (on its land) which the employee (probably a winery worker) maintained in his own time in the evenings and on weekends. The employee would receive 75 per cent of the sale price of the grapes (which of course went to Stanley), and Stanley would get (or rather keep) the other 25 per cent. During a time of labour shortage, and with quality grapes in keen demand, it worked well. Ten or so trusted men worked 15 or 20 hectares each on the scheme; planted predominantly to rhine riesling which yielded 7.5 to 10 tonnes to the hectare, it was a profitable sideline for the worker.

The degree of dependence which each company had upon the other, while reflecting a very useful trading relationship, inevitably imposed its own strains. Each company realised just how exposed it would be if the other decided to terminate the relationship. So in 1959 discussions were commenced about the possibility of the sale of Stanley to Lindemans, but in the end no agreement on price could be reached. The level of business continued, indeed increased, but each party took steps in the 1960s to develop alternative strategies.

With the appointment of Peter Weste as senior winemaker in the early 1960s, and the return of Tim Knappstein from Roseworthy Agricultural College in 1966, Stanley commenced to develop its own brands with the introduction of the Leasingham label. Special attention was given to the quality of the batches of wine which went under this label, and the quality of the rhine riesling, in particular, increased dramatically. On the other side of the fence Lindemans commenced to develop its massive Padthaway

Vineyard. Stanley could see that this was a highly economic alternative source for a substantial portion of the material which Lindemans was presently buying in the Clare Valley.

Production at Stanley continued to rise in leaps and bounds. When Mick Knappstein assumed control of the winery in 1962 the intake was 1100 tonnes a year. By 1970 it was just under 5000 tonnes, and Stanley Wines had become known across Australia. Nonetheless, this expansion programme had taken a heavy toll of capital. The taxation laws of the time meant that the handsome dividends declared to members of the family all went in taxation or were redeposited with the company to finance the expansion. The paper profits were there, but there was no cash. It was also the high point of take-over fever in the wine industry, with the multinationals leading the charge. In the two years to December 1970 Stanley received 10 serious take-over offers. The eleventh came in December 1970 when Len Evans approached Mick Knappstein to ascertain whether, indeed, Stanley was available. Knappstein replied in the affirmative and Evans introduced H. J. Heinz as the eleventh suitor.

For the first time the offer appeared to match up to all of Stanley's requirements, not the least of which was a categoric assurance that the interests of its numerous growers would be fully protected. There was no haggling over price, and in February 1971 letters of intent were exchanged for the sale of Stanley at $35 per share. The sale duly proceeded, and history records that Stanley made the right choice: the brief flings of Reed and Gilbeys (both of whom had been bidders) in the Australian wine industry brought joy to no-one.

The subsequent departure of Tim Knappstein in 1976, and the fairly acrimonious circumstances of the departure of Brian Barry 12 years later, have given rise to periodic suggestions that Stanley is run by accountants and baked-bean manufacturers. The fact that it is a subsidiary of Heinz is mentioned far more frequently than is the relationship between Philip Morris and Lindemans, Reckitt and Colman and Orlando. It is an imputation which Mick Knappstein bitterly resents. He says—and I believe it to be the case—that the winemaking team at Stanley, composed of himself, Chris Proud (chief winemaker) and Tim Adams, is given complete freedom in the fashioning of all Stanley's top-range wines.

The annual crush at Stanley is now stabilised at around 7000 tonnes a year. A large portion of this comes from the still substantial but ever-dwindling number of independent growers; but Stanley's own wineries, spread from one end of the Valley to the other, are very substantial. By 1986 all the 380 hectares will have come into full bearing; as at August 1983 63 hectares were still to come into bearing. They comprise shiraz (102 hectares), rhine riesling (99 hectares), cabernet sauvignon (40 hectares), sauvignon blanc (20 hectares), chardonnay (17 hectares), pedro ximenez (14.5 hectares), crouchen (12 hectares), traminer (10.4 hectares), grenache (10.3 hectares), malbec (9.5 hectares), chenin blanc (7.1 hectares), pinot noir (6.7 hectares), verdelho (5.3 hectares), mataro (3.7 hectares), semillon (3.5 hectares), cabernet franc (2.8 hectares), trebbiano (1.8 hectares), muscadelle (1.6 hectares), merlot (0.85 hectare), palomino (0.8 hectare) and muscat (0.8 hectare).

(Subsequent to writing the foregoing, Stanley auctioned off a substantial portion of its vineyards in March 1985.)

Since the mid-1960s Stanley's mid-range and top-of-the-range wines have been marketed under a bin number system. The number is a constant (rather than an annually changing one, in the style of Lindemans and Buring's), and is used in tandem with a varietal or generic description. Some of these bins are far more important than others; the top bins are in addition described as Winemakers' Selection wines. This means that the quantity and style of the wine is determined solely by the winemakers, and not by the requirements of the Stanley marketing team. The Winemakers' Selection wines are (or were) Bins 5, 7, 9, 49 and 56. This in turn reflects the prime importance of rhine riesling and cabernet sauvignon which dominate the Winemakers' Selection wines. But a number of the other bins have produced wines of very considerable merit, and I think that each merits description.

Bin 1 Hock Only four vintages of this wine were produced between 1978 and 1981. It was made from a blend of crouchen and pedro ximenez, with lesser and varying percentages of these riesling pressings. It was described by Stanley as being made in traditional German style, fairly dry, and with a clean finish. It is not a wine which I have any particular recollection of, and I do not think it ever aspired to greatness, nor is it ever likely to, if you have any locked away in your cellar.

Bin 3 White Burgundy Bin 3 was first made in 1970, and remains in production as an important part of Stanley's mid-range. Initially produced from a blend of semillon and crouchen (the 1980, for example, was a blend of 50 per cent crouchen, 40 per cent semillon and 10 per cent rhine riesling and verdelho), in recent years first semillon and then chardonnay have played a more important role. In coming years it is expected that the percentage of chardonnay will increase further, and that the wine will become a semillon chardonnay blend to the exclusion of the other varieties. The wine has always received some oak maturation, often in new Nevers oak puncheons, adding to the weight and complexity of the wine. I have seen one or two vintages which I did not think particularly successful, but equally it has at times been very good. It does repay cellaring.

Bin 4 Traminer Riesling A blend of approximately 50 per cent traminer (or, if you prefer, gewurtz-traminer) and 50 per cent rhine riesling. It was first produced in 1980, following the maiden commercial crop of traminer from the Leasingham vineyards. In 1984 the traminer component was absolutely out-standing, winning a gold medal at the Brisbane show in that year, and a small quantity was bottled as a straight varietal and released under a Winemakers' Selection varietal label (with no bin number).

Bin 5 Rhine Riesling After yeoman service from 1968 until 1981, Bin 5 became Leasingham Rhine Riesling in 1982 (with Bin 5 in small print) and ceased to be part of the top quality/restricted quantity Winemakers' Selection range. The first release, back in 1968, won three gold, two silver and two bronze medals together with the trophy for the best "hock" in the 1968 Adelaide show—a wine which sold for less than $1 a bottle when released.

The wine was not made in 1969, but from 1970 onwards Bin 5 and Bin 7 were made in each year. Bin 5 became established as the more forward style, made from late-picked fully ripe grapes. Its rich, estery, aromatic qualities ensured its place both in the market and the show ring. The quality of Bin 5 has been a model of consistency. It may be argued that the extra touch of residual sugar, and the fuller structure, tend to compensate for any deficiencies in fruit flavour stemming from the vintage. Be that as it may, the outstanding vintages of Bin 5 are generally agreed to be 1968, 1971, 1973, 1977, 1978, 1980 and 1984.

It is perhaps worth repeating that these wines are deliberately made to be drunk young. Every now and then a vintage will surprise by going from strength to strength in bottle, living off the richness of the fruit and the residual sugar. More frequently, however, the wines become rather broad and flabby if kept for more than five years at the outside.

Bin 6 Rhine Riesling Moselle Bin 6 has been in continuous production since 1969, and is designed to fill the gap between Bin 5 Rhine Riesling and Bin 9 Spatlese Rhine Riesling (not, as the numbering may suggest, a halfway-house between Bins 5 and 7, both of which are basically dry wines). It is, in other words, a wine with appreciable residual sugar, but is finer and more delicate than the Bin 9 Spatlese. The name moselle in Australia has unfortunate con-notations, being almost inevitably associated with the market leader, Ben Ean Moselle. Ben Ean is a technically superb product, but it is an unashamedly commercial one. Bin 6 does not deserve to be put into the same category. It has from time to time been quite outstanding, and in one or two years has shown a clean pair of heels to Bins 5 and 7. The wine usually contains around 17.5 grams per litre of residual sugar, compared with six or seven grams in the Bins 5 and 7.

Bin 7 Rhine Riesling The Bin 7 label was first introduced in 1969, although there had been earlier varietal rhine riesling releases for a number of years, and a wine was released in 1967 under a different bin number. Between 1969 and 1973 a succession of quite superb Bin 7 Rhine Rieslings appeared. The 1970 is now looked on as marginally behind the others in that group, yet won gold medals at virtually every show it was entered in, and two major trophies for best white wine of show. It took 13 years for another rhine riesling to outperform it (the 1983 Hungerford Hill Coonawarra Rhine Riesling achieved that feat).

Right from the outset, the more austere and elegant style of Bin 7 manifested itself, due in no small part to the very different pattern of picking. Bin 7 has always been a blend of early-picked grapes, high in natural acid, and with as little as 10 degrees of alcohol, combined with mid-season grapes, and a lesser quantity of fully ripe material. It is a formula which has worked wonderfully well over the years, and Stanley sees no reason to change it. Tim Knappstein, who was the architect of that success, modestly describes the wines as being startling by the standards of their time, but not by those of today. In his words:

A lot of money was continually put back into the winery and into the vineyards. In particular, much money went into the winery at the time white-wine technology was rearing its head, and really my uncles—who were the directors—gave me everything I wanted. Indeed at that time there were only four companies in South Australia who consistently won medals in the riesling classes: Leo

Buring, Lindemans, Stanley and Orlando, and sometimes Yalumba. For the time, Stanley really did have some good equipment—centrifuges, stainless steel, refrigeration and yeast propagation plants.

Consistency of quality was precisely what Stanley has always achieved with its Bin 7. If the quality dipped between 1974 and 1976, it was only in comparison to the great wines which had gone before and which were to come after in 1977, 1978, 1980, 1982 and 1984.

Bin 9 Spatlese Rhine Riesling Like Bin 6, Bin 9 has been made each year since 1969 and, until 1981, was the sweetest and richest riesling in the range. Interestingly, occasionally a little sauvignon blanc has been added to the wine to give it further lift. It is made from late-picked grapes, with a baume often over 14 and occasionally as high as 15 degrees. It is undoubtedly one of the top wines under the Leasingham label, although curiously it was not a success in 1980. The 1971 and 1972 vintages of Bin 9 are still quite magnificent, holding their fruit flavour and structure. Like the equally good 1978 vintage, these wines are rich more than luscious, with excellent balancing acid. They are very much the Clare Valley style of spatlese, at the opposite end of the style-spectrum to the botrytised spatleses of Coonawarra and Padthaway.

Bin 14 Chablis The composition of this wine has changed radically since its introduction in 1978. In that year it was blend of 50 per cent late-picked pedro ximinez and early-picked rhine riesling. Those two varieties have been progressively replaced by semillon and chardonnay; as in the case of Bin 3, it is expected that the chardonnay percentage will increase in years to come as Stanley's extensive chardonnay plantings come into full bearing. I have not always liked this wine, and have thought that its more successful vintages made a good white burgundy style. However, that in all probability merely reflects my hostility to the name chablis which, I believe, is a marketer's dream and a consumer's nightmare.

Bin 17 Rosé The first Bin 17 Rosé appeared in 1974, but Stanley had made rosés for many years previously with outstanding success, releasing them under the rather more humble Stanley Rosé label. The 1972, for example, won three gold medals in a fairly brief show career. The 1974 release was a blend of grenache and malbec, and went on to win two gold medals and the Sheppard Tankers' Trophy for the best rosé in the 1974 Brisbane show. As

from 1977 the malbec component was dropped; occasionally thereafter, until the line was discontinued after the 1981 vintage, small amounts of cabernet pressings were added for colour and complexity. Its demise was not due to any lack of quality in the wine, but rather the continuing indifference of the Australian wine-drinking public to rosés in general.

Bin 46 Cabernet Grenache An occasional release in the mid-70s (I particularly remember the 1975) which also had a little shiraz included in the blend. The grenache component was deliberately added to soften the wine and produce an early-drinking style. There have been no releases of the wine in recent years, nor will there be in the future.

Bin 49 Cabernet Sauvignon The first varietal cabernet sauvignon released by Stanley was Bin 14 of 1966, sold in 1968. At that time the red-wine boom was in full swing, and cabernet sauvignon was pitifully scarce. While it was being planted all over the country, most of the vineyards were not in production. In the manner of chardonnay in the late 1970s and early 1980s, far more of the variety was to be found on the label than in the bottle. Bin 14 was one of the rare exceptions, and the wine was nigh on unprocurable unless one visited the winery (as I did in that year). It still remains a marvellous wine: a bottle opened in August 1984 was a ripe yet not jammy wine with very good balance and structure, and bell-clear cabernet fruit flavour. It was showing no sign of tiring.

1967 saw the first release of Bin 49, a blend of 80 per cent cabernet sauvignon and 20 per cent malbec. A similar blend followed in 1968, although for some reason it was labelled Bin 73. In 1969 the numbering reverted to Bin 49, where it has remained ever since. Shiraz replaced malbec, and the cabernet sauvignon component increased to 95 per cent. This, with minor vintage variations, has remained the composition of the wine since that time. Probably the greatest Bin 49 was the 1971 vintage, which still retains the great depth of fruit for which these wines are most remarkable, yet shows great finesse and elegance. 1972 (another elegant, though oaky wine), 1975 (rich, complex and with strong American oak), 1978 (quite outstanding, with excellent varietal definition and firm, "cool" varietal cabernet evident on a long palate with a lingering finish), and 1980 (a warmer style, with sweet berry flavours and vanillan oak aromas and flavours) have been the best of the releases to so far come onto the market.

The 1982 and 1984 vintages also promise to be of high quality. The wines are usually released with at least three, and frequently four, years' bottle-age. Just how much longer they should be kept—allowing for the variations of vintage—really turns on what one looks for in a red wine: if it is maximum fruit flavour, drink the wines within six to eight years of vintage; if it is maximum complexity, but at the expense of diminished fruit, the wines may be kept for anything up to 20 years.

Bin 56 Cabernet Malbec Bin 56 is really the child of Max Schubert. It was not that Schubert was engaging in a little consulting wine work on the side, but rather that Penfolds (along with so many other major companies) was a regular purchaser of bulk wine from Stanley. In 1969 he saw and greatly admired a vat of malbec which Stanley had made and, in seeking to buy it, rather unwisely told Stanley to put its own price on it. Much impressed, Stanley decided it would not sell it at all, but bottle it. The wine was a great disappointment and was in fact never released under the Leasingham label. But Schubert's involvement did not end there; in a conversation with the Knappsteins a few months later, Schubert made the comment: "The trouble with you blokes is you don't blend enough, you don't experiment enough." Stanley took the comment to heart, and in 1970 made a blend of 75 per cent cabernet sauvignon and 25 per cent malbec, which it released under the Bin 56 label.

There are many who would put the 1971 Bin 56 among the top-dozen Australian red wines made in the period 1966 to 1976. To this day it remains a quite beautiful wine, soft round and fleshy, yet not heavy, and with a delicate astringency on the finish. It has an almost flower-like flavour. Undoubtedly it will not improve, but equally undoubtedly it is still at its peak.

1972 Bin 56 was another great success and this, too, is still a marvellous wine. The outstanding years of subsequent vintages have been 1975, 1978 and 1980. Of the three I think the 1975 is the best wine, with the 1978 only fractionally behind it. The two are in marked contrast in style, mainly due to the differing oak treatments. The 1975 has the sweet vanillan/mint flavours of American oak; the 1978 the more astringent, lemony characters of French oak. The most recent release, the 1981, is another very good wine. Winner of the trophy at the 1982 Canberra National Wine Show for best one-year-old red, it is a firm and crisp wine, with good varietal cabernet sauvignon aroma and flavour dominant, augmented by the lemony French oak. At this stage the malbec component is not obvious, although its

softening effect will undoubtedly become apparent with further bottle-age.

Bin 61 Shiraz This label first made its appearance with the 1973 vintage, and has remained in continuous production since then. The best shiraz of each year is selected for this label, which almost inevitably fails to receive the recognition it deserves. In mid-1984 the excellent 1980 vintage was still available with a recommended retail price of $4.77 and a real price no doubt well below that. Tasted "blind" against 15 or so other Clare Valley reds of all varieties and makers, it was one of my top wines: extremely full-flavoured and rich, with excellent balance and outstanding cellaring potential.

Bin 68 Cabernet Shiraz Bin 68 was first vintaged in 1968. The blend varies marginally according to the vintage, with the cabernet component usually between 75 and 80 per cent. Like Bin 61, it does not always receive the recognition it deserves; and again like Bin 61, it can be quite excellent.

At the bottom end of the bottled range of wines comes Spring Gully Riesling and Hutt Creek Claret. Spring Gully Riesling has more than once excelled itself. Both the 1976 and 1980 vintages were equal to or better than many rieslings twice the price; the wine was consistently chosen by reviewers, myself included, in comparative tastings. In those early years I imagine the wine was a blend of crouchen and rhine riesling (with a fair percentage of pressings of the latter grape), but with the sudden increase in the availability of rhine riesling, the wine is now 100 per cent Clare Valley rhine riesling. Hutt Creek Claret is a multi-grape multi-area blend, with 20 per cent cabernet sauvignon and 23 per cent malbec coming from the Barossa Valley and 36 per cent grenache and 21 per cent shiraz from the Clare Valley. Unlike Spring Gully, I do not think it has ever excelled itself, but it is at least true to its description as claret.

Finally, Stanley have been at the forefront in the development of the artificially induced botrytised rhine riesling and sauterne styles. The project at Stanley has been under the control of Tim Adams, who became assistant winemaker at Stanley having completed his Bachelor of Science (Wine Science) degree in 1981 at the Riverina College of Advanced Education. His first major winemaking project with the company was the production of two heavily botrytised wines in the 1982 vintage, using the inoculation techniques pioneered in Australia a few years earlier by Tim Knappstein and Joe Grilli.

Much is heard about botrytis these days, as it now

occurs regularly—indeed too regularly—at Coonawarra and other cool-climate regions. *Botrytis cinerea* is known as *pourriture noble* (noble rot) in the Sauternes region of France, and as the *Edelfaule* in Germany, where it is usually responsible for the great beerenauslesen and trockenbeerenauslesen wines of that country. Botrytis is a fungus which grows on the skin of the grapes and which, after several weeks of growth, punctures tiny holes in the skin which allow moisture (in the form of water) to escape from the grapes. Under ideal conditions (and even in France and Germany these occur only occasionally, say one year in every three or four) the mould does its work gradually, and over a prolonged period the sugar and acid levels in the grapes increase until they almost double. But to work in this way very precise conditions are required: cold nights to arrest the march of the mould, and short periods of high humidity and midday temperatures around the 15°C mark to permit it to work. If it is too dry (or too cold) the mould will not grow; if it is too warm or too humid the growth is too rapid, secondary infections occur, and the grapes become a mushy slush.

In many Australian regions (of which the Clare Valley is one) these conditions seldom, if ever, occur. So if you want to make a botrytised wine, nature needs considerable assistance. The Californians devised a system which, to a large extent, replaced nature altogether, and it is this system which has come to Australia. The grapes are harvested at normal optimum ripeness, when typically they will be at about 13 to 14 degrees baume and contain around six to seven grams per litre of acid. They are placed on shallow trays with a wire-netting base, and each tray is sprayed with a mixture containing a culture of active *Botrytis cinerea* which has previously been propagated in the laboratory. This culture stage can be especially difficult, as it is essential to screen out foreign moulds, many of which can closely resemble *Botrytis cinerea*.

The racks are then stacked in a framework allowing the free passage of air between each tray. The first vintage at Stanley saw the wine made in a section of the cellar, but a special insulated cool-room was erected in time for the 1983 vintage. This is entered through a double-door airlock system, rather like that used in spacecraft or infectious diseases wards. Each morning the room is filled to saturation with humid air, which is then progressively reduced throughout the rest of the day. The temperature is likewise increased and reduced. For those who recoil in horror from the in-vitro fertilisation overtones of

the procedure, the same answer is given: it is only repeating what nature should, but for reasons of its own, has failed to do. It is not an "artificial" wine in the sense that acid or sugar or other chemicals have been added; it is not "artificial" as a freeze-concentrated wine may be; and it is not artificial in the sense that the flavour has been enhanced by other chemical or mechanical manipulation. Is is not seeking to improve on nature, only to simulate what nature at its best can produce.

The process takes two and a half to three weeks, and at each vintage two lots of wine can be processed. It is an exceedingly expensive technique: not only is there a disproportionately high capital investment involved, but the risks are very high and the production very small. Thus just as Tim Knappstein lost the 1981 Enterprise vintage through vinegar flies, Stanley's 1983 Rhine Riesling was a total failure. What is more, the amount of wine produced from a tonne of grapes is less than one-quarter of that which would be made from normally processed grapes. So even though the 1982 Stanley Trockenbeerenauslese was released for $12.50 per half-bottle at the cellar door (the only sales outlet for it), the actual return to Stanley is less than for conventionally made wines.

The question remains as to how far the process of dehydration and concentration should be taken. As the grapes go over 20 degrees baume the technical difficulties progressively increase: it becomes almost impossible to press them using conventional techniques, and even to measure the sugar level. This apart, as the level of botrytis increases so does the varietal character diminish. The ultimate heavyweights are the Nederburg Edelkeurs from South Africa, and in these wines it is nigh on impossible to determine the varietal composition by taste. The other problem is control of the development of volatile acidity during fermentation. These "super stickies", as they are called in the vernacular, develop far higher levels of volatility than conventional white wine, and indeed need a certain level to prevent their becoming impossibly sweet and cloying.

Stanley has decided to brave all these problems, and take all its wines to the far end of the scale, and more power to it for so doing. I cannot praise highly enough the enterprise of the winemaking team, and the financial courage of Heinz in backing the project, simply because it offers us wine on a plane and of a style quite different from anything ever made in Australia prior to 1980.

The '82 Trockenbeerenauslese was crushed at an average of 20 degrees baume; the analysis of the finished wine is residual sugar 9.7 baume; pH 3.3; acid 9.6 grams per litre and alcohol 11.3 degrees. At a *Winestate* magazine tasting in April 1984 Brian Croser, Brian Barry and I had no difficulty in awarding it the five-star rating, with the following tasting notes. *Colour:* full yellow. *Bouquet:* exceptionally intense and powerful botrytis wine fruit. *Palate:* intense, honeyed-wine/apricot fruit with pungent, cleansing acid on a long, lingering finish.

Since 1982 Stanley has also made a sauterne from a blend of semillon and sauvignon blanc. I thought the 1982 was less successful than the rhine riesling when first released; but bottle-age should see a vast improvement, just as it has with the rhine riesling, itself a little ragged when it was marketed (in my view prematurely) at the end of 1982. More than any other white, these wines demand bottle maturation, and should still be improving at the end of 10 years.

The 1984 releases of these wines promise to be the most astonishing of all. The ideal season, and the perfect vintage conditions, gave Adams a flying start. He says:

> The almost perfect conditions of good rainfall late last year, clear, mild, sunny days and cool evenings, allowed the fruit to develop and mature at a slow, even rate. The result was that we gained rhine riesling, semillon and sauvignon blanc fruit in absolutely sound condition, with the all-important high levels of natural acid and sugar.

In the end result the sauterne had an average of 19 baume at crushing, while the rhine riesling reached the unprecedented level of 26 baume. The wine will be available from retailers, albeit in extremely restricted quantities, when released some time in late 1985.

TAYLORS
MINTARO ROAD, AUBURN

The Taylor family had had a close association with the Clare Valley for over 20 years before their 1969 decision to establish Taylors' Chateau Clare. Bill Taylor senior, and his two sons, John and Bill, were Sydney hoteliers and liquor wholesalers. Since the Second World War they had purchased substantial quantities of wine from the district, chiefly from the Clarevale Cooperative, and this had brought them into contact with Jim Barry. So it was to Barry they turned when, in 1969, the family purchased a 300-hectare property at Auburn, at the bottom end of the Valley. The winery was to be called Chateau

Clare, and the planning for it was carried out on a grand scale. There were to be just two wines: a cabernet sauvignon and a hermitage. The cabernet sauvignon was to be the standard-bearer, the wine which would make Chateau Clare as well known and respected in Australia as Chateau Mouton Rothschild in France.

In 1969 and 1970 the first 178 hectares of vines were planted, 149 to cabernet sauvignon with the balance to shiraz. In 1973 the imposing winery was built, and 1000 American oak puncheons started to find their way into the cellars. Initially the plan was to replace a quarter of these each year so that no oak would be older than four years. Partly because of the grim economics of the past five years, and partly due to the conscious choice of a lighter style of wine, few casks have been disposed of, and the percentage of new oak has diminished in consequence.

Morgan Yeatman was appointed winemaker, and produced the first 10 vintages. Success came quickly: the initial vintage of Cabernet Sauvignon (1974) won six gold medals in its first year of showing. It is decidedly ironical that this (1975) was the last year in which the Australian sales of red wine exceeded those of white. The roller-coaster was about to take off, propelling white-wine sales to a level six times greater than those of red, and signalling the end of the red-wine boom which so many (like Taylors) had geared up for. By the mid-70s vineyards across Australia were utterly out of line with the rapidly emerging trends of the marketplace. Red wines started to pile up in cellars—with long-term consequences for price—and a reshaping of those vineyards became imperative. For the Taylors the decision was the end of a dream, but there was no choice. Phase two began in 1977 and continued through until 1983. The vineyards are now fully planted, and it is unlikely their shape will change much in the foreseeable future.

Thanks both to grafting and to a significant extension in size, vineyard manager George Finn now presides over 156 hectares of red-grape vines and 131 hectares of whites. Plantings comprise cabernet sauvignon (125 hectares), shiraz (28 hectares), pinot noir (three hectares), chardonnay (55 hectares), rhine riesling (42.5 hectares), crouchen (28.3 hectares) and traminer (5.6 hectares). Six wines head the range (cabernet sauvignon, hermitage, pinot noir, rhine riesling, chardonnay and white burgundy) with three more "commercial" wines bringing up the rear.

Obviously enough output has always been very substantial, rising from 50,000 cases in the early years to around 150,000 cases at the present time, and heading towards 250,000 cases once the vineyards are in full production. Whatever the thoughts and ambitions of the Taylors at the time they conceived Chateau Clare, the subsequent positioning of the red wines (both in terms of style and of price) has reflected the difficulties inherent in establishing a major new brand in a basically oversupplied market. Thus the prices have always been very modest. In mid-1980 the 1976 Cabernet Sauvignon had a recommended retail price of $3.90, while four years later the 1980 had a recommended retail price of $6.58, but a "real" price of around $5, the cellar-door price of the time. In 1984 I have seen the wines discounted below the $4 a bottle level. Given yields of around 7.5 tonnes per hectare for cabernet sauvignon and a vineyard average of 10 tonnes per hectare, such prices leave little room for error. Which is the chicken and which is the egg, I do not know, but the style of the Taylor reds is distinctly softer and lighter than that of the Valley as a whole.

The vineyards are all fitted with drip-irrigation facilities, and over the year the equivalent of 100 to 125 millimetres of water are added to the natural rainfall of around 550 millimetres. Winemaker Andrew Tolley insists this is merely to relieve stress on the vine and cannot be regarded as irrigation. Without becoming embroiled in what is at best a semantic argument, I agree with that general proposition. Certainly the yields do not suggest the vines are being unduly forced, although the style of the wine is undeniably light. All picking is done by hand, somewhat surprising given the economies of machine harvesting. But a team of 120 allows the fruit to come into the winery in top condition and to be crushed within one hour of picking.

Taylors released its first rhine riesling from the 1979 vintage. The style has been an early-maturing one, rich and full-flavoured; overall quality has been a little variable, but usually adequate if not exciting. In the 1980s a white burgundy label was introduced from a crouchen-chardonnay blend, with the crouchen predominant. A commercial wine at best, it may prove simply to be a holding operation until the chardonnay plantings come into full bearing. The first commercial release of chardonnay will come from the 1984 vintage, with subsequent vintages providing increased quantities.

Since 1980 Taylors has produced a varietal pinot noir. The 1980, 1981 and 1982 vintages simply go to prove that pinot is a very difficult variety at the best of times, and suggest that the Clare Valley may not be the best place to grow the grape. The 1983

vintage was a radical departure, with far better colour, flavour and body. It had quite a degree of success in capital city wine shows; my reservations about the wine stem from the fact that I still do not see pinot noir varietal flavour as I would like it.

Hermitage came on-stream at the same time as the cabernet sauvignon, and has struggled somewhat in the shadow of its big brother. Looking back over the line, the 1976 and 1977 vintages stood out, but even these have not lived up to my early expectations of them. The 1976, which looked outstanding in its youth, is at its peak now, while some of the vintages either side of it have already passed their best. Certainly the line-up suggests the wines should indeed be consumed within a year or two of their release while they retain fruit freshness. Thus the 1982 and 1983 vintages both had good flavour when tasted in the early part of 1984.

Without question, Taylors has succeeded best with its cabernet sauvignons. Characteristically the wines are soft, forward styles, but they do have flavour. Every now and then a wine comes along which offers that little bit extra: the 1974 was such a wine, and the 1982 looks as if it will be equally successful.

Andrew Tolley became winemaker at the end of 1983. He intends to pay close attention to the acid balance of the wine, something he feels was overlooked in the early vintages. I agree; many of the older wines show the ravaging effects of high pH, as they have turned brown and lost fruit flavour. This balance will be achieved by acid addition at the crusher, rather than picking earlier. Tolley firmly believes that the best flavour comes from fully ripe grapes, taken from vines which are free from stress.

WATERVALE CELLARS
MAIN NORTH ROAD, WATERVALE

Watervale Cellars is presided over by Robert Crabtree, an expatriate English lawyer turned hobby winemaker (in England), trainee winemaker (in France) and full-time winemaker and vigneron (in Australia). This somewhat unlikely background, coupled with his rather academic appearance, hesitant manner of speech and, last but not least, his partnership with Rick Robertson at Watervale Cellars between 1980 and 1983, all conspire to create the impression that Crabtree is less than serious about wine and winemaking.

Nothing could be further from the truth, although even here one has to wait for proof positive in the form of wines wholly made by Crabtree. It was not until 1984 that Watervale Cellars, which had commenced business in 1977, acquired its own winery. Some quite marvellous red wines have come out under the Watervale Cellars label over the years, but almost all of these were bought in from other wineries in the district. It is true that in 1983 Crabtree had made two white wines using the "I've been everywhere, man" technique which is so peculiar to the Clare Valley. The rhine riesling was crushed at Andrew Mitchell's winery in the Skillogalee Valley, and was then moved across to Fareham Estate for fermentation. History does not relate where it was stabilised, filtered and bottled. In the same year Crabtree was also successful in assembling a few bits and pieces of semillon and chardonnay, which he oak-matured. The 1983 Rhine Riesling was a good wine, all things considered, but the 1983 Semillon Chardonnay was very heavily oaked.

As from 1984 the wines will be made in a simple but functional galvanised-iron winery at Auburn, which previously served duty as an aerated waters factory. The reds will be made entirely here; the whites will be crushed at Jeffrey Grosset's winery, literally across the road, and moved back for fermentation at the Watervale Cellars winery. For the time being almost all of the fruit will be purchased from independent growers. Crabtree has 10 hectares of vineyard land suitable for planting, and established 0.8 hectare of cabernet sauvignon in 1983 together with a trial row of cabernet franc.

WENDOUREE
SPRING FARM ROAD, CLARE

A. P. Birks' Wendouree Cellars were established in 1892 as wine fever gripped the Clare Valley. In that year Alfred Percy Birks and his brother planted a half-acre (0.2-hectare) block of cabernet sauvignon, and made a few gallons of wine from grapes presumably purchased from other growers in the district. Three acres (1.2 hectares) of shiraz were planted in 1893. Both of these plantings, together with a further half-acre of shiraz planted in 1896, remain in production, a rich heritage from the last century. By February 1896 the local newspaper, the _Northern Argus_, was able to report:

> Messrs. Birks . . . have a very nice vineyard and orchard . . . 20 acres [eight hectares] of vines are planted of the shiraz, cabernet, malbec and mataro varieties. If the proprietors cannot find a market for the latter variety they intend to graft with cabernet . . . a fair crop will be taken from them this year.

Nothing changes, it seems. Eighty years later, grenache and mataro were once again being grafted to cabernet sauvignon.

By 1903 the Birks brothers had built a small winery and storage area. They were unable to turn all their grapes into wine, but made 1000 gallons (4550 litres) and sold both it and their surplus grapes to the Stanley Wine Company. For the next 20 years Stanley remained their sole customer, either reselling the wine to the London market, or using it to bolster up some of their own lighter-bodied wines.

In 1914, with production around 18,000 litres a year, Alfred Percy Birks decided the time had come to build a proper wine cellar and to expand production. The first stone section of the cellars, which remains in use virtually unaltered to this day, was constructed. A large basket press was installed on rails set in cement running between the newly built open fermenters. It, too, remains in use, and present-day winemaker Tony Brady prefers it to the Willmes airbag press (the first of its kind in Australia) which Jim Barry bought for Roly Birks in the early 1960s. The basket press came secondhand—and cheaply— from Leslie Salter, son of the founder of Saltram, and one of the doyens of the Australian wine industry at that time. It had been built specially for him by Bagshaws, but on arrival at Saltram it was found it would not fit between his fermenters. Salter acted as a semi-consultant to A. P. Birks, who had worked for Salter as a sales representative in the 1880s, and so the press found its way to Wendouree. That it is still in use is remarkable; that Tim Knappstein uses it to press his heavily botrytised rhine riesling grapes, destined for beerenauslese and trockenbeerenauslese, is at first sight even more remarkable. But its configuration is not so different from the classic winepress of champagne, and the pressure action on a small, thinly spread load is equally gentle.

In 1917 failing health caused A. P. Birks to hand over winemaking responsibilities to his son Roly Birks, who then started a winemaking career which was to span 65 vintages. It must surely rank second only to Dan Tyrrell, who made 70 consecutive vintages between 1888 and 1958. It was a rare privilege to be able to record my conversation with Roly Birks on tape when I interviewed this remarkable 91-year-old in July 1984. Time has slowed Roly, but his spirit—and that indefinable mixture of raw Australian courage and humour—was undiminished even in the antiseptic surroundings of the geriatric ward of the Clare District Hospital.

Under Roly's direction, Wendouree's vineyards were almost immediately expanded. What became known as the Eastern Vineyard was purchased and planted over the winters of 1919 and 1920. Part of this survives: two large blocks of shiraz of four and two acres (1.6 and 0.8 hectares) respectively, and a half-acre (0.2 hectare) of bush-pruned mataro. The remaining two blocks have been grafted to cabernet sauvignon and malbec respectively, but the 1920 rootstocks remain.

The cellars were once again extended, and equipment was upgraded with one of the first must pumps in the district. In 1925 Roly Birks and his brother decided it was time to start establishing their own markets for their ever-increasing production. They would load up a truck with casks and kegs of varying sizes (never bottles) and set off on a round trip selling to hotels. Roly Birks recalls:

> We used to make the four-day trip through Burra, across to Jamestown, back to Pirie, and down through Crystal Brook every two months or so. We sold quite a bit that way. Most of the wine sold to the hotels was port, not so much sherry — that came later. But we still sold hogsheads of full-bodied dry red in Port Pirie, and later we sold our heavy dry red in Hindley Street, Adelaide. We used to sell it to the Cumberland Hotel, which I remember was one of our best customers. It used to take seven or eight hogsheads at a time, bottle it and sell it — no labels, of course, they weren't compulsory then.

In the years up to the Second World War output stayed roughly constant at half full-bodied dry red and half fortified wine. In the years after the Second World War Wendouree built up a surprising business in supplying substantial quantities of base wine for the then-infant sparkling-wine production of Wynns. By the early 1950s this had grown to between 55,000 and 65,000 litres a year.

The 1950s also marked the appearance of the respected Melbourne wine merchant W. J. Seabrook & Son. The late Doug Seabrook began purchasing substantial quantities of Wendouree wines, making a specialty of Birks' "pressings" red. Absolutely immense wines, they nonetheless had sufficient fruit and acid to balance the tannin, and soon became one of Seabrook's most important house labels. Although the wines were bought in cask by Doug Seabrook and matured for a period of time before bottling, the maker was always specified on the label.

In 1970, at the age of 77, Roly Birks decided he had had enough. His son, Peter Birks, is an entomologist with the South Australian Department of Agriculture and had no interest in taking over the winery, so Birks decided to sell. If the Knappsteins made the right choice, Birks made the wrong one. Matters were made worse by the fact that part of the

purchase price was in the form of shares in the purchasing company, which within a few years had gone into liquidation.

The period between 1970 and 1974 was an extremely unhappy one for Wendouree. The winery and vineyards ran down with frightening rapidity: by 1974 only a token 10 tonnes of grapes were crushed, and the properties were split up and offered for sale by the mortgagee. In October 1972 the two principal vineyard blocks (with the old house and winery) were purchased by Sydney businessman Max Liberman, and his son-in-law, Tony Brady, together with wife Lita were installed as managers. Brady was an Adelaide lawyer who, in his own words, barely knew how to spell the word grape, but he nonetheless tackled the project with enthusiasm. Roly Birks was retained as a consultant, and a close and enduring friendship was forged between the Bradys and Birks. A neighbour, Chris Sullivan, had recently graduated from Roseworthy and became winemaker.

The Bradys immediately began to rejuvenate the old vineyards, preserving wherever possible the oldest plantings and removing or grafting only those established to inferior varieties. Currently the vineyards are planted to shiraz (4.85 hectares), cabernet sauvignon (2.3 hectares), malbec (1.35 hectares), rhine riesling (0.75 hectare), cabernet franc (0.36 hectare) and mataro, muscat and chenin blanc (0.25 hectare in all). Production varies between 18 and 60 tonnes per year — the low 18 tonnes was recorded in the drought year of 1983.

It is not the yields, varying from pitifully low to modest, that are impressive. Rather it is the quality of the grapes, freakish by any standards and certainly by those of Australia. The combination of climate (or rather microclimate) and *terroir* produces grapes high in alcohol, high in acid and low in pH. A fairly common analysis would be 13 degrees baume, eight grams per litre of acid and a pH of 3.2 — all of this before any correction by the winemaker. These figures, confirmed independently by other (envious) growers in the district, explain the extraordinary quality of the Wendouree reds, with their ability to live and grow in bottle for astonishing periods of time. Because they are high in alcohol, and because of their immense structure and sturdiness, they run somewhat counter to the mainstream of contemporary winemaking thought and practice. Neither will they ever appeal to the faint-hearted or the impatient. It is perhaps for these reasons that the wines are among some of the most underrated and undervalued in Australia.

For anyone who wishes to buy wines which at

once offer density of colour, immensity of structure and flavour and yet avoid jamminess and the perils of over-extraction, these are the wines. For all their weight, they are at the same time wines of style and elegance. The principal releases are a shiraz, a cabernet malbec, and the occasional cabernet sauvignon. Since 1975 there has not been a poor or weak wine made; perhaps 1977 was a less successful vintage, but 1975 was magnificent and almost every other year since that time has produced outstanding wine.

The winemaking has gradually devolved on the shoulders of Tony Brady, with considerable help from Stephen George since 1980. Oak has played an increasing role in recent years, but thanks to the power of the base fruit it cannot and will not ever overwhelm that fruit. It certainly adds another dimension to the very young wines, which at 12 months of age can be formidable if not downright frightening.

I devoutly trust that Tony and Lita Brady will spend many more happy years at Wendouree making wines in precisely the same way as they do today.

WILSON'S POLISH HILL RIVER VINEYARDS
POLISH HILL RIVER ROAD, SEVENHILL

Dr John Wilson is yet another of the countless band who march—or who have marched—under the banner of vine and scalpel. In 1974 John Wilson purchased a 26-hectare triangular block of land on the floor of the Polish Hill River Valley, nestling under the lee of the hills separating it from the Clare Valley. The first vines were planted in that year; of the 1000 planted, only 100 or so survived. A replanting programme saw the gradual establishment of a 0.3-hectare block of experimental varieties, covering such oddities as emerald riesling, muller-thurgau, souzao, pinot meunière, zinfandel and sylvaner.

These in turn led to endless home winemaking trials over the ensuing years. This taught Wilson two things: the difficulties of making wine in small batches (and techniques for overcoming those difficulties) and the distinctively different nature of the Polish Hill River grapes from those grown in the Clare Valley proper. Wilson ascribes this difference in part to the acidic slate subsoil, overlain by a shallow topsoil of red-brown clay loam. Although the vineyards are at an average height of 425 to 450 metres above sea-level, little different from that of

the Clare Valley, vintage is usually two weeks later for all varieties. What is more, acid levels are higher, and winemakers on both sides of the hills agree the fruit character is markedly different. That of the Polish Hill area is finer, more delicate and less robust than that of the Clare Valley.

By 1980, and the first on-site vintage, Wilson was well aware of the differences. A basic Colorbond shed had been erected, and a limited amount of winemaking equipment installed. Limited, because the entire vintage saw less than 10 tonnes of fruit crushed and, until 1983, the small batch, handmade technique which Wilson had developed at home, was used. The principal feature of this is a modified form of carbonic maceration: the berries are removed from the stalks without being crushed and are fermented whole. As well as dispensing with the need for a crusher, this technique also results in a slower fermentation than usual. The grapes are placed in a closed vat; carbon dioxide rapidly builds up, producing an anaerobic atmosphere. Wilson departs back to Adelaide for the week, leaving the ferment to proceed untended until the following weekend.

All of John Wilson's wines so far made have caused heated debate among other winemakers and wine judges, some criticising the degree of volatile lift which many of the wines show. There is also a very characteristic meaty/gamy flavour which seems to be part and parcel of the carbonic maceration process.

One of the more successful wines so far made was the 1981 Cabernet Shiraz, the label depicting an RX-class steam-engine. An exceedingly complex wine, although fairly soft in structure, it has won a wide degree of acceptance. But to my palate the most remarkable wine of the Polish Hill River Vineyard is its pinot noir. On my first visit to the winery in 1982 I was impressed with the fruit style of the 1981 vintage, and I think the 1982 is even better. These are the most promising wines from this variety so far to come from the Clare region as a whole. The 1982 Pinot Noir has strong plum/spice/strawberry aromas and flavours, almost essency in their intensity. The wine has been accused of volatility, and I guess it does have some, but I am more interested in its flavour.

The argument regarding volatility (and the other peculiar carbonic maceration characters) spills over into the hermitage and cabernet sauvignon wines made by Wilson. This debate may well become academic with the erection of a large-scale winery in time for the 1985 vintage. After the winery has been built Wilson will approach vintage in a more conventional fashion, spending five or six weeks on-site continuously. The winery will be receiving fruit from cabernet sauvignon (two hectares), zinfandel (0.3 hectare), pinot noir (1.2 hectares), traminer (0.8 hectare), malbec and merlot (0.2 hectare each), chardonnay (0.3 hectare) and rhine riesling (3.5 hectares). Small purchases from contract-growers in the region of pinot noir, cabernet sauvignon, shiraz and malbec will also be made. The winery will have a capacity of 70 tonnes.

Fruit quality is not seriously in dispute, and I see no reason why the Polish Hill wines should not be of exemplary quality. ◖◗

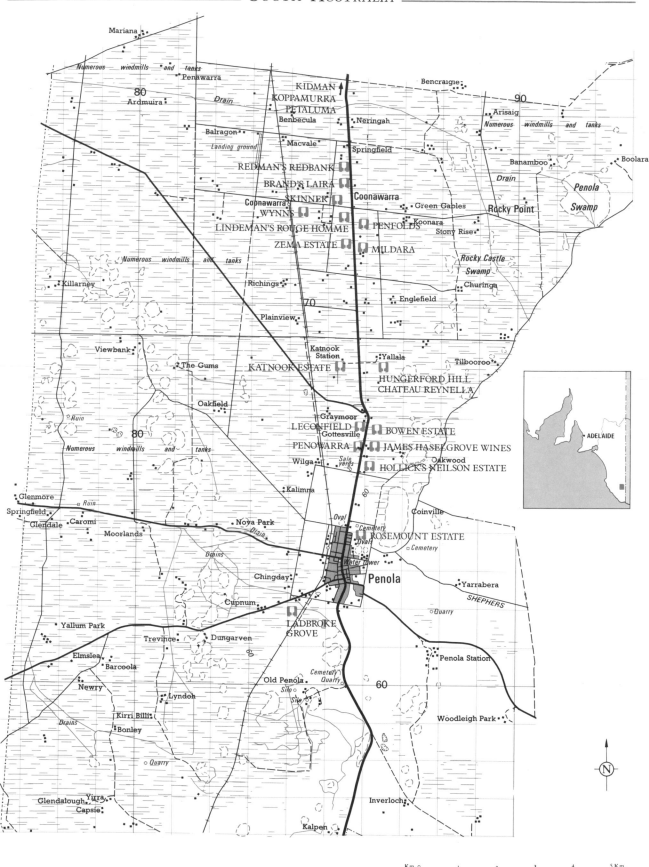

Mariana
Numerous windmills and tanks
Penawarra
80
Ardmuira
Drain
Balragon
Landing ground
Macvale

KIDMAN
KOPPAMURRA
PETALUMA
Benbecula
Neringah
Springfield

Bencraigie
90
Arisaig
Numerous windmills and tanks
Banamboo
Boolara

REDMAN'S REDBANK
BRAND'S LAIRA
SKINNER
Coonawarra
WYNNS
LINDEMAN'S ROUGE HOMME
ZEMA ESTATE

Coonawarra
Green Gables
Koonara
PENFOLDS
Stony Rise
MILDARA

Penola
Swamp
Rocky Point

Rocky Castle
Swamp
Churinga

Killarney
Numerous windmills and tanks
Richings
Plainview
70

Englefield

Viewbank
The Gums
KATNOOK ESTATE
Oakfield

Katnook
Station
Yallala
HUNGERFORD HILL
CHATEAU REYNELLA

Tilbooroo

Ruin
80
Numerous windmills and tanks

Graymoor
LECONFIELD
Gottesville
PENOWARRA
Wilga
Sale
yards

BOWEN ESTATE
JAMES HASELGROVE WINES
Oakwood
HOLLICK'S NEILSON ESTATE

Glenmore
Ruin
Springfield
Glendale
Caromi
Moorlands

Kalimna
60

Nova Park
Drain
Drains

Coinville

Oval
Cemetery
Oval
ROSEMOUNT ESTATE
Cemetery
Water Tower

Chingday
Cupnum

Penola
Yarrabera
SHEPHERS

Yallum Park
Trevince
Dungarven
Elmslea
Barcoola
Newry
Lyndoh
Kirri Billi
Bonley

LADBROKE
GROVE
Quarry

Old Penola
Cemetery
Quarry
Silo
Site
60

Penola Station

Woodleigh Park

Drains
Quarry

Glendalough
Yirra
Capsie
Inverloch
Kalpeh

ADELAIDE

Km. 0   1   2   3   4   5 Km.
Mi. 0   1   2   3 Mi.

N

Coonawarra

There are many winegrowing regions in the world that nature clearly designed for the purpose. They nestle on the foothills of nearby mountains, or in gently rolling valleys, or on riversides. There are others which are improbable areas, none more so than remote, flat and featureless Coonawarra. Driving winter rains, spring frosts and occasional searing summer heat are not prone to encourage those who find their way to this tiny dot on the map to stay, let alone plant vines.

However, Coonawarra has been occupied by white people for 145 years (and before that into the mists of recorded time by Aborigines, who provided the name, meaning honeysuckle). In that period of 145 years vine-growing has been a major and successful operation for two brief periods only: from 1890 to 1910, and from 1955 to the present time. For the remainder, "you can write failure across the face of Coonawarra", in the oft-repeated words of Bill Redman, a man who struggled longer and harder than anyone else to remove that stigma.

Solomon, Josiah and Thomas Austin were the first permanent settlers. They arrived in 1840 with a flock of merinos, and took up the 109-square-mile (280-square-kilometre) Yallum Park. Shortly afterwards they built Austin House, a stone building which still stands in remarkable condition behind the main Yallum Park homestead. The Yallum lease was sold to Thomas and Harry Wells in 1851, and was in turn purchased by the Riddoch brothers in 1861.

Scottish-born John and George Riddoch had made a fortune during the Victorian gold rush, not by digging for gold but by supplying necessities to the miners, eventually establishing a chain of stores in Beechworth, Ballarat and Geelong. When John Riddoch arrived in 1861 only 810 hectares of land were freehold. Twenty years later his holdings stretched from Coonawarra in the north to the site of the present Mount Gambier airport in the south:

51,400 hectares of freehold, 180 square kilometres of leasehold and more than 160,000 sheep. For motives that are still debated, Riddoch announced the Penola Fruit Colony in 1890. On the recommendation of a Scottish gardener called William Wilson, 464 hectares of terra rosa soil to the north of Penola were subdivided into four-hectare blocks and offered for sale at $50 per hectare, payable by instalments with interest at five per cent. Riddoch later added a further 330 hectares, making a total of 794 hectares, but they were not easy times. His original intention was to limit each landholder to a maximum of 16 hectares or four blocks; lack of takers forced him to relax that restriction, and in the end 26 "blockers" (as they came to be known) took parcels varying in size between four and 32 hectares. Yet no sooner had the Penola Fruit Colony come into being than Australia was convulsed by the great bank crash of 1893.

But Riddoch was not deterred: a marketing campaign which spread as far afield as London saw the colony quickly established. Riddoch himself planted 52 hectares of vines, chiefly shiraz and cabernet sauvignon, with small plantings of malbec and pinot noir. By 1899 the total district plantings, including both those of Riddoch and of the numerous blockers, amounted to 141 hectares, comprising shiraz (73 hectares), cabernet sauvignon (45 hectares), pinot noir (12 hectares) and malbec (11 hectares). The original 26 block-holders included a number of names still remembered: Jim Skinner, whose descendants run the Coonawarra store; Sharam, who sold to Penfolds in 1957; and Captain Stentiford, whose block passed to Eric Brand and whose ship is depicted on the Laira label.

In 1891 work started on the marvellous cellars which stand intact to this day—perpetuated on the exceptional woodcut-designed label introduced by Wynns when it bought Chateau Comaum (as it was then called) in 1951. The eastern wall, made of iron, has recently been completed in stone using identical techniques to the main, northern facade. In a few years the stone will weather, creepers will grow, and it will be indistinguishable from the front. The cellars were capacious because Riddoch had promised to buy all the blockers' grapes. They were designed to accommodate 337,500 litres, but in a few years they were holding far more than that. Catton Grasby, *Garden and Field*, gives this contemporary view of the winery:

> The cellars are an imposing structure, situated on a slight rise near the township, and comprise a basement and main floor, with a loft floor above. The climate is so good that the nights are always cool, so that the difficulties met with in other places, owing to the rise in temperature, do not arise here. In addition, the water supply is so good and cool, that the operation of fermenting wine is a comparatively simple one.
>
> The crusher is driven by a portable steam-engine. The must is run into the fermenting tanks by means of chutes. The fermenting tanks are of masonry, cemented, and cooling coils are available if necessary. Adjoining the fermenting room are the laboratory and two offices. The cellars contain a few oak casks of 1000 gallons [4550 litres] capacity but the standard size is 500 gallons [2275 litres], and the fittings leave nothing to be desired; indeed, the equipment is one of the best in South Australia.

The *Garden and Field* of November 1896 reported that the vintages of 1895 and 1896 had shown the area was capable of producing dry red wine of superior quality. The attraction of the region and of Riddoch's venture was such that in June 1898 Riddoch was able to employ Ewen Ferguson McBain as his winemaker. McBain was a Roseworthy gold medallist and was assistant South Australian government viticulturalist when he was appointed. Bill Redman has paid eloquent tribute to the influence of McBain. In a recorded conversation with Jack Neilson (then aged 90) Bill Redman (a youngster at 82) said:

> Well, all the experience I got in winemaking was under a man called McBain. He was a Roseworthy College student and a very thorough man, and he'd drill it into the heads of the lads that the best way wine could be made would be to keep everything thoroughly clean and not let any taints or anything get into the wine. This was instilled into me for about five, six or seven years. From there on up gave me an insight on the best way to go about making a red wine.

As the vines came progressively into production, so the size of the vintage increased. 1897 yielded 72,000 litres; 1898, 96,000 litres; 1899, 81,000 litres; 1900 (frost devastated), 33,000 litres; 1901, 238,000 litres; and climbing to 364,000 litres in 1903. From

here on until 1909 the vintage always exceeded 300,000 litres. In the middle of this expansion John Riddoch died, but his family showed no inclination to carry on Riddoch's great scheme. One of his daughters—Mary—married Robert Rymill at Yallum and in 1903 they moved to Old Penola Station. The other children moved out of the district (were its winters too cold?) and three trustees took over management of the estate. Massive dismemberment followed. In 1905 over 688 hectares were sold to the government for closer settlement, and in May of the following year 80 applicants secured areas ranging from 10 to 350 hectares. Only the homestead and the surrounding 910 hectares were left unsold; the house and most of the land was purchased in August 1914 by William Clifford, whose family continues to own and live in Yallum Park.

In the meantime vast quantities of unsold wine continued to accumulate. With the cellars filled well beyond their capacity, the estate was soon forced to store casks in the vast Katnook shearing sheds—a forerunner of today, when those same sheds once again store wine fermented in the stainless-steel tanks that now tower alongside them. The executors, faced with an impossible dilemma, decided to install a pot-still, and tens of thousands of gallons of fine, aged Coonawarra claret were turned into brandy. The quality of the brandy caught the eye of Chateau Tanunda, who bought the winery and vineyards towards the end of the First World War and expanded the plantings. But it soon learnt that the low alcohol content of the wine made distillation disconcertingly uneconomic. Within two years it had sold out to the Adelaide distillers Milne & Company, who ran the winery and vineyards making nothing but brandy until 1946.

In the meantime the Redman family had arrived in Coonawarra. Fourteen-year-old William Leonard Redman, accompanied by his 16-year-old brother Dick, had arrived a few months before Riddoch died, seeking work as grape-pickers. Dick left at the end of that season, but William Redman stayed on. He worked at the winery for six years; by the time he was 19, in 1907, he had become head cellarman. He returned to the family farm at Pinnaroo later that year, but returned to the district in 1908 with his family, never to leave again.

The following year the family purchased a 16-hectare block from Riddoch's executors which had proved difficult to sell, acquiring it on exceptionally advantageous terms. Almost half the total cost was recouped out of the first year's grape sales. But Redman was well aware that he could not be certain of selling his grapes every year, particularly at the price he received in 1909. However, he also realised that if he made his own wine, there was no guarantee that the Riddoch executors would take this either. He had watched as first the main cellar and then Katnook had overflowed with wine, and as blockers such as Stoney and Darwent had installed concrete tanks on their own properties. Alexander and Hoffman had gone one step further: they had begun to make wine on their own account. But they had no greater success than Riddoch in finding buyers. Eventually their wine was sold back to the main cellars for one shilling per gallon (4.5 litres) for distillation. (The one shilling was the standard price upon which the price for the grapes was determined. If the winery was able to obtain more, the excess was to be shared between it and the blockers.)

So Redman determined first to find his market, and if he were successful in doing that, he would make his own wine. He journeyed north to Adelaide and approached Douglas Tolley of Tolley Scott and Tolley at Hope Valley. Tolley said he would give Redman a trial vintage: Tolley would supply the hogsheads and take the wine at a guaranteed price of one shilling per gallon.

The first vintage was made without any wine-making equipment in the conventional sense. The grapes were pressed in an old cheese-press, and fermented in the hogsheads in which the wine was to be ultimately matured. (One end of the hogshead was removed for the vintage, and the cask was left standing upright.) From these humble beginnings sprang a tradition of red-winemaking which was to keep Coonawarra on the viticultural map. For a brief period of time in the 1930s the Redmans were joined by H. B. H. Richardson, who established what was known as Coonawarra Winery, and who made several vintages.

Although Redman had been successful in selling his wine first to Tolleys and thereafter to Colonel Fulton of Woodley Wines, Richardson was unable to find a market for his wine, and winemaking operations ceased. Much of the winemaking equipment was purchased by Chateau Comaum in 1946 when it acquired the Riddoch Winery from Milne's. The winery building stood until 1956 when Richardson's sons pulled it down; the concrete fermentation tanks remained on the land until the mid-1960s when the land was acquired by Lindemans. The tanks were then bulldozed into a nearby quarry, and no mark of the winery remains today.

At the end of 1945 it became clear that Milne & Company wished to dispose of its Coonawarra interests. J. L. Williams, a long-time lecturer in viticulture at Roseworthy College, wrote to Samuel Wynn on Christmas Eve 1945 proposing a 50-50 joint venture for the acquisition of the Milne interests. He concluded his proposal by observing that Coonawarra was "extremely good for the production of grapes for dry-winemaking, in fact I consider it is destined to become Australia's premier dry-wine area . . . Milne's vineyards and distillery have been shockingly managed but could be made into an excellent proposition with proper attention".

Wynns decided not to go ahead, concentrating instead on the development of its Modbury Estate vineyard. Woodley Wines was very much more interested; it had of course purchased all of Redman's production for more than 20 years, and needed no persuasion about the potential of the district. Tony Nelson, having acquired control of Woodley, formed Chateau Comaum and purchased the winery, the 58 hectares of vineyard and eight hectares of unplanted land for the sum of $18,000.

Bill and his son Owen Redman had already agreed that they would run the winery for Nelson and make the wine. The first task confronting the Redmans was to restore the winery into a condition adequate for making table wine. Williams had not exaggerated when he said that it had been shockingly managed — the concrete tanks were coated with thick layers of acetic acid crystals, which meant that the wine was thoroughly acetified by the end of fermentation. While this would not have helped the quality of the spirit ultimately distilled, it was not as critical for Wynns as it would have been for Woodley.

The winery restored, the Redmans divided their attentions between their own winery and that of Chateau Comaum. They continued to sell most of the production from their own winery to Nelson, and for a few years the arrangement worked well enough. Strains then began to emerge, and the Redmans announced they were not prepared to continue running the Riddoch Winery for Chateau Comaum. On the other hand they were still prepared to make the wine for Chateau Comaum at their own winery, and at one stage Tony Nelson sought to dispose of the old Riddoch Cellars to the Woods and Forest Department of South Australia. When this and other proposals came to nothing, Nelson put the property on the market for sale.

In 1951 an advertisement appeared in the *Australian Brewing and Wine* journal, and this time Wynns took a more careful look. David Wynn commissioned a report from J. L. Williams (who had in the meantime joined Wynns), and from winemakers

Ken Ward and Ian Hickinbotham. In a coldly realistic report, the committee argued that the property should be valued not as a vineyard, but as an agricultural property suited to wool and dairying. The authors observed:

> In view of the difficulties of management and labour associated with vine growing in the area, together with the hazards of frost and downy mildew, the property cannot be considered as suitable for viticulture. The justification for this argument lies in the fact that the property has had three or four owners. They have all (except the present owners) contributed something to the way of improvements not derived from the property itself, and none has managed to survive the battle against adverse conditions.

David Wynn was not deterred: on 19 July 1951 Tony Nelson accepted S. Wynn & Company's offer of £22,000 on a walk-in, walk-out basis.

The red-wine boom was still more than a decade away, and while Ronald Haselgrove brought Mildara into the district in 1955, followed by Penfolds in 1960, and eventually Lindemans in 1965, the early years were not easy for Wynns. Gradually, however, the exceptional quality of the Wynns Coonawarra Estate wines became known, and history relates that the Coonawarra vineyards and winery are now the most important part of the massive Wynn winemaking operations.

In 1952 Redman commenced to sell his wine direct to the companies who had hitherto bought it in bulk from Woodley's. The Redmans were soon supplying seven companies (including Thomas Hardy, Yalumba, Reynella, Leo Buring and Woodley) out of a total annual production of around 27,000 litres. This alone created demand pressures, which were soon exacerbated by a decision by the Redmans to bottle and release part of their production under their own label. Resort to a French dictionary came up with the loose translation of Redman: Rouge Homme (instead of Homme de Rouge). In 1954 the first vintage (1953) was released at 42 shillings a dozen. The 550 cases sold out within six months. By 1965, when Lindeman took over, 4000 cases were released annually under the Rouge Homme label.

In 1956 Redman ceased selling wine to Woodley, and one of the great chapters of Australian wine history came to a close. Anyone who has been lucky enough to taste the Woodley Treasure Chest Series covering the vintages 1949 to 1956, or even more the Woodley wines made by Redman between 1930 and 1949, has been greatly privileged. The Redman family finally elected to sell Rouge Homme to Lindemans in 1965 but, with Coonawarra Machinery

Company, history has to a large degree repeated itself. Coonawarra Machinery has in the 1970s and 1980s taken over the role of supplier to the wine industry at large which the Redman family filled in the 1950s. Those who purchase range from the biggest to the smallest; some who disclose their purchasing activities, and others who do not. Some release Coonawarra wines unblended, others use them as a disclosed component in blends, and yet others quietly use five to 20 per cent as an unmentioned blend component.

The largest purchaser is Orlando, who have made extensive and regular releases of Coonawarra rhine riesling and Coonawarra cabernet since the late 1970s. Orlando has made no bones about the fact that it sees Coonawarra as a better source of quality table wine than the Barossa Valley. Orlando's technology is second to none in the country, and predictably excellent wines have resulted. Middle-sized companies such as Mitchelton and Norman's have bought significant quantities of wine for release as Coonawarra varietals; while yet further down the scale boutique wineries such as Ashbourne and Brokenwood have been regular purchasers.

Coonawarra took a surprisingly long time to establish itself as a producer of high-quality white wine—the recognition came only in the 1980s. As the table on page 422 shows, rhine riesling is one of the two most important grape varieties, and by far the most important white variety. It is at once a strength and a weakness of Coonawarra that under the viticultural conditions which normally prevail, and with big-company economies of scale, rhine riesling can be produced and bottled for a cost of around $15 a dozen, and profitably marketed at $2.99 a bottle. Thus the standard rhine rieslings of Lindemans, Wynns, Mildara and Penfolds are uncompromisingly commercial wines.

The smaller producers have tended to produce the more exciting wines in recent years, none more so than the Petaluma botrytis wines and the 1983 Hungerford Hill Collection Rhine Riesling. These wines, of course, introduce the botrytis issue which hangs over Coonawarra. Since 1980 it has appeared in ever-increasing strength, and went close to destroying the 1983 red-wine vintage for some growers and makers. Even with rhine riesling, the grape with which botrytis is traditionally associated, there is an element of controversy. While it is almost invariably welcome in late-harvested grapes, its intrusion into grapes destined for dry rhine riesling causes much heartburn. It has led to the development of an entirely new style of rhine riesling in Australia,

GRAPE-PICKING, 1898

which at its best is rich and full of flavour, and at its worst hard and phenolic. The fruit flavours take on tropical overtones and, provided the hardness is avoided, I very much like the style, although equally I would not wish to see all rhine rieslings assume this character.

The market for luscious botrytised white wines is smaller than the newly found capacity to produce them. This, as much as anything else, holds back the production of late-harvest rhine rieslings in Coonawarra. Without question the greatest wines of this style to be made in the district have been those of Petaluma and Mitchelton, although James Haselgrove has also made a number of marvellously luscious and intense late-harvest rieslings.

No doubt largely due to the very restrictive policies of the South Australia Phylloxera Board, and to the consequent lack of adequate nursery stocks, chardonnay has taken an inordinately long time to come to Coonawarra, and any district style has been long in emerging. The wines range from the fairly light-bodied and delicate wines of Mildara through to the much richer and heavily oaked wines of Wynns. Most of the wines have indeed followed the Wynns pattern, particularly the 1983 Rouge Homme Chardonnay and the Katnook chardonnays. All of these wines have developed remarkably rapidly; it seems that even in the cool Coonawarra climate, the propensity of Australian chardonnay to develop quickly will manifest itself.

The relatively small quantities of sauvignon blanc so far made have been full of promise, with Katnook and Mildara by far the most prominent. Here again, some quite luscious flavour and structure have been achieved, demonstrating that while Coonawarra is cool, it is most certainly not excessively so.

For all the success of the whites, Coonawarra remains a red-wine region. But here the picture becomes even more confused. Cabernet sauvignon and shiraz make up just on 50 per cent of the total plantings (both red and white); and until 1976 (or thereabouts) it was a relatively easy matter to describe the flavour and style of a Coonawarra red. Since that time it has become extremely difficult as an entirely new series of flavours has manifested itself. These flavours have no parallels elsewhere in the wine world, and have been the subject of much debate. I believe the only sensible explanation lies with the results of mechanical pruning. Apart from increasing yield, mechanical pruning leads to very uneven flowering and hence ripening. When the major portion of the crop is at optimum ripeness, a certain percentage of the bunches will be grossly overripe

and virtually raisined, while a similar percentage will be green and unripe. Since mechanical harvesting is now almost universal practice in the district, there is no capacity to exclude the underripe and overripe bunches. The end result is very complex flavours, running the full gamut from green herbaceousness through to stewed-plum/mulberry flavours. To add insult to injury many of these new-generation reds have an almost gamy meat aroma and flavour.

At first blush the flavour can be very attractive. I certainly found it so when I first encountered it; I no longer do so, however. The character is not so marked when one of these wines is tasted on its own, nor for that matter in a comparative line-up of Coonawarra reds—simply because the overwhelming majority display the character. It stands out in stark relief in show tastings and other large line-ups. At least in shows, judges are becoming increasingly split in their acceptance or rejection of the flavour. The South Australian judges tend to accept it, and indeed rate the wines highly; those from other States are far less enthusiastic. This confusion does not help the public, but is understandable given the recent emergence of the character.

At this juncture it is far from certain where it will all end; the cost economies of mechanical pruning and mechanical harvesting are such that it is very difficult to see any of the medium to large companies even contemplating a reversion of hand-pruning or picking. But it may be that an element of bunch selection will have to enter the process at some stage. This could presumably be achieved by a hand crew removing the underripe and overripe bunches before picking. It would represent a significant additional cost, but it may be the only way to restore equilibrium.

Coonawarra's strength, applicable equally to white and red wines, lies in the abundant yields, with shiraz producing 15 tonnes per hectare on average, cabernet sauvignon 10.25 tonnes per hectare and rhine riesling 12.75 tonnes per hectare overall. These yields are achieved through the remarkable soil structure, with its thin layer of terra rosa overlying a thick limestone belt from which the terra rosa itself springs. Contrary to public belief, it is not a volcanic soil, but simply a weathered limestone, stained red by organic and mineral matter. The limestone overlies a watertable which the roots of the vines ultimately tap—the final blessing.

The climate, too, has long been recognised as eminently favourable, with a centigrade heat-degree day summation of 1259, and a mean January temperature of 19.4°C. Rainfall in the critical

October to March period is not high, and modern viticultural thought suggests that irrigation is essential to prevent vine stress during the intermittent periods of heat which are a pattern of most growing seasons. In years such as 1980 and 1984 irrigation may not have been necessary; in years such as 1981 it most certainly was. The major hazards come through spring frosts and—increasingly—botrytis. It was thought that modern viticultural practice had largely eliminated the danger of frost until the 1983 vintage proved otherwise. Nonetheless, the greater threat is posed by botrytis, particularly with the propensity that moulds have to build up resistance to the sprays used to combat them.

For all these difficulties Coonawarra remains the most important single region in Australia for the production of high-quality table wine, and there is little prospect of that position being challenged. The only pretender is Padathaway, but it is part of the family in any event.

BOWEN ESTATE
PENOLA–NARACOORTE ROAD, COONAWARRA

Owner-winemaker Doug Bowen has established Bowen Estate as the best (and most consistent) small red-wine producer in Coonawarra since his first vintage in 1975. In the ensuing decade he has taken up where Owen Redman and Eric Brand left off, producing wines of great elegance and style.

Bowen came to Coonawarra for the best possible reasons. As part of his studies at Roseworthy he prepared a report on Coonawarra from the viticultural point of view. He was so impressed with what he saw and learnt that he resolved to set up a vineyard and winery there at the earliest possible date. After graduating from Roseworthy at the end of 1971, he worked first at Chateau Reynella and thereafter at Lindemans' Coonawarra Winery for a number of years while his vineyard came into bearing.

The first vintage was 1975, made in a modest winery constructed from Mount Gambier stone. These early wines were produced from young vines, but won immediate recognition in the show ring. The 1975 Shiraz Cabernet won a bronze medal in Adelaide that year; the 1975 Claret won a gold medal at Melbourne in 1976 in the one-year-old Burgundy Class (Coonawarra reds have a habit of doing that), and a silver medal at Adelaide in the same year. The 1976 Claret also won a gold medal at Melbourne, and by 1977 Doug Bowen was winning trophies—the 1977 Cabernet Sauvignon was his first

of several trophy-winners.

Both vineyard and winery have been extended substantially and upgraded over the past few years. No doubt much to the despair of his wife Joy, Doug Bowen completed an imposing new winery in time for the 1982 vintage (the Bowens' house nearby remains unextended, in best winemaker's tradition). It appears to be modelled on the Penola Hotel; as the stone surface weathers it will become one of the more attractive landmarks of the Coonawarra plain. Over the past few years Doug Bowen has planted virtually all of the 13 hectares suitable for grapes (his property is 16.2 hectares in all). The vineyard comprises shiraz (five hectares), cabernet sauvignon (4.85 hectares), merlot (two hectares), rhine riesling (0.8 hectare) and chardonnay (0.4 hectare).

He makes significant quantities of rhine riesling each year with grapes bought in from other growers. The rhine riesling is a flavoursome style which will repay several years' cellaring. Bowen himself upholds that proposition by usually holding the wine back for several years before releasing it. Thus the 1982 Rhine Riesling was still the current release well into 1984. It showed even greater richness than the wines that had preceded it, with an obvious botrytis influence heightening the propensity all the Bowen Estate rhine rieslings have to fullness of flavour.

It is his estate-grown reds that have really excelled, however. While he believes in late picking to allow the full development of flavour, he adjusts the acid and the pH, and rigorously controls his fermentation temperatures. He also uses new small oak as an important part of maturation. The resultant wines are full-flavoured yet supple, and with marked cabernet herbaceous varietal character. The fruit structure epitomises the benefits of Coonawarra's cool climate, and is for me strongly reminiscent of the wines of Bordeaux. I look forward to the cabernet merlot blends of future years with keen interest.

The cabernets made between 1977 and 1980 inclusive were remarkably even, both in terms of quality and style. Whether the 1979 or the 1980 will ultimately be the greater wine, I do not know. Both show classic cool-climate cabernet aroma and flavour, with the 1980 keeping very much to the Bowen style and avoiding the tendency to jamminess which some of the wines of that vintage show. I also greatly admire the 1978 Cabernet Sauvignon, a wine of restrained power. 1981 proved that in the final analysis the winemaker is only as good as the fruit he or she gets from the vineyard. This is an immense wine, big, old-fashioned and completely at odds with the style which Bowen had developed up until that time. Very much a reflection of the general vintage conditions, it positively demands cellaring to allow the rich, deep and ever so slightly tarry flavours to come back into balance.

Over the years Bowen Estate has also released some excellent Coonawarra shiraz. The 1980 was, predictably enough, the most successful, with ripe fruit sensitively balanced by oak. The older vintages of Bowen wines (such as the 1975 Claret) put the cellaring potential of all his reds beyond question.

BRAND'S LAIRA
PENOLA–NARACOORTE ROAD, COONAWARRA

Eric Brand came to Coonawarra in 1950 when he married Nancy Redman, Owen's sister. At that stage a baker, he purchased a 24-hectare block from the Redman family which originally had been taken up by a retired sea captain called Stentiford. (Stentiford had commanded the sailing vessel *Laira*.) For the next 16 years Brand was but one of numerous blockers anonymously supplying grapes for wine that could have ended up under a dozen or so different labels. Only a little over two hectares of the block were planted to grapes; the major part was an orchard.

In the winter of 1965 Owen Redman approached Brand and suggested that instead of selling his grapes to Lindemans, he should start a small winemaking operation to supply Thomas Hardy with the shiraz that company had previously purchased from Redman. Brand agreed. A crusher was procured by Hardy's, a couple of cement tanks were installed, and Brand duly made the wine. (When I say "made the wine", Brand did so under the constant supervision of Owen Redman—Brand himself had no previous winemaking experience.) The 1966, 1967 and 1968 vintages of both Redman and Brand were made at the small Laira Winery. Both labels offered only a shiraz-based wine, and there have been suggestions (disputed by Eric Brand) that the 1966 Laira was identical to the 1966 Redman Redbank.

In 1969 Redman's own winery was opened: he sold his old casks to Eric Brand. Brand supplemented these with small new oak of his own, and also introduced a shiraz cabernet in that year. Starting in 1966, Eric had instituted a planting programme, and first made a cabernet malbec in 1974.

Eric Brand switched to stainless-steel fermenters in the early 1970s and employed cooling for the fermentations. An inexhaustible supply of very cold bore water runs in a film down the outside of the tanks, providing a virtually cost-free but very effective form of cooling. Whether it was due to this alone or whether it was a combination of factors, I do not know, but for a majority of vintages in the first half of the 1970s I thought that Brand's reds were the best to come out of Coonawarra. Certainly they had more colour and deeper fruit flavour than any of their competitors. To be sure, there were some faulty wines here and there, with volatility occasionally reaching quite unacceptable levels. And the mercaptan which appeared in the 1978 and 1979 wines carried over into some of those from 1980. It was a problem that Brand had never encountered before, and it slipped through under his guard.

Since 1981 the wines of Laira have returned to their form of old. It is reasonable to assume that this is due in part of the arrival of son Bill Brand in the winery following his graduation from Roseworthy. Bill and his brother Jim Brand are now primarily responsible for running the vineyard and winery. The vineyard is now planted to shiraz (16 hectares), cabernet sauvignon (eight hectares), malbec (one hectare), grenache (one hectare) and less than one hectare each of pinot noir and merlot; the merlot is the most recent planting.

The most senior of the Laira wines is the shiraz; senior in the sense that it has been produced longer than any of the other Laira wines, and in greater quantity. Anyone who has the 1966 or 1968 wines in their cellar will readily understand just why this variety was able to carry the reputation of Coonawarra for more than 50 years, and why the wines of Eric Brand have a favoured spot in my heart (and in my cellar). It is true that some of the intervening years were less than satisfactory; as I have said, some of the wines from the early 1970s suffered from an acute attack of volatility and those of 1978 to 1980 were all grossly flawed by mercaptan. Even the 1981 Shiraz has just the faintest touch, but the rich, deep and ripe fruit flavours more than compensate. A special "one-off" release from that year was a separate parcel made from the oldest vines on the property and released under the Original Vineyard Shiraz label. The 1982 Shiraz confirmed that the line had returned to its best form, with rich, deep fruit with hints of dark chocolate and well-integrated oak. It puts me in mind of the 1976 Shiraz, a marvellously complex wine, and the best made in the intervening years.

When Eric Brand commenced winemaking he had just a few hectares of shiraz to grow from. Thus it was not until 1971, when the first of the cabernet plantings came into production, that he was able to make and subsequently release a cabernet sauvignon. The 1971, 1972 and 1973 vintages added strength to the claim Eric Brand then had to be making the best wines in Coonawarra. Volatility struck in the 1974 vintage; 1975 was an adequate wine which has developed some camphor characters in the bottle; while the 1976, like the shiraz of that year, was one of the great vintages. 1977 produced a big, solid wine, perhaps a little one-dimensional but with strong berry fruit on both bouquet and palate. 1978 was clean enough but was rather light and soft, an ominous lead into the mercaptan-induced dip between 1979 and 1981. The line returned to its best in 1982 with a typical Laira wine: big, strong berry-fruit characters, full of flavour and even with some wood and oak tannins. Like the best Laira cabernet sauvignons from the earlier years, it demands cellaring.

Winemaking philosophies and the expectations of wine judges and drinkers have changed markedly in the 15 years since Eric Brand first started making cabernet sauvignon. On the evidence of the 1982 wine, I think that the Brand family has continued to make the wine in much the same way. The net result is that for some the wines may seem a little old-fashioned. I am not at all sure that this is necessarily a bad thing. Firstly, it certainly means that the wines require lengthy cellaring, and there are all too few of these; secondly, subject to the vagaries of vintage and to the occasional lapse in the winery, it will produce a consistent style over a long period of time, which makes for fascinating comparisons as the wines slowly evolve.

Almost as if he were looking forward to the day when the cabernet might be criticised for being a trifle simple and straightforward, Brand planted first malbec and more recently merlot. The cabernet malbec blend has made its appearance intermittently since 1974: unhappily, that wine was little short of a disaster, with volatility destroying the malbec component. The 1976 proved yet again what an outstanding vintage this was for Laira, producing by far the best wine in the series. In 1981 the quality of the fruit was such that Laira released a straight malbec. Rich, plummy and spicy, and with abundant new oak aroma and flavour, it was an outstanding wine which will only improve over the next five years. It may well be that in future vintages the cabernet sauvignon will be a cabernet-dominant blend with a little merlot and malbec, leaving enough malbec for a straight varietal release in the years which justify it.

Since 1979–80 Brand has made experimental quantities of pinot noir from the first few grapes harvested. Those early experiments gave no cause for optimism as the wines were excessively light in colour, aroma and body. He persevered, and in 1982 made one of the relatively few pinot noirs so far to be commercially produced in Coonawarra. I thought the oak was a little too obvious, a common-enough fault with the usually light-bodied Australian pinots, but underneath that oak there was clearly defined pinot noir character.

Finally, Laira's grenache is used to make a non-vintage rosé, which is usually good and sometimes outstanding.

CHATEAU REYNELLA
PENOLA-NARACOORTE ROAD, COONAWARRA

Reynella has never had a physical presence in Coonawarra, although at one time it was a sister company under common ownership with Hungerford Hill. It is history now that Rothmans did not exercise the option it had to acquire the Hungerford Hill Vineyards for Reynella, and when in 1982 Thomas Hardy & Sons acquired Reynella, the dowry was simply a grape-purchase contract which ran until 1986. Despite all of this the Reynella involvement in Coonawarra has been a very important one, and Thomas Hardy has every hope and expectation that it will continue to be so in the future.

Each year Chateau Reynella acquires around 500 to 600 tonnes of Coonawarra grapes, the actual quantity depending on the total amount produced by the old Hungerford Hill vineyards, which have now passed into the control of the Yunghanns/Rentiers Pty Limited group. In a typical year the purchases would amount to 200 tonnes of cabernet sauvignon, 200 tonnes of rhine riesling and 100 tonnes of shiraz.

These wines have been made at Chateau Reynella for a decade, most under the control of the irrepressible Geoff Merrill, Reynella's chief winemaker. It is a tribute to the power and quality of Coonawarra in general, and the Hungerford Hill Vineyards in particular that the Reynella and Hungerford Hill Rhine Rieslings have been close in terms of style and quality. Given that one line has been made in the Southern Vales of South Australia, and the other in the Hunter Valley, both by winemakers who no doubt have had quite different philosophies and winemaking techniques, the similarities must stem from the base fruit. I emphasise this only because of the publicity which the Hungerford Hill

Rhine Riesling has attracted in recent years. The Chateau Reynella wines suffered greatly in the latter years of Rothmans ownership, and inevitably there was a period of readjustment after the Thomas Hardy take-over — readjustment in terms of marketing and future direction. The 1977, 1978, 1979, 1981, 1982 and 1984 vintages have all, in their different ways, been quite outstanding.

I have to admit to a particular admiration for the older trio, which have developed magnificently. Of the younger three the 1981 holds out the greatest promise for cellaring potential, while the 1984 is an immaculately made wine. The fairly strong botrytis influence in the 1982 vintage makes me think that discretion is the better part of valour, and that the wine should be drunk rather than cellared.

The spatlese or late-harvest rhine rieslings of Reynella have always been made in the lighter, more elegant mould. The younger botrytis-affected styles suffer in comparison to other wines of similar age because of that lightness and elegance, when viewed in comparative line-ups. When separately approached or assessed, they have marvellous life and flavour. Among the older wines the 1976 amd 1978 vintages were — and are — quite magnificent.

Reynella's Coonawarra Cabernet Sauvignons have for many years been unsung heroes, selling either under their own label at ludicrously low prices or under merchant labels (Crittenden and others) at similar — sometimes higher — prices. Some of the attention they so richly deserve came in 1981 when the show cabernet sauvignon outpointed the eventual winner of the Jimmy Watson Trophy (Lindemans' St George Cabernet Sauvignon) when they confronted each other in their particular class. Only when the other judges (and the chairman) were brought in, and the other wines lined up, did the Lindeman wine edge out that of Reynella. Reynella "did a Mildara" with its 1980 Cabernet Sauvignon and made two releases — one of the show wine and the other of the standard blend. However, it did not fall into the trap of Mildara by confusing the labels.

All of the Chateau Reynella Cabernet Sauvignons have been made in the same mould. Geoff Merrill is an uncompromising supporter of early picking, and a dedicated seeker of elegance. The Chateau Reynella Cabernet Sauvignon wines are accordingly invariably crisp, delicate and with pungent grassy, herbaceous fruit. Some of Australia's most respected red-wine-makers are strongly opposed to this style of wine and to the Merrill philosophy. It is no secret that Geoff Merrill and Brian Croser have diametrically opposed views on this aspect of winemaking. The detached

observer finds it difficult to come down conclusively on one side or the other. Both have a great deal to offer the consumer, and which style of wine is ultimately chosen is in no small part a question of personal choice. Few judges, however, could quarrel with the overall quality of the Chateau Reynella Coonawarra Cabernets between 1979 and 1981. As I say, whether you like the ultra-grassy, dusty austerity of the wines is a very personal decision.

HOLLICK'S NEILSON ESTATE
RACECOURSE ROAD, COONAWARRA

The Hollick Neilson Estate label may be a new one for Coonawarra, but the Hollick name is not. Ian Hollick is a nephew of Bob Hollick, Mildara's long-serving vineyard director, and Ian was manager of the Mildara Coonawarra Vineyards and winery from 1979 until February 1983, when he left to commence his own business.

The name was chosen to commemorate the birth on the property of the poet John Shaw Neilson in 1872; prior to the adoption of the new name the vineyard had been known as Berrima Vineyards, having been established by Ian Hollick and his wife Wendy in the 1970s.

It is planted to cabernet sauvignon (five hectares), rhine riesling and chardonnay (1.6 hectares each), pinot noir (0.8 hectare) and merlot and cabernet franc (0.5 hectare). The original plantings were of the cabernet and rhine riesling, followed by the chardonnay, and more recently, merlot, cabernet franc and pinot noir. These most recent plantings have been planted on a closer spacing than has been traditional in Coonawarra, with the aim of controlling vine vigour and hopefully improving fruit quality. Yields are around the average for the district, at 11 tonnes per hectare for cabernet sauvignon and 10 tonnes per hectare for chardonnay and rhine riesling. The soil, too, is the classic terra rosa clay loam over a limestone base. Only the cabernet sauvignon is mechanically pruned, while the other varieties are pruned by hand.

The 1982, 1983 and 1984 vintages were all made at other wineries in the district; Ian Hollick's own winery was completed in time for the 1985 vintage, and all future winemaking will be carried out on the estate. The vineyard got off to a flying start with a quite magnificent 1982 Cabernet Sauvignon. Universally praised for its elegance and subtle integration of fruit and oak, it is one of the best of the very good cabernet sauvignons of 1982 to come from the district. The 1984 Rhine Riesling is a solidly flavoured wine, with the mid-palate fruit to carry it in bottle for up to five years. Future releases will also offer a chardonnay, with the merlot and cabernet franc being used in a bordeaux blend.

HUNGERFORD HILL
PENOLA–NARACOORTE ROAD, PENOLA

Following the 1983 take-over of Hungerford Hill, its presence in Coonawarra has altered radically. The previous Hungerford Hill Vineyards are now part of the Yunghanns Coonawarra Machinery group interests, and Hungerford Hill simply has a five-year grape-purchase contract which commenced in 1984. In that year Hungerford Hill moved to establish its long-term connections with the area by purchasing land on the northern outskirts of Penola, which it will commence to plant in 1985. I trace the detail of these developments at page 31. Time alone will show whether this new vineyard, which manager Doug Balnaves believes is potentially even better than the original vineyard, will lead to any change in fruit style. For the time being the continuation of the remarkably high quality of the Hungerford Hill Coonawarra wines can be confidently expected.

The 1983 Coonawarra Collection Rhine Riesling has now written itself into Australian show history, winning 11 gold medals and numerous trophies in an 18-month show career from the middle of 1983 to the end of 1984. This wine is probably the finest example of the handling of botrytised rhine riesling to make a dry wine. As other winemakers have discovered, this is an extremely difficult task: while the botrytis intensifies flavour, it also leads to unwanted hardness, oiliness and strange and unwanted aromas in dry rhine rieslings. Winemaker Ralph Fowler skirted around these difficulties to make a marvellously fragrant yet elegant and balanced wine. While this success came as a surprise to some, it most certainly did not surprise me. For a long time I have regarded the Hungerford Hill Coonawarra Collection Rhine Riesling range as undiscovered treasures. Right from the first vintage in 1976 the line was outstanding; only the 1979 dipped a little, with the 1977, 1980, 1981 and 1982 being outstanding. The 1981 and 1982 vintages served notice that Fowler had the capacity to harness botrytis, although they were admittedly rather heavier than the marvellous 1983 wine.

Hungerford Hill Coonawarra Collection Spatlese Rhine Rieslings of 1976 to 1982 were every bit as impressive. Outstanding among this line were the 1976, 1977, 1978, 1981 and 1982 vintages. The earlier wines showed little or no botrytis influence, but nonetheless have aged quite magnificently, showing that these wines benefit from at least five years' bottle-aging if one is looking for complexity. If the object is simple intensity of luscious fruit, then they may by all means be drunk within one or two years of vintage.

In the extreme botrytis conditions of 1983 Hungerford Hill also made an unusual late-harvest gewurtztraminer; one of the characteristics of botrytis is to obscure varietal aroma and flavour, and this is precisely what happened with the gewurtztraminer of that year. Magnificently sweet and luscious, it is nonetheless very difficult to tell what the variety was, and appears almost muscat-like. Earlier vintages of traminer, some made with a little residual sugar, have not been particularly successful. The 1979 vintage was the best of those earlier years. A few chardonnays have come out of the Hungerford Hill Coonawarra Collection label, and the 1982 was the most successful.

After an inauspicious start in 1975 the Hungerford Hill Coonawarra Collection Cabernet Sauvignon range sprang to life in 1978. In that year, and in every subsequent vintage to 1982, outstanding cabernets have been made. If 1979 suffered a little, it was only in comparison to the quality of the vintages which succeeded it (as well as the 1978). A hallmark of these wines is the clearly defined, no-nonsense varietal cabernet flavour and aroma. There is much less of the stewed-plum character which I have discussed in length elsewhere, and which is of such concern in Coonawarra these days.

Finally, the Coonawarra Collection Shiraz range has produced some excellent wines. The 1982 vintage was a disappointing exception, nowhere near the class of the marvellously spicy 1981 Coonawarra Collection Shiraz.

All of these wines are crushed at Katnook Estate and transported as chilled must or juice to Hungerford Hill's Pokolbin Winery, where they are made under the watchful eye of Ralph Fowler.

JAMES HASELGROVE WINES
PENOLA–NARACOORTE ROAD, COONAWARRA

James Haselgrove is the younger son of the late Ronald Haselgrove. Throughout much of the 1970s he was the Coonawarra-resident manager of Mildara; and like Ian Hollick, who succeeded him as manager,

Haselgrove decided to leave Mildara and establish his own vineyard and winery operation. This he did in 1980, joining forces with the Haig and Bagshaw families to form Haselgrove Haig Proprietary Limited. The company has a vineyard and winery in McLaren Vale, and also acquired the 12 hectares of vineyard which James Haselgrove had established in Coonawarra in the early 1970s. That Coonawarra vineyard is now planted to rhine riesling (four hectares), cabernet sauvignon (3.5 hectares), malbec and traminer (two hectares each) and shiraz and merlot (one hectare each).

Unlike Hollick, James Haselgrove Wines does not have a winery at Coonawarra, although it does have a cellar-door sales area. The Coonawarra reds are made at the Haselgrove Haig McLaren Vale Winery, while the white wines are made under contract, with help from various consultants. Overall the quality of the wines has been quite exemplary, and remarkably consistent. The 1980, 1981, 1982 and 1983 Coonawarra Rhine Rieslings all show great intensity of flavour, but also display consistent botrytis influence. While bestowing the wine with an extra degree of flavour and weight, botrytis also introduces a range of tropical-fruit aromas and flavours (and not infrequently a touch of hardness on the finish). Some wine judges find this incompatible with the basic flavour and style of what they consider to be a first-class dry rhine riesling. Whether one accepts the James Haselgrove rhine rieslings will depend very much on what is a personal decision regarding style.

Not surprisingly with botrytis evident in the dry rhine rieslings, some outstanding late-harvest spatlese and auslese rhine rieslings have come out under the Haselgrove label. These carry the intense flavours of the dry rhine rieslings one step further, and here there are few doubts about the beneficial influence of botrytis. In 1981, 1982 and 1983 James Haselgrove released an excellent traminer riesling. The 1981 was a well-made wine in which the traminer influence was fairly subdued; in 1982 the traminer was far more evident, though not aggressively so, in a finely balanced and stylish wine; in 1983 the traminer was even further to the fore, allied with marked botrytis influence, and resulting in a wine of quite remarkable flavour.

The James Haselgrove Coonawarra Cabernet Sauvignons have been equally consistent, both in style and in quality. All have been big wines by the normal standards of Coonawarra, with ripe-fruit characters and some tannin evident. The best of the wines has been the 1982 Cabernet Sauvignon, simply because it had that extra touch of style and finesse. Nonethe-less, it is a very deeply flavoured wine which will require at least five years to reach its peak — say, in 1990. Perhaps in recognition of this in 1983 James Haselgrove released a cabernet nouveau, an early-picked wine designed, no doubt, to get around the problems of botrytis which swept through the red-grape varieties that year. Out of the mainstream of the line, and no doubt a style enforced by the year, it was not a success.

KATNOOK ESTATE
OFF PENOLA–NARACOORTE ROAD, COONAWARRA

Katnook Estate is the publicly viewed tip of the iceberg of the immense landholdings and viticultural activities in Coonawarra of the Yunghanns family. The holding company for the group is Rentiers Pty Limited, with the principal viticultural operating arm being Coonawarra Machinery Company (known throughout the district as CMC) and the marketing arm being Katnook Estate.

The group has vineyards second only to those of Wynns in size. They comprise rhine riesling (220 hectares), cabernet sauvignon (122 hectares), shiraz (121 hectares), chardonnay (51 hectares), sauvignon blanc (20 hectares), traminer (nine hectares), merlot (five hectares), pinot noir (4.4 hectares), cabernet franc (3.9 hectares) and malbec (2.8 hectares). With yields varying from a low of 7.5 tonnes per hectare for malbec to a maximum of 14.8 tonnes per hectare of rhine riesling (and an overall average of 12.5 tonnes per hectare), Katnook/CMC are the major producers of grapes, must and wine for sale to the veritable forest of other wine companies who wish to purchase Coonawarra material. Eighty per cent of the crush of nearly 1000 tonnes is sold in the form of grapes, grape must or juice. Wine production for release under the Katnook Estate label accounts for only 15,000 cases, or 20 per cent of the total crush.

The winemaking operations take place in a large open-air winery adjacent to the old Katnook Estate woolshed. There is extensive refrigeration, but by harvest time Coonawarra is in any event a very cool place. What is more, the bulk of the output is moved out in the form of juice immediately it is clarified. The stainless-steel tanks are all either insulated or equipped with dimple-plate refrigeration.

Wayne Stehbens is in charge of the winery operation and Ray Stehbens is in charge of the vineyards. As neither is formally qualified, consultants have been used at various stages to assist Katnook — first Ken Ward (formerly of Wynns) and thereafter

Oenotec. With the ability Katnook has to pick and choose the very best of its grapes, it is not surprising that the Katnook wines have been of a consistently very high standard.

Since 1980 it has made one of the very best sauvignon blancs in Australia. These are invariably enormously complex wines, with far more mid-palate weight that one usually encounters in the variety. There is also a profusion of fruit and oak flavours harnessed in tandem with the undercurrent of unmistakable herbaceous/grassy sauvignon blanc character. It is a style very different from that of (say) the 1984 Taltarni Sauvignon Blanc, and makes that wine seem positively one-dimensional. I fancy that if American judges could get hold of the Katnook wine they would be ecstatic in their praise. Every release has, as I say, been excellent, but I fancy that the 1980 and 1983 have been the best of an outstanding group.

The Katnook chardonnays have showed similar fullness and complexity of flavour. Once again, they seem to me to be very Californian in their intensity and lusciousness. The fruit flavours run the full gamut from peaches to ripe figs, and the oak is invariably impeccably handled. These are the ultimate food wines, with the richness similar to that of Rosemount's best chardonnays, but with that little extra edge of cool-climate elegance.

Rhine riesling and gewurztraminer complete the Katnook white-wine releases; I have the feeling that traminer may not be a regular release. These are good wines, but lack the outstanding fruit weight and flavour of the chardonnay and sauvignon blanc.

The only red wine so far released is a cabernet sauvignon. It is a wine that has caused considerable controversy. Initially I was immensely attracted to the intense, perfumed-berry richness and complexity of the wines. Now I tend to the view that the Katnook cabernets are just too much of a good thing: that the fruit has been picked a little bit too ripe, and that there is simply too much ripe-berry flavour in the wine. Certainly they offer spectacular, no-compromise flavour and character; equally certainly, once the grapes are received in the winery they are handled with great care and given the best oak handling one could hope for. It will also be interesting to see how the wines develop with 10 or 15 years' bottle-age. I am far from certain whether they will live on the (presently) excess fruit and become absolutely magnificent, or whether they will simply become progressively portier and clumsier.

The Katnook wines are invariably at the top end of the price range. But when you pay your money you know precisely what you are getting.

KIDMAN
PENOLA–NARACOORTE ROAD, COONAWARRA

The Kidman family had been major landholders and graziers in the Coonawarra district for almost 100 years when grape fever swept Coonawarra in the 1960s. With ample land at their disposal, Ken Kidman and his son Sid determined to establish vineyards.

Meanwhile in Melbourne the wine writer and retailer Dan Murphy had been one of the first independent observers to appreciate the outstanding quality and potential of Coonawarra. In about 1970 he formed Terra Rosa Wines Limited and took up a major shareholding, with the Kidman family also having a large interest. This company runs the vineyards and markets the wines.

The plantings comprise cabernet sauvignon (23 hectares), shiraz (21 hectares) and rhine riesling (eight hectares). At no time has the entire production been made into wine. In most years between one-third and one-half of the crop is sold as grapes; while since the erection of the winery for the 1982 vintage a further substantial portion of the vintage has been contract-made for sale to other wine companies. The net result is that about 5000 cases of cabernet sauvignon and 3000 cases of rhine riesling are released each year under the Kidman label.

The first vintage made for the company was in 1974. From that year until 1982 various contract-winemakers produced the Kidman and Terra Rosa wines (the latter being a second label with a smaller price-tag), but not necessarily the same winery was used for white and red wine in each year. The flamboyant labels, with "Great Red Wine of Coonawarra" stridently emblazoned across their face, have not always matched the contents. Wine quality, particularly that of the red wines, has been variable and at times disappointing. The best of the recent red-wine releases was the 1980 Great Red Wine of Coonawarra, a blend of cabernet sauvignon and shiraz. It has marked vanillan American-oak aromas, a suspicion of mercaptan, and sweet-berry fruit on the mid-palate.

The 1982 and 1983 Rhine Rieslings were very much better than any of the earlier years. They present a remarkable contrast in style: the 1982 is firm, slightly smoky with traditional toasty, concentrated rhine riesling characters, more like a wine from a dry vintage in the Clare Valley than Coonawarra. The 1983 Rhine Riesling has intense tropical-fruit aromas, a generous palate with marked pineapple flavours and the evidence of botrytis right throughout the wine. I liked both wines.

KOPPAMURRA
NARACOORTE

Koppamurra, owned by Susan Andrews and John Greenshields, and situated at the northern end of the Coonawarra district, produced its first vintage in 1980. The 10.4-hectare vineyard is planted to cabernet sauvignon (four hectares), merlot (one hectare), cabernet franc and pinot meunière (0.3 hectare each) and rhine riesling (2.5 hectares). The rhine riesling is a recent planting, and the first commercial harvest was due in 1985.

Koppamurra does not have a winery of its own. The grapes are contract-crushed and fermented, and the wines are then returned to Koppamurra for ageing in oak before being contract-bottled. This system paid handsome dividends with the first two releases, a 1980 Cabernet Sauvignon and a 1982 Cabernet Merlot. The 1980 Cabernet Sauvignon showed full, ripe-berry aromas and flavours, tempered by just a touch of varietal astringency. Perhaps thanks to the hand-pruning, none of the stewed-plum characters were evident. The 1982 Cabernet Merlot is a firm wine, with a slight touch of astringency in the bouquet, but with most attractive sweet, minty/ berry-fruit flavours, and a finely grained tannin structure.

LADBROKE GROVE
MILLICENT ROAD, PENOLA

Ladbroke Grove was formed as a result of a chance conversation in the United Kingdom in 1982 between long-term Coonawarra resident Peter McDonald and an English friend. McDonald had the idea, and the friend had the money; the upshot was the release in 1984 of the first wines under the Ladbroke Grove label. McDonald had learnt the Coonawarra wine industry working at Brand's and at Katnook, chiefly as a cellar-hand. His idea was to purchase grapes, have the wine crushed and fermented under contract, and the red wines would then be taken back to Ladbroke Grove's cellars for maturation.

The cellars are situated in the old butter factory at Penola, and the system has worked very well. All the white wines have been made from rhine riesling purchased from Coonawarra Machinery Company and contract-made and bottled at Katnook. The highly praised releases so far have included a 1983 and a 1984 Rhine Riesling, and a 1984 Late-Harvest Rhine Riesling. The only red wines released to date have been no less successful: a 1982 Cabernet Sauvignon, which sold out almost immediately, followed by a 1982 Hermitage.

The quantity so far made has not been great: 1000 dozen were made in 1984, and a little under 1500 dozen in 1985. In the early part of 1985 it seemed unlikely that any 1983 reds would be released under the Ladbroke Grove label; the partners are understandably reluctant to imperil the sparkling start they made with their initial releases.

LECONFIELD
PENOLA-NARACOORTE ROAD, PENOLA

The Hamilton family name stands second to none in the winemaking history of South Australia. The present Dr Richard Hamilton's namesake lays claim to have been the first person to make wine in South Australia. He commenced planting his property at Marion—which he named Ewell after his erstwhile home in Surrey, England—at the end of 1837.

By 1840 Hamilton's Ewell vineyards were said to have been producing 5500 litres of wine, and went on to become one of the best-known and most highly respected wineries on the south-eastern outskirts of Adelaide. It remained in the control of the Hamilton family for well over a century. Sydney Hamilton, born in 1898, was one of the members of the family; for over 30 years he worked at Hamiltons until his retirement in the mid-1950s. But winemaking was in his blood, and at the time when most people are content to call it a day, Sydney Hamilton was formulating long-range plans to start all over again. Richard Hamilton recalls that his uncle had "always wanted to make the classic red wine". Hamilton methodically explored possible vineyard sites in places as far afield as the Hunter Valley, Clare, Tasmania, Canberra and the Victorian foothills of the Alps. One of the areas that interested him most was southern New South Wales around Canberra; he eventually decided against establishing a vineyard there because he felt the quality of the vintages would be too irregular.

Hamilton was more or less a contemporary of Bill Redman, and a life-long friend. Bill heard of Sydney's ambition to start again, and in 1974 told him of a Coonawarra dairyman with some hectares of choice red soil in the heart of Coonawarra who wished to sell. Hamilton decided to purchase the property and erected the winery with its vaguely Spanish air in time for the 1975 vintage (made from bought-in grapes). With the help of vineyard manager Gordon Bannister, he set about establishing a 12-hectare vineyard comprising roughly eight hectares of cabernet sauvignon and four hectares of rhine riesling.

In October 1981 Sydney Hamilton reluctantly bowed to family pressure, and at the age of 84 sold Leconfield to his nephew Richard Hamilton, a medical practitioner who had already established his own vineyard and winery at McLaren Vale. Richard Hamilton has extended the vineyards somewhat (he planted 1.2 hectares of merlot in 1982 and a further four hectares of cabernet sauvignon in the spring of 1984), but has otherwise changed little in either the winery set-up or the winemaking practices of his uncle.

Viticulture is uncompromisingly traditional. No herbicides are used in the vineyard, which is worked by disc plough and scarifier in the traditional way; the vines are hand-pruned; and the picking is, as one of the labels rather quaintly explains, carried out by "experienced women". Yields at 7.5 tonnes per hectare are well below district average, and may well go to explain the excellent quality and depth of flavour which the Leconfield wines have.

The winemaking methods used for the cabernet are traditional: cool fermentation in stainless steel, followed by maturation in a mixture of new-oak hogsheads and larger oak storage vats. Three wines are made: a cabernet sauvignon, a cabernet shiraz (utilising around eight tonnes of shiraz purchased from a neighbour) and a rhine riesling. The rhine riesling receives some oak maturation, an approach favoured by Richard Hamilton and used extensively at McLaren Vale. He produces a distinctive style of wine which is somewhat at odds with modern wine-making thought, and I must admit I find the white wines hard and unattractive.

The red wines are in a very different category. As at the end of 1984 Leconfield was still to release its 1982 Cabernet Sauvignon, so that all the red wines so far to come onto the market have been made at least partially by Sydney Hamilton. But as I say, I can see little reason to suspect that the style will change at all. The cabernet sauvignons made between 1977 and 1981 inclusive were, and are, quite superb. One of the hallmarks of the Leconfield style is the presence of soft but quite perceptible tannin running through the middle to back palate of the wine. Few other makers have been able to secure this in quite the same way, and I suspect it comes partly from the fruit and partly from the oak. Whatever be the answer, it adds an extra degree of structure to wines which are generously endowed with classic berry-fruit flavours.

If my theory about hand-picking is correct, it is not surprising that these wines have shown none of the stewed-plum/meaty characters which are these days common throughout the district. It is not easy to pick and choose between the cabernet sauvignons, but I think it is generally agreed that the 1978 and 1980 wines are exceptional. The 1981 release has the richness and sweet fruit one would expect from this rather difficult Coonawarra vintage, and again the grape and oak tannins are present.

LINDEMANS' ROUGE HOMME
PENOLA–NARACOORTE ROAD, COONAWARRA

In common with the other major wine companies in the 1950s, Lindemans' Wines was a substantial purchaser of bulk wine made by other, smaller wineries. While based in New South Wales, its purchasing extended through Victoria to South Australia. Since 1953 it had taken the major part of Stanley's red table wine production at Clare Valley, and was likewise Bleasdale's major customer at Langhorne Creek, both in South Australia.

In the latter half of the 1950s, under Ray Kidd's direction, Lindemans started to formulate the cellar blend styles now known as Nyrang Hermitage and Auburn Burgundy. George Fairbrother, as well as being Australia's foremost wine judge, had a substantial wine-broking business and dealt extensively with Lindemans. In the mid-1950s he offered Lindemans its first Coonawarra red (made, of course, by Redman). Ray Kidd recalls that Lindemans bottled one 500-gallon (2275-litre) cask straight and released it under the Lindemans Private Bin label then in use. Most of it, however, was used in the Hunter/Coonawarra/Clare Reserve Bin wines that were the fore-runners of Nyrang and Auburn.

As the table-wine market grew, and Lindemans' share of that market increased, so did the pressure on the supply of top-quality table wine. In 1959 Lindemans had come close to purchasing the Stanley Wine Company, but the negotiations had fallen through. Nonetheless it remained Stanley's major customer, and always had first choice of each year's wine. The situation was very different at Rouge Homme: Lindemans was but one of a number of customers clamouring for wine, and many of the other companies (notably Hardy's) had longer-established ties.

By the end of 1964 it became imperative that Lindemans secure its position. Initially it proposed that Redman substantially increase his vineyard plantings with financial support provided by

Lindemans, with a long-term wine-supply agreement guaranteeing Redman a market and Lindemans the wine it needed. When Redman declined this proposal serious negotiations for the acquisition of Rouge Homme commenced through the agency of George Fairbrother. The sale was concluded in June 1965, Lindemans acquiring the winery, all bottled and bulk-wine stocks, the homes of Don and Owen Redman, the vineyards, and of course the goodwill and the name Rouge Homme. The terms of sale included a provision that Don Redman would stay on to manage Rouge Homme until the end of 1965 and that Bill Redman would stay on as a director. In the event it was not until June 1966 that Bill Redman finally stepped down.

Philip Laffer arrived on 5 January 1966, and Lindemans was in control. It had acquired 119 hectares of red soil suitable for vines, 22 hectares of grazing country and 19 hectares of vineyards. Of that 19 hectares, 8.9 hectares were of old vines and 10 were young vines not in full production. The old vines included a previous 1.2 hectares of cabernet sauvignon on the Cellar Block, with a further 2.3 hectares of cabernet sauvignon planted between 1962 and 1964 in a thin strip down the side of Snelling's Block.

By purchasing Rouge Homme Wines Pty Limited, Lindemans acquired the Cellar Vineyard, Richardson's, Snelling's, Limestone Ridge, St Cedd's and the South Block. Lindemans (in its own right) subsequently purchased St George from Wynniatt and the Nursery Block from Childs. I should explain that Rouge Homme Wines Pty Limited and Lindemans Wines Pty Limited—both subsidiaries of Lindeman (Holdings) Limited—carry on parallel operations in Coonawarra. Rouge Homme markets district wines; Lindemans markets individual vineyard wines. Although the distinction between Rouge Homme Wines and Lindemans Wines is of importance to Lindemans, and to the marketing of the wines, I shall by and large bypass it, using the term Lindemans to encompass each of the two subsidiaries.

Planting did not get under way until 1967; between then and 1978 Lindemans laid the base for the fine range of wines it is now producing, many of which are released under the vineyard names. In this time, too, the old Rouge Homme Winery all but disappeared as massive new installations surrounded it.

The vineyard to receive most attention in recent times has been St George, planted to 12 hectares of cabernet sauvignon in 1969. It takes its name from Surgeon Major-General Hinton St George, who bought the land from Riddoch in the early 1890s. It

remained in the family until Edith Hinton sold it to Wynniatt, who in turn sold it to Lindemans in the late 1960s. The first release from the vineyard came in 1973; two more years were to pass (neither 1974 nor 1975 were easy vintages) before it made its reappearance with the outstanding 1976 version. Given the fairly prompt release of the wines (usually about three years after vintage), it seems that Lindemans regards them as reasonably quick-developing wines. This is a fair assessment, but it should not disguise the fact that the fruit flavours are very complex and in recent vintages have been complemented by some sophisticated oak handling. All of the vines on the block were clonally selected, resulting in high and dependable yields. A considerable quantity of fruit comes from the vineyard, and the output (and availability) of St George Cabernet Sauvignon will increase with each vintage.

Since I first looked in depth at the St George range almost three years ago (and indeed, all of the Lindeman flagships from the late 1970s and early 1980s), my initial enthusiasm for the wines has been tempered somewhat. Viewed on their own, or in a retrospective tasting with their fellow wines, one cannot help but be impressed by the outstanding winemaking and the exceedingly rich and complex, if somewhat unusual, flavours. It is only when these wines appear in an even larger tasting such as is encountered under standard show conditions that it becomes apparent just how unusual the flavours are. I am still in two minds: the formula, if it can be called that, works to the extent that it produces a wine of individual and, in itself, complete flavour. For most people the end result is an extremely attractive wine. For a few the question remains whether the flavours are legitimately part of what winemakers should be deliberately seeking, and whether in the longer-term perspective these characteristics will be regarded as desirable.

The first release of St George Cabernet Sauvignon was in 1973; that wine is now well past its best, with aged cigar-box/cabbage aromas and flavours, rather like an old Hunter. It was not made in 1974 nor 1975, but a big, rich and ripe wine, with smooth minty fruit on the middle and back palate, was made in 1976. It is ageing well, though near its peak. The 1977 vintage was disappointing, showing some volatility; the 1979 and 1981 vintages reflected the less favourable vintage conditions at Coonawarra, although each was a well-made wine with plenty of stylistic fruit and well-handled oak; while the 1978 and 1980 vintages were exceptionally good. The 1978 wine, with that curious mixture of herbaceous and ripe-berry characters, was a logical forerunner to the even more complex 1980 vintage, which was the winner of the Jimmy Watson Trophy in Melbourne in 1981.

I have watched the development of this wine with considerable interest: tasted immediately after it won the Jimmy Watson Trophy, the wine was redolent of cassis/mint aroma. I remember being able to smell the bouquet from the glass sitting on the table in front of me. Tasted again in May 1982 some chalky/dusty tannins were evident, with a hint of herbaceousness. By the second half of 1984 the wine had developed both softness and complexity, the rate of development once again confirming Lindemans' view that these wines will probably be at their best five to seven years after vintage. My tasting notes on the latter occasion read as follows. *Colour:* excellent purple-red. *Bouquet:* intense and extremely complex herbaceous/spice/mint aromas with a touch of tobacco. *Palate:* soft and complex meaty/spicy/herbaceous flavours on the fore-palate; soft sweet-berry mid-palate richness, characteristic of the vintage, and fairly low tannin.

Limestone Ridge was the first vineyard planted by Lindemans after the acquisition of Rouge Homme from Redman. Between 1967 and 1968 22 hectares of shiraz were planted with a strip of a little over two hectares of cabernet sauvignon down the eastern side. It was so named because the topsoil was very shallow, and the hard limestone cap caused considerable problems before the land was finally readied for planting.

This same limestone gives the wines the bony structure and long life which so distinguish them. Although the cabernet sauvignon amounts to little more than 10 per cent of the blend, it plays an important part in what is a range of excellent wines. In the course of researching my book *Coonawarra*, I tasted all of the Limestone Ridge wines made between 1971 and 1980 inclusive; at that point of time (in mid-1982) the 1976 vintage was the most recent release. If one accepts the new Coonawarra flavour, the wines of 1976 to 1980 inclusive are quite outstanding. The 1976 wine marks the first real appearance of these complex flavours, and has been the subject of many an animated discussion—indeed, argument—with a number of my winemaker and wine-judge friends. The most recent release under the Limestone Ridge label has been the 1979 vintage, put on sale midway through 1984. A little aggressive two years earlier, the wine had developed and softened beautifully over the intervening years. Its outstanding feature was the perfect balance of the palate, not to

mention the complex, rich amalgam of powdery/oak/meat/spice flavours. Of the older vintages the 1971 and 1972 wines have developed well, with the latter showing rather more weight and fruit. The 1973 vintage is tired, dull and cabbagey, and the wine was not made in 1974 or 1975.

The largest-selling lines are Rouge Homme Claret and Rouge Homme Cabernet Sauvignon. Even in Redman's time the claret occasionally had a little cabernet sauvignon in it; the 1961 and 1962 releases were labelled cabernet shiraz, but in those days this did not necessarily indicate a greater percentage of cabernet sauvignon than shiraz. Indeed it is certain that those wines had only a small percentage of cabernet sauvignon. In 1970 cabernet sauvignon made its reappearance in the wine, and since 1976 Rouge Homme Claret has had between 30 per cent and 35 per cent cabernet sauvignon. The grapes for the wine come variously from the South Block (with 2.4-hectares of old shiraz and 13.7 hectares in 1969); from the Nursery Vineyard (13 hectares planted in 1969); from Snelling's (5.3 hectares planted between 1962 and 1964 and a further 6.5 hectares in 1969); and from the Cellar Block (part old vines and part planted in 1963–64). Some part of the shiraz is presently being grafted, and future figures may well be different; but shiraz makes a great red in Coonawarra, so the decline is not likely to be dramatic.

The wines between 1965 and 1975 are by no means outstanding, reflecting the fact that, to use Ray Kidd's words, "We didn't really have a winemaker there between 1968 and 1974". Winemaking responsibilities were split between Coonawarra, Tanunda and Sydney, while it took some time to modernise the winery and winemaking equipment. Things changed with the arrival of John Vickery in 1974, but he ran into one of the worst vintages in Coonawarra's memory, so one had to wait until 1976 to really see the results. This time coincided with a new approach by the major companies to red-wine-making—in particular a new understanding of the role played by pH in red-wine quality. There is no doubt that the wines between 1965 and 1975 show more brown colour than they should, and lack the intensity of fruit flavour necessary to justify 15 or 20 years' cellaring. On the other hand they equally demonstrate Coonawarra's inherent fruit quality—that even when (by the standards of today) neglected during the winemaking process, it can produce wines of above-average quality.

The 1961, 1962 and 1963 vintages are still magnificent wines, followed not so far behind by the

1964 vintage. 1965, 1966 and 1969 were above average, and only the 1967 and 1968 lacked fruit and showed mercaptan. Another consistent run of wines was made between 1970 and 1973, with the 1970 and 1973 vintages of high quality. The 1974 and 1975 wines are best forgotten (or quickly drunk), but in 1976 the wine was literally transformed. Since that year it has gone from strength to strength. Given the volume in which this wine is made, the quality is impeccable.

The Rouge Homme Cabernet Sauvignons follow a similar path, although I respectfully disagree with the views of Penfolds' Max Schubert (who believes that Coonawarra produces better shiraz than cabernet sauvignon). I think that in Coonawarra (as in most places) cabernet sauvignon produces the better wine, and certainly produces one that ages better. The cabernet sauvignon comes from 8.5 hectares established on the Nursery Block in 1969; from two thin strips running down Snelling's and planted in 1962–63 and 1969 each (of 2.3 and 2.15 hectares respectively); from 24.3 hectares on Richardson's, dating from 1969; and finally from 8.1 hectares established on St Cedd's in 1975. The 12-hectare patch on the Cellar Block (which produced the wine until 1966) has long since been swamped in the total blend.

This vast increase in production has allowed Lindemans to hold—and in real terms decrease—the price of Rouge Homme Cabernet Sauvignon, although one would be brave to argue that the quality of the wine made between 1959 and 1963 was maintained throughout the 1960s and the early 1970s. But since 1978 the wine has gone from strength to strength: the 1978, 1980 and 1981 vintages were very good indeed. The latter is one of the best wines to come out of Coonawarra in 1981, with voluptuous ripe fruit (admittedly in the stewed-plum flavour range), allied with perfectly handled new oak. Those lucky enough to have Rouge Homme Cabernet Sauvignon from any of the vintages between 1959 and 1963 in their cellar have great Australian red wine—so great, indeed, that I think it worth providing the tasting notes from a 1982 assessment.

1963 *Colour:* light red-brown. *Bouquet:* light, lively sappy/complex fruit aromas. *Palate:* lifted berry/mint flavours; a delicate yet intensely flavoured wine, very different from both the 1962 and the 1964. (18.5/20)

1962 *Colour:* strong, deep red-brown. *Bouquet:* deep and smooth; similar to the 1959. The mint which was once so evident in the wine is now diminishing but still there. *Palate:* rich, smooth fruit with camphor/mint overtones. Of medium to full weight and holding beautifully. (18.5/20)

1961 *Colour:* medium to full depth, still holding red hue. Very good for age. *Bouquet:* crisp and clean with some mellow camphor overtones. *Palate:* of medium weight; very fresh fruit, good acid and a lovely touch of camphor/mint. What a wine for a vintage that never was. (18/20)

1960 *Colour:* very deep. *Bouquet:* fuller and a little heavier than the 1959. *Palate:* a medium-weight wine, quite fresh with a little hard acid on the finish but still drinking very well. Good fruit throughout. (18/20)

1959 *Colour:* dark red, garnet-tinged holding both depth and hue remarkably well. *Bouquet:* clean, smooth and with cool-climate dusty cabernet aroma. *Palate:* perfectly aged, smooth with a long, clean, soft tannin finish. A lovely old wine, although the cabernet varietal character is now starting to fade somewhat. (19/20)

Thereafter the quality faded away considerably. With the exception of the 1966, 1967, 1971 and 1973 vintages, the intervening wines were very poor at worst and mundane commercial wines at best. The wine was not, indeed, made in 1974 or 1976, and probably should not have been made in 1975.

St Cedd's takes its name from the Anglican church in Coonawarra, and was so christened by Philip Laffer, for a time manager at Coonawarra. It is something of a patchwork quilt, boasting 4.1 hectares of traminer, 8.1 hectares of cabernet sauvignon, four hectares of malbec (all planted in 1975) and 8.1 hectares of chardonnay planted in 1978. In 1980 a malbec (80 per cent) cabernet (20 per cent) blend was made; interestingly, the wine was bottled without the benefit of any oak maturation. It may well be used to fill out other wines (as a small component of the blend) in future years.

St Cedd's is better known in the marketplace for its gewurztraminer, of which two vintages have so far been released. This variety, it seems to me, is a fine foil for Vickery's unquestioned mastery of white-winemaking—for he turned a sow's ear into a silk purse in 1980 and again in 1982.

The Nursery Vineyard is so called because it was used for precisely that purpose in the golden days of the establishment of the Coonawarra Fruit Colony. It was planted to five varieties (all in 1969): cabernet sauvignon, shiraz, rhine riesling (5.4 hectares), crouchen (4.4 hectares) and muscadelle (4.2

hectares). Rhine riesling has been released under the Nursery Vineyard label since 1974. The fruit from the Nursery Vineyard has been something of a disappointment over the past few years. Not that the wines are bad, but in the hands of Vickery they should by rights have been sublime. Their main fault is that they lack fruit intensity; given the technology which now abounds and Vickery's track record at Leo Buring, the fault must be in the vineyard (and possibly partly with mechanical pruning and harvesting). For the time being at least, Padthaway offers far more up-front fruit flavour and intensity, although it is true the early Nursery wines promise more than does Padthaway for those who seek the complexity that the top 10- to 15-year-old Buring whites give. The 1984 Nursery Vineyard Rhine Riesling showed a partial return to form, with rather more fruit and intensity than had been apparent in prior vintages.

The Rouge Homme Rhine Riesling label has offered rather more, if only because of the sporadic appearance of spatlese and auslese styles. Since 1981 botrytis has made a contribution to these wines, although whether deliberately or otherwise Lindemans has not taken the styles to the far extremes of lusciousness and intensity of some makers. When viewed against the almost searing intensity and opulent richness of the Petaluma wines (and the Petaluma half-brothers such as Mitchelton), the wines look a little one-dimensional and old-fashioned. But not everyone enjoys the extreme intensity of heavily botrytised wines, and for those who like a more controlled sweetness and acid, the Rouge Homme Spatlese and Auslese releases of the 1980s will be the preferred style.

The most recent release from the Rouge Homme Vineyards is a 1983 Pinot Noir, the first such wine released by Lindemans from Coonawarra. While not in the class of the best of the Lindemans Padthaway Pinot Noir, it does have good fruit, with some sweet varietal pinot flavour and a nice touch of oak.

The name of John Vickery has dominated these pages because he was chief winemaker at Coonawarra between 1974 and 1982, when the vast majority of the wines discussed was made. He has now returned to Chateau Leonay in the Barossa Valley, and Greg Clayfield has taken over as chief winemaker. I do not think this will herald any significant changes in style: Rouge Homme is a massive winery, capable of handling 6000 tonnes of fruit each vintage. The role of the winemaker in such a situation is more that of a general manager/quality controller, and less that of an artist working an individual canvas. There is a

school of thought that says being a quality controller is all a winemaker should aspire to be. Eighty per cent of his or her job is simply to preserve as much natural fruit flavour as possible: only in the other 20 per cent does self-expression—in the form of deliberate modification or amelioration of wine flavour—find its place. If ever a district were to prove the wisdom of that view, it is Coonawarra.

MILDARA
PENOLA–NARACOORTE ROAD, COONAWARRA

In many ways the motivation for Mildara's entry into Coonawarra (and its subsequent years of trial and error) follow strikingly similar paths to those of Lindemans. Each company found that Coonawarra had its own peculiarities, and each took more than a decade to come to terms with the special problems of vineyard and winery. Neither, however, has had cause to regret the decision to invest, even if they (like most of us) wish they had had the wisdom of hindsight.

Elsewhere (at page 207) I have recounted how in 1950 Ronald Haselgrove decided the time had come to take Mildara away from an exclusively fortified-wine base, and to introduce red table wine into the company's range of products. What is more, he determined that he would need to look beyond Chateau Reynella and the Southern Vales to achieve the style of wine he wished to make. With a catholic eye, Haselgrove looked at Great Western where his friend Colin Preece was making wines of sublime quality (1952 saw the first, and greatest, Chalambar Burgundy); his glance then turned northwards to the Hunter Valley and in particular to the lean, lantern-jawed Doug Elliott; and last but by no means least to Coonawarra and Bill Redman.

In each case Haselgrove was looking for elegance, for a lighter style of wine than those of Saltram and Stoneyfell, good though those wines may have been. Preece had no wine to spare; but Redman did, thanks to an introduction through George Fairbrother.

Ronald's son Richard Haselgrove was just 16, a momentous year in his life because it enabled him to get his driver's licence and gain immediate employment as his father's chauffeur during long country trips. It was thus that he accompanied Ronald Haselgrove on his first trip to Coonawarra in May 1953.

Richard remembers the trip as if it were yesterday, and the wines no less clearly:

Bill Redman had set up a few samples on an old wooden table. They were incredible—these great purple things you get in young Coonawarra wines. The Shiraz all tasted like Cabernet; it didn't matter that they grew very little Cabernet at Coonawarra. The Shiraz had this great depth of character that people in those days only associated with Cabernet; the Shiraz of those times tended to be big, gutsy and jammy.

Ronald Haselgrove was singularly impressed. Not only did he take every litre Bill Redman had available—12,735 litres to be exact—but he insisted that Redman put his price up. He told Redman that wines of lesser quality from the Barossa and Hunter Valleys were bringing higher prices, and that Redman's was worth more than he (Redman) was asking. It was not a move calculated to win friends with Redman's other customers, but Haselgrove was a man of both principle and vision; vision that allowed Haselgrove to predict correctly that within a few years every major wine company in Australia would be clamouring for terra rosa country at Coonawarra.

Not only did he realise the magic of the Coonawarra climate and soil, but also that supplies of Redman wine would inevitably come under increasing pressure of demand. In August 1955, barely two years after that initial purchase, Mildara purchased its first 12.5 hectares from Smith. The first plantings were to break new ground immediately in Coonawarra: cabernet sauvignon, palomino, semillon and rhine riesling. While that initial purchase was regarded by the locals as sheer extravagance, and the subsequent accretions no less so, the price of $516 per hectare pales into insignificance with the $7500 a hectare that prime terra rosa brings now.

Between July 1960 and 1973 Mildara steadily built up its landholdings. In July 1960 it purchased 16.2 hectares from McShane; in May 1962 four hectares from Gibbs; in October 1962 16.2 hectares from Robinson; in August 1966 28.4 hectares from O'Dea; in September 1966 15.4 hectares from Munn; in October 1967 100 hectares from O'Dea; in June 1970 20.2 hectares from Alexander; and in 1973 12.5 hectares from Reschke. The price paid by Mildara rose from a little over $1000 per hectare to $1650 per hectare, and when in the late 1970s and early 1980s it disposed of some of its surplus landholdings (notably to Wynns) it did so at a very handsome profit.

Mildara's Coonawarra Winery was erected in time for the 1973 vintage, which provided the first substantial crop from the still relatively young vineyards. In that year 1250 cases of one of Australia's most famous red wines was made, 1963 Mildara

Coonawarra Cabernet Sauvignon, otherwise known as Peppermint Pattie. This nickname has been bestowed on it because of the intense peppermint character which it has exhibited all its life. Various explanations have been given for that, ranging from the new-oak casks in which it was matured through to young vine character, to the making method (the fermentation was finished in new oak), and finally simply to a quirk of vintage. The truth may well lie in a combination of all those explanations. The fact remains that the same character did not appear in the 1963 Cabernet Shiraz of that year, nor in any subsequent vintage of cabernet sauvignon.

Cabernet sauvignon has been the most important red grape for Mildara and equally its most important wine. The 70 hectares of cabernet sauvignon provide around 700 tonnes each year, the best of which goes into the Coonawarra cabernet sauvignon range and, more recently, into the cabernet merlot and cabernet merlot malbec wines. Some bottles of the 1963 Cabernet Sauvignon are starting to show distinct signs of age; but within the last two years I have shared in a number which were superb. At its best the wine has extraordinary fragrance, redolent of mint, and with mouth-filling minty/berry/tobacco flavours, with the new oak still very much in evidence. No one hundred per cent cabernet sauvignon was made in either 1964 or 1965; the 1966 vintage was initially greeted with great enthusiasm, but it seems to be tiring and losing some of its varietal fruit character.

In 1967 and 1968 Mildara ran into great problems in the winery: it proved impossible to induce the wines to undergo a malolactic fermentation, which was considered essential. In an endeavour to induce that fermentation sulphur dioxide was withheld. By the time the malolactic fermentation finally proceeded, the wines were oxidised. It was eventually realised that the conditions in the new winery were so clean that the lactobacillus population had been unable to build up.

In 1969 it was once again decided that the quality of the wine did not merit a separate release, and a single 2250-litre vat was kept for company purposes. Paradoxically it has turned out to be the best cabernet sauvignon made between 1964 and 1978. It consistently shows great power and depth, with true overtones of Bordeaux. The 1970, 1971 and 1973 vintages (the latter a trophy-winner at the 1977 Sydney show) are the best of a fairly mediocre line between 1969 and 1979. In 1978 Jack Schulz was put in charge of winemaking at Coonawarra, and wine quality immediately improved. The 1978

Cabernet Sauvignon shows the first signs of the return to high quality which has since been evidenced in the 1979, 1980 and 1981 vintages. The 1979 and 1980 wines show strong, grassy varietal fruit in their aroma and have enough ripe-berry fruit flavours on the palate to give balance and structure. The 1980 vintage, in particular, is an outstanding wine.

Running in tandem with the Coonawarra cabernet sauvignon have been two other releases: cabernet shiraz malbec, and cabernet shiraz. The cabernet shiraz malbec blend was first introduced in 1966 and has been made every year since with the exception of 1977, a gloomy year in which none of the Coonawarra red wines was of sufficient quality to be released. Once again the pattern is similar. The 1966 and 1967 vintages were good wines, and have held on remarkably well. Between 1968 and 1976 there is little to enthuse about; the best of the subsequent vintages was the 1979, with a pleasing complexity which was once described as Italianate. Attractive ripe-berry flavours mingle with some astringency, and the wine has good acid.

The Coonawarra cabernet shiraz series, first made in 1963, will probably disappear from the scene in the near future. It was always a somewhat uncomfortable blend, made up with whatever was left over after the other blends and straight varietal releases were determined. Despite that, some beautiful wines have come out under this label. In two major comparative tastings, the first in 1982 and the second in January 1985, the 1963 and 1964 vintages were remarkable. The 1963 Cabernet Shiraz still has excellent life with complex leafy/leathery/cigar aromas and flavours, and a touch of minty spice on the palate. In 1985 (although not 1982), the 1964 Cabernet Shiraz was at last starting to show distinct signs of age, with the fruit just commencing to drop out. It certainly should be drunk over the next few years. In the 1985 tasting the 1971 and 1972 vintages showed much better than they did in 1982, but it is not until 1979 that the quality of the early wines returned. The 1979 Cabernet Shiraz is a remarkable wine with considerable power and depth; the full mid-palate fruit, firm rather than ripe, will ensure a long life for the wine. The 1980 was a major disappointment; the 1981 release is very much better, although showing some ripe-plum/stewed-fruit characters.

In 1980 the first of the Coonawarra cabernet merlot blends was made, and in 1982 the first of the cabernet merlot malbec blends. The 1980 and 1981 Coonawarra Cabernet Merlot wines are both excellent, and the 1982 Bordeaux blend looks even

better. The 1980 Cabernet Merlot is the firmest and most astringent of the three wines; the 1982 the fullest and roundest, showing excellent oak handling and a most attractive amalgam of berry flavours on the palate. One assumes it is in this direction that Mildara will head in the future with its Coonawarra red-wine blends.

The 21 hectares of rhine riesling, yielding around 12.5 tonnes per hectare, are Mildara's most important white varietal planting at Coonawarra. The first release was 1967; while not in the class of the Wynns' Rhine Riesling of that year, it still retains varietal fruit and some life. The 1968 Rhine Riesling, a wine with still-perceptible sweetness from around 12 grams per litre of residual sugar, is another wine which has aged with considerable grace, and offers far more than curiosity value. Those made between 1971 and 1977 offer just that, and no more. Since 1978 the wines have been reliable, although unexciting. They are commercial wines, produced in substantial quantity, and selling for a fairly modest price. It is difficult to see that any of them should be cellared for more than a year or two at the outside.

Mildara has eight hectares of chardonnay, releasing its first wine in 1980. One imagines that the quantities available for future release will be sharply reduced, as Dominique Landragin will no doubt be staking a large claim for the Yellowglen sparkling wine. The 1980, 1981 and 1984 vintages were all very successful. Though not especially rich wines, they do show good cool-climate varietal character. The wine was not made in 1982, and the 1983 shows off-aromas and flavours which I assume derive from botrytis.

The eight hectares of sauvignon blanc go back much further; the first sauvignon blanc release was in 1974, although at that stage the trial plantings (introduced in 1963) were interplanted with some crouchen. Apart from a quite attractive 1974 vintage (somewhat like a madeirised/honeyed Hunter) the line was indifferent until 1979, and really came alive with the 1980 release. This and the 1984 were and are first-class wines. The 1980 vintage shows classic herbaceous aroma and flavour, but is rather one-dimensional compared with the far more complex 1984 wine. It manages to combine strong varietal gooseberry/grassy varietal aroma and flavour with a rich mid-palate structure. This "tongue-feel" is an important part of wine quality, but is often missing with sauvignon blanc.

Mildara is making some very good wines at Coonawarra. Do not be deceived by the frequency of the discount offerings; take advantage of them.

PENFOLDS
PENOLA–NARACOORTE ROAD, COONAWARRA

Penfolds, like Lindemans, was a substantial purchaser of bulk wine in the 1950s; like Lindemans, too, Redman was one of Penfolds' suppliers. Initially Penfolds purchased the wine from Tony Nelson at Woodley's; but after he ceased to handle Redman wine it purchased direct. Surprisingly Max Schubert recounts that it did so more out of respect for Bill Redman as a man than out of any great regard for the wine. Schubert says: "They were not particularly good wines; they were light-weight, too light for our purposes, really, and didn't have any really distinguished character."

To this day Schubert sees Coonawarra reds as blending propositions. While freely acknowledging the great elegance and freshness of the wines, he believes they are at their best when married with the fuller, softer and fruitier wines of Magill and Kalimna. In 1962 Bin 60A, 1966 Bin 620 and 1967 Bin 7 he produced powerful evidence in support of that proposition. These are widely acknowledged as three of the greatest reds produced in this country over the past two decades, with Bin 60A virtually unchallenged at the helm. What is more, Schubert leans to Coonawarra shiraz blended with cabernet from other districts, rather than vice versa.

To this day, too, Schubert believes that grapes should be allowed to ripen fully; that maximum flavour is achieved only with totally ripe grapes. "If you want to control sugar and alcohol levels, do it through choosing your district," he says. So it is hardly surprising that he should not particularly like the early-picked and rather delicate wines of Redman. Nonetheless Schubert and Jeffrey Penfold Hyland were receptive when in 1960 the Redmans approached them at Magill to discuss the proposition that Penfolds should buy Sharam's Block and that Redman would work it and make the wine for them. Agreement was reached that the block would be purchased; and that Penfolds would supply Redman with a considerable amount of additional equipment, most of it secondhand but some of it new. Further, the wine was to be made under strict specifications, not the least being the ripeness at which the grapes were picked.

The agreements entered into between Penfolds and Redman make fascinating reading. By letter dated 19 September 1960 Penfolds agreed to sell £2700 of equipment including a Whitehill crusher, a press, various pumps and generators and other incidentals. The actual management contract of October 1960 is even more extraordinary. It provided for a loan to Redman to cover the cost of the equipment, and then went on in clause 5: "Penfolds will pay Rouge Homme Wines Pty Limited the sum of five shillings for each and every gallon of wine made out of the said grape crops as provided for herein."

The sum of five shillings covered vineyard maintenance, pruning and picking as well as the winemaking. In the event Redman continued the viticultural side for only two years; thereafter Penfolds took over, and the price was reduced to two shillings and sixpence per gallon (4.5 litres).

While the agreement provided for Redman to store the wine until 1 June of the year after vintage, Penfolds usually moved it shortly after vintage to Magill, whether or not it had undergone its malolactic fermentation.

Between 1960 and 1965 all the wines were made at Rouge Homme, but in that year (which coincided with the Lindemans sale) Penfolds decided to install a crushing facility, and transported the must to Magill and Nuriootpa for fermentation. Over that five-year period Penfolds gradually planted Sharam's Block. By 1965–66 planting was complete and further acquisitions had lifted total plantings to 92 hectares, comprising 30 hectares of shiraz, 20 hectares of cabernet sauvignon, two hectares of malbec, 30 hectares of rhine riesling and 10 hectares of traminer.

From 1965 until the end of the 1970s most of the grapes were processed at the crushing station installed by Penfolds at Coonawarra. With the wide-scale advent of night mechanical harvesting, the crushing plant was closed down and the grapes transported direct to Nuriootpa. More recently still part of the harvest has been crushed (and in the case of whites, pressed) at the large and modern Katnook plant, and taken to Nuriootpa as unfermented must or juice.

Over the years Penfolds has released only one Coonawarra red every year: Bin 128. The rest of the red wine is too valuable as a blending medium. Schubert is openly contemptuous of those who decry blends simply because they are blends. This philosophy applies from Penfolds' standard-bearer Grange Hermitage down through the line. David Dunstan wrote in 1981: "It is no secret that St Henri is now almost entirely cabernet sauvignon from Coonawarra." Penfolds deny that statement, but agree there is some Coonawarra cabernet sauvignon present, the amount of which varies considerably from year to year.

Schubert's argument is that the task of the chief

winemaker (Don Ditter, now that Schubert is in retirement) is to realise to the fullest the potential of the various parcels of wine and to produce, within constant overall style specifications, the best-possible wine. Wine quality in turn depends greatly on balance. If the season in the Barossa was a hot one with high baume and low acid, the percentage of Coonawarra material should logically increase, and vice versa.

Penfolds capitalises to the full on the fact that the Coonawarra vintage commences after that of the Barossa has finished. Once the style and quality of the Barossa wine is determined, parcels of Barossa/ Eden wine (and more recently Clare Valley material) are set aside, specifically awaiting a largely pre-determined percentage of Coonawarra material. The wine-marketer, on the other hand, also wishes to preserve (on a continuous basis) his or her well-known brand names. From a different viewpoint he or she comes to the same conclusion: the presence or absence of 10 per cent or 20 per cent Coonawarra is an irrelevant distraction (within the bounds imposed by the labelling regulations under the Pure Foods Act). It has been said that all of this is a potent argument for appellation control. So it is, but only if one realises that appellation adds nothing to the quality of the wine in the bottle, and gives no guarantee of that quality. Indeed, it may detract from quality if it inhibits the choice of the wine-maker.

Bin 128 has always been a modestly priced wine, usually offering very good value for money but every now and then scaling the heights. Viewed overall it certainly evidences Penfolds' late-picking preferences. Interestingly, some of the best wines over the years have showed the ripest characters. Between 1966 and 1976 I think the overall quality of Bin 128 was significantly above that of its counterpart from Lindemans, Rouge Homme Claret. Since that time, perhaps partly because of the inclusion of some cabernet sauvignon in Rouge Homme Claret, but also because of changed winemaking techniques, the latter has outperformed Bin 128. Indeed, Bin 128 can be seen to be simply too traditional: the wines are solid, with rich, ripe, sweet-fruit flavours but lack that edge of elegance required to lift them into the highest quality of Australian red wine. For the traditionalists the style no doubt works very well. The most recent releases, those of 1980 and 1981, are typical of the line: honest, full-flavoured wines with no great pretensions, yet offering quite good prospects for cellaring. Other good vintages over the years have been the 1976, 1972, 1968, 1966, 1965, 1964 and 1963. The three great classics among these are generally reckoned to be the 1963, 1966 and 1968 vintages (1963, incidentally, was the first wine in the release).

Over the years Penfolds has released one or two "specials" from Coonawarra; clearly the best of these is 1966 Bin 620, a quite magnificent cabernet shiraz. As at the end of 1984 it was still at the peak of its form, with firm, fresh fruit, complex fruit/oak flavour, and a long, clean finish.

Penfolds have also released a Coonawarra Rhine Riesling Bin 231 each year. Curiously, it seems to receive little corporate support or publicity, but some vintages have developed magnificently and have had considerable show success.

PENOWARRA
PENOLA–NARACOORTE ROAD, PENOLA

Ray Messenger is the local bus proprietor and earth-moving contractor. His winery and vineyard are very much a sideline—visitors to the district are liable to find the simple shed which houses the winery and sale area closed as often as not.

Messenger originally established four hectares to cabernet sauvignon, shiraz, and rhine riesling. Total plantings have now increased to 16 hectares. The wine is made with equipment scrounged from here and there, and it is matured in old wood, mainly large, but with a few small casks. Over the years he has had help from many of the locals: in 1979 it was Redman; in 1980 Doug Bowen; in 1981 Ken Ward. The wines are of very uneven quality, but can be pleasant.

PETALUMA
PENOLA–NARACOORTE ROAD, COONAWARRA

The Petaluma Vineyard, a little over eight hectares in extent, was initially acquired by Len Evans and the late Peter Fox, but was soon totally integrated into the Petaluma operation. It is situated on the site of some old stockyards, and the surface soil is particularly fertile. It is in the middle of the terra rosa strip, and of course has the usual underlying limestone base. When it was acquired the vineyard was planted to equal quantities of cabernet sauvignon and shiraz; the shiraz has now been grafted to merlot (two hectares) and to cabernet sauvignon (four hectares). The merlot will feature in future releases of the Petaluma Coonawarra red.

The vines are hand-pruned, picked by hand and

the shiraz is bunch-thinned to reduce the yield and increase quality. This process involves the selective removal of up to 30 per cent of the bunches about five to six weeks before vintage.

Petaluma has so far released three vintages from Coonawarra. The 1979 Petaluma Coonawarra (as it is simply called) was a blend of 60 per cent Coonawarra shiraz, 32 per cent Coonawarra cabernet sauvignon and eight per cent Clare Valley cabernet sauvignon. It is a marvellously complex wine in which the oak is still very evident and which is still a long way from its peak. It is the fleshiest and softest of the three vintages to date, but for all that is still an outstanding cellaring proposition.

The 1980 Coonawarra is a blend of 88 per cent cabernet sauvignon and 12 per cent shiraz, all from Petaluma's own vineyard. The component parts were separately fermented, and aged for 12 months in Nevers and Limousin oak barriques prior to blending; the blend then spent a further year in wood before being bottled. Petaluma's practice, then, is to allow a further year in bottle before release, meaning that the red wines are at least three years old by the time of their release. The 1980 is clearly the best of the three wines so far released, and equally certainly has the longest future in front of it. As with all the Petaluma reds, the oak is quite marked at this early stage. Winemaker Brian Croser is confident that, given the minimum 10 years in bottle which the wine demands, the oak will come back into balance. It is also distinguished by the sweetness of the berry fruit on the mid-palate; 1980 in Coonawarra may have been a cool year, but some extraordinarily ripe-fruit flavours were obtained, and the Petaluma is no exception.

The 1981 Petaluma Coonawarra is 100 per cent cabernet sauvignon; unlike the two previous wines, no new oak was used. The wine was matured in the barriques which have been used for prior vintages of Petaluma. This decision was taken simply because the hot vintage conditions produced very soft wines which will develop far more quickly and which could not stand up to excessive oak. Petaluma believes this most attractive wine will be at its peak by 1988-89.

The 1982 Petaluma Coonawarra, which may not be released until 1986, is in my view the best of the wines made to date at Petaluma. The 1982 wine was a blend of 88 per cent Coonawarra cabernet sauvignon and 12 per cent Coonawarra shiraz. The 1983 is 100 per cent cabernet sauvignon; while the 1984, seemingly destined to be the greatest of the Petaluma reds, will contain around 25 per cent merlot once the blend is finally determined.

Petaluma's involvement in Coonawarra does not end here. The Hills Vineyard Development Company, an associate of Petaluma, has planted just under five hectares of cabernet sauvignon, four hectares of chardonnay, 3.3 hectares of merlot and 2.85 hectares each of malbec and sauvignon blanc. In what is virtually standard practice for Petaluma in cool-climate areas, the plantings are on close spacing, with a vine density of over 3000 per hectare. Petaluma will of course make all the wine to be produced from these grapes, but not all of it will appear under Petaluma labels.

The other major involvement in Coonawarra is through the extraordinary Petaluma botrytised rhine rieslings. Petaluma has entered into a long-term arrangement with the Coonawarra Machinery Company (the owners of Katnook); a designated area of Coonawarra Machinery rhine riesling vintage is hand-pruned and managed to Petaluma's specifications, with the sole object of producing heavily botrytised fruit for extremely rich dessert-style wines.

Only tiny quantities of the wine (around 450-dozen bottles, or 900-dozen half-bottles) are made each year. The 1982 wine is the best beerenausleseweight wine so far made in Australia. In February 1985 it was still developing richness, with an intense lime-juice aroma (yet distinctively riesling in character) leading onto a palate of unflawed balance. The wine has great elegance, a moselle style rather than a rheingau; the acid is intense yet not mouth-puckering; the sweetness intense but not cloying or sugary. The 1984 vintage was harvested at 22 baume, and has finished fermentation with nine baume of residual sugar, not much less than that with which most wines start their fermentation. Croser smiles contentedly as he thinks about the wine.

Petaluma is determined to produce wines which will be regarded as Australia's best—it is not doing too badly so far.

REDMAN'S REDBANK
PENOLA–NARACOORTE ROAD, COONAWARRA

Winemaking was in Owen Redman's blood, and it took him little time after the sale of Rouge Homme to Lindemans was completed at the end of 1965 to lay the basis for his new winery. He immediately purchased a nine-hectare vineyard, planted to 60-year-old shiraz and owned by Arthur Hoffman; this provided the fruit for all of the early Redbank wines, commencing with the 1966 vintage.

From 1966 to 1969 Owen Redman produced only one wine: Redman Claret, made solely from shiraz. In 1966, 1967 and 1968 Owen Redman shared Eric Brand's Laira Winery. Since 1970 a second wine — Redman Cabernet Sauvignon — has been released each year. The 1970 and 1971 releases of the cabernet sauvignon were in tiny quantities; 1972 was the first generally available commercial release.

The vineyard now comprises 23.4 hectares of shiraz and 8.9 hectares of cabernet sauvignon. The wines are made at the attractive but functional winery erected in time for the 1969 vintage.

Owen Redman's winemaking beliefs and practices can be traced directly to the lessons learnt by his father Bill between 1901 and 1907. The first and most important rule of winemaking is to keep a scrupulously clean winery. Visit Redman at vintage time and it is easy to see how rigidly this practice is followed.

For some years now Redman has crushed its grapes in the field, carrying the clean-winery concept one stage further (crushing can be one of the more messy steps, with stalks flying everywhere in a small winery). This innovation, however, was necessitated by a decision to move to mechanical harvesting. The winery is simply not big enough to handle the large skips into which mechanically harvested grapes are fed; a small crusher mounted on the back of a tractor feeding into a following tank was the only solution. With this exception Owen Redman's winemaking practices remained as they were 40 years ago, and as Bill Redman's were 40 years before that.

The grapes are fermented in open wax-lined cement tanks, each holding four tonnes. They are relatively shallow, and the heat build-up is negligible, something Wynns learnt when it took over Chateau Comaum and used header boards on their seven-tonne tanks. The skins are hand-plunged, a wearisome and time-consuming method, but resulting in good extraction of colour and tannin. The wine is then left on skins until the fermentation has finished completely.

Until recently the Redman practice of adding absolutely no sulphur at fermentation (or until the wine was 12 months old) was regarded with amused tolerance by generations of Roseworthy graduates, who were assured by their teachers that 70 parts per million of sulphur was absolutely essential for sound winemaking. A major trend in red-winemaking in the 1980s has been to lower sulphur levels significantly: a few highly advanced technological wineries have even managed to do without it altogether. Whether it is suited to the regime at Redman is another matter.

After fermentation is completed — usually about five days — the wine is run by gravity into underground tanks where it immediately goes through its malolactic fermentation while still on gross lees. How different this is from most "modern" wineries where the wine is filtered and polished bright and clean before undergoing its malolactic fermentation (if it is allowed to do so at all). Three weeks later the wine is racked off gross lees, and then transferred to the oak casks (mainly 1365 litres capacity) in which it is matured.

Owen Redman was brought up in a school in which new oak played no part in winemaking. From 1969 to 1973, as his production increased in leaps and bounds, he inevitably acquired significant quantities of new oak, and it is reflected in the excellent wines made during that time. I believe that the cabernet sauvignon in particular now suffers from not having a greater oak influence, although in exceptional years the quality of the fruit is such that the lack is not so obvious.

Redman has always picked the fruit early, relying on the higher natural acidity and lower pH that this gives, so much so that he never checked the pH nor corrected the acid. He believed that physiological ripeness is not determined on the laboratory bench, but by the taste of the grapes. Here again contemporary thought is in some ways swinging round behind him.

All of these practices have a significant impact on the wines. They are deceptively light-bodied: despite the backblending of all the pressings, they have always given the impression they will not be particularly long-lived. Nothing could be further from the truth for the older Redman wines — witness the Woodley tasting at Len Evans's in 1972 of Redman-made wines going back to 1930. Redman's wines under the new label may go back only to 1966, but tastings over the period 1977 to 1984 confirm that the wines vintaged between 1966 and 1971 have changed relatively little during that period. They are not big-bodied wines, nor are they especially rich or complex. They score fairly well because they are clean and crisp; they are beautifully balanced "light dinner clarets" — wines that 60 years ago Colonel Fulton would have approved of thoroughly.

The same cannot be said for the wines since 1971: the Redman Clarets of 1967, 1968, 1969, 1970 and 1971 are lovely wines with life in front of them. Whether they reflect a greater proportion of shiraz from Arthur Hoffman's wines — a block that Ronald Haselgrove believed always made the best wine in Coonawarra — or whether the younger wines have been picked earlier, I do not know. I think the younger wines miss out because they have insufficient weight and complexity; and from their fairly rapid colour development one must question whether they will exhibit the same keeping power of the older wines.

Worse still, the wines of more recent vintages have a depressing array of wine faults, chiefly mercaptan and not infrequently volatility. Thus the 1979 and 1980 releases, which were quite attractive as young wines, have faded badly; while the 1981 and 1982 releases are simply poor wines by any standards, and do scant justice to the standing and reputation of the Redman name.

The Redman Cabernet Sauvignons have fared better—indeed significantly better—but once again here the 1981 and 1982 releases were simply unacceptable. Given the problems of the district in 1983, it is difficult to see any return to former glory around the corner. Let us simply hope that 1984 will provide the springboard. The wine was first made in 1970, and the cabernet sauvignons of that year, 1971 and 1972 are still superb. The 1976, a trophy-winner, was another outstanding wine, while even the 1974 was a great success in an otherwise very difficult vintage.

In 1982 Owen Redman handed over winemaking responsibilities to his Roseworthy-trained son Bruce. Bruce has made it clear from the outset that he has no plans to alter either the style of the wines or the winemaking methods developed by his father.

"Three years at Roseworthy is no substitute for 80 years of district experience."

ROSEMOUNT ESTATE
PENOLA–NARACOORTE ROAD, PENOLA

Rosemount Estate acquired a 26-hectare block of terra rosa soil on the outskirts of Penola in December 1981. After various trials and tribulations, and a change of heart about certain of the varieties to be planted, it is now established to cabernet sauvignon (10 hectares), pinot noir (six hectares), chardonnay (four hectares), and shiraz, merlot and sauvignon blanc (two hectares each).

Since 1980 Rosemount has bought significant quantities of grapes from Coonawarra Machinery Company. These are crushed at Katnook and transported as chilled must or juice to Rosemount's Upper Hunter wineries, where fermentation (and, obviously enough, maturation) take place. The Rosemount Coonawarra releases have been of consistently high quality. These comprise a rhine riesling, a shiraz and

a cabernet sauvignon. The three 1982 vintage wines (released in 1984) were praised by all those who reviewed them. The outstanding wine, in pure quality terms, was the 1982 Coonawarra Shiraz, with its opulent depth of fruit flavour balanced by obvious, although well-handled, oak.

SKINNER
MEMORIAL DRIVE, COONAWARRA

The Skinner family runs the local store in Coonawarra, with four hectares of shiraz as a very profitable sideline. In a number of vintages it has had the production contract-made for it at Katnook, and some very good wine has been the result. Some of the vintages have been sold locally under the Skinner label; others have been sold in a single line to merchants in Sydney and Melbourne.

WYNNS
MEMORIAL DRIVE, COONAWARRA

The 1951 decision by David Wynn to buy Chateau Comaum and rename it Wynns' Coonawarra Estate was one for which lovers of Australian wine should be profoundly grateful. It was a decision taken 10 years before its time, and in the face of a market that as a whole displayed little or no interest in the fine claret styles at which Coonawarra excelled. Certainly the major wine companies appreciated the quality of these wines, but used them only for blending; the consumer had no idea that many of the top reds of the day had a Coonawarra component in them.

The first thing David Wynn did was to commission Richard Beck to design the classic woodcut front and back labels that still adorn the Wynns' Coonawarra Estate wines. True, so-called "marketers" have been unable to resist the temptation to update the label insidiously, so it has lost some of the simplicity and purity of its original design. But the concept remains. Next Wynn embarked on an advertising campaign in such unlikely magazines as *Quadrant* and *Meanjin*, it being always intended that the wines from Coonawarra Estate would be positioned at the very top end of the market.

Penola's newspaper, the *Pennant*, of 29 April 1954 records a visit by David Wynn to Coonawarra in which he explained the aims and philosophies of Wynns to the local growers. His company hoped to increase its crush from 300 to 1000 tonnes within a few years. Wynn was reported as saying: "My prime aim is an extensive advertising campaign in Melbourne to make Coonawarra famous. People, when thinking of claret, would then naturally think of Coonawarra. Even in a depression there would always be a demand for claret, as it is of such high quality."

But before he did all this Wynn had sent Ian Hickinbotham to take charge at Coonawarra, the first formally qualified winemaker to work in the district since Ewen McBain. Ian Hickinbotham had graduated from Roseworthy in 1950; his first job was with Wynns at their Melbourne offices. He had inherited from his father Alan Hickinbotham a deep interest in the workings of the malolactic fermentation, a fermentation of particular significance for Coonawarra. Ian made the first two vintages (1952 and 1953), and pioneered the use of far lower than traditional sulphur levels to encourage the malolactic fermentation.

Although 1952 was a miserable vintage, some great wine was made in 1953. In 1954 Norman Walker took over winemaking responsibilities; that year also saw the first vintage of Wynns' Coonawarra Estate Cabernet. 1955 was an historic year; not only did Wynns plant the first rhine riesling in the district (and commence an expansion of its cabernet sauvignon plantings) but it also produced a range of quite magnificent wines. The most exceptional of these was 1955 Michael Hermitage, a freak wine which seemingly gained much of its character from the secondhand fortified-wine cask in which it was matured. Wynns is said to have tried to repeat the success with similarly sourced casks in later years, but without success. (On the basis of the 1955 Cabernet Sauvignon, I suspect Wynns also had some great fruit to play with.)

I have tasted Michael Hermitage on half a dozen occasions over the past 15 years; every time it has shown a concentration and complexity of flavour beyond any normal bounds. It probably gave of its best at a New South Wales Wine and Food Society lunch on 28 September 1976. Six Australian reds from the 1955 vintage were lined up: Rouge Homme Claret, Orlando Cabernet, Hardy's Reserve Bin C9 Cabernet, (itself largely Redman Cabernet) Mc-William's Frederick, Wynns' Michael, Penfolds' Grange and, by way of comparison, 1955 Chateau Pontet Canet (fifth-growth Pauillac from Bordeaux). Two wines—Grange and Michael—came out on top with 19.5 points out of 20 each. My tasting notes for Michael were commendably brief: "Enormously complex on both nose and palate; intense; burgundy-like overtones" and (in block letters for reasons which now escape me), "No volatility".

But great though those early wines were, David Wynn had more than his fair share of agony in seeing the company through the initial years. It was a hard market, and the viticultural practices were much less sophisticated than those of today. Those 1955 plantings of rhine riesling, for example, did not produce their first commercial harvest until 1962. Even then there were stories circulating in the district which cast some doubt on the authenticity of the wine. In 1961 the terrible late frost that decimated much of the district entirely obliterated Wynns' harvest for that year, and no wine whatsoever was made.

In the marketplace the struggle was no less dire. But adversity of this kind had been life's blood to Samuel Wynn, and the family stood together in the hour of trial. It certainly left relatively little money to upgrade the ancient winery or even to employ qualified winemakers. Thus Jock Redman, originally the vineyard manager, without any technical qualification or training, became winemaker in 1961 and held that position until 1968. The open concrete fermenters remained in use until 1973, and all of the wood storage was in 300- and 500-gallon (1365- and 2275-litre) casks, many of them exceedingly old. It was nothing other than a tribute to the district that wines such as the '59, '60, '62 and '65 Cabernets were made.

The income tax laws of Australia in those days were little short of iniquitous in their application to private companies, forcing distribution of paper profits, and effectively preventing the level of reinvestment necessary to sustain an expanding business. It was only a question of time before Wynns went public, which they did in June 1970. In May 1972 Castlemaine Tooheys took control and subsequently amalgamated the Seaview/Glenloth/Wynns winemaking operations. These all come under the Allied Vintners Pty Limited umbrella; it in turn reports to Allied Vintners of the United Kingdom.

Whatever one's national pride may say, there can be no gain-saying the benefits to Wynns' Coonawarra Estate in terms of the development of the vineyards and winery over the past 10 years. In 1973 reconstruction and restoration of the old Riddoch Cellars commenced. A programme of replacement of the old oak storage was started, and it has gathered pace in recent years. Since John Wade's arrival as winemaker in 1978, 700 new puncheons have been acquired, and new puncheons are coming in at the rate of 180 per year. In 1973 erection of the new fermentation cellar began, housing towering rows of stainless-steel fermenters replacing the open concrete vats, which were then laboriously removed from the old building. The method of removal was old-fashioned brawn: sledge-hammers and wheelbarrows.

The fermentation cellars have been extended recently and now have a fermentation capacity of 1.2 million litres. Red grapes move one way into a brand new continuous Coq press (put into service for the 1982 vintage) with a capacity of 45 tonnes per hour. White grapes are processed at the other end of the winery and in a separate bank of presses. This system allows Wynns to crush over 6000 tonnes each vintage, all but 500 tonnes of which comes from their own vineyards. Under the guidance of vineyard manager Vic Patrick these have become the showpiece of Coonawarra. As the following table indicates, Wynns is easily the most important vigneron in this district.

PLANTED HECTARES

GRAPE	Total	Wynns	Percentage
Cabernet sauvignon	440	90	20.45
Shiraz	398	59	14.8
Grenache	34	—	—
Malbec	10	—	—
Pinot noir	32	20	62.5
Rhine riesling	458	212	46.3
Crouchen	57	2	3.5
Semillon	8	—	—
Sauvignon blanc	16	—	—
Chardonnay	59	34	57.6
All others	72	23	31.9
TOTAL	1584	440	27.7
Unplanted	262	241	
Winery	—	5	
TOTAL	1846	686	37.2

This table was prepared as at 1981; similarly detailed figures to show the current position are not available. However, Vic Patrick estimates that overall new plantings in the district in 1982 amounted to 30 hectares of pinot noir, 10 hectares of chardonnay and 10 hectares of sauvignon blanc; in 1983 40 hectares of cabernet sauvignon and 12 hectares of chardonnay; and in 1984 20 hectares of cabernet sauvignon and 12 hectares of chardonnay. It may safely be assumed that Wynns had its share of these plantings.

Together with Mildara's Bob Hollick, Vic Patrick has been responsible for the large-scale introduction of many of the new viticultural techniques to Coonawarra. Mechanical harvesting and mechanical pruning are no longer novelties, but rather standard viticultural practices in the district. Indeed Leconfield and Petaluma are the only two vineyards that claim still to hand-prune and hand-pick their vines. The new techniques encompass mechanised planting machines, enabling three workers to plant four hectares a day with a minimum of physical effort. When I think of the blood, sweat and tears that went into the planting of the first hectare at Brokenwood, words fail me. But such systems are essential when dealing with vineyards on the scale of Wynns. Thus Gartner's Block, purchased in 1976 and situated at the northern end of Coonawarra, is planted to 121.5 hectares of rhine riesling and 40.5 hectares of chardonnay. Those 121.5 hectares are the largest single planting of rhine riesling in Australia to my knowledge; in 1981 that planting was joined by another 68 hectares of rhine riesling planted on the Abbey Vineyard at the other end of Coonawarra, on the northern outskirts of Penola.

Many keen judges of the area are fiercely critical of the big companies—and particularly Wynns—for what they see as a concerted move to turn Coonawarra into a jumped-up Riverland—Australia's quality bulk-wine area. Yet talk to vineyard manager Vic Patrick as he drives you around Wynns' vast vineyards, and you get a very different viewpoint. In cooperation with Dr Richard Smart innumerable canopy-control, trellising and planting systems have been tried: east-west rows instead of the traditional north-south; movable foliage wires to promote vertical growth; the Geneva double-curtain vine-training system; close-spaced planting—the list goes on and on. And Patrick vigorously contests the notion that Wynns applies excessive irrigation to increase yields. It is used principally to aid establishment of young vines. Once they are mature, irrigation is used at the rate of around 175 millimetres per annum, lifting the average rainfall from 675 millimetres to about 850 millimetres.

In the winery John Wade points to the ever-increasing use of small oak, and to his partial adoption of French winemaking techniques following a French-funded scholarship trip to France a few years ago. This has led to his returning the red wine to barrel shortly after vintage so that it can undergo its malolactic fermentation in wood. He is also reverting to the traditional (but labour-intensive) method of leaving the casks with the bungs upright, rather than on the quarter, which means the evaporation loss (principally through the bung hole) has to be replaced by topping up at least once a week.

Wines made by him on a trial basis in the 1981 vintage using this method showed significantly greater complexity of depth and flavour than those made in the standard large-winery fashion. And the interests of Vic Patrick and John Wade coincide in the new plantings of merlot, a variety about which both men are enthusiastic.

The most recently established variety to come into commercial production is chardonnay. Wynns first planted chardonnay on a trial basis in 1974; it liked what it saw, and substantially expanded the quantity under vine in 1979 and 1980. Much of Wynns' production of chardonnay, both at Coonawarra and at Padthaway, is used to provide the base wine for its top-quality sparkling wines, notably Edmond Mazure. But in 1981 part of the crop was reserved for a still table wine. Like the Wynns' Coonawarra Rhine Riesling, it is taken to Wynns' Seaview Cellars in the form of juice and fermented there. At this point the similarity to rhine riesling ends. The wine was put into Nevers oak on July 1981, where it remained (having undergone a malolactic fermentation in the meantime) until it was bottled early in March 1982. Subsequent releases were treated in much the same way, except that a mixture of German and French oak was employed.

The Chardonnays from 1981 to 1983 inclusive have all developed remarkable richness within two years of their release. Initially the oak appeared dominant, but the fruit has quickly come up to balance that oak. Both the rate of development and the degree of richness have come as something of a surprise. On the experience of Wynns, at least, chardonnay is performing in Coonawarra in much the same way as it is in the warmer areas of Australia. Time alone will show how much this is due to the viticultural influence, how much to young vine character and how much to the winemaking techniques employed. It also remains to be seen whether these early vintages will gain a second wind in bottle.

In a comparative line-up held in July 1982 of virtually every chardonnay made in Australia in 1981, the 1981 Wynns' Coonawarra Chardonnay was ranked second overall, just behind the Roseworthy Chardonnay from David Wynn's High Eden Estate. Both it and the subsequent vintages have been consistent medal-winners at national shows, and can only be classed as a major success for Wynns.

With 212 hectares of rhine riesling planted, and with 146 hectares in bearing yielding 12.5 tonnes to the hectare, Wynns is easily the largest single producer of rhine riesling in the district. While something of a bread-and-butter line, and certainly not one ranked as one of Australia's classic whites, retrospective tastings in 1981 and 1982 showed once again that Coonawarra rhine reisling can gain unexpected depth and complexity with bottle-age. The tasting covered

the years 1964 to 1981. The 1965 vintage had entirely gone; the 1964, 1968, 1969 and 1970 showed pleasant, soft, aged rhine riesling characters, but really were little more than curiosities and did not suggest that one should make a practice of cellaring these wines for 15 years. But the 1967, and to a lesser degree the 1971, vintages were quite outstanding. The 1967 Rhine Riesling still has marvellous rich, honeyed fruit and surprising freshness. The 1971 also showed considerable life and even a suggestion that a little botrytis may have been at work in developing some lime aromas and flavours. Among the younger wines the 1979 and 1980 vintages were disappointing, but the 1981 and 1982 were both much more successful. However, there seems to me little point in cellaring these wines: the overwhelming probability is they will reach their peak in the 12 months following their release.

Like Mildara, Wynns' flagship is its Coonawarra Estate Cabernet Sauvignon. Over the many years this wine has been released some quite remarkable wines have been made. As the tasting notes that follow indicate, there have also been one or two poor ones. In 1976 Wynns gave a clear indication of just what it can achieve, even given the large-volume handling techniques it must perforce use. Its cabernet sauvignon from that year won the Jimmy Watson Trophy in Melbourne in 1977. Since that time Wynns has invested heavily and continuously in new small oak, and Coonawarra winemaker John Wade is introducing some French-oriented winemaking practices. On top of this Wynns believes its 1982 reds are the best for many, many years—thanks to some outstanding fruit from its vineyards. A tasting from cask at Coonawarra in 1984 confirmed Wynns' optimism. It will be interesting to watch the cabernet sauvignon releases over the next few years. It is also awesome to contemplate the quantities in which these wines are being made: Wynns will have well in excess of 1000 tonnes of Coonawarra cabernet sauvignon each vintage as its new plantings come into full bearing. Because of the importance of this line, and the great wines which have appeared under the Coonawarra Estate label over the years, I include tasting notes of all of the wines released up to the end of 1984. Wynns usually holds back these wines for upwards of four years before releasing them.

1980 _Colour:_ bright and clear light to medium red-purple. _Bouquet:_ crisp, clear herbaceous fruit aromas with well-handled oak. _Palate:_ a fairly light but very stylish wine, again showing herbaceous cabernet fruit flavours. Oak well integrated. A fairly forward style, for drinking before 1990. (17.5/20)

1979 *Colour:* light, bright red-purple. *Bouquet:* aromatic, fresh grassy fruit with a pleasant lift of new oak. *Palate:* rather fuller than the bouquet suggests, but with similar flavours and again well-integrated fruit and oak. The fruit flavours show little or no of the stewed-plum characters. Rather fuller in style than the 1980 wine. (18/20)

1978 *Colour:* reddish purple of medium depth; tawny rim. *Bouquet:* full, rich with a peppery tang. Fairly ripe fruit. *Palate:* full, rich, sweet fruit; a soft wine overall with low tannin on the finish. Has developed quickly. (17.5/20)

1977 *Colour:* pale brick-red. *Bouquet:* light and with cabbagey/vegetable overtones. *Palate:* lacking depth, although some recognisable cabernet character. A vintage best forgotten. (13/20)

1976 *Colour:* red-purple, not deep but of very good hue. *Bouquet:* most attractive combination of sweet-berry and green-leaf cabernet aroma. *Palate:* clean, gently sweet fruit on the middle palate. Firm finish with substantial acid and adequate tannin. Overall the wine is one of delicacy and elegance. (18.5/20)

1975 *Colour:* much lighter in colour, reddish garnet. *Bouquet:* a touch of pepper (reminiscent of the '78) intermingled with herbaceous fruit and a touch of mint/camphor for good measure. *Palate:* very French in style, with elegance, intense sappy fruit and that persistent touch of spice. (18/20)

1974 *Colour:* fairly deep red; tawny rim. *Bouquet:* distinct volatility evident, together with old-oak character. *Palate:* lacks fruit; the stale wood character together with volatility mar the wine. Never a favourite of mine. (14/20)

1973 *Colour:* deep red-brown, still with purple tints. *Bouquet:* round, rich and complex with cigar-box hints, nice oak and a touch of acceptable volatility. *Palate:* long-flavoured and quite intense, yet soft because of the low tannin profile. (17/20)

1972 *Colour:* medium red with brown rim. *Bouquet:* soft, with that vineyard pepper intermingled with an assertive wood character. *Palate:* complex fruit flavours—a curious mixture of chocolate and mushroom, yet far from unpleasant. (16.5/20)

1971 *Colour:* pale. *Bouquet:* dark, flat off-character. *Palate:* very undeveloped; lacks depth to fruit. Not in the class of the other wines. (13.5/20)

1970 *Colour:* very deep red, holding hue well.

Bouquet: abundant ripe fruit, firm and full. *Palate:* dense yet smooth wine, of medium to full weight and a firm finish. Will be long-lived. (17.5/20)

1969 Not made.

1968 *Colour:* red-brown. *Bouquet:* light, sweet caramel fruit, very ripe. *Palate:* similar to bouquet: sweet, ripe porty fruit. Finish starting to show oxidation. It is a wine going nowhere. (15/20)

1967 *Colour:* reddish, brown-tinged. *Bouquet:* not dissimilar to the 1968, but fruit much firmer and fresher. *Palate:* a ripe, chocolatey wine; firm tannin on the finish helps give balance and hold the wine together. (16.5/20)

1966 *Colour:* medium red-brown. *Bouquet:* light fruit; old-wood character dominant. *Palate:* very heavy tannin finish throws the wine out of balance. Tastes as if it were left on skins for far too long. (14.5/20)

1965 *Colour:* deep red. *Bouquet:* strong, youthful cabernet, complex and firm; outstanding for age. *Palate:* fulfils all the promise of the bouquet; very firm and fresh; excellent structure with medium tannin on the finish. (Note: bottle variation affects this wine. Some volatile. Above notes made March 1982 at Coonawarra.) (18.5/20)

1964 *Colour:* developed red-brown. *Bouquet:* dull, showing little or no varietal character. *Palate:* fruit starting to fade, although (contrary to bouquet) some cabernet flavour evident. Light, soft finish. (15/20)

1962 *Colour:* excellent for age: medium to dark red, tawny rim. *Bouquet:* marvellously complex, lifted by a touch of volatility which I love. *Palate:* outstanding old wine, wonderful fruit complexity and great varietal character. More than once have I picked it as a Bordeaux. (18.5/20)

1961 Not made.

1960 *Colour:* medium red, also excellent for age. *Bouquet:* remarkably firm and fresh with good varietal aroma. *Palate:* beautifully balanced wine with good fruit, and which will quite obviously live for many years yet. (18/20)

1959 *Colour:* brick-red of good depth. *Bouquet:* even richer than the 1960, with extraordinary fruit still evident. *Palate:* a round and complete wine at the peak of its life (November 1980). Lovely complex fruit. (18.5/20)

1958 *Colour:* developed red-brown. *Bouquet:* a big

"old-style" red with the faintest trace of mercaptan which did, however, dissipate in the glass, or was possibly just "bottle stink". *Palate:* beautifully rounded, with an ethereal finish—delicate and haunting. (18/20)

1955 *Colour:* garnet-red. *Bouquet:* remarkably clean and fresh for age, with fragrant, spicy sweet fruit. *Palate:* fulfils the promise of the bouquet, with fragrant, complex, spicy berry fruit. What a year 1955 was for Wynns. (19/20)

1954 *Colour:* brick-red. *Bouquet:* marked coffee-essence character. *Palate:* very much better; fruit still holding well, and a crisp clean finish. Would have been rated much higher if it were not for the nose. (17/20)

Wynns' Coonawarra Estate Hermitage has an equally proud history. The wines made in 1953, 1954 and 1955 are still absolutely remarkable, equal to the very greatest wines produced in Australia in those years. Tasted in 1982 and again 1984, the wines had quite exceptional fruit freshness and structure. One wine journalist on tasting the 1954 Claret (as it was then called) in 1984 commented: "I am humbled by a wine like this. It throws things into a new perspective." The 1956 and 1957 vintages have aged well, but without the power and the glory of the older wines. The 1958 and 1959 wines have gone, but 1960 produced a magnificent wine which is now at its peak. The 1962 and 1963 wines are still very attractive, and those of 1964 to 1967 are wines of character and substance which have aged well. From 1968 to 1976 (with the exception of the very pleasant 1971 vintage) the wines went through a marked dip in quality, and there is no point in cellaring these. Since 1978 fruit freshness and varietal character have returned, and, at least in some vintages, a light coating of new oak has helped. The criticism of wines such as the 1980 Hermitage is its lightness of body: while it has exceptionally attractive crushed-pepper spice aromas and flavours, it was really more of a light red or a rosé than a conventional table wine. One would also need to be exceptionally brave to cellar it.

Winemaker John Wade was well aware of the shortcomings of these wines, and has put matters to rights with the quite excellent 1982 Hermitage. The colour has returned to an appropriately deep hue; there are complex aromas of spice and berry fruits and the wine has excellent depth on the palate. At a recommended retail price of around $5 in 1984, it represented exceptional value for money.

Finally, there is the cabernet hermitage range, which seems to me to have been basically composed of the bits and pieces left over after the wine had been selected for the cabernet sauvignon and hermitage releases. It is not a wine which adds much to Wynns' reputation.

ZEMA ESTATE
PENOLA–NARACOORTE ROAD, COONAWARRA

Zema Estate is one of the newcomers on the Coonawarra scene. The Zema family, headed by Penola house-painter Dimitrio Zema, established an eight-hectare vineyard planted to four hectares of shiraz and four hectares of cabernet sauvignon. The family then established a small but functional winery on the property and employed Ken Ward as consultant winemaker.

The initial releases in 1984 comprised a 1982 Vintage Shiraz, a 1983 Rhine Riesling and a 1984 Late-Harvest Rhine Riesling. At around $6 to $6.50 a bottle at the cellar door, they offered exceptional value for money. The 1983 Rhine Riesling was, as one would expect, strongly influenced by botrytis, with an intensely aromatic and rich bouquet, and a powerful palate. As I have said again and again, whether this style appeals is a matter of personal preference. But it is not the sort of wine one can simply pass by. The 1982 vintage Shiraz was an even better wine, with magnificent spicy rich fruit, with that crushed-pepper character that I so admire. The vines are hand-pruned and hand-picked, and I believe this shows in the quality of the end product.

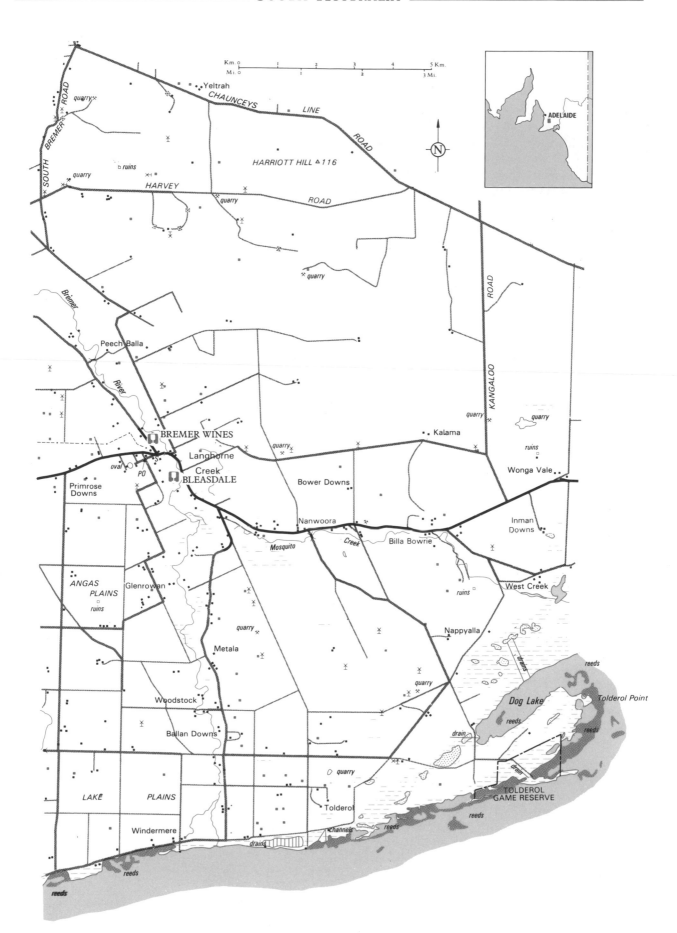

Langhorne Creek

Langhorne Creek languishes in relative obscurity 40 kilometres south-east of Adelaide on the shores of Lake Alexandrina. It is surprising it has not become better known because first of all Stoneyfell, then Lindemans and finally Wolf Blass have made extensive use of grapes grown in the region. Wolf Blass in particular finds the style of the wine ideally suited to his smooth, rich red blends designed to be at their best when released at five years of age or so.

For many years Lindemans released a shiraz oeillade claret made entirely from Langhorne Creek material. Oeillade is a synonym for cinsaut; the two parts of the wine were bought in bulk from Potts's Bleasdale Vineyards and blended and matured by Lindemans. It has, however, been discontinued. The other great wine from the region was Stoneyfell Metala, a wine developed by Bryan Dolan, which was a blend of shiraz and cabernet sauvignon. An immensely flavoured and structured wine, it is nonetheless of a style which has gone out of fashion.

BLEASDALE
WELLINGTON ROAD, LANGHORNE CREEK

The viticultural history of Langhorne Creek is essentially that of Bleasdale. It was founded by Frank Potts, who was one of the passengers on board HMS *Buffalo*, which landed the first colonists in South Australia in 1836. In 1850 he moved to the Langhorne Creek area, so named after Alfred Langhorne who had travelled overland from New South Wales in 1841 and settled in the region with his mob of cattle.

Potts planted vines and named his property Bleasdale after the Reverend J. I. Bleasdale, who was one of the major figures in nineteenth-century viticulture. The 12 hectares of vines were planted on either side of the Bremer River, the waters of which Potts diverted for the purpose of flood-irrigation, essential given the rainfall of only 350 millimetres per year. A ship's chandler by profession, he not only built the cellars but also all of the winemaking equipment in them, mostly from local red gum. The cellars and much of the remaining equipment are now classified by the National Trust. Later in his life Potts took to building paddle-steamers and racing yachts.

Until the early 1960s production was almost exclusively composed of fortified wines—port, muscat and sherry. Sales were made in bulk to local hotels and to retail bottle shops, with some larger bulk sales to the Emu Wine Company. In 1961 the first dry red table wine was made from malbec, and in 1963 the first dry red shiraz was made. Cabernet sauvignon was planted in the early 1960s, with the first shiraz cabernet blend in 1967 and the first 100 per cent cabernet varietal being made in 1971.

As the quality of the red wines became better known, so the larger wine companies came to Bleasdale to buy its wines. Quality improved further with the appointment of Iain Riggs first as vineyard manager and then winemaker. After several years Riggs moved to Hazelmere and thence to Brokenwood, to be succeeded at Bleasdale by Michael Potts, who had graduated from Roseworthy in 1980.

Bleasdale is a substantial operation; a little over 60 per cent of its annual crush of around 700 tonnes is estate-grown, the rest being purchased from local growers. The vineyards are planted to shiraz (nine hectares), verdelho, palomino and cabernet sauvignon (five hectares each), muscat gordo blanco, doradillo and rhine riesling (two hectares each), malbec and grenache (one hectare each), merlot (0.6 hectare), oeillade and frontignac (0.3 hectare each), with token quantities of crouchen and tinta madeira. The rich

alluvial loam, aided by silt deposited each year from the Bremer River floods, produces very substantial yields ranging between 10 and 15 tonnes per hectare for the premium varieties and up to 30 tonnes per hectare for doradillo.

The Bleasdale red wines sometimes suffer from mercaptan, but many of the releases are smooth, easy-drinking, if somewhat inconsequential styles. The one wine of real distinction is the very old madeira made from verdelho, one of the two varieties planted by Frank Potts in 1860. The wine is matured in small oak casks in the roof of the cellars in time-honoured tradition. Stocks are extremely limited, and cellar-door customers are limited to one bottle per head at a cost of $25 per bottle.

BREMER WINES
WELLINGTON ROAD, LANGHORNE CREEK

Bremer Wines is a small enterprise started by winemaker-owner W. L. (Bill) Davidson in 1975. The Bremer Estate vineyards comprise five hectares of cabernet sauvignon, rhine riesling and shiraz which produce a little more than half of the annual crush of around 50 tonnes. The balance is supplied from local growers.

The quality of the wines is adequate though not exciting, and most are sold at the cellar door and through the on-site restaurant. Early in 1985 it seemed probable that Bremer would discontinue its winemaking activities.

GRAPE-PICKING GANG, BLEASDALE, c. 1880

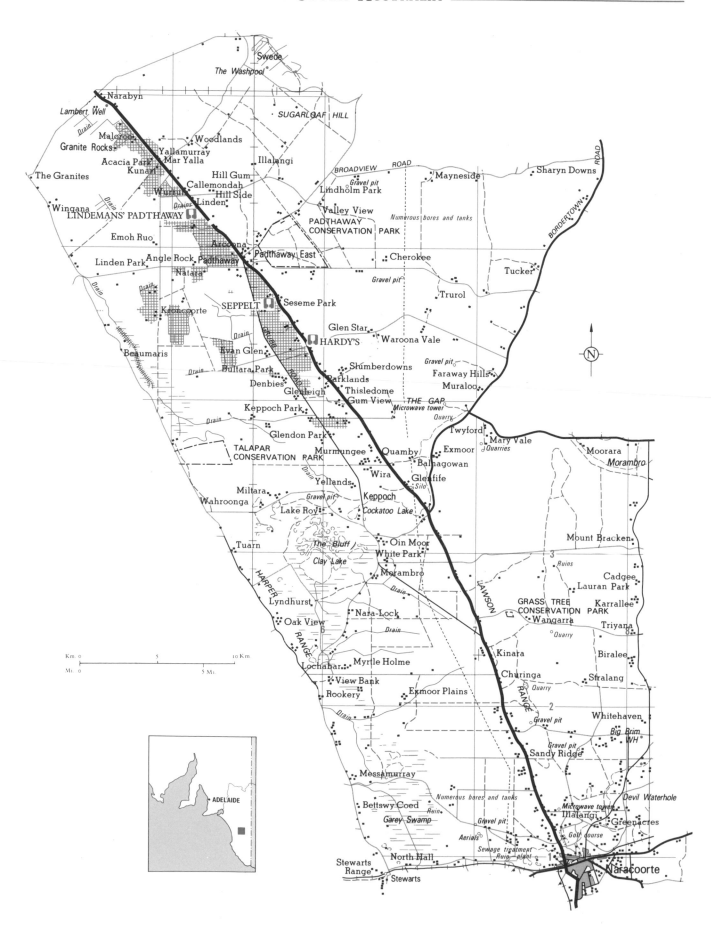

Swede

The Washpool

SUGARLOAF HILL

Narabyn

Lambert Well

Drain

Maloroo

Granite Rocks

Acacia Park

Kunari

The Granites

Woodlands

Yallamurray

Mar Yalla

Illalangi

BROADVIEW ROAD

Mayneside

Sharyn Downs

Gravel pit

Lindholm Park

Hill Gum

Callemondah

Hill Side

Wurul

Linden

Valley View

PADTHAWAY CONSERVATION PARK

Numerous bores and tanks

Wingana

Drain

Drains

LINDEMANS' PADTHAWAY

Emoh Ruo

Arcoona

Linden Park

Angle Rock

Padthaway

Natara

Padthaway East

Cherokee

Tucker

Gravel pit

Trurol

Kroncoorte

SEPPELT

Seseme Park

Glen Star

Waroona Vale

HARDY'S

Drain

Evan Glen

Bultara Park

Slumberdowns

Gravel pit

Faraway Hills

Muraloo

Denbies

Glenleigh

Parklands

Thisledome

Gum View

THE GAP

Microwave tower

Beaumaris

Drain

Keppoch Park

Quarry

Glendon Park

Twyford

Mary Vale

Moorara

Morambro

TALAPAR CONSERVATION PARK

Murmungee

Quamby

Exmoor

Quarries

Drain

Wira

Balnagowan

Glenfife

Silo

Miltara

Yellands

Keppoch

Wahroonga

Gravel pit

Lake Roy

Cockatoo Lake

Mount Bracken

Tuarn

The Bluff

Clay Lake

Oin Moor

White Park

Ruins

Cadgee

Lauran Park

Karrallee Park

Morambro

Triyana

HARPER RANGE

Lyndhurst

Nara-Lock

GRASS TREE CONSERVATION PARK

Wangarra

Oak View

Drain

Biralee

LAWSON

Kinara

Churinga

Quarry

Stralang

RANGE

Lochabar

Myrtle Holme

View Bank

Rookery

Exmoor Plains

Whitehaven

Drain

Big Brim WH

Gravel pit

Gravel pit

Sandy Ridge

Messamurray

Numerous bores and tanks

Devil Waterhole

Bettswy Coed

Ruin

Microwave tower

Illalangi

Greenacres

Garey Swamp

Gravel pit

Golf course

Aerials

Stewarts Range

North Hall

Sewage treatment plant

Ruin

Stewarts

Naracoorte

N

Km. 0   5   10 Km

Mi. 0   5 Mi.

ADELAIDE

Padthaway/Keppoch

Padthaway, also known as Keppoch, was selected as a vineyard site by Seppelt in a classic Sherlock Holmes exercise. The selection of the site both in terms of what Seppelt want from it, and in terms of pinpointing it on a map, was determined by a committee sitting around a board-room table at Seppelt's head office. The requirements were ready availability of land; a cool climate suiting the early-ripening varieties; and a readily available water supply. With these basic criteria established, Seppelt turned its attention to the south-eastern quarter of South Australia. Searches at the CSIRO and Department of Agriculture revealed a 1944 study of an area of about 8000 acres (3240 hectares) lying between Naracoorte and the Stewart Range. That report said in part:

> The soil type which occurs in numerous small patches consists of a brown sandy loam over red-brown clay over limestone. This soil type is very variable in depth and there are usually some stony portions on each of the small patches in which it occurs. It is a terra rosa soil . . . the deeper sites of the terra rosa soils should make first-class garden soils.

Only then did Seppelt's viticulturalists set foot in the area. They located a strip running for 16 kilometres along the Padthaway to Naracoorte road, varying in width from just under one kilometre to 1.6 kilometres. Importantly it fell within the narrow 550-millimetre rain belt. Just as at Coonawarra, the pioneers had selected the red earth for their main roads because of its good draining qualities. These made roads passable in winter when the surrounding grey and black soils become a quagmire. Although 500 millimetres is a modest rainfall, the south-eastern area literally floats on an underground watertable, and extensive surface-drainage systems have had to be installed to make much of it suitable for agriculture. That watertable—common to Coonawarra—is the key to the viticultural magic that both areas offer: high-quality grapes with high yields, a very rare combination. Young vines

use irrigation while they are being established, but within four or five years their roots reach down to the watertable and draw up moisture naturally. Irrigation is then used for spring frost control and to avoid stress in summer drought.

There are still no wineries at Padthaway, although Seppelt and Hardy's both have crushing facilities to enable chilled must or juice to be transported in tankers to their various wineries. Furthermore, the district plantings of 1356 hectares (compared with around 1680 hectares at Coonawarra) are dominated by four companies: Lindemans, Seppelt, Hardy's and Wynns. There is only one independent grower of importance, Don Brown. It is fair to say that while both Seppelt and Lindemans went into the area on a large scale, they were not expecting to obtain high-quality grapes; and so they have been pleasantly surprised at the quality which has been forthcoming.

If the reputation of Coonawarra is based on its red wines, that of Padthaway is based on its whites. Rhine riesling, chardonnay and sauvignon blanc have all produced table wines of well above-average quality. Traminer, verdelho, crouchen, tokay, sylvaner, semillon, chenin blanc and muller-thurgau are all also grown with varying degrees of success.

Which is the chicken and which is the egg, I do not know, but rhine riesling (accounting for by far the greatest proportion of white varieties in the region) has had the greatest success. It now provides all of the base wine for Hardy's Siegersdorf Rhine Riesling, most for Seppelt's Black Label Rhine Riesling, and of course all of the Lindemans' Padthaway Rhine Riesling range. In the case of Hardy's and Seppelt these rhine rieslings are clearly their brand leaders; the multiplicity of the Lindemans brands leaves its position a little more obscure. Orlando, large buyers of material in Coonawarra, also purchase extensively in Padthaway, and have also released some excellent rhine rieslings. Overall Padthaway rhine riesling is rather softer, fuller and slightly quicker to develop than that of Coonawarra. Quality has been much more consistent, with a mid-palate weight and flavour vaguely reminiscent of a developed Eden Valley rhine riesling. Many of the wines seem to have a soft tropical-fruit/lime overlay.

Padthaway was also the first region to produce late-harvest rhine riesling in large quantity. Botrytis has finally arrived at Padthaway too, but those early wines were, I believe, achieved using a variety of techniques including branch-cutting. Using this system the arms of the vines are severed up to two weeks before harvest, allowing the grapes to raisin slowly.

Chardonnay is put to a number of uses. The extensive Wynns plantings are basically dedicated to sparkling wine, and it is fair to assume that an increasing percentage of the production of each of the other three major companies is being used for this purpose. Lindemans (regularly) and Hardy's (intermittently) release Padthaway chardonnay varietal wines, the quality of which is exemplary. Lindemans also appears to have determined precisely the formula for handling sauvignon blanc in a fumé style. One or two of its releases have been criticised for volatility, but I have enjoyed every one of them.

The red wines have been more variable. Here Thomas Hardy has had by far the greatest success, with some outstanding cabernets and cabernet malbec blends. The red variety which (relatively speaking) most consistently succeeds is pinot noir. Once again its use is partly as a table wine and partly in sparkling-wine production. Lindemans has been the most consistent producer of varietal table wine, while Hardy's has had one or two outstanding wines.

THOMAS HARDY
NARACOORTE ROAD, KEPPOCH

Thomas Hardy purchased wine from Coonawarra for many decades. Over the years I have shared many bottles of 1955 Cabernet Sauvignon Bin C9, a Tahbilk/Redman blend and a wine of rare quality. Nonetheless, Hardy's stood back and watched as the other major wine companies carved up the dwindling supplies of Coonawarra terra rosa between them.

When Lindemans bought Redman — its traditional source of supply — Hardy's was forced to do something. In the short term it secured wine from Eric Brand, whose initial encouragement had come partly from Hardy's and who in effect had set him up in business. Indeed the Brand/Hardy link continues to this day, but Eric always had and still has a relatively

small winery. For a company the size of Thomas Hardy his wines were but a drop in the bucket.

A major move was essential, but to everyone's surprise it came not in Coonawarra but at Keppoch. It would be interesting to read the board minutes and feasibility studies that Hardy's must have commissioned, but it was fairly reticent about disclosing any detailed information on what lay behind its decision. The closest it came was a cryptic comment, "Keppoch is 50 miles [80 kilometres] north of Coonawarra where the wines in some years are excessively acid".

In any event in 1968 Hardy's purchased 240 hectares at Keppoch, of which 160 hectares were terra rosa and 80 hectares were light loam over limestone. After planting 80 hectares of shiraz and 40 hectares of cabernet sauvignon, and 10 hectares each of malbec and pinot noir, seven hectares of rhine riesling were established on a trial basis. The fruit produced by the rhine riesling was of such quality that Hardy's purchased an additional 240 hectares of adjoining land with identical soil. No doubt this ready availability of large parcels of land — at significantly lower prices than those prevailing at Coonawarra — had played an important part in the original decision to go to Keppoch rather than to Coonawarra.

The composition of the plantings has changed somewhat, with rhine riesling (115 hectares) now by far the most important variety, followed by shiraz (88 hectares), cabernet sauvignon (33 hectares), traminer (17 hectares), chardonnay (17 hectares), merlot (10 hectares), pinot noir (seven hectares), sauvignon blanc (five hectares) and malbec (2.5 hectares). It is Hardy's most important source of quality table wine, and its importance continues to grow year by year.

Hardy's has installed a large crushing/dejuicing plant at Keppoch which allows it to transport white juice and red must back to its wineries around Adelaide. When I visited it during the height of vintage it was working 24 hours a day at almost maximum capacity, handling prodigious amounts of juice.

Prior to 1981 (with the exception of the 1978 Pinot Noir) Hardy's marketed its best Keppoch varietal or Keppoch-blended wines under its Reserve Bin label: a typed style of label with each wine having a different bin number. The Reserve Bin label has remained for the top commercial releases by Hardy's, but has been joined — in terms of quality and no doubt price — by a special Keppoch label modelled on the pinot noir label. Both the Reserve Bin and Keppoch releases will be available only when Hardy's considers the wine quality is sufficiently high. Thus in both 1979 and 1980 the Keppoch Pinot Noir was not considered up to standard for the Keppoch label and was blended into the St Thomas Burgundy (which, incidentally, is of excellent quality in those two years).(Late in 1985 the labelling system for Hardy's will change once again.)

The most important contribution of Keppoch is the wine which these days makes Hardy's national brand leader, Siegersdorf Rhine Riesling. Throughout the latter part of the 1980s Siegersdorf was gradually transformed from a Barossa/McLaren Vale-based wine to a Keppoch-dominant wine, and finally in the 1980s it became 100 per cent Keppoch. The Keppoch material fits very well into the Siegersdorf style; ever since Brian Croser left a little residual sugar in the 1975 vintage (while at the same time preserving maximum fruit freshness), Siegersdorf has been one of the most popular rhine rieslings on the Australian market. Its quality, too, has been almost invariably very good. Recent releases have continued the tradition; the 1983 release showed fairly marked botrytis influence (and was for this reason a little outside the normal Siegersdorf style) but the quality was there.

Like the other major companies in the south-east, most of the chardonnay and a considerable part of the pinot noir grown by Hardy's at Keppoch goes towards sparkling wine. With Hardy's large back stocks of these wines the impact is only slowly becoming apparent, but by the end of the 1980s one assumes its wines of this style will come exclusively from Keppoch.

The range of releases is steadily increasing. In the last few years outstanding wines have included a richly flavoured 1982 Reserve Bin Chardonnay, aromatic and powerful; a 1982 Gewurtztraminer which had infinitely more flavour and style than earlier releases under this label; a truly excellent 1981 Pinot Noir, after a long absence of this label; and a very creditable 1980 Malbec with sweet spicy fruit and a nice touch of charred oak.

The most prestigious wine (at least in Hardy's reckoning) to be released from Keppoch in recent years is the 1979 Eileen Hardy Cabernet Sauvignon. I very much enjoyed the rich, ripe-fruit characters in this wine; other judges were less enthusiastic, but it was, and is, a great food wine.

LINDEMANS' PADTHAWAY
NARACOORTE ROAD, PADTHAWAY

Both Lindemans and Hardy's moved into the Keppoch/Padthaway area in 1968. Cost considerations apart, Hardy's were of the opinion that at the time significant parcels of land were not available in Coonawarra. The land that Mildara and Wynns subsequently purchased was simply not on the market when Lindemans (and thereby Hardy's) took their investment decisions. The catalyst in the case of Lindemans was (ironically) an offer to acquire Tulloch's Hunter Valley winery and vineyards. Lindemans did some figures, looked at the uncertain climate and modest yields of the Hunter, and looked, too, at the market it wished to service at that time. This market revolved around its Cawarra/Private Bin range—commercial wines produced in large quantities requiring a guaranteed grape supply at modest cost. It was painfully clear that whatever Tulloch's might offer, it was not the answer to that particular requirement. In November of the following year Tulloch's was purchased by the multinational Reed Consolidated Industries group.

Lindemans calculated that for the asking price put by Tulloch's it would be able to buy and bring into production 405 hectares of land in the south-east. Philip Laffer was directed to carry out a detailed survey of possible sites in that general area, and came up with two possible answers. One was a 2000-hectare property called Hatherley Hills on the coast at Beachport. The soil on much of it was ideal: terra rosa, with abundant water between three and six metres under the surface. The disadvantage was the proximity to the sea: Lindemans foresaw ripening and salt-burn problems, the latter of the kind which have seemingly affected the Margaret River area in Western Australia. The alternative was a 440-hectare property owned by W. (Bill) Smith at Padthaway and which was then on the market. Lindemans went over it with the intending vigneron's version of a fine-toothed comb—a two-inch (five-centimetre) auger-drill—taking soil samples on 30-metre spacings. They found the soil types varied from grey sands, through to heavier grey soils equivalent to the black soil of Coonawarra, through to terra rosa. But all were well drained (better, in Lindemans' opinion, than much of Seppelt's land purchased some years earlier), and all had access to the underlying water-table.

The decision to purchase at a cost of $200,000 was taken in 1968, but planting commenced in the winter of 1970. Both then and now Lindemans regards Padthaway as primarily a white-wine area, although several excellent pinot noirs have been released. In 1973 the adjoining 365-hectare property known as Arcoona, owned by Saddler, was acquired. The final piece in the jigsaw fell into place a year or two later when Stanfield sold Lindemans a similarly sized property.

Plantings have continued methodically each year since 1970; the bottom land was planted first, with the gentle hills which run away from the road coming next. Plantings are now virtually complete, and are made up as follows: rhine riesling (216 hectares), chardonnay (61 hectares), traminer (51 hectares), shiraz (49 hectares), grenache (42 hectares), crouchen (29 hectares), tokay (21 hectares), sauvignon blanc (19 hectares), verdelho (19 hectares), sylvaner (15 hectares), frontignac (12 hectares), semillon (12 hectares), pinot noir (10 hectares), chenin blanc (10 hectares), cabernet sauvignon (eight hectares), cinsaut (six hectares), muller-thurgau (one hectare) and experimental varieties (five hectares). The fruit is mainly processed at Lindemans' Rouge Homme although, in common with Wynns and Mildara, much of the white juice is taken elsewhere (principally to Karadoc but also to Chateau Leonay) for fermentation.

The purpose of Padthaway has at least partially changed since the original investment decision was taken. I think Lindemans is quite frankly surprised— and delighted— at the quality of the wines it has been able to make. While a significant part of the crop does end up in the Private Bin range (and incidentally keeps the value for money of those wines at an uncomfortable level for their competitors), a diverse range of very good to outstanding wines has been released.

Rhine riesling is by far the most extensively propagated variety. Thanks both to the climate and to some highly sophisticated viticultural techniques (including the cutting of fruit-laden branches, which are then left on the vine for the grapes to raisin slowly) some singular spatlese and auslese wines have been made, some released under the Lindemans banner and others under the Leo Buring label. The dry rhine rieslings so far released have been consistently pleasant wines. Both the 1981 and 1982 releases (the latter still current in early 1985) exhibit full, soft, non-botrytised fruit with those lime/vanilla aromas and flavours which are so much a hallmark of the district. With a true retail price of under $5, these are remarkable buys.

It may well be my sweet tooth, but I believe the spatlese and auslese Padthaway rhine rieslings of Lindemans have been even more impressive. The 1980 Spatlese and the 1980 Auslese were both great wines; they were also made in very substantial quantities, and had been on the market more or less continuously from 1983 through to early 1985. By the end of this time they had developed marvellous complexity, with the 1980 Auslese obviously the sweeter of the two. Remarkably the 1980 Spatlese still seemed to have time in front of it, and could be purchased for less than $5. The 1981 vintages of each of these wines are equally outstanding.

Lindemans' Padthaway Traminer, made in a dry style, has been an eminently forgettable wine: while free from fault, the releases have also been free from any real varietal character or fruit. In 1983, under the Leo Buring label, an auslese traminer was released; although the area source is not named I would be surprised if this were not at least substantially Padthaway material. It, in contrast, is a superbly luscious and rich wine, full of tropical-fruit aromas and flavours, and none of the tannic hardness which can disfigure such wines. Again in the late-harvest mould, Lindemans has released two Padthaway spatlese frontignacs. The 1980 vintage had enormous varietal flavour but a touch of hardness on the finish; the 1981 had less intense varietal flavour, but was perfectly balanced. Even though the flavour was relatively less, it was still marvellously true to the flavour of the grape.

The Lindemans' Padthaway Fumé Blanc releases of 1980 to 1983 inclusive have all been excellent wines showing very sophisticated use of oak, and with the soft Padthaway fruit character filling out the mid-palate to perfection.

A one-off release of 1982 Padthaway Zinfandel was an interesting wine, very light and fresh, but far from instantly recognisable as zinfandel. Certainly it bears no resemblance to the zinfandels of the Margaret River. Of the pinot noir releases so far, the 1980 is the outstanding vintage.

Finally, the 1984 Lindemans' Padthaway Chardonnay has swept all before it in shows in 1985, reinforcing both the quality and versatility of this area.

SEPPELT
NARACOORTE ROAD, KEPPOCH

Seppelt was the first company to establish (in 1963) a vineyard in the Keppoch area (as they prefer to call it). It was a far-reaching decision taken against the profound changes then sweeping the Australian wine industry. In the early 1960s the significant movement away from fortified wines to table wines had became apparent in wine sales. Seppelt took stock of its position, and this is what it saw. Many of its existing vineyards were ageing and in need of replanting, and two of its three winery complexes (Barossa and Rutherglen) were designed principally to handle fortified wines and brandy. After a detailed assessment of the potential for expansion in the Barossa Valley and other existing areas, Seppelt decided it was necessary to look at totally new areas.

Seppelt's assessment had extended to the impact of climate (and soil) in Europe, and it was decided to look to cooler areas. An added reason was the existing pattern of Seppelt's plantings: it had adequate supplies of the mid-season varieties such as rhine riesling, cabernet sauvignon and shiraz, but little or no access to early-ripening varieties such as pinot noir, chardonnay, pinot meunière, gewurztztraminer and sylvaner.

The decision was taken to come to Padthaway and in 1963 an 880-acre (356-hectare) property was purchased. Trial plots of a quarter acre (0.1 hectare) each were established in October of that year, covering a wide range of red and white varietals. Shortly after Seppelt acquired its Drumborg Vineyard across the border in Victoria, and the decision was taken to concentrate on white varieties there and on reds at Keppoch. Accordingly in the following few years the plantings (25 hectares in 1964 and a further 25 the following year) were of traditional red varieties.

It was not until a number of years later, when the wines made from the trial plantings were evaluated, that it became clear that the area was suited just as well—if not better—to white varieties. The pattern of plantings then changed again. Today Seppelt has a total of 169 hectares under vine, planted to rhine riesling, chardonnay, frontignac, sylvaner, pinot noir, shiraz, cabernet sauvignon, gewurztztraminer and merlot.

Certainly the rhine rieslings made by Seppelt have proved the worth of the area for whites beyond doubt. Pride of place goes to the Seppelt Black Label range, usually but not always containing more than 50 per cent Keppoch material. While these wines seem to develop full, soft flavour at an early age, and are for this reason regarded as early-maturing styles, the older releases have held together better than one might have expected.

The wines have all won numerous medals at national shows, with the 1981 (a multi-gold-medal and trophy-winner) the most successful. The 1982 vintage (comprising 80 per cent Keppoch material)

was a good wine, though not in the same class. In 1983 an outstanding spatlese rhine riesling was made, with such depth of flavour that one might have expected an auslese label. The wine was full of sweet fruit flavours, botrytis having quite clearly been heavily at work, investing the wine with overtones of peaches and apricots.

Seppelt has also had success with frontignan blanc releases, with the wines exhibiting similar intense varietal characteristics to those of Lindemans. The 1982 vintage was the best so far.

Substantial quantities of Seppelt's Keppoch rhine riesling go into the Reserve Bin range and also into the other confusing array of Seppelt's table-wine labels. There is little doubt that Seppelt class the variety as an unqualified success in the district.

The shiraz and cabernet sauvignon have also been vintaged with success from Keppoch material, but have so far been used principally as blend components. ◘

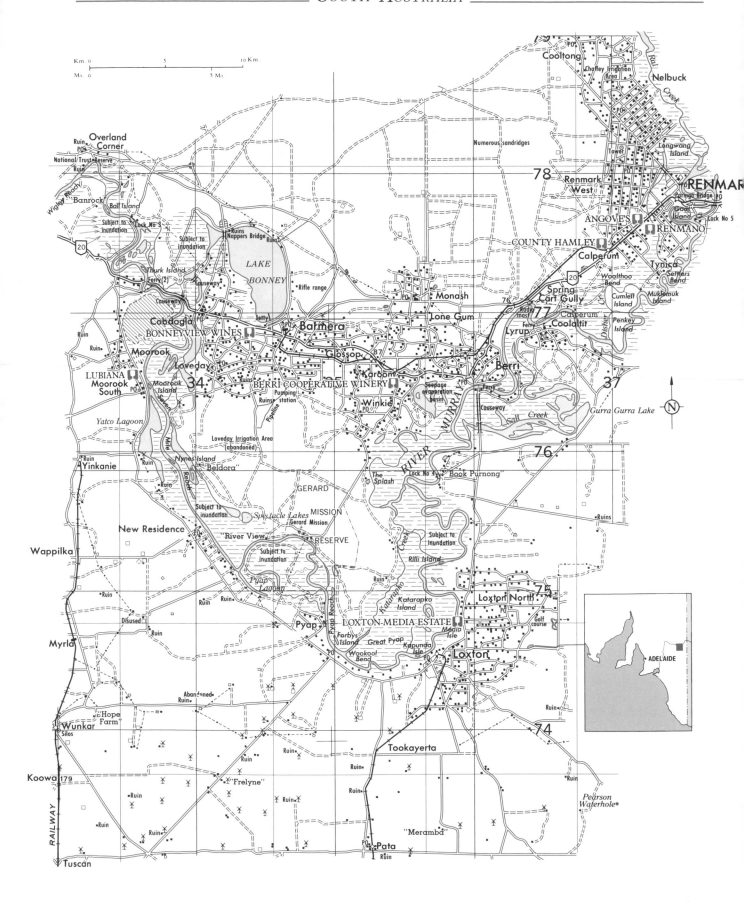

Km 0   5   10 Km
Mi. 0   5 Mi

Overland Corner
Ruin PO
National Trust Reserve
Ruin
Banrock
Ball Island
Wigley Reach
Thurk Island
Ferry (2)
Subject to inundation
Lock No 3
Causeway
Causeway
Ruins Nappers Bridge Ruin
Subject to inundation
LAKE BONNEY
Rifle range
Jetty
PO
Monash
Lone Gum
Cobdogla
BONNEYVIEW WINES
Barmera
Moorook
Glossop
LUBIANA
Moorook South
Loveday
PO
Moorook Island
34
Kardom
BERRI CO-OPERATIVE WINERY
Winkie
Berri
Ferry
Causeway
Salt Creek
37
Gurra Gurra Lake
Seepage evaporation basin
Pumping station
Ruins
Pipeline
Loveday Irrigation Area (abandoned)
Yatco Lagoon
Ruin
Yinkanie
Ruin
Nynes Island
"Beldora"
Mile
Rebeh
River View
Subject to inundation
GERARD MISSION
RESERVE
Gerard Mission
The Splash
Lock No 4
"Book Purnong"
RIVER MURRAY
76
Ruins
New Residence
Subject to inundation
Spectacle Lakes
Subject to inundation
Rilli Island
Wappilka
Pyap Lagoon
Katarapko Creek
Katarapko Island
Loxton North
Golf course
75
Ruin
Disused
Ruin
Myrla
Pyap
Pyap Reach
Forbys Island
LOXTON MEDIA ESTATE
Media Isle
Great Pyap
Kapunda Isle
Wookool Bend
Loxton
PO
Ruin
74
Abandoned Ruin
"Hope Farm"
Wunkar
Silos
Tookayerta
Ruin
Ruin
Ruin
"Meramba"
Pearson Waterhole
Koowa 179
"Frelyne"
Ruin
Ruin
RAILWAY
Ruin
Ruin
Ruin
Ruin
Pata
Ruin
Tuscan

Cooltong
PO
Chaffey Irrigation Area
Nelbuck
Numerous sandridges
Rail
Renmark Creek
78
Renmark West
Longwang Island
Tower
RENMARK
Paringa Bridge PO
ANGOVES
Goat Island
Lock No 5
RENMANO
COUNTY HAMLEY
Calperum
Woolthoo Bend
Tynica
Settlers Bend
Cumlett Island
Mukkomuk Island
Spring Cart Gully
Coolaltit
77
Calperum
Radio mast
Lyrup
Penkey Island
20
76

ADELAIDE

N

Riverland

When George Chaffey fell foul of political duplicity in Victoria in 1887, the South Australian government quickly stepped in to capitalise on the expertise he and his brother William had developed in pioneering irrigation in California. With unconditional government support the Chaffeys selected Renmark, on the west bank of the Murray, as the site for the commencement of irrigation in South Australia. With formidable energy, the brothers had quickly laid out the site of the town, with the wide streets and parklands which remain a feature to this day.

It was not long, however, before the Chaffeys were back in Victoria, developing Mildura for a by then chastened Victorian government. In 1893 the Renmark Irrigation Trust took over responsibility for the area, and for maintaining the irrigation channels which had already started to fall into disrepair. The trust has since been responsible both for the town of Renmark and for 4800 hectares of orchards and vineyards in the district; it is in turn effectively run by local landholders.

Over the years the Riverland areas have spread along the length of the Murray and are now divided into three principal sub-districts. The first is the Lower Murray area, which runs south from Waikerie—the area of vines has steadily declined over the past six years from 3300 hectares in 1979 to 2746 hectares in 1984. Production has fallen from 49,000 tonnes to 42,300 tonnes over the same period. The principal winery is Thomas Hardy and Sons' Cyrilton Winery, erected in 1921 but expanded and modernised on a number of occasions since. Hardy's has 40 hectares of vineyards in the region, planted principally to doradillo, muscat gordo blanco, grenache, palomino, pedro ximinez, rhine riesling and shiraz. As the plantings indicate, much of the material is distilled to form the base of the immense stocks of high-quality brandy which Hardy's still holds. The other large winery is the Barossa Waikerie Cooperative, now part of the Penfolds—Kaiser Stuhl marketing group.

Further upstream the Riverland is divided into the South Murray area (running along the south bank of the river) and the North Murray area (obviously enough, running along the north bank). The division seems to have importance for statistical purposes, but little other. The South Murray area is centred around Loxton; the North Murray, by far the biggest in terms of production, around Renmark. As with the case of Waikerie and the Lower Murray, both areas have shown a steady decline in plantings, although production has remained more or less constant which suggests greater efficiency in the vineyards. In 1984 the 2200 hectares of vines in the South Murray region produced 37,000 tonnes of grapes; in the North Murray 6850 hectares yielded 96,000 tonnes.

In all, the Riverland contributes a little over 175,000 tonnes to the South Australian crush of 288,000 tonnes in 1984. This handsome contribution provided 35 per cent of the entire Australian crush for the year and 61 per cent of the entire South Australian crush. The decline in production has been due in part to the salinity problems which have plagued the Murray for decades. The decline in the brandy fortified-wine markets has also had a marked impact. Nonetheless, the Riverland remains the most important grape-growing region in Australia. The alluvial sandy loams (occasionally running into heavier red clays) over limestone subsoils provide the ready drainage which vines so appreciate. Only water is required to produce yields of between 15 to 20 tonnes per hectare. Obviously the very hot and dry climate is not conducive to ultimate quality—the Riverland is principally a bulk producer of *vin ordinaire* and of base wine for distillation.

However, companies such as Yalumba (who have a 240-hectare vineyard at Oxford Landing), Seppelt (a 200-hectare vineyard at Qualco), Thomas Hardy, Renmano, Berri Cooperative and Angove's have all at various times proved that it is possible to gain that bit of extra quality with a certain portion of the crush. This relatively small percentage is bottled and released, proving that clever winemaking can produce silk purses out of sow's ears.

ANGOVE'S
BOOKMARK AVENUE, RENMARK

It may be that Angove's finds itself based solely in Renmark through default rather than by free choice, but it by no means shows in its wines. Perhaps the resumption of the Tea Tree Gully Vineyards will in the fullness of time no longer seem an injustice. For it was in Tea Tree Gully, at the foothills of the Mount Lofty Ranges, that Dr William Angove, his wife and five children settled when they arrived from England in 1886. Dr Angove had graduated from St Bartholomew's Hospital Medical School in 1875, but after a period of general practice in the United Kingdom he decided to seek a new and better life in Australia.

A medical practice—centred on Tea Tree Gully— was purchased by correspondence from England and Angove duly arrived in Australia. A man of immense energy, his many interests included grape-growing and winemaking. Initially on a small scale, with 13 hectares of vines near the Angoves' house, it became a major enterprise with the 1891 acquisition of 65 hectares of land in the nearby Hope Valley. Angove named this property Tregrehan, recalling the name of a house owned by his wife's parents in Cornwall. By the mid-1890s Angove's wines were well known, competing successfully in shows against the great names of the day.

By the turn of the century Angove's was processing 300 tonnes of grapes each year—mostly estate-grown but with small quantities bought in from local growers. Production was principally of fortified wine and brandy, but limited quantities of dry table wine were also made.

In 1899 Dr Angove's eldest son, Thomas Carlyon Angove, enrolled at Roseworthy Agricultural College and undertook the diploma course in agriculture. In those days (and indeed for a further 40 years) there was no oenology course, winemaking and viticulture being taught as subjects in the general agriculture course. During his time at Roseworthy, Thomas Angove became friends with Henry Martin of Stoneyfell, and the two were to remain close friends for the rest of their lives.

In 1910 Thomas Angove, together with his brothers Edward and Leonard, decided to establish a distillery and processing house at Renmark on the River Murray. Angove's interest had been sparked by a glut of grapes in the previous year, which had led to 400 tonnes being processed at Tea Tree Gully and turned into fortifying spirit. It was for this purpose—fortifying spirit—that the Renmark operation was established. Until that time all of the grapes grown in South Australia's Riverland had been used as table or dried grapes, so the Renmark distillery was the first winemaking venture in the Riverland.

Two years later a second winery was established at the nearby settlement of Lyrup and the first vintage was made there in 1914. The Lyrup Winery was established in partnership with Henry Martin of Stoneyfell, and from the year of its establishment until 1958 it was managed by H. H. Beams, who had joined Angove's at Tea Tree Gully at the age of 14. Both the cellars at Lyrup and those in Tea Tree Gully are still in operation, although the latter is purely a museum and tourist information centre.

Edward Angove was killed in the First World War and Leonard left the business to become a marine engineer, leaving Thomas Angove to run the business on his own. The Soldier Settlement Schemes introduced after the First World War led to a rapid expansion in the level of activity. The 1920s were a period of unequalled prosperity for the Riverland areas in all three States—exports soared with the dual incentive of the Commonwealth government bounties under the Export Development Act and the preferential tariffs introduced by the British Parliament.

When this market was threatened in 1929 with the removal of the preferential tariff and the termination of the bounty, Angove's and Stoneyfell responded by setting up their own agency in London, Dominion Wines Limited, which was instrumental in gaining continued access to the British market. Angove's was also active in Malaya, India, Canada and the East and West Indies.

St Agnes Brandy was produced at Renmark; Marko Vermouth and sweet dessert wines were made at Lyrup; while Tea Tree Gully provided dry table wines and some fortified wine. In 1940 Bob Hill joined the Renmark Winery and continues the tradition of long-serving employees. Together with Frank Newman, he is responsible for winemaking operations at Renmark.

Perhaps the most significant development was the 1968 establishment of the Nanya Vineyards, which have been increasingly oriented to the production of premium table wine. Angove's now has 480 hectares under wine, producing 35 per cent of the company's very large crush. Even now not all the vineyards are in bearing, with some varieties still under evaluation. The varieties planted include rhine riesling, sauvignon blanc, sylvaner, traminer, chardonnay, colombard, doradillo, palomino, trebbiano, cabernet sauvignon, shiraz, mataro, grenache, malbec, pinot noir, carignane and ruby cabernet.

If all that suggests that Angove's has not left much to chance, the winemaking reinforces the impression. Angove's does not disclose its total crush or production, but I would be surprised if it were much less than 15,000 tonnes a year. Production extends across the full gamut of every known wine style from fine varietal table wines to generic styles, to flagons and five-litre casks, to vermouth, ginger wine, sherries, ports, muscats and marsalas (many offered in both bottle and flagon), and finally to a range of brandies culminating in St Agnes Very Old Brandy, one of the greatest wood-aged pot-still brandies available in Australia.

But since 1979 it has been the varietal white-wine releases—and as in 1983 the red-wine varietal releases—which have been outstanding. These varietal wines do not scale the heights of absolute excellence in every year, but Angove's track record over 1983 and 1984 leaves little to be desired. In 1983 the sauvignon blanc was the outstanding varietal release, hotly pursued by the chardonnay and colombard. In 1984 the colombard, sauvignon blanc and chenin blanc were all excellent; the chardonnay was well above average, and the rhine riesling and sylvaner riesling were well-made wines which suffered only in comparison with the other releases. The hallmark of all of these wines is the technical excellence of the making, which has resulted in every last whisper of aroma and every milligram of flavour being retained. Yet I am not too sure that this technical virtuosity pales into insignificance against the achievement of the 1983 Cabernet Sauvignon. Australian white-wine-makers have become very adept at handling warm-climate fruit, with night harvesting and all of the modern gadgetry of the well-equipped winery. The 1983 Cabernet Sauvignon, with its intense cassis/berry flavours, allied with a remarkably rich and deep structure, represents a high point of achievement with red grapes grown in Riverland conditions.

All in all Angove's must be regarded as the premier producers of South Australian Riverland table wine.

BERRI COOPERATIVE WINERY
STURT HIGHWAY, KAROOM

In July 1982 Consolidated Cooperative Wineries Limited acquired the share capital of the Berri Cooperative Winery and Distillery Limited and of Renmano Wines Cooperative Limited. In so doing it has created one of the largest wine-producing companies in Australia, which provides around 15 per cent of the annual Australian domestic production. Its 1100 grape-grower shareholders delivered more than 50,000 tonnes of grapes during the 1984 vintage from over 3025 hectares of grapes.

Berri and Renmano have recently made concerted moves to gain access to the British market on a large scale. One of the wines sold is labelled Fruity Gordo and will bear the slogan "The wine from down under you will flip over". It is in fact the single-largest selling wine in Australia, with annual sales exceeding six million litres, mainly in bulk to other wine companies, but of course partly under the Fruity Gordo label. It is a style of wine at which Australia excels, and there is no reason why it should not do well in the British market.

Notwithstanding the merger the products of each of the two companies will continue to be made and marketed quite separately on the domestic market, and for this reason I have elected to deal with them as separate entities.

In 1916 the major dried-fruits processor and exporter in the district formed a subsidiary to distil the excess sultanas and raisins left over at the end of packing operations. The equipment was makeshift, and in 1918 a little winery/distillery was built. It was equipped with a small crusher and other steam-driven machinery together with one continuous still. In that year 100 tonnes of grapes were crushed.

Grape production increased rapidly after the end of the First World War with the impact of Soldier Settlement Schemes. By 1922 a substantial grape surplus was imminent and Mrs H. R. Curran and W. Gillard were instrumental in initiating moves which led to the formation of the Berri Growers' Cooperative Distillery.

For a number of years the operation produced only brandy spirit. Gradually, however, the growers were encouraged to reduce their plantings of doradillo by grubbing out or grafting over the vines to other varieties. This in turn meant the introduction of a gradual increase in the production of fortified wine. With this change in emphasis the company's name was changed to Berri Cooperative Winery and Distillery Limited in the early 1930s; throughout this time the cooperative's production steadily increased.

The most significant development came in 1958, with the decision to build a separate winery dedicated solely to the production of table wine. It led to the establishment of what is one of the most sophisticated and technologically efficient table-wine cellars in Australia.

There are now 40 million litres of storage within the winery, five million litres of which are devoted to oak hogsheads and puncheons for premium dry red, dessert wine and brandy maturation. A further six million litres of stainless-steel storage is contained inside specially constructed refrigerated cold-rooms used for cold fermentation and for general storage purposes.

In 1984 Berri crushed 38,738 tonnes under the supervision of its chief winemaker, R. J. Wilkinson. Wilkinson inherits a proud tradition; previous wine-makers have included Brian Barry (who did much to lift the quality of Berri's red wines and the public's awareness of them) and Ian MacKenzie (now chief winemaker for Seppelt). It was in no small part due to the efforts of these two men that Berri has won more than 1000 medals during the eight-year period from 1976 to 1983. It also has received a number of trophies including the Jimmy Watson Memorial Trophy, and the Most Successful Exhibitor's Trophy at the first National Wine Show in Canberra in 1977.

The Berri Estate white table wines are invariably honest, well-made wines which offer excellent value for money at the very modest prices at which they are sold. The most consistent is the rhine riesling, both dry and spatlese. The 1982 and 1984 vintages were workmanlike, early-maturing wines with initial light, aromatic fruit flavours developing fairly rapidly into a fuller, softer style. The chardonnays of recent years are obviously all receiving some oak; in 1982 the formula worked well enough, but in 1984 the oak was rather bitter and hard, and obscured the fruit. It may be that an extra year in bottle will allow the fruit to come up and the oak to soften.

The most successful wines for Berri—at least in terms of show results—have been its cabernet sauvignon, its cabernet malbec, and its cabernet malbec shiraz. The 1975 Cabernet Malbec Shiraz and the 1977 Cabernet Malbec were both prolific show winners, the final release of the latter wine being made at the end of 1984. By this time it was very developed, still retaining some of the lush, sweet-fruit characters and pronounced oak which had won it so many awards, but nonetheless starting to tire. With a release price of around $5.50, it was hard to complain about the lack of freshness. Around the same time a 1980 Cabernet Malbec Shiraz was released, which really is a lovely wine. It has that distinctive soft, ripe-fruit aroma and flavour, coupled with sophisticated oak handling, which is typical of Berri at its best. The winery works hard to get tannin back into the wine, but the styles are always soft and by 1986 this wine will start to decline.

BONNEYVIEW WINES
STURT HIGHWAY, BARMERA

Bonneyview crushes around 33 tonnes of fruit each year; if processed at a winery such as Angove's, this part of the vintage would be over in a matter of minutes. It is one of the pleasant features of the wine industry that the very small can co-exist happily with the very big, providing the consumer with an exceptionally wide range of choice. An even more striking feature of the wine industry is its ability to draw all sorts of people into its fold: owner and joint founder Robert Minns is an Oxford Bachelor of Arts and once played cricket for Kent, England.

Bonneyview started life with five shareholders and five workers; Minns is now the owner, and the initially small crush has declined even further, as Bonneyview in the future intends to rely solely on estate-grown grapes produced from its Nookamka Vineyard. Here an eclectic range of varieties has been established, although many are only just coming into production. It is planted to chardonnay, white frontignac and cabernet sauvignon (0.5 hectare each), rhine riesling and merlot (0.4 hectare each), shiraz, malbec, currant and black frontignac (0.25 hectare each), tarrango (0.2 hectare) and petite verdot (0.1 hectare).

The elaborate trellis system established the vines at two heights, 2.7 metres and three metres above the ground, and opens out on a wide "V". The open canopy thus created is intended to slow the ripening process, and hopefully invest the grapes with greater flavour. It will also permit very substantial yields, although the extent of these cannot yet be finally determined.

The wines are made by Christoper Sim, a Rose-worthy graduate, and all are sold by cellar door and mail order. The wines on offer in 1984 included a cabernet merlot, a shiraz malbec, a cabernet beaujolais, a traminer riesling, a chardonnay (very dry), a frontignac blanc (full, sweet) and a spatlese trebbiano, together with a limited range of fortified wines and a spumante.

COUNTY HAMLEY
Cnr BOOKMARK AVENUE
AND TWENTY-EIGHTH STREET, RENMARK

What better illustration of the universality of wine than to find a Hungarian-born and trained winemaker taking fruit from the Adelaide Hills, making it at Renmark in the Riverland, using an obscure fermentation technique devised by Frenchman Professor Louis Semichon, and marketing it under the County Hamley label.

Tom Bodroghy founded County Hamley prior to the 1974 vintage; he had worked at Angove's before that time. His eldest son, Michael, studied at Roseworthy College before coming back to County Hamley for the 1980 vintage.

Fruit sources are diverse: from County Hamley's own vineyards planted to chardonnay, sauvignon blanc, pinot noir and merlot; from Paracombe in the Adelaide Hills; from the Southern Vales; and also from other local Renmark growers.

The winery is determined to produce wines which are of high quality, but elects to use unconventional wine-making methods which result in unconventional wines. The County Hamley vineyards are frequently double-pruned to increase quality, albeit at the expense of yield. There is no quarrel with this technique, nor with the practice of buying grapes from the Adelaide Hills or Southern Vales. The Achilles' heel is the use of the Semichon technique, which involves covering uncrushed berries with fully fermented wine of the same variety and vintage, resulting in a prolonged and even fermentation in which the alcohol content starts (and of course remains) above four degrees at all times. This is due to the fact that fresh grapes are being continually added to the ferment. Bodroghy claims it results in "enormous fruit extraction yielding a wine far advanced in age compared to the usual system, yet one that is exceptionally long-lived and will keep improving with age". The difficulty is that it seems to induce a very high level of acetic volatility; I suspect that part of the problem may be due to the commencement of the malolactic fermentation while there is still substantial sugar in the wine.

The conventionally made wines from County Hamley are very acceptable wines.

LOXTON MEDIA ESTATE
BERRY–LOXTON ROAD, LOXTON

Loxton Media Estate is the label under which a small percentage of the production of the Loxton Cooperative Winery and Distillery Limited is marketed. The cooperative was founded in 1949, but did not begin production until four years later. The Loxton Irrigation Area had been established by the government to provide land for returned soldiers, and the cooperative was set up to process the intake from the 2400 hectares of vines which were planted.

While the major part of the production is sold in bulk to other wineries, Loxton has always produced a limited quantity for release under its own label. I have hazy memories of a cabernet sauvignon from the early 1960s, which must have been one of the first varietal cabernets from this region.

The crush is now around 26,000 tonnes, producing a wide range of wine styles and products. Not only is table wine made in bulk, but so are fortified wines and brandy, all for on-sale to other makers. Loxton has also followed in the footsteps of other major producers in the area in providing grape concentrates for sale to amateur and other winemakers both locally and overseas.

Loxton Media Estate wines are sold principally by cellar door; the white varietals, recently expanded to include chenin blanc and sauvignon blanc, are adequate but unexciting.

LUBIANA
SCHOOL ROAD, MOOROOK

It seemed as if time had stood still when I received a cellar-door pricelist at the end of 1984 offering 15 white and red varietal table wines ranging in price from $2.50 a bottle and from $2.75 to $3.10 per flagon. It is true there were two premium wines—a chardonnay and a Special Bin Cabernet Malbec Shiraz blend which were more expensive, at $3 per bottle. Finally, it must also be admitted that the pricelist was printed before the 10 per cent sales tax was imposed by our ever-considerate government.

The Lubiana family had been winemakers in Trieste for three generations, and it was not surprising that Andrea Lubiana eventually decided to turn to winemaking again after his arrival in Australia in 1950. In 1959 the family purchased the remains of the old Moorook Distillery and, with virtually no winemaking equipment, completed a 40-tonne foot-trod crush. The resultant wine was sold to the Italian community,

CONSIGNMENT OF GRAPES ARRIVING AT BERRI ESTATES, c. 1920

principally in Melbourne where Lubiana lived. The business flourished, and in 1969 it became the full-time occupation of the family, who moved to Moorook and proceeded to rebuild the old winery, with the rebuilding and extensions completed in time for the 1973 vintage.

Fifty per cent of the 1984 crush of 400 tonnes came from the family's own vineyards planted to shiraz (4.8 hectares), grenache (2.3 hectares), muscat gordo blanco (1.9 hectares), chardonnay (0.7 hectare), colombard (0.6 hectare), chenin blanc and emerald riesling (0.4 hectare each) and pedro ximinez (0.2 hectare).

All of the grapes are mechanically harvested. Winemaker Steve Lubiana uses modern winemaking techniques, cold-fermenting the white wines at around 12°C and giving varieties such as chardonnay some oak maturation.

One of the winery's best wines is its Special Bin Red, a blend of 60 per cent cabernet sauvignon, 30 per cent malbec and 10 per cent shiraz which spends 18 months in American oak before bottling, and is given further maturation before sale.

RENMANO
STURT HIGHWAY, RENMARK

As I have recounted earlier in this chapter, Renmano Wines Cooperative Limited is now one of the operating arms of Consolidated Cooperative Wineries Limited. It started life as an offshoot of Chateau Tanunda in 1914, and within two years 130 local grape-growers had raised enough money to buy the winery as a going concern. The new company, the Renmark Growers' Distillery Limited, was formed as a cooperative enterprise and was the first cooperative winery in Australia. The initial vintage took 1000 tonnes of grapes, all of which were processed into spirit.

Until the Second World War the steadily increasing production was limited to brandy and fortified wine. The establishment of the Soldier Settlement Schemes at the end of the Second World War resulted in increased production of varieties such as palomino, pedro ximinez, crouchen and shiraz. In consequence Renmano became increasingly involved in the production of table wine. This trend was accelerated by the arrival of rhine riesling and cabernet sauvignon in the late 1950s, and the production in 1962 of Renmano's first varietal cabernet sauvignon. Rhine riesling and malbec were vintaged for the first time in the following year.

Throughout the 1960s and 1970s winery equipment was progressively upgraded and expanded, and now extends to all of the facilities necessary to make high-quality white table wine in a very warm climate. Since 1970 increased emphasis has been placed on marketing part of the production under the Renmano name, which was adopted around that time. Prior to 1970 almost all of the output had been sold in bulk to other wineries. The 1984 crush of 16,000 tonnes was produced from 1000 hectares of vineyards operated by producer members.

All of the bottled wines are released under the Chairman's Selection range. These comprise Chardonnay Bin 104, Traminer Riesling (Moselle) Bin 204, Fumé Blanc Bin 504 and Rhine Riesling Bin 604, Cabernet Sauvignon Bin 460 and Merlot Bin 540. Given the price of these wines, the quality can be exceptional. Over the past three or four years the major surprises of a number of large masked tastings I have conducted for various purposes have been the Renmano Chairman Selection wines. 1981 produced some outstanding releases, with the 1981 Cabernet Sauvignon and Chardonnay both being bargains. Thus the 1981 Cabernet Sauvignon was still available in 1984 at a "real" price of less than $5 a bottle. ◄▐

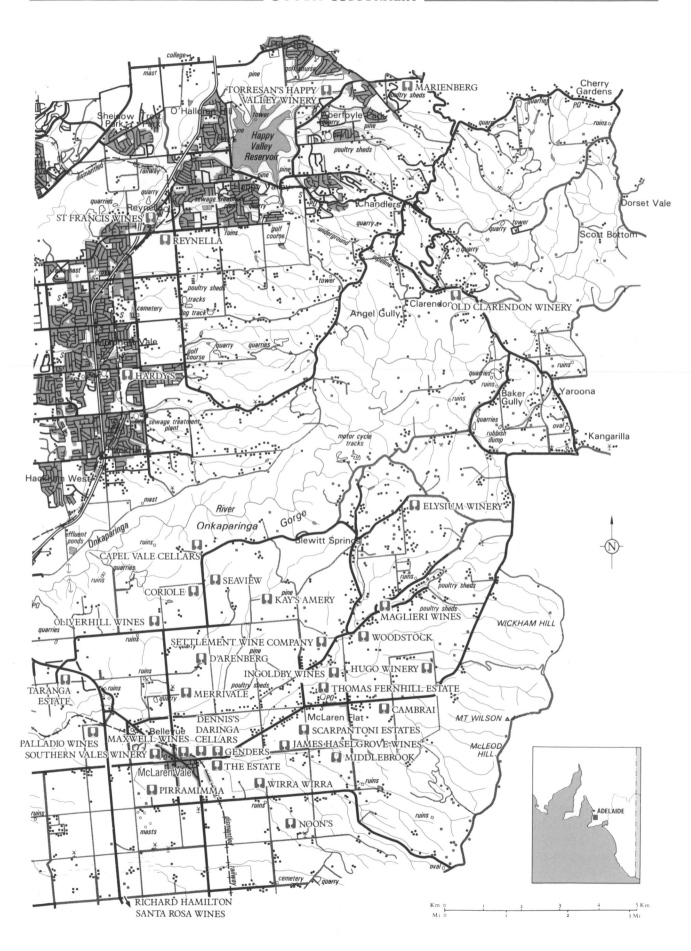

Km. 0   1   2   3   4   5 Km.
Mi. 0   1   2   3 Mi.

ADELAIDE

Southern Vales

Although John Reynell laid the foundations for Reynella in 1838, and was followed by Thomas Hardy in 1853, viticulture and winemaking in the Southern Vales region remained largely within the province of those two enterprises until the late 1880s. The district was first settled and intensively farmed in the early 1850s, with the establishment of extensive wheat fields. Development continued through that decade and the 1860s, and numerous flour mills were constructed. Just as in the Clare Valley (and the country beyond) 20 years later, unscientific and extravagant farming methods soon depleted the soil. Again, just as in the Clare Valley, numerous wheat farmers had small vineyard holdings to provide wine as part of the wages for their labourers. When the wheat fields disappeared, so the small vineyards were abandoned as the population moved out of the district. By the mid-1870s the township of McLaren Vale was very nearly deserted.

Thus it was that the major vineyards were maintained by John Reynell and Thomas Hardy; in 1876 Thomas Hardy was able to purchase the third large vineyard in the area, Tintara, which had been established by Dr A. C. Kelly over 15 years earlier. There were some other vineyards and wineries, notably George Manning's Hope Farm which was planted in 1850 and which is now known as Seaview. But it was not until 1888 that viticulture began to assume the importance it has today. From this point on what was described as vine mania swept over the whole of South Australia, with all of the major winegrowing regions reflecting its impact.

In 1887 and 1888 J. G. Kelly established the Tatachilla Vineyard, planting 124 acres (50 hectares) in just two years. In 1890 the Kay brothers established Amery: in 1891 the Johnston family established Pirramimma, and in the same year W. H. Craven purchased Hope Farm and substantially extended the cellars. In 1895 Frank Wilkinson made the first wine at Ryecroft and in 1896 H. V. Pridmore built

temporary cellars known as The Wattles, soon to become a major and more permanent base. Katunga commenced business in the same year, and in 1900 Pirramimma and Wirra Wirra made their first vintages.

In 1903 over three million litres of wine were made by the 19 wineries in the district. In order of importance they were Thomas Hardy & Sons Limited (which alone produced 765,000 litres), followed by W. Reynell, Horndale, Vale Royal, Tatachilla, The Wattles, Amery, Clarendon Vineyard, Kanmantoo, Pirramimma, Wirra Wirra, Mount Hurtle, F. Potts, Hope Vineyard, Mrs Douglas, Ryecroft, Katunga, Formby and E. Potts. The major part of the production was of full-bodied red wine, and the major market was the United Kingdom. Long after exports from other regions of Australia had declined, or had altered to sweet fortified wines, the Southern Vales continued to supply Britain with substantial quantities of dark-coloured, high-alcohol red burgundy. This trade continued on a large scale until well into the 1950s; its subsequent decline was as much due to the desire of the wineries to establish their own identity and labels as to any falling-off in demand.

McLaren Vale was ideally placed to supply the burgeoning interest in red table wine in Australia in the early 1960s. Throughout the rest of that decade, and for the first part of the 1970s, the district was a prosperous one. But with the almost overnight appearance of the cool-climate culture, the vignerons of the Southern Vales area were confronted with a wine market that had changed beyond all recognition in less than 10 years.

By 1975, when the full extent of the change had become apparent, the Southern Vales was already home to a bewildering number of small wineries. The rate of change in the ensuing 10 years is some indication of the problems the vignerons have had to confront. Akeringa, Berenyi, Elysium and Trennert are no more; Ingoldby, Merrivale, Middlebrook,

Oliverhill, Palladio, Hazelmere Estate, and Taranga Estate have all changed hands at least once, and many have changed their names. Middlebrook takes the trophy, having changed its name five times and owners seven times in all, with most of the changes in the past 15 years.

It is not all unrelieved gloom. Since 1980 Geoff Merrill, Hugo Winery, James Haselgrove, Santa Rosa, Simon Hackett and Woodstock have all commenced marketing wines; some, such as Woodstock, have been vignerons for far longer, but had previously sold their wine in bulk.

In many ways the Southern Vales region is the home of the small winery in Australia. It is a relatively easy viticultural area, with very reliable—if somewhat warm—growing conditions, well-structured soils and with a highly developed infrastructure. It is also very conveniently situated to a major market (in the form of Adelaide) and, together with the Clare Valley, has more than effectively competed with the Barossa Valley for cellar-door trade.

It is nonetheless a changing and even more competitive world. Whereas 15 years ago significant cellar-door and mailing list trade would certainly follow the establishment of a new winery, that is no longer so. The wine-buying public is infinitely more discerning, indeed, demanding, and lesser-quality wines no longer pass unnoticed. Nor can the Southern Vales compete on price against the products of the larger company offered through the local supermarket or chain-store retailer. Here technically very well-made wines will be offered for sale at prices less than the cost of production in the Southern Vales, and at half of the cellar-door sales price.

Companies such as Coriole, Pirramimma, Hazelmere Estate (now The Estate), Wirra Wirra and Woodstock are among those who have shown it is possible to produce high-quality wines which the wine-buying public wants and is prepared to pay the appropriate price for. These makers have shown that with appropriate viticultural techniques and skilled winemaking, the Southern Vales can produce excellent rhine riesling, semillon, chardonnay, sauvignon blanc, cabernet sauvignon, cabernet merlot and even pinot noir. Shiraz, of course, remains the workhorse, and if anyone wishes to see why it was the base of the Australian industry for so long, the wines of Coriole provide the answer.

The presence of the Thomas Hardy/Reynella and of the Wynns/Seaview groups in the region is also of immense significance. While it is true that both groups source only a small part of their annual crush from within the Southern Vales, their very presence provides a stabilising influence. But in the longer term only those operations which are truly professional—both in terms of winemaking and wine marketing—can expect to survive.

CAMBRAI
HAMILTONS ROAD, McLARENS FLAT

Graham Stevens knew the McLaren Vale area better than most when he founded Cambrai in 1975. Between 1962 and 1969 he worked for d'Arry Osborn at d'Arenberg, before moving to Coriole for its first vintage in 1969. He spent 10 years there, and in the last few years shared his time between Cambrai and Coriole.

The initial Cambrai releases were extremely successful in local and national shows, and the limited production was eagerly sought after. The attraction of Cambrai was heightened by the unusual varieties, reflected in the present plantings. The vineyards, which produce around 50 per cent of the annual 70-tonne crush, are planted to pinot noir (one hectare), zinfandel (0.75 hectare), cabernet sauvignon, shiraz, traminer, sylvaner and muller-thurgau (0.5 hectare each), chardonnay (0.35 hectare) and malbec and ruby cabernet (0.2 hectare each).

It may be the very limited quantities grown, or it may be that Graham Stevens simply likes to challenge conventional thinking, but the end result sees some highly unconventional blends. As long ago as 1978 he produced a cabernet sauvignon (70 per cent) pinot noir (30 per cent) blend; he now opts for a more conventional pinot noir–shiraz blend, but there is nothing conventional about the 1983 Chardonnay Sylvaner. I cannot say that I particularly liked the end result—it had a rather curious cosmetic character and a rather oily texture.

Indeed, overall I think the red wines of Cambrai are infinitely preferable to the white wines. The latter are very much at odds with the generally accepted requirements for varietal whites. Even the quality of recent red-wine releases has, overall, failed to live up to the very high standard of some of the early wines, however. Recent releases of pinot hermitage and zinfandel have not impressed; Stevens is much more consistent with his cabernet sauvignon. The 1981 release was a good wine, with clean fruit and oak aromas and flavours, with some attractive minty characters on the palate, and good overall balance.

GRAPE-PICKING, KAY BROTHERS, 1898

CHAPEL VALE CELLARS
CHAPEL HILL ROAD, McLAREN VALE

Chapel Vale Cellars is one of the smallest McLaren Vale wineries, with an annual production of around 1300 cases. The winery is owned by members of the Sellick family and the wines are marketed through the cellar door and a few restaurants. However, with plans to increase the size of the vineyards, production (and availability) will increase in the future.

The vineyards presently comprise rhine riesling and cabernet sauvignon (two hectares each), shiraz (1.2 hectares), grenache (0.6 hectare) and chardonnay (0.2 hectare). These produce around 85 per cent of the annual production, with a certain amount of additional shiraz purchased from local growers. Yields from the loam/ironstone topsoil (with a limestone base) are very low, despite the fact that one-third of the plantings have irrigation available.

Wine styles are decidedly traditional. The red wines are oak-matured for three years before bottling, and are then held for a further two or three years before release. Thus as at January 1985 a 1977 Cabernet Sauvignon, a 1977 Shiraz Cabernet and a 1979 Shiraz were all available at $6.50 per bottle.

Winemaker Robert Paul cold-settles and cold-ferments the rhine riesling to produce clean, fruit styles. The 1983 Spatlese Rhine Riesling was very successful, with a brilliant, rich golden colour and abundant soft, full, fruit flavour. The red wines are sound, smooth wines of good commercial quality.

CORIOLE
CHAFFEYS ROAD, McLAREN VALE

Coriole is owned by the Lloyd family (or, at least, seven members thereof) which is probably better known in the district for Lloyd Aviation, the regional air service replete with several helicopters. It certainly makes the Lloyd name very visible. Coriole was established in 1967 by Dr Hugh Lloyd, an Adelaide general practitioner who has followed in the footsteps of some of his enterprising nineteenth-century forebears in establishing a wide range of outside business interests. He had intended one of those businesses to be almond-growing, and it was while searching for suitable land for this purpose that he came across a run-down winery glorying under the name of Chateau Bonne Santé. The property comprised eight hectares of 60-year-old vines, a few old ironstone buildings and a dilapidated winery.

Dr Lloyd purchased the property and spent the next three years in rebuilding the winery, reviving the old plantings and extending the vineyards with additional varieties. The vineyards, which now provide around 85 per cent of the 160-tonne crush, are planted to shiraz (11 hectares), cabernet sauvignon (three hectares), rhine riesling (two hectares), chenin blanc, grenache, touriga and pinot noir (1.5 hectares each), with a small planting of chardonnay yet to come into bearing. The old shiraz and the younger vines are all planted on red loam over an ironstone or limestone subsoil and produce grapes of the highest quality. Since the first vintage in 1970 Coriole has produced some of the best red wines to come from McLaren Vale, and in recent years quality has improved even further.

Hugh Lloyd's son Mark took over winemaking responsibilities in 1979, having gained a science degree from Adelaide University and worked for a year with an English wine company which formed the basis of the English Vineyards Association. Mark Lloyd's task was to vintage parcels of grapes grown by would-be vignerons from all parts of England. With that baptism of fire it is hardly surprising that he has revelled in the task at Coriole. The releases of 1980, 1981 and 1982 have all been consistently excellent. I have judged all of these wines in large masked tastings and, without fail, have rated them at the very top of their respective classes.

The shiraz is probably the most impressive release overall, no doubt partly due to the intensity of the fruit obtained from the very old vines. Both it and the shiraz cabernet blends exhibit unusual depth of flavour, not unlike the wines of Wendouree in the Clare Valley. Like those wines, the Coriole reds have an extra dimension and depth, yet avoid jamminess or portiness.

Extensive use is also made of French and American oak hogsheads. The influence of this is again very evident in the wines, but because of the fruit depth the oak remains in balance. Yet another feature of the wines is their excellent red-purple colour. Mark Lloyd pays special attention to both pH levels and to avoiding oxidation, aiming to make red wines with genuine fruit freshness, and which will age for prolonged periods. He succeeds admirably with these aims. If all this were not enough, the wines sell for significantly less than many of their competitors, which they comprehensively outperform.

D'ARENBERG
OSBORN ROAD, McLAREN VALE

D'Arenberg was established in 1928, although the vineyards had been owned by the Osborn family since 1912 and had, indeed, been planted in the 1890s. Some of those original vines are still in production, rivalling the old vines at Kay's Amery vineyards.

Founder Francis Osborn produced two wines: a big, porty dry red, with all the pressings returned, which was sold to the Emu Wine Company for export. The most traditional of McLaren Vale styles, these immense, ferruginous wines were put to all sorts of purposes by the English wine trade and—for that matter—by the English medical profession, who were wont to prescribe them as tonics. The other wine was a vintage port, sold either to Thomas Hardy or to the Emu Wine Company. After the business had been established for some time, Penfolds became an important customer, buying bulk red for use as a base wine for Minchinbury Sparkling Burgundy.

After a prolonged illness Francis Osborn died in 1957. His son d'Arenberg (universally known as d'Arry) had joined his father in 1943, and had progressively taken over responsibility for wine-making and running the business. D'Arry determined that the time had come for the winery to establish its own brand and label. His neighbour Ben Chaffey, of Seaview, was emphatic that the label must be instantly recognisable. D'Arry felt equally that it should not look out of place in the formal surroundings of a dining-room table. The third influence came from the Houghton White Burgundy label, a familiar sight at d'Arenberg because it was given away by the Emu Wine Company as Christmas presents to its major customers. These three strands were gathered together by Donald Allnutt, a close friend of d'Arry Osborn, who designed the label with its distinctive red stripe.

Nonetheless, it was not until 1965 that the first significant release appeared under the d'Arenberg label. In that year they bottled a cabernet shiraz blend, and a burgundy. The claret label did not make its appearance until 1967, with the 1965 vintage.

The style of d'Arenberg's reds has changed little over the intervening years, simply because d'Arry Osborn has deliberately opted to continue making the style which he knows and likes, and which he believes the region is suited to producing. The only compromise has been marginal reduction in the weight of the wines by the exclusion of pressings.

The red wines, variously blends of cabernet sauvignon, shiraz and grenache, with the occasional 100 per cent cabernet sauvignon release, are given extensive oak-maturation (with minimal new-oak influence) and a further period of time in bottle before release. They are constructed with full, rich, ripe fruit which will benefit from leisurely maturation, and which will always provide fleshy, generous wines.

There is no argument with this approach. It may not make wines which fit easily into contemporary winemaking practice, but nor is it intended to. And at their best the wines can show extraordinary character. Thus the 1967 d'Arenberg Burgundy, composed largely of grenache, won seven trophies and 25 gold medals. One might think that was no mean achievement for the fourth vintage of a newly established brand, but in the following year d'Arry Osborn made a 1968 Cabernet Sauvignon which proceeded to win the Jimmy Watson Trophy at Melbourne in 1969.

Not surprisingly these wines came to the attention of the very few wine writers then on the scene, headed by Len Evans. He praised the wines for their richness and depth of flavour, and the combined effect of Evans's praise and the show successes meant that for years the d'Arenberg reds literally walked out of the cellar door.

In recent years the situation has turned around dramatically. I think this is due to two factors. The first is, of course, that the styles are unashamedly traditional. The second is that the district "cowshed" character, which used to be accepted as a regional character in the same way as it was in the Hunter Valley, is now recognised as being nothing more or less than mercaptan (or hydrogen sulphide). The older generation of wine drinkers is tolerant to the leathery, vegetable aromas and tastes which it gives rise to, and which can—against all the odds—become very pleasant when integrated into the complex aroma and taste of an old red. The young generation of wine drinkers rejects such flavours. So it is that the wines of d'Arenberg are increasingly an acquired taste. There are those who love the style, and who always will. But I suspect it is a dying race.

It may be that the style of d'Arenberg wines will slowly evolve into a more conventional pattern. D'Arry's son Chester, a Roseworthy graduate, now shares the winemaking responsibilities with his father. D'Arenberg has also from time to time purchased excellent Clare Valley rhine riesling to supplement the range of available wine.

The 1983 crush of around 550 tonnes underlines the fact that d'Arenberg is still a very substantial enterprise. Around 50 per cent was provided from the d'Arenberg vineyards, planted to shiraz (36 hectares), grenache (12 hectares), cabernet sauvignon (five hectares), rhine riesling (four hectares), and palomino and doradillo (three hectares).

D'Arry Osborn is loved and respected by everyone in and around the wine industry. It is hard to imagine a more honest, gentle and open man, or one who is more passionately devoted to maintaining the integrity of the wine industry in general and the McLaren Vale in particular. I suspect he is a little bewildered by the rate of change in the wine industry, and cannot quite believe that the old days are gone forever. I devoutly hope he can find a midway course which allows d'Arenberg to accommodate those changes without sacrificing what d'Arry Osborn undoubtedly sees as its integrity.

DENNIS'S DARINGA CELLARS
KANGARILLA ROAD, McLAREN VALE

Egerton Dennis has had a long and distinguished involvement in the wine industry. A McLaren Vale vigneron since returning from service in the Second World War, he joined with Jim Ingoldby to form McLaren Vale Wines Pty Limited in 1965 for the purpose of marketing nationally the red wines of the district. This company merged with Ryecroft Vineyards Pty Limited in 1970, and shortly thereafter the merged group was acquired by Reed International. Reed in turn merged the operations of J. Y. Tulloch and Sons, Ryecroft and McLaren Vale Wines, with Ege Dennis as managing director. He continued in this post when the group was acquired by Gilbeys, eventually retiring in 1979.

Along the way—in 1971, to be precise—he had formed a partnership with another well-known district vigneron, Ken Maxwell, to form Daringa Cellars. Daringa was built on part of the first land holding registered in the McLaren Vale district, in 1839. The winery was built on land which had been in the Maxwell family for more than three generations, but eventually it was decided that the partners should go their separate ways, Maxwell to establish Maxwell's Wines and Ege Dennis to continue with Daringa, which he purchased from the Maxwells.

In consequence of that change the Dennis name now appears more prominently on labels than does Daringa. It has also established its own vineyards, which provide all of the 65-tonne crush. These are planted to cabernet sauvignon (5.3 hectares), shiraz (4.85 hectares), chardonnay and sauvignon blanc

(1.2 hectares each) and muscat and merlot (0.5 hectare each). The special viticultural techniques employed are "the vigneron's footprints".

Peter Dennis is winemaker, although the white wines are made for Daringa at Petaluma. Wine quality is exemplary. McLaren Vale has surprised many observers with the quality of the chardonnay it produces, and the 1982 and 1983 vintages were absolutely outstanding. The rhine riesling, too, is an excellent wine, with the rich flavours which the district produces immaculately preserved and bottled.

The red wines—usually a straight cabernet sauvignon and a shiraz cabernet blend—are also of high quality. Sweet American oak is evident in both, with the full and rich fruit flavours for which the district is noted. Devoid of any semblance of "cowshed"/mercaptan characters, they are very much wines for today. The 1980 vintage was quite outstanding.

ELYSIUM WINERY
BROOKMANS ROAD, BLEWITT SPRINGS

In July 1984 Betty Harris, the winemaker at Elysium, despatched the annual newsletter with the following announcement:

> It is with mixed feelings that I send out our annual letter with the news that my husband, Frank, and I have decided to discontinue winemaking and to sell the winery later next year. We have thoroughly enjoyed our eight years of activity here, especially the cordial relations which have developed with our regular customers, but we have increasingly felt the need to spend more time with our family and to follow our own pursuits.
>
> We are retaining the name "Elysium" for sentimental reasons, so all the bottled wines on this list are the final Elysium releases. Other wines already vintaged will be sold in bulk.

Thus ends a brand which, since its inception in 1971, added significantly to the reputation of McLaren Vale as a fine producer of red wine and the occasional producer of such oddities as a liqueur chardonnay port—which constituted one of its final releases.

In the volatile environment of McLaren Vale, the future of the winery is uncertain. (Indeed it is; since writing those words, Elysium has had a temporary reprieve as a purchaser had not been found as at April 1985.)

GENDERS
RECREATION ROAD, McLAREN VALE

The Genders family, headed by Keith Genders, had been McLaren Vale grape-growers for 20 years before establishing its own winery in 1968. The business prospered during the heady days of the red-wine boom, but has since contracted considerably. The wines are sold principally by cellar door, with limited amounts being sold through organisations such as the Australian Wine Club. Both winemaking techniques and wine styles are traditional; the wine quality is mediocre.

GEOFF MERRILL
KANGARILLA ROAD, McLAREN VALE

Geoff Merrill is the highly visible and highly talented chief winemaker at Chateau Reynella, now part of the Thomas Hardy group. Young, effervescent and with a moustache which would do Kaiser Wilhelm proud, he has already had what most people would regard as a lifetime's experience in the wine industry.

It nonetheless comes as something of a surprise to find that Merrill did not attend Roseworthy (nor gain its gold medal), and that he entered the industry as a trainee winemaker with Seppelt in 1969 at the age of 17. He spent three years in the central laboratory at Seppeltsfield, and studied at the South Australian Institute of Technology, gaining a certificate in industrial studies. His three vintages at Seppeltsfield and two at Chateau Tanunda taught him the importance of quality control in wine production, the chemistry of wine, and how to correct it.

In June 1974 he left to work in South Africa with Stellenbosch Farmers' Winery, the fifth-largest winery in the world. He worked for six months in their research laboratory as a "small-scale winemaker", handling as many as 200 different parcels of grapes each vintage.

In 1975 he returned to Australia, and shortly after joined Reynella Wines as assistant winemaker. He worked the 1976 vintage at Swan Hill, and in 1977 was appointed winemaker at Reynella, becoming senior winemaker the following year. He has remained with Reynella ever since, and has happily integrated into the Thomas Hardy winemaking team, with which he quite evidently has much in common.

Thomas Hardy has what I believe to be a thoroughly enlightened and sensible approach to the aspirations of young winemakers to do their own thing. Provided that sales do not go much over 1000 cases a year, the company allows its winemakers the right of private practice, as it were. Thus Geoff Weaver has Ashbourne and Geoff Merrill has his label, trading under the name of Geoff Merrill Stratmer Vineyards.

Eventually Merrill's own vineyards and winery will be established on a 16-hectare block in Kangarilla Road, McLaren Vale. For the time being the wines are basically contract-made for Geoff Merrill at other wineries, eventually returning to Johnston's Pirramimma Winery under a complex use-and-pay scheme. Thus he owns his own stainless-steel fermenters, which are situated where the grapes are to be crushed and fermented, and also owns all of the necessary new oak for the maturation of the wines. The latter is stored at Johnston's.

Even after Geoff Merrill's own vineyards come into production, he will not hesitate to take fruit from other premium areas. Thus one of these days he may buy grapes from the Margaret River or from south-eastern Victoria.

The initial releases were a wood-matured 1981 Semillon (which spent three months in Nevers oak prior to bottling) and a 1980 Cabernet Sauvignon, the latter a blend of 60 per cent McLaren Vale fruit and 40 per cent Coonawarra material. The 1981 Semillon was made at Peter Lehmann's Barossa Winery from a mixture of Barossa Valley and Eden Valley fruit. It also had 10 per cent sauvignon blanc included for good measure.

Merrill is an uncompromising advocate of elegance in red wines. He does not believe that any particular level of alcohol must be achieved before a wine has adequate flavour and structure. There are many who disagree with these views; as in any discussion of this kind, the opposing views tend to polarise themselves and go to extremes. I personally believe his theories have considerable validity. It is, as I say, a complex argument, but if I have to choose a single position, then I will throw my vote with Merrill.

Certainly the judges seem to think so. The 1980 Cabernet Sauvignon won the Fibre Containers' Trophy for best dry red (light body) at the 1983 Adelaide show; the 1982 Cabernet Sauvignon won the same trophy in 1984, and teamed with the 1983 Cabernet Sauvignon to secure a second trophy as the most successful exhibitor in the light-bodied red classes.

The same style has, of course, been apparent in the Reynella Coonawarra Cabernet Sauvignons and in the Reynella Cabernet Malbec Merlot blends. I admire these wines greatly; it follows that I also admire the Geoff Merrill releases. Others disagree; that is their prerogative.

Geoff Merrill has the last word: "What I aim for is to be regarded as a quality winemaker. I am sick of the accountants' wines. I don't think there is any excuse for bottling a wine with faults. You have to be honest with yourself; the wine you sell reflects so much about your character and personality."

Well, not quite the last word. Elegant and light-bodied are not words I would use to describe Geoff Merrill or his noisy, rambunctious and full-fronted approach to life. Still, that is a small quibble.

HARDY'S
WILLUNGA ROAD, McLAREN VALE

Thomas Hardy stepped ashore from the sailing ship *British Empire* at Port Misery on 15 August 1850. A 20-year-old farmer from Devon in England, he had £30 in cash and a few personal possessions in a wooden box. Within a week he made a decision that set in train the weaving of a complex tapestry of events which was completed in the same month 132 years later. Hardy noted in his diary on 23 August that he had decided to accept employment as a labourer with another Devon emigré, John Reynell of Reynella Farm. Hardy went on: "Although it was low wages, I thought I had better embrace the opportunity as I have no doubt I shall soon be able to better myself . . ."

He was not wrong. Within a year he was at the Victorian goldfields; after a skirmish with the law for failing to have a miner's licence, he found a surer way of making money by driving cattle overland to feed the miners. In 1853 he returned to Adelaide and purchased a property on the River Torrens, which he called Bankside. In 1857 he made his first wine, matured in a cellar which he dug by hand at night after his day's labours in the fields. By 1859 he had exported wine to England, and was actively and effectively marketing his wine throughout the whole of South Australia. By the mid-1870s he had a firm hold on the northern market, employing hawkers who visited every farmer with offers of harvest wine at very low prices.

Hardy's success in the marketplace meant that he was the only bidder when the Tintara Winery, wine stocks and vineyard were offered for sale by the receivers of the company in 1876. Tintara had been developed by Dr A. C. Kelly, yet another physician who believed in the medicinal qualities of wine. He was also an author of note, and a less successful businessman. He had formed a syndicate with a group of influential Adelaide men, including Sir

Samuel Davenport, Sir Thomas Elder and Sir Edward Stirling, to purchase and develop a 283-hectare property at McLaren Vale. Tintara was planted in the 1850s, but suffered badly in the economic downturn of the 1860s, and ultimately went into receivership.

Hardy recouped the total purchase price out of the first year's sales of the accumulated wine stocks. From this point on the business grew rapidly. As well as crushing the large output from the company's own vineyards, Thomas Hardy was buying grapes from over 40 growers on the plains and in the foothills. In 1878 the McLaren Vale Flour Mill was converted into the Mill Cellars; in 1881 a large head office was built in Currie Street, Adelaide; in 1884 a further 195 hectares adjoining Tintara were purchased; and in 1893 new cellars were built at Mile End, to provide additional storage.

It is hardly surprising that by 1895 Hardy's had overtaken Seppelt as the largest winemakers in Australia, with a vintage of 1.5 million litres. Of this, 900,000 litres came from his Aldinga, Morphett Vale, McLaren Vale and Woodside vineyards, with the balance purchased from independent growers.

Federation in 1901 and the opening of State borders to free interstate trade offered Thomas Hardy & Sons Limited (as it had become in 1887) another major opportunity. Within weeks of Federation the company had opened offices in Sydney and Melbourne, followed by Brisbane by 1905.

Thomas Hardy died on 10 January 1912, two days before his eighty-second birthday. He was survived by one son and three grandsons. The Hardy blood runs strong, and the management of the company has always been thickly populated with members of the Hardy family. The chain of command passed through Robert to Tom Mayfield, thence to Kenneth, then Thomas Walter and now Sir James Hardy as chairman. The fourth- and fifth-generation members of the family are all involved, with the sixth generation waiting in the wings.

In the first part of the twentieth century Hardy's had extended its operation to Siegersdorf in the Barossa Valley and to Waikerie on the Murray River. But the importance of those acquisitions pales into insignificance against the move to Keppoch-Padthaway in 1968, where the company now has 307 hectares under vine, which provide it with over 30 per cent of its annual crush of around 13,000 tonnes of grapes.

The next major acquisition was Hardy's masterstroke: the take-over of the England-based Emu Wine Company group, with its Morphett Vale Winery and—far more importantly—the Houghton Wine Company in Western

Australia. It is no secret that financially the transaction rivalled that of Thomas Hardy's acquisition of Tintara 100 years earlier.

In the meantime another link with Reynella had been forged. In 1938 Colin Haselgrove was appointed technical director of Thomas Hardy & Sons Limited, a position he held until 1953 when he became managing director of Walter Reynell & Sons. In August 1982 the wheel turned full circle: Thomas Hardy & Sons Limited acquired the issued capital of Walter Reynell & Sons Limited, and has now based its entire administration at the magnificently restored Reynella complex. For once it is doubtful whether the investment will be recouped in one year (or, for that matter, in many years).

The three principal operating wineries are now situated at Reynella, McLaren Vale and Waikerie. The Tintara Winery at McLaren Vale is responsible for the production of the group's dry red table wine, vintage and tawny ports, and flor sherry. It also matures and blends Black Bottle Brandy. A small oak cooperage programme has been established, which provides for 400 new French oak hogsheads and puncheons to be introduced into insulated maturation cellars each year. Rob Dundon is in charge of the making of red wines, brandies and fortified wines, while Geoff Weaver is in charge of white wines. Geoff Merrill commutes from Reynella to supervise the making of the Reynella red wines.

Hardy's has spent $5.8 million in the acquisition and restoration of Reynella. It must now be regarded as the greatest showpiece in the Australian wine industry, but it is more than just a pretty face. One million dollars has been spent in establishing one of the most up-to-date white-table-wine wineries and cellars in Australia. A large bottling hall provides a technologically advanced bottling system and an insulated bottle maturation cellar allows for the subsequent ageing of those wines prior to release.

The Cyrilton Winery at Waikerie is dedicated to the making of base material for Black Bottle Brandy and for the production of the fairly low-key range of flagon white wines. Three pot-stills convert 80,000 litres of base wine a day into young brandy, which is then transferred to McLaren Vale for maturation in small oak casks for the next two to three years.

The wines of Chateau Reynella will continue to be made and marketed separately, and I follow the course of that company later in this chapter.

Hardy's has quietly disposed of virtually all of its McLaren Vale vineyards, with only five hectares of vines remaining. Nonetheless, it remains a substantial purchaser of grapes from the region, and has a long-term commitment to it.

Some time ago Hardy's decided to concentrate on the middle and upper sectors of the wine market, and in consequence discontinued production of wine casks. The table wines have—since 1970—been headed by the annual Eileen Hardy release. In that year it was decided to keep separate the best 4500-litre parcel (500 cases) of red wine made in the vintage, and to release it under the Eileen Hardy name. That year marked the eightieth birthday of "Aunty Eileen", the marvellous matriarch of the family who had been widowed when her husband Tom was killed in the Kyeemagh air crash of 1938, and who had raised not only her own children, but also many of the other Hardy family members.

The 1970 release was a McLaren Vale shiraz; each of the subsequent releases between 1971 and 1977 coming from McLaren Vale cabernet sauvignon. At a retrospective tasting of those wines a few years ago, the 1970 stood out as the great wine, followed by the 1971 and 1975 vintages, then the 1976. Several of the wines were marred by mercaptan, and overall the style seemed rather stolid and somewhat old-fashioned.

No Eileen Hardy was made in 1978, and in 1979 the base moved to Keppoch, from whence the 1980 and 1981 releases also come. These "new-generation" Eileen Hardy wines conform more closely to present-day expectations. They are impressive wines, still preserving the richness of fruit for which the range was noted, but with an extra degree of elegance. A percentage of malbec in the last two releases helped the mid-palate fruit structure.

Indeed, in the mid- to late 1970s I felt that Hardy's red wines generally were disappointing. Since 1980 there has been a total transformation: the quality of Nottage Hill Claret, Hardy's Cabinet Claret, McLaren Vale Hermitage, Hermitage Bin 454 and St Thomas Burgundy have been consistently good and—more often than not—underpriced.

The white wines are headed by Hardy's brand leader, Siegersdorf Rhine Riesling. The name no longer signifies any connection with the Barossa Valley; the wine is made exclusively from Keppoch grapes and made at Reynella. It cannot be said that these changes are for the worse: the 1982 has developed into a classic Australian rhine riesling style with strong, clean and firm toasty aromas and flavours. The 1983 vintage, with a botrytis influence, is an almost riotously rich and flavoury wine, with opulent lime/pineapple aromas and flavours. The excellent balancing acid gives the wine length and prevents the flavours from cloying.

A 1984 cellar maturation release of a 1975 McLaren Vale-Barossa Valley Rhine Riesling blend allowed a nostalgic look back to a great vintage for Hardy's: made by Brian Croser, it is sustained by the evident residual sugar on the mid-palate, which has kept the structure remarkably full and round. It is a fine example of an aged rhine riesling.

The white wine range now encompasses the full spectrum from wood-matured semillon through to Keppoch gewurtztraminer, Keppoch chardonnay and the usual range of generics, including the long-established Moana White Burgundy and St Vincent Chablis. All of these are well-made wines. Finally, Old Castle Riesling is made in vast quantities, which should not obscure its quality. Now made from 100 per cent rhine riesling, the 1984 vintage is an excellent wine, unequalled at its price.

Lastly, Hardy's makes one of the two consistently great vintage ports of Australia. At the end of October 1983 the Classic Wine Club held a remarkable tasting of the 1901, 1928, 1936, 1938, 1941, 1945, 1951, 1954, 1956, 1964, 1966, 1971 and 1975 vintages. The two young wines were included because they are the acknowledged classics of the 1970s, and duly showed their class. The 1975 wine is magnificently complex with cassis, spice and furry tannin on the palate, leading on to a cleansingly dry finish. It is, quite simply, as good as they come.

Of the older wines the 1956 showed extraordinary youthful fruit, in balance with its spirit and tannin, and with years still in front of it. The 1951 also showed well; while the 1945—one of the acknowledged all-time classics—possessed all the integration and balance for which the wine is legendary. The very much older wines were showing their age in different ways; the best was the 1928, although verging on a tawny style. The 1901 was a great old curio—while showing some oxidation in the bouquet, it had remarkable fruit and spirit given its age. Those present described it as a marvellous Australian sweet red.

HUGO WINERY
ELLIOTT ROAD, McLAREN VALE

Hugo Winery is not only one of the newest in the Southern Vales, but also one of the smallest. John Hugo had been a grape-grower for 12 years before deciding to venture into winemaking in a tiny way, with Wayne Thomas as consultant.

The first wine was made in 1980—250 dozen of an estate-grown shiraz which was not bottled until well into 1983. Its extensive wood-ageing had produced a wine with a clean and attractive, slightly powdery bouquet, and very soft, ripe fruit on the palate. The 1983 Rhine Riesling was a fair wine in mid-1984, with considerable depth of flavour followed by a slightly hard finish. A Muscat of Alexandria, with an orange-peel/raisin nose and deep raisined flavours was by far the most striking of the Hugo wines then available.

The 1984 crush amounted to 20 tonnes, and it is hardly surprising that all of the output is sold through the winery door in Elliott Road, McLaren Flat.

INGOLDBY WINES
INGOLDBY ROAD, McLAREN FLAT

Jim Ingoldby is one of the great characters of the McLaren Vale area. Few who heard it will forget his after-dinner speech in 1984 to the members of the Wine Press Clubs of Australia as he reminisced about his years as a student studying fine arts, in the Second World War with the RAF, and thereafter in the McLaren Vale district. My tape-recorder had had one glass of wine too many and refused to function, but I remember the best lines.

Jim Ingoldby had returned to his family's Ryecroft Vineyard in 1950, taking over as winemaker in 1957. Until that time all the wine was sold in bulk; he designed and introduced the Ryecroft label, and commenced bottling and selling the dry reds which the vineyard produced.

In 1965 he joined with Ege Dennis to form McLaren Vale Wines Pty Limited, with the purpose of buying wine from local makers and bottling it separately. Ryecroft was one of those makers. In 1970 the group was purchased by Reed Consolidated Industries. By 1975 Ingoldby had become tired of big-company politics and left to start all over again, buying eight hectares of vineyard in Ingoldby Road, McLaren Flat, and erecting a small winery. The vineyards were subsequently expanded and now comprise 14 hectares of cabernet sauvignon, 15 hectares of shiraz and eight hectares of rhine riesling.

Ingoldby remained a traditionalist to the end, leaving his wines in old oak for up to four years. Marketing difficulties led to the slow decline of the venture, and it was purchased by a syndicate formed by Bill Clappis in early 1984.

Bill Clappis has taken over as winemaker; it will be some time before the stocks of Ingoldby-made wine are depleted. No doubt the new owners will nonetheless adopt a more progressive attitude to marketing.

JAMES HASELGROVE WINES
FOGGO ROAD, McLAREN VALE

James Haselgrove Wines' major presence is in Coonawarra. James Haselgrove is a member of the Mildara Haselgrove family, but severed ties with that group to form his own Coonawarra/McLaren Vale company with two other well-known South Australian families, the Haigs and the Bagshaws.

The McLaren Vale wines are contract-made in the district at various wineries from purchased grapes. The exception is the vintage and tawny ports which are made from shiraz and grenache grown on the estate vineyards.

Recent releases have included a 1983 McLaren Vale Rhine Riesling (full, quite rich and with a slightly peppery finish) and a 1981 McLaren Vale Cabernet Shiraz (a blend of 66 per cent cabernet sauvignon with 34 per cent shiraz, a well-constructed wine with solid, sweet-berry flavours on the mid-palate and soft but persistent tannin on the finish). The outstanding release of recent times was the 1982 Vintage Port, with excellent spirit, deep minty aromas and flavours and with balancing soft tannin on the finish. James Haselgrove also releases Coonawarra-McLaren Vale blends of shiraz, a potentially synergistic mix.

Perhaps the most exciting development for the Haselgrove label has been the establishment of its Mount Gambier Vineyard, the most southerly vineyard in South Australia. Pinot noir and chardonnay have been planted with the aim of producing a *méthode champenoise* sparkling wine; the first vintage is expected in 1985.

KAY'S AMERY
KAYS ROAD, McLAREN VALE

The Kay family has remained in tight control of the Amery winery since its establishment in 1890. In that year brothers Herbert and Frederick Walter Kay built the core of the stone cellars which remain to this day, using a model exhibited at the Chamber of Manufactures. There have been only three generations of Kays as winemakers: Cuthbert (invariably known as Cud) took over on the death of his father Herbert in 1948, and he has now retired in favour of his son Colin, a Roseworthy Gold Medallist.

Subsequent extensions to the cellars have provided storage capacity for 1,000,000 litres of wine, although production has decreased somewhat in recent years with the rationalisation of the vineyards.

Since 1976 the vineyard area has been reduced from 64 hectares to 24, chiefly by the removal of very old, unproductive vines and also by removing varieties such as pedro ximinez. Some marvellous old gnarled vines remain from the original plantings, and the Kays look forward to producing a 100 per cent shiraz from these vines in their centenary year.

Plantings presently comprise shiraz (10 hectares), rhine riesling (5.3 hectares), cabernet sauvignon and traminer (2.4 hectares each), pinot noir (2.2 hectares), muscat à petit grains (two hectares), and sauvignon blanc (one hectare). Plantings are on the increase again, and present projections see 56 hectares under vine by 1995.

Such an increase will also cause the present production of around 116,000 litres to rise substantially, as 90 per cent of each year's crush is estate-grown.

These present and future vineyard changes are reflected in changes in the styles of wine coming through the winery. Until 1961, almost all of the production was sold in bulk to B. P. Burgoyne in England. The Southern Vales area provided a rich source of wine, at least some of which was put to nefarious purposes by wine merchants in England, chiefly to bolster thin and insipid French wines from indifferent vintages.

Kay's Amery offers a blend of the traditional and the new. At the same time as the immense reds were being made for the export market, Cud Kay was pioneering the planting of rhine riesling in the McLaren Vale district. He also established some of the first plantings of sauvignon blanc (outside of Thomas Hardy) and frontignac. Long before the style became popular, he successfully experimented with late-harvest styles, although production difficulties saw these go into eclipse for many years.

The red wines remain very traditional. At their best, they have the capacity to age with grace: a 1971 Reserve Bin Shiraz, a consistent bronze and silver medal winner for the first eight years of its life, eventually won its initial gold medal in 1979. Unfortunately, red wine quality is at best variable, with the wines often showing rank mercaptan. One of the best of the recent releases was a very attractive, peppery 1980 Shiraz Cabernet, a clean and balanced wine of considerable charm. The 1982 Pinot Shiraz did not give any indication that pinot noir is suited to the Kay vineyards. The 1982 Cabernet Sauvignon showed good, firm varietal fruit, although the oak was very raw and unintegrated.

The white wines are, with a few exceptions, simply not competitive in today's marketplace, although they no doubt have their supporters at the cellar

LOADING GRAPES, KAY BROTHERS, 1898

door. One notable exception was the 1984 Late Harvest White Frontignac, a rich and spicy wine, with voluminous varietal fruit, and showing surprising elegance given the overall depth of flavour.

The Tawny Port, and an immense raisined liqueur Muscat, are cellar-door specials.

MAGLIERI
13 DOUGLAS GULLY ROAD, McLAREN FLAT

The Maglieri family had been McLaren Vale grape-growers for many years before deciding to establish their own winery in 1972. Situated in Douglas Gully Road, the family initially chose the name Gully Wines for the unpretentious tin shed in which the first vintage was made. Not only has the winery been extended and received a handsome facade, but owner Stephen Maglieri has put the family name on the bottle.

The enterprise has flourished. The 1984 crush produced just under 550,000 litres of wine made from 780 tonnes of grapes. The Maglieri vineyards contribute approximately 40 per cent of the crush, with 30 hectares planted principally to shiraz and grenache, together with one hectare of rhine riesling and half a hectare of cabernet sauvignon.

The first wine made by Maglieri and entered in a show won two gold medals, and the company continues to be very successful in competitions. The 1979 Shiraz (still available for $5 a bottle at the cellar door in mid-1984) was judged the best red wine at the 1979 McLaren Vale Wine Festival, winning the Bushing King Trophy for Steve Maglieri. A very traditional, strong, slightly leathery bouquet leads on to a wine full of character on the palate, in a rich, raw-boned Australian style—or perhaps I should say, McLaren Vale style.

The 1983 Traminer Riesling won the corresponding Bushing Festival Award for the best white wine; spicy traminer dominates the bouquet, then a full spicy palate with a soft finish, and some of the oily characters that dog the footsteps of so many traminers. The Rhine Rieslings of recent vintages are very full and slightly broad wines, again fairly typical of the district.

MARIENBERG
BLACK ROAD, COROMANDEL VALLEY, BETWEEN CLARENDON AND BLACKWOOD

The gold medal awarded to a young Shiraz Cabernet at the 1970 Royal Adelaide Wine Show might well have gone largely unnoticed were it not for the fact that the wine had been made at a boutique Southern Vales winery by a relatively young and demonstrably attractive female. Women's liberation has since swept through all aspects of the wine industry, but at that time it caused a minor sensation.

The Austrian-born wife of an Adelaide stockbroker, Ursula Pridham had started the winery as a weekend hobby, carrying on the tradition of her forebears in Austria. It rapidly became apparent that Ursula Pridham was also an energetic and effective marketer as she forcefully visited the major retailers in both Melbourne and Sydney. Within a very short space of time, Marienberg had become a nationally known brand, with an importance that far outweighed its still modest production.

Since that time it has increased to a healthy 180 tonnes per year, providing between 10,000 and 13,000 cases. Ursula Pridham continues as winemaker, and the crush now comes entirely from the estate-grown grapes produced on seven hectares of rhine riesling, five hectares of cabernet sauvignon, four hectares of semillon, two hectares of shiraz and one hectare of gewurztraminer. The soils are typical McLaren Vale structure, principally gravelly loam interspersed with areas of ironstone gravel and sand over clay and alluvium. Limited use of drip irrigation produces adequate yields, varying between 6.7 and 11 tonnes per hectare.

Oak, both for fermentation and maturation, has always figured large in the Marienberg scheme of things. Oak-fermented white wines have since become an accepted part of winemaking practice, although the treatment of rhine riesling in this fashion remains an unconventional approach. This apart, it would seem that Ursula Pridham continues to make the white wines using techniques she inherited. Whatever the cause, the result is white wines which are often harsh and hard, lacking fruit aroma and flavour.

An obvious exception are the Beerenauslese (and even Trockenbeerenauslese, to the outrage of some) releases. These are late harvest wines, weighty and with considerable sweetness, although some oxidative characters are usually present.

At their best, the red wines are delicate and fragrant, and at their least, excessively thin and light.

MAXWELL WINES
24 KANGARILLA ROAD, McLAREN FLAT

Maxwell Wines was established in 1979 by Ken Maxwell and his son Mark. Ken Maxwell had worked as a winemaker in the district for many years, winning the Dan Murphy Trophy in perpetuity (having received it three times) and the Bushing King title twice (received for the best red wine at the McLaren Vale Wine Festival of that year). Notwithstanding his vast experience, he has now cheerfully handed over winemaking responsibilities to his son Mark.

The winery is established on the site of one of the first land grants in the township of McLaren Vale, granted in 1839. The historic homestead on the site was erected not long thereafter. At first sight some of the winery equipment seems to be of roughly similar vintage: in fact, it is of far more recent origin, although built from the ground up by Ken Maxwell from an unlikely assemblage of spare parts.

Thus the open concrete red fermenters are agitated by a Maxwell-devised beater system driven by washing machine motors. The crusher and press are no less original. I think it unlikely that the Maxwells have bothered to take out patent protection, but the system (and the machines) all work very well.

The 70-tonne crush is purchased from independent growers, chiefly from the Southern Vales but in recent years including Coonawarra cabernet sauvignon.

Output is basically restricted to two wines: one red and one white. The white wine is a blend of 70 per cent chenin blanc and 30 per cent rhine riesling. In 1984 I tasted each of the wines made between 1979 and 1983 according to this rather unusual formula. The tasting demonstrated the capacity these wines have to develop with age: the 1980 and 1979 were the most complete wines in the line-up, with honeyed aromas and flavours and the rich and generous palate sustained both by the relatively high alcohol and a little residual sugar. Indeed, the only marginally disappointing wine in the line-up was the 1981, which was a little coarse and heavy. These are not the greatest white wines made in McLaren Vale, but they are honest, full-flavoured and excellent food wines.

A corresponding tasting of all of the red wines made between 1977 and 1982 showed similar consistency. The four wines made between 1978 and 1981 were an unusually coherent line, with the bouquet of each almost indistinguishable from the other, clean, smooth and almost silky, with light oak and an underlying hint of powerful alcohol. All of the wines have sweet berry flavours on the palate, occasionally intermingled with some minty characters and some leafy astringent tannins.

The wines made between 1978 and 1981 were all McLaren Vale Cabernet Sauvignon; in 1982 a Cabernet Shiraz made from 35 per cent McLaren Vale cabernet, 25 per cent Coonawarra cabernet and 40 per cent McLaren Vale shiraz was made. A ripe style, it shows marked lifted berry characters. Future releases (as from 1984) will be a cabernet merlot blend. The 1984 merlot component, tasted a few months after vintage, promised a great deal. There is no doubt that merlot is a variety to be encouraged in the district.

Last, but by no means least, the Maxwells make mead throughout the year. Mark Maxwell points out that they obtain lucerne honey from Meningie, not far from Coonawarra. He therefore suggests that this is cool-climate mead. It is released in two forms, spiced (delicious served hot on a cold day), and unspiced (served chilled, or as a long drink with soda water, or lemonade or crushed ice). Both can be used to advantage in cooking. Mead is made, incidentally, using the winemaking equipment and employing fermentation techniques not dissimilar from those for wine.

MERRIVALE
OLIVERS ROAD, McLAREN FLAT

Merrivale has changed owners four times and its name twice since it was established in 1969 by Jack Starr. He purchased seven hectares of recently planted vineyard, and built a winery which the family called Southern Star. The vineyards had in the meantime been expanded to 7.4 hectares of shiraz, 3.5 hectares of rhine riesling, 3.1 hectares of grenache, 2.2 hectares of cabernet sauvignon and 0.6 hectare of brown muscat.

In 1974 Merrivale Wines Limited was incorporated as a public company, and it acquired the Starr family ownership. The family retained a major shareholding, and son-in-law Michael Bradley remained as winemaker until 1982 when the third change of ownership occurred. In that year Krondorf Wines took over ownership, with the intention of making Merrivale its boutique winery.

Some very attractive wines were released under the Merrivale label during the brief Krondorf stewardship. The 1981 Merrivale Cabernet Sauvignon was a stylish, light and elegant wine; while the 1983 Chardonnay was a total contrast, with its pungent oak and rich and powerful fruit.

Early in 1985 ownership changed once again with Dean Liebich, formerly of the Barossa's Rovalley, buying the winery from Krondorf. It represents a total change of direction for Liebich, who elected to sell his interest in Rovalley in the wake of family disagreements. In an ever-fluid McLaren Vale it will be interesting to see where Merrivale heads from this point onwards.

MIDDLEBROOK
SAND ROAD, McLAREN VALE

Merrivale seems like the veritable rock of ages compared with the changes that have taken place at Middlebrook. Since it was founded in the 1930s it has had seven changes of ownership and five changes of name. To add spice, virtually all of these changes have taken place since 1958.

If one begins at the beginning, the property passed through a 100-year cycle of ownership, commencing with the Hardy family and, after a break of 80 years, returning to it, only to pass once again out of Hardy ownership early in 1985.

In 1880 Thomas Hardy acquired the property as part of his ever-burgeoning grape-growing and winemaking interests. For the next 67 years this and the adjacent vineyard were called Glenn Hardy. In 1947 the property was acquired by an English firm of ship's chandlers, P. B. Mason & Company of Hull, who erected a winery and renamed the property Roxton. The venture was not successful, and was closed down until 1958 when it was reopened by local grape-grower Connor Sparrow. He continued to make fortified and dry red table wines for some years until John Rosato and Lorenzo Comazetto purchased the property. They extended the winery and changed the name to Valle d'Oro. They specialised in spumante-style wines, pioneering the Australian production thereof. During their ownership the vineyards were also expanded to 35 hectares.

In 1971 Dalgety Wine Estates acquired the vineyard and winery and changed the name back to Roxton. Yet another round of vineyard expansion followed, and yet another winery modernisation. As part of a "package deal" sale, the winery passed to Seagrams along with Dalgety's other wine interests; Seagrams quickly on-sold the winery to David and John Hardy in 1979.

The Hardys, following in the tradition of previous owners, once again changed the name, somewhat unwisely choosing Benelen. For some obscure reason

this incited the wrath of Lindemans, who claimed it was likely to be confused with Ben Ean. Given a total crush of a little over 200 tonnes, this might have seemed to a detached observer to be a fairly unlikely threat. Nonetheless, unwilling to become involved in protracted litigation, the name was changed once again, this time to Middle Brook. Charity has led me to ignore the final change to Middlebrook, then still under the Hardy ownership.

The estate vineyards are now planted to four hectares each of shiraz, cabernet sauvignon, rhine riesling, sauvignon blanc and semillon, 3.5 hectares of grenache, three hectares of palomino, two hectares of pedro ximinez and one hectare of pinot noir. These provided around 30 per cent of the 1984 crush of 263 tonnes.

Some excellent wines were released under the Middlebrook label, not the least being a 1983 Late-Harvest Rhine Riesling and a 1982 Hillcrest Shiraz. Both were extremely well made: the 1983 Late-Harvest Rhine Riesling is made in a style which seems to me naturally suited to McLaren Vale, with rich, deep and sweet flavour and considerable overall weight and strength. The Hillcrest Shiraz had strong, minty fruit, with sweet-berry flavours on the mid-palate, and had quite obviously been well looked after before going into bottle. A third wine of utterly individual style (and of which the declining remnants of a dozen bottles reside in my cellar) is Durus, a blend of white wine, brandy and honey. It is an utterly seductive mixer, topper or even aperitif on a cold day.

Middlebrook boasts one of the prettiest wineries and adjoining restaurants in the Southern Vales region. The spacious restaurant has a charm and atmosphere all of its own.

Early in 1985 Middlebrook changed hands once again. Oenotec was appointed consultants to the new owners, and Caroline Burston was installed as winemaker. With considerable experience at Tisdall and Capel Vale, Burston set about cleaning the winery with much vigour, and even better wines should appear under the Middlebrook label in the future.

NOON'S
RIFLE RANGE ROAD, McLAREN VALE

Adelaide schoolteacher David Noon moved with his wife Nerida and five children to McLaren Vale in 1968. The property they acquired included a five-hectare vineyard, the grapes from which had been sold to other wineries in the district.

Within a few years David Noon was experimentally making small quantities of wine for home consumption. The wines turned out well, and production increased to the point where a vigneron's licence was obtained in 1976. The Noons then erected a new storage and cellar-door sales area, together with a separate bottling facility.

Noon's specialises in red wines. Around 50 per cent of the annual crush is estate-grown, the balance coming from local growers. With help from his winemaking son Andrew, David Noon has successfully experimented with a number of winemaking techniques and styles.

His late-picked carbonic maceration grenache is, it must be admitted, as much a child of necessity as of invention. With his fermentation capacity filled with premium grape varieties, the grenache is invariably left until last. At this point of time it has often ripened and raisined to the point where it produces wine with an alcohol content of just under 16 degrees. The grapes are allowed to ferment by the carbonic maceration process for four weeks (the ferment is started by around 15 per cent of the grapes being conventionally crushed and must-seeded) and the 1983 vintage was typical of the massive wines which result. They are a long way removed from the normal concept of a carbonic maceration red, which is light, fruity and delicate. The Noon wines have the spicy nutmeg/meat aromas of the more conventional wines, but the palate is extremely powerful with very heavy tannin.

The quality of the conventionally made shiraz cabernet blends, released under the Côtes de la Vallée label (David Noon, amongst other things, teaches French), are variable in quality but can be outstanding. The 1980 vintage (still on sale in mid-1984) was such a wine, with a marvellously spicy palate, lovely oak and good balance. It bore a more than passing resemblance to a fine Rhone Valley wine.

OLD CLARENDON WINERY
MAIN ROAD, CLARENDON

David Dridan is a highly regarded South Australian landscape artist, and it is appropriate that the Skottowe Estate base should be situated in the beautiful town of Clarendon, high in the Adelaide Hills. Because the grapes for the tiny output come from grapes grown around Reynella, I have treated the winery as coming within the McLaren Vale area rather than the Adelaide Hills.

The Old Clarendon Winery is situated on one of the more historic viticultural sites in South Australia. It was first planted in 1850 by two prominent Adelaide men, John Morphett and William Lee. In 1882 the 16-hectare vineyard was sold to Joseph Gillard, a prominent Australian vigneron who managed the Penfolds Magill Vineyards until 1905. He then returned to Clarendon where first he, and then his family, managed the vineyards until they went out of production in 1935.

In the late 1960s Dridan and architect Ian Hanaford determined to restore the property. The Old Clarendon complex now offers a variety of facilities including motel units, restaurants, craft shops and David Dridan's art gallery and winery. The buildings flow down the side of the steep hill, and the motel is one of the most pleasant in the entire Southern Vales area. The development is a tribute to Dridan's imagination; Russell Drysdale once wrote of him: "He is the kind of person who can turn a mundane ten-cent bus ride into a new adventure or make a drab day memorable."

If it is true that Dridan designed the label for his wines when he was only 10 years of age—as the story goes—his artistic talents must have developed at around the same pace as the musical skills of Mozart.

The winemaking is very much an incidental part of the whole enterprise, with the basic releases comprising a rhine riesling and a cabernet sauvignon. Output is sold from the Old Clarendon Winery. It is believed that some of the wine sold is purchased as "clean skins" from other wineries.

OLIVERHILL WINES
SEAVIEW ROAD, McLAREN VALE

Oliverhill Wines was founded in 1973 by an Adelaide biologist, a virologist, a general practitioner and a wine chemist. The small winery was built and opened for cellar-door sales in 1976. Three hectares of cabernet sauvignon, rhine riesling, shiraz and sauvignon blanc provided part of the 20-tonne crush, supplemented by purchases from local growers.

In 1984 the most flamboyant figure in McLaren Vale, Vincenzo Berlingieri, purchased Oliverhill with, as usual, grand schemes in mind. Enzo (as he prefers to be called) cut a swathe during his time at Settlement Wines, one which extended from the Southern Vales, indeed, to Sydney. One of his schemes for Oliverhill is the establishment of a "portorium".

Grape-growers and would-be port-makers can bring their grapes to Oliverhill; Enzo will crush them, ferment and fortify the wine, returning it either in bulk for home bottling or in bottle, as the customer requires.

Whether the Oliverhill labels will assume the same awesome proportions as the original Settlement labels remains to be seen.

PALLADIO WINES
MARTINS ROAD, McLAREN VALE

Italian-born and trained winemaker Gianni Frada established Palladio Wines in 1974, after a nine-year stint in Australia working for various wineries. The initial production was of Italian-style sparkling wines, but the facilities and range of wines were increased during the late 1970s and early 1980s.

In the ever-changing McLaren Vale scene, Palladio was acquired by Torresan in 1984 following the subdivision of the latter's six-hectare vineyard and winery at Happy Valley for housing purposes. It is believed that the entire Torresan base will be moved to Palladio.

PIRRAMIMMA
JOHNSTON ROAD, McLAREN VALE

Pirramimma was acquired by the Johnston family in 1892; at that time there were only a few vines on the property, but the Johnstons soon had a substantial area under vine. The first vintage was made in 1900; by 1903 it was producing 81,000 litres of wine, placing it tenth among the McLaren Vale wineries.

It has remained in the family ever since, with third-generation Alex Johnston as general manager, and his cousin Geoffrey (a Riverina College of Advanced Education graduate) as winemaker. It is now a most important operation, both in terms of the quantity of the wine it produces and more so in terms of the quality. Its vineyards are extensive, providing over 80 per cent of its crush of around 450 tonnes. The vineyards comprise shiraz (13.6 hectares), grenache (10.7 hectares), pedro ximinez (8.5 hectares), rhine riesling (5.6 hectares), cabernet sauvignon (5.2 hectares), palomino (4.9 hectares), chardonnay (three hectares), cabernet franc (1.8 hectares), merlot (1.2 hectares) and mataro (1.1 hectares). Additional quantities of chardonnay, cabernet sauvignon and rhine riesling are purchased

from local contract-growers. The 1984 production resulted in 150,000 litres of white table wine, 106,000 litres of red table wine and 61,000 litres of fortified wine, while 23,000 litres were distilled into fortifying spirit.

It is only in recent times that the company has made a concerted push into premium-quality bottled table wine. Rhine riesling was not made before 1979, nor chardonnay before 1981. Indeed, until 1946 virtually the entire production was sold in bulk to W. A. Gilbey Limited of London, a trade which continued on a declining scale until 1966. It was after that year that the company moved into the bottled-wine market, initially with reds and more recently with white wines.

In these days of "chardomania" it is hardly surprising that most attention is paid to the Pirramimma chardonnays. The home vineyards were planted in 1977 and were the source block for the McLaren Vale area. The first vintage of 1981 is still drinking superbly, although its enormous fruit and oak flavour will almost certainly become broad and flabby if left much longer. The 1983 Chardonnay is a complete contrast in style; supremely elegant, with very sensitive fruit and oak handling, and very fine grapefruit/peach-fruit flavours on the palate. Part of the wine was barrel-fermented for two months, and the wine is a great success.

The Pirramimma Rhine Rieslings have also been technically excellent since their introduction in 1979. McLaren Vale provides an abundance of fruit flavour and all of the rhine rieslings in the district show this. The more difficult task for the winemaker is to invest the wines with life and elegance, a task which Pirramimma accomplishes with seeming ease. Some particularly good spatlese rhine rieslings also come out under the Pirramimma label, again proving the suitability of the area to making this style of wine.

In 1982 Pirramimma joined the carbonic maceration band-wagon and, typically enough, outperformed most others. While these are normally regarded as early-drinking styles, the wine was still a pleasure in mid-1984. The bouquet was soft and clean, spicy/nutmeg aromas led on to a soft, sweet mid-palate, low tannin and very good overall richness. It was of the same quality as the conventionally made 1981 Cabernet Sauvignon, a very clean wine, with deep and ripe minty/camphor aromas together with a well-structured palate with deep, sweet mint/berry flavours.

There is no disputing Pirramimma's position as one of the outstanding winemakers in the Southern Vales region.

REYNELLA
REYNELL ROAD, REYNELLA

John Reynell was born to a Devonshire farming family in 1809, but from an early age he turned his back on the family traditions. At the age of 16 he set out on his first business trip abroad; over the ensuing 10 years he visited Europe, the United States and Egypt. Returning to London, he observed an advertisement in the *Strand* for men and money to help build the colony of South Australia.

Reynell and a companion, Thomas Lucas, each purchased several 30-hectare allotments at $3 per hectare, and sailed to South Australia with Thomas Lucas's sister Mary, whom Reynell married shortly after they arrived in the colony. On the journey to Australia Reynell had acquired vine cuttings at the Cape of Good Hope in 1838, and planted these on his arrival, thus laying claim to being one of the first vignerons in the colony.

By 1845 he had excavated the underground cellar which was to become famous as the Old Cave Cellar and which is so much a part of the Reynella of today. In that year he also obtained a substantial supply of vine cuttings from John Macarthur's Camden Vineyard. The vines obtained included riesling, cabernet sauvignon, malbec, gouais, dolcetto, constantia, verdelho and tokay. Five years later he provided a year's employment for a newly arrived Thomas Hardy; but lack of capital was a constant problem for Reynell, who narrowly escaped bankruptcy on a number of occasions. In 1854 he decided to raise money by selling part of his landholdings for the purpose of establishing the township of Reynella. The scheme was successful. Freed of economic problems, the business flourished and was aided by Walter Reynell who was born in 1846, and by 1854 was already helping his father plough the vineyard with two bullocks.

John Reynell died in 1876, a tenacious pioneer; it was Walter Reynell who was chiefly responsible for building the business to the position of pre-eminence which it obtained. By 1903 it was the second-largest winery in the Southern Vales area, and one of the larger in the entire colony. In that vintage it produced 400,000 litres of wine, and shortly after Walter Reynell & Sons Wines Limited was incorporated.

Walter Reynell's son Carew became managing director, but enlisted in the First World War to become Commanding Officer of the Ninth Australian Light Horse Regiment. Carew Reynell was killed in action on Hill Sixty at Gallipoli in 1915. It was to set an unhappy precedent for the company, with three more members giving their lives in the Air Force in the Second World War.

Indeed, the depredations of wartime meant that much of the management passed out of the Reynell family. Colin Haselgrove became managing director in 1953, and the company was eventually acquired by Hungerford Hill in April 1970. Two years later Hungerford Hill sold a half-share of its wine interests to Rothmans of Pall Mall, which subsequently took full control of Reynella. The final move in the corporate chess game came in August 1982 when Reynella was acquired by Thomas Hardy & Sons.

The Hungerford Hill link had provided Reynella with one great benefit: long-term access to grapes grown in Coonawarra, to supplement the McLaren Vale-sourced material. Most of the latter comes from Reynella's own vineyards, planted to shiraz (19 hectares), cabernet sauvignon (12 hectares), rhine riesling (10 hectares), malbec (five hectares), merlot and traminer (three hectares each) and melon (two hectares).

The total crush of around 1300 tonnes is not large by big-company standards, but Reynella has always specialised in the top end of the wine market. During Rothmans' ownership the marketing of the company's products was little short of deplorable, with consistently fine wine sold (with equal consistency) for a fraction of its worth. Wine consumers can hardly be blamed for assuming a red wine discounted to $2 a bottle retail is of mediocre quality at best. This is the sorry spectacle which confronted the Reynella Coonawarra Cabernet Sauvignon releases from the 1976 and subsequent vintages. The rhine rieslings from the same period were only marginally more kindly treated. I have discussed the high quality of these wines at pages 403–404.

Hardy's took the only possible course when it took over. It discontinued all of the old Reynella labels, left a decent breathing space and then introduced a new range of labels (and some new wines) in the second half of 1984. The pretty, pastel-coloured labels are certainly a major break with those that preceded them, which was no doubt the intention of the designer. The top wine under the Reynella label is now the cabernet malbec merlot, first made in 1975. These wines are normally held for six years before release, and the 1978 was on the market in the second half of 1984. Its colour is absolutely extraordinary; a vibrant cherry-purple which would do justice to a top-quality two-year-old wine.

The other unusual feature is that it shows virtually no sign of the 16 months it spent in new French oak hogsheads. This is no doubt due to the extremely crisp, finely accented fruit flavours and very low pH of the wine. All of this stems from Geoff Merrill's belief in early picking to retain both varietal character and sufficient natural acid to eliminate the necessity for acid adjustment.

He has at times carried these views to extremes, and the 1978 vintage is a prime example, with only 8.8 degrees of alcohol. For the purist there may be a structural dip in the middle to back palate, but it is easier to find this flaw _after_ one has been told the wine has only 8.8 degrees of alcohol, rather than beforehand.

The base releases under the new Chateau Reynella label are the Vintage Reserve Chablis and Vintage Reserve Claret. The chablis is given significant oak treatment, and made from an assemblage of grape varieties; my only criticism of the wine is that it really should be labelled a white burgundy. The Vintage Reserve Claret is one of the best commercial reds available on the market today. The 1980 vintage, released in 1984, had a recommended retail price of $5.69 and a real price closer to $4. A wine of intense fragrance, redolent of red fruits—cherries, strawberries and mulberries—married with a touch of spicy oak on the palate, it was a striking and quite lovely wine.

The other important releases in the table-wine range are the Chateau Reynella Cabernet Sauvignon and Chateau Reynella Chardonnay, both of which uphold the high standing of the label.

Overall Reynella's greatest claim to fame lies with its vintage ports. Those who really understand vintage-port style will argue with animation about the relative merits of the vintage ports of Thomas Hardy and those of Reynella. While the argument may be intense, it invariably turns on the question of style rather than quality. Both sides agree the quality is not in dispute.

At the 1985 State Bank Royal Sydney Show the 1977 Chateau Reynella Vintage Port was one of the two finalists contending for the major port trophy. In the end it was relegated to second place by an Old Tawny Port from Saltram, but I for one would have been more than happy to see the trophy go to the Chateau Reynella wine. It has a marvellous cool elegance evocative of Portuguese vintage port at its best, with hints of minty fruit, a little oak, superb clean spirit, and just the right amount of tannin. But it is only one of a long line of superb vintage ports which do Australia proud.

RICHARD HAMILTON
MAIN SOUTH ROAD, WILLUNGA

Yet again vine and scalpel go hand in hand. Indeed, in Dr Richard Hamilton's case they go more closely than usual: he is a specialist in plastic surgery, and in particular microsurgery of the hand. He not only claims medical kinship with Dr Max Lake, but is also the great-great-grandson of one of South Australia's first viticulturalists, whose name he bears: the first Richard Hamilton founded Hamilton's Ewell Vineyards in 1837. Richard Hamilton's father was also a vigneron; while his uncle not only worked in the industry for decades with Hamiltons, but founded Leconfield in Coonawarra. This vineyard and winery is now also operated and owned by Richard Hamilton.

The Willunga property on which the Southern Vales winery is situated was first planted in 1972, the year of the first vintage under the Richard Hamilton label. In the early years the crush was provided by grapes bought in from local growers, but now all of the wines are made from estate-grown grapes.

The vineyard is a very substantial one, with 66 hectares planted to premium varieties including cabernet sauvignon, merlot, chardonnay, semillon, sauvignon blanc, chenin blanc and muscat gordo blanco. The soils are slate and gravel, over a deep-drained limestone base. Hamilton believes this premium soil structure eliminates the necessity for supplementary water, as the vines are able to obtain moisture reserves from the subsoil. Willunga is only seven kilometres from Gulf St Vincent and, being influenced by the southerly coast, has a cooler climate than Adelaide.

The original concept of the winery was to produce principally white table wines which, in the French style, had some oak maturation. Hamilton was thus a pioneer in the region, which in the early 1970s was regarded as a red-wine area rather than a white-wine one. His use of large American oak vats to ferment all the white wines, and to give some additional maturation in small oak casks, is also unusual when applied to varieties such as rhine riesling and (to a lesser degree) chenin blanc.

All of the Richard Hamilton white wines show a similarity of style. I have to admit frankly that I do not like that style, and consistently down-point the wines in masked comparative tastings. I imagine this will not cause Richard Hamilton any particular distress—the wines are undoubtedly moulded the way he desires. He has been winemaking for too long now not to know precisely what he is aiming to achieve, and how to achieve that objective.

The cabernet sauvignon can be excellent, fine, cool and elegant. Equally I have tasted some vintages which have been badly affected by mercaptan and sour tastes. The beautifully packaged range comprises a chardonnay, a semillon, a chenin blanc, a rhine riesling, a semillon white burgundy, an auslese riesling, a sauterne, a cabernet sauvignon, a dessert muscat and a vintage port.

ST FRANCIS WINES
STURT HIGHWAY, REYNELLA

St Francis Wines relies heavily on the passing tourist trade from Adelaide. Well situated on the Sturt Highway at Reynella, just south of the township, the winery occupies the building which housed the first licensed distillery in South Australia.

The operation is owned and run by Karl Lambert, who worked at Penfolds for 16 years before acquiring the St Francis property in 1970. The winery has no vineyards of its own, relying on bought-in grapes and on contract-made wine acquired from other wineries. A full range of generic table and sparkling wines is available, of unremarkable quality.

SANTA ROSA WINES
CURRENCY CREEK

Santa Rosa Wines was established by Wally and Rosemary Tonkin and family in 1969. It is established on the 1300-hectare property on which they live, and which is also devoted to a variety of farming and grazing interests.

The vineyard is located on the southern side of the Mount Lofty Ranges, in contrast to McLaren Vale which is on the northern side. Situated only six kilometres from the Southern Ocean, the climate is significantly cooler than McLaren Vale proper as it is aided by the influence of the sea-breezes which start to blow through the vineyard early each afternoon. In the end result the vintage is substantially later than McLaren Vale, and the late-harvested semillon and rhine riesling are invariably botrytised.

The vineyards are located among tall gum trees, attesting to the merit of the sandy loam over a well-drained red clay subsoil. Drip-irrigation is used to avoid summer stress.

The 1984 vintage yielded 32 tonnes of semillon, 19 tonnes of rhine riesling, eight tonnes of sauvignon blanc, 4.5 tonnes of chardonnay, 23 tonnes of shiraz,

18 tonnes of cabernet sauvignon and three tonnes of pinot noir. The white wines are all made for Santa Rosa at Petaluma; the red wines are made on the recently erected on-site winery by son Philip Tonkin, directed on a daily basis by Brian Barry.

Santa Rosa was an unknown quantity to me when I visited the McLaren Vale area with the Victorian Wine Press Club in mid-1984. They happened to be the first wines of the day, part of a large line-up. I shall not quickly forget my surprise: normally the first wines of the day come as something of a cold shower at best, and seem like vinegar at worst. These were nectar.

Distrusting my palate I turned to my neighbour, only to receive confirmation that the wines were, indeed, quite superb. It was only then that I learnt their provenance. In short, there is no question that the Santa Rosa Vineyard does produce very high-quality fruit, all of the attributes of which are preserved by the abundant winemaking skills at Petaluma.

In 1983 the drought meant that only a late-picked rhine riesling was made from Santa Rosa fruit, or Deer Park, as the vineyard is called. It was magnificently intense and balanced wine, with clearly delineated botrytis influence. The 1983 Rhine Riesling was made with grapes from the Clare Valley and from Coonawarra.

The 1984 white wines should be outstanding; the 1983 Shiraz won the Adrian Brown Trophy for the best Southern Vales dry red, and will be released at the same time. Santa Rosa wines are not widely distributed, but they are very well worth seeking out.

SCARPANTONI ESTATES
KANGARILLA ROAD, McLAREN FLAT

Domenico Scarpantoni came from a family with a long history of winemaking in Italy. When he migrated to Australia in 1952 it was more or less inevitable that he would find a place in the wine industry. After spending some years working and travelling in various parts of Australia, he moved to the Southern Vales region and worked first at Hardy's for seven years, and then as vineyard manager at Seaview for a further six years.

In 1965 the Scarpantoni family purchased the property on which its vineyard and winery are now established. The vineyard came first and is now planted to shiraz (8.3 hectares), cabernet sauvignon (5.5 hectares), rhine riesling (5.4 hectares), grenache (4.2 hectares), muscat gordo blanco (0.8 hectare), chardonnay, traminer, semillon, merlot and gamay (0.4 hectare each), with a few vines of chenin blanc and tarrango. The vines are established on a mixture of light and heavier sands, intermingled with ironstone, and are relatively low-yielding, averaging six tonnes per hectare. Supplementary water is not used, and all of the vineyard work is done by hand.

Winemaking methods are traditional: the rhine riesling is full and soft; the red wines are not bottled until they are at least three years of age. They normally spend 18 months in cask, and 18 months in tank. The 1981 Shiraz was a remarkably clean and fresh wine, given the extended period in bulk storage before bottling. The 1981 Cabernet Sauvignon is slightly leathery, but has good varietal character.

One of the most unusual offerings is a liqueur riesling, which the Scarpantonis explain "has a fruitful texture that is unlike any other wine and can only become more interesting with time".

SEAVIEW
CHAFFEY'S ROAD, McLAREN VALE

Seaview has since 1971 been part of the Allied Vintners group of companies. Allied Vintners, for the record, was a wholly owned subsidiary of Castlemaine Tooheys Limited until May 1985, when it was acquired by Penfolds. In turn the operating subsidiaries of Allied Vintners include Wynn Winegrowers Proprietary Limited, S. Wynn (SA) Proprietary Limited, Wynvale Wine Proprietary Limited, Coonawarra Estate Proprietary Limited, Edwards & Chaffey Proprietary Limited, Seaview Winery Proprietary Limited, Glenloth Wines Proprietary Limited, Killawarra Vintage Wines Proprietary Limited, J. Y. Tulloch & Sons Proprietary Limited and S. Wynn & Company (Containers) Proprietary Limited.

The three principal brands sold by the Allied Vintners group are Wynns' Coonawarra Estate, Tulloch and Seaview. Seaview is increasingly a brand rather than a product of a particular winery (least of all the old Seaview Winery) or a particular area. Seaview has four major vineyard areas in the McLaren Vale and Willunga region, known as the Seaview Home Block, Chapel Hill, Blencowe and Bethany Vineyards. These total 154 hectares and produce around 60 per cent of the grapes which go to provide the Seaview range. It is no secret that much of the material for Seaview Cabernet Sauvignon and Seaview Rhine Riesling comes from Coonawarra, while the

Seaview Sauvignon Blanc comes partly from McLaren Vale, but has a substantial Eden Valley component.

Given the quantity in which Seaview Rhine Riesling is made, little more could be asked of it. It seldom disappoints and often outperforms far more expensive wines. Both the 1983 and 1984 releases were well above average.

Seaview Cabernet Sauvignon is rather more variable; the 1980 vintage was excellent, the 1981 not so good. But again the wine has to be put into its perspective as a major brand. Indeed, it is somehow reassuring to find that vintage variation does play a role, and that the Seaview winemaking team is fallible.

The recent introduction on a substantial scale of the Seaview Sauvignon Blanc has been a welcome addition to the range. The 1984 release showed excellent varietal character, even if the acid in the wine seemed rather hard and oily.

The extent to which Seaview is a brand is underlined in part by the fact that the wine is made at the Glenloth Cellars (the old Seaview Winery is used for storage only), and in part by the late 1984 announcement of the construction of the Seaview _méthode champenoise_ cellars at Reynella. Here $16 million will be spent in building the largest _méthode champenoise_ cellars outside Europe, which will on completion replace the existing Seaview Champagne Cellars at Magill. The site is adjacent to the existing principal table-wine production facility at Reynell Road, Reynella, now called (rather confusingly) Seaview Winery, although once Glenloth.

The building concepts developed for the _méthode champenoise_ cellars involve the sinking of the buildings into the site, enabling the space between the buildings to be landscaped. All movement between the buildings is by means of underground tunnels to reduce noise and to maintain cool cellar temperatures. The buildings provide for a tirage building for storage of maturation stock; a processing building for bottling, disgorging and packaging of _méthode champenoise_ wines; a remuage and warehouse building for storage of the finished products; and an administration building for management which will also include a public sale and tasting area.

The area surrounding the cellars has been planted to chardonnay (largely for show purposes, as the great part of the premium fruit for the top-quality wines will come from Coonawarra and Padthaway); and native trees planted on the perimeter in 1982 complement the cork oaks planted along the main entrance to the site.

It is here that Seaview will make all of its _méthode_

465

champenoise and sparkling wines. These will no doubt be headed by the Edmond Mazure wine, first released in 1984 with the 1980 vintage. Made chiefly from Coonawarra pinot noir, with a little chardonnay, 1980 Edmond Mazure sets the benchmark for top-quality Australian commercial _méthode champenoise_ wines. Only 1500 cases were made, but quantity will increase with subsequent vintages. It is a magnificently balanced and constructed wine, with its aristocratic base material beautifully softened and fined by the four years it spent on yeast lees.

These wines will undoubtedly be the brand leaders for the entire Seaview operation. The quality spreads down through the range and, somewhat against the odds, Seaview has stayed aloof from the price battle waged between Seppelt and Penfolds. In the long term the benefits of this restraint will flow through to the consumer in the form of a better product.

SETTLEMENT WINE COMPANY
PENNY'S ROAD, McLAREN FLAT

The Settlement Wine Company has had something of a roller-coaster existence since 1976, when Vincenzo Berlingieri formed a partnership with Reynella general practitioner David Mitchell to make and market distinctively Australian table and fortified wines.

David Mitchell has now bought his erstwhile partner out of the operation. The flamboyant Berlingieri produced several red wines which achieved everything the partners strove for: impenetrable colour, unfathomable depth and equally extraordinary power and concentration of flavour and body. The best wines were made at the end of the 1970s; and even if the Sydney market found both the personality of Enzo Berlingieri and the strength of his wines difficult to take in large doses, small sips were great fun.

Since that time, however, Settlement has gone into something of an eclipse, and it will be interesting to see just where it heads with David Mitchell in sole control.

SIMON HACKETT
WALKERVILLE

One might be forgiven for saying that Simon Hackett is a poor man's Geoff Merrill. Certainly the course the two winemakers have adopted with their own brands is strikingly similar, although Simon Hackett

has decided to devote himself full-time to the making and promotion of the wines under his label.

Like Geoff Merrill, Simon Hackett has neither winery nor vineyards. The grapes for the releases are purchased from independent growers — chiefly in the Southern Vales district — and contract-made at other wineries. It is a formula which works well if one has the winemaking experience of either Merrill or Hackett. In other words, it sounds easy but it is far more difficult in practice.

The similarities between Hackett and Merrill do not end with their _modus operandi_. Like Merrill, the 33-year-old Hackett has already had a lifetime's experience in the industry. His father was general manager and director of the huge Tarac distillation plant at Nuriootpa. The family home was situated next door to Saltram Winery, and it was here that 17-year-old Simon Hackett obtained his first job in the industry. With Peter Lehmann as his employer, Simon Hackett graduated from washing barrels to crusher operator. Between 1970 and 1973 he worked variously in the Hunter Valley and Saltrams, before moving to the Southern Vales Cooperative in 1973, where he worked with Grant Burge.

Simon Hackett remained at Southern Vales Cooperative and was appointed chief winemaker only months before the Cooperative went into receivership in 1980. He stayed on, but with the uncertainty surrounding the operation he formed a small wine company with Adelaide orthopaedic surgeon Michael Hone. The Aldinga Wine Company laid down small quantities of wine, made by Hackett, each year for sale to selected clients.

When Hong Kong businessman George Lau purchased Southern Vales Cooperative in 1982 he appointed Simon Hackett as general manager and chief winemaker, but was happy to allow him to continue his Aldinga Wine Company business. Late in 1984 Hackett and Hone decided to expand the operation of Aldinga under the Simon Hackett label; Hackett resigned from Southern Vales, and now is winemaker and ambassador-at-large for the new label.

The initial releases of a McLaren Vale semillon (with 10 per cent of sauvignon blanc) and a 1982 Cabernet Sauvignon (75 per cent from McLaren Vale and 25 per cent from Coonawarra) were an auspicious start. Both are excellent wines, each reflecting high-quality fruit and impressive winemaking technology. The packaging, too, was immaculate, with imaginative labels and French dead-leaf green bottles.

SOUTHERN VALES WINERY
WILLUNGA ROAD, McLAREN VALE

The Southern Vales Winery has an immensely rich history, one in which the feeling of _déja vu_ runs strong. Its origins go back to 1896, in which year H. V. Pridmore established a winery known as The Wattles. He was encouraged to do so by Thomas Hardy, the purpose being to dispose of a surplus of grapes grown in the district at the time. The first cellars were temporary, but a stone storage cellar built in 1901 is still in use, with its memorial stone attesting to the fact that it was opened in February of that year.

In 1901 Pridmore moved from his home at The Wattles on Tatachilla Road into an historic home purchased from the Colton Estate. Tatachilla was for a long time part of the fabric of what became known as the Southern Vales Winery. But in 1903 both Tatachilla Winery (with a vintage of 225,000 litres) and The Wattles (with a vintage of just over 200,000 litres) were major forces in the Southern Vales area.

In 1910 Penfolds Wines Limited acquired the Pridmore interests and operated them until 1963; the wines were taken to Nuriootpa for maturation and blending at the end of each vintage.

In February 1965 185 grape-growers in the region banded together to form the Southern Vales Cooperative Winery Limited. With State government financial assistance, it purchased the Penfolds Winery and that year crushed just on 2700 tonnes of grapes.

In 1968 the cooperative purchased the Horndale Distillery at Happy Valley, enabling part of the crush to be distilled, but also providing ideal storage and maturation facilities in the massive cellars built in 1896.

Winemaking facilities were both upgraded and centralised at the principal Southern Vales Winery in 1971, and processing at Horndale ceased. Its function then reverted to pure distillation (with the wine transported in bulk from McLaren Vale) as well as storage and maturation.

In 1980 a receiver-manager was appointed to Southern Vales Cooperative; although it continued to process grapes for its existing contract markets, throughput was much reduced.

On 20 May 1982 the entire Southern Vales operation was sold as a going concern to George Lau, an Adelaide-born but Hong Kong-based businessman. The purchase price of $650,000 represented but a tiny part of the replacement cost of the assets acquired, but assets in any industry have value only if they produce a return. The problem was Southern Vales simply could not find sufficient markets for its output.

Lau has a ready-made answer to that problem: substantial exports to Hong Kong have already commenced, and he now intends that a significant proportion of production be exported to the Far East.

George Lau, aged 70, and his son Roland have already spent substantial sums in upgrading the winery and in repurchasing the vineyards which once formed part of The Wattles and Tatachilla. Part of the original Tatachilla Vineyard has been purchased, as has the original Tintara Vineyard. These moves are linked with plans for the introduction of a top-of-the-range Tatachilla label. This will be reserved for genuinely small parcels of high-priced premium wine; the principal Southern Vales labels will be marketed in the medium- to lower-price bracket.

It is these latter wines which have so far been released under the Lau regime. I have tasted the range on several occasions, both in blind tastings and otherwise, and it seems to me that domestic sales are more likely to be based on price than on quality.

TARANGA ESTATE
MAIN SOUTH ROAD, McLAREN VALE

Taranga Estate was established in 1974 by Lorenzo Comazetto, who some years earlier had sold his share in what was then called Valle d'Oro Winery to Dalgety's (the name changed successively to Roxton, Benelen and then Middlebrook). Wishing to continue in the wine industry, he purchased a 20-hectare property near the McLaren Vale township which he planted to cabernet sauvignon, shiraz, malbec and rhine riesling.

Prior to the 1975 vintage a modern winery was erected, which was extended in 1976 by the addition of a bottling cellar, warehouse and tasting and sales area. A further 16 hectares of adjoining land were purchased for vineyard extensions, but in 1977, before his dream was fully realised, Lorenzo Comazetto died. Management of the winery passed to the family, and noted winemaker Jack Davoren, who had retired from Penfolds, was retained as a consultant.

If the potential of the vineyards (established on an ideal rich loam over a limestone base) with their premium varieties, the capacity of a new winery and the skills of Jack Davoren were realised, the results did not percolate much past the cellar door. Certainly

Taranga drifted, and it came as no surprise when the enterprise was sold.

In 1984 Melbourne export consultant Daryl Ross and Adelaide soft-drink entrepreneur Jim Hayden acquired the business. The profile of Taranga has been swiftly altered: one initiative is to offer customers the opportunity of having grapes contract-grown and made into one's personalised wine. Ross also has ambitions to form a McLaren Vale consortium to enter larger export markets. These ingenious ideas and initiatives are commendable, but they are no substitute for wine quality.

THE ESTATE
KANGARILLA ROAD, McLAREN VALE

Some wineries start quietly, humbly even, with wines produced in a hastily converted tin shed and shyly offered to the public. Others start with a fanfare of trumpets, few more strident than that which greeted the initial release of the 1981 Hazelmere Estate wines.

The enterprise was planned in 1977 by Rod Scroops as a diversification of his then-ownership of the Townhouse, Adelaide. When Hazelmere Estate opened for business in 1980 half a million bricks had been used to erect a 50-seat à la carte restaurant; a 200-seat function centre; the Mews courtyard, with its fibreglass roof, allows outdoor dining for up to 300; and the motel section consisting of 30 units. The winery area, although palatial, seemed almost an afterthought. A spacious cellar-door tasting and sales area led through to the immaculately planned production area.

Oenotec was retained as consultant, and Iain Riggs joined Hazelmere Estate from Bleasdale Vineyards as winemaker. With an immaculately equipped, brand-new winery, and with Oenotec close at hand, it was hardly surprising that the Hazelmere Estate wines of 1981, 1982 and 1983 were enthusiastically received by wine writers, wine judges and the market place alike.

Although a vineyard had been planted none of the grapes came from Hazelmere itself, but were purchased throughout the Southern Vales area. Hazelmere's own vineyard, with nine hectares of rhine riesling, chardonnay, gerwurtztraminer, pinot noir and cabernet sauvignon, produced its first significant harvest in 1985.

The greatest accolades have been given to the various releases of Chardonnay between 1981 and 1983, and the Sauvignon Blanc of 1982 and 1983.

The chardonnays are typically rich and buttery, with the depth which McLaren Vale seems to provide at will, and the oak handling is very sophisticated, adding yet a further dimension. The sauvignon blanc, by contrast, is marvellously pungent, austere and crisp. The 1982 and 1983 releases of this wine were outstanding.

In 1984 the first of the high-quality red-wine releases under the Hazelmere Estate label was made, a 1982 Cabernet Sauvignon Merlot. It is an extremely elegant wine and shows fine style. The 1981 Hazelmere Estate Shiraz also reflected immaculate winemaking and fruit handling, combined with attractive, dusty, gently tannic oak.

Late in 1983 Hazelmere was sold to interests associated with Kim Peglar, and Charles Hargreaves (ex-Merrivale) was installed as winemaker. In consequence it has changed its name to The Estate, although no releases under this label had appeared before February 1985. It will be interesting to see whether the quality is maintained, and whether the style of the wines changes.

THOMAS FERNHILL ESTATE
INGOLDBY ROAD, McLAREN FLAT

Wayne and Pat Thomas established Thomas Fernhill Estate in Ingoldby Road, McLaren Flat, in 1975. Wayne Thomas had spent a lifetime as a winemaker in the district, working first for Stoneyfell, Saltram and Ryecroft, followed by a period as a consultant winemaker to others. Indeed, Thomas still continues as a consultant and runs the small Fernhill Winery at the same time.

Ninety per cent of the 1984 55-tonne crush came from grapes purchased in from local growers. The Thomas' vineyards amount to a token 0.5 hectare of cabernet sauvignon.

Until 1985 the facilities of other wineries were used to produce the white wine, but all winemaking is now centralised at Fernhill. Right from the outset Thomas has produced wines of very high quality. The red wines are invariably deep-coloured, full-flavoured and clean; the white wines started with aromatic, full-flavoured yet crisp rhine rieslings, and now extend to first-class chardonnay and sauvignon blanc.

Output remains small, but the wines do have distribution in each of the eastern States, and are well worth looking for. The 1983 and 1984 Chardonnays were among the best made in the district.

TORRESAN'S HAPPY VALLEY WINERY
MARTINS ROAD, McLAREN VALE

Gino Torresan emigrated from Treviso in the north of Italy in 1939. Torresan's father was a skilled winemaker and Gino Torresan had had a basic grounding both in viticulture and winemaking by the time he arrived in this country. Nonetheless, it was not until 1958 that he purchased a 100-year-old vineyard in Happy Valley, which had been established by Mrs Horn, one of the founders of Horndale Winery. He revived and trellised the ailing vineyard, and established a winery in partnership with the members of his family.

The business has now passed into the ownership of his sons, Emilio and John Torresan, with Stephen Clark as winemaker. Unhappily the 1984 crush of 260 tonnes was the last to take fruit from the old vineyard, which provided 25 per cent of the crush. It has fallen prey to urban pressure, and is to be subdivided for housing. This will also mean the partial relocation of the winery and, as I have recounted earlier, the Torresans have purchased Palladio Wines for this purpose.

The 1984 crush of 123 tonnes of pedro and palomino, 50 tonnes of grenache, 31 tonnes of doradillo, 28 tonnes of muscat gordo blanco, 20 tonnes of a mixed planting of shiraz and cabernet (from the old vineyard) and six tonnes of rhine riesling gives a fair indication of the wines produced by Torresan, aimed for the bulk and clean-skin markets.

WIRRA WIRRA
McMURTIE ROAD, McLAREN VALE

The original Wirra Wirra was born in the wine boom which swept the Southern Vales area around the turn of the century. In 1903 Wirra Wirra produced 76,000 litres of wine, fractionally less than Pirramimma, but substantially more than Ryecroft and Hope Vineyard (the latter ultimately to become Seaview).

By the time Wirra Wirra was re-established in 1969 by Greg and Roger Trott, the old cellars were no more than ruins. The Trotts rebuilt them using beams from a Methodist church in Adelaide. The spacious cellars and cellar-door sales area are among the most attractive in the entire McLaren Vale area, the walls featuring old handmade sandstock bricks.

Since the latter part of the 1970s Wirra Wirra has grown substantially in size and in reputation, to the point where it is now one of the most exciting small wineries in the region. This growth has coincided with increased ties with Petaluma and its associated consulting business, Oenotec Pty Limited. Oenotec is the winemaking consultant to Wirra Wirra and is a substantial shareholder, together with the Trott family. All of the grapes for Wirra Wirra's substantial output are crushed at Petaluma, and the cleaned juice is returned to Wirra Wirra for all the subsequent stages of the winemaking process.

Around 45 per cent of the annual 18,000-case output is grown on two McLaren Vale vineyards owned by Greg and Roger Trott respectively. Roger Trott's Moray Park was once owned by Thomas Hardy, but has been in the ownership of the Trott family since 1923. Situated seven kilometres north-east of McLaren Vale, and close to the foothills near McLaren Flat, it is widely regarded as one of the best vineyards in the Southern Vales. It is planted to cabernet sauvignon (5.7 hectares), shiraz (4.9 hectares, some of it up to 60 years old and the youngest 12 years), grenache (four hectares), merlot (3.85 hectares, producing its first major crop in 1985), rhine riesling (2.4 hectares) and chardonnay (two hectares). Greg Trott's Bethany Vineyards (the Southern Vales Bethany, not that of the Barossa Valley) have rhine riesling (2.8 hectares), pedro ximinez (2.2 hectares), cabernet sauvignon and sauvignon blanc (1.6 hectares each), pinot noir (1.2 hectares) and merlot (one hectare).

The remaining 55 per cent is purchased from other growers, but by no means necessarily in the Southern Vales area. Wirra Wirra has a policy of obtaining suitable material from whatever region is likely to produce the best grapes to complement the estate-grown material. Thus Wirra Wirra's sources encompass Coonawarra, the Clare Valley, the Adelaide Hills and, of course, the Southern Vales.

The winemaker is a peripatetic American, Rollin Soles, who has a Master's degree in oenology from Davis UCLA and a Bachelor of Science degree from Texas A & M. He has wandered backwards and forwards between Australia and California for a number of years now, usually working somewhere in the complex Petaluma/Oenotec operations.

The success of Wirra Wirra is due to a number of factors. Firstly, wine quality is immaculate; secondly, the wine styles made are precisely in tune with the demands of the marketplace. Thirdly, the bottles are beautifully labelled and presented; and finally, the marketing is both energetic and effective.

In the first half of 1984 I tasted the majority of the Wirra Wirra wines released over the past few years.

The lowest points I awarded any wine was 16.8 out of 20, while the top two wines (1982 Late-Picked Rhine Riesling and 1982 Clarendon Chardonnay) received 18.8.

The range of Hand-Picked Rhine Rieslings from 1979 to 1983 defy much of the conventional wisdom about the suitability of the region for rhine riesling. Certainly the wines are not fine or delicate, but their very richness of flavour, balanced by crisp acid, was their greatest strength.

A range of Chardonnays made in 1982 and 1983 from McLaren Vale and Clarendon fruit showed the radically differing style that the McLaren Vale flats provide compared with that of the Adelaide Hills. That of McLaren Vale is extremely full, rich and buttery; that of Clarendon is crisp and fine with pronounced grapefruit/citric characters. The range also included a 1982 Semillon and the 1983 Sauvignon Blanc/Semillon. Wirra Wirra's use and handling of oak is all that one could ask for, and its success with this style has continued with the subsequently made and released 1984 Sauvignon Blanc.

If the whites are excellent, so are the reds. Colour, balance and fruit freshness are the hallmarks of these wines. The Church Block Cabernet Merlot releases are outstanding, with the 1982 the best so far released. One of the most interesting red wines is the 1983 Pinot Noir, with its outstanding colour, soft cherry/plum/spice nutmeg aromas—a surprisingly firmly structured wine with seemingly good cellaring potential. Once again the wine defies accepted views of the capacity of McLaren Vale, and stands in sharp contrast to the other—admittedly few—attempts at the variety in the region.

It may be possible to make better wines in the Southern Vales area; if if is, I have the distinct feeling it will be Wirra Wirra which achieves that honour.

WOODSTOCK
DOUGLAS GULLY ROAD, McLAREN FLAT

Woodstock Wine Cellars are owned and run by the Collett family. The winery takes its name from the 100-year-old property on which it is established, with the beautiful Victorian mansion set amid towering gum trees.

The winery was established in 1974 for the purpose of contract-making wine for other producers in the district. At that time the vineyard on the property was planted to varieties suitable for distillation. The 10-hectare vineyard has now been replanted to 7.5

hectares of cabernet sauvignon, two hectares of shiraz and experimental plantings of merlot and cabernet franc. The soil is generally sand over clay, particularly suited for red grapes. The Douglas Gully area in which the vineyard is situated usually ripens grapes two or three weeks later than McLaren Vale, and benefits from higher rainfall due to the proximity of the Willunga Range.

In 1982 Doug Collett's son Scott returned to Woodstock to take over winemaking responsibilities. He had graduated from Roseworthy Agricultural College with a degree in oenology and had gained practical experience in South Australia, New South Wales, California, Italy and Germany before returning home.

One of the first decisions he took was to bottle on the estate and release under the Woodstock label around 30 per cent of each year's crush of approximately 250 tonnes. The estate vineyards produce the cabernet sauvignon and shiraz, with rhine riesling, chardonnay, muscat and sauvignon blanc purchased from other growers, one of whom is Scott Collett's brother Ian with a property at Willunga.

Doug Collett had a lifetime's experience in the wine industry, and formed the first wine consulting service in Australia in 1967. The combination of his talents with those of Scott Collett as winemaker is evidently a formidable one, for the Woodstock releases have been of the highest quality.

The first red wine released from the vineyard was one of the best McLaren Vale cabernet sauvignons I have tasted. It was overwhelmingly selected by the 22 winemakers of the district as the best red from the 1982 vintage, and constituted the first release under the McLaren Vale Winemakers' Selection label. The same wine was also released under the Woodstock label. Its gold medal at the Melbourne show in 1983 seems almost superfluous. A marvellously complex wine, with minty, herbaceous aromas and superbly balanced and constructed palate, again with beautifully modulated cabernet flavour, it was and is a triumph. The other red-wine release so far made under the Woodstock label, a 1981 Cabernet Sauvignon, is a more traditional style, soft, developed and clean, but without the intensity and elegance of the 1982.

The white wines are unmistakably products of the region. The rhine rieslings are deep and concentrated, with toasty developed aromas and a rich palate. The first chardonnay release, from 1984, is a state-of-the-art wine: clean, filtered juice was in the major part fermented in German, French and American oak barriques, backblended with a small proportion fermented in stainless steel. A more or less unintended nine grams of residual sugar fills out the palate with its citric/marmalade aromas and flavours. It is a magnificently lush food wine.

One of the most interesting releases to date has been a botrytised sweet white made from a blend of 75 per cent chenin blanc and 25 per cent rhine riesling grown at Simpsons Vineyard near Willunga. The wine was crushed at 22 baume and partially fermented in new French oak. I tasted the wine very early in its life when it showed soft, full, spicy/cinnamon/nutmeg flavours.

There is no doubt that Scott Collett is a highly talented winemaker. With a well-equipped winery, and the ability to select the best 25 or 30 per cent of each year's crush, the elegantly designed Woodstock label is one to follow closely.

Western Australia

The sailing ship _Parmelia_ arrived to found the colony of Western Australia in 1829, five years before Victoria and seven years before South Australia. The supplies on board included vine cuttings from England, and these were planted only two days after the arrival of the _Parmelia_. It is thus not surprising that the first commercial wine was made in Western Australia some years in advance of either Victoria or South Australia. That wine was made by Thomas Waters, a botanist who arrived in 1829 bringing with him rootlings packed in barrels, vine cuttings and numerous other seeds and plants including olives. Waters was granted a 20-hectare property at Guildford on the banks of the Swan River, and in 1830 he dug the lower cellar of what is now the oldest winery in Australia to have remained in continuous production. Olive Farm, as it is known, thrives under the ownership of the Yurisich family, producing some of the better wines to emanate from the Swan Valley.

Prior to Waters' arrival Charles McFaull had planted the first vineyard near what is now Hamilton Hill. The vineyard lasted only a brief time and the young vines were dug out and taken elsewhere. As with the other States, all of the early development took place in areas which now form part of the city centre or adjacent suburbs. Thus vines were established at a pilot nursery at Government House, and grew along the Swan, Canning and Helena Rivers. Part of Waters' original vineyard holding is now included in the Perth International Airport, while Olive Farm and its few remaining vines are very much part of suburban Guildford.

John Septimus Roe planted the first vines at Sandalford in 1840; however, the 1842 sale of wine by Olive Farm marks the first commercial production in the State. Thomas Waters' earlier vintages were used for domestic consumption. By 1843 local diarist Henry Camfield was able to observe that "the colony is possessed with a vine mania" although it has been rightly pointed out that this seems to have been an exaggeration. For more than a century the Swan Valley was the principal source of West Australian wine, and it was in this region that the first substantial vineyard development took place, principally after 1860. By that time vines had been successfully established in a number of areas, including Ellenbrook, Australind, Toodyay, Katanning, Glen Forest, Bakers Hill, Armadale and New Norcia.

In the 1880s viticulture spread further. F. and C. Piesse established a vineyard at Katanning, just to the north of the Lower Great Southern area. That vineyard went out of production in the First World War but Pinwernying Winery has since been re-established at Katanning and carries on production in a limited fashion.

In 1890 Ephraim Clarke planted a vineyard just south of Bunbury, at the northern extremity of

the present Margaret River area. This continued in operation well into the twentieth century, and was followed by Duce's winery at Boyanup in the interwar years, and by Sam Moleri at Yallingup and Albert Vinci at Kirup in the 1950s.

However, until the 1970s the industry was centred almost entirely in and around the Swan Valley. Even here expansion had been slow until the 1890s. In this decade the wine industry flourished in South Australia (benefiting both from the establishment of the export market on a large scale, and from the phylloxera devastation in Victoria), and so did it in Western Australia. In the period from 1895 to 1905 production increased from 225,000 litres to 837,000 litres. Two factors in particular contributed to this growth. Firstly, just as in Victoria, the discovery of gold brought both a rapid increase in population, and an equally impressive increase in disposable income. Goldminers have always lived life to the full, and alcohol was but one of their after-hours pleasures. The other factor shared with South Australia was the establishment of significant British export markets.

Just when it appeared that the momentum might falter, the years after the First World War saw the arrival of a large number of Yugoslavs who settled in the Swan Valley, many taking up viticulture. Production, which in 1920 amounted to 730,000 litres, increased to 1.4 million litres in 1930 and to 3.25 million litres in 1945. By 1953 vineyards had grown to 3690 hectares, close to the all-time peak. Of these, approximately 1000 hectares were wine grapes, the balance going to table grapes grown to support Western Australia's then very large fresh- and dried-fruit exports. In that year 3.6 million litres of wine were made, not very much less than present production.

Since the mid-1950s vineyard area has steadily declined to the point where in 1984 the total vineyard area had decreased to 2101 hectares; yet tonnes produced have increased. The reason is simple enough: in the 1950s and 1960s Western Australia's average yield per hectare was by far the lowest of any State, and less than half the national average. Even in 1973 the average yield across all vineyards (for all purposes, including table grapes) was 4.49 tonnes per hectare, compared with 9.67 for South Australia, 11.41 for Victoria and 10.63 for New South Wales, and a national average of 10.25 tonnes per hectare. Thus the increase in production reflected an increase in the average yield. On the other hand, all things are relative: the national average for vines in bearing in 1984 was 14.22 tonnes per hectare, compared with a still very low average of 6.19 tonnes per hectare in Western Australia.

These statistics tell only part of the story. In the past decade there has been an even greater change as the Swan Valley has abdicated in favour of the new areas, chiefly Margaret River and the Lower Great Southern region. The following table shows just how significant this alteration has been.

WESTERN AUSTRALIA: GRAPE PRODUCTION

| YEAR | TONNES OF GRAPES FOR WINEMAKING | | | TOTAL HECTARES |
	SWAN VALLEY	REST OF STATE	TOTAL	(Table and Wine)
1979	3868	2784	6652	2649
1980	4236	2994	7230	2579
1981	4446	3095	7541	2446
1982	3654	4288	7942	2274
1983	3496	4999	8495	2240
1984	2666	5182	7848	2101

The statistical division of Western Australia into the Swan Valley district and the rest of the State is not particularly helpful. "Rest of State" includes the Gingin area, where there are a number of independent growers, but most importantly the large Houghton Moondah Brook Estate is also included. These plantings account for over 100 hectares of the non-Swan contribution, and have flourished in recent years. Logically the area belongs more to the Swan than to the southern regions.

What is more, the Darling Ranges, or the Perth Hills, seem likely to become the State's next important winegrowing district. In the nineteenth century many vineyards were scattered through this area at a height of around 400 metres above sea-level, 30 kilometres to the east of Perth. During the last few years there has been a resurgence of interest, with over 20 hectares of grapes established and about to come into bearing. The Darling Range viticultural area runs in a narrow 15-kilometre-wide strip from the Avon River in the north to the Canning River in the south. This narrow strip has a relatively high winter rainfall of 1200 millimetres, and a centigrade heat-degree day summation of around 1550, marginally warmer than the Margaret River. Vignerons to date include Peter Fimell's Hainault Vineyards, Woodhenge Wines and Woodvale Wines.

There seems little doubt that the trend shown in the table above will continue as the importance of the Swan Valley in a viticultural sense declines and that of the other areas increases. But, for the reasons that are discussed in the introduction to Chapter 4, the Swan Valley will always have an important role in winemaking and marketing.

The major problem that confronts Western Australia is its remoteness from the eastern markets. Here, the impact of companies such as Houghton, and Evans and Tate, together with the boom status accorded to the whole of the Margaret River area, are of critical importance. Vignerons from outside the Margaret River area frequently exhibit jealousy about the publicity which it receives. In truth they should be very grateful: they fail to appreciate that Margaret River is seen as part of Western Australia, and that the State as a whole benefits. ▯

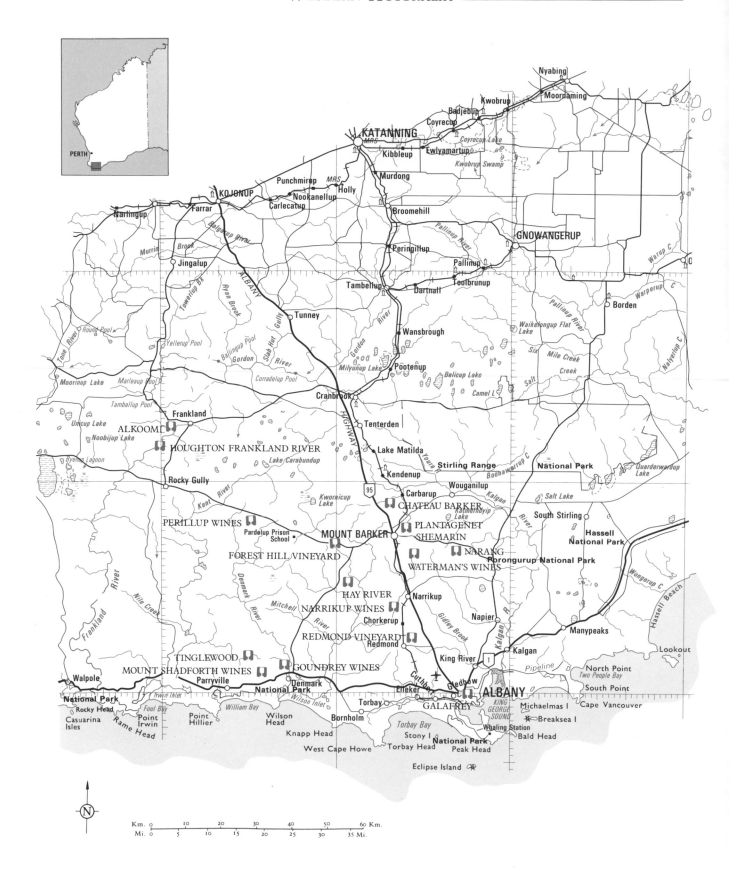

Km. 0   10   20   30   40   50   60 Km.
Mi. 0   5   10   15   20   25   30   35 Mi.

Lower Great Southern Area

The Lower Great Southern area is the largest recognised viticultural area in Australia. Largest not in terms of production, but simply in terms of the immense distances one has to cover to visit the vineyards in the area. One memorable day I made the round trip from Mount Barker, south to Albany on the coast, thence west to the town of Denmark, bearing north to Mount Barker, thence west to Frankland and back to Mount Barker. On that day I visited less than half the vineyards in the district and covered just under 400 kilometres. Not only are the distances substantial, but so is the sense of remoteness and isolation. There is not the concentration of vineyards that one finds in the Margaret River area; much of the country has been tamed only since the Second World War and settlement is far from intensive.

The viticultural potential of the region is said to have been first recognised by Maurice O'Shea; he allegedly expressed the opinion that if he had his time over again, he would establish his vineyards in this area. This was, however, an armchair exercise in a rudimentary climate and soil study, for he never in fact visited the region. The great West Australian winemaker Jack Mann did so in the years between the First and Second World Wars, not in his capacity as a winemaker but as a cricketer of some note. He, too, was singularly impressed with what he saw, although nothing came of it at the time.

Earlier still, the West Australian government had endeavoured to interest Penfolds in establishing vineyards in the Mount Barker region. The first attempts to clear the immense stands of jarrah and red gum had been made by the Muir family in a large leaseholding at Pardelup in the early years of the twentieth century. Without bulldozers and heavy equipment to help them, the scrub regenerated as quickly as it was cleared and the family eventually gave up the unequal struggle. The leasehold reverted to the government and, as Penfolds was not interested

in taking it up, it finally became the site of the Pardelup Correction Centre.

Given the vast area which the region covers, it is hardly surprising that there are a number of distinct subregions. Geographically speaking these separate themselves into the lush coastal hills around Denmark; the undulating scrub and forests of Mount Barker; and the softer areas of the Frankland River.

Overall the region is the coolest in Western Australia, with the centigrade heat-degree day summation ranging from 1553 at Albany on the coast (the Southern Ocean having a marked moderating effect) to 1410 at Mount Barker, 50 kilometres due north of Albany. Rainfall is substantial at between 1000 and 1200 millimetres per year, falling largely in winter and spring. Unlike the Margaret River region, it is often supplemented by some light summer falls generated by clouds moving in from the Southern Ocean. Cloud cover and relatively high humidity at the end of the growing season have proved to be a favourable environment for the incidence of botrytis. Generally the climate is extremely favourable for the production of high-quality grapes. The principal risks lie with spring frosts, which in years such as 1981 caused widespread damage. Salinity is also an increasing problem, particularly in areas such as the Frankland River where drip-irrigation has proved to be essential.

Yields throughout the region have remained extremely low. Initially it was thought that the low yields were simply a function of young vineyards, but further experience suggests this is not so. While the gravelly loams over clay, which make up the general soil types, are very well drained, overall they are of low fertility. The three factors of low fertility, free draining soils and low summer rainfall all induce summer stress and reduce vine vigour, in turn leading to the necessity for drip-irrigation. The great problem is to find water which is not excessively saline, and the lack of suitable water is one of the limiting factors to any substantial increase in viticulture in the area.

The potential of the region was first officially documented by a distinguished Californian viticulturist, Professor Harold Olmo. In 1955 he was invited to Western Australia by the government to advise on the status of the West Australian wine industry and its potential for development. Apart from drawing attention to the shortcomings of the Swan Valley area, he had this to say about the Lower Great Southern area:

> For the production of high-quality light table wines the south coastal area along the Frankland River, spanning the 30-inch to 35-inch (760-millimetre to 890-millimetre) rainfall zone is a very promising one. Here the summer climate is cool enough to promote slow maturity of the fruit, and the rainfall is high enough to produce a vigorous productive vine on the better alluvial soils.

In 1962 the West Australian Department of Agriculture set up a subcommittee to investigate specific areas for the expansion of viticulture. Building on the work of Professor Olmo, a site was selected in 1965 at Forest Hill, near Mount Barker, and the first successful vines were planted on the Pearses' property in 1966.

Separate work had been carried out by Dr John Gladstones of the University of Western Australia, and in the December 1965 issue of the *Journal of the Australian Institute of Agricultural Science* he published a lengthy paper entitled "The Climate and Soils of South-Western Australia in Relation to Vine Growing". It reinforced the conclusions drawn by other researchers, although its publication led not so much to the development of the Lower Great Southern area as to that of the Margaret River.

To date there has been only one major vineyard development in the area, that of Frankland River Wines. The same report which led to the establishment of the Forest Hill Vineyard went on to say:

> A particularly impressive area was seen and tested south of Frankland, on either side of the Frankland River. This area ran north from Muirs Bridge. The Frankland River soils had less gravel, appeared better drained, as shown by the soil auger and the dense erect and vigorous nature of the trees, especially Redgums. The rainfall would be higher than Mount Barker and more spread in its incidence.

This led the Frankland River Grazing Company, operated by erstwhile Adelaide Lord Mayor, John Roche, to establish a little under 100 hectares of vines on a 7400-hectare property owned by the company and called Westfield. As at 1980 the Frankland River Wines development accounted for just on 80 per cent of total vine plantings in the district. Since that time other growers have extended their plantings, and the Lower Great Southern area now has approximately 220 hectares of vines in all, although precise viticultural statistics are extremely difficult to obtain.

Much of the grapes from the region (including all of those from the Frankland River Vineyards, which have been leased for five years since early 1981 by Houghton) go to the Swan Valley for processing. There are only four operating wineries in the region, Chateau Barker and Plantagenet at Mount Barker, Goundrey's at Denmark and Alkoomi at Frankland.

There are many who believe that in the best vintages—and vintage variation plays a larger-than-normal role in the Lower Great Southern area—the greatest of Western Australia's table wines will eventually come from Mount Barker. That view may well be correct, but there is as yet little consistency. Certainly the area has proved that it can produce elegant, fine and racy cabernet sauvignon, particularly that coming from the Mount Barker subregion. The wines all have excellent colour and show considerable bottle-ageing potential—indeed, the wines tend to be rather closed and to lack aroma when young.

A very similar situation applies to rhine riesling: again the wines are steely, with high natural acid and, like the wines of the Eden Valley, need at least two years to start showing their wares. The corollary is that these wines, too, are of a potentially long-lived style. However, in some vintages the wines are altogether too fine, lacking fruit and structure.

Chardonnay clearly has great potential in the region: it ripens a full month later than at Margaret River, reaching high baume levels while still retaining substantial acid. Like all of the Lower Great Southern wines, chardonnays tend to be delicate and fine when young, but are showing the capacity to develop richer fig-like characters with age.

Pinot noir is still grown on a very small scale and the table wines so far to reach the market have been a little disappointing. It may well be that its prime use will lie in the production of high-quality sparkling wines.

The first wine commercially made in the Lower Great Southern area was a 1972 Frankland River Rhine Riesling, made by Sandalford. Thirteen years is but a speck in the sands of viticultural time, and it is not the least surprising that the excitement of the Lower Great Southern area lies in its potential more than in its achievements to date.

ALKOOMI
WINGEBALLUP ROAD, FRANKLAND

The story of Mervyn and Judi Lange's involvement in wine is a timeless one, and one that is told again and again. First came a decision to plant a few hectares of grapes to supplement the income from their 1200-hectare sheep and grain farm; followed by the vines growing and the grapes ripening, weaving their spell, which led to a burgeoning interest in wine and the idea taking hold that instead of selling their grapes they might make the wine themselves. And so it finally developed to the point where 90 per cent of the Langes' time is spent either in the winery or in the vineyard.

The first vines were planted in 1971 with the simple idea of providing an additional cash crop. At that time it was intended that plantings would eventually increase to around eight hectares, and on Department of Agriculture advice it was proposed to plant 75 per cent to shiraz and cabernet sauvignon, and 25 per cent to white varieties. In fact the vineyards have already reached 13 hectares with a roughly even balance between whites and reds. They are planted to cabernet sauvignon (five hectares), rhine riesling (2.8 hectares), shiraz (two hectares), malbec (0.8 hectare), and sauvignon blanc, merlot and semillon (0.4 hectare each).

The first Alkoomi vintage was made in 1976 by Mike and Alison Goundrey. The Langes erected their own winery in time for the 1979 vintage, and have since made all of the wine on site with assistance from Dr Michael Peterkin, a doctor turned Roseworthy graduate who runs the Pierro Winery in the Margaret River, as well as providing consultancy services to a number of winemakers.

Frost has proved to be a major problem: in 1981 Alkoomi lost two-thirds of the crop, and in 1982 one-third. But with the aid of drip-irrigation, yields are reasonable and the winery is now approaching its 100-tonne capacity with purchases from a number of the independent growers in the region.

Wine quality is a little variable, but generally excellent. A retrospective tasting at the winery of a large number of the wines made between 1978 and 1981 underlined Mervyn Lange's view of the region when he says, "I believe this area will produce good whites—but outstanding reds". He made excellent rhine rieslings in 1980 and 1981, the 1980 in particular showing surprising aroma. 1983 was obviously a very difficult vintage, for the recently released 1983 Rhine Riesling is a very ordinary wine.

The cabernet sauvignons have, again with the exception of the 1983, been of a very high standard. That latter wine is rather harsh and heavy, in total contrast to the leafy herbaceous and elegant cabernets of most other vintages. These wines really do show Bordeaux-like characters: they have backbone, and are not thin and green, yet are unmistakably the product of a long, slow and cool ripening season. The 1982 vintage won the gold medal at the 1984 Sheraton Western Australia Wine Awards at which I was a judge, and richly deserved its success. Of the earlier vintages, the 1980 was outstanding, with marked minty/berry aromas and flavours; like many of the wines of the Margaret River area of bygone days, it did not undergo a malolactic fermentation before bottling.

Alkoomi is destined to play an important role in the development of the Lower Great Southern area.

CHATEAU BARKER
ALBANY HIGHWAY, MOUNT BARKER

If the gentle slope of Mount Barker seems something of a misnomer, so is the title of "Chateau" attached to the unpretentious though functional corrugated-iron winery which is the focal point of Chateau Barker. The Cooper family is quick to point out that there are 1500 chateaux in Bordeaux alone, not all with castles as such; it is in fact, it says, the buyer's guarantee that the wine is produced on the vineyard by its proprietor.

Somewhat ironically, until 1981 the wines were made for Chateau Barker at various other wineries in the district, chiefly at Plantagenet but also at Goundrey's. The first estate-made and bottled vintage was 1981, conducted under the care of eldest son James Cooper, a Roseworthy graduate. Younger brother David trained as a cooper (of the barrel-making kind) and also works full-time at the winery. Mother Margaret Cooper was a botanist, and it is she who devised the European-style vineyard, with its relatively close spacing and trellising systems. It is also maintained on the sod system, with weeds controlled by herbicides and with little or no conventional cultivation.

Plantings were commenced in 1973 and comprise rhine riesling (six hectares), cabernet sauvignon (four hectares), together with one hectare each of gewurtztraminer, semillon, malbec, merlot, shiraz and pinot noir.

The Chateau Barker wines are released under four labels, each of which is protected by trade-mark registration. They are the Chateau Barker and Coach label, the Pyramup, Tiger's Eye and Quondyp labels. The Quondyp label is reserved for the white varietal table wines, which revolve chiefly on the rhine riesling. I have found this wine to be very well made, with a greater depth of both aroma and flavour than is usual in the region. Indeed, if there is to be a fault, it is that the wines are almost too heavy, too full of flavour. The 1981 vintage was excellent; in mid-1984 the 1982 Quondyp Rhine Riesling had developed toasty rhine riesling characters more akin to those of South Australia than Mount Barker; and the 1983 vintage was extraordinarily full, soft and almost buttery, verging on a white burgundy style if that were possible. I gave it substantially higher marks than my fellow judges at the 1984 Sheraton Awards.

Occasional traminers are also released under the Quondyp label. While most have been unremarkable, the spicy and floral 1983 wine showed the same generosity and softness as the Quondyp Rhine Riesling of that year.

The pinot noir releases under the Tiger's Eye label have been disappointing, lacking colour, flavour and fruit. The one exception was the 1979 wine, which did show character. On the other hand the Pyramup Cabernet Shiraz Malbec blends have been models of consistency, with clean, soft, aromatic berry flavours. Malbec is, I am certain, a very valuable variety in the district, adding a little flesh and roundness to the otherwise fairly austere structure of cabernet sauvignon.

The Coopers are a somewhat unconventional family, and they add substantially to the interests of the region, as well as providing some of its better wines.

FOREST HILL VINEYARD
MUIR HIGHWAY, FOREST HILL

The Pearses' Forest Hill Vineyard is the mother (and I guess the father) of all viticulture in the Lower Great Southern region. The story of its establishment is that of the establishment of grape-growing in Mount Barker.

One day in the early 1960s Tony Pearse was pruning apple trees in his orchard when, in his words, "I saw these blokes running all over the place digging little holes in the soil". No farmer likes that sort of thing going on, but peace was restored when Pearse learnt they were two senior viticulturalists from the Department of Agriculture, Bill Jamieson and Dorham Mann, looking for a site to establish a

trial vineyard. They went back to Perth and two years elapsed before they came back with a proposition to set up such a trial on the Pearses' property.

The first plantings in 1965 failed, partly through lack of attention, but two hectares (one each of rhine riesling and cabernet sauvignon) were successfully established in 1966. One of the reasons the Pearses were selected was their skill as farmers, and also because they were proprietors of one of the numerous large apple orchards in the district which provided them with much of the basic machinery required. Indeed, until the advent of the European Economic Community and the collapse of the export market, followed by the removal of the sugar-related soft-drink subsidy, the area was one of the foremost apple regions of Australia.

The vineyard was exceptionally well looked after, but the vines grew very slowly in the cool climate. It was not until 1972 that the first commercial vintage from Forest Hill grapes was made by Jack Mann at Houghton. The drought-affected '73 vintage wines (and the following two) were made by Dorham Mann, who had left the Department of Agriculture and joined Sandalford. The great '75 Rhine Riesling was made by Dorham Mann under the Sandalford label, and won nine trophies.

In 1976, after 10 years, the vineyard passed back to the absolute control of the Pearses, having in the meantime proved beyond doubt the potential of the region and having encouraged numerous other vineyards, both large and small, to follow in its path. In that year the Pearses formed a joint venture with Paul Conti which covered the making, bottling and marketing of the wines, an association which continued until 1983.

In 1975 the Pearses planted a further 18 hectares, extending the rhine riesling and cabernet plantings and establishing some traminer. In 1979, 0.4 hectare of chardonnay was established and, with the success of the wine made from it in 1982 and 1983 by Paul Conti, a further 1.6 hectares were planted in 1985. Sauvignon blanc, 0.4 hectare, has also been established. The only further planting on the horizon is an increase of a little under three hectares of rhine riesling, reflecting the outstanding success of rhine riesling grown on the Forest Hill Vineyard.

In 1984 Forest Hill Vineyard (formerly known as Conti Forest Hills) severed the relationship with Paul Conti, and established its own identity and brand. The wines were made for it by Rob Bowen at Plantagenet: 500 cases of a 1984 Rhine Riesling and 250 cases of a 1984 Cabernet Sauvignon which as at February 1985 was still in new French oak. The

1984 Rhine Riesling won the trophy for the best West Australian rhine riesling at the 1984 Royal Perth Show and took the corresponding trophy at the Mount Barker show of the same year. Bowen also made small quantities of a traminer (which topped its class at both Perth and Mount Barker) and a ruby port, generally regarded as the best light vintage port made in Western Australia in 1984. All of these successes helped Forest Hill to the trophy for most successful small producer at the Mount Barker show.

Nonetheless, the importance of Forest Hill rests more on its reputation as a high-quality grape-producer. In 1983 and 1984 the Mitchelton Winery in Victoria purchased substantial quantities of rhine riesling, and in the second year also purchased cabernet sauvignon. A wine made from the cabernet sauvignon won a gold medal at the Melbourne show of that year. Mitchelton's outstanding success both with the wines made (and with the logistics of the 48-hour refrigerated truck transportation of the grapes in small cartons) has encouraged others in the eastern States to look to the Mount Barker region. Although Mitchelton wished to continue the rhine riesling production, in 1985 (and very probably in future years) the grapes were purchased by Plantagenet.

GALAFREY
LOWER STERLING TERRACE, ALBANY

Ian and Linda Tyrer moved from Melbourne to Mount Barker in 1975, seeking an alternative—and hopefully better—lifestyle. Like so many others, they have found progress painfully slow and I doubt whether they now have too many romantic illusions about the life of a vigneron.

The vineyard has gradually increased in size and in terms of plantings—if not production—is quite substantial. There are 3.5 hectares each of rhine riesling and cabernet sauvignon, 1.5 hectares each of pinot noir and chardonnay, 1.2 hectares of muller-thurgau, and one hectare each of cabernet franc and merlot. The vineyard is established on the typical gravelly loam over clay which runs throughout the region, and limited supplementary water is used. Nonetheless, the 1984 crush provided only 11 tonnes of grapes, and of this 20 per cent was purchased from other growers.

The first wine was made under contract in 1981, employing fruit purchased from the Frankland River Vineyard. The winery is now established in a converted factory in Albany. The Tyrers found cellar-door sales almost non-existent in the isolation of their vineyard, and this in part prompted the move to Lower Sterling Terrace in Albany.

Ian Tyrer is still learning the winemaking trade, and while fruit quality from the vineyard is good, wine quality has not been exciting.

GOUNDREY WINES
11 NORTH STREET, DENMARK

Mike and Alison Goundrey are now senior citizens among the winemaking fraternity of the Lower Great Southern region. Their seniority stems not from their age—they still have a young family—but from the fact that they planted their first vines in 1971 and Mike Goundrey made his first wine in 1976.

What started as a sideline has now become a full-time business. In 1971 Alison was a schoolteacher, and Mike was a grazier and part-time shearer running his property, Sheldon Park. They both enjoyed drinking wine, and it seemed like fun to establish a half-hectare or so of vineyard. Mike Goundrey relates: "Then we realised we could not look after the vineyard with hand tools, and that it would need machinery. We thought this was too costly for such a small planting, so we decided to double it."

One thing led to another. The 1975 vintage was made by Plantagenet under contract; the 1976 was made by Mike Goundrey at Plantagenet using equipment from that winery, Goundrey having spent the two previous vintages learning the trade in the Swan Valley. The 1977 was made at Ellendale, where Goundrey had trained; and the 1978 vintage was made under primitive conditions at Sheldon Park.

In November 1978 they purchased the old butter factory at Denmark, which had stood empty and unused for the previous 14 years. By the time they had finished renovating it the Goundreys had spent $150,000 in establishing Goundrey Wines. The factory, set on the side of a hill, makes a particularly attractive but also highly functional winery, facilitating the use of gravity and allowing ample space.

The 1984 crush of just under 60 tonnes came exclusively from the two properties which the Goundreys own or lease. Their vineyards comprise six hectares of cabernet sauvignon, five hectares of rhine riesling and one hectare each of shiraz, sauvignon blanc and chardonnay. The latter two varieties are yet to come into bearing, and the releases so far have centred around rhine riesling and cabernet sauvignon.

The rhine rieslings show intermittent signs of oxidation, always a problem in the small winery, and particularly so given the fairly basic winemaking equipment which is oriented more to red wine than white-wine production.

The red wines have shown far more promise, with excellent cabernet sauvignon made in 1976 and again in 1981. But running through virtually all of the other reds is a consistent overlay of mercaptan; it seems it is a character which Mike Goundrey either tolerates or is simply not sensitive to. Tasted on their own, the wines show considerable depth and complexity, but in comparative line-ups the mercaptan is very intrusive. If this relatively simple winemaking fault were to be corrected, the strength and style of the underlying fruit would produce some of the most attractive reds in the district.

HAY RIVER
DENMARK ROAD, MOUNT BARKER

In an area in which the problems of isolation and lack of expertise are evident both in viticulture and winemaking, the Hay River Vineyard comes as a very considerable surprise. Not only is it many kilometres from any other viticultural development, but it is the most immaculately maintained of the smaller vineyards.

The hillside site of this substantial grazing property was originally chosen because it was known that attempts to establish dams on this part of the property had failed. The soil was too well drained to hold water, with the corollary that it was considered ideal for viticulture. It is leased to a syndicate headed by Robert Ruse, who had become friendly with David McNamara during the time McNamara was winemaker at Plantagenet. McNamara is one of the most senior figures in the area, and has been something of a godfather to a number of the newer ventures.

The 6.5-hectare vineyard was established in 1974, planted entirely to cabernet sauvignon. In 1981 a wine was made on site by Jane Paull, who has subsequently worked for the Oenotec winemaking team both in South Australia and at Capel Vale in the south-west coastal plain area. With power supplied from a generator which broke down at the most crucial stages of vintage, and with the most basic of winemaking equipment, Jane Paull nonetheless made a quite lovely cabernet sauvignon, crisply elegant and with most attractive varietal berry characters. New oak added a dimension of complexity to the wine.

With Jane Paull's departure, commonsense prevailed and in subsequent years the wine has been made under contract for Hay River by Rob Bowen at Plantagenet. The 1983 Cabernet Sauvignon showed much of the same fruit character: smooth, with sweet-berry flavours, and very soft tannin, it was deliberately made as an early-drinking style. Equally it is somewhat outside the normal structure of the region's cabernets.

HOUGHTON FRANKLAND RIVER
Off FRANKLAND-ROCKY GULLY ROAD, ROCKY GULLY

As I have recounted in the introduction to this chapter, the Frankland River Vineyards now leased by Houghton were initiated as the result of a major study conducted between 1962 and 1965. Four varieties were planted on a trial basis near the Westfield Homestead in the late 1960s; the vineyard proper was commenced in 1970 on the southern boundary of the property.

Initially the Roche family had intended to erect a winery and make its own wine. In the outcome it decided to concentrate on grape-growing, and between 1972 and 1978 Sandalford took all but a few tonnes of the production. The first wine was made in 1972, winning a gold medal; the 1973 and 1975 Sandalford Mount Barker wines are still drinking superbly with exceptional fruit and acid balance.

In 1978 Houghton purchased a large part of the cabernet sauvignon, and followed up in 1979 by virtually replacing Sandalford as the sole purchaser. So pleased was Houghton with the quality of the wines that in 1981 it negotiated a five-year lease of the vineyard, guaranteeing itself exclusivity and dismaying a number of the small vignerons who had been buying fruit from the Frankland River Vineyard over the years.

The 95-hectare vineyard is planted primarily to rhine riesling, shiraz and cabernet sauvignon. This is reflected in the fact that the Houghton Frankland River releases comprise a rhine riesling, a late-harvest rhine riesling (in some years), a shiraz and a cabernet sauvignon.

Planting continued until 1979, with two hectares of semillon, two hectares of chardonnay, 1.3 hectares of pinot noir, one hectare of sylvaner, 0.8 hectare of zinfandel and 0.4 hectare of sauvignon blanc established in that year. Small quantities of malbec (3.9 hectares), traminer (2.7 hectares) and chenin blanc (0.6 hectare) had been established in earlier years. The vineyards produced 650 tonnes in 1984, at a yield of around seven tonnes per hectare.

In 1983 Houghton laid down its first *méthode champenoise* wine made from Frankland River fruit: 70 per cent chardonnay, 20 per cent chenin blanc and 10 per cent pinot noir. The wine is due for release towards the end of 1985 or early 1986.

The Houghton winemaker, Jon Reynolds, is extremely gifted; and the Houghton Winery has been progressively upgraded and rationalised in the wake of the closure of Valencia. Right from the outset the Houghton Frankland River wines have been of first-class quality, and with the improvement in white-winemaking facilities at Houghton, they can only get better.

Houghton Frankland River Rhine Riesling is almost invariably extremely delicate when first released, with diminished aromatics. The wine appears delicate, pale and almost insipid. With two, or preferably three years bottle-age the wine fills out, gaining richness in the bouquet and in particular on the palate. The zesty, almost citric fruit flavours are heightened by the pronounced acid on the finish, which can sometimes appear hard.

The Houghton Frankland River Shiraz can show superlative varietal aroma and flavour, with rich, spicy/crushed-pepper overtones to strong cherry/berry-fruit flavours. I regarded the 1982 vintage as quite outstanding, although other judges did not fully share my enthusiasm.

The Houghton Frankland River Cabernet Sauvignons have shown a consistent style, with marked cool-climate characteristics. The aromas and flavours fall in the capsicum/herbaceous/leather/cedar range. The body is not especially big, and the wines appear to reach their peak between three and five years after vintage.

Perhaps the most impressive releases have been some of the late-picked rhine rieslings, with the 1981 among the best. The fine acid which so characterises the wines of the region has given the wine balance as it mellows and ages. Future, more heavily botrytised versions should turn out to be even better.

MOUNT SHADFORTH WINES
MT SHADFORTH DRIVE, DENMARK

There are few more beautiful vineyards than that of Mount Shadforth: high on the crown of a hill above the town of Denmark, it cascades down the mountainside with sweeping panoramic views of the country-

side and the Southern Ocean beyond.

The 1.6-hectare vineyard was established by a local medical practitioner, Dr Kevin Keeley, and is planted to rhine riesling, malbec and cabernet sauvignon. The wines are made for Keeley by Mike Goundrey, and an excellent 1984 Rhine Riesling demonstrated the quality of the fruit.

NARANG
WOODLANDS, PORONGURUP

Narang was established in 1980 by Campbell McGready. Two hectares of rhine riesling have been planted on the small property at Porongurup, 19 kilometres east of Mount Barker. The longer-term plans are both to increase the plantings and establish a winery, one of the McGreadys' daughters having undertaken the winemaking course at the Riverina College of Advanced Education.

NARRIKUP WINES
Off ALBANY HIGHWAY, NARRIKUP

Narrikup is part of a very mixed farming operation conducted by Doug and Ruth Coxall, ranging from goat-breeding to grape-growing. The small hillside vineyard was established in 1977 with some advice and assistance from the Department of Agriculture, although some highly unconventional viticultural methods were used in its formative years. In consequence the vines have assumed a shape quite unlike any others I have ever seen. The 1.2-hectare vineyard is planted principally to rhine riesling, which is made under contract at Plantagenet.

The quality of the few wines I have seen was not especially good, and the enterprise probably lacks long-term commercial viability. Once again, isolation is an enormous problem, particularly given the dependence on cellar-door sales which such operations have.

PERILLUP WINES
PAPES ROAD, ROCKY GULLY

Isolation takes on an altogether different dimension when one visits Perillup. It rivals Chateau Hornsby of Alice Springs in terms of remoteness; it also has what must be the most unusual tasting and sales facilities in Australia. To reach this one has to walk across an unmarked paddock, climb over a fence, proceed around the back of the farm dam and there, built into the sides of the retaining wall, is a tiny sales and tasting area-cum-cellar. This, I might say, is achieved after one has left the main road halfway to Rocky Gully, and proceeded along a dirt track called Papes Road and found the unmarked entrance to the property of owner Lindsay Smith.

The 1.5-hectare vineyard is but a tiny portion of the 600-hectare grazing property. The roughly equal quantities of rhine riesling and shiraz are, once again, made for the Smiths at Goundrey, and returned to Perillup once they are bottled and labelled. There is nothing at all amiss with wine quality, and the wines are—as one might expect—modestly priced at the cellar door. But, once again, it is very hard to see a long-term future for ventures such as this.

PLANTAGENET
46 ALBANY HIGHWAY, MOUNT BARKER

Plantagenet is not only the most senior winery in the Lower Great Southern area, but by far the most professional. With both experience and skill has come ever-increasing success, culminating in 1984 when gold, silver and bronze medals were won at the Brisbane, Melbourne and Perth shows. The latter was a happy hunting ground for Plantagenet, which won the trophy for the best riesling in Open and Premium Classes; the trophy for the most successful West Australian producer in all classes; and the trophy for the most successful exhibitor in the West Australian Small Winemakers' Class.

Plantagenet was the first commercial vineyard in the Lower Great Southern area, or, to be more precise, in the Shire of Plantagenet, one of the five shires in the region. Earlier plantings at the Pearses' Forest Hill Vineyard had been established by the Department of Agriculture, but the syndicate of Tony Smith, M. F. Meridith-Hardy and R. W. Devonish was the first truly commercial venture. One hectare each of cabernet sauvignon and shiraz grapes were planted at the Bouverie Vineyard at Denbarker, followed by 3.2 hectares of rhine riesling and 1.8 hectares of malbec at the Wyjup Vineyard in 1971. Plantings have subsequently been extended to a total of seven hectares each of rhine riesling, cabernet sauvignon and shiraz, two hectares of chardonnay and one hectare each of gewurztraminer and pinot noir.

Approximately 85 per cent of the 1984 crush of 130 tonnes was produced from the two vineyards. The remaining 15 per cent was purchased, including an acquisition of chenin blanc from Bindoon (60 kilometres north of Perth) which provided the gold-medal-winning white wine at the 1984 Sheraton Awards.

In 1974 the partners purchased a disused apple-packing shed on the outskirts of the township of Mount Barker. It provides a spacious and functional winery, first presided over by David McNamara and then by Rob Bowen since 1978. Bowen is a Roseworthy graduate who has built for himself and for Plantagenet a high reputation.

The top releases of the vineyard are now released under the King's Reserve label, trading heavily on the Plantagenet name. Indeed, they are not only labelled King's Reserve, but also "Reserve du Roi" for good measure. These include the first chardonnay (of which a total of 50 cases was made) and a gewurztraminer. The gewurztraminer has a far better palate than bouquet, with considerable weight and style, though it is held back by a slightly thick finish. The skill of Rob Bowen as a winemaker is readily apparent with the 1984 Bindoon Chenin Blanc, in which all of the available fruit aroma and flavour was captured in the bottle in the best style of modern winemaking.

Nonetheless, it is the red wines for which Plantagenet should be most honoured. Over the years some magnificent spicy hermitage releases have appeared, and since a few errant mercaptan overtones apparent in the 1970s have been eliminated, the wines have gone from strength to strength. Both the 1982 and 1983 releases were exceptional, with the 1982 my preferred wine. It had an extra dimension of intensity to the pungent peppery shiraz in both its aroma and palate; the same character in the 1983 was not so marked in the aroma, although the wine explodes into life on the palate.

The cabernet sauvignon releases have also been of the highest quality. The 1976 is still drinking beautifully, with generous fruit on the mid-palate and most attractive tobacco/cigar aromas. The 1981 and 1983 releases were of similar quality. The 1982 was not considered good enough for release, and was disposed of elsewhere, a potent indication of the commitment to quality which the winery has. The 1983 more than made up for the gap: deep, marked cool-climate cabernet on the bouquet leads on to a rich and silky wine of great complexity, showing very well-handled oak.

Plantagenet's contribution to the region does not stop with its own wines. It is a contract winemaker for a number of other vineyards, recently adding the Pearses' Forest Hill Vineyard to its portfolio.

Plantagenet, both through its own wines and through its contract-making activities, is the major force in the region today.

REDMOND VINEYARD
REDMOND ROAD, REDMOND

Redmond Vineyard was established in 1975 by Robert Sippe on his family's 243-hectare farm. The cuttings were obtained from the Pearses' Forest Hill Vineyard, and the well-kept vineyard now contains 2.1 hectares each of cabernet sauvignon and rhine riesling, 0.2 hectare of traminer and 0.1 hectare of sauvignon blanc.

Production from the 1979 and 1980 vintages was sold to Plantagenet; in 1981 the first Redmond Vineyard wines were made by Rob Bowen at Plantagenet for the Sippe family. The 1981 Redmond Rhine Riesling received the trophy for the best rhine riesling at the Mount Barker show of that year, receiving one of the four gold medals awarded in the entire show. The 1983 Rhine Riesling won the same trophy in its year, and was once again awarded one of the rare gold medals at the Mount Barker show.

I believe the Redmond Rhine Rieslings deserved every bit of success they achieved: impeccably made, they show an extra dimension of fruit flavour and aroma and are still drinking superbly. I should perhaps add that the 1982 Rhine Riesling won a bronze medal at the National Wine Show in Canberra, and was only marginally behind the quality of the 1981 and 1983 releases.

If all this were not enough, the 1981 Cabernet Sauvignon won the Stewart Van Raalte Trophy for the best West Australian dry red in Premium and Commercial Classes at the 1983 Royal Perth Show. In addition it won a gold medal at Mount Barker in 1983 and silver and bronze medals at the Canberra National Wine Show in 1982 and 1983 respectively. A generously flavoured wine with beautifully modulated ripe (but not overripe) fruit, augmented by sensitive oak handling.

The decision to lease the vineyard to Alkoomi for the 1984 and 1985 vintages is, to put it mildly, a surprise. The wines were elegantly packaged, and the style and presentation of the mailing-list offerings were an object lesson for other small vignerons. Nonetheless, Robert Sippe had to accept the reality of the demands of an important job with the government in Perth and of the strains imposed on a weekend vigneron commuting such distances. Once again, the isolation factor raises its head.

SHEMARIN
PLANTAGENET, 46 ALBANY HIGHWAY, MOUNT BARKER

In 1980 Rob and Denise Bowen purchased a small property 20 kilometres from Mount Barker on which they have established two hectares of sauvignon blanc and 0.4 hectare of chardonnay. This forms the nucleus of the still fairly embryonic Shemarin label under which Rob Bowen "does his own thing".

Like Geoff Weaver and Geoff Merrill, Bowen is very careful not to compete with his employer, Plantagenet. He does this in a number of ways. Firstly, Tony Smith of Plantagenet has in effect a right of first refusal on any wine which Rob Bowen makes and which is tentatively designated for the Shemarin label. If Plantagenet wants it, it can have it. Secondly, output is extremely limited (a matter of hundreds of cases) and will never rise above 1500 cases. Thirdly, Rob Bowen makes certain he does not use the same marketing systems or retail outlets, selling wines chiefly through one retailer in Sydney and one in Melbourne.

So far Shemarin has released wines made from purchased grapes, the estate plantings only recently coming into bearing. These releases have included a zinfandel in a number of years and a cabernet shiraz. In 1984 Rob Bowen made a Bowen/Bowen blend, buying shiraz from Doug Bowen at Coonawarra. The two have decided they must be related because they both live in similar organised chaos.

TINGLEWOOD
DENMARK

Tinglewood is in the lush countryside at the back of Denmark. Giant karri forests soar overhead and the vineyard has been placed on the site of a recently cleared patch of forest. That it was established at all is a powerful testimonial to the perseverance of owner Bob Wood.

The property is a weekend retreat for the Wood family; during the week Bob Wood works for the local shire. He cleared the forest from the 1.6-hectare vineyard block; a local timber company took the logs, leaving Wood with the job of clearing the rest. There were 50 truckloads of granite rock and boulders; one tonne of explosives was used to remove the tree stumps; and it took two years to drive the 60 end-posts in with a 180-kilogram hammer sinking them three millimetres with each blow—and that was after holes had been drilled in the ground. Bob

HAND PRESS, PRE-1920

Wood estimates it cost him $7000 to clear the 1.6 hectares and that estimate does not include any allowance for the immense amount of time invested by the Wood family in the project.

Not surprisingly, the vines have grown very slowly in this inhospitable environment. It reminded me more of a lunar landscape than a conventional vineyard, with granite outcrops in several places throughout the vineyard. A high trellis has been used, and that has probably not helped much. Birds have wreaked havoc; and only token quantities of wine have so far been made for Tinglewood by Mike Goundrey. The varieties planted are principally rhine riesling, cabernet sauvignon and shiraz.

Tinglewood takes its name from a eucalypt which grows in the so-called Valley of the Giants, a magnificent forest to the west of Denmark. There are two species of this eucalypt: red and yellow. Bob Wood intends to market his white wine as Yellow Tingle and his red as Red Tingle. It is to be hoped the derivation of the names is explained—there is obvious scope for misunderstanding.

WATERMAN'S WINES
34 ALBANY HIGHWAY, MOUNT BARKER

Waterman's is established on the side of an ironstone outcropping hill with extensive views over the rolling plains to one of the few real mountains in the Mount Barker region. It is planted to two hectares each of rhine riesling, traminer and cabernet franc, and one hectare each of chardonnay and merlot, all of which are in bearing, having been planted in 1976. Other more recent plantings are yet to come into production.

The owners are Ron and Jan Waterman; Ron Waterman worked for a time as vineyard manager at Petaluma's Coonawarra Vineyard. Up until 1984 the wine was made for Waterman's by Rob Bowen at Plantagenet. In 1985 the wine was made at Capel Vale, with input from Oenotec. It is likely that this arrangement will continue in the future. ▯

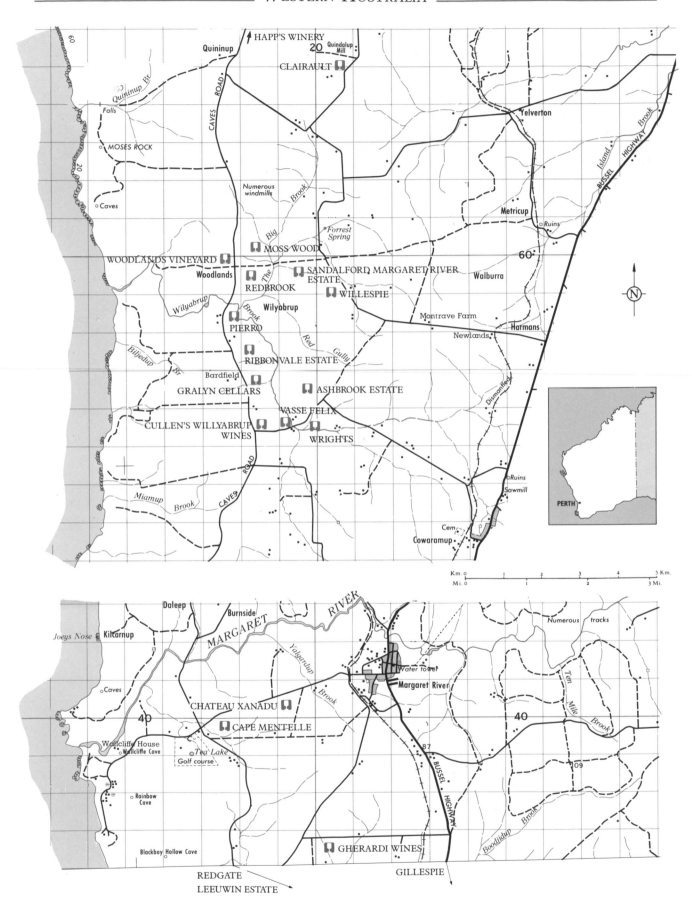

Margaret River

The Margaret River area has had a fairytale rise to national prominence since Dr Tom Cullity, a Perth heart specialist, planted the first vines at Vasse Felix in 1967. The area's success has caused a certain amount of heartburn to vignerons in other districts, some of whom believe their own livelihood has been damaged by the Margaret River, and many of whom are jealous of the attention paid to it. Those of the Swan Valley are acutely conscious of their own rapidly declining market share and production contribution; while those of the Lower Great Southern area struggle unsuccessfully to create the regional identity which has come so effortlessly to the Margaret River.

The simply facts are that the Margaret River has proved itself very well suited to the propagation of a wide range of varieties and a substantial number of vignerons have commenced active winemaking within a relatively short space of time and within a relatively small geographic area. A number of them have proved adept at publicising the area and the majority of them have produced wines varying in quality from good to magnificent, the equal of anything produced elsewhere in Australia.

Unlike the Lower Great Southern area, grapes were grown and wine made—albeit on a small scale—in the last century. The grandfather of Dr Kevin Cullen (of Cullen's Willyabrup Wines) established a vineyard at Bunbury in 1890. Ephraim Clarke continued viticulture and wine production until his death in 1921, whereupon it passed to his son, but subsequently disappeared into the suburban sprawl of Bunbury. The cellars in Clarke Street remain to this day, and the output (all of fortified wine) was sold through the Clarkes' general store. Other vineyards were also conducted to the south at Yallingup and at Boyanup.

However, the direct stimulus to the spectacular development of the late 1960s and 1970s came from Dr John Gladstones' paper. While Professor Olmo in 1955 and the Department of Agriculture Committee in 1962 had recognised the potential of the area, it was these words from Dr Gladstones that caught the attention of Dr Cullity:

> The climate is essentially that of the west coast rather than the south coast, being characterised by a high winter rainfall and a dry, warm, sunny summer. The south coastal influence, characterised by cool southerly winds, cloudiness, and an appreciable summer rainfall, is felt only to the south of Margaret River. Being virtually frost-free, and having a much lower ripening period, cloudiness, rainfall, and hail risk than Manjimup and Mount Barker, it has distinct advantages over both those areas, and indeed over all other Australian vine districts with comparable temperature summations . . . The temperature summations, probably about 1540 day degrees immediately to the north of Margaret River, should be ideal for table wines generally. Not only should excellent quality be obtainable with choice grape varieties, but the district might also be very suitable because of its equable climate for higher-yielding, but still good quality varieties, such as Shiraz and Semillon.

Subsequent events have proved Dr Gladstones right in every way. The area has a high rainfall of up to 1100 millimetres, but almost all falls in winter. The soils are to all intents and purposes ideal: the gravelly and sandy loams of the surface permit good drainage, while the heavy clay subsoil holds the winter moisture and sustains the vines through most of the usually completely dry growing seasons. Because of the extreme vigour in the early and middle stages of the growing season, stress can develop towards the end of the season and it is clear that more sophisticated viticultural techniques than those hitherto generally practised are desirable. A large-scale vineyard in the area in the course of establishment has retained Oenotec, and it is likely that we shall see close spacing employed, coupled with a less conventional trellis system.

The major viticultural problem so far encountered

CRUSHING GRAPES, PRE-1920

has been wind damage, and in particular winds blowing from the nearby Indian Ocean. It is believed that the salt-spray carried by the winds has been largely responsible for the coulure problems, which in a number of vintages have sharply reduced the eventual crop. The spray breaks down the natural protective wax coating on the vine buds, and fungal spores then enter to abort the flowering and subsequent fruit-set.

Birds caused untold havoc in the early days, and are still the major problem for many vineyards. If the gums blossom early—or if the vintage is late—they prefer their natural food and generally leave the grapes alone. They follow a migratory pattern (which explains the importance of the sequence of the flowering of the gums and the ripening of the fruit), which also means that Mesurol (a spray applied to the grapes which gives the birds an acute attack of indigestion) is largely ineffective. New waves of birds are constantly arriving, unaware of the uncomfortable after-effects in store for them. In the early years entire vintages were lost; more recently the damage has been less, but is occasionally severe.

Plantings now exceed 500 hectares and, with a number of new vineyard developments, are continuing to increase. Virtually all of the noble grape varieties are grown extensively, and all have succeeded to a lesser or greater degree. Perhaps the one disappointment has been rhine riesling, both from a viticultural and oenological viewpoint. It seems particularly susceptible to the coulure problems, and in the bottle fails to compete effectively against the classic areas of Australia. Why this should be so is not clear: it is grown to great effect in far warmer climates and one cannot blame the winemakers, for Vasse Felix and Leeuwin Estate are two of the major growers. Whatever be the reasons, the wines are solid and honest, with only the occasional late-harvest wine rising to any heights.

Semillon has been an unqualified success. Not only does it provide a far higher yield than other varieties grown under similar conditions in the region (up to 15 tonnes per hectare compared with a district all-varieties average of around six tonnes per hectare), but it produces wines of excellent flavour and structure. Moss Wood, Redbrook and Cullen have been particularly successful, and the blend with chenin blanc and sauvignon blanc has also proved synergistic.

That latter variety—sauvignon blanc—has produced some outstanding wines, particularly from Cullen. The Margaret River sauvignon blancs are able to marry the grassy/gooseberry aromas and

flavours which are regarded as an essential part of the style with a surprisingly rich mid-palate. In many areas of Australia one or other of these two characteristics is achieved, but only at the expense of the other.

Chardonnay has proved as difficult as rhine riesling from a viticultural viewpoint, but has produced some of the wines which have taken the Margaret River area to world prominence. Leeuwin Estate is, obviously enough, the leader, but both Moss Wood and Cullen have produced some strikingly rich and generous wines.

The cabernet family—headed by cabernet sauvignon, but with substantial help from merlot, and to a lesser degree cabernet franc and malbec—has provided the greatest number of outstanding wines so far to come from the region. The style of these cabernets varies surprisingly, from the elegant, fine and gently sappy Vasse Felix wines, to the austerity and power of Cullen's Willyabrup, to the tremendous strength and complexity of richness of Cape Mentelle and finally to the almost voluptuous roundness and smoothness of Moss Wood. In recent times some of the newer, smaller vineyards, such as Woodlands, Redgate, Clairault and Gillespie, have added a further dimension to the reputation of the region—and there are others.

Pinot noir has proved an elusive quarry. In one magic year Moss Wood captured it, making one of the three best pinot noirs so far to come from Australia. On the evidence to date there may be easier ways to make great wine in the Margaret River area, but no doubt vignerons will continue to make the effort. Even the humble shiraz has produced some lovely wine, notably Wrights and—until it was removed—Leeuwin Estate.

Apart from the quality of its wines, the Margaret River has made one other major contribution to Australian wine. In 1978 the Margaret River Grape Growers' Association joined with the Western Australian Department of Agriculture to establish the first regional wine-origin certification system in Australia. Twelve months later the Lower Great Southern area joined the scheme.

It works this way: the weight of the crop is declared by the grower from picking buckets and weighbridges, having been—usually inaccurately—assessed by Department of Agriculture officers while still on the vines. Once the wine is made and taken off gross lees, the producer declares the precise varietal composition and volume of each container. The volume is checked by a Department of Agriculture oenologist, and once the wine is bottled random samples are taken to Perth for assessment by a panel of three judges: the Department oenologist, a consumer show judge and a winemaker from another area. The panel is instructed that the wine "must be sound, 100 per cent regionally authentic and should not fail to impress a consumer of reasonable discrimination of the value of the certificate".

Thus many of the wines you see from the Margaret River will have the statement "Certified Margaret River origin" running diagonally across the corner of the label between parallel bars (and a similar marking on many Mount Barker region wines stating "Certified Great Southern origin"). You may rest assured that the wine deserves its rating, and that it will be a wine which is indeed representative of one of Australia's finest wine areas.

There is no question that the major advantage of the certification system lies in the marketplace, and that in the Margaret River as elsewhere in Australia it has no magical effect on wine quality. But then, in the case of the Margaret River, it has no need to.

ASHBROOK ESTATE
HARMANS SOUTH ROAD, WILLYABRUP

Ashbrook Estate was established in 1976 by the Devitt family. Tony Devitt, one of the shareholders of Ashbrook Estate Pty Limited, is a senior viticulturalist with the Western Australian Department of Agriculture. In a nice irony, one of his major responsibilities has been to advise and assist those who set up operations such as Ashbrook. The resident manager is brother Brian Devitt, a schoolteacher at nearby Busselton. Brian has the day-to-day (or rather weekend-to-weekend) care of the 7.3-hectare vineyard, planted to 2.2 hectares of cabernet sauvignon, 1.6 hectares each of semillon and chardonnay, 1.2 hectares of verdelho, 0.4 hectare of sauvignon blanc, and token quantities of cabernet franc and merlot.

The first experimental vintage was made in 1979 and the first commercial vintage in 1980. These were made in the lovely winery that the Devitt family built. The frame and roof were erected first; clay was then taken from a nearby creek and large air-dried clay bricks were made under the roof of the winery. The 30-centimetre-thick bricks act as totally effective insulators, and the winery is both aesthetically pleasing and extremely functional.

Production to date has been very small, accentuated by the fact that Ashbrook has elected to hold back a number of its wines for several years before releasing

them. Those so far to come onto the market have been of variable quality, with a number showing oxidation problems associated with the extreme difficulties of small-batch white-winemaking.

Production since 1984 has increased substantially; in that year 50 tonnes were crushed, of which three-quarters came from the Ashbrook vineyards and the remaining quarter purchased from local growers. Future vintages will be larger, and Ashbrook wines will soon be more readily available in the eastern States.

CAPE MENTELLE
WALLCLIFFE ROAD, MARGARET RIVER

In the somewhat unlikely event that any Australian wine-lover was unaware of the Margaret River, Cape Mentelle must surely have brought the region to the awareness of everyone. In 1983 it became the first small winery since Graeme Miller's Chateau Yarrinya (in 1978) to win the country's most desired red-wine trophy, the Jimmy Watson Trophy at the Melbourne show. Wolf Blass might make a habit of winning such a trophy more than once, but no-one else is expected to do so, thus when Cape Mentelle repeated the exercise in 1984 those who had suggested it was a sheer aberration were quickly silenced. For good measure the 1982 wine took its second major trophy at the same show.

The Cape Mentelle wines achieved their success because of their unusual complexity, unusual both for the Margaret River and by the standards of other Australian regions. They have always had this complexity, but I at least have felt that many of them were marred by traces of mercaptan. This view is not one which winemaker and part-owner David Hohnen shares, but then that is hardly surprising.

Hohnen is not only one of the relatively few qualified winemakers in the district, but also came to it with a wealth of winemaking experience. After a year with Stoneyfell in 1969, he went to California and studied oenology and viticulture for two years. He then returned to Australia, and played a key role in establishing the Taltarni Vineyard in Victoria. This led to his establishing a close friendship with Dominique Portet of Taltarni, one that is reflected in their common approach to red-winemaking and in their perceptions of red-wine style.

Both men believe that a cabernet sauvignon should have the structure and strength to repay prolonged cellaring, and that this in turn is derived in no small part from tannin. Hohnen invests his wines with tannin from two sources: firstly, he frequently leaves the wine in contact with the skins after the primary fermentation has completed, borrowing the practices of the Bordelaise; and secondly, through maturation in new oak. At least some of his oak-handling techniques have derived from the vintage he spent with Dominique Portet's brother, Bernard, at Clos du Val in California in 1978. Hohnen's winemaking thus reflects the influences of three countries: France, North America and Australia.

He also spends considerable time in determining the final assemblage of his wine. This is not so much a blending exercise (until his recent merlot plantings come into bearing he is restricted in the choice of material) as determining precisely what casks will be included, what excluded; how long the wine will be left in oak before bottling; and what fining techniques will be used.

The 10,000-case output comes through a 120-tonne crush. Eighty per cent is estate-grown, 20 per cent bought in from other growers of the region; the purchases are principally of semillon and rhine riesling.

The vineyards are planted to cabernet sauvignon (six hectares), shiraz, merlot, semillon and sauvignon blanc (two hectares each), zinfandel (1.5 hectares) and chenin blanc (one hectare). Yields from the lateritic gravels on which the vineyards are established are at the fairly modest district average of around six tonnes per hectare, and are not given supplementary water.

Five wines are released each year: a cabernet sauvignon, a hermitage, a zinfandel, a rhine riesling and a semillon/chenin blanc/sauvignon blanc wood-matured blend.

If there were ever any doubt—and in truth there was not—the cabernet sauvignon is now firmly established as the most important release. In mid-1983 I participated in a fascinating masked tasting of all of the cabernet sauvignons made by the "Big Four" of the Margaret River area: Cape Mentelle, Moss Wood, Vasse Felix and Cullen's. The tasting established, first and foremost, just how different the style of each of the four wines is, and just how consistently the respective winemakers have applied their own techniques and philosophies. More particularly, the colour of each of the Cape Mentelle wines in the five years in which it was represented (1977 to 1981 inclusive) was consistently the darkest, freshest and best. When the other wines were showing signs of development, those of Cape Mentelle had the liveliest red-purple hues. The next obvious connecting link for the Cape Mentelle wines was the more robust

tannin structure, frequently allied with marvellously rich and round sweet-berry flavours on the mid-palate, coupled with marked oak influences.

The 1979 and 1980 vintages suffered from mercaptan; even the 1981 showed a trace. The 1978 Cape Mentelle is a marvellous wine by any standards, and was my top-pointed wine among the first 16, and equal top for the entire tasting (at 19 points out of 20). The colour is excellent red-purple; the bouquet redolent of rich, ripe, complex fruit and sweet oak; the palate has great depth, complexity and richness with the round, ripe-fruit flavours of most of the Cape Mentelle wines; and the tannin has now softened to the point where it is perfectly in balance with the complete wine. The 1977 vintage, too, showed very well with similar fruit flavours allied with a touch of coconut in the bouquet. It was ranked second among the four 1977 wines.

It goes without saying that Cape Mentelle has gone from strength to strength with its subsequent releases, which have brought together all of the best features of the earlier wines.

The hermitage releases have from time to time been very good, none better than the powerfully spicy 1982 vintage. Hohnen is an uncompromising opponent of the blending of shiraz and cabernet, which he describes in unprintable words. Very good though the hermitage can be, my second preference (after the cabernet sauvignon) goes to the zinfandel. The wines mature more quickly than either the hermitage or the cabernet sauvignon, as a retrospective tasting at the vintage some years ago showed. In that line-up the 1979 was outstanding; since then the exhilarating 1982 Zinfandel has been released. I suppose that as with the previous releases it will mature reasonably quickly, but it showed little sign of that in late 1984. The colour is typical Cape Mentelle, dense purple-red. The bouquet is deep, solid and clean with slightly dusty/powdery fruit; the palate is rich and concentrated, with voluptuous spicy/berry flavours. All in all it is an exceptional wine which shows just why this grape variety, rare in Australia, has held such a sway over the Californian industry for so long.

The wood-matured semillon blend is Cape Mentelle's most popular white, and invariably sells out quickly. It is a complex wine but, for me at least, is not in the class of the reds. One of the best vintages was the 1983 release of the wine; as so often happens in cooler climates, the wine had aromas and flavours in the gooseberry/grapefruit spectrum, more reminiscent of sauvignon blanc than either semillon or chenin blanc. I suspect that the sauvignon blanc component was very small, and that the fruit flavours in fact derived from the other two varieties. Whatever the cause, the result was certainly very pleasant.

CHATEAU XANADU
Off WALLCLIFFE ROAD, MARGARET RIVER

Chateau Xanadu is one of the newest of the Margaret River wineries; like so many of the others it is owned by a medical duo, Dr John Lagan and Dr Eithne Sheridan. The vineyard is planted to just under four hectares each of cabernet sauvignon, semillon and chardonnay, and one hectare of cabernet franc.

In 1983 Chateau Xanadu appointed Theodore Radke as winemaker. Radke is a Roseworthy graduate, and is in charge of a crush which in 1984 was around 30 tonnes of cabernet sauvignon, 15 tonnes of semillon and a lesser quantity of chardonnay.

The principal releases to date have been of cabernet sauvignon and semillon. Wine quality has been variable, with some of the cabernet sauvignon suffering badly from mercaptan. I found the most impressive release so far is the 1982 Cabernet Sauvignon. Nevers oak combines with full cherry/berry aromas; the palate is very complex, and the wine will need at least three and probably five years for the tannin, oak and fruit to come into balance. But the wine does have complexity, and the fruit backbone to carry it.

CLAIRAULT
PUSSEYS ROAD, MARGARET RIVER

Clairault—or, as it is more correctly known, Cape Clairault—came into national prominence in late 1984. At the Canberra National Wine Show its 1982 Cabernet Sauvignon was awarded the *Canberra Times* Trophy for the best dry red table wine (firm finish) in the Premium Classes. In doing so it disposed of 51 other entries in its class, all of which had won qualifying medals at other Australian wine shows during the year. The competition ranged through all of the major wine companies (Lindemans, Penfolds, Orlando, Mildara, Seppelt) to Wolf Blass, Krondorf, Tyrrell, Mitchelton and finally to the small wineries. Many of the particular wines entered were famous wines, with any vintage being permitted.

I happened to be on the judging panel for that particular class; it received its top rating because of the great depth and strength of the varietal cabernet aroma and flavour. It shows strong, intense grassy/ herbaceous aromas, yet avoids the stalky, green characters which sometimes accompany wines of the style. The palate is an exercise in elegance, with sweet berry/cherry flavours on the mid-palate, and overall it is not as aggressively herbaceous as the bouquet would suggest. Beautiful balance and structure are the chief features of an outstanding wine. Yet it is but one of a number of quite outstanding cabernet sauvignons made in the Margaret River area in 1982, and underlines just how suited the district is to this variety.

Nonetheless, it was an astonishing achievement for a winery with an output of between 1000 and 1500 cases in total, and which in 1984 crushed only 15 tonnes of cabernet sauvignon (and of course even less in 1982). The 1984 crush of 21 tonnes was completed with four tonnes of rhine riesling and two tonnes each of semillon and sauvignon blanc.

When the Lewises purchased the 66-hectare property (at which they now live) in 1976 they had had no previous experience with viticulture or winemaking. Ian Lewis is a geologist, and Arni Lewis a schoolteacher who specialised in the care of autistic children, first in her native South Africa and thereafter in the United Kingdom.

The small winery, built in Cape Dutch style with white gables, offers something quite different in the Margaret River scene. It is surrounded by the 6.6 hectares of vineyards, planted to cabernet sauvignon (2.4 hectares), sauvignon blanc (1.5 hectares), semillon (1.4 hectares), rhine riesling (0.8 hectare) and merlot (0.5 hectare). The soils are typical of the region, with lateritic gravelly loam interspersed with a covering of heavier loam. The white varieties are drip-irrigated; bunch-thinning is practised in some years to reduce crop loads and increase quality.

In 1981 the Lewises provided the fruit for a joint venture with Erl Happ to produce a jointly made 1981 Vintage Port of quite remarkable elegance and freshness. Since that time all of the wines have been made by the Lewises at Clairault. They have certainly learnt their winemaking well.

The white wine is released under a blanc de blanc label; the semillon and sauvignon blanc are blended together, and it is a wine which needs some time in bottle to develop character and complexity.

Interestingly, Clairault divided its 1982 cabernet production into two halves: one which received the trophy at the National Wine Show and the other released as a light-bodied cabernet sauvignon. It, too, was a beautifully made wine, with soft, sweet, spicy cabernet but uncompromisingly light in body. I assume it is devoid of the pressings which were presumably returned to the trophy wine.

CULLEN'S WILLYABRUP WINES
CAVES ROAD, WILLYABRUP

The Margaret River of today was built upon the efforts of three doctors: Cullity (Vasse Felix), Pannell (Moss Wood) and Cullen (Cullen's Willyabrup). For some reason it seemed to me that for a while Cullen's lived quietly in the shadow of the other two wineries; certainly the early newspaper and magazine articles dealing with the region concentrated on the other two. Whether or not that is true, Cullen's has emphatically established its entitlement to be treated on equal grounds with the best wineries in the region.

The Cullens had been long-term residents of the Margaret River when their thoughts turned to viticulture. Dr Kevin Cullen had had a busy medical practice in the district for over 30 years, and by 1970 Kevin and Diana Cullen's six children were all well into their schooling. With Dr Tom Cullity as their guide and mentor, the Cullens toured the district, talking to farmers and analysing soil types and structures.

In 1971 they took the plunge and commenced the establishment of what is now a substantial vineyard. It comprises cabernet sauvignon (7.9 hectares), rhine riesling (2.9 hectares), chardonnay (2.8 hectares), sauvignon blanc (2.6 hectares), merlot (1.4 hectares), pinot noir (one hectare), chenin blanc (1.5 hectares) and cabernet franc (0.4 hectare). These provided a 1984 crush of around 115 tonnes, and a substantial range of wines.

The motivation for establishing the vineyard had been basically that of a long-term interest in fine wine, although there was the added attraction of diversifying the substantial grazing interests they were already involved in. Winemaking commenced with red wines, the first being a 1975 Cabernet Sauvignon. It and the ensuing few vintages were very much a joint effort between Kevin and Diana Cullen; however, as Diana Cullen's children grew less dependent on her, she gradually assumed more responsibility for the winemaking, and has been the sole winemaker since about 1980.

The principal releases from Cullen's are the cabernet sauvignons and the cabernet merlots, the latter having been made since 1979. The blend has indeed included a percentage of malbec in some years. I have been lucky enough to participate in a number of retrospective tastings of the Cullen cabernet sauvignons, several within recent years. The following notes show how the wines had developed up till the end of 1983.

1975 _Colour:_ dark red with just a touch of garnet on the rim. _Bouquet:_ very complex fruit and oak integration, with the oak still very evident. A touch of bottle-developed lift. _Palate:_ a big, strong yet smooth wine, with considerable complexity, and holding fruit structure very well indeed. Has years in front of it, but will never be any better. (18/20)

1976 _Colour:_ excellent red, still tinged with purples. _Bouquet:_ sweet, berry aromas, with slightly edgy oak. _Palate:_ a touch of bottle-developed camphor flavours to a round, sweet and soft fore-palate, followed by a long, slightly dusty finish with soft but persistent tannin. (17.5/20)

1977 _Colour:_ red-purple of light to medium depth. _Bouquet:_ rather aggressive, slightly stalky herbaceous aromas. _Palate:_ firmly structured and textured, but rather green and stalky, with an aggressive bite. The least of the Cullen wines, which may or may not soften with further age. (15.5/20)

1978 _Colour:_ deep red still tinged with purple. _Bouquet:_ solid and firm, with a trace of minty/camphor aromas, but still developing. _Palate:_ a youthful, deep and complete wine with a very long finish, with soft tannin evident. Will seemingly live for decades. (18/20)

1979 _Colour:_ again excellent hue with purple still dominant. _Bouquet:_ very firm, with some stalky/chalky/dusty characters, bordering on hardness. _Palate:_ aggressive, youthful fruit with some chalky characters again evident, together with green tannin characters. Pronounced acid. A wine that certainly needs time, but has great strength. (17/20)

1980 _Colour:_ lively, bright red-purple. _Bouquet:_ another fairly firm wine, clean with crisp characters. _Palate:_ firm and youthful with excellent cabernet varietal character, although the finish is fairly astringent and the wine needs time to soften. (17/20)

1981 _Colour:_ strong purple-red. _Bouquet:_ much softer, with quite rich cherry/berry fruit aromas. _Palate:_ a firm, fresh, strongly structured wine with good fruit and oak tannins and strong, rich sweet-berry fruit. (18/20)

1982 _Colour:_ dark purple-red. _Bouquet:_ spotlessly clean, strong herbaceous varietal cabernet with well-integrated oak. _Palate:_ very similar to bouquet, with strong varietal berry flavours, allied with some pleasing astringency. The wine has great structure and depth, and finishes with good acid and soft drying tannin. Outstanding cellar potential; at least five years. (Tasted mid-1984.) (18.5/20)

There is no question that overall the Cullen Cabernet Sauvignons are the firmest of the major Margaret River makers, and indeed may be seen as too firm by some wine-lovers. I like the strength, and believe that the older wines do show that patience will be rewarded. However, the cabernet merlot blends made since 1979 may be seen as a more attractive style. The moderating influence of the merlot is not especially marked, it must be acknowledged, and the wines are still unmistakably Cullen.

Diana Cullen has developed her own very distinctive style of winemaking, which is particularly evident with the white wines. All are oak-fermented, and she has had outstanding success with several vintages of sauvignon blanc. Her view of this wine is that it really should be made like a cabernet sauvignon, invested with mid-palate weight and pronounced oak. 1980 and 1982 were both very successful realisations of this theory. It does not always work, however, for small-oak fermentation of white wines is a demanding regime. What is more, they are often very difficult to assess when young, needing some time to develop fruit character. This is particularly so in the Margaret River area, where the aroma levels are often reduced and the fruit obscured by the naturally high acid of the young wines.

Diana and Kevin Cullen are two of the most charming people I know; it is appropriate that they produce some of Western Australia's best wines.

GHERARDI WINES
GNARAWARY ROAD, MARGARET RIVER

Peter Gherardi is employed by the Western Australian Department of Agriculture as a viticulturalist and oenologist, having completed his degree in applied science (wine) at the Riverina College of Advanced Education. Together with his wife, Jennifer, he commenced the establishment of a small vineyard in 1979, with plantings continuing through to 1982. It now comprises cabernet sauvignon (2.4 hectares), sauvignon blanc (1.4 hectares), semillon (1.2 hectares), chenin blanc (one hectare), merlot and chardonnay (0.8 hectare each) and cabernet franc (0.4 hectare).

The first commercial vintage was made in 1984.

GILLESPIE
DAVIS ROAD, WITCHCLIFFE

The Gillespie family commenced the development of their beautiful vineyard in 1976. Set in a valley, it is surrounded by forested hillsides, a haven for birds but attractive nonetheless. The vineyard is planted to cabernet sauvignon (4.5 hectares), semillon and rhine riesling (2.5 hectares each) and sauvignon blanc (one hectare). The first commercial vintage was made in 1980, although both it and 1981 resulted only in small quantities of wine.

Winemaking is carried out at the winery erected on the property by the family; Alastair Gillespie is winemaker. He had commenced working with Houghton in 1976 before moving to Vasse Felix in 1978 to assist David Gregg. Alastair's brother works full-time in the vineyard and assists in the winery.

Both red and white wines so far released have shown good style and depth of flavour. The semillons (and particularly the 1983) have exhibited grassy, almost sauvignon-blanc-like flavours, and the same style is evident in the cabernet sauvignons. The 1982 is almost raw in its youth and varietal herbaceous aggression (particularly in the bouquet), although the palate is less aggressive with attractive berry flavours on the mid-palate.

GRALYN CELLARS
CAVES ROAD, WILLYABRUP

Merilyn and Graham Hutton do not readily fall into the established pattern of Margaret River vignerons. They have elected not to join the local association; absent is the Aboriginal or local name for the enterprise; and present is a certain amount of kitsch in the tasting room in their somewhat unusual winery. Most significantly of all, they have elected to specialise in fortified wines, releasing first shiraz-based vintage ports, and in 1984 adding a white port made from fortified rhine riesling.

The Huttons established the 4.5-hectare vineyard in 1975 on their beef-farming property. The 2.5 hectares of cabernet sauvignon, 1.25 hectares of rhine riesling and 0.75 hectare of shiraz were all established on gentle undulating hills with a one-metre-deep gravel/loam topsoil overlaying a clay base. The country had had a long history of pasture improvement and the vines have always grown well, with above average yield.

The Huttons built the winery themselves, completing it in time for the 1978 vintage. It is unusual in that it is constructed around a 55,000-litre concrete water tank, which was already in place. The theory was that they needed to cover the tank for winery use, and that it would act as a form of air-conditioning in warm weather, reducing the need for costly insulation.

The Huttons are self-taught winemakers, although Merilyn Hutton completed the short Roseworthy wine quality control course. Wine quality is solid rather than brilliant.

HAPP'S WINERY
COMMONAGE ROAD, YALLINGUP

Erland Happ has had a remarkably varied and active career, a testimony to his seemingly endless array of talents. Until 1976 he was an economics teacher; the offer of promotion to headmaster at a new school prompted him to resign and become a potter and winemaker, devoting half his time to each. He established the vineyard in 1978, building winery, pottery and house himself and using local materials with marvellous effect. His ingenuity is limitless. The main frames of the building are telegraph poles; the cross members were used to clad one of the walls of the living room to great effect.

The vineyard is planted to 1.25 hectares each of cabernet sauvignon, shiraz and merlot (all in bearing, the merlot only partially so), 0.9 hectare of verdelho, 0.5 hectare of chardonnay and a total planting of 0.7 hectare of the three classic Portuguese port varieties, touriga, souzao and tinta cao. The chardonnay, verdelho and the Portuguese varieties are yet to come into bearing. Both soils and yields are standard for the region.

Erl Happ learnt his winemaking in various ways. First he read all the books he could find. Next he spent part of the 1979 vintage working at Moss Wood with Bill Pannell. Finally he spent several vintages experimenting with half-tonne purchases of grapes bought in from other vineyards. In these experimental vintages his flair and imagination were once again apparent. Instead of being content to make a red wine and seeing how it turned out, he divided the parcel into three lots. Various radically different winemaking techniques were employed with the lots, and Happ then monitored the progress of the wine over subsequent years.

It is no doubt this early experience which led him to make his 1982 Cabernet Sauvignon employing a full carbonic maceration technique, fermenting uncrushed berries. It is an interesting wine, with an unusually aggressive structure for a carbonic maceration wine. The 1983 Cabernet Sauvignon was far more successful, a richly flavoured wine with noticeable oak.

But there is no doubting that Happ has had greater success with his vintage ports. In 1980, again in 1981 and then in 1983 he produced quite lovely wines. The most recent release is perhaps the biggest in terms of body, but still has the freshness and life which so distinguished the earlier releases. It will indeed be interesting to see how the Portuguese varieties fare in the relatively cool climate of the Margaret River region. One thing seems certain: Happ will extract the best from them.

LEEUWIN ESTATE
GNARAWARY ROAD, MARGARET RIVER

Leeuwin Estate has been created with one thing in mind: to produce the very best wine, regardless of cost. It has also been conceived and executed with flair and style by owner Denis Horgan. It is true that Horgan has been in the happy position of not having to count the cost, but mere money cannot of itself produce excellence.

The atmosphere of Leeuwin Estate is very similar to that of the best Californian boutique wineries. This is somehow fitting, for Robert Mondavi played a key role in the original selection of the site and in the early days of the establishment of the vineyard. Bob Mondavi's son worked for some time at Leeuwin. However, that association terminated many years ago and the Leeuwin Estate of today is strictly the result of the almost single-minded obsession of Denis Horgan to create a lasting landmark in this beautiful region.

The development of the vineyard commenced in 1974, with the establishment of a vine nursery and the clearing of the timbered country on which it was to be planted. The 89-hectare vineyard was largely planted in the 1975 and 1976 seasons; an additional nine hectares of chardonnay in 1978, and the 1982 grafting of three hectares of shiraz to sauvignon blanc have been the only significant subsequent additions. The vineyard now comprises rhine riesling (30 hectares), cabernet sauvignon (28 hectares), chardonnay (17 hectares), pinot noir (five hectares), sauvignon blanc (four hectares), gewurztraminer (3.5 hectares) and malbec (1.5 hectares). Virtually all of the plantings are on red gravelly loam soil; Leeuwin has not opted for the use of supplementary water and yields are, in consequence, very low.

Indeed, for chardonnay they rival those of the Hunter Valley at only 3.5 tonnes per hectare. Pinot noir is only marginally better at 3.8 tonnes per hectare, while none of the other varieties exceeds 5.2 tonnes per hectare. Most provide exactly five tonnes.

The Margaret River region has proved a surprisingly difficult one from a viticultural viewpoint. Particularly in the early part of the growing season the vines exhibit tremendous vigour, giving the impression that they will produce very heavy grape crops. But wind has proved a deadly foe, with fruit-set more or less constantly impaired. Leeuwin has embarked upon a long-range scheme of planting windbreaks and, pending the full establishment of the trees, has planted cereal rye in every second row. The rye grass grows to the same height as the vines, giving a substantial measure of protection.

The grass has, however, also acted as an alternative food source to birds, the other significant viticultural problem in the region. This approach has been extended by planting sunflowers adjacent to the vineyards, again to provide an alternative food source. Once the marri, karri, jarrah and blackbutt trees in the windbreaks have been established, these, too, will provide nectar in those years when the gums flower before the grapes ripen. Birds have proved particularly troublesome in the years in which the grapes have ripened first, however. Leeuwin carries the ecological approach to viticulture to its logical conclusion by eliminating pesticides and fungicides; only weedkillers are used to control under-vine growth.

Winemaker Bob Cartwright presides over a winery equipped with every conceivable aid to winemaking. It has not one, but two, Willmes tank-presses, the second not really required for the 440-tonne crush, but kept close at hand just in case the first breaks down. Once again the isolation problems of the Margaret River and Lower Great Southern areas manifest themselves: it may be a day or longer before expert mechanics arrive from Perth to attend to malfunctioning machinery at vintage time.

The white varieties (other than chardonnay) and the reds are conventionally fermented in jacketed stainless-steel fermentation tanks, allowing for a precise control of fermentation temperatures. All the white wines, including chardonnay, are cold-settled before fermentation at low temperatures.

All the wines, both white and red, show a fruit power and concentration which logically goes back to the very low-yielding vineyards. By the very nature of the winemaking process, little or none of the potential fruit is lost in the winemaking process.

Thus the rhine rieslings (released both under a standard and Private Bin label) are solidly powerful wines which seldom offer much in terms of aroma or delicacy, but which do age with grace. Every now and then a little backblending of a small percentage matured in oak gives further complexity. Even the occasional late-picked release does not vary much from the general pattern, with none of the intense botrytis aromatics of the late-picked rhine rieslings of other regions.

The Leeuwin Estate Cabernet Sauvignon is no less concentrated and powerful. I find the wines sometimes border on the extractive—immense and sledge-hammer-like in their impact. Time will tell whether they will gain complexity and elegance as they soften. The risk is they will always remain big, rather dumb wines. Nonetheless, there is no doubting their parentage, nor the integrity with which they are made.

Any reservations disappear with the Leeuwin Estate Chardonnay. Each of the 1980, 1981 and 1982 releases has been quite magnificent, the 1982 deservedly ranking first in a major tasting of 70 chardonnays from around the world organised by the English *Decanter* magazine in late 1984. The price of the wine (around $24 for the 1982) offends some, but I believe it is justified both in terms of the cost of production and—more importantly—in terms of its quality. As ever, the base quality and style of the wine stems from the grapes, and the low yield obviously contributes to the end result. But wine-making techniques are also very important. The wine is given varying periods of skin contact in the Willmes tank-press before pressing commences; the length of the contact will depend on the style and chemical composition of the fruit. After pressing and cold-settling approximately 80 per cent is returned to new Limousin barrels for fermentation. The remaining 20 per cent is conventionally fermented in stainless steel, allowing for options in the backblending to strike a balance between fruit freshness and complexity. The wine is then bottled around the middle of the year following vintage, allowing between nine and 12 months in oak.

All three releases have demonstrated a depth of fruit flavour greater than virtually any other Australian, or even Californian, chardonnay. The fruit characters range in the grapefruit/melon spectrum, seemingly gaining richness and sweetness with bottle age. The 1982 vintage, released in the second half of 1984, is a more elegant wine than the two which preceded it, and holds out more promise of cellaring potential. Both the 1980 and 1981 releases have developed quickly, although it is still too early to make any definitive statement about their future. As for that 1982 vintage, well, I cheerfully purchased a case at the full retail price, and these days I tend to be fairly selective with my acquisitions of Australian wines in general and chardonnays in particular. Along with the 1982 Petaluma, it is one of the truly great chardonnays to be made in Australia, achieving, if not transcending, the Horgan aim of excellence.

MOSS WOOD
METRICUP ROAD, WILLYABRUP

If I were to be marooned on a desert island, and given the choice of one Margaret River vineyard, it would rest with Moss Wood. The quality of its cabernet sauvignon is consistently brilliant, while it has produced one of the greatest pinot noirs to surface so far in Australia. The wood-matured semillons are full of flavour and develop with great style, while the occasional chardonnay takes the peaches-and-cream style into another dimension.

Bill Pannell is another of the endless stream of doctors who populate the vineyards of the southern regions of Western Australia. A lifetime's love of wine led him to establish his own vineyard in 1969. Curiously he had originally intended to locate it in the Mount Barker region; it was Ross Heinze of Seppelt who pointed him to the Margaret River. Once arrived, he emulated Dr Max Lake by digging holes up and down the district, seeking the perfect soil structure. This technique certainly worked for Max Lake, and it has worked equally certainly for Bill Pannell.

The initial plantings were of cabernet sauvignon, and throughout the 1970s this was the only wine released. It was made by Bill Pannell during his hard-earned annual holidays, with the weekends given over to tending the wine and the vineyards. Eventually a long-suffering wife, Sandra, and their children threatened rebellion, so Bill Pannell employed Roseworthy graduate Keith Mugford as his assistant. Mugford has now completely taken over the wine-making responsibilities, and carries on the great tradition, leasing the winery from Pannell. Bill Pannell has in consequence had time to make extensive tours of Burgundy, probing further the secrets locked in the heart of pinot noir and chardonnay.

The vineyard is planted to cabernet sauvignon (4.8 hectares), pinot noir (1.9 hectares), semillon (1.6 hectares) and chardonnay (1.4 hectares). As I

say, Pannell did his hole-digging to good effect: the non-irrigated gravelly soils yield 8.6 tonnes per hectare of cabernet sauvignon and 14.8 tonnes per hectare of semillon. It must be admitted that the yields of pinot noir and chardonnay are around those of Leeuwin, at 4.9 and 3.7 tonnes respectively.

The Moss Wood Cabernet Sauvignons must surely be the most elegant, rounded and supple made anywhere in Australia. What is more, they have demonstrated their capacity to age with grace for at least 10 years, with the future as yet uncharted. Yet it is not only the quality of these wines that is remarkable, but also their consistency. As with the other major Margaret River producers, I have participated in a number of retrospective tastings; here are the results:

1974 *Colour:* holding exceptionally well for age, with excellent depth and hue. *Bouquet:* incredibly rich amalgam of coconut oak/cassis/mint/berry aromas. *Palate:* sweet, perfumed cassis fruit, followed by pronounced tannin. A giant, ripe wine, very oaky and crammed full of all sorts of flavours. (18/20)

1975 *Colour:* strong red. *Bouquet:* an equally complex wine, with rich mint aromas intermingled with herbaceous cabernet. *Palate:* a very long, fine and elegant wine with some herbaceous varietal cabernet flavours developing classic tobacco overtones. (19/20)

1976 *Colour:* strong red, with a touch of garnet on the rim. *Bouquet:* follows in the tradition, with complex camphor/cassis/berry aromas. *Palate:* a marvellously round and supple wine, with great complexity and fruit depth. In almost perfect harmony. (19/20)

1977 *Colour:* deep, although some signs of browning on the rim. *Bouquet:* very strong with complex mint/herbaceous characters proclaiming its cool-climate origin. *Palate:* a wine of weight, complexity and length, extremely stylish and mouth-filling. (18.5/20)

1978 Wine not released; not considered up to standard.

1979 *Colour:* strong red-purple, starting to show signs of development, however. *Bouquet:* very lively and fresh, with clean, gently grassy varietal cabernet aroma. *Palate:* similar to the bouquet with beautifully modulated grassy herbaceous flavours, very elegant and fresh. (18.5/20)

1980 *Colour:* lively red-purple, though with the

purples diminishing and the red hue intensifying. _Bouquet:_ ultra-smooth, with perfect weight, balance and integration between sweet oak and berry fruit. _Palate:_ seductive mulberry/berry fruit flavours, round and sweet; a marvellously smooth yet complex wine with great palate feel and richness. (18.5/20)

1980 Reserve _Colour:_ deep, dense purple-red. _Bouquet:_ rich, deep and harmonious spicy oak and strong classic cabernet aroma. _Palate:_ an extra dimension of depth with strong peppery oak imparting some extra tannin structure. The fruit, however, has the style and power to balance the oak. A quite remarkable wine. (A special one-off release which spent an extra year in oak.) (19/20)

1981 _Colour:_ dark red-purple. _Bouquet:_ clean, strong oak with a touch of spice; complex berry fruit aromas. _Palate:_ an outstanding young red with strong sweet-berry characters balanced by soft oak tannins. As ever, the ripeness and subtlety of the fruit is a triumph. (18.5/20)

In 1981 Moss Wood made an all too few bottles of an Olympian pinot noir. Unlike so many Australian pinots, it immediately proclaims its varietal origin, yet has the softness, subtlety and mid-palate richness which equally mark it as a Moss Wood wine. The pinot flavour is not the boiled-lolly variety, effeminately sweet, but in the sappy/racy mould of the great wines of Vosne Romanee. Rumours circulate from time to time that some bottles underwent a malolactic fermentation after release; those that I have shared in have given no evidence of such problems.

In 1980, and again in 1983, Moss Wood produced chardonnays of very nearly similar quality. The 1983, in particular, was showing fairly assertive oak when released at around 18 months of age. Like all of Moss Wood whites, and in particular the semillons, it really needs time in bottle to show its best. But, like the 1980 wine, the 1983 has unusual flesh and richness.

PIERRO
CAVES ROAD, WILLYABRUP

Pierro has one of the prettiest locations in an area which offers much, even at its most mundane. A creek passing between the vineyard and the A-framed winery has been dammed, creating an azure lake. The vineyard is on one of the steeper hills in the region, running down to the lake's edge.

Owner and winemaker is yet another medical practitioner, although a somewhat unusual one.

Michael Peterkin graduated from medical school in 1973, and during his time at university he became fascinated with wine. Having determined to start a vineyard in the Margaret River area, he also realised there was a dearth of technical expertise in the district. Accordingly, having gained a remission from the first year of the three-year Roseworthy course thanks to his medical degree, he undertook the Roseworthy degree course in 1976 and 1977.

It must have been a busy time; he worked as a locum at weekends, but still managed to spend the 1976 vintage at Sandalford and the 1978 vintage at Enterprise with Tim Knappstein. He then returned to the Margaret River to enter into medical partnership with Dr Kevin Cullen, eventually entering into an altogether different partnership (marriage) with Kevin Cullen's eldest daughter. He also found time to set up a consulting practice to a number of wineries in the Margaret River and Lower Great Southern areas. The 10-hectare vineyard was commenced in 1980 and includes chardonnay, sauvignon blanc, rhine riesling, chenin blanc and pinot noir. A winery was built in 1981, constructed from the rammed-earth walls which are so common in the district (used at Cape Mentelle, for example) and a steeply pitched wooden roof. It was commissioned in time for the 1982 vintage.

Dr Peterkin made the first Pierro wines in 1980 from rhine riesling purchased in the Frankland River and Mount Barker areas; they were vintaged at Capel Vale. They were very good, brilliantly coloured and with outstanding aroma and flavour. The subsequent white-wine releases from Pierro have been utterly inconsistent with Michael Peterkin's background and training. The 1983 Chardonnay, 1983 Sauvignon Blanc and 1983 Rhine Riesling were all ravaged by oxidation, and were virtually undrinkable. I can only speculate that something went badly wrong in the bottling process. Unhappily the 1980 Cabernet Sauvignon, made from Margaret River grapes, was only marginally better, with excessive raw and unintegrated oak and a trace of volatility.

REDBROOK
METRICUP ROAD, WILLYABRUP

Redbrook was the third vineyard established by Evans and Tate; I pay due homage to their contribution to the wines of Western Australia and, in particular, of the Swan Valley, in Chapter 4.

However, the 1974 purchase of 27 hectares of land at Willyabrup has seen the subsequent concentration of the firm's activities in this region. The vineyard is now fully planted, with cabernet sauvignon (8.2 hectares), semillon and chardonnay (3.6 hectares each), merlot (1.8 hectares), shiraz (1.7 hectares) and sauvignon blanc and traminer (one hectare each). Many of the plantings are still coming into full production, but the vineyards produced just under 80 tonnes of fruit in the 1984 vintage. Ever seeking quality, owner John Tate and winemaker Bill Crappsley employ both bunch-thinning and hedging as standard viticultural practice.

Winemaker Bill Crappsley made such an impact on Swan Valley red-wine style because he picked the grapes far earlier than any other winemaker in the region. He convincingly demonstrated it was possible to make clean, elegant and fresh wines in an area which had taken roasted and jammy reds as an inevitable consequence of the very hot climate.

It seems to me that when Bill Crappsley made the first two Redbrook vintages (1979 and 1980) he followed the same approach. The resulting wines were brilliantly clean, highly polished and elegant, with crystal-clear fruit flavours early in their life, but had insufficient middle palate to support the longer-term cellaring necessary for the wines to gain complexity. In a sense this is no bad thing: the wines were certainly very attractive at two or three years of age, and there is no reason why every red wine should be put away for 10 or more years. It may be I am doing Bill Crappsley an injustice, and that the far greater weight of the 1981 Cabernet Sauvignon is simply a function of more mature vines. Whatever the answer, it has clean, markedly varietal fruit aromas, with good oak, on the bouquet; these lead on to a medium- to full-bodied wine with clean, sweet berry flavours on the mid-palate, then a long, smooth and gently astringent finish.

The Redbrook Hermitage releases have continued in a slightly lighter mood, exhibiting a spotlessly clean fruit and beautiful balance which are so much the hallmark of Bill Crappsley's winemaking. These wines, too, are released at about three years of age, and seem to be constructed for early drinking. All that will happen with cellaring is a loss of fruit freshness and sparkle.

At first blush the Redbrook Semillons may be seen to have followed down a similar path, and some people have criticised the wines for lack of distinct varietal character and mid-palate flesh. But I am very attracted to the clean elegance of the wines, and I suspect they will repay short- to medium-term cellaring. Crisp acid and balanced fruit have been features of all of the releases.

As the other noble varieties of Redbrook come into bearing, the reputation of the vineyard cannot help but grow.

REDGATE
BOODJIDUP ROAD, MARGARET RIVER

Redgate was established in 1977 by Perth-based civil engineer Bill Ullinger. His interest in viticulture and wine sprang in part from his family, graziers in Western Australia for four generations, and in part from a period of service in South Australia during the Second World War.

Planting commenced in 1967 with four hectares each of rhine riesling and cabernet sauvignon, with the vineyard subsequently expanded to 12 hectares through plantings of semillon, chardonnay, sauvignon blanc, merlot and cabernet franc.

The 1981 and 1981 vintages were produced in a temporary winery, replaced by a more permanent structure in 1983. The limited releases to date have shown considerable potential. The 1982 Cabernet Sauvignon is a rich and full wine, with strong charred-oak aromas and a very strong, fairly astringent palate, and with a Cape Mentelle-like complexity and similar tannin structure.

Two white wines from the 1983 vintage were also commendable: a wooded semillon, with a complex amalgam of smoky oak and grassy fruit; and a rich and soft, if slightly sweet, rhine riesling.

RIBBONVALE ESTATE
LOT 5, CAVES ROAD, WILLYABRUP

Ribbonvale Estate is well named: the block is 150 metres wide and 1.5 kilometres long. A kindly neighbour acceded to John James's pleas and subdivided the unused edge of his property.

The vineyard was established in 1978, with two hectares of semillon and one hectare each of sauvignon blanc and cabernet sauvignon. Despite its modest frontage, plantings were ultimately increased to 10 hectares. The limited production is contract-made; an early release of an attractively packaged semillon/sauvignon blanc showed good fruit flavour and style.

SANDALFORD MARGARET RIVER ESTATE
METRICUP ROAD, WILLYABRUP

Like Evans and Tate's Redbrook, the Margaret River Estate of Sandalford has no winemaking facilities. All of the grapes are carted back to the Swan Valley for processing. Five hundred and sixty tonnes of the total 830-tonne 1984 crush of Sandalford came from the Margaret River; as the newer plantings come into bearing the Margaret River Estate's contribution to Sandalford production will increase further.

The vineyard has been steadily expanded over the past few years, and plantings now comprise rhine riesling (64.6 hectares), cabernet sauvignon (27.9 hectares), verdelho (15.4 hectares), chardonnay (11.2 hectares), shiraz (9.9 hectares), semillon (3.2 hectares), chenin blanc (2.4 hectares) and traminer (0.6 hectare). As at 1984 the chardonnay, chenin blanc and sauvignon blanc plantings were still to come into bearing, and others were still only producing small crops.

There is no doubting that Sandalford's best wines come from the Margaret River Estate. These are headed by three special-release limited-quantity wines, a gewurztraminer, a graves-style semillon and an auslese rhine riesling. Then follow the standard Margaret River Estate varietal releases, comprising a rhine riesling, a late-harvest rhine riesling, a verdelho, a cabernet sauvignon and a vintage port.

The recent white varietal releases under the various Sandalford Margaret River labels have been very impressive, with the rhine riesling being outstanding. The verdelho also produces a very attractive and full-flavoured wine, far more weighty than the usual Margaret River style. The cabernet sauvignon seems to suffer frequently from the mercaptan which so dogs the footsteps of this winery.

VASSE FELIX
HARMANS ROAD SOUTH, COWARAMUP

Perth cardiologist Dr Tom Cullity was the father of viticulture in the Margaret River area. He has always given full credit to the work done by Dr John Gladstones, but of course identifying an area as suitable for viticulture through the minute analysis of climatological and physical data is one thing, and actually commencing a wine industry is another. Scepticism on the part of the locals and the unexpected viticultural problems of the area made the life of the vigneron seem more than usually difficult.

So while Vasse Felix has done as much as any other winery to forge the reputation of the region, the early years following its establishment in 1967 were far from easy. One of the major problems of the early years is perpetuated on the label: the silvereye, or "greenie", was such a problem that Cullity even tried falconry to combat it—and with typical wry Australian humour it is depicted on the label. The establishment of other vineyards at least gave the birds additional targets, and Vasse Felix has used similar techniques to those other vineyards in offering alternative food sources. These come in the shape of fig trees planted around the edge of the vineyard.

David Gregg, an English food technologist, joined Cullity in 1973 and has remained ever since. David and his wife Ann now lease the vineyard from Cullity and have total control of both viticulture and winemaking. Twelve years after arriving the highly intelligent and motivated David Gregg is still hard at work in the vineyard, experimenting with trellis systems, canopy control and summer hedging.

The vineyard is planted to cabernet sauvignon (six hectares), rhine riesling (two hectares), shiraz (one hectare) and malbec (one hectare). Yields are at or around the district average of seven tonnes per hectare; supplementary water is not used, but other techniques are employed to alleviate vine stress.

The first wine was produced in 1971; in Tom Cullity's words it was "bottled before December out of stainless-steel kegs, had a malolactic fermentation in bottle and was eventually drunk by friends". The 1972 vintage was harvested by the birds; the 1973 was a great wine, but even Cullity has none left; the 1974 he considers to be big and jammy. In 1975 Vasse Felix came of age, and has not looked back since.

Vasse Felix has produced the most interesting rhine rieslings out of the region, employing a wide diversity of styles according to the dictates of the vintage. The 1972 is still remembered with great affection; the 1977, 1979 and 1981 wines were all beautifully constructed. But, as the plantings indicate, it is the cabernet sauvignon upon which the fortunes of Vasse Felix rest. As the following notes indicate, it has nothing to fear.

1974 *Colour:* extraordinary depth and density for a 10-year-old wine. *Bouquet:* strong chalky/dusty cabernet varietal aromas with just a suggestion of bottled-developed volatility. *Palate:* again some volatility evident; a rather stalky fore-palate, then rich, ripe fruit on the mid-palate, followed by strong drying tannin on the finish. A strong but somewhat unbalanced wine. (16/20)

1975 *Colour:* strong red. *Bouquet:* voluminous fruit with a slightly mawkish sweetness evident. *Palate:* lovely soft fruit on the fore- and mid-palate followed by a touch of bitterness on the finish. (16.5/20)

1976 *Colour:* strong red, with only a hint of garnet on the rim. *Bouquet:* a big, fairly ripe wine with some alcohol showing. *Palate:* a strong, very ripe style with rich mulberry fruit flavours and a long finish. (17/20)

1977 *Colour:* light to medium red with some browning evident. *Bouquet:* light and rather sappy with green merlot-like characters. *Palate:* not successful; the fruit has cracked and broken. (15/20)

1978 *Colour:* light to medium in depth but excellent red-purple hue. *Bouquet:* aromatic and lively with sappy/berry aromas, clean and most attractive. *Palate:* comes from a lighter mould than the other Margaret River wines of the same year, with lively, light berry flavours and soft oak. (17.5/20)

1979 *Colour:* strong red-purple. *Bouquet:* full, soft and round fruit with beautifully handled oak and good varietal cabernet underneath. *Palate:* an almost velvety soft and accessible wine, with soft, sweet-berry flavours and an attractive touch of camphor on both bouquet and palate. A wine of great elegance. (18.5/20)

1980 *Colour:* lively, bright red-purple. *Bouquet:* oak tends to sit on top of and slightly diminish the fruit. *Palate:* a very firm wine with a trace of green-fruit bitterness on the finish and some tannin evident. (17/20)

1981 *Colour:* excellent purple-red. *Bouquet:* a lively wine with crisp herbaceous cabernet varietal aroma; not heavy. *Palate:* of light to medium weight with very good gresh cabernet fruit flavours, simply lacking the final weight and richness of the bigger Margaret River wines. (17.5/20)

As the notes indicate, the cabernet sauvignons of Vasse Felix are lighter and more elegant than many of the other wines of the region. I do not believe for one moment that this is a criticism, or that David Gregg would want it any other way.

WILLESPIE
HARMANS MILL ROAD, NORTH-EAST of COWARAMUP

Willespie is a week-end retreat for the headmaster of a local primary school. The Squances purchased a 40-hectare block in 1976, and commenced to plant the vineyard in 1977. Between that year and 1981 all of the grapes were sold to local winemakers, chiefly Cape Mentelle. The 1981 Cape Mentelle Verdelho was made wholly from Willespie fruit, as the label of the wine indicates.

Since 1982 the production of the 3.5-hectare vineyard, planted to rhine riesling, verdelho, semillon and cabernet sauvignon, has been made under contract at Cape Mentelle and marketed under the Willespie label. I did not find the three white varietal releases from 1983 to be at all attractive; it may be that the wines have been subjected to extreme heat during the journey from Western Australia. Certainly they had a broken, almost chemical character, which was not apparent in the same wines tasted separately by others in Sydney.

WOODLANDS VINEYARD
CAVES ROAD, WILLYABRUP

The 3.5-hectare Woodlands Vineyard was established by David Watson in 1974. It is planted chiefly to cabernet sauvignon, with lesser quantities of cabernet franc, merlot, malbec and pinot noir. The first four varieties go into a cabernet sauvignon-dominant wine (labelled simply cabernet sauvignon, as it contains more than 80 per cent of this variety) which since 1980 has achieved great show success.

The style of Woodlands' Cabernets has varied quite substantially with the vintage. The 1979 wine showed the intense, rich, minty characters which reappeared in 1981, the latter a quite marvellous wine. Dark purple in colour, the clean and deep bouquet is redolent of minty fruit; the palate follows on logically, with intense sweet minty/berry/cassis flavours which are neatly balanced by crisp acid on the finish. The 1982 wine is a complete contrast in style, with fine, astringent, herbaceous cabernet aromas and flavours augmented by lemony oak.

The output of Woodlands is not great, but the quality more than compensates.

WRIGHTS
MIAMUP ROAD, COWARAMUP

Wrights may not be the most fashionable of the Margaret River wineries, but it consistently produces excellent wines which completely belie the fact that the Wrights came into viticulture more by default than anything else, and without any formal training or background in wine. Equally, however, when they came to Australia from the furthest corner of Kenya, it never crossed their minds to seek a job in the city. Henry Wright had been a district officer with the Colonial Civil Service, and the open air was in his blood. At first he and Maureen Wright ran a mixed grazing farm (cattle, sheep and pigs) on the "other" side of Cowaramup, but increasingly their thoughts turned to wine.

Before Kenya became independent—the cause of their departure—its capital Nairobi had been a marvellous cosmopolitan city, with fine food and fine wine very much to the fore. This introduced the Wrights to wine and the taste stuck. In 1974 they decided to become full-time viticulturalists, and sold their farm. Their initial intention was simply to grow grapes. They were in a premium area, had established premium varieties and, not unreasonably, expected premium prices. The hard economic facts soon became apparent (outside the irrigation areas there is little money to be made from making wine, but even less from growing grapes) and in 1977 they changed course.

They visited numerous wineries seeking practical input, read winemaking books avidly and began construction of a winery. In 1978 they made a small amount of wine, preferring to sell most of their crop to other makers in the district. In 1979 they made their first commercial vintage of 10,000 litres, and all the wines achieved success. Subsequently Maureen Wright completed the laboratory quality control course run by the Western Australian Department of Agriculture, and is Henry Wright's laboratory assistant.

The vineyard now comprises 3.3 hectares of shiraz, three hectares each of cabernet sauvignon and rhine riesling, and one hectare each of semillon and chardonnay. The latter two varieties will come progressively into bearing over 1985-86.

Wrights' Cabernet Sauvignon has always shown marked cool-climate herbaceous aroma and flavour, with good mid-palate weight and balancing tannin on the finish. The consistency of the style is wholly commendable, although not designed for early drinking. The oak is often fairly obtrusive at first.

For my palate the outstanding wine of the vineyard is the Hermitage, as it is labelled. Here beautiful crushed-pepper/spice aromas and flavours permeate the wine; the Wrights either have a very good clone of hermitage, or the _terroir_ is particularly suited. The most recent release (from 1982) was a particularly outstanding example.

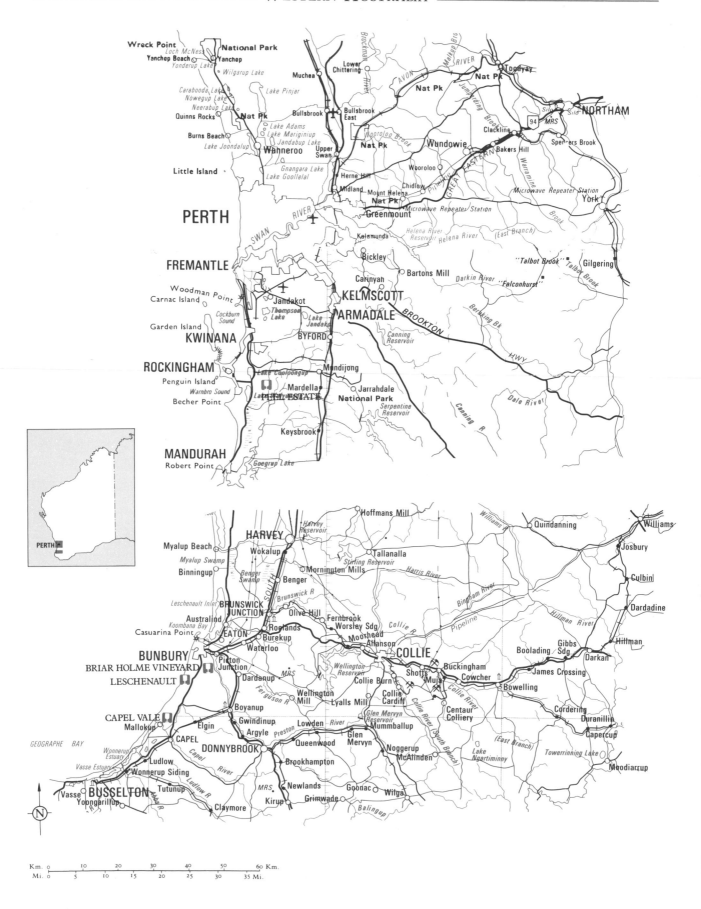

South-West Coastal Plain

The south-west coastal plain is a region born as much by default as by necessity. All wineries except Peel Estate have "dual citizenship" — Conti, Hartridge and Luisini with the Swan Valley; Briar Holme, Capel Vale and Leschenault with the Margaret River. All, however, share the feeling that they are not really part of their "alternative" region. Leschenault, Briar Holme and Capel Vale are physically separated; Conti (particularly), Hartridge and Luisini make wines of a distinctively different style from the remainder of the Swan Valley. The reason for that difference is in turn the connecting link which brings the vineyards together: the tuart sands on which they are established.

A more unlikely soil type for vineyards is hard to imagine. Four-wheel-drive vehicles are necessary in dry weather and only when it rains can ordinary vehicles be used. The soil colour varies from almost white through to grey; it is not easy for the layperson to distinguish the soils from the poorer sands with which they are interspersed. The easiest method is to look at the surrounding trees: the magnificent tuart gums are a sure sign of good sandy soil.

At Peel Estate heavy limestone rocks underlie the sand, and underneath them again is a watertable. At both Leschenault and Peel Estate irrigation is necessary to establish young vines. The deep silica soils at Briar Holme, rich in minerals, produce minute yields of grapes, even though the vines are now 10 years old. Capel Vale, I should add, is the exception to all of this: its soils are rich, dark, sandy alluvial loam, and the vines grow at a prodigious rate.

The area is generally frost-free, and rain or hail at vintage time is rare. With an annual rainfall of over 750 millimetres, the vines grow freely. The reds are light- to medium-bodied, with a crisp, fresh fruit flavour. The whites are fewer and more disparate in character and style.

BRIAR HOLME VINEYARD
CROWD ROAD, GELORUP

One might be cynical and say that Gil Thomas proves the value of being in the right place at the right time. Thomas is a third-generation Bunbury pharmacist whose business interests extend even to icecream parlours; he strayed into winemaking quite by accident. In 1973 Dr Bill Pannell of Moss Wood asked Gil Thomas's wife Janet, a medical practitioner, to be his locum while he attended to vintage. At about the same time Thomas met John Hanley whose "enthusiasm for wine was very catching", says Gil. During the following vintage Pannell again asked Janet Thomas to stand in for him; Gil Thomas agreed on condition that he could keep an eye, not on his wife, but on Bill Pannell making his wine.

Since then Gil has spent the two weeks of vintage living in a caravan parked outside the winery, helping Pannell and learning. In 1976 he took the obvious step of establishing his own vineyard, planting 1.6 hectares of pinot noir on a small block he owned at Gelorup. Thomas cannot remember who persuaded him that the block was suitable for grape-growing, but reckons he owes that adviser no favours.

One difficulty succeeded another as Gil Thomas strove to harvest his first commercial crop. Finally in 1983 125 cases of pinot noir were made, and the first commercial release from Briar Holme followed in early 1985. The wine was matured in five new French barriques, at substantial cost, and Thomas was most unhappy with the wood character the barriques imparted. It has a particular hessian-like character which winemakers know and which seems to appear for no apparent reason in some new casks.

The 1984 vintage produced 250 cases, and the by-now once-used casks had settled down so that Gil Thomas is more than happy with the wine. During the long wait Thomas purchased grapes from Moss Wood between 1978 and 1980. Thereafter Moss Wood's production increased to the point where Thomas was forced to find supplies elsewhere; in 1984 and 1985 he purchased excellent cabernet sauvignon from a new vineyard at Donnybrook, in the apple country not far inland from Bunbury.

Gil Thomas is a talented winemaker: he has twice won the trophy for the best Western Australian red wine in recent years. Output is still tiny and sold by cellar door and through a few Perth retailers.

CAPEL VALE
LOT 5, CAPEL NORTH WEST ROAD, STIRLING ESTATE, CAPEL

Capel Vale was established in 1975 by—yes—yet another medical practitioner, Dr Peter Pratten and his wife Elizabeth. The vineyard, on the banks of the quiet waters of the Capel River, was the site of a famous orchard of years gone by. It was selected by Dr Pratten for this very reason, and the growth of the vines on the alluvial loam over limestone soils exceeded even his optimistic expectations.

Indeed, during the early years controlling the vigour of the vines turned out to be a major viticultural problem, as were some of the extravagant yields. Since 1983 Oenotec has been retained as consultants, and complex viticultural techniques have been employed to tame the vigour successfully. Increased bud numbers and a wide-spread parallel fruiting wire, coupled with a modified form of Geneva double-curtain training, have had the desired results of reducing shading and further increasing fruit quality from its initially impressive levels. The secret to this vigour is the unique soil structure: rich alluvial soil over a limestone-bearing sand base, and underneath that a permanent watertable. The soil is very acid, with a pH of 5.3, which has a favourable impact on the finished wines, all of which in turn have a low pH.

The vineyard is now planted to chardonnay (three hectares), rhine riesling (2.5 hectares), cabernet sauvignon (two hectares), shiraz and traminer (one hectare each) and sauvignon blanc (0.5 hectare). Overall the vineyard yields around seven tonnes per hectare, and produces 95 per cent of each year's crush. A little extra cabernet sauvignon is purchased from the Margaret River area.

The quality of Capel Vale wines is consistently and formidably high. Every wine made in 1983 and 1984 has won a medal at a major show, with the 1983 and 1984 Chardonnays being outstandingly successful and winning the trophy for best white wine at the Mount Barker show two years running, and the younger wine being runner-up to the Adelaide trophy-winner.

So far it has been the white wines that have shone. However, as in the early part of 1985 the first of the 1983 vintage reds were released. While Oenotec has been in theory retained only for white wines, it might be assumed there will have been some impact on the red wines. Whatever the reason, the 1983 Cabernet Sauvignon is the bast Capel Vale red wine so far released, and of equal quality to its whites.

The actual winemaking responsibilities are shared between Peter Pratten and a qualified winemaker: in 1983 Jane Paull, and in 1984 Caroline Burston. Allan Johnson joined Capel Vale prior to the 1985 vintage; having gained practical experience working in New Zealand with McWilliam's, he returned to Australia to complete the Roseworthy degree course before moving to Western Australia. He inherits a formidable track record.

PAUL CONTI
529 WANNEROO ROAD, WANNEROO

Paul Conti has done as much as any other winemaker to change the face of the reds and whites of the Swan Valley. Curiously he has achieved this from what can only be described as a fairly conservative base, and without any evangelical drive or desire for innovation. This is due in part to the fact that he is an instinctive winemaker with a naturally delicate touch. The other reason is that the major part of his intake comes from his two vineyards, both of which are situated on tuart sands.

The first and oldest of these is Mariginiup with 2.8 hectares of shiraz and 2.8 hectares of very old white frontignac vines. The second, and newer vineyard is on the coast near Yanchep; here 2.8 hectares of chardonnay produced their first crop in 1983, and 0.8 hectare of sauvignon blanc will provide the first harvest in 1986.

For many years Paul Conti also made the Forest Hill wines from the Pearses' vineyard. This arrangement terminated after the 1983 vintage, and in consequence the crush has been halved from around 200 to 100 tonnes. Over 80 per cent of this comes from estate-grown grapes. The principal variety purchased is Swan Valley chenin blanc, with locally grown rhine riesling replacing that of Mount Barker as from the 1984 vintage.

I have been a long-term admirer and supporter of Paul Conti's wines. His spatlese white frontignac, made from Mariginiup fruit, is invariably absolutely delicious. Similarly his touch with the Mariginiup hermitage has been consistently deft and assured. The fruit from this vineyard provides wines which have vibrant, light cherry flavours, delicate fragrance and crispness, and low tannin. In four years out of five Paul Conti captures all of these characters in the bottle, and most certainly did so in 1982.

With the more recent availability of chardonnay another fine wine has been developed under the Conti label. The 1984 vintage in particular showed a lovely balance between fruit and oak, with a most attractive touch of peachy fruit flavour to a wine which had good structure and was not propped up by residual sugar.

Some of the Mount Barker rhine rieslings suffered from oxidation; whether this was due to problems associated with bringing the fruit to the Conti winery at Wanneroo for crushing and fermentation, I do not know. In any event that line of wines is now finished. So, I should add, are the Mount Barker cabernet sauvignons, some of which showed a rather distressing level of mercaptan.

The labels have had a face-lift, and the business name changed from Contiville to Paul Conti, but the quality and style of the wines remain reassuringly the same.

HARTRIDGE
LOT 36, 35 KM PEG, WANNEROO ROAD, WANNEROO

Hartridge is unobtrusive as the furthest viticultural outpost of Wanneroo Road, sharing the tuart sands with Paul Conti's vineyard. A few vines surrounded by flowering gums are the only visible signs from the road; a twisting drive leads into the house and winery, set well back and enjoying total privacy. The only sign that the Perth metropolitan area is but 15 minutes' drive away is the inground pool between the house and winery.

Hartridge was established by Jim Yates, a chemical engineer with the Swan Brewery. Yates won the trophy for best small winemaker red wine with the first wine he made, a 1978 Cabernet Sauvignon. The fruit for this came from the small Hartridge vineyard.

In 1981 Hartridge was purchased by Perry and Faye Sandow; Faye Sandow comes from a South Australian wine family and is related to the Sobels.

Perry Sandow is a commercial photographer, and in the early stages relied on consulting advice from Jim Yates.

The vineyard is planted to two hectares of cabernet sauvignon, 1.5 hectares of chenin blanc, and a few rows of pinot noir and malbec. Hartridge is making some attractive varietal white wines, with its Fisher's Patch Chenin Blanc of particular quality. On the other hand an attempt at a late-harvest chardonnay in 1984 was an unqualified failure. 1983 Hartridge Cabernet Sauvignon was full-flavoured, but very heavy and rather extracted. The very limited output is all sold by cellar door and through retailers in Perth.

LESCHENAULT
LAKES ROAD, BUNBURY

Leschenault is owned by yet another medical family. Dr Barry Killerby's interest in wine developed during his years as a medical student in Adelaide. A tradition was that the students took one of their specialist consultants to dinner once a term: he paid for the meal and they produced the wine, and some great bottles were shared. A love of the land also developed early. Killerby spent most of his school holidays helping his father clear and fence a 300-hectare cattle property in the Busselton area. The skills learnt then were put into effect when the time came to build a winery, which Killerby largely did himself— only the brickwork was subcontracted.

Leschenault's vineyard is only one kilometre from the sea on the flat, sandy, coastal plain between Capel and Bunbury. It is most unlikely country for a successful vineyard, but once again the fine grey tuart sands work their remarkable magic. They do receive assistance, however: the vineyard has drip-irrigation installed throughout. Bores tapping the underground watertable provide unlimited water, which is not salty but rather rich in iron.

The vineyards are now planted to four hectares each of shiraz and cabernet sauvignon, 2.5 hectares of traminer, two hectares each of semillon and chardonnay, and 1.5 hectares of pinot noir. Yields are modest—the 1984 crush of 50 tonnes produced around 3000 cases of wine. The winery is built into a small slope and has been cleverly designed to facilitate one-person winemaking. Members of the family have over the years provided most of the winery labour: labelling and despatch is usually done after dinner, and Dr Killerby's wife, Betty, presides over the well-appointed sales and tasting area.

Wine quality has been variable. At their best the wines of Leschenault show sparkling fruit flavour, with the typically light, elegant structure which the tuart sands seem to provide. Other wines show evidence of oxidation, and not infrequently the amount of oak overwhelms the fairly delicate fruit.

LUISINI
17 KM PEG, WANNEROO ROAD, WANNEROO

Luisini was for many years the biggest privately owned winery in Western Australia. However, its vineyards on the Wanneroo sands have fallen prey to commercial developments of various kinds, and production has decreased in consequence. The vineyards are now reduced to six hectares of shiraz, which provide 20 per cent of the annual crush of just under 100 tonnes.

The winery is in one of several immense rambling iron buildings constructed more than 50 years ago. Following the arrival of David Cooper as winemaker in 1981, the equipment was modernised and reorganised, and Luisini is now producing some very pleasant white varietal wines from grapes purchased locally and in the Swan Valley. A 1984 Chablis, sold at the cellar door only in flagons, showed good fresh fruit at the 1984 Sheraton Awards, outpointing many far more exalted wines. At $4 a flagon, the consumer was certainly receiving value for money.

As at the second half of 1984 no less than seven vintage dry reds from the 1969, 1970 and 1971 years were on sale for $3.75 a bottle. A similar range of old fortified wines was also available; these were also exhibited at the Sheraton Awards and were showing their age. Luisini has no pretensions to premium or boutique status; the emphasis is on price and on a wide range of fortified wines sold chiefly in bulk.

PEEL ESTATE
FLETCHER ROAD, BALDIVIS, near MANDURAH

The name (and the family crest on the label) come from Sir Robert Peel, whose son Thomas Peel was granted one million acres (404,860 hectares) along the coastal plain south of Perth by the Crown in 1834. Thomas Peel, who arrived with an entourage from England to take up his entitlement, was apparently totally unprepared for both the climate and the work required to put the country into shape for farming, and quickly retired to the beach to drink gin and tonic (or its equivalent) under the protection of umbrellas. The government was understandably unimpressed and three-quarters of the grant was revoked. Nonetheless, Thomas Peel was left with one-quarter of a million acres (101,215 hectares); this founded what became known as the Peel Estate, from which the vineyard takes its name.

The fine grey-white sands are heavily impregnated with limestone, but in dry weather are only accessible by four-wheel-drive vehicles (when it rains the ground firms up enough to allow ordinary vehicular traffic). A five-metre watertable allows drip-irrigation to be used to establish the vines in their early years: a 318,000-litre dam was simply scooped out, which constantly refills itself and supplies more than 3000 millions litres of crystal-clear water each year. As the vines become fully established, they will no doubt reach that water table, which may reduce the need for irrigation.

When Will Nairn first planted three hectares of shiraz in 1974, he was a farmer with 400 hectares of lucerne and 80 hectares of cattle country. He had no previous grape-growing or winemaking experience, but his grandfather had founded the Perth Wine and Food Society with Bill Jamieson. It was Bill Jamieson and Paul Conti (who purchased Nairn's grapes until 1979) who persuaded Nairn to commence the plantings, which have been steadily expanded each year since. There are now 12.6 hectares of vineyard, planted to chenin blanc (four hectares), chardonnay (two hectares), cabernet sauvignon and sauvignon blanc (1.2 hectares each), zinfandel and verdelho (0.4 hectare each) and semillon (0.2 hectare). Only the chenin blanc and the shiraz are in full bearing; the chardonnay provided a token three tonnes in 1984, and the sauvignon blanc is only now coming into bearing. The beautifully designed and well-constructed winery was erected in time for the 1980 vintage and the Nairns' home nearby was completed just prior to Christmas 1981. It is an idyllic setting.

The Peel Estate has made something of a specialty with its wood-matured chenin blanc. Nairn started experimenting with the marriage of chenin blanc and oak at a time when it was far from conventional to do so. I wish I could say that the attempts have always been greeted with success; they have not. Periodically the wines suffer from pinking in colour and from numerous telltale signs of oxidation. When they are good, they are very good.

The red wines, too, have been somewhat variable. The fruit structure is once again totally consistent with that produced from other vineyards on the tuart sands. The wines are fragrant, aromatic and with a typically low tannin structure. They are clearly very fragile, and are very sensitive to oak. Thus the 1981 Shiraz was really too oaky for the fruit, while the marvellously spicy 1982 Shiraz had marked traces of volatility.

For all that the Peel Estate wines do have a certain style and flair, and can from time to time scale the heights of excellence.

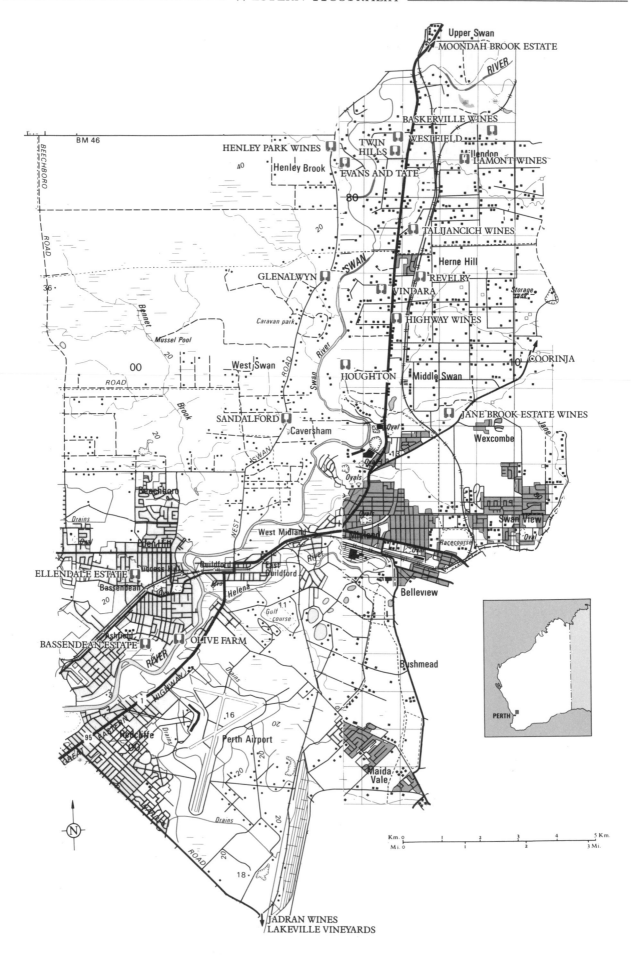

Upper Swan
MOONDAH BROOK ESTATE
RIVER

BM 46

BASKERVILLE WINES

HENLEY PARK WINES
TWIN HILLS
WESTFIELD
Henley Brook
EVANS AND TATE
Ilendon
LAMONT WINES

TALIJANCICH WINES

GLENALWYN
SWAN
Herne Hill
REVELRY
VINDARA
Caravan park
HIGHWAY WINES

West Swan
ROAD
Bennet
Mussel Pool
00
COORINJA
HOUGHTON
Middle Swan

SANDALFORD
JANE BROOK ESTATE WINES
Caversham
Oval
Wexcombe

Beechboro
Oyals
Swan View

Drains
West Midland
Midvale
Pool

Eden Hill
Racecourse
ELLENDALE ESTATE
Uddess
Guildford
East Guildford
River
Bassendean
Helena
Belleview

Golf course

BASSENDEAN ESTATE
OLIVE FARM
RIVER
Bushmead

HIGHWAY
Perth Airport

Redcliffe
Perth Airport

Maida Vale

PERTH

JADRAN WINES
LAKEVILLE VINEYARDS

Km. 0   1   2   3   4   5 Km.
Mi. 0   1   2   3 Mi.

N

Swan Valley

At one time the number of wineries in the Swan Valley exceeded that of any other viticultural region in Australia, with the result that Western Australia had more wineries than either New South Wales or Victoria. In common with New Zealand, the vast majority of the vignerons were Yugoslavs; and, as in New Zealand, the second and third generations continue to provide at least a numeric base for the industry. While the largest companies are either publicly owned or form part of larger corporate groups, the small winery has a strong ethnic orientation, both in terms of its ownership and of its markets. The role and function is very similar to that played by the Italian community in the Riverlands areas of the eastern States.

Indeed, the Swan Valley can be said to have three wine industries. The first is based on the extraordinary number of backyard vignerons selling their wine in bulk to local buyers. In this chapter I have attempted to cover only the more important of these: if one drives out along the Great Northern Highway or the West Swan Road, many others can be found. All of the production is sold by cellar door and the customers are almost invariably first- or second-generation Australians.

The second of the three industries has a foot in both worlds, as it were. While the Yugoslav influence is still dominant on the ownership and winemaking side, the market is more broadly based and centres around own-brand bottled wines. Relatively few of these wines, however, find their way out of Western Australia to the eastern States. Qualified exceptions would be the wines of Paul Conti and of Olive Farm; a major exception would be Evans and Tate. Until recently many of these small- to medium-sized wineries with a better-than-basic product marketed much of their wine in flagons.

Two factors are operating to change this. First, it has become impossible to compete on price terms with the flagons and casks from the east offered through the major liquor stores. Secondly, the quality and range of Swan Valley wines are steadily increasing as is the population of informed wine-drinkers. Thus the better-quality bottled wines now disappear rapidly from the winery, and a significant number of wineries have abandoned flagon sales.

The third industry comprises the large companies, with the Houghton group absolutely dominant, supported by Sandalford. With their superior marketing abilities—created by their much greater production—these companies have hitherto made the greatest impact in the eastern States. They also provide a solid foundation of technical expertise for an industry which otherwise might have found great difficulty in maintaining the viability, and credibility, of what was essentially a cottage industry governed by folklore more than by science.

It is hardly surprising, therefore, that a great diversity exists in the style of Swan Valley wines. This reflects both differing structures and the effects of technological change. It is even less surprising that differing opinions are held about wine style and quality. The chief spokesperson for the old school was Jack Mann, who was magnificently eloquent in his support of the old-style whites and reds, and equally vehement in his condemnation of the characterless wines (his expression) now made. In 1981 he regaled me with his views of winemaking: "Wine should be resplendent with generosity; unless it can be diluted with an equal volume of water, it wasn't worth making in the first place . . . I never picked grapes unless the vines had reached the stage where they would not nourish them any more."

No-one would doubt that the Swan Valley owes more to Jack Mann than to any other winemaker, past or present. He was a creative genius who made wines in the 1930s and 1940s which were way ahead of their time. In 1973 Len Evans in his *Australia and New Zealand Complete Book of Wine* introduced a chapter on Western Australian wine with these

515

LOADING AN EXPORT CONSIGNMENT, HOUGHTON'S, PRE-1920

observations: "The Swan Valley around Perth has long been a centre for winemaking. Today it is probably best known for Houghton's famous White Burgundy."

For more than 20 years after the Second World War Houghton's White Burgundy was the only Western Australian wine regularly selling on the Sydney market. With equal consistency it proved its ability to age marvellously in bottle, and for many years was the benchmark example of the white burgundy style.

But times have changed, even if Jack Mann's perception of wine style has not. Increasingly winemakers ask themselves whether the grapes they receive are truly suited to the style of wine they are endeavouring to make. Winemakers are no longer content simply to produce the best-possible wine from a particular load of grapes or from a particular vineyard. In other words the increasing tendency is to look elsewhere—possibly to non-estate vineyards but more probably outside the particular region—for the right grapes. Then, if the same winemaking skills are applied, the end result will be better than that of an estate-grown-and-made policy.

In this context the Swan Valley has a long-term future as a fortified-wine producer, and possibly as a producer of late-harvest white wines. I say possibly, because the late-harvest styles will derive their flavour from the simple effects of raisining and concentration of the grapes through heat; botrytis (or, at least, vineyard botrytis) will not play a role. Whether the wine-drinkers of the year 2000 will see non-botrytised sweet table wines as unacceptably old-fashioned is a question which only time will answer.

There is also little doubt that Swan Valley plantings of chardonnay, chenin blanc, semillon and verdelho will be maintained, and in certain instances increased. Houghton for one has proved that very good table wine can be made from these varieties and, what is more, that economic yields can be obtained. For a variety of reasons, sourcing grapes from other regions may simply be impracticable. So from small and large makers alike, substantial quantities of white varietal table wines from these varieties will be made. How successfully they will be marketed will depend very much on the skills of the maker. For the undeniable facts are that the Swan Valley is one of the hottest grape-growing regions in the world, with a centigrade heat-degree day summation approaching 2200. The remaining vineyards do have the advantage of being largely situated on deep alluvial loam and clay loam soils; those planted on the poorer sands have by and large been removed.

The wines also are supported by a high winter rainfall of around 860 millimetres, although even here problems occur with winter waterlogging, thanks to the impervious clay subsoils. These serve a useful purpose in spring and early summer as the vines are able to tap the trapped moisture reserves. Quite obviously ripening is never a problem, and in the dry heat fungal sprays are seldom, if ever, necessary.

The enduring strengths of the Swan Valley are not dissimilar to those of the Barossa Valley and of the Hunter Valley. It has a long-established infrastructure; it is close to a major market and will benefit increasingly from wine tourist travel; and even though its reputation is being reappraised, it is sustained by 100 years of tradition.

BASKERVILLE WINES
LOT 35, HADDRILL ROAD, BASKERVILLE

Baskerville was taken over by a syndicate of wine lovers with diverse interests in the early days of the wine boom. Somehow or other it has struggled on since, although one imagines that the romance of winemaking is now wearing a little thin.

Whatever else one may say about it, Baskerville is certainly different. The hound menacing one from the label does not, however, do justice to the friendly and informal way the operation is run. Output is limited, and on my last exposure to the wines a couple of years ago I found the quality to be variable, to say the least. It probably does not matter too much: the syndicate members and their friends take most of the output, and what is left sells readily enough through the cellar door and by mailing list.

Baskerville has changed hands several times since it was founded by Oscar Boghesi in 1951. Whether it continues under its present ownership will depend more on the continued involvement and commitment of its syndicate owners than on the acceptance of its wines in the marketplace.

BASSENDEAN ESTATE
147 WEST ROAD, BASSENDEAN

Bassendean Estate is only a part-time occupation for owner-winemaker Laurie Nicoletto, although wife Moira Nicoletto is usually to be found behind the cellar-door sales counter. In the 1960s Laurie Nicoletto took over the winery and vineyard which his father had founded in 1951, and almost immediately achieved success. He entered his first wine in the Perth show of 1968 and won a gold medal. Consistent show success at all levels has since come to Bassendean.

The winery is situated at the end of a suburban street only two minutes' drive from the central business district of Perth. Not surprisingly the River-side Vineyard which surrounds it is relatively small: only two hectares, planted to shiraz. Grape intake is thus supplemented by purchases from the Swan Valley, although total intake is still a fairly modest 50 tonnes.

The winemaking practices of Nicoletto are as basic and traditional as the winery equipment. Concrete fermentation tanks and large, old storage vats go hand-in-glove with a very basic crusher and press. Small oak casks of any age are not employed, let alone new oak. Yet for all this the Bassendean wines have always had an elegant softness about them. The only explanation is that Laurie Nicoletto has the winemakers' equivalent of "green fingers"—that touch of flair and understanding which a few lucky people have without knowing just how they do it. Perhaps it was handed down by his father, who had in turn learnt winemaking from his parents in Italy.

Whatever is the cause, the Bassendean style came through with distinction at the 1984 Sheraton Awards. One of the other features of the winery is that the reds are sold when fully mature, and thus a 1979 Shiraz, a 1980 Burgundy and a 1981 Cabernet Shiraz were all exhibited at the Sheraton Awards and were all on sale at the winery at the end of 1984. The sweet, minty/cherry fruit flavours, coupled with a touch of surprisingly complex spice in the 1981 Cabernet Shiraz, ran through all of the wines. That minty character was particularly pronounced; I had not previously noticed it. Clearly it is a fruit- and not an oak-derived characteristic, and it provides that little bit of lift.

The legendary Jack Mann once assessed Bassendean's Chenin Blanc as being one of the best, if not *the* best, coming from the Swan Valley. But I think that is a judgement which was part of its day.

COORINJA
BOX 99, TOODYAY ROAD, TOODYAY

Coorinja is a region all of its own, but its closest neighbours are the vineyards of the Swan Valley, 50 kilometres to the south-east. It is set in rolling hill country, just south of Toodyay. The land was first occupied in 1840 and vines were planted in 1870. The back section of the winery was built then and

the front, or lower, section was added in 1893. The only addition since then was a storeroom erected in 1936. Coorinja came into the ownership of the Wood family in 1919, and has passed through the family to the present owner/winemakers, Doug and Hector Wood. They have certainly looked after their inheritance. Perched on a steep hillside which runs down to a creek, the winery is well worth the trip from the Swan Valley. The large old oak casks and smaller barrels have been well kept, their painted ends adding a splash of colour to the atmospheric interior of the old winery.

Vintage runs from late February to the very end of March, reflecting the somewhat cooler climate in this region than in the Swan. Inadequate rainfall, however, is a problem in many years—a five-year drought to the end of 1981 substantially slowed the establishment of a new eight-hectare vineyard commenced in the 1970s.

The original or home vineyard has 30 hectares of vines, chiefly muscat, with shiraz, grenache, pedro ximinez and a little malbec and semillon. Even in the new vineyard traditional grape types—shiraz, grenache and muscat—are being planted, reflecting the Woods' belief in traditional wine styles.

The crush of 80 tonnes is all estate-grown except in drought years, when small supplementary purchases are made from the Swan Valley. The emphasis is on a range of old fortified wines, many of which have some age and complexity. A basic non-vintage claret and burgundy are also offered, which are smooth, pleasant wines. Cellar-door prices are ridiculously low.

ELLENDALE ESTATE
18 IVANHOE STREET, BASSENDEAN

John Barrett-Lennard's approach to winemaking and marketing is distinctly casual, as if he were seeking to divert attention from the fact that he is a vastly experienced professional winemaker (after graduating from Roseworthy he worked successively at Houghton, Stanley and Loxton Cooperative); a wine-show judge; and, for good measure, a member of one of Western Australia's pioneer families.

The last fact has its significance for Ellendale Estate (until recently known as Sveta Maria). Barrett-Lennard is a part-owner of the 1200-hectare Belhus Estate at the top end of the Swan Valley. At one stage it had more than 130 hectares of wine grapes and the largest table-grape vineyard in Australia, the latter based on the British export market. Only 27 hectares of wine grapes remain, providing Ellendale's intake, but Belhus has the distinction of being one of the oldest surviving vineyards in continuous production in the State. The vineyard is planted to chenin blanc (10 hectares), zinfandel and muscadelle (five hectares each), shiraz (four hectares) and muscat gordo blanco (two hectares).

Barrett-Lennard's relaxed attitude to winemaking is best illustrated by the photograph which appeared (with his full knowledge and consent) in a Western Australian newspaper—it showed him standing on the top of a stainless-steel tank adding oak chips from a plastic bag. Few winemakers will even privately admit to using oak chips; fewer still publicly acknowledge it; only John Barrett-Lennard, so it seems, will go on stage to demonstrate their use. His point is, of course, that what matters is the quality of the wine in the bottle and the price at which it is sold. Oak chips are a highly economical way of adding oak flavour, and if the choice lies between oak chips and no oak at all (in reds), oak chips are better than nothing.

The winery offers a wide range of bottled and flagon wines at the cellar door in effective competition—in terms of price—with the local supermarket. The basic wines are just that: basic. The specialities of the winery are the fortified styles and, in particular, a wine which to my knowledge is unique to Ellendale. Ripe muscat gordo blanco (which is known in Western Australia as muscat of Alexandria) is allowed to ferment from around 12 or 13 baume to six baume, and then fortified with six degrees of alcohol, giving a total alcohol content of 12 degrees. It is labelled White Liqueur Muscat, and a vintage is made each year. It produces a striking and full-flavoured wine, which not surprisingly has a very loyal following at the cellar door, where all the wines are sold.

EVANS AND TATE
GNANGARA ROAD, WEST SWAN

It is impossible to overstate the importance of the contribution made by Evans and Tate to the cause of Western Australian wine. Not only did Evans and Tate fundamentally reshape the perceptions of easterners about the style and quality of wine which could be made in the Swan Valley, but they marketed the wines with a panache and flair which was equally arresting. Immaculately presented press releases, beautifully labelled bottles and a constant flow of information all contributed to an awareness of Evans and Tate which was totally disproportionate to its

production, and absolutely remarkable given its relative isolation from the eastern markets. The bottom line, as it were, was a recognition that there were winemakers in the Swan Valley who were committed to consistently producing wines of the highest quality and which needed no apology when placed against the best wines of the eastern States.

It all started in 1971 when two business partners, John Evans and John Tate, established a small vineyard on the Evans family farm at Bakers Hill. The following year they purchased an old-fashioned winery called Gnangara Wines in the west Swan Valley, with its surrounding four-hectare vineyard. The Bakers Hill Vineyard, named Côte de Boulanger, had only 0.8 hectare of cabernet sauvignon and, given the partners' policy of only using estate-grown grapes, it was a curiously small base for a winery which soon marked itself as having such lofty ambitions.

Yet right from the outset the partners made it clear they were interested only in quality. They ripped out the old muscat and grenache vines at Gnangara and replanted them with shiraz; and they completely renovated the winery, installing refrigerated fermenters and an air-conditioned storage shed for the maturation of wines both before and after bottling. They also designed some of the cleanest and most striking labels then in use in Australia; and at a time when it was very uncommon to do so, bought expensive French burgundy bottles in which they put their wine. Next the partners turned their attention to the Margaret River area, acquiring their Willyabrup property, Redbrook. It is from this source that the vast bulk of their wine now comes, and I discussed this in greater length in Chapter 2.

In 1975 Evans and Tate exhibited their first wine, 1974 Gnangara Shiraz. It won medals in the Open Classes at Sydney, Canberra and Melbourne that year, setting a precedent for the exceptional show success and critical acclaim that the winery has since enjoyed. The 1977 Gnangara Shiraz was the most successful dry red table wine in the history of Western Australian winemaking, having won 14 medals and two trophies in capital city wine shows. The winery won the trophy for the best Western Australian red in the Perth show for three years in a row, and in the first six years of operation Evans and Tate won over 100 medals in national wine shows.

In 1977 the team was strengthened by the arrival of Bill Crappsley as winemaker. He had had a career stretching back to 1964, working first with Houghton, then d'Arenberg, Redman, Tulloch, Renmano and Basedows. Bill Crappsley's winemaking philosophies coincided exactly with those of John Evans and John Tate, and the style of the wines has not altered. Elegance, fruit freshness and balance are the three characteristics which Crappsley most admires in wine, and which in turn distinguish the Evans and Tate releases.

There have, however, been changes in the 1980s. John Tate and his wife are now the sole owners, and the Côte de Boulanger Vineyard has gone. To mark its passing Evans and Tate released a 1982 Three Vineyards Cabernet which was made, as its name suggests, from a blend of cabernet sauvignon grown at Bakers Hill, Gnangara and Redbrook. (There are a few vines of cabernet sauvignon at Gnangara.) The Margaret River component of the wine was very evident; beautiful oak, crisp fruit with cherry fragrances and flavours. It was a fitting farewell.

The same deft touch has always distinguished Gnangara Shiraz; the wine has between five to 10 per cent of cabernet sauvignon, and also shows the sophisticated use of both French and American oak. Particularly successful vintages have been the 1976, 1977, 1979 and 1981.

GLENALWYN
WEST SWAN ROAD, WEST SWAN

When George Pasalich purchased the nine-hectare vineyard at Glenalwyn in 1933 he was content to retain the Welsh name bestowed on it by its previous owners. Pasalich left Yugoslavia after phylloxera destroyed the family vineyard, and came to Australia via Belgium in 1926. Winemaking remained in his blood and it was only a matter of time before he purchased a property and established a vineyard.

The vineyard is now planted principally to chenin blanc, shiraz and cabernet sauvignon, with much smaller plantings of grenache, pedro ximinez, verdelho and several varieties of muscat. The business has now passed to George Pasalich's son, Len, a gregarious man who was for some time president of the Swan Valley and Regional Winemakers' Association.

Len Pasalich's spotless and scrupulously tidy winery specialises in fortified wines. While he has had occasional success with white and red table wines, certainly the range of Glenalwyn wines shown at the 1984 Sheraton Awards left no doubt that his wine-making strength does indeed lie in the fortified-wine arena. The Glenalwyn 1979 Vintage Port is an extremely good wine.

HENLEY PARK WINES
SWAN STREET, WEST SWAN (near HENLEY BROOK)

Henley Park was established by the Yujnovich family in 1935. The small vineyard is planted on some of the richest soil in the Swan Valley, known to be over 13 metres deep in places. Chenin blanc (one hectare), cabernet sauvignon and shiraz (1.2 hectares each), muscadelle (0.4 hectare) and rhine riesling (0.25 hectare) produce up to 50 tonnes a year with the yields varying between 11 tonnes per hectare for the red varieties and 20 tonnes per hectare for chenin blanc. Semillon and chardonnay (0.5 hectare) have also recently been planted, but are yet to come into full bearing.

Winemaker Mark Yujnovich was once described by Jack Mann as "the magician", a generous recognition on the part of Jack Mann of the flavour which Yujnovich is able to obtain in his wines. Recent white table wine releases have not impressed, but the fortified wines have. Good though the 1979 Glenalwyn Vintage Port may be, I think the Henley Park Vintage Port of the same year is absolutely outstanding: rich, tangy and peppery with lovely spicy flavours on the palate.

HIGHWAY WINES
GREAT NORTHERN HIGHWAY, HERNE HILL

The Bakranich family run a small but very neat and well-ordered winery on the Great Northern Highway, from which it takes its name. Grape varieties used and the wine styles made are traditional, and in every way the winery is at the heart of Swan Valley winemaking.

The 11-hectare vineyard is planted to shiraz and grenache, with a little semillon and muscadelle. Part of the 150-tonne crush comes from grapes purchased from local growers. Virtually all of the production is sold in bulk or by flagons through the cellar door.

HOUGHTON
WEST SWAN ROAD, CAVERSHAM

Houghton stands unchallenged as the most important winery in Western Australia, making 37 per cent of the total State production in 1984. It is also one of the oldest—although not *the* oldest as is often claimed—vineyards and wineries. Much of its long and rich history can be felt in the old underground cellars. The original vineyard formed part of a grant of 3240 hectares made to Revitt Henry Bland on 10 January 1835. A few years later the major part of the grant was sold to a syndicate of three British Army officers serving in India—Houghton, Lowis and Yule. As Colonel Houghton was the senior of the three, the property was named after him although he never came to Australia. It was managed on behalf of the syndicate by Yule, who subdivided it further.

In 1859 Dr John Ferguson, the colonial surgeon, purchased the home block with its small cottage and vineyard. He made 135 litres of wine in that year, some of which was offered for sale. The property, and particularly the vineyard and cellars, flourished under the control of C. W. Ferguson, Dr Ferguson's second son. The grand cellars incorporate that first tiny cottage, and offer one of the major wine attractions of the Swan Valley. The property remained in the possession of the Ferguson family for almost 100 years, finally being sold to the Emu Wine Company Limited in 1950 when it became apparent that no member of the family wished to continue the business.

However, long before then the Mann family had joined forces with the Fergusons as winemakers. In 1920 George Mann left Chateau Tanunda and become winemaker at Houghton; in 1922 he was joined by his son Jack, who became chief winemaker in 1930, a position he held until his (temporary) retirement in 1972. His tally of 51 successive vintages is dwarfed only by Dan Tyrrell, with 70, and by Roly Birks of Wendouree. Under the supervision of Jack Mann Houghton's wines became famous across Australia. His two specialities were, incongruously, white burgundy and fortified wines. His sherries, tokays and muscats were second to none; while the blue stripe of Houghton's White Burgundy heralded a revolution in the hitherto commonly accepted concepts of dry white wine.

The vehicle which the Emu Wine Company used to acquire Houghton was in fact Valencia Vineyards Pty Limited; Emu had acquired this historic vineyard and winery in 1945. Valencia had once ranked with Houghton in terms of importance, and the combination of the two vineyards and wineries was a potent one. The strength of the group was increased with the 1968 establishment by Valencia of its Gingin Vineyard, some 80 kilometres north of Perth.

In 1976 Thomas Hardy and Sons acquired the Emu Wine Company and with it, its extensive Western Australian holdings. A major process of rationalisation followed over the ensuing decade. The engine room of the Houghton winery has been completely replaced; what is to all intents a new working winery has been installed, with every piece of winemaking equipment appropriate to white and red table-wine production in a very hot climate.

At the same time the historic buildings have been preserved and refurbished. As the visitor approaches Houghton he or she has a strong sense of the history of the place, with the historic buildings sitting quietly in immaculately kept lawns and parklands. The new winery is largely out of sight around the back, as it were. It stands absolutely unchallenged as the showpiece of the Swan Valley.

Following the return of Bill Hardy to South Australia, Jon Reynolds has moved from his long-term position as white-winemaker to chief winemaker, responsible for all of the Houghton and Moondah Brook Estate wines. Reynolds is a winemaker of exceptional talent, who for many years has demonstrated his ability to produce white wines and rosés of the highest class. There is no reason to suppose he will not achieve precisely the same success with red wines.

Indeed, in 1983 Jon Reynolds was able to make two cabernet sauvignons from grapes purchased respectively in the Margaret River and Mount Barker areas, giving Houghton the ability to market wines made from grapes grown in each of the five major regions of Western Australia. The early indication is that those cabernets have beautiful berry character, generous flavour and soft tannins.

Around 85 per cent of Houghton's crush of 2960 tonnes comes from its 270 hectares of vineyards in three locations—the Swan Valley, Gingin and the Frankland River. The Moondah Brook and Frankland Vineyards and wines are discussed separately; while there is inevitably some crossblending, by and large there is a product/vineyard link, with the Moondah Brook Estate Wines, in particular, being differentiated from those of Houghton.

The Houghton Vineyard is planted to chenin blanc (24 hectares), muscadelle (13 hectares), shiraz and grenache (nine hectares each), cabernet sauvignon and malbec (six hectares each), verdelho and pedro ximenez (five hectares each), rhine riesling (three hectares), and semillon, muscat and madeleine (two hectares each).

The Houghton brand leader, and one of the largest-selling middle/upper-quality table wines in Australia, is Houghton White Burgundy. The shape of the wine has changed very significantly since the days of Jack Mann; yet it has done no more than keep pace with the changes in white-winemaking and philosophy at large. Thus even though the Houghton White Burgundy of 1980 bears little resemblance to that of 1960, its relationship to other wines on the market is roughly the same. In other words it remains uncompromisingly a white burgundy, with an extra degree of flavour and mid-palate softness. Whereas the white burgundy of Jack Mann was immensely high in alcohol, high in free sulphur dioxide, was fermented on unclarified juice and took no assistance from new oak, that of today has more chenin blanc and less muscadelle (or tokay, as it is often called) in the blend, unashamedly employs the extra dimension of new oak, is clean-fermented and protected not so much by sulphur as by modern winemaking techniques.

Both approaches have served their masters well. The new generation of Houghton White Burgundy has been no less successful than the old. The 1980 vintage is a quite magnificent wine, which has won innumerable gold medals at national shows across Australia, and is simply going from strength to strength. In early 1985 it seemed to be approaching its peak, but will undoubtedly hold for many years yet.

Houghton also releases a chablis, another wine which draws heavily on oak (which is, as in all the Houghton wines, well handled) but which, in all honesty, seems to me to be a rosé (or rather a white burgundy) by any other name. Its composition of chenin blanc and muscadelle from the Moondah Brook and Houghton Vineyards certainly does not differentiate it from its big brother. Nonetheless, as with all the Houghton wines it is a well-made, flavoursome drink.

The varietal releases now extend to a rhine riesling, an auslese rhine riesling, a chardonnay, a wood-aged chenin blanc, a late-picked verdelho, and an autumn harvest semillon. There is not a bad wine among these, perhaps the most striking being the wood-aged chenin blanc and the autumn harvest semillons. The latter are often available in back-release form, covering a span of vintages. Thus in late 1984 wines from the 1977, 1980 and 1982 vintages were available. Bottle-age adds a further dimension of complexity to these wines, which are produced in a climate well suited to the style. Nonetheless, of those three vintages the 1982 was by far the best, with intense and concentrated raisined lusciousness, balanced by adequate, though fairly soft acid.

One of Houghton's most celebrated wines is its cabernet rosé. This is not an easy style of wine to make; in fact, it is a very difficult wine to make. Houghton have so mastered the art that it is seemingly able to produce a brilliant wine every year, regardless of the vagaries of vintage. The vibrant fuchsia colour, crisply aromatic nose and perfectly balanced palate are invariably technically flawless, but, more importantly, provide one of the most enjoyable of all table wines on the market.

Next there is a standard Houghton cabernet sauvignon release, offering solid, honest and rich flavour. Future years will no doubt see the release of specials from the Mount Barker and Margaret River areas.

Finally there are the Houghton fortified wines, offering vintage port and Centenary Port, followed by the two old fortified wines drawing upon stocks going back for 40 years or more—liqueur tokay and liqueur frontignac. Released in tiny quantities, these wines show great flavour, although Houghton has been careful to blend in sufficient young material to give fruit freshness and aroma. They are thus in the lighter mould, albeit with a backbone of complexity and lusciousness which comes only from the very old material in the blend.

JADRAN WINES
445 RESERVOIR ROAD, ORANGE GROVE

Jadran Wines is a substantial operation, established in 1927 and now under the tight control of wine-maker-owner Steve Radojkovich. Although the major part of the substantial volume of wine sold through the cellar door is of non-vintage generic style, offered variously in bottle and flagon, Jadran has from time to time shown its ability to rise to better things. Thus in 1975 Jadran received the trophy for the most successful Western Australian producer in the under 90,000 litres class at the Perth show. Subsequently Jadran purchased rhine riesling from the Lower Great Southern area, and made some excellent wine from it in the early 1980s. In yet another seeming flight of fancy, it used imported French burgundy bottles for its then-current chenin blanc releases.

I understand that Jadran no longer bothers with the show system, and has discontinued its purchases of Lower Great Southern and Margaret River material. Instead it is concentrating on its more traditional cellar-door clientele and styles. Radojkovich knows his market well: he spends half a day a week behind the sales counter for this very purpose. So the reasons for the change of direction are no doubt well based.

JANE BROOK ESTATE WINES
TOODYAY ROAD, MIDDLE SWAN

Jane Brook Estate is the new name of Vignacourt, which was purchased by David and Beverley Atkinson in 1972. Vignacourt had been established by its previous owner in 1955, and until 1984 the Atkinsons were content to trade under the old name. In a major change of identity the new name and striking new labels were introduced, which were said to have won a label competition in Italy. Just what relevance this has to the consumer I am not sure, although I have always had a lurking suspicion that many wine lovers are label drinkers at heart.

When they acquired Vignacourt the Atkinsons were, to use their words, "thrown in the deep end". They had had no previous experience in viticulture or winemaking; and although the previous owner stayed on for a year to teach them basic winemaking techniques, it was very much a matter of trial and error. Over the years they received advice and encouragement from the Department of Agriculture, and have from time to time attended wine industry technical conferences. These modest exceptions to one side, David Atkinson's winemaking skills have been learnt on the job.

It was a system which worked well: Vignacourt did not have a high reputation when the Atkinsons purchased it, and in the ensuing decade they did much both to increase the quality of the wine and likewise to increase production. Output has declined somewhat from the highpoint of the early 1980s. The 1984 crush of 83 tonnes was around half that of five years earlier. This was no doubt partly due to a radical reshaping of the estate vineyards; only 20 per cent of the 1984 crush came from the estate, reflecting the replanting programme. With the recent acquisition of an adjoining block of land there are now 12 hectares surrounding the winery, of which 10.5 hectares will be planted by 1987.

As at 1984 shiraz (two hectares), cabernet sauvignon (one hectare), grenache (one hectare), sauvignon blanc (one hectare) and tokay (one hectare) were in bearing, with the grenache grubbed out in 1985. In that year one hectare of semillon, 0.5 hectare of chardonnay and 1.5 hectares of verdelho were planted, with a further one hectare each of cabernet franc, semillon and tarrango planned for 1986. With trickle-irrigation the new plantings are expected to yield not less than 10 tonnes per hectare, lifting the estate-grown crush from around 15 tonnes at present to 100 tonnes.

The Atkinsons have for many years purchased grapes both in the Swan Valley and from the Mount Barker areas, resulting in a wide range of table wines, including wood-matured chenin blanc, late-harvest chenin blanc, Mount Barker cabernet sauvignon, vintage port and liqueur muscat. For a time the quality of the wines was really very good. By 1981 Vignacourt (as it then was) had won 50 medals and several trophies, being runner-up to Olive Farm as the most successful exhibitor in the Small Winemakers' Classes of the 1981 Perth show. Since that time the wines have been very disappointing, exhibiting a wide range of very obvious winemaking faults. Why this should be so, I simply do not understand; but it is very difficult to argue with the wines in the bottle.

LAKEVILLE VINEYARDS
1921 ALBANY HIGHWAY, MADDINGTON

Lakeville is a small, family-run and owned winery struggling to survive against dual threats: increasing commercial and industrial development around it, and competition from conventional liquor outlets, one of which has been established directly across the road from it.

The Lakeville winemaking equipment is, to put it mildly, traditional and the cellar facilities are limited. Output is all sold in flagons and the clientele is drawn exclusively from the neighbourhood.

LAMONT WINES
BISDEE ROAD, MILLENDON

Lamont Wines was founded in 1978 by Neil and Corin Lamont. It is a small winery at the northern end of the Swan Valley, which in 1984 produced around 45 per cent of its 26-tonne crush from its own vineyards. The vineyards are planted to cabernet sauvignon (one hectare), navera (0.5 hectare), verdelho (0.45 hectare), and muscadelle and semillon (0.35 hectare each). There is nothing remarkable in any of that until one finds that Corin Lamont is Jack Mann's daughter, and that the legendary Jack Mann, now in his eighties, is winemaker.

Virtually all of the wine is sold by cellar door, and all too few wine drinkers have the opportunity of tasting for themselves wines which are "resplendent in their generosity".

MOONDAH BROOK ESTATE
GINGIN

The very large property upon which Moondah Brook Estate is established was purchased in 1968, and developed jointly by the Valencia and Houghton operations of the then Emu Wine Company Limited. Seventy kilometres north of the Swan Valley, the Gingin area had been identified by Dr John Gladstones in his 1965 study as suited "for expanded production of wine types made in the Swan Valley, especially sweet dessert wines and sherries . . . considering the fact that there are fairly large areas of highly suitable soils at Gingin, a place might also be found for production of sweet and full-bodied dry table wines, of the types now made on the Swan." The surprising feature of the subsequent extensive development is that Gingin has in fact proved itself most suitable for the production of dry white table wines, albeit in the white burgundy mould.

The 86-hectare vineyard is planted to chenin blanc, muscadelle, verdelho, rhine riesling, chardonnay, shiraz, cabernet sauvignon and malbec. Recent grafting of shiraz to chardonnay, together with some vine removal, has seen the vineyard area decline from a peak of 112 hectares five years ago.

Moondah Brook has a number of special advantages. The soils consist of deep, red, fine sandy loams of extreme fertility; there is unlimited water for irrigation; and overall the vineyard averages 12 tonnes per hectare, with some varieties producing up to 20 tonnes per hectare. Finally the climate is cooler than that of the Swan Valley, thanks to cool late-afternoon sea-breezes.

The Moondah Brook chenin blanc and Moondah Brook verdelho are consistently excellent. Every now and then the wines excel themselves, such as the 1983 Moondah Brook Chenin Blanc, a magnificently complex wine with beautifully handled oak. The early releases of chardonnay, too, have shown great promise. All have a weight and viscosity on the palate which lends itself to small-oak treatment, something which winemaker Jon Reynolds is well aware of and takes full advantage of.

The Moondah Brook Estate cabernet sauvignon, while perhaps not rising to the heights of the Moondah Brook chenin blanc, can be a very good wine. Here astute winemaking preserves acid and freshness, and the Moondah Brook cabernets can often stand out in masked line-ups above all other Swan Valley reds to take their place with their counterparts from the Margaret River and Lower Great Southern areas.

OLIVE FARM
77 GREAT EASTERN HIGHWAY, SOUTH GUILDFORD

As I recounted earlier, Olive Farm is the oldest winery to have remained in continuous use since its establishment in 1829. In that year Thomas Waters acquired what was then a 20-hectare block situated on the banks of the Swan River at Guildford. He had brought with him grape vines and olive cuttings from South Africa, and planted both on the property— hence the name. In 1830 Waters dug his wine cellar which remains at the core of the present-day winery; he was in production by 1834, and in the 1840s was selling wine from the vineyard for two shillings a gallon (4.5 litres). After Waters' death in 1869 the property passed through a series of owners; when Ivan Yurisich purchased it in 1933 for the sum of £900, the vineyard had to be replanted so great was the neglect.

Since Yurisich's first vintage of 1000 litres, the enterprise has grown continuously in both size and reputation. It now produces around 90,000 litres of good table and fortified wines each year. It is run by Vince Yurisich and his son Ian, who, since graduating from Roseworthy, has taken over the winemaking responsibilities.

The winery of today has been equipped with everything necessary to make high-quality white table wine as well as the more traditional red and fortified wines. But underneath the refrigerated stainless-steel fermentation tanks and somewhat sterile surroundings of the modern ground-level winery, the old cellars live on, still in use and holding stocks of some excellent fortified wines.

Olive Farm is now enclosed in suburban sprawl and bounded on one side by the Perth International Airport. The land has progressively shrunk in size, but there are still three hectares of recently replanted cabernet sauvignon vines surrounding the winery and providing a peaceful background to the cellar-door sales area. Cabernet sauvignon, shiraz, chenin blanc, verdelho, semillon, chardonnay and muscat gordo blanco are all purchased from independent growers through the Swan Valley.

The most consistent wines in the Olive Farm range are the varietal white table wines (with a series of attractive wines made in 1984) and the Olive Farm fortified wines. Foremost among these are its oloroso sherry and old madeira, both of which are of well-above-average quality.

REVELRY
200 ARGYLE STREET, HERNE HILL

Revelry was established in 1930 by the Illich family. The 40-tonne crush comes from estate-grown grapes; the vineyard is planted to cabernet sauvignon, shiraz, pinot noir, grenache, muscadelle, chenin blanc and pedro ximinez. All wines are sold by cellar door, principally in flagons.

SANDALFORD
WEST SWAN ROAD, CAVERSHAM

John Septimus Roe was one of the first settlers in Western Australia, arriving on the *Parmelia* in 1829. It may be this that has led some writers to bestow on Sandalford (the property he was granted in 1840) the incorrect title of oldest vineyard in Western Australia. It is not the oldest and, indeed, although the property remained in the sole control of the Roe family until 1971, winemaking only became a commercial venture after the Second World War. Until then the viticultural activities were restricted to table grapes and currants, with a small amount of wine made for consumption by the family.

In the postwar years Septimus Roe's grandsons decided to start commercial winemaking: the vineyards were replanted under the control of John Roe, and David Roe became the winemaker. In 1969 David Roe's unexpected death left a major gap which was finally filled by the formation of a private company to acquire the Sandalford wine interests in 1971. John Roe and a Western Australian merchant bank became the principal shareholders, and the funds became available for the expansion and upgrading of winemaking facilities and, even more importantly, the acquisition of a large property in the Margaret River area. The property was purchased in 1972 and contains the largest plantings in the Margaret River. By 1980 125 hectares were under grape, three times greater than the Swan Valley plantings of Sandalford. There is accordingly no question that the future of Sandalford lies in the Margaret River.

In 1973 Sandalford took another major step by securing the services of Dorham Mann as winemaker. Dorham, son of Jack Mann, had spent some years as an extension oenologist-viticulturalist with the WA Department of Agriculture. The move brought immediate success; at the Perth show of that year Sandalford won trophies for the best Western Australian white and red wines.

In 1979 the Inchcape group of the United Kingdom purchased the shares not held by the Roe family; Taylor Ferguson (also in the Inchcape group) now handles the distribution of Sandalford outside Western Australia.

The Swan Valley-sourced wines are released under the Caversham Estate label. Caversham Estate (and of course the Margaret River Estate) provide Sandalford with all of its annual production of around 600,000 litres; unlike many of the larger companies, Sandalford does not buy grapes from contract growers. Caversham Estate is planted to pedro ximinez (10 hectares), cabernet sauvignon (8.5 hectares), chenin blanc (8.1 hectares), semillon (2.4 hectares), shiraz and verdelho (two hectares), muscadelle and zinfandel (1.2 hectares), together with smaller plantings of a number of other varieties totalling five hectares.

The Caversham Estate range comprises a chablis, Parmelia moselle, Parmelia riesling, verdelho, white burgundy, Matilde rosé, cabernet sauvignon and zinfandel. The range is priced beneath that of the Margaret River releases. Like those of the Margaret River, quality is variable and mercaptan is an intermittent problem with the red wines. However, there could be no criticism of wines such as the 1983 Caversham Estate Zinfandel, a massively constructed red wine in the traditional Californian mould.

TALIJANCICH WINES
121 HYEM ROAD, MILLENDON

In a move which runs counter to the normal trend, Peters Quality Wines recently changed its name to Talijancich Wines. One does not imagine that the glossy corridors of high-powered advertising agencies or public relations firms would reverberate with joy at such a change.

As both the old and new name acknowledge, the enterprise was founded by Peter Talijancich, in 1955. Talijancich senior turned from log-haulier and marketgardener to fortified-winemaker with very considerable success. In 1960 and again in 1961 he made liqueur muscats which have been released from the winery in recent years. Both vintages show extreme complexity, richness and—obviously enough—age. Indeed, I agree wholeheartedly with those who suggest that the 1961 should be freshened up with a little younger material. Blending is an integral part of old fortified-wine styles, and vintage purity is not always an advantage.

Winemaking is now in the hands of James Talijancich, who has initiated a move to earlier picking of the grapes in an effort to freshen and lighten the wine style. Eighty per cent of the 50-tonne crush comes from the family's vineyards, planted to shiraz (3.5 hectares), verdelho and semillon (0.5 hectare each), and muscadelle and grenache (0.25 hectare each). Pedro ximinez and chenin blanc are purchased from contract growers. The recent vintages of table and fortified wines have, by and large, been very disappointing.

TWIN HILLS
GREAT NORTHERN HIGHWAY, BASKERVILLE

Twin Hills, at the top end of the Swan Valley, is a medium-sized winery specialising in bulk sales, although bottles are available. It was founded in 1937 by the Kraljevich family; control has now passed to the founders' sons, Mark and Eddie.

The vineyard was originally established in the foothills of the Swan Valley and moved to its present location in 1947. It is not named, as one might suspect, after those foothills, but in honour of "twins' hill", an oblique reference to a celebrated pregnancy. The 27-hectare property is planted to a mixture of wine- and table-grape varieties. The wine-grape varieties comprise grenache, shiraz, chenin blanc, verdelho, pedro ximinez and muscat. The soil is very fertile—the table grapes, which are irrigated, yield 40 tonnes to the hectare in one area. Yields for winemaking are deliberately controlled at between 7.5 and 10 tonnes per hectare, with bunch-thinning where necessary.

In traditional Swan Valley fashion, the grapes are picked when very ripe, at around 14 baume. A wide range of table and fortified wine is made; the same wine is sold in bulk, in flagons and in bottles. The quality is surprisingly good.

VINDARA
NORTHERN HIGHWAY, HERNE HILL

Established in 1978, Vindara is one of the smaller and newest traditional-style Swan Valley wineries. Ivan Viskovich came to Australia in 1959; his family had made wine in Yugoslavia, although he was a builder-carpenter by trade. It was inevitable that he would become a cellar-hand at Houghton, combining all his skills and interests, and that he would make wine for himself from the old vines that surrounded the house he bought in 1960.

He has replanted part of the vineyard with better varieties, and it now produces a mixture of table, dried and wine grapes. Most of the crush comes from the four-hectare vineyard surrounding the house, which is planted principally to shiraz, grenache, muscat, semillon and rhine riesling. A small amount grown on relatives' vineyards is bought in each year.

Once the wine grapes were fully established, Viskovich built himself a new, small, brick winery and made his first commercial vintage in 1978. The winemaking equipment is basic, indeed primitive, and the wines have a character all their own.

WESTFIELD
Cnr MEMORIAL AVENUE and
GREAT NORTHERN HIGHWAY, BASKERVILLE

John Kosovich is held in universally high regard by his fellow Swan Valley winemakers. His wines are consistent show winners, and Westfield has won the trophy for most successful Western Australian exhibitor in the under 130,000-litre section—not a bad effort for a winery with a production of around 30,000 litres a year.

As so often happens, the reason for this success is based in the vineyard. The vines are established on typical fertile Swan Valley loam over clay subsoil, but Kosovich becomes most unhappy if cabernet sauvignon yields go over 7.5 tonnes per hectare and he aims for five tonnes. Semillon, a variety he particularly favours as a viticulturalist, can run up to 10 tonnes per hectare. If the vines look as if they are carrying an excessively heavy crop, he resorts to bunch-thinning, a sophisticated and relatively rare form of crop control.

The 50-tonne crush comes entirely from the eight-hectare vineyard which is planted to cabernet sauvignon (two hectares), chardonnay and verdelho (1.5 hectares each), shiraz, rhine riesling and semillon (0.5 hectare each) and merlot and chenin blanc (0.4 hectare each). Kosovich employs modern winemaking techniques in the winery: the whites are all allowed to cold-settle overnight before fermentation commences. He is also one of the few small winemakers to produce his own bottle-fermented sparkling wine, using cabernet sauvignon as the base grape. (Some of the largest sparkling-winemakers in the country are also using a percentage of cabernet sauvignon.)

The winery is spacious; in 1977 the main structure was built over the top of the old winery, which was then pulled down. The underground cellars and tasting area remain the same, however, featuring the hand-hewn beams cut with an axe by John Kosovich's father when he built the cellar in 1922.

Recent white-wine vintages have had significant critical acclaim; I must admit to being less taken by the white varietals than other tasters have been. However, some very well-made varietal red and fortified wines have come from Westfield in the past few years. Overall there is no doubting the fact that John Kosovich deserves his high reputation.

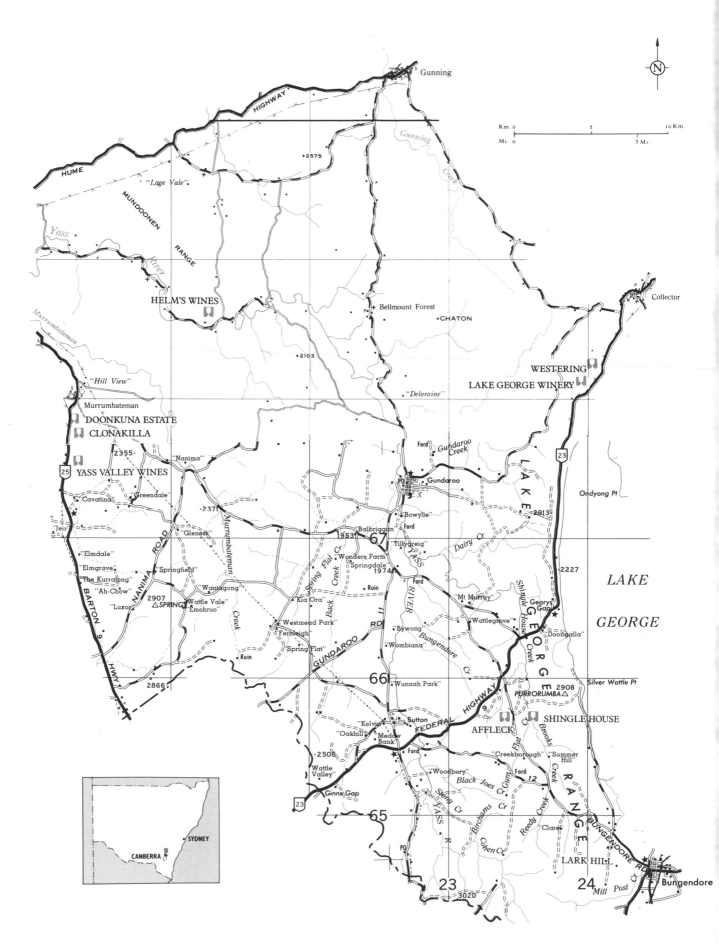

Canberra District

I t is, I suppose, fitting that all of the vineyards and wineries owned by the vignerons who are members of the Canberra District Vignerons' Association should be situated outside the Australian Capital Territory. But what is at first sight a classic piece of political double-speak has a very sensible—indeed, necessary—foundation.

The only known vineyard to have been established within the Australian Capital Territory was planted at Narrabundah in the early 1950s to rhine riesling and muscat. Wine was made from the 0.4-hectare planting for some years, but the vineyard was then absorbed in residential development. The fact is that all rural land within the Australian Capital Territory is held on short-term lease; the ever-present possibility of land resumption for urban or government use acts as a powerful deterrent to those who might otherwise have established vineyards within the Territory.

Thus it is that the 20 or so members of the Canberra District Vignerons' Association have all established their vineyards and wineries immediately across the border in New South Wales. In recognition of the urban pressure from Canberra, and ever-alert to increased rates and taxes revenue, many of the surrounding shires have permitted subdivision into relatively small blocks ranging from two to 80 hectares in size. This availability of smaller holdings is one of two key factors operating to provide potential long-term support to viticulture in the Canberra region. The other is the ready market that exists within a very short distance of production. Neither of these two attributes applies in the other tableland areas of New South Wales which might be equally suited to viticulture.

Nonetheless, the rate of development has been slow. Apart from that early Narrabundah planting, the first planting in the region was in 1971 when Edgar Riek planted the first rootlings at his Cullarin vineyard. Other plantings followed, although in those early days few would-be vignerons knew of the intentions of their brethren. It was not until November 1974 that the Canberra District Vignerons' Association was formed.

There are two main sub-regions in the district. The first is the Yass Valley area surrounding the town of Murrumbateman. The wineries in this region include Doonkuna Estate, Middleton's Murrumbateman, Clonakilla, Helms Wines and Yass Valley Wines. The other region spreads for the 30-kilometre length of Lake George, again with five wineries: Lake George Winery, Westering, Shingle House, Affleck and Lark Hill.

All of the wineries are weekend operations for Canberra residents, many of them working either for the government or the CSIRO. All are conducted on a doll's-house scale, although several are ambitious and have every intention of increasing the scale of operations.

There are many misconceptions about the Canberra region, not the least being that it is too cool to grow grapes. This is simply not true: it is undeniably cold in winter, but the summers are (relatively speaking) warm. Its six-month centigrade heat-degree day summation of around 1250 is similar to that of Coonawarra and Bordeaux. It is distinctly warmer than that of Burgundy, and very much warmer than the Rhine Valley. Nor do frosts present insuperable problems. Spring and autumn frosts do occur, and appropriate viticultural techniques will always be needed to guard against them. In truth the major viticultural limitation lies in the very dry spring and summer months. Thus at nearby Queanbeyan, in the period from 1901 to 1965, there were 28 spring-summer droughts lasting from four to seven weeks; 20 lasting eight to 11 weeks; 16 lasting 12 to 15 weeks; four lasting 16 to 19 weeks; and four lasting 24 to 38 weeks. It was one of those latter four that ended a small vineyard which I and several others attempted to establish near Bungendore in the early 1970s.

Experience has shown that supplementary water in the form of drip-irrigation is, to all intents and purposes, essential if vineyards are to be established. The slowness in the pace of development to date has been due to resistance to irrigation, because of prejudice against it and because it was not initially realised to be essential. Now virtually all of the fledgling vineyards are supplied with drip-irrigation to supplement the substantial deficit between spring-summer rainfall and the vines' base requirements. It is not generally realised that moisture is essential for proper ripening of the grapes: in a total drought situation the grapes may neither fill out nor ripen. Experience shows that in the Canberra district it is water availability more than temperature which has inhibited satisfactory ripening.

Nonetheless, even with adequate moisture parts of the Canberra district must be accepted as marginal for late-ripening varieties, such as cabernet sauvignon, and more suited to early ripening varieties, such as pinot noir. Yet even in 1984 cabernet sauvignon and cabernet franc ripened satisfactorily (as they also did in 1983 and 1982); while in some years pinot noir has ripened too soon and suffered from the same lack of flavour common to pinot noir growing in warmer climates.

Inevitably enough the *terroir* varies substantially, with vineyards established on flats, on slopes, in protected valleys, exposed plains and at widely differing altitudes. The subsoils also vary substantially, although all tend to be relatively poor and acid. Climate is likewise variable: those vineyards situated near Lake George benefit from the moderating influence of this large volume of water, while those established on north-facing slopes are least prey to frost. The diversity extends to viticultural practices; most of the vignerons have very definite views on viticulture, although not all have been able to translate theory into reality.

Wine quality is, to say the least, variable and fully reflects the difficulties of small-scale winemaking. At the end of 1984 I attended a tasting of almost 30 wines organised by the Vignerons' Association—the wines came from most of the wineries in the area and spanned the years from 1981 to 1984. There is no question that the red wines are far more successful than are the white wines. I do not believe that this reflects any inherent superiority of the region for red grapes: indeed, the reverse is almost certainly the case. Rather it is due to the difficulties of small-scale white-winemaking, particularly given the fairly basic equipment with which all of the wineries have to contend. If a fully qualified winemaker were given an adequately equipped winery, there is no reason why very good (if not outstanding) chardonnay, sauvignon blanc, rhine riesling and possibly even semillon could not be made.

In theory the district should produce excellent pinot noir in a majority of (though not all) years. As I have already suggested the problem here is too much warmth, rather than too little. The cabernet family—cabernet sauvignon, cabernet franc and merlot—has already demonstrated its potential, and even the very late-ripening shiraz has performed creditably in some locations.

One of the problems of assessment has been the tendency of some of the vignerons to blend their estate-grown material with grapes purchased from other districts. Sometimes these districts have been similar (such as Young), whereas other vignerons have been less particular in their grape sources.

Whatever the vignerons of the district may lack, it is not intelligence nor is it enthusiasm. They are still learning and if the Vignerons' Association took the bold step of retaining a trained consultant, the occasional sparks of brilliance might well ignite a sizeable fire. ▢

AFFLECK
BUNGENDORE

Affleck was established in 1976 by Ian and Sue Hendry with a little over one hectare of vines. I have not so far tasted any of its tiny output.

CLONAKILLA
CRISPS LANE, off GUNDAROO ROAD, MURRUMBATEMAN

Dr John Kirk's interest in wine developed at an early age and in somewhat unorthodox circumstances. When he was 14 he was placed in charge of the wine cellar at the family hotel in the west of Ireland. Just how seriously he took his responsibilities, and quite how he discharged them is not recorded. Suffice it to say that when he moved to Canberra in 1968 he immediately commenced the search for a suitable vineyard area.

He found what he was looking for in 1971, selecting a property in the Yass Valley about 18 kilometres south of the township of Yass near the Barton Highway. Plantings commenced in 1971 and continued in 1972, reaching almost two hectares. The advent of the 1972–73 drought (which terminated my own modest efforts in the area) led to a hurried reappraisal. Discouraged but not daunted, Dr Kirk started again, albeit more slowly.

The one-hectare vineyard is planted to two-thirds white varieties (principally rhine riesling) and one-third red (principally cabernet sauvignon). On average the one hectare provides around three tonnes of grapes. Dr Kirk has recently successfully sunk a bore, making trickle-irrigation possible, and has plans to increase the vineyard to four hectares. Once this is achieved and the vines come into full bearing, John Kirk proposes to cease being a research scientist and become a full-time vigneron and winemaker. He is presently taking the degree course in wine science at the Riverina College of Advanced Education as an external student, and will have completed that course by the time he takes up full-time winemaking.

His winemaking philosophy is already formulated: to interfere with the wine as little as possible, and in particular to filter neither white wines nor reds. He also believes that the Yass Valley is ideally suited to late-harvest rhine rieslings and, with the recent advent of botrytis, I am certain he is correct in this belief.

The wines made include a rhine riesling, a cabernet sauvignon and a muscat. The muscat is a blend of muscat of Alexandria purchased from Mildura, blended with a small percentage of brown muscat grown on the estate. The solera was first laid down in 1978 and is supplemented from year to year. The muscat is clean, light and fairly youthful, but obviously has little or nothing to do with the Canberra district. The 1983 Rhine Riesling exhibited the problems of small-scale winemaking, but the oxidation did not obscure some attractive fruit richness in the bouquet.

Kirk's real long-term ambitions lie with the making of a long-lived, Bordeaux-styled claret, fermented on the skins to dryness for maximum tannin extraction. He comments that, "At present, in deference to predominant public taste, a somewhat lighter style is produced".

The great wines of Clonakilla are still to be made.

DOONKUNA ESTATE
BARTON HIGHWAY, MURRUMBATEMAN

Doonkuna Estate was begun in 1973 by Harvey and Betty Smith and by 1978 two hectares were under vine. In that year the present owners acquired the property, and their names appear at the foot of the label as B. S. and J. Murray, Doonkuna Estate, Murrumbateman, New South Wales. They are in fact His Excellency Rear-Admiral Sir Brian and Lady Murray, and Sir Brian is better known as the current Governor of Victoria.

The vineyards are established adjacent to the Barton Highway in Murrumbateman, close to Clonakilla and approximately 18 kilometres south-east of Yass. The 4.5 hectares planted comprise chardonnay, rhine riesling, sauvignon blanc, pinot noir, cabernet sauvignon and shiraz, together with a little semillon and valdiguie. The plantings have been expanded significantly since Sir Brian and Lady Murray acquired Doonkuna, and are still coming into bearing. It is expected that the annual crush will reach 40 tonnes once the vines do come into full production.

The vineyard and winery are managed by Roland Kaval, the district's only fully qualified winemaker, who has an honours degree in science from Monash University and a Bachelor of Applied Science (Wine Science) from Roseworthy Agricultural College. As one might expect, some good wines have appeared under the Doonkuna label. Until 1980 the grapes were sold to other growers, but wine has been made since that time and most significantly since the arrival of Kaval as winemaker in 1982.

A pinot noir from that year showed great flavour, but was rather over-oaked and a little extractive. The 1984 Pinot Noir, tasted when only six months old, showed excellent, light, spicy varietal pinot flavour, although it seemed that some acid reduction would be necessary to soften its impact. The best of four Doonkuna wines tasted was the 1983 Shiraz, a big, sweet, ripe and minty wine with a generous bouquet and very full-flavoured palate, with pleasingly soft tannin. It is very interesting to observe how shiraz grown in cool climates follows one of two quite different tracks: it either develops a strong eucalypt-mint aroma and taste, or a strong crushed-pepper character. The two are utterly divergent; we still have a lot to learn about cool-climate winemaking in this country before we understand why and how these characters emerge from the one grape.

The 1983 Doonkuna Cabernet Sauvignon had that typical profile of the variety, with a distinct dip in the mid-palate flavour, followed by a very firm tannin finish. Finally, the 1984 Sauvignon Blanc confirmed the potential the area has for the variety, with the well-balanced palate in sharp contrast to that of Cullarin.

Doonkuna wines are available chiefly through the cellar door and mailing lists; Florentino's Restaurant in Melbourne lists its pinot noir. On any view of the matter Doonkuna is entitled to be regarded as the senior winery of the district.

HELM'S WINES
BUTT'S ROAD, MURRUMBATEMAN

Ken Helm comes closest of all the Canberra vignerons to being a professional viticulturalist: he is a senior technical officer at the CSIRO, currently researching the biology and control of phylloxera, and with 16 years of orchard and vineyard research behind him. He established his Nanima Creek vineyard in the Yass Valley in 1973 on the site of the old Towal Public School, founded in 1888 but long since passed into history. The school gave rise to the school bell which features as the emblem on the label.

The soils of the Yass Valley are mostly shale over clay with little topsoil, but some of Ken Helm's vines are established on the gravelly alluvium of the Nanima Creek flats.

Helm's viticultural experience is reflected in his installation of automatic frost-control sprinklers (essential for the flats), drip-irrigation and sod culture, the latter involving the use of weedicides under the vines and mown grass between the rows. The establishment of the vineyard also marked the return of the Helm family to viticulture; Ken Helm's great-grandfather was one of the vine-dressers and grape-growers who were brought from Germany to help run J. T. Fallon's Murray Valley vineyards in Albury in 1854.

The estate vineyards comprise 0.5 hectare each of rhine riesling, gewurztraminer, muller-thurgau and cabernet sauvignon. For some years now Helm has encouraged his neighbours to plant grapes, with 11 hectares now under vine and contracted to Helm's. The 1984 crush of 25 tonnes was the largest in the district and upwards of 50 tonnes were expected in 1985.

The winery incorporates both old and new, with a 100-year-old press from Rutherglen working alongside modern filters, stainless-steel tanks and well-equipped laboratory.

The 1984 Gewurztraminer was light and clean, but virtually devoid of varietal character. Traminer is a very difficult variety to grow and vinify successfully, producing wines which seem to vary from one extreme to the other. The 1984 Muller-Thurgau was more successful, although the limitations of this very mundane variety were evident. The wine was well enough made; I simply doubt the long-term worth of the variety.

The 1984 blend of late-picked traminer and rhine riesling was once again a well-enough-made wine, but lacked varietal character and fruit. By far the most successful was the 1983 Cabernet Sauvignon, which won the trophy for the best red wine of show at the 1983 Cowra Show. It has crystal-clear cherry/cassis-berry aroma and flavour, low tannin and very well-balanced acid.

Ken and Judith Helm are some of the most committed vignerons and winemakers in the district. As the vines mature and as the Helms learn to maximise fruit flavour in the aromatic white varietals, some very good wines will appear under the Helm label.

LAKE GEORGE WINERY
FEDERAL HIGHWAY, COLLECTOR

The Lake George Winery (formerly Cullarin Vineyard) is owned by the *eminence grise* of the Canberra district vignerons, Dr Edgar Riek. Riek is perhaps best known as the driving force behind the Canberra National Wine Show, which in the six years since it was initiated has gone from strength to strength and lays claim to being the country's major show.

Yet another doctor of philosophy (in science), and another of the hyperintelligent vignerons, Edgar Riek is also the most iconoclastic of his peers. Whereas the others all blindly assume that Canberra variously is or is destined to be a great wine region, Riek looks at it this way:

> If the Canberra district wines of the future are to be distinctive and outstanding, they will have to compare favourably with the pinot noir and chardonnay wines from Tasmania, the south-west of Western Australia and some of the cooler areas of southern Victoria; the cabernet wines from Coonawarra and the south-west of Western Australia; the rhine rieslings from Watervale; the semillon and shiraz wines from the Hunter; and outstanding wines from other yet to be recognised regions. It is a challenge.

It is Riek, more than anyone else, who argues that far from being too cool, the Canberra district may be too warm. But in doing so I think he is trying more to stimulate discussion than establish a point of view.

Not only is the vineyard one of the two oldest in the region, it is one of the largest. It is situated on an east-facing slope at the north-western end of Lake George, planted on a variety of soils ranging from a pan outwash of metamorphic sediments, to black soil, to the remnants of a former shingle shoreline of the lake. The varieties planted are chardonnay (one hectare), pinot noir (one hectare), cabernet sauvignon, cabernet franc and merlot (one hectare collectively), sauvignon blanc (0.4 hectare), rhine riesling (0.3 hectare), semillon (0.2 hectare) and various experimental varieties, including such oddities as viognier, melon, furmint, ehrenfelser and numerous other varieties. The "unpretentious shed", in which Riek makes the wine each year, limits the size of the crush to 10 tonnes whether or not additional grapes are available.

Even though he has been making wine for 10 years now, Edgar Riek remains Socrates dissatisfied; or perhaps it is simply his scientific bent which leads him to continuing experimentation. Thus even though he succeeds with a given variety in producing the style he sought in a given year, next vintage he is as like as not to do something entirely different (and which may not succeed).

It was this enquiring mind which led to a searingly acid 1984 Sauvignon Blanc. Riek calmly explained, once my tastebuds had regained some of their equilibrium, that he had wanted to find out how much varietal character he could capture if he picked the wine "rather early". The answer is a considerable amount, even if it is at the risk of life and limb for the unwary taster.

For all this he has produced the best wines to come so far from the district. The 1982 Cullarin Pinot Noir, the 1982 Cabernet (a blend of 50 per cent cabernet sauvignon and 50 per cent cabernet franc) and 1981 Cabernet Sauvignon (with the oak flavour induced through oak chips and oak essence) are wines which would stand out in any company. Learning from his early games that oak chips and oak essence were not really the answer, Riek put his 1984 Chardonnay into a new French oak barrique to produce a masterly wine, albeit heavily wooded.

Good though the wines are, they are all but unprocurable unless one is a member of the appropriate club in Canberra or visits the few restaurants which list the wines. I suppose there have to be some compensations for living in Canberra.

LARK HILL
RMB 281, GUNDAROO ROAD, BUNGENDORE

Lark Hill claims to be the highest vineyard in New South Wales, at an altitude of 860 metres on the top of an escarpment overlooking Lake George. One of the newer arrivals on the Canberra scene, it was established by Sue Carpenter and her husband Dr David Carpenter, both of whom are science graduates (David Carpenter has the almost mandatory Doctor of Philosophy degree). Sue Carpenter is undertaking the Bachelor of Applied Science degree in oenology at the Riverina College of Advanced Education. The Carpenters have also gained extensive practical experience working for several vintages at Brokenwood in the Hunter Valley.

The vineyard comprises one hectare each of rhine riesling, chardonnay and pinot noir, and 0.5 hectare each of cabernet sauvignon and semillon. The pinot

VINES AT DAWN

noir was planted in 1984 and is yet to produce a crop.

Grape intake has been supplemented by rhine riesling, cabernet sauvignon and semillon purchased from the Moppity Park Vineyard in Young. On the label of their wines the Carpenters have been very careful to disclose which are 100 per cent estate-grown and which are blended. With the 1984 crush of 21 tonnes and an estimated 30 tonnes in 1985, the Carpenters have wasted no time. What is more, the quality of the wines, both red and white, has probably been more consistent than those of any other winery in the region.

The 1984 Late-Harvest Rhine Riesling was by far the best aromatic white wine made in the district in that vintage. Only the Cullarin Chardonnay has the potential to challenge it, but of course it is an entirely different style of wine in any event. The 1984 wine, with its rich lime/botrytis aromas and flavours, follows in the footsteps of two prior vintages of equal stature. The 1983 Lark Hill Rhine Riesling won the trophy for the best white wine of the Forbes Wine Show, while the 1982 Late-Harvest Rhine Riesling won a bronze medal at the 1982 Canberra National Wine Show. The Lark Hill Rhine Rieslings have the depth of fruit flavour and varietal character which seem to be absent in many of the other aromatic white wines of the district.

The Lark Hill Cabernet Sauvignon has, if anything, been even more consistent. Each vintage has won medals, none being more successful than the 1983 Cabernet Sauvignon, which in 1984 was placed first in the Forbes Wine Show and first in its class at the Cowra Wine show, and was also runner-up for the trophy for best wine of show (which went to the 1983 Helm Cabernet Sauvignon).

In winning its class at Cowra, Lark Hill disposed of wines from Montrose, Miramar (from Mudgee) Elliotts and Marsh Estate (from the Hunter Valley) and the Riverina College of Advanced Education. It is a blend of 60 per cent Lark Hill cabernet and 40 per cent Moppity Park cabernet. It is probably the presence of the the latter wine that gives the blended wine the extra depth on the mid-palate; it has attractive minty flavours and a soft tannin finish to give the wine balance and length.

David and Sue Carpenter are young and enthusiastic. Both have a broad-based understanding of the great wines of the world, and I have the feeling they will not rest on their laurels.

MIDDLETON'S MURRUMBATEMAN
BARTON HIGHWAY, MURRUMBATEMAN

Jeff and Trish Middleton acquired their Murrumbateman property in 1970, intending to establish a vineyard and eventually a winery. The first vines were planted in 1973, but the rate of development in the early years was slow, reaching 1.8 hectares by 1979. There are now three hectares under vine, comprised of one hectare each of shiraz and cabernet sauvignon and 0.5 hectare each of chardonnay and sauvignon blanc. The 20-tonne crush is supplemented by shiraz from Young and traminer from Griffith.

The winery, with its attractive sales and function area, was opened in 1980, the first commercial winery in the district to open its doors on a full-time basis. Although small, the winery has become one of the more popular tourist attractions in the Yass district. Mead is made between vintages, utilising the winemaking equipment, and the function centre is frequently used by Canberra-based groups seeking a night in the country. A haunch of beef is spit-roasted and served with Murrumbateman wines.

Wine quality is not exceptional; the winery relies on its other attractions as much as the inherent quality of the wine to gain custom.

SHINGLE HOUSE
BUNGENDORE

Max and Yvonne Blake established their Shingle House Vineyard in 1973; at one stage almost four hectares were under vine, but this amount has since been significantly reduced because of recurrent frost problems.

A 1983 Mataro tasted at the end of 1984 was apparently undergoing a malolactic fermentation and was very difficult to assess.

WESTERING
FEDERAL HIGHWAY, COLLECTOR

Dr Geoffrey Hood, another man of science, commenced planting his Westering vineyard close to Cullarin in 1973, and now has almost three hectares under vine.

A 1981 Chardonnay had seen better days when tasted at the end of 1984, and a 1983 Shiraz had characters which one more frequently associates with the Hunter Valley (in other words, mercaptan). Perhaps these two wines were not representative.

YASS VALLEY WINES
CRISPS LANE, MURRUMBATEMAN

Situated next-door to Clonakilla in Crisps Lane, Murrumbatemán, Yass Valley Vineyard (formerly Telofa Vineyard) was first planted by Peter Griffiths in 1978. The small vineyard is planted to rhine riesling, chardonnay, traminer and cabernet sauvignon, supplemented by shiraz and semillon purchased from Young. The 1984 vintage totalled only five tonnes, with only 0.4 hectare of vineyard in full bearing.

The principal output of Yass Valley Wines is an estate-grown rhine riesling and a rosé made "by the traditional methods" from shiraz grapes. I have not tasted the wines.

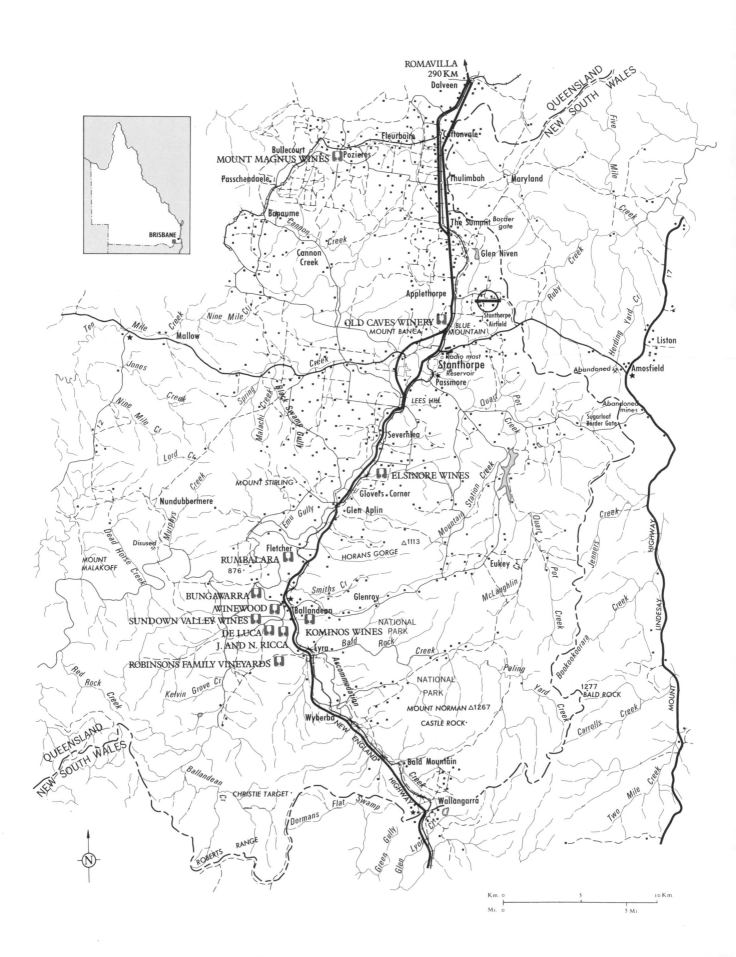

Queensland

The Queensland wine industry of today centres around Stanthorpe in the so-called Granite Belt. Its outposts extend to the Atherton Tableland, west of Cairns, where the Foster family produce wines at Herberton, thence to the unlikely outskirts of Roma, halfway between Brisbane and Charleville, and finally through the southern fringes of Brisbane itself, where Peter Love had his small Elsinore vineyard and winery before re-locating to the Granite Belt.

The activities of the Fosters are on a small scale, and primarily directed at the tourist trade, the wines are made from the American vitis labrusca grapes. The peculiar foxy flavour of the wines is an acquired taste, whether they be grown in the cold of New York State or the warmth of the Atherton Tableland. Roma, however, is a different story, for it was here that the Queensland wine industry started and it was here (and only here) that it survived on a continuous basis until the revitalisation of the Granite Belt in the latter part of the 1960s.

Romavilla was founded in 1863 by a 23-year-old Cornish man, Samuel Bassett. Bassett had arrived in New South Wales in 1856 to work for his uncle at East Maitland, before moving on to Maranoa in Queensland in 1858. What prompted his move to Roma, and his decision to establish a vineyard in such an inhospitable spot, is not known. One factor may well have been the availability of grape cuttings from his uncle's Maitland property, 1000 of which were brought by bullock dray from Toowoomba to Roma shortly after his arrival. Even that part of the journey took two months, and by the time the cuttings arrived, many had already sprouted or died. Three hundred survived, to provide the base for what was to become a thriving wine industry.

By 1874 Bassett had 25 hectares of vineyard, and was marketing his wine locally under the Romavilla label. He was evidently self-taught; and in deference both to the climate and to his winemaking abilities, all of the wine made and sold was fortified. After an unsuccessful attempt to sell Romavilla in 1879, Bassett continued to develop the operation, purchasing grapes from six other growers in the region.

Not surprisingly phylloxera has never come to Roma, and by the late 1890s Samuel Bassett suddenly found himself in charge of a winery which was of national significance in terms of production. The property was by now 180 hectares in extent, with a vineyard of over 170,000 vines, producing wines which in 1901 won 10 of the 11 medals awarded at the Royal Brisbane Show. By this time he had extended his winemaking to a full range of both table and fortified wines; the 1903 price-list offered port, muscat, amontillado, burgundy, madeira, chablis, hock, claret, sherry, champagne and sauterne.

Substantial improvements had been made in the vineyards. In recognition of the rainfall of less than 500 millimetres, irrigation was introduced into the vineyards which lifted yields to five tonnes per hectare. Samuel Bassett arranged for his son William to learn winemaking from Leo Buring, and on Samuel's death in 1912 William Bassett took over the winery. A teetotaller, he demanded total abstinence from all of the winery workers, although it was no doubt difficult for him to watch all of them all of the time. A district identity, he owned the first motorcycle in the district, a marvellous contraption with a large wicker-basket sidecar.

A little-known side-light was that throughout the 1950s substantial quantities of lightly fortified burgundy (sold as Bassett's Fruity Burgundy) were purchased by Mick Morris as a blending base for the Morris ports.

In 1973 William Bassett died; although his four children were all on the land none had any interest in continuing the winery's operations. For a time it appeared it would disappear, but in 1975 a Sydney-based syndicate purchased it, 112 years after it was founded.

Meanwhile in 1878 an Italian-born Roman Catholic priest at Stanthorpe established a vineyard and urged his parishioners to follow suit. Father David planted his first vines near his presbytery, and later established what became known as Vichie's Vineyard. The remains of the cellar he established can still be seen.

The Granite Belt around Stanthorpe has a very different climate and *terroir* from that of Roma. It has for long been one of the leading stone-fruit and deciduous-fruit-growing areas of Queensland, and inevitably attracted Italian migrants who had been used to growing crops and fruit in their home country. It was around these migrants that the very substantial table-grape industry flourished, but it was not until 1928 that Constanza and Musumeci constructed winemaking facilities to permit wine to be made from table grapes.

Until the mid-1960s winemaking was almost exclusively limited to the use of table grapes which had failed to find a market and which were consequently damaged and overripe. The resultant wines were high in alcohol, which was appreciated by the Italian clientele, and it was also fortunate in providing some measure of protection against bacterial disease. The use of sulphur was all but unknown, and the wines were prone to oxidation from the day they were made. Most were sold in bulk for consumption prior to the next vintage.

In 1965 the first wine grapes (one hectare of shiraz) were planted, and the Granite Belt region of today began slowly to take shape. It is, indeed, highly suited to viticulture, thanks entirely to its altitude, with virtually all the vineyards lying between 750 and 900 metres above sea-level. This altitude results in a centigrade heat-degree day summation which averages 1706, and provides a mean January temperature of 20.4°C, the same as that for Margaret River. In exceptional years such as 1984 the heat-degree summation fell to 1592, and the mean January temperature to 19.26°C. All of this makes Stanthorpe one of the cooler Australian regions.

Wine consultant John Stanford, one of the most experienced in the Australian wine industry, has been proclaiming the virtues of the Granite Belt for over a decade now. The hilly terrain allows considerable scope for site selection, with vast differences in *terroir* from one slope to the next. There are a number of vineyards with a significantly lower heat summation than the district average. Annual rainfall is around 780 millimetres per year, falling principally between October and January, but sometimes extending through to March with cyclonic influences. Vintage-time rain can accordingly be a major viticultural problem. On the other hand, the relatively high humidity and summer cloud-cover reduces vine stress during the vintage period. The soils consist of decomposed granite; they are well drained and easily worked.

Wineries such as Bungawarra, Rumbalara, Mount Magnus and Robinsons are determined to establish the fact that the Granite Belt can produce table wines of a quality comparable to those of the principal southern winemaking regions. They have some way to go yet to achieve that objective consistently, but one or two wines from the region have been outstanding.

BUNGAWARRA
MARSHALLS CROSSING ROAD, BALLANDEAN

Bungawarra was established by Angelo Barbagello in the 1920s, producing wines from table grapes for sale in bulk at the local Italian communities in southern Queensland and northern New South Wales. The winemaking equipment was basic, and wine quality such that it was highly desirable it be drunk within three months of vintage (or not at all).

When Alan Dorr and Phillip Christensen purchased Bungawarra in 1976, the vineyard comprised four hectares of table grapes (muscat, waltham cross, purple cornichon and servante) between 10 and 40 years of age. These have now been replaced by shiraz (2.4 hectares), cabernet sauvignon (two hectares), muscat (1.8 hectares), chardonnay (one hectare), semillon (0.8 hectare), servante (0.4 hectare) and traminer (0.2 hectare), with the annual crush supplemented by shiraz and cabernet sauvignon purchased in from local growers. From a 1984 crush of 57 tonnes, the partners (joined in 1982 by Ian Mathieson, and in 1983 by Jon Davies, Harry Eastment, Allan Edwards and Greg Lamerton) are aiming at an eventual crush of 90 tonnes.

The vineyard is established on typical coarse-grained, decomposed granite on a north-facing slope. Fruit quality from the vineyards is good; and prior to the 1982 vintage the winery was both substantially expanded and modernised. In that vintage Bungawarra produced two magnificent wines from shiraz— they were redolent of crushed pepper and spice and evocative of the Rhone Valley at its best. As outstanding as these wines were, so the white wines were exceedingly disappointing. I shall be watching the future releases of shiraz from Bungawarra with more than passing interest.

DE LUCA
SUNDOWN ROAD, BALLANDEAN

Dick De Luca established a substantial vineyard between 1970 and 1979, with 15 hectares under vine. Plantings were chiefly shiraz, but also included rhine riesling, cabernet sauvignon, mataro and jacquez.

De Luca produced some excellent wine in this time, with a 1976 Shiraz winning a gold medal at the Brisbane show of that year, and several years later receiving the Champion Award at the Redland Bay Wine Show. However, at the end of the 1970s De Luca sold all but two hectares of shiraz and cabernet sauvignon, and output has declined in consequence.

ELSINORE WINES
SEVERNLEA

Elsinore Wines was established in 1973 by Peter Love, at one time an employee of the Queensland branch of the Wine Information Bureau. The first vineyard source was a small planting established by Love on the southern outskirts of Brisbane, the initial vintage following in 1978.

Recently, Love moved to the Granite Belt, purchasing an already established vineyard at Severnlea. He is in the process of removing the table grapes and replacing them with selected white and red varieties. Future vintages will be made in a winery established on the property.

KOMINOS WINES
Off THORNDALE ROAD, SEVERNLEA

Stephen Comino's introduction to wine came in 1959 when he visited Murray Tyrrell in the Hunter Valley. He was impressed not only with the wine, but with Murray Tyrrell's enthusiasm and evident commitment to his products. In an ever increasingly competitive market, Stephen Comino believes that the same commitment and enthusiasm remain an essential prerequisite for success.

Nonetheless, it was not until a 1973 campervan trip through Europe with his wife Penelope that Comino started to think seriously about one day making his own wine. A sojourn in his native Greece provided first-hand experience in winemaking in the traditional Greek peasant style. The seeds were sown, and in 1976 the family bought land at Severnlea (11 kilometres south of Stanthorpe) at a height of 840 metres. Shortly thereafter their son Tony commenced an agricultural science degree, and the first small plantings of chenin blanc and shiraz were made.

On completing his degree Tony Comino went to work for the Department of Agriculture in Tasmania for two years, leaving Stephen and Penelope Comino to continue tending the vineyard at weekends. Tony Comino returned three years ago, and the pace of the development picked up. The home vineyard now has 0.4 hectare of chenin blanc and 0.2 hectare of shiraz in bearing, with a further 1.2 hectares each of chardonnay and cabernet sauvignon to come into bearing over 1986 and 1987.

In 1984 the family purchased another vineyard, established some years earlier by Lex Ferris, on the New England Highway at Severnlea, comprising two hectares of shiraz and a total of 0.8 hectare of semillon, rhine riesling and cabernet sauvignon. The grapes had been sold to Bungawarra in the years up to 1984 and had contributed to the excellent Bungawarra reds.

1985 saw the erection and equipping of the Kominos winery and the first full-scale vintage. Substantial quantities of a dry red shiraz were made, together with a very promising cabernet sauvignon as well as the Cominos' version of the district Nouveau.

Tony Comino is presently completing the Riverina College wine science degree course and the family is clearly committed to establishing a significant commercial enterprise.

MOUNT MAGNUS WINES
DONNELLY'S CASTLE ROAD, POZIERES

Mount Magnus Wines throws in its claim to be the highest vineyard in Australia, with plantings lying between 890 and 910 metres above sea-level. Mount Magnus is the new name for Biltmore Cellars, recently purchased from the Zanatta family by John and Debbie Matthews.

Biltmore was the largest and one of the oldest wineries in the district, having been owned by the Zanatta family for more than 50 years. The first winemaking was from the table-grape varieties of muscat, isabella, waltham cross and purple cornichon. But commencing in 1972 20 hectares of vineyards were established, comprising shiraz, cabernet sauvignon and rhine riesling. Up until the first few years of the 1980s Biltmore continued to make and market traditional Italian styles, such as vino rosé made from the frolla table grape. Its last few years were troubled ones, and the operation was in a somewhat neglected state when acquired by the Matthews.

Kevin McCarthy is winemaker with a Bachelor of Science degree from Monash University and an oenology degree from Roseworthy Agricultural College. He has also had experience working with Orlando, Taltarni, Rothbury and Tisdall.

In 1984 and 1985 a vigorous replanting programme was commenced, with the introduction of chardonnay, malbec and emerald riesling, and the expansion of the plantings of cabernet sauvignon and shiraz. The existing vineyards have also been reworked, with fruiting-wires being established at two metres above the ground level. This high trellis system has a number of purposes: to assist in drying out after summer rains, a period of heavy humidity; to avoid reflected heat from the light-coloured sandy granite soil in summer; and to try to lift the young shoots above the frost level, with damaging frosts occurring as late as November.

The 1985 vintage resulted in the production of a quantity of nouveau-style wine made from shiraz grapes; the style is seen as being particularly suited to the Queensland market. Late in 1985 a French-oak-matured semillon and a traminer were scheduled for release.

OLD CAVES WINERY
NEW ENGLAND HIGHWAY, STANTHORPE

Old Caves Winery is situated at Applethorpe, a few kilometres north of Stanthorpe. Established by David Zanatta, it is one of the newest wineries in the district. David Zanatta is a son of Gino Zanatta of Biltmore (now called Mount Magnus Wines), and decided to establish his own winery at the end of the 1970s, making his first vintage in 1979.

The vineyards comprise three hectares planted to shiraz and chardonnay, with the annual crush supplemented by shiraz, rhine riesling and cabernet sauvignon purchased from three contract-growers. A white wine destined for the local market is also made from the table grape servante.

Zanatta has recently shown the ability to make red wines of excellent quality.

J. AND N. RICCA
SUNDOWN ROAD, BALLANDEAN

The Ricca vineyard, situated in Sundown Road at Ballandean, directly opposite Angelo's, is one of the oldest in the region. Still visible is the concrete crushing pit installed in 1935, rather like a Portuguese lagar, and used for foot-crushing the grapes. Part of the existing winery dates from 1949, although the principal operational portion was not completed until May 1981.

The Ricca family continued the practice of the former owners when they acquired the property in 1960. Wine was made in the traditional Italian style from the plantings of muscat, and sold in bulk for consumption within months of vintage. In 1965 one hectare of shiraz was planted; the 18 hectares of table and wine grapes now include shiraz, cabernet sauvignon, rhine riesling and semillon.

All wine is produced for sale in bulk; the red is a blend of muscat and a small proportion of shiraz fermented with natural yeast. It is most assuredly the style which has a local following and, equally assuredly, would not be understood by markets further afield.

ROBINSONS FAMILY VINEYARDS
LYRA CHURCH ROAD, LYRA, BALLANDEAN

John and Heather Robinson established Robinsons Family Vineyards in 1969, selecting a site 20 kilometres south of Stanthorpe on the New England Highway at Lyra in the Ballandean district. John Robinson is a solicitor, and was motivated to found the vineyard by his love of fine table wine. It is now the most important winery in the Granite Belt region, with its products distributed nationally by Rhine Castle Wines and produced from a crush of just on 90 tonnes. The estate vineyards are the largest plantings of many of the premium varieties in Queensland and are comprised of chardonnay (seven hectares), cabernet sauvignon (five hectares), pinot noir (two hectares), malbec and traminer (one hectare each) and a total of two hectares of merlot, sauvignon blanc and rhine riesling. All are established on the typical decomposed gravelly granite soils of the region, with yields varying between five tonnes and eight tonnes per hectare.

John Robinson has taught himself the art of winemaking partially through the school of necessity, but also by undertaking external courses at the Riverina College of Advanced Education and in-depth study tours to the wine regions of Bordeaux, Burgundy and the Napa Valley. For a while Robinson lived in France in the Burgundy region.

The attractively designed modern winery is fully equipped to facilitate the making of high-quality white and red table wines. Ample refrigeration allows for cold fermentation of chardonnay, which is then matured in French Nevers oak.

The releases typically consist of a chardonnay, a somewhat unusual chardonnay traminer, a cabernet sauvignon, a pinot noir and a shiraz cabernet. The winery has been a consistent winner of medals at the Brisbane show since first exhibiting in 1975, and the recent releases show just why this should be so. The wines are usually technically well made, but as yet there are no clearly defined varietal characters emerging. Whether this will come with more mature

vines and a greater understanding of the viticultural and oenological requirements of the district remains to be seen.

ROMAVILLA
NORTHERN ROAD, ROMA

I have followed the fascinating history of Bassett's Romavilla Winery in the introduction to this chapter; the vineyard and winery is now in the sole ownership of David Wall and his family. David is the brother of Peter Wall, the chief winemaker at Yalumba, and had spent much of his working life in and around the wine industry before moving to Roma in 1975. He had five years in the Barossa Valley working with veteran winemaker Ray Ward and at Yalumba. Subsequently he spent eight years managing a substantial Sydney hotel, which gave him experience in the "other side" of winemaking. The early years at Romavilla were made more difficult by a protracted partnership dispute with his brother-in-law and sister, an acutely unhappy time for all concerned.

Romavilla has, of course, always been best known for its fortified wines. The vineyards, which have declined substantially from the high-water mark at the turn of the century, still reflect that production, although David Wall has increased the plantings of rhine riesling and cabernet sauvignon. The existing 24 hectares include those varieties together with an exotic range of traditionally named (and no doubt) technically incorrectly named) varieties such as red muscat, white muscat, black muscat, black cluster, mataro, solverino, syrian and portugal.

The last three varieties are said to have been brought to Roma by Henry Trident, the descendant of a Swiss family commissioned by the Russian Czar to grow grapes on the Black Sea for the royal court. Trident was one of a group of viticulturalists invited by the Queensland government to improve and extend the State's wine industry in the late 1800s, an initiative which, not surprisingly, was largely unsuccessful.

The exterior of the buildings remains largely unchanged, looking more like a set from a Wild West film than anything else. The front of the main winery is emblazoned with the words "The Romavilla Vineyards Ltd Wine Vaults. Est. 1863". The wine vaults reference reflects the fact that the cellars are basically constructed on two underground levels; only the madeira-style fortified wine is stored under the galvanised-iron roof and walls at ground level. Inside the winery David Wall has modernised winemaking methods and equipment. Extensive refrigeration now permits must-cooling and cold fermentations; the aim here is to complement the traditional fortified-wine styles with a range of table wines.

These efforts have so far met with limited success. The real strength of Bassett's lies in its fortified-wine range, with its unique blending stocks up to 50 years old. Indeed, if there must be a criticism of the madeira, muscat or port releases, it is that they show too much evidence of age. It is clear that some of the old material was not very well looked after, and errant signs of volatility and oxidation intrude. Nonetheless, Romavilla adds substantially to the fabric of the Queensland wine industry.

RUMBALARA
FLETCHER ROAD, FLETCHER

Rumbalara provides the winery operation for the Granite Belt Vignerons partnership which encompasses three vineyards: Rumbalara, Girrawheen and Excelsior. The partnership arrangement was a complicated one, and the marketing arrangements more so. It has now been decided to concentrate on the Rumbalara label, and to phase out that of Girrawheen, although the vineyard identities will be preserved. Thus in the future we are likely to find labels such as Rumbalara Girrawheen Vineyard Semillon.

Winemaking responsibilities are shared by Bob Gray and his son Chris Gray. Bob Gray, an erstwhile civil engineer, is a graduate of the Riverina College, and has in addition spent time learning winemaking first-hand in Europe.

The Grays have substantial vineyard sources to draw on. The home Rumbalara vineyard has six hectares of cabernet sauvignon, shiraz, rhine riesling and pinot noir. The Girrawheen vineyards (established in 1973 by Doug Custance and Doug Hall) comprise 10 hectares of cabernet sauvignon, cabernet franc, shiraz, pinot noir, rhine riesling, semillon, chardonnay, sylvaner, traminer and muscat gordo blanco.

The Girrawheen and Rumbalara wines have always done well in local shows, but Bob Gray is on record as saying, "Of course it's nice to win any competition, but I prefer to win in wider based shows". Shortly after he made that statement, he achieved precisely the recognition he was seeking. The 1984 Semillon made by Granite Belt Vignerons was the top-pointed semillon in the 1985 international View Wine Exhibition in Melbourne. In a class of 119 wines,

dominated by some magnificent chardonnays and outstanding sauvignon blancs, it won a very creditable silver medal. I happened to be one of the judges of the class in which it was entered, and can personally vouch for the richness and style the wine achieved. Given the poor reputation of the 1984 vintage, the showing was all the more notable.

Rumbalara is one of the vineyards certain to establish the credibility of the Granite Belt south of the border.

SUNDOWN VALLEY WINES
SUNDOWN ROAD, BALLANDEAN

The Puglisi family are third-generation farmers in the Granite Belt region. In 1970 31-year-old Angelo Puglisi became the first vigneron this century to propagate wine grapes specifically dedicated for winemaking. In that year he commenced to replant an old table-grape vineyard, initially establishing six hectares of shiraz and cabernet sauvignon. The vineyard now extends to 14 hectares planted to cabernet sauvignon, shiraz, mataro, rhine riesling, semillon, chenin blanc and sylvaner.

The 1974 Shiraz produced by Puglisi was the first wine made in the district from anything other than table grapes. Three years later Angelo Puglisi was awarded a Churchill Fellowship to study overseas winemaking techniques in Europe, signalling the determination on the part of the Puglisi family to lift the quality of the locally produced wine. Originally sold under the Sundown Valley label, Angelo now proudly markets his wines under his own name.

The vineyard specialises in dry reds, which Puglisi believes the vineyard is particularly suited to. He is not lacking in confidence and goes so far as to say that the region is capable of producing some of the great red wines of Australia. However, he can also claim success with wood-matured white wines, producing a series of full-flavoured oak-matured semillons, one of which was the champion wine at the 1980 Stanthorpe show. Overall, however, Puglisi acknowledges that the white wines tend to be fairly broad and soft.

Angelo's has one of the few fully equipped laboratories in the region, shared by other makers. Overall the clean and well-ordered winery employs a higher level of technical sophistication than is commonly found in the district. He was also one of the first to install formal tasting facilities for vineyard visitors.

WINEWOOD
SUNDOWN ROAD, BALLANDEAN

Ian Davis is yet another relative newcomer with technical qualifications to the Granite Belt area. He completed the two-year Roseworthy Agricultural College Wine Marketing Course (a course which nonetheless involves a significant degree of oenology training) in 1977. In 1979 he acquired an old vineyard at Ballandean from Dick de Lucca, planted to a mixture of table and wine grapes. However, he moved outside the narrow confines of the wine industry to work as a high school teacher in Southport between 1979 and 1984.

During those five years, he and his wife made the 550-kilometre round trip from Southport to Ballandean on most weekends, gradually replanting the table grapes, installing appropriate trellis systems and generally reviving what was a fairly rundown vineyard. Virtually all the work was done by hand, even the placement of the strainer posts.

In 1984 a long awaited transfer to Stanthorpe High School was approved, and the Davises have now committed themselves to a commercial winery. In 1984 they purchased a further 12 hectares of vineyards opposite the original plantings, with semillon and shiraz of already proven quality. In all, the Davises now have 1.6 hectares of shiraz, 0.4 hectare each of cabernet sauvignon and semillon, and 0.2 hectare of mataro at their disposal. These plantings produced a 14-tonne crush in 1985, the first vintage of Winewood.

A basic winery was erected at the end of 1984, and stainless steel fermenters obtained from South Australia. The crusher was borrowed for the first vintage, and it will be some little time before the winery is fully equipped.

The 1985 vintage resulted in 425 dozen of a conventionally made dry red, principally shiraz (but with a little cabernet sauvignon and mataro included), and 225 dozen of Nouveau.

Ian Davis believes the Granite Belt region is ideally suited to produce fuller styles of white wine, and is particularly interested in experimenting with verdelho and marsanne. However, he laments Queensland's strict quarantine laws (designed to prevent the introduction of phylloxera) which have significantly limited the availability of suitable rootstock, holding the industry back in much the same way as that in South Australia was affected for many years. To this end he has started his own rootstock propagation programme, but concedes that development will nonetheless be slow.

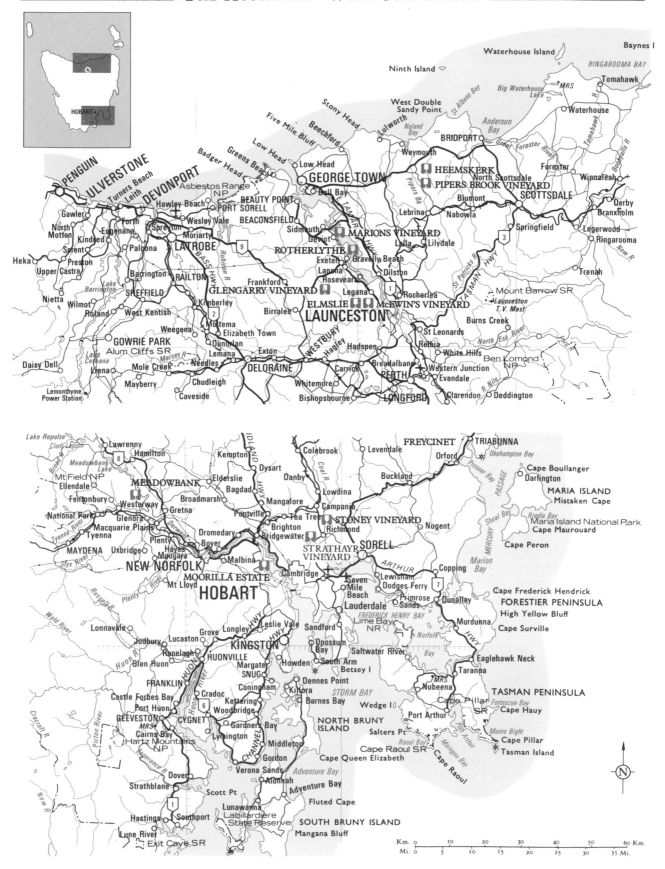

Tasmania

It is a quite astonishing fact that Tasmania can claim to have founded both the Victorian and South Australian wine industries. Wine was being commercially made and sold in Tasmania several years before vines were planted in either of the other two States, and it was the source of the first vines for those States. When William Henty sailed from Launceston to Portland on board the schooner *Thistle* in 1834, his personal effects included "one cask of grape cuttings and one box of plants". John Hack planted the first vines in South Australia in 1837; both he and John Reynell (who followed suit in 1838) obtained their cuttings from Port Arthur.

Like their mainland counterparts, the Tasmanian settlers planted vines in much the same way as other staple-food-producing plants. Many of these "domestic" vines—dating from the period 1825 to 1850—still survive in gardens spread all over the island. A number of these have been identified as chasselas, a variety which is regarded as a table grape in France but which in very cool areas—principally Switzerland—is used for making wine. No wonder that it adapted well to Tasmania, or that it has survived so long there.

The first commercial vineyard was established by Bartholomew Broughton in 1823 at Prospect Farm, New Town. The following year the press reported that "the produce of grapes this year is expected to be greater than has been known since the formation of the colony", while in 1827 Broughton publicly advertised that he had 300 gallons (1365 litres) of the 1826 vintage for sale.

The quality of the wine was evidently impressive, even making allowances for parochial pride. A Dr Shewin, who had tasted the wine made by Gregory Blaxland in 1822 at Brush Farm, on the Parramatta River near Sydney, pronounced Broughton's wine to be "as far superior as fine Port to Blackstrap". Blaxland's wine was the first to be exported from Australia, and had won a large silver medal from the Royal Society of Arts in England.

Broughton died in 1828 and his property was purchased by a Captain Swanston who proceeded to expand production significantly. In 1848 he made 1600 gallons (7280 litres) and stated he hoped to be producing 5000 gallons (22,750 litres) annually within the next five to six years. His sale catalogue for 1848 offered two-year-old champagne at 40 shillings per dozen; three-year-old bottled sherry; and red wine in bulk offered at eight shillings a gallon (4.5 litres).

By 1827 commercial nurseries were offering rooted vine cuttings for sale, and commercial vineyards were subsequently established at Windemere at East Tamar, Eustone Park near Falmouth, Marchington at Breadalbane and Claremount at Moonah. The government garden at the Queen's Domain site was also an important source of cuttings, and distributed vines over much of the

island. Its 1857 list records 29 grape varieties; by 1865 the number had grown to 45. Included were the finest types: pinot noir, cabernet sauvignon, malbec, shiraz, pinot blanc and sauvignon blanc.

But despite this seemingly promising start the industry had all but disappeared by the end of the 1860s. Captain Swanston died in 1850, ruined by the bank crash, while Tasmania suffered in the same way as the rest of rural Australia at the hands of the Victorian gold rush—there was literally no-one left to tend the vineyards. Other factors contributing to the decline were the refusal of the government to permit distillation to provide brandy for fortification, thanks to the temperance movement; lack of suitable sprays; and simple ignorance of proper viticultural and winemaking techniques.

There was a brief renaissance in the 1880s with the establishment of a vineyard on Maria Island. Diego Bernacchi acquired cabernet sauvignon cuttings from de Castella's St Hubert's Vineyard in the Yarra Valley, and exhibited a wine at the Melbourne Centennial Exhibition of 1888–89. Bernacchi was rumoured to have attached artificial bunches of grapes to his vines in an attempt to attract investors; whether or not this is true, his venture had failed by 1890.

For the next 70 years all was quiet. Even on the mainland grape-growing was concentrated in the warmer regions, and it became the official view of the Tasmanian Department of Agriculture that the island was unsuited to the commercial production of wine. Two men with a European background were the first to challenge that view. Between 1956 and 1960 Jean Miguet, a Frenchman working on a civil engineering project in Tasmania, established a one-hectare vineyard at Lalla, north of Launceston and just to the east of the Tamar River. In 1958 Claude Alcorso planted vines on the banks of the Derwent River on the northern outskirts of Hobart. Miguet did not persevere, but returned to France in 1974 and died not long afterwards. Claude Alcorso, however, did persevere and can legitimately be regarded as the father of the present-day industry.

At the end of 1984 leading Hobart wholesale and retail wine-and-spirit merchants, Aberfeldy Cellars, pieced together an accurate picture of the present-day Tasmanian industry. This was no easy task, for even in a State as small as Tasmania it is not easy to keep track of the new vineyards springing up like mushrooms after autumn rain.

In 1985 Tasmania will crush fewer grapes than Taltarni Vineyard in Victoria, enough to produce around 20,000 cases of wine in all. On the other hand this will come from almost a dozen wineries, with a similar number of additional vineyards whose owners harbour ambitions to make their own wine one day. What is more, the big three of the wineries, Moorilla Estate, Heemskerk and Pipers Brook, have a reputation that cannot be assessed by reference to their admittedly small production.

Another little-appreciated fact is that wine is made in a number of regions in Tasmania; only the wild mountains of the west remain untouched by vines. The following table shows the six principal regions with their 1984 and 1985 contributions to total production.

DISTRICT	VINEYARDS	JUNE 1984/ha	JUNE 1985/ha (est)	JUNE 1986/ha (est)	1984 tonnes
Pipers Brook	6	36.4	48.4	51.4	181
Tamar Valley	11	16.6	23.1	37.1	33
East Coast	3	8.9	11.9	11.9	15.25
Coal River Area	5	6.5	7.6	8.1	4.5
Derwent Valley	2	4.5	7.25	8	13.5
D'Entrecasteaux Channel	2	1	1	9.5	2
North-West Coast	2	0.4	0.5	0.6	—
TOTAL	31	74.3	99.75	126.6	249.25

Possibly the most important lesson learnt so far is that Tasmania is not too cool for grape-growing. Thus Pipers Brook has a centigrade heat-degree day summation of 1150, compared with around 1100 for Dijon in Burgundy. With appropriate site selection and viticultural techniques, growers across the length and breadth of the island have satisfactorily ripened most varieties in most years.

Harvest usually occurs between late March and early May, not so different from that of mainland cool-area vineyards. This was so even in the very cool 1984 vintage, with the last grapes harvested in mid-May. Indeed, in that year and prior years the major viticultural problem in the central and southern regions had been lack of rainfall. In almost every way Tasmania contradicts the commonly held mainland views of its potential.

As at June 1984 the 74 hectares of vineyards in the State were planted to cabernet sauvignon (28.1 hectares), chardonnay (15.05 hectares), pinot noir (13.3 hectares), rhine riesling (12.05 hectares), traminer (3.1 hectares) and miscellaneous varieties (2.7 hectares). Obviously the early-ripening varieties, with pinot noir and chardonnay to the fore, are the most prevalent. Heemskerk, Moorilla Estate and Pipers Brook have all made outstanding wines from these varieties which compete with ease against the best mainland examples. Pipers Brook and Heemskerk have also produced a series of remarkable cabernet sauvignons.

There are numerous vineyards which have so far not produced wine on a commercial scale, although one or two have produced homemade experimental quantities. These include Austwick Vineyard at Swansea on the east coast planted by dentist Dr John Austwick in 1979. There are two hectares of grapes planted to the classic varieties; small quantities of wine have been made since 1982 and a winery is planned.

Bellingham Vineyard at Pipers Brook is owned by Dallas Target, with 12 hectares planted between 1984 and 1985 and with the possibility of a further six hectares in 1986. Varieties include cabernet sauvignon, chardonnay and rhine riesling. The Richardson family, St Patrick's Vineyard and the Leigh Vineyard have all been established in the Pipers Brook area, with a total of six hectares planted to premium varieties.

At the extreme south of Tasmania, and possibly the southernmost vineyards in the world, Elsewhere Vineyard and Panorama Vineyard have been established. Eric and Gette Phillips established a trial vineyard in Glaziers Bay on the D'Entrecasteaux Channel in 1978, and planned to increase the vineyard to eight hectares over 1985–86. Nearby the Ferencz family own Panorama Vineyards, established in 1977 and planted to one hectare of cabernet sauvignon, pinot noir, chardonnay and rhine riesling. Two tonnes were crushed in 1984 yielding 1600 litres of wine. As from the 1985 vintage it is anticipated that the wine will be available for commercial sale, and that the vineyard will be progressively extended over the years to 1987.

The oldest vineyard in Tasmania is La Provence, owned by Stuart Brice and his family. Close-planted on a 1.2 by one-metre spacing by Jean Miguet on a clay soil on a north-facing hillside, it produces high-quality grapes which are being sold to Heemskerk. Stuart Brice, a viticulture and winemaking graduate of Riverina College of Advanced Education, has recently moved from Sydney to live permanently on site, and the vineyard is being extended by an additional two hectares of pinot noir and chardonnay. In future vintages the wine will be made and marketed by Brice.

The Tasmanian industry may as yet be small, but no-one should underestimate its potential.

ELMSLIE
LEGANA, TAMAR VALLEY

Elmslie, situated near Legana in the Tamar Valley, was established in 1972 when trial quantities of cabernet sauvignon, rhine riesling and a hybrid, barco noir, were planted on a steep, stony, chocolate-brown soil hillside. Owner/winemaker Ralph Power has now grafted the barco noir and the rhine riesling to chardonnay. At the same time he has increased the vineyard to 0.75 hectare, planted with equal quantities of cabernet sauvignon, pinot noir and chardonnay.

Approximately 500 litres of wine were made from the 1984 vintage and were offered for sale at the cellar door.

FREYCINET
TASMAN HIGHWAY, BICHENO

Geoffrey Bull has had a varied career, working for 12 years as a journalist before becoming a full-time abalone diver on Tasmania's east coast at Bicheno. This profitable but arduous occupation has now in turn been replaced by that of full-time vigneron and winemaker, with assistance from his wife, Suzanne Bull.

The vineyard presently comprises 1.9 hectares of cabernet sauvgnon, pinot noir, chardonnay, muller-thurgau, sauvignon blanc and rhine riesling, all planted in 1981 on well drained stony loam over clay soils. Vineyard spacing is conventional at 3.5 by 1.5 metres, and a high "T" trellis is used. Inter-row sod culture is practised. The vineyard is 16 kilometres inland near Bicheno, and although there are hills between it and the seas the moderating influence of the ocean is still apparent. Geoff Bull believes that the vineyard is too warm for pinot noir and muller-thurgau as the grapes reach almost 13 baume by the end of March.

A further four hectares of vineyard land have been prepared and will be planted in 1985 and 1986. The first commercial vintage was made in 1984 by Julian Alcorso at Moorilla Estate, but the 1985 and future vintages will be made at Freycinet by Geoff Bull.

GLENGARRY VINEYARD
LUKE ROAD, GLENGARRY, TAMAR VALLEY

Glengarry, in the Tamar Valley, was established by Gavin Scott in 1980; there are now 1.6 hectares of cabernet sauvignon and 1.1 hectares of pinot noir, with a further 1.6 hectares to be planted in 1985 and 1986. The vines are planted on a three-metre by 1.3-metre spacing on grey sandy loam over clay and limestone. It is intended to propagate only red varieties on the site.

Glengarry fulfils the function of a mini cooperative, with the produce of both McEwin's Vineyard and Rotherlythe Vineyard being vinified at Glengarry. Fourteen tonnes of grapes in all were processed at the winery in 1984 from the three vineyards, yielding 8000 litres of wine. Each of the three vineyards' wines are kept and marketed separately. Those of Glengarry will be available for sale at the cellar door and through selected Tasmanian retailers.

HEEMSKERK
PIPERS BROOK

Heemskerk is now the largest of the Tasmanian wineries, crushing 40 per cent of the State's production in 1984. It is a totally professional operation in all its aspects and, together with Pipers Brook and Moorilla Estate, has put the credibility of the Tasmanian wine industry beyond dispute.

It was also the second commercial winery to be established in Tasmania after Moorilla Estate. Its origins were at Legana near Launceston, where winemaker/founder Graham Wiltshire joined forces with Michael Curtis of Hobart to establish a small pilot vineyard. Wiltshire had been experimenting with vines at Underwood near Lillydale, close to the original Jean Miguet plantings, while Curtis was doing the same at Legana. The two men consolidated their interests at the latter site and the vineyard was ultimately expanded to 1.2 hectares, planted principally to cabernet sauvignon and rhine riesling.

Graham Wiltshire took over the operation in the early 1970s and established a small winery. The quality of the early experimental wines made at Heemskerk came to the notice of Bill Fesq, the well-known Sydney wine merchant, and Colin Haselgrove, who had then recently retired as managing director of Walker Reynell & Sons Pty Limited. In 1973 they started discussions with Wiltshire, which led to an extensive search throughout Tasmania for a suitable location for a far larger operation planned for the future. In 1975 a consortium was formed between Wiltshire, Barry Larter of Launceston and the Fesq and Haselgrove families. Fesq, Haselgrove Wiltshire & Company Pty Limited was incorporated and acquired a substantial property at Pipers Brook, abutting the one purchased by Andrew Pirie the year before.

Up until 1980 all of the commercially released Heemskerk wines came from the Legana Vineyard. The rhine riesling wine was not persevered with, and cabernet sauvignon alone was made. The first release of any significance was 1976; it and every subsequent release were to win gold and silver medals at national wine shows, principally in Hobart. The wines were of great importance in establishing the credibility of Tasmania. Each of the cabernets showed pungent herbaceous varietal aroma and flavour, and stood out at a time when such characters were not common. With a fuller perspective it is possible to see just why the partners felt there might be better sites on the island and, in particular, areas that would produce wines with greater mid-palate weight.

The Pipers Brook Vineyard now has 16 hectares of cabernet sauvignon and chardonnay, with smaller plots of traminer, pinot noir, rhine riesling and sylvaner in production. It is to be increased by annual plantings of five hectares in each of the years between 1985 and 1988. The Legana Vineyard has in consequence been leased.

Prior to the 1984 vintage a substantial and very beautiful winery was erected using one of the most rare of building timbers, celery-top pine. The Adelaide-based consultancy firm Oenotec was involved for a period, and the wines of Heemskerk are going from strength to strength. Good though the wines of the late 1970s were, they are not in the class of those produced since 1982.

The 1982 Cabernet Sauvignon won a gold medal at the Royal Melbourne Show in 1982 and was in serious contention for the Jimmy Watson Trophy; the 1982 and 1983 Chardonnays were also outstanding. The 1982 Cabernet Sauvignon is a vibrant cherry-red-purple in colour, with fresh minty fruit and a haunting hint of spice, no doubt imparted by the oak; the palate is marvellously elegant, crisp and with the same minty characters evident in the bouquet. The extraordinary success to date has been with the chardonnays; both the 1982 and 1983 vintages have utterly unexpected richness and weight. These high-quality wines challenge the best mainland cool-climate examples of the style.

Finally, some very promising pinot noir has been made; the releases so far have been very good,

although Pipers Brook and Moorilla Estate have, at their best, produced the most exciting wines from this variety.

In April 1985, Heemskerk announced a joint venture with the French champagne house of Louis Roederer, a move which will add much credibility to the Tasmanian industry as a whole.

McEWIN'S VINEYARD
LEGANA, TAMAR VALLEY

McEwin's Vineyard is the name now given to the original Heemskerk property, which has been taken on a long-term lease from Heemskerk by Gavin Scott of Glengarry Vineyard and Steven Hyde of Rotherlythe. It now comprises one hectare of cabernet sauvignon and 0.2 hectare of pinot noir.

The production of approximately 10 tonnes of grapes each year is now vinified at Glengarry; the 500 dozen bottles of wine are marketed separately through Glengarry.

MARIONS VINEYARD
FORESHORE ROAD, DEVIOT, TAMAR VALLEY

One of the most obvious features in the development of the Tasmanian industry to date has been the very slow rate at which the vineyards have come into production. A major exception is that of Marions Vineyard, established by the Semmens family at Deviot in 1980. Three hectares of cabernet sauvignon, pinot noir, chardonnay and mullerthurgau were planted in that year.

The first wines were made in 1983 and the 1984 vintage produced 16 tonnes of grapes resulting in almost 12,000 litres of wine. Understandably the Semmens have been encouraged to expand the plantings, which over the next three years will be increased to a total of 8.5 hectares. Wines will be available at the cellar door and also through agents in Tasmania and interstate.

MEADOWBANK
GLENORA, DERWENT VALLEY

In 1974 the Ellis family planted one hectare each of cabernet sauvignon and rhine riesling, together with a little shiraz, at Glenora in the Derwent Valley, approximately 75 kilometres north-west of Hobart. The vineyard, established on podsolic sandy loams, flourished and plantings have now been increased to two hectares. Additional plantings of around 0.7 hectare per year are planned for the next five years, which will bring the vineyard to approximately seven hectares by 1989. The existing vineyards are established on conventional spacing, but the new plantings will see the distance between the vines shortened from 1.6 to 1.3 metres. Likewise a new one-metre-wide "T" trellis will be employed with those new plantings.

Notwithstanding the limited production (the 9.5 tonnes of cabernet sauvignon and riesling in 1984 was the largest harvest to date), the wines of Meadowbank are known to a considerable number of wine lovers. This is due to the Hickinbotham family of Anakie, Victoria, who have purchased all of the fruit since 1981 and vinified and released the Meadowbank wines separately. The grapes are packed in small waxed-cardboard boxes for the 24-hour trip to Victoria.

The 1983 Cabernet Sauvignon was by far the best red so far to be made from the vineyard, while the rhine riesling has been consistently good. Future plantings of chardonnay and merlot will widen the choice, and the Ellis family have long-term plans to establish their own winery at the vineyard. Fruit quality is not in doubt.

MOORILLA ESTATE
655 MAIN ROAD, BERRIEDALE

Claudio (for some reason almost always called Claude) Alcorso is not only the father of the present-day Tasmanian industry, but one of its greatest characters. Now in his seventies, he still enjoys life to the full, a life which has always been rich and varied. The connecting thread, or rather threads, have been a life-long interest in music, art, wine and textiles, the latter forming the base of Alcorso's business since he arrived in Australia after the Second World War.

When Claudio Alcorso planted half a hectare of assorted grape varieties on the banks of the Derwent River, just north of Hobart, in 1958, he had no idea that Jean Miguet had established a vineyard two years earlier. Alcorso believed he was the first person to endeavour to grow grapes in Tasmania this century. He was moved to do so because of his European upbringing, which treated wine as part of everyday life and which had also taught him that vines flourished in climates no warmer than that of Tasmania.

Despite that, it was a frustrating and lonely time. The official attitude of the Tasmanian Department of Agriculture at the time was that the island was unsuited to grape-growing, an attitude with echoes in the past. In the previous century the government had refused to permit the distillation of wine into brandy, helping to precipitate the demise of the industry. Even in mainland Australia there was very little understanding of the specialised requirements of cool-climate viticulture, and both here and in winemaking the isolation factor was acute. Birds, too, were delighted to find a new food source, methodically destroying entire vintages until the embryonic vineyard was totally enclosed in nets.

The end result was that for many years grapes were produced in tiny quantities and the wines were made under the most difficult of circumstances. Wine faults were common, but every now and then a spark of brilliance would emerge. Alcorso gradually gained the interest of and assistance from the CSIRO, the University of Tasmania, the Australian Wine Research Institute and ultimately professional consultancy services from mainland vignerons. Since the latter part of the 1970s Moorilla Estate has been transformed with a substantial modern winery; a major interest in the Bream Creek Vineyard on the east coast; and the retention of Oenotec as consultants.

The grapes for the still very small 1984 crush of 15 tonnes came from three sources. The first is the "home" vineyard on the banks of the Derwent River with 1.5 hectares (predominantly pinot noir, with a little rhine riesling and traminer) in bearing. A further one hectare of pinot noir was planted in 1985. The Alcorsos believe they have finally found the appropriate clone of pinot noir after years of experimentation, and have likewise established that European close spacing (1.5 metres by one metre) coupled with "U" trellising produce grapes of the highest quality.

The second vineyard is that of Bream Creek, established by a syndicate of Hobart businessmen in 1974, and which is now largely owned by the Alcorso family. Five hectares are in bearing, planted on a heavy clay loam looking out over the Tasman Sea. Even on a grey, rainy day it is a beautiful place.

Cabernet sauvignon is the dominant variety, with smaller plantings of pinot noir, rhine riesling and chardonnay. All of the vines are planted on a high vertical-trellis system on largely conventional spacing. By 1986 an additional three hectares will have been planted. The third source of fruit is the Sandford Vineyard run by J. Chancellor as an experimental research station.

Julian Alcorso has now assumed full responsibility for winemaking, with assistance from Tony Jordan of Oenotec. The recent releases of pinot noir, and in particular those of 1983 and 1984, lend credence to the view that the Derwent River Vineyard is now perfectly set up to produce the variety. Intense varietal character is evident, with a steely backbone that is lacking from the majority of mainland pinot noir.

Similar intensity is evident in the 1983 Moorilla Chardonnay, of which only 1000 bottles were made. Brilliant green-yellow in colour, it has an intensely pungent grapefruit aroma and a similarly intense almost citric-like grapefruit flavour. It is one of those rare wines that combine intensity and elegance with generosity.

The most successful cabernet sauvignon to date was the 1980 vintage, which won the trophy for the best small vineyard red wine at the Canberra National Wine Show. Nonetheless, I think that future vintages will be even better.

PIPERS BROOK VINEYARD
PIPERS BROOK

The site for Pipers Brook Vineyard was selected in 1972 following a feasibility study carried out in Sydney, using scientific methods to locate a region in Australia which could produce European-style wine. The study also resulted in owner/winemaker Andrew Pirie obtaining Australia's first Doctor of Philosophy degree in viticulture from Sydney University.

The *terroir* and climate of the hilly site were considered so perfect that the logistical disadvantages of moving from the mainland were ignored. With over 7.5 sunshine hours per day, and a centigrade day heat-degree summation of around 1150, compared with 1100 for Burgundy, it appeared ideally suited to cabernet sauvignon, chardonnay, gewurtztraminer and pinot noir. All of these varieties were planted on an ultraclose-spaced vineyard (1.8 by 1.1 metres) which now comprises 10.3 hectares. There are approximately 2.5 hectares of each of the four

varieties. Nonetheless, experience has shown that *terroir* is no less important in Tasmania than in France, and that certain portions of certain of the slopes are far more suited to one variety than another. Wind, too, presents its problems for some varieties.

Pirie has one of the few "over-the-vine" tractors in Australia, and the vines are cane-pruned and summer-hedge-trimmed in the French manner. The immaculately tended vineyards are one of the showpieces at the forefront of Australian viticultural practice.

Pipers Brook is now a very substantial operation, with 74 tonnes of grapes in the 1984 vintage yielding 48,500 litres of wine. Production in prior years was much smaller, but I have not the least hesitation in rating the Pipers Brook wines as the best to come so far from Tasmania. In 1984 I was treated to a retrospective tasting of all the wines so far made; it was one of the most memorable tastings of that year, even though the number of wines was necessarily limited.

Production of pinot noir rose to 200 dozen in 1984; in 1983 it had been 23 dozen, in 1982 20 dozen, and in 1981 a total of 35 bottles of wine were made. I treasure an empty bottle of 1981 Pinot Noir as a souvenir of the best Australian pinot noir I have tasted to date. By 1984 it had developed exceptional burgundian characters; soft, sappy mulberry aromas leading on to a soft, velvety-structured palate with the slightly sappy-green pinot flavours one finds at the southern end of the Côte de Nuits. It is truly a magnificent wine; there are unfortunately only two bottles remaining at the winery.

The 1982 Pinot Noir inevitably suffered a little in comparison with the sublime 1981; the fruit quality is certainly there, but the oak is rather heavy at the moment. The 1983 is by far the lightest of the three wines, refecting the vintage conditions, but has some of the burgundian characters of the 1981. The bouquet is powdery and spicy; the palate has crisp fruit and acid, augmented by a touch of cinnamon-spice flavours from the oak. It will be very interesting to watch the development of this excellent wine.

The cabernet sauvignons from 1981 to 1983 were overall even more impressive. Here the outstanding vintage was the 1982, with a deep, briary, complex aroma and a touch of cassis, leading on to a palate of extraordinary concentration and quite marked tannin. It is a wine of power and breed, destined for a very long life. The 1983 is a total contrast in style, with light sweet-berry fruit flavours and a light herbaceous overlay. A fresh, vibrant wine, it will be the first to mature of the three wines. The 1981 Cabernet

Sauvignon has a first-class bouquet, smooth, full and rich; the palate is very well balanced, but rather lighter than the bouquet suggests. There are some distinct cool-climate herbaceous fruit flavours; these are not overdone and the palate has enough sweet-berry flavours to give it balance.

The 1984 Sauvignon Blanc, tasted early in its life (one of 35 half-bottles), was a distilled essence of sauvignon blanc grown in the Loire Valley, penetrating and cleansing, with high acid and intense varietal characters. It was in total contrast to the 1982 Rhine Riesling which had soft lime/pineapple aromas and was surprisingly forward on the palate.

The packaging of the Pipers Brook wines is immaculate. The labels have no equal in Australia (or even California) and are worthy of the wine in the bottle.

ROTHERLYTHE
GRAVELLY BEACH, BLACKWELL, TAMAR VALLEY

Between 1972 and 1973 Bill Mitchell planted 0.1 hectare of pinot noir and cabernet sauvignon on the western river bank of the Tamar Valley, some 20 kilometres from Launceston. The vineyard was then known as Tamarway, and I have one bottle of cabernet sauvignon from that era given to me by Bill Mitchell's daughter, Jill.

In 1984 failing health forced Bill Mitchell to lease the Tamarway vineyard to Dr Steven Hyde, who has named it Rotherlythe. He expanded the operation by planting four hectares of pinot noir, chardonnay and cabernet sauvignon in 1985.

The wines are made by Gavin Scott at Glengarry; Scott also made the wine during Bill Mitchell's ownership. The old plantings produce approximately half a tonne of cabernet sauvignon and half a tonne of pinot noir each year, and are offered separately through Glengarry.

STONEY VINEYARD
CAMPANIA, COAL RIVER

George and Priscilla Park established Stoney Vineyard in 1973, when they planted a half-hectare vineyard to a kaleidoscopic array of varieties including cabernet sauvignon, pinot noir, shiraz, zinfandel, rhine riesling, traminer, sylvaner and four other varieties.

George Park is a senior officer with the Hydro-Electric Commission, and is a self-taught winemaker. His tiny winery adjacent to the house bears mute

witness to the total lack of understanding on the part of the local health authorities when he applied for permission to establish a winery in the mid-1970s. In the outcome both George Park and the authorities agreed that the initial requirements were appropriate for a 1000-tonne winery, but hardly appropriate for one with an annual output of around 200 to 300 cases of wine.

Whatever bureaucratic difficulties George Park may have had, he learned his winemaking well. From the first uncertain vintages in 1975 and 1976 he has produced some of the best wines so far to come from the State. So much so that for several years the tiny vineyard has dominated the Tasmanian classes at the Royal Hobart Show. The extent of his success is even more remarkable given the minute quantities in which the wine has been made. After 10 years of experimentation and having proved to his entire satisfaction that shiraz and zinfandel, for example, ripen handsomely and make excellent wine, George Park is rationalising the vineyard to allow for the production of larger quantities of particular wines. He will in the future concentrate on cabernet sauvignon and pinot noir, an understandable decision although I regret the passing of the zinfandel and shiraz.

I tasted a large number of his wines at the winery in 1984, and after a lovely 1983 Rhine Riesling (which was surprisingly full, soft and honeyed, with deep fruit and good acid), the first red wine was a 1982 Zinfandel. At that time I had not long returned from California, and I was immediately taken back in my mind to the top of Storybook Mountain at the upper end of the Napa Valley above Calistoga, where I had tasted a similarly flavoured and styled zinfandel. The bouquet is clean, spicy and perfumed, with the crisp palate showing very similar spice and lively flavour.

George Park has found that over the years his pinot noir has abundant weight and style, with the capacity to improve in bottle for five years or more. The 1983 Pinot Noir showed why he has come to this view. Strong purple-red, it has a spicy/leathery bouquet with real French overtones; the palate is powerful and tightly knit; there are sweet-berry flavours on the mid-palate but it has a rather hard finish. The 1982 Pinot Noir was a warmer style than the 1983, with sweet cherry-fruit characters and a rather softer structure.

The best wines of Stoney are the cabernet sauvignons of 1982 and 1983. The 1982 is generally regarded as the better wine, with an illustrious show record and critical acclaim from winemaker and writer Maynard Amerine. Fine, elegant and bordeaux-like, it is a truly excellent wine. However, I preferred the intense perfumed cassis/berry richness, indeed opulence, of the 1983 Cabernet Sauvignon. The palate of this wine is soft yet intense, with deep, lingering, sweet-berry flavours.

George Park intends to double the size of his vineyard at some time in the future, presumably when he retires from the Hydro-Electric Commission. Even then the wines of Stoney Vineyard will be rarer than diamonds, and of similar quality.

STRATHAYR VINEYARD
RICHMOND, COAL RIVER

Strathayr Vineyard was established in 1975 by Bill Casimaty in the Coal River area, not far from Stoney Vineyard. One hectare of cabernet sauvignon, pinot noir, riesling and chardonnay was planted on sandy loam soils with closer-than-average spacing (three metres by one metre). The vineyard has now been expanded to 2.5 hectares, with rhine riesling, cabernet sauvignon, chardonnay, traminer and pinot noir being the principal varieties and with a small planting of sauvignon blanc.

Up until 1984 birds harvested all of the grapes. In that year a small quantity of experimental wine was made by the current managers, Tom Crossen (former lecturer at Roseworthy College) and Hobart restaurateur Berti Tuccero. It is intended that as from 1985 small quantities of wine will be made for sale, and there are tentative plans to extend the plantings by a further one hectare in 1985–86.

Glossary

Acetaldehyde: The principal aldehyde of wine, occurring in amounts of up to about 100 parts per million.

Acetic acid: A volatile acid present in virtually all table wines in small quantities. The legal limit is 1.2 grams per litre; the flavour threshold is around 0.5 to 0.6 grams per litre. A wine described as volatile suffers from an excess of acetic acid.

Acid: A generic term used to denote the three principal acids present in wine—tartaric, malic and citric. In dry table wine the levels usually fall between 5.5 and seven grams per litre. Acid plays an essential role in preventing bacterial spoilage, providing longevity and giving flavour balance.

Aggressive: An unpleasantly obvious component of wine flavour, for example, aggressive tannin.

Albillo: An incorrect name for the grape variety chenin blanc.

Alcohol: One of the principal components of wine and derived from the action of yeast on grape sugar during the fermentation process. Most table wines have between 10 and 14 degrees of alcohol; if all of the available grape sugar is fermented, each degree baume of sugar will produce one degree of alcohol.

Aldehyde: A volatile fluid deriving from the oxidation of alcohol, present in most wines but undesirable in any appreciable quantity; hence, aldehydic.

Aleatico: A grape of the muscat family from Italy and grown in Australia chiefly in the Mudgee region. Produces red or fortified wine.

Alicante Bouschet (or **Bouchet**): A French hybrid red grape grown extensively in France and, to a lesser degree, California. High-yielding but inferior quality grapes are produced. Limited plantings in Australia, chiefly north-east Victoria.

Alvarelhao: A Portuguese grape variety once propagated in tiny quantities in southern New South Wales and northern Victoria. Has little or no future.

Amontillado: A wood-matured sherry, slightly fuller in body and slightly sweeter than fino sherry.

Amoroso: A very old, fully sweet wood-matured sherry. Similar in weight and style to a fortified muscat or tokay.

Ampelography: The science of the identification and classification of grape vines.

Anthocyanin: A colouring pigment found in grape skins and playing an important part in both the colour and keeping qualities of a red wine.

Appellation Controlée: A system of laws which guarantees the authenticity of a wine with a given label, extending both to region, grape variety, methods of viticulture and (occasionally) methods of vinification.

Aroma: The scent or smell of the grape variety; aroma decreases with age as bouquet builds.

Astringency: Sharpness or bitterness deriving usually from tannin and sometimes from acid; particularly evident in a young wine, and it can be an indication of the keeping potential of such a wine.

Aubun: An extremely rare red-grape variety from the Mediterranean region of France; a few vines still exist at Bests Great Western Vineyards.

Aucerot: Incorrect name for montils.

Auslese: In Australian usage, a sweet white wine made from late-harvested grapes, often affected by botrytis.

Balance: The harmony or equilibrium between the different flavour components of wine, and the first requirement of a great wine.

Barbera: The principal red-wine grape of Italy, grown in tiny quantities in Australia, chiefly in Mudgee but also in the Murrumbidgee Irrigation Area. Noted for its high acidity and low pH.

Barrique: An oak barrel containing 225 litres of wine, used almost exclusively in Burgundy and Bordeaux in France for maturation of wine, and increasingly used throughout Australia.

Bastardo: A red-grape variety from Spain, incorrectly called cabernet gros in South Australia. Of minor importance.

Baume: A scale for the measurement of grape sugar. One degree baume equals 1.8 per cent sugar, or 1.8 degrees brix. (See also Alcohol.)

Beerenauslese: As with auslese, the term has no precise meaning in Australia. Adopted from the German, and applied to heavily botrytised, extremely sweet white table wine.

Biancone: A white grape of Corsica; the highest-yielding variety in commercial propagation in Australia, regularly achieving 30 tonnes per hectare in the relatively small plantings in South Australia's Riverland area.

Big: Used to describe a wine with above-average flavour, body and/or alcohol. By no means necessarily a favourable description.

Bitter: A fault detectable at the back of the palate, usually deriving from skin, pip or stalk tannins.

Blanquette: Synonym for clairette.

Blue imperial: Synonym for cinsaut.

Body: A term used to describe the weight or substance of a wine in the mouth and deriving from alcohol and tannin. Softens and mellows with age.

Bonvedro: A red grape of Portugal, grown principally in South Australia with a little in New South Wales and Victoria. Produces a relatively light-bodied wine; not an important variety.

Botrytis: *Botrytis cinerea* (called *pourriture noble* in France and *Edelfaule* in Germany) is a microscopic fungus or mould that attacks first the skin and then the pulp of grapes in certain very specific climatic conditions, causing the pulp to lose its water and the grape to soften and shrink with a corresponding concentration of the remaining components of the grape, notably sugar and acid. The grey-brown grapes look extremely unattractive, and the juice first pressed from them equally so, but juice settling and subsequent fermentation produces the great sweet wines of the world.

Botrytised: Grapes or wine affected by botrytis.

Bouquet: The smell of the wine (as opposed to simply the aroma of the grape) produced by the volatile esters present in any wine. Bouquet becomes more complex during the time the wine needs to reach full maturity and finally softens and dissipates with extreme age. Much work still remains to be done to understand fully the very complex chemical changes which take place in a wine as it matures and which contribute to the changing bouquet.

Bourboulenc: A white-grape variety from the Mediterranean region of France, included in the Busby importation of 1832 but now restricted to a few vines in central and northern Victoria. Unlikely ever to be of significance in Australia.

Breathing: The process of allowing a wine to come in contact with air by drawing the cork (and possibly decanting) prior to serving. Enhances the development of the bouquet. The optimum period of time is frequently the subject of fierce debate among experts, but one or two hours is a safe estimate for young or semi-mature wines.

Brix degrees: An alternative measure of the approximate sugar content of wine; most grapes are harvested between 19 and 24 brix, one degree brix produces one degree of proof spirit.

Broad: A term used to describe wine which is softly coarse, lacking in refinement.

Brown frontignac: Incorrect name for muscat à petits grains.

Brown muscat: Incorrect name for muscat à petits grains.

Brut: The driest of the sparkling-wine styles, though in fact containing some sugar.

Bung: The wooden or silicon-rubber stopper in a wine barrel.

Buttery: A term encompassing the aroma, taste and texture of a white wine, usually oak-matured, but which can also develop from long bottle-age. Typically found in semillon and chardonnay.

Cabernet: In Australia, simply an abbreviation for cabernet sauvignon; also used to denote the cabernet family (see below).

Cabernet franc: An important red-grape variety in Bordeaux and the Loire Valley in France; also extensively propagated in Italy. Until recently, little attention was paid to the variety in Australia but it is now assuming greater importance for top-quality reds. Produces a wine similar to but slightly softer than cabernet sauvignon.

Cabernet gros: Incorrect name for bastardo.

Cabernet sauvignon: The great red grape of Bordeaux and, with pinot noir, one of the two most noble red varieties in the world. As at 1984 there were 3764 hectares in Australia which produced 23,672 tonnes. It has become the most important top-quality red-wine grape in Australia only during the last two decades; prior to that time it was grown in small quantities.

Carignan, Carignane: A grape variety of Spanish origin but very widely propagated in the south of France to produce _vin ordinaire_. Also extensively grown in California for similar purposes. Some South Australian plantings of an unidentified grape are incorrectly called carignane; the grape is not commercially propagated in Australia.

Cassis: A dark purple liqueur made from blackcurrants, chiefly near Dijon in Burgundy. The aroma of cassis is often found in high-quality cabernet sauvignon as the smell of sweet blackcurrants.

Cépage: A French word for grape variety, but increasingly used to denote the varietal composition of a wine made from a blend of several varieties (hence, _cépagement_).

Chaptalisation: The addition of sugar to partly fermented wine to increase the alcohol level, permitted in France but illegal in Australia.

Character: The overall result of the combination of vinosity, balance and style of a wine.

Chardonnay: The greatest white grape of France (Burgundy and Champagne), grown extensively throughout the world and in particular in California. All but unknown in Australia before 1970, it has had a meteoric rise since, with 1920 hectares in 1984 producing 8515 tonnes of grapes (reflecting the high proportion of recent plantings still to come into production). As elsewhere, it provides rich table wines and fine sparkling wines.

Chasselas: The principal white-wine grape of Switzerland, and also extensively propagated in France and Italy. Both in Europe and in Australia it is used both for winemaking and as a table grape. In the last century it was called sweetwater; the principal area of propagation in Australia is at Great Western in Victoria.

Chenin blanc: The principal white grape of the Loire Valley in France, grown in relatively small quantities in Western Australia, South Australia

and Victoria and for long incorrectly identified variously as semillon and albillo. Seldom produces wines of the same character as in the Loire Valley, but the plantings have recently shown a modest increase. Can produce great botrytised wines.

Cinsaut: A red-grape variety from the Mediterranean region of France. Frequently called blue imperial in north-east Victoria, black prince at Great Western and confused with oeillade in South Australia. Produces agreeable soft wines with good colour but low in tannin.

Clairette: A once very important white-grape variety in the south of France, grown in relatively small quantities in Australia where it is often called blanquette (particularly in the Hunter Valley). A difficult wine to make and of no great merit.

Clare riesling: Incorrect name for crouchen.

Classic: A wine conforming exactly to style and of the highest quality.

Clean: The absence of any foreign (or ''off'') odour or flavour, an important aspect of a wine of quality.

Cloudy: Colloidal haze and gas particulate matter in suspension leading to a hazy or milky appearance.

Cloying: A sweet wine without sufficient balancing acid.

Coarse: Indicates a wine with excessive extract of solids, particularly tannins, and probably affected by oxidation during the making process.

Colombard: A white grape extensively grown in France, used both for table-winemaking and also in the production of brandy. Extensively propagated in California where it is known as French colombard. Has been planted extensively in Australia's warm irrigated regions because of its excellent acid-retention capacity. Used both in blends and in varietal white wines.

Complete: Denotes a wine which has all of the requisite flavours and components in harmony and balance.

Condition: A technical term to describe the clarity of a wine; a cloudy wine is described as being out of condition.

Corked: A wine tainted by microscopic moulds growing in the pores of the cork. A corked wine will smell and taste sour, mouldy or possibly earthy.

Coulure: A disease leading to the flowers or immature berries falling from the vine with a consequent reduction in crop level.

Crouchen: A white grape originally from France but now propagated only in South Africa and Australia. The substantial plantings in this country have been consistently incorrectly identified for a century, being called Clare riesling in the Clare Valley, semillon in the Barossa Valley, and firstly Clare riesling and then semillon in South Australia's Riverland, before being finally identified as crouchen. A relatively high-yielding variety, producing wines of modest quality; of declining importance, although plantings still exceed 1000 hectares.

Crusher: A machine to remove the berries from the stalks prior to fermentation, forming a must which will be pressed shortly thereafter if it is a white wine, and pressed at the end of fermentation if it is a red wine.

Crust: Sediment adhering to the inside of bottles of wine, usually red; consists mainly of pigment and tartrate crystals.

Decant: The careful pouring of the contents of a bottle into a carafe or decanter to leave behind the crust or other deposits.

Deep: Indicates both complexity and profundity when applied to aroma; indicates depth (or intensity) of hue when applied to colour.

Developed: Showing the effects of ageing in bottle, usually but not invariably beneficially so.

Dolcetto: A red grape from Piedmont in Italy, grown in tiny quantities in South Australia and Victoria. Many of the old classic Saltram reds contained small quantities of the variety.

Doradillo: An extremely important white grape in Australia but of little significance elsewhere, which was brought to Australia by James Busby from Spain. As at 1984 there were 1484 hectares in production in Australia, producing 27,467 tonnes. Grown principally in the Riverland areas for distillation into brandy and for the production of sherry.

Downy mildew: One of the two principal vine fungi, which can be devastating if not checked.

Dry: A wine without apparent sweetness or residual sugar; in fact many wines contain minute traces of sugar, and it is difficult to detect at levels of up to five grams per litre.

Dull: Denotes a wine either cloudy or hazy in colour, or with a muted or flawed bouquet or palate.

Dumb: A wine showing either no aroma or distinct varietal taste or no development.

Durif: A variety first propagated in the Rhone Valley only a century ago, and called petite sirah in California. Grown in tiny amounts in Australia, notably in north-eastern Victoria by Morris.

Earthy: Bouquet and flavour reminiscent of certain soil types; a smell of fresh earth can often be identified in young vintage port.

Esparte: Synonym for mataro.

Esters: Flavourful and usually volatile substances formed by the combination of acids with alcohols. Wine probably contains over 100 different esters.

Extract: Soluble solids adding to the body and substance of a wine.

Extractive: A coarse wine with excessive extract from skins and pips.

Fading: A wine past its peak, losing its bouquet, flavour and character.

Farana: A white grape from the Mediterranean region grown in tiny quantities in the Barossa Valley, where it was previously confused with trebbiano.

Fermentation: The primary winemaking process in which the sugar (in the form of glucose and fructose) in grapes is converted to alcohol and carbon dioxide by the action of yeasts.

Ferruginous: A wine tasting of iron, possibly derived from the soil type.

Fetayaska: A white grape grown in tiny quantities in north-east Victoria and South Australia to make a white table wine of no great significance.

Filter pad: A synthetic woven sheet used to remove suspended solids and bacteria from wine. Incorrect treatment may lead to a particular cardboard-like taste being imparted to the wine, often referred to as paddy.

Finesse: A term denoting a wine of high quality and style.

Fining: A method of clarifying young wines before bottling by the addition of beaten egg white, bentonite or other fining agent.

Finish: The flavour or taste remaining after the wine leaves the mouth.

Fino: A Spanish-derived term for the driest and most delicate type of sherry made by the flor-yeast process.

Firm: A term usually applied to the finish of a wine, and denoting the impact of tannin and possibly acid.

Flabby: A wine without sufficient acid and freshness, often due to excessive age but sometimes to poor winemaking.

Flat: Similar to dull and flabby; a lack of freshness, character, or acid.

Fleshy: A youthful wine with full-bodied varietal flavour.

Flowery: The aroma reminiscent of flowers contributed by certain aromatic grape varieties.

Folle blanche: A still important white-grape variety used in the production of brandy in France. The supposed Australian plantings have now been identified as ondenc.

Foxy: The unpleasantly cloying, sweet aroma of wines produced from *Vitis labrusca* grapes.

Free-run: Wine that separates without pressing from grape skins after fermentation and which is generally more fruity and lower in tannin than the pressings that follow.

Fresh: An aroma or taste free from any fault or bottle-developed characters, usually found in a young wine but occasionally in old wines.

Frontignac: Incorrect name for muscat à petits grains.

Fruity: The pleasant aromatic taste of a young wine with strong varietal character.

Furmint: The white grape used to make the famous Hungarian tokay. Introduced into Australia by James Busby; a few vines exist at Great Western and one or two boutique wineries have experimental plantings.

Gamay: Gamay is the red grape which produces beaujolais in France; it is also grown extensively in the Loire Valley. Two attempts to introduce the variety into Australia from California have failed. The first introduction turned out to be pinot noir, the second valdigue. Still grown only in tiny quantities; it seems inevitable that further attempts to propagate it in the future will be made.

Gassy: A wine with small bubbles of carbon dioxide, often mistaken for a form of secondary fermentation. Undesirable (particularly in red wines) but tolerated in Australia.

Gewurtztraminer: Synonym for traminer.

Glory of Australia: A black grape from the Burgundy region of France, from which it disappeared after phylloxera; frequently mentioned in the nineteenth-century accounts of the vineyards of Geelong. A few vines survive at Great Western. Also called liverdun, la gloire, but correctly called troyen.

Glycerine: A byproduct of fermentation which adds to the texture of a white wine. Sometimes (improperly) added to white wine, particularly chardonnay.

Gouais: A minor white-grape variety from the centre of France, extensively propagated in Victoria in the nineteenth century but now largely disappeared except from areas around Rutherglen.

Graciano: A red variety of importance in Spain's Rioja area. Called morrastel in France, but unrelated to the variety once called thus in South Australia (which is in fact mataro). Grown in small quantities in north-eastern Victoria. Produces strongly coloured wines, rich in tannin and extract, which age well.

Green: Term applied to a young wine which is unbalanced because of excess malic acid deriving from unripe grapes.

Hard: An unbalanced and unyielding wine suffering from an excess of tannin and/or acid (if red) and acid (if white).

Harsh: Usually applied to red wine suffering from excess tannin, often when young.

Hárslevelü: A white grape of Hungary used in making Hungarian tokay. Tiny plantings in Australia.

Hermitage: An incorrect name for shiraz.

Hogshead: A barrel of 300 litres capacity, once the most widely used small barrel in Australia but progressively replaced by barriques and puncheons.

Hollow: Applies to a wine with fore-taste and finish, but with no flavour on the middle palate.

Honeyed: Denotes both the flavour and the structure (or feel in the mouth) of a mature white wine, particularly aged semillon but also sauterne.

Hunter River riesling: Incorrect name for semillon.

Hybrid: A cross between an American and a European vine achieved by cross-pollination as opposed to grafting.

Hydrogen sulphide: The smell of rotten eggs found in red wines resulting from the reduction of sulphur dioxide or elemental sulphur. Detectable in tiny quantities (one part per million); when bound into the wine it becomes mercaptan.

Irvine's white: Incorrect name for ondenc.

Jacquez: An American variety thought to be a naturally occurring hybrid between the species *Vitis aestivalis* and *Vitis vinifera*. Small quantities grown in the Murrumbidgee Irrigation Area and the Hunter Valley where it is usually called troia. It has a strong, unusual flavour less unpleasant than those of the species *Vitis labrusca*.

Jammy: Excessively ripe and heavy red-grape flavours, sweet but cloying.

Lactic acid: Seldom present in grapes but formed during the alcoholic and malolactic fermentations. Also occurs in faulty wines as a result of bacterial decomposition of sugars; the slightly sickly sour-milk aroma is very unpleasant.

Lees: Deposit of bacteria, tartar, yeast and other solids found on the bottom of vessels containing wine.

Light: Lack of body, but otherwise pleasant.

Long: Denotes the capacity of the flavours of the wine to linger in the mouth and palate after the wine has been swallowed.

Madeira: (i) Island off the coast of Spain famous for its dessert wines.
(ii) General term for wines resembling those produced on the island.
(iii) Incorrect name for verdelho.

Madeirised: Oxidative change in white wines brought about by prolonged storage in warm conditions.

Malbec: A red-grape variety grown chiefly in and around Bordeaux and also in the Loire Valley where it is known as cot. Grown on a vast scale in Argentina (over 50,000 hectares) and in a minor way throughout Australia. Has been confused with dolcetto and tinta amarella; actual area in Australia is uncertain but is probably around 400 hectares. Ideal for blending with cabernet sauvignon which it softens and fills out.

Malolactic fermentation: A secondary fermentation, usually taking place after the primary fermentation, involving the decomposition of malic acid in wine to lactic acid and carbon dioxide. Considered essential for most red wines, and increasingly used in the making of wines such as wood-matured chardonnay. Softens and adds complexity to the flavour of wine.

Mammolo: A red-grape variety once of minor importance in Tuscany, Italy; a few vines exist in Mudgee, and there have apparently been some other isolated recent plantings. The wine is said to have an aroma resembling the scent of violets.

Marc: The residue of grape skins and seeds after the pressing process has been completed; can be distilled into a spirit bearing the same name.

Marsanne: A white-grape variety of declining importance in the Rhone Valley of France, grown in relatively small quantities in the Goulburn Valley, north-east Victoria and the Hunter Valley. Around 50 hectares in production. Once famous in the Yarra Valley, where tiny plantings also still exist.

Mataro: A red grape of major importance in Spain, where it is called morastell or monastrell. Once one of Australia's most important red grapes in terms of production, but now declining with 1047 hectares in 1984 producing 11,166 tonnes. Called balzac at Corowa and esparte at Great Western. Yields well and produces a neutrally flavoured but astringent wine which is best blended with other varieties.

Melon: A white grape which originated in Burgundy but is now propagated principally in the Loire Valley, where it is known as muscadet. Significant plantings in California are called pinot blanc. Only small quantities are propagated in Australia, chiefly in South Australia.

Mercaptan: Produced by ethyl mercaptan and ethyl sulphides in wine deriving from hydrogen sulphide and produced during the fermentation process. It manifests itself in a range of unpleasant odours ranging from burnt rubber to garlic, onion, gamy meat, stale cabbage and asparagus. While hydrogen sulphide can easily be removed, once mercaptan is formed it is much more difficult to eliminate.

Merlot: One of the most important red-grape varieties in the Bordeaux region, dominant in St Emilion and Pomerol. A relatively recent arrival in California, and even more recent in Australia, where the small commercial plantings to date have been disappointing from a viticultural viewpoint. Poor fruiting has caused some experimental plantings to be abandoned. However, others are persevering and plantings are on the increase.

Metallic: A taste of metal, sometimes encountered in red wines which have been treated with copper sulphate to remove mercaptan.

Méthode champenoise: The method of making sparkling wine employed in champagne in which the all-important second fermentation takes place in the bottle in which the wine is ultimately sold.

Meunière: A red grape almost invariably known under its synonym pinot meunière in Australia. Also called Miller's burgundy at Great Western. A naturally occurring derivative of pinot noir and grown principally in France in Champagne. The upsurge in interest in sparkling wine in Australia may see an increase in the presently small and isolated plantings, chiefly in Victoria.

Miller's burgundy: Incorrect name for meunière.

Monbadon: A white variety of declining importance in Bordeaux and Cognac; grown on a small scale in the Corowa–Wahgunyah area of north-eastern Victoria.

Mondeuse: A red grape of minor importance in the east of France, grown chiefly by Brown Brothers at Milawa in north-eastern Victoria. Introduced to Australia at the suggestion of Francois de Castella in the aftermath of phylloxera. Produces a very strong, tannic wine ideal for blending with softer varieties.

Montils: A white grape grown in small quantities in Cognac. Small plantings in the Hunter Valley where it is also known as aucerot; the aucerot of north-eastern Victoria is a separate and, as yet, unidentified variety. Produces a wine with low pH and high acidity, and would appear to have at least as much potential as colombard, but little commercial interest has so far been demonstrated.

Moschata paradisa: A white-grape variety grown in tiny quantities in Mudgee, but so far its overseas source has not been identified. Australia's most unusual grape.

Mouldy: "Off" flavours and aromas derived from mouldy grapes or storage in a mouldy cask or from a bad cork.

Mousy: A peculiar flat, undesirable taste resulting from bacterial growth in wines, most evident after the wine leaves the mouth. Its precise cause is not yet known.

Muller-thurgau: A cross, bred by Dr Muller in 1882 and put into commercial propagation in 1920 in Germany; now that country's most important grape. Originally thought to be a riesling/silvaner cross, but now believed to be a cross of two riesling grapes. Propagated in limited quantities in Australia; produces a fairly uninteresting wine. The most important white grape in New Zealand, where it is generally known as riesling sylvaner.

Muscadelle: The white grape which is the third and least important component of the wines of Sauternes. Grown across Australia, and usually known as tokay. The largest plantings are in South Australia, but in north-east Victoria extremely ripe, raisined grapes are used to make the famous fortified tokay of that region. The grape is not used for this purpose anywhere else in the world.

Muscadet: Synonym for melon.

Muscat à petits grains: A grape variety grown over much of Europe and which is called by a wide variety of names both there and in Australia, not surprising given that it appears in three colour variants—white, rose and red. The coloured forms mutate readily from one to the other, while chimeras, in which the genetic make-up of the berry skin differs from that of the flesh, also exist. Confusion regarding names and identification makes statistics unreliable, but there appear to be around 500 hectares in Australia, half grown in South Australia and the rest divided between New South Wales and Victoria (most frequently called white, red or brown frontignac). The white variety is common in South Australia, the red in north-eastern Victoria, where it is known as brown muscat (or brown frontignac) and used to make the great fortified wines of that region. The white variant is used to make table wine of very high flavour, often used in small percentages with other more noble varieties such as rhine riesling.

Muscat gordo blanco: A white-grape variety, originating in Spain but grown in many countries. A very important variety in Australia with 4252 hectares in 1984 producing 71,224 tonnes for winemaking and 2140 tonnes for drying and table-grape use. Widely called muscat of Alexandria, it is a high-yielding multi-

purpose grape. For winemaking it is used for fortified sweet wines such as cream sherry and also in cask and flagon wines, often in combination with sultana.

Muscat of Alexandria: Synonym for muscat gordo blanco.

Must: In white-winemaking, unfermented grape juice; in red-winemaking, the mixture of grape juice, skins and seeds before fermentation. During fermentation it is known as fermenting must.

Nose: The scents and odours of a wine, encompassing both aroma and bouquet.

Nutty: Characteristic pungent flavour and aroma of sherry, due in part to wood age and to the presence of acetaldehyde.

Oeillade: Incorrect name for cinsaut.

Oenology: The science of winemaking.

Oidium: *Oidium tuckeri*, commonly known as powdery mildew.

Oily: Oils deriving from grape pips or stalks and not desirable in wine.

Olfactory: Pertaining to the sense of smell.

Oloroso: A Spanish term for old, rich, sweet, full-bodied sherry.

Ondenc: An obscure white grape from France, travelling both there and in Australia under a confusingly large number of names. Probably brought to this country by James Busby as piquepoule, but then became known as sercial in South Australia and Irvine's white in Victoria at Great Western. In France it is used for brandy-making; in Australia for sparkling wine (because of its neutrality), chiefly by Seppelt at Great Western and Drumborg.

Orange muscat: A highly aromatic white-grape variety, also known in France as muscat fleur d'orange, grown chiefly in north-eastern Victoria.

Organoleptic: The analytical appreciation, by use of the senses, of wine (or food).

Oxidised: Refers to a wine that has been exposed to too much oxygen, resulting in loss of flavour and development of coarseness.

Palomino: A white grape from Spain providing virtually all the raw material for sherry. Grown on a very large scale in South Africa (around 19,000 hectares) and an important variety in Australia (with around 1100 hectares). Very similar to pedro ximinez and statistically grouped with pedro ximinez. Used chiefly for fortified wine in Australia, and in particular dry sherry.

Pedro ximinez: Another Spanish variety used to produce both dry and sweet fortified wines. Extensively propagated in Argentina (20,000 hectares), and with around 1300 hectares in Australia (although decreasing). Grown chiefly in the Riverland areas, it is used in the making of sherry, but also to provide flagon and cask white wine.

Peloursin: An ancient grape variety from the east of France but of little or no commercial significance. Survives in Australia and California interplanted with durif, which it resembles.

Peppery: May refer to a raw, harsh quality in immature wine, but increasingly recognised as a characteristic of cool-climate shiraz with pepper/spice aromas and flavours.

Petit meslier: An extremely obscure, although still permitted, white-grape variety in Champagne in France; a few vines survive amongst ondenc plantings at Great Western.

Petit verdot: A minor red grape of Bordeaux of declining importance in that region. The once significant Hunter Valley plantings have disappeared since 1930, but a few tiny plantings have since been established elsewhere in Australia by those seeking to emulate the great wines of Bordeaux.

Petite sirah: Incorrect name for durif used throughout America.

pH: Literally, the power of hydrogen. In simple terms it is a logarithmic expression of the measurement of free hydrogen ions in solution. The lower the pH number, the higher the level of hydrogen ions and, in turn, the greater the available or useful acid. Table wine usually has a pH of between 3.1 and 3.6; white wines tend to have a slightly lower pH than reds. Low pH wines will usually age better than those with a higher pH.

Phylloxera: A microscopic insect, introduced into Europe and thence to Australia from America in the second half of the nineteenth century, which devastated the vineyards of Europe and of Victoria. Feeds chiefly by sucking the sap from the roots of the vine.

Pinot blanc: The true pinot blanc is a white variant of pinot noir, seemingly grown only in Alsace, Germany and Italy. Varieties grown elsewhere and called pinot blanc are variously chardonnay, chenin blanc or melon.

Pinot chardonnay: Incorrect name for chardonnay.

Pinot de la Loire: French synonym for chenin blanc.

Pinot gris: Another colour variant of pinot noir similar to pinot blanc. Grown in Alsace, Germany (where it is called rulander) and northern Italy.

Pinot meunière: Synonym for meunière.

Pinot noir: The classic red grape of Burgundy, grown in practically every country in the world but only producing wine of real quality in cool climates. In 1984, 473 hectares in Australia produced 2049 tonnes; plantings are expected to increase substantially with increasing use of the variety for sparkling wine.

Piquepoule noir: A minor red-grape variety from the Chateauneuf-du-Pape region of France, surviving as a few vines at Great Western.

Pressings: Wine recovered from pressing the skins, stalks and pips after fermentation. It is higher in tannin and may be deeper coloured. Often backblended into free-run wine to add strength and colour.

Puncheon: An oak barrel usually between 450 and 500 litres in capacity.

Pungent: Refers to a very aromatic wine with a high level of volatiles.

Punt: Indentation at the base of a bottle originally introduced to strengthen it.

Racking: Drawing off or decanting clear must or wine after allowing the lees to settle.

Rancio: Distinctive developed wood character of an old dessert wine stemming from a degree of oxidation. Highly desirable.

Residual sugar: Unfermented grape sugar remaining in white wine in the form of glucose and fructose. Can be tasted at levels in excess of five grams per litre. Many so-called dry rhine rieslings have six to seven grams per litre of residual sugar.

Rhine riesling: Simply known as riesling in its native Germany, where it is the most highly regarded white grape. Grown extensively around the world; known as white riesling or Johannisberg riesling in California and by a host of names in other countries. In 1984, 4694 hectares in Australia produced 36,201 tonnes of grapes; while it has fallen from public favour in Australia, it still remains the most important high-quality white grape. The widespread advent of botrytis has meant that both dry and

very sweet wines of excellent quality can be made from it.

Riesling: (i) Preferred name for rhine riesling.
(ii) A dry white wine which may or may not be made from or contain a percentage of rhine riesling in it.

Rkatitseli: A Russian white grape propagated chiefly in the Murrumbidgee Irrigation Area by McWilliam's and others.

Rootstock: The type of vine root onto which a scion or bearing grape vine is grafted. The scion, and not the rootstock, determines the grape type.

Rough: Astringent, coarse tannin taste in red wines indicating lack of balance and maturity.

Round: A well-balanced, smooth wine showing good fruit characters.

Roussanne: A white grape grown in the Rhone Valley and usually blended with marsanne. Also a minor component of some (red) Chateauneuf-du-Pape wines. Experimental plantings at Yeringberg in Yarra Valley.

Rubbery: The most common manifestation of hydrogen sulphide in the form of mercaptan.

Rubired: An American-bred red hybrid producing wines of startlingly intense colour and very useful for blending in small quantities for this purpose. Propagated on a limited scale in Australia.

Ruby cabernet: Another red hybrid bred by Professor Olmo at the University of California. Grown on a very limited scale in Australia.

Rulander: German synonym for pinot gris.

Sappy: A touch of herbaceous or stalky character often found in young wines, particularly pinot noir, and usually a sign of potential quality.

Scented: A wine having a highly aromatic smell, usually associated with flowers or fruits.

Semillon: The major white grape of Bordeaux and the second most widely grown in the whole of France. Outside of France it is propagated chiefly in the southern hemisphere (Chile has 17,000 hectares) with 2810 hectares producing 31,905 tonnes in Australia in 1984. Has been confused with chenin blanc in Western Australia and crouchen in South Australia; Barnawartha pinot of north-eastern Victoria is semillon. The classic white grape of the Hunter

Valley; produces wines which are extremely long-lived and often need five or 10 years to reach their peak. Now also matured in new oak to produce a different style, and increasingly used for the production of sauterne-style wines in South Australia.

Sercial: Incorrect name for ondenc.

Shepherds riesling: An incorrect (and no longer used) name for semillon.

Shiraz: A red grape coming from the Hermitage area of the Rhone Valley, the origins of which are obscure and hotly debated. Frequently called hermitage in Australia (particularly in New South Wales and Victoria); 6387 hectares produced 56,260 tonnes in 1984. For long the mainstay of the Australian red-wine industry, and still the most widely propagated red grape. The fact it can produce wines of the very highest quality is frequently forgotten; a very versatile variety which can do well in all climates and soil types. Also useful for blending with cabernet sauvignon.

Silvaner, Sylvaner: A vigorous, high-yielding white grape extensively grown in Germany, producing rather neutral-flavoured wines. Even in cool-climate areas such as Drumborg and Keppoch it produces an unexciting wine in Australia. The modest plantings are not likely to increase.

Smooth: Agreeable and harmonious; opposite of astringent, harsh or rough.

Soft: Wine with a pleasing finish, neither hard nor aggressive. May indicate fairly low acid levels, but not necessarily so.

Sour: Excessively acid, a character usually manifesting itself on the back of the palate.

Souzão: A minor red grape grown in the Douro Valley of Portugal.

Sparge: To saturate.

Spatlese: A German term for naturally sweet late-harvested wines, but appreciably less sweet than auslese.

Spritzig: A German term indicating the presence of some carbon dioxide bubbles in the wine, frequently encountered in Australian white wine and occasionally in reds. Often an unintended consequence of protecting the wine from oxidation during storage and/or bottling. Can be felt as a slight prickle on the tongue.

Stabilisation: The chilling of a white wine to near-freezing point to precipitate tartaric crystals.

Stalky: Bitter character deriving from grape stalks, mainly appearing in red wines and indicative of poor winemaking.

Steen, Stein: Incorrect names for chenin blanc used in South Africa.

Sulphide: The generic term given to hydrogen sulphide and mercaptans.

Sulphur dioxide (SO_2): An anti-oxidant preservative used in virtually every wine—red, white or sparkling. In excessive quantities it imparts a disagreeable odour and may artificially retard the development of the wine. Dissipates with age.

Sultana: A white grape which originated in Asia Minor or the Middle East, and which is principally used both in Australia and elsewhere as a table grape. In California, where it is known as Thompson's seedless, it is grown on a very large scale and significant quantities are used for white-winemaking. In Australia in 1984 17,912 hectares produced 74,641 tonnes for winemaking, 298,914 tonnes for drying and 9038 tonnes for table-grape purposes. If used for white-winemaking it produces a very neutral wine with quite good acidity.

Supple: A lively, yet round and satisfying wine.

Sylvaner: See **Silvaner**.

Synonym: An alternative, though not officially preferred, grape variety name.

Syrah: Synonym for shiraz.

Tannin: A complex organic constituent of wine deriving chiefly from grape pips and stalks, and occurring in greater quantities in reds than in whites. Plays an important part in the self-clearing of young wines after fermentation, and thereafter in the period of maturation the wine requires: a full-bodied red, high in tannin, requires a longer period than does a lighter-bodied wine. Easily perceived in the taste of the wine by the slightly mouth-puckering, drying, furry sensation, particularly on the side of the tongue and on the gums. Some red-winemakers add powdered tannin to wine to increase the tannin level artificially.

Tarrango: A red hybrid grape bred by the CSIRO. Chiefly used in the production of nouveau-style reds by Brown Bros and others; has considerable promise.

Tart: A wine with excess acid.

Tartaric acid: The principal naturally occurring acid in grapes, and added in powdered form to the vast majority of Australian white and red wines to compensate for the usually naturally deficient acid levels in ripe grapes.

Tawny: (i) The colour of an old red wine.
(ii) A wood-matured port.

Tempranillo: The most highly regarded of the red-grape varieties grown in Spain's Rioja, and known as valdepenas in California. A small planting by that name in the Upper Hunter Valley is presumably tempranillo. The wine matures extremely quickly.

Terret noir: A grape grown in the Languedoc area of France, appearing in three colour combinations—white, grey and black. A small planting of the latter type exists in the Barossa Valley.

Thin: Lacking in body, almost watery and probably excessively acid.

Thompson's seedless: American synonym for sultana.

Tinta amarella: A red grape widely grown in the Douro Valley of Portugal and used in vintage port. There are about 30 hectares in South Australia, where the variety is known as portugal. It has from time to time been confused with malbec.

Tinta Câo: A red grape grown in the Douro Valley in Portugal and important in the making of vintage port. Only experimental plantings in Australia.

Tokai friulano: A white grape closely related to sauvignon blanc and grown extensively in the Friuli-Venezia-Giulia region of north Italy. Grown on a large scale in Argentina where it is called sauvignon. Isolated vines exist in Mudgee, the Goulburn Valley and Great Western, sometimes in surprisingly large numbers. The wine has a definite bouquet and a slight bitterness, as its sauvignon blanc heritage would suggest.

Tokay: See **Muscadelle**.

Touriga: The most important red grape in the Douro Valley in Portugal, used extensively in vintage port. Small plantings have been grown for many years in the Corowa region, and there have been small recent plantings on the floor of the Barossa Valley. It is used to make high-quality vintage port, and a modest increase in plantings can be expected.

Traminer: An ancient white-grape variety derived from the primitive wild grapes of Europe. The main European plantings are in Alsace and Germany, and also northern Italy. Produces a highly aromatic wine which can quickly become overbearing and overblown. Contrary to public belief, there is no viticultural or other distinction between traminer and gewurtztraminer, although the latter is supposedly more spicy in aroma and taste.

Trebbiano: The leading white grape of Italy, and now dominant in the Cognac region of France where it is known as St Emilion, although the official French name is ugni blanc. It is known by both these names in Australia and also (incorrectly) as white shiraz or white hermitage. It is grown in virtually all Australian wine regions, bearing well to produce a neutral and rather hard table wine and an excellent distillation base for brandy.

Trockenbeerenauslese: A German term for ultra-sweet white table wine made from hand-selected and picked berries, although in Australia there are no legal limits to its use.

Ugni blanc: French synonym for trebbiano.

Ullage: The air space present in a bottle of wine between the cork and the surface of the wine. In old wines it is a fairly reliable indication of likely quality: the greater the ullage, the more suspect the wine.

Valdepenas: Californian synonym for tempranillo.

Varietal: (i) Character of wine derived from the grape.
(ii) Generic term for wines made from a single or dominant variety and identified by reference to that variety.

Vat: A container in which wine is fermented, made of stainless steel, concrete or oak.

Verdelho: A white grape from Portugal, grown on the island of Madeira where it is used to make fortified wine, and in small quantities in the Douro Valley. The Australian plantings of under 100 hectares are divided between Western Australia, South Australia and New South Wales. Produces a very distinctive, full-bodied table wine, and can also be used to make fortified wine. Many judges would like to see more of the variety planted.

Vinification: The process of making wine.

Vinosity: A term relating to the strength of the grape character in a wine (though not necessarily the varietal character) and linked to the alcoholic strength of the wine. Denotes a desirable characteristic.

Viognier: A white grape grown chiefly at the northern end of the Rhone Valley to produce distinctive and highly flavoured although relatively quick-maturing wine. Experimental plantings in Australia show some promise.

***Vitis aestivalis* and *Vitis labrusca*:** Species of vine native to North America with natural resistance to phylloxera and used as rootstocks in Europe and elsewhere.

***Vitis vinifera*:** The species of vine responsible for virtually all the wines of the world.

Volatile: A wine spoiled by an excess of acetic acid.

Volatile acid: A group of acids comprising acetic, carbonic, butyric, propionic and formic.

Volatility: Relating to the release of acetic acid and other esters, and which may be present to excess in a faulty wine.

White frontignac: Synonym for muscat à petits grains.

White hermitage: Incorrect name for trebbiano.

White shiraz: Invalid name for trebbiano.

Yeast: Single-cell organism responsible for the fermentation of sugar into alcohol.

Zinfandel: A grape variety grown chiefly in California, but may be related to the widely propagated primitivo variety of Italy. Grown in small quantities in Australia, chiefly in Western Australia and South Australia. Can produce a wine deep in colour and rich in soft, spicy flavour.

Index